The appearance of the third edition of *Introduction to Biblical Interpretation* (much more than a mere introduction!) stands as testimony to the book's lasting influence and significance. The authors engage ongoing scholarship in biblical studies as they provide readers necessary principles and guidelines that impact the discipline of hermeneutics. Importantly, they also point readers to the fact that we must not be content merely to "master" the biblical text; rather, we must strive to let it master us. The book will greatly benefit those willing to invest the time to wrestle with its insights.

Bryan E. Beyer, Dean of the College of Arts and Sciences,
Columbia International University

Long a foundational resource for the study of the Scriptures, *Introduction to Biblical Interpretation* now appears in a third edition. With updated discussions, footnotes, and bibliographies this work constructively engages developments in areas treated in previous editions and interacts with more recent approaches that bring fresh questions to the text. Deeply committed to the Bible as holy writ, the authors present guidelines for its careful study and application to life. Detailed yet practical, this valuable tool proves its worth for a new audience.

M. Daniel Carroll R., Blanchard Chair of Old Testament,
Wheaton College

With this new edition, Klein, Blomberg, and Hubbard demonstrate the excellence of their previous editions while bringing their discussion up to date in light of contemporary hermeneutical theory. Clearly defending the appropriateness of author-centered interpretation, they provide students with a comprehensive set of tools for understanding the Bible in its ancient context and also the means for contextualizing its message today. Written with clarity and an awareness of the needs of students, this will remain an essential work for many years to come. It deserves to have pride of place in courses on hermeneutics, but ought also to be on the shelves of those who faithfully seek to interpret the Bible in a range of settings today.

David G. Firth, Old Testament Tutor and Academic Dean,
Trinity College, Bristol

I heartily welcome the third edition of a textbook I have used for more than twenty years as the primary text in an introductory seminary course on hermeneutics. This new, updated edition retains the breadth of topics, the well-conceived practical approach to interpretation, and the clarity of presentation of its two predecessors. Its discussion of literary genres and crucial theological and philosophical concepts that affect interpretation is first-rate and up-to-date.

The volume is a treasury of interpretive methods that equip students with the key skills for discovering the riches in a biblical text; this is especially important given the vast array of genres found in both testaments. The joy students experience from a thorough study of a particular text gives them confidence to preach and teach God's Word enthusiastically. The volume includes a thorough discussion of approaches for moving from the discovery of the message of a text to making it relevant to the current culture.

John E. Hartley, Distinguished Professor of Old Testament Emeritus,
Azusa Pacific Seminary

Retaining the best of the previous two editions, this classic textbook is updated with new material relevant to the interpretive issues of our day. No other work has surpassed the comprehensive study of biblical interpretation Klein, Blomberg, and Hubbard have produced. Tested by time, this new edition deserves a place in the library of every serious student of the Bible.

Karen H. Jobes, Gerald F. Hawthorne Professor Emerita of New Testament
Greek and Exegesis, Wheaton College & Graduate School

Long one of the most thorough, comprehensive, and practical textbooks for biblical interpretation, *Introduction to Biblical Interpretation* has now been expanded and further improved.

Craig S. Keener, F. M. and Ada Thompson Professor of Biblical Studies,
Asbury Theological Seminary

I have often used Klein, Blomberg, and Hubbard's excellent *Introduction to Biblical Interpretation* as a textbook since it originally appeared over twenty years ago. This readable and profound book covers all the important topics of interpretation with great skill. I am very excited about the publication of the third edition that takes into account recent scholarship. I recommend it to all who want to deepen their ability to read Scripture well.

Tremper Longman III, Robert H. Gundry Professor of Biblical Studies,
Westmont College

Earlier editions of this title have served a generation of students well, and this third substantially revised and updated edition continues to provide not only a reliable entry point to the art and science of biblical interpretation but also a competent introduction to the contemporary currents in the field of hermeneutics. As a product of three experienced teachers and able interpreters of the ancient texts, it deserves a place on the shelf of serious students of the Bible.

David W. Pao, Professor of New Testament and Chair of the
New Testament Department, Trinity Evangelical Divinity School

A third edition of a tried and true book on hermeneutics by wise and veteran scholars is to be warmly welcomed. The new edition considers the latest issues on hermeneutics, and at the same time the authors expertly explain what students need to understand to interpret the Scriptures.

Tom Schreiner, The Southern Baptist Theological Seminary

For over twenty years *Introduction to Biblical Interpretation* has set the standard for evangelical hermeneutics textbooks. It is remarkably comprehensive, clear, accurate, and balanced. This third edition is most welcome.

Mark L. Strauss, Professor of New Testament, Bethel Seminary San Diego

The first two editions of this book have become the standard textbook on biblical interpretation among evangelical circles, and this new edition should be a welcome addition to the bookshelf of any student of the Bible. It is the fruit of a model cooperation over several decades by the same authors who specialize in three different areas: doctrine, the NT, and the OT. The revision is thorough and comprehensive and covers current postmodern questions such as reader-response criticism, narrative criticism, and deconstruction.

David Toshio Tsumura, Professor of Old Testament, Japan Bible Seminary

INTRODUCTION TO
BIBLICAL
INTERPRETATION

THIRD EDITION

WILLIAM W. KLEIN
CRAIG L. BLOMBERG
ROBERT L. HUBBARD, JR.

ZONDERVAN

Introduction to Biblical Interpretation
Copyright © 1993, 2004, 2017 by William W. Klein, Craig L. Blomberg, and Robert L. Hubbard, Jr.

This title is also available as a Zondervan ebook.

Requests for information should be addressed to:
Zondervan, 3900 *Sparks Dr. SE, Grand Rapids, Michigan 49546*

Library of Congress Cataloging-in-Publication Data

Names: Klein, William W. (William Wade), author | Blomberg, Craig L., 1955- author. | Hubbard, Robert L., Jr., 1943- author.
Title: Introduction to biblical interpretation / William W. Klein, Craig L. Blomberg, Robert L. Hubbard, Jr.
Description: Third edition. | Grand Rapids, MI : Zondervan, [2016] | Includes bibliographical references and indexes.
Identifiers: LCCN 2016039056 | ISBN 9780310524175 (hardcover)
Subjects: LCSH: Bible—Hermeneutics.
Classification: LCC BS476 .K545 2016 | DDC 220.601—dc23 LC record available at https://lccn.loc .gov/2016039056

Cover design: Rick Szuecs Design
Cover image: ® Valentin de Boulogne
Interior design: Kait Lamphere
Interior imagery: © Rashad Ashurov/Shutterstock

Printed in the United States of America

---

18 19 20 21 22 23 24 25 26 27 28 /DCI/ 16 15 14 13 12 11 10 9 8 7 6 5 4 3 2

Dedicated to our esteemed mentors:
Donald W. Burdick (†)
D. A. Carson
David A. Hubbard (†)

And to our beloved wives:
Phyllis Klein
Fran Blomberg
Pam Hubbard

TABLE OF CONTENTS

Abbreviations 15
Preface to Third Edition 27
Preface to Second Edition. 29
Introduction 33

PART I—THE TASK OF INTERPRETATION

CHAPTER 1–THE NEED FOR INTERPRETATION 39
  Why Hermeneutics? 40
  Hermeneutics Defined 42
    The Art and Science of Interpretation 42
    The Role of the Interpreter 44
    The Meaning of the Message 45
      The Text 47
      The Author and the Audience 49
  Some Challenges of Bible Interpretation 53
    Distance of Time 53
    Cultural Distance 56
    Geographical Distance. 57
    Distance of Language 58
  Eternal Relevance—The Divine Factor 59
  The Goal of Hermeneutics 61
  Conclusion 63

CHAPTER 2–THE HISTORY OF INTERPRETATION 66
  Jewish Interpretation 66
    Inner-Biblical Allusion. 66
    Post-Biblical Interpretation: The Transition. 69
      Hellenistic Judaism. 70
      The Qumran Community 72
      Rabbinic Judaism 73

The Apostolic Period (ca. AD 30–100) 77
The Patristic Period (ca. AD 100–590) 80
 The Apostolic Fathers (ca. AD 100–150) 81
 The Alexandrian School (ca. AD 150–400) .83
 Church Councils (ca. AD 400–590) 86
The Middle Ages (ca. AD 590–1500) 88
The Reformation (ca. AD 1500–1650) 92
The Post-Reformation Period (ca. AD 1650–1750) 96
The Modern Period (ca. AD 1750–Present) 99
 The Nineteenth Century 99
 The Twentieth Century 102
 Post-World War I 104
 Post-World War II 106
 The Twenty-First Century 111

CHAPTER 3–LITERARY AND SOCIAL-SCIENTIFIC
APPROACHES TO INTERPRETATION 117
 Literary Criticism 118
 Narrative Criticism 119
  Applications 120
  Critique 125
 Poststructuralism/Postmodernism 126
  Reader-Response Criticism 128
  Deconstruction 131
 Social-Scientific Approaches to Scripture 134
 Classification 135
  Social History 135
  Application of Social-Scientific Theories 140
 Advocacy Groups 144
  Liberation Hermeneutics 145
  Cultural Criticism 148
  Feminist Hermeneutics 155
  LGBT Hermeneutics 161
 Conclusion 163

CHAPTER 4–THE CANON AND TRANSLATIONS 165
 The Biblical Canon 165
 The Canon of the Old Testament 166
  The Development of the Canon 166
  The Order of the Canon 171
 The Canon of the New Testament 172

The Development of the Canon 172
The Order of the Canon 177
Criteria of Canonicity 178
Canon Criticism 180
Texts and Translations 183
Textual Criticism 184
Techniques of Translation 191
The Major English Translations 192
Choosing a Translation 196

PART II—THE INTERPRETER AND THE GOAL

CHAPTER 5–THE INTERPRETER 201
Qualifications of the Interpreter 202
A Reasoned Faith in the God Who Reveals 202
Willingness to Obey Its Message 205
Illumination of the Holy Spirit 206
Membership in the Church 208
Willingness to Employ Appropriate Methods 209
Presuppositions for Correct Interpretation 210
Presuppositions about the Nature of the Bible 211
Divinely Inspired Revelation 211
Authoritative and True 213
A Spiritual Document 217
Characterized by Both Unity and Diversity 218
An Understandable Document 220
Forming the Canon of Holy Scripture 221
Presuppositions about Methodology 222
Presuppositions about the Ultimate Goal of Hermeneutics 224
Preunderstandings of the Interpreter 226
Definition of Preunderstanding 227
The Role of Preunderstanding 228
A Philosophy of Interpretation as Preunderstanding 231
Testing Preunderstandings 236
A Christian Preunderstanding 237
Preunderstandings Change with Understanding 239
Preunderstandings and Objectivity in Interpretation 241

CHAPTER 6–THE GOAL OF INTERPRETATION 244
Speech Acts 244

Levels of Meaning 247
   Does the Text Have One Fixed Meaning or Several Levels
    of Meaning? 247
Author-Centered Textual Meaning 263
   Author-Centered Textual Meaning Is the Goal of Interpretation. . . .263
     Definition of Author-Centered Textual Meaning. 265
     The Challenge of Reader-Oriented Interpretation 266
     The Bible as Literature 268
     The Question of Historicity 269
The Place of the Reader in "Constructing" Meaning 271
   Baptism 272
   Millennium 274
   Assessment. 276
Validating Our Interpretation 280
   Agree to Disagree: "That They May Be One" 289

PART III—UNDERSTANDING LITERATURE

CHAPTER 7–GENERAL RULES OF HERMENEUTICS: PROSE 293
The Literary Context 294
   The Importance of Literary Context 295
     Context Establishes the Flow-of-Thought. 295
     Context Provides Accurate Meaning of Words 296
     Context Delineates Correct Relationships among Units:
      Words, Sentences, Paragraphs 297
   Principles of Interpretation Relating to Literary Context 298
   Circles of a Literary Contextual Study. 300
     Immediate Context. 301
     Literary Context of the Entire Bible 305
     Context of the Entire Bible. 308
Historical-Cultural Background 312
   The Significance of the Historical-Cultural Background. 313
     The Issue of Perspective 313
     The Issue of Mindset 314
     The Matter of Contextualization 314
   Principles for Historical-Cultural Interpretation 315
     The Original Historical-Cultural Background. 315
     The Original Impact 317
     The Correct Expression 318
     The Priority of the Plain Sense. 319

Retrieving Historical-Cultural Background. 321
Exploring the General Background of the Book. 321
Examining the Historical-Cultural Factors of a Specific Passage. . .323
Word Meanings 324
Crucial Matters about the Nature of Words. 325
Words are Arbitrary Signs. 325
Words Have a Range of Meanings 327
Word Meanings Overlap 328
Word Meanings Change Over Time .329
Words Have Connotative and Denotative Meanings 331
Steps for Performing Word Studies 332
Grammatical-Structural Relationships 344
The Importance of Grammatical Relationships 346
Steps for Discovering Structural Relationships. 351
Natural Divisions 351
Flow of Thought. 352
Verbs. 355
Connectives 357
Adjectives and Adverbs. 358
Pronouns 359

CHAPTER 8—GENERAL RULES OF HERMENEUTICS:
BIBLICAL POETRY. 361
The Dynamics of Poetry 362
The Sounds of Hebrew Poetry. 364
Rhyme and Meter. 364
The Sounds of Poetic Words. 368
The Structure of Hebrew Poetry 373
Parallelism 373
Basic Units of Parallelism 375
How Parallelism Works 378
Types of Parallelism 379
Other Poetic Structures 389
The Language of Poetry. 395
Imagery 396
Devices of Poetic Language 396
Similes and Metaphors 396
Other Poetic Devices 401
Interpreting Poetic Language. 408
Larger Units of Poetry 409
Sense Units 409

PART IV—UNDERSTANDING BIBLE GENRES

CHAPTER 9–GENRES OF THE OLD TESTAMENT 417
The Nature of Genre 418
Narratives 420
  Old Testament Narrative Genres 421
    Reports 422
    Principles of Interpretation—Reports 424
    Heroic Narrative 425
    Prophet Story 428
    Principles of Interpretation—Heroic Narratives
      and Prophet Stories 429
    Comedy 429
    Principles of Interpretation—Comedy .430
    Farewell speech 431
    Principles of Interpreation—Farewell Speech 431
    Interpreting a Sample Narrative: Judges 7:1–15 432
  Embedded Genres 433
    Popular Proverbs and Blessings 434
    Riddles, Fables, and Parables 434
    Songs 436
    Lists 436
    Principles of Interpretation—Embedded Genres 437
Law 438
  Forms of Old Testament Legal Material 439
    Casuistic Law 439
    Unconditional Law 440
    Legal Series 441
    Legal Instruction 442
    Principles of Interpretation—Law 443
    A Sample Legal Text: Exodus 21:7–11 .449
  Deuteronomy 449
    Principles of Interpretation—Deuteronomy 450
Poetry 451
  Types of Old Testament Poetry 451
    Prayers 451
    Songs 454
    Liturgies 456
    Wisdom Psalms 457
    Principles of Interpretation—Poetry 458
    Principles of Interpretation—Psalms 459

The Books of the Psalms: An Overview. 459
Prophecy. 462
  Basic Types of Prophecy. 463
    Prophecy of Disaster. 463
    Prophecy of Salvation 464
    Woe Speech 465
    Prophetic Dirge 466
    Prophetic Hymn. 467
    Prophetic Liturgy 468
    Prophetic Disputation. 470
    Prophecies Against Foreign Nations 471
    Prophetic Vision Report 472
    Prophetic Narratives 473
  General Principles for Interpreting Old Testament Prophecy. 474
    Interpreting Prophetic "Forthtelling" .475
    Interpreting Prophetic "Foretelling" .479
    The Many Ways of Fulfillment 482
    Specific Principles for Interpretation—Prophecy 487
    A Sample Prophetic Text: Isaiah 5:1–7 488
  Apocalyptic Prophecy 491
    Principles of Interpretation—Old Testament Apocalyptic 492
Wisdom 493
  Types of Wisdom Literature. 494
    Proverbs 494
    Principles of Interpretation—Proverbs 496
    Instruction 497
    Principles of Interpretation—Instruction 498
    Example Story and Reflection 498
    Principles of Interpreation—Example Story and Reflection 499
    Disputation Speeches 500
    Principles of Interpretation—Job 502
    A Sample Wisdom Text: Proverbs 30:24–28. 504
Conclusion 505
How to Write a Structural Outline 505

CHAPTER 10–GENRES OF THE NEW TESTAMENT. 510
Gospels. 510
  Implications for Interpretation. 512
    Historical Trustworthiness. 512
    Reading Horizontally and Vertically. .514
    The Gospels' First Audiences 518

Key Theological Issues. 519
   The Kingdom of God. 519
   The Ethics of Jesus 522
The Forms within the Gospels. 523
   Parables. 524
   Miracle Stories 528
   Pronouncement Stories. 530
   Other Forms. 531
Acts. 532
Implications for Interpretation. 533
   Thinking Vertically 533
   The Significance of Pentecost. 536
   Acts as Narrative. 538
Epistles 541
Implications for Interpretation. 541
   General Considerations 541
   Specific Considerations. 545
   Distinctives of Hebrews and the General Epistles. 549
Individual Forms in the Epistles 551
   Creeds and Hymns. 551
   The Domestic Code 552
   Slogans 552
   Vice and Virtue Lists 554
Key Theological Questions for the Pauline Epistles 555
   Is There a Center of Pauline Theology? 555
   Is There Development in Paul's Writings? 557
Revelation. 558
Revelation as an Epistle 558
Revelation as Prophecy. 561
Revelation as Apocalyptic 562
Conclusion 567

PART V—THE FRUITS OF INTERPRETATION

CHAPTER 11—USING THE BIBLE TODAY 571
To Gain Information and Understanding .572
To Motivate and Enrich Worship. 573
To Create Liturgy. 576
To Formulate Theology 578
   How Biblical and Systematic Theology Differ 580

The Problem of Preunderstanding 581
Must We Choose Between Biblical and Systematic Theology?. 583
How to Formulate Theology: Key Principles 584
What about Church Tradition? 587
To Preach 589
To Teach 591
To Provide Pastoral Care 583
To Promote Spiritual Formation in the Christian Life 595
To Enjoy Its Beauty as Literature 600
Summary 601

CHAPTER 12—APPLICATION 602
The Importance of Application 603
Avoiding Mistakes in Application 605
Total Neglect of Any Context 605
Partial Neglect of the Literary or Historical Context of a Passage . . .607
Insufficiently Analogous Situations 608
A Four-Step Methodology for Legitimate Application. 609
Determine the Original Application(s). 611
Evaluate the Level of Specificity of the Original Application(s) 613
Identify the Cross-Cultural Principles 629
Levels of Authority 630
Find Appropriate Applications that Embody the Broader Principles. . .632
The Role of the Holy Spirit 635

Annotated Bibliography—Hermeneutical Tools .637
Indexes
Scripture Index 683
Extra Biblical Literature Index. 698
Subject Index. 699
Author Index 709

ABBREVIATIONS

Abbreviations in the following lists occur throughout the text of the book and in the footnotes. Abbreviations are also found in the concluding bibliography, which lists extensive sources.

BOOKS OF THE BIBLE AND RELATED WORKS

Hebrew Bible / Old Testament

Gen	Genesis	Song	Song of Songs (Solomon)
Exod	Exodus	Isa	Isaiah
Lev	Leviticus	Jer	Jeremiah
Num	Numbers	Lam	Lamentations
Deut	Deuteronomy	Ezek	Ezekiel
Josh	Joshua	Dan	Daniel
Judg	Judges	Hos	Hosea
Ruth	Ruth	Joel	Joel
1–2 Sam	1–2 Samuel	Amos	Amos
1–2 Kgs	1–2 Kings	Obad	Obadiah
1–2 Chr	1–2 Chronicles	Jonah	Jonah
Ezra	Ezra	Mic	Micah
Neh	Nehemiah	Nah	Nahum
Esth	Esther	Hab	Habakkuk
Job	Job	Zeph	Zephaniah
Ps / Pss	Psalm / Psalms	Hag	Haggai
Prov	Proverbs	Zech	Zechariah
Eccl	Ecclesiastes	Mal	Malachi

New Testament

Matt	Matthew	1–2 Thess	1–2 Thessalonians
Mark	Mark	1–2 Tim	1–2 Timothy
Luke	Luke	Titus	Titus
John	John	Phlm	Philemon
Acts	Acts	Heb	Hebrews
Rom	Romans	Jas	James
1–2 Cor	1–2 Corinthians	1–2 Pet	1–2 Peter
Gal	Galatians	1–2–3 John	1–2–3 John
Eph	Ephesians	Jude	Jude
Phil	Philippians	Rev	Revelation
Col	Colossians		

Deuterocanonical Works

Tob . . . . Tobit

Jdt. . . . . Judith

Wis . . . . Wisdom of Solomon

Sir . . . . Sirach / Ecclesiasticus

Bar . . . . Baruch

Ep Jer . . . . . Epistle of Jeremiah

Add Dan . . . Additions to Daniel

Sus . . . . Susanna

1–2 Macc . . 1–2 Maccabees

1 Esd . . . . . . 1 Esdras

Pr Man . . . . Prayer of Manasseh

3 Macc . . . . 3 Maccabees

2 Esd . . . . . . 2 Esdras

4 Macc . . . . 4 Maccabees

Josephus

Life . . . . Life

Ag. Ap. . . . . Against Apion

Ant. . . . . Jewish Antiquities

J.W. . . . . Jewish War

Talmud

b. B. Bat. . . . Baba Batra

b. Sanh. . . . . Sanhedrin

Apostolic Fathers

1–2 Clem. . . 1–2 Clement

Barn. . . . . . . Barnabas

Did. . . . . . . Didache

Eus . . . . Eusebius

Ign. . . . . Ignatius

Latin Works

Strom . . . . . Miscellanies

Hist. eccl. . . . Ecclesiastical History

Ancient Texts

DSS . . . . . . Dead Sea Scrolls

LXX . . . . . . Septuagint

MT . . . . Masoretic Text

VERSIONS AND EDITIONS OF THE BIBLE

ASV   American Standard Version (1901)

BHS   *Biblia Hebraica Stuttgartensia* (1983)

CEV   *Holy Bible: Contemporary English Version* (Copyright © 1995; American Bible Society)

ESV   *Holy Bible: English Standard Version* (Copyright © 2001; Crossway)

GNB   *Good News Bible* (NT © 1966, OT © 1976; American Bible Society)

GNT   Greek New Testament

HCSB   *Holman Christian Standard Bible* (NT 1999, complete 2006; © 1999, 2000, 2002, 2003, 2009; Holman Bible Publishers)

JB   *Jerusalem Bible* (Copyright © 1966; Darton, Longman & Todd Ltd. and Doubleday and Company Ltd.)

KJV	Holy Bible: King James Version (1611)
LB	*The Living Bible* (Copyright © 1971; Tyndale House Publishers, Inc.)
NCV	*The New Century Version Bible* (Copyright © 2005; Thomas Nelson)
NA[28]	*Novum Testamentum Graece*, 28th ed. (Copyright © 2012; Erwin Nestle, Barbara Aland, and Kurt Aland)
NAB	*New American Bible* (Copyright © 1970; Confraternity of Christian Doctrine)
NASB	*New American Standard Bible* (Copyright © 1960, 1962, 1963, 1968, 1971, 1972, 1973, 1975, 1977, 1995; The Lockman Foundation)
NEB	*New English Bible* (Copyright © 1961, 1970; Cambridge University Press and Oxford University Press)
NET	*New English Translation* (Copyright © 1996–2006; Biblical Studies Press, L.L.C.)
NIV	*Holy Bible: New International Version* (Copyright © 1973, 1978, 1984, 2011; Biblica, Inc.®)
NJB	*New Jerusalem Bible* (Copyright © 1985; Darton, Longman & Todd, Ltd. and Doubleday)
NKJV	*Holy Bible: New King James Version* (Copyright © 1982; Thomas Nelson)
NLT	*Holy Bible: New Living Translation* (Copyright © 1996, 2004, 2007, 2013; Tyndale House Foundation)
NRSV	*Holy Bible: New Revised Standard Version* (Copyright © 1989; National Council of the Churches of Christ in the United States of America)
Phillips	*New Testament in Modern English* (Copyright © 1960, 1972; J. B. Phillips)
REB	*Revised English Bible* (1989)
RSV	*Holy Bible: Revised Standard Version* (Copyright © 1946, 1952, 1971; National Council of the Churches of Christ in the United States of America)
TEV	*Today's English Version* (Copyright © 1992; American Bible Society)
TNK	*Tanakh: The Holy Scriptures: The New Jewish Publication Society Translation According to the Traditional Hebrew Text* (1988)
UBS[5]	*The Greek New Testament*, 5th ed. (2014); United Bible Societies)

JOURNALS, MAJOR REFERENCE WORKS, AND SERIALS

AB	Anchor Bible
ABD	*The Anchor Bible Dictionary*. Edited by David Noel Freedman. 6 vols. New York: Doubleday, 1992
AcBib	Academia Biblica
ACCS	Ancient Christian Commentary on Scripture
AIL	Ancient Israel and Its Literature

AJEC	Ancient Judaism and Early Christianity
AnBib	Analecta Biblica
ANEA	*The Ancient Near East: An Anthology of Texts and Pictures*. Edited by James B. Pritchard. Princeton: Princeton University Press, 2010
ANEP	*The Ancient Near East in Pictures Relating to the Old Testament*. 2nd ed. Edited by James B. Pritchard. Princeton: Princeton University Press, 1994
ANET	*Ancient Near Eastern Texts Relating to the Old Testament*. 3rd ed. Edited by James B. Pritchard. Princeton: Princeton University Press, 1969
AnOr	*Analecta Orientalia*
ApOTC	Apollos Old Testament Commentary
AsTJ	*Asbury Theological Journal*
ATANT	Abhandlungen zur Theologie des Alten und Neuen Testaments
ATD	Das Alte Testament Deutsch
AThR	*Anglican Theological Review*
AUSS	*Andrews University Seminary Studies*
AYBRL	Anchor Yale Bible Reference Library
BA	*Biblical Archaeologist*
BBR	*Bulletin for Biblical Research*
BBRSup	*Bulletin of Biblical Research, Supplements*
BCBC	Believers Church Bible Commentary
BCOTWP	Baker Commentary on the Old Testament Wisdom and Psalms
BDAG	Danker, Frederick W., Walter Bauer, William Arndt, and F. Wilbur Gingrich. *Greek-English Lexicon of the New Testament and Other Early Christian Literature*. 3rd ed. Chicago: University of Chicago Press, 2000
BDB	Brown, Francis, S. R. Driver, and Charles A. Briggs. *A Hebrew and English Lexicon of the Old Testament*
BDF	Blass, Frederick, Albert Debrunner, and Robert W. Funk. *A Greek Grammar of the New Testament and Other Early Christian Literature*. Chicago: University of Chicago Press, 1961
BECNT	Baker Exegetical Commentary on the New Testament
BETL	Bibliotheca Ephemeridum Theologicarum Lovaniensium
Bib	*Biblica*
BibInt	*Biblical Interpretation*
BibInt	Biblical Interpretation Series
BibSem	The Biblical Seminar
BJRL	*Bulletin of the John Rylands University Library of Manchester*
BNTC	Black's New Testament Commentary
BRev	*Bible Review*
BSac	*Bibliotheca Sacra*
BSNA	Biblical Scholarship in North America
BST	Bible Speaks Today

BT	*The Bible Translator*
BTB	*Biblical Theology Bulletin*
BZ	*Biblische Zeitschrift*
BZAW	Beihefte zur Zeitschrift für alttestamentliche Wissenschaft
CAH	Cambridge Ancient History
CBAA	Catholic Biblical Association of America
ConBNT	Coniectanea Biblica: New Testament Series
CBQ	*Catholic Biblical Quarterly*
CBQMS	Catholic Biblical Quarterly Monograph Series
CC	Continental Commentaries
CHB	*Cambridge History of the Bible*
CHJ	*Cambridge History of Judaism*. Edited by William D. Davies and Louis Finkelstein. 4 vols. Cambridge: Cambridge University Press, 1984–2006
ChrCent	*Christian Century*
CSR	*Christian Scholar's Review*
CT	*Christianity Today*
CTJ	*Calvin Theological Journal*
CTR	*Criswell Theological Review*
CurBR	*Currents in Biblical Research* (formerly *Currents in Research: Biblical Studies*)
Did	*Didaskalia*
DOTHB	*Dictionary of the Old Testament: Historical Books*. Edited by Bill T. Arnold and H. G. M. Williamson. Downers Grove, IL: InterVarsity Press, 2005
DOTP	*Dictionary of the Old Testament: Pentateuch*. Edited by T. Desmond Alexander and David W. Baker. Downers Grove, IL: InterVarsity Press, 2003
DOTWPW	*Dictionary of the Old Testament: Wisdom, Poetry, and Writings*. Edited by Tremper Longman III and Peter Enns. Downers Grove, IL: InterVarsity Press, 2008
EBC	*Expositor's Bible Commentary*
ECC	Eerdmans Critical Commentary
EcR	*Ecclesiastical Review*
EDNT	*Exegetical Dictionary of the New Testament*. Edited by Horst Balz and Gerhard Schneider. 3 vols. Grand Rapids: Eerdmans, 1990–1993
ERT	*Evangelical Review of Theology*
EvQ	*Evangelical Quarterly*
EvT	*Evangelische Theologie*
ExAud	*Ex Auditu*
ExpTim	*Expository Times*
FAT	Forschungen zum Alten Testament

FOTL	Forms of the Old Testament Literature
FRLANT	Forschungen zur Religion und Literatur des Alten und Neuen Testaments
GBS	Guides to Biblical Scholarship
GNTE	Guides to New Testament Exegesis
GTJ	*Grace Theological Journal*
HACL	History, Archaeology, and Culture of the Levant
HALOT	*The Hebrew and Aramaic Lexicon of the Old Testament.* Edited by Ludwig Koehler, Walter Baumgartner, and Johann J. Stamm. Translated and edited under the supervision of Mervyn E. J. Richardson. 4 vols. Leiden: Brill, 1994–1999
HBT	*Horizons in Biblical Theology*
HDR	Harvard Dissertations in Religion
Herm	Hermeneia Commentary
HeyJ	Heythrop Journal
HSM	Harvard Semitic Monographs
HTR	*Harvard Theological Review*
HUCA	*Hebrew Union College Annual*
IB	*Interpreter's Bible.* Edited by George A. Buttrick et al. 12 vols. New York, 1951–1972
IBMR	*International Bulletin of Missions Research*
ICC	International Critical Commentary
IDB	*The Interpreter's Dictionary of the Bible.* Edited by G. A. Buttrick. 4 vols. New York: Abingdon, 1962
IDBSup	*Interpreter's Dictionary of the Bible: Supplementary Volume.* Edited by Keith Crim. Nashville: Abingdon, 1976
Int	*Interpretation*
ISBE	*International Standard Bible Encyclopedia.* Edited by Geoffrrey W. Bromiley. 4 vols. Grand Rapids: Eerdmans, 1979–1988
ISBL	Indiana Studies on Biblical Literature
ITQ	*Irish Theological Quarterly*
IVPNTC	InterVarsity Press New Testament Commentary
JAAR	*Journal of the American Academy of Religion*
JBL	*Journal of Biblical Literature*
JBR	*Journal of Bible and Religion*
JETS	*Journal of the Evangelical Theological Society*
JHebS	*Journal of Hebrew Scriptures*
JLT	*Journal of Literature and Theology*
JPT	*Journal of Pentecostal Theology*
JPTSup	Journal of Pentecostal Theology Supplements
JSJ	*Journal for the Study of Judaism in the Persian, Hellenistic, and Roman Periods*

JSJSup	Journal for the Study of Judaism in the Persian, Hellenistic, and Roman Periods Supplements
JSNT	*Journal for the Study of the New Testament*
JSNTSup	Journal for the Study of the New Testament Supplements
JSOT	*Journal for the Study of the Old Testament*
JSOTSup	Journal for the Study of the Old Testament Supplements
JTI	*Journal for Theological Interpretation*
JTISup	*Journal for Theological Interpretation* Supplements
JTS	*Journal of Theological Studies*
KBL	Koehler, Ludwig, and Walter Baumgartner. *Lexicon in Veteris Testamenti libros*. 2nd ed. Leiden, 1958
L&N	Louw, Johannes P., and Eugene A. Nida, eds. *Greek-English Lexicon of the New Testament: Based on Semantic Domains*. 2nd ed. New York: United Bible Societies, 1989
LHBOTS	The Library of Hebrew Bible/Old Testament Studies
LNTS	The Library of New Testament Studies
LSJ	Liddell, Henry George, Robert Scott, Henry Stuart Jones. *A Greek-English Lexicon*. 9th ed. with revised supplement. Oxford: Clarendon, 1996
MM	Moulton, James H., and George Milligan. *The Vocabulary of the Greek New Testament*. London, 1930. Repr., Peabody, MA: Hendrickson, 1997
MNTC	*Moffatt New Testament Commentary*
NAC	New American Commentary
NBBC	New Beacon Bible Commentary
NCB	New Century Bible
NCBC	New Cambridge Bible Commentary
NCHB	New Cambridge History of the Bible
NEA	*Near Eastern Archaeology*
NEAEHL	*New Encyclopedia of Archeological Excavations in the Holy Land*. Edited by Ephraim Stern. 4 vols. Jerusalem: Israel Explorations Society & Carta; New York: Simon & Schuster, 1993
NICNT	New International Commentary on the New Testament
NICOT	New International Commentary on the Old Testament
NIDB	*New Interpreter's Dictionary of the Bible*. Edited by Katharine Doob Sakenfeld. 5 vols. Nashville: Abingdon, 2006–2009
NIDNTT	*New International Dictionary of New Testament Theology*. Edited by Colin Brown. 4 vols. Grand Rapids: Zondervan, 1975–1978
NIDNTTE	*New International Dictionary of New Testament Theology and Exegesis*. Edited by Moisés Silva. 5 vols. Grand Rapids: Zondervan, 2014
NIDOTTE	*New International Dictionary of Old Testament Theology and Exegesis*. Edited by Willem A. VanGemeren. 5 vols. Grand Rapids: Zondervan, 1997

NIGTC	New International Greek Testament Commentary
NIVAC	The NIV Application Commentary
NovT	*Novum Testamentum*
NovTSup	Supplements to *Novum Testamentum*
NSBT	New Studies in Biblical Theology
NTA	*New Testament Abstracts*
NTC	New Testament Commentary
NTL	New Testament Library
NTS	*New Testament Studies*
OEANE	*The Oxford Encyclopedia of Archaeology in the Near East.* Edited by Eric M. Meyers. 5 vols. New York: Oxford University Press, 1997
OECS	Oxford Early Christian Studies
OTA	*Old Testament Abstracts*
OTG	Old Testament Guides
OTL	Old Testament Library
OTS	Old Testament Studies
OtSt	*Oudtestamentische Studiën*
PNTC	Pillar New Testament Commentary
PRSt	*Perspectives in Religious Studies*
RelSRev	*Religious Studies Review*
ResQ	*Restoration Quarterly*
RevExp	*Review and Expositor*
RSP	*Ras Shamra Parallels*
SAP	Sheffield Academic Press
SBET	*Scottish Bulletin of Evangelical Theology*
SBLDS	Society of Biblical Literature Dissertation Series
SBLMS	Society of Biblical Literature Monograph Series
SBLSP	Society of Biblical Literature Seminar Papers
SBT	Studies in Biblical Theology
SBTS	Sources for Biblical and Theological Study
SemeiaSt	Semeia Studies
SFSHJ	South Florida Studies in the History of Judaism
SJOT	*Scandinavian Journal of the Old Testament*
SJT	*Scottish Journal of Theology*
SNTSMS	Society for New Testament Studies Monograph Series
SP	Sacra Pagina
SSN	Studia Semitica Neerlandica
StBibLit	Studies in Biblical Literature (Lang)
STDJ	Studies on the Texts of the Desert of Judah
STJ	*Stulos Theological Journal*
SUNT	Studien zur Umwelt des Neuen Testament

SVTQ	*St. Vladimir's Theological Quarterly*
SwJT	*Southwestern Journal of Theology*
TB	Theologische Bücherei
TDNT	*Theological Dictionary of the New Testament.* Edited by Gerhard Kittel and Gerhard Friedrich. Translated by Geoffrey W. Bromiley. 10 vols. Grand Rapids: Eerdmans, 1964–1976
TDOT	*Theological Dictionary of the Old Testament.* Edited by G. Johannes Botterweck and Helmer Ringgren. Translated by John T. Willis et al. 8 vols. Grand Rapids: Eerdmans, 1974–2006
THAT	*Theologisches Handwörterbuch zum Alten Testament.* Edited by Enrst Jenni, with assistance from Claus Westermann. 2 vols. Munich: Chr. Kaiser Verlag; Zürich: Theologischer Verlag, 1971–1976
Them	*Themelios*
THNTC	Two Horizons New Testament Commentary
Theol	*Theology*
TJ	*Trinity Journal*
TLOT	*Theological Lexicon of the Old Testament.* Edited by Ernst Jenni, with assistance from Claus Westermann. Translated by Mark E. Biddle. 3 vols. Peabody, MA: Hendrickson, 1997
TLZ	*Theologische Literaturzeitung*
TNTC	Tyndale New Testament Commentaries
TOTC	Tyndale Old Testament Commentaries
TU	Texte und Untersuchungen
TWOT	*Theological Wordbook of the Old Testament.* Edited by R. Laird Harris, Gleason L. Archer Jr., and Bruce K. Waltke. 2 vols. Chicago: Moody Press, 1980
TynBul	*Tyndale Bulletin*
UBC	Understanding the Bible Commentary Series
USQR	*Union Seminary Quarterly Review*
VE	*Vox Evangelica*
VT	*Vetus Testamentum*
VTSup	Supplements to *Vetus Testamentum*
WAW	Writings from the Ancient World
WBC	Word Biblical Commentary
WMANT	Wissenschaftliche Monographien zum Alten und Neuen Testament
WTJ	*Westminster Theological Journal*
WUNT	Wissenschaftliche Untersuchungen zum Neuen Testament
WW	*Word and World*
ZAW	*Zeitschrift für die alttestamentliche Wissenschaft*
ZBK	*Zürcher Bibelkommentare*
ZECNT	Zondervan Exegetical Commentary on the New Testament

ZNW	*Zeitschrift für die neutestamentliche Wissenschaft und die Kunde der älteren Kirche*
ZPEB	*Zondervan Pictorial Encyclopedia of the Bible.* Edited by Merrill C. Tenney. 5 vols. Grand Rapids: Zondervan, 1975

GENERAL ABBREVIATIONS

abbrev.	abbreviated
ad loc.	*ad locum,* at the place discussed
ANE	ancient Near East
ca.	*circa*
c.	century
cf.	*confer,* compare
ch(s).	chapter(s)
contra	in contrast to
diss.	dissertation
ed(s).	edition, edited by, editor(s)
e.g.	*exempli gratia,* for example
enl.	enlarged
esp.	especially
et al.	*et alii,* and others
ET	English translation
f(f).	and the following one(s)
fem.	feminine
FS	*Festschrift*
Ger.	German
Gr.	Greek
Heb.	Hebrew
Hiph.	Hiphil
Hith.	Hithpael
idem	the same
i.e.	*id est,* that is
lit.	literally
loc.	locative
loc. cit.	*loco citato,* the place cited
MS(S)	manuscript(s)
masc.	masculine
n.d.	no date
niph.	niphal
no(s).	number(s)
n.s.	new series

NT	New Testament
orig.	original
OT	Old Testament
p(p).	page(s)
pace	with due respect to, but differing from
par.	parallel (to)
para.	paragraph
passim	here and there
pl.	plural
Q	*Quelle* (Ger. "sayings" source for the Gospels)
repr.	reprint(ed)
rev.	revised, reviser, revision
sing.	singular
s.v.	*sub verbo*, under the word
trans.	translator, translated by
UBS	United Bible Societies
unpubl.	unpublished
upd.	updated
v(v).	verse(s)
viz.	*videlicet*, namely
vol(s).	volume(s)
vs.	versus
X	times (as in 3X = three times)

PREFACE TO
THIRD EDITION

We three authors are enormously gratified that a third edition of our book is warranted. The first edition appeared in 1993 to be followed about a decade later in 2004 by edition two. Now, after an elapse of a little more than another decade, we are pleased to offer this third edition to a new generation of students. The subject of hermeneutics—biblical interpretation—continues to occupy prominence in the fields of biblical and theological studies. That assessment is certainly borne out in the ongoing flood of articles, essays, and books that appear—some, like this one, in multiple editions. That should be no surprise: what the Bible *means* by what is written, and what its significance is to the church and individual believers, are not insignificant issues. In fact, they are paramount!

We followed the process of composing this edition in the same ways as in the preceding editions, and we ask readers to review the "Preface to Second Edition" for that process. Happily, Robert Hubbard returned to live in Denver a few years ago, so we have enjoyed, again, the opportunity for in-person engagement in our writing and editing (and warm friendship). This book represents one of the delights of scholarly collaboration—the chance to work together as friends and colleagues, as well as to pool our scholarship for the sake of Christ's church.

Like the edition before it, this third edition reflects some important changes due to developments in the extensive fields that we attempt to cover. For example, we give much more space to speech-act theory than in the former edition. Beyond that, we have updated the discussions on two fronts. First, what we three veteran Bible teachers write here builds on more than one hundred years of combined teaching and study. We believe our refinements in this volume reflect our more mature (and we hope more adequate and correct) thinking about this crucial task. Second, we have witnessed many advances as well revisions in various scholars' thinking and writings about the topics we engage; we need to interact with these scholars in our goal to be faithful interpreters of God's Holy Scriptures. These advances, we believe, require that we revisit and refine some of the things we said a dozen years ago.

As with the previous editions, we continued to profit from many colleagues both at Denver Seminary (Blomberg and Klein), and at North Park University (Hubbard). Some of their insights appear at various places, as well as in the footnotes—though often without specific acknowledgement. In addition, we have benefitted from our students in our classes and from colleagues in various institutions who have used the book—both in their teaching and studying. Many of these scholarly colleagues are also reflected in the footnotes and bibliography of the book. These resources are extensive and expansive, our conscious tactic that we hope will allow interested readers to pursue in more detail some of the matters that we are able to pursue far too briefly (although students might complain that the book is too large already!). And we repeat what we acknowledged in the previous preface: many people have influenced our thinking and ways of expression in ways that we can no longer recall or properly document. We give them our grateful thanks nonetheless. As well, books do not land on publishers' lists without the significant efforts of editors. We wish to thank Katya Covrett, Executive Editor of Zondervan Academic, for encouraging us to produce this edition.

As before, we acknowledge three mentors who blazed some trails of biblical interpretation for us to follow: Donald W. Burdick, D. A. Carson, and David A. Hubbard. We thanked them previously and do so again. But to this trio of men we add a trio of women. With this edition we gratefully honor our three wives from whom we have also learned much about the nature and importance of biblical interpretation, each in their own ways. So thank you: Phyllis Klein, Fran Blomberg, and Pam Hubbard. You have blessed us with your godly examples and faithful discipleship in the ways of Christ. While Paul wrote his words about two women in Philippi, well do we apply them to our wives, ". . . these women since they have contended at [our] side in the cause of the gospel . . . whose names are in the book of life" (Phil 4:3).

William W. Klein
Craig L. Blomberg
Robert L. Hubbard, Jr.

February 2016

PREFACE TO
SECOND EDITION

M uch has happened within the discipline of biblical interpretation in the years since the first edition of this book appeared in 1993. Many worthy volumes and innumerable articles, essays, and chapters have appeared steadily over the years. Clearly this remains a "hot topic," as it should. In addition, the landscape of biblical studies and biblical interpretation has changed in many ways. We are faced with new understandings of how language functions, the rise and demise of several approaches to evaluating texts, differing attempts to assess the nature of meaning, and the increased influence of postmodernism, to name a few. Several important translations and versions of the Bible have appeared.

We have been gratified to witness the widespread use of the first edition of this book since it was published. It has served as a textbook in many classes in colleges and seminaries. It has been translated into several other languages and is used widely. But, given the changes over these past years, we welcomed the opportunity to alter the way we said some things, to rearrange some of the parts, to bring some issues from the appendix into the main text, and, *very importantly*, to bring the discussions of many issues, the footnotes, and the annotated bibliography up to date. We have read many reviews of the book and have learned from reviewers and users their assessments of its strengths and weaknesses. As we approached the process of revision, we solicited and received targeted and extremely helpful comments from several valued colleagues in other institutions who have used the book regularly in their classes. We appreciate very much the time and effort they gave us in their assessments.

We offer this volume to advance the practice of biblical interpretation—also called hermeneutics—in this generation. A comprehensive yet readable text, it covers all the key issues in interpreting the Bible. We have incorporated insights from beyond biblical studies themselves—philosophy, linguistics, the social sciences, and literary criticism, among others. We have written this book not merely to collate and report others' findings—though we have certainly done much of that—but also to propose our own strategy for this crucial venture of interpretation. The book brims with biblical examples to demonstrate the principles under discussion. We strive to show students not merely what interpretation is all about, but *how* to interpret.

How did such a book emerge, and how do three authors write a book together?

Initially Dr. Klein proposed the idea of a new volume on hermeneutics and wrote the original outline. Soon he realized how formidable a task this would be, so he recruited three colleagues, all professors at Denver Seminary, and they divided the tasks of research and writing equally among themselves. Unexpectedly, other Seminary responsibilities forced Dr. Kermit Ecklebarger to withdraw from the project. He was able to provide input for the chapters on the history of interpretation, general rules of hermeneutics, and application. The task fell to the remaining three—Dr. Klein and Dr. Blomberg covered the New Testament field, and Dr. Hubbard represented Old Testament studies.

To maximize the value of our backgrounds and expertise, we decided that all three would be involved in everything produced. So each wrote his assigned sections and then read the others' drafts. We made extensive comments and suggested revisions, deletions, or insertions. Where genuine differences and disagreements surfaced we discussed the issues until a consensus was reached; we wanted to produce a text that all could affirm. Ultimately, Dr. Klein served as the final editor with freedom to alter and edit as necessary to produce the final manuscript.

Since the first edition appeared, Robert Hubbard moved from Denver to take up a teaching post at North Park Theological Seminary in Chicago. Drs. Blomberg and Klein remain at Denver Seminary. We three employed the same approach in this revision as we did in the initial writing. We returned each chapter to its original author to perform the initial revision—taking into consideration all the reviews and comments we received. We circulated each revised chapter to the other two authors for comments, critique, suggestions for revisions and corrections, and then returned it to the author for a rewrite in view of these reactions. We were more ruthless with each other than before. When we were satisfied that we had the best product, William Klein again did the final editing. We hope that the resulting volume weds the best of our individual and joint competencies. We have verified the truth of the proverb, "As iron sharpens iron, so one man sharpens another" (Prov 27:17). By absorbing each other's critical comments, we grew to appreciate one another's abilities and understanding of God's truth. We have remained good friends, and we believe our joint efforts have produced a volume that will yield a rich harvest of faithful interpreters and doers of God's Holy Word.

We wish to thank Wayne Kinde, Director of Reference and Professional Books at Thomas Nelson, for enthusiastically agreeing to produce this second edition. As well, it was a pleasure to work directly with Lee Hollaway, Managing Editor of Nelson Reference & Electronic Publishing, who helped oversee the project in a hands-on way. We were again assisted and blessed by the efforts of several colleagues at Denver Seminary—with research assistance by Prof. Elodie Emig and the word processing and indexing skills of Ms. Jeanette Freitag. Our research also benefited from sabbaticals granted by our schools, from their fine libraries and expert staffs, and from the input of teaching assistant Paul Corner of North Park Theological Seminary. We also thank the theological faculty of the University of Tübingen, Germany, for its hospitality and the use of its excellent libraries during one sabbatical.

No book surfaces apart from the contributions of numerous people beyond the author or, in this case, authors. Dr. Timothy P. Weber graciously read the chapter on the history of interpretation. Dr. M. Daniel Carroll R. provided extensive comments on the chapters on the Old Testament. Our numerous references readily acknowledge the work of our colleagues in the scholarly arena. No doubt many others contributed to our thinking, but we were unaware of their input, gained as it was over the years, and are unable to acknowledge it beyond this admission. Yet four individuals—not adequately featured in the footnotes—have made a lasting impression on our lives. They were our first mentors in graduate biblical studies. They not only honed our skills in interpretation, but they also ignited an enduring love for the Bible. Each stressed the need to know not only *what* the Bible says, but also what the Bible *means* by what it says. We pray that we can pass on the same mindset to our students. We rededicate this second edition to these mentors, three of whom now reside in the presence of their Lord. So we laud Donald W. Burdick (†), D. A. Carson, David A. Hubbard (†), and A. Berkeley Mickelsen (†). Well might the writer of Hebrews have spoken of this quartet when he admonished:

> Remember your leaders, who spoke the word of God to you. Consider the outcome of their way of life and imitate their faith. (Heb 13:7)

Thank you, brothers, for what you have meant to us.

William W. Klein
Craig L. Blomberg
Robert L. Hubbard, Jr.
31 October 2003

INTRODUCTION

Almost daily, the average Christian is challenged to obey God's Word. How well we sense the urgency of Jesus' words to that Israelite woman of long ago, "Blessed rather are those who hear the word of God and obey it!" (Luke 11:28 NRSV). And James' words ring out in our minds: "Do not merely listen to the word, and so deceive yourselves. Do what it says" (Jas 1:22). The Psalmist assures us, "Your word is a lamp to my feet, a light for my path" (Ps 119:105). We believe we can grow in our relationship with God, we can develop into more spiritually-wise disciples, and we can become increasingly useful servants of God—if we will believe and follow God's instructions in the Bible. How much more effective we could be—how much more Christ-like—if we would make Bible study and application integral parts of our lives. We face the challenge to become *biblical* Christians: Christians who learn what God's Word says, and who humbly, obediently, put it into practice. In an era of increasing biblical illiteracy, this appeal becomes ever more urgent.

But how are we to learn what the Bible says? How do we mine its resources? What are we to learn and how are we to respond? Can we know if we have understood the message correctly? Our goal in writing this book is to help answer these questions, to unravel some of the mysteries of biblical interpretation.

Admittedly, it can be daunting to face a voluminous Bible full of alien genealogies, barbaric practices, strange prophecies, and eccentric Epistles. It would be so much simpler if the "experts" would simply assemble God's instructions for us in a nice systematic list. But God did not provide a mere list of principles and practices. Dare we reduce the Bible to such a level? However much we might prefer that God's revelation came in a different form, we bow to his wisdom in giving us the Bible as it stands. We are convinced that when we understand the nature of the Bible and what God has done in providing it, we will see that it cannot be reduced to a list of beliefs to espouse, attitudes to adopt, actions to pursue, nor the corresponding opposites to avoid. In his wisdom, God has given his people the kind of revelation he decided would be best for us. Our task is to understand and respond to what God has communicated in ways that demonstrate our obedience and faithfulness to that revelation. We have to come to terms with the Bible *as it is*! And that is precisely what we intend to help the reader accomplish.

But in order to execute the task of correct biblical interpretation, we must first understand what biblical interpretation is. Thus, in *Part I* we define hermeneutics

33

and demonstrate the crucial need for careful and valid hermeneutical principles. To understand how to interpret the Bible today requires an appreciation of our predecessors in the biblical faith. So we investigate the various approaches and techniques people have employed to understand Scripture throughout history. We want to learn from them—appropriating what is valid and valuable while avoiding their mistakes and pitfalls.

In recent years, some biblical scholars and interpreters have issued a call for a radical shift in the focus of interpretation. Several new, and in some cases esoteric, methods have arisen in both literary-critical (e.g., deconstruction) and social-scientific (e.g., feminist hermeneutics) studies. While some readers of this textbook may not add all of these tactics to their arsenals of interpretative methods, they offer some definite assistance to interpreters. In addition, their presence on the modern scene requires us to provide students with some assessment of their procedures and usefulness.

A most valuable legacy of our spiritual ancestors is the biblical canon. We provide insight and perspective on the formation of the Bible. In addition, we will consider the phenomenon of Bible translation and seek to help readers navigate through the maze of competing versions available today.

In *Part II* we consider first the interpreter—the qualifications and presuppositions that are necessary and appropriate for the task of biblical interpretation. Hermeneutics has long been concerned with unraveling the meaning of the ancient texts. But until recently sufficient attention was not given to those seeking to understand that meaning—to the interpreters themselves. Interpreters are not blank slates or empty sponges; who they are contributes greatly to the entire enterprise of understanding. So beyond qualifications and presuppositions, we investigate the concept of "preunderstanding"— what interpreters bring with them to the task of interpretation. Having described the interpreter, we will then raise the question of the *goal* of interpretation—what it is that we seek. Is the goal to determine the meaning the authors intended, the meaning in the texts themselves, or the meaning produced when text and modern interpreter interact? Can we say that a text has (or produces) only one possible meaning, or should we seek different meanings or levels of meaning within it? Or, to change the question, can texts have meanings that their authors intended while containing an additional meaning or meanings placed there by the Holy Spirit to be recovered by subsequent readers? Can we assure that our interpretations are valid? These are foundational questions, and their answers have enormous implications for our task because issues of life and eternity are determined by a proper understanding of God's message.

In *Part III* we proceed to establish basic, commonly accepted principles for understanding how literature—both prose and poetry—functions. The Bible is fundamentally a literary document, and we must understand it as such. We survey the various literary, cultural, social, and historical issues involved in interpretation. Since languages function according to specific rules and principles, interpreters must understand these rules in order to study the texts properly. The goal is not to complicate matters, but to achieve better understanding. We aspire to the greatest precision and accuracy in the process of interpretation.

Part IV introduces the reader to the specific kinds of literature (or genres) found in the Bible, and gives an overview of the appropriate methodologies for understanding the meaning conveyed by each. We describe each genre—Law (the Bible's legal material), OT historical narrative, poetry, prophecy, wisdom literature, OT apocalyptic, Gospels, NT historical narrative (Acts), Epistles, and Apocalypse—and show how the interpreter needs to study each one to comprehend its message fully.

Undoubtedly, readers have a variety of reasons for wanting to study the Bible. *Part V* seeks to make accessible the practical wealth of the Bible by investigating, briefly, the various ways it ministers to God's people. Whether they use the Bible to help others (in teaching, preaching, or counseling a friend), or to seek for personal spiritual encouragement, or simply to worship the God of the universe, the Bible has proved its value since its origin. What is more, the Bible serves as the source book for the church's theology—for its understanding of God's perspective on life and his will for his people.

In essence, the Bible is God's written revelation to his people. It records in human words what God has mandated for them. Thus, a significant question for every student of the Bible is: How can we *apply* the Bible to our lives today? *Part V* considers this essential question of personal application. This task is not always easy, for the biblical message moves across centuries and cultures. And precisely because the Bible came to people within their own cultures and experiences thousands of years ago, modern Christians are not always sure how literally they should implement what the Bible commands. They are puzzled about how to move from the principles in a passage to appropriate modern application. When we read what God required of the ancient Israelites or the first-century Christians, we puzzle over his expectations for us today. If pork and shrimp were forbidden for God's people in 1200 BC (Lev 11:7, 10–12), on what basis, if any, can we rescind that prohibition today? If Paul required women in the Corinthian church of AD 57 to wear appropriate head coverings (1 Cor 11:4–6, 13), may twenty-first-century women disregard his instructions? Christians insist on following Jesus' instructions to his disciples to celebrate the Lord's Supper: "This is my body given for you; *do this* in remembrance of me" (Luke 22:19; emphasis added). Should we not also perform another clear instruction: ". . . you also should wash one another's feet. I have set you an example that *you should do* as I have done for you" (John 13:14–15; italics added)? These are pivotal issues for the Christian who sincerely wants to apply the Bible correctly to his or her life.

To aid biblical interpreters, whether novice or experienced, we have provided an Annotated Bibliography of suggested helps. As carpenters, programmers, or surgeons require tools to do their work, so interpreters need specific tools. Throughout the book we argue for a responsible approach to discerning the meaning of the biblical texts. That approach often requires insights and information accumulated by specialists.

In this final section we list those resources we feel interpreters will find most useful in the full range of tasks needed for effective interpretation. The Bibliography is a practical list for students to *use* in Bible interpretation. For the more technical details and documentation of the approach to biblical interpretation developed in this book, readers can consult the footnotes at appropriate points.

We have a final word to teachers who employ this as a textbook: each chapter was designed to be self-contained in scope. The chapters can be assigned for study in various sequences, for each can stand on its own. This also means there is some minor overlap and repetition in the discussions of a few topics. We usually cross-reference topics to alert readers to locations where an issue receives more detailed discussion.

Part I

THE TASK OF
INTERPRETATION

1

THE NEED FOR
INTERPRETATION

M aking sense of Scripture is an arduous and often puzzling task. We may readily explain what the Bible *says*, but have more difficulty in agreeing about what it *means* by what it says. And, often even more troublesome, modern Christians differ wildly on how the Bible's words should influence their lives today, if at all. Consider some of the difficult tensions we face in this task:

- The Bible is God's Word, yet it has come to us through human means. The commands of God appear to be absolute, yet they are set in such diverse historical contexts that we are hard-pressed to see how they can be universally normative.
- The divine message must be clear, yet many passages seem all too ambiguous.
- We acknowledge the crucial role of the Holy Spirit, yet scholarship is surely necessary to understand what the Spirit has inspired.
- The Scriptures present the message God wants us to hear, but that message is conveyed within a complex literary landscape with varied genres and over a huge span of time.
- Proper interpretation requires the interpreter's personal freedom, yet that freedom comes with considerable risks of bias and distortion. Is there some role for an external, corporate authority?
- The objectivity of the biblical message seems essential to some readers, yet on the one hand presuppositions surely inject a degree of subjectivity into the interpretive process, while on the other postmodernity calls the very concept of objectivity into question.[1]

Every student of the Bible could add his or her own list of troublesome and perplexing issues. How can we be successful in our attempts to understand the Scriptures correctly? We need a well-thought-out approach to interpreting the Bible. And that is precisely where hermeneutics comes in.

The meaning of this term can be ambiguous in current usage, so we need to explain the sense in which we will use it in this book. *Hermeneutics* describes the task

---

1. Adapted from M. Silva, *Has the Church Misread the Bible? The History of Interpretation in the Light of Current Issues* (Grand Rapids: Zondervan, 1987), 37–38.

of explaining the meaning of the Scriptures. The word derives from the Greek verb *hermēneuō* that means "to explain, interpret or to translate," while the noun *hermēneia* means "interpretation" or "translation." Using the verb, Luke informs us that Jesus *explained* to the two disciples on the Emmaus road what the Scriptures said about him (Luke 24:27). Paul uses the noun in 1 Corinthians 12:10 to refer to the gift of *interpretation* of tongues. In essence, then, hermeneutics involves interpreting or explaining. In fields like biblical studies or literature, it refers to the task of explaining the meaning of a piece of writing.[2]

Hermeneutics describes the principles people use to understand what something means, to comprehend what a message—written, oral, or visual—is endeavoring to communicate.

WHY HERMENEUTICS?

But what does hermeneutics have to do with reading and understanding the Bible? Haven't God's people through the millennia read and understood the Scriptures without recourse to hermeneutics? Actually, the answer to this second question is no. For though we might not always be conscious of it, unless certain things are in place we would not be able to comprehend anything.

Think of normal everyday life. We engage in conversations or read a book, and we unconsciously interpret and understand the meanings we hear or read. When we watch a television program, listen to a lecture, or read a blog or an article about a familiar subject in our own culture and language, we interpret intuitively and without consciously thinking of using methods. Though unaware of the process, we employ methods of interpretation that enable us to understand accurately. This explains why

---

2. Two points require clarification here. First, in this book we are using the term hermeneutics in what might be called its traditional sense: a systematic study of principles and methods of interpretation. Seminal thinkers like Schleiermacher, Dilthey, Heidegger, Fuchs, Ebeling, Gadamer, Ricoeur, and others use hermeneutics in a more philosophical sense to identify how something in the past can "mean" today or become existentially significant in the modern world. The term "new hermeneutic" describes this program to move hermeneutics from mere rules for understanding texts to a more far-reaching understanding of understanding. Its practitioners would say they have shifted hermeneutics out of the realm of merely explaining, to providing an in-depth understanding of human existence. To fathom the intricacies of the "new hermeneutic" requires a separate discussion that lies beyond our scope here, although some further perspectives will be presented in the chapters that follow. We refer readers to A.C. Thiselton, *The Two Horizons: New Testament Hermeneutics and Philosophical Description with Special Reference to Heidegger, Bultmann, Gadamer, and Wittgenstein* (Exeter: Paternoster; Grand Rapids: Eerdmans, 1980); A. C. Thiselton, *New Horizons in Hermeneutics* (Grand Rapids: Zondervan, 1992); A. C. Thiselton, *Hermeneutics: An Introduction* (Grand Rapids: Eerdmans, 2009); E.V. McKnight, *Meaning in Texts: Historical Shaping of a Narrative Hermeneutics* (Philadelphia: Fortress, 1978); and K. J. Vanhoozer, *Is There a Meaning in This Text?: The Bible, the Reader and the Morality of Literary Knowledge*, anniv. ed. (Grand Rapids: Zondervan, 2009). Second, readers will sometimes encounter the singular term "hermeneutic." Typically, this refers to a specific and self-acknowledged standpoint or frame of reference that an interpreter adopts to interpret a text or utterance. Usually this approach implies an established ideology, specific attitudes, and a definite approach. Thus, a "feminist hermeneutic" will adopt a way of reading a text that conforms to the premeditated confines of a feminist ideology. Substitute "womanist," "African-American," "Marxist," "*mujerista*," "liberationist," "queer," or "Freudian" for the word "feminist" and you can see how adopting a frame of reference will program a reading or hermeneutic of the text.

normal communication "works." If there were no system, understanding would occur only randomly or occasionally, if at all.[3]

But is reading the Bible like this? Can we understand the Bible correctly merely by reading it? Some people are convinced that we can. One seminary professor tells how a distraught student once interrupted a seminar on principles for understanding the Bible. Fearful that he might have offended the student, the teacher asked if anything was wrong. Mournfully, the student responded, "I feel so sorry for you."

"Why do you feel sorry for me?" The professor was perplexed.

"Because," said the student, "it is so hard for you to understand the Bible. I just read it and God shows me the meaning."

How Illumination of the Holy Spirit Helps Believers Understand Scripture
Convinces reader the Bible is true
Gives the ability to apprehend, not comprehend, the meaning
Leads to conviction that enables reader to embrace its meaning

Does the Holy Spirit tell people what the Bible means? While this approach to biblical interpretation may reflect a commendable confidence in God, it reveals a simplistic (and potentially dangerous) understanding of the illumination of the Holy Spirit and the clarity of Scripture—important issues that we will take up in due course. As we will argue, the role of the Spirit in understanding God's Word is indispensable. The Spirit convinces God's people of the truth of the biblical message and then convicts and enables them to live consistently with that truth. However, apart from extraordinarily rare and unusual circumstances, the Spirit does not inform readers of Scripture's *meaning*. That is, the Spirit's help does not replace the need to interpret biblical passages according to the principles of language communication.

Through the centuries, if people have correctly understood God's Word, it is because they have employed proper principles and methods of interpretation. That does not mean, of course, that they all had "formal" biblical training. Rather, they were good readers—they used common sense and had enough background to read accurately. Equally, others seriously misunderstood what the Bible meant, sometimes with lamentable results. *What this book aspires to do, then, is to uncover and explain what makes a "good reader" and to provide the principles to enable Bible readers to read accurately while avoiding mistakes.*

The need for such principles becomes more obvious when one is in an unfamiliar domain—such as a lecture on astrophysics or with a highly technical legal document. Terms, allusions, and concepts are strange and perhaps incomprehensible. We immediately perceive a need for help in deciphering the message. How are we to make sense of antiquarks, the weak anthropic principle, or neutrinos? Who can tell us how

---

3. To introduce OT genres (chap. 9) and the idea of "interpretive competence," we provide four examples of texts that we easily identify using hermeneutics.

to distinguish a *habeas corpus* from a *corpus delicti*? We cannot simply make up our own meanings, or merely ask a random person who might be nearby. We need the help of specialized resources or an expert. Taking a physics class might help in the first situation, while consulting a lawyer would be helpful in the second.[4]

At times understanding even the most straightforward communication is not so clear-cut. For example, to understand a father's statement to his daughter, "You will be home by midnight, won't you?" will probably require decoding various cues beyond the simple meanings of individual words. To determine whether this is an inquiry, an assumption, or a command will require a careful analysis of the entire situation. How much more complicated this task is when one seeks to make sense of an ancient text written by people in centuries past! What does Genesis 1:2 have in mind when it says, "Now the earth was formless and empty, darkness was all over the surface of the deep . . . ?" What did Jesus mean when he said, ". . . for they make their phylacteries broad and their fringes long" (Matt 25:3)? We might kindly ask the distraught student mentioned above, "Will the Holy Spirit tell you what phylacteries are, or must you use some source to supply the meaning?" The great distances of time and culture between those ancient writers and us require some bridges if we are to gain understanding.

But beyond the meaning of the text itself (what it meant in the original context for authors and recipients), faithful biblical readers also want to know the significance of that text for themselves. They ask, "What is this text saying to me and what difference should it make in my life, if any?"

If the goal is correct understanding of communication, we need an approach and methods that are appropriate to the task. Hermeneutics provides the means for understanding the Scriptures and for applying that meaning responsibly. To avoid interpretation that is arbitrary, erroneous, or that simply suits personal whim, the reader needs methods and principles for guidance. A deliberate procedure to interpret based on sensible and agreed-upon principles becomes the best guarantee that an interpretation will be accurate. When we consciously set out to discover and employ such principles, we explore hermeneutics—biblical interpretation.[5] *Thus, the basic goal of this book will be to establish, explain, and demonstrate guidelines and methods to guide those who want to understand and apply Scripture correctly.*

HERMENEUTICS DEFINED

The Art and Science of Interpretation

Interpretation is not *either* an art *or* a science; it is *both* an art *and* a science. Every form of communication uses "codes" of some sort—cues in sounds, spelling, tone

---

4. Of course, in today's world online search engines can give us a rough and ready answer for many such questions.

5. We will use the terms hermeneutics and biblical interpretation interchangeably in what follows.

of voice, etc.—to convey meaning. We use rules, principles, methods, and tactics to "decode" messages we hear, see, or read. Yet, human communication cannot be reduced solely to quantifiable and precise rules. No mechanical system of rules will ever help one understand correctly all the implications or nuances in the three words "I love you" as spoken by a teenage girl to her boyfriend, a husband to his wife of twenty-five years, a mother to her child, or an aging baby boomer to his mint-condition '57 Chevy. This is where the "art" of interpretation enters in. Adults may think they understand the words "awesome," "sweet," or "dude"[6] (or any popular teenage word), but without knowing the codes of a specific youth subculture, they may be wide of the mark. Similarly, youth may find words of their grandparents like "far out" or "smashing"—words common in their youth—unintelligible.

In light of this, how much more must modern biblical interpreters seek to bridge the linguistic, historical, social, and cultural gaps that exist between the ancient and modern worlds so that they may understand what texts mean? We assume that people communicate in order to be understood, and this includes the authors of the Scriptures. Hermeneutics provides a strategy that will enable us to understand the meaning and significance of what an author or speaker intended to communicate.

Are we presuming that there is only one possible meaning of a text or utterance and that our goal is to understand the author's intention in writing that text? Alas, an answer to this question is not so simple. Perhaps, given a specific text, we must ask whether it has only one correct meaning or whether it may accommodate several or many possible meanings (perhaps at different levels). On one end of the spectrum, some say that the only correct meaning of a text is that single meaning the original author intended it to have.[7] On the other end stand those who argue that meaning is a function of readers, not authors, and that any text's meaning depends upon the readers' perception of it.[8] Readers, they say, actually "create" the meaning of a text in the process of reading it. Between the two poles stand other options. Perhaps meaning resides independently in the texts themselves, regardless of what the author meant or of what later readers understand from them. Or perhaps meaning results from some dynamic, complex dialogue between a reader and a text. These issues are crucial because our definition of the task of hermeneutics will depend on our answer to where meaning resides—in the author's mind, in the text, in the mind of the reader, or in some combination of these. We will return to these questions in the chapters that follow.

---

6. Is a "dude" a cowboy, a guy, or merely a sentence starter akin to "man" in "Man, is that a cool shirt"? It all depends on the context.

7. The name often associated with the stress on meaning as a function of authorial intention is E. D. Hirsch. He articulates and defends this view in *Validity in Interpretation* (New Haven: Yale University Press, 1967) and *The Aims of Interpretation* (Chicago: University of Chicago, 1976). An early proponent in the field of biblical studies was K. Stendahl, "Implications of Form Criticism and Tradition Criticism for Biblical Interpretation," *JBL* 77 (1958): 33–38.

8. A key figure among the several we could mention is S. E. Fish, *Is There a Text in This Class? The Authority of Interpretive Communities* (London and Cambridge, MA: Harvard University Press, 1980).

The Role of the Interpreter

What role does the interpreter play in the hermeneutical process? We must realize that just as the biblical text arose within historical, personal processes and circumstances, so interpreters are people in the midst of their personal circumstances and situations. For example, the phrase "white as snow" makes perfect sense to a resident of Colorado where we live, though it may be rather inconsequential. For skiers or snowboarders, details about the nature of the snow on wintry slopes are more important. In contrast, the phrase will be completely incomprehensible to a tribesman from Kalimantan who has no idea what snow is, much less its color. Then the resident of Chicago will have another perspective, wistfully recalling what used to be white while grumbling about the dirty, rutted, frozen snow that impedes the commute to work.

In other words, people understand (or misunderstand) "white as snow" based on what they already know or have experienced. Does this mean that because we live in an age and location far removed from people of the Bible we are doomed to misunderstand its message? No, but we need approaches and tools that will guide us to interpret it as accurately as possible—that is, to become better readers. But we also need to take into account the presuppositions and preunderstandings we bring to the task of interpretation. To fail to realize what interpreters bring to the task of Bible reading opens them to distortion and misunderstanding.

Thus, while hermeneutics must give attention to the ancient text and the conditions that produced it, responsible interpretation cannot ignore the circumstances and the understanding of those who attempt to explain the Scriptures today. No one interprets in a vacuum; everyone has presuppositions and preunderstandings. Dr. Basil Jackson, a leading Christian psychiatrist, learned this hermeneutical lesson during his youth when a Plymouth Brethren elder in Ireland told him, "Wonderful things in the Bible I see, most of them put there by you and me."[9] This is truer than we wish it to be.

Of course, one cannot interpret without some preunderstanding of the subject.[10] Yet no one should approach biblical interpretation assuming that their current preunderstanding is sufficient to guide them. It is understandable for a sincere Christian to affirm, "the Bible was written *for* me," but that does not mean that it was written *to* her or him. In effect we are reading someone else's mail! The authors and the original recipients lived long ago. If we seek to understand the Bible strictly through the lenses of our own experiences, we run the risk of misunderstanding the message. One extreme example was reported by a Christian counselor. A woman explained to her therapist that God had told her to divorce her husband and marry another man (with whom she was romantically involved). She cited Paul's command in Ephesians 4:24 (KJV), "Put on the new man," as the key to her "divine" guidance. As humorous

---

9. B. Jackson, quotation from a lecture at Denver Seminary, March 1991.

10. On these points see the classic article by R. Bultmann, "Is Exegesis Without Presuppositions Possible?" in *Existence and Faith,* ed. S. Ogden (London: Hodder and Stoughton, 1961), 289–96.

as this sounds, she was absolutely serious.[11] Although modern translations clarify that Paul was instructing believers to replace their sinful lifestyle with a Christian one, this woman, preoccupied with her marital problems, read her own meaning into the passage. Yet far less obvious examples of this error occur regularly when people read or teach the Bible. We want to show why this approach is wrong.

However, an accurate analysis of the Bible is not simply a matter of applying with scrupulous honesty and accuracy certain precise techniques. Things are not so simple. When we try to understand each other's communication, scientific precision seems to elude our grasp. In fact, even the so-called objective or hard-science researchers recognize the influence of values. How a researcher frames a question may determine the nature of the results that emerge. To raise a controversial question: Is there some "objective" way to answer the question of when human life begins? Values (preunderstandings) play a huge role in the answers. What one brings to the question colors one's answer. David Tracy observes, "Former claims for a value-free technology and a history-free science have collapsed. The hermeneutical character of science has now been strongly affirmed. Even in science, we must interpret in order to understand."[12]

No one comes to the task of understanding as an objective observer. All interpreters bring their own presuppositions and agendas, and these affect the ways they understand as well as the conclusions they draw.[13] In addition, the writer or speaker whom the interpreter wishes to understand also operates with a set of presuppositions. We humans mediate all our understanding through a grid of personal history and bias. Our prior experiences and knowledge—our total background—shape what we perceive and how we understand. So can we study Scripture texts objectively and accurately? Though we will argue that objective *certainty* in interpretation will always elude our grasp, we propose a critical hermeneutical approach that will provide standards and tactics to guide us in navigating through the variable and subjective human factors to enable us to arrive at the most likely understanding of the biblical texts' meaning.

The Meaning of the Message

At this point, it will help to explain our approach to language by using some of the categories of speech act theory. Consider how any type of oral or written communication involves three elements:

---

11. H. L. Bussell, *Unholy Devotion: Why Cults Lure Christians* (Grand Rapids: Zondervan, 1983), 119.

12. D. Tracy, *Plurality and Ambiguity: Hermeneutics, Religion, Hope* (San Francisco: Harper, 1987), 33.

13. To take just one obvious example, those who believe that women should be ordained as ministers have no difficulty detecting those biblical passages that emphasize the crucial role women played in the Bible and throughout church history. Yet those who argue for a view of the role of women in the church that precludes ordination point to those passages they believe teach the subordination of women. Among other issues, no doubt, presuppositions and agendas clearly influence what evidence interpreters value more highly and what weight they give to various kinds of evidence. A classic documentation of this phenomenon occurs in W. Swartley, *Slavery, Sabbath, War, and Women: Case Issues in Biblical Interpretation* (Scottdale, PA: Herald Press, 1983). For defenders of the two views mentioned see the various essays in J. R. Beck, ed., *Two Views on Women in Ministry*, rev. ed. (Grand Rapids: Zondervan, 2005).

1. *Locution.* This refers to what is spoken or written: the words, sentences, in a given statement or discourse. A simple example consists of Jesus' assertion, "You are the light of the world" (Matt 5:14).

2. *Illocution.* This identifies the intention the speaker or writer has by using those specific words. What do the words actually accomplish? What energy does the author employ? What "content" does the author convey? This focuses what the author was seeking to "do" to or for the readers. We might say that Jesus intended to *encourage* his disciples to "brighten up" their world by doing "good deeds" (Matt 5:16). Or perhaps he wanted to *inform* them of their identity as his disciples: they are to be lights in a world characterized by darkness.

3. *Perlocution.* This refers to what the speaker or writer envisioned the outcome or results to be for the listener or reader. Probably Jesus intended that the disciples engage in all manner of good works that show their commitment to God's kingdom priorities. The world would be a brighter place because of their deeds. This may be Jesus' intended outcome. Of course, we can often never know to what extent an outcome was achieved.[14]

All this is related to but separate from the additional factors of the *meaning* of what is said (what do the words "light" and "world" and the phrase "light of the world" mean?), how a given hearer or reader actually understands the message, and how he or she responds, if at all. All these combine to determine "meaning."[15] Authors' words may convey more than they intended, but the point is that authors normally determine *what* they will say, *how* they will encode their message to accomplish their intention, and what *results* they hope to achieve.

When we seek to understand the meaning of a biblical text, we possess only the words on a page. The author is no longer available to explain what was "meant." The first hearers or readers remain equally inaccessible, so we cannot ask them to tell us how they understood the message. Only by means of the written text itself (the locution) in its context can we hope to reconstruct the meaning of the utterance (considering both illocution and perlocution) the author most likely intended. Recognizing these "speech act" distinctions remind us that we must consider more than only the words

14. We will have more to say about the various features of so-called speech act theory below. John H. Walton and D. Brent Sandy, *The Lost World of Scripture* (Downers Grove: InterVarsity, 2013), 41, use a simple example of a wedding vow to illustrate these terms. "When the bride and groom say 'I do' they are using a very basic *locution*—words that could be used in any number of contexts with varieties of meaning. But in this context they are used for a specific *illocution*: a lifetime vow of faithfulness and commitment. The resulting *perlocution* is the implementation of that vow throughout life" (emphasis added). See also the section in J. K. Brown, *Scripture as Communication. Introducing Biblical Hermeneutics* (Grand Rapids: Baker Academic, 2007), 32–35. Brown also uses the example of the couple's words, "I do."

15. Following a more semantically based model, G. B. Caird investigates the phenomenon of meaning in some detail in *The Language and Imagery of the Bible* (Philadelphia: Westminster, 1980), especially pp. 32–61. Under "meaning" he assesses referential meaning, sense, value, entailment, and intention. These overlap somewhat with our three categories. The meaning encoded in the text itself (in our example, "light of the world") probably relates most closely to his referential meaning, though that in no way exhausts what a text "means." For a valuable discussion of these semantic relations see J. Lyons, *Linguistic Semantics: An Introduction* (Cambridge: Cambridge University Press, 1996).

on the page (locution) and what they mean. Any appraisal of "meaning" must take into consideration this complex interplay of text, author, and audience.

The Text

How can the utterance or text itself help in discovering the message the author intended to convey or the message the hearers understood? Clearly, one basic factor is to determine the meanings of the terms that are used. We must adopt an approach to understanding the meaning of words that considers precisely their referential, denotative, connotative, and contextual meanings.

Type of Word Meaning	Definition	An Example
Referential	What a word "refers to"	"Tree" refers to the large plant outside my office
Denotative	Precise or direct meaning of the word	"Tree" denotes a woody perennial plant, at least several feet high with an erect main stem and side branches[16]
Connotative	Special suggestive sense that grows out of its denotative meaning in some way	Jesus died on a "tree" (1 Pet 2:24), meaning, the cross
Contextual	Specific sense suggested by a word's use in a specific context that limits it to one of the above.	In the sentence, "I love that apple tree," the sense required by the context is the denotative meaning.

Briefly, *referential* meaning specifies what some words or terms "refer to." In other words, one meaning of the word "tree" is (or refers to) a large woody and leafy plant growing outside that bears apples in the fall. Denotative and connotative meanings speak of complementary aspects of a word's meaning. Words may denote a specific meaning. A biologist could provide a specific, scientific definition of tree that would represent its *denotative* meaning. But in a specific instance the word "tree" might take on special meanings or *connotations*, as when Peter observes that Jesus died on a *tree* (1 Pet 2:24; ESV, NET, NASB). In that instance the term has a unique significance for Christians for whom "tree" graphically recalls that Jesus was crucified. Connotations, then, include a word's emotional overtones—the positive or negative associations it conjures up beyond what the word strictly denotes. The "hanging tree" used for executing criminals also conveys connotative meaning—a sad, sober feeling for crimes, their perpetrators, and their victims. In these uses, "tree" means more than the biologist's explanation, just as that scientific explanation pales before the

---

16. Of course, this is only the botanical meaning of the word "tree." The word also occurs with different denotative meanings as in linguistics where we may find a "tree diagram." We also use the word in "family tree" and "shoe tree," to name a few others.

view of a spreading chestnut tree under which the village smithy stands.[17] Peter's use also illustrates *contextual* meaning, for when we read his words we quickly conclude that he does not refer to a literal tree at all. In the context, tree means "cross," which is how the NIV and NRSV, among others, render the word.[18]

Words do not occur in isolation in a text. All languages present their words in a system of grammatical and literary structures—sentences, paragraphs, poems, discourses, and whole books. We must understand how the biblical languages function if we are to understand what the writers meant by their words. A crucial dimension involved in understanding an utterance is the specific literary genre and writing style the author employed to convey his or her message. We interpret the words in a poem differently from those in a letter or a story. We expect ambiguity or figures of speech to convey a meaning in poetry that differs from the more concrete sense of words in a historical narrative.

In fact, much recent study has focused upon the literary dimensions of the Bible, of both individual passages and whole books, and any responsible procedure to interpret Scripture must address this dimension.[19] When we receive a business letter in the mail, we expect it to follow a fairly standard format. For the most part, the biblical writers also used and adapted literary forms and conventions that were standard when they wrote. Thus, in order to understand the books of the Bible as literary documents and to appreciate the various dimensions—both cognitive and aesthetic—of what we read in the Scriptures, we need to employ the insights and methods of literary criticism. The use of literary-critical (and historical) methods to understand the biblical writings is crucial. The uniqueness of Scripture pertains to its content as God's revelation and to the process God employed to convey his truth through human instruments. That process included the use of specific and varying literary features. Those literary features are culturally based in the ancient world and require our critical analysis to achieve understanding.

What does it mean to study the Bible from a literary-critical standpoint? Leland Ryken provides some help. Speaking of the literary dimensions of the NT, he argues that we must be "alive to the images and experiential concreteness of the New Testament" (and the OT, we would hasten to add) while resisting "the impulse to reduce literary texts to abstract propositions or to move beyond the text to the history behind it." He adds, "this means a willingness to accept the text on its own terms and to concentrate on reliving the experiences that are presented."[20] To take a literary approach to the Bible means entering, living, and understanding its world before we move beyond it to abstract meaning. It also means that we study the texts in terms of their genre, that is, in keeping with their

---

17. Or compare the metaphorical use of "tree" by John the Baptist: "The ax is already at the root of the trees, and every tree that does not produce good fruit will be cut down and thrown into the fire" (Matt 3:10). For an OT example, recall the "flourishing tree" to which someone who wisely meditates on Torah compares (Ps 1).

18. Of course, this raises the question about the task of translators when they attempt to convey in English what the Greek *means*. Which is more "literal" (a loaded term), to render the Greek word *dendron* as "tree" or "cross"? Which conveys the sense better to a modern reader? We will have more to say about this in the chapter on translations.

19. We will take this up in detail in our later chapters on prose, poetry, and genres.

20. L. Ryken, *Words of Life: A Literary Introduction to the New Testament* (Grand Rapids: Baker, 1987), 22–23.

own conventions and intentions. It requires that we appreciate the artistry and beauty of texts, that we savor the nuances of language, and that we apply appropriate techniques for teasing out the meaning in the extensive poetic sections.[21] Ryken summarizes his principle in the formula "meaning through form." In a nutshell, "we cannot derive the meaning of the New Testament (or the OT) without first examining its form."[22]

To conclude, part of the meaning recorded in the Bible derives from the forms the authors employed in their writing. We risk missing much of significance if we attempt merely to formulate abstract propositions from the texts we analyze. As we noted above, the meaning of a text embodies not merely "content," but how it is constructed (locutions) and to what ends (illocutions and perlocutions). How much of the meaning of passages such as Psalm 23 or 1 Corinthians 13 will we miss if we extract only theological statements? To grasp the text fully—and, more importantly, to *be grasped* by it fully—means to enjoy the "pleasure of the text," to engage it joyfully and adventurously with our mind, emotions, and imagination.[23]

The Author and the Audience

Although we cannot ask the authors directly for clues to the meaning they intended to convey, an examination of their respective contexts (historical setting, general social values and conditions, and specific life circumstances), when known, can provide helpful information for interpretation.[24] Similarly, knowing as much as possible about the conditions that surround the recipients of the original message provides further insight into how they most likely understood the message,[25] as does the relationship, if any, between the author and recipients at the time of writing.[26]

Of course, if we are seeking the meaning the author/editor intended for the

---

21. This same "nuance-savoring" approach also applies to OT narratives, especially in their use of characterization, plot, dialogue, and other features.

22. Ryken, *Words of Life*, 24.

23. We borrow the phrase from R. Barthes, *The Pleasure of the Text* (New York: Hill & Want, 1975).

24. This principle also extends to the compilers and editors we credit with finishing OT books, e.g., Psalms, Proverbs, Deuteronomy, Jeremiah, etc. More on this below.

25. Through his analysis of Mark's Gospel, R. H. Stein, "Is Our Reading the Bible the Same as the Original Audience's Hearing It?" *JETS* 46 (2003): 63–78, identifies six key features that describe its intended readers. One crucial finding, one that interpreters often forget, is that Mark's audience originally consisted of *hearers*; they did not read the Gospel silently (as you are now reading this footnote). Of course, this is true for most of the books in the Bible: they were composed to be heard aloud; after all, most people were illiterate within these oral cultures. How might this affect how we interpret? Among other points, Stein suggests that this likely precludes all the very elaborate structures that scholars sometimes "find" in the biblical books (e.g., book-length chiasms). Normal, unlearned, common believers in the first century had "to process the information being read to them, *as it was being read*" (p. 74). On the other hand, Stein may be overly pessimistic here. If books were designed to be read and reread repeatedly, the author could choose to embed subtler, even elaborate, structures. Each biblical book needs to be assessed on its own terms.

26. For example, the situation of some NT Epistles is simpler than, say, that of OT prophetic oracles. In the former we may be able to isolate such information to aid our understanding of the written text. In the latter we may have little or nothing to help us understand the relationship between a prophet and the original audience who heard his or her spoken message, not to mention the final "product" that emerged in written form perhaps decades or even centuries later. Likewise, we may be able to discover little if anything about the relationship between the editor of the final form of a book and the readers—whether it be Deuteronomy, Isaiah, or John's Gospel. These points illustrate the larger problem with which we must deal as interpreters.

original recipients, that meaning *must* be what they could have understood at that time, not some meaning later readers would determine based on later historical and theological (or scientific) understanding. Obviously, we have access to the full canon of Scripture. We know how the whole story turned out, so to speak. We also have the benefit of creeds and councils and two millennia of theological reflections.[27] In seeking to understand the meaning of a given text in Scripture, we cannot impose insights that derive exclusively from this later information.

What we have just said raises, however, an important question about the "movement" that we describe briefly at the conclusion of chapter 2 below: Theological Interpretation of Scripture (TIS). This program consists of "those readings of biblical texts that consciously seek to do justice to the perceived theological nature of the texts and embrace the influence of theology (corporate and personal; past and present) upon the interpreter's enquiry, context, and method."[28] They see their program as a return to those approaches that characterized the study of Scripture prior to the Enlightenment, especially in the church fathers.[29] Adherents of TIS have reacted against the hegemony of the historical-critical methods and what they perceive as its sterile results and seek to return the locus of interpretation to the church and the believing community. As opposed to the academic scholars who stand "over" the text and subject it to their critical analyses, the TIS positions the interpretive task as standing "under" the Scriptures as God's communication to his people. Readers will see below how these values correspond with many of the presuppositions that we will defend in chapter 5.

But TIS often embraces a tactic that troubles us. It's best to quote proponent R. R. Reno here: "Insofar as theological analysis claims to be faithful to Scripture and yet draws upon material and makes formulations not found within the literal sense of Scripture, it functions as a kind of spiritual interpretation, an extension beyond the literal sense."[30] In other words, in TIS the meaning of a text may need to be explained not by the historical intention of the human author in composing that text, but by the larger canon of Scripture and by how the church has come to understand that text. This is troublesome to us, for it puts the putative meaning of a biblical locution not in the illocution and perlocution intended by the author (under the inspiration of the Holy Spirit), but in the way readers (even ancient ones) seem to have come to understood that. The danger is that TIS puts the authority of a text of the Bible not

---

27. However, the divergence of "theological systems" shows there is no consensus about many things. As a result, later readers are liable to read their own conclusions into the texts.

28. D. C. Spinks, *The Bible and the Crisis of Meaning: Debates on the Theological Interpretation of Scripture* (London: T&T Clark, 2001), 7. For a thorough review of both the benefits and pitfalls in this movement see G. R. Allison, "Theological Interpretation of Scripture: An Introduction and Preliminary Evaluation," *SBJT* 14 (2010): 28–36; and D. A. Carson, "Theological Interpretation of Scripture: Yes, But . . . ," in *Theological Commentary: Evangelical Perspective*, ed. R. M. Allen (London: T&T Clark, 2011), 187–207.

29. One seminal article was D. C. Steinmetz, "The Superiority of Pre-Critical Exegesis," *Theology Today* 37 (1980): 27–38.

30. R. R. Reno, "From Letter to Spirit," *International Journal of Systematic Theology* 13 (2011): 468.

in that divine text itself but in how the church fathers, or the creeds, or some church community understands the meaning of that text. As we will argue in more detail below, the *meaning* of the text for study is the meaning the author intended for his readers. At the same time, the *significance* of that text may need to be understood within the larger context of the entire canon and the trajectory of that message for the church's existence. The assignment of that significance may well be understood by the guidance of the Holy Spirit (or apart from the Spirit), but that is different than saying that the biblical text *means* what later interpreters construe it to mean. This may turn out to be a version of "reader-response" interpretation. But more on all this in later sections.

It would be out of bounds to read in information from the NT in interpreting the original illocution (the author's intention) of an OT text. It would not have been available to the author, and the first readers could never have discerned that information. Again, we cannot impose on a biblical author information that we possess because of our accumulated current knowledge—whether historical, astronomical, or theological—or expect that an ancient writer possessed our knowledge. If we read into the biblical texts information the authors could not have possessed, we distort their meaning. For example, when Isaiah speaks of the "circle of the earth" (Isa 40:22), he may well employ a flat-earth model (that is, as seen from God's heavenly throne, the earth looks like a flat, round disk). To hear him on his terms requires that we resist the temptation to impose our scientific, spherical cosmology upon the text. Because we know "the rest of the story," we have to make a special effort to recreate how the writers understood things and the impact their words had on their original recipients who lacked our knowledge.

This also works on another level because the Bible contains not only the words of the final author or editor of each book but also the words of people whose stories they report—and in some cases the results of, perhaps, generations of tradition that was passed on.[31] We may be intensely interested in what the historical Jesus said on specific occasions, but we do not have transcripts of the actual words he spoke (probably in Aramaic).[32] We have only the evangelists' Gospels, originally written in Greek and now translated into modern languages. To achieve their purposes for writing (illocutions and perlocutions), they selected and recast Jesus' words and actions in their unique ways (their locutions). This need not mean that the evangelists distorted or misconstrued what Jesus said, nor, as some Bible scholars suggest, that the evangelists actually attributed words to Jesus that he never said. Our point is simply that at all points we must take the Bible as it is—the final form of the Hebrew, Aramaic, and Greek texts we possess.

---

31. Walton and Sandy, *The Lost World*, 30, discuss the origin of some biblical books composed under the authority and aegis of an original figure and subsequently added to, compiled, and then "published" as final written texts—perhaps many years later. They defend this proposition: "Expansions and revisions were possible as documents were copied generation after generation and eventually compiled into literary works." See their important elaboration on pp. 30–38.

32. "Red letter" editions of the Gospels may give the (mistaken) impression that we have direct quotes of Jesus, though quotation marks in other Bibles may leave the same impression. What may be worse is that red letters tend to reinforce the mistaken notion that Jesus' words are somehow *more* inspired or authoritative than all other Bible verses.

The report that God sent Saul an "evil spirit" (1 Sam 16:14–16; etc.) illustrates how easily we may read later information into our reading of the OT.[33] In the NT an "evil spirit" is a demon (e.g., Mark 1:26 par.), so we might presume that the same phrase identifies the tormentor of Saul as a demon. This assumption overlooks two points of background: to read the OT phrase as "an evil spirit from God" implies that God sends demons on people—a conclusion that conflicts with the biblical teaching that God does not associate with "evil." In addition, it wrongly assumes that the OT has an awareness of the demonic world, which does not seem to be the case. Instead, we might better translate the Hebrew as "bad spirit" or "harmful spirit" (ESV), i.e., "foul mood," "depression" or "a tormenting spirit that filled him with depression and fear" (NLT; cf. Judg 9:23[34]). The error consists in imposing a meaning on the locution (the actual words used) that may well conflict with the illocution (the author's intent given his own understanding).[35]

Jesus' parable of the Good Samaritan also illustrates the danger of reading a later understanding into our interpretation of biblical texts. When we call the Samaritan "good," we betray how far removed we are from sensing the impact the parable had on the Jewish legal expert who first heard this memorable story (Luke 10:25). We must remember that the Jews despised the Samaritans as half-breeds. How shocked the lawyer would be when Jesus made a hated Samaritan the hero of his story—as shocked as Jews of today would be if one of their storytellers portrayed a Palestinian as more heroic or sympathetic than leading Jewish figures! The Samaritan may be "good" to us, but not to the original hearers. Jesus' intention, his illocution, was to use the Samaritan in the story to jolt the lawyer into a reconsideration of his view of the command to love. Accurately understanding the Bible requires that we take into account any preconceptions we carry that could distort the text's meaning. Our goal remains to hear the message of the Bible as the original audiences would have heard it.

We must avoid the tendency to regard our own experience as the grid through which we see and read. All of us suffer from the same propensity: to view our own perceptions of the world as normative, valid, and true. Naturally, we are apt to read the Bible through the lens of this tendency. For example, though today we readily see slavery as an abhorrent evil, it is amazing how many leading Christians defended this inhuman institution prior to the US Civil War. Using the book of Philemon, J. H. Hopkins defended slavery in the nineteenth century saying,

---

33. For a helpful discussion of the issues in this passage see D. Tsumura, *The First Book of Samuel*, NICOT (Grand Rapids: Eerdmans, 2007), 426–28.

34. For additional insight on the use of "evil spirit" in this text, see D. I. Block, *Judges, Ruth*, NAC 6 (Nashville: Broadman & Holman, 1999), 322–24.

35. We acknowledge that our example here of an evil spirit is notoriously complex, as examples elsewhere of a "deceiving spirit" (e.g., in 1 Kgs 22:19–23; cf. 2 Chr 18:18–22) also portray. Our point is not to solve such complex problems as to warn against reading in a later development into an earlier text. On 1 Kgs 22 see P. R. House, *1, 2 Kings*, NAC 8 (Nashville: Broadman & Holman, 1995), 236–38; and Simon J. DeVries, *1 Kings*, 2nd ed., WBC 12 (Dallas: Word, 2003), 268.

He [Paul] finds a fugitive slave, and converts him to the Gospel, and then sends him back again to his old home with a letter of kind recommendation. Why does St. Paul act thus? Why does he not counsel the fugitive to claim his right to freedom, and defend that right . . . ? The answer is very plain. St. Paul was inspired, and knew the will of the Lord Jesus Christ, and was only intent on obeying it. And who are we, that in our modern wisdom presume to set aside the Word of God . . . ?[36]

Based on his own worldview and experiences, Hopkins believed slavery was a commendable and biblically sanctioned institution.

Like Hopkins, we may unconsciously assume that our own experiences parallel those of the ancients—that life and landscape parallel things "back then." In one sense this is natural. But when we simply allow our unchallenged feelings, values, and observations to misunderstand or determine whether consciously or unconsciously what the Bible means, our experiences have become the measure for what a text can intend.[37] We must adopt an approach to interpretation that confronts this danger, for Scripture alone constitutes the standard of truth for Christians, and we must judge our values and experiences based on its precepts, not vice-versa. It follows, then, that any valid approach to interpretation must concern itself with two crucial dimensions: (1) an appropriate methodology for deciphering what the text is about and what it meant to its first audience; and (2) a means of assessing and accounting for our present situation as readers as we engage in the interpretive process. We must account for both ancient and modern dimensions.

SOME CHALLENGES OF BIBLE INTERPRETATION

Hermeneutics Needed to Overcome Barriers Caused by Our Distance From the Worlds of Ancient Texts	
Distance of Time	Geographical Distance
Cultural Distance	Distance of Language

Distance of Time

A word that captures one of the greatest challenges (and frustrations) the Bible interpreter will face is *distance*. Consider first the distance of *time* between the ancient texts and our modern world. The writings and events in the Bible span many centuries, but more than 1,900 years have passed since its last words were written. Not only

---

36. J. H. Hopkins, *A Scriptural, Ecclesiastical, and Historical View of Slavery, from the Days of the Patriarch Abraham, to the Nineteenth Century* (New York: W. I. Pooley & Co., 1864), 16, as quoted in Swartley, *Slavery, Sabbath, War, and Women*, 37.

37. To take one example, in the First World we face the danger of reading the Bible through our experience of prosperity. We may view our wealth as the blessing of God on our faithfulness with the result that we rationalize our materialism. But, are Christians in the Majority World much less faithful, and thus, much less prosperous? We must read Heb 11 to review how some faithful followers of God were treated; some prospered, but others were sawed in two! Or consider the differing impact the story of the raped and murdered concubine (Judg 19) has on men versus women due to what they *bring* to the text.

has the world changed in substantial ways, but most of us lack essential information about the world "back then" or the process involved in producing the Bible's various and diverse "books" within oral cultures. We may be at a loss to understand what a text means because it involves subjects far removed in the past. Even a cursory glance at Hosea 10 points to many references that remain incomprehensible to most modern readers: calf-idol of Beth Aven (v. 5); Assyria (v. 6); Ephraim (v. 6); "Israel will be ashamed of its foreign alliances" (v. 6); "the high places" (v. 8); "the evil doers in Gibeah" (v. 9); "a trained heifer" (v. 11); and "Shalman devastated Beth Arbel on the day of battle" (v. 14). What was a calf-idol or high places? Where were Beth Aven, Assyria, or Ephraim located? Are they within or outside Israel? What's this about Gibeah or a trained heifer? How do we determine the meaning behind historical features that are so distant in time?

Consider also the possible gaps that existed—more or less in various places—between the time the Bible events occurred and the time when those events were written down in the texts we now possess. Since the chronology in Genesis goes all the way to the death of the patriarch Joseph, earlier sections like Genesis 12–25 probably were composed, passed down orally, and eventually written into a text after their main character, Abraham, died.[38] At the creation of universe (Gen 1), God was the only sentient being, and since Hebrew as a distinct language probably emerged ca. 1000 BC, obviously someone composed the creation account after that date.[39] We may locate the ministry of the prophet Amos in the mid-eighth century BC, but it is very likely that his oral messages were preserved and then eventually collected into the biblical book bearing his name by someone else at a later date.[40] Though Jesus' ministry probably spanned the years AD 27–30, our Gospels were not written until several decades later. Jesus' words were preserved (mostly) orally and then translated into Greek before being committed to the writings we call the Gospels.

This means that our interpretations must reckon with *both* the situation at the

---

38. Richard Hess informs us that there is evidence for ancient written sources. A cuneiform tablet was discovered from ancient Hebron and dated to the early/middle second millennium BC. There is also evidence for writing in Abraham's and Jacob's neighborhood roughly contemporaneous with them. For more on the evidence of sources behind Genesis see the various articles in R. Hess and D. T. Tsumura, eds., *"I Studied Inscriptions from Before the Flood": Ancient Near Eastern, Literary, and Linguistic Approaches to Genesis 1–11*, SBTS, vol. 4 (Winona Lake, IN: Eisenbrauns, 1994).

39. For more on the nature of orality in the ancient world and the resulting production of the OT written books see Walton and Sandy, *The Lost World*, 17–74. Among other sources also see S. Niditch, *Oral World and Written Word* (Louisville: Westminster John Knox, 1996); and K. van der Toorn, *Scribal Culture and the Making of the Hebrew Bible* (Cambridge, MA: Harvard University Press, 2007).

40. D. Stuart, *Hosea–Jonah*, WBC 31 (Dallas: Word, 2002), 288, writes, "Quite conceivably Amos' oracles were gathered and published in response to the threat to Israelite orthodoxy posed by the Assyrian incursions during the second half of the eighth century." R. F. Melugin, "Amos," in *Harper's Bible Commentary*, ed., J. L. Mays (San Francisco: Harper & Row, 1988), 720, adds, "Almost no one doubts that the book of Amos grew over time, but it remains difficult to reconstruct precisely the stages of development." For a fuller explanation of the possible stages see T. E. McComiskey and T. Longman III, "Amos," *The Expositor's Bible Commentary: Daniel–Malachi*, rev. ed., ed. T. Longman III and D. E. Garland (Grand Rapids: Zondervan, 2008), 8:350–55.

time Amos or Jesus originally spoke *and* the circumstances in which later people preserved, passed on, compiled, and, finally, wrote down their words.[41] Certainly, both Jews and Christians cared deeply about preserving and transmitting their traditions accurately. Yet the believing communities (Israel and the church), as well as the final authors' unique perspectives and their goals for writing, influenced what they felt was important, what deserved emphasis, and what might be omitted.[42] In this process the writers were mindful of their readers and the effects they hoped to produce in them (illocutions and perlocutions).

Certainly, some of the biblical "authors"[43] were eyewitnesses and wrote out of their own experiences (e.g., Isaiah, Paul). Others incorporated additional sources into their eyewitness accounts (Acts). Still others had little or no personal contact with the people and events about which they wrote (Luke, in the case of the third Gospel).[44] Once we recognize that many of the biblical writers employed or edited preexisting materials (and sometimes, several renditions alongside each other), then we must evaluate the roles and motives of these editors (again, think about their own illocutions and perlocutions).

So, for example, after learning from one biblical historian that Solomon, not David, would build the temple (2 Sam 7:12–13), and reading that he did so four years after David's death (1 Kgs 2:10; 6:1), the Chronicler's long report of David's extensive preparations for the temple's construction and worship system comes as a complete surprise (1 Chr 22–26; 28–29; cf. 2 Chr 8:14; 29:25; 35:15).[45] Apparently, while the editor of Kings omitted David's temple preparation, the Chronicler makes David the virtual founder of temple worship, in our view, to root restored, post-exilic temple worship in the Davidic covenant.

Similarly, if we surmise that Matthew hoped to persuade Jews in his locale not to repeat the mistake of Jesus' Jewish contemporaries by rejecting Jesus as Messiah,

---

41. For the additional phenomenon whereby the OT incorporates both original texts and their adaptations by later writers or editors, see our discussion of Inner-Biblical Allusion in the next chapter.

42. The compilers of Kings and Chroniclers cite sources on which they drew for their histories, thereby excluding other materials (1 Kgs 15:23, 31; 1 Chr 29:29), and the Evangelist John was certainly aware that his Gospel omitted many things that Jesus did (John 21:25).

43. We put "authors" in quotes simply to acknowledge that we don't readily know who were responsible for the final form of some of the biblical books, especially in the OT. We may view some of them to be editors of preexisting materials that may bear some connection to the "name" given to the books themselves (as in the "Books of Moses") or perhaps, no connection (as with "Ruth").

44. Luke admits this in his introduction to the third Gospel (Luke 1:1–4) where he informs Theophilus that he ". . . carefully investigated everything from the beginning." In our estimation, the "we" sections in Acts (16:10–17; 20:5–15; 21:1–18; 27:1–28:16) indicate that Luke participated with Paul in some of the incidents recorded there. If we adopt the commonly accepted explanation of the origin of the gospels, we must conclude that when writing their Gospels both Luke and Matthew employed several sources. See R. H. Stein, *Studying the Synoptic Gospels: Origin and Interpretation*, 2nd ed. (Grand Rapids: Baker, 2001) for a sane appraisal of this issue. For a more succinct discussion see A. D. Baum, "Synoptic Problem," *Dictionary of Jesus and the Gospels*, ed. J. B. Green, J. K. Brown, and N. Perrin, 2nd ed. (Downers Grove: IVP Academic, 2013), 911–19.

45. Notice also that the Chronicler, writing two centuries after the completion of Kings (ca. 350 BC), seems aware that his portrait of David differs from that of the latter because he twice takes pains to explain that David made those preparations because of Solomon's youth and experience (1 Chr 22:5; 29:1).

we have a better appreciation of his constant use of OT quotes and allusions.[46] His message to that particular audience shouts that Jesus is the Messiah. Thus, we can deduce Matthew's perlocution: that his Jewish readers acknowledge Jesus as the Promised One. The books of the Bible are literary pieces, carefully crafted to achieve their purposes, not transcripts or merely cut-and-paste collections put together naively, haphazardly, or even chronologically.

Cultural Distance

Another challenge of distance is the *cultural* distance that separates us from the world of the biblical texts. The biblical world was essentially agrarian, made up of landowners and tenant farmers using machinery that was primitive by our standards and methods of travel that were slow and wearying. On the pages of the Bible we encounter customs, beliefs, and practices that make little sense to us. Why would people in the ancient world anoint priests and kings, and sick people, with oil? What is the sandal custom for the redemption and transfer of property mentioned in Ruth 4:6–8? What was the point of the Levitical purity laws or the many other seemingly pointless requirements? For example, Leviticus 19:19 seems to rule out most of the garments we wear today: "Do not wear clothing woven of two kinds of material." What about today's polyester and wool blends? And why were tattoos forbidden in Leviticus 19:28? Are they still? In addition to factors such as these, we hasten to add a feature mentioned earlier: these people existed as parts of oral cultures. A majority of people in the ancient world were illiterate; only a minority, especially among the elites or scribes, knew how to read, with a fewer number able to write.[47] It's virtually impossible for us in literary, digital, visual, and electronic worlds to comprehend a world with few or no written texts, and the inability of most people to read those that did exist.

In addition, how we think about certain things may so color our understanding of ancient customs that we miss their significance. For example, what does "head covering" mean in 1 Corinthians 11:4–16? Are we to understand this in terms of some kind of head scarf? After reading some translations we may assume that Paul refers to veils, so we envision the veil or hijab that Middle Eastern Muslim women wear today. Yet some commentators insist that hairstyles, not veils are in view here.[48] We need more information to understand properly how Paul viewed this issue and

46. See C. L. Blomberg, "Matthew," in *Commentary on the New Testament Use of the Old Testament*, ed. G. K. Beale and D. A. Carson (Grand Rapids: Baker, 2007), 1–110.

47. See Alan Millard, *Reading and Writing in the Time of Jesus* (New York: New York University Press; Sheffield: Sheffield Academic, 2000) for a survey of the evidence. In addition, W. M. Schniedewind, "Orality and Literacy in Ancient Israel," *RelSRev* 26 (2000): 327–31, argues that, while Israel was primarily an oral culture, during the late monarchy a shift toward a broader literacy beyond the scribal class occurred in Judah, significantly transforming Judean society; cf. Schniedewind, *How the Bible Became a Book* (New York; Cambridge: Cambridge University Press, 2004) for thorough history of writing in ancient Israel.

48. See R. E. Ciampa and B. S. Rosner, *The First Letter to the Corinthians*, PNTC (Grand Rapids: Eerdmans, 2010), 503–41, for a helpful analysis.

why it was important. Likewise, a western concern for cleanliness might not help (it might even hinder) our understanding of the Pharisees' practice of ceremonial washing (Mark 7:3–5). We must inform ourselves if we are to understand properly the customs and concepts of the biblical world that are foreign to us. We cannot simply pick up the Bible and read it like a familiar book.

Finally, we must be aware that the grid of our cultural values and priorities sometimes may inadvertently lead us to adopt an interpretation that is not present in the text.[49] For example, in the Western world individualism pervades our thinking. As a result we may impose an individualistic framework on texts that that author intended to have a corporate meaning.[50] For instance, readers familiar with modern contests between individuals might view the battle between the boy David and the Philistine Goliath as simply two enemies going "one-on-one" (1 Sam 17). In fact, the episode follows the ancient custom of "representative combat" in which armies let a winner-take-all contest between two soldiers decide the victorious army rather than slaughter each other on the battlefield. Each contestant competes as if he were the whole army. Similarly, some readers conclude that in 1 Corinthians 3:16–17 Paul's reference to God's temple instructs individual Christians. As a result, they explore how Christians can build proper spiritual qualities in their personal lives (certainly not a bad practice). Yet this reads individualism into the passage despite clear indicators that Paul is referring to the corporate body of Christ as a temple in which God's Spirit dwells. Christians together form one temple—on a local or worldwide level.[51] In the metaphor, Paul cooperates in building the church (1 Cor 3:10). He urges his readers to exert their efforts to unity, to build up the body of Christ, the church, not tear it down through their divisions. He does use the same metaphor individually in 6:19, but we should not read that meaning back into chapter 3.

Geographical Distance

Another challenge to correct Bible interpretation is *geographical* distance. Unless we have had the opportunity to visit the places mentioned in the Bible, we lack a mental, visual databank that would aid our understanding of certain events. Of course, even if we could visit all the accessible sites (and many Christians have), few of them retain the look (and none, the identical culture) they had in biblical times. We have seen satellite dishes stationed next to Bedouin tents in the Negev! In other words, we have difficulty picturing why the Assyrians came "up" from Lachish to Jerusalem (2 Kgs 18:17) and why the NT speaks of people going "up" to Jerusalem

---

49. For a handy and now classic introduction to the cultural values of the U.S. in the latter decades of the twentieth century, see R. Bellah, et al., *Habits of the Heart: Individualism and Commitment in American Life*, new preface ed. (Berkeley: University of California Press, 2007).

50. For further insight on corporate elements in the Bible see, e.g., E. Best, *One Body in Christ* (London: SPCK, 1955); B. J. Malina, *The New Testament World*, 3rd ed. (Louisville: Westminster John Knox, 2001); and W. W. Klein, *The New Chosen People: A Corporate View of Election*, rev. and exp. ed. (Eugene, Oregon: Wipf & Stock, 2015).

51. See A. C. Thiselton, *The First Epistle to the Corinthians*, NIGTC (Carlisle, UK: Paternoster; Grand Rapids: Eerdmans, 2000), 316.

from Caesarea (Acts 21:12) or "down" from Jerusalem to Jericho (Luke 10:30) unless we know the differences in elevation. Perhaps less trivial, though in many parts of the world graves are excavated "down" into the earth, in Palestine graves often were dug into limestone outcroppings (or existing caves were used and were scaled with a stone). So the phrase, "he was gathered to his people/fathers" (Gen 49:29, 33; 2 Kgs 22:20), may have originated from the practice of collecting the bones of the deceased after the flesh had decomposed and putting them in a location with those of the ancestors (perhaps in an ossuary, though this is not certain). Likewise, knowledge of geography helps us understand why Jonah, in seeking to avoid God's call to prophesy against Assyria (to the northeast of Israel), headed for Tarshish (far to the west of Israel).

Distance of Language

The *language* gap between the biblical world and our own further challenges the task of biblical interpretation. The writers of the Bible wrote in the languages of their day—Hebrew, Aramaic, and Hellenistic Greek—languages that are inaccessible to most people today even though they may have their modern descendants.[52] Hebrew and Greek have different forms for masculine and feminine nouns, pronouns, and verbs, so English "you" hides whether the Hebrew or Greek word it translates is singular or plural and masculine or feminine. The plural "they" could also be either gender, as is true in English.

We are also relatively unfamiliar with the literary conventions of the ancient authors. We depend upon trained biblical scholars to translate the biblical languages and their literary devices into our native tongues, but their work is necessarily interpretive. Paul's words in 1 Corinthians 7:1 present a puzzle for translators. The NIV and ESV render the final clause, "It is good for a man not to have sexual relations with a woman."[53] Compare this with the KJV, NRSV, and NASB: "It is good (or well) for a man not to touch a woman"; Phillips, "It is a good principle for a man to have no physical contact with women"; and NEB, "it is a good thing for a man to have nothing to do with women."[54] You may well ask whether the Greek is that inconclusive. The verb translated "touch" does mean that, but it was also a common euphemism for sexual intercourse (cf. "sleep with" today), so the versions that capture that point are likely to be correct. Since these versions diverge so markedly, how would an English reader understand what Paul really meant apart from some help with the cultural situation? And the appeal for what is most "literal" is unhelpful. "Touch" may be a

---

52. Modern Greek and Hebrew are much altered from their ancient versions. C. C. Caragounis, *New Testament Language and Exegesis: A Diachronic Approach* (Tübingen: Mohr Siebeck, 2013), however, argues that there was more change between classical and Hellenistic Greek in the five centuries leading up to the time of the NT than there has been in the twenty centuries since.

53. This greatly alters (and corrects) the 1984 version of the NIV which read, "It is good for a man not to marry." On this point see G. D. Fee, *The First Epistle to the Corinthians*, 2nd ed., NICNT (Grand Rapids: Eerdmans, 2014), 301–07; and Thiselton, *The First Epistle to the Corinthians*, 499–501.

54. The REB has changed this to read, "It is a good thing for a man not to have intercourse with a woman."

literal translation of the Greek verb, but "have sex" or "sleep with" may more literally capture the meaning today.

In addition, the desire to supply "gender neutral" or "inclusive" versions makes the translation process even more complex. In both Hebrew and Greek the word translated "man" (masc. sing.) often refers to both males and females, as was formerly true in common English usage. Yet when Paul says, "God forbid: yea, let God be true, but every *man* a liar (Rom 3:4 KJV; also NASB), he clearly does not have only males in view. So one may rightly translate the phrase, "Let God be true, and every *human being* a liar" (e.g., NIV, NET, CEB) or "*everyone* a liar" (ESV, HCSB, NRSV). The same problem appears if we compare Deuteronomy 19:16 KJV, NKJV, NASB (if a false witness rises up against any "man") with most all other translations ("person" or "someone"). In short, the distances between the various biblical worlds and our own require careful historical study if we are to understand the meaning of words in the Bible.

In summary, we need a systematic approach to interpreting Scripture because the Bible was originally written:

- to somebody else
- who lived a long time ago
- in another part of the world
- where they spoke a different language
- and had different cultural values.

ETERNAL RELEVANCE—THE DIVINE FACTOR

Though the Bible originates through human agents in the normal circumstances of life, it is fundamentally God's word to his people; it has an "eternal relevance."[55] While we have described the humanness of the Bible and have emphasized that we must treat it in many ways like other books, this does not diminish its quality as a divine book. We assert that critical methods of interpretation alone will never do complete justice to Scripture if they exclude from consideration its theological and spiritual dimensions. To affirm that the Bible is God's Word does not mean God dictated a series of propositions out of heaven for people simply to transcribe verbatim. The presence of the many writing styles and genres within its pages refutes any such conclusion.

Historically, Christians have affirmed that God inspired human authors to compose the Scriptures as a means to convey his message, albeit through the matrix of human words reporting human circumstances and events, and through diverse kinds of literature. Echoing the image of Genesis 2:7, Paul speaks of the Scriptures as "God-breathed" or inspired (2 Tim 3:16), while Peter insists that in Scripture people

---

55. G. D. Fee and D. K. Stuart, *How to Read the Bible for All Its Worth,* 4th ed. (Grand Rapids: Zondervan, 2014), 25.

spoke God's message as they were "carried along" by the Holy Spirit (2 Pet 1:21). Verses like these assert the Bible's divine factor, God's sovereign shaping of *all* its dimensions—human, theological, and spiritual. Historical and rational methods of interpretation have a proper place in unfolding its human dimension; however, they can take us only so far in the interpretive process. When we discuss the qualifications of the interpreter below, we will consider those factors we believe will enable readers better to appreciate and understand the "spiritual dimensions" of the biblical text.

No doubt, the mere mention of historical and rational methods of interpretation raises questions in the minds of some sincere Christians. They may believe with some justification that some scholars using their historical-critical methods have damaged the reputation of the Bible and the faith of countless people. They may view scholarship as a subtle threat or even as a hostile enemy. At best, some perceive it as largely irrelevant to the faith of believers and the mission of the church in the world. No doubt, many academics contribute to this perception, for they do their work with no concern for the faithful who believe that the Bible is God's Word. Some may even see that their mission is to dispel religious myths and to show that the Bible is merely a human book that records the religious beliefs and aspirations of a disparate array of ancient Jewish and Christian writers.[56]

However, the fact that some scholars employ critical methods in such ways should not drive us to reject all such methods. The culprit (if there is one) is not historical or rational methods per se, but rather the *presuppositions* of some of those who use them. Believers, we assert, must not ignore the insights that accurate and precise critical methods bring, for Christians are committed to the truth. Historical methods aim to discover what happened in history. We believe that biases that distort the texts' meanings must be acknowledged and jettisoned.[57]

Some scholars have biases that cause them to reject the presence of the supernatural, while others have biases that accept them. Some exclude any role for a God who interacts with his creation and with his people, while others strongly affirm such a deity. As we will examine in more detail below, all interpreters come with preunderstandings and presuppositions. No one comes to interpret with "disinterested objectivity." An overlooked danger, however, is that some sincere believers may refuse to acknowledge their own biases and the usefulness of any scholarly achievements.[58] This is the "throw out the baby with

---

56. One of the avowed objectives of the Jesus Seminar is to wrest the Bible from dogmatic (superstitious) interpretations. It seeks to determine using its preferred critical scholarly methods which of the 176 events in the gospels that record words and deeds of Jesus actually occurred. Their consensus is that only 16% of the deeds and 18% of the words did. See R. W. Funk, *The Acts of Jesus: The Search for the Authentic Deeds of Jesus* (San Francisco: HarperCollins, 1998). As well, Bart Ehrman has made debunking what he considers the myths of the Bible one of his key objectives. For example, see his *How Jesus Became God: The Exaltation of a Jewish Preacher from Galilee* (New York: HarperOne, 2014) and *Jesus, Interrupted: Revealing the Hidden Contradictions in the Bible (And Why We Don't Know About Them)* (New York: HarperOne, 2010).

57. For the recent emergence of canonical criticism, a positive, theological approach to critical studies, see the next chapter.

58. Some conservative scholars appear to decry the very presence of historical criticism. An example is R. L. Thomas and F. D. Farnell, ed., *The Jesus Crisis: The Inroads of Historical Criticism into Evangelical Scholarship*

the bathwater" syndrome. Instead, we suggest that they should welcome valid historical and rational methods that unpack the meanings of the biblical texts. From all sides, we believe it is important to control the impact of unwarranted and truth-distorting biases lest they blind us to the divine reality of which the texts may be speaking.

When critical methods uncover what is true, we are committed to welcome and incorporate these findings into own interpretations.[59] On the other hand, we may deem unacceptable other conclusions or conjectures where an interpretation accounts for features of the text in purely rationalistic terms (e.g., when a report of a miracle of healing, the presence of a demon, or Paul's encounter with the risen Lord on the road to Damascus are reduced to psychological explanations). We believe valid interpretation must account for the "divine factor" of the biblical text (i.e., all its dimensions) and accept what God says through it to his people. Though we do not condone believing what is untrue, we affirm that rationalistic scholarship that discounts the divine factor cannot fully understand the meaning of the Bible's message.

THE GOAL OF HERMENEUTICS

As students of the Bible, we cannot limit hermeneutics to the factors and issues that concern our understanding of the ancient text. People do not usually read or study the Bible as a mere intellectual exercise. Certainly, the biblical authors never intended their writings to be only objects of such study. Normally, historians aspire to understand the causes or the results of certain historical events, but they rarely, if ever, attempt to apply what they discover to their personal lives.[60] However, Christian believers study the Bible precisely because they believe it does have something to say to their lives. Indeed, we intend to argue that one cannot thoroughly understand the Bible's message simply through the exercise of historical and grammatical methods that disclose the original meaning of a text. We insist that the goal of hermeneutics

(Grand Rapids: Kregel, 1998). See also R.L. Thomas, *Evangelical Hermeneutics: The New Versus the Old* (Grand Rapids: Kregel, 2003) for his "in-house" critique of evangelicals who have embraced critical methodology. When one sees how the vast majority of reputable conservative biblical scholars are demonized by their rhetoric, it becomes clear how misguided his approach is. An even more recent and unfortunate example of this same approach, with numerous factual errors on top of it, appears in N. L. Geisler and W. C. Roach, *Defending Inerrancy: Affirming the Accuracy of Scripture for a New Generation* (Grand Rapids: Baker, 2012). For Geisler and Roach, staunch inerrantist Darrell Bock and archskeptic Bart Ehrman are alike rejected as inconsistent with their personal interpretation of the International Council of Biblical Inerrancy's statement!

59. Admittedly, a key question arises: how do we determine what is true? Certainly, a scholarly consensus contributes to assurances that results are true or correct. When accepted historical or literary methods display results that honest and thoughtful scholars acknowledge, we can have confidence that they are likely to be true. But we must remain aware of the influence of presuppositions (discussed more fully later). In other words, when some scholars say that the miracles attributed to Elijah in 1 Kgs 17–18 can only be myths or legends, we must protest. Similarly, we object when some scholars conclude that Jesus could never have predicted that Jerusalem would be devastated (recorded in Luke 21:20–24 par.) and that such words were only read back onto Jesus' lips after the events occurred. Given our presuppositions, we believe genuine history can include miracles, and genuine prophecy of future events can occur (even though others with rationalistic commitments will not accept the validity of such conclusions).

60. Of course, later military strategists may indeed study the tactics of previous military generals and apply useful principles of warfare.

must include detecting how the Scriptures can affect readers today. This means that true interpretation of the Bible combines *both* an exercise in ancient history *and* a grappling with its impact on our lives. Indeed, to understand fully what a text meant to its original recipients requires that we grasp something of that original impact ourselves, to the extent we are able.

At the same time, if we admit that "applying" the Bible is a primary reason people read or study it, then we must answer a crucial question: how do we know *what* to apply and how do we apply it? In other words, if Christians believe that the Bible is God's Word to all people (see our discussion of this presupposition below), then to say to ourselves or to those we teach, "The Bible says . . ." carries the implication that in some sense this is what God says. And if we have heard a word from God, we must believe it and comply, or reject his[61] will to our own peril. This is no inconsequential matter. It becomes exceedingly critical to understand accurately what God intends to reveal in the Bible. We must understand correctly so we can believe and act correctly. There is no benefit to following—even with great and earnest sincerity—a mistaken point of view.

Because proper hermeneutics helps us understand God's will, it is crucial to faithful application. Satan tried to convince Jesus to misapply Scriptures in one of the temptations (Luke 4:9–12). Quoting from Psalm 91:11–12, the devil urged Jesus to apply the Scriptures literally and throw himself down from the highest point of the temple, all with the assurance that God's Word promised divine protection. In effect, in his reply Jesus accused Satan of employing bad hermeneutics. Jesus indicated that Satan did not interpret the text in view of the context of God's promise; Satan needed to understand Psalm 91 in light of the principle of not putting God to the test (see Deut 6:16). Neither extraordinary faith nor great sincerity will necessarily save a person who jumps from a tall precipice from a tragic death. Psalm 91 promised God's protection when unexpected or accidental harm threatened (and even then not *always*), not from self-inflicted foolishness.[62] Since Satan misconstrued the intention of Psalm 91, the application of a bad interpretation could have had unfortunate—even deadly—results. Thus, since we desire to obey God's will, we need to understand how to interpret the Scriptures, which reveal his will, correctly.

---

61. Perhaps this is a good a place to explain our use of masculine pronouns for the Deity in some places. Of course, God is neither male nor female; humans, male *and* female were made in God's image (Gen 1:26–27). English pronouns must be either male or female, and the indefinite "it" does not appropriately describe God. Using "he" or "him" is purely a convention of convenience that we sincerely hope will not trouble our readers. We find it easier for stylistic reasons in some contexts to write, e.g., "he" rather than continually to repeat "God," or to use "himself" rather than the awkward "Godself."

62. M. E. Tate, *Psalms 51–100*, WBC 20 (Dallas: Word, 1998), 456, explains: "The angels of Yahweh will be given charge over the faithful ones to protect them in all their 'ways,' i.e., in their activities and conduct of life, though some commentators argue that the reference here is to actual travel, 'ways' in the sense of journeys. He adds, "'Ways' is more probably used here in the sense found in such references as Pss 1:1, 6; 10:5; 26:4; 39:2; 51:15; Prov 3:6."

CONCLUSION

The proper use of hermeneutics is essential for a valid interpretation of the Bible. Instead of piously insisting that we will simply allow God to speak to us from his word, we contend that to insure we hear God's voice rather than our culture's voice or our own biases we need to interpret the Scriptures in a systematic and careful fashion. We need to practice correct principles and methods of interpretation. We conclude with several reasons why this is the case.

1. *To discern God's message.* If we are to understand God's truth for ourselves (and also to teach or preach it to others), we must discover precisely what God intended to communicate. A careful system of hermeneutics provides the means for the interpreter to arrive at the text's intention, and more importantly, to understand what God intended to communicate through human minds and hands (both illocution and perlocution). Some conservative Christians abuse the Bible by their one-dimensional "proof-texting." They use the Bible like a telephone database of individual texts and cite chapter and verse in a vain attempt to prove their viewpoint—with little or no regard for the contexts in which those verses appear. This leads to many distortions and errors that using appropriate methods will avoid. A systematic approach to hermeneutics safeguards the Scriptures against misuse by people who, deliberately or not, distort the Bible for their own ends. Proper hermeneutics provides the conceptual framework for interpreting correctly by means of accurate exegesis.[63] Exegesis puts into practice one's theory of interpretation. Thus good hermeneutics will generate good exegetical methods and in turn a proper understanding of the text.

2. *To avoid or dispel misconceptions or erroneous perspectives and conclusions about what the Bible teaches.* Ideally, correct interpretation undermines erroneous teachings that people use to support aberrant beliefs and behavior. One encounters all too often in the news sincere and well-meaning parents who withhold medical intervention for their children because with the best of motives they believe they should trust God for healing. Or they refuse immunization for their children holding, in our view, a misguided trust in God's protection. Though we do not deny God's ability to heal today or his invitation to pray for what we need, we believe that a correct interpretation of the relevant biblical texts mandates prayer for healing *and* medical prevention and intervention. God can use a variety of means to effect healing. Failure to seek appropriate medical help may be akin to jumping from the temple—with similar disastrous results! Or for a more controversial issue, we should ask whether Christians should be more concerned to support the nation of Israel (based on such

---

63. As used in biblical studies "exegesis," from the Greek word *exēgeomai*, means to "explain" the meaning of a text or passage by using appropriate tactics. The standard Greek lexicon gives these two precise meanings to the Greek word: (1) to relate in detail, tell, report, describe, and (2) to set forth in great detail, expound (BDAG, 349). We heartily agree with G. R. Osborne, *The Hermeneutical Spiral*, 2nd ed. (Downers Grove: InterVarsity, 2006), 21, who says, "Hermeneutics is the overall term, while exegesis and 'contextualization' (the cross-cultural communication of a text's significance for today) are the two aspects of that larger task."

texts as Gen 12:3; 27:29) or Palestinian Christians who happen to live in that land today (Matt 10:42; 25:40, 45). How one interprets these texts should drive one's conclusions and actions. Genesis 12:3 does not mention the political state of Israel, only Abraham's seed or descendants, and Paul clearly equates Abraham's seed with Christians, whether Jews or Gentiles (e.g., Rom 2:28–29; 4:16; Gal. 3:29; 6:16)! A majority of Christians in Israel today happen to be Palestinian,[64] but of course Jew and Gentile in Christ should be treated equally.

3. *To be able to apply the Bible's message to our lives.* God has chosen to reveal most of his truth through the medium of written language, and this message is both univocal and analogical.[65] As Carnell puts it, "terms may be used in one of three ways: with but one meaning (univocally), with different meanings (equivocally), and with a proportional meaning—partly the same, partly different (analogically)."[66] In other words, in places the Bible speaks to us univocally. Though its message was written to ancients, many features remain the same—human existence, the realities of angels, demons, God, Jesus as God's Son, and forgiveness on the basis of Jesus' death, to name a few. As Paul notes concerning truth in the Scriptures, certain factual affirmations about past events always remain true (1 Cor 15:3–5). These statements are univocal, having the same meaning for Paul as for us, though we may apply that single meaning in a variety of ways. More on application appears in the final chapter.

At the same time, in places the Bible conveys truth to us analogically in its didactic sections, poetry, apocalypses, and narratives, even though they were written to people long ago. We learn by analogy when we discover that truth in the Bible applies to life and situations in the modern world in ways parallel to their original intentions (perlocutions). As noted above, Jesus told his followers, "You are the light of the world" (Matt 5:14). Since people in Bible times and people today both have an understanding of how a light functions to provide illumination to everyone in the house (whether by means of candles, olive oil lamps, torches, electric or battery-operated lights, or LEDs), we understand the analogy. We learn that Jesus wants his followers to "brighten up" their world, which Jesus elaborates to mean, among other things, doing good deeds (Matt 5:16).

Today we read about God's actions and those of his people in the past, and because certain parallels and commonalities link the worlds of the ancients and ours, we can comprehend the analogies and learn from them. Our task is more difficult in places where an author or speaker does not clearly spell out the lesson to be learned or the

---

64. On this controversial point see, G. Burge, *Whose Land? Whose Promise?: What Christians Are Not Being Told about Israel and the Palestinians*, rev. ed. (Cleveland, OH: Pilgrim Press, 2013); and G. Burge, *Jesus and the Land: the New Testament Challenge to "Holy Land" Theology* (Grand Rapids: Baker, 2010).

65. We don't discount nor are we unaware of the nature of the oral record and traditions that preceded the eventual fixed written texts of Scripture. We have more to say on that issue below.

66. E. J. Carnell, *An Introduction to Christian Apologetics* (Grand Rapids: Eerdmans, 1948; Eugene, OR: Wipf & Stock, 2007), 144. Univocal meaning is single, having only one sense. We learn by analogy when we make inferences from what we learn or know in one sphere and apply it to another sphere.

nature of the analogy. For example, we might wonder what we might learn from the following possible analogies:

- The story of Joseph's life and his exploits in Egypt.[67]
- The inspiring narratives about David's friendship with Jonathan.
- The accounts of Nehemiah's rebuilding the walls of Jerusalem.
- Israel's circumstances and the church's.
- The psalms written by an ancient king to express his frustrations or joys in life.
- The erotic love poems in the Song of Songs.

The basic goal of this book is to help readers discover God's message to Christians today from the teachings and stories "back then."[68]

---

67. Equally, the later circumstances in the lives of Daniel and Esther.

68. Indeed, we wish to take seriously Paul's words to his Roman readers, "For everything that was written in the past was written to teach us, so that through the endurance taught in the Scriptures and the encouragement they provide we might have hope" (Rom 15:4).

2

THE HISTORY OF
INTERPRETATION

As is now apparent, we believe one must interpret Bible passages in their original historical context—a view that descends from a long line of intellectual ancestors, both Jewish and Christian, who have sought to interpret the Bible properly. A brief survey of the history of Bible interpretation is beneficial in several ways. First, it introduces key issues that are pertinent to Bible interpretation, which, in turn, prepares the student to understand the approach to these issues that we present.

Second, it sensitizes readers to the opportunities and pitfalls involved in trying to contextualize Bible teachings in the present. A critical assessment of the major interpretive methods practiced throughout history challenges readers to develop a personal approach to Bible interpretation that maximizes the opportunities and minimizes the pitfalls. Finally, knowledge of the history of interpretation cultivates an attitude of humility toward the interpretive process. Certainly we want to avoid the methods that history has judged as mistaken or faulty. At the same time, the history illustrates how complex the process is and how inappropriate is arrogance in the pursuit of it.[1]

JEWISH INTERPRETATION

The Bible's first interpreters were those who first possessed its writings—ancient Israelites who studied and edited what later became the Hebrew Scriptures. Their identity and the history of their work remain obscure, but the Hebrew Scriptures still show the thumbprints of their work.

Inner-Biblical Allusion

Recent scholarship has recognized that Jewish interpretation of Scripture begins with a phenomenon called inner-biblical allusion, a process that precedes and eventuates

---

1. With a few exceptions, our survey limits itself to the history of interpretation by Western Christianity or, after the Reformation, primarily to Protestant interpretation. For a good overview of the most relevant features of Eastern Christianity for evangelicals, see G. R. Osborne, "The Many and the One: The Interface between Orthodoxy and Evangelical Protestant Hermeneutics," *SVTQ* 39 (1995): 281–304. Cf. E. J. Pentiuc, *The Old Testament in Eastern Orthodox Tradition* (New York: Oxford University Press, 2014).

in the completion of the canon of Scripture.[2] Over time, ancient Israel came to accept certain writings as authoritative, texts that later writers and editors sought to revise, update, amend, or rewrite so that those source texts could address the new challenges and new realities faced by each reviser's own generation and perhaps by future ones. Soon, the reworked texts achieved the same authority as their sources—in other words, the scribes ceased to be revisers and became authors. Interestingly, later generations retained both source and revised texts as if, by clarifying the source text, its revision reinforced the authority of the former. Eventually, the canonical text included both authoritative texts, and that is why our Bibles have, for example, both 1–2 Kings (source text) and 1–2 Chronicles (a reinterpretation of Kings from a post-exilic perspective).

At the simplest level, later interpreters simply supply brief parenthetical explanations to clarify an unfamiliar (and possibly Canaanite) place-name. Genesis 23:2 records that Sarah "died at Kiriath Arba (that is, Hebron)," updating the source text with the place name by which their readers knew the city. Longer parenthetical comments similarly seek to explain something old and unfamiliar to a later audience—for example, the apparently passé sandal-exchange custom in Ruth 4:7. Some editorial comments introduce or conclude longer literary sections. Like a colophon (or brief notation) appended to clay tablets in the ancient Near East, Leviticus 14:54–57 wraps up the detailed regulations of Leviticus 13–14, while Proverbs 25:1, written by editors working for King Hezekiah (late eighth c. BC), prefaces the book's second collection of Solomonic proverbs (Prov 25–29).[3] In Hosea 14:9 (MT 10) an editor ends the prophecy with an exhortation that sounds a lot like Proverbs, in essence urging readers to interpret Hosea both as prophecy and as a guide to acquiring wisdom. An anonymous writer ended Deuteronomy with this interpretation of the unique significance of Moses: "Since then no prophet has risen in Israel like Moses, whom the LORD knew face to face . . ." (Deut 34:10).

Finally, the reinterpretation of Jeremiah's Seventy Years theme, one by Jeremiah himself and one by the Chronicler two centuries later, illustrate inner-biblical allusion at work. Compare the following texts:

---

2. We think the term inner-biblical allusion better describes the phenomenon than the earlier, more familiar name inner-biblical exegesis; cf. R. L. Hubbard, Jr., "Reading Through the Rearview Mirror: Inner-Biblical Exegesis and the New Testament," in *Doing Theology for the Church: Essays in Honor of Klyne Snodgrass*, ed. R. A. Eklund and J. E. Phelan, Jr. (Eugene, OR: Covenant Press/Wipf & Stock, 2014), 126–27, who also supplies additional bibliography and excellent overviews of the phenomenon, (125–39). For OT examples, see M. Fishbane, *Biblical Interpretation in Ancient Israel* (Oxford: Clarendon, 1984); for NT examples, see R. B. Hayes, *Echoes of Scripture in the Letters of Paul* (New Haven: Yale University Press, 1989). Recent studies include G. Gakuru, *An Inner-Biblical Study of the Davidic Covenant and the Dynastic Oracle*, Mellen Biblical Press Series 58 (Lewiston, NY: Mellen, 2000); R. Nurmela, *Prophets in Dialogue: Inner-Biblical Allusions in Zechariah 1–8 and 9–14* (Åbo: Åbo Academis Förlag, 1996); and S. L. Harris, *Proverbs 1–9: A Study of Inner-Biblical Interpretation*, SBLDS 150 (Atlanta: Scholars Press, 1995).

3. Interestingly, the title presumes a source text (an inventory of Solomonic proverbs now to be "collected" together in writing) and some unstated need for Solomon's voice to address Hezekiah's generation. Meinhold notes that, like his contemporary Isaiah, the king sought to foster the importance of wisdom in Jerusalem, perhaps to inform palace deliberations over Judah's response to the decades-long Assyrian threat; cf. A. Meinhold, *Die Sprüche. Teil 2: Sprüche Kapitel 16–31*, ZBK (Zürich: Theologischer Verlag Zürich, 1991), 416.

Jeremiah 25:11–12 Preexilic (605 BC)	Jeremiah 29:10 Exilic (ca. 597 BC)	2 Chronicles 36:21 Postexilic (ca. 400 BC)
[11] This whole country will become a desolate wasteland, and these nations will serve the king of Babylon seventy years. [12] "But when the seventy years are fulfilled, I will punish the king of Babylon and his nation, the land of the Babylonians, for their guilt," declares the LORD, "and will make it desolate forever."	[10] This is what the LORD says: "When seventy years are completed for Babylon, I will come to you and fulfill my good promise to bring you back to this place."	[21] The land enjoyed its sabbath rests; all the time of its desolation it rested, until the seventy years were completed in fulfillment of the word of the LORD spoken by Jeremiah.

Jeremiah 25:11–12 (605 BC) comprises an oracle of doom addressed to preexilic Judah. In it the seventy years demarcate two events—the length of time that Judah will suffer destruction and exile and the endpoint of exile through divine judgment on Babylon. The latter implies (but does not announce) hope of return for Judah. But nearly a decade later (ca. 597 BC) in a letter to exiles in Judah, the prophet himself reuses that seventy-year motif to make explicit to exilic Judah the hope of return implicit in the earlier oracle (Jer 29:10). A conciliatory tone has replaced the condemnation of the latter. Two centuries later (ca. 400 BC) the closing chapter of Chronicles (2 Chr 36:21) also interprets the seventy-year motif of Jeremiah for a new audience and in a new way. For the Chronicler, the end of the seventy years coincides with the beginning of Persian rule, the power with whose decree authorizing the Jews to return home 2 Chronicles 36 ends. The Chronicler's new slant comes by reading Jeremiah's seventy-year motif through the lens of another authoritative text, Leviticus 26:34–35:

> Then the land will enjoy its sabbath years all the time that it lies desolate and you are in the country of your enemies; then the land will rest and enjoy its sabbaths. All the time that it lies desolate, the land will have the rest it did not have during the sabbaths you lived in it.

For the Chronicler, the seventy years are ten sabbath years mandated by Leviticus 26: "The land enjoyed its sabbath rests; all the time of its desolation it rested, until the seventy years were completed in fulfillment of the word of the LORD spoken by Jeremiah." Rhetorically, the echo of prophetic threats of doom in Jeremiah 25 and Leviticus 26 subtly warns the Chronicler's contemporaries, now back in the land, to avoid another seventy-year national debacle. It also offers hope, as if to say, "For Israel, the rest period is over. Time to get back to work—time to rebuild our country." In sum, the afterlife of Jeremiah's oracle about the seventy years illustrates the process of inner-biblical allusion and how it sought to apply then-extant biblical materials to contemporary concerns.

Post-Biblical Interpretation: The Transition

The first interpreters known by name were Levites who assisted Ezra the scribe on the solemn occasion that Nehemiah 8:7–8 reports. As Ezra publicly read the Mosaic law (in Hebrew), Levites explained to the crowd (in Aramaic) what they were hearing. According to rabbinic tradition, this incident spawned a new Jewish institution, the Targum (i.e., reading and interpretation), an occasion one scholar deems "the birthday of Judaism" with the reading and explaining of the law of Moses at its center.[4]

In fact, that institution was one of two formative activities involving biblical interpretation in late intertestamental Judaism. In that period Jewish worship included the oral Targums—i.e., the translation and interpretation of Hebrew scripture readings in Aramaic, the common spoken language of that day. Eventually, scribes reduced these oral Targums to writing in order to perpetuate their use, which continues to the present.[5] At the same time, scribes and rabbis vigorously pursued the study and teaching of the Hebrew Scriptures, especially the Pentateuch. They worked to solve problems raised by the texts, explaining obscure words and reconciling conflicting passages. More important, they sought to apply the Scriptures to the issues of daily life raised by their contemporaries.[6]

A grave cultural crisis fueled their intensive Scripture study. In the late intertestamental era, domination by the Hellenistic and Roman empires forced Jews to define and preserve their own religious identity in the face of foreign cultural values and religions. They found refuge in the study of their ancient Scriptures. In the process, they honed their methods of interpretation to a fine edge. As Kugel points out, the influence of these largely anonymous figures proved far-reaching:

> They established the basic patterns by which the Bible was to be read and understood for centuries (in truth, up until the present day), and, what is more, they turned interpretation into a central and fundamental religious activity.[7]

---

4. *Palestinian Talmud, Megillah* 4, 74d; M. J. McNamara, *Targum and Testament Revisited*, 2nd ed. (Grand Rapids: Eerdmans, 2010), 50 (quote), 51; cf. G. Stemberger, "From Biblical Interpretation to Rabbinic Exegesis," in *The New Cambridge History of the Bible: From the Beginnings to 600*, 3 vols., ed. J. C. Paget and J. Schaper (Cambridge: Cambridge University Press, 2013), 1:190–217 (henceforth, *NCHB* 1).

5. For general background on Targums, see P. V. M. Flesher, B. Chilton, and P. V. McCracken, *The Targums: A Critical Introduction* (Waco, TX: Baylor University Press, 2011). Some scholars suggest that, since the returned exiles spoke the Aramaic of Babylon instead of the Hebrew of their Scriptures, the Levites' explanations involved both translation of the text into Aramaic and interpretation of its content. More likely, Jews in Judah during Nehemiah day were bilingual in Hebrew and in the local Aramaic dialects of their non-Jewish neighbors (McNamara, *Targum*, 88).

6. As McNamara, *Targum*, 51, observes, "It will be the task of the religious leaders in the following centuries [post Ezra] to see to it that all Israel will be acquainted with both the text and the meaning of the Law of Moses."

7. J. L. Kugel, "Early Interpretation: The Common Background of Late Forms of Biblical Exegesis," in *Early Biblical Interpretation*, ed. J. L. Kugel and R. A. Greer (Philadelphia: Westminster, 1986), 13; cf. McNamara, *Targum*, 52–55.

By the NT period, amid this intense hermeneutical activity three distinctive approaches to Scripture began to coalesce. Each approach was associated with a geographical center of Jewish religious life and a different school of thought. For our purposes, their importance lies in the background they provide on the way NT writers interpreted the OT.[8]

Hellenistic Judaism

In 331 BC Alexander the Great completed his conquest of the Persian Empire including Palestine. He and his successors began to impose Greek culture throughout their domain. Greek influence proved to be particularly strong on the large Jewish community in Alexandria, the city in Egypt named for the great emperor. There, Hellenistic Judaism flourished, a movement which sought to integrate Greek philosophy, especially that of Plato, with Jewish religious beliefs.[9]

Eventually, Greek replaced Aramaic as the common language among Jews outside of Palestine. So about 285 BC, Alexandrian Jewish scholars produced a remarkable Greek translation of the Pentateuch (the remaining Hebrew Scriptures were translated later).[10] Eventually called the Septuagint (i.e., "70"; abbrev. LXX) because, according to tradition, seventy scholars translated it, it later became the Bible of the early church.[11] More important for our purposes, in the fertile intellectual soil of Alexandria flowered a major school of biblical interpretation, one that enjoyed wide influence among Jews scattered throughout the Roman Empire and in Jerusalem itself.

The major distinctive of this "school" was its allegorical method, which was rooted in platonic philosophy. Plato taught that true reality actually lay behind what appeared to the human eye.[12] Applied to literature, this view of reality suggested that

---

8. A comprehensive collection of interpretations by these (and other) schools is available in L. H. Schiffman, *Texts and Traditions: A Source Reader for the Study of Second Temple and Rabbinic Judaism* (Hoboken, NJ: KTAV, 1998), 121–761. For a useful introduction to the variety of literature produced by Jews outside the Hebrew Bible, see L. R. Helyer, *Exploring Jewish Literature of the Second Temple Period* (Downers Grove: InterVarsity, 2002). Besides introducing subjects like the apocrypha, pseudepigrapha, apocalyptic, Dead Sea Scrolls, Mishnah, Targums, Josephus, and Philo, it also shows their value for students of the NT.

9. Kugel, "Early Interpretation," 40–44. For an overview of Hellenistic Judaism, see M. Hengel, *The Hellenization of Judaea in the First Century After Christ* (London: SCM, 1989).

10. The translation of the Pentateuch was particularly remarkable because the very process of its completion created, in the words of Lamarche, "a whole religious language . . . that would find its culmination in the New Testament and in the works of the Fathers"; cf. P. Lamarche, "The Septuagint: Bible of the Earliest Christians," in *The Bible in Greek Christian Antiquity*, ed. P. M. Blowers (Notre Dame: University of Notre Dame, 1997), 18 (quote); L. Greenspoon, "Hebrew into Greek: Interpretation in, by, and of the Septuagint," in *A History of Biblical Interpretation: The Ancient Period*, ed. A. J. Hauser and D. F. Watson (Grand Rapids: Eerdmans, 2003), 102–8.

11. The alleged story of its origin and purpose told in the *Letter of Aristeas* is now thought unreliable by scholars; cf. Lamarche, "The Septuagint: Bible of the Earliest Christians," 15–33. For excellent introductions, see J. K. Aitken, ed., *The T&T Clark Companion to the Septuagint* (London; New York: Bloomsbury T&T Clark, 2015); T. M. Law, *When God Spoke Greek: The Septuagint and the Making of the Christian Bible* (Oxford: Oxford University Press, 2013); and K. H. Jobes and M. Silva, *Invitation to the Septuagint*, 2nd ed. (Grand Rapids: Baker, 2015).

12. To illustrate, in *The Republic* (514a–520a) Plato compared human perception of reality to the experience of being in a dimly lit cave. There one sees only shadowy figures (the "forms"), but true reality (the "ideas") lies behind them; cf. S. L. R. Clark, "Ancient Philosophy," in *The Oxford History of Western Philosophy*, ed. A. Kenny (Oxford: Oxford University Press, 1994), 22–28.

a text's true meaning lay behind the written words. That is, the text served as a kind of extended metaphor that pointed to the ideas hidden behind it.[13] With respect to the Hebrew Scriptures, the master practitioner of allegory was the brilliant Alexandrian Jewish thinker, Philo (ca. late-first c. BC–mid-first c. AD), who sought to reconcile the Hebrew Scriptures with the philosophy of Plato.[14]

For Philo, a Bible passage was like a human being; it had a body (i.e., a literal meaning) and a soul (an allegorical meaning).[15] He accepted the literal meaning of many Scriptures (e.g., observance of the Mosaic law), but he also believed that only the allegorical method could reveal the true inner meaning that God had encoded in them. He developed a set of rules to recognize when a text's allegorical meaning was its true meaning. In his view, one could disregard a text's literal meaning when it (1) said anything unworthy of God, (2) contained some insoluble difficulty, unusual grammar, or unique rhetoric, and (3) involved an obvious allegorical expression.

Further, Philo believed that hidden meaning lay behind numbers and names. More ingeniously, he also found meaning by playing with the many possible senses of the same word and by regrouping the words of a biblical passage. In Philo's interpretation of Genesis 2:10 ("A river watering the garden flowed from Eden; from there it was separated into four headwaters"), he determined that the Edenic river represented goodness, while the other four headwaters were the four great virtues of Greek philosophy—prudence, temperance, courage, and justice.[16] In other words, the number four in the biblical text suggested to him four items from Greek philosophy.[17]

From hindsight, the strengths and weaknesses of Philo's approach appear evident. On the one hand, he rightly recognized the limitations of human language to convey the profound mysteries of spiritual reality and the nature of God, and he attempted to integrate biblical ideas with those of the dominant philosophy of his day in order to relate biblical faith to contemporary culture—a difficult challenge people of faith in every generation must face. On the other hand, from a modern viewpoint, Philo's approach too often seems dependent on subjectivity, arbitrariness, and artificiality. One might ask, for example, why the Edenic river represents goodness and its tributaries four other virtues. To someone else, the former might represent the stream of human

---

13. The Greeks had honed this interpretive method to a fine edge from the sixth century BC. It allowed them to find value in Greek classical literature (e.g., Homer, etc.), some of whose ideas (e.g., the morality of the gods) the philosophers found offensive. The Platonists at Alexandria used allegory to teach platonic philosophy from classical Greek literature.

14. For Philo's life and thought, see C. Mondesért, "Philo of Alexandria," in *The Cambridge History of Judaism: The Early Roman Period*, 3 vols., ed. W. D. Davies, et al. (Cambridge: Cambridge University Press, 1984–1999), 3:877–900 (henceforth *CHJ III*). Concerning Philo as an exegete, cf. P. Borgen, "Philo of Alexandria as Exegete," *A History of Biblical Interpretation: The Ancient Period*, ed. Hauser and Watson, 114–43; P. Borgen, *Philo of Alexandria: An Exegete for His Time*, SNTSMS 86 (Leiden: Brill, 1997).

15. *De Vita Contemplativa*, x. 78. For a translation, see C. D. Yonge, *The Works of Philo: Complete and Unabridged* (Peabody, MA: Hendrickson, 1995).

16. *Legum Allegoriarum*, 1.63–64.

17. On the other hand, in keying on insoluble textual difficulties, by appealing to the multiple meanings of single words, and by rearranging words, Philo's method closely resembles that of midrash (about which we say more below).

life and the latter four major ethnic groups of humanity. Again, Philo tends to ignore the real differences between biblical ideas and those of Greek philosophy. It is hard to escape the conclusion that ultimately Philo's interpretation depended more upon platonic philosophy than upon the Bible.[18] Nevertheless, one scholar rightly judges him as "probably the most influential Jewish biblical scholar and theologian of the ancient Jewish diaspora."[19]

The Qumran Community

A branch of Judaism—probably the Essenes—flourished at Qumran, a site on the northwestern shore of the Dead Sea, about 150 BC–AD 68. Its now famous literary legacy, the Dead Sea Scrolls, reveals the community's self-identity and reason for being. It regarded the Judaism centered in Jerusalem as apostate. So, led by its founder, a mysterious figure called the Teacher of Righteousness, its members withdrew to the wilderness of Judea to form a monastic community to prepare for the coming of the messianic age. Specifically, they awaited God's imminent judgment, which they expected to fall on their apostate religious competitors, and they anticipated his renewal of the covenant with the only true, pure Israel—themselves. They saw themselves as the final generation about whom biblical prophecy speaks.[20]

The interpretation of Hebrew Scriptures played a prominent role at Qumran.[21] If the law of Moses entranced the rabbis, the OT prophets preoccupied the Qumran sectarians. Alleging special divine inspiration, the Teacher of Righteousness claimed to show that events of that day, especially those involving the Qumran community, fulfilled OT prophecies. This explains why so many of the scrolls consist of copies of OT books and why Qumran produced so many commentaries on them. For our purposes, the latter are most important, for they show the principles of biblical interpretation that the community followed.

---

18. Whether Philo's thought owes more to Greek philosophy than to Judaism or vice versa remains a hotly-contested issue among scholars. For a convenient summary, see D. Hagner, "Philo," in *New Dictionary of Theology*, ed. S. B. Ferguson and D. F. Wright (Downers Grove: InterVarsity, 1988), 509–10.

19. R. E. Olson, *The Story of Christian Theology: Twenty Centuries of Tradition and Reform* (Downers Grove: InterVarsity, 1999), 49. For Philo's influence on later patristic interpreters, see F.Ó. Fearghail, "Philo and the Fathers: The Letter and the Spirit," in *Scriptural Interpretation in the Fathers: Letter and Spirit*, ed. T. Finan and V. Twomey (Dublin: Four Courts Press, 1995), 39–59. A less philosophical hermeneutical approach appears in the writings of Philo's Jewish contemporary, Josephus (AD 37–100?), whose principal works are *The Antiquities of the Jews* and *The Jewish Wars*. As an apologetic mainly for Jewish detractors, his interesting paraphrastic retelling of biblical texts occasionally seems to rewrite them. For a comprehensive study of his biblical materials, see L. H. Feldman, *Studies in Josephus' Rewritten Bible*, JSJSup 58 (Leiden: E.J. Brill, 1998); cf. also S. Mason, *Josephus and the New Testament*, 2d ed. (Peabody, MA: Hendrickson, 2003).

20. Kugel, "Early Interpretation," 61–62. For an English translation of the scrolls, see M. O. Wise, M. G. Abegg, Jr., and E. M. Cook, *The Dead Sea Scrolls: A New Translation*, rev. ed. (San Francisco: HarperSanFrancisco, 2005). For background to interpretation, see Peter W. Flint, *The Dead Sea Scrolls* (Nashville: Abingdon Press, 2013); George J. Brooke, *The Dead Sea Scrolls and the New Testament* (Minneapolis: Fortress Press, 2005).

21. For an overview of their interpretive methods, see P. R. Davies, "Biblical Interpretation in the Dead Sea Scrolls," *A History of Biblical Interpretation: The Ancient Period,* ed. Hauser and Watson, 144–66; M. Berstein, "Interpretation of Scriptures," in *Encyclopedia of the Dead Sea Scrolls*, 2 vols., ed. L. H. Schiffman and J. C. VanderKam (Oxford: Oxford University Press, 2000), 1:376–83.

To be specific, the community practiced a method called *pesher*.[22] Three interpretive techniques typified this approach. Interpreters might actually suggest a change in the biblical text (textual emendation) to support an interpretation. They would select a known alternate textual reading of the phrase in question and offer the interpretation. Lacking an existent variant, Qumran interpreters were not averse to creating one that suited their interpretive purposes! For example, Habakkuk 1:13a reads, "Your eyes are too pure to behold evil, and you cannot look on wrongdoing" (NRSV). The Pesher rightly comments that the words address God and describe his holiness. One expects a similar treatment for v. 13b: "Why then do you tolerate the treacherous? Why are you silent while the wicked swallow up those more righteous than themselves?" But the commentary interprets the "you" pronouns as plural, not singular, and as such they refer not to God but to the house of Absalom—a religious group that the Qumranians disliked.[23]

Again, commentators might contemporize a prophecy, claiming to find its fulfillment in events either of their own day or of the immediate future. For example, one writer sought to contemporize Habakkuk 1:6, "For I am raising up the Babylonians, that ruthless and impetuous people . . . ." Originally, the line predicted that the Babylonian army would come to punish sinful Judah, but according to the Pesher, "this refers to the Kittim [Romans] who are indeed swift and mighty in war . . . ."[24] In other words, the commentator interpreted the ancient prophecy about the Babylonians as predicting the coming of Qumran's enemies, the Romans.

Finally, interpreters might use an atomization approach, dividing the text into separate phrases, then interpreting each one by itself regardless of the context. For example, in explaining Habakkuk 2:4 (literally "Look, his soul shall be swollen . . ."; cf. NIV: "puffed up") the Pesher says, "they will pile up for themselves a double requital for their sins . . . ." The idea of double punishment derives from the word "swollen" (Heb. *'pl*), which the commentator arbitrarily reads as "to be doubled" (Heb. *kpl*).[25]

Rabbinic Judaism

Centered in Jerusalem, this branch of Judaism promoted obedience to the Hebrew Scriptures, especially the Torah, in the face of mounting pressure to accommodate to Greco-Roman culture.[26] The interpretive approach of rabbinic Judaism is evident in

---

22. On the nature of *pesher*, see M. P. Horgan, *Pesharim: Qumran Interpretations of Biblical Books*, CBQMS 8 (Washington, D.C.: The Catholic Biblical Association, 1979), 229–59.

23. Horgan, *Pesharim*, 15, 32–34; W. H. Brownlee, *The Midrash Pesher of Habakkuk*, SBLMS 24 (Missoula, MT: Scholars, 1979), 91–98.

24. Brownlee, *Midrash Pesher*, 59–62; Horgan, *Pesharim*, 13, 26.

25. The translation follows Brownlee, *Midrash Pesher*, 122–24 ("a pun"); cf. Horgan, *Pesharim*, 17, 39 ("probably an interpretation").

26. For a convenient introduction, see S. J. D. Cohen, *From the Maccabees to the Mishnah* (Louisville, KY: Westminster John Knox, 2006). For a useful topical survey, cf. D. Instone-Brewer, *Traditions of the Rabbis from the Era of the New Testament*, 6 vols. (Grand Rapids: Eerdmans, 2004–). G. Boccaccini, *Roots of Judaism: An Intellectual History from Ezekiel to Daniel* (Grand Rapids: Eerdmans, 2002), explores the roots of the rabbinic system in the

the massive amounts of literature it inspired. It contains two basic types of content. *Halakah* (Heb. "rule to go by") involves the deduction of principles and regulations for human conduct derived specifically from OT legal material. *Haggadah* (Heb. "a telling"), by contrast, draws on the whole OT offering of stories and proverbs to illustrate biblical texts and to edify readers.[27]

Rabbinic Judaism produced three main literary works. The Mishnah presents the once-oral teachings of leading rabbis from the time of the famous competitors, Hillel and Shammai (late first c. BC to early first c. AD). Published about AD 200, the Mishnah presents many individual tractates arranged under six topics (e.g., feasts, women, holy things, etc.).[28] About fifty years later, another document called Abot (lit., "the Fathers") affirmed that what the Mishnah writers taught was part of the oral law received by Moses at Mount Sinai. Most of its content is halakah.

The Palestinian and Babylonian Talmuds (ca. AD 400 and 600, respectively) essentially offer commentary (also known as Gemara) on the Mishnah by later rabbis. Topically organized, each Talmudic section quotes a section of Mishnah, which is followed by citations of rabbis and portions of Scripture. The frequent citation of Scripture implies that the Talmud's purpose was to give biblical support for the interpretations of the Mishnah.[29] At times like modern biblical commentaries but often very different, the midrashim (from Heb. *darash* "to search") provide interpretation of biblical books, sometimes explaining passages almost verse-by-verse while often addressing only selected verses. The commentary—which may provide parallel or even competing perspectives—follows the quotation of a verse or phrase from Scripture. Though written no earlier than the second century AD, some of their interpretive material probably derives from the pre-Christian era, and most of their content is haggadah.[30]

The interpretation of Scripture in rabbinic Judaism shows several distinct features. First, it depends heavily upon rabbinic interpretive tradition. Interpretation amounts to citing what earlier revered rabbis say about a passage. For example, consider how the

Second Temple period (BC 515–AD 70), a system that in his view (xiv–xv) came to prominence no earlier than the third century AD.

27. *Halakah* and *haggadah* also refer to the genres of rabbinic traditions themselves, whether they are legal or narrative in form; cf. Kugel, "Early Interpretation," 67–72. For an introduction to Rabbinic literature, see J. Neusner, *Rabbinic Literature: An Essential Guide* (Nashville: Abingdon Press, 2005). For in-depth treatment of the literature's development, cf. R. Nikolsky and T. Ilan, eds., *Rabbinic Traditions between Palestine and Babylonia*, AJEC 89 (Leiden; Boston: Brill, 2014).

28. For a standard edition, see J. Neusner, *The Mishnah: A New Translation* (New Haven: Yale University Press, 1988). Cf. also the general comments and examples in J. Neusner, *From Testament to Torah: An Introduction to Judaism in Its Formative Age* (Englewood Cliffs, NJ: Prentice Hall, 1988), 45–65.

29. Cf. the excellent introduction with examples in Neusner, *From Testament to Torah*, 72–99. Schiffman (*Texts and Traditions*, 619–70) offers additional examples.

30. Kugel, "Early Interpretation," 78; B. Chilton, "Varieties and Tendencies of Midrash: Rabbinic Interpretation of Isaiah 24.23," in *Studies in Midrash and Historiography*, vol. 3 of *Gospel Perspectives*, ed. R. T. France and D. Wenham (Sheffield: JSOT Press, 1981), 9–11. Conveniently, G. G Porton, "Rabbinic Midrash," *A History of Biblical Interpretation: The Ancient Period*, ed. Hauser and Watson, 198–224, and Neusner, *From Testament to Torah*, 100–15, provide useful overviews and examples.

Mishnah cites two ancient rabbis to resolve a possible conflict between two important OT legal teachings.[31] The Law taught that the people of Israel must not work on the Sabbath (Deut 5:12–15) and must circumcise newborn sons on their eighth day of life (Lev 12:3; cf. Luke 1:59; 2:21). But suppose the eighth day falls on a Sabbath? The Mishnah resolves the conflict by appealing to rabbinic tradition:

> R. Eliezer says, "If one did not bring a utensil [used for circumcision] on the eve of the Sabbath, he brings it openly on the Sabbath." And in time of danger, one covers it up in the presence of witnesses. And further did R. Eliezer state, "They cut wood to make coals to prepare an iron utensil [for circumcision]." An operative principle did R. Akiba state, "Any sort of labor [in connection with circumcision] which it is possible to do on the eve of the Sabbath does not override [the restrictions of] the Sabbath, and that which it is not possible to do on the eve of the Sabbath does override [the prohibitions of] the Sabbath."[32]

Second, rabbinic commentators often interpret Scripture literally (Heb. *peshat*, "plain sense"). At times, taking the plain sense of Scripture produced a rather wooden interpretation. For example, Deuteronomy 21:18–21 legislated the legal recourse of Israelite parents who have a rebellious son. By taking the text quite literally, the Mishnah defined the circumstances under which an accused son would escape condemnation:

> [If] one of them was (1) maimed in the hand, (2) lame, (3) dumb, (4) blind, or (5) deaf, he is not declared to be a rebellious and incorrigible son, since it is said, *Then his father and his mother will lay hold of him* (Dt. 21:20)—so they are not (1) maimed in their hands; *and bring him out*—(2) so they are not blind; *and they shall say*—(3) so they are not dumb; *"This is our son"*—(4) so they are not blind; *"He will not obey our voice"*—(5) so they are not deaf.[33]

The central feature of rabbinic interpretation, however, is the practice of *midrash*. Basically, midrash aims to uncover the deeper meanings that the rabbis assumed were inherent in the actual wording of Scripture. Ultimately, their motives were pastoral—to give logical biblical teaching for situations not covered directly by Scripture. To do so, the rabbis followed a system of exegetical rules (Heb. *middot*) carefully worked out over the years. Hillel listed seven such rules by which an interpreter might draw inferences from a passage.[34] Most of the rules employed assumptions that we still

---

31. Two studies explore in-depth the rabbinic interpretation reflected in the Mishnah; cf. J. N. Lightstone, *Mishnah and the Social Formation of the Early Rabbinic Guild: A Socio-Rhetorical Approach*, Studies in Christianity and Judaism 11 (Waterloo, ON: Wilfrid Laurier University Press, 2000); and A. Samely, *Rabbinic Interpretation of Scripture in the Mishnah* (Oxford: Oxford University Press, 2002).

32. Shabbat 19.1 (from Neusner, *The Mishnah*, 202).

33. Sanhedrin 8.4 (from Neusner, *The Mishnah*, 601).

34. For Hillel's list, see C. K. Barrett, "The Interpretation of the Old Testament in the New," in *The Cambridge History of the Bible: From the Beginnings to Jerome*, 3 vols., ed. P. R. Ackroyd and C. F. Evans (Cambridge: Cambridge University Press, 1970), 1:201 (henceforth, *CHB I*). Tradition also attributes lists of thirteen and thirty-two rules to later rabbis. Cf. the excellent treatment of midrashic interpretation in I. Jacobs, *The Midrashic Process: Tradition*

deem valid—e.g., the use of analogous words, phrases, or verses from biblical cross-references to illumine the text under study. On the other hand, they sometimes used cross-references in ways that we consider questionable (e.g., citing words, etc., without regard to their context).

As the Mishnah and midrashim attest, the application of these rules resulted in a fragmentary approach to exegesis. Interpreters first break up the Scripture quotation into separate short phrases, then interpret each one independently without regard for its context. Thus, they tend to make much of a text's incidental details that may or may not have been intended to convey such meanings. For example, one Gemara in the Mishnah biblically defends Jewish agricultural practices as follows:

> How do we know of a garden bed, six handbreadths square, that five different kinds of seed may be sown in it, four on the sides and one in the middle . . . ? Since it says, *For as the earth brings forth her bud and as the garden causes seeds sown in it to spring forth* (Is. 61:11). *Its seed* is not said but *Its seeds*.[35]

By breaking down Isaiah 61:11 into parts, the Gemara explains why Jews should sow five kinds of seed in the same small garden:

> R. Judah said: "The earth bringeth forth her bud"; "bringeth forth"—one; "her bud"—one; making two. "Seeds sown" means (at least) two more; making four; "causeth to spring forth"—one; making five in all.[36]

Such interpretations may strike modern readers as ingenious manipulations of Scripture. In fairness, however, one must remember that the rabbis had a high view of Scripture: they assumed that divine truth resided both within and behind its words. Further, their motive was the same as that of any modern pastor—to apply Scripture to the pressing problems of a contemporary audience. On the other hand, the rabbis were the first to model the cross-reference strategy in biblical interpretation. In that respect, modern Bible students remain in their debt.[37]

---

and Interpretation in Rabbinic Judaism (Cambridge: Cambridge University Press, 1995); R. N. Longenecker, *Biblical Exegesis in the Apostolic Period*, 2nd ed. (Grand Rapids: Eerdmans, 1999), 18–24.

35. Shabbath 9.2; cf. (from Neusner, *The Mishnah*, 190).

36. Shabbath 9.2 n. 8 (from H. Danby, *The Mishnah* [London: Oxford University Press, 1933], 108).

37. A common scholarly claim is that Paul occasionally interpreted the OT in midrashic ways similar to those of the ancient rabbis. An oft-cited example is Gal 3:16, where he bases his interpretation of the word "seed" in the Abrahamic promise (e.g., Gen 12:2–3; 17:1–11) as a reference to Christ on one detail—the fact that the word is singular (i.e., "seed" not "seeds")—in apparent violation of the original context (i.e., "seed" means collectively "descendants"). However common, this claim is anachronistic, since Paul wrote long before the Midrashim and Targumim reached written form. Further, it fails to reckon sufficiently with two facts: 1) Paul's interpretation accords well with some Jewish tradition that interpreted "seed" as a reference either to Israel as a nation or to a specific individual (i.e., Isaac), and 2) Gal 3:29 shows Paul's awareness of the collective sense of "seed." Instead, Paul probably appeals to the biblical understanding of corporate solidarity, whereby Jesus the Messiah represents both Abraham's true descendant and Israel as a nation; cf. R. N. Longenecker, *Galatians*, WBC 41 (Dallas: Word, 1990), 131–32. For a specifically messianic reading of Paul's argument, see D. H. Juel, "Interpreting Israel's Scriptures in the New Testament," in *A History of Biblical Interpretation: The Ancient Period*, ed. A. J. Hauser and D. F. Watson (Grand Rapids: Eerdmans, 2003), 292–96.

In sum, Judaism sought to relate its ancient Scriptures to the realities of its contemporary experience. Rabbinic Judaism found in the application of the Mosaic law a refuge to protect Jewish identity. Rather than resist outside influences, Hellenistic Judaism tried to accommodate its beliefs to those of platonic philosophy. And the ascetic Qumran sectarians mined OT prophecies to explain their involvement in the events of their own day. In part drawing on this rich, complex stream of interpretation, and in part parallel to it, flowed a new interpretive current—Christian interpretation.[38]

THE APOSTOLIC PERIOD (CA. AD 30–100)

Continuity and discontinuity mark the comparison between Jewish and early Christian interpretation. As devout Jews, the first Christian interpreters—the apostles—regarded Jesus as Israel's promised Messiah and the small religious community he left behind as the true fulfillment of Judaism's ancient hopes. They appealed to the OT Scriptures to support their beliefs, interpreting them by many of the same principles as other Jewish religious groups.[39] On the other hand, they revered Jesus as the new Moses and the authority of Jesus as superior even to that of the law of Moses—a decisive departure from their Jewish roots. Also, they interpreted the OT from a radically new perspective—in light of the Messiahship of Jesus and the new age inaugurated by his coming.[40]

How the Apostles Interpreted the Old Testament
Literal Interpretation
Literal-contextual Interpretation
Principle/application Interpretation

Indeed, Jesus' *literal fulfillment* of OT prophecy was their fundamental hermeneutical principle. In this they followed the example of Jesus himself.[41] Jesus launched his ministry by claiming in a Galilean synagogue that he personally fulfilled Isaiah 61:1–2 (Luke 4:18–21; cf. Mark 1:15). Later, when John doubted that Jesus was the Messiah, Jesus appealed to his healing of the blind, the lame, and the deaf just as Isaiah 35:5–6 had forecast (Luke 7:21–23). Along those same lines, the apostles found the prophetic fulfillment of the OT in Jesus and his teaching about the kingdom of God. In other words, they understood the OT christologically. According to Paul, to

---

38. On this transition, cf. J. J. Collins and C. A. Evans, eds., *Christian Beginnings and The Dead Sea Scrolls*, Acadia Studies in Bible and Theology (Grand Rapids: Baker Academic, 2006).

39. R. A. Greer, "The Christian Bible and Its Interpreters," *Early Biblical Interpretation*, ed. J. Kugel and R. A. Greer,128; cf. the nuanced, comparative study in Juel, "Interpreting Israel's Scriptures in the New Testament," 283–303. For details and examples, see Longenecker, *Biblical Exegesis in the Apostolic Period*, 36–198.

40. Cf. Barrett, "Interpretation," 399–401.

41. D. Dockery, *Biblical Interpretation Then and Now* (Grand Rapids: Baker, 1992), 23–26, summarizes interpretation of the OT, especially as regards Jesus himself.

read the law of Moses without Christ is like reading it through a veil (2 Cor 3:14–16; cf. Exod 34:33–35). The reader simply cannot see what it really means.

To remove that veil of ignorance, however, the apostles did not limit themselves to the literal interpretation of OT prophecies; in fact they employed at least three other interpretive approaches. First, they often mined OT historical and poetic sections to find predictions of the work of Christ and the church. Their method was that of *typological* interpretation—to find events, objects, ideas, and divinely inspired types (i.e., patterns or symbols) represented in the OT that anticipate God's activity later in history.[42] The assumption is that the earlier event/object/idea repeats itself in the later one. This technique sought to persuade the apostles' first-century Jewish audience of the similarities between the OT and NT ideas and events as well as the superiority of the latter to the former. The point was to show Christianity as the true culmination of the OT worship of God.[43]

Two NT books, Matthew and Hebrews, best illustrate the typological approach. For example, Matthew 2:17 writes that Herod's killing of young Jewish boys fulfills Jeremiah 31:15:

> A voice is heard in Ramah,
>   weeping and great mourning,
> Rachel weeping for her children
>   and refusing to be comforted,
> because they are no more.

In the context of Jeremiah, the verse refers to the exile of Israel to Babylon in the sixth century BC. It invokes the ancient image of Rachel, the Israelite mother par excellence (cf. Ruth 4:11), as a symbol of corporate Israel's intense maternal grief. Matthew believed Herod's violence fulfilled the lines from Jeremiah in a typological sense: history had, as it were, repeated itself in that both the earlier and later events shared similar features indicating God's sovereign hand at work in both events. This repetition signaled to Matthew that Herod's bloodshed fulfilled Jeremiah's words and thus implied that Jesus was the Messiah.[44]

---

42. Cf. conveniently, D. L. Baker, *Two Testaments, One Bible: The Theological Relationship between the Old and New Testaments* (Downers Grove: IVP Academic; Nottingham: Apollos, 2010), 169–90; J. J. O'Keefe and R.R. Reno, *Sanctified Vision: An Introduction to Early Christian Interpretation of the Bible* (Baltimore: Johns Hopkins University Press, 2005), 69–88. Cf. G. K. Beale, *Handbook on the New Testament Use of the Old Testament: Exegesis and Interpretation* (Grand Rapids: Baker Academic, 2012); G. K. Beale and D. A. Carson, eds., *Commentary on the New Testament Use of the Old Testament* (Grand Rapids: Baker Academic; Nottingham: Apollos, 2007). The classic study of NT typology remains L. Goppelt, *Typos: The Typological Interpretation of the Old Testament in the New* (Grand Rapids: Eerdmans, 1982). We engage the topic of typology in more detail in ch. 6.

43. In fact, studies have shown that, in using typology, the NT writers followed an approach evident within the OT itself; cf., F. Ninow, *Indicators of Typology Within the Old Testament: The Exodus Motif* (Frankfurt am Main: P. Lang, 2001); C. Seitz, *Figured Out: Typology and Providence in Christian Scripture* (Louisville: Westminster John Knox, 2001). More on this to follow.

44. Cf. D. A. Hagner, *Matthew 1–13*, WBC 33a (Dallas: Word, 1993), 38, who believes that the tradition of Rachel's burial near Bethlehem "was initially responsible for [Matthew's] utilization of the quotation."

A second apostolic approach that departed from seeking only how Jesus fulfilled the OT literally could be called *literal-contextual* interpretation. This approach interpreted OT Scriptures more broadly according to their normal meaning within their original contexts. Here again, their method followed Jesus' example. Jesus rebutted Satan's clever but twisted use of OT passages with straightforward OT quotations (Deut 6:16 in answer to Ps 91:11–12; cf. Matt 4:4, 7). Twice Jesus invoked the normal sense of Hosea 6:6 ("For I desire mercy, not sacrifice") to answer the Pharisees' criticism of him or his disciples (Matt 9:13; 12:8).

The Epistles offer several examples of this approach. Primarily, the apostles cited OT texts interpreted literally (that is, their normal senses in context) to support their instruction on Christian morals.[45] In Romans 12 Paul teaches his readers not to seek revenge on those who have wronged them (vv. 17–21). To back up his point, he cites Deuteronomy 32:35 ("It is mine to avenge; I will repay") and Proverbs 25:21–22 ("If your enemies are hungry, give them bread to eat . . ." NRSV) according to their natural meaning. Along the same line, Peter instructs believers to treat each other with humility, quoting Proverbs 3:34 for support: "God mocks proud mockers but shows favor to the humble" (1 Pet 5:5). If you do this, he concludes (v. 6), God "may lift you up in due time."

A third apostolic method is *principle/application*. In this method they did not interpret an OT passage literally; rather, they interpreted it by applying its underlying principle to a situation different from, but comparable to, the one in the original context. For example, Paul sought to prove that God wants to save both Jews and Gentiles by quoting Hosea 2:23:

> I will call them "my people" who are not my people;
> and I will call her "my loved one" who is not my loved one.
> (Rom 9:25; cf. 9:26 with Hos 1:10)

Originally, Hosea's words referred to the nation of Israel—specifically to Israel's reconciliation with God after a period of divine rejection. "Not my people" and "not beloved" were actually the names of Hosea's children that symbolized that rejection (cf. Hos 1:6, 9). To make his case, Paul extracts a theological principle from Hosea's words—God can lovingly make those into his people who were not so before—then he uses that principle to justify the full membership of Gentile believers in the people of God.

Paul's defense of the apostles' right to earn a living from their ministry provides another classic example of this approach (1 Cor 9:9; cf. 1 Tim 5:17–18). This practice may have needed justification because Jewish custom prohibited rabbis from receiving payment for their services.[46] He quotes Deuteronomy 25:4 ("Do not muzzle an ox

---

45. Barrett, "Interpretation," 396–97; for specifically Pauline practice, see Longenecker, *Biblical Exegesis in the Apostolic Period*, 98–109.

46. Greer, "The Christian Bible," 130. According to Longenecker, *Biblical Exegesis in the Apostolic Period*, 109–110,

while it is treading out the grain"), a text that, one's initial impression notwithstanding, actually contributes to the theme of Deuteronomy 24–25—in Thiselton's words, "*human* sensitivity and *humane compassion* toward the suffering or defenseless."[47] On one level, from the ox citation Paul defends apostolic financial support ("whoever plows and threshes should be able to do so in the hope of sharing in the harvest," 1 Cor 9:10). For Paul, the underlying principle is: if human labor benefits anyone (and gospel ministry *does*), it should at least benefit those who perform it (here, the apostles). On another more important level, however, understood as originally promoting human compassion, the citation also serves Paul's wider, long-term purpose—to cultivate the mature, Christ-like character that God desires of the entire Christian community.

In summary, apostolic interpretation both compares with and departs from the contemporary Jewish interpretive method.[48] The apostles' primary method is typology, especially when defending the messiahship of Jesus and the ministry of the Christian church. Significantly, they are the last notable interpreters with Jewish roots. From here on, Greco-Roman influences displace Jewish ones and dominate Christian biblical interpretation.

THE PATRISTIC PERIOD (CA. AD 100–590)

The death of the last apostle, John, ushered in a new era for the church. It lasted until Gregory I became pope in AD 590. We call it the "patristic period" because it features the contribution of the so-called church fathers—the prominent leaders during the initial four centuries after the apostolic period.[49] During most of the patristic period, the writings of the apostles circulated among the churches but had not yet been collected into a canonical companion to the OT. Thus, while the church considered many of the books and letters that later became our NT to be on a par with the OT, it still regarded the OT as its primary authoritative collection of Scriptures.[50]

As we shall see, however, during this period another authority—church tradition—began to exercise significant influence on the definition of church doctrine. Indeed, this development definitively shaped the practice of biblical interpretation until the Protestant

Paul's method here is allegorical in that it subordinates the OT's literal sense in order to tease out an additional meaning. But Thiselton persuasively argues that Paul's application of Deut 25:4 actually pursues "a more complex hermeneutical strategy"; cf. A. C. Thiselton, *The First Epistle to the Corinthians*, NIGTC (Grand Rapids: Eerdmans, 2000), 686.

47. Thiselton, *First Corinthians*, 686 (his italics), on whose careful discussion (686–88) our comments here draw.
48. Cf. D. C. Allison, Jr., "The Old Testament in the New Testament," *NCHB* 1, 479–502.
49. For convenient overviews, see J. C. Paget, "The Interpretation of the Bible in the Second Century," *NCHB* 1, 549–83; and C. Kannengiesser, *Handbook of Patristic Exegesis: The Bible in Ancient Christianity*, Bible in Ancient Christianity 1 (Leiden; Boston: Brill, 2004); C. A. Hall, *Reading Scripture with the Church Fathers* (Downers Grove: InterVarsity, 1998); R. P. C. Hanson, "Biblical Exegesis in the Early Church," *CHB I*, 412–53. More detailed treatment appears in E. Grypeou and H. Spurling, eds., *The Exegetical Encounter Between Jews and Christians in Late Antiquity*, Jewish and Christian Perspectives Series 18 (Leiden; Boston: Brill, 2009).
50. For further study of biblical interpretation by the early church fathers we commend the emerging Ancient Christian Commentary on Scripture series edited by T. C. Oden (InterVarsity, 1998–). The series projects thirteen volumes for the OT, two for the apocrypha, and twelve for the NT, each providing a kind of *glossa ordinaria* (on this see below)—the biblical texts artfully elaborated with ancient reflections and insights.

Reformation fourteen hundred years later. When church councils finally agreed on the precise contents of the Christian canon of Scripture, this period came to an end.[51]

The Apostolic Fathers (ca. AD 100–150)

The era of the apostolic fathers marks the first of three main subperiods within the patristic period. The apostolic fathers give us a glimpse of biblical interpretation during the first half-century after the apostle John's death. Our sources are the writings of early church leaders like Clement of Rome, Ignatius, Polycarp, and a pseudonymous writer who calls himself Barnabas. Other important writings include the Didache (from Gk. "teaching"), the Shepherd of Hermas, the Epistle to Diognetus, and various fragments that help round out the picture.[52] The fathers address two primary audiences—Christians in the churches and Jews opposing them—and their writings serve two corresponding purposes: to instruct believers in Christian doctrine and to defend the faith against Jewish arguments.

Several methods of interpretation are evident among the early church fathers.[53] Occasionally, they use *typology* to relate the OT to the NT, especially with regard to teachings about Jesus. For example, the Epistle of Barnabas (12:1–7) sees two OT passages as types of the cross of Christ—the outstretched arms of Moses, which gave Israel victory over Amalek (Exod 17), and the bronze serpent, which Moses lifted up in the wilderness (Num 21; cf. John 3:14). The Christian writer implies that both of these types teach that there is no hope of salvation outside of Jesus. Similarly, according to 1 Clement, a letter from the church in Rome to the church in Corinth, the scarlet color of the cloth that Rahab hung in Jericho to signal Joshua's spies foreshadowed the blood of Jesus (1 Clem. 12:7). In this letter's view, by choosing that signal, the spies showed that "through the blood of the Lord redemption will come to all who believe and hope in God."[54]

On other occasions, typology helps the writer to teach about Christian living from the OT. So, the Epistle of Barnabas 10:3 finds in Moses' prohibition against eating pork a warning against associating with inconsistent Christians. The reason is that, like pigs, "when they are well off, they forget their Lord, but when they are in need, they acknowledge the Lord . . . ."[55]

The most popular interpretive approach among the fathers, especially when

---

51. Cf. the illuminating history of this period with implications for the Restoration Movement (see below) by E. Ferguson, *The Early Church and Today* (Abilene: Abilene Christian University Press, 2012–2014).

52. For translation and commentary see M. W. Holmes, ed., *The Apostolic Fathers*, 3rd ed. (Grand Rapids: Baker Academic, 2007). Cf. J. Trigg, "The Apostolic Fathers and Apologists," in *A History of Biblical Interpretation: The Ancient Period*, ed. Hauser and Watson, 304–33. For convenient overviews, cf. C. N. Jefford, *Reading the Apostolic Fathers: A Student's Introduction* (Grand Rapids: Baker Academic, 2012); and D. J. Bingham, ed., *The Routledge Companion to Early Christian Thought* (London; New York: Routledge, 2010).

53. Greer, "Biblical Interpretation," 137–42. For a more detailed, classic treatment of the larger period, see also J. Pelikan, *The Emergence of the Catholic Tradition (100–600)* (Chicago: University of Chicago Press, 1971).

54. The translation is from Holmes, *The Apostolic Fathers*, 61. Cf. also his treatment of the epistle's author and background (33–39).

55. Holmes, *The Apostolic Fathers*, 411.

handling the OT, was that of *allegory*.[56] Apparently, several factors led them to adopt this approach. They wanted to support their teachings from the OT Scriptures, presumably to give their doctrine more credibility, and at the time, the allegorical method was the most popular way to interpret literature in general. Hence, it was natural for them to take up the accepted literary method of the day and apply it to the Scriptures. Despite some awareness of the history of interpretation, modern readers tend to do the same thing.

Consider, for example, the interpretation that Barnabas 8:1–7 cites for the OT ritual of the red heifer (Num 19). Typical of allegory, it draws great spiritual significance from the details of the procedure. So, the writer says the red heifer represents Jesus, and the children who sprinkle its ashes "are those who preached to us the good news about the forgiveness of sins . . . , those to whom he [Jesus] gave the authority to proclaim the gospel" (i.e., the apostles). Similarly, for Barnabas the seven days of creation provide the interpretive key to the future of history. The six days symbolize that the world will last six thousand years, the seventh day symbolizes the second coming of Christ, followed by the eighth day—"the beginning of another world" (15:3–9).[57]

At times the early fathers employ a midrashic interpretive approach reminiscent of the rabbis and the Qumran sectarians. The interpretation of Genesis 17:23–27 in Barnabas 9:7–8 provides a classic example. Here Barnabas cites as "scripture" a brief paraphrase of the Genesis report of Abraham's inauguration of the observance of circumcision, arbitrarily including in the citation the number 318 from Genesis 14:14 as the total number circumcised that day. By clever (though to us opaque) midrashic treatment of the number 318, Barnabas surprisingly finds a reference to Jesus and his cross:

> Now the (number) 18 (is represented) by two letters, J = 10 and E = 8—thus you have "JE," (the abbreviation for) "JEsus." And because the cross, represented by the letter T (= 300), was destined to convey special significance, it also says 300. He makes clear, then, that JEsus is symbolized by the two letters (JE = 18), while in the one letter (T = 300) is symbolized the cross.[58]

Finally, the fathers show early signs of an interpretive principle that was to dominate biblical interpretation until it was rejected during the Reformation. In the second century, an increasing number of heretical groups arose within the church. Most prominent among them were the gnostics who, like the others, supported their unorthodox views by appealing both to the Scriptures and to so-called sayings of Jesus—sayings they claimed Jesus taught his disciples in private.[59] The lack of a

---

56. In our view, this is certainly evident in A. Louth, ed., *Genesis 1–11*, ACCS OT 1 (Downers Grove: InterVarsity, 2001). That allegory was less popular in commentary on the NT, however, seems also evident in, e.g., G. Bray, ed., *1–2 Corinthians*, ACCS NT 7 (Downers Grove: InterVarsity, 1999).

57. Translation of Holmes, *The Apostolic Fathers*, 405, 427–29.

58. Translation of R. A. Kraft, *The Apostolic Fathers*, 4 vols., ed. R. M. Grant (New York: Nelson, 1964), 1:109.

59. Cf. W. Löhr, "Gnostic and Manichaean Interpretation," in *NCHB* 1, 584–604; C. A. Evans, "The Interpretation

finished, canonical collection of apostolic writings placed leaders of the orthodox branch of the church at a disadvantage. They felt that their only recourse to rebut the heresies was to appeal to the authority of tradition handed down from the apostles.

This established a new hermeneutical principle in the church called *traditional interpretation*. The church came to regard the traditional interpretation of a biblical passage (that which the churches taught) as its correct interpretation.[60] Without a completed canon of Scripture, church tradition offered the only firm basis for explaining what the apostles had taught. It enabled the church to defend its teaching against the gnostics and the early heretics. Later, even with a settled canon in place, traditional interpretation still served positively as a kind of interpretive "rule of thumb" to explain what biblical texts meant.[61] The danger, of course, is that in practice church tradition may (and did) attain a status almost equal with that of Scripture as the church's ultimate authority for doctrine. Further, by making church leaders official adjudicators of the apostolic tradition, the practice froze their doctrinal rulings as the correct interpretation of many biblical passages. Eventually, abuses of the otherwise useful principle of traditional interpretation (e.g., its application to support the payment of medieval indulgences) contributed to the rise of the Protestant Reformation.

The Alexandrian School (ca. AD 150–400)

With the passing of the early church fathers from the scene, the patristic period entered its second main era as a new generation took up the task of interpreting the Bible, especially the OT, to meet the needs of the Christian community. Though not a clear-cut "method" per se (the early church, in fact, lacked such), its approach was to interpret all of Scripture in light of one single key theological idea.[62] At the Christian catechetical school at Alexandria that prevailing theme was the person of Christ.[63] Among the reading strategies available from the fathers it adopted that of allegory, the exegetical method of the Alexandrian Jewish scholar, Philo, and one long promoted by Alexandrian thinkers among Jews and neo-Platonic philosophers.

---

of Scripture in the New Testament Apocrypha and Gnostic Writings," in *A History of Biblical Interpretation: The Ancient Period*, ed. Hauser and Watson, 430–56. See also M. Meyer, *The Gnostic Discoveries: The Impact of the Nag Hammadi Library* (New York: HarperCollins, 2005); and R. Roukema, *Gnosis and Faith in Early Christianity: An Introduction to Gnosticism* (Harrisburg, PA: Trinity International Press, 1999).

60. Cf. W. H. C. Frend, *The Rise of Christianity* (Philadelphia: Fortress, 1984), 134–39, 231; and Pelikan, *The Emergence of the Catholic Tradition*, 7–10.

61. The so-called "rule of faith" taught by Irenaeus (AD 120–200)—i.e., the rejection of any view that did not agree with the preaching of the apostles—articulates this idea; cf. Paget, "The Interpretation of the Bible in the Second Century," *NCHB* 1, 564–66.

62. We gratefully acknowledge the conceptual and bibliographic advice of Dr. D. Fairbairn, a patristics scholar and our former student, in an earlier revision of this section.

63. I.e., ". . . the person of Christ, the revelation of Christ, and the ecclesial reality established by Christ constitute the fundamental and indispensable hermeneutic principle and method for the complete and perfect interpretation and understanding of the prophecy of Isaiah and any other Old Testament prophecy"; cf. Metropolitan D. Trakatellis, "Theodoret's Commentary on Isaiah," in *New Perspectives on Historical Theology: Essays in Memory of John Meyendorff*, ed. B. Nassif (Grand Rapids: Eerdmans, 1996), 341. This christological principle also applied to the interpretation of non-prophetic OT books.

With the prestige of Alexandria as a center of learning behind it, the use of allegory came to dominate Christian biblical interpretation until the dawn of the Renaissance later (AD fifteenth c.). By adapting the interpretive methods of their contemporaries, Christian teachers at Alexandria undoubtedly hoped to gain credibility for their interpretations among their non-Christian peers. More important, they regarded the method as the best way to bring Scripture to bear in a positive way on the life of the expanding church and its members.[64]

Two articulate spokesmen present the case for reading the Bible allegorically. The first is Clement of Alexandria, who taught there from AD 190 until 203 when the persecution of Christians by the Roman emperor Septimius Severus drove him into exile.[65] Like Philo, Clement taught that Scripture has a twofold meaning: like a human being, it has a body (literal meaning) as well as a soul (spiritual meaning hidden behind the literal sense). Clement regarded the hidden, spiritual sense as the more important one. His allegorical method is evident in his interpretation of the parable of the prodigal son.[66] Typical of those who allegorize, he attributes Christian meaning to the story's various details. So, the robe that the father gave to the returned prodigal represents immortality; the shoes represent the upward progress of the soul; and the fatted calf represents Christ as the source of spiritual nourishment for Christians. In Clement's view, therefore, a text's literal sense is but a pointer to its underlying spiritual truth.

The second spokesman is Clement's successor, the distinguished scholar Origen (AD 185–254). In his extensive writings, Origen argued that just as humans consist of body, soul, and spirit, so Scripture has a threefold meaning.[67] Origen expanded Clement's twofold body and soul view by separating the soul into soul and spirit, adding a third or "moral" meaning: ethical instructions about the believer's relationship to

---

64. Cf. F. Young, "Alexandrian and Antiochene Exegesis," in *A History of Biblical Interpretation: The Ancient Period*, ed. Hauser and Watson, 334–54. Here we follow recent patristics scholarship that no longer contrasts the "Alexandrian" and "Antiochene" schools as proponents of, respectively, allegorical (thought "bad") and grammatical-historical methods (thought "good"). The idea of a unique Antiochene school of interpretation proves in reality to have been the creation of nineteenth-century scholarship, whereas the current consensus believes both Alexandrians and Antiochenes shared a common approach, albeit with identifiable differences. For details, see D. Fairbairn, *Grace and Christology in the Early Church* (New York; Oxford: Oxford University Press, 2003); B. Nassif, "'Spiritual Exegesis' in the School of Antioch," in Nassif, *New Perspectives*, 343–77; and F. Young, "The Rhetorical Schools and Their Influence on Patristic Exegesis," in *The Making of Orthodoxy: Essays in Honour of Henry Chadwick*, ed. R. Williams (Cambridge; New York: Cambridge University Press, 1989), 182–99. For an earlier view of Alexandria and Antioch, cf. K. Froehlich, *Biblical Interpretation in the Early Church* (Philadelphia: Fortress, 1984), 19–20.

65. Cf. Paget, "The Interpretation of the Bible in the Second Century," *NCHB* 1, 571–72; M. Edwards, "Figurative Readings: Their Scope and Justification," *NCHB* 1, 722–23; Grant and Tracy, *Short History*, 52–56. For further in-depth discussion, see E. Osborn, "The Bible and Christian Morality in Clement of Alexandria," in *The Bible in Greek Christian Antiquity*, ed. P. M. Blowers (Notre Dame: University of Notre Dame Press, 1997), 112–30.

66. A. R. Roberts and J. Donaldson, eds., *The Ante-Nicene Fathers*, 10 vols. (New York: Charles Scribner's Sons, 1913), 2:581–82 (sermon fragment). Though Philo undoubtedly influenced Clement, a recent assessment concludes that the great Jewish exegete shaped his interpretation of Scripture very little (Osborn, "The Bible and Christian Morality in Clement of Alexandria," 114).

67. G. Dorival, "Origen," in *NCHB* 1, 605–28; R. Heine, "Reading the Bible with Origen," in *The Bible in Greek Christian Antiquity*, ed. Blowers, 135–39; cf. also J. W. Trigg, *Origen* (London: Routledge, 1998), 32–35.

others. He also refined the idea of a spiritual sense into a doctrinal sense, i.e., truths about the nature of the church and the Christian's relationship to God.

Thus, said Origen, the wise interpreter of Scripture must move from the events of a passage (its literal sense) to find the hidden principles for Christian living (its moral sense) and its doctrinal truth (its spiritual sense). As an example, consider Origen's interpretation of the sexual relations between Lot and his daughters (Gen 19:30–38).[68] According to Origen, the passage has a literal sense (what actually happened), but its moral meaning is that Lot represents the rational human mind, his wife the flesh inclined to pleasures, and the daughters vainglory and pride. Applying these three elements yields the spiritual (or doctrinal) meaning: Lot represents the OT law, the daughters represent Jerusalem and Samaria, and the wife represents the Israelites who rebelled in the wilderness.

From a modern perspective, such interpretation seems to play fast and loose with the text. One might argue that Origen is simply reading his own Christian ideas into the text rather than drawing them from it. Anticipating such criticism, Origen contended that God had inspired the original biblical writers to incorporate the allegorical meaning into their writings. Thus, what Origen considered the highest meaning of Scripture—its deeper spiritual truth—was already implicit in Scripture, not something invented by the interpreter. Of course, Origen's was not the only view at this time; voices asserting alternate views were occasionally heard. For example, the later Alexandrian, Cyril (AD 378–444), understood the anachronistic and arbitrary tendencies of allegory and rejected the method in favor of a more grammatically-based approach.[69] Similarly, Theodore of Mopsuestia (ca. AD 350–428), thought to be the greatest interpreter among those associated with Antioch, wrote that only four psalms (2; 8; 45; 110) truly contained messianic prophecy about the incarnation of Christ and the church. He also departed from the traditional allegorical interpretation of the Song of Songs as symbolizing Christ's love for the church or the Christian's devotion to Christ, reading it instead as a love poem written by Solomon to celebrate his marriage to an Egyptian princess.[70] Nevertheless, Origen's allegorical approach would shape Christian interpretation for more than a millennium.[71]

---

68. "Genesis Homily V," in *Origen: Homilies on Genesis and Exodus*, The Fathers of the Church 71 (Washington, D.C.: Catholic University of America Press, 1982), 112–20. For Origen's interpretation of Jesus' triumphal entry that sought to reconcile differing gospel accounts, see D. L. Dungan, *A History of the Synoptic Problem*, ABRL (New York: Doubleday, 1999), 78–80.

69. J. O'Keefe, "Christianizing Malachi: Fifth-Century Insights from Cyril of Alexandria," *Vigiliae Christianae* 50 (1996): 138–39. Cyril's interpretation of Malachi illustrates two phenomena typical of this period: how a single theological concern (i.e., the life of the Christian community) dominated biblical interpretation, and how both Alexandria and Antioch shared a common concern about the excesses of allegory.

70. For more on Theodore, although from an older scholarly perspective, see M. F. Wiles, "Theodore of Mopsuestia as Representative of the Antiochene School," *CHB I*, 489–510. Trakatellis ("Theodoret's Commentary on Isaiah," 313–42) claims to find a synthetic interpretive approach, albeit with obvious differences, in the commentaries of Theodore's student, Theodoret (ca. AD 393–460), and in the sermons of John Chrysostom (ca. AD 347–407). For a very nuanced discussion of the hermeneutical idea of *theoria* (Gk. "insight") among the so-called "Antiochenes," see Nassif, "'Spiritual Exegesis,'" 345–77; cf. also Young, "Alexandrian and Antiochene Exegesis," in *A History of Biblical Interpretation: The Ancient Period*, ed. Hauser and Watson, 347–50.

71. Most modern interpreters feel ambivalence, if not antipathy, toward this approach. But for a recent, balanced

Church Councils (ca. AD 400–590)

The era of the church councils marks the third and final phase of the patristic period. With the conversion of the Roman emperor Constantine in AD 312, politics exercised a profound influence on the church's interpretation of Scripture. In the emperor's view, doctrinal disputes between the orthodox mainstream and its heretical tributaries threatened the empire's political stability. So he pressured the church to settle its differences and to standardize its disputed doctrines. This proved to be a difficult task for two reasons. First, simple appeals to Scripture in defense of orthodoxy produced nothing but a doctrinal stalemate. The reason was that the unorthodox groups also supported their views from Scripture, often very persuasively. That fact led the early church father Tertullian (ca. AD 200) to question their right to such appeals since in his view the Scripture belonged only to a church holding to apostolic teaching.[72] The church desperately needed some authority to determine with finality the meaning of Scripture. It found the answer in the apostolic succession of church leadership.

Above, we noted how the apostolic fathers appealed to traditional interpretation in response to heresies like Gnosticism. Under Constantine, orthodox church leaders took up that argument again, affirming their "apostolicity"—i.e., that only they, the apostles' successors, were the true interpreters of Scripture since only they had directly received the apostolic teaching. To implement this principle, church leaders convened a series of church councils to define official church doctrine.

Their decisions defined correct Christian beliefs and defended orthodox views against those of the heretics. Since all sides cited Scripture as support, the conciliar pronouncements tried to spell out what, according to apostolic tradition, was the correct interpretation of the Scriptures and wherein lay the heretics' misunderstandings. The importance of the councils lies in their description of "orthodoxy," the mainstream Christian beliefs consistent with properly interpreted Scripture and the apostles' teaching. Those beliefs distinguished orthodoxy from the views of the heretics.

Early in this period, the great church leader Augustine became the first orthodox Christian in the Western church to articulate an original and comprehensive approach to hermeneutics.[73] His complex, nuanced interpretive approach emerges in his sermons, biblical commentaries, the famous *Confessions*, and especially his *Christian*

Roman Catholic assessment of patristic exegesis as the stream of tradition that also shapes modern Catholic exegesis in some ways, see O'Keefe and Reno, *Sanctified Vision*, 69–88; P. S. Williamson, *Catholic Principles for Interpreting Scripture*, Subsidia Biblica 22 (Rome: Pontificio Istituto Biblico, 2001), 137–47.

72. Dockery, *Biblical Interpretation*, 71.

73. C. Harrison, "Augustine," *NCHB* 1, 676–96; R. A. Norris, Jr., "Augustine and the Close of the Ancient Period of Interpretation," in *A History of Biblical Interpretation: The Ancient Period*, ed. Hauser and Watson, 380–408; F. Van Fleteren, "Principles of Augustine's Hermeneutic: An Overview," in *Augustine: Biblical Exegete*, ed. F. Van Fleteren and J. C. Schnaubelt (New York: P. Lang, 2001), 1–32; cf. T. Williams, "Biblical Interpretation," in *The Cambridge Companion to Augustine*, ed. E. Stump and N. Kretzmann (Cambridge: Cambridge University Press, 2001), 59–70. Augustine's commentaries on Genesis and Psalms offer especially important clues to his interpretive approach.

Instruction (AD 397). Augustine's first principle of interpretation specifies that it aims to lead readers to love God and other people (i.e., the goal of Scripture itself).[74] Proper interpretation seeks to cultivate a proper, ethical, and devout Christian life. According to Augustine, to interpret the Bible properly one must focus on a text's literal or historical meaning, by which he meant its "real meaning" or what the text intended to say.[75] But what does one do when Scripture does not make good literal sense? For example, taken literally, the phrase "the image of God" (Gen 1:26) might imply that God has some physical substance, if not a physical body just like humans.[76] In such cases, Augustine (a highly trained rhetorician) seeks a figurative or allegorical meaning in the text (e.g., that "image" refers to humanity's spiritual side). To guard against the subjective excesses of allegory, he offered three interpretive principles for finding the figurative meaning of difficult texts.

First, one consults what other, clearer passages of Scripture say on the subject, and second, one consults the "rule of faith" or the apostolic interpretation of the major doctrines of Scripture. Third, if conflicting views meet both criteria, one should consult the context to see which view best commends itself. One cannot overstate Augustine's momentous contribution to the study of the Bible. His thought profoundly influenced later thinkers (e.g., Aquinas, Erasmus, Luther), and Bible students still follow his principles of proper interpretation.[77]

Another important event toward the close of the patristic period involving another influential thinker merits mention. Church leaders finally persuaded the learned scholar Jerome (AD 331–420) to translate the OT and NT, as well as the Apocrypha, into Latin.[78] This translation from Hebrew and Greek manuscripts, known as the Vulgate (from the Latin word for "common"), became the official Bible of the Western church. Its unique contribution was to provide the Latin-speaking world a translation of the OT based on the original text rather than on a translation (i.e., the Septuagint or

74. *On Christian Doctrine*, I, 40–41. For translation and commentary, see J. E. Rotelle, ed., *The Works of Saint Augustine: A Translation for the 21st Century*, Vol. 11 (Hyde Park, NY: New City Press, 1996). For an introduction to Augustine's theology, see M. Levering, *The Theology of Augustine: An Introductory Guide to His Most Important Works* (Grand Rapids: Baker Academic, 2013).

75. Van Fleteren, "Principles of Augustine's Hermeneutics," 10; Augustine, *On Christian Doctrine*, 1.41. Cf. the convenient overview of Augustine and his thought in Hall, *Reading Scripture with the Church Fathers*, 116–25; and G. Bonner, "Augustine as Biblical Scholar," *CHB I*, 541–63.

76. Indeed, according to Hall (*Reading Scripture with the Church Fathers*, 119–20), Augustine's North African contemporaries held such a materialistic view of God based on a wooden, literal hermeneutic. Augustine found temporary intellectual refuge among the more flexible (but heretical) Manichees, but eventually the preaching of Ambrose with its allegorical approach won his return to the ecclesiastical mainstream. Later he rebutted the Manichees' criticisms of orthodox hermeneutics and interpreted Genesis' figures of speech in his *Two Books on Genesis against the Manichees* (Hall, 122–23).

77. Cf. Van Fleteren's characterization of him ("Principles of Augustine's Hermeneutic," 22) as "the philosopher-theologian upon whom the West was constructed."

78. A. Kamesar, "Jerome," *NCHB* 1, 653–75; D. Brown, "Jerome and the Vulgate," in *A History of Biblical Interpretation: The Ancient Period*, ed. Hauser and Watson, 355–78. Jerome received a rigorous education in classics at Rome and later learned Greek and Hebrew (cf. Dockery, *Biblical Hermeneutics*, 129: ". . . the most learned person in the Latin-speaking church of the late fourth century"). In a letter, he once described himself as "trilinguis, Hebraeus, Graecus, Latinus" (quoted from Hall, *Reading Scripture with the Church Fathers*, 110).

LXX).[79] Unfortunately, from that time the Western church's study of the Bible in the original Hebrew and Greek ceased for all practical purposes until it revived during the Renaissance. Instead, the Western church came to depend upon the Vulgate translation for all doctrinal discussions. In some instances, Jerome's dynamic-paraphrase method of translation gave renderings that were not as accurate in reflecting the original languages as they could have been (e.g., in Luke 1:28, "Hail Mary, full *of grace . . .*" [cf. Gk. "favored one"; NRSV; NIV "you who are highly favored!"]). Thus the Western church moved still another step away from dependence upon the original Scripture text itself as the source for its teachings.[80]

THE MIDDLE AGES (CA. AD 590–1500)

As the name implies, the Middle Ages is the millennium that falls between the patristic period, dominated by church fathers and councils, and the new courses charted by the Reformation. In a sense, it constitutes a transitional phase between the two. The Middle Ages mark the decline of some features of the former and lay the groundwork for the emergence of the latter. Popular impression sees the period as a dark, oppressive one, and that portrait is largely consistent with historical reality.[81] Ignorance plagued both Christian clergy and laity, and morally bankrupt church leaders stopped at nothing to preserve their ecclesiastical power. At the same time, and usually hidden behind cloister walls, a millennium-long, lively, and rich dialogue with the Bible quietly advanced and produced tools for its continuing study that profoundly shaped the practice of biblical interpretation in the following centuries.[82]

Three approaches typify biblical interpretation in the Middle Ages. Interpreters continued to depend heavily upon *traditional* interpretation—the views of the fathers passed down over centuries. The primary resource for this method remained the written *catena* (Lat. "chain") or chain of interpretations, i.e., long collections of interpretive comments compiled from the commentaries of the church fathers.[83] Significantly, while pre-medieval catenae cited a variety of commentators, medieval ones featured fathers

79. The offspring of his monumental work, the Vulgate, includes the later Wycliffe (fourteenth c.) and Douai (sixteenth c.) English versions.

80. J. N. D. Kelly, *Jerome: His Life, Writings, and Controversies* (New York: Harper and Row, 1975), offers in-depth biographical treatment of him; cf. also H. D. F. Sparks, "Jerome as Bible Scholar," *CHB I*, 510–40. More recently, see A. Cain, *The Letters of Jerome: Asceticism, Biblical Exegesis, and the Construction of Christian Authority in Late Antiquity*, OECS (Oxford; New York: Oxford University Press, 2009).

81. For an overview, see J. Fried, *The Middle Ages*, trans. P. Lewis (Cambridge, MA; London: Belknap Press, 2015). Cf. also J. H. Lynch and P. C. Adamo, *The Medieval Church: A Brief History* (London; New York: Routledge/Taylor & Francis Group, 2014).

82. For an insightful survey of the contours of this dialogue, see C. Ocker, "Medieval Exegesis and the Origin of Hermeneutics," *SJT* 52 (1999): 328–45. For additional background touching medieval biblical interpretation, see A. J. Hauser and D. F. Watson, "Introduction and Overview," in *A History of Biblical Interpretation, Volume 2: The Medieval Through the Reformation Periods*, ed. A. J. Hauser and D. F. Watson (Grand Rapids: Eerdmans, 2009), 1–85.

83. R. E. McNally, *The Bible in the Early Middle Ages* (Atlanta: Scholars Press, 1986), 30–32. The *Catena Aurea* compiled by medieval scholar, Thomas Aquinas, exemplifies this practice; cf. the English translation in M. F. Toal, *The Sunday Sermons of the Great Fathers* (San Francisco: Ignatius Press, 2000). Cf. the wide-ranging, detailed

like Augustine and Jerome, who expressed the church's accepted doctrinal views. In other words, interpreters using catenae tended to conform their interpretations to the church's doctrinal norms. As McNally puts it, during this period "[e]xegesis became almost synonymous with tradition, for the good commentator was the scholar who handed on faithfully what he had received."[84]

The catena spawned one important interpretive offspring during the Middle Ages. Medieval monks developed the practice of the *interpretive gloss*, Scripture annotations or commentaries from the fathers that were written in the margins or between the lines of the Bible (eighth–ninth c.). By the late eleventh century, this practice became widespread in medieval schools, eventually took on a uniform design, and finally saw publication in glossed Bibles in Paris (ca. 1220). About the same time, the *Glossa Ordinaria* (lit. "ordinary tongue") also appeared, a massive multi-volume compilation of comments and glosses on individual biblical books that soon became the standard medieval commentary on the Bible.[85]

As noted earlier, of all the methods of biblical interpretation in the Middle Ages, the *allegorical* method dominated. Indeed, in contrast to Origen's threefold sense of Scripture, many medieval scholars believed every Bible passage had four meanings. A popular rhyme (in Latin, that is) that circulated widely in the Middle Ages summarizes them:

> The letter teaches deeds;
> allegory, what you should believe;
> the moral sense, what you should do;
> and the anagogical sense, what to hope for.[86]

Thus, the Bible's four senses are: literal (or historical), allegorical (or doctrinal), moral (or tropological), and anagogical (or eschatological). For example, medieval Bible scholars might understand Israel's crossing of the Red Sea to have four senses:

Literal: the actual crossing by Moses and Israel
Allegorical: the Christian's baptism and new life in Christ
Moral: the obedient Christian crosses from life's difficulties to earthly blessings
Anagogical: the Christian's final crossing from death to eternal life[87]

treatment of the Bible (and Bibles) during this period in R. Marsden and E. A. Matter, eds., *The New Cambridge History of the Bible. Vol. 2, From 600 to 1450* (Cambridge: Cambridge University Press, 2012; henceforth, *NCHB* 2).

84. McNally, *The Bible in the Early Middle Ages*, 29. For a major, more positive recent assessment, see H. De Lubac, *Medieval Exegesis: The Four Senses of Scripture*, 3 vols. (Grand Rapids: Eerdmans, 1999–2009).

85. B. Smalley, *The Study of the Bible in the Middle Ages* (Oxford: Blackwell, 1952), 46–66 (with a photograph); Ocker, "Medieval Exegesis," 329–32, who notes its "tremendous influence within scholastic exegesis" (332). For a convenient discussion of its history, see J. Swanson, "The *Glossa Ordinaria*," in *The Medieval Theologians*, ed. G. R. Evans (Oxford: Blackwell, 2001), 156–67, who calls the *Glossa* "an intermediate textbook" that schooled students and enabled scholars to develop their own interpretations (166–67, quote 167). For further developments in scholastic exegetical literature (i.e., the improvements on the *Glossa Ordinaria* in the *Historia Scholastica*, the *postilla* [a kind of running commentary], and Latin Bible concordances), see Ocker, "Medieval Exegesis," 332–36.

86. Williamson, *Catholic Principles*, 172, who credits the couplet to Augustine of Denmark (13th c.). For a slightly different, rhyming version, see Grant and Tracy, *Short History*, 85.

87. Both the expansion to a four-fold sense of Scripture and Jerusalem as an example go back to the writings

This suggestion of Scripture's "senses" might strike the modern reader as a cliché, if not plain nonsense. But Ocker rightly reminds us that this apparent cliché rests on an important (and obvious) assumption—the depth and complexity of Scripture—in other words,

> . . . that biblical texts and nouns yielded historical meanings more remote from the reader or the reader's world and other meanings that touched on present religious life—the church, the moral condition of the soul, the future. The four-fold sense indicated a process of abstraction and the possibility of lithe movement, seldom if ever a procedure for chopping Bible passages into quarters.[88]

The third method of medieval interpretation was *historical* interpretation. Some medieval interpreters sought to find the historical sense of Scripture by consulting with Jewish authorities. The biblical commentaries written by Andrew of St. Victor (twelfth c.), abbot of an English abbey at Wigmore, exemplify this approach.[89] Unlike his contemporaries, Andrew excluded spiritual commentary and theological questions from his interpretation. Instead, he concentrated on a text's historical or literal sense, drawing often on Jewish interpretation. Though a minority figure on the larger historical landscape, Andrew reminds us that some medieval scholars kept alive the tradition of earlier exegetes like Jerome and Augustine for whom Scripture's literal or historical sense was primary.

Eventually a more influential proponent of the literal/historical approach emerged, the movement called *scholasticism*.[90] Scholasticism was a pre-Renaissance intellectual awakening in Europe that began in the monastic schools and later spread to the universities (twelfth to thirteenth c.). Its main concern was to sort out the relationship between the Christian faith and human reason. Two factors provided the fertile seed bed from which this movement sprouted and spread.

First, Europe enjoyed several centuries of relative political stability and peace that allowed scholars to pursue their questions without distraction. Second, the rediscovery of pre-Christian classical philosophers, especially Aristotle, provided the intellectual tools for the task. Aristotelian philosophy was the primary tool.[91] Forerunners of scholasticism like Anselm and Peter Abélard (eleventh c.) used the methods of logical analysis and syllogisms to raise great "cathedrals of ideas" on various theological

---

of John Cassian (early fifth c.); cf. Ocker, "Medieval Exegesis," 338–39. For a detailed discussion of this approach from a modern Catholic perspective, see Williamson, *Catholic Principles*, 161–215.

    88. Ocker, "Medieval Exegesis," 339; cf. the similar sentiment in R. A. Muller and J. L. Thompson, "The Significance of Precritical Exegesis: Retrospect and Prospect," in *Biblical Interpretation in the Era of the Reformation*, ed. R. A. Muller and J. L. Thompson (Grand Rapids: Eerdmans, 1996), 344.

    89. Smalley, *Study of the Bible*, 120–72.

    90. C. Ocker, "Scholastic Interpretation of the Bible," in *A History of Biblical Interpretation, Volume 2: The Medieval Through the Reformation Periods*, ed. Hauser and Watson, 254–79. Cf. also treatments in Olson, *The Story of Christian Theology*, 311–15; and J. González, *The Story of Christianity*, 2 vols. (San Francisco: Harper and Row, 1984), 1:301–23.

    91. Interestingly, some access to Aristotle came through Arabic and Syriac translations of his Greek writings.

topics.[92] More importantly, Aristotle's theory of causation (i.e., that events may have multiple causes) subtly reshaped the thought-world of exegetes in the late Middle Ages (fourteenth c.). Applied to the Bible, it led them to consider the possibility of multiple causes behind the Bible itself (e.g., God, the human authors, their intentions as determiners of textual meanings, etc.). Further, they began to see that, in Ocker's words, "a quality of thought *beyond* speech [i.e., the basis for multiple senses] in fact was a quality of thought *of* speech."[93] That insight ultimately undermined the long-held distinctions assumed between Scripture's various "senses" and led to a more holistic understanding of its meanings. Indeed, discussions of the day point to "growing confidence in the ability of the literal text as such, even at its most obscure and bizarre figurative moments, to convey religious and philosophical knowledge."[94]

The most articulate spokesman for scholasticism was the brilliant Christian thinker, Thomas Aquinas (thirteenth c.).[95] His massive *Summa Theologica* synthesized the intellectual fruits of three centuries of intense academic discussion. It gave the Christian faith a rational, systematic expression, and eventually became the standard summary of theology in the Roman Catholic Church. More than any of his contemporaries, Aquinas propounded the importance of the literal meaning of Scripture. For him it represented the basis on which the other senses (allegorical, anagogical, etc.) rested. Indeed, he argued that the literal sense of Scripture contained everything necessary to faith.[96]

In summary, practitioners of allegory still abounded in the church of the Middle Ages, and dependence upon traditional interpretation remained heavy.[97] At the same time, the long hegemony of these two methods within the church declined, various other approaches to interpretation flourished, and a reformulation of how the supposed four senses interrelated emerged. The scholastic application of philosophical tools to theology also tended to anchor the interpretation of Scripture to more rational, objective moorings. As Muller and Thompson observe, "an increasing interest in both the text and its literal sense" positioned medieval exegesis "along a trajectory pointing toward the Reformation rather than away from it."[98] The intellectual stage, thus, was set for the next step in the long saga of how the church would interpret its Bible.

---

92. This phrase comes from Olson, *The Story of Christian Theology*, 312, who also offers an illuminating discussion of these two theologians (316–30); cf. G. R. Evans, "Anselm of Canterbury," and L. O. Nielsen, "Peter Abélard and Gilbert Poitiers," in *The Medieval Theologians*, ed. Evans, 94–101 and 102–14 (respectively).

93. Ocker, "Medieval Exegesis," 341. We are indebted to his remarkably insightful discussion and citation of medieval writers reflecting this changed outlook (338–44).

94. Ocker, "Scholastic Interpretation of the Bible," 267.

95. Olson, *The Story of Christian Theology*, 331–47, who judges Aquinas to be "the single greatest theologian of the Western Catholic tradition between Augustine in the fifth century and Karl Rahner of Austria in the late twentieth century" (331); cf. F. Kerr, "Thomas Aquinas," in *The Medieval Theologians*, ed. Evans, 201–20.

96. G. Bray, *Biblical Interpretation Past and Present* (Downers Grove: InterVarsity, 1996), 152–53.

97. Perhaps the epitome of the persistence of the allegorical method in this period is the eighty-six sermons on the Song of Songs by the mystic, Bernard of Clairvaux (12th c.); cf. Bray, *Biblical Interpretation*, 160–64.

98. Muller and Thompson, "The Significance of Precritical Exegesis," 344.

THE REFORMATION (CA. AD 1500–1650)

Despite popular impression, the step from the Middle Ages into the Protestant Reformation was neither as radical nor as obvious as is often thought. The historical forces that caused it are many, but one in particular merits mention because of its relevance to our subject.[99] During the late Middle Ages, conflict arose between the more traditional scholastics and the so-called new learning of Christian humanists like Erasmus.[100]

With some justification, the latter derided what he deemed the hair-splitting, convoluted logic of scholastic theology.[101] According to the humanists, such theology offered no spiritual food for hungry Christian souls, and many writers openly yearned for the simple faith and devotion of the early church. Erasmus proposed that the regnant theology of sterile speculation give way to what he called the "philosophy of Christ," genuine spirituality and concern for ethics centered on the teaching of Christ.[102] Since scholastic systematic theology provided traditional orthodoxy with its rational buttress, many saw scholasticism as a fortress that needed to fall.

Further, a renewed interest in studying the Bible in its original Hebrew and Greek languages provided scholars with a fresh glimpse of the Scriptures. In 1506 the controversial philologist Johann Reuchlin published a rudimentary Hebrew grammar, thereby founding the modern study of Hebrew.[103] In 1516 Erasmus published the first modern edition of the Greek NT with a fresh Latin translation appended to it. This increasing interest in the early manuscripts exposed many translation errors in the Latin Vulgate and undermined the absolute authority it had enjoyed in supporting church doctrine. Since the Catholic Church had staked its own authority in part on the Vulgate, doubts concerning the authority of the latter also cast shadows of doubt on the authority of the former.[104]

---

99. D. MacCullough, *The Reformation: A History* (New York: Viking, 2004), 3–102, ably illuminates the historical setting of the Reformation (1490–1517 AD).

100. "Humanists" were scholars who devoted themselves to the study of classical literature during this period; cf. MacCullough, *The Reformation*, 73–84; E. Rummel, "The Renaissance Humanists," in *A History of Biblical Interpretation, Volume 2: The Medieval Through the Reformation Periods*, ed. Hauser and Watson, 280–98. For an excellent discussion of the continuity and discontinuity between medieval and reformation interpretation, see R. A. Muller, "Biblical Interpretation in the Era of the Reformation," in *Biblical Interpretation*, ed. Muller and Thompson, 8–16. For an insightful analysis of the crucial paradigm-shifts in intellectual thought that contributed to the Reformation and later to modern biblical criticism, see Dungan, *Synoptic Problem*, 146–58. In addition, what follows draws on O. Chadwick, *The Reformation* (Baltimore: Penguin Books, 1972), 29–39.

101. He described his opponent as "academic theology, corrupted as it is by philosophic and scholastic quibbling"; quoted from M. Hoffmann, *Rhetoric and Theology: The Hermeneutic of Erasmus* (Toronto: University of Toronto Press, 1994), 7. Hoffmann offers a thorough, rigorous assessment of Erasmus' approach to biblical interpretation (esp. 95–167, 211–27). More recently, see C. C. von Wedel, *Erasmus of Rotterdam: Advocate of a New Christianity*, Erasmus Studies (Toronto: University of Toronto Press, 2013); cf. also the brief treatment in MacCullough, *The Reformation*, 94–102.

102. Olson, *The Story of Christian Theology*, 315, 362; cf. the expanded treatment of J. L. Carrington, "Desiderius Erasmus," in *The Reformation Theologians*, ed. C. Lindberg (Oxford: Blackwell, 2002), 37–39.

103. B. K. Waltke and M. O'Connor, *An Introduction to Biblical Hebrew Syntax* (Winona Lake, IN: Eisenbrauns, 1990), 38–39. For details concerning the larger context, see Rummel, "The Renaissance Humanists," 282–87.

104. Rummel ("The Renaissance Humanists," 281) cites one telling example of how Erasmus' translation undermined traditional Catholic theology and shaped that of the Reformation: "In Matt 4:17, he changed the

Again, growing dissatisfaction with the allegorical method fueled a desire for a better interpretative approach. At the end of the fifteenth century, a man named Geiler of Kaiserberg observed that abuse of the allegorical method had made Scripture a "nose of wax" to be turned interpretively any way the reader wanted.[105] Many rued the arbitrary, speculative nature of allegory.

According to a popular saying in the sixteenth century, "Erasmus laid the egg and Luther hatched it."[106] Indeed, Martin Luther was one of two figures whose careful exegesis aligned the best of the medieval approach with the new ecclesiastical reality of the sixteenth century and led Christian hermeneutics into new paths. First, Luther affirmed that only Scripture has divine authority for Christians. In so doing, Luther broke with the long-held principle that church tradition and ordained church leaders held virtually the same weight of doctrinal authority as the Bible.[107] He thus laid down the foundational premise of the Reformation, the principle of *sola scriptura* (Scripture alone). As a corollary, Luther also affirmed the principle that Scripture itself is its own best interpreter; consequently, readers no longer needed to depend as heavily as before on patristic commentary and church authorities to understand the Bible.

Second, Luther followed those medievalists who rejected the allegorical method of interpretation because, in his view, it amounted to empty speculation. Instead, with Aquinas he affirmed that Scripture had one simple meaning, its historical sense. This is discerned, Luther said, by applying the ordinary rules of grammar in the light of Scripture's original historical context. At the same time, Luther echoed a theme of the church fathers and the medievalists: he read the Bible through Christocentric glasses, claiming that the whole Bible—including the OT—taught about Christ.[108] Thus, while rejecting allegory, Luther took up again the typological interpretation typical of the NT.

But Luther stressed that proper interpretation also has a subjective element. By this he meant that the illumination of the Holy Spirit guides Christians in applying their

---

Vulgate translation *poenitentiam agite* ("do penance") to *resipiscite* ("repent"), shifting the emphasis from works to faith, a point elaborated by Luther in his *Ninety-Five Theses* . . . ." Dungan (*Synoptic Problem*, 185–90) details the history of how Erasmus' Greek NT, despite its flaws, won acceptance as the *textus receptus*—"the received (i.e., only true) text" from which the King James Version was translated—and how the emerging method of textual criticism eventually undermined the Vulgate's credibility (191–97).

105. B. Hall, "Biblical Scholarship: Editions and Commentaries," in *Cambridge History of the Bible: The West from the Reformation to the Present Day*, ed. S. L. Greenslade (Cambridge: At the University Press, 1963), 48 (henceforth *CHB III*).

106. Olson, *The Story of Christian Theology*, 367. Cf. the treatment of Luther's life in MacCullough, 111–58. The classic biography of Luther remains R. Bainton, *Here I Stand: A Life of Martin Luther* (New York: Mentor Books, 1950).

107. Cf. M. D. Thompson, "Biblical Interpretation in the Works of Martin Luther," in *A History of Biblical Interpretation, Volume 2: The Medieval Through the Reformation Periods*, ed. Hauser and Watson, 299–318; cf. E. Cameron, *The European Reformation* (Oxford: Oxford University Press, 1991), 136–37.

108. Thompson, "Biblical Interpretation in the Works of Martin Luther," 304–6, 314–15; Cameron, *The European Reformation*, 137–38, 140. The doctrine of justification by faith, a central theme in Luther's thought, also influenced his reading of Scripture. This interpretive lens in part accounts for his well-known characterization of the Epistle of James as "an epistle of straw."

personal experience to biblical interpretation. It enables the Bible reader to understand accurately what a given passage teaches about Christ. The resulting interpretation is, thus, a truly "spiritual interpretation."[109]

The other figure that led the hermeneutical transition was John Calvin.[110] Like Luther and Aquinas, Calvin rejected allegory in favor of a historical interpretation of Scripture. With Luther, he also affirmed Scripture as the church's only ultimate authority, an authority to be accepted by faith. Again, Calvin believed in a subjective element in interpretation—what he called "the internal witness of the Holy Spirit." In Calvin's view, this witness served not to illuminate the process of interpretation but to confirm in the Christian's heart that an interpretation was correct.[111]

In brief, the Reformation further developed the emphasis of some medievalists on the primacy of Scripture's literal sense. Also, while cherishing and often invoking church tradition and the interpretations of church fathers, the Reformers set the teachings of Scripture over both as their ultimate authority. They affirmed that the Bible itself was both "perspicacious" (i.e., clearly understandable) and its own best interpreter. If many past exegetes applied allegory to dig out Scripture's alleged multiple meanings, the Reformers followed Aquinas in accepting Scripture's plain, simple, literal sense as the basis for all its treasury of meanings. Small wonder, then, that both Luther and Calvin produced commentaries on numerous biblical books, commentaries still prized by Bible students today.

The Reformers' consensus on "how" to understand Scripture, however, proved no guarantee of their concurrence on "what" it says. In fact, they disagreed on the meaning of many biblical texts. For example, at a now famous meeting in 1529, Luther and H. Zwingli, a leading Swiss reformer, failed to agree on what the Bible taught about the Lord's Supper.[112] Indeed, the episode anticipated the many interpretive

---

109. Thompson, "Biblical Interpretation in the Works of Martin Luther," 310–12, who suggests (312) that the roots of this aspect of Luther's thought "lie in a long tradition of *lectio divina*, 'sacred reading,' . . . joined to the academic study of Scripture by the scholars of the Abbey of St. Victor in Paris . . . ." For more on Luther's spiritual interpretation, see R. C. Gleason, "'Letter' and 'Spirit' in Luther's Hermeneutics," *BSac* 157 (2000): 468–85. K. Hagen, "*Omnis homo mendax*: Luther on Psalm 116," in *Biblical Interpretation* (Muller and Thompson), 85–102, offers an illuminating glimpse of Luther as exegete, highlighting elements of his continuity and discontinuity with medieval exegesis and calling into question any ties of Luther's work to Enlightenment approaches.

110. For an overview of his life and work, see MacCullough, *The Reformation*, 230–45; R. C. Zachman, "John Calvin (1509–1564)," in *The Reformation Theologians*, ed. Lindberg, 184–97. For his hermeneutics, see B. Pitkin, "John Calvin and the Interpretation of the Bible," in *A History of Biblical Interpretation, Volume 2: The Medieval Through the Reformation Periods*, ed. Hauser and Watson, 341–71. Cf. also the biographies of H. J. Selderhuis, *John Calvin: A Pilgrim's Life*, trans. A. Gootjes (Downers Grove: IVP Academic, 2009); and B. Cottret, *Calvin: A Biography*, trans. M. W. McDonald (Grand Rapids: Eerdmans, 2000).

111. T. H. L. Parker, *Calvin: An Introduction to His Thought* (Louisville: Westminster/John Knox, 1995), 24–27; cf. Zachman, "John Calvin," 191, 193. More recent relevant studies include J. L. Thompson, "Calvin as a Biblical Interpreter," in *The Cambridge Companion to John Calvin*, ed. D. K. McKim (Cambridge: Cambridge University Press, 2004), 58–73; and D. K. McKim, *Calvin and the Bible* (Cambridge: Cambridge University Press, 2006).

112. Both rejected *transubstantiation*, the Catholic teaching that in the Mass the bread and wine become literally the body and blood of Christ and automatically convey grace when consumed. Luther argued that communion comprised a sacrament involving Christ's "real presence" in the sacrament, while Zwingli believed that, since the physical Christ was in heaven, communion was a symbolic sacred meal (later called an "ordinance"); cf. MacCullough, *The Reformation*, 240–45, 340–43; Olson, *The Story of Christian Theology*, 404–8; Hauser and

differences that soon divided "Lutherans" and "Calvinists" in the post-Reformation era, divisions that remain today. Such disagreements, however, both confirm the complexity of the process of interpretation (including the fact that interpreters still work within traditions) and affirm the centrality of the Bible as the primary source of Christian doctrine.

Indeed, like most movements, the Reformation also birthed a more extreme expression—the so-called "Radical Reformation."[113] Regarding hermeneutics, groups like the Anabaptists and Mennonites took seriously the Reformation principles of *sola scriptura* and of the perspicacity of Scripture, although they applied them in ways that other Reformers strongly opposed. They gave priority to the NT, which they read literally, appealing to the Holy Spirit for illumination, and they sought to establish relatively autonomous Christian communities patterned after the NT church. They only baptized adults by immersion, appointed Spirit-led lay leaders, separated themselves from both the world and the established churches, and refused to pay taxes or serve as soldiers. Thought rebellious and seditious by other Christians at the time, thousands of them were cruelly martyred—in retrospect truly a dark day for the Reformation.[114] They bequeathed to Christendom, however, a vibrant fifth stream of western Bible interpretation and Christian community alongside the more established Catholic, Lutheran, Calvinist, and Anglican ones. More tellingly, they put the Bible and its interpretation in the hands of lay leadership and, through the groups' community gatherings, made the Bible an ongoing part of the lives of ordinary Christians.[115]

Ironically, in the late sixteenth century the spiritual children of Calvin and Luther seemed to lapse back into a Protestant form of scholasticism.[116] Esoteric doctrinal disputes bordering on hair-splitting tended to preoccupy the emerging Lutheran and Calvinist churches. For example, in Geneva the idea of predestination preoccupied Calvin's successor, Theodore Beza, who led speculation by theologians concerning the

Watson, "Introduction and Overview," in *A History of Biblical Interpretation, Volume 2: The Medieval Through the Reformation Periods*, ed. Hauser and Watson, 46; G. J. Miller, "Huldrych Zwingli," in *The Reformation Theologians*, ed. Lindberg, 161–63.

113. G. H. Williams, *The Radical Reformation*, 3rd ed. (Kirksville, MO: Sixteenth Century Journal Publishers, 1999).

114. The well-known story of the German town of Münster illustrates the extremes to which this movement could go. Claiming prophetic inspiration, a series of authoritarian leaders took over the town, compelled the populace to accept rebaptism or else, executed dissenters, and attempted to set up a "New Jerusalem" patterned, in this reconstruction, mainly after the OT, including the practice of polygamy. Only a siege organized by the local bishop ended the Anabaptist rule sixteen months later (1534–1535). MacCullough, *The Reformation*, 199–206, narrates the sad story and its aftermath.

115. For details see S. Murray, "Biblical Interpretation among the Anabaptist Reformers," in *A History of Biblical Interpretation, Volume 2: The Medieval Through the Reformation Periods*, ed. Hauser and Watson, 403–27. We say, "tellingly," because putting the interpretation of the Bible in the hands of laypersons led to its own mixed outcomes. For an interesting take on this see S. Hauerwas, *Unleashing the Scripture: Freeing the Bible from Captivity to America* (Nashville: Abingdon, 1993).

116. Olson, *The Story of Christian Theology*, 455–60; Hall, "Biblical Scholarship," 76–77; and N. Sykes, "The Religion of the Protestants," *CHB III*, 175–76. R. A. Muller, *Post-Reformation Reformed Dogmatics*, vol. 1 (Grand Rapids: Baker, 1987), 13–97, examines the development of the doctrines of God and Scripture after the Reformation.

logical order of God's decrees.[117] To outside observers, the Reformed churches departed from Luther and Calvin in one respect: they appeared to place more importance on intellectual agreement with Protestant dogma than on the practice of warm, lively, personal piety. In their preoccupation with Protestant orthodoxy, they sadly seemed to resemble the very scholasticism against which the Reformation movement had revolted. Their shared piety failed to bridge the doctrinal chasms between them. On the broader scene, Catholicism still held sway in Spain, France, Italy, Austria, and Poland; in England the newly formed Anglican Church, a stepchild of the Reformation, ruled; Lutherans dominated Germany, Denmark, Sweden, Norway, and Finland; Calvinists controlled Scotland and most of Switzerland; and the Anabaptists held small pockets in Germany, Poland, and Hungary.[118]

The Reformation also had another important effect: the reaction of the Catholic Church. The decisions of the Council of Trent (1545–63) marked the official Catholic response to the Reformation—often called the Catholic (or Counter-) Reformation.[119] Against the Protestant principle of *sola scriptura*, it reaffirmed, among other things, the Roman Catholic tradition of biblical interpretation that combined Scripture and tradition, the latter including the doctrinal decisions of popes and church councils. It also upheld the authenticity of the Vulgate and forbade anyone to interpret Scripture out of harmony with church doctrine.[120] As a result, from the momentous events of the sixteenth century flowed two distinct streams of biblical interpretation, one Protestant and one Catholic. Nearly four centuries would pass before their approaches drew closer together again.

THE POST-REFORMATION PERIOD (CA. AD 1650–1750)

The Reformation was not the only revolutionary movement spawned by the late Middle Ages. The Renaissance (1300–1600) featured a reborn interest in classical Greek and Roman art and philosophy. The revived interest in Hebrew and Greek that aided the Reformation derived from the spirit of the Renaissance. If renewed Christian faith drove the Reformation, an increasing reliance on human reason spurred

---

117. Beza argued for *supralapsarianism* (Lat. *supra* "before" + *lapsus* "fall"), the idea that God's decree to predestine the salvation/damnation of humans logically preceded his decrees to create and to allow them to fall into sin. By contrast, according to *infralapsarianism* (Lat. *infra* "later"), the former decree follows the latter two decrees.

118. See the illuminating map in S. Ozment, *The Age of Reform 1250–1550* (New Haven: Yale University Press, 1980), 373.

119. For details of the story, cf. MacCullough, *The Reformation*, 294–303; G. Bedouelle, "Biblical Interpretation in the Catholic Reformation," in *A History of Biblical Interpretation, Volume 2: The Medieval through the Reformation Periods*, ed. Hauser and Watson, 428–49.

120. Ozment, *The Age of Reform*, 407–9; cf. also Chadwick, *The Reformation*, 273–81. In fairness, Trent's decisions also responded positively to Protestant criticisms, authorizing bishops to pastor their flocks more closely and promoting active, personal spirituality among laity. On the other hand, on the heels of Trent, Catholic biblical scholars sadly retreated to the safety of patristic and medieval interpretive paths and showed little originality for three hundred years (Bray, *Biblical Interpretation*, 208–9).

on the Renaissance. Consequently, important movements flowing from both the Reformation and the Renaissance influenced the interpretation of the Bible in the post-Reformation period.

From the Reformation emerged the movement called *pietism*. Pietism began in Germany in the seventeenth century and later spread to Western Europe and America.[121] It represented a reaction to the arid intellectual dogmatism of Protestant scholasticism and the sterile formalism of Protestant worship services. Pietism sought to revive the practice of Christianity as a way of life through group Bible study, prayer, and the cultivation of personal morality. Centered in the German city of Halle, its leader was Philip Jacob Spener (1635–1705), a German pastor who preached the necessity of personal conversion to Christ and an intimate, personal relationship with God. Against the purely doctrinal interests of their contemporaries, Spener and the German pietists stressed the devotional, practical study of the Bible. Their method featured a literalistic, "common sense" approach applied to careful grammatical study of the ancient Hebrew and Greek texts, always, however, with an eye for their devotional or practical implications. In England, another pietistic movement, the Methodism of John Wesley (1703–91), also sought to recover a vibrant personal piety and holy life through Bible study and prayer.[122] Both movements took advantage of a groundbreaking innovation of the early Renaissance—the translation of the Bible into the spoken languages of the people (e.g., the KJV in 1611). Today's widespread practice of small-group Bible studies and prayer groups continues their practice.

The renowned New England preacher Jonathan Edwards (1703–1758) represents pietism in America. Like Spener and Wesley, Edwards approached the Bible with an eye both for its practical application as well as for its doctrinal teachings. As for method, Edwards resorted to typology to draw out practical applications from Scripture. Consider, for example, his interpretation of Genesis 29:20: "So Jacob served seven years to get Rachel, but they seemed like only a few days to him because of his love for her." In enduring hard work out of love for Rachel, according to Edwards, Jacob was a type of Christ who endured the cross out of love for the church.

In the seventeenth century, the spirit of the Renaissance gave birth to the Enlightenment (also called the Age of Reason) and the important intellectual movement called *rationalism*.[123] Rationalism regarded the human mind as an independent

---

121. Olson, *The Story of Christian Theology*, 473–92; González, *The Story of Christianity*, 204–16. Cf. recently, D. H. Shantz, ed., *A Companion to German Pietism, 1660–1800*, Brill's Companions to the Christian Tradition 55 (Leiden; Boston: Brill, 2015); and R. E. Olson and C. Collins Winn, *Reclaiming Pietism: Retrieving an Evangelical Tradition* (Grand Rapids: Eerdmans, 2015).

122. For a scholarly reassessment of the Wesleyan movement, see J. Kent, *Wesley and the Wesleyans* (Cambridge: Cambridge University Press, 2002); cf. also González, *The Story of Christianity*, 209–16; and Olson, *The Story of Christian Theology*, 510–16. A very useful telling of the story of Wesley and his movement is found in R. P. Heitzenrater, *Wesley and the People Called Methodists* (Nashville: Abingdon, 1995).

123. Cf. the balanced, in-depth historical analysis of J. Sandy-Wunsch, *What Have They Done to the Bible? A History of Modern Biblical Interpretation* (Collegeville: Liturgical Press, 2005). For shorter surveys see Sykes, "Religion of the Protestants," 193–98; and W. Neil, "The Criticism and Theological Use of the Bible 1700–1950," *CHB III*, 128–65.

authority capable of determining truth. The roots of rationalism lay in the Christian humanism of scholars like Erasmus who, in the service of the church, employed human reason to study the Bible in its original languages. They also believed that the use of reason to investigate the Bible helped Christians to establish their faith. In the seventeenth and eighteenth centuries thinkers applied this tool of reason not only against the authority of the church but also against the Bible itself. Subtly, their work set the stage for the complete overthrow of both.

In Neil's words, rationalism "was not a system of beliefs antagonistic to Christianity, but an attitude of mind which assumed that in all matters of religion reason is supreme."[124] Three thinkers, two of them philosophers, illustrate the approach of seventeenth-century rationalism to the Bible. In his *Leviathan* (1651), the Anglican philosopher Thomas Hobbes argued from internal evidence that Moses lived long before the Pentateuch was completed and, hence, could not be its author.[125] In his *Critical History of the Old Testament* (1678), the French secular priest Richard Simon reached a similar conclusion, stating that some parts of the OT reflect confusion in chronology.[126]

The thoughts of Jewish philosopher Bernard Spinoza, however, most significantly undercut the authority of Scripture.[127] In his originally anonymous *Tractatus Theologico-Politicus* (1670), Spinoza argued for the primacy of reason in the interpretation of Scripture. In other words, Scripture should be studied like any other book—by using the rules of historical investigation. For example, reason understands scriptural claims to God's direct intervention in history to be simply a common Jewish way of speaking, not actual revelation. Miracle stories thus become nothing more than a powerful way to move ignorant people to obedience. By implication, Spinoza subjected Scripture to the authority of the human mind rather than the other way around.

Thus, the post-Reformation period brought the fragmentation of approaches to biblical interpretation among Protestants. On the one hand, the pietists continued to search the Scriptures to feed their hungry souls and to guide their quest for virtuous lives. On the other hand, whereas Aquinas had sought the integration of philosophy and theology, the rationalists promoted the radical divorce of each from the other. Though rationalism had declined in popularity by the mid-eighteenth century, it spawned a series of influential biblical handbooks written along the critical lines of Spinoza and enjoyed an even greater flowering in the next century.[128]

---

124. Neil, "Criticism and Theological Use," 239. Cf. also the useful historical analysis in Dungan, *Synoptic Problem*, 171–76.

125. T. Hobbes, *Leviathan*, III, chap. 33. This denial, of course, ran counter to the longstanding opinion of the day.

126. Sykes, "Religion of the Protestants," 194; Bray, *Biblical Interpretation*, 239–40. Later scholars would look back to Simon as the father of modern biblical criticism.

127. Grant and Tracy, *Short History*, 105–8. For a detailed analysis of Spinoza's thought, including his political agenda to promote modern secular democracy, see Dungan, *Synoptic Problem*, 198–260; cf. D. Boerman, "The Significance of Spinoza for Biblical Interpretation," *ResQ* 51 (2009): 93–106.

128. Influential writings during this period included the introduction to the NT by J. D. Michaelis (1750) and an introduction to the OT by J.G. Eichhorn (1780–1783); cf. Bray, *Biblical Interpretation*, 245, 248.

THE MODERN PERIOD (CA. AD 1750–PRESENT)

The Nineteenth Century

On many fronts, the nineteenth century was a revolutionary one, particularly its unprecedented expansion in missions,[129] but ironically, at the same time it witnessed a skeptical repudiation of Christianity among intellectuals.[130] Radical advances in human science created popular confidence in the scientific method, which in turn produced a revolutionary and more scientific method for studying history. Also, in the nineteenth century, *developmentalism*—the idea that evolving historical progress underlies everything—became widespread as the dialectical philosophy of G. W. F. Hegel, which shaped the social philosophy of Karl Marx, and the evolutionary theory of Charles Darwin attest.

The Bible did not escape the impact of these changes. Scholars, especially those teaching in German universities, sought to approach the Bible similarly through so-called objective, scientific means.[131] Thus was born the approach known as *the historical-critical method*, an interpretive method guided by several crucial philosophical presuppositions.[132] It inherited the rationalistic assumption from its seventeenth-century intellectual ancestors that the use of human reason, free of dogmatic limitations, is the best tool with which to study the Bible. Therefore, scholars treated the Bible as they would any other literature, not as God's special revelation to humanity.

In addition, the historical-critical method presupposed a naturalistic worldview that explained everything in terms of natural laws and excluded the possibility of supernatural intervention. Thus, scholars accounted for biblical miracles by means of the laws of physics, biology, and chemistry. Again, the approach believed that all history happens as an evolutionary process of development. Thus, its practitioners interpreted the history that the Bible reports along that line, viewing earlier eras as "primitive" and later ones as "advanced." The historical-critical method further regarded the Bible's ideas as time-bound truths, not timeless ones (the Bible merely records what people thought at the time). Finally, scholars assumed that the Bible's greatest contribution lay in its moral and ethical values, not in its theological teachings or historical claims.

These presuppositions brought about two decisive shifts in the focus of biblical interpretation. First, rather than seek to discern what a text meant, many scholars

---

129. Cf. González, *The Story of Christianity*, 239–93, whose excellent treatment especially tracks the expansion in America, Latin America, and Europe.

130. Cf. Sandy-Wunsch, *What Have They Done to the Bible?* 219–79.

131. For details, see ibid., 281–331; cf. more briefly, Neil, "Criticism and Theological Use," 255–65; González, *The Story of Christianity*, 282–93.

132. Cf. the summary in Bray, *Biblical Interpretation*, 251–53. According to Harrisville and Sundberg, as the offspring of the political chaos birthed by the Reformation, the purpose of historical criticism was "to nullify the arbitrary political power of those [i.e., princes and priests] who used the Bible to legitimate their authority"; cf. R. A. Harrisville and W. Sundberg, *The Bible in Modern Culture: Theology and Historical-Critical Method from Spinoza to Käsemann* (Grand Rapids: Eerdmans, 1995), 264–66 (quote 266).

sought instead to discover the sources behind it—the method called *source criticism*.[133] Second, rather than accept the Bible as divine revelation, some scholars sought to retrace the historical development presumed to underlie it. The work of three influential German scholars illustrates these shifts in biblical interpretation.

F. C. Baur, professor of historical theology at the University of Tübingen (1826–1860), argued that Paul's letters reflect a deep division in apostolic Christianity.[134] On one side, said Baur, stood the church of Jerusalem (led by Peter and other original disciples) that taught a Jewish form of Christianity. On the other stood Paul and his Gentile converts who insisted that the gospel actually abolished the legalistic demands of Judaism. More important, Baur inferred that NT books that did not reflect this division in early Christianity must be post-apostolic in origin. On this premise he dated both Acts and the Gospels to the second century, in effect denying their authority as sources of information for the life and ministry of Jesus and the apostles. In short, Baur and his disciples, the so-called Tübingen School, applied only critical human reason to the study of the NT and claimed to find a historical scenario implicit in the NT that differed from the impression the documents themselves gave. The resulting portrait of the history of early Christianity departed radically from portraits commonly accepted by their contemporaries.[135]

In OT studies, Julius Wellhausen concluded a long scholarly discussion about the written sources of the Pentateuch. In his monumental *Prolegomena to the History of Israel* (1878), Wellhausen argued that behind the Pentateuch stood four separate sources written between 850 and 550 BC.[136] Several crucial implications derived from that claim: (1) Moses could not have written any of the Pentateuch; (2) the Law originated *after* the historical books, not *before* them; and (3) the actual history of Israel differed markedly from the history the OT books narrate.[137]

The last German scholar whose work typifies nineteenth century thought is Adolf von Harnack. Probably more than any other book, his *What Is Christianity?* (1901)

---

133. For a detailed history of this method and its assumptions as applied to the origin of the Gospels, see Dungan, *Synoptic Problem*, 302–41. More recently, cf. J. Barton, *The Nature of Biblical Criticism* (Louisville: Westminster John Knox, 2007).

134. R. A. Harrisville and W. Sundberg, *The Bible in Modern Culture: Theology and Historical-critical Method from Spinoza to Käsemann*, 2nd ed. (Grand Rapids: Eerdmans, 2002), 104–22; more briefly, Bray, *Biblical Interpretation*, 321–24. For a larger account, see the still-valuable volume by P. C. Hodgson, *The Formation of Historical Theology: A Study of Ferdinand Christian Baur* (New York: Harper and Row, 1962). B. E. Shields, "The Hermeneutics of Alexander Campbell," *ResQ* 43 (2001): 169–72, 178–79, briefly compares the hermeneutical principles of Baur with those of his American contemporary, Alexander Campbell, leader of the Restoration Movement.

135. More positively, the application of source criticism in NT studies produced the now widely accepted theory that two main documents (Mark and a collection of Jesus' sayings called "Q") lay behind the present Synoptic Gospels.

136. Originally in German, its English translation appeared as J. Wellhausen, *Prolegomena to the History of Israel* (Edinburgh: Adam and Charles Black, 1885; Atlanta: Scholars Press, 1994). For recent assessments, see M. Weinfeld, *The Place of the Law in the Religion of Ancient Israel*, VTSup 100 (Leiden; Boston: Brill, 2004); and E. Nicholson, *The Pentateuch in the Twentieth Century: The Legacy of Julius Wellhausen* (Oxford: Clarendon Press; Oxford; New York: Oxford University Press, 2002).

137. For a review of pentateuchal scholarship, see the essays in T. B. Dozeman, K. Schmid, and B. J. Schwartz, eds., *The Pentateuch: International Perspectives on Current Research*, FAT 78 (Tübingen: Mohr Siebeck, 2011).

summarized the liberal theology that dominated nineteenth century Protestantism and shaped its biblical interpretation.[138] Harnack called for Protestants to return to the religion of Jesus, the religion he claimed lay hidden behind the church's later portrait of him in the NT. For Harnack, three essential teachings summarize Jesus' religion: (1) the coming of the kingdom of God; (2) the fatherhood of God and the infinite value of the human soul; and (3) the commandment of love.

In sum, Baur, Wellhausen, and Harnack claimed that historical criticism unearthed a complex literary and religious history behind sections of the present Bible. As many critics pointed out, if true, their views severely undermined the historical reliability of the Bible and, hence, its authority as a document of divine revelation. More important, their work radically redefined the object of biblical interpretation. For them, its purpose was not to determine the meaning of the present text but to find the sources and history lurking behind it. The implication was that only at the earliest stages of the tradition behind the present texts could one encounter accurate and authoritative history.

Though dominant, their views did not pass unchallenged. As one would expect, German confessional scholars strongly criticized the rationalism of the new historical criticism and promoted academically credible alternative interpretations of both Testaments.[139] Other scholars, including the highly respected H. Ewald and M. Kähler, similarly charted their own interpretive paths in opposition to their more radical colleagues.[140] In the United Kingdom, the academic stature of S. R. Driver and W. Robertson Smith, who wrote the preface to the English translation of Wellhausen's *Prolegomena*, helped the latter's views gain entry there, but J. B. Lightfoot's now-classic translation of *The Apostolic Fathers* (1885–1890) disproved several of Baur's key assumptions and essentially discredited his theory.

In North America, figures like B. B. Warfield, W. H. Green, and W. J. Beecher not only ably critiqued the assumptions of the new criticism but promoted an alternative, vibrant new criticism of their own, thus winning a standoff if not actually reversing

---

138. The English translation of the German original is A. von Harnack, *What Is Christianity?* (New York: Putnam, 1901); cf. P. Kennedy, *Twentieth-Century Theologians: A New Introduction to Modern Christian Thought* (London; New York: I.B. Tauris, 2010), 17–30. For liberalism, see A. Richardson, "The Rise of Modern Biblical Scholarship and Recent Discussion of the Authority of the Bible," *CHB III*, 311–18.

139. Certainly the formative leader in OT studies was E. W. Hengstenberg (cf. his *Christology of the Old Testament: and a Commentary on the Messianic Predictions*, 4 vols., trans. T. Meyer (vols. 1–2) and J. Martin (vols. 3–4) [Edinburgh: T. & T. Clark, 1861–1868]), but others sympathetic and contributory included C. F. Keil, J. C. K. von Hofmann, and Franz Delitzsch. In fairness, however, one must state that these scholars represented a spectrum of views and degrees of openness to the method; cf. the definitive study by J. Rogerson, *Old Testament Criticism in the Nineteenth Century: England and Germany* (London: SPCK, 1984), 79–90 (Hengstenberg, Keil), 104–20 (von Hofmann and Delitzsch); cf. the more recent assessment of von Hofmann in Harrisville and Sundberg, *The Bible in Modern Culture*, 2nd ed., 123–45. Significant opposing NT scholars included A. H. Cremer (1834–1903), J. P. Lange (1802–84), B. Weiss (1827–1918), and M. Baumgarten (1812–1889); cf. Bray, *Biblical Interpretation*, 332–33, 335.

140. Rogerson (*Old Testament Criticism*, 91) regards Ewald as "one of the greatest critical Old Testament scholars of all time" and devotes an entire chapter to his contribution (91–103). Another example is C. C. J. von Bunsen (Rogerson, *Old Testament Criticism*, 121–29). For Kähler, see Bray, *Biblical Interpretation*, 335.

the inroads of European criticism.[141] Against the latter's skepticism, they defended their straightforward inductive approach to biblical interpretation by appealing to the epistemology of the so-called Scottish Common Sense philosophy—the view that common sense rightly recognizes some ideas as true and needing no defense.[142] Meanwhile, away from academia the Anabaptist theme of a return to primitive NT Christianity reappeared in two new movements that, as one might expect, gave new priority to the NT in interpretation. The Restoration Movement led by Barton W. Stone and Alexander Campbell based itself on the interpretation of Acts and the Epistles, with Campbell developing a hermeneutical approach that remarkably anticipates that of twentieth century evangelicals.[143] At the same time, Pentecostal revivals in the late nineteenth century convinced many that God had supernaturally baptized them in the Holy Spirit and that their supernatural experiences had recovered the essence of the NT church.[144] How their experiences related to the interpretation of the Bible would become a topic of discussion among their spiritual descendants in the next century.

The Twentieth Century

The dawn of this century witnessed the flowering of two interpretive approaches that grew out of the late nineteenth century. The first was that of the *history of religions*.[145] Baur and Wellhausen had claimed to uncover the "true history" of the Israelite and Christian religions through internal biblical evidence. But during the nineteenth century, archaeologists had unearthed numerous written texts from ancient Egypt, Syro-Palestine, Babylonia, and Assyria. These texts gave scholars fresh new insights into religions contemporary to the Bible. Inevitably, scholars came to compare them

---

141. Cf. Bray, *Biblical Interpretation*, 324–25; M. A. Noll, *Between Faith and Criticism: Evangelicals, Scholarship, and the Bible in America*, SBL Confessional Perspective Series (San Francisco; Cambridge, UK: Harper & Row, 1986), 11–31, 62–90. Prominent among the casualties were Presbyterian scholars C. A. Briggs, H. P. Smith, and A. C. McGiffert, who either lost a denominational judicial hearing for their views or chose to resign to avoid one. In Scotland, W. R. Smith also lost his professorial post but retained his ordination in the Free Church of Scotland. Noll's concluding assessment of the American scene (31) is that, as the nineteenth century ended, both the "strongholds of the new criticism" and "conservative evangelical scholarship" remained secure, the latter maintaining its place in the wider academic world and its "theological grounding"—a situation not true a generation later.

142. Cf. M. A. Noll, "Common Sense Traditions and Evangelical Thought," *American Quarterly* 37 (1985): 216–38; and his criticism of evangelical dependence on this philosophy in M. A. Noll, *The Scandal of the Evangelical Mind* (Grand Rapids: Eerdmans; Leicester: InterVarsity, 1994), 94–107.

143. Cf. Shields, "The Hermeneutics of Alexander Campbell," 175–79; and T. H. Olbricht, "Hermeneutics in the Churches of Christ," *ResQ* 37 (1995): 1–24. Present-day Disciples of Christ, the Christian Church, and the Churches of Christ trace their roots to this movement. For recent discussion of this movement's inductive method of hermeneutics and its possible response to postmodernism, see D. L. Little, "Inductive Hermeneutics and the Early Restoration Movement," *Stone-Campbell Journal* 3 (2000): 5–18. Cf. the retrospective essay on scholarship in the movement by J. M. Tucker, "The Ministry of Scholarship: The Jubilee History of *Restoration Quarterly*," *ResQ* 50 (2008): 3–14.

144. J. C. Poirier and B. S. Lewis, "Pentecostal and Postmodernist Hermeneutics: A Critique of Three Conceits," *JPT* 15 (2006): 3–21; K. J. Archer, "Pentecostal Hermeneutics: Retrospect and Prospect," *JPT* 4 (1996): 64.

145. J. Riches, *A Century of New Testament Study* (Valley Forge, PA: Trinity Press International, 1993), 14–49, reviews its impact on NT studies. For developments since World War II, see P. D. Miller, *The Religion of Ancient Israel* (London: SPCK; Louisville: Westminster John Knox, 2000).

with biblical religion. Such comparisons soon gave birth to the history-of-religions approach, a method that tried to trace the historical development of all ancient Near Eastern religions. Specifically, it professed to show how ancient neighboring religions had profoundly influenced the religious practices of the Israelites. Sometimes its adherents went to unwarranted extremes in their approach, as when Friedrich Delitzsch famously argued that the OT contained nothing more than warmed-over Babylonian ideas.[146]

The history-of-religions approach left two lasting influences on biblical interpretation. First, its comparative research suggested that many biblical ideas had originated earlier than scholars like Wellhausen had thought. For example, the discovery of ancient law codes implied that at least some of the OT's ethical demands might be ancient, perhaps even derived from Moses, rather than from the religious creativity of the prophets. Second, it firmly established what came to be known as "the comparative principle." Henceforth, proper biblical interpretation would require consultation with relevant cultural evidence from the ancient world of the Bible in order better to tune into its cultural milieu.[147]

The second interpretive approach was the new literary method called *form criticism*.[148] The father of form criticism was Hermann Gunkel, a German OT scholar best known for his study of the Psalms.[149] Form criticism sought to recover the shorter oral compositions from which the Bible's written sources supposedly derived. It also aimed to determine the specific cultural life-setting in which each originated. Gunkel and his disciples claimed that the original setting of most of the psalms was the temple in Jerusalem.

Eventually, OT form criticism began to focus more on the literary types of the present written text rather than on the Bible's oral pre-stages.[150] For that reason form criticism remains an invaluable method in the toolbox of all serious Bible students. Our survey of OT literary genres later in this book bears witness to the lasting legacy of Gunkel's approach, and, as we shall see, in the hands of NT scholars it also profoundly shaped the interpretation of the Gospels in the twentieth century.[151]

---

146. F. Delitzsch, *Babel and Bible* (New York: G. P. Putnam's Sons, 1903).

147. Though written four decades ago, the critique of Krentz still rings true. He rightly pointed out the sinister downside of late nineteenth century "scientific" thought, both history of religions and historical criticism in general. By elevating historical knowledge in opposition to Christian faith, such thinking removed the academic study of the Bible from any accountability to the church and denigrated Christian use of the Bible that was not "historical" by its definition; cf. E. Krentz, *The Historical-Critical Method*, GBS (Philadelphia: Fortress Press, 1975), 28–30.

148. Cf. M. A. Sweeney, "Form Criticism," in *Dictionary of the Old Testament: Wisdom, Poetry, and Writings*, ed. T. Longman III and P. Enns (Downers Grove: IVP Academic, 2008), 227–41; M. A. Sweeney and E. Ben Zvi, eds., *The Changing Face of Form Criticism for the Twenty-First Century* (Grand Rapids: Eerdmans, 2003).

149. Sweeney, "Form Criticism," 229–30.

150. Gunkel's own definitive research on the Psalms certainly reflects this change. An English translation of his introductory work is available in H. Gunkel, J. Begrich, and J. Nogalski, *Introduction to the Psalms: The Genres of the Religious Lyric of Israel*, Mercer Library of Biblical Studies (Macon, GA: Mercer University Press, 1998); cf. also his classic study of narratives, *The Stories of Genesis* (Richland Hills, TX: D & F Scott Publishers, 1998).

151. Cf. the recent assessment of the method's application to the study of parables in the NT by C. L. Blomberg. *Interpreting the Parables*, 2nd ed. (Downers Grove: InterVarsity, 2012), 82–118. For OT examples of its application,

Post-World War I

To a great extent, the twentieth century's two world wars provide the key markers in biblical interpretation during that century. The disastrous events of World War I devastated Europe and destroyed the naive optimism that had supported liberal theology. The horrors of the war also seemed to stir up both a reaction against the exclusive hegemony of science and an increasing interest in the existentialist philosophies of figures like Søren Kierkegaard and Martin Heidegger.

Like the proverbial phoenix, new directions in biblical interpretation arose from the ashes of world conflict. Two towering figures, men who today still cast long shadows of influence, initially charted those new directions. The first was the Swiss country pastor, Karl Barth (1886–1968), whose commentary on Romans (1919) severely critiqued the mistakes of liberalism and sought to reassert long-lost emphases of his Reformation heritage.[152] Specifically, he reemphasized the authority of Scripture as the Word of God and the necessity of a personal encounter with the living God of whom it speaks. The idea of such a personal encounter reflected the influence on Barth of Kierkegaard. Barth's later multi-volume *Church Dogmatics* fueled a lively renaissance in Protestant systematic theology and exemplified how penetrating biblical interpretation could enrich theology.[153]

The second imposing shadow on the twentieth-century landscape was the noted NT scholar Rudolf Bultmann (1884–1976).[154] As Kierkegaard helped to shape Barth's theology, so Heidegger's brand of existentialism formed the philosophical foundation of Bultmann's work. The history of biblical interpretation remembers Bultmann for two distinct developments. First, he applied the method of form criticism to the study of the Gospels and their historical development. As Gunkel had done magisterially with the Psalms, Bultmann classified the Gospels' individual episodes (pericopes) into various literary types (e.g., miracle story, pronouncement story, etc.) and suggested an original setting for each.[155] Bultmann also judged the historical reliability of certain

---

see the volumes in the Forms of Old Testament Literature (FOTL) series published by Eerdmans. For NT form criticism, see below.

152. For an English translation based on the sixth German edition, see K. Barth, *The Epistle to the Romans* (London: Oxford University Press, 1968). Cf. Richardson, "The Rise of Modern Biblical Scholarship," 319–23; S. Neill and T. Wright, *The Interpretation of The New Testament 1861–1986*, 2nd ed. (Oxford: Oxford University Press, 1988), 215–27.

153. The English translation is K. Barth, *Church Dogmatics*, 4 vols. (Edinburgh: T&T Clark, 1956–1969). For an overview of Barth's thought, see G. W. Bromiley, *An Introduction to the Theology of Karl Barth* (Edinburgh: T&T Clark, 2000). For an assessment of Barth's hermeneutics, see S. E. Porter and J. C. Robinson, *Hermeneutics: An Introduction to Interpretive Theory* (Grand Rapids: Eerdmans, 2011), 214–25. Cf. also B. L. McCormack and C. B. Anderson, eds., *Karl Barth and American Evangelicalism* (Grand Rapids: Eerdmans, 2011); B. L. McCormack, *Orthodox and Modern: Studies in the Theology of Karl Barth* (Grand Rapids: Baker Academic, 2008).

154. Cf. the appreciative treatments in Harrisville and Sundberg, *The Bible in Modern Culture*, 2nd ed., 217–48; and Neill and Wright, *The Interpretation of the New Testament*, 237–51. T. Larsson, *God in the Fourth Gospel*, CBNT 35 (Stockholm: Almqvist and Wiksell, 2001), 168–212, assesses his influential work on the Gospel of John.

155. For a translation of the ground-breaking work originally published in 1921, see R. Bultmann, *The History of the Synoptic Tradition* (New York: Harper & Row, 1963). Cf. also the influential form critical work of Bultmann's contemporary, M. Dibelius, *From Tradition to Gospel* (New York: Charles Scribner's Sons, 1965 [Germ. orig. 1919]).

literary forms depending upon their setting. He especially doubted those types that, in his view, seemed colored by the later beliefs of the early Christian community. Thus, in Bultmann's hands, form criticism raised serious questions concerning the historical reliability of the Gospels. Bultmann distinguished between the "Jesus of history" (the person who actually lived) and the "Christ of faith" (the person in Christian preaching).[156] On the other hand, using modern historical-critical methods, British scholars like C. H. Dodd, T. W. Manson, and V. Taylor ably defended the substantial historical reliability of Gospel accounts.

Second, Bultmann sought to "demythologize" the Bible, to recover the *kerygma* or "message" currently couched in its (in his view) outmoded mythological worldview.[157] Like Barth, Bultmann was concerned that the Bible speak to the needs of modern people. He wanted to make the Bible's message understandable and relevant to his contemporaries. In his view, the prevailing scientific worldview had undermined the faith of many intelligent Christians. They had trouble believing the Bible because of what he called its mythological language—for example, its three-storied universe, its claims that Jesus "descended" from and "ascended" to heaven, and its miracles.

Bultmann's approach requires that one read the Bible with an existentialist hermeneutic.[158] Most readers expect to derive objective information from the Bible, and Bultmann conceded that the text does provide much of that, but he also allowed that readers may disregard anything they deem as prescientific (e.g., primitive cosmology, myths, etc.). Further, he argued that one should read the Bible subjectively to let its understanding of human existence clarify one's own existential predicament. Indeed, Bultmann affirmed that the Bible becomes revelation when it confronts us with such a challenge. He determined that people can understand the Bible only when they understand what he called their "unauthentic existence" and the possibilities of making it more authentic. In other words, he proposed a primarily subjective, existentialist reading of the Bible—one uprooted from any first-century historical event.

Between the two world wars, the work of Barth and another Swiss theologian, Emil Brunner, spawned a new theological movement called *neo-orthodoxy* (or dialectical theology). Three basic metaphysical assumptions guided the approach of neo-orthodox theologians to biblical interpretation. First, God is regarded as a subject not an object (i.e., a "Thou" not an "It"). Thus, the Bible's words cannot convey knowledge of

---

E. V. McKnight, *What Is Form Criticism?* (Philadelphia: Fortress, 1969) remains a convenient introduction to the method.

156. For a classic explication of the origin of this distinction see M. Kähler, *So-Called Historical Jesus and the Historic-Biblical Christ* (Philadelphia: Fortress, 1964; orig. German edition, 1892).

157. The translation of the 1941 German original is R. Bultmann, "New Testament and Mythology," in *Kerygma and Myth*, vol. 1, ed. H. W. Bartsch (London: SPCK, 1957), 1–44; cf. also his *Jesus Christ and Mythology* (New York: Charles Scribner's Sons, 1958). Porter and Robinson (*Hermeneutics: An Introduction to Interpretive Theory*, 226–38) and Neill and Wright (*Interpretation of the New Testament*, 241–51) provide insightful retrospective assessments of Bultmann's hermeneutics.

158. Hence, the chapter title, "The Development of An Existential Interpretation of the Bible," in *Riches, A Century of New Testament Study*, 70–88; cf. Richardson, "Modern Biblical Scholarship," 327–39.

God as abstract propositions; one can only know him in a personal encounter. Such encounters are so subjective, mysterious, and miraculous that they elude the objective measurements of science. Second, a great gulf separates the Bible's transcendent God from fallen humanity. Indeed, he is so transcendent that only myths can bridge this gulf and reveal him to people. Thus, rather than read biblical reports of events as historical in some sense, neo-orthodoxy interpreted them as myths meant to convey theological truth in historical dress. Critics, of course, pointed out that the effect of this approach was to downplay the historicity of biblical events.

Third, neo-orthodox theologians believed that truth was ultimately paradoxical in nature, so they accepted apparently conflicting statements in the Bible as paradoxes for which a rational explanation would be both inappropriate and unnecessary. By accepting apparently opposite biblical ideas as paradoxes, critics noted, neo-orthodoxy in effect seemed to cast doubt on the assumption that rational coherence underlies and binds together the diverse ideas of Scripture.

Post-World War II

If World War I gave birth to both neo-orthodoxy and demythologizing, World War II also fathered significant offspring. In postwar America, a flood of publications showed a revival of interest in biblical theology, a revival that many have called the *Biblical Theology Movement*.[159] In 1947 the journal *Interpretation* began publication to promote positive reflection on theology and the Bible. Three years later SCM Press launched its scholarly series Studies in Biblical Theology. While historical-critical matters had formerly dominated biblical commentaries, now the commentaries featured discussions of the theology and message of biblical books.

According to Childs, five major emphases typified the movement: (1) the rediscovery of the Bible's theological dimension; (2) the unity of the whole Bible; (3) the revelation of God in history; (4) the distinctiveness of the Bible's mentality (i.e., a Hebrew way of thinking in contrast to a Greek way); and (5) the contrast of the Bible to its ancient environment. Though criticism of the movement cast doubt on some of those emphases, in the late 1960s it nevertheless served to revive study of the theological dimension of the Bible, a dimension that had become a casualty of historical criticism in the late nineteenth century.[160]

---

159. The term "biblical theology" refers to the theology that the Bible itself shows as opposed to that of philosophers or systematic theologians. B. S. Childs, *Biblical Theology in Crisis* (Philadelphia: Westminster, 1970), 13–60, provides details on the Biblical Theology Movement. But see also J. D. Smart, *The Past, Present, and Future of Biblical Theology* (Philadelphia: Westminster, 1979), 22–30, who denied enough discrete features to label the developments a "movement."

160. For recent assessments of Childs' work, see C. R. Seitz and K. H. Richards, eds., *The Bible as Christian Scripture: The Work of Brevard S. Childs* (Atlanta: Society of Biblical Literature, 2013); and D. R. Driver, *Brevard Childs, Biblical Theologian: For the Church's One Bible* (Grand Rapids: Baker Academic, 2012). Oddly enough, at the time Childs pronounced the Biblical Theology Movement "dead" and proposed that the canon provides the only viable context for Christian exegesis and theology (on his "canon criticism" see below). Nevertheless, as Mark Twain might say, news of biblical theology's demise seems premature. From 1977 to 2005, The Overtures to Biblical Theology series published forty volumes (most recently, L. G. Perdue, *Reconstructing Old Testament Theology: After*

The postwar era also saw the birth of what proved to be an influential new method. The nineteenth century passed on interpretive methods that tended to highlight the Bible's diversity and disunity. With source criticism, for example, biblical interpretation amounted to a kind of academic autopsy. It was enough for the interpreter simply to catalog the parts of the textual cadaver. Again, by focusing on individual forms and their transmission, form criticism tended to bog down in a similar tedious analysis. In both cases, scholars simply ignored the larger literary context (the present, final text of the Bible) of which the sources and forms were a part.

But in the mid-1950s, *redaction criticism* emerged as a complementary discipline to form criticism. Essentially, redaction criticism seeks to discern the distinctive theological and thematic emphases that the individual biblical writers or editors gave their materials.[161] It assumes, for example, that—however it came to be—each context or book reflects the editorial design of its author/editor, a design that aims to emphasize certain themes. Redaction criticism first appeared in studies of the Gospels,[162] but OT scholars have used a similar approach in studying sections of the Hebrew canon.[163]

Two other postwar interpretive developments trace their intellectual genealogy to the work of Bultmann. The first is the movement among Bultmann's students called the "new quest for the historical Jesus."[164] They reacted vigorously against his

---

the Collapse of History [Minneapolis: Fortress, 2005]), and the journal *Ex Auditu* still publishes the papers of the annual Theological Symposium held at North Park Seminary in Chicago. Two of Childs' former students (B. C. Birch and D. L. Petersen) and scholars T. E. Fretheim and W. Brueggemann recently published a second edition of their new genre, *A Theological Introduction to the Old Testament*, 2nd ed. (Nashville: Abingdon, 2005). Evangelicals stand at the forefront of this lively field of study, as attested by the recent major work by G. K. Beale and B. L. Gladd, *Hidden But Now Revealed: A Biblical Theology of Mystery* (Downers Grove: InterVarsity, 2014). Since 1995, the New Studies in Biblical Theology series edited by D. A. Carson, the successor to the earlier, discontinued Studies in Biblical Theology (SBT), has produced thirty-seven volumes (most recently, L. M. Morales, *Who Shall Ascend the Mountain of the Lord? A Biblical Theology of the Book of Leviticus* [Downers Grove: InterVarsity, 2016]). Obviously, scholarly interest in biblical theology remains very much alive.

161. For the method, see the older introduction by NT scholar N. Perrin, *What is Redaction Criticism?* (Philadelphia: Fortress Press, 1969); for a more recent treatment, see M. Goodacre, "Redaction Criticism," in *Searching for Meaning: An Introduction to Interpreting the New Testament*, ed. P. Gooder (Louisville: SPCK/Westminster John Knox, 2009), 38–46. Cf. recent evaluations of its subsequent refinement and application by evangelical scholar C. L. Blomberg, *Interpreting the Parables*, 119–50.

162. E.g., W. Marxsen, *Mark the Evangelist: Studies on the Redaction History of the Gospel* (Nashville: Abingdon, 1969); and H. Conzelmann, *The Theology of Saint Luke* (New York: Harper & Row, 1961).

163. E.g., most recently, M. Hallaschka, "Interpreting Zechariah's Visions: Redaction-Critical Considerations on the Night Vision Cycle (Zechariah 1:7–6:8) and its Earliest Readers," in *'I Lifted My Eyes and Saw': Reading Dream and Vision Reports in the Hebrew Bible*, ed. E. R. Hayes and L.-S. Tiemeyer, LHBOTS 584 (London and New York: Bloomsbury T&T Clark, 2014), 149–68; and T. S. Hadjiev, *The Composition and Redaction of the Book of Amos*, BZAW 393 (Berlin; New York: De Gruyter, 2009).

164. The expression derives from the book title of J. M. Robinson, *A New Quest of the Historical Jesus*, SBT 25 (London: SCM; Naperville, IL: Allenson, 1959), a title that echoes the English title of an important earlier book by A. Schweitzer (*The Quest of the Historical Jesus* [New York: MacMillan, 1910; recently, New Orleans: Cornerstone Book Publishers, 2014]). For recent assessments of the quest, see J. van der Watt, ed., *The Quest for the Real Jesus*, BibInt 120 (Leiden: Brill, 2013); and from an evangelical viewpoint, J. D. G. Dunn, *A New Perspective on Jesus: What the Quest for the Historical Jesus Missed*, Acadia Studies in Bible and Theology (Grand Rapids: Baker Academic, 2005). For recent discussion of broader issues, see L. T. Johnson, ed., *Contested Issues in Christian Origins and the New Testament: Collected Essays*, NovTSup 146 (Leiden; Boston: Brill, 2013).

rigid denial that one could know much of anything historical about Jesus. They (and many others) asked how one could have an authentic Christian faith without an actual historical Jesus. They wondered whether Bultmann's agnosticism about Jesus might actually undermine the faith. So, in the 1950s and 1960s they cautiously sought to sketch from the Gospels what they thought could be known historically about Jesus.[165] Bultmann's critics had accused him of Docetism, the heresy that Jesus only appeared to suffer and die but did not actually do so because he was not human. Consequently, his students paid particular attention to the history of the crucifixion because of its importance in Christian theology. Outside of the passion narrative, however, they focused primarily on individual teachings of Jesus more than his deeds, and honed specific criteria of authenticity to help them adjudicate which they would accept as historical. Conservative scholars might regard their conclusions as rather meager, but they at least narrowed the gap between the "Jesus of history" and the "Christ of faith."[166]

The second development, the so-called *new hermeneutic*, also involved Bultmann's academic children.[167] From the field of linguistics it drew on new views about human language. Specifically, it understood language to be an actor (i.e., something that sets things in motion) rather than a label one attaches to passive objects. Thus, each use of language brings a new entity into being—what movement spokesmen like E. Fuchs and G. Ebeling call a "word-happening" or "language-event." Each speech-event communicates its own unique truth—and this is the crucial point—in light of the hearer's own experience.

Applied to biblical interpretation, this new concept of language implied a different view of the biblical text. Up to now, interpreters presumed it to be an object that passively responded to their interpretive questions, an object over which they were master. By contrast, the new hermeneutic assumed that, when read, the text created, as it were, a new language-event that mastered the reader. In other words, the biblical text interprets the reader, not vice versa, confronting him or her with the Word of God at that moment. Thus, in the new hermeneutic the text, not the interpreter, guides biblical interpretation. In interpretation, the text and its intention must grip the reader rather than the reader's questions controlling the text.

The new hermeneutic made several positive contributions to biblical interpretation.

---

165. The monograph by Robinson (*A New Quest of the Historical Jesus*) pointed the way. Other important contributors included the 1953 lecture by E. Käsemann, "The Problem of the Historical Jesus," published in translation in his *Essays on New Testament Themes*, SBT 21 (London: SCM; Naperville: Allenson, 1964), 15–47; and G. Bornkamm, *Jesus of Nazareth* (New York: Harper & Row, 1960).

166. A "Third Quest" for the historical Jesus has since 1980 superseded both the "first" (i.e., A. Schweitzer's) and the "new" quests. Its distinctives are: (1) use of extrabiblical evidence to reconstruct the cultural milieu of Jesus; (2) a renewed interest in Jesus' Jewishness; (3) discussion about why Jesus was crucified; (4) an interest in Jesus' deeds and not just his words; and (5) holistic questions and explanations about Jesus' aims and self-understanding. See below.

167. For an overview, see W. G. Doty, *Contemporary New Testament Interpretation* (Englewood Cliffs, NJ: Prentice-Hall, 1972), 28–51; and the essays in J. M. Robinson and J. B. Cobb, eds., *The New Hermeneutic* (New York: Harper & Row, 1964). The movement's master theoretician is H. G. Gadamer, *Truth and Method* (London: Sheed and Ward, 1975).

First, it stimulated a refreshing revival of theoretical reflection on the subject. Biblical hermeneutics used to focus on the various interpretive techniques a reader employed to draw out meaning from a text. The new hermeneutic, however, underscored the complex relationship that links readers and written texts. Second, it rightly drew attention to the effect a text has on the reader. Previously the assumption was that the interpreter controlled interpretation, that the text was a passive object to be analyzed. Now the interpreter is challenged to reckon with the scrutiny that the text imposes on him or her. In essence, by drawing readers into its world, the text actively interprets their world. This idea lays a stepping stone toward today's so-called *reader-response* approach to hermeneutics and its discussion of the role that the reader plays in the interpretive process.

Third, the concept of language-event in the new hermeneutic properly emphasized that Scripture must relate to the meaningful existence of its contemporary audience. In other words, besides defining what the text meant originally, interpretation also entails relating the historical meaning of Scripture to the issues of contemporary life.

As for its weaknesses, the new hermeneutic tended to deemphasize a text's historical meaning and its contribution to the language-event. Hence, it runs the risk of losing its roots in the biblical text, a risk that also faces extreme forms of reader-response criticism. Again, while opening up new interpretive insights, in effect its existentialist orientation limits what a text can say to the reader, namely, it can only offer insights into human existence. Readers may not gather biblical insights, for example, into history, science, culture, the nature of God, etc.

The postwar Biblical Theology Movement also left a methodological offspring: *canon criticism.* To remedy the movement's weaknesses, B. S. Childs proposed a new context for doing theology—the canonical status of the Bible.[168] Canon criticism regards biblical books as canonical, that is, as the authoritative writings of the Jewish and Christian communities. It also presumes that theological convictions guided those who compiled these books. Hence, it seeks to find their theological meaning by analyzing their canonical shape—the editorial design of their present form.[169] More on this below.

Finally, the late twentieth century saw the emergence of two important new developments whose influence still continues. First, academic discussions of hermeneutics from a Pentecostal perspective began to appear. In 1979 the Society for Pentecostal Studies launched a major journal, *Pneuma* (Leiden: E. J. Brill), as a forum for international scholarly discussion of pentecostal and charismatic issues. In 1992,

---

168. Childs, *Biblical Theology in Crisis,* 99–107. For an introduction to the approach, see J. A. Sanders, *Canon and Community: A Guide to Canonical Criticism* (Philadelphia: Fortress, 1984). See our further analysis in ch. 3.

169. Childs himself pursued this task in his *Introduction to the Old Testament as Scripture* (Philadelphia: Fortress, 1979), his *The New Testament as Canon: An Introduction* (Philadelphia: Fortress, 1984), and his *Biblical Theology of the Old and New Testaments* (London: SCM, 1992). For further developments and examples, see C. Seitz and K. Greene-McCreight, eds., *Theological Exegesis: Essays in Honor of Brevard S. Childs* (Grand Rapids: Eerdmans, 1999). Cf. the assessment of Childs' work in Harrisville and Sundberg, *The Bible in Modern Culture,* 304–28.

Sheffield Academic Press began the *Journal of Pentecostal Theology* (*JPT*) to promote constructive theological discussion across many faith traditions. The resulting lively discussion has surfaced several key questions: Is the use of a rational evangelical hermeneutic helpful or harmful to experience-based Pentecostal life? How does the experienced work of the Holy Spirit relate to biblical interpretation? According to the NT, is the central authority of the Christian community to be the Bible or Christ addressing it through the Spirit?

Second, beginning in the early 1980s the appearance of several major studies on Jesus led some NT scholars to hail them as the "Third Quest for the Historical Jesus."[170] New archaeological data concerning first-century Palestine, refinements in scholarly methods, and newly discovered manuscripts like the *Gospel of Thomas* provided new perspectives from which to interpret him. The Jesus Seminar, a self-appointed, select group of North American scholars, developed a set of highly controversial criteria allegedly necessary to differentiate what Jesus actually said or did from later embellishments.[171] Recent publications by a spectrum of scholars have portrayed Jesus in a variety of ways (i.e., as an itinerant Cynic philosopher, an eschatological prophet, a prophet of social change, a wise sage, a marginal Jew, and a Jewish messiah). The lively discussion continues and, along with the "heat" of controversy, has shed some new "light" on our understanding of Jesus. The long-term significance of this "quest" remains to be seen. Today, a few scholars, most notably Paul Anderson, have been calling for a Fourth Quest, one that takes the most historically authenticable material from John's Gospel and gives it equal weight as the most trustworthy Synoptic material in reconstructions of the historical Jesus.[172]

In conclusion, the twentieth century saw the emergence of new methods of interpretation as well as rigorous philosophical and theological reflection on the nature of the interpretive process.[173] In its last two decades, other new methods joined the ranks of those discussed above. Literary approaches—the new literary criticism, reader-response criticism, and deconstruction—generated intriguing interpretations and lively scholarly discussion. Sociological approaches, including explicit hermeneutics

---

170. For a convenient introduction and helpful evaluation, see B. Witherington III, *The Jesus Quest: The Third Search for the Jew of Nazareth* (Downers Grove: InterVarsity, 1995). Recent discussion includes J. Charlesworth and B. Rhea, eds., *Jesus Research: New Methodologies and Perceptions* (Grand Rapids: Eerdmans, 2014); J. K. Beilby and P. R. Eddy, eds., *The Historical Jesus: Five Views* (Downers Grove: InterVarsity, 2009); J. Schroter, "New Horizons in Historical Jesus Research? Hermeneutical Consideration Concerning the So-called 'Third quest' of the Historical Jesus" in *The New Testament Interpreted: Essays in Honour of Bernard C. Lategan*, ed. C. Breytenbach, J. C. Thom, and J. Punt, NovTSup 146 (Leiden; Boston: Brill, 2006), 71–85. The most detailed and wide-ranging collection of all is T. Holmén and S. E. Porter, eds., *Handbook for the Study of the Historical Jesus*, 4 vols. (Leiden: Brill, 2010).

171. Chronologically, the Jesus Seminar was a contemporary of the Third Quest, but many critics allege that it used methods that were a throwback to the New Quest. Seminar members accepted primarily sayings material, were not concerned to root their Jesus in first-century Palestinian Judaism, and failed to ask the integrative questions about his aims or what prompted his crucifixion. See esp. N. T. Wright, *Jesus and the Victory of God*, Christian Origins and the Question of God, vol. 2 (Minneapolis: Fortress Press, 1996), 28–82.

172. Cf. P. N. Anderson, *The Fourth Gospel and the Quest for Jesus* (London and New York: T&T Clark, 2006).

173. Here we refer readers to the definitive discussion of contemporary biblical interpretation in A. C. Thiselton, *New Horizons in Hermeneutics* (Grand Rapids: Zondervan, 1992).

adopted by various advocacy groups (e.g., feminist and liberationist hermeneutics), also gained a wide hearing. The ascendancy of these methods has been so rapid, and in some early twenty-first century circles have become so dominant, that we devote the entire next chapter to them.

The Twenty-First Century

The nearly two decades of the new century have seen continued interest and significant developments in hermeneutics, some that follow threads that appeared toward the end of the previous one and others that mark new innovations on the subject. Introductions to the practice of hermeneutics aimed at students continue to appear,[174] and interest in theories of hermeneutics also remains high, especially retrospective evaluations of significant theoreticians of the previous century and the promotion of responsible interpretation for the future.[175] Remarkably, during this period Zondervan launched and completed a new eight-volume series (Scripture and Hermeneutics) to treat state-of-the-art issues in interpretation.[176] Literary criticism (i.e., the "new literary criticism") continues to attract scholarly attention although occasionally with a broader focus and a more cross-disciplinary methodology than in the past.[177] Familiar voices from the perspectival approach to biblical interpretation also continue to offer sophisticated reflection, particularly those from liberationist, ethnic (e.g. Latino/a, Asian), global, and post-colonial perspectives.[178]

---

174. A. C. Thiselton, *Hermeneutics: An Introduction* (Grand Rapids: Eerdmans, 2009), who traces the history of the subject; H. A. Virkler and K. G. Ayayo, *Hermeneutics: Principles and Processes of Biblical Interpretation*, 2nd ed. (Grand Rapids: Baker, 2007); W. C. Kaiser, Jr. and M. Silva, *Introduction to Biblical Hermeneutics: The Search for Meaning*, 2nd ed. (Grand Rapids: Zondervan, 2007); G. R. Osborne, *The Hermeneutical Spiral: A Comprehensive Introduction to Biblical Interpretation*, 2nd ed. (Downers Grove: InterVarsity, 2006). Cf. also A. C. Thiselton, *Thiselton on Hermeneutics: Collected Works With New Essays* (Grand Rapids: Eerdmans, 2006); and C. G. Bartholomew, *Introducing Biblical Hermeneutics: A Comprehensive Framework for Hearing God in Scripture* (Grand Rapids: Baker Academic, 2015). For a convenient, popular historical summary through select readings, see W. Yarchin, ed., *History of Biblical Interpretation: A Reader* (Grand Rapids: Baker Academic, 2011).

175. E.g., S. E. Porter and M. R. Malcom, eds., *The Future of Biblical Interpretation: Responsible Plurality in Biblical Hermeneutics* (Downers Grove: IVP Academic, 2013); and Porter and Robinson, *Hermeneutics: An Introduction to Interpretive Theory*.

176. The capstone volume is D. L. Jeffrey and C. S. Evans, eds., *The Bible and the University* (Grand Rapids: Zondervan, 2015).

177. Cf. K. Smelik and K. Vermeulen, eds., *Approaches to Literary Readings of Ancient Jewish Writings*, SSN 62 (Leiden; Boston: Brill, 2014), which includes literary essays on both the Hebrew Bible and other ancient Jewish writings, on the one hand, and essays that bridge the disciplinary gaps between linguistics and literary studies and between rational exegesis and intertextuality, on the other. Cf. the review of other methods of interpretation in S. L. McKenzie and J. Kaltner, *New Meanings for Ancient Texts: Recent Approaches to Biblical Criticisms and Their Applications* (Louisville: Westminster John Knox, 2013); and P. Gooder, ed., *Searching for Meaning: An Introduction to Interpreting the New Testament* (Louisville: SPCK; Westminster John Knox, 2009). Cf. R. Hamborg, *Still Selling the Righteous: A Redaction-Critical Investigation of Reasons for Judgment in Amos 2:6–16*, LHBOTS 555 (New York: T&T Clark, 2012).

178. Cf. C. M. Maier and C. J. Sharp, eds., *Prophecy and Power: Jeremiah in Feminist and Postcolonial Perspective*, LHBOTS 577 (London: Bloomsbury, 2013); R. C. Bailey, et al., eds., *They Were All In One Place? Toward Minority Biblical Criticism*, SemeiaSt 57 (Atlanta: Society of Biblical Literature, 2009); A. F. Botta and P. R. Andiñach, eds., *The Bible and the Hermeneutics of Liberation*, SemeiaSt 59 (Atlanta: Society of Biblical Literature, 2009); F. Lozada, Jr. and F. F. Segovia, eds., *Latino/a Biblical Hermeneutics: Problematics, Objectives, Strategies*, SemeiaSt 68 (Atlanta: SBL Press, 2014). From an Asian perspective, see A. Yong, *The Future of Evangelical Theology: Soundings from the Asian*

Further, the proliferation in this century of new, distinctive approaches to Bible interpretation is nothing short of stunning. One recent volume of essays introduces twenty-three such approaches![179] One prominent new voice in the hermeneutical conversation concerns interpretation from the perspective of gender orientation, a prominence born of the larger public conversation about it in this century. *Queer hermeneutics* is now an accepted academic discipline with its practitioners of biblical interpretation and increasing list of publications.[180] Other useful studies approach the topic of gender orientation and its implications for biblical hermeneutics from an explicitly religious perspective.[181]

Two new approaches, in our view, mark extensions of the reader-response approach (see below). In biblical studies, *intertextuality* studies the interrelationship between texts within the biblical canon. Its concern is how (or whether) a chronologically later text quotes, alludes to, echoes, or reflects the influence of an earlier one and how that interrelationship affects the interpretation of the former.[182] Though only recently prominent, the technique of cross-referencing texts in interpretation was actually among the principles articulated by the ancient rabbis (see above). Today, the approach guides discussions of the use of OT texts by NT writers as well as proposed connections with the OT and NT themselves. Still unsettled, however, is a consensus as to what constitutes "intertextuality" and how to identify its examples (e.g. how do "echoes" and "allusions" differ?). For readers seeking an author's intended

American Diaspora (Downers Grove: IVP Academic, 2014). Cf. also K. H. Smith, et al., eds., *Evangelical Postcolonial Conversations: Global Awakenings in Theology and Praxis* (Downers Grove: InterVarsity, 2014); C. Keener and M. D. Carroll R., eds., *Global Voices: Reading the Bible in the Majority World*, with a foreword by E. Yamauchi (Peabody, MA: Hendrickson Publishers, 2013); G. O. West, *Reading Other-wise: Socially Engaged Biblical Scholars Reading with their Local Communities*, SemeiaSt 62 (Atlanta: Society of Biblical Literature, 2007); and R.S. Sugirtharajah, ed., *Voices from the Margin: Interpreting the Bible in the Third World*, 3rd ed. (Maryknoll: Orbis Books, 2015). For a one-volume biblical commentary, see T. Adeyemo, ed., *Africa Bible Commentary* (Nairobi, Kenya: WordAlive Publishers; Grand Rapids: Zondervan, 2006).

179. P. Gooder, ed., *Searching for Meaning*. Cf. the sixteen approaches—some standard, some newer—in J. B. Green, ed., *Hearing the New Testament: Strategies for Interpretation* (Grand Rapids: Eerdmans, 2010).

180. E.g., A. R. Heacock, "Queer Hermeneutics and the David and Jonathan Narrative," *Jonathan Loved David: Manly Love in the Bible and The Hermeneutics of Sex*, Bible in the Modern World 22 (Sheffield: Sheffield Phoenix Press, 2011); R. C. Bailey, "Reading Backwards: A Narrative Technique for the Queering of David, Saul, and Samuel," in *The Fate of King David: The Past and Present of a Biblical Icon*, ed. T. Linafelt, LHBOTS 500 (New York: T&T Clark, 2010), 66–83; T. J. Hornsby, "Queer Criticism," in *Searching For Meaning*, ed. P. Gooder, 144–51; D. Guest et al., eds., *The Queer Bible Commentary* (London: SCM, 2006). Cf. M. Nissinen, *Homoeroticism in the Biblical World: A Historical Perspective*, trans. K. I. Stjerna (Minneapolis: Fortress Press, 2004).

181. Two New Testament scholars have provided a recent very popular resource; cf. D. O. Via and R. A. J. Gagnon, *Homosexuality and the Bible: Two Views* (Minneapolis: Fortress Press, 2009). Cf. also A. C. Thistelton, "Can Hermeneutics Ease the Deadlock? Some Biblical and Hermeneutical Models," in *The Way Forward? Christian Voices on Homosexuality and the Church*, 2nd ed., ed. T. Bradshaw (Grand Rapids: Eerdmans, 2004), 145–96. Cf. also K. Stone, "Queer Criticism" in *New Meanings for Ancient Texts*, ed. McKenzie and Kaltner, 154–76.

182. C. A. Evans and J. J. Johnston, eds., *Searching the Scriptures: Studies in Context and Intertextuality*, LNTS 543 (New York: T&T Clark, 2015); R. B. Hayes, S. Alkier, and L. A. Huizenga, eds., *Reading the Bible Intertextually* (Waco, TX: Baylor University Press, 2009); J. T. Hibbard, *Intertextuality in Isaiah 24-27: the Reuse and Evocation of Earlier Texts and Traditions*, FAT 16 (Tübingen: Mohr Siebeck, 2006); M. A. Sweeney, *Form and Intertextuality in Prophetic and Apocalyptic Literature*, FAT 45 (Tübingen: Mohr Siebeck, 2005). For an example of extra-biblical intertextuality, see M. J. Gilmour, *The Significance of Parallels Between 2 Peter and Other Early Christian Literature*, AcBib 10 (Boston: Brill, 2002).

meaning, the question of which examples are intentional or accidental (i.e. the product of original writers or of later writers) looms large. The second new approach interprets the Bible retrospectively through its *reception history*. It traces how the Bible's contents have been "received"—incorporated, used, influenced—in diverse arenas (e.g., art, music, poetry, narrative, film, politics, popular culture, other religions, etc.). Rather than ask "What does this text mean?" (i.e., exegesis), reception history asks "What can this text do?" (i.e., its reception).[183] Oxford University has established the Centre for the Reception of the Bible, and nine of the projected thirty-volume major reference work, the *Encyclopedia of the Bible and Its Reception* (*EBR*), have appeared thus far.[184] Granted, reception history may enrich one's interpretation of Bible, but we still accord the Bible's pre-reception contents as unique and of ultimate, superior authority.

Academic discussions of hermeneutics from a Pentecostal perspective that emerged in the late twentieth century continue to thrive and find publication in journals. Founded in 1979, the journal *Pneuma* (Brill) published its thirty-seventh volume in 2015, while the *Journal of Pentecostal Theology* (now published by Brill) that same year issued Volume 24 and has also produced a supplementary series of scholarly monographs now numbering forty.[185] A distinguished record of publications has established Professor Amos Jong as a leading voice in discussions from this perspective (and from a global one, as well).[186] He co-edits (with J. K. A. Smith) the Pentecostal Manifestos series (Eerdmans), whose volumes reflect creative, distinctly Pentecostal scholarly engagement with themes and concerns of contemporary Christian thought.[187]

Both OT and (to a lesser extent) NT scholars continue to apply the approach of canon criticism proposed by the late Professor Brevard Childs. A collection of essays responds to criticism levelled against the method, and another explores the implications of canon for interpretation of various biblical texts and for theological interpretation

---

183. B. W. Breed, *Nomadic Text: A Theory of Biblical Reception History*, ISBL (Bloomington, IN: Indiana University Press, 2014); R. Evans, *Reception History, Tradition and Biblical Interpretation: Gadamer and Jauss in Current Practice*, Scriptural Traces 4 (London: Bloomsbury T&T Clark, 2014); cf. W. J. Lyons and E. England, eds., *Reception History and Biblical Studies: Theory and Practice*, Scriptural Traces 6 (London: T&T Clark International, 2015); M. Lieb, E. Mason, and J. Roberts, eds., *The Oxford Handbook of the Reception History of the Bible*, Oxford Handbooks in Religion and Theology (Oxford: Oxford University Press, 2011).

184. H. Spieckermann, et al., eds., *Encyclopedia of the Bible and Its Reception*, 30 vols. (Berlin; New York: DeGruyter, 2009–).

185. E.g., W. Ma and R. P. Menzies, eds., *The Spirit and Spirituality: Essays in Honour of Russell P. Spittler*, JPTSup 24 (London and New York: T&T Clark International, 2004); S. Solivan, *The Spirit, Pathos and Liberation: Toward an Hispanic Pentecostal Theology*, JPTSup 14 (Sheffield: Sheffield Academic Press, 1998).

186. Cf. the wide-ranging, multi-faceted interaction with his work in W. Vondey, ed., *The Theology of Amos Yong and the New Face of Pentecostal Scholarship: Passion for the Spirit*, Global Pentecostal and Charismatic Studies 14 (Leiden: Brill, 2013). For his rigorous interaction with science as a pentecostal, see Amos Yong, *The Spirit of Creation: Modern Science and Divine Action in the Pentecostal-charismatic Imagination*, Pentecostal Manifestos (Grand Rapids: Eerdmans, 2011).

187. Cf. most recently, the seventh volume in the series, M. J. Cartledge, *The Mediation of the Spirit* (Grand Rapids: Eerdmans, 2015). In addition, volumes of the Pentecostal Commentary continue to appear, most recently, T. Grizzle, *Ephesians: A Pentecostal Commentary* (Blandford Forum, UK: Deo Publishing, 2012).

in general.[188] Meanwhile, studies applying the approach continue to appear.[189] Also, during this period the *inductive method* of Bible study that originated in the late nineteenth century as an alternative to higher criticism (see above) and is thought to have influenced Childs, found a new institutional home at Asbury Theological Seminary in Kentucky.[190] Organizations like InterVarsity and Bible Study Fellowship have long used the method effectively with university students and large lay groups, respectively. In 2014, from its base at Asbury, the method also found a new scholarly voice, the *Journal of Inductive Biblical Studies*, with three volumes now in print.[191]

One especially fascinating development this century is the emergence of a movement broadly known as the *Theological Interpretation of Scripture* (TIS) and associated with the works of K. J. Vanhoozer, C. G. Bartholemew, and D. J. Treier.[192] Interestingly, the movement is led primarily by Christian theologians, not biblical scholars, and in a sense represents an attempt to recover the Bible from the centuries-long hegemony of scholarly skepticism since the Enlightenment. At heart, the movement desires to recover the Bible's theological voice and to demonstrate the ongoing intellectual and practical viability of interpreting Scripture theologically. So, with Childs, its practitioners study the Bible as the Christian canon and also welcome pre-critical interpreters, long dismissed by critical scholars, back into the hermeneutical conversation. The movement's members also recognize the importance of the Bible's historical ecclesiastical context—its role in shaping the church's creeds, its worship, its liturgy, and its spiritual practices.

Three new commentary series reflect the movement's theological interests and depart from ones typically written by biblical specialists. The first series, written primarily by theologians, is the Brazos Theological Commentary on the Bible of

---

188. C. G. Bartholomew, et al., eds., *Canon and Biblical Interpretation*, Scripture and Hermeneutics 7 (Grand Rapids: Zondervan, 2006).

189. P. Sumpter, *The Substance of Psalm 24: An Attempt to Read Scripture after Brevard S. Childs*, LHBOTS 600 (London and New York: Bloomsbury T&T Clark, 2015); H. J. Keener, *A Canonical Exegesis of Psalm 8: YHWH's Maintenance of the Created Order through Divine Reversal*, JTISup 9 (Winona Lake:, IN Eisenbrauns, 2014); C. E. Shepherd, *Theological Interpretation and Isaiah 53: A Critical Comparison of Bernhard Duhm, Brevard Childs, and Alec Motyer*, LHBOTS 598 (London and New York: Bloomsbury T&T Clark, 2014); G. M. O'Neal, *Interpreting Habakkuk as Scripture: An Application of the Canonical Approach of Brevard S. Childs*, StBibLit 9 (New York: Peter Lang, 2007).

190. For a history of the inductive Bible study movement and the method's distinctions, see conveniently D. R. Bauer, "Inductive Biblical Study: History, Character, and Prospects in a Global Environment," *AsJ* (2013) 68:6–35. During the twentieth century, the movement founded Biblical Seminary in New York and later played a prominent curricular role at Presbyterian seminaries like Princeton and Union Seminary in Virginia.

191. Cf. http://place.asburyseminary.edu/jibs/. For a full presentation of inductive biblical study, see D. R. Bauer and R. A. Traina, *Inductive Bible Study: A Comprehensive Guide to the Practice of Hermeneutics* (Grand Rapids: Baker Academic, 2011).

192. K. J. Vanhoozer, *Is There a Meaning in This Text?*; K. J. Vanhoozer, ed., *Dictionary for Theological Interpretation of the Bible* (London: SPCK; Grand Rapids: Baker Academic, 2005); D. J. Treier, *Introducing Theological Interpretation of Scripture: Recovering a Christian Practice* (Grand Rapids: Baker Academic, 2008); C. G. Bartholomew and M. W. Goheen, *The Drama of Scripture: Finding Our Place in the Biblical Story* (Grand Rapids: Baker Academic, 2014); C. G. Bartholomew, et al., eds., *Canon and Biblical Interpretation*; and S. Fowl, ed. *The Theological Interpretation of Scripture: Classic and Contemporary Readings* (Oxford: Blackwell, 1997).

which, to date, twenty-one volumes have appeared.[193] Second, volumes in the Ancient Christian Commentary on Scripture compile comments gleaned on biblical texts from an enormous treasury of patristic writings (see above).[194] Their unique value is the pre-critical and pre-reformation perspective from which those cited write and their obvious passion for the church. The project reflects recent public interest in the doctrine and practice of the early church, including its Orthodox branches. Finally, to date eight of a projected twenty-eight volumes in the Reformation Commentary on Scripture have appeared.[195] In each volume, theologians and church historians compile interpretation chapter-by-chapter gleaned from Reformation-era writers.

Two other significant, recently proposed hermeneutical approaches round out this history of interpretation. In a stimulating book William Webb proposes what he calls a *redemptive-movement hermeneutic*.[196] It offers a sophisticated method to distinguish in Scripture what is timeless and what is cultural—to help readers with integrity resolve dilemmas that arise when what the Bible says seems out-of-keeping with either mature common sense or other biblical teachings. Webb's view has sparked controversy among some evangelicals, especially since it challenges a complementarian model of gender roles.[197] Further, in this book we argue that application is an intrinsic part of proper hermeneutics—that interpretation is incomplete without it. Y. S. Kim takes this idea a step further, speaking in his *hermeneutic of transformation* more comprehensively of "transformation" rooted in self-knowledge and self-criticism rather than simply "application."[198] His challenge is that Christians should do theology by abandoning individualism in favor of solidarity with readers worldwide, even those with whom they disagree.[199]

Finally, one notable beginning trend parallel to the theological interpretation of Scripture movement merits mention—conversations about the relationship between exegesis and ancient spiritual practices such as *lectio divina*. J. Vanier and F. Young

---

193. R. Reno, ed., The Brazos Theological Commentary on the Bible, 30 vols. (Grand Rapids: Brazos Press, 2005–). Recent volumes include R. E. Barron, *2 Samuel* (2015) and E. T. Charry, *Psalms 1–50* (2015).

194. T. C. Oden, ed., Ancient Christian Commentary on Scripture, 29 vols. (Downers Grove: InterVarsity, 2001–); cf. also A. Di Berardino, *Encyclopedia of Ancient Christianity*, 3 vols., trans. J. T. Papa, et al. (Downers Grove: IVP Academic, 2014). For an appreciation of patristic biblical interpretation, see J. Childers, "Reading the Bible with Old Friends: The Value of Patristic Bible Interpretations for Ministry," *ResQ* 45 (2003): 69–89.

195. See most recently, B. Kreitzer, *Luke*, Reformation Commentary on Scripture, New Testament 3 (Downers Grove: IVP Academic, 2015).

196. W. J. Webb, *Slaves, Women & Homosexuals: Exploring the Hermeneutics of Cultural Analysis* (Downers Grove: InterVarsity, 2001).

197. Cf. W. J. Webb, "A Redemptive-Movement Model," in *Four Views on Moving Beyond the Bible to Theology*, ed. G. T. Meadors, Counterpoints (Grand Rapids: Zondervan, 2009). For the spectrum of responses and Webb's replies, see his "A Redemptive-Movement Hermeneutic: Encouraging Dialogue Among Four Evangelical Views," *JETS* 48 (2005): 331–49.

198. Y. S. Kim, *Biblical Interpretation: Theory, Process, and Criteria* (Eugene, OR: Pickwick Pub., 2013); cf. his *Truth, Testimony, and Transformation: A New Reading of the "I Am" Sayings of Jesus in the Fourth Gospel* (Eugene, OR: Cascade, 2014), and *A Transformative Reading of the Bible: Explorations of Holistic Human Transformation* (Eugene, OR: Cascade Books, 2013).

199. Kim also is both the founding editor of the new online *Journal of Bible and Human Transformation* and (since 2014) editor of the *Journal of Race, Ethnicity, and Religion*.

articulate a "dynamic model of interpretation"—serious interaction between the objective and subjective dimensions of interpretation as exemplified by Vanier's work on the Gospel of John.[200] If, as Thompson proposes, the practice of *lectio* positively shaped Luther's hermeneutics, the great reformer would likely regard this new conversation as in fact the renewal of a very old one—and smile his approval.[201] We engage this use of the Bible in more detail in chapter 11.

200. J. Vanier and F. Young, "Towards Transformational Reading of Scripture," in *Canon and Biblical Interpretation*, ed. Bartholomew, et al., 236–54.

201. Cf. Thompson, "Biblical Interpretation in the Works of Martin Luther," 312.

3

LITERARY AND SOCIAL-SCIENTIFIC APPROACHES TO INTERPRETATION

Much of this book considers what one might call traditional hermeneutics, that is, common-sense wisdom for interpreting the Bible in ways people typically interpret other acts of human communication, combined with the methodological precision given to that wisdom by the last two centuries of modern biblical criticism.[1] As we saw in chapter two, it also embraces the more sophisticated tools of source, form, and redaction criticism—tools whose foundational concepts substantially predate the terms themselves. In recent decades, however, many Bible scholars, particularly those outside of evangelical circles, have called for nothing less than a paradigm shift in hermeneutics.[2] They found the old ways sterile, limiting, or misleading and believed it was time to do something new. The suggestions they have made for replacing the more common approach to interpretation—traditional historical-grammatical analysis—primarily revolve around two areas of study: (1) modern literary criticism and (2) social-scientific analysis.[3] The first of these in certain aspects recovers a healthy emphasis on the literary nature of the Bible and the second on its communal or corporate nature that have been lost in our scientific and individualistic age. We dispute that it is a case of *either* the old ways *or* the new ways; indeed, scholarship as a whole is increasingly realizing this.[4] We grant that these new arenas of study can afford important insights to supplement traditional hermeneutics, but they also offer dangerous pitfalls when abused.

---

1. Cf. J. K. Brown, *Scripture as Communication: Introducing Biblical Hermeneutics* (Grand Rapids: Baker, 2007).

2. The concept comes originally from T. S. Kuhn, *The Structure of Scientific Revolutions*, 4th ed. (Chicago: University of Chicago Press, 2012). A paradigm shift occurs when one model of interpreting data is almost entirely replaced by a quite different model.

3. For an excellent example, see C. H. Talbert's unnecessarily scathing review of J. Fitzmyer (*The Gospel According to Luke*, AB 28–28a, 2 vols. [Garden City: Doubleday, 1981–85] in *CBQ* 48 [1986]: 336–38), in which Talbert essentially faulted Fitzmyer for having written a traditional, historical-critical commentary of a kind that Talbert believed was now passé, that is, in an age when he thought literary-critical paradigms should predominate. For a more positive call for a paradigm shift to a social-scientific perspective, see B. J. Malina, *Christian Origins and Cultural Anthropology* (Atlanta: John Knox, 1986; Eugene, OR: Wipf & Stock, 2010).

4. An excellent defense and discussion of the complementarity of historical and literary methods appears throughout M. A. Powell, *What Is Narrative Criticism?* (Minneapolis: Fortress, 1990). For the blend of historical and social-scientific methods, see J. H. Elliott, *What Is Social-Scientific Criticism?* (Minneapolis: Fortress, 1993).

LITERARY CRITICISM

"Literary criticism" means different things to different people. Aída Spencer has compiled a list of no less than fifteen distinct definitions, many of which are best treated under different headings. Such topics include analysis of authorship, date, place of writing, original audience, linguistic style, sources, tradition and redaction, integrity, and purpose.[5] All of these are necessary components of the analysis of any work of literature. But while all at various times in the past have been considered a part of literary criticism, now they are usually treated under *historical* criticism. What critics who have called for a shift in biblical studies usually mean by literary criticism today is largely *ahistorical* in nature—methods that require an examination only of the final form of the text. We treat two such methods later in this volume: genre criticism, which analyzes the literary classification of an entire biblical book, and that portion of form criticism that describes the form or subgenre of a given part of a biblical book. Under genre criticism we note also the growing tendency to classify the nature of the rhetoric of the writer—what is often called rhetorical criticism.[6] This still leaves three major areas of literary criticism, however, that we need to discuss: narrative criticism, reader-response criticism, and deconstruction.

The history of literary criticism correlates closely with the three dimensions of hermeneutical analysis we introduced in chapter one—the author, the text, and the reader. While traditionally literary critics have attempted to determine an author's original intent, the approach in the first half of the twentieth century of "formalism" or "new criticism" in literary studies more generally focused on a coherent interpretation of the text in its entirety apart from any historical background information. Seeking to avoid committing what they called the "intentional fallacy," such critics stressed that readers usually do not have access to the mental states or intentions of authors, often long separated in time and place from contemporary readers. In addition, the written, historical information that does exist about the circumstances of the composition of a document may not be adequate to enable us to discern authorial intention. Moreover, authors may write something other than what they mean to say or there may be additional dimensions of the meanings of their texts than those they recognized initially.[7]

Focusing on texts independent of their authors then spawned two sub-disciplines—narrative criticism and structuralism. Narrative criticism focused on a close reading of what became known as the surface structure of a text—elements like plot,

---

5. A. B. Spencer, "Literary Criticism," in *New Testament Criticism and Interpretation*, ed. D. A. Black and D. S. Dockery (Grand Rapids: Zondervan, 1991), 235–36. Not surprisingly, the second edition of this volume has an entirely different article under this heading by a different author.

6. A term first given widespread currency and used in a broader context, to overlap with some of the concerns we will treat under narrative criticism, by J. Muilenburg, "Form Criticism and Beyond," *JBL* 88 (1969): 8.

7. See, classically, W. K. Wimsatt and M. C. Beardsley, "The Intentional Fallacy," in *The Verbal Icon*, ed. W. K. Wimsatt (Lexington: University of Kentucky Press, 1954), 2–18. More on these matters appears in a subsequent chapter.

theme, motifs, characterization; or, in poetry, meter, rhyme, parallelism, and so on. Structuralism analyzed the so-called deep structures of a text—consistent elements perceptible beneath the surface of the narrative, related to, for example, how a "sender" attempts to communicate an "object" to a "receiver" by means of "subject," who may be aided to by a "helper" and/or hindered by an "opponent." Or it might analyze how narratives, especially in religious myths, try to mediate between and resolve the conflict generated by pairs of opposites. In biblical studies this method generated an intense flurry of specialized studies in the 1970s and 1980s, but the highly esoteric terminology and the sense that few exegetical insights resulted not already available by other methods led to its demise. Today one finds very few scholars doing much of anything with structuralism.[8]

Instead, attention has turned to two kinds of "poststructuralism" or postmodernist hermeneutics—reader-response criticism and deconstruction—which focus on the role of the reader in the interpretive process. Narrative criticism, however, continues to generate considerable interest; hence the three main subheadings of this half chapter on literary criticism.[9]

Narrative Criticism

Narrative criticism is that branch of modern literary criticism that most closely resembles what readers of the world's great literary classics have done for centuries. Its predecessor was the study of the Bible as literature, a profitable exercise that has often been undertaken in public school and university settings.[10] Studying the Bible as literature focuses on the questions one would ask of Shakespeare or Cervantes, Sophocles or Cicero, Aesop or Goethe. Of particular value for works of narrative genre, this approach analyzes plot, theme, motifs, characterization,[11] style, figures of speech, symbolism, foreshadowing, repetition, speed of time in narrative, point of view, and the like. It focuses more on an appreciation of the artistic or aesthetic value of the work than on its theological or moral value. If the latter are studied too, one still approaches the work only from the point of view of a sympathetic outside

---

8. For representative surveys of applications in OT and NT studies, respectively, see D. Jobling, *The Sense of Biblical Narrative: Structural Analyses in the Hebrew Bible*, 2 vols., JSOTSup 39 (Sheffield: JSOT, 1986); R. F. Collins, *Introduction to the New Testament* (Garden City: Doubleday, 1983), 231–71. The scholar in the U.S. who perhaps did the most with the method was D. Patte. For an introduction to his approaches, see his *What Is Structural Exegesis?* (Philadelphia: Fortress, 1976). For sample applications, see his *Structural Exegesis: From Theory to Practice* (Philadelphia: Fortress, 1978).

9. For an excellent, thorough overview of these three periods of attention to author, text, and reader in literary criticism and biblical studies, see S. E. Porter, "Literary Approaches to the New Testament: From Formalism to Deconstruction and Back," in *Approaches to New Testament Study*, JSNTSup 120, ed. S. E. Porter and D. Tombs (Sheffield: Sheffield Academic Press, 1995), 77–128.

10. An example serving these settings is K. R. R. Gros Louis, ed., *Literary Interpretations of Biblical Narratives*, 2 vols., The Bible in Literature Courses (Nashville: Abingdon, 1974–1982).

11. Characterization has received particularly detailed and helpful scrutiny. See esp. A. Berlin, *Poetics and Interpretation of Biblical OT Narrative* (Sheffield: Almond, 1983; Winona Lake, IN: Eisenbrauns, 1994); and C. Bennema, *A Theory of Character in New Testament Narrative* (Minneapolis: Fortress, 2014).

observer, not as the devotee of a particular religion, and hence it can be a legitimate topic for the public high school or state university context.[12]

Narrative Criticism
Places the focus on plot, theme, motifs, characterization, style, figures of speech, point of view, etc.
Good examples: Story of Samson (Judg 13–16); Nicodemus (John 3:1–15; 7:50–52; 19:39)

Applications

A narrative-critical approach to a portion of Scripture can have great value. Noting how a character is developed may help one understand whether the author wants readers to identify with that character or to avoid imitating that person. In other instances, characterization may be deliberately ambiguous. Thus, it is arguable that, despite the complexities of characterization, Samson's heroic death, like his repeated filling by the Holy Spirit throughout his life (Judg 13–16), marks him out ultimately as someone to emulate, though not in every aspect of his life. Conversely, for all of Saul's redeeming characteristics, Scripture ultimately seems to portray him as a tragic figure, losing what he could have had while knowing better, and thus someone not to emulate (1 Sam 9–2 Sam 1).[13] In between these two stands Nicodemus who appears three times in the Fourth Gospel (John 3:1–15; 7:50–52; 19:39). But here the reader is not given enough data to know if Nicodemus, like Joseph of Arimathea with whom he finally appears (19:38), eventually became a disciple of Jesus or not. He can be viewed as a model of someone who came to faith against the pressure of his peers, and hence more slowly and secretively than others, or as one who failed to make a decisive break from his past, which true discipleship requires. Perhaps John deliberately refuses to satisfy our curiosity so that we might take whatever steps are necessary to enter the kingdom, whether or not Nicodemus did.[14]

Focusing on the surface features of plot, theme, episode, and so on, can also demonstrate the unity of a text, which older historical criticism often segmented into complex layers of tradition and redaction. David Clines, for example, broke

---

12. Good introductions to the method include Powell, *What Is Narrative Criticism?*; and Y. Amit, *Reading Biblical Narratives: Literary Criticism and the Hebrew Bible* (Minneapolis: Fortress, 2001). Perhaps the best anthology is R. Alter and F. Kermode, eds., *The Literary Guide to the Bible* (Cambridge, MA: Harvard University Press, 1987). From an explicitly evangelical perspective, cf. esp. L. Ryken and T. Longman III, eds., *A Complete Literary Guide to the Bible* (Grand Rapids: Zondervan, 1993). Also very helpful is L. Ryken, *Words of Delight: A Literary Introduction to the Bible* (Grand Rapids: Baker, 1987). On individual testaments, see M. D. Coogan, *The Old Testament: A Historical and Literary Introduction to the Hebrew Scriptures*, 3rd ed. (Oxford: Oxford University Press, 2013); and J. L. Resseguie, *Narrative Criticism of the New Testament: An Introduction* (Grand Rapids: Baker, 2005).

13. For both of these assessments see D. M. Gunn, *The Fate of King Saul*, JSOTSup 14 (Sheffield: JSOT, 1980).

14. Cf. esp. J. M. Bassler, "Mixed Signals: Nicodemus in the Fourth Gospel," *JBL* 108 (1989): 635–46; and R. Hakola, "The Burden of Ambiguity: Nicodemus and the Social Identity of the Johannine Christians," *NTS* 55 (2009): 438–55. For a striking contrast between Nicodemus in John 3 and the Samaritan woman in John 4, see C. L. Blomberg, "The Globalization of Biblical Interpretation—A Test Case: John 3–4," *BBR* 5 (1995): 1–15.

fresh ground with his study of themes in the Pentateuch by showing how the five books of Moses were united by the common theme of the partial fulfillment of the promise to or blessing of the patriarchs—which in turn contained the three aspects of posterity, divine-human relationship, and land. In so doing Clines undermined important bases that had led critics to postulate J, E, D, and P (Jahwist, Elohist, Deuteronomist, and Priestly writers), among whom the Pentateuch could be parceled out.[15] So too, Alan Culpepper, in his fine literary analysis of the unity of style and literary features of John, appears to have superseded his earlier work on a Johannine school as the composite author through several successive stages of redaction of the Fourth Gospel.[16]

Of course, this kind of narrative criticism may presuppose an earlier tradition history in which a text gained its current form over a long period, but it may also offer a more radical challenge. As G. W. Coats explains in his analysis of the Joseph narrative (Gen 37–50), if "the story stands as a unit in at least one stage of its history . . . the burden of proof lies therefore on the person who wants to argue that the unity is synthetic" (i.e., brought about by a redactor imposing that unity on disparate sources).[17] And even when literary critics do not recognize this point, their concern to focus on the final, unified form of the text makes possible many discussions across theological lines (most notably evangelical-mainline), since historical questions are simply bracketed as irrelevant for the matters at hand. In other words, even if one scholar may accept that a certain narrative tells the story as it actually happened, while another may dispute that claim, both may agree on what the story means and how it functions.

Studying the Bible as literature further helps students focus on major emphases and not get sidetracked with peripheral details. For example, once we understand the theme of the Pentateuch as the partial fulfillment of God's promises despite various obstacles, apparent digressions such as Abraham's twice-aborted attempts to pass Sarah off as his sister (Gen 12:10–20; 20:1–18) make more sense in their context. Along this line, neither story has a particular "moral" in its own right—for example, to speak for or against half-truths or deceiving an enemy. Rather, thematically, they reflect potential impediments to the fulfillment of God's desire to bless Abraham with the holy land and promised seed. As Abraham's schemes fail, we learn more of God's sovereignty and how he is working to assure that his promises do not fail.[18]

---

15. D. J. A. Clines, *The Theme of the Pentateuch*, 2nd ed., JSOTSup 10 (Sheffield: Sheffield Academic Press, 1997). The suggestion that Genesis through Deuteronomy is actually a compilation of the works of four different anonymous authors (usually called J, E, D, P), centuries after the life of Moses, represents the famous "documentary hypothesis," which has dominated the last hundred years of Pentateuchal criticism but waned in influence in recent decades.

16. R. A. Culpepper, *Anatomy of the Fourth Gospel* (Philadelphia: Fortress, 1983). Cf. R. A. Culpepper, *The Johannine School* (Missoula: Scholars, 1975).

17. G. W. Coats, *From Canaan to Egypt: Structural and Theological Context for the Joseph Story*, CBQMS 4 (Washington, DC: CBAA, 1976), 60.

18. B. K. Waltke with C. J. Fredricks, *Genesis: A Commentary* (Grand Rapids: Zondervan, 2001), 212–17, 282–89. Particularly helpful in interpreting OT historical narrative is J. Goldingay, *Approaches to Old Testament Interpretation*, 2nd ed. (Toronto: Clements, 2002).

Yet again, this kind of literary criticism can explain the purposes of repetition better than traditional source criticism. For example, two passages that might have been viewed as doublets (two similar sounding accounts believed to reflect only one original, historical event, which was then narrated differently in two or more different documents) and as clues to discerning separate sources, can now both be seen to be authentic. Thus, the similarities between Isaac's meeting Rebekah and Jacob's first encounter with Rachel, both at a well, involving the watering of flocks, and leading ultimately to a return to the woman's home and a betrothal, fit into a conventional "type-scene" of ancient oral and literary narrative.[19] In other words, as in form criticism, because of the currency of stereotypic forms in which people expected those stories to be told, they often sounded more similar than they would have had additional details been narrated. This means, then, that Bible readers should not assume that only one historical event has been repeated in two or more different ways. Rather, the similarities in the stories help them to recognize the "form" or "sub-genre" of the passage and thereby how to interpret it (see our chapter on OT genre criticism). Then, to discover the unique emphasis of any given text, readers should pay attention to those areas in which the stories, notwithstanding convention, diverge. With this strategy in mind, the reader will see how Jacob is much more assertive than Isaac, a feature that continues throughout the patriarchal narratives. Conversely, Rebekah proves more discerning than Rachel. These observations fit the greater prominence given to Jacob (Rebekah's co-conspirator for the blessing) than to either his father or his wife. Thus, the narrative gives clues as to the characters with whom we should most identify and from whom we should most learn.

A careful study of plot and character development also helps us to identify the climax or most important idea of a passage. Too, we may recognize where a surprise or shock effect would have driven home certain truths with extra force or poignancy to the original biblical readers. Dan Via helpfully categorized the parables as comic or tragic based on their endings.[20] ("Comic" here refers to a positive resolution of a plot conflict, not to a sense of humor.) Hence, even though the parables of the wedding banquet (Matt 22:1–14) and the wicked tenants (Matt 21:33–46) have similar structures and much of the identical imagery, the former ends on a note of destruction and the latter on a note of victory. Modern teaching based on these passages should reflect similar emphases: warning those who too glibly think that they are right with God and encouraging those who fear that God's purposes may fail.

We can similarly categorize the Minor Prophets. Although many of them preach judgment throughout a majority of their books, often a climactic, final look to the eschatological restoration of God's people reverses the reader's focus to the ultimate "good news" beyond the "bad news" (e.g., Hos 14:4–8; Amos 9:11–15; Zeph 3:14–20).

---

19. See esp. R. Alter, *The Art of Biblical Narrative,* rev. ed. (New York: Basic, 2011), 61–67.

20. D. O. Via, Jr., *The Parables: Their Literary and Existential Dimension* (Philadelphia: Fortress, 1967; Eugene, OR: Wipf & Stock, 2007).

The amount of discussion of a topic may not prove as significant as the placement of that discussion within a given book. On the other hand, Micah seems consistently to alternate between sections of good and bad news, as if to balance them.[21]

Literary criticism has done many other things. It identifies characters as flat, stock, or round, or as agents, types, or full characters, depending on how complex and lifelike they are portrayed.[22] Those developed the most—as with Jacob, Joseph, and his brothers in Genesis 37–50—are most likely the characters on which the story's writer wanted his audience to center most attention.[23] In 2 Kings 5 Naaman evokes sympathy because of the complex or round nature of his character. Elisha too is round, alternately tolerant and intolerant, which makes the reader hold him at arm's length. Literary criticism delineates ways in which writers attempt to achieve empathy, as with the introduction and conclusion to the story of Judah's revenge for the rape of Dinah (Gen 34), or to "justify God's ways to man."[24] Gehazi as a "flat" representative of mere greed inspires only antipathy.[25] Plot analysis can dovetail with redaction criticism in helping to understand the outline and ideological emphases of a narrative author. The central plot of Matthew's Gospel, for example, unfolds around the growing hostility of the Jewish leaders against Jesus.[26] Matthew's placement of certain passages, different from the other Gospels, then makes sense against this backdrop.[27] But what is today increasingly called "narrative criticism," while adopting all of these devices from the study of Bible as literature, usually goes one important step further.

Narrative criticism typically adopts an analytical framework that distinguishes the *real author* of a particular writing from the *implied author,* who is again distinguished from the *narrator.* The real author is the person who actually wrote the text. The implied author is the picture of the real author that emerges from the text without any additional background information. The narrator is the person in the narrative who actually tells the story. Similarly, one may separate the *real readers* from the *implied readers* (the picture of the readers emerging from the text alone) and the *narratées* (the persons in the text to whom the story is told). The real author and readers are often inaccessible from the written text alone.[28] Narrators and narratées might well be

---

21. Cf. M. J. Buss, "Tragedy and Comedy in Hosea," *Semeia* 32 (1984): 71–82; and N. K. Gottwald, "Tragedy and Comedy in the Latter Prophets," *Semeia* 32 (1984): 83–96.

22. For the Gospels, see esp. D. Rhoads and K. Syreeni, eds., *Characterization in the Gospels,* JSNTSup 184 (Sheffield: Sheffield Academic Press, 1999). Cf. also T. Wiarda, *Interpreting Gospel Narratives: Scenes, People, and Theology* (Nashville: B&H, 2010).

23. W. L. Humphreys, *Joseph and His Family: A Literary Study* (Columbia: University of South Carolina Press, 1988), 68–92.

24. See, respectively, M. Sternberg, *The Poetics of Biblical Narrative* (Bloomington: Indiana University Press, 1985), 445–75, and 484.

25. D. Marguerat and Y. Bourkin, *How to Read Bible Stories* (London: SCM, 1999), 61–62.

26. R. A. Edwards, *Matthew's Story of Jesus* (Philadelphia: Fortress, 1985).

27. See the suggested outline and headings in C. L. Blomberg, *Matthew,* NAC 22 (Nashville: Broadman, 1992).

28. Most scholars credit the development of this method in literature more generally to W. Iser, *The Implied Reader: Patterns of Communication in Prose Fiction from Bunyan to Beckett* (Baltimore: The Johns Hopkins University Press, 1974).

fictional characters, as, for example, with the narrator, Ishmael, in Herman Melville's *Moby Dick*. Thus, those who believe that Luke-Acts was not written by Paul's "beloved physician" but by a second-or third-generation Christian to an end-of-the-first-century or early second-century church might distinguish between the real author and readers (as just described), the implied author and readers (the picture of Luke derivable from the text, who was perhaps purporting to write to a pre-AD 70 congregation), and the narrator and narratée (the historical Luke and Theophilus).[29]

For an OT example, in the Minor Prophets several different real authors seem to resemble one and the same implied author; several groups of real readers correspond to one implied reader.[30] Thus, it is not so crucial to determine the exact historical settings of books like Joel and Obadiah, which pose notorious problems for traditional historical critics. The real authors (or editors) are not concerned to divulge much information about themselves because they share a common, almost timeless concern—to warn God's people about particularly well-entrenched patterns of sin. They prophesy judgment with the possibility of subsequent restoration contingent on repentance. In this instance literary criticism allows Bible students more closely to approximate the interpretations of average Bible readers who never bothered with much historical background in the first place. There are obviously strengths and weaknesses to such an approach. But when students discover proposals of modern narrative criticism that fit with the results of more traditional historical criticism, they may be able to accept both with greater degrees of confidence.

In still other cases, narrative criticism reminds us to distinguish between the presumably reliable narrator of a biblical book and an unreliable speaker whose words are reported within that book. The apparent contradiction between 1 Samuel 31, in which Saul has his armor bearer help him commit suicide, and 2 Samuel 1, in which an Amalekite boasts that he has killed Saul, is resolved when we understand that the Amalekite was lying in hopes of gaining some reward from David, who he assumed would be grateful to learn of his archenemy's death. In other instances, it is harder to be sure of what the narrator is doing. It is interesting, for example, to compare the quite different analyses by Y. Amit, on the one hand, and Gunn and Fewell, on the other hand, of the role of Judah in Genesis 38 where he has sex with Tamar, believing her to be a prostitute. Depending on which elements one focuses, Judah can be seen as thoroughly ignoble or somewhat redeemed.[31]

---

29. New Testament narrative criticism has largely focused on the Gospels and Acts, with one pioneering study dominating the analysis of each of the four evangelists: J. D. Kingsbury, *Matthew as Story*, 2nd ed. (Philadelphia: Fortress, 1988); D. Rhoads, J. Dewey and D. Michie, *Mark as Story*, 3rd ed. (Minneapolis: Fortress, 2012); R. C. Tannehill, *The Narrative Unity of Luke-Acts*, 2 vols. (Philadelphia and Minneapolis: Fortress, 1986–90); and Culpepper, *Anatomy*.

30. Sternberg, *Poetics*, 75. The Minor Prophets are not, for the most part, historical narratives, but many narrative critics apply their methods to all genres of literature.

31. For the more positive take, see Amit, *Reading Biblical Narratives*, 91–92. For the negative take, see D. M. Gunn and D. N. Fewell, *Narrative in the Hebrew Bible* (Oxford: Oxford University Press, 1993), 34–45.

Critique

To the extent that narrative criticism engages in a close reading of texts with a view to understanding their plot, theme, characterization, and other features of the "surface structure" of a biblical story as literature, we may enthusiastically welcome the discipline. Additionally, in avoiding both the intentional and affective fallacies (which affirm, respectively, that meaning is wholly in the mind of an author or wholly in the perception of readers), narrative criticism offers a more sophisticated and valid model of where the meaning of a text resides—namely, in that text! We may speak of authorial intention as a key to interpreting stories only to the extent that real authors have been transparent in equating their narrators with their implied authors and making both reveal substantial information about the real authors themselves. We may speak of readers creating meaning only to the extent that real readers correctly identify the roles of narratée and implied readers.[32] As Stephen Mailloux puts it, intentions are best described or defined in terms of "the intended structure of the reader's response."[33] Moreover, narrative criticism's focus on the final form of the text, taken as a unity, and with an intentional analysis of how narratives work, all comport well with evangelical theology *for theology as well as method*.[34] After all, it is the final literary form of any biblical book we believe to be inspired and therefore authoritative.

But there are serious pitfalls with narrative criticism, whether in its more traditional form as "the Bible as literature" or in its more rigorous, recent analytical form of distinguishing various kinds of authors and readers. Narrative critics often assume when they study the Bible as literature that the texts must be viewed as fiction.[35] This seems to result, however, not from the nature of the method itself but from a misunderstanding of the number of features that historical and fictional texts share in common. Students of ancient historiography helpfully stress how few literary characteristics actually enable a reader to preclude the identification of a work as a well-written, interesting history.[36] Indeed, completely realistic historical fiction as we know it didn't really exist in antiquity; novelists often tipped their hands by including clearly anachronistic or inaccurate information.[37] Or else they "focused on

---

32. Cf. further C. L. Blomberg, *Interpreting the Parables,* 2nd ed. (Downers Grove: InterVarsity; Nottingham: Apollos, 2012), 175–78, and the literature there cited.

33. S. Mailloux, *Interpretive Conventions: The Reader in the Study of American Fiction* (Ithaca: Cornell University Press, 1982), 112.

34. F. Watson, "Literary Approaches to the Gospels: A Theological Assessment," *Theol* 99 (1996): 125–33.

35. E.g., D. A. Robertson, *The Old Testament and the Literary Critic* (Philadelphia: Fortress, 1977); D. A. Templeton, *The New Testament as True Fiction* (Sheffield: Sheffield Academic Press, 1999; London and New York: T&T Clark, 2004).

36. See esp. C. H. Gempf, "Historical and Literary Appropriateness in the Mission Speeches of Paul in Acts" (PhD thesis, University of Aberdeen, 1988); cf. C. H. Gempf, "Public Speaking and Published Accounts," in *The Book of Acts in Its Ancient Literary Setting*, ed. B. W. Winter and A. D. Clarke (Carlisle: Paternoster; Grand Rapids: Eerdmans, 1993), 259–303. From the perspective of modern literature, cf. T. J. Roberts, *When Is Something Fiction?* (Carbondale, IL: Southern Illinois University Press, 1972).

37. Classically, see the OT apocryphal works of Tobit and Judith and cf. D. J. Harrington, *Invitation to the Apocrypha* (Grand Rapids: Eerdmans, 1999), 11, 28–29. Cf. also E. Auerbach, *Mimesis: The Representation of Reality*

ethnographically or geographically remote subjects not easily checked." They might include major, well-known locations, "but many were inconsistent or uninterested in local color."[38] Norman Petersen, finally, has applied literary criticism to the Epistle to Philemon, showing how even the nonfictional and nonnarrative material we find in a letter can have an unfolding plot, point of view, climax, and so on.[39] Thus, it does not follow that narrative and fiction must be synonymous.

Moreover, some narrative critics depreciate the religious value of a text in favor of its aesthetics, sometimes to correct a past imbalance in the other direction. But again, it seems this abuse can be divorced from the method itself. A genuine appreciation of the beauty, power, and style of a biblical book should lead a believer in its inspiration and canonicity to treasure it that much more.[40]

In general, narrative criticism holds the most promise of all of the sub-disciplines of literary criticism since it focuses on the "surface structure" or literary features of the final form of the text with which all readers have to come to grips. Sadly, many literary critics have not stopped here, however, but have moved on to the discipline known as "poststructuralism," part of today's larger postmodernist movement and increasingly referred to simply as postmodern criticism or hermeneutics. Here we cannot be as enthusiastic about scholarly developments. But in some circles, poststructuralism or postmodernism is so popular that serious Bible students must familiarize themselves at least briefly with its methods.

Poststructuralism/Postmodernism

Poststructuralism refers to developments that built on but went beyond structuralism (and, for that matter, narrative criticism). Increasingly, post-structuralism is linked ideologically to postmodernism in general. Postmodernism is a broad term, used in different ways by different authors. But it usually involves a cluster of such convictions and values as: 1) an ideological pluralism in which no one religion or worldview contains absolute truth; 2) the impossibility of objectivity in interpretation and the treasuring of value-laden approaches; 3) the importance of human communities in shaping ourselves and our interpretive perspectives; 4) a rejection of the negative modernist evaluation of religion and spirituality; 5) an emphasis on the aesthetic, the symbolic, and ancient tradition; 6) the formative role of narrative in understanding our own life-pilgrimages and those of others, along with the rejection of the existence of any overarching meta-narrative that can give meaning to all individual stories; and 7) language as determinative of thought and meaning.[41] Both poststructuralism

---

in Western Literature, (ed. W. R. Trask (Princeton: Princeton University Press, 2003 [orig. 1953]), 40–49; and E. M. Blaiklock, *Jesus Christ: Man or Myth?* (Homebush West, Anzea; Nashville: Nelson, 1984), 38–47, 68–78.

38. C. S. Keener, *Acts: An Exegetical Commentary,* 4 vols. (Grand Rapids: Baker, 2012–15), 1:99.

39. N. R. Petersen, *Rediscovering Paul: Philemon and the Sociology of Paul's Narrative World* (Philadelphia: Fortress, 1985).

40. Powell, *What Is Narrative Criticism?,* 88–89.

41. For a clear, succinct introduction to modernism vs. postmodernism, with closely parallel features discussed, see B. Kristanto, "The Bible and Our Postmodern World," *ERT* 37 (2013): 153–65.

in literary analysis and postmodernism as a worldview share a concern to move beyond methods and conclusions that see meaning as at all fixed and residing in a text. Rather, they find meaning as largely or wholly the product of individual readers or interpretive communities.[42]

Clearly postmodernism offers evangelicals a mixed bag of bane and blessing.[43] We should welcome the rejection of modernism's dependence on human autonomy, reason, science, and technology as the be-all and end-all of life, for in its most thoroughgoing forms it led inexorably to skepticism and atheism. Christians in general and the Bible in particular have historically valued narrative, symbolism, the aesthetic, a value-laden interpretation, and the importance of community. Christians once too enamored with modernism are increasingly recapturing many of these dimensions thanks to postmodernism.

On the other hand, we must dispute the postmodernists' denial of absolute truth, their claim that no religion or ideology can ultimately be superior to any other, much less the "one true way," their denial of any overarching meta-narrative (like the one portrayed in the Bible), and the inability of humans to transcend their cultural or linguistic conditioning. One of the major problems with respect to hermeneutics, to which postmodernism has called attention, is the impossibility of human interpreters ever to fully capture (or to know they have fully captured) someone else's meaning in any communicative act. This much Christians should readily accept because of our beliefs that humans are both finite and fallen. But there is a middle ground between claiming absolute objectivity and denying that in many cases we can attain *adequate* understanding of the meaning of a text. Ben Meyer and N. T. Wright have both argued persuasively that interpreters should embrace "critical realism," an approach that involves the dialogical process between interpreter and texts in which one successfully approximates true meaning, even if never comprehensively capturing it (or knowing that one has).[44] The image of a hermeneutical spiral—like a cone-shaped tornado zeroing in on one small spot on the ground—or that of an

---

42. For introductions to postmodernism as a worldview more generally, see C. Butler, *Postmodernism: A Very Short Introduction* (Oxford: Oxford University Press, 2003); H. White, *Postmodernism 101: A First Course for the Curious Christian* (Grand Rapids: Brazos, 2006); and S. Sim, ed., *The Routledge Companion to Postmodernism*, 3rd ed. (London and New York: Routledge, 2011).

43. Many critiques have appeared; particularly helpful on the strengths of postmodernism are S. Grenz, *A Primer on Postmodernism* (Grand Rapids: Eerdmans, 1996); and C. Raschke, *The Next Reformation: Why Evangelicals Must Embrace Postmodernity* (Grand Rapids: Baker, 2004). On its weaknesses, see esp. D. R. Groothuis, *Truth Decay: Defending Christianity against the Challenges of Postmodernism* (Downers Grove: InterVarsity, 2000). An anthology of various responses that cumulatively captures perhaps the right balance is D. S. Dockery, ed., *The Challenge of Postmodernism: An Evangelical Engagement*, 2nd ed. (Grand Rapids: Baker, 2001). For a creative but representative application of postmodernism to a specific biblical passage (Luke 4:14–30), see H. S. Pyper, *New Meanings for Ancient Texts: Recent Approaches to Biblical Criticisms and Their Applications*, ed. S. L. McKenzie and J. Kaltner (Louisville: Westminster John Knox, 2013), 117–36.

44. B. F. Meyer, *Critical Realism and the New Testament* (Pittsburgh: Pickwick, 1989); J. J. Collins, *The Bible after Babel: Historical Criticism in a Postmodern Age* (Grand Rapids: Eerdmans, 2005). For an overview of its applications across the disciplines of human knowledge, see M. Hartwig, ed., *Dictionary of Critical Realism* (London and New York: Routledge, 2007).

asymptote of a hyperbola, coming very close to the vertical or horizontal lines of its axes without ever actually touching them, helps us to visualize this model.[45] The flip side of this approach is that while we may not always be able to determine one and only one correct or even simply the most correct interpretation of a given text, we can usually rule out many as improbable.[46]

Poststructuralism / Postmodernism	
Reader-Response Criticism	Claims that meaning is the product of individual readers in interaction with texts; there is no objective meaning in a text itself
Deconstruction	Seeks to show how all texts deconstruct (undermine) themselves; texts make no absolute claims on readers

Returning to literary criticism more narrowly, the two major categories of postmodern or poststructural analysis are reader-response criticism and deconstruction. Reader-response criticism is the less radical of the two, affirming that meaning derives from the interaction between a text and its readers. Deconstruction, when consistently applied, despairs of finding coherent meaning at all, apart from readers' own diverse perceptions and experiences. Interestingly, there are some circles that are declaring all postmodern thinking to have peaked and to be on the wane.[47] This seems premature, though it may well be true for deconstruction, as the more radical of the two.

Reader-Response Criticism[48]

As the label suggests, reader-response criticism focuses primarily not on authors' intentions or the fixed meaning of texts but on the diverse ways readers respond to a text (see also our discussion in ch. 6). Reader-response criticism itself breaks down into two major approaches, though they are not always clearly distinguished from each other (just as narrative criticism sometimes includes both text- and reader-centered approaches).[49] A more conservative form was pioneered by Wolfgang Iser, who also

---

45. Cf., respectively, G. R. Osborne, *The Hermeneutical Spiral*, 2nd ed. (Downers Grove: InterVarsity, 2006); A. O. Bellis, "Objective Biblical Truth vs. the Value of Various Viewpoints: A False Dichotomy," *HBT* 17 (1995): 30.

46. See esp. U. Eco, *Interpretation and Overinterpretation* (Cambridge: Cambridge University Press, 1992). R. Hendel ("Mind the Gap: Modern and Postmodern in Biblical Studies," *JBL* 133 [2014]: 422–43) helpfully distinguishes between a weak and a strong form of postmodernism. The strong form is totalizing, which lands it squarely in a self-contradictory position. The weak form recognizes the corruption of all rationality, embedded in culture and entangled with power. But it can learn and it can be self-correcting.

47. E.g., I. Huber, *Literature after Postmodernism: Reconstructive Fantasies* (Basingstoke and NY: Palgrave Macmillan, 2014).

48. Good introductions to reader-response criticism appear in J. L. Resseguie, "Reader-Response Criticism and the Synoptic Gospels," *JAAR* 52 (1984): 307–24 (limited to the Gospels); R. M. Fowler, "Who Is 'The Reader' in Reader Response Criticism?" *Semeia* 31 (1985): 5–23 (on Scripture more generally); and J. P. Tompkins, ed., *Reader-Response Criticism* (Baltimore: Johns Hopkins University Press, 1980) (on literature more generally).

49. J. Barton, "Thinking About Reader-Response Criticism," *ExpTim* 113 (2002): 147–51; K. J. Vanhoozer, *Is There a Meaning in This Text?: The Bible, the Reader, and the Morality of Literary Knowledge* (Grand Rapids: Zondervan, 2009), 152.

developed the concepts of implied authors and readers (see above), thus generating further overlap between methods. But the distinguishing feature of "conservative" reader-response criticism is that the text still provides important constraints on interpreters. This form of analysis may try, for example, to reproduce the experience of a first-time reader of a passage, so that what one learns from a later portion of a text cannot yet influence the understanding of an earlier portion.

Robert Fowler comes close to a traditional evangelical hermeneutic when he refuses to endorse a popular, modern reading of the feedings of the 5000 and 4000 (Mark 6:30–44; 8:1–10) as Eucharistic because the Last Supper (Mark 14:12–26) had not yet occurred at the time of those miracles. A reader may use the feeding miracles to interpret the Last Supper but not vice versa. But Fowler is not applying historical criticism to limit the interpretation of an event to data derived from previous events; he is taking the point of view of a reader coming to Mark for the first time, who has not yet read of the Last Supper.[50]

Interestingly, this strategy of sequential reading perhaps agrees better with the standard process in the ancient world in which written texts were read aloud to gathered groups. Hearing a text only once afforded the listener no luxury to look ahead to the end or to reread a section already forgotten. Perhaps traditional historical-grammatical analysis, with all its cross-references to uses of words and concepts throughout a document, has often found too much meaning in texts, which a one-time listener could not catch![51]

A more conservative reader-response criticism, further, helpfully explores the "gaps" in a text, in which a reader must supply his or her own meaning. For example, why does the account of David's sin with Bathsheba begin with kings going out to war while David (the king) stays home (2 Sam 11:1)? Why does David send Uriah home to sleep with his wife after David has committed adultery with her? When Uriah refuses to go, is it because he knows what David has done and refuses to participate in his attempted cover-up? Or is it just that he is so virtuous he will not avail himself of any privileges that his fellow soldiers still on the battlefield cannot share, as he explicitly claims (v. 11)? When he does not go home, does David suspect that Uriah knows his ploy? At each stage of this narrative, the reader must make some assumptions to fill in these "gaps." How we answer these questions will considerably color our perspectives on the main characters in the story.[52] If Uriah is being less than straightforward with David, then we cannot identify with him quite so much as the innocent victim. If we had additional historical information to enable us to answer these kinds of questions,

---

50. R. M. Fowler, *Loaves and Fishes: The Function of the Feeding Stories in the Gospel of Mark*, SBLDS 54 (Chico, CA: Scholars, 1981), 140–41.

51. S. D. Moore, *Literary Criticism and the Gospels* (New Haven: Yale University Press, 1989), 84–88. R. H. Stein, "Is Our Reading the Bible the Same as the Original Audience's Hearing It?" *JETS* 46 (2003): 63–78, also makes this point.

52. Sternberg, *Poetics*, 193–213. Cf. M. Garsiel, "The Story of David and Bathsheba: A Different Approach," *CBQ* 55 (1993): 244–62.

we would be engaging simply in historical criticism. Absent these, we must make inferences from other features of the text itself, so that the process becomes part of literary criticism.

A more *radical* reader-response criticism focuses on meaning as that which is entirely, or almost entirely, the product of the individual reader. Meaning (like beauty) is in the eye of the beholder. The only reason similarities and interpretations arise in the first place, according to this view, is because various readers belong to "interpretive communities" with shared conventions that lead them to read texts in similar ways. But apart from these shared conventions, there is no objective meaning in the symbols of the texts themselves. Stanley Fish is usually credited with being the founder of this wing of reader-response criticism that delights in showing how even texts that seem most clearly to communicate objective, recoverable meaning can be plausibly understood in quite different ways.[53] For example, one could read the story of God's interactions with Saul and David as a largely secular "novel" of an arbitrary, capricious God who raises up and brings down rulers without good reason—a story that Jews and later Christians then domesticated into an edifying religious tale.[54] One might understand the parable of the prodigal son so that the prodigal, his father, and the older brother correspond respectively to Freud's understanding of id, ego, and super-ego.[55] We do not encounter a large number of such readings of biblical texts, apart from readings by interpreters who identify with specific advocacy movements, which we discuss in the second half of this chapter.[56]

The main weaknesses of more radical reader-response criticism lie in its relativism. On the one hand, if nothing more than shared interpretive conventions account for similarities in readings of given texts, reader-response critics should not object to readings very different from their own, and yet many still attempt to defend their interpretations as better than others! And those that do not do so, but just put theirs forward as one legitimate reading among others, at least want people to understand their intended meaning in normal kinds of human discourse—and almost always also in the articles or books they write denying authorial intention as a key to meaning! One could further argue, theologically, that all humans—created in God's image—share common interpretive conventions and hence are part of a single interpretive community that requires meaning to transcend the perceptions of individual readers or interpretive communities. In the former scenario, reader-response criticism is self-defeating; in the

53. S. E. Fish, *Self-Consuming Artifacts: The Experience of Seventeenth-Century Literature* (Berkeley: University of California Press, 1972); S. E. Fish, *Is There a Text in This Class? The Authority of Interpretive Communities* (Cambridge, MA: Harvard University Press, 1980).

54. K. L. Noll, "Is There A Text in This Tradition? Readers' Response and the Taming of Samuel's God," *JSOT* 83 (1999): 31–51.

55. M. A. Tolbert, "The Prodigal Son: An Essay in Literary Criticism from a Psychoanalytic Perspective," *Semeia* 9 (1977): 1–20.

56. For some of the main reasons, see S. E. Porter, "Why Hasn't Reader-Response Criticism Caught on in New Testament Studies?" *JLT* 4 (1990): 278–92. Cf. the response by P. R. Noble, "Fish and the Bible: Should Reader-Response Theories 'Catch On?'" *HeyJ* 37 (1996): 456–67.

latter it collapses back into some more traditional text-centered hermeneutic. What is more, radical reader-response criticism cannot account for how texts transform readers, generating interpretations and behavior that cut against the grain of their preunderstandings, presuppositions, and social conditioning.

In some cases, what pass for competing *interpretations* should probably be viewed as alternative *applications*. As we will argue, original meaning remains fixed, even as contemporary significance varies. Alternately, using the language of "speech act theory,"[57] we may say that God's illocutionary acts (what he accomplishes by the very act of speaking) is always consistent with his intended perlocutions (the intended results or effects of his speaking).[58] At the very least, reader-response criticism has done all interpreters a service in reminding them of the truly significant influence of their preunderstandings (as we will discuss further below). But we must subject our cherished preconceptions of the meanings of texts to the challenges of new data and new perspectives that acknowledge the potential of a considerable measure of objectivity, as in critical realism.[59]

Deconstruction

Even more widespread in literary circles, including biblical studies, is the second brand of poststructuralism: deconstruction. Ideologically, deconstruction derives from the nineteenth-century nihilist philosopher Friedrich Nietzsche and his recent disciple, Jacques Derrida. It is an anarchistic, hyper-relativistic form of criticism designed to demonstrate how all texts, indeed all human communication, ultimately "deconstructs" or undermines itself.[60] In the words of T. K. Seung, its avowed purpose is one of "generating conflicting meanings from the same text, and playing those meanings against each other."[61] Nor is this just a new variation on the old theme of pointing out

---

57. For an excellent introduction to the discipline and its application to biblical studies, see R. S. Briggs, "The Uses of Speech-Act Theory in Biblical Interpretation," *CurBR* 9 (2001): 229–76. We have more to say about the uses of speech act theory below.

58. Vanhoozer, *Is There A Meaning in this Text?*, 261. Of course, though the divine author always accomplishes what he intends when communicating, this does not mean that readers always respond to his message as he desires.

59. For as appreciative a critique as exists among evangelicals, but one that nevertheless points out some of these and other problems with reader-response criticism, see A. C. Thiselton, "Reader-Response Hermeneutics, Action Models, and the Parables of Jesus," in *The Responsibility of Hermeneutics*, ed. R. Lundin, A. C. Thiselton, and C. Walhout (Grand Rapids: Eerdmans, 1985), 79–113. From a Roman Catholic perspective, cf. esp. T. J. Keegan, "Biblical Criticism and the Challenge of Postmodernism," *BibInt* 3 (1995): 1–14. We too adopt a somewhat open stance, while insisting on the constraints we defend under the concept of "validation" below, in ch. 6.

60. Two standard introductions to deconstruction in literature more generally are J. Culler, *On Deconstruction: Theory and Criticism after Structuralism*, rev. ed. (Ithaca: Cornell University Press, 2007); and C. Norris, *Deconstruction: Theory and Practice*, 3rd ed. (New York: Methuen, 2002). R. Briggs ("Gnats, Camels and Aporias: Who Should Be Straining Out What? Christianity and Deconstruction," *VE* 25 [1995]: 17–32) adopts a less sweeping definition of deconstruction as merely an approach that asserts the existence of meaning that cannot finally be pinned down to the words that carry it. He is thus able to find more virtue in it than most evangelicals have, but his does not seem to be the most common understanding of the concept.

61. T. K. Seung, *Structuralism and Hermeneutics* (New York: Columbia University Press, 1982), 271. For application to biblical studies, see A. K. M. Adam, *What Is Postmodern Biblical Criticism?* (Minneapolis: Fortress, 1998).

apparent contradictions in Scripture (or in any other works of history, theology, or literature).[62] Rather, deconstruction normally seeks subtle, often unwitting, ideological inconsistencies or ambiguities in a text that seem hard to resolve and that prevent interpreters from claiming that it has a fixed meaning. Motives for such analysis range from an innocuous desire to be creative to a preoccupation with denying any absolute claims of the text over interpreters.

Obviously, no one with anything like a traditional Christian view of Scripture's inspiration, accuracy, clarity, or authority should accept deconstruction as an ideological package. Still, focusing on underlying tensions in a text may surface some part of its meaning, particularly in the more cryptic parts of Scripture—even if we might wish to go on to propose resolutions to those tensions. For example, it is intriguing to read how Esther, in essence, has to "lose" her Jewishness in order to save it. Only as the Persian queen, hiding her ethnic identity from her husband-king, can she rescue the Jewish people from the pogrom Haman planned for them.[63] Perhaps this presents a salutary reminder of the ambiguities and compromises inherent in trying to live life as a person of God in the political arena of fallen humanity.

Again, consider Job. After all the many speeches of Job and his counselors, God ultimately vindicates Job against his friends: "I am angry with you and your two friends, because you have not spoken of me what is right, as my servant Job has" (Job 42:7). His friends, in essence, have tried to vindicate God as justly punishing sinners and rewarding the righteous, whereas Job has repeatedly protested that God is unfairly persecuting him. However, if God is right in supporting Job, then God must be unjust because Job seemed to accuse him of being unjust.[64] The solution may be that when God declares Job right, he is not referring to every single thing that Job said. Again we are cautioned against imitating Job's friends with too facile or simplistic explanations of why people suffer.

Here is one more example on the very conservative end of the deconstructive spectrum (which, by definition, is not very conservative!). Werner Kelber has helpfully called attention to how John's Gospel comprises words about "the Word" (*ho logos*) incarnate, who is Jesus. Careful attention to these words and the Word will direct oneself away from written (or oral) words to a Person. The more one takes seriously the medium of John's message, the more one will be pointed away from that message to a living relationship with the one about whom the message is spoken.[65] To a certain

---

62. Though in some instances, this is how the term gets applied. See esp. D. Seeley, *Deconstructing the New Testament*, BibInt 5 (Leiden: Brill, 1994).

63. D. J. A. Clines, "Reading Esther from Left to Right," in *The Bible in Three Dimension*, JSOTSup 87, ed. D. J. A. Clines, S. E. Fowl, and S. E. Porter (Sheffield: JSOT, 1990), 31–52.

64. D. J. A. Clines, "Deconstructing the Book of Job," in *What Does Eve Do To Help? And Other Readerly Questions to the Old Testament*, JSOTSup 94 (Sheffield: JSOT, 1990; London: Bloomsbury T. & T. Clark, 2009), 106–23.

65. Kelber is cited in Moore, *Literary Criticism and the Gospels*, 152–57, which refers to a forthcoming work by Kelber in which this discussion is to appear. Apparently the work never appeared.

degree, the text undermines its own unique authority. And doubtless, some Christians do need regular reminders that they worship a Person and not a book.[66]

Far more characteristic of deconstruction, however, are its much more radical applications. Dominic Crossan, for example, has written quite a bit about the parables in which his own cleverness rather than validity in interpretation seems to be his goal, as summarized by his term, "freeplay."[67] In one place he declares, "Since you cannot interpret absolutely, you can interpret forever."[68] Thus, he reads the parable of the prodigal son (Luke 15:11–32) as an allegory of Western consciousness' path from mimetic (realistic) to ludic (playful) allegory.[69] He sees the parable of the treasure in the field (Matt 13:44) as teaching, among other things, that one must abandon all for the sake of the kingdom, which includes abandoning the parable, and, ultimately, abandoning abandonment![70] Quite understandably, D. A. Carson critiques this type of deconstruction by calling it "so anachronistic as to make a historian wince,"[71] to which Crossan would probably reply, "Of course, I wasn't attempting to please a historian!" Even more bizarre is Stephen Moore's entire book on Mark and Luke that uses the wordplays (in English!) between Mark and "mark" as the stroke of a letter on a piece of paper, and between Luke and "look," meaning "to see." Moore then proceeds to discuss Mark and Luke in association with a wide range of modern literature as two Gospels that stress written marks and the art of seeing, respectively.[72]

From an OT perspective, Peter Miscall argues that any attempt to assess the positive or negative characterizations of David and his associates in 1 Samuel 16–22 runs aground on conflicting data so that it is impossible to make definitive statements about the significance of these characters or the events with which they were involved.[73] If Miscall is right, then we cannot identify characters whose behavior we are to emulate or avoid quite as easily as most readers have thought.

Advocates of deconstruction ought to ask where all this would lead us if adopted on a widespread scale. Those who have replied to this question do not give us satisfying

---

66. Cf. G. A. Phillips, "'You Are Either Here, Here, Here, or Here': Deconstruction's Troublesome Interplay," *Semeia* 71 (1995): 193–213. Phillips argues that if deconstruction attends to texts to discover evidence for and disclose more about the fullness and depth of meaning beyond an original author's intent or audience's understanding, then it can lead us back to "the Other behind the text" that modernism and strictly author-or text-centered approaches disallowed.

67. See esp. J. D. Crossan, *Cliffs of Fall: Paradox and Polyvalence in the Parables of Jesus* (New York: Seabury, 1980; Eugene, OR: Wipf & Stock, 2008), 25–104.

68. Ibid., 102.

69. Ibid., 101.

70. J. D. Crossan, *Finding Is the First Act: Trove Folktales and Jesus' Treasure Parable* (Philadelphia: Fortress, 1979), 93.

71. D. A. Carson, "Matthew," in *The Expositor's Bible Commentary: Matthew-Mark*, rev. ed., ed. T. Longman III and D. E. Garland (Grand Rapids: Zondervan, 2010), 9:376.

72. S. D. Moore, *Mark and Luke in Poststructuralist Perspectives: Jesus Begins to Write* (New Haven and London: Yale University Press, 1992). For a deconstruction of John, see P. C. Counet, *John—A Postmodern Gospel: Introduction to Deconstructive Exegesis Applied to the Fourth Gospel*, Biblical Interpretation 44 (Leiden: Brill, 2000).

73. P. D. Miscall, *The Workings of Old Testament Narrative* (Chico, CA: Scholars; Philadelphia: Fortress, 1983). For a deconstruction of a prophetic work, see E. K. Holt and C. J. Sharp, eds., *Jeremiah Invented: Constructions and Deconstructions of Jeremiah*, LHBOTS 595 (London: Bloomsbury T. & T. Clark, 2015).

answers.[74] Although some argue that deconstruction is here to stay, ordinary people do not and cannot live as if human conversation were ultimately relativistic and self-defeating. More likely, poststructuralism will prove to be a passing fad, as we saw some have suggested it already is. Deconstruction will one day deconstruct itself altogether. The rapid decline in the number of studies from this perspective in the early years of the twenty-first century (as compared to the prior decade) suggests this is already starting to happen. But what will take its place?

Supporters of poststructuralism reject the idea of a giant eclecticism or metacriticism in which the valid insights of all the various new critical tools will cooperate with more traditional hermeneutics. But it seems to us that we need something precisely like this. Cultural anthropologists, for example, have for nearly two decades renounced relativism in favor of seeking meta-models that remain valid atop cross-cultural diversity.[75] Interestingly, the method that some hail as the next panacea for biblical criticism is a social-scientific analysis that draws heavily on anthropological models.[76] To date, such analysis has not always accepted its place as one limited method among many. As with new ideas more generally, its supporters tend to hail it as the best approach of all. But in time, less grandiose claims will no doubt prevail. Meanwhile, we must survey this new methodological arena of biblical scholarship and see what promise it offers a study of hermeneutics.[77]

SOCIAL-SCIENTIFIC APPROACHES TO SCRIPTURE

Many of the same factors that spawned discontent with traditional historical-critical methods and gave rise to literary criticism of the Bible have also led scholars to propose new, social-scientific models of interpretation. Discontent with the status quo, a realization of the modern presuppositions imported into historical criticism, opportunities for creativity and fresh insights, and the growing interdisciplinary dialogue in the universities all have contributed. Hence, many biblical scholars are

---

74. Most notably, Moore, *Literary Criticism and the Gospels*, 171–78.

75. P. G. Hiebert, "Critical Contextualization," *IBMR* 11 (1987): 104–12.

76. Note particularly how B. J. Malina ("Reader Response Theory: Discovery or Redundancy?" *Creighton University Faculty Journal* 5 [1986]: 55–66) sees social-scientific analysis as the appropriate successor to a bankrupt reader-response criticism.

77. Additional key literature on modern literary criticism of the Bible, not already mentioned in the preceding footnotes of this section, includes T. Longman III, *Literary Approaches to Biblical Interpretation* (Grand Rapids: Zondervan, 1987)—an evangelical survey and sympathetic critique; N. Frye, *The Great Code: The Bible and Literature* (New York: Harcourt, 1982; New York: Mariner, 2002)—a major study of archetype and symbol by a leading literary critic; E. V. McKnight, *The Bible and the Reader* (Philadelphia: Fortress, 1985)—a survey of reader-centered approaches, but including structuralism and more traditional forms of literary criticism as well; S. Bar-Efrat, *Narrative Art in the Bible* (Sheffield: Almond, 1989; Edinburgh: T&T Clark, 2004)—on narration, characters, plot, time and space, and style in the Hebrew Bible; A. K. M. Adam, ed., *Postmodern Interpretations of the Bible—A Reader* (St. Louis: Chalice, 2000)—deconstructive or reader-response analyses of all the major sections of the Bible; D. Jobling, T. Pippin, and R. Schleifer, eds., *The Postmodern Bible Reader* (Oxford: Blackwell, 2001)—a more thematically organized collection of similar studies; and J. B. Gabel, C. B. Wheeler, A. D. York and D. Citino, *The Bible as Literature*, 5th ed. (Oxford: Oxford University Press, 2005)—a classic, wide-ranging introductory textbook.

delving deeply into the study of sociology, anthropology, economics, and political science, using the findings of their studies to add new dimensions to the discipline of biblical hermeneutics.

Classification

Social–Scientific Approaches to Interpretation	
Social History	Seeks to illuminate texts through understanding the social worlds in which they emerged
Social–Scientific Theories	Seeks to apply current models of analysis to texts from the ancient world

These social-scientific studies fall into two broad categories: research that illuminates the social history of the biblical world, and the application of modern theories of human behavior applied to scriptural texts.[78]

Social History

This category could easily comprise a special branch of historical background research. But, for the most part, modern students of the Bible have not focused on the significantly different social worlds and dynamics of Bible times. Today we in the West live in a highly individualistic culture with many opportunities for choices in life—concerning spouses, jobs, places to live, and so on. More often than not, ancient Middle Eastern cultures were rooted more strongly in the various groups to which an individual belonged, and these—family, ethnicity, gender, occupation—usually limited the opportunities for choosing a spouse or changing a career or place of residence (or in the case of women, even having education or a career "outside the home"). Careful attention to the social world explicit or implicit in various biblical texts often casts new light on them and/or calls into question popular misinterpretations.[79]

This obvious but often neglected truth captured the attention of one of us in a conversation about married life that he had with a Singaporean friend in graduate

---

78. Good overviews of research include, for the OT, T. W. Overholt, *Cultural Anthropology and the Old Testament* (Minneapolis: Fortress, 1996); C. E. Carter and C. L. Meyers, eds., *Community, Identity, and Ideology: Social Science Approaches to the Hebrew Bible*, Sources for Biblical and Theological Study 6 (Winona Lake: Eisenbrauns, 1996); C. E. Carter, "Opening Windows onto Biblical Worlds: Applying the Social Sciences to Hebrew Scripture," in *The Face of Old Testament Studies: A Survey of Contemporary Approaches*, ed. D. W. Baker and B. T. Arnold (Grand Rapids: Baker; Leicester: Apollos, 1999), 421–51. For the NT, see Elliott, *What is Social-Scientific Criticism?*; P. F. Esler, *The First Christians in Their Social Worlds: Social-Scientific Approaches to New Testament Interpretation* (London and New York: Routledge, 1994); D. G. Horrell, ed., *Social-Scientific Approaches to New Testament Interpretation* (Edinburgh: T&T Clark, 1999); and J. B. Tucker and C. A. Baker, eds., *T&T Clark Handbook to Social Identity in the New Testament* (London and NY: T&T Clark, 2014). For both testaments, see J. Johnson, *The Biblical World through New Glasses: Seeing the Bible through Its Cultural Context* (Dallas: Saint Paul Press, 2011).

79. Particularly helpful in stressing these points, in his application of "group/grid" analysis to modern versus biblical cultures is Malina, *Christian Origins and Cultural Anthropology: Practical Models for Biblical Interpretation* (Atlanta: John Knox, 1986; Eugene, OR: Wipf & Stock, 2010), 28–67.

school. The author marveled at how he could speak so calmly and pleasantly about extended families living together—including newlyweds moving into the home of one of their parents! He ventured to tell him that the Bible suggested a different model—"a man will leave his father and mother and be united to his wife" (Gen 2:24). The Singaporean quickly replied that this could not mean physical, geographical separation, since Bible cultures more often than not resembled his experience in traditional Chinese society. Rather, this verse must refer to a change in ultimate allegiances (after one marries, the interests of spouse supersede those of parents even if all live under the same roof). The author left the conversation feeling rather foolish.

Sensitivity to this kind of social history can illumine numerous other passages. Mark 3:31–35, for example, then stands out as remarkably radical. Jesus lived in a culture that prized familial loyalties above all other human relationships (a virtue often lacking today). So for him to ignore his biological family while teaching the crowds that his disciples ("whoever does God's will") were "my brother and sister and mother" would have shocked and offended many of his listeners. What is more, these words suggest that Jesus was creating not only new, intimate personal relationships with his followers but also an extended family that would involve detailed obligations for care and commitment among these new "family" members (what sociologists often call "fictive kinship").[80] An understanding of kinship ties can also explain how entire households were converted simultaneously (e.g. Acts 16:14–15, 31–34). Modern missionaries, encountering non-Western tribes or clans in which religious commitments made by leaders were binding on whole groups of people, have been too slow to recognize the validity and biblical precedent for such response.[81] Conversion must be personal, but it is not always individual.[82]

Modern American separation of church and state also clouds our understanding of ancient cultures that knew no such divisions. To say, for example, that Jesus brought a spiritual message without political implications—or that religion is purely a private matter—would introduce a division foreign to the first century (and to many people today). The various Jewish authorities combined governmental and religious roles in their communities and nation. If they perceived Jesus as a threat to their authority in the one realm, that threat naturally carried over to the other. Conversely, Rome (more naturally associated in modern eyes with the political authority) would eventually include within its purview religious claims ("Caesar is Lord"). Christians could not offer the imperial sacrifice, even though the rest of the empire viewed these claims as little more significant than our pledge of allegiance or salute to the flag. For first-century Christians, such "patriotism" implied blasphemous associations of deity with

---

80. See esp. D. M. May, "Mark 3:20–35 from the Perspective of Shame/Honor," *BTB* 17 (1987): 83–87.

81. See esp. D. Tidball, *Social Context of the New Testament: A Sociological Analysis* (Grand Rapids: Zondervan, 1984), 84–85.

82. A concept particularly associated with the modern church growth movement and pioneered by D. McGavran, first in *Bridges of God: A Study in the Strategy of Missions* (New York: Friendship; London: World Dominion, 1955; Eugene, OR: Wipf & Stock, 2005).

human emperors. Consequently, their "civil disobedience" led to numerous outbreaks of persecution and to the writing of several NT documents (e.g., Hebrews, 1 Peter, and Revelation).[83]

Indeed, a burgeoning area of NT study involves reading various NT books against the backdrop of imperial claims and threats. "Empire criticism" at one point or another has claimed that virtually every part of the NT might have been viewed as subversive by someone particularly loyal to Rome because of the absolutizing claims made about Jesus, his epiphany, good news (gospel), proclamation, offers of peace, miraculous powers, and the needs for his followers to render him total allegiance.[84] This trend is an important reminder to those who think of religion only as a private matter, as it is too often in today's world, that first-century readers would have always reflected on the socio-political significance of religious claims.

On the other hand, it is likely that readers of Romans, in the capital city of the empire, would have more quickly compared Jesus with Caesar than readers of Galatians, far from any centers of the imperial cult, would have done.[85] As with so many critical tools, one must evaluate each proposal on a case-by-case basis rather than make sweeping generalizations about what "everyone" thought or believed.[86] The same is true for those inherently suspicious of empire criticism. Because postcolonialism (see below) tends to reject all empires with equal animosity, some have swung the pendulum to the opposite extreme and not seen any imperial critique in the Scriptures. But to acknowledge that Jesus and his followers were at times very critical, even implicitly, of the first-century Roman Empire does not automatically mean that every empire throughout history shared the identical weaknesses (or strengths).[87]

The number of areas in which a better understanding of the social history of the biblical cultures can illuminate the text is almost endless.[88] The large topic of honor and shame helps us understand why a man rousted from his sleep by a midnight visitor would be so concerned to provide hospitality for him, even if it required considerable inconvenience (Luke 11:5–8); his reputation in the village is at stake.[89] Jephthah

---

83. For the various points in this paragraph, cf. esp. R. A. Horsley, *The Liberation of Christmas: The Infancy Narratives in Social Context* (New York: Crossroad, 1989; Eugene, OR: Wipf & Stock, 2006). It is worth asking if "Christian patriotism" or appeals to the second amendment to the U.S. Constitution today ever elevate country above God.

84. W. Carter has taken this tack as consistently and emphatically as anyone. See esp. his *Matthew and Empire: Initial Explorations* (Harrisburg, PA: Trinity Press International; 2001); and *John and Empire: Initial Explorations* (London and New York: T&T Clark, 2008).

85. S. Kim, *Christ and Caesar: The Gospel and the Roman Empire in the Writings of Paul and Luke* (Grand Rapids: Eerdmans, 2008).

86. Usually judicious in this endeavor is S. McKnight and J. B. Modica, eds., *Jesus is Lord, Caesar is Not: Evaluating Empire in New Testament Studies* (Downers Grove: InterVarsity, 2013).

87. A. C. Hebert, "God and Caesar: Examining the Differences between Counter-Imperial and Post-Colonial Hermeneutics," *CTR* 11 (2014): 91–100.

88. For a wide-ranging survey, see R. L. Rohrbaugh, ed., *The Social Sciences and New Testament Interpretation* (Peabody: Hendrickson, 1996; Grand Rapids: Baker, 2010).

89. V. H. Matthews and D. C. Benjamin, "Social Sciences and Biblical Studies," *Semeia* 68 (1994): 7–21, offer an excellent summary of applications of these concepts.

shows the seriousness of his commitment to defend the honor of his people against their enemies by vowing to sacrifice "whatever comes out of the door" of his house to meet him when he returns triumphantly from battle (Judg 11:31). Tragically, that turns out to be his daughter, whose striking reply (v. 36) shows her understanding of the need to keep a vow, however rash it may have been.[90]

Issues of ritual purity dominated the life of ancient Israel, which explains the highly symbolic divisions of the tabernacle and the Jerusalem temple into progressively more sacred space as one drew closer to the holy of holies and as fewer people could enter each successive court.[91] A particularly damaging form of impurity resulted from a curse. One interesting belief widely held in ancient Mediterranean cultures (and still present in places to this day) was that certain people had the ability to cast a spell on others merely with the power of a malignant stare—known as "the evil eye." In several places in the Gospels, the literal translation of the text refers to this belief. For example, in Matthew 6:23 Jesus speaks of those whose eyes are evil, corrupting their entire selves. To avert the curse, one must seek to look at the world in wholesome ways, and then one's entire life will be pure (vv. 22–24).[92]

The social system of patronage, in a world largely without the concept of state-sponsored welfare, linked well-to-do benefactors with groups of clients for whom periodic employment and financial care were provided in return for private favors and public, political support. Paul's care not to ask for or accept money for ministry except in very specific situations (see esp. 1 Cor 9:1–18) stems from his concern not to be perceived as giving his supporters anything that might compromise his freedom to preach and minister precisely as he believed God was leading him. The reciprocal expectations of patron-client relations also explain why Paul avoids too direct an expression of thanksgiving in Philippians 4:10–20. He does convey his gratitude to the Philippian church for their monetary gift, but he does not want to be perceived as becoming indebted to them in any inappropriate fashion or with promises he could not make good on while languishing in prison.[93]

To understand some dynamics in ancient Israel requires an awareness of cultural practices of the surrounding nations. Many aspects of Elisha's healing ministry could have conjured up images of shamanism in other ancient Near Eastern (ANE) cultures, but Elisha clearly attributed his powers to Yahweh, the God of Israel.[94] The patriarchy

---

90. V. H. Matthews and D. C. Benjamin, *Social World of Ancient Israel 1250–587 BCE* (Peabody: Hendrickson, 1993), 19–21. This is not to say that Jephthah *should* have kept his vow, since child sacrifice is an abomination to God (Lev 18:21, 20:2–5; Jer 32:35). See B. G. Webb, *The Book of Judges*, NICOT (Grand Rapids: Eerdmans, 2012), 336.

91. For the OT background, cf. P. P. Jenson, *Graded Holiness: A Key to the Priestly Conception of the World*, JSOTSup 106 (Sheffield: JSOT Press, 1992).

92. Cf. further J. H. Elliott, "The Evil Eye and the Sermon on the Mount," *BibInt* 2 (1994): 51–84.

93. For the most recent book-length treatments of honor in Corinth and Philippi, respectively, see M. T. Finney, *Honour and Conflict in the Ancient World: 1 Corinthians in Its Greco-Roman Social Setting* (London and New York: T&T Clark, 2012); and J. H. Hollerman, *Reconstructing Honor in Roman Philippi* (Cambridge: Cambridge University Press, 2005).

94. T. W. Overholt, *Cultural Anthropology and the Old Testament* (Minneapolis: Fortress, 1996), 24–68.

of the OT was considerably muted compared to that of the nations around Israel, and the Song of Songs depicts the woman's right to initiate and experience sexual delight with her beloved in a way that stands out even within the OT.[95] The political and economic dimensions of sexual behavior in other texts must also be noted. Amnon's rape of Tamar is not merely a case of incest but a claim on David's throne, which also explains the extent to which Absalom, the rival claimant, goes to avenge his brother's sin (2 Sam 13).[96]

Like other items of historical background, the value of a study of the history of social interaction in a given culture depends directly on the accuracy of the data and the appropriateness of their application to specific texts. Scholars agree on most of the above examples. In other cases, interpretations prove more controversial. For example, many people assume that Jesus and his followers came from the substantial majority of the Galilean populace who were poor, marginalized, peasant workers. Recent study has reassessed the role of tradesmen like carpenters and masons in Galilean villages. Such study focuses attention on details such as the mention in Mark 1:20 that Zebedee's family had "hired men" or servants. A growing number of scholars thus suggests that Jesus and his troupe may have included a fair number of the tiny middle class of their society (though even then we may not import the affluence attributed to Western middle class people into our picture of first-century life).[97] Equally groundbreaking but less secure is the attempt to divide the prophets into Ephraimite and Judean categories, in which the former are identified as "peripheral" to their society, and working for social change and the latter as "central" to their human environment, working for social stability.[98] Given that appeals to the laws of Moses dominate the messages of both groups of prophets, one wonders if theological emphases do not overshadow sociological distinctives.[99]

Perhaps the most valuable upshot of the new interest in studying social history

---

95. D. Bergant, "'My Beloved is Mine and I Am His' (Song 2:16)": The Song of Songs and Honor and Shame," *Semeia* 68 (1994): 23–40.

96. Matthews and Hamilton, *Social World of Ancient Israel*, 182–86.

97. See the discussion of past and present study in J. P. Meier, *A Marginal Jew*, AYBRL, 5 vols. to date (New York; London: Doubleday, 1991–), 1:278–85. There is also a fair consensus today that a significant minority of the first Christians came from the smaller middle and upper classes of the Roman Empire, especially as the Jesus movement spread into predominantly Gentile territories.

98. R. R. Wilson, *Prophecy and Society in Ancient Israel* (Philadelphia: Fortress, 1980).

99. Good resources now exist to familiarize students with the most secure results of social-historical analysis of the biblical world. For OT study, pride of place must go to P. J. King and L. E. Stager's *Life in Biblical Israel* (Louisville and London: Westminster John Knox, 2001). A distinctively evangelical survey, only slightly less comprehensive, and occasionally more speculative, is Matthews and Benjamin's, *Social World of Ancient Israel 1250–587 BCE*. More selective still is the anthology of M. D. Carroll R., *Rethinking Contexts, Rereading Texts: Contributions from the Social Sciences to Biblical Interpretation* (Sheffield: Sheffield Academic Press, 2000), but the essays are well-conceived and Carroll's own overviews provide an excellent introduction to the literature. For NT study, A. A. Bell, Jr., *A Guide to the New Testament World* (Scottdale and Waterloo: Herald, 1994) provides a succinct, introductory overview, while D. A. de Silva's *Honor, Patronage, Kingship and Purity: Unlocking New Testament Culture* (Downers Grove: InterVarsity, 2000) covers a wide swath of key cultural issues. Finally, K. C. Hanson and D. E. Oakman's *Palestine in the Time of Jesus: Social Structures and Social Conflicts,* 2nd ed. (Minneapolis: Fortress, 2008) offers a thorough introduction to the first-century world of Israel and relevant background for studying the Gospels.

is that it gives interpreters new sets of questions to ask of the biblical texts. Howard Kee helpfully enumerates a long list of these; sample items include: to what groups do various individuals in the Bible belong? What are the social dynamics of those groups? What are their goals? How might they accomplish them? What are the roles of power within the group and the means of attaining them? Are age groups or sex roles defined? What are the key formative experiences of the group, including initiation, celebration, and stages of transition? What are the boundaries of acceptable behavior that one may or may not transgress? And there are many more.[100] Asking new questions of a text will certainly elicit new answers and yield fresh insights.

Application of Social-Scientific Theories

Under this heading we turn to a different kind of social-scientific analysis. Here scholars use theories about human behavior developed in modern studies of various cultures, including the so-called primitive cultures, to shed fresh light on what may have been the dynamics of social interaction in biblical times. In other words, even where we have no reliable data from the Bible or other ancient texts about the ways in which people interacted in certain settings, perhaps analogies from other cultures in other times and places can enable us to make plausible inferences as to those dynamics.

So, for example, scholars have expended much energy in the attempt to account for the social forces involved in the rise of ancient Israel as a political state, from a loose confederation of tribes to a people who demanded and received a king (the story narrated in 1 Sam–2 Kgs). The three most popular theories have proposed analogies, respectively, from the later development of the Greek nation out of independent city-states, from peasant revolts in other ancient cultures, and from the rise of modern socialism or communism.[101] From the Greek concept of "amphictyony" (an association of neighboring states) has come the hypothesis that during the days of the judges Israel was a very loose confederation of tribes unified only by the single Shiloh sanctuary. An alternate explanation of the settlement period theorizes that "Israel" came into being by a rebellion of nomadic tribesmen already living in Canaan who overthrew their urban oppressors. On a quite different front, studies of ritual taboos in traditional cultures have offered widely accepted explanations for why certain animals were considered unclean in ancient Israel: they deviated from some established norm that was the symbol of ritual purity.[102]

Again, the study of Melanesian "cargo" cults in the South Pacific led to a popular

---

100. H. C. Kee, *Knowing the Truth: A Sociological Approach to New Testament Interpretation* (Minneapolis: Fortress, 1989), 65–67.

101. These three views are classically associated, respectively, with M. Noth, *The History of Israel*, rev. ed. (New York: Harper & Row, 1960); G. E. Mendenhall, *The Tenth Generation: The Origins of the Biblical Tradition* (Baltimore: Johns Hopkins University Press, 1973); and N. K. Gottwald, *The Tribes of Yahweh: A Sociology of the Religion of Liberated Israel 1250–1050 B.C.E* (Maryknoll: Orbis, 1979).

102. See esp. M. Douglas, *Purity and Danger: An Analysis of Concepts of Pollution and Taboo* (London: Routledge & Kegan Paul, 1966); cf. M. Douglas, *Leviticus as Literature* (New York; Oxford: Oxford University Press, 2001). There is, however, no universally agreed on origin for the dietary laws.

proposal about a people's response to "failed prophecy" (a bit of a misleading term), as when the OT prophets repeatedly predicted "the Day of the LORD is at hand" (see esp. Zephaniah), even though centuries passed without its fulfillment. Perhaps this phenomenon recurred in the experience of first-generation Christians who may have expected Christ's return within their lifetime (see esp. 2 Thess). Among other things, this proposal suggests that a religious group whose members discover that "the end" has not come as soon as they first believed "saves face" by engaging in more vigorous proselytizing or evangelism. As more people flock to the movement, then, it regains its credibility and can revise its expectations without threatening the existence of the group.[103]

Study of recurring patterns of institutionalization in the development of religious groups or sects has proved influential in accounting for the development of the first-century church. Itinerant charismatics often give way to more settled and organized forms of leadership. Office replaces charisma. Many NT scholars identify such a pattern of institutionalization in the movement from Jesus and his first followers (the "wandering charismatics"), to Paul (who promoted settled charismatic worship—1 Cor 12–14), to post-Pauline literature (esp. 1 Tim 3, with its criteria for office-holding, believed by most to be written a generation later than Paul; or Jude 3, seen as a classic example of "early catholic" institutionalization of "the faith that was once for all entrusted to the saints").[104] In the OT, some suggest that charismatic prophets eventually yield to forces that institutionalize or "routinize" their leadership. The latest writing prophets (e.g., Haggai, Malachi) thus may resemble the preachers in the emerging synagogue more than their iconoclastic predecessors (e.g., Amos, Jeremiah).[105]

Employing sociological analysis, many view the divisions at Corinth (1 Cor 1:10–17) in light of socio-economic divisions, in which the more wealthy apparently bring extra to eat and drink but do not share enough of their provisions with the poor who come empty-handed (cf. 11:20–21).[106] Some see 1 Peter as an extended tract encouraging the church to become "a home for the homeless" (referring to literal refugees).[107] Others view miracle-stories in the Gospels and Acts as responses to the frustration of a marginalized existence in this life.[108]

---

103. Cf. esp. J. G. Gager, *Kingdom and Community: The Social World of Early Christianity* (Englewood Cliffs, NJ: Prentice-Hall, 1975); and R. P. Carroll, *When Prophecy Failed: Reactions and Responses to Failure in the Old Testament Prophetic Traditions,* rev. ed. (London: SCM, 1996).

104. Cf. esp. G. Theissen, *The Sociology of Early Palestinian Christianity* (Philadelphia: Fortress, 1978). Theissen builds on the more wide-ranging studies of the growth of religions from sect to institution by M. Weber.

105. R. E. Clements, "Max Weber, Charisma and Biblical Prophecy," in *Prophecy and Prophets,* ed. Y. Gitay (Atlanta: Scholars, 1997), 89–108; J. Blenkinsopp, "The Social Roles of Prophets in Early Achaemenid Judah," *JSOT* 93 (2001): 39–58.

106. G. Theissen, *The Social Setting of Pauline Christianity* (Philadelphia: Fortress, 1978), 145–74. Cf. also B. D. Smith, "The Problem with the Observance of the Lord's Supper in the Corinthian Church," *BBR* 20 (2010): 517–43.

107. J. H. Elliott, *A Home for the Homeless: A Sociological Exegesis of 1 Peter* (Philadelphia: Fortress, 1981; Eugene, OR: Wipf & Stock, 2005). See also his *1 Peter,* AB 37b (New York; London: Doubleday, 2000).

108. H. C. Kee, *Miracle in the Early Christian World* (New Haven: Yale University Press, 1983).

How should the biblical interpreter respond to this plethora of proposals? Numerous items are certainly worthy of consideration, but we must subject this program to careful analysis by asking key questions. First, is the specific sociological theory reductionistic or deterministic?[109] That is to say, does it rule out God, the supernatural, or human freedom as primary or even possible agents? Several of the explanations for the establishment of the Israelite nation or for belief in Jesus' miracles involve precisely such presuppositions. The open-minded inquirer cannot accept those that rule out God or human freedom.

Second, does the theory require rejecting part of the biblical text as it stands or reconstructing a set of historical events at odds with the claims of the text itself? Many of the theories involving the transition from judges to kingship assume that the data of Scripture are almost wholly unreliable and must be replaced with a different reconstruction of events.[110] Theissen's view that Jesus' first followers in Palestine were almost exclusively itinerant charismatics requires that we trust only a handful of Q-sayings as the oldest and most authentic portion of the gospel tradition, often *at the expense* of other sayings. To the extent that such theories assume the unreliability of the Bible as we have it, we believe that they are ill-founded.

Third, is a given proposal based on a valid theory commonly accepted by other social scientists? A popular view of the rise of apocalyptic literature proposes that it stems from times of acute social crisis among the communities in which it arises. But more careful study has shown that what is most crucial is the *perception* of crisis—which may or may not correspond to reality. In this case we may not speak with as much confidence about the social origins of every scriptural use of apocalyptic as consistently due to the oppression of the people of God.[111] A popular explanation for group dynamics in OT times has been the notion of "corporate personality" (hence, e.g., all Israel could be punished for the sins of Achan—Josh 7),[112] but more recent research suggests that while corporate responsibility (as in the Achan story) may indicate some kind of corporate *solidarity*, it does not necessarily require the "psychical unity" often postulated as a unique feature of the ancient Hebrew mind.[113]

Fourth, if the theory is valid elsewhere, are the parallels or analogies with the biblical

---

109. A criticism frequently leveled by E. Yamauchi in his important analytical survey, "Sociology, Scripture and the Supernatural," *JETS* 27 (1984): 169–92.

110. W. G. Dever, *What Did the Biblical Writers Know and When Did They Know It? What Archaeology Can Tell Us about the Reality of Ancient Israel* (Grand Rapids: Eerdmans, 2001).

111. See esp. A. Y. Collins, *Crisis in Catharsis: The Power of the Apocalypse* (Philadelphia: Westminster, 1984). On the origins of OT apocalyptic, see classically P. D. Hanson, *The Dawn of Apocalyptic: The Historical and Jewish Roots of Apocalyptic*, rev. ed. (Philadelphia: Fortress, 1975).

112. Due in large measure to H. Wheeler Robinson, "The Hebrew Conception of 'Corporate Personality' in the Old Testament," in *Werden und Wesen des Alten Testaments* (Berlin: Töpelmann, 1936), 49–62; rev. and repr. as *Corporate Personality in Ancient Israel* (Philadelphia: Fortress, 1980; Edinburgh: T&T Clark, 1999).

113. See esp. J. W. Rogerson, "The Hebrew Conception of Corporate Personality: A Re-examination," *JTS* 21 (1970): 1–16. For helpful correctives to Rogerson see R. A. di Vito, "Old Testament Anthropology and the Construction of Personal Identity," *CBQ* 61 (1999): 217–39; and J. S. Kominsky, "The Sins of the Fathers: A Theological Investigation of the Biblical Tension between Corporate and Individualized Retribution," *Judaism* 46 (1997): 319–33.

material close enough to warrant its application to this new context? Twentieth-century South Pacific islanders may be too far removed in time and space from the ancient Middle East to provide much help for interpreting the missionary movements in ancient Judaism and early Christianity!

Fifth, does the theory fit the biblical data as well as do alternatives that are more traditional? For example, one may read 1 Peter as a call to "seek the welfare of the city" (cf. Jer 29:7) at least as plausibly as a mandate to care for the needy within the church.[114] Neither is necessarily a summary of the entire letter. For a different example, it is hard to find much fit at all between peasants' revolts within a nation and the Israelites' establishment of themselves in the land from outside.[115] The story of exodus, covenant, wilderness wandering, and conquest, however one conceives it, seems far more plausible.

Notwithstanding all of these caveats suggesting that we may need to temper, if not reject outright, some of the more popular social-scientific theories, numerous proposals do improve on older, commonly held opinions. Viewing ritual cleanliness and uncleanliness in light of religious taboos or an understanding of order versus disorder seems more appropriate than the popular view that these laws reflected some kind of primitive understanding of hygiene.[116] Wayne Meeks's research on "the first urban Christians," a study of the major cities in which Paul ministered, helpfully compares and contrasts Pauline churches with other socio-religious groups, including trade guilds. He demonstrates that the church might often have been perceived as a similar voluntary association that held the potential, from the viewpoint of Roman leadership, to be subversive to the state.[117] Because of the abundance of written material on life in ancient Greece and Rome from extrabiblical sources, theories here are much more likely to be valid than those, say, relating to periods of Israelite history for which little but ambiguous archeological evidence exists to confirm or contest biblical detail. William Herzog applies research into the social stratification of ancient and modern pre-capitalist empires to show the probable percentages of people in each of the socio-economic brackets of the Roman world.[118]

---

114. See esp. D. L. Balch, *Let Wives Be Submissive: The Domestic Code in I Peter*, SBLMS 26 (Chico, CA: Scholars, 1981); B. Winter, *Seek the Welfare of the City: Christians as Benefactors and Citizens* (Carlisle: Paternoster; Grand Rapids: Eerdmans, 1994), 11–23.

115. As, e.g., in N. P. Lemche, *Early Israel: Anthropological and Historical Studies on the Israelite Society before the Monarchy*, VTSup 37 (Leiden: Brill, 1985). See instead esp. the relevant chapters in B. T. Arnold and R. S. Hess, *Ancient Israel's History: An Introduction to Issues and Sources* (Grand Rapids: Baker, 2014), and the literature there cited.

116. See esp. the appropriation of Douglas' research throughout G. J. Wenham, *The Book of Leviticus*, NICOT (Grand Rapids: Eerdmans, 1979).

117. W. Meeks, *The First Urban Christians: The Social World of the Apostle Paul*, 2nd ed. (New Haven: Yale University Press, 2003). Cf. P. A. Harland, *Associations, Synagogues, and Congregations: Claiming a Place in Ancient Mediterranean Society* (Minneapolis: Fortress, 2003). For a further update, see T. D. Still and D. G. Horrell, eds., *After the First Urban Christians: The Social-Scientific Study of Pauline Christianity Twenty-Five Years Later* (London: Bloomsbury: T&T Clark, 2009).

118. W. R. Herzog II, *Parables as Subversive Speech: Jesus as Pedagogue of the Oppressed* (Louisville: Westminster John Knox, 1994), 53–73. Herzog's comparison is compelling because the model largely fits what primary source

These kinds of evaluations or "judgment calls" obviously require some familiarity with the social sciences. We advise theological or pre-seminary students to take introductory courses in sociology, psychology, anthropology, economics, and the like in order to be familiar with the basic terms and theories that these disciplines employ. They will still need to rely on helpful literature that evaluates the methods employed in these disciplines, especially when applied to the Bible.[119] But even the relative novice can sift theories that incorporate biblical data as valid source material from those that depend largely on reconstructions of ancient history that contradict or ignore the testimony of Scripture.[120] In our judgment, even the most valid social-scientific study will never replace the classic historical-grammatical tools of analysis, but it can provide important supplementary information and correctives to past mistakes in interpretation.

Advocacy Groups

Within the broad arena of social-scientific interest in the Bible several subdisciplines have taken on whole lives of their own, both in the sheer volume of literature published and in the ideological stances they represent. Traditionally, biblical scholarship promoted a certain detachment by its practitioners as a laudable goal. Precisely because the use of the Bible in church and synagogue usually involved theological motives and biases, scholars in academic institutions tried to distance themselves from particular ideologies as they study Scripture. But various practitioners of social-scientific analysis have more recently sought to reverse this trend. In the 1970s and 1980s the two main representatives of this perspective were those who practiced liberation and feminist hermeneutics. In the 1990s and 2000s the former largely gave way to broader forms of cultural criticism, especially what has come most often to be called postcolonialism, while the latter has continued unabated. Each of these movements shares a common commitment to the liberation of the disenfranchised of this world and views goals or claims of "detached objectivity" as both a myth and a weakness for interpreters. In

---

data we do have from the Roman Empire itself, on which see B. W. Longenecker, "Exposing the Economic Middle: A Revised Economy Scale for the Study of Early Urban Christianity," *JSNT* 31 (2009): 264.

119. Cf. esp. B. Holmberg, *Sociology and the New Testament: An Appraisal* (Minneapolis: Fortress, 1990). To date, no comparable, comprehensive critique of the methodologies of a broad cross-section of OT sociology exists. For a good anthology, however, see D. Chalcraft, ed., *Social-Scientific Old Testament Criticism: A Sheffield Reader* (Sheffield: Sheffield Academic Press, 1997).

120. For NT study a series of like-minded works in commentary format provides easy access to a wide range of hypotheses that should be tested. See B. J. Malina and R. L. Rohrbaugh, *Social-Science Commentary on the Synoptic Gospels*, 2nd ed. (Minneapolis Fortress, 2003); B. J. Malina and R. L. Rohrbaugh, *Social-Science Commentary on the Gospel of John* (Minneapolis: Fortress, 1998); B. J. Malina and J. J. Pilch, *Social-Science Commentary on the Book of Acts* (Minneapolis: Fortress, 2008); B. J. Malina and J. J. Pilch, *Social-Science Commentary on the Letters of Paul* (Minneapolis: Fortress, 2006); B. J. Malina and J. J. Pilch, *Social-Science Commentary on the Deutero-Pauline Letters* (Minneapolis: Fortress, 2013); and B. J. Malina and J. J. Pilch, *Social-Science Commentary on the Book of Revelation* (Minneapolis: Fortress, 2000). A few of the interpretations prove problematic but a significant number provide valuable, legitimate insights. Some of Malina's takes on Revelation form the only really idiosyncratic part of the series. For the OT, the only partly comparable volume is J. van Seters, *The Pentateuch: A Social-Science Commentary*, rev. ed. (London: Bloomsbury T&T Clark, 2015).

other words, if one is not part of the solution, one is part of the problem! If biblical scholars do not join the marginalized in their quest for full equality, human rights, and a decent life for all, irrespective of gender, race, sexual orientation, nationality, and so on, then they de facto remain aligned with the inhumane, oppressive, sexist, and racist powers of this world. In the last dozen years, lesbian-gay-bisexual-transgendered (LGBT) interpretation has grown from being a very small to a very significant piece of the hermeneutical mosaic, so it merits assessment as well. There are, of course, numerous other strands of Christian theology, both traditional and avant-garde, that remain activistic in nature.[121] But no other systems of thought employ so unique a set of hermeneutical axioms nor remain as influential internationally as the following four. So we turn to each briefly for some special analysis.

Advocacy Groups	
Liberation Hermeneutics	Feminist Hermeneutics
Cultural Criticism	LGBT Hermeneutics

Liberation Hermeneutics

Liberation theology initially developed as an engaged, Roman Catholic response in Latin America to centuries of oppression of the impoverished majority of poor, mostly indigenous residents by ruling élites in government, society, and even the church.[122] Liberation hermeneutics developed a three-part agenda. In opposition to the stated objectives of many forms of classical theology, experience takes precedence over theory. The dominant experience of a majority of people in the Majority World, in which liberation theology emerged, is the experience of poverty—suffering, malnutrition, lack of access to basic human rights, education, clean water, health care, and the like. Hence, first, a liberation hermeneutic begins with the experience of the injustice of poverty. Second, it attempts to analyze or assess the reasons for this impoverished existence. Third, actions take precedence over rhetoric. Liberationists seek to determine a course of corrective measures based on their previous observation, insight, and judgment.[123] In the liberationist hermeneutic, the Bible does not normally come into play at the beginning in step one but only to aid in steps two and three. Particularly by focusing on the biblical narratives of liberation from oppression, with the exodus

---

121. E.g., one thinks, respectively, of mainstream Protestant liberal reformers and proponents of New Age or pantheistic worldviews.

122. The widely acknowledged founder of this movement is G. Gutiérrez, with his *A Theology of Liberation: History, Politics, and Salvation*, 2nd ed. (Maryknoll: Orbis, 1988 [orig. Spanish 1968]).

123. A good, detailed introduction to liberationist hermeneutics (as distinct from liberation theology more generally) is C. Rowland and M. Corner, *Liberating Exegesis: The Challenge of Liberation Theology to Biblical Studies* (London: SPCK; Louisville: Westminster John Knox, 1989). Cf. also A. R. Ceresko, *Introduction to the Old Testament: A Liberation Perspective*, rev. ed. (Maryknoll: Orbis, 2001); A. Botta and P. R. Andiñach, eds., *The Bible and the Hermeneutics of Liberation*, SemeiaSt 59 (Atlanta: SBL, 2009); and T. Hanks, *The Subversive Gospel: A New Testament Commentary of Liberation* (Cleveland: Pilgrim, 2000; Eugene, OR: Wipf & Stock, 2009).

as the OT paradigm and a socio-political understanding of God's kingdom as the NT paradigm, the liberationist takes heart from his or her conviction that God has a "preferential option for the poor."[124] God sides with the oppressed against their oppressors and calls believers today to do the same in working for a more humane society on this earth.

How to bring about this new society, God's kingdom, remained a topic on which liberationists disagreed. Some labored within the framework of Western democracies but believed that we needed more socialist checks and balances on a capitalism run amok.[125] Some strongly eschewed violence but endorsed social protest and civil disobedience à la Martin Luther King, Jr.[126] Still others endorsed both violence and Marxism as necessary means to more desirable ends.[127] Most all agreed that, without some form of outside intervention, the current disparities between haves and have-nots would continue to widen, as they have so considerably under various forms of capitalism. Most all also believed that the Bible itself promotes peace and justice in ways that require a modification of current economic and political structures in society.

As clearly as any liberationist writer, José Miranda equated Christianity with communism, believing that it is taught throughout the Bible.[128] It is indeed striking that both "haves" of Marx's manifesto come straight from the book of Acts: "from each according to his ability" (Acts 11:29) and "to each according to his need" (4:35). The OT Jubilee laws were designed to prevent the perpetuation of extreme disparities in the distribution of wealth, as debts had to be forgiven in the Sabbath and jubilee years. A major theme of the Law and Prophets is the denunciation of injustice against the powerless and a call to help the poor. The communal living and redistribution of goods depicted in Acts 2:42–47 and 4:32–5:11 serve as indictments of contemporary Western forms of Christianity. And Luke's summary statements make it clear that he viewed this fellowship as exemplary and not the mistake (2:47, 5:14) some modern-day Christians have thought it was. Paul too outlines radical requirements for Christian stewardship of money (2 Cor 8–9), in which, following the model of God's provision of manna in the wilderness, "he who gathered much did not have too much, and he who gathered little did not have too little" (2 Cor 8:15; Exod 16:18). The goal was "that there might be equality" (2 Cor 8:13).[129]

---

124. A slogan that emerged in the late 1960s from Vatican II and subsequent Catholic bishops' conferences as the rallying cry and starting point for the vast majority of liberation theology.

125. Cf. the excellent survey by S. E. Heaney, *Contextual Theology for Latin America: Liberation Themes in Evangelical Perspective* (Milton Keynes: Paternoster; Eugene, OR: Wipf & Stock, 2008).

126. E.g., R. J. Cassidy, *Jesus, Politics and Society: A Study of Luke's Gospel* (Maryknoll: Orbis, 1978; Eugene, OR: Wipf & Stock, 2015); and J. M. Ford, *My Enemy Is My Guest: Jesus and Violence in Luke* (Maryknoll: Orbis, 1984; Eugene, OR: Wipf & Stock, 2010).

127. E.g., J. H. Cone, *A Black Theology of Liberation*, 4th ed. (Maryknoll: Orbis, 2010); J. L. Segundo, *The Liberation of Theology* (Maryknoll: Orbis, 1976).

128. J. P. Miranda, *Communism in the Bible* (Maryknoll: Orbis, 1982; Eugene, OR: Wipf & Stock, 2004). For a survey of approaches, see R. Boer, "Twenty-Five Years of Marxist Biblical Criticism," *CBR* 5 (2007): 298–321.

129. From a non-Communist perspective, see C. L. Blomberg, *Neither Poverty nor Riches: A Biblical Theology of Possessions*, NSBT (Leicester and Downers Grove: InterVarsity, 1999); cf. also C. L. Blomberg, "'Your Faith Has

We observe two major problems, however, with a hermeneutic that proceeds from the conviction that Christianity is inherently socialist, at least in the forms that have evolved since the days of Marx. First, such a hermeneutic tries to impose on society ethics that were originally limited to God's people. Neither in OT Israel nor in the NT church were believers mandated to make God's laws or principles the laws of every nation. Second, the liberationist hermeneutic usually plays down the voluntary nature of NT giving (2 Cor 9:7; cf. Acts 4:32). Texts like these show that the Christians retained personal property much as Job did in the OT. In short, as with the good news of the kingdom itself, no one is forced to be a good steward of his or her God-given resources who does not want to![130] But, having said this, many Bible scholars, evangelicals included, now agree with liberationists that models of Western church life have much to learn from the paradigms of fellowship and stewardship of the Bible. As well, in certain respects the Bible's paradigms may more closely approximate socialist (or social democratic) rather than purely capitalist structures.[131]

Liberationist hermeneutics pose other problems. They often do not seem adequately to preserve the spiritual element of salvation. Mark 8:36 stands out poignantly: "What good is it for someone to gain the whole world, yet forfeit their soul?" They may overlook that "the poor" in Scripture are consistently not *all* the physically dispossessed or oppressed but those who in their need turn to God as their only hope.[132] Liberationists often create a de facto canon within the canon and ignore or deem as not as authoritative those texts that do not support their agenda. At the same time, too often more traditional forms of theology have at times proved even more blind to the parts of Scripture the liberationists stress. So as a corrective to one imbalance, though not as the sum total of the scriptural witness, liberation theology proves extremely significant.

Rereading other Scriptures from a perspective of a commitment to help the disenfranchised of this world can thus shed significant new light on them. The exodus account reminds us that God is concerned about sociopolitical as well as spiritual freedoms.[133] The Jewish midwives engaged in civil disobedience when they refused to obey Pharaoh's law mandating that they kill the newborn Hebrew boys (Exod 1:15–21). We may rightly see Esther as a model of one who risked the penalties of civil disobedience to stand up for her people rather than as one who was duly submissive

---

Made You Whole': The Evangelical Liberation Theology of Jesus," in *Jesus of Nazareth, Lord and Christ*, ed. J. B. Green and M. Turner (Grand Rapids: Eerdmans, 1994), 75–93.

130. For important critiques of liberation hermeneutics, cf. E. A. Nuñez, *Liberation Theology* (Chicago: Moody Press, 1985); R. C. Hundley, *Radical Liberation Theology: An Evangelical Response* (Wilmore, KY: Bristol Books, 1987); and H. Belli and R. H. Nash, *Beyond Liberation Theology* (Grand Rapids: Baker, 1992).

131. Cf., e.g., T. D. Hanks, *God So Loved the Third World: The Biblical Vocabulary of Oppression* (Maryknoll: Orbis, 1984; Eugene, OR: Wipf & Stock, 2010); A. Kirk, *The Good News of the Kingdom Coming: The Marriage of Evangelism and Social Responsibility* (Downers Grove: InterVarsity, 1983).

132. See esp. W. Heard, "Luke's Attitude toward the Rich and the Poor," *TrinJ* 9 (1988): 47–80; cf. S. Gillingham, "The Poor in the Psalms," *ExpTim* 100 (1988): 15–19.

133. See esp. J. S. Croatto, *Exodus: A Hermeneutics of Freedom* (Maryknoll: Orbis, 1981).

to the authorities in her world.[134] We should view Jesus, as already noted above, as a challenge to political as well as religious authorities and structures in his society.[135] And in perhaps the most important biblical document that requires us to wrestle with the liberationist agenda, the Epistle of James, we discover a community of largely poor, Christian day-laborers being oppressed by their wealthy, often absentee landlords—a frightening parallel to the situation of many Majority World laborers today. Many of them are Christian believers denied a decent wage and basic human rights by the large multinational corporations or corrupt national governments that employ them as virtual slave labor.[136] Yet many conservative Christians explicitly and implicitly continue to support right-wing regimes and ultra-capitalist policies that only exacerbate the physical suffering of their Christian brothers and sisters. Whatever else we may question in a liberationist hermeneutic, we obviously have much still to learn from it. We must listen to the voices of the disenfranchised, test each claim against the Scriptures, and see if either their or our presuppositions have obscured the true meaning or significance of the text.[137]

Cultural Criticism

The collapse of Communist regimes in Eastern Europe and Asia at the beginning of the 1990s dealt a near death blow to those forms of liberationist hermeneutics that were closely wedded to socialist economics.[138] For the next fifteen years, comparatively little was written under the explicit banner of liberation theology. Also, at the grassroots level, the poor in Latin America have been converting to evangelical, and especially Pentecostal, Christianity in large numbers. As these branches of Christianity mature in their recognition of a holistic gospel—meeting needs of body and soul alike—the impetus swings away from liberation theology as well. What remains of a liberationist hermeneutic appears far more toned down, but perhaps that much more balanced and legitimate as a result.[139] For example, E. Tamez, in her commentary on Ecclesiastes, reads from a context of "hopelessness" of many Majority World poor at the start of the twenty-first century and derives four major principles from the text that afford hope for the future: (1) there is a time and season for everything (3:1–8); (2) real life has a rhythm to it that dehumanizing social forces ignore; (3) one must fear God as one recognizes the finite limited human condition (13:13–14); and (4) discernment

---

134. O. E. Costas, "The Subversiveness of Faith: Esther as a Paradigm for a Liberating Theology," *EcR* 40 (1988): 66–78.

135. Cf. further H. C. Waetjen, *A Reordering of Power: A Socio-Political Reading of Mark's Gospel* (Minneapolis: Fortress, 1989; Eugene, OR: Wipf & Stock, 2014).

136. See esp. P. U. Maynard-Reid, *Poverty and Wealth in James* (Maryknoll: Orbis, 1987; Eugene, OR: Wipf & Stock, 2004); and E. Tamez, *The Scandalous Message of James: Faith without Works Is Dead*, 2nd ed. (New York: Crossroad, 2002).

137. A good anthology to help in such a process is R. S. Sugirtharajah, ed., *Voices from the Margin: Interpreting the Bible in the Third World*, 3rd ed. (Maryknoll: Orbis, 2006).

138. Cf. D. B. Forrester, "Can Liberation Theology Survive 1989?" *SJT* 47 (1994): 245–53.

139. Cf. S. K. George, "From Liberation to Evangelization: New Latin American Hermeneutical Keys," *Int* 55 (2001): 367–77.

and wisdom in everyday tasks can lead to a solidarity with fellow sufferers that encourages God's people in the midst of a radically individualistic, "save-your-own-skin" world.[140]

In recent years, however, liberation theology has started to make a comeback.[141] Miguel de la Torre is one articulate spokesman. His "thick Hispanic Jesús" [the Spanish name], which alone, de la Torre claims, can save Hispanics, is born homeless, into poverty, as an undocumented immigrant. He dwelled among us, came from the *barrio*, and lived a life of poverty. He was perceived to be *mestizo* (of mixed race), tempted by Satan with power, possessions, and privilege, and was not afraid to reinterpret the Scriptures. He is willing to learn from his margins, proclaims his mission statement for the oppressed, and challenges basic neoliberal principles. He links salvation with praxis, calls the privileged to repent, and saves oppressors who do so. He rejects repressive religiosity, lives as the Good Shepherd, and makes an evangelistic call.[142] Not all of these are quite historically accurate; for example, as we have seen, by his adulthood Jesus would have been more akin to a lower middle-class blue collar worker of purely Jewish ethnicity. But the overall package is collectively closer to the Jesus of history than to the Jesus of many North American white people of privilege.

At the same time, however, has come the upsurgence of a flood of biblical and theological studies under the rubric of "cultural" or "intercultural" criticism.[143] Common to such study is an emphasis on reading Scripture through the eyes of those raised in traditionally marginalized cultures. Some cultural criticism closely resembles liberationist exegesis in that it selectively accepts those portions of Scripture that it believes humanize or give dignity to the oppressed, while rejecting parts believed to be inherently dehumanizing. Randall C. Bailey, for example, studies the OT polemic against the Canaanite peoples for their sexual sin. He believes it functions to dehumanize Israel's enemies to pave the way for their (unjustifiable) genocide.[144] Somewhat paradoxically, this approach uses Judeo-Christian morals found in certain parts of Scripture to critique and even condemn the contents of other parts, and it

---

140. E. Tamez, *When the Horizons Close: Rereading Ecclesiastes* (Maryknoll: Orbis, 2000), 143.

141. See esp. T. Cooper, ed., *The Reemergence of Liberation Theologies: Models for the Twenty-First Century* (New York: Palgrave Macmillan, 2013). Cf. also M. A. de la Torre, *Liberation Theology for Armchair Theologians* (Louisville: Westminster John Knox, 2013), and C. Rowland, ed., *The Cambridge Companion to Liberation Theology* (Cambridge: Cambridge University Press, 2007).

142. M. de la Torre, "A Thick Hispanic Jesús," *PRSt* 40 (2013): 131–42.

143. For both of these terms, see F. F. Segovia: "And They Began to Speak in Other Tongues: Competing Modes of Discourse in Contemporary Biblical Criticism," in *Reading from this Place*, 2 vols., ed. F. F. Segovia and M. A. Tolbert (Minneapolis: Fortress, 1995), 1:7; and F. F. Segovia, "Toward Intercultural Criticism: A Reading Strategy from the Diaspora," in *Reading from this Place*, 2:303–30. For an excellent and representative anthology, see F. Lozada and G. Carey, eds., *Soundings in Cultural Criticism: Perspectives and Methods in Culture, Power, and Identity in the New Testament* (Minneapolis: Fortress, 2013). For the whole Bible, see H. de Wit and J. Dyk, eds., *Bible and Transformation: The Promise of Intercultural Bible Reading* (Atlanta: SBL, 2015). Most cultures involve races or ethnic groups, but they may also group people together due to some other minority feature. See, e.g., N. Junior and J. Schipper, "Disability Studies and the Bible," in *New Meanings for Ancient Texts*, 21–37.

144. R. C. Bailey, "They're Nothing but Incestuous Bastards: The Polemical Use of Sex and Sexuality in Hebrew Canon Narratives," in *Reading from this Place*, 1:121–37.

still presupposes the modernist conception that some absolute truths exist, in this case that genocide is always wrong.

Increasingly, however, cultural criticism is joining hands with postmodernism so that the former exists not only as a subset of social-scientific analysis but also as one category of reader-response criticism. Here claims that are more modest surface. Practitioners suggest readings merely as viable alternatives to traditional ones, not as inherently correct or even better.[145] But this perspective leaves inadequately addressed questions such as: "Why should liberating interpretations be preferred to oppressive ones?" The very approach undercuts convictions that biblical texts should aid in the advocacy of certain causes versus others.

Some cultural criticism appears merely as a form of application of biblical texts and themes to cultures and contexts not often previously addressed. For example, the apostles in Acts 6:1–7 seek to redress the neglect of the Hellenist widows in the early church in Jerusalem by having the Hellenist branch of the church appoint its own leaders to address it. Here is a possible mandate for doing all we can to empower indigenous leadership in each new culture that accepts the gospel.[146] Likewise, the situation of repatriated Jewish exiles presupposed by Isaiah 56–66 closely parallels the experiences of Chinese Christians in Hong Kong after its return to China. They have a measure of freedom that most others in the larger nation that encompasses them do not, but they are still ruled by what amounts to an empire, so lessons from these chapters apply quite directly in this contemporary context.[147] But these are merely cross-cultural applications or contextualizations[148] of the Bible, a practice followed in varying ways throughout church history and one to which we will return in a later chapter, but hardly a new hermeneutical method.

One important branch of cultural criticism that has been widely discussed is postcolonialism. Whereas liberation theology initially grew out of the distinctive Latin American political history, postcolonialism has emerged in former Asian and African colonies. Liberation for them was politically achieved in most cases by no later than the 1960s, but Western religious and economic forces still keep them from being fully decolonized in those arenas. One definition of the task of postcolonialism in the late 1990s could have been a central objective of liberation theology in its heyday:

> to ensure that the yearnings of the poor take precedence over the interests of the affluent; that the emancipation of the subjugated has primacy over the freedom of the powerful; and that the participation of the marginalized takes priority over the perpetuation of a system which systematically excludes them.[149]

---

145. Again, see esp. F. F. Segovia throughout his contributions to *Reading from this Place*, 2 vols. Cf. F. F. Segovia, *Decolonizing Biblical Studies: A View from the Margins* (Maryknoll: Orbis, 2000).

146. J. L. González, "Reading from My Bicultural Place: Acts 6:1–7," in *Reading from This Place*, 1:139–47.

147. A. C. C. Lee, "Exile and Return in the Perspective of 1997," in *Reading from This Place*, 2:97–108.

148. On which, see esp. T. E. van Spanje, "Contextualization: Hermeneutical Remarks," *BJRL* 80 (1998): 197–217.

149. R. S. Sugirtharajah, "A Postcolonial Exploration of Collusion and Construction in Biblical Interpretation,"

But postcolonialism often goes one distinctive step further—accepting a pluralism among religious worldviews[150] which paradoxically (and seemingly unwittingly) relativizes its own claims. M. W. Dube, for example, objects to the "one-way" theology of the Gospel of John, with its emphasis on Jesus' unique divinity and absolute claims on the world. This sounds too much like the ideology that supported colonization, she argues, and so it must be rejected.[151] Sugirtharajah provocatively identifies the various saviors in religions that have influenced Asia as all on the side of good versus the Satanic dehumanizing forces of secularism:

> In a multireligious context like ours, the real contest is not between Jesus and other savior figures like Buddha or Krishna, or religious leaders like Mohammed, as advocates of the "Decade of Evangelism" want us to believe; it is between mammon and Satan on the one side, and Jesus, Buddha, Krishna, and Mohammed on the other. Mammon stands for personal greed, avariciousness, accumulation, and selfishness, and Satan stands for structural and institutional violence. The question then is whether these religious figures offer us any clue to challenge these forces, or simply help to perpetuate them, and how the continuities rather than contrasts among these savior figures may be experienced and expressed.[152]

Less radically, G. M. Soares-Prabhu compares the Great Commission of Matthew 28:18–20 to a famous Buddhist Scripture that commands monks to go into the world with the teaching of the *ehamma*—the good in the beginning, middle, and end of everything—as "the Lord" does. Its basis lies in the spiritual liberation the monk has experienced, and its driving force is compassion for the world and for the happiness of many. By juxtaposing two such partly parallel mandates, the differences also stand out more clearly. The Asian familiar with Buddhism will recognize more readily even than Christians from other contexts would the distinctive Christological (Christ-centered) rather than anthropological (person-centered) focus of Jesus' commission.[153]

Larry Hurtado reflects perceptively on what he calls "fashions" in the history of biblical interpretation. These are new methods that an influential writer or school of thought outside of biblical scholarship per se develops and that make genuine contributions to various disciplines of human knowledge, which a small group of biblical

---

in *The Postcolonial Bible*, ed. R. S. Sugirtharajah (Sheffield: Sheffield Academic Press, 1998), 113. This is an excellent, representative anthology of postcolonial studies, to which should now be added F. F. Segovia and R. S. Sugirtharajah, eds., *A Postcolonial Commentary on the New Testament Writings* (London and NY: T. & T. Clark, 2009).

150. R. S. Sugirtharajah, *Postcolonial Criticism and Biblical Interpretation* (Oxford: Oxford University Press, 2001), 71, 100, 115.

151. M. W. Dube, "Savior of the World but Not of This World: A Postcolonial Reading of the Spatial Construction in John," in *The Postcolonial Bible*, 118–35.

152. R. S. Sugirtharajah, *Asian Biblical Hermeneutics and Postcolonialism: Contesting the Interpretations* (Maryknoll: Orbis, 1998), 119.

153. G. M. Soares-Prabhu, "Two Mission Commands: An Interpretation of Matthew 28:16–20 in the Light of a Buddhist Text," *BibInt* 2 (1994): 264–82.

scholars latches on to.[154] Convinced that these methods form the key to advancing or improving biblical scholarship, they promote them vigorously through publications, organize conferences to study them, and convince a few high-profile institutions or societies to privilege them. But the methods never demonstrate widespread, lasting, or highly significant value across the academy, and especially not outside of it. So they seldom outlive those who propound them so vigorously and perhaps a few of their students. Hurtado focuses on structuralism as a classic example (recall our comments above).[155] He might well have added canon criticism (see ch. 4) or certain subdisciplines, like support for the Griesbach hypothesis within source criticism (recall ch. 2), which when William Farmer died dropped out of sight almost at once. Hurtado suspects postcolonialism may prove to be another such fashion, not least because it is largely the purview of Western scholars and others transplanted to the West rather than owned by large numbers of scholars and churchgoers in the Majority World and in literal postcolonial contexts themselves.[156]

The most valid and helpful results of cultural (or multicultural) exegesis, therefore, involve the recognition of genuine dimensions of meaning or background of biblical texts that more closely parallel the biblical world than typical Western culture. This often enables readers, particularly from the Majority World, to pick up something that other readers miss or unwittingly distort.[157] African readers of the OT, for example, will probably recognize that polygamy in the biblical world, as on their continent, was not primarily about sex but about social status, about having large families to provide for basic needs, and even about achieving peace between rival tribes through intermarriage.[158] African-Americans are more likely to recognize a theological and literary unity to the book of Daniel because of their historic appeal both to Daniel's this-worldly salvation in chs. 1–6 and to its other-worldly rescue in the more apocalyptic chs. 7–12. Both sections speak powerfully to people marginalized in society; no historical-critical dissection into separate documents need be postulated, as white and politically liberal scholars so often have done.[159]

Turning to the NT, Spanish readers will quickly observe the links between "righteousness" and "justice" because they have only one word to use—*justicia*—to

---

154. L. W. Hurtado, "Fashions, Fallacies and Future Prospects in New Testament Studies," *JSNT* 36 (2014): 299–324.

155. Ibid., 300–2.

156. Ibid., 317.

157. See esp. C. Keener and M. D. Carroll R., eds., *Global Voices: Reading the Bible in the Majority World* (Peabody: Hendrickson, 2013); and H. de Wit, et al., eds., *Through the Eyes of Another: Intercultural Readings of the Bible* (Amsterdam: Institute of Mennonite Studies, 2004). Cf. also C. H. Cosgrove, H. Weiss and K.-K. Yeo, *Cross-Cultural Paul: Journeys to Others, Journeys to Ourselves* (Grand Rapids: Eerdmans, 2005); and D. Rhoads, ed., *From Every People and Nation: The Book of Revelation in Intercultural Perspective* (Minneapolis: Fortress, 2005), though this last work also has some postcolonial essays in it.

158. K. Holter, *Yahweh in Africa: Essays on Africa and the Old Testament*, Bible and Theology in Africa (New York: Peter Lang, 2000), 77–90.

159. J. Kampen, "The Genre and Function of Apocalyptic Literature in the African American Experience," in *Text and Experience: Toward a Cultural Exegesis of the Bible*, ed. D. S. Christopher (Sheffield: Sheffield Academic Press, 1995), 43–65.

translate the one Greek word *dikaiosunē*. They are more likely to understand, when Paul speaks of imputing God's righteousness to believers, that he employs a holistic concept that involves spiritual salvation and social justice. As the Spirit then works in believers' lives, they should be equally concerned with both tasks.[160] Likewise, Majority World readers of Revelation 17–18, accustomed to economic oppression by the minority of well-to-do people in their society, including those in political and religious positions of power, will more quickly note the economic dimensions of the exploitation by the great, evil, end-times empire depicted in these chapters. They will thus more likely point to the increasingly anti-Christian, enormously wealthy West and its multinational corporations with their exploitative sweatshops in Majority World countries than to largely impoverished Middle Eastern or formerly Soviet countries for the closest contemporary parallels.[161]

Of course, even contemporary cultures more akin to biblical ones are not identical, and the danger remains of interpreting an ancient text in light of current cultural practices, however traditional, where the ancient and modern cultures do not match. Thus while it is fascinating to consider traditional African taboos on counting as bringing bad fortune as possible background for why God condemned David's census (2 Sam 24:1),[162] it was probably the practice of counting people for the sake of military conscription in Israel that displeased God when he had not commanded David to go to war (thus explicitly v. 2). Even more clearly mistaken is the attempt to make *Yahweh Elohim* ("the Lord God") in the OT mean "Yahweh [is] the gods" in a polytheistic context, just because that is what it could mean in certain African contexts and might well have meant even in various ancient Near Eastern contexts.[163] The significant differences between Israel and the nations even in the earliest stages of its developing monotheism, not to mention consistent OT usage, are overlooked in the process.

Thus we may study traditional cultures analogous to biblical ones to identify a correct interpretation of a scriptural text. On the flip side we can use such parallels to expose an incorrect interpretation found among Western commentators. This challenges the common tendency to read into the text modern and alien (to the Bible) cultural prejudices. Stereotypes concerning African slaves in American history may lead white readers to assume blindly that Onesimus was a runaway who had committed some crime, perhaps stealing Philemon's goods. In fact, that is only one of

---

160. Cf. E. Tamez, *The Amnesty of Grace: Justification by Faith from a Latin American Perspective* (Nashville: Abingdon, 1993; Eugene, OR: Wipf & Stock, 2002). Interestingly this English title actually better captures this holism than the title of the Spanish original: *Contra todo condenado* ("Against Everything Condemned").

161. D. R. Fernández, "The Judgment of God on the Multinationals: Revelation 18," in *Subversive Scriptures: Revolutionary Christian Readings of the Bible in Latin America*, ed. L. E. Vaage (Valley Forge, PA: Trinity Press International, 1997), 75–100.

162. So S. Githuku, "Taboos on Counting," in *Interpreting the Old Testament in Africa*, ed. M. Getui, K. Holter, and V. Zinkuratire (New York: Peter Lang, 2001), 113–17.

163. T. L. J. Mafico, "The Divine Name Yahweh Elohim from an African Perspective," in *Reading from This Place,* 2:21–32. Cf. the comparative study of ancient Near Eastern deities in M. S. Smith, *God in Translation: Deities in Cross-Cultural Discourse in the Biblical World* (Grand Rapids: Eerdmans, 2010).

several possible inferences from the text. Some commentators suggest that Onesimus may have gone to Paul in Rome voluntarily as a respected friend and mediator for both parties, following an ancient Roman convention for resolving conflict. If so, then Onesimus may not have been at fault at all.[164]

An additional unique contribution comes from African and African-American cultural analysis. While no one can argue fairly that East Asians, Latin Americans, or native Americans appear in the Bible, set as it is in the ancient Near and Middle East, there are certainly black and African characters in Scripture who are not necessarily so recognized by white readers—or even by black readers trained by white teachers! Cain Hope Felder, perhaps the most prolific African-American practitioner of cultural criticism, has a helpful survey of these characters, including Hagar, Egyptian pharaohs, Moses' Cushite wife, Eli's son Phineas (the Nubian), Zephaniah son of Cushi, the Queen of Sheba, Candace Queen of Ethiopia, Simeon called Niger in the church at Antioch, the Ethiopian eunuch, and so on. Some of these characters are positive; others, negative, so one can scarcely use them for purposes of reverse discrimination. But there clearly is a positive black presence in the Bible that readers must recognize. Even the color and features of Jews in the first century, prior to centuries of intermarrying with Europeans, would have been more akin to contemporary Palestinian or Lebanese peoples. Using the terminology of modern polls and censuses, Jesus would have checked a box marked "non-white." But centuries of Euro-American artwork have portrayed all biblical characters, and especially Jesus, more as members of their own white cultures, so few readers of the Bible really have a true picture in their minds.[165]

On top of all the strengths and weaknesses of the various methods of cultural and intercultural criticism that we have surveyed, perhaps the most significant consequence of the movement is the reminder that all interpreters are the products of their own cultures and subcultures. Thus we must always be aware of imposing an alien culture onto the biblical text. Norman Gottwald suggests that theological students in particular should self-consciously reflect on the following eighteen factors that have shaped their experiences: (1) their denominational history or tradition, (2) norms or standards valued besides the Bible; (3) their working theology, (4) ethnicity, (5) gender, (6) social class, (7) educational background, (8) community priorities, (9) explicit political position, (10) implicit political stances, (11) customary exposures to the Bible,

---

164. For the evidence for both sides, see in detail J. A. Fitzmyer, *The Letter to Philemon*, AB 34 (New York; London: Doubleday, 2000), 12–24. The African-American scholar A. D. Callahan (*Embassy of Onesimus: The Letter of Paul to Philemon* [Valley Forge: Trinity Press International, 1997]) goes one step further, arguing that the references to slavery in Philemon are metaphorical and that Philemon and Onesimus are actually blood brothers in need of reconciliation. This view, in the end, does not do justice to the grammar or use of *doulos* ("slave") in Philemon, but the suggestion was worth considering. Interpreters not attuned to the issues of a culture afflicted with slavery might not have even made the proposal in the first place.

165. Cf. C. H. Felder, *Troubling Biblical Waters: Race, Class, and Family* (Maryknoll: Orbis, 1989). Of course, art in all cultures often portrays Jesus in culturally compatible terms, so we are not picking only on Christians in the West. For a discussion of all the ways Africans and Africa appear in the Bible, see E. M. Yamauchi, *Africa and the Bible* (Grand Rapids: Baker, 2004).

(12) Bible translations used, (13) use of other Bible study tools, (14) past exposure to biblical preaching, (15) orientation toward biblical scholarship, (16) family influences, (17) life crises, and (18) spirituality and divine guidance.[166] Students may then reflect on how they have consciously or unconsciously prioritized these various factors in their lives and how these factors may help or hinder valid biblical interpretation.

Experience-Shaping Factors that Influence How We Interpret the Bible	
1. denominational history or tradition	2. norms or standards valued besides the Bible
3. working theology	4. ethnicity
5. gender	6. social class
7. educational background	8. community priorities
9. explicit political position	10. implicit political stances
11. customary exposures to the Bible	12. Bible translations used
13. use of other Bible study tools	14. past exposure to biblical preaching
15. orientation toward biblical scholarship	16. family influences
17. life crises	18. spirituality and divine guidance

Feminist Hermeneutics

Feminism may be viewed as one particular branch of liberation theology or cultural criticism, but it too has developed a life and literature all its own. Indeed, depending on which writers one reads, it may be considered as a subset of social-scientific analysis or as an alternative to it. It may also function as one of many viable readings of a passage, in keeping with postmodern, pluralist versions of reader-response criticism. Or it may be viewed as the most viable, most necessary reading of a text, in keeping with modernism. In the 1980s, Rosemary Reuther identified three major directions in contemporary feminism: liberal, socialist/Marxist, and romantic/radical. The liberal element saw a model of progress within capitalist society and worked for political reform, equal rights, and improved working conditions. It tended to benefit middle-class women more than poor or minority women. The socialist feminists who followed Marxist assumptions believed that women could achieve full equality only by the full integration of labor and ownership. They argued that capitalism in typical patriarchal cultures placed a double burden on working women: not only did they work outside the home, they also remained the major source of domestic labor. The romantic or radical view upheld the notion of women and feminist values as inherently superior to men and patriarchal values.[167] Still other writers advocated some combination of two or three of these positions.

---

166. N. K. Gottwald, "Framing Biblical Interpretation at New York Theological Seminary: A Student Self-Inventory on Biblical Hermeneutics," in *Reading from This Place*, 1:251–61.

167. R. Reuther, *Sexism and God-Talk: Toward a Feminist Theology*, rev. ed. (Boston: Beacon, 1993), 41–45, 216–32.

With the demise of Communist socialism in so many parts of the world, feminist studies in the 1990s and 2000s, like liberation theology, has turned largely to different emphases. A better categorization of more recent feminist studies involves the role the Bible and Christianity play in their hermeneutics. Evangelical or biblical feminists believe that Scripture, at least in Genesis 1–2 (before the fall) and in the NT (after redemption), promotes full equality of the sexes and does not delineate any unique, timeless roles for husband vs. wife or male vs. female.[168] Nonevangelical Christian feminists agree with more traditional Christians that parts of the Bible, even before the fall or after redemption, promote patriarchalism and bar women from certain roles in the family and in the church (e.g., Eph 5:22–33; 1 Tim 2:11–15). But because of their prior commitment to a worldview that permits no such discrimination and seeks human liberation from all forms of oppression, these feminists will not accept such portions of Scripture as authoritative. Instead, they focus on other texts that do teach complete equality (e.g., Gen 1; Gal 3:28), regarding them as more "programmatic." They believe that "biblical revelation and truth are given only in those texts and interpretative models that transcend critically their patriarchal frameworks and allow for a vision of Christian women as historical and theological subjects and actors."[169] A third category of feminists finds Scripture so irredeemably chauvinist that they have abandoned any recognizable forms of Judaism or Christianity in favor of other religions, most notably, reviving an interest in the goddess worship of many ancient pagan cults.[170]

We may divide nonevangelical Christian feminism, which produces by far the largest quantity of feminist biblical scholarship, into three categories. The first is the "revisionist" or "neo-orthodox," well represented by Letty Russell and Rosemary Reuther, who distinguished the central contents of Scripture from its larger patriarchal form and believe that God speaks *through* the text of the Bible but that not all of Scripture is itself inspired. The second category involves those who hold to a "remnant" perspective, as particularly with Phyllis Trible, retrieving texts overlooked or distorted by patriarchal hermeneutics while recognizing that a majority of Scripture does (unacceptably, in their view) promote male headship in the domestic and religious spheres. Finally, there is the "reconstructive" or "liberationist" approach of Elisabeth

---

168. E.g., G. Bilezikian, *Beyond Sex Roles: What the Bible Says about a Woman's Place in Church and Family* (Grand Rapids: Baker, 2006); and A. B. Spencer, *Beyond the Curse: Women Called to Ministry* (Nashville: Thomas Nelson, 1985). A major organization, Christians for Biblical Equality, was organized to reflect this perspective. Cf. esp. R. M. Groothuis, R. W. Pierce, and G. D. Fee, eds., *Discovering Biblical Equality: Complementarity Without Hierarchy*, 2nd ed. (Downers Grove: InterVarsity, 2005).

169. E. Schüssler Fiorenza, *In Memory of Her: A Feminist Theological Reconstruction of Christian Origins*, 2nd ed. (New York: Crossroad, 1994), 30. Schüssler Fiorenza is generally held to be the primary founder of this wing of feminist hermeneutics. She has arguably also been its most prolific spokesperson, continuing to publish into her retirement. See also her *Wisdom Ways: Introducing Feminist Biblical Interpretation* (Maryknoll: Orbis, 2001).

170. Most notably, N. R. Goldberg, *Changing the Gods: Feminism and the End of Traditional Religions* (Boston: Beacon, 1979), from a Jewish background; and M. Daly, *Quintessence: Realizing the Archaic Future—A Radical Elemental Feminist Manifesto* (Boston: Beacon, 1998), from a Roman Catholic background. But both authors have virulently renounced their religious roots.

Schüssler Fiorenza, which views the societies of OT Israel and NT Christianity as more liberating than the later Jewish and Christian communities that grew out of them. So, they view more repressive portions of Scripture as stemming from transitional periods in which these liberating dimensions were already starting to be lost.[171]

Ironically, nonevangelical Christian feminists rarely ever acknowledge the existence of evangelical feminism, but lump all conservatives together (usually calling them fundamentalists) as hopelessly loyal to the entrenched patriarchy of the Bible. Conversely, those evangelicals who do believe the Bible promotes male headship as a timeless absolute often label evangelical feminists simply as liberals, without recognizing the vast difference in their use of Scripture as compared with nonevangelical feminists.[172] One of those huge differences is the general refusal of the evangelical feminists to speak of God as female even while recognizing feminine metaphors for God here and there in Scripture.[173] Thus biblical feminists become doubly marginalized. Even the term "feminist" has become so misleading that some who embraced it two or three decades ago now simply prefer to be called "egalitarian"—supporting the equality of the sexes. To compare liberal and evangelical feminist perspectives, under whatever label, on any given passage of Scripture, read the treatments of those texts in the one-volume women's Bible commentaries now available from those two scholarly communities: from a more liberal perspective see C. A. Newsom and S. H. Ringe, eds., *Women's Bible Commentary: Expanded Edition*,[174] and from a more conservative perspective C. C. Kroeger and M. J. Evans, eds., *The IVP Women's Bible Commentary*,[175] though these distinctions are by no means absolute.[176]

Feminists of all these various classifications have challenged numerous traditional interpretations of Scripture. They have argued that a better translation of "a helper suitable for" Adam (Gen 2:18) is "a partner corresponding to" (or even "superior to") him.[177] They have interpreted 1 Timothy 2:11–15 in the context of women teaching heresy, promoting fertility rites, or murdering men, and hence not mandating a timeless

---

171. E.g., C. Osiek, "The Feminist and the Bible: Hermeneutical Alternatives," in *Feminist Perspectives on Biblical Scholarship*, ed. A. Y. Collins (Chico, CA: Scholars, 1985), 93–105. This categorization continued to be endorsed, e.g., in E. K. Wondra, "By Whose Authority? The Status of Scripture in Contemporary Feminist Theologies," *AThR* 75 (1993): 83–101; and J. O. H. Amador, "Feminist Biblical Hermeneutics," *JAAR* 66 (1998): 39–57. Our summary is a synthesis of the taxonomies found in these three sources.

172. See esp. the various writings of W. Grudem, most explicitly articulated in *Evangelical Feminism: A New Path to Liberalism?* (Wheaton: Crossway, 2006).

173. See esp. V. R. Mollenkott, *The Divine Feminine: The Biblical Imagery of God as Female* (New York: Crossroad, 1983; Eugene, OR: Wipf & Stock, 2014).

174. 3rd ed. (Louisville: Westminster John Knox, 2012).

175. (Downers Grove: InterVarsity, 2002).

176. Evangelicals who believe in some form of male headship today prefer the less pejorative term "complementarian," believing that men's and women's roles complement each other while not remaining identical. A major anthology of complementarianism is J. Piper and W. Grudem, eds., *Recovering Biblical Manhood and Womanhood: A Response to Evangelical Feminism*, rev. ed. (Wheaton: Crossway, 2006). For two articulate defenses apiece of both major perspectives within evangelicalism, see J. R. Beck, ed., *Two Views on Women in Ministry*. rev. ed. (Grand Rapids: Zondervan, 2005).

177. Spencer, *Beyond the Curse*, 25.

prohibition that women are "not to teach or have authority over men" (v. 12).[178] They have called upon Bible readers to focus on the women in various texts, to read their stories through feminine eyes, so that we agonize over the rape of Tamar (2 Sam 13) or the dismemberment of the unnamed woman of Judges 19[179] or so that we reflect theologically on metaphors involving divine violence directed toward promiscuous women in the OT.[180] They ask us to question why five women appear in Matthew's genealogy of Jesus (Matt 1:1–18), all of whom are famous in Scripture for finding themselves in morally ambiguous situations.

One plausible answer to this last question—with which we agree—suggests that Matthew intends to stress that even the Messiah had such women in his ancestry and came to identify with and remove the stigma attached to them.[181] Feminists point out paradigms of wisdom, leadership, and authority like Ruth, Deborah, and Huldah, inviting readers to identify with the desire of these women for justice or their loyalty to family.[182] They may even come up with solutions to otherwise baffling problems, as with Lot's bizarre behavior in offering his virgin daughters to an unruly and seemingly homosexual mob. Was this an attempt to do something so jarring that it would defuse tension in a setting in which Lot knew the crowd was not interested in the young women but in which he also had the obligation to protect his heavenly sent houseguests (Gen 19:1–38)?[183]

As with liberation theology more generally, a feminist hermeneutic combines certain (to us) objectionable features with other highly commendable ones. When non-evangelical feminists create a canon within a canon to reject the authority of texts with which they disagree, they replace the Bible with some other external standard as their ultimate authority and, hence, differ from the perspective on Scripture we have defended in this volume. When evangelical feminists argue for lexically dubious interpretations of certain words (such as "suitable" meaning "superior" or "have

---

178. C. C. Kroeger promoted each of these views in a succession of articles. All may be found together in her book, co-authored with R. C. Kroeger, *I Suffer Not a Woman: Rethinking 1 Timothy 2:11–15 in Light of Ancient Evidence* (Grand Rapids: Baker, 1992). The Kroegers concluded that the best option for rendering 1 Tim 2:12 is "I do not allow a woman to teach nor to proclaim herself the author of man" (p. 103). For the complementarian side, see esp. A. J. Köstenberger and T. R. Schreiner, *Women in the Church: An Analysis and Application of 1 Timothy 2:9–15*, 2nd ed. (Grand Rapids: Baker, 2005).

179. P. Trible, *Texts of Terror: Literary-Feminist Readings of Biblical Narratives* (Philadelphia: Fortress, 1984).

180. J. C. Exum, "The Ethics of Biblical Violence against Women," in *The Bible in Ethics*, ed. J. W. Rogerson, M. Davies and M. D. Carroll R. (Sheffield: Sheffield Academic Press, 1995), 248–71.

181. C. L. Blomberg, "The Liberation of Illegitimacy: Women and Rulers in Matthew 1–2," *BTB* 21 (1991): 145–50. Cf. J. Schaberg, *The Illegitimacy of Jesus: A Feminist-Theological Interpretation of the Infancy Narratives*, rev. ed. (Sheffield: Sheffield Phoenix, 2006), 33, who, much more implausibly, goes on to argue that Jesus was in fact illegitimately conceived by Mary and another man (not Joseph). It also bears mentioning that three of the five are foreigners, an indication of Jesus' international ancestry and an advanced hint that the Gospel holds the door of the kingdom wide open for all peoples to enter it (Matt 28:19–20).

182. T. Cavalcanti, "The Prophetic Ministry of Women in the Hebrew Bible," in *Through Her Eyes: Women's Theology from Latin America*, ed. E. Tamez (Maryknoll: Orbis, 1989; Eugene, OR: Wipf & Stock, 2006), 118–39.

183. L. M. Bechtel, "Boundary Issues in Genesis 19.1–38," in *Escaping Eden: New Feminist Perspectives on the Bible*, ed. H. C. Washington, S. L. Graham, and P. Thimmes (Washington Square, NY: New York University Press; Sheffield: Sheffield Academic Press, 1999), 22–40.

authority" meaning "to engage in fertility rites"), they raise suspicions that their eagerness to make the text say something other than what they find objectionable has overwhelmed exegetical rigor, not to mention common sense. More liberal feminists have also rightly criticized more conservative ones for so stressing the liberating strands of the NT that the OT—and Judaism more generally—appear in an unnecessarily and inappropriately negative light.[184] On the other hand, when some of the more strident complementarians reject a demonstrably legitimate translation of a word (e.g., "assume authority" in 1 Tim 2:12) solely on the grounds that, from their perspective, it will be impossible to appeal to this text to argue for their point of view (which in this case is simply false),[185] then one realizes that a desire to buttress one's already established viewpoints rather than letting the biblical text speak for itself has become an interpreter's "bottom line." Gary Hoag, however, may well have demonstrated that the views associated with the worship of Artemis that would make 1 Timothy 2:11–15 situation-specific in its application, identified by the Kroegers but not previously found before the early third century, existed already by the middle of the first-century (in *Ephesiaca* by Xenophon of Ephesus).[186]

A new generation of evangelical egalitarians is quickly becoming much more responsible in its scholarship, avoiding some of the least persuasive suggestions of their predecessors. Some men and women alike are calling for a third way, neither classically complementarian nor classically egalitarian. Michelle Lee-Barnewall, for example, argues persuasively for a kind of servant leadership that stresses servanthood before leadership rather than simply using "servant" as an adjective to temper the noun "leadership," while they still focus primarily on leadership privileges and prerogatives as both complementarians and egalitarians typically have.[187] Indeed, one of us has repeatedly staked out positions that appear so centrist that he has been assured by

---

184. E.g., J. Plaskow, "Anti-Judaism in Feminist Christian Interpretation," in *Searching the Scriptures*, 2 vols., ed. E. Schüssler Fiorenza (New York: Crossroad, 1993), 1:117–29.

185. Wayne Grudem ("The English Standard Version [ESV]," in *Which Bible Translation Should I Use? A Comparison of 4 Major Recent Versions*, ed. A. J. Köstenberger and D. A. Croteau [Nashville: B&H, 2012], 72) insists that "the NIV committee failed to appreciate that evangelical feminists who want to become pastors are not going to take 'assume authority' in a positive sense at all. They will uniformly take it to prohibit wrongful 'self-assumed authority' and then say they are not 'assuming authority' on their own but just accepting it from the church. Consequently, 1 Timothy 2:12 in the NIV has become useless in the debate over women's roles in the church. In any church that adopts the 2011 NIV, no one will be able to answer their argument using this English Bible." This last sentence seems completely unfounded. All that is needed is a simple explanation about how scholars are divided on the meaning of *authentein* in this passage. Some think it refers only to the exercise of some wrongful kind of authority; others, to a positive use of authority as well. The Committee on Bible Translation for the NIV chose this particularly happy translation because one can "assume authority" both in a right way and when it is not one's to assume at all. Even the KJV rendered the verb "usurp authority," while John Calvin's commentary on this verse is translated "assume authority" in a context where the expression clearly has its positive sense! See the translation of his *Commentary on 1 Timothy* 2:12, accessed at http://www.ccel.org/ccel/calvin/calcom43.iii.iv.iv.html. His Latin translation of the text that he follows reads for v. 12: *Docere autem mulieri non permitto, neque auctoritatem sibi sumere in virum, sed quietam esse.*

186. G. G. Hoag, *Wealth in Ancient Ephesus and the First Letter to Timothy*, BBRSup 9 (Winona Lake: Eisenbrauns, 2016), 61–99.

187. M. Lee-Barnewall, *Neither Complementarian nor Egalitarian: A Kingdom Corrective to the Evangelical Gender Role Debate* (Grand Rapids: Zondervan, 2016).

others who are classic complementarians that he is most assuredly egalitarian and by classic egalitarians that he is most assuredly complementarian![188]

In any event, all Bible students would do well to reread Scripture through the windows of various feminist perspectives. They must be open to see if they have read texts in light of their own prevailing, patriarchal cultural biases (that is, traditionalists have preunderstandings, too, as we will discuss in ch. 5). For example, when biblical writers use the term "sinner" to describe men, no particular sin necessarily comes to mind. So why did traditional readings of Luke 7:36–50 almost automatically assume that the female "sinner" who anoints Jesus is a prostitute? The text itself scarcely demands that interpretation.[189] They must learn to hurt where oppressed women hurt and work together with them for a more just and compassionate world. They have to ask if elements of passages traditionally assumed to be universally timeless are indeed culture-bound instead.

That is quite different, however, from applying an interpretive canon-within-a-canon. We seek to acknowledge *every* text of Scripture as inspired and authoritative but recognize that both interpretations and applications often vary from one culture to the next. Today most Christians do not believe it is necessary for women to keep their heads covered while praying in church, any more than that all believers ought literally to wash each other's feet. Might there be equally good reasons for insisting that women have opportunities for teaching or having authority over men? The principles taught by each text must be applied today in culturally appropriate ways (see further our chapter on application).

Just as importantly, we need to recognize that women may read the Bible differently than men. Both may discover unique insights that emerge more clearly because of their specific gender. Both, too, may be blinded in some contexts because of their gender.[190] In other words, there are two issues at stake. First, the biblical texts themselves are culturally conditioned by the overwhelmingly patriarchal societies of their day. They reflect the world as it existed "back then." Interpreters must consider when this conditioning coincides with normative, divinely intended values and when it does not. Second, all readers are conditioned by their culture and gender and must exercise great care not to impose anachronistic, alien grids from high profile agenda items of modern society onto ancient texts.[191]

---

188. See C. L. Blomberg, "Neither Hierarchicalist nor Egalitarian: Gender Roles in Paul," in *Paul and His Theology*, Pauline Studies 3, ed. S. E. Porter (Leiden and Boston: Brill, 2006), 283–326; C. L. Blomberg, "Gender Roles in Marriage and Ministry: A Possible Relationship," in *Reconsidering Gender: Evangelical Perspectives*, ed. M. Habets and B. Wood (Eugene, OR: Pickwick, 2011), 48–62.

189. Thus rightly T. J. Hornsby, "Why Is She Crying? A Feminist Interpretation of Lk 7.36–50," in *Escaping Eden*, 91–103.

190. We have more on this in the discussion of "preunderstandings" in chap. 5.

191. For additional important works of feminist biblical interpretation, see L. M. Russell, ed., *Feminist Interpretation of the Bible* (Philadelphia: Westminster, 1985); A. L. Laffey, *An Introduction to the Old Testament: A Feminist Perspective* (Philadelphia: Fortress, 1988); L. Schottroff and M.-T. Wacker, eds., *Feminist Biblical Interpretation: A Compendium of Critical Commentary on the Books of the Bible and Related Literature* (Grand Rapids: Eerdmans,

LGBT[192] Hermeneutics

Many of the same points could be made about the approaches taken by lesbian, gay, bisexual and transgendered scholars and hermeneutics. Indeed, although no one to our knowledge has done so, it would appear that the identical taxonomy used with feminist hermeneutics of more liberal vs. more evangelical LGBT approaches along with the various subdivisions of the more liberal approaches could be meaningfully replicated for LGBT scholarship. The entire denomination known as the Metropolitan Community Church, for example, was founded in large part to provide a safe, supporting place for LGBT Christians. Apart from their understanding of the key biblical passages on homosexual behavior, the rest of their doctrine and ethic follows historic evangelical contours, and we acknowledge our spiritual kinship with them. Those who do not find all LGBT sexual behaviors sinful can likewise be subdivided into those who believe that classic interpretations of the key biblical texts are either mistaken or were meant to be applied in less than a timeless fashion to all homosexual relationships and those who believe that they do proscribe all gay sex in a timeless fashion but simply reject the Bible's teaching on that topic.

When evangelical feminism was younger, many of its critics predicted that it would just be a matter of time before the identical arguments would be applied to LGBT issues and used that prediction as one reason not to seriously consider feminism. They have turned out to be correct, even though the issues are by no means entirely the same. William Webb's book, *Slaves, Women, and Homosexuals*, which we mentioned in the last chapter and discuss more fully in our chapter on application, showed already in 2001 that there are various issues on which one can trace what he calls a redemptive trajectory throughout God's progressive revelation to humanity from the oldest parts of the OT to the end of the NT.[193] In the case of slavery, it is never commanded but is legislated for in the OT with what are often much more humane laws than in all the surrounding nations. In the NT it is never formally abolished, but the seeds are sown for its abolition in 1 Corinthians 7:21 and the letter to Philemon.[194]

In the case of women's roles, while it is arguable that women always were granted more dignity in ancient Israelite religion than many acknowledge, even on fairly traditional understandings of OT times, they are certainly more often given greater freedoms, responsibilities and leadership roles in the NT. In stark contrast, every reference to homosexual practice (as opposed to orientation) in both testaments

2012); and A. Sloane, ed., *Tamar's Tears: Evangelical Engagements with Feminist Old Testament Hermeneutics* (Eugene, OR: Cascade, 2012).

192. Often the acronym is enlarged to LGBTQ (lesbian, gay, bisexual, transgender, queer). Sometimes IA or IAA are also added, for intersex, asexual and ally.

193. W. J. Webb, *Slaves, Women, and Homosexuals: Exploring the Hermeneutics of Cultural Analysis* (Downers Grove: InterVarsity, 2001).

194. See esp. S. S. Bartchy, ΜΑΛΛΟΝ ΧΡΗΣΑΙ: *First-Century Slavery and 1 Corinthians 7:21* (Missoula: Scholars, 1973), repr. as *First-Century Slavery and 1 Corinthians 7:21* (Eugene, OR: Wipf & Stock, 2003); L. G. Lewis, "An African American Appraisal of the Philemon-Paul-Onesimus Triangle," in *Stony the Road We Trod*, ed. C. H. Felder (Minneapolis: Fortress, 1991), 232–46.

uniformly disapproves of it. Even if one adopted every interpretation that takes the key texts as referring only to homosexual rape, pederasty, ritual prostitution, or promiscuity, there still are no passages that even hint at LGBT sex as desirable or even permissible. The Bible lacks any portrayal of exemplary individuals in such relationships (for our view of the David-Jonathan example see below), although we do not deny the possibility that they may exist today. Instead, it seems clear to us that, while the patriarchs and Israelite kings practiced polygamy, the Bible subsequently assumes monogamous heterosexual marriage as typical and the required prerequisite to sexual relations (cf. Gen 2:24). Though by today's standards that pattern seems quaint and antiquated, in fact millions of heterosexual men and especially women throughout the centuries have remained celibate because they had no opportunity to marry, or even have a sexual partner.[195]

Of course, the phenomenon of human sexuality is complex and at times mysterious, and God's people should lament that we live in a fallen world where many people's desires on a wide range of deeply seated convictions remain unmet. Of course we should empathize with and support those, both heterosexuals and non-heterosexuals, who struggle to live as believers. Nevertheless, it seems quite unwise to set aside Scripture's teachings on sexual sin as somehow outmoded.[196] We do better to obey NT teachings and refrain from sex outside of monogamous, heterosexual marriage.

Permit us to comment on some recent interpretations of classic biblical themes and theology. In recent years an entire branch of "Queer" theology and hermeneutics has developed. The term "queer," once viewed as very derogatory, has been rehabilitated by the very community that not too many years ago took serious offense at it. In part the term serves to embrace all of the sexual minorities under one label and in part it is to mine the interpretive possibilities of the concept of queer (meaning strange) when applied to just about any strange or unusual feature of human behavior in Scripture. The biblical portraits of Jesus and Paul as standing apart from the norms of married life, deeply entrenched in ancient Judaism, have been said to make them queer. Misunderstandings of the nature of deep, loving, same-sex friendships like Ruth and Naomi, David and Jonathan, and even Jesus and his "beloved disciple" (probably the

---

195. If one points to the comparatively rare OT exceptions to standard marital ethics with polygamy, levirate marriage, and mandated divorce of pagan wives, one needs also to realize that there are *no* exceptions of these kinds for the NT Christian. Also, the OT exceptions all apparently concern only heterosexual relationships, and the first two are driven, respectively, by legitimate ancient concerns for having large families (i.e., enough "hands" to keep society alive and well) and for protecting inheritance rights (and perhaps the continuing existence of deceased ancestors). Additional rationales may have included the protection of women who would otherwise have been left without a male guardian, the need for more workers within an extended household's labor force, and the desire to preserve a family line.

196. See further esp. R. A. G. Gagnon, *The Bible and Homosexual Practice: Texts and Hermeneutics* (Nashville: Abingdon, 2001); L. L. Belleville, *Sex, Lies, and the Truth: Developing a Christian Ethic in a Post-Christian Society* (Eugene, OR: Wipf & Stock, 2010); J. Hallmann, *The Heart of Female Same-Sex Attraction: A Comprehensive Counseling Resource* (Downers Grove: InterVarsity, 2008); S. L. Jones and M. A. Yarhouse, *A Longitudinal Study of Religiously Mediated Change in Sexual Orientation* (Downers Grove: InterVarsity, 2007); and M. A. Yarhouse, *Understanding Gender Dysphoria: Navigating Transgender Issues in a Changing Culture* (Downers Grove: InterVarsity, 2015).

apostle John), lead to their relationships being labeled homosexual. Sometimes any stories that champion the outcast or marginalized, or that depict people behaving in countercultural or unusual ways, or that even use the language of "coming out" in contexts having nothing to do with sexuality (e.g., Lazarus coming out of his tomb) are said to promote queer theology.[197]

Classic Christian doctrines are also truncated, selectively defined, and redefined so that God is defined as the sending forth of radical love; revelation, as God's "coming out" as radical love and dissolving the boundaries between divine and human, weak and strong, conventional and deviant. In queer theology, sin becomes the rejection of this radical love, including the rejection of the legitimacy of all chosen forms of consensual self-expression among adults. Hospitality, in fact, may at times demonstrate love by offering one's body to another for sex, apart from any ongoing commitment to that individual. Atonement turns into the abolition of the barriers caused by scapegoating and the rejection of God's radical love. The church then becomes responsible to embody this love to the world. Classic biblical teaching on rewards and punishments in a life to come must be rejected or redefined so that the people most punished are those who reject queer hermeneutics and the radical redefinitions of historic teaching on which they insist.[198] We hasten to add that our inclusion of the above survey aims not simply to denigrate such interpretive views but to raise the question as to whether or not proper hermeneutical method supports them.

CONCLUSION

It is inevitably difficult for readers for whom some or all of these ideas under the various advocacy groups are new or possibly scandalous not to reject them out of hand without careful study of the rationales offered by those who propose them. In many cases, liberationist and feminist hermeneutics emerge out of suffering of a kind and scale that most Americans, particularly white males, have never experienced or even observed firsthand. When writers reflect the double marginalization of "womanist" (African-American feminism) or *"mujerista"* (Hispanic or Latina feminism) or other Majority World feminist theology, white men and women alike in the privileged West should try to read with great empathy, whether or not they ultimately agree with every hermeneutical or exegetical detail.[199] Historically, Christians and especially theologically conservative ones, have not expressed God's love well to those who identify themselves as LGBT. On the other side, sexual minorities (and majorities!) have often missed

---

197. For the most comprehensive treatment of biblical texts available, see D. Guest, et al., eds., *The Queer Bible Commentary* (London: SCM, 2006).

198. See further P. S. Cheng, *Radical Love: An Introduction to Queer Theology* (New York: Seabury, 2011); and P. S. Cheng, *From Sin to Amazing Grace: Discovering the Queer Christ* (New York: Seabury, 2012).

199. See esp. M. J. Smith, *I Found God in Me: A Womanist Biblical Hermeneutics Reader* (Eugene, OR: Cascade, 2015); A. M. Isasi-Díaz, *Mujerista Theology: A Theology for the Twenty-First Century* (Maryknoll: Orbis, 1996); M. W. Dube, *Other Ways of Reading: African Women and the Bible* (Atlanta: SBL; Geneva: WCC, 2001); and K. Pui-lan, *Introducing Asian Feminist Theology* (Cleveland: Pilgrim, 2000).

the fact that God's unconditional love for his people does not mean that he approves of everything they do. Neither does our unconditional love for a brother or sister in Christ, whether heterosexual or not, mean that we are absolved of the responsibility of gently pointing them back to God's Word and lovingly challenging what we deem to be foolish choices that will hurt them and perhaps others in the long run. We must nevertheless accept that before God we are all sinners unworthy of God's love and humbly leave final judgment to God who alone will judge all of us perfectly justly.

All the writers of this textbook can personally testify that extensive travel and living in Majority World cultures, or among the urban or rural poor of North America, along with our ever increasing experiences with women and sexual minorities has often made us question standard but culturally biased interpretations of various passages.[200] For example, one of us was particularly challenged by a Majority World Christian who called his attention to the oft-abused passage, "the poor you will always have with you" (Mark 14:7)—a quote by Jesus of a text from the Law commanding generous care for the poor (Deut 15:11). Even the most sensitive North American Christian is likely to read this text from the viewpoint of the benefactor—we always have time and obligation to help the needy. Quite differently, the impoverished Majority World Christian living in a regime that abuses human rights will more likely see it as a tragic reminder that there will always be oppressors in the world for God to judge! We must take the time to listen to divergent readings of Scripture from our Christian brothers and sisters around the globe, and particularly from women, various kinds of minorities, and the poor. As we do so, we will be both convicted and renewed.[201] And in some instances, we will have our traditional understandings strengthened and reinforced. Not all traditions need be wrong; if they were, then today's novelties would also all be wrong once they become entrenched and thus traditional!

Like the literary readings surveyed in the first half of this chapter, we will have to assess each social-scientific reading, whether of social history or from one of the advocacy movements, on a case-by-case basis according to its own merits. Not all will prove legitimate or helpful, but those that do can expand our horizons of biblical understanding considerably. If our footnotes have been a little fuller in this chapter than in a number of other parts of our book, it is to help readers begin to embark on precisely that enterprise.

---

200. Cf. esp. E. R. Richards and B. J. O'Brien, *Misreading Scripture with Western Eyes: Removing Cultural Blinders to Better Understand the Bible* (Downers Grove: InterVarsity, 2012).

201. See also the ongoing series of commentaries from Sheffield Academic Press entitled A Feminist Companion to the Bible; the newly unfolding Africa Bible Commentary Series from Zondervan, Word Alive, ACTS and Hippo Books; and the one-volume commentary, B. Wintle and H. Dharamraj, eds., *South Asia Bible Commentary* (Grand Rapids: Zondervan, 2015).

4

THE CANON AND TRANSLATIONS

THE BIBLICAL CANON

The word "canon" comes from the Greek *kanōn*, meaning "list," "rule," or "standard." The canon of Scripture refers to the collection of biblical books that Christians accept as uniquely authoritative. We accept it, but how do we know we have the right collection of books? Why do these sixty-six writings command our (i.e., Protestant) attention but not others? Did any other books ever compete for inclusion in the canon, and if so, why were they excluded? The question of which books belong in the Bible becomes crucial for a study of hermeneutics that asserts that certain documents, and only those documents, remain normative for all believers. Our discussion becomes all the more urgent because Protestants, Catholics, and Orthodox Christians have never agreed on the extent of the OT. What is more, many Christians from mainline denominations today suggest that, although all branches of Christianity traditionally have agreed on the contents of the NT (since at least the fourth c.), the criteria for that agreement may no longer be acceptable. Some would argue that other ancient Christian and even gnostic writings are as valuable as parts of the canonical NT.[1] In the first half of this chapter we will sketch, in turn, the rise of the OT canon, the development of the NT canon, the criteria of canonicity, and the implications for hermeneutics of the methodology known as canon criticism.

The Biblical Canon: The Central Questions
What is the "standard" for determining what God has revealed?
What constitutes Scripture?[2]

---

1. The most notable recent development along these lines is the publication of *A New New Testament: A Bible for the Twenty-First Century*, ed. H. Taussig (Boston: Houghton Mifflin Harcourt, 2013). Nineteen self-appointed "spiritual leaders" (scholars, pastors, and rabbis) created a "New Orleans Council" to discuss non-canonical works they believed were written by AD 175 and voted to add ten of them, nine of which were largely gnostic, to the 27 traditional books to create an enlarged canon.

2. B. D. Sommer argues that what constitutes "Scripture" is largely a question within Christianity (especially Protestant Christianity), for in Judaism it is a more fluid category, including not only the *Tanakh* (what Christians call the OT) but also rabbinic literature. See B. D. Sommer, ed., *Jewish Concepts of Scripture: A Comparative Introduction* (New York; London: New York University Press, 2012), 2–14.

THE CANON OF THE OLD TESTAMENT

The Development of the Canon

Since the Reformation, Protestants have accepted the thirty-nine books, from Genesis to Malachi, that appear in the standard editions of the Bible in print today. Roman Catholics and Eastern Orthodox Christians, however, preserve various so-called apocryphal (from the Greek word for "hidden") or deutero-canonical (a "second canon") books that were influential throughout the first 1500 years of church history.[3] These books include such works as 1 and 2 Esdras, Tobit, Judith, the Wisdom of Solomon, Ecclesiasticus (also called the Wisdom of Jesus ben Sira[ch], and not to be confused with Ecclesiastes), Baruch, the Letter of Jeremiah, the Prayer of Azariah and the Song of the Three Young Men, Susanna, Bel and the Dragon, the Prayer of Manasseh, and 1 and 2 Maccabees. Some of these works are historical in nature: 1 and 2 Maccabees describe the history of key portions of second-century BC Israel, while 1 Esdras largely reduplicates material found in Chronicles, Ezra, and Nehemiah. Second Esdras is an apocalypse of secret revelations purportedly given to Ezra. The two books of Wisdom somewhat resemble the canonical book of Proverbs. Baruch resembles parts of the prophecy of Jeremiah, and the Letter of Jeremiah could be characterized as an impassioned sermon based on the canonical text of Jeremiah 11:10. The two Prayers represent devotional literature. The remaining books are (at least partially) legendary novels illustrating virtue and vice by means of their main characters. The three works known as Susanna, the Prayer of Azariah and the Song of the Three Young Men, and Bel and the Dragon all appear as subsections within a longer form of the book of Daniel. Apocryphal additions to Esther also exist.[4]

Protestants have defended the shorter OT canon, asserting that these thirty-nine books were the only books that the Jews of the time of Christ and the apostles accepted as their canon of Scripture. The other books, presumably though not demonstrably all of Jewish origin (some exist now only in Greek or Latin and not Hebrew), date from the intertestamental period after the time of Malachi. The Jews never believed they were inspired in the same way as the earlier biblical books. In fact, widespread testimony in later rabbinic literature (primarily from the second through fifth centuries after Christ), as well as in Josephus (a first-century Jewish historian), outlines the Jewish belief that prophecy (or at least divinely inspired writings) ceased after the time of Ezra, Nehemiah, and the latest of the Minor Prophets: Haggai, Zechariah,

---

3. For a complete list of the OT canons of the Roman Catholic Church and each of the various Eastern Orthodox churches, see H. P. Rüger, "The Extent of the Old Testament Canon," *BT* 40 (1989): 301–8.

4. A standard edition of the Apocrypha can be found in the *The New Oxford Annotated NRSV Apocrypha*, 4th ed., ed. M. D. Coogan (New York: Oxford University Press, 2010). Three excellent introductions and surveys of these books are D. J. Harrington, *Invitation to the Apocrypha* (Grand Rapids: Eerdmans, 1999); D. A. de Silva, *Introducing the Apocrypha* (Grand Rapids: Baker, 2002); and O. Kaiser, *Introduction to the Old Testament Apocrypha* (Peabody: Hendrickson, 2004). Two major commentary series, The Anchor Bible (Garden City: Doubleday) and Hermeneia (Minneapolis: Fortress) are somewhat unique in including volumes on the Apocrypha as well as the OT and NT. The smaller *New Interpreter's Bible Commentary* (Nashville: Abingdon) does also.

and Malachi (see esp. Josephus, *Ag. Ap.* 1.40–41; b. Sanh. 22a).[5] This means that no book dated later than about 450–400 BC could be considered part of the Hebrew Scriptures, and, therefore, part of the Christian OT. Such claims should not unduly denigrate the apocryphal books, for they provide valuable information about historical and theological developments between the testaments and often prove inspiring, even if not inspired, reading (for the evidence for the actual contents of the OT canon, see below). One should remember that Roman and Orthodox belief in some of these works as authoritative stems from a later period, removed by at least a century from the NT era, when Christianity had largely lost sight of its Jewish roots.[6]

Since the pioneering work of A. C. Sundberg, however, it is often argued that, because the NT reflects widespread use of the Septuagint (the Greek OT, abbreviated LXX), which included much of the Apocrypha, first-century Christians must therefore have believed in the canonical status of apocryphal works.[7] However, the NT authors never quote these works directly as they do the rest of the OT. With LaSor, Hubbard, and Bush, "it is probably safe to assume that the Old Testament they used [in terms of the books it contained] was identical with that known today."[8] The evidence of Philo and Josephus points in the same direction. Lee McDonald disputes these claims, citing numerous possible allusions to the Apocrypha in the NT,[9] but none appears as unequivocally as the numerous direct quotations of undisputed OT literature. What is more, not even the fairly obvious allusions to apocryphal books (e.g., Wis 15:7 in Rom 9:21 or Sir 51:23–27 in Matt 11:28–30) convincingly prove that early Christians viewed these works as canonical. Paul, for example, alluded to Greek poets and prophets (Acts 17:28; Titus 1:12), and Jude quoted the pseudepigrapha (other Jewish intertestamental literature) on two different occasions (vv. 9, 14), even though Christians never claimed canonicity for any of these sources.[10]

The LXX, which contains the Apocrypha, originated among Greek-speaking Jews in Egypt. It probably became popular among early Christians because they could read Greek but not Hebrew. So they naturally became familiar with the Apocryphal books.

---

5. Josephus also suggests that the Scriptures did not contain insuperable contradictions, that they were inspired by God, and that they therefore functioned authoritatively. See P. D. Wegner, T. L. Wilder, and D. L. Bock, "Do We Have the Right Canon?" in *In Defense of the Bible: A Comprehensive Apologetic for the Authority of Scripture*, ed. S. B. Cowan and T. L. Wilder (Nashville: B&H, 2013), 402.

6. The fullest exposition of the traditional Protestant defense within the past generation is R. Beckwith, *The Old Testament Canon of the New Testament Church* (Grand Rapids: Eerdmans, 1985), to which this paragraph is largely indebted.

7. A. C. Sundberg, Jr., *The Old Testament of the Early Church* (Cambridge, MA: Harvard University Press, 1964).

8. W. S. LaSor, D. A. Hubbard, F. W. Bush, *Old Testament Survey* (Grand Rapids: Eerdmans, 1982), 21. Curiously, the 1996 edition so revises the treatment of canon that this sentence never appears.

9. L. M. McDonald, *The Formation of the Christian Biblical Canon*, 2nd ed. (Peabody: Hendrickson, 1995), 45, 259–67 (this list also contains possible allusions to the Pseudepigrapha—other intertestamental Jewish literature never canonized by anyone). A more modest and convincing list and discussion of possible allusions appears in B. M. Metzger, *An Introduction to the Apocrypha* (New York: Oxford, 1957), 158–70.

10. For a response to the view that the earliest church fathers viewed the Apocrypha as canonical, see Beckwith, *Canon*, 386–95.

The Jewish canon, however, seems to have been decided by rabbis in Palestine, so Jews there never even got to know these works. But Christians often came to value the Apocrypha for hermeneutically illegitimate reasons. Even as early Christian interpreters often read into OT texts allegorical and Christological meaning that the original authors could not have intended (see ch. 2), so also the apocryphal books were often preserved and cherished because of "Christian readings" of them, which in retrospect we can see were not valid. For example, the Wisdom of Solomon contains the verse, "Blessed is the wood through which righteousness comes" (14:7). In context, it refers to Noah's ark, but early Christians prized it as an apparent prediction of the cross of Christ. Baruch 3:36–37 speaks of God who "found the whole way to knowledge," which "afterward appeared on earth and lived among people." In context, the author personifies God's knowledge as a woman, much as wisdom appears in Proverbs 9, but many church fathers interpreted the passage as a reference to Christ's incarnation. From the second century onward, a majority of them increasingly accepted the Apocrypha as canonical, although a minority (including esp. Jerome) argued for following the Jewish canon. But the sixteenth-century Reformation returned resoundingly to the Jewish Bible of Jesus and the apostles (and of Jerome).

The patristic misreadings of the Apocrypha already noted seem harmless enough, but in other instances the question of whether or not the Apocrypha should be viewed as canonical takes on greater significance. Probably the most famous example comes from 2 Maccabees 12:44–45, which extols the virtue of praying for the dead to help make atonement for them. From this text, more than from any other, developed the Roman Catholic practice of praying for those who died in hopes of speeding their way through purgatory and on to heaven. No NT text, however, clearly speaks of the existence of purgatory, so Protestants typically reject its existence.[11] Both Paul (Phil 1:23) and one of the men next to Jesus on the cross (Luke 23:43) expected to be with Christ immediately after death.

Modern scholars, Protestant and Catholic alike, often admit that some ancient Christian uses of the Apocrypha were inappropriate.[12] Nevertheless, many still challenge the inviolability of the Protestant canon.[13] Again, particularly since Sundberg, many claim that the Jews of Jesus' day did not have a fixed collection of authoritative Scriptures.[14] All agree that the five books of the Law (Genesis to Deuteronomy) became canonical at least by the time of Ezra's reading of the Law or the time of the Samaritan schism with Israel (because Samaritans accepted only the Law as canonical) ca. 500–400 BC. The writings of the Prophets, which included Joshua, Judges,

---

11. An important exception is evangelical J. L. Walls, *Heaven, Hell, and Purgatory: Rethinking the Things that Matter Most* (Grand Rapids: Brazos, 2015).

12. See esp. the introductions and annotations to the apocryphal books and the above-cited texts in Coogan, ed., *Apocrypha*. This edition is accepted by Protestants and Catholics alike.

13. See, e.g., most of the contributors to the section on OT canon in L. M. McDonald and J. A. Sanders, eds., *The Canon Debate* (Peabody: Hendrickson, 2002).

14. Sundberg, *Old Testament*, 107–69.

Samuel, and Kings, as well as Isaiah through Malachi (minus Daniel), were probably all recognized as uniquely authoritative at least by 200 BC. All appear, for example, among the Dead Sea Scrolls at Qumran, which date from that time onward. They were translated into Greek (the Septuagint or LXX) as part of the Hebrew Scriptures by this same time, and the prologue to Ecclesiasticus, probably written no later than the mid-100s BC, refers to both Law and Prophets as Scripture.[15] Certainly, conservatives and liberals differ widely as to the authorship and therefore dating of many of the OT books.[16] But even if the dates of the acceptance of the Law and Prophets are as late as the critical consensus outlined here claims, they still well predate Jesus and the apostles, and the traditional Protestant argument remains persuasive.[17]

More intense controversy attends the third traditional division of the Hebrew Scriptures: the Writings. This catchall category includes all of the books not classified as Law or Prophecy: Ruth, Chronicles, Ezra, Nehemiah, Esther, Job, Psalms, Proverbs, Ecclesiastes, Song of Songs, Lamentations, and Daniel. Many argue that the Writings may have included at different times any or all of the Apocrypha, and that the canon of the OT was not limited to the books Protestants now accept until after the proceedings of a Jewish council at Jamnia (also spelled Jabneh or Javneh) in approximately AD 90 (and perhaps considerably later than that).[18] In other words, some assert that the OT canon was not decisively determined within Judaism until the end of the writing of the NT books. This view may agree that it is logical to follow Jesus' lead in treating as Scripture what he, with Jews of his day, accepted as Scripture. However, they insist that we simply cannot know which books he would have had embraced.

Though this view of the OT canon often prevails in many scholarly circles today, it is improbable. A closer examination of what occurred at Jamnia shows that, more likely, discussions there dealt with challenges to and questions about books that were already widely established as canonical.[19] A variety of quotations from writers no later than the mid-first century AD strongly suggests that the Writings as well as the Law and Prophets were already fixed in number at an earlier time. Josephus speaks of "only 22" books "containing the record of all time and justly accredited" (*Ag. Ap.* 1.38–41). He goes on to specify the five books of Moses (the Law) and thirteen books of prophecy and history, which from later Jewish lists we can reconstruct as Joshua, Judges and Ruth (as one book), 1 and 2 Samuel (as one), 1 and 2 Kings

15. See esp. E. E. Ellis, *The Old Testament in Early Christianity: Canon and Interpretation in the Light of Modern Research* (Tübingen: Mohr, 1991; Grand Rapids: Baker, 1992).

16. E.g., contrast the evangelical text by R. B. Dillard and T. Longman, III, *An Introduction to the Old Testament*, 2nd ed. (Grand Rapids: Zondervan, 2006) with the liberal counterpart by J. J. Collins, *Introduction to the Hebrew Bible* (Minneapolis: Fortress, 2004).

17. The fullest survey of proposals appears in S. B. Chapman, *The Law and the Prophets: A Study in Old Testament Canon Formation*, FAT 27 (Tübingen: Mohr Siebeck, 2000). Chapman also argues that a core of the Law and Prophets began to emerge together as canonical Scripture already in the mid-sixth century BC.

18. See, e.g., A. C. Sundberg, Jr., "The Septuagint: The Bible of Hellenistic Judaism," in *Canon Debate*, 68–90.

19. See esp. J. P. Lewis, "Jamnia after Forty Years," *HUCA* 70–71 (1999–2000): 233–59.

(as one), 1 and 2 Chronicles (as one), Ezra and Nehemiah (as one), Esther, Job, Isaiah, Jeremiah and Lamentations (as one), Ezekiel, Daniel, and the Twelve Minor Prophets (as one). "The remaining four books," Josephus concludes, "contain hymns to God and principles of life for human beings." These would be Psalms, Proverbs, Ecclesiastes, and Song of Songs.

Luke 24:44 recognizes a similar threefold division of the Hebrew canon ("the Law of Moses and the Prophets and Psalms"), as does the earlier first-century Jewish writer Philo ("the Laws, and Oracles given by inspiration through the Prophets, and the Psalms and the other books whereby knowledge and piety are increased and completed"; *On the Contemplative Life*, 25). The Greek prologue to the important apocryphal book of Jewish Wisdom, Ecclesiasticus, already in the mid-second century BC specified "the Law and the Prophets and the other books of the fathers." At Qumran copies of all of the undisputed OT books (except Esther) have been found, but only three of the Apocrypha—Tobit, small fragments of Ecclesiasticus and a few lines of the Letter of Jeremiah—though of course the existence of a book within the Dead Sea sect's library does not by itself prove (or disprove) its canonicity. And one of the most recently translated Dead Sea Scrolls (4Q397) refers to the need to understand "the books of Moses [and] the book[s of the pr]ophets and Davi[d . . .]." Of course, we cannot be sure of the exact contents of those sections summed up as "David" (or in Luke or Philo as "the Psalms").

The interpretation of this and other evidence remains disputed, but Sid Leiman, from a Jewish perspective, followed by Roger Beckwith from a Christian perspective, sets out all the texts in great detail, including many later rabbinic discussions.[20] Leiman and Beckwith plausibly conclude that the entire twenty-two book canon (following Josephus's enumeration) was already well established before the writing of Ecclesiasticus in the mid-second century BC. Even more common are references to twenty-four books, but ancient lists make it clear that this number results simply from dividing Judges and Ruth, and Jeremiah and Lamentations, into two parts. Attempts to deny the significance of widespread belief in the cessation of prophecy (again found as early as the second century BC in, e.g., 1 Macc 9:27) point out that not every Jew shared this belief.[21] But such attempts do not successfully dislodge the convincing Protestant claim that most first-century Jews recognized no inspired and canonical writers after the fifth-century BC.[22] Less certain, but still plausible, is the additional proposal of Leiman and Beckwith that the final collection of these books and the separation of the Prophets and Writings into distinct categories occurred at the time of and under the influence of the great Jewish revolutionary hero, Judas

---

20. S. Z. Leiman (*The Canonization of Hebrew Scripture: The Talmudic and Midrashic Evidence*, 2nd ed. [New Haven, CT: Connecticut Academy of Arts, 1991], 51–124) lays out all the rabbinic texts. Beckwith (*Canon*, 16–104) discusses the nature of the witnesses and their sources.

21. See esp. F. E. Greenspahn, "Why Prophecy Ceased," *JBL* 108 (1989): 37–49.

22. See esp. B. D. Sommer, "Did Prophecy Cease? Evaluating a Reevaluation," *JBL* 115 (1996): 31–47.

Maccabeus, in the 160s BC (cf. 2 Macc 2:13–15).[23] Second Maccabees 2:14–15 refers to Judas collecting the books that had been lost because of the war against Antiochus Epiphanes; the most natural interpretation is that these would have been the Jews' Scriptures, many copies of which had been destroyed.[24]

On this view, later rabbinic debates focus more on matters of interpretation than of canonization. The five books that appear in those discussions are Proverbs, Ecclesiastes, Ezekiel, Song of Songs, and Esther. Rabbis raised questions about these books because of the apparent contradiction in Proverbs 26:4–5, the tension between Ezekiel's picture of the new temple (Ezek 40–48) and early biblical commands about God's sanctuary, the seeming "secularity" of Ecclesiastes and Song of Songs, and the lack of reference to God in Esther coupled with its institution of a new, non-Mosaic festival (Purim). The only apocryphal book discussed was Ecclesiasticus, which the Rabbis deemed too late to be canonical.[25] To be sure, in later centuries, after the writing down and codification of the Oral Law (first in the Mishnah about AD 200 and then in the greatly expanded Jerusalem and Babylonian Talmuds of the fourth and sixth centuries), there was a sense in which these works too were treated as canonical. But all this substantially postdates NT times, and even then most rabbis apparently still accorded a privileged place to the original written Torah (our OT).[26]

The Order of the Canon

It is reasonable, therefore, to conclude that the Jews agreed upon the boundaries of the Hebrew canon in NT times. The order of its books, however, is less clear, largely because at that time individual documents were still written on separate scrolls. One ancient Jewish tradition, possibly the oldest, puts the order as: the Law (Genesis-Deuteronomy), the Prophets (Joshua, Judges, Samuel, Kings, Jeremiah, Ezekiel, Isaiah, and the Twelve Minor Prophets), and the Writings (Ruth, Psalms, Job, Proverbs, Ecclesiastes, Song of Songs, Lamentations, Daniel, Esther, Ezra-Nehemiah, and Chronicles) (see the Talmud tractate: b. B. Bat. 14b). This arrangement sometimes proceeds chronologically (Joshua–Kings; Daniel–Nehemiah), and sometimes thematically (Ruth ends with David's genealogy, a fitting introduction for the Psalms of David; Chronicles sums up almost all of OT history).

Modern Hebrew Bibles preserve the order, Law, Prophets, and Writings, but

23. Leiman, *Canonization*, 29; Beckwith, *Canon*, 152. S. Dempster ("'An Extraordinary Fact': Torah and Temple and the Contours of the Hebrew Canon," *TynBul* 48 [1997]: 23–56, 191–218) has pointed to phenomena particularly at the beginning and end of each of the three parts of the Hebrew canon that suggest one discrete stage of conscious, thematic editing of a final, canonical form of the Hebrew Bible at the end of the biblical period itself. Even allowing for a late date for Daniel, this, too, would place us no later than the mid-second century BC. Cf. also his "Canons on the Right and Canons on the Left: Finding Resolution in the Canon Debate," *JETS* 52 (2009): 47–77.

24. A. van der Kooij, "Canonization of Ancient Hebrew Books and Hasmonaean Politics," in *The Biblical Canons*, ed. J.-M. Auwers and H. J. de Jonge (Leuven: Leuven University Press, 2003), 27–38.

25. Beckwith, *Canon*, 283–91, 318–23.

26. D. Kraemer, "The Formation of Rabbinic Canon: Authority and Boundaries," *JBL* 110 (1991): 613–30.

change the sequence of some of the books within the last two categories.[27] English Bibles are based on the arrangement of the Greek translation of the OT (LXX), in which the Prophets and Writings are interspersed within each other in order to create a past-present-future sequence: Genesis through Esther describes the history first of the human race and then of Israel from creation to the fifth century BC; Job through Song of Songs includes psalms and wisdom for present living; and Isaiah through the Twelve preserves that form of prophecy that is mostly proclamation (foretelling and forthtelling) rather than historical narrative.[28] The order of these books of prophecy sometimes follows chronological considerations and sometimes decreasing length of the documents.

THE CANON OF THE NEW TESTAMENT

The Development of the Canon

Clearly one may not appeal to the teaching of Jesus to determine which books belong in the NT even if he did hint of future Spirit-inspired Scripture (a possible inference from John 14:26; 15:26). One might expect, therefore, less agreement among Christians as to the boundaries of the NT than to the limits of the OT, but in fact, historically, there has been much more unanimity. Still, agreement did not appear instantly in the formation of the NT canon.[29]

Since the first Christians inherited a "complete" Bible from the Jews, it might seem surprising that they were willing to add *any* books to what they termed Scripture. But in viewing Jesus as the fulfillment and authoritative interpreter of the Hebrew Scriptures (based on Jesus' own claims in Matt 5:17–20), they already had relativized somewhat the value of those writings. Increasingly, the story of Jesus and the preaching of the gospel took on greater significance. So it was natural for them to write down the story and message about Jesus and, within a generation or two, to view them at least as authoritatively, if not more so, than the previous writings that they believed had prepared the way for that gospel. OT history provided a precedent with Deuteronomy and the Prophets as commentators or "appliers" of the earlier Laws of Moses.[30] The concept of covenants proved instructive, too. Jeremiah had prophesied about a coming new covenant (Jer 31:31–34), which Jesus and the NT

---

27. For details, see F. F. Bruce, *The Canon of Scripture* (Leicester and Downers Grove: InterVarsity, 1988), 29.

28. The reason Jews could include historical books as part of "prophecy" stems from their understanding of a prophet more broadly, as an accredited teacher of moral law. See esp. J. Barton, *Oracles of God: Perceptions of Ancient Prophecy in Israel After the Exile* (Oxford: Oxford University Press, 1986). For one plausible explanation of the sequence of the Twelve Minor Prophets, see P. R. House, *The Unity of the Twelve* (Sheffield: Almond, 1990), 63–109. House sees a progression from the themes of covenant and cosmic sin in Hosea through Micah to covenant and cosmic punishment in Nahum to Zephaniah climaxing in hope for restoration in Haggai to Malachi.

29. The best overviews are Bruce, *Canon*; D. G. Dunbar, "The Biblical Canon," in *Hermeneutics, Authority, and Canon*, ed. D. A. Carson and J. D. Woodbridge (Grand Rapids: Zondervan, 1986), 315–42; and B. M. Metzger, *The Canon of the New Testament: Its Origin, Development, and Significance* (Oxford: Clarendon, 1987).

30. The independence of the OT writing prophets from the Law has often been asserted, but see B. S. Childs, *Biblical Theology of the Old and New Testaments* (Minneapolis: Fortress, 1992), 174–75.

writers claimed that his death established (Luke 22:20; 2 Cor 3:6; Heb 8:8–13). If the older covenant with Moses led to a collection of written Scriptures, it would be natural to expect God to guide Christian writers to inscribe a newer collection of Scriptures. This kind of reasoning seems to be implied by the discussions near the end of the second century in Tertullian (*Against Marcion* 4:1) and Clement of Alexandria (*Miscellanies* 1:9; 3:11; 4:21; 5:13).

1 Timothy 5:18 cites Luke 10:7 as authoritative (cf. 1 Corinthians 9:14):
"The worker deserves his wages."
2 Peter 3:16 considers some of Paul's writings as Scripture:
"He [Paul] writes the same way in all his letters, speaking in them of these matters. His letters contain some things that are hard to understand, which ignorant and unstable people distort, as they do the *other Scriptures*, to their own destruction."

Yet belief in the Gospels, Acts, Epistles, and Revelation as Scripture began to emerge much earlier than the second century. Two of the later NT writings refer to earlier Christian works as Scripture (1 Tim 5:18, quoting Luke 10:7;[31] 2 Pet 3:16, referring to an unknown number of Paul's Epistles). Although some critics date 1 Timothy and 2 Peter well into the second century, a fair number of scholars recognize that late first-century dates are more probable, and in our view the traditional views that put them in the sixties still commend themselves.[32]

The earliest noncanonical Christian literature dates from about AD 90 through the mid-second century and is referred to as the Apostolic Fathers.[33] (This title is somewhat misleading because it refers to the generations immediately *following* the apostolic era.) These works include numerous epistles from early church leaders to various Christian individuals or communities.[34] Like the NT Epistles, these letters give instruction concerning various aspects of Christian living. For the most part they follow the teaching of the NT writers, though newer developments emerge, for example, a growing preoccupation with the virtue of martyrdom or an increasing

31. Some would argue that "Scripture" applies only to the quotation of Deut 25:4 in the first half of 1 Tim 5:18, but this is not a natural reading of the verse. I. H. Marshall (*A Critical and Exegetical Commentary on the Pastoral Epistles*, with P. H. Towner, ICC rev. [Edinburgh: T&T Clark, 1999], 615) comments, "for the author the second citation had equal authority with the OT."

32. For the Pastorals, see esp. L. T. Johnson, *Letters to Paul's Delegates* (Valley Forge: Trinity Press International, 1996); expanded in L. T. Johnson, *The First and Second Letters to Timothy*, AB (New York; London: Doubleday, 2001). For 2 Peter, see J. D. Charles, *Virtue amidst Vice: The Catalog of Virtues in 2 Peter 1*, JSNTSup 150 (Sheffield: Sheffield Academic Press, 1997), 11–37; G. L. Green, *Jude and 2 Peter*, BECNT (Grand Rapids: Baker, 2008), 139–50.

33. The best introduction and translation is that of M. W. Holmes, trans. and ed., *The Apostolic Fathers in English*, 3rd ed. (Grand Rapids: Baker, 2006). For the Greek text see, M. W. Holmes, *The Apostolic Fathers: Greek Texts and English Translations*, 3rd ed. (Grand Rapids: Baker Academic, 2007).

34. E.g., from Clement of Rome to Corinth; from Ignatius to Ephesus, Magnesia, Tralles, Rome, Philadelphia, Smyrna, and to St. Polycarp; from Polycarp to the Philippians; from an unknown author to one Diognetus; and from an unknown author taking the pseudonym of Barnabas to a general Christian audience.

emphasis on an episcopal church hierarchy. Additional works include a more or less historical narrative of the Martyrdom of Polycarp; a manual called The Teaching of the Twelve Apostles (or the Didache) on church order, especially regarding baptism, the Eucharist, and false prophets; and a series of commands, parables, and visions allegedly given by God to a Christian writer known as Hermas the Shepherd, replete with instruction on the themes of purity and repentance.

In various parts of the Roman Empire, the writings of Barnabas, Hermas, and perhaps Clement and the Didache seem to have gained a brief following among some Christians who prized them as highly as other books that eventually became part of our NT. Yet this status never included a majority of Christians and was relatively short-lived. A study of many of the Apostolic Fathers in fact reveals that their authors were conscious that they lacked the authority of the apostolic writings.[35] In addition, they liberally quoted and alluded to those earlier books in ways that acknowledged their greater authority and, at times, their scriptural status. For example, Ignatius, bishop of Smyrna, wrote to the Trallians in the early second century, "I did not think myself qualified for this, that I . . . should give you orders as though I were an apostle" (3:3). A generation or two later 2 Clem. 2:4 quoted Mark 2:17 verbatim, after a citation of Isaiah, with the introduction "another Scripture says." Not surprisingly, the Apostolic Fathers most often cited the words of Jesus in ways that suggested they viewed them as of the highest authority.[36]

In the middle of the second century, the first major impetus to the explicit discussion of a Christian canon came from the heretic Marcion.[37] Marcion believed that Jesus and the God of the OT were opposites, and that anything in Christian writings that smacked of Judaism ought to be expunged. He therefore promoted a "canon" of edited versions of the Gospel of Luke and various Epistles of Paul, but nothing else. The rise of gnostic writings, also beginning about the mid-second century, provided a further stimulus. Many of these purported to contain secret revelations from Jesus, following his resurrection, to one or more of his followers (most notably James, Peter, John, Thomas, Philip, and Mary).[38] In addition, as persecution against Christians intensified, especially toward the close of the second century and periodically in the third, it became more crucial for Christians to agree on what books they were willing to die for (when they defied orders to burn all their holy books). Thus, beginning about AD 150, and continuing without complete agreement for another 200 years, they produced a series of lists of Christian books to be treated as Scripture. But the

---

35. The evidence for the last three sentences is scattered throughout each of the works cited in n. 29. See esp. Dunbar, "Canon," 323–28. More generally, cf. Metzger, *Canon*, 39–73.

36. The significance of the evidence of the Apostolic Fathers has regularly been exaggerated by conservatives and unduly denigrated by liberals. Particularly balanced, though somewhat limited in scope, is D. A. Hagner, "The Sayings of Jesus in the Apostolic Fathers and Justin Martyr," in *Gospel Perspectives V: The Jesus Tradition Outside the Gospels,* ed. D. Wenham (Sheffield: JSOT, 1984; Eugene, OR: Wipf & Stock, 2003), 233–68.

37. See Bruce, *Canon*, 134–44.

38. The standard collection and translation is M. W. Meyer, ed., *The Nag Hammadi Scriptures: The Revised and Updated Translation of Sacred Gnostic Texts* (New York: HarperOne, 2007).

testimony of Irenaeus, during this period in which the false teachers were "perverting the Scriptures" (see esp. *Against Heresies* 3.12.12), suggests an already existing canon even before the publication of the various lists.

Probably the earliest of these lists is the so-called Muratorian fragment from the late second century.[39] It includes the four Gospels, Acts, all thirteen letters attributed to Paul, two letters of John, the letter of Jude, and Revelation. It also curiously refers to the Wisdom of Solomon, and it notes that in Rome the Apocalypse of Peter was read, though some questioned it, as in fact some did the Apocalypse of John (Revelation). Around this time Irenaeus, bishop of Lyons, recognized a similar collection with the addition of 1 Peter.[40] At the turn of the third century, Tertullian first used the Latin *testamentum* in referring to a NT. He was translating the concept of a Greek *diathēkē* ("covenant") and should not be interpreted, as we often understand "testament" in English, as referring to a will. Tertullian recognized twenty-three of our NT books as authoritative, omitting James, 2 Peter, and 2 and 3 John, about which he mentions nothing.[41] Early in the third century, Origen refers to all twenty-seven, but notes that six are disputed: Hebrews, James, 2 Peter, 2 and 3 John, and Jude (as quoted in Eusebius, *Hist. eccl.* 6:25.8–14).[42] This situation seems to have persisted until the fourth century.

Like the rabbinic discussions about certain OT books, however, questions about these six writings focus more on internal evidence (issues arising from the texts themselves) than on external evidence (doubts about their inspiration or the conditions under which they were written). The one exception is Hebrews. Some believed it came from Paul; others proposed different authors or pled ignorance. In the case of James, then as later, questions focused on harmonizing his view of faith and works with that of Paul. Doubts about 2 Peter focused on the differences from 1 Peter in style and contents. Arguably, some deemed 2 and 3 John too personal to be universally relevant. Jude's quotation of the intertestamental Jewish apocalypse known as 1 Enoch and his apparent allusion to an apocryphal work known as the Assumption of Moses puzzled some. These internal problems, thus, led some to doubt the inspiration and canonicity of these last six books mentioned. A seventh book also came under some fire, as the millennial theology of Revelation troubled many who were becoming increasingly amillennial in outlook.

Athanasius, bishop of Alexandria, in his Easter-time festal letter of AD 367, is

---

39. For its contents and significance, see Bruce, *Canon*, 158–69. G. M. Hahneman, *The Muratorian Fragment and The Development of the Canon* (Oxford: Clarendon, 1992), has defended a fourth-century date for this fragment. But see the rebuttal by C. E. Hill, "The Debate over the Muratorian Fragment and the Development of the Canon," *WTJ* 57 (1995): 431–52.

40. Irenaeus nowhere gives one definitive list of these works, but one may be pieced together from a variety of references presented and discussed in Bruce, *Canon*, 170–77.

41. Again, Tertullian's views reflect a mosaic of sources. See Bruce, *Canon*, 180–83. Around the same time, Clement of Alexandria may have begun to use the Greek *diathēkē* in the same way.

42. At the same time, Eusebius himself accepted Hebrews but not Revelation. Origen doubted the Pauline authorship of Hebrews, but not its inspiration.

the earliest-known Christian writer to endorse without hesitation the twenty-seven books that now comprise our NT. The subsequent Councils of Hippo (AD 393) and Carthage (AD 397) ratified his views. Only minor debates persisted after that time. Due to these debates, some writers argue that the NT canon was not closed until the time of the Protestant Reformation and the Roman Catholic Council of Trent in the mid-1500s, if even then.[43] Such a position leaves the door open for certain groups, most notably Mormons, to add their own formative documents to the canon.[44] But while it is true that one cannot prove either Christian or Jewish canons ever to have been so conclusively closed as to preclude all further discussion, it is abundantly clear that no later sectarian literature could ever pass the early church's criteria for canonicity (see below). Most obviously, such writings could not meet the criterion of widespread use from the earliest days of the faith to the present.

Even though the NT canon has remained well established since the fourth century, numerous voices today clamor for a reconsideration of its boundaries. Particularly noteworthy are those students of ancient Gnosticism who argue that texts like those found at Nag Hammadi (esp. the Gospel of Thomas, the Gospel of Truth, the Apocryphon of James, the Gospel of Philip, and the Treatise on the Resurrection) preserve traditions of Jesus' teaching at least as valuable as those found in our canonical Gospels and that they date from at least as early a first-century time period.[45] Almost certainly, these scholars date every one of these non-canonical sources (except Q) at least seventy-five years too early! No clear evidence for the existence of those documents predates the mid-second century, and a careful comparison of their teachings with those of the Gospels shows them to be mostly later than and, where they run parallel, dependent on the canonical four. It is possible, to be sure, that otherwise unparalleled but authentic sayings of Jesus may have occasionally been preserved in these texts, but a substantial percentage of them reads more like later gnostic revisions and corruptions (if not outright fabrications) of earlier traditions of Jesus' words and deeds.[46]

Even more specious are the claims that the NT was simply the result of a power

43. It is of course important to recall the Reformers' emphasis on the witness of the Holy Spirit and the self-attestation of the Scriptures. Protestants do not ultimately rely on the decision of any ancient church council or more recent Reformation emphasis. See esp. M. J. Kruger, *Canon Revisited: Establishing the Origins and Authority of the New Testament Books* (Wheaton: Crossway, 2012). But the degree of subjectivity involved at this point requires that additional criteria for canonicity be applied as well.

44. See esp. S. E. Robinson, *Are Mormons Christians?* (Salt Lake City: Bookcraft, 1991), 45–56.

45. In addition to Taussig, *A New New Testament*, see R. W. Funk, R. W. Hoover, and the Jesus Seminar, *The Five Gospels: The Search for the Authentic Words of Jesus* (New York; Oxford: Macmillan, 1993); R. W. Funk and the Jesus Seminar, *The Acts of Jesus: The Search for the Authentic Deeds of Jesus* (San Francisco: HarperSanFrancisco, 1998).

46. See C. Tuckett, *Nag Hammadi and the Gospel Tradition* (Edinburgh: T. & T. Clark, 1986); J. P. Meier, *A Marginal Jew: Rethinking the Historical Jesus*, AYBRL, 5 vols. to date (New York: Doubleday, 1991-), 1:112–66. J. H. Charlesworth and C. A. Evans, "Jesus in the Agrapha and Apocryphal Gospels," in *Studying the Historical Jesus: Evaluations of the State of Current Research*, NT Tools and Studies, ed. B. Chilton and C. A. Evans (Leiden: Brill, 1994), 479–533; and C. E. Hill, *Who Chose the Gospels? Probing the Great Gospel Conspiracy* (Oxford: Oxford University Press, 2010).

play on the part of the "orthodox," who ousted the hapless Gnostics from what had been a credible place in the development of Christianity and then rewrote the history of the movement to make it look like they had dominated all along.[47] This scenario might just be credible if the major developments in the establishment of the canon began only in the fourth century when Constantine became the first Christian emperor and gave the religion its first power base, as Bart Ehrman and others have claimed. But most of the developments in the establishment of the canon had already occurred by this time, and the encyclopedic-sized body of Christian literature known as the ante-Nicene fathers from which we learn about the various movements within the first three centuries of Christianity had already been written by then.[48] The NT books' unbroken existence throughout the history of the church, along with a fair amount of the sectarian literature that was rejected, shows that no widespread suppression of dissident voices ever occurred in these days. The oldest of the patristic writers do not even show any awareness of the heterodox literature, either by way of support or by way of protest.

The Order of the Canon

As with the OT, the final arrangement of NT books combined chronological and topical concerns with issues of length of documents.[49] The Gospels were naturally placed first, as they described the origins of Christianity in the life of Jesus. Matthew assumed first place because, as the most Jewish of the Gospels, it provided the clearest link with the OT.[50] Then Mark, Luke, and John most commonly followed in the order in which presumably they were composed.[51] Even though Acts was Luke's second volume, it was separated from his Gospel by John's work when the four Gospels were all grouped together. But it naturally came next as the historical sequel to the events of Jesus' life.

After Acts came the Epistles. As Paul was the premier apostle to the Gentile world and the most prolific epistle writer, his letters were naturally placed first. As the order of the books became increasingly standardized, Paul's Epistles were then divided into letters to churches (Romans–2 Thessalonians) and letters to individuals (1 Timothy–Philemon). Within these two sections the Epistles were arranged in order of decreasing length, except that books written to the same church or person were

---

47. E.g., B. D. Ehrman, *Lost Scriptures: Books That Did Not Make It into the New Testament* (Oxford: Oxford University Press, 2003), 2; D. L. Dungan, *Constantine's Bible: Politics and the Making of the New Testament* (Minneapolis: Fortress, 2007), 120–21.

48. Alexander Roberts, ed., *The Ante-Nicene Fathers*, 10 vols. (Peabody: Hendrickson, 1994).

49. As in the OT, early groupings of NT books took a variety of orders, though as far as we know the Gospels, Epistles of Paul, and General Epistles were always discrete groupings, despite variations in sequence within each section. Interestingly, at first Acts was often put at the head of the General Epistles. For key lists, see Metzger, *Canon*, 295–300.

50. Some would also argue that it was written first, though that discussion is beyond our scope. See the NT introductions in the bibliography at the end plus the standard commentaries on the Synoptic Gospels.

51. Cf. M. Hengel, *The Four Gospels and the One Gospel of Jesus Christ* (London: SCM; Harrisburg: Trinity Press International, 2000), 38–47.

kept together even when this pattern was broken (1 and 2 Thessalonians, 1 and 2 Timothy).[52] Even though it is just slightly shorter, Galatians may have been placed before Ephesians as a frontispiece to the collection of Prison Epistles (Ephesians, Philippians, Colossians) because of its use of the term *kanōn* or "rule" (Gal 6:16).[53] Hebrews was placed immediately after the avowedly Pauline Epistles because many thought it came from Paul, but it was not placed within the collection since it was anonymous, and many others disavowed Pauline authorship. The writings of James, Peter, John, and Jude were then added in that order, also in generally decreasing length but probably also in descending order of the prominence of their authors in the earliest church. James the brother of Jesus also was originally the head of the Jerusalem church (Acts 15). Eventually, after Peter arrived in Rome, he supplanted James in empire-wide significance, but in the earliest years he seems to have been subordinate to James.[54] John the son of Zebedee was another one of Jesus' inner three apostles (with Peter and James his brother). Jude, another brother of Jesus, clearly figures least prominently in early Christian writings. Finally, Revelation, with its focus on the end of history, formed a fitting conclusion to the canon.[55]

CRITERIA OF CANONICITY

The reasons the Jews came to accept the thirty-nine books of the Hebrew Scriptures as arranged in modern enumeration are largely lost in antiquity. The main reason given in the rabbinic discussions revolves around their inspiration. Yet this only throws the question back one stage—i.e., why were these books believed to be inspired or "God-breathed" (cf. 2 Tim 3:16)? Conservative scholars have often tried to link inspiration and canonicity to prophecy. God gave the Law to Moses, they argue, and he was also called a prophet and was largely responsible for the composition of the Pentateuch. Moses, they claim, anticipated a succession of divinely accredited prophets (Deut 18:17–19) who composed the books the Jews included among the Prophets. What is more, even many of the Writings come from prophetic authors (e.g., David [cf. Acts 2:30] and, for some of the Psalms, Asaph the seer).[56] Yet this view fails to account for all of the biblical books and probably pushes the evidence for prophetic authorship (even of the books it does account for) further than is defensible. Why assume that God can inspire only prophets and not also sages and priests?

---

52. Metzger, *Canon*, 297.

53. This last point is by far the most dubious but is a plausible suggestion of W. R. Farmer in *The Formation of the New Testament Canon*, with D. M. Farkasfalvy (New York: Paulist, 1983), 79–81.

54. Numerous studies have rehabilitated the historical James to the place of prominence he once held. Many of these are conveniently summarized in H. Shanks and B. Witherington, III, *The Brother of Jesus* (San Francisco: HarperSanFrancisco, 2003), 89–223.

55. See esp., R. W. Wall, *Revelation*, NIBC (Peabody: Hendrickson, 1991; Grand Rapids: Baker, 2011), 25–32, who takes an explicitly canon-critical approach (on which see below).

56. See esp. R. L. Harris, *Inspiration and Canonicity of the Bible*, 2nd ed. (Grand Rapids: Zondervan, 1969; Eugene, OR: Wipf & Stock, 2008).

A second view links canonicity to the concept of covenant. The Law established God's covenant; the historical narratives described Israel's obedience and disobedience to the covenant; the prophets called people back to a proper relationship to the covenant; and the Wisdom Literature expanded the theme of obedience to it.[57] This theory has fewer holes in it than the previous one, but it also remains rather broad in nature and without much ancient testimony to corroborate it. While plausible, it must remain a theory. Christians will probably have to rest content with the traditional Protestant argument outlined above. To state it rather colloquially, "What was good enough for Jesus (as a representative Jew of his day) is good enough for us."

Criteria for New Testament Canonicity		
• Apostolicity	• Orthodoxy	• Catholicity

More evidence survives that suggests criteria for the canonicity of the NT. Again, inspiration is more a corollary of canonicity than a criterion of it.[58] Nevertheless, other criteria may helpfully be classified under three headings: apostolicity, orthodoxy, and catholicity. All of the NT writings were believed to have apostolic connections. Though not necessarily written by one of the original twelve apostles (this would apply only to Matthew, John, and Peter), they came from the apostolic age (first c.) and could be closely associated with those who were considered apostles (including Paul), or closely associated with Jesus (such as the Epistles of his brothers, James and Jude). Thus, Mark was traditionally associated with Peter, Luke with Paul, and Hebrews, if not from Paul himself, then with one of his intimate companions.[59] Although many of these traditional authorship claims are widely disputed today, a cogent case can still be made for each of them.[60]

Second, Christians believed that the theology and ethics promoted by the NT books as a whole cohered in shared orthodoxy—beliefs not held by most of the gnostic challengers. To call all the NT writings orthodox does not preclude a wide measure of diversity among them, but it does imply that none of the texts actually contradicts another one. Although this claim is widely rejected today,[61] it remains thoroughly

---

57. See esp. M. G. Kline, *The Structure of Biblical Authority*, 2nd ed. (Grand Rapids: Eerdmans, 1989; Eugene, OR: Wipf & Stock, 1997).

58. Bruce, *Canon*, 268.

59. Suggestions from the first centuries of the church's history include Paul, Barnabas, Luke, and Clement of Rome; at the time of the Reformation, Luther suggested Apollos; A. Harnack in the nineteenth century suggested Priscilla and Aquila. Modern scholars have added several other proposals.

60. See esp. D. A. Carson and D. J. Moo, *An Introduction to the New Testament*, 2nd ed. (Grand Rapids: Zondervan, 2005); and A. J. Köstenberger, L. S. Kellum, and C. L. Quarles, *The Cradle, the Cross, and the Crown: An Introduction to the New Testament* (Nashville: B&H, 2009), both ad loc. Some would argue today that the other criteria for canonicity are adequate so that not as much depends on authorship for the modern church as for the ancient church. For the issues that are pressing today, their supporters, and an excellent response, see M. J. Kruger, *The Question of Canon: Challenging the Status Quo in the New Testament Debate* (Downers Grove: InterVarsity, 2013).

61. Just about every nonevangelical NT theology is predicated on the assumption of irreconcilable diversity. Of recent works, cf. esp. U. Schnelle, *Theology of the New Testament* (Grand Rapids: Baker, 2009); and F. J. Matera, *New Testament Theology: Exploring Diversity and Unity* (Louisville: Westminster John Knox, 2007).

defensible.[62] The canon came *after* the preaching of the gospel and the instruction of the faithful and accepted only what cohered with that inaugural tradition.

Third, books were preserved that had proved useful for a large number of churches from the earliest generations of Christianity. Closely related was the widespread recognition of a book's authority. One can only speculate as to why the first letter Paul wrote to the Corinthians, before our 1 Corinthians (see 1 Cor 5:9), was not preserved. It obviously was apostolic and presumably orthodox, but quite plausibly was not as relevant for other groups of believers outside of Corinth. Christians often ask the tantalizing question, "What would happen if such a letter were discovered and proved highly relevant?" This question is in fact just a specific form of the broader question: "Is the Christian canon open or closed?" Now since we believe that no church tradition is on a par with Scripture, so that authoritative church pronouncements of the fourth and fifth centuries cannot ultimately determine the canon, we must say that the canon *theoretically* remains open—if some additional document could meet all the criteria for canonicity. However, *practically,* the canon is closed, since a work that had not been used for nearly twenty centuries could not meet the criterion of catholicity and would almost certainly not command the acclaim of more than a minority of Christians today.[63]

A Crucial Distinction:	The process of canonization did not grant biblical books their authority.
	Rather, books that were recognized as authoritative were admitted to the canon.

CANON CRITICISM

In response to the often-atomistic approaches of traditional historical criticism, a new form of biblical analysis developed, particularly in the 1980s and 1990s, known as canon or canonical criticism (recall our discussion in ch. 2). Initially due to the extensive writings of Yale professor Brevard Childs, canon criticism seeks to move beyond standard source, form, and redaction criticism, and to interpret the biblical texts in their "canonical shape" (i.e., their final form).[64] Canon criticism does not reject the reconstructions of modern historical criticism as to how the various documents developed, but it finds little value in these methods for preaching or ministry in the

---

62. For detailed demonstration of this defensibility, see I. H. Marshall, *New Testament Theology: Many Witnesses, One Gospel* (Downers Grove: InterVarsity, 2005); and F. Thielman, *Theology of the New Testament: A Canonical and Synthetic Approach* (Grand Rapids: Zondervan, 2005). For methodological discussion, see P. Balla, *Challenges to New Testament Theology,* WUNT 2.95 (Tübingen: Mohr, 1997).

63. See esp. Metzger, *Canon,* 271–75.

64. See esp. B. S. Childs, *Introduction to the Old Testament as Scripture* (Philadelphia: Fortress, 1979); B. S. Childs, *The New Testament as Canon: An Introduction* (Philadelphia: Fortress, 1984). For additional background, see ch. 2 above.

life of the church. Rather, it calls the Christian community to accept the wisdom of its ancestors and to interpret passages and books of Scripture as they finally took shape. Many of these developments may be welcomed.

In some instances, canon criticism focuses on agreements rather than disagreements among allegedly divergent texts. Again, the claims of more critical scholars are not rejected but simply set to one side. Childs, for example, believes with many that the two Gospel infancy narratives (Matt 1–2 and Luke 1–2) contradict each other in numerous places. Instead of following redaction critics who focus on those distinctives as keys to Matthew's and Luke's emphases, he prefers to stress the features the texts have in common: the Spirit-influenced virgin birth, the child who is to bring salvation, the fulfillment of OT prophecy, and the need to accept and adore the Christ-child.[65]

Canon criticism also tempers the urge to absolutize one of two or more competing strands of biblical theology. Exodus, for example, presents a supernatural view of God's intervention in the lives of his people, whereas Genesis provides a much more "naturalistic" understanding of God's providence acting in ordinary human events (Gen 50:20).[66] Liberals have often rejected the former picture and conservatives have often neglected the latter. Canon critics, however, call interpreters to balance the two.[67] Again, evangelicals may reject the claims that such examples really involve outright contradiction, but they should welcome a renewed emphasis on the unity of the Scriptures and a balanced appropriation of their diverse themes and theological perspectives.

Sometimes, for canon critics the final form of the text does not mean the final form of an individual book of Scripture; rather, the final form indicates its theological role in the context of the later, completed canons of the OT and NT. That is, canon criticism brackets *all* historical issues. Thus, Acts can be studied not as the sequel to Luke's Gospel as it was originally intended, but as an introduction to the Epistles that follow. For example, Acts may well describe and legitimize the ministries of Paul to Gentiles as well as of James and Peter to Jews, even while showing how "Paul's Gospel" ultimately became more dominant. This reading paves the way for an understanding of the legitimacy of the Epistles of both Paul and James, but it also explains why, historically, Paul enjoys more prominence, even as the position of his letters in the NT canon suggests.[68] So, too, in the OT, even though many of the psalms originally were composed in unrelated contexts, their position in the collection of the 150 may shed some light on how the "canonical community" interpreted them. Most obviously, Psalm 1, with its classic contrast of righteous and wicked, seems

---

65. Childs, *New Testament*, 161–65.

66. In fact, some suggest that a gradually diminishing role of God's direct intervention in human affairs is a unifying feature of the narrative of Genesis itself. See R. Cohn, "Narrative Structure and Canonical Perspective in Genesis," *JSOT* 25 (1983): 3–16.

67. J. A. Sanders (*Canon and Community* [Philadelphia: Fortress, 1984], 50) gives the humorous example of Balaam's talking donkey. Liberals denied the donkey could really talk; conservatives defended that it could, but neither asked the more important question of what the account was meant to teach in the context of Num 22–24!

68. R. W. Wall, "The Acts of the Apostles in Context," *BTB* 18 (1986): 1–31.

to establish the theme for the entire collection. Psalms 144–150, all praise psalms, form a fitting climax and point to activity that should be the culmination of the life of all God's people.[69]

In sum, canon criticism's focus on the "final form" of a text can mean two quite different things. It can refer to what the actual author or final editor of a given book wrote or put together—roughly equivalent to what we mean by the "autograph" of a particular biblical document. To the extent that evangelical doctrines of inspiration focus on the autographs alone and not on their previous tradition-histories,[70] this preoccupation of canon criticism offers a welcome corrective to those who find only certain, supposedly oldest layers of a text authoritative or most significant (e.g., the most authentic words of Jesus in a given Gospel or the oldest Jahwist stratum in a book of the Law).[71]

But when "final form" or "canonical shape" refers to how a completed book of Scripture was interpreted centuries after its composition, when it was combined with other Scriptures, then we simply have an observation, often rather speculative, from the history of exegesis.[72] More often than not, these interpretations deflect attention from the original intention of the texts. As Metzger helpfully explains, the canon is "a collection of authoritative texts," not an "authoritative collection of (authoritative) texts."[73] In other words, the canonical placement of the books was not inspired; only the writing of the books was.[74] But to the extent that such study helps us focus on the biblical books as literary unities, on the biblical canon as a theological unity, or on important details within individual texts that might not otherwise be stressed, then it is most surely to be welcomed.[75]

James Sanders practices a quite different form of canon criticism, one that probably

---

69. For these and other examples from the Psalms, see G. H. Wilson, "The Qumran Psalms Manuscripts and the Consecutive Arrangement of Psalms in the Hebrew Psalter," *CBQ* 45 (1983): 377–88. N. deClaissé-Walford, R. A. Jacobson, B. LaNeel Tanner, *The Book of Psalms*, NICOT (Grand Rapids: Eerdmans, 2014), 21–38, helpfully summarize a plausible perspective concerning the Psalter's shape.

70. The evangelical OT scholar who has most extensively employed this form of canon criticism is J. H. Sailhamer, esp. his *Introduction to Old Testament Theology: A Canonical Approach* (Grand Rapids: Zondervan, 1995). The two evangelical NT scholars who have worked the most with this kind of canon criticism are R. W. Wall and E. E. Lemcio, esp. their *The New Testament as Canon: A Reader in Canonical Criticism*, JSNTSup 76 (Sheffield: JSOT, 1992).

71. Cf., respectively, J. Jeremias, *New Testament Theology: vol. 1: The Proclamation of Jesus* (London: SCM; NY: Scribner, 1971), esp. 3–37; and H. Bloom, *The Book of J* (New York: Grove Weidenfeld, 1990), esp. 3, 16, 316–22. The former is a common approach among certain NT scholars; the latter, more unusual for OT commentary.

72. See several of the chapters in Wall and Lemcio, *NT as Canon*, that speculate on the interpretive significance of juxtaposing the collections of Gospels and Letters or by placing Acts in between them, or by grouping Paul's and others' Epistles into separate collections.

73. Metzger, *Canon*, 282–84.

74. This is not to deny that the various placements of the books in the earliest collections of the Old and New Testaments are important for understanding the way in which their compilers valued them. At times, they almost formed a mini-commentary on those texts.

75. For a more philosophical critique of canon criticism, see esp. P. R. Noble, *The Canonical Approach: A Critical Reconstruction of the Hermeneutics of Brevard S. Childs*, BibInt 16 (Leiden: Brill, 1995). For a more appreciative study of Childs' method, see C. R. Seitz and K. H. Richards, eds., *The Bible as Christian Scripture: The Work of Brevard S. Childs*, BSNA (Atlanta: Society of Biblical Literature, 2013).

ought to have a different name.[76] Sanders's study focuses on canon not so much as a *product* but as a *process*. Canonical hermeneutics, in this program, refers to the way in which one biblical writer read, rewrote, and/or reapplied earlier Scripture, for example, Deuteronomy's reworking of the laws of Exodus and Leviticus, the Chronicler's rewriting of parts of the Samuel-Kings narrative, or the NT quotations of and allusions to the OT. But these topics are not new, and they are probably best studied under other headings such as redaction criticism, midrash criticism, and the history of exegesis.

What may be more significant is Sanders's claim that the hermeneutics used in these scriptural interpretations themselves should be normative for believers. This question surfaces, for example, whenever one asks, Can Christians today interpret the OT in the same way the NT writers did? Sanders believes the answer is clearly, yes. We offer our qualified agreement, though we often disagree with him in his actual assessment of the methods employed (see ch. 6 below).

In recent years, NT canon criticism has increasingly received less attention, though a valiant corps of past and present professors at Seattle Pacific University has attempted to keep it vibrant within evangelical circles.[77] OT canon criticism, especially following the legacy of Childs, is healthier. It is possible that the most valuable insights of the discipline will be subsumed under various branches of literary criticism and the more speculative suggestions will fade from view. One of the lasting contributions of canon criticism, surely, is the legitimacy it has again given to interpreting a whole book or section of the Bible as a unified, complete entity with important theological topics meriting serious scholarship.[78]

TEXTS AND TRANSLATIONS

Ideally, students would interpret the autographs of Scripture—the original documents penned by the various biblical writers. However, since none of these exists, the next best choice is to read and interpret the modern critical editions of the Hebrew, Aramaic, and Greek texts: the *Biblia Hebraica Stuttgartensia* (*BHS*, now in its 5th edition) for the OT, and the Nestle-Aland (28th edition) or United Bible Societies' (5th edition) *The Greek New Testament* (UBS[5]). The *BHS* follows the text of Codex Leningradensis—a well-preserved tenth-century AD manuscript of the Masoretic family of texts, the dominant orthodox Hebrew tradition of scribal activity from

---

76. For an article-length autobiographical reflection on his method, see J. A. Sanders, "Scripture as Canon for Post-Modern Times," *BTB* 25 (1995): 56–63. For fuller treatment, see esp. J. A. Sanders, *Canon and Community*; and J. A. Sanders, *From Sacred Story to Sacred Text* (Philadelphia: Fortress, 1987).

77. In addition to Wall and Lemcio, *The New Testament as Canon*, and their individual writings, cf. the various works of D. R. Nienhuis, esp. *Not by Paul Alone: The Formation of the Catholic Epistle Collection and the Canon* (Waco: Baylor University Press, 2007). See also R. W. Wall and D. R. Nienhuis, *A Compact Guide to the Whole Bible: Learning to Read Scripture's Story* (Grand Rapids: Baker, 2015).

78. See, e.g., C. R. Seitz, *Prophecy and Hermeneutics: Toward a New Introduction to the Prophets* (Grand Rapids: Baker, 2007).

ca. AD 600–900. A critical apparatus presents textual variants in the footnotes, including readings of older Hebrew texts (primarily the Dead Sea Scrolls [DSS]) and other older translations (esp. the LXX). The GNT chooses from among all the ancient manuscripts and versions of the NT to reconstruct what those autographs most likely contained. However, many Bible interpreters do not have the language skills to read these documents either, so they must rely on translations of Scripture into their native tongues. How then does one choose among the many available translations? Students should consider two factors. First, to what extent does a given translation utilize the most reliable findings of modern textual criticism reflected in works like the *BHS* or UBS[5]? Second, what kind of translation is it? Is it highly literal, highly paraphrastic, or somewhere in-between? To help the student answer these two questions we will discuss several pertinent issues.

Texts and Translations: The Key Questions
• How did we get from the initial "autographs" of the biblical writers or editors to the abundance of manuscripts and versions of the Bible?
• Can we have confidence in our modern versions?

Textual Criticism

Since this is not a manual on exegesis (interpreting the Bible in its original languages), we will discuss textual criticism only briefly.[79] Much of the work of textual critics involves tedious and painstaking comparisons of dozens of ancient OT manuscripts and versions, and hundreds (thousands if one includes small fragments) of portions of Greek NT texts from the early centuries of the Christian era.[80] The vast majority of the differences between the manuscripts stem from the mechanics of copying by hand the contents of a written document. A brief introduction to that process will enable readers to understand why manuscripts were not always copied perfectly.

Ancient writing on scrolls and codices (manuscripts in book form) did not look much like print in modern books. In the oldest manuscripts, words were written in

---

79. Helpful introductory guides include E. R. Brotzman, *Old Testament Textual Criticism: A Practical Introduction*, 2nd ed. (Grand Rapids: Baker Academic, 2016); and J. H. Greenlee, *The Text of the New Testament: From Manuscript to Modern Edition* (Peabody: Hendrickson, 2008). More technical but more thorough studies are E. Tov, *Textual Criticism of the Hebrew Bible*, 3rd ed. (Minneapolis: Fortress, 2012); E. Würthwein, *The Text of the Old Testament*, rev. and exp. A. A. Fischer, trans. E. F. Rhodes, 3rd ed. (Grand Rapids: Eerdmans, 2014), 157–205; D. B. Wallace, *Laying a Foundation: A Handbook on New Testament Textual Criticism* (Grand Rapids: Zondervan, forthcoming 2018) and the web site of the Center for the Study of New Testament Manuscripts: csntm.org; and K. Aland and B. Aland, *The Text of the New Testament*, 2nd ed. (Grand Rapids: Eerdmans; Leiden: Brill, 1989).

80. Bart Ehrman (*Misquoting Jesus: The Story behind Who Changed the Bible and Why* [San Francisco: HarperSanFrancisco, 2005], 89) speaks of there being perhaps as many 400,000 textual variants. But these are spread across more than 25,000 ancient manuscripts in Greek and other languages into which the NT was translated, leaving less than 16 *unique* variants per manuscript. The vast majority of these are variations in spelling. Less than 10,000 are deemed worthy of note in NA[28], less than 1,500 in the USB[5], and an average of 300–400 in the footnotes of most modern-language translations.

capital letters with no use of lower case and no spacing between words, punctuation, hyphenation, paragraphing, section headings, or any of the other devices of modern writing.[81] In addition, in the case of Hebrew and Aramaic, generally only consonants were written out. The later Masoretic scribes supplied the vowels by symbols underneath or above the consonants centuries after the books were written and the canon was complete. To imagine what this might look like for an English reader, we might conceive of the NIV of Genesis 1:1–2 as appearing:

NTHBGNNNGGDCRTDTHHVNSNDTHRTHNDTHRTHWS
FRMLSSNDMPTYDRKNSSWSVRTHSRFCFTHDPNDTHSPRTFGDW
SHVRNGVRTHWTRS

John 1:1–2 would not look quite so strange because vowels were included in Greek manuscripts:

INTHEBEGINNINGWASTHEWORDANDTHEWORDWASWITHGO
DANDTHEWORDWASGODHEWASWITHGODINTHEBEGINNING

Naturally, one wonders how anybody could read such writing. But those who read these languages had learned the method from childhood, and in the case of Hebrew had learned what vowels should be added to the consonants mentally or orally. Nevertheless, modern readers do well to remember that the original Scripture texts looked quite different from our own. No one dare claim inspiration for chapter and verse references (these were added in the middle ages),[82] punctuation and NT word division (which began about the sixth c.), or Hebrew vowels (finalized in writing in about the tenth c.).

When manuscripts began to be copied, many of the differences among them, therefore, resulted from the ambiguities of the older documents, especially with respect to word division. However, the context usually clarified the correct reading. Yet unintentionally, scribes introduced other mechanical errors: letters, words, or whole lines were accidentally omitted or repeated as the copyist's eye jumped back to the wrong place in the text being copied. Spelling variations or mistakes intruded when two adjacent letters were reversed, or when one letter was substituted for another that was similar in appearance. Sometimes scribes intentionally altered texts they copied—e.g., in the direction of "orthodoxy" or to harmonize a text with another one. Nevertheless, most of these errors are trivial, detectable, and correctable, and do not significantly affect the overall meaning of the larger passages in which they appear.

---

81. This is demonstrable for the oldest NT documents. For OT texts, even the oldest existing copies (the DSS) indicate word division in various ways, but scholars are divided as to whether the originals would have used spacing between words. Both the practice of Phoenician inscriptions and the numerous Hebrew variants based on variant word divisions support an original text without spaces between words. On the other hand, the kind of uneven and ambiguous spacing found at Qumran could also have generated these variants. See Tov, *Textual Criticism of the Hebrew Bible*, 196–97.

82. Chapter divisions were introduced by the Archbishop of Canterbury, Stephen Langton, at the beginning of the thirteenth century; verses, by Robert Estienne (Stephanus), in the mid-sixteenth century.

Occasionally there are interesting exceptions. For example, should 1 Thessalonians 2:7 read "we were *gentle* among you" or "we were *little children* among you?"[83] The two readings in the Greek differ only by an additional *n-* to begin the second word: *egenēthēmen ēpioi* ("we became gentle") vs. *egenēthēmen nēpioi* ("we became infants").[84] Is it more likely that a scribe accidentally (or intentionally) added or omitted the *n-*?[85]

Or should Genesis 49:26 read, "Your father's blessings are greater than the blessings of the ancient mountains" or ". . . greater than the blessings of my progenitors" (i.e., "those who conceived me")? The phrase "the ancient mountains" (הַרְרֵי עַד; *harre ad*) in Hebrew looks similar to "those who conceived me" (הוֹרֵי עַד; *horay ad*), if one letter (ר; *r*) is replaced with a similar looking letter (ו; *ô*).[86]

Obviously, textual variants in verses of great doctrinal significance introduce important ambiguities. Usually Psalm 2:12 has been seen as messianic, in keeping with the traditional rendering of the Hebrew (נַשְּׁקוּ־בַר; *naššequ-bar*), as "Kiss [i.e., reverence] his son" (NIV; cf. HCSB, ESV, NASB). But the last two letters (בר, *br*, reading from right to left) are not the normal Hebrew for "son" (which is בן, *bn*, as in verse 7), and the LXX translates the command into Greek as "take hold of discipline," which cannot be extracted from these Hebrew letters at all. Modern translators, therefore, have sometimes supposed that these six letters, along with those of the preceding two words, were at some point rather dramatically rearranged from an original *naššequ beraglayw biradah* to the existing MT *wegiylu biradah naššequ-bar* (נַשְּׁקוּ־בַר וְגִילוּ בְּרֶעָדָה). They propose a non-messianic rendering: "Kiss his feet" (referring to God). Thus instead of "Serve the LORD with fear and rejoice with trembling, Kiss the son," Psalm 2:11–12a then reads, "Serve the LORD with fear, with trembling kiss his feet" (RSV; cf. NRSV, NJB, CEB).[87]

Less complex, but equally significant, is a NT example from Luke 22:19b–20. Did a later scribe add the words, ". . . given for you? This do in remembrance of me. And likewise the cup, after supper saying, this cup is the new covenant in my

---

83. Most modern English translations adopt the former, but most textual critics favor the latter. See now, however, the updated NIV (2011), which follows the textual-critical consensus. See also the NET and NLT.

84. Recall that originally these were written in all capitals with no spaces. They would differ only in the presence of an extra *n-*. Compare *EGENHQHMENHPIOI* ("we were gentle") with *EGENHQHMENNHPIOI* ("we became infants").

85. The standard source for explaining the cases for and against the major textual variants in the New Testament is B. M. Metzger, *A Textual Commentary on the Greek New Testament*, 2nd ed. (New York: United Bible Societies, 1994). Particularly useful is Metzger's description of how the five-member committee that produced the fourth edition of the UBSGNT arrived at its decisions to rank a certain reading with an {A}, {B}, {C}, or {D} level of confidence. In this particular example, the committee adopted the reading *nēpioi* (infants) and gave it a {B} rating indicating that the text is almost certain. (An {A} indicates that the text is certain; {C} that the committee had difficulty in deciding which variant to place in the text; and {D} that the committee had great difficulty with its decision, an option occurring rarely.) A comparable reference work is not yet available for the fifth edition.

86. On which, see e.g. V. P. Hamilton, *The Book of Genesis, Chapters 18–50*, NICOT (Grand Rapids: Eerdmans, 1995), 682–83, n. 19. The former reading lies behind the LXX; the latter, the Hebrew (MT).

87. For details and alternative proposals see C. Vang, "Ps 2, 11–12—A New Look at An Old Crux Interpretum," *SJOT* 9 (1995): 162–85; and S. Olofsson, "The Crux Interpretum in Ps 2, 12," *SJOT* 9 (1995): 185–99. The NET takes *bar* as an adjective meaning "pure" and translates, "Give sincere homage," avoiding both "feet" and "son" (cf. also NAB, TNK).

blood shed for you"? Or were these words accidentally omitted in the exemplar (an influential manuscript widely copied for a large number of other manuscripts) behind the manuscripts that lack this material, and so the scribe merely added what he thought ought to be present?[88] We could multiply examples. Still, we insist that no doctrine of Christianity rests solely on textually disputed passages.[89] There are numerous other messianic psalms and prophecies besides Psalm 2:12, and there are three other accounts of Jesus' words at the Last Supper, one of which very closely agrees with the wording of Luke's disputed text (cf. 1 Cor 11:24–25).

The science of textual criticism nevertheless has a crucial place in proper hermeneutics. All of the other methods described in this book are somewhat inconsequential if we cannot determine with reasonable probability what the original words of the Bible actually were. The good news is that the vast majority of the Bible is textually secure.[90] Readers of English translations, especially of the NT, need not wonder if textual variants lurking behind every verse they read would drastically change the meaning of the passage. Estimates suggest that more than 99 percent of the original NT can be reconstructed from the existing manuscripts with a high degree of probability.[91] The percentage for the OT is lower, but even a very cautious figure would be well above 90 percent.[92] But good editions of the various modern English translations contain footnotes that alert readers to most of the significant textual variants (as well as important alternate translations). Serious students of the Bible would be wise to obtain such editions of the Scriptures.[93]

Even with all of this help, Christians often ask two important questions for which there are no simple answers. First, why did God in his providence not insure that an inerrant, inspired original was also inerrantly *preserved*?[94] Second, how do we as Christians deal with those portions of traditional translations (like the KJV) that modern discoveries have shown were not part of the original autographs? The first question takes on added significance in light of other religions that claim, however

---

88. For details, see B. S. Billings, *Do This in Remembrance of Me: The Disputed Words in the Lukan Institution Narrative (Luke 22.19b-20): An Historico-Exegetical, Theological and Sociological Analysis*, LNTS 3/4 (London: T&T Clark, 2006).

89. For this and related points, and for an excellent introductory survey to the theological issues surrounding textual criticism for the evangelical, particularly with reference to the more difficult OT issues, see B. K. Waltke, "How We Got the Hebrew Bible: The Text and Canon of the Old Testament," in *The Bible at Qumran: Text, Shape, and Interpretation*, ed. P. W. Flint (Grand Rapids: Eerdmans, 2001), 27–50.

90. Brotzman (*Old Testament Textual Criticism*, 23) notes that much of the OT text exists without any variation.

91. J. E. Komoszewski, M. J. Sawyer, and D. B. Wallace, *Reinventing Jesus: What* The Da Vinci Code *and Other Novel Speculations Don't Tell You* (Grand Rapids: Kregel, 2006), 259.

92. Paul D. Wegner, *A Student's Guide to Textual Criticism of the Bible: Its History, Methods & Results* (Downers Grove: InterVarsity, 2006), 37.

93. Translation footnotes usually draw on the four major text traditions that figure in textual criticism: the Masoretic Text (MT), the Septuagint (LXX), the Dead Sea Scrolls (DSS), and the Aramaic Targums.

94. The fact that no two known manuscripts are identical refutes any claim that God did preserve an inerrant manuscript. To identify any particular manuscript as without error is an act of sheer faith that all the empirical evidence contradicts. See esp. D. B. Wallace, "The Majority-Text Theory: History, Methods and Critique," *JETS* 37 (1994): 185–215.

speciously, that their sacred writings have been better preserved (most notably the Book of Mormon and the Qur'an). To be sure, we do not know God's hidden motives. Certainly, the first Christians were more concerned to get their message transmitted and/or translated to put in the hands of as many people as possible rather than making superhuman efforts to copy every last "jot and tittle" flawlessly. Moreover, NT citations of the OT suggest that they used (and at times abridged) wording from several ancient versions much as we might select particular wording from a modern translation that best expresses our sermonic point (see below). Perhaps, too, God did not want us to idolize a book but to worship him as the One who became incarnate in Jesus. Leaving the transmission of Scriptures to fallible human beings parallels leaving the proclamation of those Scriptures to sinful and potentially rebellious disciples. God does not choose to override free will in either case, and he reveals and inspires only at particular moments in human history. At the same time, we can discern his providence in the amazing extent to which the texts have been preserved.

The second question becomes particularly acute with regard to the two longest passages (printed in most Bibles) that almost certainly did not appear in the original manuscripts: Mark 16:9–20 (an additional account of Jesus' resurrection) and John 7:53–8:11 (the story of the woman caught in adultery). The necessary approach should be clear—whatever was most likely in the original texts should be accepted as inspired and normative; what was not in those texts should not be given equal status. Application, however, proves more difficult. As noted elsewhere in this book, John 7:53–8:11 may be a true story, from which we can derive accurate information about Jesus' view of the Law, even if it did not originally form part of John's Gospel. On the other hand, there is almost no evidence to support Jesus ever having said, "He that believes and is baptized shall be saved" (Mark 16:16; as if baptism were necessary for salvation), or for the promise that believers may pick up snakes, drink their venom, and yet not be harmed (Mark 16:18). One unnecessarily risks suicide by treating that text as normative! But in both Mark and John, the textual evidence is very strong for rejecting these passages as inspired Scripture.[95]

The OT creates different problems. Some books are so different in Hebrew and Greek forms that we probably must speak of two different editions of these books. The clearest example is Jeremiah, in which the LXX is nearly one-sixth shorter than the MT. Now that fragments of a Hebrew copy of Jeremiah that resemble the LXX have been found among the DSS, it seems likely that the Hebrew version of Jeremiah underwent successive revisions (expansions) that account for its longer length. But whatever we make of this process of development, there is no evidence that Judaism (i.e., the compilers of the MT in Palestine, the DSS) ever treated the shorter Jeremiah as authoritative once the longer revised version was available. So it

---

95. The UBSGNT gives an {A} rating (its highest) for not including this material in each instance.

is this final Jeremiah, on which our English translations are based, that we should continue to treat as canonical.[96]

In other instances, however, the DSS have provided textual variants—sometimes completely new, sometimes matching the LXX—that probably reflect the original autographs more closely than the MT. English translations like the NIV, ESV, and NRSV periodically include in their footnotes references to readings found among the DSS. Probably the most celebrated example involves an additional text at the beginning of 1 Samuel 11 in the Qumran text 4QSam[a] that seems likely to have been original and later accidentally omitted.[97] The NRSV has thus added it in, rendering it:

> Now Nahash, king of the Ammonites, had been grievously oppressing the Gadites and the Reubenites. He would gouge out the right eye of each of them and would not grant Israel a deliverer. No one was left of the Israelites across the Jordan whose right eye Nahash, king of the Ammonites, had not gouged out. But there were seven thousand men who had escaped from the Ammonites and had entered Jabesh-gilead.

These changes remind us again that our knowledge of the original text of the Bible is not 100 percent secure, and new discoveries may lead to still more revisions. But it is also important to stress that our ability to reconstruct the probable original far outstrips that of any other document from the ancient world.[98]

A different kind of hermeneutical issue raised by textual criticism involves verses in which the NT quotes the OT but follows the Septuagint even though the meaning in the Greek translation does not accurately reflect the Hebrew of traditional OT manuscripts. These differences prove more difficult to assess. As we have noted, the traditional Hebrew versions (the MT) date from no earlier than the AD 800–1000s. The existing LXX manuscripts go back an additional half a millennium or more. It is possible, therefore, that at times the LXX accurately translated a Hebrew original that later became corrupted. Portions of OT books found among the DSS from as long ago as 200 BC suggest that occasionally, though not often, this was exactly

---

96. See esp. Tov, *Textual Criticism of the Hebrew Bible*, 286–94. For the more general debate regarding method when OT texts or passages seem to have existed in different forms from very early on, see K. H. Jobes and M. Silva, *Invitation to the Septuagint*, 2nd ed. (Grand Rapids: Baker, 2015), 128–55. This book is also perhaps the best introduction to the LXX more generally.

97. Tov, *Textual Criticism of the Hebrew Bible*, 311–13.

98. For some comparative data, see C. L. Blomberg, *Can We Still Believe the Bible? An Evangelical Engagement with Contemporary Questions* (Grand Rapids: Brazos, 2014), 35–37. Various versions of the Qur'an existed at the time of Muhammad's death; but only one was preserved, to try to unite the different factions with Islam. As a result, we cannot even guess at how close the one that was preserved is to the original, and one can only speculate that the reason for preserving only one tradition was that there were some considerable differences that mattered a lot to the competing factions at that time. Even in the early history of copying the one ('Uthmān) version that was preserved, numerous variants were introduced, as early Islamic history freely acknowledged (though this is not widely acknowledged among Muslims today). See esp. K. E. Small, *Textual Criticism and Qur'ān Manuscripts* (Lanham, MD: University Press of America, 2011).

what happened. Compare, for example, Hebrews 1:6, which quotes a longer form of Deuteronomy 32:43 found only in the LXX and DSS.[99]

Aramaic Targums, which combined free translation with occasional explanatory additions and commentary, may at times also account for NT renderings of OT texts. Interpreters, for example, have often wondered how to account for the end of Ephesians 4:8, "he gave gifts to his people," when the Hebrew of Psalm 68:18 that Paul quotes reads "receiving gifts from people" (NRSV). Yet at least one early Targum contains Aramaic wording that parallels how Paul rendered this verse, so it is quite possible that Paul is following a similar tradition. Jews and Christians have often speculated that God received tribute in order to return those gifts as blessings to his people. Whether or not Paul reasoned in this way—or even used some now-lost fragment—the Targum at least shows that Paul based his interpretation on an acceptable Jewish reading and did not simply manipulate the psalm willy-nilly.[100]

Because the LXX was the common Bible for first-century Jewish readers outside Israel, in some instances the NT may quote from it even when it differed from the Hebrew, so long as it did not mitigate the point at stake. Thus, James in Acts 15:17 quotes the LXX of Amos 9:11–12 in which the Greek, "that the remnant of men may seek the Lord, and all the Gentiles who bear my name," is quite different from the Hebrew, "so that they may possess the remnant of Edom and all the nations may hear." Yet James' point can be justified from either version—when God restores Israel, Gentiles will become an integral and united part of his new chosen people along with Jews.[101] Of course, not every NT use of the LXX can be explained in these ways. (For additional discussion, refer to the section on the use of the OT in the NT in ch. 6).

Perhaps the most important hermeneutical principle to learn from textual criticism is that one must not derive theological or ethical principles solely from passages that are textually uncertain. When significant textual variants appear in a given passage, the sensible Bible reader will derive interpretations and applications that can be defended no matter which version of the text one follows. Therefore, too, students should always base syntheses of biblical doctrine and practice on textually certain passages, and then ponder how the latter enrich our understanding theologically.

---

99. On which, see esp. J. de Waard, *A Comparative Study of the Old Testament Text in the Dead Sea Scrolls and in the New Testament*, STDJ 4 (Leiden: Brill, 1965), 13–16; G. L. Cockerill, "Hebrews 1:6: Source and Significance," *BBR* 9 (1999): 51–64.

100. For this and other attempts to resolve the problem, see P. T. O'Brien, *The Letter to the Ephesians*, PNTC (Grand Rapids: Eerdmans; Leicester: InterVarsity, 1999), 289–93. For more detail on the use of Ps 68:19 in early non-rabbinic sources see H. H. Harris, III, *The Descent of Christ: Ephesians 4:7–11 and Traditional Hebrew Imagery* (Leiden: Brill, 1996; Grand Rapids: Baker, 1998), 96–122. On this specific passage, cf. T. G. Gombis, "Cosmic Lordship and Divine Gift-giving: Psalm 68 in Ephesians 4:8," *NovT* 47 (2005): 367–80; and W. N. Wilder, "The Use (or Abuse) of Power in High Places: Gifts Given and Received in Isaiah, Psalm 68, and Ephesians 4:8," *BBR* 20 (2010): 185–99.

101. This is the approach frequently taken and well defended by D. L. Bock, *Proclamation from Prophecy and Pattern: Lucan Old Testament Christology*, JSNTSup 12 (Sheffield: JSOT, 1987). For the textual details here, cf. D. W. Baker, "Language and Text of the Old Testament," in *Interpreting the Old Testament: A Guide for Exegesis*, ed. C. C. Broyles (Grand Rapids: Baker, 2001), 79.

Techniques of Translation

Translation techniques constitute the second criterion by which readers ought to evaluate modern versions of the Bible. It helps to plot the various English translations at points on a two-dimensional graph that takes both accuracy and clarity into account.[102] Some versions prioritize preserving the form and structure of the original text over what is the most intelligible English, though of course they still want to be understood by readers. We call these *formally equivalent* translations. The (N)KJV and NASB are prime examples, and to a certain extent also the ESV and NRSV. The NASB, for example, renders the theologically rich Romans 3:25 as "whom God displayed publicly as a propitiation in His blood through faith. *This was* to demonstrate His righteousness, because in the forbearance of God He passed over the sins previously committed." This is a very "literal" (i.e., formally equivalent) translation but not one that all English readers can readily understand. At the other end of the spectrum we find versions that seek to prioritize clarity over grammar and syntax while still being true to the meaning of the text. We call these *dynamically* (or functionally) *equivalent* translations (e.g., GNB, NLT, CEV, NCV). These versions are less concerned to consistently translate a given Greek or Hebrew word with the same English word if a given context suggests a different meaning for that word. Dynamically or functionally equivalent translations often reword a sentence with a passive-voice verb into an equivalent one with an active-voice verb, reflecting better English style ("I was hit by the baseball" would become "the baseball hit me."). For example, "Blessed are those who mourn, for they shall be comforted" (Matt 5:4), becomes in the GNB, "Happy are those who mourn; God will comfort them!" Idioms and figures of speech often become more intelligible by means of modern equivalents or nonidiomatic language (e.g., "kick against the goads" in Romans 16:4 becomes "fight against my will").

Between these, *optimally equivalent* translations (e.g., NIV, HCSB, CEB) prioritize neither clarity over accuracy nor accuracy over clarity but seek to attain as much of each as possible in every passage, recognizing that sometimes one may end up being favored slightly and sometimes another. What exactly did the man asking his neighbor for bread at midnight demonstrate in Luke 11:8? The Greek word *anaideia* appears only here in the Bible.[103] The KJV suggested it was the man's "importunity" (but how many people know what that means today?). The ESV rendered it correctly as "impudence," but many English speakers don't know that term either. At the other end of the spectrum, the NCV is clear with "boldness" but loses the edginess of the original Greek. The NIV uses "shameless audacity," which may capture the best

---

102. On the theory and practice of translation, see esp. E. A. Nida, *Toward a Science of Translating* (Leiden: Brill, 1964); J. Beekman and J. Callow, *Translating the Word of God* (Grand Rapids: Zondervan, 1974); J. de Waard and E. A. Nida, *From One Language to Another: Functional Equivalence in Bible Translating* (Nashville: Thomas Nelson, 1986); and S. E. Porter and M. J. Boda, eds., *Translating the New Testament: Text, Translation, Theology* (Grand Rapids: Eerdmans, 2009).

103. BDAG give this meaning: "lack of sensitivity to what is proper, carelessness about the good opinion of others, shamelessness, impertinence, impudence, ignoring of convention" (63).

of both worlds—clear and accurate by introducing the idea of shame. The CEB'S "brashness" similarly seems very useful as a translation. In short, our discussion here sets the translation options in perspective so readers can make an informed choice. Most important, we underscore (with Brunn, see below) that the overall commonalities of all the standard translations far outstrip their distinctives—that all will serve readers quite well.

The Major English Translations[104]

Since its completion in 1611, the King James Version of the English Bible has dominated the field. The first "authorized" version, after previous efforts by men like John Wycliffe, Miles Coverdale, and William Tyndale, ran aground of ecclesiastical authorities, the KJV was a masterpiece of formal equivalence rendered into the common vernacular of seventeenth-century England. A team of scholars commissioned by James VI bypassed the Latin Vulgate, which had dominated Christianity for 1,000 years, compared prior English translations with the best couple dozen Hebrew and Greek manuscripts available to them, and produced a painstaking, monumental version of the Scriptures. Imagine: a Bible translation that is still around after 400 years![105] But the English language has changed dramatically since then, and the discovery of many, new Bible manuscripts much older than those available in 1611 make the KJV far less valuable today. The KJV, of course, has been revised frequently; no edition in print today reads exactly like the original. The most famous twentieth century edition of the KJV, the Scofield Reference Bible, contains numerous marginal notes to indicate where it updates obscure English. The New King James Version (NKJV) offers an even more thorough rewrite.

The textual base in each of these editions and versions of the KJV, however, remains unchanged. A handful of textual critics continues to defend the so-called Majority Text (the 80 percent or so of NT manuscripts that roughly agrees with the KJV). They argue that if this were not the earliest text-form, it would not have survived in so many manuscripts.[106] But, in fact, most of these manuscripts come from the Byzantine family of texts (a collection of manuscripts with similar readings and geographic origins suggesting that they all derived from one or a few exemplars) associated with the world power that ruled from Constantinople (formerly called Byzantium) after the fall of Rome. So naturally, their manuscripts of the NT were most widely copied and well preserved. But none of the oldest, second-through-fifth

---

104. For surveys of many of these, see J. P. Lewis, *The English Bible from KJV to NIV*, 2nd ed. (Grand Rapids: Baker, 1991); B. M. Metzger, *The Bible in Translation* (Grand Rapids: Baker, 2001); and D. Brunn, *One Bible, Many Versions: Are All Translations Created Equal?* (Downers Grove: InterVarsity, 2013).

105. On the incredible production and achievement of the KJV, also called the Authorized Version (AV), see A. Nicolson, *God's Secretaries: The Making of the King James Bible* (New York: HarperCollins, 2003); and L. Ryken, *The Legacy of the King James Bible: Celebrating 400 Years of the Most Influential English Translation* (Wheaton: Crossway, 2011).

106. See esp. Z. C. Hodges and A. L. Farstad, eds., *The Greek New Testament According to the Majority Text* (Nashville: Nelson, 1982).

century manuscripts, most of which were discovered since 1611, come from this tradition, and so our knowledge of what the biblical writers themselves actually wrote has improved greatly since the production of the KJV. We now have nearly 5,800 pre-Gutenberg, hand-copied documents of part or all of the NT, in addition to the DSS supplementing the MT for the OT. We really ought to be thankful, for example, that Mark did not write the KJV rendering of Mark 16:18 (see above), but readers who limit themselves to the KJV will never know this. Readers of the NKJV will find slightly clearer and more up-to-date English, and they will know about the differences among manuscripts, if they read the footnotes, but they will naturally conclude that the better readings are those of the KJV, because those are the variants chosen for translation within the text itself. For this reason, we cannot endorse the widespread use of these versions when more accurate alternatives are available.[107]

Revision of the KJV based on new textual discoveries in both testaments began with the British Revised Version (RV) in 1885 and the American Standard Version (ASV) in 1901. But the most dramatic manuscript discoveries, including the DSS, occurred since then. The first truly modern translation, still very formally equivalent but abreast of the scholarly state of the art, was the Revised Standard Version (RSV) completed in 1952. Unfortunately, it received unduly negative press in some conservative circles because of occasional controversial renderings. Most famous was its use of "young woman" instead of "virgin" in Isaiah 7:14. Others criticized the RSV because of its somewhat liberal use of conjectural emendation (proposing different consonants in the Hebrew text, even when no known variants support those proposals) in seemingly garbled OT passages (as in the illustration from Ps 2:12 above).[108] But when it appeared, the RSV was far superior in fluency and accuracy to any other English version available. The RSV was updated in 1971, and in 1990 a New Revised Standard Version (NRSV) appeared. One of the prominent changes was the use of inclusive language instead of masculine nouns and pronouns when both men and women are in view.

After the RSV first appeared, many English and American readers began to feel the need for versions of Scripture that were easier for the average, biblically illiterate person to read. Paraphrases,[109] produced by individuals rather than the larger committees that worked together on the other versions, began to appear. J. B. Phillips published his NT in England in 1958. An American, Ken Taylor, published his "Living Letters" in 1962 and eventually completed the Living Bible Paraphrased (LBP) in 1971. Phillips and Taylor were often harshly criticized for taking undue liberties with the

---

107. For a detailed defense of these claims, see D. A. Carson, *The King James Version Debate: A Plea for Realism* (Grand Rapids: Baker, 1979); and J. R. White, *The King James Only Controversy: Can You Trust Modern Translations?* 2nd ed. (Minneapolis: Bethany, 2009).

108. For a good summary of most of the complaints that led certain evangelicals to seek new, alternate translations to the RSV, see P. J. Thuesen, *In Discordance with the Scriptures: American Protestant Battles over Translating the Bible* (Oxford: Oxford University Press, 1999), 67–144.

109. Paraphrases add explanatory words or phrases that do not correspond to anything in the original text and are not necessary to preserve the original sense of the passage, but give the text added freshness and impact.

text. In the LBP, Psalm 119:105 (usually translated, "you are a lamp unto my feet") became, anachronistically, "Your words are a flashlight to light the path ahead of me." Phillips's rendering of Acts 8:20 (usually translated, "May your money perish with you") became shocking to many ("To hell with you and your money!"), even though Phillips correctly comments in a footnote that this is a quite defensible and a highly accurate translation of the Greek. In the 1990s, however, the publishers of the LBP convened a large committee of scholars to revise Taylor's work to make it a legitimate, functionally equivalent translation. This New Living Translation (NLT) first appeared in 1996.[110]

On the other hand, Eugene Peterson's *The Message* (completed in 2002) is a far freer paraphrase than even the original LBP, but a group of scholars (chaired by W. W. Klein and R. L. Hubbard, Jr.) assessed it for theological accuracy, and it has proved very popular because of its strikingly fresh language. Critics often overlooked that these versions were not produced to replace translations that are more traditional; rather, they aimed to make the Bible come alive and to be read by people who would not otherwise read Scripture at all. To that extent they succeeded remarkably. More distinctive is the Amplified Bible, which often places several synonyms for particular words in parentheses right in the text itself. Unfortunately, uninformed Bible readers may think that all of these words are equally plausible translations or that the original terms actually meant everything that appears in parentheses simultaneously! Neither of these is true, of course.

Translations that sought dynamic equivalence include, most notably, Today's English Version (TEV) of the NT (1966), which ten years later was expanded to become the Good News Bible (GNB), along with most of the newer translations being published by the United Bible Societies in languages other than English. The British produced the New English Bible (NEB; NT in 1961 and OT in 1970), which falls somewhere between dynamic equivalence and paraphrase but often relies on idiosyncratic textual criticism. Improvements, revisions, and the addition of some inclusive language to the NEB resulted in the Revised English Bible (REB) of 1990. The American Bible Society has issued a new translation entitled the Contemporary English Version (CEV, completed in 1995). A widely used children's Bible proved so popular with adults that it was revised and "upgraded" for a wider audience as the New Century Version (NCV). It, too, employs inclusive language for people, dynamic equivalence translation principles, and uses the simplest English of all the new versions.

Many evangelicals were unhappy with one or another feature of the first efforts to improve on the KJV and ASV. Either they suspected liberal bias or found paraphrases

110. For several years running, the NLT has ranked fourth in international sales, after the NIV, KJV, and NKJV, in that order. These are the only translations to have consistently captured more than 10 percent of the share of the Bible market in the last decade. The ESV has been fifth, hovering at around 9 percent, and the NRSV, a distant sixth, at about 3 percent.

too free, but they agreed that updating was desperately needed. So two translations stemming from evangelical teams of scholars were produced—the first by Americans, the second by an international group. The former, a revision of the ASV, was called the New American Standard Bible (NASB) and was completed in 1971; the latter, the New International Version (NIV), was finished in 1978. The NASB is very formally equivalent, to the point of being rather stilted at times. The NIV is optimally equivalent and has become far and away the translation of choice in evangelical circles, much as NRSV is in ecumenical circles.[111] A simplified version known as the New International Readers' Version (NIrV) particularly geared for children or adults just learning to read has proved very popular.

The most controversial issue concerning Bible translation in evangelical circles involved inclusive language for humanity. In 1996, Hodder and Stoughton in London issued the NIV Inclusive Language Edition (NIVI), which consistently used substitutions like "brothers and sisters" for "brothers"; "person" for "man"; and even "they" or "you" for "he" when the terms in question were deemed generic in their original contexts. Vigorous protests from certain very conservative American evangelicals led to the suspension of plans to publish a highly similar American edition.[112] But the NIV's "Committee on Bible Translation" (CBT) continued to work and in 2002 released Today's NIV (TNIV) with similar revisions. Sadly, criticism of the TNIV was often based on misunderstandings of linguistics in general and of the CBT's philosophy of translation in particular[113] and somewhat polarized the evangelical community in the U.S. into two large groups, who were either staunchly opposed or solidly in favor of the methodology. Those opposed produced their own more formally equivalent and gender-exclusive translations, most notably the English Standard Version (ESV in 2001). A uniquely Southern Baptist venture called the Holman Christian Standard Bible (HCSB in 2009) was more like the NIV in trying to attain optimal equivalence but also more gender exclusive than the NIVI or TNIV. [114]

---

111. The importance of these two translations has led to entire books about their production: K. L. Barker, ed., *The NIV: The Making of a Contemporary Translation* (Grand Rapids: Zondervan, 1986); and B. M. Metzger, R. C. Dentan, and W. Harrelson, *The Making of the New Revised Standard Version* (Grand Rapids: Eerdmans, 1991).

112. See further C. L. Blomberg, "*Today's New International Version*: The Untold Story of a Good Translation," *BT* 56 (2005): 187–211.

113. For overviews of the debate, contrast D. A. Carson, *The Inclusive Language Debate: A Plea for Realism* (Grand Rapids: Baker; Leicester: Intervarsity, 1998) (generally favorable to inclusive language for humanity) with V. S. Poythress and W. A. Grudem, *The Gender-Neutral Bible Controversy: Muting the Masculinity of God's Words* (Nashville: Broadman and Holman, 2000) (generally opposed).

114. We could say much more about other modern translations. Briefly, in Roman Catholic circles the two most important are the New Jerusalem Bible (NJB) and the New American Bible (NAB). Both break with the traditional Catholic practice of following the Latin Vulgate and go back instead to the Greek and Hebrew. The NAB is reasonably similar to the NIV as an optimal translation; the NJB is closer to the REB as more dynamically equivalent. In Judaism, The Tanak (TNK) is a significant modern rendering of the Hebrew Scriptures into contemporary English and the Complete Jewish Bible is a Messianic Jewish translation. The New English Translation pioneered storyboarding of study notes in its online version. The New World Translation of the Jehovah's Witnesses is widely known because of its unjustifiable translations of passages that teach Christ's deity or the personality of the Holy Spirit (both of which the Jehovah's Witnesses deny). The Joseph Smith Translation of the Mormons at times includes changes and

An updated NIV was released in 2011, after the CBT commissioned the London-based Collins Dictionary Group to search the world's largest database of English documents (4.4 million words) of all different topics and genres, including but scarcely dominated by evangelical Christian writings and sermons, to determine the frequency of use of a whole host of specific constructions. Perhaps the most dramatic finding was that about 84 percent of time speakers and writers used the "singular they" to follow up on a generic antecedent, and it has been deemed desirable by academic societies of English professors and writers. That figure continues to grow annually. Proverbs 17:5a can be chosen virtually at random as an illustration: "Whoever mocks the poor shows contempt for *their* Maker." An optimally equivalent translation produced by a mainline Protestant publisher in 2011 with both mainline and evangelical translators is the Common English Bible (CEB), which uses contractions and other colloquialisms, while still staying reasonably close to the meaning of the text.

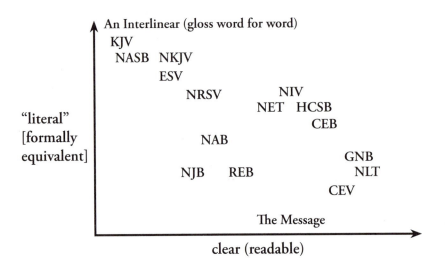

Choosing a Translation

Which translation is the best to use?[115] The basic answer is that it depends on your purpose or occasion. If, for the sake of doing word studies or outlining a passage, you want a version that generally tries to reflect the actual structure of the biblical language and that translates key terms with the same English word as often as possible, then follow the NASB or, with a few more exceptions, the ESV or NRSV. Deciding among those three might depend on your view of the inclusive language issue. If you

---

expansions unjustifiable from the original texts that were supposedly given to Smith by direct inspiration from God. But the official Bible of the Church of Jesus Christ of Latter-day Saints is the KJV.

115. See further G. D. Fee and M. L. Strauss, *How to Choose a Translation for All Its Worth: A Guide to Understanding and Using Bible Versions* (Grand Rapids: Zondervan, 2007); and A. J. Köstenberger and D. A. Croteau, eds., *Which Bible Translation Should I Use? A Comparison of 4 Major Recent Versions* (Nashville: B&H, 2012).

are looking for an accurate translation with fresh thoughts and insights for a young or inexperienced reader in simple and vivid language, or someone learning English as a second language, consider the NLT or the NCV. For sheer arresting paraphrase and innovation, check out *The Message*.[116] For the best overall combination of accuracy and readability, consult the updated NIV (or at a slightly lower reading level, the CEB or, with slightly less accuracy, the HCSB). For dramatic and poetic readings in classic Elizabethan English, dust off the KJV!

Above all, whenever you are serious about studying a passage intensively, especially when you are teaching it to others or dealing with controversial exegetical or theological issues, consult more than one translation. For memorization, choose the translation you prefer and use it consistently. Nevertheless, for valid interpretation, if you cannot read the biblical languages, you must compare several versions lest you miss an important possible nuance. Indeed, comparing translations is probably the best way to discover where significant textual differences or ambiguous wording occurs in the Hebrew or Greek originals. Numerous computer programs also allow for the quick comparison of standard texts and translations.[117]

---

116. A revision to this popular version is in the works.

117. Logos Bible Software, BibleWorks, and Accordance are three of the perennially most popular, but many other publishers offer a wide range of Bible versions in their packages. Online, see esp. www.biblegateway.org.

Part II

THE INTERPRETER
AND THE GOAL

⋙ 5 ⋘

THE INTERPRETER

Suppose two people decided to conduct a similar chemistry experiment. One had a PhD in chemistry, years of research experience, and carefully followed the experimental design with accuracy and precision. The other had only one high school chemistry course, worked carelessly, and failed to follow the procedures or make the measurements precisely. Which of these two "chemists" would obtain the more valid results? Without doubt, the one who worked with accuracy and precision would get the nod. The same is true of Bible interpretation. If interpretation is to succeed, the interpreter must possess certain competencies and must work with correct and accurate methodology. Careful and accurate work by skilled practitioners produces the best results. It is our goal in this book to present responsible, careful methods for accurate interpretation and understanding of the Scriptures. Those who practice these methods with rigor and care will have the best possible prospects of success in this endeavor. The best techniques are most likely to furnish the most accurate insights.

However, we are still faced with a dilemma, for in addition to accurate methodology, the interpreter's set of convictions or presuppositions about the nature of Scripture and about the precise nature of the task of interpretation profoundly affects his or her work. In chapter 1 we stressed that interpretation was both a science and an art. An experienced art critic who analyzes a painting will observe the focus of attention, mood, lighting, perspective, and the use of color and shadow, in addition to the more technical or mechanical details. But that critic's own commitments will affect the assessment of these features. Likewise, to cite an obvious example, the biblical interpreter who rejects the existence of demons will explain all biblical references to them as myth or legend—certainly not as literal history. An interpreter's presuppositions will cause him or her to accept or reject the possibility that sentient demons might oppress or possess a person. So the two topics, qualifications and presuppositions, go hand in hand. In this chapter we will discuss *qualifications* first and then consider *presuppositions*. Then, building on that foundation, we will study the role of *preunderstanding* in the interpretive process.[1]

---

1. K. J. Vanhoozer, *Is There a Meaning in This Text?*, 376–77, lists three additional "interpretive virtues" that we will assume without explicitly defending them: honesty (acknowledging one's personal stance and commitments), openness (willingness to hear and consider others' views), and attention (having a focus on the text). We agree these are crucial.

QUALIFICATIONS OF THE INTERPRETER

We believe there is a set of qualifications that puts the interpreter in the best position to obtain valid interpretations of the biblical text.

Qualifications for the Interpreter of Scripture
A Reasoned Faith in the God Who Reveals
Willingness to Obey Its Message
Willingness to Employ Appropriate Methods
Illumination of the Holy Spirit
Membership in the Church

A Reasoned Faith in the God Who Reveals

All understanding requires a framework or context within which to interpret. Thus, to understand a lecture about the properties of the Higgs boson, one must have at least some knowledge of theoretical physics. The more knowledge the listener has about particle physics, the more understanding he or she will gain from the lecture. Returning to the art world, the more one understands the effects and uses of lighting, perspective, textures, the other works of a period or school, the more qualified that person will be to appraise a painting. Likewise, if the Bible is God's revelation to his people, then *the essential qualification for a full understanding of the Bible is to know God and to believe that he is speaking through it.* One must have a relationship with God in order to fully understanding the book God has authored.

The Bible uses the term "faith" to describe the essential element in this relationship: "And without faith it is impossible to please God, because anyone who comes to him must believe that he exists and that he rewards those who earnestly seek him" (Heb 11:6).[2] Only the one who believes and trusts in God can truly understand what God has spoken in his Word, the Scriptures. This makes sense, for how can one understand a text from the Bible that purports to be a word from God if one denies that there is a God or that the Bible is a message from God? We doubt that one can fully grasp the Bible's message if he or she claims that the Bible is merely a human religious book.[3]

Paul makes clear in 1 Corinthians 2:14 that the ability to apprehend God's truth in its fullest sense belongs only to the "spiritual person." This is true because the material is "spiritual" in nature—i.e., it concerns and derives from God who is spirit—and

---

2. Having a "relationship" with God may be popular language, but the concept is expressed in various ways through the Bible. For a few examples: Moses was called "the man of God" (Josh 14:6) and often spoke face-to-face with the Deity; James calls Abraham God's friend (Jas 2:3); David was a "man after God's heart" (Acts 13:22; cf. 1 Sam 13:14). Micah writes about walking humbly with God (Mic 6:8).

3. We do not imply here that simply because one is a "believer," that she or he will *fully* grasp the Bible's meaning, any more than a seasoned art critic will fully grasp the meaning of a specific painting by van Gogh.

so requires a reader who can tune in to that dimension. So while excellence in methodology is a necessary qualification, we allege that tactical precision alone does not suffice for understanding the Bible. Such understanding comes only through possessing the spiritual sensitivity that belongs to those who have faith in God, to those who believe. Thus, in the sense we are using it here, faith is foundational for a full comprehension of the Scriptures. It is not the only qualification, nor does it guarantee correct interpretation.

Do not misunderstand. We do not arrogantly assert that one who is not a believer cannot understand anything about the Bible. Unbelievers, even skeptics, can grasp much of its meaning. They may discover what it asserts or claims, even when their own beliefs or value systems lead them to deny those claims. Thus, a competent, unbelieving scholar may produce an outstanding technical commentary on a biblical book—perhaps even better on some of the details of the text than many believing Christian scholars could write. But that unbelieving scholar cannot understand and portray the true *significance* of the Bible's message, for he or she is not ultimately committed to the Bible as divine revelation.[4] On the other hand, we do not assert that a believing interpreter will always be right in an interpretation. The believer must be able to defend his or her specific interpretation and demonstrate its validity to believer and non-believer alike.

We simply argue that even when scholars apply the same methodology, their differing presuppositions will open the way to potentially different results. If a reader says, "Though the Gospel story reports that a man was possessed by a demon, we know demons don't exist so there must be a psychological or physiological explanation for the man's behavior," that person's modern values or philosophical positivism has led to a rejection of the historical nature of this specific account. On the other hand, those who accept the Bible as God's revelation expect it to provide true information, and they would not utter such a statement. They may puzzle over what the Bible teaches; they may disobey its instructions; but they are bound to acknowledge it as the true word of God.

If interpreters choose to work within the Bible's own framework (e.g., the existence of an all-powerful, all-knowing God; the reality of the supernatural; and the fact that God speaks in the Bible), the results will be of one kind. That is, interpretations will correspond to the affirmations the biblical writers themselves make. However, if an interpreter operates within a modern, secular, naturalistic viewpoint, then he or she

---

4. The difference between the findings of unbelieving versus believing readers is often one of volition, not cognition. Through their careful work, both may come to the same understanding of a text's *meaning*. But due to their different faith commitments, only the believer will *perceive* the text's true *significance* and *be willing to obey* the truth conveyed. We take this perspective partly from our understanding of 1 Cor 2:14, on which see C. L. Blomberg, *1 Corinthians*, NIVAC (Grand Rapids: Zondervan, 1995), 63–68; A. C. Thiselton, *The First Epistle to the Corinthians*, NIGTC (Grand Rapids: Eerdmans, 2000), 267–71; and D. E. Garland, *1 Corinthians*, BECNT (Grand Rapids: Baker, 2003), 100–1. We discuss the important distinction between meaning and significance later. In addition, one's faith commitment opens a believer's mind to engage the text personally under the guidance of the Holy Spirit—which is often the Bible's objective! See the next point.

will exclude certain categories out of hand. Or from a postmodern point of view, a supernatural reading of the Bible may be "valid," but no more so than a psychological or existentialist one. Read it any way you want, so long as you are consistent and creative!

In other words, two scholars, believer and unbeliever, might both research literary elements in the Gospel narratives. They might come to similar conclusions about most issues—say the background of the pericope in the life of Jesus, the editorial work of an Evangelist, etc. But how would they handle the mention of "demons"? The conservative scholar is disposed to admit the existence of such beings, if for no other reason than that the Bible affirms their reality and contemporary testimony and experience back it up.[5] The other scholar may state that ancient peoples attributed certain infirmities to demons, but today we "know" better and ascribe them to psychological or medical causes. And rejection of what the Bible teaches may go even farther than merely discounting supernatural accounts. For if the Bible is not divine revelation, then others of its teachings may be reasonably rejected as out of touch with modern findings.

Modern science cannot confirm or disconfirm alleged biblical miracles for they are beyond its orbit. Thus scholarship built solely on the foundation of rationalism and science is compelled to find naturalistic explanations for the biblical accounts of miracles. No amount of protesting can dislodge the naturalists, for, according to their presuppositions, miracles do not occur.[6]

*Faith*ful readers, on the other hand, accept the miraculous in the Bible as factual, not as the result of naïve fideism or dogmatic pronouncements, but after critical investigation and reasoning.[7] As evangelicals, we are committed to being logical and to engaging in careful historical argumentation to show that the biblical accounts are defensible and historically credible, even if in the end they cannot be scientifically proven.[8] We bind ourselves to the facts of history, but we insist this does not

---

5. See, e.g., the kind of evidence that C. Keener amasses in his lengthy appendices A and B on exorcisms in C. Keener, *Miracles: The Credibility of the New Testament Accounts*, 2 vols. (Grand Rapids: Baker, 2011), 2:769–856.

6. For further study see Keener, *Miracles*, as well as C. L. Blomberg, *Can We Still Believe the Bible?: An Evangelical Engagement with Contemporary Questions* (Grand Rapids: Brazos, 2014), esp. 179–212.

7. We discuss the phenomenon of miracles in the chapter on the Gospels genre below. See key literature in C. L. Blomberg, *Historical Reliability of the Gospels*, 2nd ed. (Downers Grove: InterVarsity, 2007), 104–51.

8. In addition to the literature cited above in defense of Scripture's truthfulness, see for the OT, I. Provan, V. P. Long, and T. Longman III, *A Biblical History of Israel*, 2nd ed. (Louisville: Westminster John Knox Press, 2015); B. T. Arnold and R. S. Hess, eds., *Ancient Israel's History: An Introduction to Issues and Sources* (Grand Rapids: Baker Academic, 2014); K. A. Kitchen, *On the Reliability of the Old Testament* (Grand Rapids; Cambridge: Eerdmans, 2003); G. A. Klingbeil, "Historical Criticism," in *Dictionary of the Old Testament: Pentateuch*, ed. D. T. Alexander and D. W. Baker (Downers Grove: InterVarsity Press, 2003), 401–20 (for the Pentateuch); S. L. McKenzie, "Historiography, Old Testament," in *Dictionary of Old Testament: Historical Books*, ed. B. T Arnold and H. G. M. Williamson (Downers Grove: InterVarsity, 2005), 418–25 (for the historical books); V. P. Long, D. W. Baker, and G. J. Wenham, eds., *Windows into Old Testament History: Evidence, Argument, and the Crisis of "Biblical Israel"* (Grand Rapids: Eerdmans, 2002); and W. G. Dever, *What Did the Biblical Writers Know and When Did They Know It? What Archaeology Can Tell Us about the Reality of Ancient Israel* (Grand Rapids: Eerdmans, 2001). For a helpful introduction to the role of the historical method in NT studies see D. A. Hagner, "The New Testament, History, and the Historical-Critical Method," in *New Testament Criticism and Interpretation*, ed. D. A. Black and D. S. Dockery (Grand Rapids: Zondervan, 1991), 73–96. Hagner concludes his essay with several valuable modifications

obligate us to a nonsupernatural explanation of reality or the biblical record.[9] Since, in our view, the sources prove reliable where they can be tested, we give them the benefit of the doubt where they cannot be. We insist that to hold such evangelical presuppositions is neither to commit intellectual suicide nor to relegate ourselves to a hopelessly obscurantist dogmatism. The evangelical faith is committed to a defensible, historically credible explanation of the Bible—within the bounds of the Bible's own claims about itself and its origins. Rather than reject logic and reason, the evangelical study of the Bible welcomes any method or approach that enables the Bible's meaning and significance to be understood.

Willingness to Obey Its Message

A second requirement for a valid interpretation of the Bible, following close upon the requirement of faith, is the *willingness to put oneself "under" the text, to submit one's will to hear and respond the text in a faithful manner.* The truly faithful reader seeks to obey what God reveals in Scripture. As readers, we must not lose sight of the significant (often spiritual) issues the original biblical authors were trying to communicate, and be willing to obey. N. Lash states the point forcefully, "If the questions to which ancient authors sought to respond in terms available to them within their cultural horizons are to be 'heard' today with something like their original force and urgency, they have first to be 'heard' as questions that challenge us with comparable seriousness."[10]

We cannot genuinely understand what a text meant without allowing it to affect our lives in the ways the text intends. Interpretation involves a crucial dialectic between the historical origin of a text and the perspective of the modern reader or interpreter. To focus *only* on the former consigns the Bible to the status of an ancient (but irrelevant) artifact. Yet to abandon the historical reference and seek only for some felicitous significance for today is equally misguided. Scripture loses all normativeness if all "readings" of its text can claim equal validity. Genuine interpretation requires a fusing of the ancient and modern horizons where the meaning of the ancient text helps interpreters come to new understandings of themselves.[11] As Lash properly

---

of the historical-critical method that will counter its unwarranted negative conclusions (89–91). On the historical veracity for the Gospels, see C. L. Blomberg, *The Historical Reliability of the Gospels*; C. L. Blomberg, *The Historical Reliability of John's Gospel: Issues & Commentary* (Downers Grove: InterVarsity, 2001); I. H. Marshall, *Luke: Historian and Theologian*, 3rd ed. (Downers Grove: InterVarsity, 1998); and P. R. Eddy and G. A. Boyd, *The Jesus Legend: A Case for the Historical Reliability of the Synoptic Jesus Tradition* (Grand Rapids: Baker, 2007).

9. As an example, see the massive weight of the historical evidence for Jesus' miracles in the gospels defended by J. P. Meier, *A Marginal Jew: Rethinking the Historical Jesus*, vol. 2 (New York: Doubleday, 1994), esp. 509–644. On the historicity of the most foundational yet questioned of all miracles, Jesus' resurrection, see N. T. Wright, *The Resurrection of the Son of God* (Minneapolis: Fortress, 2003); and M. L. Licona, *The Resurrection of Jesus: A New Historiographical Approach* (Downers Grove: InterVarsity, 2010).

10. N. Lash, "What Might Martyrdom Mean?" *Ex Auditu* 1 (1985): 17.

11. We borrow the image of the fusing of horizons from A. C. Thiselton, *The Two Horizons. New Testament Hermeneutics and Philosophical Description* (Grand Rapids: Eerdmans, 1980), who in turn builds on the work of H.-G. Gadamer, particularly his *Truth and Method* (New York: Continuum, 2004; first German edition, 1960).

insists, "the articulation of what the text might 'mean' today is a necessary condition of hearing what that text 'originally meant.'"[12] Though Lash does not take the point this far, we insist that full understanding comes only to the sincere follower of the God who revealed—the follower who diligently seeks to practice the message of the text studied.[13]

Illumination of the Holy Spirit

The third qualification, related to the previous two, is to allow the Holy Spirit to complement the process of exegesis. For his part, God provides the resource for an obedient understanding of his truth: the regeneration of the Holy Spirit.[14] A consequence of the Spirit's presence in a believer's life is the *illumination of the Holy Spirit*. That is, the Bible speaks of a work that God's Spirit performs in people once they have committed their lives in faith to Jesus as Lord. This internal capacity enables believers to perceive and apprehend spiritual truth, an ability unavailable to unbelievers (cf. 1 Cor 2:6–16; 2 Cor 3:15–18). This illuminating work of the Spirit does not circumvent nor allow believers to dispense with the principles of hermeneutics and the techniques of exegesis. That is, the Spirit does not reveal the meanings of texts "out of the blue," as it were. Illumination refers to a dynamic comprehension of the *significance* of Scripture and its *application to life* that is uniquely available to those indwelt by the Holy Spirit.

Though we may possess an arsenal of methods and techniques with which to decipher the meaning of the biblical texts, interpretation falls short of its true potential without the illumination of the Spirit. Methods alone are not sufficient to understand profoundly and exactly the true meaning and significance of Scripture. And neither methodology nor the Spirit operates in isolation from the other. We need to see how methodology and illumination are linked.

First, consider whether one can depend solely upon the Holy Spirit for understanding the Bible apart from methods and techniques. The reasoning often goes like this: if the Holy Spirit inspired the original writers, then certainly the Spirit can unlock the texts' meaning without recourse to historical or grammatical study. C. H. Spurgeon (1834–92), England's best-known preacher for most of the second half of the nineteenth century, countered such pretension with some advice to budding preachers in "A Chat about Commentaries":

---

12. Lash, "Martyrdom," 18.

13. The writer of Ps 119:97–104 exemplifies the perspective of the obedient believer. The psalmist desires that God's commands be "ever with me." Speaking to God, his practice remains to "meditate on your statutes," and he seeks to "obey your precepts." "I have not departed from your laws," he says to his God.

14. Paul speaks of this transformative work of the Spirit using these words: "He saved us through the washing of rebirth and renewal by the Holy Spirit" (Titus 3:5). Some versions substitute the word "regeneration" for the NIV "rebirth." BDAG (752) defines *palingenesia* here as: "experience of a complete change of life, *rebirth* of a redeemed person" (their italics).

Of course, you are not such wiseacres as to think of ways that you can expound Scripture without assistance from the works of divines and learned men who have labored before you in the field of exposition. If you are of that opinion, pray remain so, for you are not worth the trouble of conversion, and like a little coterie who think with you, would resent the attempt as an insult to your infallibility. It seems odd, that certain men who talk so much of what the Holy Spirit reveals to themselves, should think so little of what he has revealed to others.[15]

In the pulpit today this error may sound like this:

Dear friends, I have consulted no other books, human sources, or worldly wisdom. I have considered no commentaries. I have gone right to the Bible—and only the Bible—to see what it had to say for itself. Let me share with you what God showed me.

As Bernard Ramm, who invented a similar quote, observes, "This sounds very spiritual," but in fact "it is a veiled egotism" and a "confusion of the inspiration of the Spirit with the illumination of the Spirit."[16] The Spirit's work of illumination does not impart new revelation.[17] Unfortunately, some deeply spiritual people have declared some obviously incorrect interpretations of the Bible. Being indwelt by the Spirit does not guarantee accurate interpretation. Though we have no desire to diminish the Spirit's role, it does not work apart from sound hermeneutics and exegesis.

The Spirit provides sincere believers that indispensable ability to comprehend the text's significance for themselves (that "Aha!" enlightenment) by working within and through methods and techniques.[18] The Spirit enables readers to apprehend the message of the Bible as a word of God *for them*. As the Apostle Paul put it, "God works in (or among) his people both to will and to act . . ." (our translation of Phil 2:12). Both the willingness and the capacity to act on what believers discover are gifts of God to his people. An encounter occurs between the Spirit of the Word and the human spirit. Swartley says, "In the co-creative moment, text and interpreter experience life by the power of the divine Spirit. Without this experience, interpretation falls short of its ultimate potential and purpose."[19]

---

15. C. H. Spurgeon, *Commenting and Commentaries* (New York: Sheldon & Company, 1876), 11. Of course, in his day virtually all biblical scholars and preachers were "men."

16. B. Ramm, *Protestant Biblical Interpretation,* 3rd ed. (Grand Rapids: Baker, 1970), 17–18.

17. One of the striking features of most heresies or cults is their use of Jesus' words recorded in John 14–16, esp. 14:26, 15:26, and 16:5–16. In fact, Jesus does not promise that the Holy Spirit will provide new truth or revelation to all succeeding Christians throughout the Church Age. Rather he refers to the inspiration of the Spirit in providing the NT canon of Scripture through the apostles. The Spirit's role in relationship to believers today is not to reveal new truth; he did that in producing the Bible. His role now is to speak through Scripture to enable believers to apprehend and apply its truth. A. J. Köstenberger, *John,* BECNT (Grand Rapids: Baker Academic, 2004), 442, helpfully observes: "The Spirit will not provide qualitatively new or independent revelation . . . but will bring to light the true meaning and significance of the revelation imparted by Jesus." For more on these Johannine texts also see D. A. Carson, *The Gospel According to John,* PNTC (Grand Rapids: Eerdmans, 1991), 505–6, 527–30, and 533–43.

18. We do not wish to deny that God works in the lives of unbelievers, even through the Scriptures. We merely stress the Holy Spirit's illumination in the lives of believers in keeping with 1 Cor 2:14–16.

19. W. Swartley, *Slavery, Sabbath, War, and Women* (Scottdale, PA: Herald Press, 1983), 224.

Certainly, we cannot "program" this creative encounter; it requires a stance of faith and humility before the Lord who has revealed his truth on the pages of Scripture. Yet by seeking to hear God's voice, the interpreter becomes open to true understanding and allows the text to fulfill God's purposes for it. *Prayer puts one in the position to hear and understand.* For the Christian, prayer is an indispensable ingredient for the proper understanding of Scripture. We must ask God to assist our study and to speak to us through it so that we might understand his truth and will for our lives. But we do not substitute prayer for diligent exegetical work. We pray that we will do our work well, that we will be sensitive to the Spirit's direction, and that we will be obedient to the truth we discover. We openly admit our bent to sin, error, and self-deception, and our finitude; we ask for an openness to receive what God has revealed and a willingness to learn from others throughout the history of interpretation.

Membership in the Church

We believe there is a fourth qualification that enables one to interpret well. Bible interpreters must be wary of the traps of individualism and tribalism (exaltation of my tribe, sect, church, or denomination above other groups). *We need to recognize our membership in the Body of Christ, the church.* By *church* we mean local *as well as* global body of Christ. It serves as the antidote to both individualism and tribalism. First, the church is the arena in which many of the significant requirements for truly hearing the text can be nurtured. Interpreters should not work in a vacuum; people across the centuries and across the continents have puzzled over the meaning of the Bible. We require the enrichment, efforts, and assistance of our fellow believers to check our perceptions and to affirm their validity. That is, if we can't communicate our interpretations to ordinary laypeople in ways that will ring true to at least an important cross-section of them, there's a good chance we haven't understood the text quite correctly. Even when convinced of our views, we do well to listen humbly to fellow believers in the church with an open ear to the voice of God possibly speaking through them. Likewise, our conclusions, if they are correct, have importance for others. The church throughout its history, constituted and illumined by the Spirit, provides accountability; it offers the arena in which we can formulate and implement our interpretations.

Such accountability guards against maverick, individualistic, and sectarian interpretations.[20] It provides a check against selfish and self-serving conclusions by those who lack the perspective to see beyond their own circumstances and prejudices. And since the church of Jesus Christ is a worldwide fellowship, it crosses all cultural boundaries and insular interests. This is a crucial reality we deny if we limit our interpretations and formulations of God's truth to personal (or parochial) attempts to understand Scripture. If we discover the meaning of God's revelation, it will make sense or ring

---

20. For a provocative appeal to situate interpretation in the community, see S. Hauerwas, *Unleashing the Scripture: Freeing the Bible from Captivity to America* (Nashville: Abingdon, 1993).

true to others in Christ's worldwide Body when they openly assess the evidence we used to reach our conclusions.

Willingness to Employ Appropriate Methods

The fifth and final qualification for interpretation has been assumed to this point, but we wish to make it explicit: *we need methods that are appropriate to the task of interpretation.* This task requires diligence and commitment, hard work and discipline. It requires the pursuit of excellence and learning in all dimensions (e.g., language, history, culture, literature, theology) that relate to the study of the Scriptures.

If the best interpretation involves a merging of the horizons of the ancient text and those of the modern interpreter, then interpreters must be aware of the worlds of the texts—of the ancient Near East for nearly two millennia before Christ for the OT, and the Roman Empire of the first century AD for the NT. There is no substitute for diligent study and the use of available tools. The interpreter must cultivate a sensitivity to hear and learn from all the research and data available. This requires study and practice.

Interpreters cannot settle issues that concern factual matters by an appeal to prayer or the illumination of the Holy Spirit. Prayer will not reveal to a Bible student that Baal was a fertility god worshiped by the Canaanites or that the Jews of Jesus' day regarded Samaritans as hated half-breeds. One cannot determine the identity of the "sons of God" in Genesis 6:1–4 or the "spirits in prison" in 1 Peter 3:18–22 simply by reading and rereading these texts in a prayerful and humble way. One must study history and culture to discover the nature of the "high place" at Bethel (2 Kgs 23:15) and the "head coverings" in first-century Corinth (1 Cor 11:2–16). Today Bible interpreters have numerous, excellent tools that provide facts and information about the ancient world and the biblical texts. Capable interpreters become acquainted with such research tools and use them to the best of their ability. If the first goal of interpretation is to determine the meaning the text had for its original author and recipients, then the diligent interpreter must be committed to using historical sources critically.

As well, since the Bible comes to us as literature—and in a variety of literary genres—those who seek to understand its message must become competent readers of literature. We must apply methods that will unpack for us what each level of the text and each kind of genre requires for understanding—whether historical narrative, epic, parable, prophetic denunciation, epistle, or apocalypse. On the lowest levels of language, we must understand lexicography and syntax and then proceed to the levels of paragraph, discourse, genres, literary analysis, book, and finally to an understanding of the entire canon.

Does this mean that no one can understand God's message in the Bible without a competence in biblical languages and a mastery of all the critical historical and linguistic tools? We do not think so, for no one possesses complete proficiency in these matters, and even were it obtainable, it would not guarantee correct interpretation.

We believe there are degrees of proficiency, and readers should strive for as much competency as their situation in life allows:

- A simple, sincere, and uneducated believer can comprehend the central truths of the Bible—and profit greatly from applying what they have learned to their lives.[21]
- The diligent Christian with an average education who is willing to study, and who has access to the fine tools now available,[22] can arrive at the central meaning of virtually every passage in the Bible.
- The believer who can acquire expertise in the biblical languages in addition to further training in biblical studies, history, culture, and theology will become that much more qualified to explain the meaning of most verses and even many of the more obscure or controversial texts.
- Finally, the scholars who have advanced training and specialized skills are able to perform closely reasoned and technical studies, write commentaries, engage in textual criticism to determine the original texts, translate and evaluate ancient literature that sheds light on the Bible, and produce modern translations of the Bible.

PRESUPPOSITIONS FOR CORRECT INTERPRETATION

The computer industry popularized a basic truth, immortalized in the acronym, GIGO—"garbage in, garbage out." That is, what you get out depends on what you put in.[23] This principle is certainly true in interpretation. The aims and presuppositions of interpreters govern and even determine their interpretations. When cartoon-character Charlie Brown expected to find the shapes of ducks and sheep in the clouds overhead, voila, he found them! Like Charlie Brown, many interpreters find in a text precisely the meaning, and *only* the meaning, they expected (and wanted!) to find—as anyone who has read or listened to debates over biblical scholarship will attest.

No one interprets anything without a set of underlying assumptions. When we presume to explain the meaning of the Bible, we do so with a set of preconceived ideas or presuppositions. These presuppositions may be examined and stated, simply embraced unconsciously, or in some combination. But anyone who claims to have no presuppositions and who studies the Bible objectively and inductively is either deceived or naïve. We argue that interpreters should discover, state, and consciously

---

21. This is what the Reformers meant is speaking of the perspicuity of Scripture. See M. D. Thompson, *A Clear and Present Word: The Clarity of Scripture*, NSBT (Downers Grove: InterVarsity, 2006). They affirmed the clarity of Scripture for matters of faith and practice.

22. We include an extensive bibliography of sources in the final chapter of this book.

23. Paul comprehended that principle well in expressing his counsel to the Philippians: ". . . whatever is true, whatever is noble, whatever is right, whatever is pure, whatever is lovely, whatever is admirable—if anything is excellent or praiseworthy—think about such things" (Phil 4:8).

adopt those assumptions they agree with and can defend, or else they will uncritically retain those they already have, whether or not they are adequate and valid.[24]

Interpretation is affected not only on the qualifications of interpreters (as we have just seen) but also upon their presuppositions. Thus, the development of an approach to hermeneutics involves an essential set of *presuppositions* that constitutes its starting point. Such a strategy will also require some means of verifying that the preferred interpretation is superior to the alternatives. We will take up this next step in subsequent chapters.

We need to consider the assumptions or presuppositions that we believe are necessary for an accurate interpretation of the Bible. Not all interpreters or readers will align themselves with this position, though we hope that many do (and that others will be persuaded to). We will outline these in several categories.

Presuppositions about the Nature of the Bible

Those who seek to interpret the Bible certainly come with specific presuppositions about the object of their inquiry. The view of the nature of the Bible that an interpreter holds will determine the method an interpreter will adopt. What do we presuppose about the nature of the Bible?

Evangelical Presuppositions for Interpretation	
	A Divine / Human book—Product of Divine Revelation
	Authoritative and True
Presuppositions About the *Nature* of the Bible	A Spiritual Document
	Unified and Diverse
	Understandable
	Forming a Canon as Holy Scripture

Divinely Inspired Revelation

We believe the Bible owes its origin to a divine all-powerful being who has revealed his message via human writers; it is *revelation inspired by God*. If an interpreter adopts an alternate explanation of the Bible's origin and nature, then he or she will view the text only as a human document, as inspiring as it might be.[25] We believe *the Bible is a supernatural book, God's written revelation to his people given through prepared and*

---

24. This has some parallels to what D. A. Carson calls "distantiation," the need to stand back from the text to study it critically, in *Exegetical Fallacies*, 2nd ed. (Grand Rapids: Baker, 1996), 23–24. The failure to undertake this step often leads to *eisegesis*—the "reading into" a text the meaning the interpreter prefers rather than "drawing out" (*exegesis*) what the author intended.

25. If the Bible records the religiously inspired thinking of pious Jews and Christians but is not divine revelation itself, then interpreters may feel free to handle it precisely and only as they do other ancient religious or philosophical books. Such interpreters may seek to explain on the basis of sociological or anthropological models (among others) how the Jewish or Christian religious communities came into existence and how they formulated foundational myths such as the crossing of the Red Sea (Sea of Reeds) or Jesus' resurrection to explain their religious experiences

selected spokespersons by the process of inspiration. This has been the church's nearly universal creed throughout its history, though modern liberalism has eroded this in certain circles.[26]

This assertion derives from the Bible's view of itself. Paul describes the OT as "inspired," using a term literally meaning "God-breathed" (2 Tim 3:16), a probable allusion to Genesis 2. Peter further affirms that the Holy Spirit carried along the writers as they spoke the words of God (2 Pet 1:20–21). The OT language supports divine inspiration with quotations like, "The LORD says, . . ." (e.g., Gen 6:7; 26:2; Exod 6:2; 12:43; 1 Sam 9:17; 1 Kgs 9:3; Zech 4:6), indicating that the speakers believed they were uttering God's message, not simply their own. When the NT writers quote the OT, they demonstrate their belief that the OT derives from God himself (e.g., 2 Cor 6:16; Matt 19:5/Gen 2:24; Acts 4:25/Ps 2:2; Rom 9:17/Exod 9:16).

In addition, various NT writers' views of other portions of the NT disclose their verdicts about the nature of these sections. Peter clearly viewed Paul's writings or letters in the same category as the "other scriptures" (2 Pet 3:16). After employing the introductory formula, "for Scripture says," Paul proceeds to quote from both Deuteronomy and (possibly) Luke (1 Tim 5:18/Deut 25:4; cf. Luke 10:7).[27] In places Paul seems to express the recognition that the apostles' teaching parallels that of the OT writers (1 Cor 2:13). John identifies his words with the "true words of God" (Rev 19:9).[28]

Of course, we do not argue that because the Bible claims to be God's Word, the question is settled. That would simply beg the question. Most religious groups make grandiose claims about their holy books. Though someone claims to be a fish, he or she remains a human. We cannot conduct the necessary apologetic defense of the Scriptures here, but we do argue that the general reliability of those historical portions of Scripture that can be verified lends credence to the Bible's overall truthfulness. Further, Jesus accepted the authority of the OT (John 10:35), and we are inclined to follow his lead.[29]

---

and longings. They may dismiss its claims as outdated, inaccurate, or even dangerous. The most extreme example of this is H. Avalos, *The End of Biblical Studies* (Amherst, NY: Prometheus, 2007).

26. For a vigorous defense of this statement, see J. D. Woodbridge, *Biblical Authority: Infallibility and Inerrancy in the Christian Tradition* (Grand Rapids: Zondervan, 1982, 2015).

27. Admittedly, Paul's quotation of the words that appear in Luke may derive from a collection of Jesus' oral (or written) sayings, rather than a written version of Luke's gospel itself. See G. W. Knight, III, *Pastoral Epistles*, NIGTC (Grand Rapids: Eerdmans, 1992), 233–35, who suggests that the source of Paul's quotation may well have been Luke's Gospel (234).

28. For a thorough treatment of how biblical writers viewed their writings as Scripture, see W. A. Grudem, "Scripture's Self-Attestation and the Modern Problem of Formulating a Doctrine of Scripture," in *Scripture and Truth,* ed. D. A. Carson and J. D. Woodbridge (Grand Rapids: Zondervan, 1983), 19–59. See also M. J. Kruger, *Canon Revisited: Establishing the Origins and Authority of the New Testament Books* (Wheaton, IL: Crossway, 2012).

29. On these two points in defense of Scripture's truthfulness see (1): K. A. Kitchen, *On the Reliability of the Old Testament* (Grand Rapids: Eerdmans, 2006); C. Armerding, *The Old Testament and Criticism* (Grand Rapids: Eerdmans, 1983); E. M. Yamauchi, *The Stones and the Scriptures* (Grand Rapids: Baker, 1981); Hess and Arnold, eds., *Ancient Israel's History*; C. L. Blomberg, *Historical Reliability of the Gospels*; C. L. Blomberg, *Historical Reliability of John's Gospel*; C. J. Hemer and C. H. Gempf, ed., *The Book of Acts in the Setting of Hellenistic History* (repr., Winona

We accept, then, that the Bible is God's Word in written form—that it records God's self-disclosure, as well as his people's varied responses to his person and his acts in history. Certainly human writers composed the Scriptures in the midst of their own cultures and circumstances, writing out of their own experiences and with their own motives for their readers. The Bible is a human book. Yet, somehow, God superintended their writing so that what they wrote comprised his message precisely. The Bible is God's Word, and the Holy Spirit speaks through it. As S. Grenz and J. Franke rightly underscore, "We acknowledge the Bible as scripture in that the sovereign Spirit has bound authoritative, divine speaking to this text. We believe that the Spirit has chosen, now chooses, and will continue to choose to speak with authority through the biblical texts."[30] This leads us to our next presupposition about the nature of the Bible.

Authoritative and True

It follows from the first presupposition that *the Bible is authoritative and true.* Being divine revelation through which God speaks, the Bible possesses ultimate authority.[31] For this reason, it must constitute the standard for all human belief and behavior. It speaks truthfully about who we are and how we are to live, so that rejecting the intent of the Bible means rejecting the will of God.[32]

What God says must be true, for God cannot lie nor will he mislead.[33] Some conservative scholars have maintained the view that inspiration implies inerrancy—that what God authored of necessity must contain no errors.[34] This has become

Lake, IN: Eisenbrauns, 1990); C. S. Keener, *Acts,* 4 vols. (Grand Rapids: Baker, 2012–15); and (2): J. Wenham, *Christ and the Bible,* 2nd ed. (Grand Rapids: Baker, 1994); and several of the chapters in *The Enduring Authority of the Christian Scriptures,* ed. D. A. Carson (Grand Rapids: Eerdmans, 2016).

30. S. J. Grenz and J. R. Franke, *Beyond Foundationalism. Shaping Theology in a Postmodern Context* (Louisville: Westminster John Knox, 2001), 65.

31. For a comprehensive defense of the veracity of the Bible see T. L. Wilder and S. B. Cowan, *In Defense of the Bible: A Comprehensive Apologetic for the Authority of Scripture* (Nashville: B&H, 2013). Other discussions of an evangelical view of the Bible include: N. T. Wright, *Scripture and the Authority of God: How to Read the Bible Today,* rev. ed. (New York: HarperOne, 2013); W. W. Klein, "Authority of the Bible" in *The Oxford Encyclopedia of Biblical Interpretation,* 2 vols., ed. S. L. McKenzie (Oxford and New York: Oxford University Press, 2013), 1:52–60; D. S. Dockery, *Christian Scripture: An Evangelical Perspective on Inspiration, Authority and Interpretation* (Nashville: B&H, 1995); P. E. Satterwaite and D. F. Wright, eds., *A Pathway into the Holy Scripture* (Grand Rapids: Eerdmans, 1994); C. F. H. Henry, "The Authority of the Bible," in *The Origin of the Bible,* ed. P. W. Comfort (Wheaton: Tyndale House, 1992), 13–27; and A. E. McGrath and D. Wenham, "Evangelicalism and Biblical Authority," in *Evangelical Anglicans: Their Role and Influence in the Church Today,* ed. R.T. France and A. E. McGrath (London: SPCK, 1993).

32. Paul makes this very point when writing to the Thessalonian Christians: "Therefore, anyone who rejects this instruction does not reject a human being but God, the very God who gives you his Holy Spirit" (1 Thess 4:8).

33. The author of Num 23:19 distinguishes between God and humans in their ability to lie: God does not. See also 1 Sam 15:29; Titus 1:2; and Heb 6:18. Jas 1:13 asserts that God never tempts people to do evil. Rather, God does only what is good. Assuming, then, that the entire Bible is God's revelation, this revelation cannot mislead, nor can it present what is untrue. R. Nicole provides a helpful appraisal of how both testaments present the nature of truth as factuality, faithfulness, and completeness: "The Biblical Concept of Truth," in *Scripture and Truth,* ed. Carson and Woodbridge, 287–98.

34. The classic exposition is B. B. Warfield, *Revelation and Inspiration* (Oxford: Oxford University Press, 1927). Another example of this position is C. F. H. Henry, *God, Revelation, and Authority,* 6 vols. (Waco: Word, 1976–79). More recently see M. J. Erickson, *Christian Theology,* esp. 196–259.

a lightning rod for various sides, since the term inerrancy is subject to numerous definitions and qualifications depending upon usage. Part of the problem is defining what constitutes an error. Are Matthew's and Luke's reversals of the second and third of Jesus' temptations an example of an error? Do the conflicts between the divine words quoted at Jesus' baptism in Matthew and Luke constitute an error? What about the differences in the accounts of Samuel, Kings, and Chronicles? Are there many errors, a few errors, or no errors? It depends on the criteria invoked; too often modern standards of precision are imposed on ancient texts anachronistically.[35]

Because they are unable to accept that everything in the Bible is without error, some shun the term and emphasize the Bible's "infallibility," its Spirit-driven ability to achieve God's purposes. Thus they allow for some degree of imprecision in the Bible.[36] Sometimes this amounts to "limited inerrancy," in which the biblical authors did not err in what they intended to teach theologically or ethically but may have erred in other incidental (to their purposes) matters, such as history or science.[37] Such readers may locate the authority of the Bible in what it accomplishes in readers rather than in the biblical text itself.[38] The so-called neo-orthodox theologians argue that the Bible only becomes the Word of God as believers faithfully read, preach, and apprehend its message.[39]

In keeping with our earlier distinctions based on speech act theory, some argue that the locutions (recall, those are the actual words on the page), may contain "errors" of various kinds—due to the need to accommodate cultural conventions or because of the genre involved—but the illocutions (the intent behind those words) do not err or fail to convey God's message. In this understanding, for example, a text may give a very large number (locution) for the Israelites who left Egypt as "six hundred thousand men on foot, besides women and children" (Exod 12:37). Yet the number may not be precisely accurate, especially given that they lived in eras that had different standards for "accuracy." Nevertheless, the illocution, the intention of the author, is trustworthy: it was a very large number. The use of such numbers fits how the ancients made their points; the intent was not to give a nose count, nor does it deceive the readers.[40] In cases like this Walton and Sandy go so far as to affirm, "To

---

35. See C. L. Blomberg, *Can We Still Believe the Bible?* chaps. 4–5.

36. See, e.g., I. H. Marshall, *Biblical Inspiration* (Grand Rapids: Eerdmans, 1982), 66. Another who argues for authority but eschews the "inerrancy" label is J. D. G. Dunn, *The Living Word*, 2nd ed. (Minneapolis: Fortress, 2009).

37. J. B. Rogers and D. K. McKim, *The Authority and Interpretation of the Bible. An Historical Approach* (New York: Harper, 1979).

38. Vanhoozer denies that "all parts of Scripture need be factually true" (*Is There a Meaning in This Text?* 425). He prefers to speak of the Bible's efficacy: "the power to produce results" (427). Grenz and Franke take a similar position: "It is not the Bible as a book that is authoritative, but the Bible as the instrumentality of the Spirit; the biblical message spoken by the Spirit through the text is theology's norming norm" (*Beyond Foundationalism*, 69).

39. K. Barth remains the prime example: *Church Dogmatics* (New York: Bloomsbury T&T Clark, 1936, 1956, 2010) I/1, 98–140; I/2, 457–537. For a helpful appraisal of how Barth puts his treatment of Holy Scripture within his larger treatment of the word of God, see G. W. Bromiley, *An Introduction to the Theology of Karl Barth* (Grand Rapids: Eerdmans, 1979), 3–53; esp. 34–44.

40. See the very useful discussion of some of these issues in J. H. Walton and D. B. Sandy, *The Lost World*

say there are errors in the Bible is to read Scripture anachronistically."[41] Their point, with which we agree, is that one can charge the Bible with "error" in such instances only if its locutions are judged by modern standards rather than the customs and standards of its day.

These various views (and there are others) also occur in various combinations, especially given the different genres within the Bible. John Goldingay, for example, argues that Scripture as "witnessing tradition" best fits narrative material, law and instruction form an "authoritative canon," an "inspired word" best applies to prophecy, and wisdom and poetry can be characterized as "experienced revelation."[42] These are the points to grasp, he says, not whether a text is inerrant or not. Finally, some affirm only that the Bible is great, inspired religious literature on a par with other examples of the world's great literature. Hence, they accord it no divine status or privileged claim to truth and study it alongside other ancient (religious and other) documents.[43] For some of them the Bible has at best only limited authority (perhaps no more than other classic documents or writings). Peter Enns and Kenton Sparks in different ways defend what might be called accommodationism. Instead of trying to defend the Bible (and claim it is inerrant), they insist we should simply read the Bible as it is and learn what we can from it (Enns). In the Bible God accommodated himself to the errors that humans invariably commit in its composition (Sparks). [44]

For us, the Bible is a trustworthy communication by Spirit-guided authors and is true in all it intends to teach. We are drawn to the virtues of a speech act theory understanding that recognizes the distinction between locution (the actual words on the page) and its illocution and perlocution (the purposes of the authors for those words and what the authors intended as the outcomes in the readers). The Bible's statements convey what is factual and true given its literary conventions/genres and its cultures; its record is faithful and reliable. This includes all its individual parts as well as its overall message. This is not the place for an exhaustive defense of the Bible's truthfulness, but several NT texts, in our estimation, assume this conclusion (e.g., John 10:35; 17:17; Titus 1:2; Matt 5:18). The psalmist likewise affirms that God's commands are utterly perfect (Ps 119:96). We believe that this represents the

of Scripture: Ancient Literary Culture and Biblical Authority (Downers Grove: InterVarsity, 2013), 44–48, whose perspective we are generally following here.

41. Walton and Sandy, *The Lost World*, 196. These authors soundly affirm their belief in the inerrancy of Scripture. The feeding of the 5,000 (Matt 14:21 par) and 4,000 (15:38 par) may also illustrate this phenomenon. At the same time, we insist that not any numbers will do. In our view, a locution that says that Jesus fed 5,000 men plus women and children cannot be taken to mean, e.g., that he fed only about 75 people in all, and that the evangelist simply picked a wildly inflated number to impress his readers.

42. J. Goldingay, *Models for Scripture* (Grand Rapids: Eerdmans, 1994).

43. An example of this is J. Barr, *Holy Scripture: Canon, Authority, Criticism* (Philadelphia: Westminster, 1983); cf. J. Barr, *Escaping from Fundamentalism* (London: SCM, 2012). An important anthology of non-evangelical approaches to inspiration and authority is W. Brown's *Engaging Biblical Authority. Perspective on the Bible as Scripture* (Louisville: Westminster John Knox, 2007).

44. P. Enns, *The Bible Tells Me So: Why Defending Scripture Has Made Us Unable to Read It* (New York: HarperOne, 2015); K. L. Sparks, *God's Word in Human Words: An Evangelical Appropriation of Critical Biblical Scholarship* (Grand Rapids: Baker, 2008).

position of the church throughout its history.[45] We also believe this presupposition does justice to the Bible's character and its claims of truthfulness.

We realize that not all who call themselves Christians nor do all scholars today hold this presupposition. Yet it is normal for thoughtful, believing Christians worldwide— among both scholars and laypersons—and throughout church history. How do we handle apparent contradictions or errors? One approach is to distinguish between the locution and illocution of a text or texts. Is the problem on the surface of the language (locution), but given the intention of the text (illocution), the conflict or "error" dissolves? The point of the text does not mislead; only the surface locution seems problematic.

For another obvious example, interpreters must always consider the literary form of the text they are seeking to understand. Though the locution may assert ". . . all the trees of the field will clap their hands" (Isa 55:12), given the nature of the genre of the prophet's words, no interpreter would accuse the text (the locution) of error if she found one tree that did not clap, or if she objected that trees don't possess hands. The illocution is true: it will be a time of jubilation. We could compound examples.[46] On the level of the locutions, two proverbs seem to contradict each other: "Do not answer a fool according to his folly, or you yourself will be just like him"; and "Answer a fool according to his folly, or he will be wise in his own eyes" (Prov 26:4–5). But on the illocutionary level, we readily grasp their distinct intentions.[47] No one, we aver, should accuse the Bible of error on the basis of this example.

Can illocutions conflict? That is, do biblical texts intend to teach contradictory messages? Our position is that God's intentions throughout the biblical record do not contradict one another or teach what is untrue. Following our supposition of truth, we would look for viable solutions or in rare instances admit that with the present state of our knowledge we cannot find a solution. This does not mean that no solutions exist. When responsible exegesis can suggest a possible solution, we claim some vindication, even if we cannot be confident that our solution is certain. It means that the charge of "error" is not mandated. And when possible solutions seem contrived or tendentious (as has sometimes happened in well-meaning attempts to defend a rigid definition of inerrancy), we frankly admit that at present we do not know the best way to solve the problem.

In fact, in the vast majority of cases, plausible solutions to alleged problems or contradictions *do* exist so that our withholding judgment in certain instances is not

---

45. L. Morris, *I Believe in Revelation* (Grand Rapids: Eerdmans, 1976), defends the view that the Bible was seen as authoritative throughout the church's history.

46. To take another, what if we compare the order of Jesus' temptations in Matthew's and Luke's accounts (Matt 4:1–11; Luke 4:1–13)? On the level of the locutions they conflict, but the intention (illocution) of the temptation narratives governs how each writer presents the material. Each Evangelist may have a different motive for ordering the narrative; they don't deceive in so doing. We object to considering such reordering of narratives as errors.

47. B. Waltke observes, "The rationale for the admonition not to answer a fool according to his folly (4a) is to avoid the negative consequence of becoming like the fool (4b)" and "The rationale for answering a fool according to his folly (5a) is to avoid the negative consequence that the fool arrogantly replaces the Lord's heavenly wisdom with his own (5b)" (in B. K. Waltke, *The Book of Proverbs, Chapters 15–31*, NICOT [Grand Rapids: Eerdmans, 2005] 349).

simply special pleading.[48] This is no more presumptuous than assuming a modern, positivist, critical omniscience about such questions.[49] Our presupposition of truthfulness disposes us to reject the position that the Bible errs and to assume, rather, in such instances that the data, our knowledge, or our theory to explain the evidence remains deficient. In many cases what appears to be a conflict between two passages appears only when we try to generalize each beyond their original applications. See Chapter 12 for our discussion of application of Scripture.[50]

A Spiritual Document

We adopt another presupposition about the nature of the Bible: it is a spiritual document. Because God has revealed his message in the Bible, *the Bible manifests unparalleled spiritual worth and a capacity to transform lives.* The Bible has the unique power to change the reader spiritually. Scripture is the living word of the living and all-powerful God, a word that has inherent power (see particularly Isa 55; Heb 4:12–13). This makes the Bible a unique book in human history—useful in ways unlike any other book.[51] Various individuals (the average Christian reader, theologian, professor, preacher, Bible School teacher) use the Bible in different ways and for different purposes (e.g., devotion/nurture, corporate worship, preaching, teaching, ethical guidance; see more on this in ch. 11 below). As we will argue, Christian interpreters share many hermeneutical principles and methods with those who study other kinds of literature. But we recognize a spiritual dimension for the Bible that sets it apart from other writings, and we seek to take this into account in interpreting (rather than deny its presence as do some readers).

By terming the Bible "spiritual," we affirm the role of the Holy Spirit who authored and who applies its message to readers. With the Spirit's aid we explore the Scriptures and find life-giving and life-changing meaning. The Bible has an animating and uplifting effect as the Spirit of God uses its truth in the lives of the faithful. As we respond in faithful obedience, we grow in maturity; we worship and praise the God of the Bible. The Spirit-energized reading of the Scriptures gives direction to our thoughts and guidance to our lives. To treat the Bible in any other way (like merely an inspiring book) robs it of its central purpose as God's revelation to his creatures.

---

48. To see how often this is the case in the Gospels, see Blomberg, *Historical Reliability*; C. L. Blomberg, *Can We Still Believe the Bible?* (Grand Rapids: Brazos, 2014).

49. D. R. Hall, *The Seven Pillories of Wisdom* (Macon, GA: Mercer University Press, 1990), provides an excellent and witty exposure of how much faulty reasoning occurs in the guise of scholarship.

50. We hasten to add what we believe happens when most Christians come to read the Bible. They don't, first, invest careful study in verifying the Bible's trustworthiness, then read its contents and decide whether or not to believe it. For the most part, they come to faith in Jesus first, either through Bible reading, the preaching of the gospel, or through the nurture of a local Christian community. In short, they give the Bible the benefit of the doubt, encounter Jesus personally (with or without the Bible), and then take on the Bible as a whole.

51. Of course, this is not to say that other books are not "inspiring" in different ways. Our point here is that the Bible is uniquely God's written Word. Through it we actually hear God's voice addressing us personally.

Characterized by Both Unity and Diversity

We also affirm as a presupposition that the Bible is a unity, yet its contents are diverse.[52] Throughout most of the history of the church, Christians assumed the unity of Scripture and downplayed or overlooked its diversity. The assumption was that it spoke with one voice, the voice of its author. Readers harmonized conflicts or tensions within the Bible, or resorted to typology, allegory, or the principle of the *regula fidei* ("the rule of faith") to interpret difficult texts in the light of clearer ones.[53] Since the Enlightenment, however, many scholars regularly deny the unity of the Bible and, especially in the last two centuries, claim there are irreconcilable conflicts among the authors of Scripture that preclude any claims to unity. Today only theologically conservative Christians and advocates of canonical criticism defend a unity in Scripture. First, we comment on the Bible's unity.

As for the OT, various proposals have emerged to identify a unifying center. Some defend the prevalence of a single theme, for example: covenant, promise, the mighty acts of God, communion, the life of God's people, dominion, justice, or righteousness. Others find pairs of themes, for example: law and promise, election and obligation, creation and covenant, the rule of God and communion with humankind, or salvation and blessing. Other suggestions involve polarities, such as the presence versus the absence of God, or the legitimation of structure versus the embracing of pain. Some writers point simply to Yahweh, or God, as the sole unifying element within the older Testament.[54] Some even find within its pages competing theologies rooted in different social settings.[55]

On the NT side, some suggest single themes as a center for the NT: kingdom, gospel, righteousness, justification, reconciliation, faith, new creation, salvation or

---

52. On many of these points see C. L. Blomberg, "Unity and Diversity of Scripture" in *New Dictionary of Biblical Theology*, ed. T. D. Alexander and Brian S. Rosner (Downers Grove: InterVarsity, 2000), 64–72. What follows draws upon this analysis. Cf. P. Enns, *Inspiration and Incarnation: Evangelicals and the Problem of the Old Testament*, 2nd ed. (Grand Rapids: Baker Academic, 2015), 61–102; and J. Goldingay, *Theological Diversity and the Authority of the Old Testament* (Grand Rapids: Eerdmans, 1987).

53. Michael Graves, *The Inspiration and Interpretation of Scripture: What the Early Church Can Teach Us* (Grand Rapids: Eerdmans, 2014) has an important chapter with the title "Usefulness," 17–41, in which he argues that the commitment to this essential value of the Bible was foundational in the history of interpretation—for both the rabbis and Christians. So, for example, since the church fathers were convinced of the profitableness of Scripture, they handled it in various ways to demonstrate how it could be useful in the lives of believers. Graves concludes: ". . . if one were to insist on the equal usefulness of every passage of Scripture . . . this could potentially require complex and even convoluted reading strategies, depending on how hard the idea was pressed" (p. 22).

54. Good surveys and introductions by evangelicals are available in K. J. Vanhoozer, ed. *Theological Interpretation of the Old Testament: A Book-by-Book Survey* (Grand Rapids: Baker Academic, 2005); and R. Routledge, *Old Testament Theology: A Thematic Approach* (Downers Grove: IVP Academic, 2008). From a mainline perspective, cf. B. C. Birch, et al., eds., *A Theological Introduction to the Old Testament* (Nashville: Abingdon, 1999). A rich single-volume by a distinguished evangelical is B. K. Waltke (with C. Yu), *An Old Testament Theology: An Exegetical, Canonical, and Thematic Approach* (Grand Rapids: Zondervan, 2007). The reader will find additional resources in the Annotated Bibliography chapter at the end of this book.

55. E. Gerstenberger, *Theologies in the Old Testament*, trans. J. Bowden (Minneapolis: Fortress, 2002). From an evangelical perspective, a good introduction to the OT's main theological traditions (e.g., creation, priestly interpretation, wisdom) is J. Kessler, *Old Testament Theology: Divine Call and Human Response* (Waco: Baylor University Press, 2013).

salvation history, reconciliation, eschatology, Israel or the new Israel, the cross and/or resurrection, the love of God, existential anthropology, covenant, and, most common of all, Jesus (or Christology more generally). Others suggest various combinations of themes, often some kerygmatic summary of essential Christian doctrine.[56]

Assessing the unity of the *entire Bible*, the most common suggestions are promise-fulfillment, type-antitype, salvation history, the mission of God, a relationship with the living God, intertextuality, and Christology. Some defend narrower themes such as monotheism, God's covenant faithfulness, God's reign, righteousness, the covenants, election, grace and the response of obedience, the people of God, exodus and new exodus, creation and new creation, or sin and salvation. We also encounter multiplex solutions, for example, the existence of God, God as creator of a good world, the fall of humanity, and the fact of election. P. Stuhlmacher offers the following narrative summary of the story of both Testaments:

> The one God who created the world and chose Israel to be his own people has through the sending, the work, and the death and resurrection of his only Son, Jesus Christ, sufficiently provided once and for all the salvation of Jews and Gentiles. Jesus Christ is the hope of all creation. Whoever believes in him as Reconciler and Lord and obeys his instruction may be certain of their participation in the kingdom of God.[57]

This last suggestion, treating the Bible as *narrative*, offers a useful model for seeing the unfolding unity and diversity within Scripture. We may summarize the plot line of the story, recognizing that various literary genres of Scripture occur within this larger "historical" framework. Despite their diversity, the books within Scripture present a rather coherent chronological sequence, each building upon what precedes in an apparently conscious and straightforward fashion. The four major periods in the Bible's overall narrative portray the creation, the fall, redemption, and the consummation of all God's purposes. In line with this, the non-narrative portions of the Bible—the law, the prophets, the wisdom, and the epistolary literature—depict how God's people should conduct themselves as this narrative proceeds to fulfillment.[58]

On the other hand, the Bible exhibits marked *diversity*.[59] This takes several forms. It exists as two very different "testaments" written in three languages, in different

---

56. For example, see A. M. Hunter, *Introducing New Testament Theology* (London: SCM, 1957), 66. We could list numerous recent NT theologies to illustrate the variety of options. We will, instead, refer the reader to the Annotated Bibliography chapter at the end of this book.

57. P. Stuhlmacher, *How to Do Biblical Theology* (Allison Park: Pickwick, 1995), 63.

58. A thorough and convincing portrayal of the Bible's over-arching narrative around the theme of mission is C. J. H. Wright, *The Mission of God: Unlocking the Bible's Grand Narrative* (Downers Grove: InterVarsity, 2006). See also C. G. Bartholomew and M. W. Goheen, *The Drama of Scripture: Finding Our Place in the Biblical Story* (Grand Rapids: Baker, 2004). Finally, G. K. Beale, *A New Testament Biblical Theology: The Unfolding of the Old Testament in the New* (Grand Rapids: Baker, 2011), presents a variation of narrative showing how the NT builds onto Israel's story in the OT. C. H. H. Scobie, *The Ways of Our God: An Approach to Biblical Theology* (Grand Rapids: Eerdmans, 2003) is also an excellent, detailed biblical theology of both testaments.

59. See esp. J. Goldingay, "Diversity and Unity in Old Testament Theology," *VT* 34 (1984): 153–68; and

cultures, over a vast span of time. The Bible embodies a diverse collection of kinds or genres of literature: legal, historical, poetic, prophetic, gospel, epistolary, and apocalyptic. Added to all this, the various authors write with distinct purposes, to different audiences, on different topics, and with varying emphases. The Bible alleges to tell the story from the creation of the world to the consummation of history in the new heavens and earth.

As well in places, different portions of Scripture so closely parallel each other that most readers postulate a literary relationship between them and assume that their differences are motivated theologically, politically, or to achieve stylistic variation. Deuteronomy consciously modernizes various laws of Exodus and Leviticus for a later time. Chronicles rehearses significant portions of the Deuteronomistic history (and adds episodes not found there), focusing more on life in the southern kingdom (Chronicles also parallels Kings). The four Gospels clearly adopt individual perspectives on the common features of Jesus and his ministry. The letter of 2 Peter appears to revise and adapt Jude for a different situation. All of this, and more, illustrates numerous differences as one compares writings within a testament and between testaments, not to mention across the centuries. Now no one would question the fact of the Bible's diversity; that it would have unity is more difficult to imagine.[60]

In conclusion, we acknowledge both the Bible's unity and its diversity, and hold them in the proper balance, if not tension. Often scholars who are more conservative emphasize the former almost to the exclusion of the latter, while scholars who are more liberal do the opposite. We suggest we must uphold both. The Bible's unity provides the authoritative foundation for Christian faith and practice; this has been the historic Christian perspective. Yet acknowledging the Bible's diversity allows interpreters to appreciate each text, book, and author on its own terms, thereby differentiating what God intended to say to his people at each point in their history.[61] If, for example, God gave us four Gospels, then he expected us to hear the message of each in its own integrity before rushing to harmonize the four into a giant whole that does not correspond to what he actually inspired. Scripture's unity also helps circumscribe what is the "Christian faith," in contrast to alternatives; its diversity reminds the church that different expressions of that "faith" may have a claim to legitimacy.

An Understandable Document

As a fifth presupposition about the nature of the Bible, we affirm that the Bible is *understandable*; it is an accessible book that God authored to provide his word to

---

J. D. G. Dunn, *Unity and Diversity in the New Testament*, 3rd ed. (London: SCM, 2006). Cf. W. C. Kaiser, Jr., *The Promise-Plan of God: A Biblical Theology of the Old and New Testaments* (Grand Rapids: Zondervan, 2008).

60. One helpful attempt is Scott J. Hafemann and Paul R. House, eds., *Central Themes in Biblical Theology: Mapping Unity in Diversity* (Grand Rapids: Baker, 2007).

61. W. Brueggemann, *Theology of the Old Testament* (Minneapolis: Fortress, 1997), 731–33, makes a forceful plea for Christians to allow the OT to stand on its own while acknowledging the appropriate Christian program to embrace the OT as part of its own Bible and to affirm the connections between the testaments.

his creatures. It presents a clear enough message to anyone willing to read it. This explains why people throughout history have understood and followed its teachings. This does not imply that it is a simple book or that anyone may grasp easily everything it contains. As noted above, the doctrine of the perspicuity or clarity of the Scriptures, so stressed in the Protestant Reformation, always referred to that which was essential for right doctrine or living—not to every sentence of the Bible.[62] Its profundity exhausts the human mind, for it derives from God himself and deals with the most important and urgent issues of human existence, now and eternally. Yet, the Bible is not a puzzle or cryptogram whose solution remains hidden from all but an elite group who know the code.[63] Written so that common people could apprehend its truth, the Bible's central message speaks clearly to human hearts even after scores of intervening centuries. The role of the Holy Spirit is, of course, central to this.

Forming the Canon of Holy Scripture

Finally, we presuppose that *the sixty-six books of the Protestant canon constitute God's scriptural record to his people.* The word "canon" has the figurative sense of "ruler" or "measuring rod," and refers to a norm or standard.[64] We use it here to speak of the list of authoritative books that comprise Holy Scripture. Though not a very tidy matter, canonicity affirms that, guided by the Spirit through various historical processes over a span of several centuries, the church settled on certain books as authoritative Scripture due to their apostolic origin or basis in Jesus' life and ministry.[65] They canonized these books because they were useful for specific purposes (e.g., preaching, catechetical training, refuting heretics, worship) and because of their consistency with the orthodox teaching of Jesus and of the apostles. Added to the completed "Old Testament" canon (established by the church's Jewish predecessors), this process enabled the church to fix the extent of the canon. The canon marks the boundaries of God's written revelation. The process recognized and thus "canonized" those books that were deemed authoritative, divine revelation. Canonization acknowledged the books' inherent authority; it did not grant them authority. It also affirmed the church's commitment to live guided by them.

---

62. See J. P. Callahan, "*Claritas Scripturae*: The Role of Perspicuity in Protestant Hermeneutics," *JETS* 39 (1996): 353–72; J. P. Callahan, *The Clarity of Scripture* (Downers Grove: InterVarsity, 2001); and W. Grudem, "The Perspicuity of Scripture," *Themelios* 34 (2009): 288–308.

63. This underscores the essential fallacy in such works as M. Drosin and D. Vitstum, *The Bible Code* (New York: Simon and Schuster, 1998) and countless others in this genre. Often certain "Bible teachers" or "prophecy experts" act as if they alone hold the keys that unlock the codes of certain prophetic or apocalyptic portions of the Bible. Unwittingly, and ironically, theirs is the ultimate in reader-response interpretation of which we say more below.

64. Roman Catholics and Orthodox Christians, of course, include the so-called deuterocanonical books in their canon. Occurring in the LXX and Vulgate but not in the Hebrew OT, Catholics deemed these "second canon" books to possess a level of divine and canonical authority at the Council of Trent (1548) and reaffirmed at the First Vatican Council (1870). For additional details, see our discussion of canon and textual criticism in ch. 4 and the literature cited in the footnotes.

65. See one useful assessment in L. M. McDonald, *The Biblical Canon: Its Origin, Transmission, and Authority* (Grand Rapids: Baker, 2006). He lays out the options for understanding how we got the Bible.

According to Christian orthodoxy, with the writing of the book of Revelation the process of Scripture formation was completed despite the further claims of groups like the Mormons or Islam.[66] In interpretation the church does not seek new revelation that would add to the Bible. Rather, the church seeks to understand what was revealed and collected in the canon. As a hermeneutical starting point, this implies we give priority to these sixty-six books in interpretation and in authority; they form the literary and theological context—the "boundary," as it were—in which to interpret any given passage.

Presuppositions about Methodology

The qualification of a "reasoned faith" and the presuppositions about the nature of the Bible naturally lead to this next item, already hinted at: methodology. *We believe that students of the Bible should employ all useful methods or techniques that enable them to discover the meaning of a text,* regardless of who developed or perfected them.[67] In short, we believe Bible students should use whatever methods yield accurate understanding.

Yet we must qualify this. Because we believe the Bible owes its origin to the inspiration of the Holy Spirit, it would be illegitimate to subject it to methods that by their nature deny or subvert its divine status. A literary example that parallels one we used earlier will illustrate. A poetic line in Psalm 96:12 reads: "Let all the trees of the forest sing for joy." Form criticism recognizes that one cannot apply all the methods for interpreting one kind of literature (say historical narrative) to another (poetry). One might get an "interesting" reading by a "nonpoetic" interpretation of that line from the psalm, but it would be beyond the bounds of what the text seeks to accomplish (its illocution) and how the author wants the readers to respond (the perlocution). In the true sense of the word, that would not be a *valid* reading of the poem.[68] Similarly, we believe that our presuppositions about the nature of Scripture preclude avenues of study that deny its essential character as God-breathed. But this also obtains for historical issues.

We affirm that the Bible is a human document that we must read and study like other human documents (given the presupposition above about its character as a spiritual document). A key question emerges, however: did all the events the Bible records actually happen as recorded—even when they involve the supernatural? Israel remembered her past, especially the miraculous exodus and the conquest of Canaan, *as genuine history* (see Deut 26:5–9; Josh 24:2–13; Ps 78). Likewise, Paul insisted that the record of Jesus' resurrection was true and factual history (1 Cor 15:3–8, 17–20). Taken at face value, these assertions are not mere myths. We assume, therefore, that the honest historian ought to be free of preconceived notions that simply deny the possibility that an all-powerful God could act in human history to rescue Israel from

---

66. An older but useful volume remains F. F. Bruce, *The Canon of Scripture* (Downers Grove: InterVarsity, 1988).

67. We add this caveat because a handful of very conservative scholars avoid using critical tools developed by scholars whose presuppositions they reject. As examples, see E. Linnemann, *Historical Criticism of the Bible* (Grand Rapids: Kregel, 2001); and R. L. Thomas and F. D. Farnell, ed., *The Jesus Crisis: The Inroads of Historical Criticism into Evangelical Scholarship* (Grand Rapids: Kregel, 1998).

68. A valid interpretation in this sense means understanding a text in the manner intended by the author.

Egypt or to vindicate Jesus as Messiah by raising him from the dead. Likewise, we must be open to all alleged miracles and supernatural explanations of biblical reports. This need not be circular reasoning. Rather, it constitutes an attempt to understand the Bible on its own terms.[69]

It follows that an interpreter who operates with our presuppositions about the nature of the Bible may employ certain techniques of form or redaction criticism to discover the unique perspectives of the OT story of Joseph or of one of the Gospels. However, that same interpreter will reject the results of these same methods in the hands of some scholars who presume that a "miraculous" incident that appears in a gospel account cannot be historical but originated decades later in early church tradition. Such a form critic, guided by this ideology, may reject accounts of the miraculous out of hand. These issues are decided on the presuppositional level. So, if a method or technique is "neutral" and productive (obvious and noncontroversial examples are grammatical and lexical analyses), we do not object to using it to understand the meaning of a text.[70] However, where the use of a method adopts a basic stance or presupposition that is inconsistent with our presuppositions about Scripture, then we find *that use* of the method unacceptable or at least requiring modification. Some rational methods without a substructure of (what we deem to be) proper presuppositions will yield results antithetical to a divine view of Scripture. We reject any methods that we find unacceptable—including those deriving from the humanistic or naïve (often fundamentalist) position that insists that strictly scientific or presuppositionless interpretation is desirable or even possible.

We embrace historical methods in our investigation of the meaning of Scripture.[71] Since faith is connected to what happened in history, we commit ourselves to know biblical history, even where it conflicts with subsequent church tradition.[72] We position

---

69. We stressed this point above. Additionally, N. T. Wright mounts an impressive campaign to demonstrate that the NT writers' presentations are historically credible when understood in light of first-century Jewish and Greco-Roman worldviews: *The New Testament and the People of God* (Minneapolis: Augsburg Fortress, 1992); *Jesus and the Victory of God* (Minneapolis: Fortress, 1996); *The Resurrection of the Son of God* (Minneapolis: Fortress, 2003); and *Paul and the Faithfulness of God* (Minneapolis: Fortress, 2013). At the same time, we do not take all literature "on its own terms," as, for example, the "legends" contained in extra-biblical literature (e.g., *The Infancy Gospel of Thomas*). There is historical evidence to support making these kinds of distinctions, as we have already noted.

70. As examples, Robert Funk and Walter Bauer were extremely liberal in their theologies yet their grammar and lexicon, respectively, have become standards that all scholars employ. See the bibliography at the end for details.

71. D. A. Hagner puts it well: "Because revelation comes to us in and through history, historical criticism is not an option but a necessity. 'Criticism' here means the making of informed judgments. In this sense no one who attempts to interpret or explain the Bible in any way can avoid the 'critical' method" ("The New Testament, History, and the Historical-Critical Method," 75). For another discussion of historiography from an evangelical viewpoint, see V. P. Long, *The Art of Biblical History* (Grand Rapids: Zondervan, 1994). Cf. A. R. Millard, J. K. Hoffmeier, and D. W. Baker, *Faith, Tradition, and History: Old Testament Historiography in Its Near Eastern Context* (Winona Lake, IN: Eisenbrauns, 1994).

72. The Catholic Church's historical claim that the Gospels' apparent identification of Jesus' brothers and sisters (e.g., Mark 3:31–34 parallels; 6:3; John 7:3–5; cf. 1 Cor 9:5) refers, in fact, to cousins, not siblings, derives, we argue, from its dogma concerning Mary's perpetual virginity, rather than a precise understanding of the texts' meanings. See the frank assessment of that issue from Catholic scholar J. P. Meier, *A Marginal Jew. Rethinking the Historical Jesus* (New York: Doubleday, 1991), 1:318–32. He concludes, "if . . . the historian or exegete is asked to render a judgment on the New Testament and patristic texts we have examined, viewed simply as historical sources,

ourselves with the writer of 2 Peter 1:16: "we did not follow cleverly devised stories . . ." Thus, historical and literary methods become essential to understand and explain the biblical record. We reject the kind of "faith" that simply believes what it wants to believe. Faith and history need not be at odds; they ought to and do inform each other.[73] If Jesus did not physically rise from the dead, then the Christian faith, Paul argues correctly, is groundless and fraudulent![74] It certainly offers no hope for an afterlife or meaning for a present life.

This means that as Christian interpreters we walk a tightrope, but we do it self-consciously and openly. No interpretation occurs apart from presuppositions. We approach the Bible with commitments, and they influence our choice of methods. We affirm the Bible's uniqueness, and we acknowledge this commitment before we begin the process of interpretation. At the same time, we drink deeply at the well of rational methods and seek to exegete each passage with integrity, accuracy, and sincerity. We want to employ whatever techniques help us understand the Bible accurately. Therefore, we reject a gullible naïveté that simply believes what it wants to believe or has been taught. The bulk of this volume seeks to expound those crucial techniques for interpretation.

Presuppositions about the Ultimate Goal of Hermeneutics

We also adopt a presupposition about what we seek to do when we interpret. We are convinced that the goal of hermeneutics is to enable interpreters to arrive at *the meaning of the text that the biblical writers or editors intended their readers to understand.* This is so crucial yet controversial that we will devote the next chapter to explore this more adequately. But we offer some brief comments here.

The biblical authors and editors produced literature of various kinds. Adopting our view of the nature of the Bible, we believe that God communicates with his people through the Bible, a book that resulted from a divine/human concursive activity. Thus, all biblical texts convey meaning through both their human and divine dimensions. Yet to understand the original "historical meaning" of the text is not the sole goal of the hermeneutical process. We have two points to make.

the most probable opinion is that the brothers and sisters of Jesus were true siblings" (331). Of course, this is not merely a Catholic problem; Protestants sometimes succumb to the same errors. For example, some deny that Matthew 16 makes Peter the leader of the apostles in *any* privileged way because they already *know* he can't be the first pope. So they propose doubtful interpretations like it is Christ who is the rock or it is Peter's confession that is the rock. Yet the whole power in Matthew's narrative is that the rock quickly becomes a stumbling stone; for that to work, Peter needs to be both. See J. Nolland, *The Gospel of Matthew*, NIGTC (Grand Rapids: Eerdmans, 2005), 667–70; and most recent commentaries on Matthew for confirmation.

73. Marshall, *Luke. Historian and Theologian*, defends this third Gospel against the charge that theology and history are mutually exclusive categories. For OT history, see the essays in Long, Baker, Wenham, eds., *Windows into Old Testament History*.

74. This is not the view of M. J. Borg and J. D. Crossan, *The Last Week: What the Gospels Really Teach about Jesus's Final Days in Jerusalem* (New York: HarperOne, 2007), who find they can embrace what is for them a valid understanding of the Jesus' life and teaching—and even his resurrection—while rejecting the fact that Jesus actually rose bodily from the dead. For a robust defense of the historicity of Jesus' resurrection see N.T. Wright, *Resurrection*. Also see the lively debate in R. B. Stewart, ed., *The Resurrection of Jesus: John Dominic Crossan and N. T. Wright in Dialogue* (Minneapolis: Fortress, 2005).

In our view, biblical interpretation succeeds, first, when it enables modern readers to understand the meaning of the original biblical texts (and here we include locution, illocution and perlocution)—the meaning the people at the time of the texts' composition (author, editor, audience, readers) would have most likely understood—and only then seeks its significance for Christians today. In some instances the original meaning is readily apparent. Without much help a reader of the Bible can understand the narration: "One day Elisha went to Shunem. And a well-to-do woman was there, who urged him to stay for a meal. So whenever he came by, he stopped there to eat" (2 Kgs 4:8). It would fill out our understanding to know more about the prophet Elisha, where Shunem was located, or how the woman came to be "well-to-do," but even apart from such insights the text makes clear sense.

In other places we may need a detective's extraordinary skills to discern a text's meaning, as in the section that informs us that Christ ". . . was put to death in the body but made alive in [by] the Spirit [spirit]. After being made alive, he went and made proclamation to the imprisoned spirits . . ." (1 Pet 3:18–19; brackets inserted to show several interpretive options). In any case, the goal is to understand the meaning of this text. Only when we grasp the meaning the author intended, to the best of our ability, may we proceed to the second crucial component of the hermeneutical enterprise: to investigate its significance for us today.

It follows as a presupposition for us that God's design in inspiration assures that the Bible spoke not only to its original readers or to hearers, *but it also speaks to us today.*[75] An inspired and authoritative Bible has significance and relevance beyond its original circumstances and intentions. Further, we assume that the significance God wants it to have today *grows out of the original meaning* and is not something we tack on to the text. On the basis of the solidarity of the human race and the spiritual plight we share, as well as the Bible's nature as God's ongoing revelation to his people, the ancient meanings will speak more or less directly to the human condition as they are applied appropriately today. The questions the Bible addresses concern ultimate issues, the "Grand Narrative" of salvation-history as we hinted above, in addition to merely localized or immediate matters. As we learn God's mind, expressed by human authors long ago, we find understanding and significance for our concerns today. Any quest for other "meanings" from the Bible lacks that objectifying basis in God's revelation. The meaning found in the text alone provides this foundation. Vanhoozer terms it "determinative textual meaning."[76]

So, presuppositions are a fact of life for all interpretation. In conclusion, we suggest the following steps in view of what we have stated above. This is now *your* task as biblical interpreters.

---

75. Paul affirmed as much about the OT to his Roman readers: "For everything that was written in the past was written to teach us, so that through the endurance taught in the Scriptures and the encouragement they provide we might have hope" (Rom 15:4). The principle applies to the NT as well.

76. Vanhoozer, *Is There a Meaning in This Text?*, 300.

Engaging the Fact of Presuppositions
• *Admit* that you have presuppositions
• *Identify* those presuppositions that you bring to the task
• *Evaluate* or *assess* your presuppositions
• *Embrace* those presuppositions you believe are valid
• Take steps to *jettison* those presuppositions you deem invalid

PREUNDERSTANDINGS OF THE INTERPRETER

Snow falls regularly during the winter months in Colorado where we live. Some years ago we found it humorous when one of our newly arrived African students expressed shock at seeing snow fall from the sky during our first snowstorm in Denver that autumn. Her only previous encounter with snow had been in pictures, and she assumed that snow somehow came up out of the ground like dew. Arguably, it was a logical assumption, though it turned out to be false. Similarly, we all have certain views of the world based upon our prior experience, training, and thinking, and we interpret our experiences based on these premises. They may be true or false—or partly true and partly false—but they filter or color everything we encounter. Knowingly and unknowingly, we construct a body of beliefs and attitudes that we use to interpret or make sense of what we experience. These beliefs and attitudes are called preunderstandings, and they play a significant role in shaping our view of reality. Along with presuppositions, no one is free from preunderstandings; it is impossible to interpret reality in a "totally objective" way. But here is a critical point: it does not follow that what readers bring to a text *determines* the meaning of that text. It may color how they interpret that text. We believe that the textual meaning is fixed (the text means what it meant); but readers bring more or less baggage to their pursuit of that meaning.

All we know has been molded in some way by the preunderstandings that we bring to the process of interpretation. In the past, the discipline of hermeneutics concentrated almost solely on the ancient world of the texts and the techniques for understanding what texts meant "back then." Now we recognize that we must give as much attention to what the interpreter brings to the interpretive process. We need to know ourselves, as well as the object of our inquiry. Thiselton observes, "historical conditioning is two-sided: *the modern interpreter, no less than the text, stands in a given historical context and tradition.*"[77] He adds, "Hermeneutics cannot proceed without taking account of the existing horizons of the interpreter."[78] Borrowing the metaphor of "horizon" from Gadamer (the limits that a point of view or understanding presents), Thiselton argues that "the goal of biblical hermeneutics is to bring about an active

---

77. Thiselton, *Two Horizons,* 11 (emphasis his). He goes on to observe, "Everything is understood in a given context and from a given point of view" (105).

78. Ibid., 237.

and meaningful engagement between the interpreter and text, in such a way that the interpreter's own horizon is re-shaped and enlarged."[79]

Definition of Preunderstanding

The term *preunderstanding* describes what the interpreter brings to the task of interpretation. D. S. Ferguson provides a succinct definition: "Preunderstanding may be defined as a body of assumptions and attitudes which a person brings to the perception and interpretation of reality or any aspect of it."[80] It is the basic and preparatory starting point for understanding. Preunderstanding is desirable and essential.[81] Certain background knowledge and experiences are pertinent to understanding other experiences or situations. For example, most of us can make only limited sense out of a medical prescription. We know it prescribes that an exact quantity of a specific medication should be taken at definite times, but apart from that limited preunderstanding, we are probably in no position to understand more about the medical terms and symbols, much less about the chemicals it prescribes or how they work to remedy our ailments. Possessing a more complete preunderstanding, a medical doctor or pharmacist gains from the text more meaning. Similarly, our African friend understands pictures of snow better because her firsthand experiences of falling snow enlarged her preunderstanding.

We need to outline the various elements that constitute preunderstanding and how they are derived. Preunderstanding consists of the total framework of being and understanding that we bring to the task of living including such things as our language, social conditioning, gender, intelligence, cultural values, physical environment, political allegiances, and even our emotional state at a given time. These elements construct and govern our individual worlds. They formulate the paradigm that helps us function in and make sense of the world.

Categories of Preunderstanding	
Informational	Ideological
Attitudinal	Methodological

Ferguson helpfully discerns four categories of preunderstanding: (1) *informational:* the information one already possesses about a subject prior to approaching it; (2) *attitudinal:* the disposition one brings in approaching a topic, also termed prejudice, bias, or predisposition; (3) *ideological:* both generally, the way we view the total complex

---

79. Ibid., xix. We disagree with his mentor, Gadamer, *Truth and Method*, 359, however, who infers that since meaning is a "fusion" of the horizons of the text and interpreters, a text does not have a single correct interpretation. We believe meaning resides in the text, not merely in a given "reading" of a text. We have more to say on this in the next chapter.

80. D. S. Ferguson, *Biblical Hermeneutics: An Introduction* (Atlanta: John Knox, 1986), 6.

81. Of course, preunderstanding cannot always be distinguished from bias or prejudice. Indeed, bias is only one element of a person's preunderstanding. We will take up these distinctions further below.

of reality (world view, frame of reference) and particularly how we view a specific subject (point of view, perspective); and (4) *methodological:* the actual approach one takes in explaining a given subject. Possible approaches include scientific, historical, and inductive. Different approaches will influence the type of results obtained, though in another sense interpreters employ specific methods precisely to guard against undue interpretive bias.[82]

We cannot avoid or deny the presence of preunderstanding in the task of biblical interpretation. Every interpreter comes to study the Bible with preconceptions and prior dispositions. If we ask about the origin or basis of our preunderstanding, we will find it in our prior experiences, conditioning, and training—political, social, cultural, psychological, and religious—in short, all our lives up to this point. Even our native language influences our view of reality. All these color and in many senses determine how we view the world. Each individual processes all these factors unconsciously when interpreting.[83] Preunderstanding in a specific arena may help us understand further, but it provides no guarantee that we will interpret accurately. As Thiselton puts it, ". . . it offers no more than a *provisional* way of finding a bridge or starting point toward further, more secure understanding. From the very first it is *capable of correction* and *readjustment.*"[84] We will develop the idea of the "hermeneutical spiral" as a way of explaining this further in our discussion below.

The Role of Preunderstanding

The Role of Preunderstanding
• Colors, if not determines, what we can see in a text
• May turn out to be an *asset*—aiding or enabling what interpreters find in a text
• May turn out to be a *culprit*—prohibiting or retarding what one is able to see

Obviously, preunderstanding plays an enormously influential role in the process of interpretation. For example, as we noted above, those whose *ideology* (to use Ferguson's third category) allows science alone to settle all matters of fact will tend to reject supernatural explanations of the biblical record.[85] Thus, scientism's ideology influences the interpretive results, just as adopting the Bible's own worldview allows

---

82. Ferguson, *Biblical Hermeneutics*, 12. He admits there are degrees of overlap among them and that a single act of preunderstanding contains elements of all four.

83. For this reason, P. J. Leithart, *Deep Exegesis: The Mystery of Reading Scripture* (Waco, TX: Baylor University Press, 2006), argues that "even the most rigorously exegetical readers are eisegetical" (117). He means that none can avoid bringing much to the text to "illuminate the text with light from outside" (117), a point with which we agree. But most teachers of hermeneutics use *eisegesis* in a negative way, the tendency to read our own preferred meanings into a text rather than reading *out of the text* the author's intended meaning.

84. A. C. Thiselton, *Hermeneutics: An Introduction* (Grand Rapids/Cambridge, UK: Eerdmans, 2009), 13 (his emphasis).

85. It should be clear here that our prior discussion of presuppositions overlaps that of preunderstanding. Presuppositions constitute part of the total preunderstanding an interpreter brings to the task.

for alternative explanations of the data. Speaking of the epistemological stance of the scientific method, David Tracy observes, "Scientism has pretensions to a mode of inquiry that tries to deny its own hermeneutical character and mask its own historicity so that it might claim a historical certainty."[86] All interpretation occurs within a context; scientists are not exempt from this constraint. On the other hand, some postmodern interpreters do not object to supernatural "readings" of a biblical text since there are no privileged or correct readings anyway. Readers make whatever sense of a text they wish.

To take another example falling into the realm of ideology, some readers start their reading of the Bible by looking for conflicts within it, and others by looking for ways to harmonize any apparent conflicts. Many blogs and websites appear to go out of their way to point out any time two writers don't say exactly the same thing in the same way (in a way those same critics would not want their own writing scrutinized). Others are inclined to give the biblical writers more latitude. Some readers almost by nature gravitate toward an assumed parallel between a biblical text and an ANE or Greco-Roman myth while others when confronted with those parallels immediately highlight the divergences. One's interpretation is sometimes influenced by one's ideology.

On the *attitudinal* dimension of preunderstanding, some argue that Wellhausen's anti-Judaism led him to denigrate the law in the OT.[87] It seems likely that Hegel's ideological influence underlay Wellhausen's view that Israel's history evolved through three distinct phases.[88] Gunkel's form criticism—a *methodological* element—significantly affected a whole generation of OT scholarship.[89] Dever catalogs what he sees as huge biases affecting how many contemporary OT scholars read the evidence of archaeology.[90]

In an extremely insightful essay, "Our Hermeneutical Inheritance," Roger Lundin traces the historical and philosophical roots of contemporary approaches to understanding.[91] He compares the deductive approach of Descartes with the more inductive one of

---

86. D. Tracy, *Plurality and Ambiguity: Hermeneutics, Religion, Hope* (San Francisco: Harper & Row, 1987), 31. For many scholars this "certainty" excludes the possibility of the miracles recorded in both Testaments, as we saw in our consideration of presuppositions above.

87. See Lou H. Silberman, "Wellhausen and Judaism," *Semeia* 25 (1982): 75–82; and M. Weinfeld, *Getting At the Roots of Wellhausen's Understanding of the Law of Israel on the 100*th *Anniversary of the Prolegomena* (Jerusalem: Institute for Advanced Studies, 1979).

88. R. N. Whybray, *The Making of the Pentateuch: A Methodological Study,* JSOTSup 53 (Sheffield: JSOT, 1987), 43.

89. D. A. Knight, "The Pentateuch," in *The Hebrew Bible and Its Modern Interpreters,* ed. D. A. Knight, et al. (Philadelphia: Fortress; Chico, CA: Scholars, 1985), 264, who observes, ". . . it is now inconceivable to conduct critical exegesis without attention to form, genre, *Sitz im Leben* and intention."

90. W. Dever, *What Did the Biblical Writers Know?*, 23–52.

91. In R. Lundin, A. C. Thiselton, and C. Walhout, *The Responsibility of Hermeneutics* (Grand Rapids: Eerdmans; Exeter: Paternoster, 1985), 1–29. See also Lundin's essay, "Hermeneutics," in *Contemporary Literary Theory. A Christian Appraisal* (Grand Rapids: Eerdmans, 1991), 149–71; Vanhoozer, *Is There a Meaning in This Text?* 16–35; and D. A. Carson, *The Gagging of God* (Grand Rapids: Zondervan, 1996), 57–92. The most exhaustive treatment is A. C. Thiselton, *New Horizons in Hermeneutics* (Grand Rapids: Zondervan, 1992). Cf. Thiselton's more concise survey in *Hermeneutics.*

Bacon. He then shows how American Christians in the nineteenth century combined Scottish common-sense realism with the scientific approach of Bacon to develop their basic hermeneutical approach. Lundin observes, "To get at the meaning of the Bible, they merely employed the inductive techniques exploited with considerable success by the natural scientists."[92] He argues that "inductive Bible study" was very much the product of historical processes, particularly the assimilation of Enlightenment thought in America, and not necessarily the only, or a self-evident and universally superior, method.[93] Interestingly, Lundin observes how this fascination with the inductive approach to biblical interpretation opened the door for any individual, group, denomination, or cult to sanction its beliefs based on its own exacting study of the Scriptures.[94]

Lundin concludes that, in reality, no one reads Scripture—or any literature, for that matter—in a completely disinterested way, even though "many of us cling stubbornly to our belief that we can approach a text with Cartesian cleanliness and Baconian precision."[95] Alluding to the philosophical tradition of Heidegger, Wittgenstein, Gadamer, and Ricoeur, Lundin concludes, "The idea of a disinterested interpretation of a literary text becomes an impossible one for hermeneutical theory."[96]

It would seem, then, that one may view preunderstanding as either a desirable asset or a treacherous culprit. Alas, asset or culprit may be in the eye of the "preunderstander"! Of course, to the extent that the interpreter requires some preunderstanding prior to coming to a text, it is indispensable. How could one understand something of the nature of the H_2O molecule without some background in atomic theory and chemistry? But equally, the preunderstanding may distort the reader's perception of reality and function like an unconscious prejudice adversely affecting the interpreter's ability to perceive accurately. It surely affects how someone will interpret the Bible unless something challenges that initial understanding.[97]

We do not always consciously adopt or even recognize our preunderstandings or the role they play in the interpretive process. As the proverbial goldfish remains unaware of the water in which it swims, we are not always conscious of our views of reality or the effects they have on what we see. Nor do we realize how extremely

---

92. Lundin, Thiselton, and Walhout, *The Responsibility of Hermeneutics*, 21.

93. We do not mean to imply here that we reject the possibility of an inductive approach to Bible study, nor do we declare that an interpreter should not be systematic and methodical in study. We argued for appropriate methods above and will defend them in more detail below.

94. Lundin, Thiselton, and Walhout, *The Responsibility of Hermeneutics*, 22. This leads Hauerwas to opine that we need to take the Bible out of the hands of individual Christians in North America who think they are qualified to interpret the Bible on their own and leave that task to "spiritual masters who can help the whole church stand under the authority of God's word" (*Unleashing the Scripture*, 16).

95. Lundin, Thiselton, and Walhout, *The Responsibility of Hermeneutics*, 23.

96. Ibid., 24; also see Lundin, "Hermeneutics," 158–63.

97. E. R. Richards and B. J. O'Brien, *Misreading Scripture with Western Eyes: Removing Cultural Blinders to Better Understand the Bible* (Downers Grove: InterVarsity, 2012) illustrate how our own culture may distort our reading of the Bible.

idiosyncratic *our own* (or our group's) preunderstandings may be—no one else sees the world as we do.

These preunderstandings may exert more or less influence on the process of interpretation depending upon their relevance to the issue at hand. For example, our African student's misunderstanding of the origin of snow probably made little difference in her understanding of the text, "Though your sins are like scarlet, they shall be as white as snow" (Isa 1:18). On the other hand, an ideology—like Wellhausen's anti-Judaism on the one hand or a politically correct aversion to any anti-Judaism on the other—will exert a major influence on how one interprets the accounts of Jesus' negative critique of certain "Jews" as reported in the Gospels. The one may be prone to conclude that all Jews are "bad guys." The other may dismiss the Evangelists as anti-Semites and seek to cleanse the accounts of such stains (and modern translations that persist in retaining such "biases"). These two examples also illustrate that some preunderstandings may have more far-reaching implications than others may. One affects (and risks distorting) our reading only of texts that concern snow. The other regulates how we read every incident or claim in both testaments that speaks negatively about Jews.

In the face of new evidence, our African student did not hesitate to adjust her erroneous preunderstanding about the origin of snow. One of our challenges as interpreters is not simply to identify and take into account our preunderstandings but also to adjust or revise them, embrace new ones, or courageously jettison those that distort our view or prove to be erroneous. We must learn to recognize our preunderstandings and to evaluate their worth. We must have a basis on which to amend them or judge them satisfactory.

A Philosophy of Interpretation as Preunderstanding

All who seek to interpret the Bible must make a decision about the basic stance they will embrace. When most people think of biblical interpretation, they think of deciphering ancient documents. After the Enlightenment and up until the 1940s or so, the essential concerns of hermeneutics were to investigate the world of the biblical author or editor, the resulting texts, and the original readers of those texts. That is, biblical interpretation was preoccupied with the historical locus of the text— what happened in the ancient world that resulted in what was written in the text back then. More recently, however, scholars have come to understand that *historical methods* are too limiting in seeking only what happened or was written in the past. If one chooses to ignore, or at least bracket, historical concerns and focus on the text only—particularly the interaction between text and reader—then different methods are needed and different conclusions will follow.

Robert Morgan responds to this issue in one way. While he does not intend that a multi-faceted approach should supplant or deny the results of historical or linguistic study, he argues that in today's pluralistic and rationalistic world, literary (i.e., not author/text-based) approaches "allow a large range of legitimate interpretations of the Bible."[98] Morgan believes that to attempt to find "the single correct answer" (i.e., *the* correct interpretation of a text) would result in a hopelessly fragmented Bible that "would offer from the distant past various pieces of information with little relation to the present."[99] In other words, he implies that because people bring to the Bible various preunderstandings and they use the Bible for various purposes, no one has the right to say only one approach is valid, true, or even better. But we ask, are we left with a kind of hermeneutical cafeteria where we must grant legitimacy to every method of interpretation and to all interpreters—*and to all results*? May people simply choose how they want to read the Bible, employ their preferred methods, and finally display their conclusions? It seems as if many are embracing some form of this approach.

Since in this pluralistic age we live with many truth-claims—those of the Buddhist, Muslim, Jew, and Christian, to name a few—Morgan believes it is invalid to claim arrogantly that a correct historical reading of the Bible supports solely one's own religious perspective. Thus, he argues, if we read the biblical accounts as literature, religious people can simply affirm their views and positions on other grounds and not make a historical use of the Bible serve that apologetic function. Morgan does not want to expunge historical-critical exegesis; rather, he seeks to relegate it to its proper place of fine tuning existing theological formulations and keeping honest those who already base their religion on the Bible.

As noted above, someone may adopt a certain philosophical position and proceed to interpret through that grid. For example, building on a framework of existentialism,[100] Heidegger and Bultmann argued that the biblical texts have meaning only when we as subjects can engage those texts and their significance for our being.[101] Though their point has clear merit, they severely limit truth or reality to what transforms our personal experience. Their vantage point (preunderstanding) *determines* what the text means, rather than giving the author the right to mean what he or she intended. What can justify such a presumption? Of course, a reader can do anything he or she wishes with a text. But as we will argue in the next chapter, this willy-nilly tactic is

---

98. R. Morgan with J. Barton, *Biblical Interpretation* (Oxford: Oxford University Press, 1998), 286.

99. Morgan with Barton, *Biblical Interpretation*, 286.

100. For a rather exhaustive treatment of these existential approaches, including Gadamer and Bultmann, see Thiselton, *Two Horizons*. Also consult the review of *Two Horizons* by W. W. Klein in *TrinJ* 2 (1981): 71–75.

101. Thiselton cites Bultmann's declaration that "it is valid in the investigation of a text to allow oneself to be examined by the text, and to hear the claim it makes" (Thiselton, *Two Horizons,* 191). This is true to a point, but does the historicity of a text make a difference in what claim it makes on us? Apparently not for Bultmann, who argues that to believe in the cross of Christ "does not mean to concern ourselves . . . with an objective event (*ein objektiv anschaubares Ereignis*) . . . but rather to make the cross of Christ our own, to undergo crucifixion with him" (211). Finally, Thiselton says, "Bultmann insists that through history the interpreter comes to understand *himself.* His relationship to the text is not theoretical but *existentiel.* Only thus does the text 'speak'" (287). Rightly Bultmann has been criticized because he places so much emphasis on the existential dimension that for him it matters little if any objective or historical events recorded in the NT even occurred. This is a serious flaw for, though Christ's resurrection may be an inspiring mythical event, how can it speak to a Christian's own resurrection if it did not actually occur in history (cf. 1 Cor 15:17)?

not the appropriate way to read a text, especially the Bible. To retrieve its resident meaning as God's authoritative revelation should be our goal.

As we saw in Chapter 2, metaphysical assumptions shaped the understanding of hermeneutics in the so-called *new hermeneutic*.[102] For example, it asserted that only myths (not historical narratives) could effectively convey truths about a transcendent God to fallen humanity. Devaluation of the historicity of biblical events was the result. Instead of employing a methodology or process for determining the meaning of texts (i.e., what they historically intended to communicate), practitioners of the new hermeneutic focused attention on the modern situation—how the ancient text sparks fresh, personal encounters with God today.

Similarly, *process theologians* adopt a stance or preunderstanding through which they view the Bible. Following philosopher A. N. Whitehead, they understand reality as a process, a maelstrom of causes and effects in which humans make sense out of their world.[103] George Lucas suggests, "Process philosophy is distinguished from other movements by its stress on the primacy of change, becoming, and the event character of reality, in opposition to what Whitehead termed the static or 'vacuous' actualities of traditional substance metaphysics."[104]

According to these theologians, language is fluid, imprecise, and capable of a variety of meanings. Thus, understanding language cannot be exact for it conveys reality by way of abstraction. Since all reality exists in such a state of flux, the meaning of a text in Scripture cannot be precise or authoritative. Neither the author's intention nor some historical meaning of a text determines the goal of understanding for process hermeneutics. Process interpreters do not search for propositional truth; they simply process what the reader has encountered in the text. Their preunderstanding is clearly self-conscious and becomes a grid through which they understand the Bible.[105] Process theology is now largely passé, though perhaps the lingering effect of this philosophy

---

102. Representatives include J. M. Robinson and J. Cobb, eds., *The New Hermeneutic* (New York: Harper & Row, 1964); R. W. Funk, *Language, Hermeneutic and Word of God* (New York: Harper & Row, 1966); and G. Ebeling, *God and Word* (Philadelphia: Fortress, 1967). For a short explanation and critique of the new hermeneutic see D. A. Carson, "Hermeneutics: A Brief Assessment of Some Recent Trends" *TynBul* 5 (1980): 14–17.

103. Some representatives include J. B. Cobb and D. R. Griffin, *Process Theology: An Introductory Exposition* (Philadelphia: Westminster, 1996); and A. N. Whitehead, *Science and the Modern World* (New York: Macmillan, 1927). J. S. Feinberg, *No One Like Him: The Doctrine of God. The Foundations of Evangelical Theology* (Wheaton, IL: Crossway, 2001), 170–79, provides a brief review and assessment of process theology. Again we risk, yet attempt to avoid, caricatures in what follows.

104. G. R. Lucas, *The Genesis of Modern Process Thought: A Historical Outline with Bibliography* (Metuchen, NJ: Scarecrow Press and the ATLA, 1983), 5, which provides a basic survey of process thinking with extensive bibliographies. See also G. R. Lucas, *The Rehabilitation of Whitehead* (Albany: The State University of New York Press, 1989); T. Trethowan, *Process Theology and the Christian Tradition* (Petersham, MA: St. Bede's Publications, 2002), who argues that the idea of an eternal yet changeable God is part of the Christian heritage; and B. G. Epperly, *Process Theology: A Guide for the Perplexed* (New York: Bloomsbury T&T Clark, 2011).

105. In R. Nash, ed. *Process Theology* (Grand Rapids: Baker, 1987), various evangelical scholars respond to different facets of process philosophy and theology. They provide helpful assessments that compare process theology to classical theism and various theological and philosophical issues and offer personal judgments of the usefulness of process thought.

is seen in open theism, the view that it is logically impossible for God to know the future actions of free, human agents.[106]

Liberation theology also illustrates the importance of preunderstanding. From that vantage point, the role the church should perform in bringing justice to the poor (initially in Latin America) determines their reading of the Bible (recall our comments in ch. 3). These theologians do not simply study the Bible based on a set of principles; they interpret the Bible based on an agenda with the goal of justice for the poor. Often though not necessarily Marxist, this ideological base becomes for these theologians the preunderstanding for interpreting the Bible and for developing their political agenda. In a similar vein some readers now welcome postcolonial, feminist, and womanist readings.[107] Some defend gay (or queer) readings of the Bible that apply the tools of "queer theory" and gender studies to biblical texts.[108] Such studies assert a new (often termed "more accurate") understanding of the biblical texts that challenges the Bible's own biases (not to mention those of traditional interpreters), such as its proscription of homosexual behavior. Self-consciously and unashamedly, these readers apply their preunderstandings of reality to their interpretation of the Bible.

What we have described under these various developments signals a distinct shift in the practice of biblical interpretation—part of the movement sometimes termed postmodernism. They illustrate the swing from author- and text-centered interpretation to reader-centered approaches. In fact E. V. McKnight contends that the nature of the modern reader's preunderstanding has led to a fundamental shift in the hermeneutical task. In his view, "A *reader-oriented approach* acknowledges that the contemporary reader's 'intending' of the text is not the same as that of the ancient author and/or ancient readers."[109] He observes, further, "Biblical texts are perceived and interpreted in quite different ways as a result of changes in world view and in social surroundings within any given world view."[110] In a later paragraph he summarizes: "Readers *make* sense. Readers may perform their role constrained by their cultural contexts and critical assumptions and remain unaware of their potential as creative

---

106. See G. A. Boyd, *God of the Possible: A Biblical Introduction to the Open View of God* (Grand Rapids: Baker, 2000) and C. H. Pinnock, *The Openness of God: A Biblical Challenge to the Traditional Understanding of God* (Downers Grove: InterVarsity, 2010).

107. For a helpful overview see R. S. Sugirtharajah, *Voices from the Margin: Interpreting the Bible in the Third World*, 3rd ed. (Maryknoll, NY: Orbis, 2006).

108. See our comments and the literature cited in chs. 2 and 3 above. Key texts include J. Rogers, *Jesus, the Bible, and Homosexuality, Revised and Expanded Edition: Explode the Myths, Heal the Church* (Louisville: Westminster John Knox, 2009); and M. Achtemeier, *The Bible's Yes to Same-Sex Marriage: An Evangelical's Change of Heart* (Louisville: Westminster John Knox, 2014). For a critique of this hermeneutical stance see S. J. Grenz, *Welcoming but Not Affirming: An Evangelical Response to Homosexuality* (Louisville: Westminster John Knox, 1998). Two studies that seek to present both sides in an irenic fashion are R. A. J. Gagnon, *Homosexuality and the Bible: Two Views* (Minneapolis: Fortress, 2009); and J. V. Brownson, *Bible, Gender, Sexuality: Reframing the Church's Debate on Same-Sex Relationships* (Grand Rapids: Eerdmans, 2013). On a more popular level see K. DeYoung, *What Does the Bible Really Teach about Homosexuality?* (Wheaton, IL: Crossway, 2015).

109. E. V. McKnight, *Postmodern Use of the Bible: The Emergence of Reader-Oriented Criticism* (Nashville: Abingdon, 1988), 150 (our emphasis).

110. McKnight, *Postmodern Use*, 149.

readers."[111] For McKnight, the modern interpreter's ability to read the biblical texts "creatively" is a major gain. Such readers attain a new freedom because they are "no longer constrained by traditional dogmatic and/or historical-critical goals of reading and interpretation."[112]

Clearly, McKnight's postmodern view greatly relativizes the Bible's teachings. Since for McKnight and many others the Bible's teachings are the product of a series of ancient cultures and their primitive or precritical worldviews, they can have no necessarily abiding authority for modern people. In this view whatever authority or application the Bible may have for people today must pass through this grid: the Bible comprises culturally and historically conditioned documents, and its cultures and ours today are radically different. For many postmodern interpreters, the reader's perception of the text, *not the text itself,* is the ultimate basis of authority for the meaning of the text.

But we hasten to ask: What about the message conveyed in the Bible? Does the message composed by the author (locution, illocution, and perlocution) make any valid claim upon a modern reader? Should readers not focus their interpretation on *that* message? Ferguson's critique of such postmodern approaches is well-founded:

> What, for example, happens to history as a means of God's self-disclosure? Once again, it would appear that the content of the *kerygma* as an object of faith has been obscured. There is little recognition that the crucifixion and resurrection are historical events themselves creative of language, not merely 'language events.' Language as the only hermeneutical guide fails to do full justice to history.[113]

We conclude that these calls for a hermeneutic more committed to pluralistic and postmodern openness leave interpreters liable to the grave danger of subjectivism and relativism. If the greatest virtue is tolerance or avoiding interpretations that offend those of other religions, cultural background, or gender orientations, do we simply abandon the search for truth? Do we set aside the Bible's message of redemption for all people?[114] Certainly, some ideas like anti-Semitism or racism are simply very bad ideas that, if left unchallenged, threaten society with dangerous consequences. Morgan recognizes this inherent danger but calls only for the critical voice of well-trained

---

111. McKnight, *Postmodern Use*, 161.

112. Ibid. For a similar affirmation see R. Crosman, "Do Readers Make Meaning?" in *The Reader in the Text*, eds. S. R. Suleiman and I. Crosman (Princeton: Princeton University Press, 1980), 149–64.

113. Ferguson, *Biblical Hermeneutics*, 174.

114. Historically, Christianity has claimed that it is uniquely true—that in Jesus we have the way, truth, and life, the only way to God (John 14:6; Acts 4:12). In a well-reasoned book H. A. Netland defends this wildly unpopular assertion of Christian exclusivism. He asserts, "Where the claims of Scripture are incompatible with those of other faiths, the latter are to be rejected as false," in *Dissonant Voices: Religious Pluralism and the Question of Truth* (Grand Rapids: Eerdmans; Leicester: Inter-Varsity, 1991), 34. Netland's point is *not* that all the claims or teachings of other religions are false, or that they possess no value, or that Christians can learn nothing from them. Rather, when religions make conflicting claims to truth, the Christian position is the true one. Netland's work presents a compelling defense of the historic Christian faith. All missiologists and philosophers of religion need to examine what Netland has presented. See also P. Copan, *True for You, But Not for Me: Overcoming Objections to Christian Faith*, rev. ed. (Minneapolis: Bethany House, 2009); and D. A. Carson, *The Intolerance of Tolerance* (Grand Rapids: Eerdmans, 2012).

historians and linguists "to call rubbish by its name."[115] But it is not clear how, if all literary approaches are equally welcome and readers make meaning, the historians and linguists can sufficiently label as rubbish a specific "literary reading" of a text. For if the historical perspective—what the author intended the text to mean at the time written—does not have the major and controlling influence, then various "readings" might be termed equally legitimate, and even desirable, whatever predetermined stance from which they emerge.[116]

Postmodernists may welcome this state of affairs because this approach puts the reader in charge. Don't mishear us: we wish to welcome and employ literary methods that enable us to understand and appreciate the Bible's literary dimensions. We, too, recognize readers as key participants in the process of understanding texts. And we acknowledge that we all come to the Bible with preunderstandings. But in using such literary methods we should not abandon the texts' historical moorings. We insist that the "historical" focus provides the best avenue to a legitimate "literary" reading. We do not want an either-or approach.[117] We reject any preunderstandings that replace the historical meaning of a text with a modern "reading" of it.

Testing Preunderstandings

How can we know if our preunderstandings are valid and will be assets in the process of biblical interpretation? One test of our preunderstandings is whether they correspond to the biblical data. Yet a critic may ask why the Bible assumes the role of ultimate authority. We discussed above our presupposition that the Bible is authoritative and true, so only a brief summary must suffice.

We believe that accepting the Bible's truthfulness is not merely our prejudiced dogmatism, an undefended presuppositionalism that simply assumes its starting point. That is to say, we do not position ourselves in the camp of those whom apologists technically call "presuppositionalists" (e.g., C. Van Til). In this view, one starts by assuming such tenets as God's existence or the truthfulness of revelation in the Bible.[118] In contrast, we embrace a modified evidentialist or verificationalist stance.[119] N. T.

---

115. Morgan with Barton, *Biblical Interpretation*, 289.

116. We will take up below our understanding and defense of author-based textual meaning as the primary goal of hermeneutics.

117. To be fair, Morgan does not argue for literary methods to replace historical ones. He realizes how subjective any interpretation can be, even those that purport to be "historical." He wants a historical framework to govern only those studies whose aims are historical (*Biblical Interpretation*, 287). But, argues Morgan, where one's aims are religious or theological, other methods (i.e., literary) need to provide the framework. History, for Morgan, takes the back seat. But, we protest most strongly: theological beliefs *must* also be rooted in history, as the Apostle Paul argues concerning Jesus' resurrection in 1 Cor 15:13–23. More follows.

118. C. Van Til, *The Defense of the Faith* (Philadelphia: Presbyterian and Reformed Publishing Co., 1955) took issue with his colleague B. B. Warfield, who taught that apologetics was a prior and separate discipline to establish the truth of Christianity before one moved to the other theological subjects. At this point we find ourselves more in sympathy with Warfield than Van Til.

119. See E. J. Carnell, *An Introduction to Christian Apologetics* (Grand Rapids: Eerdmans, 1948), 103–21, for a helpful discussion of what constitutes verification in apologetics; cf. D. Groothuis, *Christian Apologetics: A Comprehensive Case for Biblical Faith* (Downers Grove: InterVarsity, 2011), 45–72.

Wright calls such an approach "critical realism," and with him we agree.[120] That is, we believe we must start with certain hypotheses that we test and either accept or reject. We must evaluate the evidence for the Christian claims in light of all the alternative truth claims.

We believe that such an approach establishes the viability and defensibility of the historic Christian faith. It explains the issues of existence and reality with fewer difficulties than the competing alternatives. We do not claim proof in any scientific senses especially since, as we noted above, science itself is hardly a valueless enterprise. Nevertheless, in Carnell's words, "the Christian finds his system of philosophy in the Bible, to be sure, but he accepts this, not simply because it is in the Bible, but because, when tested, it makes better sense out of life than other systems of philosophy make."[121] We soundly reject a view that the Christian position is merely a "leap in the dark" opinion, no better (or worse) than alternatives that many people "sincerely believe." Postmodern western culture exalts relativism and pluralism as great virtues, almost nonnegotiable axioms rooted in its preunderstanding of the nature of human freedom. We believe, in contrast, that absolute truth exists, and that "truth" cannot be relativized so that contradictory claims are accepted as equally valid. We believe that to accept the Bible's veracity best accords with the evidence.

A Christian Preunderstanding[122]

As responsible interpreters we seek to employ whatever rational methods will enable us to understand the correct meaning of the biblical texts. But when it comes to making judgments about the theological meaning (and significance) of those texts, we must go beyond our analytic methods. Though we employ many of the critical methods in common with secular historians, we do so with our own preunderstanding of the significance of the documents we are studying.

Secular historians, anthropologists, and sociologists may view the Bible only as a collection of ancient religious texts. To treat it as such—which occurs regularly in academia—is unlikely to lead to what we consider to be valid conclusions about the religious value or significance of the Bible. In fact the results may seem sterile compared to those of believing Christians (which explains, often, their aversion to the scholars). However, we believe that the Bible is the divine Word of God. From

120. Wright, *New Testament*, 32–46.
121. Carnell, *Introduction*, 102.
122. As we have indicated at various points already, we position ourselves theologically in the evangelical tradition, within the framework described, for example, by the Lausanne Covenant [http://www.lausanne.org/content/covenant/lausanne-covenant] or the basic affirmations of the National Association of Evangelicals [http://www.nae.net/]. Sister organizations are the National Black Evangelical Association [http://www.the-nbea.org/] and the National Hispanic Christian Leadership Conference [http://nhclc.org/]. Those espousing such evangelical beliefs are found in many other sectors of Christendom as well. Thus, what follows need not be limited to our circle of Christians. Others will, we suspect, agree with most if not all of what follows. The principles and methods we employ will yield, we believe, valid understanding regardless of the practitioner, though readers with differing presuppositions and preunderstandings will accept or reject our results in varying ways. To the extent that methods are neutral (and we insist most are), the results will be similar.

that stance we will use our historical and critical methods and arrive at theologically meaningful and pertinent results. Hirsch puts it forcefully: "An interpreter's notion of the type of meaning he confronts will powerfully influence his understanding of details."[123] We posit that our stance provides the best basis for a valid understanding of the biblical texts. Richardson makes this point succinctly, "That perspective from which we see most clearly all the facts, without having to explain any of them away, will be a relatively true perspective. Christians believe that the perspective of biblical faith enables us to see very clearly and without distortion the biblical facts as they really are: they see the facts clearly because they see their true meaning."[124]

We are members of the world-wide evangelical community (theologically defined).[125] We have committed ourselves to the faith understood as traditionally Christian, though we cheerfully acknowledge there are many Christians not under the evangelical umbrella. This informs our preunderstanding and provides the boundaries for our reading of the Bible. Though we must always submit to the teachings of the Bible as our sole and final authority, our actual presupposition of the Bible as God's revelation guides our interpretation of its pages. We insist, as well, that our commitment to the authority of the Bible derives from our prior conviction of its truthfulness and our assumption of its divine inspiration. This is an informed circularity, an outgrowth of "critical realism," to borrow again Wright's phrase.

We believe we must be willing to critique and correct our preunderstandings even though they so completely encompasse all that we are. If Christians are committed to being thoroughly biblical, then one tactic is to subject our views to the scrutiny of Scripture.[126] That is, we can aspire to have a biblically based and determined preunderstanding. In other words, where beliefs and commitments derive from our culture that contradict or oppose biblical values, we must identify them, and, somehow, control their effects in the interpretive process. Beyond our own conversation with the biblical text, we must engage in the search for valid interpretation with the larger Christian community, guided by the Spirit, for it comprises the optimal arena for such self-analysis. We will have more to say on this point in the next chapter.

We must anchor our subsequent discussion of how to understand texts to this conversation about preunderstanding. A document consisting of words on a page remains an inert entity. The significance we give to those words depends to a large extent upon us: what significance do we *want* to give to the words? Postmodern

---

123. E. D. Hirsch, Jr., *Validity in Interpretation* (New Haven: Yale University Press, 1967), 75.

124. A. Richardson, *Christian Apologetics* (New York: Harper & Row, 1947), 105.

125. We repeat this clarification because we are aware that "evangelical" is a widely used and abused term that often identifies cultural or political features more than it does a biblical/theological orientation—the one we intend here.

126. Since "all truth is God's truth" (a quote attributed to many sources from Augustine to Arthur Holmes), we are also committed to learn what is true from any other sources, and to correct our preunderstandings on the basis of new truth. To repeat Paul's apt words, "Finally, brothers and sisters, whatever is true, whatever is noble, whatever is right, whatever is pure, whatever is lovely, whatever is admirable—if anything is excellent or praiseworthy—think about such things" (Phil 4:8).

readers can do anything they please; no court of law restricts how texts can be used or abused by anyone else (though, of course, libel—a defamation of someone that appears in print—is punishable by the courts). We must decide if we want to hear the Bible's words in terms of what they most likely meant at the time they were written, or whether we will use, or handle, or employ them in other ways. The authors, editors, or communities that formulated the biblical texts obviously cannot voice objections. Nor can the first readers be consulted for their input.

As ongoing debates in political circles about interpreting the U.S. Constitution illustrate, people today decide how they will use old documents.[127] The biblical texts or the creeds of the church may well claim inspiration for the Scriptures, but interpreters today still decide how they will handle those claims—both what they mean and how to respond to them. Are theology and Christian practice to be based upon what the biblical texts intend to communicate, or upon the objectives, concerns, and agendas of the modern community that interpret those authors, or upon some combination of the two? Evangelicals may insist first (correctly, we believe) upon a focus on the original meanings of the biblical texts and then upon the implications of those meanings for contemporary concerns. However, as we have seen, the history of interpretation clearly demonstrates the pervasive (and sometimes harmful) influence of the interpreters' agendas when the original meanings do not have priority. What is the optimum Christian preunderstanding? For us it is the one that derives from the set of presuppositions listed earlier in this chapter.

Preunderstandings Change with Understanding

When we speak of preunderstanding, we mean this to be a starting point at a location in time. Here's where we begin our Bible study. But our grasp of the Bible's teaching and its significance will never be static, nor should it be if we are growing as Christians in our spiritual understanding due to our engagement with the Bible. Interpreters approach the Bible with questions, biases, and preunderstandings. Inevitably, those influence the answers they obtain. But their preunderstandings are subject to revisions as a result of their honest and Spirit-led study. Bible study, if pursued responsibly, affects the interpreter: the text interprets the interpreter who becomes not only the subject interpreting but the object interpreted. We affirm this goal as our goal as interpreters: *to aspire to an ever-growing, biblically oriented preunderstanding that enables increasingly valid insights into the meaning of the texts.*

Recall our African student with her preunderstandings about snow. Once she

---

127. Is our concern to apply the Constitution in the way its original framers intended, or in view of current understandings and realities? Parallel to the phenomenon of postmodern biblical interpretation, some argue that today the courts have usurped from the Constitution the authority for governing. The courts determine what is legal or not in how they interpret the founding documents of the republic in the current era. For this view, see the musings of the editors, "The End of Democracy? The Judicial Usurpation of Politics" and "To Reclaim Our Democratic Heritage," *First Things* 69 (1997): 25–28. Such debates are ongoing. J. Pelikan, *Interpreting the Bible and the Constitution* (New Haven: Yale University Press, 2004), shows just how parallel the interpretive controversies surrounding the Constitution and those surrounding the Bible actually are.

realized that snow descends from the sky rather than emerges out of the earth, she revised her understanding about this type of precipitation. In her adjusted understanding it fit in the same category as rain, rather than in the category of dew. It transformed her interpretation of pictures of snow.

This process has led some interpreters to speak of a hermeneutical circle, or better, a *hermeneutical spiral*.[128] We believe that is a useful analogy. Every interpreter begins with a preunderstanding. During and following an initial study of a biblical text (using all the tactics and resources available and as a result of the working of the Holy Spirit), the interpreter discovers that the text has effected changes in his or her understandings. Now the preunderstandings are no longer what they were. As Paul might phrase it, they have been "transformed by the renewing of [their] mind" (Rom 12:2). Subsequently, as the newly interpreted interpreter proceeds to engage the text further, additional—perhaps, different—questions and answers emerge, changing the interpreter yet again. New (pre)understanding results. And so on, the process continues. The interpreter does not merely go around in circles. This is not a vicious circle but rather a progressive spiral of growth in understanding. The meaning of the text has not changed; the change has occurred in the interpreter's ability to understand it more adequately and to apply it more effectively.

HERMENEUTICAL SPIRAL

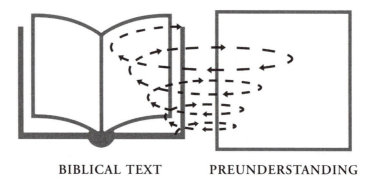

BIBLICAL TEXT   PREUNDERSTANDING

---

128. Many scholars now recognize the importance of this way of understanding the task of interpretation. One author makes it the title of his book: G. Osborne, *The Hermeneutical Spiral*, 2nd ed. (Downers Grove: InterVarsity, 2006). For some of the ways he unpacks the image see pp. 22, 31–32, 139, 351, 417–18, and 456. Cf. Thiselton, *Hermeneutics*, 13–16; W. J. Larkin, Jr., *Culture and Biblical Hermeneutics* (Grand Rapids: Baker, 1988), 302; and R. C. Padilla, "Hermeneutics and Culture: A Theological Perspective," in *Gospel and Culture,* ed. J. R. W. Stott and R. T. Coote (Pasadena: William Carey Library, 1979), 63–78. Carson, *The Gagging of God*, 121–22, proposes a mathematical model, the asymptote. Our knowledge can increasingly approximate though never attain complete (divine) knowledge. For still another image, David Starling, *Hermeneutics as Apprenticeship* (Grand Rapids: Baker Academic, 2016), 13–16, proposes the snowball. The more it rolls downhill, the more layers of snow it accumulates. The more one's preunderstandings are tested and reshaped, the more confidence we gain in our perspectives and, like the snowball that gets bigger and faster, the harder it is to stop it (i.e., change our minds)!

Admittedly, there is the danger that interpretation will be only a circle rather than a spiral—that one will come out where one went in. Indeed, there is an inevitable circularity once one has settled on his or her positions. When we posit the requirement of faith to understand the Bible fully and then we go to the Bible in order to understand God's self-revelation in Christ in whom we have faith, the process is self-reinforcing. But this process need not remain circular. We insist that an appropriate level of preunderstanding is necessary to begin any inquiry. This, as we have seen, is the nature of all investigation. One must have some knowledge of God even to arrive at the preunderstanding of faith. Then that stance of faith enables the Christian to study the Bible to come to a deeper understanding of God and what the Scriptures say. The use of the best tools, methods, and resources places believers in a position to learn, grow, and change their understanding, not merely to reinforce preexisting ideas. But, here is the key: one must be open to change and correction as a result of new discoveries.

As we learn more from our study of Scripture, we alter and enlarge our pre-understandings in more or less fundamental ways. It's possible for Calvinists to become Arminians, and vice-versa! Complementarians might become egalitarians or dispensationalists embrace covenant theology, or vice-versa! In essence, this process describes the nature of all genuine learning: it is interactive, ongoing, and continuous. When believers study the Bible with open minds and hearts, and interact with its texts and with its Author over time, they increase their understanding. They come to know more of God and his Word and the process of transformation continues. And lest readers surmise that God's word may transform only people's understandings, we insist that God uses our emerging understandings to transform our behaviors, attitudes, and actions—so that we love God and our neighbors as God desires.

Preunderstandings and Objectivity in Interpretation

Following such a discussion of preunderstanding, some may still wonder if interpreters are doomed to subjectivity. Can we ever interpret the Bible in an objective fashion, or do we simply detect in its pages only what we want or are predisposed to see? Must we say with the postmodernists that we discover only what is "true for me" and despair of or abandon the quest to find what the biblical authors intended to communicate? These questions hinge on the validity of our presuppositions that the Bible communicates a message that can be discovered by critical methods and that this message is worth the effort to find it.

We believe that God has revealed truth in the Bible, and that it is reasonable to posit that he has made us capable of apprehending that truth, or at least some measure of it. Further, we believe that we ought to seek God's message when we read the Bible, not merely our own reading of it. Thus, though we inevitably bring preunderstandings to the texts we seek to interpret, this does not mean that we cannot discover the meaning the texts intend to impart. Particularly if our goal is to discover the meaning the texts conveyed at the time they were written, we have some objective criteria to validate our interpretations.[129]

Thus we rebuff any charge that our view is simply another version of seeing what we want to see in the Bible. We will not jettison an objective assessment of the facts or data of the text and its situation in the interests of our preferred reading. Possessing preunderstandings does not doom us to a closed circle—that we find in a text what we want to find in a text—though that looms as an ever-present danger. The honest, reflective, humble interpreter remains open to change, even to a significant transformation of preunderstandings and resulting behaviors. This is the hermeneutical *spiral*. Since we accept the Bible's authority as mediated through the Spirit, we remain open to correction by its message. There are ways to verify interpretations or to validate some interpretive options as more likely than others. It is not a matter of simply throwing the dice or picking the one we prefer. This book will present useful methods to help interpreters find what the original texts most likely meant to their initial readers. Every time we alter our preunderstanding as the result of our interaction with the text we demonstrate that the process has objective constraints, otherwise, no change would occur; we would remain forever entombed in our prior commitments.

William Larkin makes the valid point that because God made people in his own image they have the capacity to "transcend preunderstanding, evaluate it, and change it."[130] People are not so captive to their preconceptions that they cannot transcend them. One of the tactics, Larkin believes, that fosters the process of evaluating and transcending our preunderstanding as interpreters is to "seek out the definite and fixed meaning intended by the author of the text and to use Scripture as the final critical authority for judging extrabiblical thought-patterns."[131] We agree; this is our goal.

The hermeneutical spiral illustrates a very positive experience as God through his Holy Spirit brings new and more adequate understanding of his truth and its application to believers' lives. If the Bible is true (one of our presuppositions), then subscribing to its truth constitutes the most adequate starting point for interpreting its content.

---

129. See the section on "reading and critical realism" in Wright, *New Testament,* 61–69.

130. Larkin, *Culture and Biblical Hermeneutics,* 299.

131. Ibid., 300. Related to this point also see W. K. Wimsatt and M. C. Beardsley, "The Intentional Fallacy," in *The Verbal Icon: Studies in the Meaning of Poetry* (Lexington: University Press of Kentucky, 1954), 3–18. Their objection was to knowing the author's intention in poems and poetry, not necessarily in texts written to specific audiences for specific purposes—such as is the case in most of the Bible. We argue that we can know much of the authors' intentions given the texts they produced. Sounding a different note, V. S. Poythress, "Dispensing with Merely Human Meaning: Gains and Losses from Focusing on the Human Author, Illustrated by Zephaniah 1:2–3," *JETS* 57 (2014): 481–99, argues that we should give up our focus on the human authors and their intentions in writing Scripture. He wants to focus on the divine author whom we know rather than the human author whom we do not. But this is not an either-or proposition. We believe that our concentration on the *text* puts us in the best position to grasp the Author's/author's meaning. Also, Larkin may be overly optimistic when he assures us, "interpreters who consciously set aside their cultural preunderstanding can be confident that the grammatical-historical-literary context will enable them to find the plain and definite meaning of the text" (301). Whether we can set aside our cultural preunderstandings as confidently as Larkin surmises remains a huge question. A good starting point is simply to try to identify them and to assess their influence.

But alone that would be insufficient to comprehend the Bible. To understand the Bible's message adequately demands appropriate methodology and the willingness of interpreters to allow the Bible to alter or clarify their preunderstandings. As Ferguson has said: ". . . all knowledge is elusive, and to grasp it demands a great deal of effort on our part, not the least of which is keeping a watchful eye on our own personal and societal forms of preunderstanding."[132] The metaphor of a spiral suggests the healthiest approach to an adequate comprehension of the Bible.

132. Ferguson, *Biblical Hermeneutics*, 17.

6

THE GOAL OF
INTERPRETATION

When people communicate, they seek to convey a message that will accomplish some purpose. Normally, the recipients of that message will seek to understand its meaning. Even so simple a message as, "Hello; how are you doing?" has some purpose, even if it's not that the speaker really wants a progress or medical report. The purpose of the words may simply be to make a friendly connection. Communication succeeds when the meaning understood corresponds to the meaning intended. As mentioned previously, human communication comprises what is called a "speech act."[1]

SPEECH ACTS

When an author composes a text (this is what Austin called the "locution," the act of writing), he or she engages in a communicative act. As a communicative act, the text has content, energy, or power ("illocutionary force"), with the intention of accomplishing some outcome ("perlocutionary effect"). To communicate an author or speaker encodes some message in a specific literary or oral form. The form (for example, a genre) may well be chosen because it is the best "container" to convey the energy and content to accomplish the desired purpose, that is, to produce the intended effect in the readers, whether to persuade, promise, inform, warn, guide, exhort, etc. To explain the "meaning" in a text requires an understanding of these aspects of

---

1. Speech act theory was developed by J. L. Austin, *How To Do Things with Words*, ed. J. O. Urmson and M. Sbisa, 2nd ed. (Cambridge, MA: Harvard University Press, 1975), and J. Searle, *Speech Acts: An Essay in the Philosophy of Language* (Cambridge, UK: Cambridge University Press, 1969). To "say" or "write" is in reality something that is "done." So they argued we must analyze what a text does if we are to discern appropriately its meaning. See the perceptive application to biblical studies provided by J. H. Walton and D. Brent Sandy, *The Lost World of Scripture* (Downers Grove: InterVarsity, 2013), 41–52; J. K. Brown, *Scripture as Communication: Introducing Biblical Hermeneutics* (Grand Rapids: Baker Academic, 2007), 32–35, 111–14; and K. J. Vanhoozer, "The Semantics of Biblical Literature," in *Hermeneutics, Authority, and Canon*, ed. D. A. Carson and J. D. Woodbridge (Grand Rapids: Zondervan, 1986), 49–104. For more on speech act theory and biblical studies, see the entire issue of *Semeia* 41 (1988); A. C. Thiselton, *New Horizons in Hermeneutics* (Grand Rapids: Zondervan, 1992), 283–312; the various articles that address these issues in C. Bartholomew et al., ed., *After Pentecost: Language and Biblical Interpretation* (Grand Rapids: Zondervan, 2001); and R. S. Briggs, *Words in Action: Speech Act Theory and Biblical Interpretation* (Edinburgh: T&T Clark, 2001).

communication. The meaning of a text cannot be derived simply by unpacking the meanings of words and grammar (as important as that task is), but how the message is presented and to what intended purpose.

Speech Act Theory: The Three Elements
• Locution: the words in a text
• Illocution: the communicative intent; the energy and form employed in order to accomplish the intent
• Perlocution: the author's desired or intended response from the readers; what the author wanted the readers to do if the purpose is successfully realized.

To recap in simplest terms, *locution* describes what is actually spoken or written: the words, sentences, genre, etc. *Illocution* refers to the intention the speaker or writer has by using those specific words in a particular form with the kind of energy employed. Finally, *perlocution* describes what the speaker or writer envisioned the outcome or results to be for the audience or readers. Jeannine Brown calls this the "perlocutionary intention."[2] Of course, when we read the Bible, we usually can't know whether the outcome was achieved, for that depends, among other things, on whether the hearers understood the message and were inclined to respond one way or the other.

Within the scope of written communication, we can talk about three potential aspects of meaning in a locution: (1) the meaning the author intends to convey (combining illocution and perlocution), (2) the grammatical and lexical meaning of the words configured on the page, and (3) the meaning the reader understands—whether or not it corresponds to the author's illocution and perlocution. We may want to assume that what an author intends to communicate corresponds precisely to the meaning of the text.[3] However, an *author* may not frame the message correctly, so the *reader* may misconstrue the intention. In these cases, the author's intended meaning will match only to a certain degree what the words on the page mean. Likewise, what a reader understands or how he or she responds will not necessarily correspond with either the author's intention or the text's meaning. For these reasons we wish to distinguish among authorial intention, textual meaning, and perceived meaning.

---

2. Brown, *Scripture as Communication*, 111. Cf. K. J. Vanhoozer, *Is There a Meaning in This Text? The Bible, the Reader, and the Morality of Literary Knowledge* (Grand Rapids: Zondervan, 2009), 255.

3. Some object that we may never get at the intention of an author—as if we can enter someone's mind, but that is beside the point. N. Wolterstorff (*Divine Discourse. Philosophical Reflections on the Claim that God Speaks* [Cambridge: Cambridge University Press, 1995], 93) makes a crucial observation: "The myth dies hard that to read a text for authorial discourse is to enter the dark world of the author's psyche. It's nothing of the sort. It is to read to discover what assertings, what promisings, what requestings, what commandings, are rightly to be ascribed to the author on the grounds of her having set down the words that she did in the situation in which she set them down. Whatever be the dark demons and bright angels of the author's inner self that led her to take up this stance in public, it is that stance itself that we hope by reading to recover, not the dark demons and bright angels."

Potential Meanings in a Text
• The meaning the author *intends* to convey
• The meaning a reader *understands*
• The *actual* meaning conveyed by the words and grammar of the text

Though one may never completely understand all dimensions and nuances of a specific speech act, normally the reader or hearer seeks to understand what the author/speaker intended. Yet, when we read a literary text or listen to an oral message, we cannot read the author's or speaker's mind; we have only the written or verbal message. In biblical interpretation, when we have only the written text to assess, our goal is to understand the meaning (again, purpose, content, energy, and intended effect) of that text. Each individual text was written at some time in history in a specific culture by a person with a personal framework of preunderstandings. The author or editor encoded a message for a specific audience to accomplish some purpose. We believe that our goal is to discover that meaning of the text in those terms.[4]

This common-sense approach to interpreting assumes that meaning resides in the message or text and that the author (editor) or speaker encoded this meaning in that text. While meaning concerns the interaction between human beings, our role as interpreters of a document (as in a biblical text) is auxiliary to that of the original author or editor; this is not a two-way communication. The author encoded the meaning in the text, and our objective is to discover it—at least to the extent that we are able to recover it in the text—not to take the text and do something inventive with it that the author never intended. In Vanhoozer's words, "What an act counts as is not a matter of how it is taken, but of how it was meant."[5] This is true, because, he goes on, "the author is the one whose action determines the meaning of the text—its subject matter, its literary form, and its communicative energy."[6] Osborne puts it this way, "the implied author and the implied reader in the text provide an indispensable perspective for the intended meaning of a text."[7] The whole point of developing an arsenal of appropriate interpretive methods and skills is that we become listeners or receivers of an intentional message. The author is not irrelevant. The message is not haphazard or without point. Nor do we create the message; rather, we seek to discover what is already there—whether consciously or unconsciously intended by the authors or editors.

---

4. Attempting to comprehend written texts gives us as much access as possible to their authors' intended meanings. On the other hand, authors may write more than they intended, for modern studies have shown that much of what humans communicate occurs unconsciously (e.g., body language). So, again, finding textual meaning is the most responsible and worthy goal.

5. See Vanhoozer, *Is There a Meaning in This Text?* 229.

6. Ibid., 230.

7. G. R. Osborne, *The Hermeneutical Spiral*, 2nd ed. (Downers Grove: InterVarsity, 2006), 519. See also W. R. Tate, *Biblical Interpretation*, 3rd ed. (Peabody, MA: Hendrickson, 2014), 2–3, for his discussion of "Author-Centered Interpretation" and for what he subsequently does in the tactics for discovering the "World Behind the Text" (11–88).

These points may seem rather straightforward to most readers, but as we have seen above, not all interpreters agree with them. Of course, the biblical writers are not present to insist that we seek only the meaning they intended, nor can they verify that after all our efforts we have interpreted the meaning correctly. This leads us to several pointed questions in our discussion of the goal of interpretation. Can a modern reader discover "new meaning" in a biblical text (or any text, for that matter)? Are texts capable of more than one meaning, even if their authors intended only a single meaning? And is the author's intention any more significant than other possible meanings in a text—even if we grant that others may exist?

Obviously, modern interpreters can do anything they please with a text. Even if the author were present to protest, we could play with a text, unknowingly misconstrue it, or manipulate it in any way we chose. We could impose on it modern categories or could view it through a grid of our own choosing, as we saw in the previous chapters. We could ask alien questions of it or demolish and reconstruct it to our liking. We could try to find meaning in the patterns of blank spaces on the printed page. But the issue we must decide is: what is our objective as evangelical interpreters in handling the biblical texts? If we seek to hear what God has conveyed through Scripture, and thus what the biblical text means, then we believe this determines our approach and our methods of interpretation. That is, if our goal is author/text centered, then historical, grammatical, literary, and cultural methods (to name some representatives) must be central. To help us establish an accurate methodology of interpretation we need to consider some strategic questions that relate to the meaning of the text.

LEVELS OF MEANING

Does the Text Have One Fixed Meaning or Several Levels of Meaning?

Does a text have only one possible meaning, several meanings, or an infinite number of meanings? Some scholars insist that the only correct meaning of a text is that meaning (or that set of meanings) the original author intended it to have—the position that we will come to defend. E. D. Hirsch, Jr. mounts a vigorous defense of meaning as a function of authorial intention.[8] In this view, meaning precedes interpretation. As we noted above, however, others argue that meaning is a function of readers not authors, and that any text's meaning depends upon the readers' perception of it. Representatives of those who defend such reader-response approaches to meaning

---

8. See esp. E. D. Hirsch, Jr., *Validity in Interpretation* (New Haven: Yale University Press, 1967); and E. D. Hirsch, Jr., *The Aims of Interpretation* (Chicago: University of Chicago Press, 1976). We should note here that Hirsch vacillated between seeking meaning in what the author intended versus what the text meant. We will opt for the latter, though with all possible constraints based on the former. Our goal is the text's meaning because that is all that we have access to. At the same time, we hope that textual meaning provides a fair approximation of the author's/editor's intention. That is a better goal than the alternatives, as we shall argue.

include Jacques Derrida, Roland Barthes, and Stanley Fish, among others.[9] In their approaches, meaning does not reside within a text because the author put it there; rather, readers bring meaning to or create meaning in their engagement with a text. Thus, a text's author does not predetermine meaning, for readers may decipher a variety of possible meanings from a written text. Most of these postmodern critics do not argue that readers can make a text say anything they please, but rather that a text may have many possible meanings. Such interpreters reject any concept of a single or normative meaning of a biblical text.

The question for us is, what is the appropriate tactic for biblical interpretation? One may interpret the utterance, "Fire," in many ways, but if someone shouts that word in a crowded room, it is crucial that we understand it as the warning that is intended and not as an invitation to cozy up to the fireplace. Illocution and perlocution matter greatly.

It is helpful here to revisit briefly an observation made in the previous chapter. Robert Morgan rightly argues that interpretation needs the checks provided by history, exegesis, and other rational controls to keep it from becoming arbitrary. Yet he espouses a potentially problematic view when he contends that "without the possibility of finding new meaning in a text, an authoritative scripture stifles development."[10] In other words, to encourage hermeneutical creativity he posits the need to continually find new meanings in the biblical texts. For Morgan, to deny the possibility of finding new meaning increases the likelihood that "theologically motivated scholars are likely to become either biblicist conservatives opposed to any development or ultra-liberals who have little use in their own theologies for what they learn from the Bible."[11] For Morgan these are equally abhorrent extremes to avoid. But *we* do wish to espouse biblicism, and by that we mean that we seek the intention of the biblical text. That is precisely where we position ourselves! We seek to be conservative in the sense of retaining what the biblical texts actually *mean*, rather than imposing modern (and perhaps alien) and ever-changing meanings upon them. With the meaning in hand, we then seek that text's *significance and application* for Christian belief and practice. Morgan seeks to retain "theological flexibility," and this requires what he calls "hermeneutical creativity." But at what price come such flexibility and creativity? Does the Bible present normative truth? Is meaning constant or is it only in the eyes of the beholder? Where are the checks and balances?

---

9. We have more to say about this methodology below. For examples see J. Derrida, *Of Grammatology* (Baltimore: Johns Hopkins Univ. Press, 1976); R. Barthes, *S/Z* (London: Jonathan Cape, 1975); and S. Fish, *Is There a Text in this Class? The Authority of Interpretive Communities* (Cambridge, MA; London: Harvard University Press, 1980).

10. R. Morgan with J. Barton, *Biblical Interpretation* (Oxford: Oxford University Press, 1988), 182.

11. Ibid., 182. We doubt that "development," to use Morgan's term, is a desirable item on the interpreter's agenda. Where the goal is to understand God's revelation—as it is for us—development smacks of adding to Scripture, an enterprise that for the last book of the Bible, at least, was specifically condemned (Rev 22:18–19). If development means to enlarge our understanding of the text's meaning and its various significances, we embrace the idea.

What is the Meaning of "Meaning"?	
When we say that a text conveys *meaning* to its readers, what do we mean by "meaning"?	• Is it tied to the intention of the author?
	• Is it language-based—words, grammar, genre, etc.?
	• Does it describe what a reader sees in or brings to the text?

Let us focus the question further. Suppose someone reads a text and then presents to its author a meaning that the reader had "discovered" in the text. The author might protest that the "discovered" meaning was not intended, even though the reader found it in the text. The text then means more than the author intended. Does this episode imply that when language leaves the mind of an author it is in the public domain and capable of meaning a number of different things depending upon who reads it? Does the meaning of a text rest in what the author consciously intended to convey, or does meaning somehow result from the interaction between the text (language) and the reader? We must invoke speech act theory again and insist that the illocution (purpose, content, energy) and perlocution (intended outcome for the reader) matter in the process of interpretation. Those are not irrelevant to biblical interpretation.

The biblical authors or the creeds of the church claim inspiration and authority for the Scriptures, but modern interpreters still decide how they will handle those claims.[12] Will we base theology and Christian practice upon what the Spirit communicates through biblical texts or upon the current objectives, concerns, and agendas of the modern individuals and communities that interpret them? The history of interpretation clearly demonstrates how often the latter has been the case. Indeed, some argue it should be the case, or that it cannot be otherwise. How we define the task of hermeneutics depends, therefore, on determining our goal. Where does meaning reside? Is it in the speech act of the biblical text or in the reader's creative interaction with it?

Before we can proceed, we must consider the possibility of *multiple meanings* within a biblical text. Some argue that multiple meanings exist in a text when they see how some NT writers employed OT texts. For example, when Matthew says that Jesus' protection from Herod's murderous designs *fulfills*[13] the prophecy, "Out of Egypt I called my son" (Matt 2:15; cf. Hos 11:1), did he presume that Hosea's words themselves contained that meaning? The author of Hosea referred to a past event: God's rescue of Israel from Pharaoh. But Hosea's use raises multiple questions. Do his words (also) *mean* to be a reference to God's "son" predicting a circumstance in

---

12. On the thorny topic of biblical authority see W. W. Klein, "Authority of the Bible," in *The Oxford Encyclopedia of Biblical Interpretation*, 2 vols., ed. S. L. McKenzie (Oxford and New York: Oxford University Press, 2013) 1:52–60. Cf. N. T. Wright, *Scripture and the Authority of God: How to Read the Bible Today*, rev. and exp. ed. (New York: HarperOne, 2013).

13. The verb "fulfill" also occurs in Matt 2:17, 23. In fact, it occurs five times in chs. 1–2. All present problems for understanding Matthew's use of the OT. For an explication of these and Matthew's other uses see C. L. Blomberg, "Matthew," in *Commentary on the New Testament Use of the Old Testament*, ed. D. A. Carson and G. K. Beale (Grand Rapids: Baker, 2007), 1–111.

the Messiah's life? Did Matthew think that Hosea was speaking of Christ or did he just invent a new meaning that he imposed on the Hosea's text? Did Matthew convey or perhaps uncover a meaning the Holy Spirit intended even though Hosea was not aware of this meaning? How did Matthew arrive at his interpretation? It seems we have several options to consider. The following table will introduce how we will proceed.

Options for Potential Meanings Within a Text
1. A text has only one meaning—the one intended by the author
2. A text may have multiple meanings (whether intended by the author or not)
3. A text has only one intended meaning, but a later reader may read another meaning into the text not intended by the author (reader-response)
4. A text has one meaning intended by the author, but the Holy Spirit may encode another meaning(s) not intended by the human author (a *sensus plenior*)
5. A text has only one intended meaning, but a later inspired biblical author may disclose additional meaning(s) not intended by the original author

1. *Only one meaning resides in a text: the meaning the author intended.* In this case, the original, historical meaning (the author's illocution and perlocution) is the only meaning in a text and is, then, the legitimate object of exegesis. In the example above, Hosea's intent focused on God's rescue of Israel (the historical meaning). He had a specific purpose for his words and intended a specific outcome for his readers. That's all he meant! But this raises a question: did Matthew discover a *different* meaning in this OT text than what Hosea intended? Walter Kaiser insists that the answer must be, no. He argues that NT writers always discover and explain the *meaning* that the OT writers intended—the same goal we should have in interpreting the Bible.[14]

Though some may agree with Kaiser's position, it raises major questions. Perhaps most troublesome to Kaiser's view are the data themselves. We doubt he can demonstrate that all NT uses of the OT disclose only that meaning the original OT author actually intended. Though Kaiser has done an admirable job of defending his case in several problematic texts, we doubt that it is possible to demonstrate that the OT writers did in fact intend only the meanings that NT writers later found.[15] We are convinced, with most, that there are instances where NT authors attribute meaning to or use an OT text in ways that the OT author did not intend.

Note, for example, how the writer of Hebrews speaks as if Psalm 45:6–7 were

---

14. For Kaiser's defense and explanation see, esp., *The Uses of the Old Testament in the New* (Chicago: Moody, 1985; repr. Eugene, OR: Wipf and Stock, 2001). For a view different from Kaiser's see C. A. Evans and J. A. Sanders, *Early Christian Interpretation of the Scriptures of Israel* (Sheffield: Sheffield Academic Press, 1997). Also see K. Berding and J. Lunde, eds., *Three Views on the New Testament Use of the Old Testament* (Grand Rapids, Zondervan, 2008). Contributors include W. Kaiser, D. Bock, and P. Enns, who also critique each other's views. For a truly outstanding survey of all the issues involved in this complex question see G. K. Beale, *Handbook on the New Testament Use of the Old Testament: Exegesis and Interpretation* (Grand Rapids: Baker Academic, 2012).

15. D. J. Moo evaluates Kaiser in "The Problem of *Sensus Plenior*," in *Hermeneutics, Authority, and Canon,* ed. D. A. Carson and J. D. Woodbridge (Grand Rapids: Zondervan, 1986), esp. on pp. 198–201.

specifically written about Jesus: "But about the Son he says, 'Your throne, O God, will last for ever and ever; a scepter of justice will be the scepter of your kingdom. You have loved righteousness and hated wickedness; therefore God, your God, has set you above your companions by anointing you with the oil of joy'" (Heb. 1:8–9). Some argue that Psalm 45 might contain messianic overtones,[16] but what can we say about, more astonishingly, the quote in Hebrews 1:6 (from Deut 32:43 found in the LXX and the Dead Sea Scrolls): "And again, when God brings his firstborn into the world, he says, 'Let all God's angels worship him'"? Surely the ancient text(s) do not refer to Jesus.

To cite a different writer, Peter employs Psalms 69:25 and 109:8 as predicting what Judas did and the apostles' need to replace him in their company: "'For,' said Peter, 'it is written in the Book of Psalms: "May his place be deserted; let there be no one to dwell in it," and, "May another take his place of leadership."'" (Acts 1:20). We doubt that these OT writers *intended* these references to the Messiah or Judas when they wrote their words. We certainly have no means to discover that they did. This option seems highly unlikely.

Though we affirm that an author intends a single meaning (illocution and perlocution) in a given text, we must still account for those instances where it appears a later biblical writer assigns a meaning beyond that historical sense. What other options do we have?

2. An author may intend a text to convey multiple meanings or levels of meaning—for instance, a literal level and a spiritual level.[17] Some argue for such multiple meanings in apocalyptic literature and predictive prophecy. In both Daniel and Revelation, the same mythical beasts convey meanings about different nations and leaders. Also, Isaiah's prophecy of an upcoming birth (Isa 7:14) was fulfilled on two levels: in the immediate future, in our view (Isa 8:1–10), and in the distant future (Matt 1:23). Are these examples of authors who *intended* multiple meanings?

In fact, when a later writer finds additional significance in an earlier prophecy (as Matthew did with Isa 7:14), we cannot prove that the original text contained addition meaning—whether intended by Isaiah or not. There may be a few instances where contextual clues may signify multiple meanings. Yet, we know of no successful methods to uncover multiple levels apart from explicit statements, or at least very marked clues by the author in the text.[18] Apart from clear cues that exegetical methods uncover from the written text, this proposal, too, provides little help for the process of interpretation.[19]

---

16. See M. J. Harris, "The Translation of *Elohim* in Psalm 45:7–8," *TynBul* 35 (1984): 65–89.

17. Recall our discussion about the church fathers like Origen. For very sympathetic treatments of how the fathers operated see M. Graves, *The Inspiration and Interpretation of Scripture. What the Early Church Can Teach Us* (Grand Rapids: Eerdmans, 2014); and J. J. O'Keefe and R. R. Reno, *Sanctified Vision: An Introduction to Early Christian Interpretation of the Bible* (Baltimore: The Johns Hopkins University Press, 2005).

18. For some examples of such contextual clues see C. L. Blomberg, "Interpreting Old Testament Prophetic Literature in Matthew: Double Fulfillment," *TrinJ* 23 NS (2002): 17–33, esp. 20–21.

19. Of course, a writer might agree to a "meaning" that a later reader found in the author's work, as we noted

But some may object, "Can't a text have different meanings in different situations?" As we will proceed to argue, a text can be legitimately *applied* in different situations and contexts. But this is a different than saying that the text itself encodes *multiple meanings*. When we try to make the Bible relevant today, we are not agreeing that the Bible can have multiple meanings—the original that the author intended and the ones we find pertinent for ourselves. A text bears the meaning its author intended it to have. In isolation or apart from a context, a text may conceivably have a variety of possible meanings. But if the author were present to adjudicate, the "correct" meaning of a text would be that which he or she intended for it. It is the single meaning the author intended that can have a variety of valid applications for different readers who read it in their own time and place. An example will help explain this.

Jesus told many parables during his ministry. Subsequently, the evangelists incorporated various ones in their Gospels to serve their purposes for their readers. Throughout the history of the church countless interpreters have employed these same parables, as people do today in their study and teaching. Does the meaning that Jesus intended when he spoke a specific parable change throughout its history? No, we argue, though that meaning impacts different situations in distinct ways.[20] For example, the parable of the workers in the field (Matt 20:1–16) is truly puzzling. How outrageous to pay the same wage to workers who worked one hour and to those who had labored the entire day! True, one denarius for a day's work was fair, but do not those who worked more hours deserve more pay? What was Jesus' point? What *meaning* did he intend? In Jesus' context it is likely that he wanted to show that salvation is undeserved; God gives his grace to those who do not deserve it.

In the context of Matthew 19–20, though, the author juxtaposes this parable with the disciples' faithfulness in serving Christ. Peter had said, "We have left everything to follow you! What then will there be for us?" (19:27). The frames at both ends of this parable make essentially the same point: the first will be last and the last will be first. The meaning Matthew intended for his audience may be that disciples ought to assess their motives in serving Christ. Alternatively, perhaps the issue for Matthew's community was the increasing priority and quantity of Gentiles as compared to Jews in the emerging church.[21] What were the Christians, especially Jewish ones, to make of this development? The meaning is single—God gives rewards at his discretion—but that point can be *applied* in a variety of ways. Ryken notes, "In the kingdom of God where generosity is the foundational premise, ordinary human standards have been abolished."[22] Matthew's single meaning is capable of several possible applications through history.[23]

---

above. But this clearly was not part of the author's illocution or perlocution.

20. A. C. Thiselton, "Reader-Response Hermeneutics, Action Models, and the Parables of Jesus," in R. Lundin, A. C. Thiselton and C. Walhout, *The Responsibility of Hermeneutics* (Grand Rapids: Eerdmans, 1985), 79–113, recasts this in terms of multiple speech acts or multiple perlocutions in one speech act.

21. On this point see D. A. Hagner, *Matthew 14–28*, WBC 33b (Dallas: Word, 1995), 566–72.

22. L. Ryken, *Words of Life. A Literary Introduction to the New Testament* (Grand Rapids: Baker, 1987), 70.

23. Of course, the meaning of parables may involve several points, each of which may find a variety of applications.

Our point should now be clear. Though a text may find a wide variety of applications or significances—both in the original context and forever after—we cannot confuse *significance* with *meaning*. In other words, unless we can demonstrate that the authors *intended* multiple meanings for a text, we can never assume they did. The possibility and presence of multiple applications or significances must be distinguished from what authors or speakers intend to communicate. Apart from clear clues in the context or the genre employed, we must expect that authors intend single meanings.[24] What other options should be considered?

3. A later reader could simply invent or read into a biblical text a meaning not intended by the original author. In other words, in the process of reading a text, interpreters may introduce some meaning that suits their purposes. We have seen above how various scholars defend this option. But also on a popular level of Bible study, this happens regularly. The Bible becomes a wax nose that can be twisted this way or that to suit the reader's whim. Returning to Matthew's use of Hosea, in this view Matthew simply used Hosea's text as a jumping-off point for him to devise his own (and perhaps minimally connected) meaning. Hosea's intention becomes relatively irrelevant—except, perhaps for the mention of Egypt or the concept of preservation there. The sole inquiry for interpreters is what Matthew wrote.

Some interpreters believe this is the only way to understand how people actually read texts.[25] Once texts exist in writing, readers not only can, but do treat them as they please. Understanding involves text plus reader, and each reader produces a different reading. Note what W. G. Jeanrond says:

> The reading of a text is, rather, a dynamic process which remains in principle open-ended because every reader can only disclose the sense of a text in a process and as an individual. This signifies in its turn that reading is in each case more than the deciphering of the signs printed on paper. Reading is always also a projection of a new image of reality, as this is co-initiated by the text and achieved by the reader in the relationship with the text in the act of reading.[26]

In this view, given the conventions of the interpretive community of which he was a member (Jewish-Christian), Matthew simply read Hosea in ways that were appropriate for his concerns.[27] That is, through that group's Christian and Christological glasses, he read Hosea and saw Christ as the Son whom God also protected in Egypt.

We discuss later both how to interpret and how to apply parables. For further help see C. L. Blomberg, *Interpreting the Parables*, 2nd ed. (Downers Grove: InterVarsity, 2012).

24. An example of a double meaning identified in the context occurs in John 3:3 in Jesus' use of *anōthen* with its double entendre "again" and "from above." The Greek word *pneuma* "wind" and "spirit" continues the scheme. Clearly these are intentional. See D. A. Carson, *The Gospel According to John*, PNTC (Grand Rapids: Eerdmans, 1991), 189–90; cf. BDAG, 92, on the multiple senses of *anōthen*.

25. Such an approach is one of several, often termed "reader-response" criticism, which we mentioned above.

26. W. G. Jeanrond, *Text and Interpretation as Categories of Theological Thinking* (New York: Crossroad, 1988), 104.

27. S. Fish defends this perspective: "It is interpretive communities, rather than either the text or the reader, that produce meanings and are responsible for the emergence of formal features" (*Is There a Text?*, 14).

Interpreters today enjoy the same privileges, such reader-response critics insist. One may put on Marxist, liberationist, gay, or feminist glasses to discover different, equally legitimate readings of a text.[28]

In a spirited reaction to this interpretive agenda, David Steinmetz asserts, "Indeed, contemporary debunking of the author and the author's explicit intentions has proceeded at such a pace that it seems at times as if literary criticism has become a jolly game of ripping out an author's shirt-tail and setting fire to it."[29] We agree that readers cannot simply ignore the author or the historical meaning of the ancient text and make it mean what they want. Yet we cannot ignore the modern reader's role either, for it is only in the process of reading that the meaning of a text emerges.

Once more we stress an important point: meaning is not indeterminate awaiting some reader to produce it. The meaning of a text (a locution with an illocution and perlocution) was encoded in the author's speech act. That is true even though that meaning is not discerned until a reader understands it. As we saw earlier, Anthony Thiselton employs a useful image in entitling his book on hermeneutics, *The Two Horizons*.[30] Understanding occurs when the horizon of the text fuses with the horizon of the modern interpreter, but only after some "distantiation" occurs—unlike the no-holds-barred approach that occurs with many reader-response critics. It is worth quoting Carson at length where he defines more carefully what is at stake.

> Whenever we try to understand the thought of a text . . . , if we are to understand
> it critically . . . we must first of all grasp the nature and degree of the differences
> that separate our understanding from the understanding of the text. Only then
> can we profitably fuse our horizon of understanding with the horizon of under-
> standing of the text—that is, only then can we begin to shape our thoughts by
> the thoughts of the text, so that we truly understand them. Failure to go through
> the distantiation before the fusion usually means there has been no real fusion:
> the interpreter thinks he knows what the text means, but all too often he or she
> has simply imposed his own thoughts onto the text.[31]

The historical meaning of the text must play the controlling role. Stephen Moore affirms this crucial point saying, "If our texts do not contain such [i.e., invariant, historically anchored] properties, what prevents interpretive anarchy in the academy (or in general)?"[32] We cannot simply dispense with the historical sense and do what we please with texts.

---

28. Some pointed examples include L. M. Russell, ed., *Feminist Interpretation of the Bible* (Philadelphia: Westminster, 1985); and L. D. Richesin and B. Mahan, eds., *The Challenge of Liberation Theology: A First-World Response* (Maryknoll: Orbis, 1981). See our more careful assessment above.

29. D. Steinmetz, "The Superiority of Pre-Critical Exegesis," *Theology Today* 37 (1980): 38.

30. A. C. Thiselton, *The Two Horizons. New Testament Hermeneutics and Philosophical Description* (Grand Rapids: Eerdmans, 1980).

31. D. A. Carson, *Exegetical Fallacies*, 2nd ed. (Grand Rapids: Baker, 1996), 23–24.

32. S. D. Moore, *Literary Criticism and the Gospels. The Theoretical Challenge* (New Haven and London: Yale University Press, 1989), 68.

Returning to Matthew and Hosea, if Matthew did not engage in some arbitrary reader-response reading of Hosea, what did he do? Is it possible in any way to replicate his methods? Before we respond to these questions we have further options to consider.

4. Along with the literal sense intended by the human author, the Holy Spirit may encode a hidden meaning not known or devised at all by the human author. Proponents of this approach argue that in the process of writing his gospel, Matthew became aware of a meaning the Holy Spirit embedded *in Hosea's prophecy* even though Hosea did not intend that meaning. Matthew recognized that "fuller" sense, sometimes called the *sensus plenior*. In J. Robertson McQuilkin's thinking, "The second (hidden or less apparent) meaning . . . might have been only in the mind of the Holy Spirit, who inspired the author."[33] The question, then, is whether (some) OT texts possess a surface intentional meaning (intended by the human author) and an additional underlying meaning or meanings—a *sensus plenior*—intended by the Holy Spirit and unknown to the human author.

That leads to several other questions. Can Scripture more generally be said to have this "deeper level" of meaning? And, if all texts do not have this *sensus plenior*, how do we know which ones do? Is there a "fuller sense" intended by the divine author beyond what the human author intended that a modern interpreter of the Bible might discover? If so, how? Almost by definition, traditional historical, grammatical, and critical methods of exegesis cannot detect or understand an alleged fuller sense. That is, such methods can distinguish only the meaning of the text the human author intended, not some secret embedded sense.

In reply, one option is to simply reject the existence of a *sensus plenior* and confine exegesis to what we can defensibly study.[34] If there are no satisfactory answers to the questions posed in the previous paragraphs, we are safer simply to reject that possibility altogether. Safer, to be sure, but we have no way of knowing if we have thus lost an opportunity for legitimate fuller understanding.

A second option is to admit, provisionally, the existence of such a sense *but* to insist that only inspired NT writers, under the guidance of the Holy Spirit, could find a fuller sense present in the OT and only in the texts they used. This position must still verify the existence of a deeper level of meaning in the Bible, even when it admits our inability to replicate what the NT writers did with the OT texts. To our way of thinking, not even this much has been accomplished. How can we know they found a *sensus plenior*? In any case, this way is not open to us.

A third option is to admit the possibility of a deeper meaning to some Scripture, to

---

33. J. R. McQuilkin, *Understanding and Applying the Bible*, 2nd ed. (Chicago: Moody, 1992), 45.

34. In various places W. C. Kaiser rejects the concept of *sensus plenior*: e.g., "Legitimate Hermeneutics," in *Inerrancy*, ed. N. L. Geisler (Grand Rapids: Zondervan, 1979), 117–47; *Uses of the Old Testament*; and "The Current Crisis in Exegesis and the Apostolic Use of Deuteronomy 25:4 in 1 Corinthians 9:8–10," *JETS* 21(1978): 3–18. For an analysis of Kaiser's position see D. L. Bock, "Evangelicals and the Use of the Old Testament in the New," part 1, *BSac* 142 (1985): 210–12.

find it, defend it, and explain it. Scholars who defend the existence of a *sensus plenior* range from Roman Catholics to evangelicals.[35] Roman Catholics typically limit the presence of this fuller sense to what is confirmed either by revelation in subsequent Scripture (viz., the NT) or via the authority of the Roman Catholic Church. Protestants typically limit their admission of a fuller sense to subsequent revelation in the NT alone, though D. A. Oss, adopting a canonical approach, attributes the fuller sense to what derives from a given text's organic relation to the rest of the canon.[36]

How is it possible, when God inspired writers of Scripture, that he intended (and encoded) a sense separate and different from what the human authors conceived and intended? In reply Douglas Moo argues vaguely that God could "have intended a sense related to but more than that which the human author intended."[37] Larkin goes even further in asserting that "many uses of the OT material in the New seem unrelated to the meaning intended by the original writer."[38] But, we ask in reply, does this prove that the Spirit encoded an additional or deeper meaning, or is it that the NT writer invented one? And, are these the only two options?

William LaSor asks, "Is it not possible for God to present to the author a revelation which by its very nature contains a deeper significance?"[39] LaSor insists that the human author intended only one meaning. "But at a later date," he argues, "in the light of further revelation, the fuller meaning becomes clear to readers under the influence of the Spirit who inspired the original author."[40] But here our distinction between "meaning" and "significance" comes into play. If LaSor means that later readers see additional *significance* in a text, we agree; but that is different from saying that a text

---

35. A leading Catholic proponent was R. Brown, *The 'Sensus Plenior' of Sacred Scripture* (Baltimore: St. Mary's University, 1955; Eugene, OR: Wipf & Stock, 2008); R. Brown, "The History and Development of the Theory of a *Sensus Plenior*," *CBQ* 15 (1953): 141–62; and R. Brown, "The *Sensus Plenior* in the Last Ten Years," *CBQ* 25 (1963): 262–85. Evangelicals include Moo, "*Sensus Plenior*," 175–212; J. D. Kunjummen, "The Single Intent of Scripture—Critical Examination of a Theological Construct," *GTJ* 7 (1986): 81–110; D. A. Oss, "Canon as Context: The Function of *Sensus Plenior* in Evangelical Hermeneutics," *GTJ* 9 (1988): 105–27; and W. S. LaSor, "Interpretation of Prophecy," in *Hermeneutics*, ed., B. Ramm (Grand Rapids: Baker, 1987), 94–117. Finally, see Steinmetz, "Pre-Critical Exegesis," who traces how belief in a fuller sense of Scripture characterized many scholars throughout the history of exegesis.

36. Oss, "Canon as Context," 107–8. J. DeYoung and S. Hurty, *Beyond the Obvious. Discover the Deeper Meaning of Scripture* (Gresham, OR: Vision House, 1995), seek to demonstrate that Christians today can duplicate Matthew's kind of reading of the OT. They believe we can discover new meaning as we are sensitive to the revelatory work of the Holy Spirit in interpreting the Bible, in keeping with its overarching theme—which they deem to be the kingdom of God. While their enterprise is admirable in many ways, they admit their case is very sketchy at present, and, despite their attempts, their method supplies no real interpretive controls. Such an approach runs the risk of miring the interpretive enterprise in subjectivism, for who can either prove or question whether an interpreter's new meaning is genuinely a product of new revelation from the Spirit?

37. Moo, "*Sensus Plenior*," 204. Of course, the question is not whether God could have intended a deeper sense, but whether he did and whether we have any means to verify such an intention.

38. W. J. Larkin, *Culture and Biblical Hermeneutics* (Grand Rapids: Baker, 1988), 257. He goes on to cite such examples as Matt 27:9–10/Zech 11:12–13 and Jer 32:6–9; Acts 15:16–17/Amos 9:11–12; Rom 10:6–8/Deut 9:4 and 30:12–14; 1 Cor 2:9/Isa 64:4; 1 Cor 9:9/Deut 25:4; Heb 3:7–11/Ps 95:7–11. Of course, simply because the meanings seem rather unrelated is no reason to account for the new sense as a *sensus plenior*. As well, we wonder if Larkin really means the NT writers' uses of the OT texts are *completely unrelated* to the sense intended by the OT writers.

39. LaSor, "Interpretation," 108. Again, possibilities are not the issue here.

40. Ibid.

has two meanings: one intended by the human author and the other encoded by the Holy Spirit (of which the human author was unaware).

Moo admits that the construct of *sensus plenior* does not handle all the NT's use of the OT. At times the NT writers appeal to what the OT human author said,[41] even though the meaning the NT author derives is not apparent to us after we subject the OT text to traditional historical methods. And we believe that LaSor mitigates his view of a deeper sense instigated by the Holy Spirit when he also attributes a fuller sense to great poets, philosophers, and other creative thinkers who express a meaning that their disciples more fully develop into schools or systems of thought.[42] This does not support a deeper meaning in the texts intended by the Holy Spirit. If LaSor is correct, the fuller sense merely develops further implications or consequences of what the author originally meant. This is what we term *significance*.

In a very intriguing article, Kit Barker uses speech act theory as a way to understand *sensus plenior*.[43] While our concern here is not the total impact of his article, he proposes a useful way of salvaging *sensus plenior* by positing that both the human and divine authors of Scripture employ speech acts in a given text. Thus, a human author may use a locution to accomplish specific illocutionary and perlocutionary purposes, which may or may not correspond at that time to the Spirit's purposes.[44] God may also intend that locution to have further illocutions and perlocutions at a later stage. Barker points to the level of the canon to illustrate this. So, e.g., in the progress of the history of redemption, the cultic demands of the sacrificial system (found in the OT) can no longer have their original illocutionary purposes. But taking the entire canon into play, the Spirit can use such texts as illocutionary acts beyond their original intentions. Barker says, "In this case, the *sensus plenior* is simply that the primary illocutionary act of the OT text ceases to be performed and an attendant illocutionary act becomes primary for the new covenant community."[45] This strikes us, however, as saying that in a subsequent reading of a text the Spirit may lead a reader to find additional significance in the text, an illocution not intended by the original author. But that need not mean that in the original text the Spirit encoded a deeper meaning.

While this is a very fruitful line of inquiry, it also returns us again to the complicated discussion of how the NT writers used the OT about which we say more below. Barker's explanation provides genuine insight on the illocutionary level within the

---

41. Moo cites the example of Peter's use of Ps 16 in his Pentecost sermon (Acts 2:25–28) in *"Sensus Plenior,"* 204. We doubt that the human David was speaking about Jesus' resurrection.

42. LaSor, "Interpretation," 108.

43. K. Barker, "Speech Act Theory, Dual Authorship, and Canonical Hermeneutics: Making Sense of *Sensus Plenior," JTI* 3 (2009): 227–39.

44. Barker makes this allowance since some texts, e.g., in the Psalms, are directed to God. In such uses, the psalmist's purposes may differ from God's. David's request for a clean heart, or a psalmist's request for God to destroy his enemies, can't have the same purposes for both the writer and the Spirit. In such cases the Spirit's illocution may be affirming that "You should pray like this in these kinds of situations" (234).

45. K. Barker, "Speech Act Theory," 238.

canon, but his insights don't help us in our own work as interpreters of the Bible. We may allow that the Spirit can appropriate an OT text and use it for new purposes in the hands of a NT writer, but our task remains understanding what each biblical writer intended by his or her specific locution, whether or not that locution had a prior history in the prior testament.

5. *An OT author may have intended a text to have only a single meaning, but the later NT author* discovered *an additional meaning in that text.* This final option itself consists of multiple elements. In other words, if Matthew was performing strict historical-grammatical exegesis of Hosea's words, he could never assert that they spoke of the Messiah. But, unlike the previous option (in which the Holy Spirit encoded a hidden meaning that bore such messianic overtones), this option posits that Matthew used a creative exegetical method that devised or uncovered the additional sense. If so, what is the origin of this additional meaning? How is this different from the reader-response option 3 above? And, importantly, is this method open to modern interpreters?

In our opinion, this option provides the best explanation for the origin of the additional meaning NT writers found in some OT texts. In other words, at such places NT writers used interpretive techniques derived from their Jewish background to envision new meanings. Specifically, they used some of the methods of the rabbis or the interpreters at Qumran, such as midrash and pesher.[46]

Scholars do not easily arrive at definitions of these practices, but several comments will help us understand them better. J. Goldin says of midrash, "All Midrashic teaching undertakes two things: (1) to explain opaque or ambiguous texts and their difficult vocabulary and syntax . . . ; (2) to contemporize, that is, so to describe or treat biblical personalities and events as to make recognizable the immediate relevance of what would otherwise be regarded as only archaic."[47] To further clarify the nature of midrash: "It was a way of delving more deeply than the literal meaning of the word of Scripture, and a method of linking the various parts of the Bible together by the discovery of typological patterns, verbal echoes, and rhythms of repetition."[48]

---

46. For an introduction to these and other Jewish methods, see our earlier discussion of Jewish interpretive methods. Key literature includes M. Henze, ed., *A Companion to Biblical Interpretation in Early Judaism* (Grand Rapids: Eerdmans, 2012); J. L. Kugel, ed., *Studies in Ancient Midrash* (Cambridge, MA: Harvard University Press, 2001); M. A. Fishbane, ed., *The Midrashic Imagination: Jewish Exegesis, Thought, and History* (Albany, NY: State University of NY Press, 1993); J. L. Kugel and R. A. Greer, *Early Biblical Interpretation* (Philadelphia: Westminster, 1986), esp. 52–106; R. Kasher, "The Interpretation of Scripture in Rabbinic Literature," in *Mikra*, ed. M. J. Mulder and H. Sysling, *Compendia Rerum Judaicarum ad Novum Testamentum*, sec. 2, pt. 1 (Philadelphia: Fortress, 1988), 560–77; R. T. France and D. Wenham, eds., *Gospel Perspectives, Vol. 3: Studies in Midrash and Historiography* (Sheffield, UK: JSOT, 1983); C. L. Quarles, *Midrash Criticism: Introduction and Appraisal* (Lanham, MD: University Press of America, 1997); and B. D. Sommer, ed., *Jewish Concepts of Scripture: A Comparative Introduction* (New York; Oxford: New York University Press, 2012). In his helpful discussion, Beale, *Handbook on the New Testament Use of the Old Testament*, 1–6, outlines the nature of the debate about how much, if at all, the NT writers employed some of the standard Jewish features of interpretation.

47. J. Goldin, "Midrash and Aggadah," in *The Encyclopedia of Religion*, ed. Mircea Eliade, 16 vols. (New York: Macmillan, 1987), 9:512.

48. R. J. Z. Werblowsky and G. Wigoder, eds., "Midrash," *The Encyclopedia of the Jewish Religion* (New York: Holt, Rinehart and Winston, 1965), 262.

Several possible examples of the use of midrashic methods appear in the NT. One is the well-known technique of *gezerah shawah* (combining features of various texts that have some verbal correlations) as in Acts 2:25–34.[49] Or note the many uses of the kind of argumentation called *qal wahomer* (from the lesser to the greater) as at Luke 11:13; 12:28; and Matthew 10:25. At times such methods seem completely responsible and reflect good common sense. In other instances in the hands of rabbis, they opened the door to rather fanciful connections and interpretations.[50]

The method of pesher had a distinctive trait: "The authors of the *pesharim* believed the scriptural prophecies to have been written for their own time and predicament, and they interpreted the biblical texts in the light of their acute eschatological expectations."[51] Hence their use of the introductory phrase, "Its interpretation refers to . . ." or more precisely, "This is that." The Qumran sectarians who produced the Dead Sea Scrolls were particularly enamored of the pesher technique, as evidenced in their Habakkuk commentary. Longenecker describes their tactic: "Biblical interpretation at Qumran was considered to be first of all revelatory and/or charismatic in nature. Certain of the prophecies had been given in cryptic and enigmatic terms, and no one could understand their true meaning until the Teacher of Righteousness [Qumran's founder and early leader] was given the interpretive key."[52]

In their view the Teacher alone qualified to explain certain prophecies. What were the techniques that characterized the pesher method? F. F. Bruce answers: "The biblical text was atomized in the *pĕšārîm* so as to bring out the relevance of each sentence or phrase to the contemporary situation. . . . It is in this situation, not in the logical or syntactical sequence of the text, that coherence was found."[53] Some of the interpretations boggle the imagination of a modern reader.[54]

Peter may have employed (or at least been influenced by) this technique when he cited Joel in his Pentecost sermon: "*This is what* was spoken by the prophet Joel . . ." (Acts 2:16; emphasis added). Jesus may have engaged in something like pesher in his sermon recorded in Luke 4:16–21 where, quoting Isaiah 61:1–2, he says, "Today this scripture is fulfilled in your hearing" (4:21).[55]

We believe that the use of such methods explains how some uses of the OT by NT writers departs dramatically from what the OT appears to mean on the surface.[56]

---

49. Peter brings together Pss 16:8–11 and 110:1 to support Jesus' resurrection because both employ the phrase "at my right hand."

50. For examples see Longenecker, *Biblical Exegesis*, 21–24.

51. Werblowsky and Wigoder, eds., "Midrash," 298. See our brief treatment of Qumran exegesis in ch. 2.

52. The "Teacher of Righteousness" was the putative leader of the Qumran Sect during the composition of much of its literature. See G. J. Brooke, "Prophetic Interpretation in the *Pesharim*," in M. Henze, ed., *A Companion to Biblical Interpretation*, 235–254; cf. Longenecker, *Biblical Exegesis*, 29.

53. F. F. Bruce, "Biblical Exposition at Qumran," in *Gospel Perspectives*, 3:81.

54. Bruce provides examples of their conclusions, "Biblical Exposition," 81–96.

55. See Longenecker, *Biblical Exegesis*, 54–58, 83–87, 113–116, where he makes a convincing case for further possible examples in the NT.

56. On the other hand, one point that the various articles in *Gospels Perspectives, vol. 3*, make repeatedly is, "very little that can confidently be traced back to the first century AD is 'midrash proper'" (France, "Postscript,"

Clearly the writers of the NT were convinced that they had entered a new era in redemptive history with the coming of Jesus. Naturally, they read the OT in a new light, a process Jesus himself encouraged (e.g., Luke 24:25–27).

Though the NT writers may have borrowed some methods of their Jewish counterparts, they spurned others. That is, the NT writers, like Jewish interpreters, "appropriated" OT texts for their new situations—for example, "straightforward identification of one situation or person with another, modification of the text to suit the application, and association of several passages."[57] We reject, though, that in these uses the NT authors were totally unconcerned about the original meaning of the OT texts.[58] They did not engage in disconnected "reader-response" readings. The NT writers were aware of the literary contexts, and sometimes the historical contexts of the OT texts that they employed in various ways.[59] And we cannot lump together the apostles, the Qumran exegetes, and the rabbis as if they all operated in the same way. Where the apostles' interpretations seem to parallel methods of their Jewish forebears, their uses generally appear extremely restrained.

To the Jewish methods of midrash and pesher we must add another: *typology*. In fact, typology may be the best way to explain how NT writers most often used the OT.[60] R. T. France sets out a clear definition of typology: "the recognition of a correspondence between New and Old Testament events, based on a conviction of the unchanging character of the principles of God's working."[61] Klyne Snodgrass prefers to describe this phenomenon as "correspondence in history" to distinguish it from abuses of the term typology.[62]

---

291). Thus, France goes on to express "real surprise that 'midrash' has been taken to be a major factor in the search for the literary affinities of the gospels" (291). We might add, "and for the rest of the NT."

57. Moo, *"Sensus Plenior,"* 194. Their approach was restrained and guided by the historical events of their experience, though not by the historical events of the original text. France, "Postscript," 296, observes about the Gospel writers, "But the point where we have found it necessary to dissent from the attribution to the gospel writers of a 'creative midrash' which produced unhistorical stories in historical form out of the Old Testament texts is in the observation of the *secondary* role of the Old Testament texts in relation to the gospel traditions." That is, the historical events of Jesus' life and ministry provided the touchstone; the Evangelists did not creatively employ the OT to invent "history."

58. Clearly, in a textbook like this we cannot pursue the intricacies and implications that a thorough analysis of this issue requires. We must again direct the reader to the various essays in *Gospel Perspectives, vol. 3*, for the necessary clarification and defense of these assertions. See also S. E. Porter and C. A. Evans, ed., *The Scrolls and the Scriptures* (Sheffield, UK: Sheffield Academic Press, 1997).

59. On this point see the comments of Beale, *Handbook on the New Testament Use of the Old Testament*, 12–13.

60. For a very succinct and useful discussion of the nature of typology see Beale, *Handbook on the New Testament Use of the Old Testament*, 13–27. He gives a very full definition on p. 14 and explains several clear examples of the use of typology on pp. 59–66.

61. R. T. France, *The Gospel According to Matthew*, TNTC (Grand Rapids: Eerdmans, 1985), 40, quoting G. Lampe. His discussion is very helpful. Also, see C. S. Seitz, *Figured Out: Typology and Providence in Christian Scripture* (Philadelphia: Westminster John Knox, 2001); D. A. Carson, ed., *The Scriptures Testify about Me: Jesus and the Gospel in the Old Testament* (Wheaton, IL: Crossway, 2013); L. Goppelt, *Typos: The Typological Interpretation of the Old Testament in the New* (Grand Rapids: Eerdmans, 1982); and G. von Rad, "Typological Interpretation of the Old Testament," in *Essays on Old Testament Hermeneutics*, ed. C. Westermann and J. L. Mays (Richmond: John Knox, 1963), 17–39. See the important assessment of the NT uses in G. Schunack, "τύπος," *EDNT*, 3:372–76.

62. K. Snodgrass, "The Use of the Old Testament in the New," in *Interpreting the New Testament: Essays on Methods and Issues*, ed. D. A. Black and D. S. Dockery (Nashville: Broadman and Holman, 2001), 215.

The use of typology rests on the belief that God's ways of acting are consistent throughout history. It was natural for the NT writers to explain phenomena in the new Messianic era in terms of their OT precursors. That is, they believed that many of God's former actions with Israel (recorded in the OT) were "types" of what he was now doing in Christ. For example, Peter speaks of the water that "saved" Noah and his family as a "type" of baptism that now saves Christians (1 Pet 3:20–21).[63] This does not imply that the OT authors actually intended, in some prophetic kind of way, the type that the NT writer later discovered. Typology is more a technique of the later writer who "mines" prior Scripture for similarities, patterns, or categories to explain God's present activities.[64] Far from a no-holds-barred reader-response reading of the OT, they discover what they see as God's typical patterns of working.

Moo responsibly puts the subject of typology within the larger "promise-fulfillment" scheme for understanding the relationship between the testaments. Thus, he says, "New Testament persons, events, and institutions will sometimes 'fill up' Old Testament persons, events, and institutions by repeating at a deeper or more climactic level that which was true in the original situation."[65] If this is true, then the OT writers were not always, if ever, conscious that what they were writing had typological significance. At the same time, NT writers assumed that God intended that his actions on behalf of Israel would one day find a kind of analogy or fulfillment in Christ and the church.[66] Humanly speaking, the OT texts only had one level of meaning: the single meaning the human authors intended to convey. Yet God was writing a larger narrative, and God's past actions set the stage for what later writers would see as patterns of his working with people.[67]

This does not mean that the OT authors intended more than one meaning, nor even that the texts they wrote contained more than one meaning. Rather, it means that the OT as a whole (hence the value of canonical criticism) had a forward-looking dimension to it, sometimes (perhaps, usually) unknown to the writers. Because God was at work in Israel and in the lives of his people, their writings reflected what he

---

63. More precisely, Peter says that the water of baptism is the "antitype" (Greek: *antitypos*) of the water that saved Noah (2 Pet 3:21).

64. Snodgrass notes, "Later writers use exodus terminology to describe God's saving his people from Assyria (Isa 11:6) or salvation generally. The suffering of a righteous person (Ps 22) finds correspondence in the crucifixion of Jesus (Mt 22:39–46)," in "Use of the Old Testament," 215. It's fair to note, however, that in the discussion of typology, some scholars do posit that the OT reference had some kind of forward-looking element to it (see Beale, *Handbook on the NT Use*, 13–14).

65. Moo, "*Sensus Plenior*," 196.

66. We do not presume here to know God's mind or intentions. Rather, we believe that NT texts refer back to OT incidents as types. As divine author of the Bible, the Holy Spirit directed the human authors to see the correspondences.

67. T. L. Howard, "The Use of Hosea 11:1 in Matthew 2:15: An Alternative Solution," *BSac* 143 (1986): 314–28, convincingly defends typology as the best approach to our example. He speaks of this as "analogical correspondence." In contrast, J. H. Sailhamer, "Hosea 11:1 and Matthew 2:15," *WTJ* 63 (2001): 87–96, argues that Matthew did not employ typology; he believes that clues in the larger context of Hosea were the bases for what Matthew subsequently said about Jesus. Readers will find a helpful discussion of the issues at stake here in R. B. Gaffin, Jr., "The Redemptive-Historical View," in *Biblical Hermeneutics: Five Views*, ed. S. E. Porter and B. M. Stowell (Downers Grove: InterVarsity, 2012), 102–8.

was doing. The subsequent writers of the NT perceived these divine patterns and made the typological connections. Craig Evans affirms this point, "The life, death, and resurrection of Jesus became for early Christians the hermeneutical key for their interpretation and application of the Jewish Scriptures. Since the Scriptures could be relied on for clarification of eschatological events, and since Jesus was the eschatological agent, there could be no doubt that the Scriptures were fulfilled in him."[68]

This view of typology helps us understand what often occurs when NT writers use the OT in what appear to be strange ways. Certainly they use the OT in ways that we do not recommend to students today! As the background to typology, the followers of Jesus consciously considered their experiences to match the patterns of God's redemptive history that began with Israel. As they read the OT they became aware of the correspondences, even though their uses of the OT did not correspond—in such non-straightforward uses—to what the original writers probably intended, nor do they explain the historical-grammatical meanings of the texts themselves. And, we add again, Jesus himself commended this reading of the OT when Luke writes, "'How foolish you are, and how slow to believe all that the prophets have spoken! Did not the Messiah have to suffer these things and then enter his glory?' And beginning with Moses and all the Prophets, he [Jesus] explained to them what was said in all the Scriptures concerning himself" (Luke 24:25–27).

Do these "Jewish methods" (use of midrash, pesher, or typology) imply that the meaning discovered by the NT writers was *actually in* the OT? We would say, only in some very limited fashion (and probably not a conscious intention of the OT author). We find that the NT writers appropriated the OT because they observed some correspondences between an OT text and their new experiences in Christ. In this narrow sense that meaning was discernible in the OT (though, of course, we have no way to demonstrate this). But we allege that the meaning the NT writer discovered in the OT was *not* present in the sense that the original OT author intended to refer to later realities. The protection of Jesus in Egypt was *not* the intention of Hosea, though it did represent for Matthew a pattern (type) of how God protects his sons.

In our view, no reader contemporary to Hosea—or any OT text so used—would have seen that later meaning. More probably, the NT writers brought their interpretations to the OT texts in light of their experiences in Christ and the emerging Christian tradition developing in the Christian community—taught and led by the apostles, including, perhaps, those who did not write NT books. Surely their christocentric preunderstanding disposed them to see meanings that were not intended by the OT

---

68. C. A. Evans, "The Function of the Old Testament in the New," in *Introducing New Testament Interpretation*, ed. S. McKnight, GNTE (Grand Rapids: Baker, 1990), 193. Our stance in this, however, is not without objectors. Indeed, there is a movement championing the "theological interpretation of Scripture" that finds many Christological readings in the OT. For more on this enterprise see the various essays, M. A. Rae, J. Goldingay, C. J. H. Wright, R. W. Wall, and K. Greene-McCreight, "Christ in/and the Old Testament," *JTI* 2 (2008): 1–22. On the task more broadly see K. Berding and J. Lunde, ed., *Three Views on the New Testament Use of the Old Testament* (Grand Rapids: Zondervan, 2008). The writers give their views on the possibility of *sensus plenior*, typology, and whether the NT writers used Jewish exegetical methods, among other things.

writers. The sequence could be explained in this way: their belief in Jesus as the Christ, the discovering of OT background anticipations of that reality, and then their emerging formulations of an accepted Christian tradition that was then passed on.

Where does this leave us, then? Do biblical texts have one fixed meaning or several levels of meaning? We have set out the choices and clearly hinted what approach we support. A summary of the options we have covered would be helpful before we conclude:

1. Biblical authors intended *only one meaning* (illocution and perlocution), and this historical meaning remains the sole legitimate object of exegesis. This is essentially the best option available to modern interpreters.
2. Biblical authors intended to convey *multiple meanings* or levels of meanings in at least some of their writings. These texts have several meanings that readers may subsequently discover. NT writers who used the OT discovered one of the intended meanings. We found this difficult to defend, much less to replicate.
3. Biblical authors intended only one meaning, but that need not limit how later readers understand a text since perception always involves a creative interaction between text and reader. Since all interpretation is a *reader-response* enterprise, later readers—like the writers of the NT in their use of the OT—may discover meanings never intended by the author. We reject this approach.
4. Biblical authors intended only one sense, but unknown to them the Holy Spirit encoded in the text additional and hidden meaning (what is called the *sensus plenior*). When NT writers employed OT texts, in places they were drawing out this fuller sense. Such a process may or may not be repeatable for modern interpreters. We found this difficult to defend, much less to replicate.
5. Biblical authors intended only one sense, though later readers may employ *creative exegetical techniques* to discover additional valid meanings not intended by the original authors. In some of their uses of the OT, NT writers apparently employed techniques such as midrash, pesher, or typology. There was some possible connection between original text and later sense, though the connection may appear arbitrary, if not undecipherable, to others. The process may or may not be repeatable today.

Where does this discussion leave us? The answer is not simple; indeed it is complex! But we believe biblical interpretation must center in the text (locution) and what the human author intended to accomplish through that text (illocution and perlocution). What follows is our attempt to demonstrate that.

AUTHOR-CENTERED TEXTUAL MEANING

Author-Centered Textual Meaning Is the Goal of Interpretation

Given our assumption that Scripture constitutes God's word to people through human authors, our goal in reading it is to discover the authors' meanings encoded in the texts they wrote. Following basic speech act theory, we believe the authors wrote texts to convey content and to effect responses in their readers. We believe God intended the Bible to function not as a mirror reflecting the readers and their meanings, but as a window into the worlds and meanings of the authors and the texts they produced. Therefore we posit the following: *the author-encoded historical meaning of these texts is the central objective of hermeneutics.* We assume that the writers or editors of the Bible intended to communicate to their readers in the same way people normally communicate.

We believe the biblical authors intended their messages to have a single meaning. Several options above affirm this point. Of course, the authors or editors did use various genres and literary devices, but they used such devices to convey their single meaning. They may have encoded their messages in metaphor, poetry, allegory, or apocalyptic, in addition to more straightforward techniques, but they selected appropriate ways to convey their intended meaning (illocution and perlocution). If the authors intended double or hidden meanings in their words, we have no means of discovering these apart from their own clues, or perhaps from analogies based upon other examples in Scripture.[69] But this remains a problematic task. We must desist from affirming other levels of meaning without objective evidence.

Clearly, interpreters may disagree about what a given text means, and an author may admit that a reader "found" a meaning that that author did not consciously intend. Texts may indeed be polyvalent or polysemous.[70] A well-known example is: "Flying planes can be dangerous."[71] Its meaning would differ radically if said by a flight instructor to a new student pilot or by King Kong as he desperately clung to a precarious spot on the Empire State Building.[72] But we cannot allow these realities to cloud the essential task of interpretation. Speech act theory supports the view that intention is paramount.

In our study of the Bible we seek to understand God's revelation. The original biblical texts were inspired; those texts were encoded in the original historical contexts. Though a given passage may be capable of being understood in several ways, our goal is to determine which of those various possible meanings the text most likely would

---

69. For example, only with great reluctance do scholars offer possible explanations of John's code number 666 in Rev 13:18. Whatever the author intended to denote remains debatable at best to modern readers. Many conjecture it may be some kind of takeoff of the perfect digits 777 or a gematria pointing to Nero Caesar or to someone else. For various takes on this see G. E. Ladd, *A Commentary on the Revelation of John* (Grand Rapids: Eerdmans, 1972), 186–87; R. H. Mounce, *The Book of Revelation*, NICNT, rev. ed. (Grand Rapids: Eerdmans, 1998), 261–63; D. E. Aune, *Revelation 6–16*, WBC (Nashville: Nelson, 1998), 770–73; G. K. Beale, *The Book of Revelation*, NIGTC (Grand Rapids: Eerdmans; Carlisle, UK: Paternoster, 1999), 718–28; and G. R. Osborne, *Revelation*, BECNT (Grand Rapids: Baker, 2002), 518–21.

70. That is, texts, as well as words, may be capable of more than one meaning or sense. The word "solution" affords a clear example on the lexical level. It can refer to either a liquid substance or the answer to a problem.

71. Another example of an ambiguous sentence is the sports headline that appeared in the 2000s in the sports section of the *Denver Post*, "Holy Family Crushes Sacred Heart." As well, *The New Yorker* (June 8, 1992, 96) provided a humorous example from a flyer announcing a topic in the Lunch and Learn Series at Auburn University, Alabama: "Disciplining Children: Concrete Helps."

72. From the famous Hollywood movie originally made in 1933 and remade in 1976 and 2005.

have meant by its author and to its original readers. This is why people communicate: they expect and hope that what they express will be understood as they intended it. Furthermore, in light of the options of meanings noted above, *if we can determine* that the original text intended to convey more than one meaning, then those multiple meanings also comprise the goal of exegesis.[73]

Definition of Author-Centered Textual Meaning

What do we mean by textual meaning? The meaning of a text (a locution) is *that which the words and grammatical structures of that text disclose about the probable intention of its author/editor (the illocution and perlocution) and the probable understanding of that text by its intended readers.*[74] It is the meaning those words would have conveyed to the readers at the time they were written by the author or editor.

Of course, we do not know with certainty who wrote many of the biblical books. Furthermore, the composition of some books was probably due to a series of editors or redactors who put their own touches on the books until at some point the books acquired their canonical shape.[75] Truly, in some biblical texts we may have several layers of authors. And though we encounter sayings of Jesus in the Gospels, in places we must distinguish Jesus' original point from the Evangelists' purposes as evidenced in their editing and placement (as we saw earlier). Further, where the Evangelists were not eyewitnesses to Jesus' remarks, presumably they obtained their material from other sources.[76]

In spite of these theoretical problems, we may conveniently speak of the person (or even group) who put the biblical book into its final form—the form the canon

---

73. Readers will note that we used "the NT use of the OT" as a kind of litmus test of what the OT can do, and therefore what the Bible does more generally.

74. We are intentionally combining two options that some theorists split apart: an author-centered focus and a text-centered focus. We see liabilities in any attempt to select one of these over against the other as the sole focus of hermeneutics. We say more below.

75. The Pentateuch provides a clear example. We do not know who or how many editors put these books in the final form we now read. Clearly it was not Moses alone, since Deut 34 records his death and other indicators point to later times (e.g., Gen 12:6; 14:14; 22:14; 36:31). For a discussion concerning the origin of the Pentateuch, see T. D. Alexander, *From Paradise to the Promised Land: An Introduction to the Pentateuch*, 3rd ed. (Grand Rapids: Baker Academic, 2012), 3–111; J. Barton and J. Muddiman, eds., *The Pentateuch*, The Oxford Bible Commentary (Oxford: Oxford University Press, 2010), 16–53; G. Wenham, "Pondering the Pentateuch: The Search for a New Paradigm," in *The Face of Old Testament Studies*, ed. D. W. Baker and B. T. Arnold (Grand Rapids: Baker, 1999), 116–44; cf. also the enlightening study by D. Garrett, *Rethinking Genesis: The Sources and Authorship of the First Book of the Pentateuch* (Grand Rapids: Baker, 1991). Or we might ask, who wrote Ruth, and when was it written? Though the story derives from the period of the judges (1:1), internal references—such as the need to explain the sandal ceremony (4:7) and the genealogy at the end (4:18–22)—indicate that it was written much later to bolster the Davidic monarchy. See R. L. Hubbard, Jr., *The Book of Ruth*, NICOT (Grand Rapids; Eerdmans, 1988). For the NT, the writers of the Gospels provide examples of editors who wove together the works and words of Jesus into coherent narratives.

76. On some of the issues that constitute the synoptic problem, see R. H. Stein, *Studying the Synoptic Gospels: Origin and Interpretation* (Grand Rapids: Baker, 2001); and D. L. Dungan, *A History of the Synoptic Problem: The Canon, the Text, the Composition, and the Interpretation of the Gospels*, AYBRL (New York: Doubleday, 1999). The method of redaction criticism particularly focuses on the Evangelists as editors of the Gospels. Cf. the relevant articles in J. B Green, J. K. Brown, and N. Perrin, eds., *Dictionary of Jesus and the Gospels*, 2nd ed. (Downers Grove: InterVarsity, 2013).

preserves. We likewise assume, along with most Christian confessions of faith, that this final form alone possesses the status of inspired revelation. Our goal is to understand the meaning of the book (or texts) the human writer (the shaper of the book's final form) produced, while at the same time asserting that God's intention is communicated through that inspired text. We assume that in the divine/human concursive activity of inspiration, God's influence assured that all biblical texts do indeed express the divine author's intentions.[77] God's purposes were furthered not frustrated when the human authors or editors produced the biblical texts. Of course, whether or not those purposes accomplished the author's or God's desired outcomes (perlocutions) is another question.

To repeat, in establishing the meaning of the biblical texts as our goal, we do not deny that some kinds of literature have meaning(s) beyond the surface level of the text, as in poetry or metaphorical language. In that case an author still intends a single meaning, but that meaning is conveyed through metaphors or symbols. Thus, a parable might appear to have two levels of meaning, the literal story and the spiritual lesson, but the author intends to convey some specific meaning by employing that vehicle. Of course, that specific meaning might consist of several points or more than one lesson.[78] The parable's literal story conveys the author's intended meaning—the lesson(s). We seek only this intended meaning. In certain instances (what Norman Perrin calls "tensive symbols"), metaphorical discourse may be deliberately open-ended or polyvalent.[79] Still, this results from an author's deliberate intention.

Author-Centered Textual Meaning Is the Central Goal of Interpretation
• All we have for study is the biblical text from which we can discern the author's intended meaning
• God's intended meaning is conveyed through this text
• In interpreting the text using the normal canons of exegesis, we can arrive at God's message for people

The Challenge of Reader-Oriented Interpretation

Obviously the interpreter or reader plays a crucial role in discovering meaning. But when the role of the author is set aside, readers are able to create meaning by reading

---

77. The classic texts on inspiration—2 Pet 1:20–21 and 2 Tim 3:16–17—do not even begin to exhaust the Bible's testimony to itself and to its divine origin and status as God's Word. For a detailed list and discussion of many such biblical texts see W. Grudem, "Scripture's Self-Attestation and the Problem of Formulating a Doctrine of Scripture," in *Scripture and Truth*, ed. D. A. Carson and J. D. Woodbridge (Grand Rapids: Zondervan, 1983), 19–64.

78. See Blomberg, *Interpreting the Parables*, esp. 188–93; and K. R. Snodgrass, *Stories with Intent: A Comprehensive Guide to the Parables of Jesus* (Grand Rapids: Eerdmans, 2008), 24–31 ("some parables make one point, and some make several points," 29).

79. N. Perrin, *Jesus and the Language of the Kingdom: Symbol and Metaphor in New Testament Interpretation* (Philadelphia: Fortress; London: SCM, 1976).

in to the text their specific needs, interests, or preunderstandings. Readers do *use* texts as mirrors and project their own meanings onto them. As we have seen, for some, our intention to restrict the goal of interpretation to an author-based textual meaning appears excessively and unnecessarily confining. McKnight observes that people have used the biblical writings throughout history to discover and create meaning for themselves.[80] We have argued, however, that this is not a legitimate way to read the Bible.

By way of review, a reader-oriented approach pays more attention to the role of the modern reader in the work of analyzing texts. In this view, interpretation is "in part a creative construction of the reader, a construction of cause, which is a result of the effect of the text in the first place."[81] The original causes behind a text are relativized and placed in balance with what modern readers do with the text to create meaning. Instead of simply looking for facts from the Bible with which to create or inform theological systems, the reader-oriented approach attempts to create a new world within the reader in the process of reading the Bible, albeit a world that intersects with the world of the texts he or she is reading.

Many rightly champion the perceived values and virtues in such an approach. It places the center of attention on Bible *readers*, who, allegedly, ought to serve as the focal point of interpretation. Too readily do author- or text-based approaches get lost in the ancient world, as if having described the origin and world of a text or identified the text's form, we have completed the task. In addition, reader-centered approaches take seriously what readers bring to the process of interpretation: they often do so unashamedly and intentionally to produce their unique readings of a text.[82] And this has opened up biblical studies to other voices, both ideological and geographical, and facilitated greater attempts to contextualize the fruits of those studies. Thus feminist or liberationist readings (to name just two) have helpfully and rightly directed attention to important issues of justice that might not have surfaced had not readers approached texts with such ideological concerns. Employing a hermeneutic of suspicion, they have questioned long-standing interpretations, assuming (rightly in some instances) that for too long Western, Northern, and male ideologies have controlled the outcomes of biblical interpretation.

Despite some of these benefits, we have registered pointed objections. A variety of reader-response approaches may find diverse meanings in a text, pointing out the subjectivity of the stance, but the presence of such diversity points out its inherent liability. Where lies a biblical text's authority? It has been jettisoned. In contrast, we affirm that only the author-encoded meaning of the text, not one's reading of it, has

---

80. E. V. McKnight, *Postmodern Use of the Bible: The Emergence of Reader-Oriented Criticism* (Nashville: Abingdon, 1988), 170.

81. Ibid.

82. Even when such reader-centered approaches function unconsciously (as often done in conservative circles where readers avow they are merely reading what the Bible itself says), the result in a lively engagement with the text and a serious attempt to put its "message for me" into practice.

any legitimate claim to acceptance as God's actual, authentic, and Spirit-inspired message. We can apply interpretive controls, assuming that accuracy and legitimacy are worthy goals, only if we seek as our primary aim the meaning that would have made sense to the original writer and readers. Though complete objectivity or certainty may elude all readers, the *textual meaning* represents the most worthy ideal or target. All other meanings may be subjective and merely reflect the fancy of the interpreter. In a postmodern climate that may be acceptable and indeed desirable for some, but not for interpreters seeking to understand the biblical texts as divine revelation. Only author-centered textual meaning represents the speech act of the author.

The Bible as Literature

Does an author-centered, text-centered approach preclude studying the Bible as literature? No, it requires it. We have no desire to deny a legitimate place for literary studies of the Bible that complement historical approaches. We agree that some readers want to study and appreciate only the literary dimensions of the text rather than seeking its historical-critical meaning.[83] And it is true that various literary theories and methods contribute immensely to our understanding and appreciation of Scripture. Morgan rightly notes, "One mark of great literature is its capacity to illuminate and enlarge the experience of successive readers in new social contexts."[84] We may read the Bible to obtain the information it contains, and we may read it for other purposes—for enjoyment, inspiration, courage, solace, or pleasure—that may go beyond the authors' original intentions. These remain valid uses of the Bible. But there is a further point to be underscored.

Literary studies are not merely optional programs, only for some; they are essential tasks in the process of interpretation. We must study the various genres as well as parallel forms of literature of the ancient world in order to shed light on the original meaning or intention of biblical texts. Indeed, a large part of this book is devoted precisely to that agenda. So if interpreters seek the historical meaning of the text, they will compare it with Jewish and Greco-Roman rhetoric, ancient near Eastern sagas, law codes, biographies, letters, or plays, etc., to gain insight into what ancient

---

83. We give considerable space to deciphering the literary dimensions of the biblical texts, and particularly literary criticism. See ch. 3. For additional insight see such works as A. Jefferson and D. Robey, eds., *Modern Literary Theory*, 2nd ed. (London: B.T. Bratsford; Totowa, NJ: Barnes & Noble, 1986); and F. Lentricchia, *After the New Criticism* (London: Methuen, 1980). L. Ryken, *Words of Delight: A Literary Introduction to the Bible*, 2nd ed. (Grand Rapids: Baker, 1992), provides good examples of how literary criticism works. For an introduction to OT narratives, see L. D. Hawk, "Literary/Narrative Criticism," in *Dictionary of the Old Testament: Pentateuch*, ed. T. D. Alexander and D. W. Baker (Downers Grove: InterVarsity, 2003), 536–44; and Y. Amit, "Narrative Art of Israel's Historians," in *Dictionary of the Old Testament: Historical Books*, ed. B. T. Arnold and H. G. M Williamson (Downers Grove: InterVarsity, 2005), 708–15; cf. J. T. Walsh, *Old Testament Narrative: A Guide to Interpretation* (Louisville: Westminster John Knox, 2009); D. Gunn and D. N. Fewell, *Narrative in the Hebrew Bible* (Oxford: Oxford University Press, 1993); and for poetry, see S. E. Gillingham, *The Poems and Psalms of the Hebrew Bible*, Oxford Bible Series (Oxford: Oxford University Press, 1994). T. Longman, III, *Literary Approaches to Biblical Interpretation* (Grand Rapids: Zondervan, 1987), furnishes a clear general introduction.

84. Morgan with Barton, *Biblical Interpretation*, 10–11.

authors—including those of the Bible—developed and produced in their writing.[85] All of this is to say that we will direct our literary critical analyses into three areas: (1) focus on the author's intent in composing the text, (2) the conventions of the text that reflect that intent, and (3) the readers' response to the text.

Thus, we view literary approaches to studying the Bible not as mutually exclusive to historical concerns centered in the world of the author and text, but as complementary and equally important. We must inquire about the historical basis of a text and its author's intentions in writing it; *and* we may seek to appreciate that author's writing as a literary product and how the act of writing conveyed the author's intentions. Since the texts function as speech acts, we seek to employ all tactics that uncover what they mean. To accomplish that we must take seriously their authors' intentions, seeking to understand their illocutions and perlocutions. Literary readings must enhance and clarify, but not take over or subvert the meaning the author intended to convey.

The Question of Historicity

We have just argued that the biblical writings are literature; for this reason literary methods are appropriate to understanding their author's intentions. But they are also historically situated documents—since they derive from writers who penned the documents long ago. But, it is fair to ask, when they report events and circumstances, do they report history as it happened? Can we know whether the events occurred as recounted, or that the reports are accurate? How are we to understand the historical nature of the Bible?

If an author writes an account as a *historical* report in the normal conventions of the time, then, assuming the author is a good historian, we are predisposed to accept it as true and interpret it in that light. If the account belongs to a different genre (say a poem, a parable, or a fable) and its message is conveyed via the conventions consistent with that genre, then we interpret it on those terms.[86] Recall our discussion of speech act theory: we aim to understand the text's propositional content, manner of presentation (e.g., genre), and the author's desired outcome or effect on the readers. Whether historical record, epistle, or apocalypse, we seek the author's intention (illocution and perlocution) as reflected in the specific text (locution).

Our goal as interpreters is to retain the appropriate balance in evaluating the Bible in its character as literature. Literary approaches yield interesting and important insights into the nature of the documents. But literary criticism does not negate the purpose of the biblical documents when they report genuine history.[87] Of course,

---

85. Three important works in this regard are D. E. Aune, *The New Testament in Its Literary Environment* (Philadelphia: Westminster, 1987); J. H. Walton, *Ancient Israelite Literature in Its Cultural Context: A Survey of Parallels Between Biblical and Ancient Near Eastern Texts* (Grand Rapids: Zondervan, 1989); and J. H. Walton and D. Brent Sandy, *The Lost World of Scripture. Ancient Literary Culture and Biblical Authority* (Downers Grove: InterVarsity, 2013). See also our bibliography.

86. Even these non-historical genres arise in a specific historical setting and may comment on historical matters, albeit indirectly.

87. Simply because the Bible is a religious document need not imply that it cannot report events as they really

on the surface level of language, genuine history and historical fiction may appear indistinguishable. For example, did Nathan's story of the ewe lamb (2 Sam 12:1–4) really happen? What about the parable of the sower (Matt 13:3–8 par.)? Is the narrative of Job or the story of Jonah literal history or historical fiction that mixes both historical and nonhistorical elements? Are the early chapters of Genesis poetry or narrative? Are Luke's reports of the speeches of Peter and Paul in Acts verbatim accounts, faithful epitomes, or pure fiction? What criteria help the interpreter decide? We must study the literary conventions as well as the accounts themselves for further clues.

Suppose we envision a continuum whose endpoints we label simplistically as "literal historical reports of events as they happened" and "pure fiction."[88] A snapshot records an event as it happened. A fantasy is pure fiction. A portrait may be somewhere in the middle, as an artist takes liberties to portray what he or she sees.

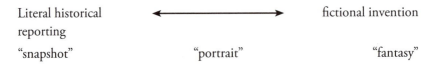

Literal historical reporting		fictional invention
"snapshot"	"portrait"	"fantasy"

We must analyze each allegedly historical account to discern where it falls along this continuum. The key issue is how the original writer intended the account to be read—how he or she and the first readers would have understood it. Individual narratives may fall somewhere along the continuum, sometimes involving both factual and creative elements. If a passage purports to record genuine history according to the literary and textual conventions of the day, then we infer that the story actually happened. If, on the other hand, the literary and textual cues of genre point to inventiveness, then we place the story toward the endpoint of fiction. In all cases the literary features as well as the historical context of the text unfold our conclusions about the historical nature of the text.[89]

We insist upon this historically plausible understanding because of our presumption that we must embrace the biblical authors' writings *on their terms*. This is a matter of integrity with the authors' texts. We would be just as misguided to insist that something intended as fictional (or somewhere in the middle of the continuum above) is strictly historical as it would be to relegate something intended as historical to the

---

happened. Of course, neither may we merely assert that because the Bible records events, they happened as recorded. Historicity must he established on neutral grounds. We contend that history and theology need not be mutually exclusive categories.

88. D. Tovey, *Narrative Art and Act in the Fourth Gospel*, LNTS 151 (Sheffield, UK: Sheffield Academic Press, 1997), also employs this way of portraying the situation.

89. For insight into the complex issues of how narratives function, see R. Alter, *The Art of Biblical Narrative*, 2nd ed. (New York: Basic Books, 2011); A. Berlin, *Poetics and Interpretation of Biblical Narrative* (Sheffield: Almond Press, 1983); M. A. Powell, *What Is Narrative Criticism?* Guides to Biblical Scholarship (Minneapolis: Augsburg Fortress, 1991); J. P. Fokkelman, *Reading Biblical Narrative: An Introductory Guide* (Louisville: Westminster John Knox, 2000); and James L. Resseguie, *Narrative Criticism of the New Testament: An Introduction* (Grand Rapids: Baker, 2005).

category of fiction. Both would misconstrue the writer's intentions and impose alien readings on the text, thereby making our modern preunderstanding the authority rather than the biblical text.

Our approach will seek the meaning of the biblical texts that reflect the authors' intentions as reflected in the texts themselves. We believe that our task is to decode these speech acts in the ways language normally functions in order to understand correctly their meaning. We will employ the usual exegetical procedures using all the appropriate tactics of historical and literary criticism. We will strive for the interpretation of texts that is most plausible historically, given all the available data.

THE PLACE OF THE READER IN "CONSTRUCTING" MEANING

We seek the meaning the texts had at the time they were written—the meaning the author/editor intended and that the original readers would most likely have acknowledged. Yet our assessment of how NT writers employed the OT raised the question of the reader's role in reading a text. In our earlier discussion we noted that in places the NT writers found meanings in texts that the OT authors never intended—meanings that would not have occurred to the original readers of those OT texts. Is such an option open to Bible students today?

We have seen that readers bring themselves to the interpretive process. At the risk of misunderstanding, we posit that when they engage the biblical text readers do construct meaning.[90] Though we have been largely negative in our assessment of the reader-response approach to biblical interpretation, because it has such potential for abuse, at this point we need to acknowledge that some insights of this approach merit thoughtful consideration. What do we mean?

Understanding a biblical text is a generative enterprise, much like a conversation between friends. In a conversation each person is involved not only in analyzing (albeit subconsciously) the precise meanings of words and grammatical constructions, but also in understanding the other person (including non-verbal cues). How each participant reads the other will depend upon prior experiences as well as upon their individual situations. This is true in reading the Bible.[91] In Tate's words, "Individual interpretations . . . are individual conversations with the text and are always situated within some context. Interpretation is relational and involves understanding the text in light of who we are, and understanding ourselves in light of the text."[92] As we

---

90. This is a point made well by P. J. Leithart, *Deep Exegesis: The Mystery of Reading Scripture* (Waco, TX: Baylor University Press, 2009), 114–19. He says that texts are like jokes: to make sense of them you need to bring other knowledge derived from outside the text (or joke).

91. We will develop some of the implications of this more fully in the later chapter on uses of the Bible, particularly in the process of spiritual formation.

92. Tate, *Biblical Interpretation*, 268–69.

insisted above, readers ought not change an author's meaning, but different readers may perceive it differently, partly because of the preunderstandings they bring.

But interpreters who remain committed to the Bible as divine revelation operate with some constraints in the range of possible perceptions they can allow. The sky is not the limit for possible meanings, and, again, we set ourselves apart from post-modern reader-response critics' work. Properly informed, readers may understand a text only in ways related to the intention of the author, i.e., its historical meaning. We believe Christians operate under the constraints of Jesus Christ—who he is, what he has done, and the community he has created—and the Holy Spirit, who inspired Scripture and illumines readers. Biblical texts must be understood within the context and confines of the believing community in which each interpreter resides, though admittedly, these interpretations will differ among communities. What accounts for this phenomenon—when different faith communities come to different understandings of a biblical text? We hope some examples will help.

Baptism

The NT presents the practice of baptism in the Gospels where John the Baptist requires this rite of those repenting. In Mark's words, "And so John the Baptist appeared in the wilderness, preaching a baptism of repentance for the forgiveness of sins" (Mark 1:4). Jesus continued and encouraged the practice (John 3:22; 4:1–2; Matt 28:19–20), and it became a central rite in the developing church (Acts 2:38, 41; 8:12, 38; 9:18; 10:47–48; 16:15, 33; 18:8; 19:5; etc.). Some texts may imply a certain method of baptism (e.g., John's baptism in the Jordan River and Acts 8:38–39 are cited to defend immersion), though most do not. The historical precedent among the Jews was (and still is) immersion in a *mikvah* (i.e., a pool of water for ritual purification).[93]

Nevertheless, Christian communities have come to understand the relevant texts in divergent ways, viewing the mode of baptism in light of their community's reading of the relevant texts. Various immersionist groups appeal to the historical precedent of immersion as the rite of cleansing and initiation for the Jews: Jews still immerse proselytes. They insist that, while the spiritual message is of paramount importance, no other mode of baptism correctly represents the biblical pattern.

Others emphasize the spiritual significance of the rite, or its link to circumcision, and treat the mode—whether immersion, sprinkling, or pouring—as a secondary issue (though even some of these groups practice a single mode, e.g., sprinkling). Some will

---

93. Though no archaeological evidence for these ritual immersion pools antedate Hellenistic times, Jewish tradition asserts that the practice of ritual cleansing in water goes back to Adam and was required for all Jews prior to meeting God at the giving of the law at Sinai; was practiced in the "well of Miriam" in the desert; was performed at the induction of Moses and Aaron and subsequent priests into the priesthood; was central to the ongoing temple cult in Jerusalem; and became a requirement for all proselytes to Judaism. Traditionally, and up to the present time, immersion in water is a central feature of Jewish religious practice. See R. Slonim, *Total Immersion: A Mikvah Anthology* (Northvale, NJ: Jason Aronson, 1996); and A. Kaplan, *Waters of Eden: The Mystery of the Mikvah* (New York: NCSY/Union of Orthodox Jewish Congregations of America, 1976).

baptize only those old enough to express their faith in Jesus, while others will sprinkle, dab, or immerse babies. Some groups even allow for multiple modes—sprinkling babies if the parents prefer, or immersing people subsequent to their confession of faith.

Do some texts "clearly" denote immersion, while others "clearly" teach sprinkling or pouring so that the groups pick the ones they prefer or reject the others? Or, to complicate the discussion, do some texts teach the baptism of *believers* while other texts teach the baptism of *infants*? Some proponents of one side or the other often insist upon affirmative answers, but the issues are not so simple. One matter is certain: various church traditions have decided what the relevant texts will *mean for them*. To cite a couple examples, some Presbyterians decide to baptize infants and adult converts by sprinkling only; others sprinkle or immerse infants and adult believers. Coming from a Lutheran background in the old country, Evangelical Covenanters will baptize infants or adults, whatever the parents or converts prefer. Baptist and similarly minded groups typically insist upon the immersion of believers, though they must decide what "belief" means, especially in instances where children of a rather young age seek baptism. Some groups struggle over what to do if potential church members were baptized as believers but by the "wrong" mode, or even by the "right" mode, but in another denomination. Those who sprinkle babies often point to the analogy of the OT practice of circumcision of infants and the parallel covenants to enter Israel (Abraham) and the church (Christ). They note, too, the historical precedent for a variety of modes: the church has employed the methods of sprinkling and pouring since the first or second century.

While some paedobaptists may admit that the pattern for baptism in the NT was immersion (sprinkling of infants is never explicitly taught in the Scriptures), they argue that is because the NT writers never addressed the issue of children of believing parents.[94] They argue that infant baptism developed as a legitimate theological inference from other clear biblical teachings.[95] Or, says Bromiley, "The inclusion of the children of adult converts is so much in line with the thought and practice of the OT that it is taken for granted in the New, as the household baptisms of Acts suggest even if they do not prove."[96] He continues, "Quite apart from the external evidence, the New Testament itself offers plain indications that the children of Christians are regarded as members of the divine community just as the children of Old Testament Israel were. In these circumstances the inference of an accepted practice of infant baptism is undoubtedly legitimate if not absolutely or bindingly so."[97] Thus, such people interpret

---

94. For a truly comprehensive treatment see E. Ferguson, *Baptism in the Early Church: History, Theology, and Liturgy in the First Five Centuries* (Grand Rapids: Eerdmans, 2013). On infant baptism see G. W. Bromiley, *Children of Promise. The Case for Baptizing Infants* (Grand Rapids: Eerdmans, 1979); and R. R. Booth, *Children of the Promise: The Biblical Case for Infant Baptism* (Phillipsburg, NJ: Presbyterian and Reformed, 1995).

95. For a useful collection of essays on relevant biblical and church practice see S. E. Porter and A. R. Cross, ed., *Baptism, The New Testament and The Church: Historical and Contemporary Studies In Honour of R.E.O. White* (Sheffield, UK: Sheffield Academic Press, 1999).

96. Bromiley, *Children of Promise*, 2.

97. Ibid., 4.

the texts concerning baptism with their preunderstandings. Biblical texts, principles and analogies, and historical tradition all weigh heavily in their interpretation.[98]

Correspondingly, those who teach the immersion of believers also rely on biblical texts and their traditions. Opposing the baptism of infants, Beasley-Murray insists, "It is not only that the New Testament is silent on the practice of infant baptism, but that the thought and practice of the primitive communities, as reflected in the New Testament documents, appear to be contrary to the ideas and practices that accompany infant baptism in the later churches."[99] Indeed, he insists that "infant baptism originated in a capitulation to pressures exerted upon the church both from without and from within."[100] His take on the NT and historical issues seems radically different from Bromiley's. Does the Bible support all these groups' varying practices of baptism? While each group insists upon an affirmative answer, each one finds different *meanings* in the same baptismal texts. How can we explain such differences of opinion?

In essence: neither those who baptize infants nor those who insist upon the immersion only of believers disregard the Bible in defending their views. Apparently equally committed, sincere, and able interpreters in these two traditions arrive at different conclusions about the *meaning* of the biblical texts—not merely their application. Certainly, constraints must apply. For example, paedobaptists typically insist upon the need for each individual's personal faith in Christ. Many do not teach that an infant's baptism secures his or her personal salvation, although some may (so-called baptismal regeneration). Salvation, most affirm, depends upon each person's trust in Christ. In other words the total Bible's teaching about relevant issues provides the guidelines and restraints within which all legitimate interpretations must lie. Nor do most immersionists affirm that baptism itself is essential for salvation. Salvation depends upon personal faith. Thus, the thief on the cross joined Jesus in paradise because of his faith in Jesus despite the absence of any kind of baptism (Luke 23:43).

Millennium

Another pertinent illustration arises within the theological topic of eschatology, which concerns the future or what are called the "end times." Since the earliest days of the church, Christians have debated the meaning of various biblical texts concerning the intricacies of end-time events. What did the biblical writers intend to teach about future events, especially the conclusion of history? Let us use this topic to illustrate a point about the nature of meaning in the process of interpretation.[101]

---

98. On some of the historical sources for infant baptism see J. Jeremias, *Infant Baptism in the First Four Centuries* (London: SCM, 1960). For the case against infant baptism from a Reformed theological position see P. K. Jewett, *Infant Baptism and the Covenant of Grace* (Grand Rapids: Eerdmans, 1978).

99. G. R. Beasley-Murray, *Baptism in the New Testament* (Grand Rapids: Eerdmans, 1973), 352. On believer's baptism also see T. R. Schreiner, *Believer's Baptism: Sign of the New Covenant in Christ* (Nashville: B&H Academic, 2007).

100. Beasley-Murray, *Baptism*, 352.

101. Here we must limit our discussion to the views of those Christians who believe that biblical prophecies

The so-called millennium refers to the thousand-year reign of Christ.[102] Some Christian theologians accept the view that this will entail an actual period of time (whether or not it spans precisely one thousand years). In one view, following his second coming, Christ himself will reign with believers on this present literal earth.[103] Others view the millennium more symbolically: they believe Christ and his followers currently reign in his kingdom, and at his glorious return Christ will bring history to a conclusion and usher in the eternal state, or age to come.[104] Proponents of a third but smaller group, adopting a view similar to the first, believe that this Church Age will develop into a final actual period of time—the millennium—after which Christ will return to begin the eternal state.[105]

As a test of these interpretations, we may scrutinize what some scholars say concerning Revelation 20:4–5, where the writer says of a group of people, "They came to life and reigned with Christ a thousand years. (The rest of the dead did not come to life until the thousand years were ended.) This is the first resurrection."

Premillennialist George Ladd argues that the phrase "came to life" refers to the literal resurrection of these believers and that "it is not used of any 'spiritual resurrection' of the souls of the righteous at death."[106] Thus, he continues, "At the beginning of the millennial period, part of the dead come to life; at its conclusion, the rest of the dead come to life."[107] In his support of an actual future millennium following Christ's return, Grant Osborne adds, "Satan is chained and sealed in the abyss so he cannot 'deceive the nations,' a statement that does not fit Satan's activity in the present world. It is better to see 20:1–10 as a future event and not as a present reality. In light of this, it is still more viable to see the 'coming to life' in 20:4–5 as physical resurrections at the parousia (believers) and last judgment (unbelievers)."[108]

Yet in his commentary on these same verses amillennialist William Hendriksen presents this view succinctly: "In this entire passage there is not a single word about

---

sketch out a future eschatology. For others who believe the Bible's teachings about the future to be incomplete or absent, this example will be irrelevant.

102. For a helpful introduction to the major competing options among conservative scholars, see R. Clouse, ed., *The Meaning of the Millennium: Four Views* (Downers Grove: InterVarsity, 1989); and C. A. Blaising, ed., *Three Views on the Millennium and Beyond* (Grand Rapids: Zondervan, 1999). For sane analyses of the options see S. J. Grenz, *The Millennial Maze* (Downers Grove: InterVarsity, 1992); and M. J. Erickson, *A Basic Guide to Eschatology: Making Sense of the Millennium*, rev. ed. (Grand Rapids: Baker, 1999).

103. For obvious reasons such interpreters are called premillennialists. Christ returns to earth prior to his reign during the millennium.

104. Sometimes such theologians are called amillennialists, though that may be a misnomer. They do not deny a millennium; rather, they prefer to view it as realized in church history following Christ's victory over Satan at the cross. They expect no future millennium. Other amillennialists equate the millennium with the future state—the new heavens and the new earth.

105. We call these interpreters postmillennialists. According to this view, Christ returns following a literal millennium. This view was predominant in nineteenth-century American Protestantism, spawned various reform movements, and is a feature of the movement called Christian Reconstructionism.

106. Ladd, *Revelation*, 265.

107. Ibid., 266.

108. G. R. Osborne, *Revelation*, 718.

a resurrection of *bodies*."[109] To him, "the thousand year reign takes place in *heaven*."[110] As to the binding of Satan during this millennial reign, "This work of *binding the devil* was begun when our Lord triumphed over him in the temptations in the wilderness, Matt 4:1–11; Luke 4:1–13."[111] For Hendriksen and other amillennialists, Satan is now bound in this age—the millennial age in which Christ rules in heaven with his victorious saints.[112]

Meanwhile, Robert Mounce seems to say something in-between. He distinguishes between the *form* of what the text of Revelation says and the *content* of meaning the author attempted to convey to his readers—an analysis that mirrors the distinction we have made between locution and illocution (though Mounce does not use these terms). Mounce observes, "In short, John described the millennium in temporal terms, but its essential meaning cannot be restricted to the form in which it was communicated."[113] In other words, the author may well have employed language that seems to indicate a literal period of time, and this probably originated in the dominant religious conceptions of the time of the author. But the "essential truth of prophecy" could well mean, says Mounce, that "we will cease to find in Revelation 20 the prediction of an *eschatological* era."[114] Such divergent views naturally raise hermeneutical questions. Are the relevant passages of the Bible so unclear that sincere interpreters cannot agree whether they teach a future actual, lengthy reign of Christ on this physical earth, or if it exists, whether Christ will return before or after such a period?

Assessment

How do such divergent views as these on baptism and the millennium develop? Is it because of a lack of *biblical evidence*? Are the data so obscure, imprecise, or minimal that any interpretation of what the biblical writers intended is a stab in the dark? Can the data be assembled in several defensible ways? Is there not enough information to overturn any of the differing interpretations with certainty? One or more of these may certainly be true.

We must attribute the variety of interpretations to the *interpreters*. What is going on? First, interpreters want, perhaps even unconsciously, to read the evidence in certain ways. Second, for various reasons they may be blinded to other alternatives. Or perhaps it is a bit of *both*. Earlier we discussed the influence of preunderstandings.

---

109. W. Hendriksen, *More Than Conquerors: An Interpretation of the Book of Revelation* (Grand Rapids: Baker, 1965), 230, his emphasis. Other commentaries written from an amillennial perspective include D. E. Johnson, *Triumph of the Lamb: A Commentary on Revelation* (Phillipsburg, NJ: Presbyterian & Reformed, 2001); S. J. Kistemaker, *New Testament Commentary: Exposition of the Book of Revelation* (Grand Rapids: Baker, 2001); and G. K. Beale, *The Book of Revelation*. In each case see the pages devoted to 20:4–5.

110. Hendriksen, *Conquerors*, 231, his emphasis.

111. Ibid., 225, his emphasis.

112. Ibid., 229.

113. Mounce, *Revelation*, 370.

114. Ibid., 369, his emphasis.

These factors explain many of the conclusions about debatable issues in biblical studies. Still, there may be a third explanation that merits consideration here.

Perhaps one or more parties to these kinds of discussions is creatively interpreting the texts and coming up with different *meanings*. This does not deny the role of preunderstandings, but rather may legitimize the view that several conclusions about meaning are not only possible but also valid in such interpretive stalemates. We are not advocating a position in which interpreters can simply read anything into any text, but at least in these two examples, variant interpretations have enjoyed long tenure in the history of the church's interpretation—virtually since the writing of the NT itself. Certainly the substance and the spirit of the biblical revelation must constrain any meaning discovered within its pages. Patterns of God's working in the past and the significance of Christ in redemption as seen on the Bible's pages (recall our earlier discussion of typology), for example, circumscribe allowable meaning.

But we stress again that meaning always results from an encounter or conversation between two partners, in this case the biblical text and the interpreter. The preunderstanding and presuppositions of the interpreter contribute enormously to the results of the interpretive process. They influence the results significantly. In our first example, both paedobaptists and immersionists claim a correct interpretation. In the second, premillennialists and amillennialists both profess legitimacy.[115] But can both be right without opening the Pandora's box of postmodernism's text as simply a mirror of the interpreter?

In some ways the process is circular, or as we prefer to call it, a hermeneutical spiral. Interpreting texts helps us formulate our understandings and systems. Out of those preunderstandings we continue to work at interpreting texts and in the process revise our preunderstandings and systems.[116] No interpretation occurs apart from preunderstandings—which inevitably influence the outcomes of the interpretive process. They enable us to see, and yet they color what we see. Accordingly, we construct an interpretation of what we find in the text. Reformed theologians tend to discover that the Bible teaches infant baptism and amillennialism. Given their prior commitments and their historical traditions, they construct that understanding of the relevant texts. Readers in other traditions bring their preunderstandings and

---

115. Most Christian individuals and groups sense that we cannot allow such squabbles to divide us—almost as if to say that we acknowledge both our own inadequacies in getting at truth and an unwillingness to pass judgment on others by saying they are wrong, at least about such issues. How striking that major interdenominational evangelical agencies, including those affiliated with the National Association of Evangelicals and those who identify with Lausanne, agree that both of the debates we have used as illustrations will not be included in the otherwise detailed list of crucial doctrinal affirmations. On the other hand, some denominations and entire wings of historic Christendom refuse the Lord's Supper to anyone not baptized under their aegis.

116. Of interest to some, in the early 1990s it became apparent that some dispensationalists were significantly revising their system. To chart some of the shifts compare, for example, early versions of the *Scofield Reference Bible* (New York: Oxford University Press, 1909); L. S. Chafer, *Systematic Theology* (Dallas: Dallas Seminary Press, 1948); C. Ryrie, *Dispensationalism Today* (Chicago: Moody, 1965); C. A. Blaising and D. L. Bock, *Progressive Dispensationalism* (Grand Rapids: Baker, 2000); and H. W. Bateman, *Three Central Issues in Contemporary Dispensationalism: A Comparison of Traditional and Progressive Views* (Grand Rapids: Kregel 1999).

commitments to the process of interpreting the Bible, so their interpretation of the texts generates alternate outcomes.

A given scholar or Bible student may argue that one of the positions in any debate provides a better or more likely understanding of the historical meaning of the relevant biblical texts and the intentions of their authors. We have argued that the historical meaning of the text should be our primary objective in interpretation. But as the writers of the NT did not always limit themselves to the literal historical sense of the OT texts they interpreted, we must be open to the creative use of biblical texts. Surely texts with a single illocution (author's purpose) can generate multiple perlocutions or effects even beyond the one the original author intended. Or with the renewed interest in *Wirkungsgeschichte*, we might speak about the "history of the effects" of a text ". . . as it is read in various situations over time and across places. These effects accumulate through language and affect subsequent readings—intentionally or unintentionally, for good or ill."[117]

What can we learn from how the writers of the NT approached their reading of the OT? Klyne Snodgrass provides wise words of counsel on this issue: "We have not completed the interpretive task until we have determined how a text does or does not correspond with Jesus' ministry or the ministry of the church. The writers of the New Testament seem to have looked for patterns of God's working in the Hebrew Scriptures, in the life of Jesus, and in their own experience. Our reading of the Scriptures should do no less."[118]

Christ and his church provided structures and trajectories for a new understanding of the events and texts in the OT Scriptures. They reread these texts and saw patterns (types) and significance not apparent to non-Christians. In their Christian experience they perceived similarities to what God did with his covenant people in previous generations as recorded in the OT. So they interpreted those OT texts in light of these new insights. More than merely re-applying the OT texts to new situations, they saw new *meaning* in those texts. The promised kingdom had arrived in the ministry of Jesus, and that made all the difference.

Both paedobaptists and believers-only immersionists have correctly perceived how God has worked with his people throughout history and how he is working among them today. They have taken the original author's meaning of the text (the author's locution and illocution) and affirmed different perlocutions beyond the author's. Perhaps many of the relevant eschatological texts may be explained as a-, pre-, or postmillennial, depending upon what trajectories a reader chooses to follow.

---

117. D. J. Treier, *Introducing Theological Interpretation of Scripture: Recovering a Christian Practice* (Grand Rapids: Baker Academic, 2008), 131. For examples of the use of this approach in NT studies see the essays in M. F. Bird and J. R. Dodson, eds. *Paul and the Second Century*, LNTS 412 (London: T&T Clark, 2011). They explore the "variety of ways that Paul was received, interpreted, and even used in the second century" (p. xi). The Wiley-Blackwell Commentary series, slowly emerging, deals with selections from the entire history of interpretation of both OT and NT books.

118. Snodgrass, "Use of the Old Testament," 427.

This may proceed along the lines of typology, as advocated above, but to admit that several options may claim validity suggests we have placed in the actions of *readers* the ability to generate perlocutions (outcomes, effects) that go beyond the texts' original intentions, as typically happens in many speech acts.

If we are open to this, then we can follow in the footsteps of the biblical writers' exegesis, though the process requires due care and important controls. As we become aware of God's working and purposes, we may read texts in new lights and craft our plausible interpretations of the biblical texts we are studying, even though such interpretations were not strictly intended by the biblical authors. *The fresh interpretation must be consistent with the text's historical meaning* (and with the Bible's total teaching— given our view of the Bible's unity), *but it need not be limited to the original perlocution.*

Using our previous example above, some argue that the likely historical meaning of the texts on baptism—based on the lexical meaning of *baptizō* (meaning "dip" or "immerse") and the historical Jewish precedents of immersing proselytes and performing ritual cleansing by immersion—points to the practice of immersion in water of a convert who has chosen to repent and believe. Taking this as their cue, in these faith communities baptism functions as the rite of initiation and to baptize means "to immerse one who has expressed faith in Christ."

But in certain other faith communities the nature of God's covenant with his people—entrance into which was symbolized by the circumcision of sons in ancient Israel—plays a major role in their understanding of their relationship with God. These sons were still expected to exercise faith in the God of Israel at some point. Taking the analogy of circumcision and the importance of the covenant as their cues, for paedobaptists baptism means "to sprinkle an infant who is joining the covenant community of believers." Since modes of baptism other than immersion (that is, pouring and sprinkling) can be traced back to early church practice, these communities feel justified in asserting that some of the pertinent NT texts could well be understood as using modes other than immersion.[119]

In such a scenario, what have we witnessed? Given their preunderstandings and community commitments, both groups embrace their own perlocution of specific texts. For one, when John baptized Jesus, he plunged him under the water (Matt 3:13–17 par.), and so the group baptizes by immersing believers in a pool of water, a lake, or a river. The other community envisions that Jesus and John were standing knee-deep in the Jordan, and John dipped a pot into the river and poured water on Jesus' head. So they baptize by pouring or sprinkling water (omitting here the issue of whether candidates ought to be believers or not). Is one interpretation of the incident correct and the other in error? (In the next chapters of this book we will discuss all the tactics of analysis that might help address this historical question.) Of course, a video of the event would show what really happened (or whether it happened in

---

119. One has only to consult iconography and other church art to see how frequently Jesus' baptism in the Jordan River is portrayed as John pouring water out of some vessel onto Jesus' head.

some way that differs from these two possibilities). If the hermeneutical spiral and our understanding of critical realism are to guide us, then the historical meaning of the text remains the central goal for all exegesis. The gospel writers intended some specific meaning, and historically, a specific event occurred in the Jordan on that occasion. These, we believe, must be the goals of interpretation. But historically, different faith communities have understood that meaning differently. They claim validity given the history of the church.

Let us sum up this discussion on baptism and the millennium in this way. We believe that the authors' or texts' locutions are clear, but their extended illocutions and perlocutions prevent us from excluding the alternative practices as heterodox or sub-biblical (i.e., none of the views promotes heresy).[120] However, some parties in the debates may have gone beyond the clear authorial/textual intent and created additional meanings typically consistent with their historical and doctrinal trajectories. Precisely for these reasons, interpreters will need to agree to disagree in love on such topics and continue to fellowship and minister together.

At the same time, we believe there are only two logical options concerning the historical meaning of texts, though epistemologically we may never be able to determine which applies in a given situation. Either (1) there *are* sufficient textual and historical data to support one view as more probable than another, in which case we ought to prefer that view even while allowing others to disagree without charging them with heresy or worse; or (2) there *are not* sufficient data to defend one view in which case we should admit that, refrain from passing judgment on others, and allow for the alternate options. Differing interpretations of texts (such as occurs in the examples of baptism and the millennium that we have used) show that whatever the historical meaning of texts, faith communities have become vested in their own illocutions and perlocutions. While we acknowledge that phenomenon, our goal as biblical interpreters ought to be to minimize departures from the historical meanings while recognizing that we will never be able to do so completely. The goal of interpretation ought to be to determine the meaning the author intended.

VALIDATING OUR INTERPRETATION

In light of this discussion, it seems appropriate to ask whether we can ever know if our understanding of a passage is correct, or whether one interpretation has a stronger

---

120. For example, Luke writes, "At that hour of the night the jailer took them and washed their wounds; then immediately he and all his household were baptized" (Acts 16:33). The locution, the jailer and his household were baptized, is clear enough. The purpose for the ritual was probably to solidify their commitment to Jesus and initiate them into the family of faith, the church. We can't know the mode, although there is a spot now by the stream near Philippi that commemorates the event. Did the entire group trek to the stream for immersion? Or did a pot of water in the jailer's household suffice? Did the "household" consist of adults, or were children included? Did they all profess a personal faith in Jesus (as the jailer evidently did) or was this household baptism a case of corporate solidarity: when the head of household makes the decision, they all comply? The NIV translation of v. 34 keeps it open: ". . . he was filled with joy because he had come to believe in God—he and his whole household."

claim to validity than a competing one. Can we ever be assured that we have perceived a text's meaning and an author's intention accurately? Or where some have proceeded to follow in the footsteps of the biblical writers in arriving at other perlocutions (outcomes, effects) of a text, how can we know whether they lie within the boundaries of acceptability? Indeed, are there such boundaries? We cannot ignore these questions. Even for Christian interpreters who affirm that the Bible is God's revelation, what value is an authoritative text if we cannot know that we have interpreted it correctly?

As noted above, in the absence of the author whom we might consult, we are unable to assert with absolute confidence that we have understood precisely an author's intention in a given text. Nor can we in any way determine how a text was originally understood. We have argued that neither of these points implies that texts have no fixed meaning. Authors do determine meaning when they write. So we set as our goal the historical meaning of the text that the author or editor intended. Inevitably, we must deal in approximations. Given all the evidence we survey and all the factors we assess, we must ask a range of questions: (1) Which interpretation is more likely to represent the text's original meaning? (2) Which interpretations fall within the reasonable limits of a text's meaning for various faith communities? (3) When might an interpretation suggest that a faith community has veered from orthodox moorings?[121] To verify an interpretation requires weighing two types of data: (1) evidence pertaining to the text itself and (2) evidence involving the interpreters.

E. D. Hirsch addresses the first concern.[122] He suggests four criteria to establish an interpretation as probable. The most probable reading:

- is possible according to the norms of the language in which it was written;
- must be able to account for each linguistic component in the text;
- must follow the conventions for its type of literature;
- must be coherent—it must make sense.[123]

In other words, the most probable interpretation of a text is the one that is consistent with the language and the literary genre in the ways that people typically use and

---

121. This perennial problem faces interpreters: When is it proper to break out of the interpretive strictures of one's (or another's) faith community? For example, Protestants insist that Luther was correct in rejecting Rome's interpretations of several texts' current meaning and their resulting practices. Recent rapprochements between Catholics and evangelicals on the one hand, and Catholics and Lutherans on the other, appear to vindicate the correct biblical understanding of justification by faith alone. Catholic theology in the pre-reformation period may well have lost its biblical moorings in the relevant texts' historical meanings. Or take Jesus' example of labeling some Pharisees' restrictive interpretations as old wineskins that were defective (Matt 9:17; par). We argue that both Luther and Jesus were justified on the basis of the historical meanings of the relevant texts. In these instances, the opposing "faith communities" had departed from the acceptable boundaries of Scripture's teachings. They needed to be challenged and their erroneous views jettisoned. On what constitutes heresy in the NT, see C. L. Blomberg, "The New Testament Definition of Heresy (or When Do Jesus and the Apostles Really Get Mad?)," *JETS* 45 (2002): 59–72.

122. Recall that his book is entitled *Validity in Interpretation*. He discusses "Verification" on pp. 235–44, which he views as a procedure for establishing that a given reading or interpretation is more probable than any competing alternatives.

123. Hirsch, *Validity*, 236.

understand them—at the time the texts were written.[124] We seek to understand a text in the normal and clear sense in which humans ordinarily communicate by that type of literature.[125] Indeed, Vanhoozer rightly affirms, "Scripture is composed of 'ordinary' language and 'ordinary' literature."[126]

Validating Our Interpretation
Weigh all the evidence pertaining to the **text's** most probably meaning and the **interpreter's** personal biases

Much of what is presented in this book expands and illustrates precisely those elements that enable interpreters to arrive at that "ordinary" meaning. We address the issues of lexical analysis, historical and cultural background, literary criticism, genre, Hebrew and Greek grammar, and the like. We consider, as well, the texts' contents, purposes, and force. An interpretation that seems at first to be coherent may turn out to be incorrect because we have misconstrued the evidence. But an incoherent or anachronistic interpretation is most certainly not correct. The more we know about the ancient world and the Bible itself, the more we increase the probability that we can select the correct interpretation from among the various viable alternatives. And if our interpretation is correct, others will be able to assess our process and agree with the conclusion.

Validating Our Interpretation	
As to personal biases, we must seek to account for these issues:	• Prejudice and parochialism
	• Sin and depravity
	• Social, sexual, racial, political, economic, and religious factors

The second locus of validation is the interpreters themselves. First, there are the inevitable factors of human prejudice and parochialism, sinfulness and depravity, and our propensity to exonerate ourselves and blame others. Second, we acknowledge all the social, sexual, racial, political, economic, and religious factors that color our thinking. These indicate that no individual interpreter is in a position to judge rightly

---

124. K. J. Vanhoozer, "Semantics," 80, suggests, "Genre thus enables the reader to interpret meaning and to recognize what kinds of truth claims are being made in and by a text." While recognizing the importance of the modern reader's situation, Vanhoozer's magisterial *Is There a Meaning in This Text?* vigorously defends the crucial role of the author for establishing the meaning of a text.

125. See B. Ramm's clarification of sense in *Protestant Biblical Interpretation*, 3rd ed. (Grand Rapids: Baker, 1970), 119–27.

126. Vanhoozer, "Semantics," 85. His explanation of how literature "works" to communicate is fresh and provocative. Vanhoozer suggests than any analysis of biblical literature must take into account four crucial factors: (1) what the text is about—facts or issues; (2) why the text was written—its function or intention; (3) the form in which the message is "incarnated"; and (4) the power or force of the text that results from the combination of the first three elements (91–92). So, "As Christian readers, we ought to be interested not only in the propositions themselves but in the manifold ways these propositions are presented for our consideration" (92).

all the time, even given the above criteria. But that naturally leads to several questions: Is there a way to take into account our prejudices and preunderstandings so they don't skew the evidence? Can we recognize them and take them into consideration in the interpretive process? Can we adopt some hermeneutic of distrust or suspicion that forces us to be aware of our biases and circumvent or account for them, at least as much as possible?

Validating Our Interpretation: Accounting for Personal Biases
Read and listen to others
Assess whether the interpretation works in real life and in the praxis of the church
Consult with other believers: both near and far
Agree to disagree when committed, faithful interpreters come to different conclusions

We think the answer to these questions is, "Yes, if we are willing." Clearly, one tactic is to consider carefully what others say about the text.[127] No reputable interpreter excludes the wisdom of interpreters at the present but also throughout the centuries. Those who want to understand Scripture must read widely and assess judiciously what others have learned about a text. Students must consider the findings of other reputable interpreters—scholars, preachers, teachers, and those who write various articles and other studies—all the while recognizing that not all of them share one's own presuppositions. While interpreters need to learn all they can from others, they must be skeptical of any author (or speaker) who exclaims, "No one has ever discovered this truth about this passage before." Equally, interpreters should be cautious even when others *agree* with their preferred conclusions—until the evidence leaves no alternative. To paraphrase a proverb, "As iron sharpens iron, so one interpreter sharpens another" (cf. Prov 27:17). Indeed, to ensure "sharpening," we recommend that interpreters make it a practice always to consult others with whom they may *disagree* in order to test the validity of their conclusions.[128]

But considering what others say goes beyond reading only the experts. Swartley suggests two other processes that can also help validate an interpretation. He proposes, first, that interpretations be validated in the "praxis of faith."[129] This criterion asks whether a proposed understanding of the text is workable in the lives of believers. Swartley suggests that interpreters apply this test "through personal and corporate

---

127. We assume here, of course, that we do not simply celebrate our ideological stances and selectively read sources that confirm our prejudices. We retain our objective to understand the historical, author-centered meaning of the texts.

128. An invaluable source for seeing how the earliest Christians interpreted biblical texts is the ongoing Ancient Christian Commentary on Scripture series, gen. ed. T. C. Oden (Downers Grove: InterVarsity, 1998–). A corresponding series, Reformation Commentary on Scripture, has now begun to appear from InterVarsity.

129. W. Swartley, *Slavery, Sabbath, War, and Women: Exploring the Hermeneutics of Cultural Analysis* (Scottdale, PA: Herald Press, 1983), 223. He builds here upon the "hermeneutic of consent" articulated by P. Stuhlmacher, *Historical Criticism and Theological Interpretation of Scripture: Toward a Hermeneutic of Consent* (Philadelphia: Fortress, 1977).

meditation upon Scripture, through the witness of *preaching*, and through *living* the love, righteousness, reconciliation, and peace of the gospel."[130] Of course, this criterion alone cannot guarantee the accuracy of a given interpretation, for the history of the church demonstrates that erroneous understandings can also be made to work, though usually they do not meet all Swartley's tests.[131] But, given the nature of Scripture as God's Word to his people, correct understandings must work, and so this test can help validate them.[132]

Second, Swartley suggests that interpreters need to secure the discernment of the believing community to check their conclusions. He says, "The community, whether the local congregation or a churchwide body, assesses an interpretation's coherence with the central tenets of its traditional beliefs, its relationship to wider Christian beliefs, or the way the interpretation accords or conflicts with how the community discerns the Spirit to be moving."[133]

In other words, maverick, novel, or parochial interpretations must be subjected to the critique of the corporate body of Christian believers. They must ring true in the church.[134] Here is where theological acceptability (the slippery term "orthodoxy") informs the process. Interpretive communities draw boundaries around what they will admit. Rather than dismissing or denying this phenomenon, interpreters can take advantage of it. They insist that interpretations be orthodox, that they conform to the community's preunderstanding. They will also understand why other communities adopt differing positions, "in spite of the clear evidence." Interpreters validate their understandings of the Bible in keeping with who they are.[135] It also means the church rejects heresy.[136] The goal must always be the best interpretation.

---

130. Swartley, *Slavery*, 215; his emphasis.

131. With striking citations Swartley, *Slavery*, shows how thoughtful Christians employed the Bible to defend both sides of the four issues in his book: slavery, Sabbath, war, and the role of women. In some sense both sides of each of these debates were made to work in the history of the church. And the biblical view of the role of women in ministry continues to be a topic of debate and division in churches (cf. J. R. Beck, ed., *Two Views of Women in Ministry*, rev. ed. [Grand Rapids: Zondervan, 2005]).

132. On a practical level, if an interpreter cannot convince his or her Sunday School class that an alleged meaning of the text is at least an option, then it probably is not—unless the teacher is, for example, a lone evangelical in a liberal church setting, or a "progressive evangelical" in an independent, fundamentalist church!

133. Swartley, *Slavery*, 215.

134. Tragically, the guild of professional biblical scholars often ignores this criterion. It stands accountable to no one, usually in the name of objectivity. Increasingly this is now seen for what it is—arrogant modernism and elitism—and it has renewed interest in so-called pre-critical exegesis with its firm moorings in church life. See the challenge to go beyond historical criticism in theological education by D. B. Martin, *Pedagogy of the Bible: An Analysis and Proposal* (Philadelphia: Westminster John Knox Press, 2008); cf. the illuminating essays in R. A. Muller and J. L. Thompson, *Biblical Interpretation in the Era of the Reformation* (Grand Rapids/Cambridge: Eerdmans, 1996), especially the editors' concluding chapter (335–45); and J. J. O'Keefe and R. R. Reno, *Sanctified Vision: An Introduction to Early Christian Interpretation of the Bible*.

135. See J. Schreiter, *Constructing Local Theologies* (Maryknoll: Orbis, 1985), for one study of the role of the community in adopting and shaping theology.

136. Some interpretations go beyond differing perlocutions (as in our discussions of baptism or the millennium above). So, for example, orthodox Christians reject as heretical the view of Jesus that Jehovah's Witnesses teach. Mainstream Christians refuse to admit interpretations of John 1:1 that suggest that Jesus was only "a god" (see the Jehovah's Witnesses' *New World Translation*). In other words, some creative interpretations lie outside acceptable bounds; heresy is always intolerable even if some faith community accepts it (Colossians and 1 John were written

Yet this does not mean any interpretation is valid if some faith community adopts it.[137] Even well-accepted interpretations need to be subjected to the bar of the world-wide Christian community, as well as the classic Christian creeds that the church has embraced over the centuries.[138] One way to examine the potentially distorting influence of our own preunderstandings is to listen to the insights of Christian brothers and sisters elsewhere, particularly those who differ from us. In the North American (or another so-called First World) context, this must include listening to the insights of believers who are poor, disenfranchised, persecuted, and oppressed. Likewise, Majority World interpreters can learn from their First World colleagues. Correspondingly, male and female interpreters, those of different races, those who live in inner cities and those in the suburbs, the urban and rural, the rich and poor, the white collar and blue collar, etc.—all need to listen to each other.

Christian interpreters can gain insights from Jewish interpreters[139] and Jewish interpreters can gain insights from Christian interpreters. In some instances unbelievers might shed crucial light on the *meaning* of biblical texts that believers might miss. But *significance* or *application* is another matter. Seeing the Bible's full significance for belief, life, and ministry belongs to believers.[140] We must seek to exert all efforts to minimize our preferences and prejudices to the extent they blur our vision and obstruct our ability to see the meaning in the Scriptures. The history of the interpretation of the Bible will dramatize to any reader just how easily even well-intentioned and pious believers can "squeeze the text into their own molds," to paraphrase translator J. B. Phillips's rendition of Romans 12:2.

Individuals as well as communities of faith embrace their interpretations of texts, but upon sane reflection and interaction with believers in other places, they might

---

to champion the truth in the face of proto-gnostic teachings). Orthodox Christians might admit the possibility of alternative explanations of baptism or eschatology, as we saw above, but they agree that a Jesus who is less than deity is unacceptable. In fact, they seek to persuade Jehovah's Witnesses of the truth about Jesus' deity using the very hermeneutical principles presented in this textbook. In our view, the Bible itself functions as the determiner of the select doctrines that *must* be defended. Sadly, even some Christian denominations now question positions that have been viewed as essential orthodoxy throughout the history of the church (e.g., Jesus' bodily resurrection or that salvation comes solely through faith in Jesus and by Jesus' substitutionary atonement).

137. Ironically, some Christian fundamentalists fall prey to this error in the guise of faithfully reading the biblical text. That is, like the academic guild they scorn, some exercise iron-clad community restraints on what texts can be allowed to mean. Their interpreters listen only to each other and ignore the scholarly consensus, even mainstream evangelicals, on many issues. They unwittingly adopt a reader-response reading of texts that allows the Bible to mean only what they want it to mean. A blatant example of this occurs in the essays in R. L. Thomas and F. D. Farnell, ed., *The Jesus Crisis: The Inroads of Historical Criticism into Evangelical Scholarship* (Grand Rapids: Kregel, 1998); or N. L. Geisler and F. D. Farnell, *The Jesus Quest: The Danger from Within* (Maitland, FL: Xulon, 2014). In our opinion these represent as close-minded a fideism as does the Jesus Seminar on the opposite end of the spectrum. The better way is to embrace all good research to seek the truth.

138. We readily think of the Apostles' Creed and the Nicene Creed that have found their foundational places in many Christian denominations over the centuries.

139. A prime example is the writings of Amy-Jill Levine. See, for example, her study of Jesus' parables: *Short Stories by Jesus: The Enigmatic Parables of a Controversial Rabbi* (New York: HarperOne, 2014).

140. We confess there are times when unbelievers point out the church's hypocrisy where it does not live up to its claims of what the Bible teaches. Of course, unbelievers can also recognize valid applications, but they aren't prepared to implement them.

decide that their views are prejudiced and ill-founded. They might even adjust their interpretations in keeping with the hermeneutical spiral. Honest and spiritually motivated reassessment of existing views can lead to their alteration if not abandonment. No individual or interpretive community is doomed to retain the errors of the past, no matter how passionately these views were embraced and defended. History also amply illustrates how individuals, communities, and even entire denominations have made such shifts. The topics in the title of Swartley's book, slavery, Sabbath, war, and women, are examples of such shifts in views.

What should interpreters do when they disagree? How should we proceed when well-intentioned Christians come to different interpretations about the meaning of a text or passage? First, we should set out precisely the nature of the difference—where, specifically, the views depart from each other. Second, we should itemize the elements in the process of study that led each interpreter to his or her view. That is, returning to our textual criteria above, did either interpreter misconstrue some evidence, engage in shoddy reasoning, or ignore some key data, or were there other flaws in the process that indicate one of the positions must be relinquished?

Third, as we evaluate the options we must determine which one relies more on the historical meaning of a text using all the principles of sound hermeneutics, in contrast to those relying on more creative extrapolations. The view that more readily emerges from the historical sense of the text has preference. The *most historically defensible interpretation has greatest authority*. That is, interpreters can have maximum confidence in their understanding of a text when they base that understanding on the most historically defensible arguments. If we are convinced that one interpretation precludes all alternatives (even if others adopt one or more of them), we may well reject the other views even if we do not believe the issue is central enough to make a big deal about it.

On the basis of these same hermeneutical criteria, however, we may conclude that Scripture does not provide enough data to exclude all competing views. At this point we acknowledge that differing interpretive communities produce their differing meanings (perlocutions) largely on the basis of their own systems. We accept this as long as the interpretations and the systems remain orthodox and biblical, that is, based on rigorous exegesis and consistent with the consensus of historical Christianity. What kind of alternatives might have a claim to such validity?

Matthew's use of Hosea 11:1 might not have reflected the prophet's intention (illocution and perlocution) for the original readers, but it fit Matthew's community typologically. That is, the Hosea text did express God's actions to protect his favored ones and to bring them out of Egypt, and Matthew saw that this divine intention was true for the Messiah and his parents, as it was for Jacob and his family.[141] Thus,

---

141. In other words, as we argued above, were the historical meaning of a text the only legitimate one, we might deem Matthew's use of Hos 11:1 in Matt 2:15 as illegitimate. Therefore, the Bible seems to admit of two interpretations

we consider a creative interpretation, such as Matthew's use of Hosea, as valid if it meets four criteria:

Four Criteria for Testing the Potential Validity of an Interpretation
it expresses or conforms to orthodox Christian theology[142]
it corresponds to typical paradigms of God's truth or activity as clearly revealed in historically interpreted sections of the Bible[143]
it works in the crucible of Christian experience—producing godliness and other valid Christian qualities, and advancing God's kingdom
it finds confirmation along the full spectrum (racial, sexual, socio-economical, etc.) of Christians within an orthodox faith-community

Where a creative interpretation meets these criteria, we believe it has a claim to validity—not as the historical meaning of the text, but as a valid perlocution, that is, an additional effect. Where one surfaces in isolated sectors of the church or derives from individual interpreters, it must remain seriously suspect and probably be rejected until it can meet the criteria.[144]

What do we mean by "a claim to validity?" An original reader of Hosea 11:1 would interpret the text in a valid way if he or she understood it to speak of God's care for the nation Israel.[145] That was its historically valid meaning. Matthew's interpretation in Matthew 2:15 was, by canonical definition, valid too, but not in the same historically defensible way. His was a creative "meaning" in light of God's protection of the Messiah, his son. We conclude that it met the four criteria above.

In conclusion, we suggest another such perlocution to illustrate our point, but only in rough fashion. No NT writer quotes Psalm 3. The psalmist writes:

---

of Hos 11:1: the text's original historical meaning and Matthew's creative understanding and application of the text to the Messiah.

142. In our view this excludes the Jehovah's Witnesses' interpretation of John 1:1 where they say the Word was "a god." It also excludes medieval Rome's inadequate understanding of justification by faith, against which the Reformers objected. And it excludes a postmodern interpretation of Jesus' resurrection as existential rather than physical.

143. An acceptable interpretation must fit with how God works with his people, how the church operates to accomplish God's mission in the world, and how Jesus exercises his Lordship.

144. Another example of an interpretation of selected texts that we put into the category of "must be rejected" is the so-called health and wealth message popular in some groups. We argue that it fails all four tests we set out above. It is not orthodox in its theology, for the Bible and Christian history readily attest that God does not prefer health and wealth for his faithful people. It does not depend upon typical patterns but elevates isolated miracles of healing to the status of the norm of how God treats his children if they simply had enough faith. It often does not promote godliness but promotes a seeking after God's gifts more than God himself. And, clearly, it lacks confirmation across the spectrum of orthodox Christians. Alas, its practitioners remain undaunted, and, we fear, dupe many. For an excellent presentation and critique see D. W. Jones and R. S. Woodbridge, *Health, Wealth and Happiness: Has the Prosperity Gospel Overshadowed the Gospel of Christ?* (Grand Rapids: Kregel, 2010).

145. D. Stuart, *Hosea–Jonah*, WBC 31 (Dallas: Word, 2002), 177, says, "Yahweh's words in Hos 11:1 are best understood in light of Exod 4:22–23, the commission from Yahweh to Moses at the very beginning of his journey to Egypt to lead the exodus: "Israel is my firstborn son . . . Let my son go. . . .""

[1]O Lord, how many are my foes!
   Many are rising against me;
[2]many are saying to me,
   "There is no help for you in God."   *Selah*
[3]But you, O Lord, are a shield around me,
   my glory, and the one who lifts up my head.
[4]I cry aloud to the Lord,
   and he answers me from his holy hill.   *Selah*
[5]I lie down and sleep;
   I wake again, for the Lord sustains me.
[6]I am not afraid of ten thousands of people
   who have set themselves against me all around.
[7]Rise up, O Lord!
   Deliver me, O my God!
For you strike all my enemies on the cheek;
   you break the teeth of the wicked.
[8]Deliverance belongs to the Lord;
   may your blessing be on your people! (NRSV)

When we read the psalm, we find images of enemies, divine protection, prayer, sleep, sustenance, deliverance, and blessing. All these themes find parallels in other psalms that the NT writers use typologically of Jesus. Likewise, when we read Paul's letters and Luke's accounts in Acts of Paul's exploits, we observe God's manifold presence with Paul in many of these same ways. Thus an exposition of Psalm 3 for Christians, after explicating the historical intent (illocution and perlocution) of the psalm, could point out parallels in the lives of Jesus and the Apostle Paul as part of the fuller meaning of the psalm. We might say the psalm describes God's presence with his son and with the great apostle on the basis of these typological parallels. At the same time, there are no unique dimensions to this psalm that necessarily point beyond what a faithful Jew then (or faithful Christian today) could experience, so, to repeat, any typological applications to Christ should not be our sole applications of the text. We have no warrant to proclaim that Psalm 3 is a messianic psalm.

Preachers, teachers, and authors of books on biblical hermeneutics are all too aware of their own limitations as well as their skeptics and detractors. Where interpreters have committed errors of methodology or judgment, they must be willing to learn and change their interpretations. As we have said already, and will continue to echo throughout this volume, determination and sincerity are no substitutes for accuracy. Nor are determination and sincerity rendered acceptable when mixed with large doses of piety! Biblical interpretation cannot remain at the what-it-means-to-me level. Correct interpretation of the author's intended meaning in the text must always be the primary goal.

Agree to Disagree: "That They May Be One"

But once we have eliminated erroneous interpretations, what do we do when sincere believers adopt different or, in some cases, conflicting explanations of the meaning of the same text? Here Christian grace must prevail. We must listen to each other and appreciate why others have arrived at alternative explanations.

Consider again the baptism example. One of the views may be more historically defensible. That is, it may better reflect the historical meaning of the relevant texts. But various competing meanings are certainly acceptable within their respective interpretive communities and within the shared interpretive community of historic orthodox Christianity. The communities could make their claims that their views meet the four criteria for valid interpretation.

That being the case, and given our mandate to maintain and promote the unity of the body of Christ, when alternative interpretations (or perlocutions) meet the requisite criteria, Christians should agree to avoid using such interpretations of texts to divide the body of Christ. Sadly, some Christian sects make an industry out of defining themselves by whom they are against and by separating from everyone else who does not agree with them. Beyond simple arrogance, as the history of interpretation shows, separating from other members of Christ's church over these kinds of disputed texts causes great damage to Christ's witness in the world. Amillennialist and premillennialist Christians need to embrace each other and their postmillennialist fellow-believers, as should those who baptize infants and those who baptize those old enough to profess faith in Christ. One may say,

> I don't agree with your conclusions, but in light of your membership in your community of faith, in light of how these biblical texts have been interpreted throughout history, and in light of the diligence and care with which you attempt to understand and live in conformity to the Bible's teachings, I accept your interpretation. You have responded to the Bible in a faithful manner.

Certainly this is preferable to accusing our brothers and sisters of shoddy work (at best) or dishonesty or heresy (at worst), and separating from them as if they were enemies.[146] We ought to exert every effort to keep in line with Jesus' words: "whoever is not against us is for us" (Mark 9:40),[147] not to mention his prayer "that they may be one as we are one—I in them and you in me—so that they may be brought to complete unity. Then the world will know that you sent me and have loved them even as you have loved me" (John 17:22–23). If the cliché "Blood is thicker than water" has any validity, then even more valid should be the truth that "Faith is thicker than

---

146. We recall how some conservative Christians shunned the ministry of the Rev. Dr. Billy Graham because he allowed "liberals" on the platform to share in his evangelistic meetings. They did this under the guise of "separation" from sin, their apparent perlocution of certain biblical texts that conflicted with Dr. Graham's perlocution.

147. Of course, these words are not universally true for the words preceding this quotation make clear the context of Jesus' statement: "'Do not stop him,' Jesus said. 'For no one who does a miracle in my name can in the next moment say anything bad about me, for whoever is not against us is for us'" (Mark 9:39–40).

either blood or water!" The landscape of Christian history exhibits tragic evidence of Christian brothers and sisters damaging each other and the witness of Christ in the world over their preferred interpretations of the Bible. Hear us well: our plea is not to condone heresy, error, or harmful teaching in the guise of Christian toleration. Nor do we excuse shoddy exegesis. Rather, we plead for humility and the grace to treat other Christians as siblings and fellow seekers for God's truth.[148] Where sincere Christians come to two different interpretations (after meeting the criteria outlined above), we should admit that both options are possible, agree to disagree, and support each other as brothers and sisters in the life of faith and in the spread of the Gospel message.[149]

---

148. This is a major plea in the article, W. W. Klein, "Exegetical Rigor with Hermeneutical Humility: The Calvinist-Arminian Debate and the New Testament," in *New Testament Greek and Exegesis. Essays in Honor of Gerald F. Hawthorne*, ed. A.M. Donaldson and T.B. Sailors (Grand Rapids: Eerdmans, 2003), 23–36.

149. D. L. Bock, *Purpose-Driven Theology: Getting Our Priorities Right in Evangelical Conversations* (Downers Grove: InterVarsity, 2002), echoes these sentiments.

Part III

UNDERSTANDING
LITERATURE

7

GENERAL RULES OF
HERMENEUTICS: PROSE

Since the fundamental goal of interpretation is to discover the meaning the authors intended in the biblical texts, our next task is to identify and explain the principles and procedures that are necessary to discern accurately that meaning. We need to understand how language communication works, particularly written communication. The writers of Scripture expressed their inspired messages in their own languages in various genres of literature. To know what they meant to convey to their readers, we have to understand the ways people ordinarily use language to communicate. In this chapter, we introduce the rules for interpreting texts written in prose.

It seems obvious that the biblical writers intended for their original audiences to understand what they wrote. They did not convey their thoughts through secret codes. Though they occasionally used a riddle, parable, or apocalyptic symbol that might puzzle and challenge the reader, they intended to communicate clearly even through these.

Confident that the biblical authors adequately communicated the message, we have the obligation to interpret it correctly by following the conventions of language communication. In normal conversation we quickly understand what we hear with hardly a conscious thought. Our mental computer, the mind, automatically processes the information we hear. Whenever we receive some message we do not automatically understand, we have to stop and think about it. We must deliberately analyze the unclear message according to the principles of language communication that normally function unconsciously. Intentional interpretation of the Bible requires that we raise the routine patterns of subconscious communication to the level of conscious analysis. This basic premise underlies most of the principles of biblical interpretation that we will present in this book. Each hermeneutical guideline arises from and addresses some essential facet of overcoming language barriers to understanding the Bible.

The process of arriving at an accurate interpretation of written texts like the Bible involves an understanding of five essential items: (1) literary context (that is, the context that surrounds a specific text within the larger document); (2) historical-cultural background; (3) word meanings; (4) grammatical relationships; and (5) literary genre (the global literary context of which the text is a part: letter, apocalyptic, narrative, parable, etc.). Along with these, in keeping with the discussion of speech act theory, we need to grasp what the author is doing in the communicative act (illocution): informing, exhorting, encouraging, telling a story, establishing basic beliefs or worldview, threatening, connecting, soliciting, celebrating, etc. In other words, what is the author's tactic in the communicative act; what is he or she seeking to accomplish? Finally, what does the author hope will be the effects or outcomes for the readers (perlocution)? Understanding how poetry works poses additional and unique challenges, and we take them up in the next chapter.

A Correct Interpretation is the Meaning Required by:
The constraints of the text's literary context
The facts of the historical and cultural background in which the text appears
The normal meanings of the words employed in such contexts
The rules of grammar and how the text is structured
The specific literary genre the author employs to convey the message

Writers normally communicate their thoughts through contextually coherent statements that use words according to their natural meanings in ways that are consistent with the historical-cultural setting in which the author and readers reside. Each word's impact on the total thought of the sentence arises from its grammatical relationship to the other words. Therefore, regardless of the literary genre (a topic we will address in subsequent chapters), to discover what a writer meant one must concentrate on four things: literary context, historical-cultural background, words, and grammar. An interpretation that does not account for each of these is unlikely to be the meaning the writer intended. We will consider each one.

LITERARY CONTEXT

Prose texts comprise a series of interconnected sentences, so our first question is, how should we interpret a sentence, or verse, or paragraph in the Bible? A basic principle of biblical hermeneutics is that *the intended meaning of any passage is the meaning that is consistent with the sense of the literary context in which it occurs.* Hence, the first test that all proposed interpretations must pass is this: Is it consistent with the literary context? In literature, the context of any specific passage is the material that comes immediately before and after it. The context of a sentence is its paragraph, the context of a paragraph is the series of paragraphs that precede and follow it, and the context of a chapter is the surrounding chapters. Ultimately, the whole book in which a passage appears is its controlling context. In interpreting a passage in the Bible, the Testament in which a passage occurs and finally the canon of all sixty-six books provide the largest literary contexts in which every passage must be understood.[1]

---

1. See further development of the role of literary context in C. L. Blomberg with J. F. Markley, *A Handbook of New Testament Exegesis* (Grand Rapids: Baker Academic, 2010), 93–116.

Definition of literary context	*Context* is the whole of which some piece is a part. In terms of literature, *context* is the larger whole within which a specific text or passage is located.

The Importance of the Literary Context

Most of us know from personal experience the frustration of having something we said taken out of context. Political leaders and public officials frequently complain that the news media have misrepresented their views. While acknowledging that the reporter's direct quote was technically accurate, a politician protests that her statement was misconstrued because the context was omitted. In a politician's case, the taken-out-of-context excuse may be a vain attempt to cover up an embarrassing slip of the tongue or to back off from an unpopular position. Nevertheless, the principle involved remains valid. Misunderstandings can certainly arise when people hear only part of what was said and base their understanding on it. The same is true of the Bible. Asserting that the Bible teaches "There is no God" by wrenching those words out of the context of Psalm 14:1 clearly violates the intention of the quotation—"Fools say in their hearts, '*There is no God.*' They are corrupt, they do abominable deeds; there is no one who does good" (NRSV; cf. Ps 53:1).

In fact, were the biblical writers alive they would undoubtedly protest loudly that they are taken out of context frequently when Christians quote individual Bible verses and apply them in violation of the biblical context. Misconstruing the context of a biblical passage has serious implications. We must interpret every passage consistent with its context for three main reasons.

The Three Principles of Literary Context
1. Context Establishes the Flow-of-Thought
2. Context Provides Accurate Meaning of Words
3. Context Delineates Correct Relationships among Units: Words, Sentences, Paragraphs

Context Establishes the Flow-of-Thought

First, taking a passage out of context violates the writer's flow-of-thought. A flow-of-thought describes the series of related ideas an author organizes to communicate a specific concept. Most meaningful communication involves some type of logical thought-flow in which one thought leads naturally to the next in keeping with the genre of literature employed.[2] A statement prepares for the one that comes after it. The words that follow grow out of what precedes and lead to what follow. People

---

2. Of course, the kind of literature will determine the nature of the progression of thoughts. Certainly, the lines of poetry are connected differently than those of carefully reasoned prose, a narrative, or a riddle.

communicate not with a series of randomly selected ideas but with related ideas linked together in a logical pattern. For example, consider this confusing account:

> I heard an interesting story on the news the other night. The quarterback faded back to pass. Carbon buildup was keeping the carburetor from functioning properly. The two-inch-thick steaks were burned on the outside but raw on the inside. Ten-feet-high snowdrifts blocked the road. The grass needed mowing. The elevator raced to the top of the one-hundred-story building in less than a minute. The audience booed the poor performance.

The words make sense. The sentences follow the rules of good English grammar. The sentences occur together as you might expect in a paragraph, but there is no evident logical continuity to link them; they are totally unrelated. Our point: people do not communicate ideas like this. Normally all sentences in a paragraph strive to develop a common theme. Each sentence carries or builds on the thought expressed in the previous sentence. Taken together, the sentences provide a continuity of subject matter that unifies the whole.

Since we normally communicate by a series of related statements, each sentence must be understood in light of the other ideas expressed in the larger context—in terms of the writer's train of thought. Any interpretation of a text that violates the principle of context is not likely to be the true one. It contradicts and ignores the normal way people use language to communicate.

Context Provides Accurate Meaning of Words

We will say more about words in a later section, but here, the second reason why an interpretation must agree with the general message of the context derives from the nature of words. Most words have more than one meaning.[3] The literary context presents the most reliable guide for determining its most likely meaning in that use. In normal circumstances our minds automatically adopt the one meaning that best fits the context at hand. Confusion or misunderstanding occurs when the literary context is vague or when several meanings fit equally well. Then a person must deliberately stop and think about the words' various possible meanings or analyze the context more carefully. Then he or she must select the one most likely intended by the writer.

For example, if we hear only the exclamation, "That was the largest trunk I ever saw!" we do not possess a literary context to know what kind of trunk is meant. Does it refer to a type of luggage, the main stem of a tree, the rear storage area of a car (in American English), or the long nose of an elephant? Suppose, however, we read the statement in a book about animals at the zoo. Then we automatically picture an elephant's trunk. Given an article about the virtues of various automobiles, the image of a car's storage compartment would emerge. Yet neither of these meanings will come

---

3. Actually, semanticists say that words cover a field of meaning, or they have a semantic range of meaning.

to mind if we are reading about the largest trunk seen in a California redwood forest. The literary context defines the precise meaning of the word.

Interpreters are not free to pick whichever meaning they choose for multiple-meaning words. We must understand each term according to the meaning that is consistent with the other ideas expressed in the literary context. This is how successful language communication works.

Context Delineates Correct Relationships among Units: Words, Sentences, Paragraphs

The third reason why correct interpretation must be consistent with context is that most biblical books (or parts, such as Psalms) were written and preserved as complete documents intended to be read as a unit. Biblical writers composed or edited individual sentences and paragraphs as parts of larger documents. The sentences and paragraphs comprise individual units of larger literary works, and interpreters must understand them according to their relationship to the whole argument of the book.

A book like Proverbs may appear to be an exception in that it groups many different sayings that originated independently. Apart from a few sections, we may see little connection between the proverbs that occur in sequence. But even here, while the immediate literary context before and after a given proverb may give little help in understanding its meaning (obviously Proverbs 31 is one exception), the context of the whole book becomes particularly important because the writer scattered many proverbs on the same topic throughout the book.[4] Thus, the combined teaching of the book on each theme becomes the key to understanding the individual wisdom saying.

Ironically, the usually helpful chapter and verse divisions in our Bibles constitute one of the hurdles to the process of Bible interpretation. We must remember that these divisions were not in the original documents. Some verse divisions were in place in the early centuries AD, though they fluctuated widely in various places. By the ninth and tenth centuries AD, verse divisions began to appear in the Hebrew Bible of the Jewish Masoretes. F. F. Bruce says, "The standard division of the Old Testament into verses which has come down to our own day and is found in most translations as well as in the Hebrew original was fixed by the Masoretic family of Ben Asher about AD 900."[5] He adds, "The division into chapters, on the other hand, is much later, and was first carried through by Cardinal Hugo de Sancto Caro in 1244."[6] Others attribute the division into chapters to Stephen Langton, professor at the University of Paris and later Archbishop of Canterbury, in AD 1228. Three centuries later, in 1560, Robert Estienne (Stephanus), a Parisian printer and publisher, added the current verse numbering in his fourth edition of the Greek NT (which also contained two

---

4. Recent studies, however, have suggested that more design may underlie the collections in Proverbs than was previously thought. For details, see the introductory section on structure in B. K. Waltke, *Proverbs*, 2 vols., NICOT (Grand Rapids: Eerdmans, 2004–5), 1:9–29.

5. F. F. Bruce, *The Books and the Parchments* (London: Pickering & Inglis, 1950), 118.

6. Bruce, *Books*, 118.

Latin versions).[7] His edition of the Latin Vulgate of 1555 was the first Bible of the modern era to use both the chapter and verse divisions. The Geneva Bible (1560) was the first English version to incorporate both the modern chapter and verse divisions. Although these divisions were meant to be helpful, even a casual reading of the Bible reveals that verse and chapter divisions are frequently poorly placed; new verses often begin in the middle of sentences,[8] and chapter changes occasionally interrupt the thought in a paragraph.[9]

The chapter and verse references help us identify and locate passages quickly, but unfortunately, they also contribute to the widespread practice of elevating individual verses to the status of independent units of thought. Readers are tempted to read each *verse* like a complete expression of truth, like randomly picking one of the restaurant reviews from a website. Then, it has no connection to what precedes or follows—each is a "quote for the day" or prooftext—and considered in isolation from its biblical context. This poses a grave danger, for in isolation a single verse might be as misleading as "There is no God." It is very crucial to know who made this promise in the Gospels: "I will give you all this domain and its glory, for it has been handed over to me, and I give it to whomever I wish" (Luke 4:6; NASB). Context matters! There is simply no justification for routinely treating individual verses as independent thought units that contain autonomous expressions of truth. Readers must understand biblical statements as integral parts of the larger units in which they occur. Detached from their contexts, individual verses may take on meanings never intended by their writers. To qualify as the text's intended meaning, an interpretation must be compatible with the flow of thought and the specific intention of the immediate context and the larger book context.

Principles of Interpretation Relating to Literary Context

Three important principles guide our practice of interpretation.

1. *Each statement must be understood according to its natural meaning in the literary context in which it occurs.* This is probably the single most important principle of hermeneutics since literary context is at the heart of all language communication. It affects the reader's understanding of both the meaning of individual

---

7. Cf. B. M. Metzger, *The Text of the New Testament,* 3rd ed. (New York; Oxford: Oxford University Press, 1992), 103–4.

8. Metzger cites the no-doubt apocryphal story that "Stephanus marked the verse divisions while journeying 'on horseback,' and that some of the infelicitous divisions arose from the jogging of the horse that bumped his pen into the wrong places" (*Text,* 104).

9. For example, in light of the Servant Song that spans Isa 52:13–53:12, dividing a new chapter at 53:1 is completely unwarranted. If a new chapter is required, it should occur before 52:13 or after 53:12. Second Corinthians 2:1 falls in the middle of a paragraph explaining why Paul has not already made a return trip to Corinth. In modern versions that supply paragraphs, one notes how often the paragraphs do not correspond with either chapter or verse divisions. See how the beginnings of new chapters in Jeremiah come in the middle of paragraphs (e.g., 41, 42, 43). Cf. the NIV paragraph divisions at 1 Cor 11:2 (not 1); 12:31b (not 13:1); 2 Cor 7:2 (not 1); and Phil 4:2 (not 1) for other examples.

words and the meaning of the complete statement. This principle requires an interpreter to focus not only on the words of a passage but also to consider carefully the contribution of each passage to the literary work as a whole. It requires taking account of the speech act dimensions of the context—what the author is seeking to accomplish in this context. It seeks to preserve the integrity of the line of thought being developed throughout the text.

2. The corollary principle is that *a text without a context may be a pretext.* Although an extension of the previous guideline, this principle puts it negatively and focuses on a serious abuse of Scripture. Here we define a "pretext" as an alleged interpretation that only appears to be valid; in reality it obscures the real state of affairs. This principle serves as a warning against the popular tendency to engage in invalid prooftexting: quoting biblical passages to prove a doctrine or standard for Christian living without regard for the literary context. How ridiculous to employ Jesus' words, "What you are about to do, do quickly" (John 13:27), as a pretext for speeding in an automobile.[10]

   Unfortunately, other prooftexting does not appear so ridiculous but is equally invalid. Such prooftexts are merely pretexts when the interpretation fails the principle of literary context. There is nothing wrong with quoting verses to prove a point provided we understand them according to their contextual meaning (under the correct circumstances prooftexting can be valid). Before listing any verse in support of a position, we should first check the literary context to insure that the passage is about the same subject and really does have the meaning that proves the point. Otherwise the interpretation is only a pretext, using a passage that seems on the surface to prove some point when in actuality it does not. Such a pretext carries no divine authority for it subverts what the author intended to convey through the text.

3. The third principle (really a caution) is that *the smaller the passage being studied, the greater the chance of error.* Short texts usually contain less information about the general theme of the larger passage. They provide fewer data about their meaning. Indeed, a phrase or a single sentence by itself could well convey several different meanings. Paul's words in Romans 8:28 provide a ready example: "And we know that in all things God works for the good of those who love him . . . ." If someone were to assess the verse apart from its context in Romans 8 (see Paul's reference to present sufferings in v. 18, weakness in v. 26, and the litany of adversities in vv. 35–39), he or she might incorrectly use it to convince a parent whose child has just died that the death was a good thing, since Paul promises good results from all things or circumstances. The surrounding context, however, provides crucial details

---

10. More common but egregious examples of taking verses out of context are Matt 7:1 ("Do not judge"); Matt 18:20 ("Where two or three gather in my name, there I am with them"); and Jer 29:11 ("I know the plans of have for you . . . plans to prosper you"). They must be read in context to understand their authors' intentions.

about the subject that enable the reader to reject such an erroneous meaning. For Paul, all things are not good, but God will accomplish his salvific purposes (which are good) for his people in all things—even though and when they suffer greatly. Larger passages provide more facts about the topic and thus give the interpreter a clearer perspective for understanding each statement within it.[11]

Simply stated, large passages have a built-in literary context; short passages do not. Normally speaking, the paragraph constitutes the basic unit of thought in prose.[12] Focusing on the meaning of a *paragraph* rather than solely a verse, phrase, or single word (which unfortunately is the practice of some Bible teachers) increases the odds of discovering the accurate meaning of all of its parts. Only by concentrating on the theme of a paragraph and noting how each sentence contributes to the development of that theme can one discern the real meaning and significance of the individual sentences.

In summary, the task of interpretation requires readers to discern the author's literary strategy in producing the text that we seek to understand. We can summarize that task in the following table.

Interpreting a Passage Consistent with the Author's Literary Strategy
• What is or are the main themes in the passage? What is the passage about? What is its content?
• What is the intention of the *message* or *argument* of the passage? How does it fit logically with the preceding and following passages to advance the argument of the entire book?
• How is the passage designed to produce that effect?

Circles of a Literary Context Study

To interpret a passage in its literary context one must examine different domains or circles of context:

- the immediate context
- the book context
- the author's corpus of writings context (where available)
- the pertinent Testament context
- the Bible context

---

11. For a wise correction based on a better understanding of the context, see how the New International Version (1978) rendition of Phil 4:13 ("I can do everything through him who gives me strength") was revised in the NIV (2011): "I can do all this through him who gives me strength."

12. Of course, for poetry we must adopt other ways to distinguish complete thought units. Those might be, for example, couplets, stanzas, or the entire poem. For other genres we would think of entire oracles, epics, parables, or ballads, to name a few.

While these contextual domains interact, they need to proceed in this order of priority. Each provides significant insight into the intended meaning of the passage, but a decreasing amount of insight emerges as one moves from immediate context to the context of the entire Bible.

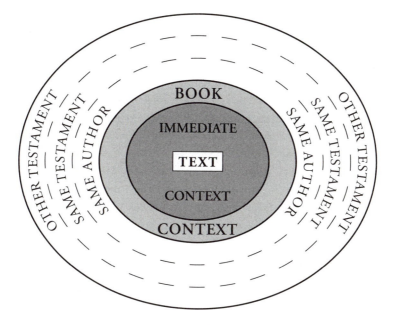

Circles of Context

Immediate Context

The immediate context exerts the most important control over the meaning of a specific text or passage. We define the immediate context as the material presented immediately before and after the passage under study. In some instances this will be the preceding and succeeding sentences or the paragraph in which the text occurs. In others it may be a subsection in the author's presentation, or possibly a major division of a book—whether or not it was identified as a chapter. The tactic of outlining a book helps the interpreter to discern its natural divisions and to establish the specific immediate context in which a passage occurs. A sequence of ideas links the ideas. The proximity of the materials to each other and the correlation of the materials with each other make the immediate context a more critical indicator of meaning than either the whole book, the Testament, or the whole Bible.

The investigation of the immediate context focuses on two things: *theme* and *structure.* To discover the *theme* or central idea of the entire section of the book where the passage under study occurs, the student must first determine the theme of the preceding section, the passage itself, and the following passage. Of course, this assumes that the passage for study does not occur at the beginning or end of a unit of thought. If it does, one can evaluate only what follows or precedes, respectively. Then the student must analyze these subjects to find the common theme that holds them together. This theme of the immediate context regulates the meaning of the individual words, phrases, clauses, and sentences within the specific passage under study.

Like any skill, learning how to recognize the main theme of a passage takes practice. The following steps illustrate the process. First, carefully read the passage to determine the dominant subject. Do this for the passage that precedes and the one that follows. That is, find the topic to which everything in that paragraph or section refers. Second, write a topic sentence or summary in your own words. A good topic sentence is both precise and concise. It is not enough to say that the theme of a passage is "love." Obviously, one passage does not tell everything there is to know about love. A precise topic sentence contains a brief summary of what the passage says about love. For example: "Love is more than a feeling, because it must be demonstrated by actions." In the interest of precision and brevity, the theme should be restricted to one sentence. Repeat this process for each part of the immediate context and then for the combined book context.

The second focus of the immediate context is *structure*. Passages are linked not only by a common theme but also by structure. A thorough interpretation investigates not only what a text says but also how the writer organizes the material. First, determine how the specific passage for study grows out of the preceding section and prepares for the following one. How does each paragraph contribute to the development of thought in the immediate context? These insights enable the interpreter to explain the relationship between the passage being studied and the surrounding paragraphs or sections. Just as one must understand each sentence in a passage consistent with the general theme of the immediate context, so also one must interpret that sentence according to the paragraph's structural relationship with the adjoining material.

Types of Structural Relationships
• Chronological Sequence
• Thematic Sequence
• Logical Sequence
• Abrupt Transition
• Psychological Sequence

To arrange passages in sequential order writers employ many different structural relationships. In some sections paragraphs are arranged *chronologically*. Historical narratives typically proceed in this way, reporting events in the order in which they occurred. For example, note the beginning words in these paragraphs: "After they came down from . . . "; "Then Samuel took a flask . . ."; "Then you will go on . . . "; "After that you will go to . . . " (1 Sam 9:25; 10:1, 3, 5). Writers normally indicate such successions of events by temporal adverbs and conjunctions that indicate continuation:

now, then, later, while, and afterwards. The OT books of Joshua, Kings and Chronicles narrate chronologically, whereas the patriarchal narratives (Gen 12–36) present loosely related episodes in a broad chronological structure.

Other texts group materials together in a context based on *thematic continuity.* For example, the Gospel writers sometimes clustered events or teachings that were similar in nature even though they did not happen at the same time. The writer of Matthew probably gathered the parables in chapter thirteen to exemplify Jesus' teaching ministry.[13] The editor of Leviticus assembles diverse cultic contents in thematic sections, while Judges sounds its main theme (Judg 2:6–23), illustrates it in the exploits of the judges (Judg 3–16), and offers other episodes to suggest that Israel needs a king (17–21).

Logical order, another organizing principle, accounts for most of the sequential arrangement in the OT prophets, NT Epistles, and Bible speeches. The logical arrangement of material takes many forms. Some of the more important structural patterns authors use in developing a logical line of thought are:

1. Introduction   preparing for what follows
2. Explanation   clarifying the meaning
3. Illustration   citing an example or instance
4. Causation   showing cause and effect
5. Instrumentation   demonstrating the means to an end
6. Interrogation   giving a question and answer
7. Evidence   proving the stated point
8. Particularization   stating the details
9. Generalization   drawing a general principle from details
10. Interchange   alternating sequence
11. Crucial   a point of special import or significance
12. Climax   indicating progression from lesser to greater
13. Continuation   extending an idea
14. Continuity   restating the same idea
15. Repetition   restating the same words for emphasis
16. Comparison   showing similarity to something else
17. Contrast   showing difference from something else
18. Summarization   reviewing main points briefly
19. Conclusion   drawing inferences or bringing to an end

Often conjunctions at the beginning of a paragraph indicate these logical connections. The writer's use of a specific logical connective between paragraphs simplifies

---

13. The parallel reports of some of these parables in the other Gospels show that they were not all taught during one phase of Jesus' ministry or necessarily in the order in which Matthew arranged them. The Sermon on the Mount in Matt 5–7 may indicate a similar thematic arrangement. Note how Luke 15:1–2 introduces the theme for the parables that follow in vv. 3–32: "Now the tax collectors and sinners were all gathering around to hear Jesus. But the Pharisees and the teachers of the law muttered, 'This man welcomes sinners and eats with them.'"

the identification of the structural relationship, but, unfortunately, writers do not always use these logical connectives. In addition, only the most woodenly literal translations render all of the connectives because of the bad English style that can result. But the author's flow of thought can be lost in the process. In those cases the interpreter has to infer the type of logical relationship from the nature of the contents (by checking other versions or the original languages, if possible). By determining how each paragraph functions in the logical flow of thought in the context, the interpreter gains perspective for appreciating the true significance of the passage.

Literary *genre* provides another clue to the organizational pattern of biblical materials. Biblical writers employed a wide variety of distinct types of literature that existed in biblical times. In recent years, scholars have become increasingly aware of how much each different literary genre influences the meaning of the message it communicates. We present the features of these specific literary formats and their significance for meaning in the subsequent chapters on literary genres.

In some instances, the relationship between adjoining paragraphs may not be readily apparent. The student may discern no reason for the sequence of ideas—whether chronological, thematic, logical, or relative to the literary genre. Some apparent "jumps" in thought between passages may owe to a phenomenon called *psychological transfer.* This occurs when one subject triggers a psychological switch in the author's thinking to a different subject. The connection between the thoughts is more psychological than logical. The relationship was clear to the writer but may not be immediately apparent to the reader. Before accusing the writer of a mental lapse in writing, the student should attempt to discover the writer's frame of reference and the likely connection.

An example of this may occur at 2 Corinthians 6:13. Following the paragraph of vv. 11–13, which ends with Paul's appeal that the readers "open wide your hearts also," he appears to interject a seemingly unrelated section, 6:14–7:1, that begins, "Do not be yoked together with unbelievers." Then at 7:2 he resumes where he left off at 6:13, repeating, "Make room for us in your hearts." The connection between sections may be psychological in nature. If you are to make room for me, Paul tells the Corinthians, you cannot "make room" for unrighteous associations with unbelievers. Paul believes their current unholy associations will subvert a genuine reunion between himself and the Corinthians.[14]

Finally, we may encounter an *abrupt transition* from one paragraph to another. When a writer introduces a new topic, a break in the thought flow will occur. Sometimes the writer prepares the reader for the transition;[15] at other times there is

---

14. On this see C. K. Barrett, *The Second Epistle to the Corinthians,* BNTC (London: Black, 1973; Peabody, MA: Hendrickson, 1993), 193–95; cf. 11–12. For an extensive discussion of the issues surrounding 6:14–7:1 in the context of 2 Corinthians, see V. P. Furnish, *II Corinthians,* AB 32a (Garden City, NY: Doubleday, 1984), 359–83. On how 6:14 connects to Paul's larger context see M. J. Harris, *The Second Epistle to the Corinthians: A Commentary on the Greek Text,* NIGTC (Grand Rapids: Eerdmans; Milton Keynes: Paternoster, 2005), 497–502. For an alternative appraisal that proposes a chiastic structure see C. L. Blomberg, "The Structure of 2 Corinthians 1–7," *CTR* 4 (1989): 3–20.

15. Such an announced transition occurs at 1 Cor 7:1 where Paul moves specifically to answer questions his

no warning.[16] In interpreting a passage in a manner that is consistent with its context, interpreters must recognize the possibility of an abrupt transition either before or after the text. This protects the interpreter from creating forced contextual insights that the writer never intended.

Literary Context of the Entire Book

The book in which the Bible passage occurs is the second most important literary context in determining the author's intended meaning. To understand a passage correctly means to understand it in terms of the entire book in which it occurs.[17] Read shorter books carefully and repeatedly. Try to read through longer books in one sitting, more than once if possible. Work out a tentative outline of the book's structure and then make use of reference works that summarize or outline their message.[18] Three kinds of information about the entire book are significant for proper understanding of any given passage within that book:

1. The book's purpose(s) or controlling theme(s)
2. The basic outline of the book
3. Parallel passages within the book that deal with the same subject

It is helpful, first, to understand the *book's purpose(s) or controlling theme(s)*. Knowing why the writer composed the book sets limits on the meaning for its individual parts. We assume that individual statements or sections contribute in some way to the writer's goal. Sometimes the writer makes it easier for interpreters by explicitly stating the purpose for the book. For example, at the beginning of his Gospel, Luke precisely states his aim:

> Seeing that many others have undertaken to draw up accounts of the events that
> have reached their fulfilment among us, as these were handed down to us by those
> who from the outset were eyewitnesses and ministers of the word, I in my turn,
> after carefully going over the whole story from the beginning, have decided to

---

readers had raised. In the OT editors may announce to readers their intentions as sections develop, e.g., Gen 22:1; and 1 Sam 23:1, 8.

16. To return to 1 Corinthians for examples, a transition does not always occur between the various topics Paul sequentially considers (see e.g., 5:1; 6:1; and 6:12). To come back to the OT, after listing David's final words (1 Sam 23:1–7) and David's mighty men (23:8–39), the writer resumes the narrative with a simple, "Again the anger of the LORD . . ." (24:1). At first glance the Judah-Tamar episode (Gen 38) seems to disrupt the narrative, but recently scholars have recognized, among other things, its anticipation of Judah's crucial, leading role later (e.g., 43:3, 8; 44:14, 16, 18; 46:28).

17. Long before compilers of our canon divided them into the books familiar to us, Joshua to 2 Kings probably comprised a major Israelite historical work, the so-called Deuteronomic History (DtH), with Deuteronomy as its introduction. Thus, for purposes of interpretation, both the individual canonical books and Deut–2 Kings as a whole constitute a "book" circle of context. Also, students may interpret Deut–2 Kings as a whole as the work of a single author (commonly called "the Deuteronomic Historian" or "DtH") or the individual books as his works just as one would handle, say, Luke-Acts or the Pauline Epistles.

18. The chief helps on this score come from books called introductions. See the bibliography for suggestions for both testaments.

write an ordered account for you, Theophilus, so that your Excellency may learn how well founded the teaching is that you have received. (Luke 1:1–4, NJB).

The author of Acts lived in a day when multiple written records and oral reports were creating confusion about the details of Jesus' life. Thus, he purposed to confirm for Theophilus the credibility of the information about Jesus' life by providing a carefully investigated and orderly record. By way of contrast, the author of the Fourth Gospel waited until near the end of his book to indicate that his purpose was to promote eternal life by generating and sustaining belief in Jesus (John 20:30–31). Other books like Romans and 1 Corinthians have multiple purpose statements at various places in the book.

For OT books, explicit purpose statements are more difficult to discover (if we can discover them at all). The first two verses of Joshua probably encapsulate the subject matter of the book: the crossing of the Jordan River and the conquest of ". . . the land I am about to give to them—to the Israelites" (Josh 1:1–2). But if we inquire *why* the writer composed the book, that is more difficult to answer. Perhaps we discover the answer in the book's conclusion with all its warnings and reminders to be faithful in serving the Lord—to follow the example of Joshua and Israel during his life. That is, the writer's purpose could well be to encourage a later generation of Israelites to "Be very strong; be careful to obey all that is written in the Book of the Law of Moses, without turning aside to the right or to the left" (23:6). They needed to affirm along with Joshua's contemporaries, "We will serve the LORD our God and obey him" (24:24).

When books lack formal purpose statements, interpreters must infer them from the contents. They must observe what the author or editor accomplishes in the book, and then deduce the purpose from that information. While this approach may prove reasonably accurate in finding the writer's goal, it remains conjectural. Rather than speculate about questionable, inferred purposes, we suggest that in such cases interpreters identify the dominant themes of the books. The end product will not differ much on either approach. Interpreters can discover the controlling themes by noting those topics the author emphasizes in the book. For example, in a short book like Obadiah, the dominant theme of God's judgment against Edom and his vindication and blessing of the house of Jacob is readily discernible. For the longer book of Galatians, Paul seeks to champion the principle of justification by faith in Christ alone, against the teachings of some "Judaizers" who apparently insisted that the converting Gentiles must follow the Jewish law. Then the student can discern how each passage contributes to one or more of those subjects.

The *basic plan* of the book is another important part of the literary context of the book. The contribution an individual passage makes to the total message of a book depends primarily on its location. For longer books this involves two main elements: the *general* train of thought of the entire book and the *specific* train of thought of the section of the book where the passage occurs. By discovering the theme of each of the main divisions of the book, the interpreter can determine whether there is any significance in their order. Once an interpreter understands how the theme of each major division fits into the book's overall flow of thought, the focus narrows to a closer look at the specific section containing the passage for study. To summarize, an interpretation is more likely to be the correct one when it explains the passage in a way that is consistent with the theme of the section in which the passage occurs. Then the likely interpretation shows how that section contributes to the overall progress of the book itself.

The final item considered in studying the literary context of the whole book concerns *parallel passages* in the book that deal with the same subject as the specific passage under study. When a writer refers to a subject more than once in a book, one or more of the passages may clarify vague aspects in another one. The procedure for this study is straightforward. Skim or quickly read the book to locate other passages that deal with the same subject and then study them to discover what they contribute to the understanding of the passage under study.[19]

So, for example, to understand "the Day of the Lord" in Joel 2:31 (part of the section that Peter quotes on the day of Pentecost, Acts 2:20), the student must investigate what else Joel says about the Day of the Lord in his prophecy (e.g., 1:15; 2:1, 11; 3:14) or other places where that theme emerges even when the specific vocabulary does not occur.[20] Likewise, for insight into what James means by "saving faith" in the section that starts with 2:14, the student must gain insight from other references to faith in the letter (1:3, 5–8; 2:1; 5:15).

But a word of caution is in order. Students must always make sure that the passages are truly parallel before allowing them to inform each other. Sometimes passages use identical words but with different meanings for those words. This would be only an *apparent* parallel. Even when both passages are true parallels, one cannot simply read the ideas of one passage into the other without proper defense. We must always observe the goal of interpretation—the author's intention as reflected in the text at hand. We become liable to serious errors when we interpret a passage in light of another while ignoring the immediate context of each passage. As a precaution, always interpret each parallel passage according to its own immediate context and the entire book context before comparing the passages. Once we know the contextually valid meaning for each parallel passage, we can compare the passages to see if any of them sheds light on specific details in the passage under study.

So for both the examples cited above—from Joel and James—the interpreter

---

19. Often a concordance helps in this task, though students must be careful not to trust merely the co-occurrence of common words to locate parallel passages or theological matches. This would be a grave error, as we will discover later in the discussion of words. See the bibliography for suggestions on concordances.

20. Israel's prophets shared a common tradition of themes, language, and an understanding of history. So, after studying one prophet's wording or development of a theme, one may also check its occurrence in other prophets, especially ones who ministered in the same century.

would need to be sure that the authors were using the concepts in truly parallel ways before simply imposing the other texts' features onto the passages under study. Do Joel's other references to the "Day of the Lord" have historical (for Joel's time) or eschatological (at some time in the future) significance? We need to be sure of the answer before simply forcing their meanings on his use at 2:31. Does James use "faith" uniformly in his letter? Students must investigate each passage individually to determine whether the definition of faith in 2:14–26 is the sense that James employs elsewhere. And certainly, James uses "faith" in a sense that differs from Paul's typical use, so students need to avoid trying to understand James by simply importing Paul.[21]

Context of the Entire Bible

This final element is more controversial and more difficult to control. As we argued earlier, the Bible possesses an overall unity despite its diversity of human authors. Scripture's divine inspiration gives continuity of thought to books written over a 1,500-year period. As Vanhoozer succinctly puts it, ". . . taken together, the various books of the Bible constitute the Word of God."[22] Furthermore, the Bible's human authors participated in the same ongoing Judeo-Christian religious tradition. On a larger scale, the sweep of the Bible's overall story displays God's grand narrative of redemption to seek and save lost humanity.[23] Some later writers knew books written previously and drew heavily upon them. In 2 Peter 3:15–16 the author refers to letters written by Paul, even implying their status on a par with "other Scriptures" (i.e., the OT). The OT book of Chronicles probably drew upon Samuel and Kings to some extent, supplementing them with other materials available to the Chronicler. Psalms 105–106 appear to depend upon sections from the Pentateuch.[24] The most popular theories of Gospel composition suggest that one or more depended upon others. Luke's prologue (1:1–4) cited above implies that very fact. Most likely the author of 2 Peter borrowed from Jude.

Because of this unity, the entire Bible provides a literary context for all passages in it. But here comes the controversy and the difficulty. How do we allow individual authors and editors their unique perspectives—the Bible's diversity—and yet affirm the Bible's unity? We do not expect that all biblical writers on an issue will have the same perspective or present their views in the same ways. They will have different

---

21. On Paul's view of faith, D. Lührmann ("Faith: New Testament," trans. F. W. Hughes, *ABD*, ed. D. N. Freedman, 6 vols. [New York: Doubleday, 1992], 2:753), says, "For Paul *pistis*, along with *pisteuein* in the aorist, means conversion to the proclamation of God, who raised Jesus from the dead, a new God for people who were previously pagans, the same God for Jews."

22. K. J. Vanhoozer, *Is There a Meaning in This Text?: The Bible, the Reader, and the Morality of Literary Knowledge* (Grand Rapids: Zondervan, 2009), 349.

23. The best treatment of this is C. J. H. Wright, *The Mission of God: Unlocking the Bible's Grand Narrative* (Downers Grove: InterVarsity, 2008).

24. This assumption has opened up a fruitful area of inquiry in biblical studies called intertextuality, the study of the various ways later biblical writers employ earlier biblical texts (e.g., see what Joel 3:10 does with Isa 2:4 / Mic 4:3). Cf. our treatment of Inner-Biblical Allusion in ch. 2.

slants and distinct emphases depending upon their purposes for writing. But due to the Holy Spirit's inspiration of the entire Bible, we posit that the correct meaning of every portion of Scripture will be *consistent* with the rest of the teaching of the Bible on that subject. One passage will not contradict the clear teaching of the rest of the Bible on that subject.[25]

Three groupings of biblical books should be consulted in interpreting a passage according to the context of the entire Bible. First, we study parallels in other books attributed to the *same author*. These writings come from the same mind energized by the Holy Spirit, thus promising the highest level of linguistic and conceptual continuity. There is the highest degree of probability that the same person talking about the same subject in a similar way means the same thing. Furthermore, each biblical writer has a personal understanding of an aspect of God's truth and a fairly consistent pattern for articulating it. Thus, to comprehend Paul's understanding of faith in Romans 3:22, the interpreter is wiser to consult passages in Galatians (e.g. 2:16; 3:8, 11, 24) than passages in James. This applies not merely to the words used but even more to the ideas they represent.[26]

Parallels in books by different writers in the *same testament* rank second in significance. Writers from the same testament have the most in common with others writing from or about the same phase of God's redemptive program. OT writers used the Hebrew (or Aramaic) language and reflected a Semitic culture in a primarily Israelite setting. They shared a focus on the nation of Israel as God's special people, on exclusive loyalty to Yahweh as an expression of that relationship, and on the prophetic promises of future blessings. That gave them, diverse as they were, a unique camaraderie.[27] NT writers, by contrast, employed the Greek language and resided in the predominantly Hellenistic culture of the Roman Empire. They lived in the age of messianic fulfillment and proclaimed the good news of God's grace made available through the death and resurrection of Jesus.[28] Antecedent writings in the same testament likely known by a later author take precedence over later writings not yet known to that author.

---

25. A challenge constantly facing the interpreter who shares this presupposition of unity, however, is to interpret each text on its own terms, especially when distinct texts seem to conflict with each other. We must avoid glossing over these places in our attempts to preserve *what we view* as biblical consistency. We must let the texts speak for themselves even if the results are not as harmonious as we would prefer.

26. Students must employ the same guidelines and cautions about using parallel passages we noted above. Although reading the same author, we are now in different books. We must assure ourselves that the passages are truly parallel before simply imposing meaning from one place to another. In addition, an author's ideas may develop over the years.

27. On the harmony of OT theology see B. K. Waltke, *An Old Testament Theology: An Exegetical, Canonical, and Thematic Approach* (Grand Rapids: Zondervan, 2007).

28. On the unity of NT theology see esp. G. E. Ladd, *A Theology of the New Testament*, rev. by D. A. Hagner (Grand Rapids: Eerdmans, 1993); I. H. Marshall, *New Testament Theology: Many Witnesses, One Gospel* (Downers Grove: InterVarsity, 2004); G. K. Beale, *A New Testament Biblical Theology: The Unfolding of the Old Testament in the New* (Grand Rapids: Baker, 2011); T. R. Schreiner, *New Testament Theology: Magnifying God in Christ* (Grand Rapids: Baker Academic, 2008); and F. S. Thielman, *Theology of the New Testament: A Canonical and Synthetic Approach*, 2nd ed. (Grand Rapids: Zondervan, 2005).

Since the writing of the OT covers more than a thousand years, interpersonal relationships were rare among its writers. So the help that other writers or books can provide for interpreting individual passages might appear to be considerably diminished from what we can discover in the NT. Yet a common religious legacy, shared convictions, and a reverence for the Mosaic tradition and the Davidic monarchy on the one hand, and the writings of earlier prophets on the other, provided some unity and sense of continuity. The unique nature of the OT requires us to nuance this point slightly. According to Jeremiah 18:18, the OT incorporates three main schools of thought or "traditions" whose influences we see evident both in single books and across several books. They are: "instruction" (or "law") as the province of priests (e.g., the Pentateuch), the "word" as the province of the prophets (e.g., the prophetic books), and "wisdom" as the province of the wise teachers (e.g., Job, Proverbs, Ecclesiastes). Further, the OT evidences other historical and theological traditions—e.g., creation, the ancestral promise, the exodus, the Sinai events, God as warrior, etc.—that also reappear in many OT (and NT) books. All these traditions comprise part of the *same testament* circle of context when interpreting the OT.

Studying OT parallels requires paying close attention to the time when the writers lived and when the OT books became complete. For example, since the ministries of Hosea, Amos, Isaiah, and Micah overlapped (eighth century BC), the interpreter can learn about the religious apostasy of Israel and Judah at the time by comparing parallel passages. They provide helpful commentaries on each other at certain points.

The writers of the NT experienced a different situation. Joining as members of the church that included believers from many nationalities, they composed the NT books over a brief period of about fifty years. The authors, a select group of apostles and their close associates, often had contact with each other. Of course, this does not mean they always agreed with each other, as the conflict between Peter and Paul shows (Gal 2:11–14). However, even allowing for diverse expressions of Christianity within the NT, interpreters can expect a high degree of continuity in the way these early Christians understood their faith.

The final type of parallel passages consists of those from the *other testament*. OT parallels for NT studies prove highly valuable as background for understanding. Because most NT writers were Jews who knew the OT well, they borrowed theological language and categories from it. After all, the Bible of the early church was the OT, most often its Greek translation, the Septuagint (LXX). Just as the English language shows the influence of the Bible,[29] so the NT language reflects Greek Septuagintal expressions.[30] In fact, some of the arguments in the book of Hebrews depend upon

---

29. For example, even completely secular people refer to their "thorn in the flesh," "going the extra mile," or being a "good Samaritan."

30. On the influence of the LXX on the language of the NT, see K. H. Jobes and M. Silva, *Invitation to the Septuagint*, 2nd ed. (Grand Rapids: Baker; 2015), 200–27. In various places readers will encounter the term "Semitisms" to describe possible Semitic influences or elements in the NT. Semitisms may come from the Hebrew OT, the LXX, or the infusion of Aramaic and possibly Hebrew terms or constructions, say, from everyday life in

the formulation of the OT in the LXX version (e.g., 1:6 cf. Deut 32:43; 10:5–7 cf. Ps 40:6–8). Furthermore, the NT writers' entire thought-world—especially the religious concepts in which they formulated their belief system: monotheism, covenant, election, people of God, atonement, and sin, to name a few—derived from OT theological convictions.

Obviously, in the other direction the NT did not influence the writing of the OT, but NT parallels to OT texts help readers find the total teaching of the Bible on a subject and may draw out further implications.[31] This demonstrates the relevance of the OT teaching as it unfolds, for example, in Jesus' ministry where he fulfills OT texts.[32] In Luke 4:18–21 Jesus explicitly identifies his ministry as the fulfillment of Isaiah 61:1–2. In Matthew 11:4–5, however, when Jesus says, "Go back and report to John what you hear and see: The blind receive sight, the lame walk, those who have leprosy are cleansed, the deaf hear, the dead are raised, and the good news is proclaimed to the poor," his answer more implicitly expands Isaiah 35:4–6 and 61:1.

At the same time, interpreters must exercise extreme caution to avoid an undue Christianizing of the OT. Parallel NT passages should not be used to make OT passages teach NT theology. The early church had the tendency—one continued by Protestants after the Reformation—to read NT theological concepts back into OT passages. We should avoid this error; our first task is always to understand each text on its own terms—as its writer intended and its readers would have understood it.[33] Only after we understand the meaning of the OT text can we address the canonical issue of how the two testaments complement each other to fill out the entire biblical teaching.

We heard of an incident that shows how tempting and prevalent this error is among Christians. After a visiting speaker preached a sermon on Jeremiah's call in which he stressed insights for responding to God's leading today, a parishioner bluntly admonished him at the door, "Young man [a clear sign of trouble], preach Christ!" The confident, "But I did, sir!" did not reassure the indignant parishioner who felt that every OT passage had to serve as a springboard for a Christ-centered gospel message. Unfortunately, he, and many others like him, failed to realize that God's message in the OT for the church today must grow out of the intended meaning of the text itself. Its *significance* for our lives may differ greatly from its significance

---

first-century Palestine. For a full, though older, treatment of the Semitisms in the NT see J. H. Moulton and W. F. Howard, *A Grammar of New Testament Greek: Accidence and Word-Formation*, 2 vols. (Edinburgh: T. & T. Clark, 1963), 2:412–85.

31. As noted above, when one interprets Joel 2:28–32, it helps to read Acts 2:14–36 to see what Peter does with the Joel text.

32. Like the modern colorizing of old black and white movies, fulfillment in this messianic age adds depth and new perspectives to OT passages. Christians cannot read OT messianic passages apart from their understanding of the texts' fuller revelation in Christ.

33. A point recently reiterated by J. Goldingay, *Do We Need the New Testament?: Letting the Old Testament Speak for Itself* (Downers Grove: InterVarsity Press, 2015).

to its original readers, but *not its essential meaning.* Many people fail to discover the great truths about God's character and his relationship with his people in the OT because of their well-intentioned but misguided belief that every part of the Bible must convey NT realities. Primarily, the OT must stand on its own terms. We must interpret its passages in keeping with the intention of its texts; that constitutes the essential goal of OT interpretation.[34]

Interpreting passages in light of the context of the entire Bible has a limited scope. Check parallels to see if they contribute to the understanding of the meaning of the passage. The careful use of parallels gives the Bible student an ability to appreciate the contribution that the text under consideration makes to the total teaching of the entire Bible on a given theme.

HISTORICAL-CULTURAL BACKGROUND

Historical–Cultural Background	
History	• Record of events that occurred in the past: *Sitz im Leben*
Culture	• Way of Life: • Customs • Value System • Economy • *Sitz im Glauben*

Biblical passages not only express a writer's train of thought but also reflect a way of life—one that in most ways differs radically from that of present-day readers. The literature and events recorded in the Bible originated thousands of years ago. Beyond reflecting ancient languages, cultures, and lifestyles, the biblical writers wrote their messages for people different from us. Consequently, every time we study a Scripture text, we must be aware of these cross-cultural and epoch-spanning dimensions. Each passage was God's Word to other people before it became God's Word to us. In a sense, the Bible always comes to us secondhand, through others who lived at different times and in different places. This is the basis of an important principle of hermeneutics: *The correct interpretation of a biblical passage will be consistent with the historical-cultural background of the passage.* There are three reasons why this principle is important: perspective, mindset, and contextualization.

---

34. W. C. Kaiser, Jr., *Toward An Exegetical Theology* (Grand Rapids: Baker, 1981), rightly expresses a principle that he calls the "analogy of [antecedent] Scripture"—that one may deduce the original *meaning* of a passage only on the basis of what it says or on the basis of texts that *preceded* it in time, even if later scripture may expand or extend its *significance* (136–37). For a responsible way to see how Christ is and isn't prefigured in each biblical book, see M. Williams, *How to Read the Bible through the Jesus Lens* (Grand Rapids: Zondervan, 2013).

The Significance of the Historical-Cultural Background[35]
The Issue of Perspective

First, the circumstances in which communication occurs substantially control, if not determine, meaning. We need to comprehend the *perspective* of the original communicators—author and readers—to understand the correct meaning. Because both the writer and the recipients shared the same cultural background and information and lived at the same time in history, they rarely make explicit their perspective. This tendency is true even today. If someone shows us a personal letter, even if the letter comes from a mutual friend, some things may need explanation because they refer to an experience known only by the writer and recipient. Lacking this information—this correct perspective on the situation—another reader has difficulty making sense out of these references.[36]

For example, such "over-the-shoulder" reading describes the situation of present-day readers of the NT Epistles. Apostles or others sent these letters to specific people living in certain places concerning particular circumstances in their lives in the first-century AD. In most instances the writer and recipients had shared familiar experiences; they spoke the same Greek language and possessed common information about each other and their world. To interpret correctly these books today, the reader needs to understand as much as possible about the details of this historical and cultural background.

The same applies equally to the majority of biblical books that are not letters. Many of the psalms of ancient Israel reflected experiences of worshipers living in a monarchy in a world replete with kingdoms and empires. The writer of Judges characterizes the days prior to the monarchy in a closing statement: "In those days Israel had no king; everyone did as they saw fit" (Judg 21:25). They were "wild and woolly" times to be sure—unquestionably and literally worlds apart from the modern era. Likewise, the apocalyptic prophecies grow out of a worldview and use literary techniques largely foreign to our experience.[37]

Because our life setting differs so radically from virtually every biblical situation, it is no wonder that at first glance many Bible statements make a different impact on us than that intended by the original writer.[38] Present-day Bible interpreters need to put themselves in the sandals of the writer and initial recipients; that is, we must read the texts from the perspective of people who lived long ago. Biblical writers did not have our situations in mind.

---

35. See the chapter on this also in C. L. Blomberg with J. F. Markley, *A Handbook*, pp. 63–92.

36. Alternatively, read a political cartoon in a newspaper or magazine from another city or, better, a different country. Unless one comprehends the issues or persons in view, the cartoon remains a mystery. J. K. Brown, *Scripture as Communication* (Grand Rapids: Baker Academic, 2007), parallels a number of the thoughts of this chapter and is well worth consulting.

37. Of course, we provide specific help in understanding these and other various genres in following sections.

38. Speaking in terms of speech act theory, we can miss their energy and intended effects even if we grasp the content.

The Issue of Mindset

The second reason why we must interpret a passage consistent with its historical-cultural setting grows out of the possibly subtle factor of *mindset*. A mindset describes a mental attitude or inclination. Speech acts not only communicate content; they do it in certain ways, for specific purposes, and with certain intended *emotional impact*. Each culture exhibits a system of values and a way of looking at the world that regulates this affective or feeling dimension of discourse. The effect of a statement may vary from culture to culture, depending on each culture's standards of right and wrong or scale of values.[39] For example, when Jesus called Herod Antipas a fox (Luke 13:32), his hearers understood a "fox" to represent a certain value.[40] To call someone a fox today would have different meanings or values, depending upon the culture (or subculture) involved.[41] If a reader simply imposed a current value for "fox," the original intent would be obscured or even lost. In some cultures, fox might have no connotative value, and the meaning would simply be opaque.[42] Biblical revelation was communicated within cultures. It could not be otherwise, for all human language is culturally conditioned.

To become aware of the mindset of people in biblical times, we need to study the historical-cultural background of their world, because an interpretation must make sense for the people "back then," even if it remains foreign to us. Eating horsemeat seems foreign to many North Americans, but it is common in places in Europe. Guinea pig meat is eaten in Peru. We have to resist the temptation to sanitize the Bible so it conforms to our values and mindset.[43] Once we understand what a passage *meant*, we can apply that meaning in light of today's cultural values so that it can have the appropriate impact and emotional effect on us.

The Matter of Contextualization

The third reason why we must interpret a passage consistent with its historical-cultural background goes to the very heart of the interpretive task. While the first two reasons, perspective and mindset, stress the importance of knowing the historical-cultural background for discovering the meaning intended for the original recipients, our third point focuses on expressing that message accurately in today's world. The word *contextualization*

---

39. We here limit the discussion to values at this point. Obviously, a culture's mindset may include other dimensions. Individuals also have unique mindsets that we can learn something about if we know them well enough or read enough of their writing. Otherwise, this is somewhat elusive.

40. According to I. H. Marshall, *The Gospel of Luke*, NIGTC (Exeter: Paternoster; Grand Rapids: Eerdmans, 1978), 571, in rabbinic literature a fox typified low cunning, but it was also an insignificant creature in comparison to a lion. Most commentaries on Luke point to either cunning or insignificance as the point of the "fox" reference.

41. Connotations today might include clever, crafty, sly, and sexually attractive.

42. Bible translators need to discover such things and make appropriate adjustments.

43. A comparison between English word usage in the seventeenth and twenty-first centuries illustrates the point about mindsets. The KJV translators did not hesitate to use the word "piss" (e.g., 2 Kgs 18:27; Isa 36:12), while most modern versions consider this term beyond the bounds of acceptable contemporary diction and use "urine." Words have affective values that grow out of a culture's mindset. Mention the words "evolution," "abortion," or "homosexual" in certain conservative Christian subcultures and their mindset will emerge.

helps capture this perspective.[44] Contextualizing biblical truth requires interpretive bifocals. First, we need a lens to look *back* into the background of the biblical world to learn the intended meaning. Then, we need another lens to see the foreground before us to determine how to best express—contextualize—that sense for today's world. We stress this dimension given our conviction that biblical interpretation must never remain an exercise merely about the ancient world. The Bible is God's Word to us.

The astute interpreter straddles two worlds: the ancient biblical world and modern society.[45] The Bible was fashioned within specific ancient cultures; in contrast, we are the products of our modern and increasingly postmodern cultures. These two horizons comprise the alternating foci of the perceptive interpreter.[46] Effective exegesis not only perceives what the message meant originally but also determines how best to express and apply that meaning to one's contemporaries. The process of contextualization expresses anew the ideas presented in a biblical passage in the language of today so that they convey the same impact to modern hearers.

The interpreter has to know both the biblical and the modern worlds in order to bridge their differences. Because our present culture has molded how we understand things (our preunderstanding), we risk fashioning our perception of the biblical message in terms of our way of life without first understanding it according to its own historical-cultural setting. If we succumb, the message we hear from Scripture may not correspond to what the text in fact means; we may simply have recast it according to *our* meanings. Our task must lead to application, but not before we have understood clearly the text's meaning.

Principles for Historical-Cultural Interpretation
The Original Historical-Cultural Background
Several principles guide the interpreter in taking proper account of the historical-cultural backgrounds of the biblical worlds. First, *we must understand each passage consistently with its historical and cultural background.* For any interpretation to qualify as the intended meaning of a text, it must be the most likely meaning given the circumstances of the original writing and reading of the passage. Any suggested explanation of a passage that would have been inconsistent with, inconceivable in, or anachronistic in the historical or cultural setting of the author and recipients cannot

---

44. Arising in missiological circles, the term *contextualization* describes the process of packaging biblical truth in ways that are relevant to the diversity of current cultures. Missiologists, in general, welcome the insights of anthropology and sociology in their quest to impact cultures with the gospel.

45. From the preacher's perspective, this concept is foundational. See J. R. W. Stott, *Between Two Worlds: The Art of Preaching in the Twentieth Century* (Grand Rapids: Eerdmans, 1978); R. C. Chisholm, *From Exegesis to Exposition: A Practical Guide to Using Biblical Hebrew* (Grand Rapids: Baker, 1999); S. D. Mathewson, *The Art of Preaching Old Testament Narrative* (Grand Rapids: Baker, 2002); S. Greidanus, *The Modern Preacher and the Ancient Text* (Grand Rapids: Eerdmans, 1988); and H. W. Robinson, *Biblical Preaching: The Development and Delivery of Expository Messages,* 3rd ed. (Grand Rapids: Baker, 2014). For a specific example using African historical, cultural, and traditional imagery in order to communicate the gospel more effectively see J. W. Z. Kurewa, *Preaching & Culture Identity: Proclaiming the Gospel in Africa* (Nashville: Abingdon, 2000).

46. A. C. Thiselton, *The Two Horizons: New Testament Hermeneutics and Philosophical Description* (Grand Rapids: Eerdmans, 1980), emphasizes this dimension.

be valid. One must ask, given the original circumstances, what interpretation fits most naturally in this culture at this time? This principle means that an interpreter must understand the historical and cultural setting as accurately as possible and must interpret the biblical message consistently with that picture.

Fortunately, archaeological findings, historical research, and sociological and cultural studies have provided a vast reservoir of information for this task.[47] So impressive is the material available that Russell Spittler boasted, "Advances in lexicography and archaeology have put us in a place to know more about the ancient world than it knew about itself."[48]

While there is much truth in this statement, we must take care not to overestimate our knowledge of the biblical world. We now have access to such highly developed academic disciplines as anthropology, sociology, linguistics, history, and psychology that shed light on the routine experiences of daily existence in the ancient world. Despite of all the detailed insights gained by these studies, our knowledge of some of the details of the interrelated components of each Bible story remains extremely limited. Consequently, we must always make modest and realistic claims for any of our historical-cultural reconstructions—and the interpretations that depend on them.

Understanding each passage according to its background involves determining how the biblical setting was like ours and how it differed from ours. There will always be some similarity between our lives and theirs. These common elements provide reference points that help present-day audiences understand the meaning. Differences, on the other hand, must be studied carefully to provide the interpreter with information that can remove ambiguities in the text.

The letter to the church at Laodicea (Rev 3:14–22) provides an intriguing example. In the Lord's description of this church, he condemns it for being "neither cold nor hot." He goes on to state, "I wish you were either one or the other!" (v. 15). He finds no reason to commend the people of this church; they are completely useless—neither like hot water (as in a comfortable bath) nor like cold water (as in a refreshing drink). Apart from insight growing out of archaeological studies, interpreters might seriously misconstrue the point. That is, we must interpret "hot" and "cold" in light of the historical context of Laodicea, which was located close to both hot springs (by Hierapolis) and a cold stream (by Colossae). Now both hot and cold water are desirable; both are useful for distinct purposes. But lukewarm water is not refreshing to drink nor is it comfortable as a bath. Jesus is *not* saying that active opposition to him (an incorrect interpretation of "cold") is better than being a lukewarm Christian.[49]

---

47. The bibliography provides a list of helpful resources.

48. R. Spittler, "Scripture and the Theological Enterprise: View from a Big Canoe," in *The Use of the Bible in Theology / Evangelical Options*, ed. R. K. Johnston (Atlanta: John Knox, 1985), 75.

49. A succinct analysis of the evidence occurs in C. J. Hemer, *The Letters to the Seven Churches of Asia in Their Local Setting*, JSNTSup 11 (Sheffield, UK: JSOT, 1986), 186–91. Also see several recent commentaries on Revelation.

The Original Impact

The second principle moves from the factual information about the biblical setting to the emotional dimension: *We must determine the impact that the biblical message would have had in its original setting.* This principle involves the factor of mindset. Interpreters should seek to know, where possible, how the original recipients would have reacted to what was written (related to the author's desired perlocution: outcome or effect). Clearly, we are not always in a position to know this with any degree of certainty, nevertheless, one window into to this is to seek, through our historical research, to discover if a text would conflict or agree with the readers' value systems and to identify whether their feelings about it would resemble or differ from ours.

The book of Amos can illustrate this point. As "the LORD roars from Zion" (1:2), he pronounces judgment against Israel's (the Northern Kingdom's) neighbors (1:3–2:5). One can sense the people of Israel gloating in self-satisfaction and complacency as the list of judgments against the neighbors proceeds. No doubt those other nations deserved God's judgment, they thought. But then the lion roars in Amos's pronouncement of God's final judgment—against Israel! Israel will not escape, and the book proceeds to detail God's case against her.

Equally, modern readers can sense the emotional impact of Amos 4:1 where the prophet calls the self-indulgent women of Israel "cows of Bashan."[50] Modern readers who live in urban areas must strain to feel the urgency of a prophecy that pronounces plagues and blights upon fields and gardens in that agrarian culture, which was totally dependent upon what the people could produce in their fields (5:16–17). Sometimes we get a hint when we experience or read about drought conditions in Africa or California. But can we empathize with the original readers what it would be like to hear God's assessment of our worship: "I hate, I despise your religious festivals; your assemblies are a stench to me" (5:21)? Imagine how you would feel if the Lord pronounced these words on your church's meetings.

The parable of the *good* Samaritan provides another example. We have "Good Samaritan" hospitals and "Good Samaritan" laws. The phrase strikes us positively. To Jesus' Jewish listeners, however, Samaritans were anything but good; they were despised. Yet Jesus makes a despised enemy the hero of his story about true neighborliness—in contrast to the religious leaders whom the Jewish listeners respected. Can we feel the discomfort, even the rage, of the audience?

This emotive angle of interpretation fosters a fuller appreciation of a passage's intended meaning. It supplies insight into the effect of the message as well as a comprehension of its concepts or ideas. It gives us a feel for the ideas and an understanding of them.

---

50. Bashan was famous for its fine cattle (cf. Ezek 39:18; Ps 22:12).

The Correct Expression

The third principle relates to the contextualization aspect of historical-cultural interpretation: *We must express in our language conclusions from our study in ways that most closely correspond to those ideas in the biblical culture.* The challenge for the interpreter is to find adequate contemporary idioms to articulate the intention of the passage so that people today will sense the meaning and impact that the original readers sensed. Certainly the NIV does a commendable job of capturing the thought of Romans 12:2: "Do not conform any longer to the pattern of this world." But readers have continued to appreciate J. B. Phillips's rendition: "Don't let the world around you squeeze you into its own mould . . . ."[51] These words express Paul's concept in a memorable idiom that a contemporary English speaker can easily understand. Eugene Peterson puts it this way: "Don't become so well-adjusted to your culture that you fit into it without even thinking."[52] Again, the paraphrase expresses the meaning more clearly for us. This principle naturally applies to the work of translators, but no less to interpreters who desire to understand and communicate the Bible's meaning to contemporary audiences or readers.

Those wishing to interface the biblical message with our contemporary culture face significant challenges and risks. One perennial danger concerns syncretism. Generally, "The term *syncretism* is used by anthropologists and historians to refer to the blending of religious beliefs."[53] But it comes to have a pejorative sense as Arnold goes on to say, "For Christians throughout history, the notion of syncretism has had largely negative connotations and is sometimes associated with heresy. This is due to the fact that assimilation is often perceived as a departure from the purity of the original."[54] So, for Christians syncretism denotes the merger of biblical and nonbiblical beliefs to form a hybrid, and thus unacceptable, religion. Most Christians view syncretism negatively, for the mixing of Christian beliefs with tenets of other belief systems results in an amalgam that is non-Christian.

In 1 Kings 13–14, we find that Jeroboam committed this error. He served as the first monarch of the Northern Kingdom of Israel after the ten tribes seceded from the Southern Kingdom of Judah. Fearing that his subjects' religious pilgrimages to Jerusalem to offer sacrifices would cause their loyalty to revert to King Rehoboam of Judah, Jeroboam established an alternate religion with worship centers within his own country. While preserving many of the features of the Mosaic beliefs and worship, his new religion, which focused worship on two golden calves, also embraced idolatrous elements from neighboring religions. While the new hybrid may have been more attractive to the king and his subjects, the Lord forcefully condemned this syncretistic

---

51. J. B. Phillips, *The New Testament in Modern English,* 2nd ed. (London and Glasgow: Bles and Collins, 1960), 332. Or see the equally paraphrastic approach of the NLT: "Don't copy the behavior and customs of this world."

52. E. H. Peterson, *The Message: The Bible in Contemporary Language* (Colorado Springs: NavPress, 2002), 328.

53. C. E. Arnold, "Syncretism," in *Dictionary of the Later New Testament and Its Developments,* ed. R. P. Martin and P. H. Davids (Downers Grove: InterVarsity Press, 1997), 1146.

54. Arnold, "Syncretism," 1146.

religion by sending a prophet to denounce it on the very day the king attempted to offer sacrifices at the new shrine at Bethel.

Like Jeroboam of old, many today blend their understanding of the Christian faith with the best elements of the religions in their contemporary culture. Describing this approach, William Larkin says, "Though the Bible still has a role to play, it is now placed in dialectical relationship with the contemporary context."[55] Evangelicals reject this approach to contextualization because it contradicts the gospel's claim to be the one and only saving faith.[56] We believe that proper contextualization uses concepts from the contemporary culture to communicate the *Bible's own message* effectively in a way that avoids diluting or subverting it—that is, syncretism.[57] When seeking to convey the Bible's message, interpreters must take care not to choose words or other features from the culture that would involve the assimilation of elements incompatible with the Christian faith. Indeed, they may need to apply the biblical message in a cogent way to correct the thought-forms of a culture.

Proper contextualization requires that the interpreter be sensitive to both the biblical and the current cultures. The ultimate goal of good interpretation is a clear, accurate, and relevant explanation of the text's intended meaning in language that is meaningful to one's contemporaries. Bridging the gap between the biblical culture and modern culture requires knowing the language, values, and significant symbols of modern society. While all translation involves interpretation, valid interpretation must take the next step: contextualizing the message. Traditionally, biblical interpreters have been better trained and skilled in exegeting Scripture than in exegeting contemporary culture. Since the agenda of hermeneutics includes developing principles for discovering the text's meaning and its relevance of the Bible for today's world, that must include guidelines for exegeting culture.

The Priority of the Plain Sense

The ever-present need for balance and perspective alerts us to the cart-before-the-horse syndrome. A final word of counsel for historical-cultural exegesis is a negative warning: *Do not allow features of the historical-cultural background to sabotage the main task of understanding the meaning of the text.* Sometimes interpreters become so preoccupied with the historical-cultural insights that they identify the main point of a passage as something that is inconsistent with what the author means to convey. This requires caution for there is an inevitable circularity involved. The historical

---

55. W. J. Larkin, *Culture and Biblical Hermeneutics* (Grand Rapids: Baker, 1988), 140.

56. Indeed, the Lausanne Covenant of 1974 states, "We also reject as derogatory to Christ and the Gospel every kind of syncretism and dialogue which implies that Christ speaks equally through all religions and ideologies," "The Lausanne Covenant," in *Let The Earth Hear His Voice*, ed. J. D. Douglas (Minneapolis: World Wide Publications, 1975), 4. For a good appraisal and critique, see D. Flemming, *Contextualization in the New Testament: Patterns for Theology and Mission* (Downers Grove: InterVarsity, 2005).

57. This challenge confronts evangelists and church leaders who look for ways to make Christianity appealing to outsiders. In the process they must avoid truncating the message so it becomes subchristian.

and cultural details enable us to understand the text, but the words of the text point to the historical issues at stake.

A good illustration is the interpretation of the parable of the unjust steward (Luke 16:1–13). This passage has troubled many Christians because Jesus appears to compliment a dishonest action. Some interpreters unravel the historical situation to suggest that the businessman for whom the steward worked probably charged his creditors' exorbitant and illegal interest rates. The steward's reducing the creditors' bills simply eliminated the unethical padding of the original bills.[58] This feature of the background may well be a clue to its meaning. Thus, for one group of readers, when this boss commends his fired employee for cutting in half all his creditors' debts, he concedes the justice of this action. For such interpreters, the lesson of the parable becomes one of justice, the righting of wrongs when that is in one's power. While this explanation has the advantage of reversing the troublesome impression of Jesus' compliment—he's commending justice, not dishonesty—is this correct?

Actually, the owner compliments his former manager for his *shrewdness*, not his justice. A second interpretation builds on this observation. Nothing in the context or in Jesus' application of the parable suggests the theme of justice. Nowhere does the passage state or imply that the owner had charged excessive interest. Whether he did or did not is not an explicit part of Jesus' story, and we cannot be sure Luke's readers (or Jesus' audience) would have understood that background. Furthermore, the surprise element, now recognized as a major characteristic and indicator of meaning in many of the parables of Jesus,[59] supports a focus on shrewdness, not justice. Receiving notice of his impending termination, the steward used the occasion to prepare for his long-range needs. Now that is shrewd.[60]

Jesus' application to the disciples underscores this point. Like the clever, dismissed bookkeeper, they too should act shrewdly in using present financial resources to make friends for eternity. The historical information about ancient loan practices may prove valuable for understanding the parable. Indeed, it may explain one facet of the fired employee's shrewdness. He may have known that the boss did not dare take him to

---

58. Defenders of this basic explanation include J. A. Fitzmyer, "The Story of the Dishonest Manager (Lk 16:1–13)," *Theological Studies* 25 (1964): 23–42; and K. E. Bailey, *Poet and Peasant* (Grand Rapids: Eerdmans, 1976), 86–110.

59. F. H. Borsch, *Many Things in Parables: Extravagant Stories of New Community* (Philadelphia: Fortress, 1988), 14–15, uses the terms "exaggeration" and "extravagance." Cf. B. B. Scott, *Hear Then The Parable* (Minneapolis: Fortress, 1989); and J. D. Crossan, *In Parables* (San Francisco; Harper & Row, 1973). E. Linnemann, *Parables of Jesus* (London; SPCK, 1966), 28, terms them *unusual features* "which do not result from a natural context in the representation in the parable narrative, [but] take their origin from the reality of which the narrator wishes to speak." See our fuller discussion of the genre of parables below.

60. The definitive defense of this view appears in D. J. Ireland, *Stewardship and the Kingdom of God: An Historical, Exegetical, and Contextual Study of the Parable of the Unjust Steward in Luke 16:1–13* (Leiden: Brill, 1992). D. L. Mathewson, "The Parable of the Unjust Steward (Luke 16:1–13): A Reexamination of the Traditional View in Light of Recent Challenges," *JETS* 38 (1995): 29–40, defends this same perspective against several more recent, and odder, alternatives. In addition, see A. J. Hultgren, *The Parables of Jesus: A Commentary* (Grand Rapids: Eerdmans, 2000), 146–57; and K. R. Snodgrass, *Stories with Intent: A Comprehensive Guide to the Parables of Jesus* (Grand Rapids: Eerdmans, 2008), 401–18.

court for canceling half of the debts owed him because he had given tacit agreement to the unethical charges. But we cannot be sure.

Thus, while knowledge of the historical-cultural setting is important for discovering the intended meaning, it should always serve the supportive role of aiding one's understanding of the text itself. It must never supplant the plain meaning of the text. Authors communicate messages through the words of the text. Background material should help us understand the meaning of the text; it must not become an additional message that contravenes that meaning.

Retrieving the Historical-Cultural Background

Exploring the world of the biblical setting involves two distinct studies: (1) studying the background of a biblical book and (2) studying the background of specific passages in the book. Background information learned about the entire book gives insight into its overall setting and provides a general perspective for each passage. It becomes a historical-cultural backdrop for understanding the individual sections within the book. But each individual passage also requires special analysis to explain the historical-cultural factors that are pertinent to it.

Exploring the General Background of the Book

Before studying a particular biblical passage, the Bible student should become familiar with the historical-cultural background of the book in which it occurs. This includes pertinent facts about the writer/editor, recipients, date, and purpose of the book. Detailed personal research will probably not be necessary every time the student begins analyzing passages in a given book. Undoubtedly, the student will already be familiar with much of the historical-cultural background through information received through reading or at church, college, or seminary. The student may need only to review (or perhaps, supplement) what he or she already knows about the book. Those students who have not had the opportunity of prior studies should consult sources such as Bible-survey and introduction books, commentaries, Bible dictionaries, and encyclopedias.[61] At times even the brief introductions in many recent study Bibles can provide a helpful start.[62]

When relying on these secondary sources, students should look up the pertinent biblical references to acquaint themselves with the specific evidence in the book itself and in other parts of the Bible, both for better understanding and to assess the validity of others' claims. Besides insight about its composition, original audience, date, and purpose, good reference works also include valuable facts drawn from ancient, extrabiblical literary sources and archaeology.

When time permits, the following supplemental strategy to studying a book's background will pay rich dividends. Students should read through the book at one

---

61. For a list and description of the best resources for this study, see the bibliography.
62. Pride of place goes to the *NIV Zondervan Study Bible*, ed. D. A. Carson (Grand Rapids: Zondervan, 2015).

sitting (perhaps several times) and record everything they find about the writer, recipients, date, and purpose of the book. After they analyze and review this material (preferably prior to consulting other sources), the articles in the reference works will become more meaningful.

Concerning the *author, editor,* or *writer,* the student will want to research matters of identity, characteristics, position among God's people, relationship with the recipients, and circumstances at the time of writing. This information will help the student understand the book from the perspective of the writer. Of course, such material may be more accessible for some books than for others. We cannot obtain information about who wrote many books of the Bible for they are anonymous; for others the authorship is uncertain. In such cases, the inductive insight we gain from reading the book itself may be all we can say about the writer.

Where possible, knowing about the *recipients*—their characteristics, circumstances, and community—sheds light on a passage, particularly how and why the writer develops specific subjects. For many books in both testaments, we have little information available about the recipients. In some prophetic books the situation is complex in that the audience addressed by the prophet may differ from the city or nation about whom the prophecy is made. For example, Obadiah prophesied about God's judgment against Edom though he addressed the book to Israel to provide encouragement. Prophetic books require careful attention since their texts may address a pre-exilic, exilic, or postexilic audience.

Date is another key historical-cultural factor. Knowing when a book was written or compiled enables the student to include in the analysis historical information from other sources for that period. For some biblical books there is insufficient evidence to determine a precise or reliable date. The historical facts included in the book may fit several periods equally well. In the case of the OT, we may be able to set a book only within a given century at best. In such situations the main emphasis should be on the general circumstances in that period of time in that part of the world. For example, Jonah's prophecy is set in the eighth century BC during the reign of the violent Assyrians. We then understand that brutal militarism of these hated pagans explains Jonah's reluctance to go to Nineveh to prophesy. For interpretive purposes, knowing the characteristics of a given period of time provides more insight than knowing a specific date.

For many NT books we can be fairly confident about locating their time of composition, at least within five to ten years. So, knowing that Paul exhorted the Romans to submit to the governing authorities during the early part of Nero's reign sheds light on his words (Rom 13:1–5). When Paul wrote (c. AD 56), that infamous emperor had not yet exhibited the cruelty he demonstrated in later years. We might even speculate whether Paul would have framed his instructions differently were he writing during Nero's atrocious pogroms against Christians in the middle 60s. In historical books, Psalms, Proverbs, and some prophecies, interpreters may need to distinguish, if possible, between the time when the material was (or began to be) collected, and the time when a writer or editor published the book in its final form. In the case of the Gospels, we must recognize the gap between Jesus' ministry in Palestine and his audience there (c. 27–30), and the time when the Evangelists composed their books for their differing audiences decades later after a period during which the sayings and deeds of Jesus were passed on by oral tradition.

Examining the Historical-Cultural Factors of a Specific Passage

After setting the entire book into its historical-cultural context, the student next moves to the specific passage for study. Determining the meaning of a passage requires interpreting each feature consistent with its natural meaning in its specific, original situation. First, determine whether historical information learned about the book as a whole applies in a particular way to the specific passage under scrutiny. A proposed interpretation of a passage must fit the historical-cultural background of the whole book.

Beyond this, individual passages within the book may contain special historical-cultural features that are pertinent to the meaning of that passage. While this background information may not surface in a study of the setting of the whole book, it is absolutely essential for the meaning of this text. Though a student may learn much about the background to the book of Amos, all that insight will not help interpret the meaning of the words in Amos 5:26, "Kaiwan your star-god" (NRSV) or "star of your God, Kaiwan" (NJB).[63] The student may understand the background for the writing of Matthew's Gospel without having a clue about the wide phylacteries worn by the Pharisees (Matt 23:5).[64] Thus, the student of Scripture also must research the specific historical and cultural details mentioned in the passage.

On the cultural side, the student should identify and seek to understand features reflected in the text. What kinds of features should the student be alert to? Look at the following range of categories. Which appear in your passage? What more can you learn about them that will shed light on your understanding of the passage?

- worldview: values, mindset, or outlook of the writer/editor, recipients, other people mentioned in the text, or in society at large
- societal structures: marriage and family patterns, roles of men and women, or racial issues
- physical features: climate and weather, structures, implements, or ease and means of transportation

---

63. All standard commentaries wrestle with the meaning of this reference. The NIV translates it as "the star of your god." For further help consult the commentaries listed in the bibliography chapter. M. D. Carroll R., *Amos—The Prophet and His Oracles: Research on the Book of Amos* (Louisville: Westminster John Knox, 2002), provides a compendium of research on issues in Amos.

64. For a succinct explanation see R. S. Fagen, "Phylacteries," in *ABD*, 6 vols., ed. D. N. Freedman (New York: Doubleday, 1992), 5:368–70 and other standard biblical dictionaries or encyclopedias (see bibliography). Wearing phylacteries (Aramaic *tĕpillîn*) began at least by the first century (Josephus, *Ant.* 4.8.13 mentions them). Black boxes containing Scripture texts, they are fastened to the left arm and forehead during prayer (Deut 6:4–9).

- economic structures: means of making a living, issues of wealth and poverty, slavery, or economic mobility
- political climate: structures, or loyalties, including actual personnel
- behavioral patterns, dress, or customs
- religious practices, power centers, convictions, rituals, or affiliations.

After identifying such items in the text, the student must attempt to discover additional information that can clarify how the original writer and readers would construe them. The first resource to consult is the Bible itself—often via concordance searches for the same word or feature. References in other parts of the specific Bible book, in other writings by the same author (or OT theological tradition) or to the same audience, in other parts of the Bible in general, or in specific parallel accounts of the same event often help to reconstruct the original situation. Beyond the Bible, other sources provide the principal and necessary means to secure background information. Many specialized works, not to mention introductions, Bible dictionaries, encyclopedias, and commentaries contain helpful material for clarifying historical or cultural references.[65]

Then we seek to explain the meaning and importance of the text in light of this historical-cultural reconstruction of the original setting. To the extent that we enter the world of the biblical setting, we can grasp the meaning of the passage. An interpretation that accurately reflects the original setting has a better claim to validity than one that does not.

The goal of historical-cultural research is to *reconstruct,* or at least to comprehend, the historical setting and cultural features of the specific passage as clearly as possible. To recap, this task involves explaining: (1) the situation of the writer, especially anything that helps explain why he or she wrote this passage; (2) the situation of the people involved in the text and/or its recipients of the book that can help explain why the writer penned this material to them; (3) the relationship between the writer and audience or the people involved in the text; and (4) the specific cultural or historical features mentioned in the text.

WORD MEANINGS

By its very nature, communication in language employs words. People transmit ideas by combining words together into larger units of thought. Without words, people would be limited in their ability to express their thoughts precisely. They would be restricted to nonverbal sounds, symbols, and pictures. The centrality of words in language communication underscores the importance of the lexical foundation of

---

65. See the bibliography—especially the sections "History of the Ancient World" and "Customs, Culture, Society"—for further help in locating useful sources. Other sections list dictionaries, encyclopedias, and commentaries. For those able to search the Bible electronically, searches of terms, people, places, or short phrases—e.g., "altar," "Moab," "Caiaphas," "shepherd's rod," etc.—often yield much useful information.

hermeneutics: *The correct interpretation of Scripture is the meaning required by the normal meaning of the words in the context in which they occur.*

On the surface words seem so simple. They make up such a routine part of our lives that we seldom stop to think about their complexity. To appreciate fully what is involved in the normal meaning of words, we must first understand several characteristics of words: nature, range of meaning, semantic fields, change of meaning, and nuances of meaning.

Crucial Matters about the Nature of Words

Basic Features of Words
• Words are Arbitrary Signs
• Word Meanings Overlap
• Words Have a Range of Meaning
• Word Meanings Change Over Time
• Words Have Denotative and Connotative Meanings

Words are Arbitrary Signs

Simply stated, a word is a combination of sounds or letters that is meaningful in a language. A more precise definition is that a word is a semantic sign—a combination of symbols or sounds that represents an idea.[66] Spoken words are a combination of sounds that stand for a specific idea; written words combine letters or other graphic representations of those sounds to symbolize a concept. The idea designated by any given word can be communicated either orally or visually. To study words we must understand their characteristics. First, words are usually *arbitrary signs*.[67] Why a word means what it does is mostly a matter of convention. That's just the way it is!

How do words become signs indicating a specific idea? Suppose someone were to ask the question, "How is your 'kebof'?" Probably all English speakers would be puzzled. "What on earth is my 'kebof'?" they would ask. Why? Is there something wrong with the word "kebof"? It sounds and looks like a perfectly good word. It combines consonants and vowels in proper syllables. It is easily pronounceable. It has

---

66. The reader who wishes more detailed help into the intricacies of the modern study of words, especially in light of linguistic studies, should consult: P. Cotterell and M. Turner, *Linguistics and Biblical Interpretation* (Downers Grove: InterVarsity, 1989); M. Silva, *Biblical Words and their Meaning: An Introduction to Lexical Semantics*, rev. ed. (Grand Rapids: Zondervan, 1995), J. P. Louw, *Semantics of New Testament Greek* (Philadelphia: Fortress, 1982); E. A. Nida and J. P. Louw, *Lexical Semantics of the Greek New Testament* (Atlanta: Scholars, 1992); J. F. A. Sawyer, *Semantics in Biblical Research: New Methods of Defining Hebrew Words For Salvation* (London: SCM, 1972); and S. Shead, *Radical Frame Semantics and Biblical Hebrew* (Leiden: Brill, 2011).

67. As M. Silva puts it, "the association of a particular word with a particular meaning is *largely* a matter of convention," in *Biblical Words*, 103–4, emphasis his. We say that words are usually arbitrary signs because in some instances where words sound like sounds (a dog's bark, "woof, woof"), the association between word and meaning is not simply arbitrary.

all the attributes of a good word, except for one—it conveys no meaning, at least not in English! On the other hand, another five-letter word, "maple," immediately brings to mind a type of tree. While several English-speaking people may envision different shapes of trees, depending upon their experience with maples, if any, they all acknowledge that "maple" refers to a type of tree, or to the wood that comes from a maple tree.[68]

What makes "maple" different from "kebof"? Throughout the development of a language, users of that language arbitrarily assign meanings to the words they use. By common practice English speakers associate "maple" with a certain meaning. When English speakers hear the word "maple," their minds automatically identify one member of the kind of plants commonly known as trees. But since English speakers have not assigned a meaning to "kebof," it represents nothing and thus calls nothing to mind.

This illustrates the most foundational fact about words: each word comes to represent a given idea (or ideas) only by its repeated *use* within a common language group. Thus, if two people wish to communicate, they both must use words in a similar way. From the standpoint of hermeneutics, accurate interpretation requires that we understand a word in the same way the writer used it.

What is a word?
A sound or its written representation that marks out a field of meaning at a given time

To illustrate, American English makes only a minor distinction between "pants" and "trousers." One may sound more formal. However, in British English these two words refer to two different garments. Trousers correspond their American counterpart while pants denote "underpants."[69] To secure a "two-legged outer garment that extends from waist to ankle" in Aberdeen, Scotland, a wise American purchaser would ask the clerk for trousers, not pants. Understanding and using words the way other speakers of the language use them is critical for effective communication.

Needless to say, this complicates the task for Bible students. Since the original writers wrote in ancient languages that are foreign to us, we do not know intrinsically the meanings of the terms they used. To begin with, we need translators to render the meaning of the biblical texts into English. Fortunately, scholars carefully study the biblical languages and do their best to convey the precise meaning of the biblical words in English. A hermeneutical point clearly emerges from this information. *Interpreters must deliberately pursue what the original words of a passage meant at the time they were written in the context in which they occur.* The correct meaning of the words, not what ideas may occur to us when we read the passage, is the goal for word

---

68. For the sake of simplicity, we avoid other senses of "maple" such as someone's last name or a flavor of syrup or ice cream.

69. British friends tell us this distinction is now breaking down due to the pervasive influence of American television and tourists.

studies. We must always remember that the biblical writer selected certain words to express specific thoughts. Our aim is to recover the ideas that the writer sought to communicate by means of those words.

Words Have a Range of Meanings

To complicate matters further, a word may have more than one meaning. In fact, most words have a *range of meanings*.[70] The very same word, spelled identically, may take on several vastly different meanings.[71] Take for example the English word "hand." The "hand" that is a part of the human body is not at all like the "hand" on a clock, the "hand" held by a card player, a unit of measurement for horses, a worker, as in "All 'hands' on deck," or the idea expressed by the request to "Give them a 'hand'!"[72] In each case the word remains the same, but the meaning changes. These different meanings constitute at least part of the range of meanings of the word "hand." Normally such multiple meanings of a word do not cause any confusion or misunderstanding. Sometimes they aid in making jokes when we recognize that the right word is in the wrong place. Aided by the context, native speakers usually pick the right meaning without any trouble. The ideas expressed in the larger message of the literary context within a given historical-cultural context usually clarify the intended meaning.

These facts also hold true for the ancient biblical languages. Both the Hebrew word *shalom* and the Greek *eirēnē*, often translated "peace" in English, have a range of meanings. For the Hebrew *shalom* the range includes "absence of strife" in the sense of prosperity, completeness, wholeness, harmony, and fulfillment. So it denotes a sense of well-being where relationships are unimpaired. In addition, it means the state of fulfillment that results from God's presence and righteousness; its source is God and comes as his gift. Finally, *shalom* can mean the eschatological state of eternal peace.[73]

The range of meaning for the Greek *eirēnē* includes an external absence of hostility, an internal tranquility, and the first Hebrew sense of well-being.[74] To understand what a biblical author means by "peace" in a specific text, one must determine which of these potential meanings best fits the context. A reader can neither pick a meaning arbitrarily, one he or she prefers, nor collect several. One has only to return to the word "hand" to see how silly it would be to assign the wrong meaning in a specific context. No less is true in our study of biblical words.

Several times during the Upper Room Discourse Jesus promised "peace" to the

---

70. We saw that the range of meaning of "pants" is broader in American English (able to denote trousers and underpants) than in British English (only denotes underpants). Consider English words like "run" or "ball" to get a feel for how wide a range some words can have. Some dictionaries have dozens of meanings for "run."

71. Recall our previous example of the many meanings of the word "trunk."

72. Interestingly, note how even this sentence is ambiguous. It could mean, "Give them applause," or "Help them." In addition, in using "hand," we introduce only instances where it functions as a noun. "Hand" also occurs as a verb ("*Hand* me a book.").

73. See P. J. Nel, "שָׁלוֹם," *NIDOTTE*, 4:130–35; and G. von Rad, "שָׁלוֹם" in the OT," *TDNT*, 2:402–6.

74. While these three meaning categories are not all listed as such in any one of the major Greek lexicons, a comparison of BDAG, 287–88, with L&N, 1:22.42, 25.248, suggests this range of meanings.

apostles (John 14:27; 16:33). It is doubtful that Jesus meant "absence of hostility," or he was sorely mistaken. In fact, he ended the discourse with the warning that in this world they would have trouble (16:33). He was not promising them trouble-free lives. In fact, though they would encounter considerable hostility, Jesus went on to say, "But take heart! I have overcome the world" (16:33), which makes clear that he was promising the apostles inward tranquility or an ultimate sense of their own well-being. So, the fact that many words have a range of meaning complicates language communication. To know the message intended by a speaker or writer, interpreters must discern which meaning makes the best sense in its context.

Word Meanings Overlap

The third factor to know about the nature of words is that *each distinct meaning of a word exists as part of a semantic field or domain.*[75] One meaning of "hand," we will call it "hand$_1$," resides in the domain of "parts of the human body." Another meaning, "hand$_2$," occurs in the semantic domain of "ways to show appreciation in a public setting" (along with "applause," "cheers," "clapping," and "ovation"). "Hand$_3$" is in the domain of "parts of a physical clock." Put simply, a number of words in the same language exhibit meanings similar to or closely related to other words. Often we call these words synonyms. Clearly, "hand$_2$" is closer in meaning to "applause" than it is to "hand$_1$" or "hand$_3$."

Two (or more) words are synonyms when, out of their total range of meanings, at least one of the meanings of one word overlaps with one of the meanings of the other word. "Run" is synonymous with "unravel" in the sentence, "These tights are guaranteed not to _____," but not (usually) in "She is ready to _____ the race."[76] Note, only one meaning of "hand" overlaps with "applause." They are synonyms in only a portion of their ranges of meaning.

Consider these two sentences: "The audience gave her a hand," and "The audience gave her an ovation." Though the two words are synonymous in these uses, they do not convey exactly the same meaning.[77] Here "hand" is probably less formal than "ovation" (and maybe implies greater strength or enthusiasm—perhaps even higher praise than "hand"). The comedian gets a rousing hand from the audience while the soprano merits a standing ovation. Most English speakers probably use "ovation" less frequently and usually only following "standing." They reserve it for specific occasions. By seeing which part of a semantic field a specific word occupies, one is

---

75. Silva, *Biblical Words*, has a brief treatment of the basic concepts (161–63). For more technical introductions, see J. Lyons, *Semantics*, 2 vols. (Cambridge: Cambridge University Press, 1977), 1:230–69. A language divides the total conceptual sphere at a given time into fields, as a kind of mosaic. Within each semantic field words have meaning in relationship to the other words in that field. Consider the field designated as "furniture" or more narrowly, "furniture to sit on." In it reside: stool, lounger, hassock, chair, couch, etc.

76. We say *usually* here because one could always envision a setting when even an odd word could be made to fit. We are discussing normal usage.

77. We will take up this element of connotation later.

able to define the meaning of each term used within that field more precisely. This helps the interpreter to recognize the specific nuances of a word that distinguish it from other terms.

In studying the Greek word for "peace" (*eirēnē*), Louw and Nida say that it belongs to two different semantic fields: first, domain 22, containing words used to express trouble, hardship, relief, or favorable circumstances;[78] and second, domain 25, listing terms for attitudes and emotions.[79] These two fields of meaning differ greatly. In the first category "peace" is one of six words in the subdomain indicating "favorable circumstances or state" (22:42–22:47), whereas the other uses of the word belong to the subdomain including "worry, anxiety, distress, peace" (25:223–25:250). The same word may refer to external circumstances free from hostility or to a psychological state of inward tranquility. Knowing this distinction enables the interpreter to watch for clues in the context to decide between the two.[80]

Word Meanings Change Over Time

Word meanings do not remain fixed; they change over time. New meanings develop through usage, and old ones become obsolete.[81] The KJV readily illustrates this phenomenon. Revered for numerous qualities, including its poetic beauty and its familiarity, the venerable translation frequently shows how English words no longer mean what they did when it emerged in 1611. In some places the wording merely causes confusion; in others, the present meaning differs drastically from that of the original Elizabethan English. Look at the KJV's uses of the word "conversation" (2 Cor 1:12; Gal 1:13; Eph 2:3; 4:22; Phil 1:27). These texts have little to do with what we think of when we use the word "conversation"; so modern versions replace "conversation" with "conduct" or "way of life" to convey the Greek texts' original intent, because the meaning of the English word has changed over time.

Then again, consider the passage promising the rapture of saints to meet Christ at his second coming. The KJV renders 1 Thessalonians 4:15, "We who are alive and remain until the coming of the Lord will not *prevent* those who have fallen asleep." In 1611 "prevent" more closely followed its Latin derivation and conveyed the idea "to go before." Today it means "to stop" or "to hinder." Because the meaning of the English word has changed, what served as a good translation in the seventeenth century no longer communicates Paul's original meaning. Hence, most modern versions substitute the word "precede" for the KJV's "prevent."

---

78. L&N: 1:242–248.

79. Ibid., 1:288–320.

80. Interestingly, the student who only used the Bauer lexicon would not be aware of the use of *eirēnē* meaning freedom from worry and anxiety, because this meaning is not listed. The closest they come is the sense of "a state of well-being, peace" (BDAG, 287–88).

81. E. Weiner and J. Simpson, eds., *Oxford English Dictionary*, 3rd ed., 20 vols. (Oxford: Oxford University Press, 2010), is the standard and monumental tool for tracing the changes of the meaning of English words over time.

Don't Be Misled by False Etymologies		
Word	Original Language	Meaning Based on Original Language
Present	*prae* + *esse* (Latin)	"to be in front"
Preside	*prae* + *sedire* (Latin)	"to sit in front"
Prevent	*prae* + *venire* (Latin)	"to come first"
Ekklesia (church)	*ek* + *kaleō* (Greek)	"called out ones"
All of these "meanings" based on their words' etymologies are false.		

The same principle holds true for the biblical languages. Words changed their meanings over the centuries. The original meaning of a word or the meaning derived from a word's etymology or root may be of no more than historical interest to the interpreter.[82] Past meanings may be interesting and even colorful, but we must always resist the temptation to believe that past meanings exert some residual influence on current usage. One may not simply discover a meaning for a word that existed in classical Greek, for example, and assume that meaning could occur at the time of the NT.[83] Many will allege that Classical Greek made a distinction between two words for knowing: *oida* and *ginōskō*.[84] The first denoted an acquired knowledge of facts or people; it had a kind of certainty about it. The second referred to the procurement of knowledge, an experiential knowledge often with the sense of "come to know." However, in the Hellenistic period during which the NT came into existence, Greek speakers did not always comply with the classical distinctions. Indeed, in their lexicon, Moulton and Milligan confidently assert, "The distinction between *oida*, 'to know' absolutely, and *ginōskō*, 'come to know' cannot be pressed in Hellenistic Greek."[85] Burdick believes that Paul normally followed the classical distinctions, though not always. But, he wisely observes, "Each occurrence must be evaluated on its own merits."[86] Silva's analysis is considerably more linguistically nuanced.[87] He rightly concludes that Paul's uses of these verbs may be heavily influenced by stylistic as well as semantic factors.

---

82. An array of scholars has repeated this point. The earliest voice was probably J. Barr, *Semantics of Biblical Language* (Oxford: Oxford University Press, 1961), 107, 109. It is echoed in D. A. Carson, *Exegetical Fallacies*, 2nd ed. (Grand Rapids: Baker Academic, 1996), 27–64.

83. This would be as inappropriate as for a modern male to call a woman a "hussy" with the defense that its original meaning was positive—a diminutive for "housewife." Today it conveys a lewd and derogatory message. Original meanings may have no significance for current usage. The same applies to biblical studies.

84. See H. Seesemann, "οἶδα," *TDNT* 5:116–19; and R. Bultmann, "γινώσκω,etc." *TDNT* 1:689–719, esp. 689–92. The former, *oida*, had more the sense of "to have experienced, learned to know." On the second, Bultmann stresses that in Greek usage the sense was the intelligent comprehension of an object or matter: "to experience, to perceive" (689). This sense of the act of comprehension may fade into the background so the sense is merely: "to know or understand." Both authors recognize that these distinctions were not hard and fast, and that often the words appear to occur synonymously.

85. J. H. Moulton and G. Milligan, *The Vocabulary of the Greek New Testament* (Grand Rapids: Eerdmans, 1963; Peabody, MA: Hendrickson, 1997), 439. See the careful, sober analysis in D. W. Burdick, "*Oida* and *Ginōskō* in the Pauline Epistles," in *New Directions in New Testament Study*, ed. R. N. Longenecker and M. C. Tenney (Grand Rapids: Zondervan, 1974), 344–56.

86. Burdick, "*Oida*," 354.

87. Silva, *Biblical Words*, 164–69.

That is, not only were the distinctions of meaning from the classical period of Greek in the process of breaking down, but certain constructions sounded or worked better than others. For example, the phrase "standing ovation" works better in English than "standing hand." If we want to indicate that an audience demonstrated its approval by clapping while standing on its feet, we are virtually locked into using "ovation" rather than "hand," semantic considerations aside.

In the same way Bible students must determine the range of meanings that was in common use at *the time a book was written.* In the case of the NT, interpreters err in attempting to retain the distinctions of classical Greek as if the NT writers were obligated to observe them (or even knew them). They must scrupulously avoid the archaic meanings of an earlier phase of the language. A similar caution applies to the use of Semitic cognate languages to illumine the meaning of Hebrew words. Broadly speaking, priority in such comparisons should go to languages most closely related to Hebrew (e.g., Ugaritic, Phoenician, Aramaic, Moabite, Edomite) and secondarily to its more distant relatives (Akkadian, Arabic; but see below).[88]

Conversely, they must avoid another version of anachronism—reading into the biblical text meanings that emerged in later periods. The fallacy of anachronism occurs even more blatantly when we read later meanings *in English* into an earlier use of a biblical word. A serious contemporary example of this abuse occurs when a preacher defines the first century Greek word for power, *dynamis*, using a commodity invented in the nineteenth century, namely dynamite, simply because the words look and sound similar and because the English word derived from the Greek![89] Paul did not intend to say that the gospel is the dynamite of God.

Words Have Connotative and Denotative Meanings

A fifth characteristic of words is that they may convey significance in addition to their explicit denotative reference.[90] This may include a *connotative* or a figurative meaning. While the word "dog" *denotes* a four-legged, hairy animal, when used figuratively of a person in the statement, "You dog!" it usually communicates an emotive sense of disapproval. Goliath considers it a huge insult—treatment as if he were a mere *dog* rather than a great warrior—that the teenager David dares confront him (1 Sam 17:43; cf. 24:14; 2 Sam 16:9). Some OT speakers call

---

88. Advanced students will want to consult commentaries and reference works discussed below.

89. D. A. Carson, *Exegetical Fallacies,* 33–34, cites this fallacy, in addition to a number of others interpreters commit in their well-intentioned attempts to interpret Scripture. We highly commend Carson's little volume. Every interpreter needs to heed his cautions. For more sophisticated linguistic analyses of the Greek of the NT see S. E. Porter, *Linguistic Analysis of the Greek New Testament: Studies in Tools, Methods, and Practice* (Grand Rapids: Baker Academic, 2015) and C. R. Campbell, *Advances in the Study of Greek: New Insights for Reading the New Testament* (Grand Rapids: Zondervan, 2015).

90. D. A. Black observes, "Linguists distinguish between *denotation,* or the meaning a word has for all who hear it, and *connotation,* or the special meaning the same word may have for a limited group of speakers," in *Linguistics for Students of New Testament Greek* (Grand Rapids: Baker, 1988), 131. To illustrate, he contrasts the denotation of "children," persons between infancy and adulthood, and its connotation, which might range from awkward, immature, obstinate, to impulsive.

themselves a *dog* to express extreme self-deprecation before someone in authority (2 Sam 9:8; 2 Kgs 8:13). When Paul warns the Christians at Philippi, "Watch out for those *dogs*, those evildoers, those mutilators of the flesh" (Phil 3:2), the word carries a noticeable derogatory force. First-century Jews considered canines despicable creatures (as do some cultures today). Thus they expressed their dislike of the Gentiles by calling them "dogs." In Philippians Paul criticizes certain Jewish troublemakers by throwing back at them their own contemptuous use of the term "dog." This connotation is not necessarily present in other uses of "dog" in the OT and NT. "Dog" is not always used figuratively of humans. An example occurs in Jesus' parable of the rich man and Lazarus in which "dog" refers simply to an animal (Luke 16:21; cf. Exod 11:7; Judg 7:5). Interpreters, therefore, must study words carefully to discern not only their denotative meaning but also whether words are used as figures or with some connotative subtlety that the original recipients would have sensed.

Type of Word Meaning	Definition	An Example: Tree
Referential	What a word refers to	"Tree" refers to the large plant outside my office
Denotative	Precise or direct meaning of the word	"Tree" denotes a woody perennial plant, at least several feet high with an erect main stem and side branches[92]
Connotative	Special suggestive sense that grows out of its denotative meaning in some way	Jesus died on a "tree" (1 Pet 2:24), meaning, the cross
Contextual	Specific sense suggested by a word's use in a specific context that limits it to one of the above.	In the sentence, "I love to climb that apple tree," the sense required by the context is the denotative meaning.

Steps for Performing Word Studies

Determining the meaning of any given biblical word is a multifaceted task. Because of the complex nature of words, we must examine several types of information to discover a word's contextually appropriate meaning. The steps outlined below are a useful guide to follow in this process.

1. *Select Words that Require Detailed Analysis*

We cannot understand a passage without knowing what the words in it mean. Now not all of the words in a passage will require further study, for the meanings of most terms will be clear enough. Those students who have facility in the biblical

---

91. Of course, this is only the biological meaning of the word "tree." The word also occurs with different denotative meanings as in linguistics where we may find a "tree diagram." We also use the word in "family tree" and "shoe tree," to name a few others.

languages will have access to more insight into the meanings of the words. However, some words do require more careful analysis.

Select Important Words to Study
• Difficult Words
• Crucial Words
• Theologically Loaded Words
• Rare Words
• Figurative Words

How does the student choose the words that require further study? One category includes words the student does not understand in English. If the student does not have a church background, many words may fit this category. Even for the majority of readers, some words will be puzzling at first. So these words, like covenant, Jubilee, ephod, redeemer, justify, or yokefellow, need to be studied, some in more detail than others. All interpreters need to know the meaning of crucial terms to assure they know their meaning in a given context. Words whose meanings are decisive for a passage or that are theologically significant warrant careful study. It is better to do a preliminary study of a term and then rule out more exhaustive study than to overlook a term whose meaning makes a crucial impact upon a passage.

Study rare words, particularly those that occur only once, especially if they are crucial in a passage.[92] Then, too, a word that a writer repeats is often significant and worth further study, especially to clarify its function in the passage.[93] The student should take particular care to investigate figures of speech in order to understand the sense implied. If English translations diverge on the meaning of a word, the interpreter should investigate to discover the most accurate sense of the word.

2. Determine the Range of Meaning for the Word

Because words cover a field of meaning, the student must do research in *lexicons* to determine the range of meaning the word had at the time of the author.[94] What are the options for its meaning in this passage? Weighing these possible meanings of the word in the context and in keeping with the historical background enables the interpreter to make a preliminary selection of the best meaning here. While many lexicons assist in making this choice by listing biblical references under the various meanings of a specific word, the interpreter should always weigh the contextual evidence for him or herself rather than simply accept this opinion.

Simply put, the interpreter seeks to take the place of the original readers to sense

---

92. Technically, we call a word that occurs only once in the Bible a *hapax legomenon*, from the Greek meaning "being said once." For Hebrew words, students may consult F. E. Greenspahn, *Hapax Legomena in Biblical Hebrew*, SBLDS 74 (Chico, CA: Scholars Press, 1984).

93. The use of "head" in 1 Cor 11:2–16 is an example. It occurs with different meanings here.

94. In semantics this is called synchronic analysis. Though words may have an interesting array of meanings over their history (thus diachronic analysis), interpreters must discover what words mean at the time in question.

how they would hear the words of the passage. This involves securing as much information as possible about the words and concepts of the time. Lexicons serve students well at this point, for they provide information about the possible meanings of words throughout the history of time the lexicon covers.

But where do lexicons get their information? Various kinds of lexicons research one or more fields of study and catalog their findings. Typically, they investigate various ancient literary sources—documents, published works, and letters, for example. Beyond that, some lexicons include nonliterary materials like epitaphs on tombs, receipts, or inscriptions on buildings and other places. Often they compare parallel or languages cognate to the biblical languages—particularly for the study of the OT. Of course, previous Scripture provides a prime source for discovering meanings of words, so NT lexicons may survey the Septuagint (LXX). This provides help, at times, since it shows how the Jews at that time rendered the Hebrew into Greek.[95] Lexicons do not neglect current Scripture. That is, they also seek to understand the meanings of words by evaluating the uses they discover either in the OT or the NT. Searching the lexicons is a fact-finding mission. What options exist for the crucial words in a passage? We know the options only by surveying actual uses.

At this juncture, we acknowledge two kinds of students: those who do not or cannot have facility in the biblical languages, and those who do—at least to some degree. For the first group of interpreters several works provide access to the meanings of words: J. D. Douglas, et al., *Zondervan Illustrated Bible Dictionary*;[96] R. F. Youngblood, and F. F. Bruce, eds. *Nelson's Illustrated Bible Dictionary*;[97] T. Longman, ed., *Baker Illustrated Bible Dictionary*;[98] M. A. Powell, ed., *HarperCollins Bible Dictionary*;[99] G. W. Bromiley, ed., *International Standard Bible Encyclopedia Revised*, 4 vols.;[100] M. C. Tenney and M. Silva, ed., *The Zondervan Encyclopedia of the Bible*, 5 vols.;[101] D. N. Freedman, ed., *The Anchor Bible Dictionary*, 6 vols.;[102] T. C. Butler, ed., *Holman Bible Dictionary*;[103] W. D. Mounce, *Mounce's Complete Expository Dictionary of Old and New Testament Words*;[104] and D. N. Freedman, ed., *Eerdmans Dictionary of the Bible*.[105] These comprise a fine range of sources in which students who do not work

95. This does not mean, however, that if we seek to know what a Greek word meant, we can simply see what Hebrew word it translated in the LXX and then find the meaning of the Hebrew word. As we have seen, the specific Hebrew and Greek words could have more than one meaning. Which translated which? In addition, there never is a one-to-one overlap between languages; often the LXX paraphrases rather than translates, and frequently the LXX was motivated by theological or practical concerns in how it renders the OT.

96. 3rd ed. (Grand Rapids: Zondervan, 2011).

97. New enhanced ed. (Nashville: Nelson, 2014).

98. (Grand Rapids: Baker, 2013).

99. Rev. upd. ed. (San Francisco: Harper, 2011).

100. Rev. ed. (Grand Rapids: Eerdmans, 1979–86).

101. Rev. ed. (Grand Rapids: Zondervan, 2009).

102. (New York: Doubleday, 1992).

103. (Nashville: Broadman, 1991).

104. (Grand Rapids: Zondervan, 2006), a significant revision of the venerable *Vine's Dictionary*.

105. (Grand Rapids: Eerdmans, 2000).

in Hebrew and/or Greek (and those who do) can learn valuable insights into words in both testaments.[106]

Students who know the biblical languages to some degree have the advantage of access to further important resources. At the same time, even students with limited or no knowledge of Hebrew or Greek might want to make use of these more advanced resources from time to time. Particularly with the use of interlinear Bibles, computer programs, and other helps, many fine insights are accessible to those willing to do some hunting. How would this work in practice? The following examples will illustrate the procedure and clarify the types of information the student is seeking. We will start with a study of OT words and then proceed to the NT.

For OT studies L. Koehler and W. Baumgartner, *The Hebrew and Aramaic Lexicon of the Old Testament* (abbreviated *HALOT*) surveys the range of meanings for words in light of the most recent scholarship for those able to find the appropriate Hebrew word.[107] F. Brown, S. R. Driver, and C. A. Briggs, *A Hebrew and English Lexicon of the Old Testament* (BDB) also provides help for studying the range of meanings for words, though again one must be able to find the appropriate Hebrew term.[108] Though less up-to-date than *HALOT,* the entries in BDB tend to be a little more complete, many listing every occurrence of a word. Another source, more convenient to use, provides very important discussions of key Hebrew words: W. A. VanGemeren, *New International Dictionary of Old Testament Theology and Exegesis,* 5 vols. (*NIDOTTE*). One advantage of *NIDOTTE* is its combination of articles about individual Hebrew words and various topical articles that include comments on the appropriate Hebrew words.[109] Finally, the most exhaustive source for OT words studies is the multi-volume set edited by G. J. Botterweck and H. Ringgren, *Theological Dictionary of the Old Testament* (*TDOT*).[110]

As a beginning, these sources help students discover the basic range of meaning for a Hebrew word through its history. This often includes a word's etymology, but students must recall that a word's history may offer little or no clues to its current meanings. For example, in Genesis 9 and 12 the word "covenant" figures prominently. A quick check in Einspahr's *Index* shows that "covenant" is the translation of the

---

106. See the bibliography for further discussion and information about these sources.

107. (Leiden: Brill, 2000).

108. (Peabody, MA: Hendrickson, repr. 1996). It codes words to *Strong's Exhaustive Concordance* (New York: Hunt Eaton; Cincinnati: Cranston Curts, 1894; and subsequently reprinted by Hendrickson, Nelson, and most recently with revisions and improvements, Zondervan as *The Strongest Strong's Exhaustive Concordance of the Bible,* 2001), which lists the English words of the KJV. In addition, B. Einspahr compiled an *Index to Brown, Driver and Briggs Hebrew Lexicon* (Chicago: Moody, 1976), employing the NASB in its references. Using this *Index* one can locate where a Hebrew word occurs in the OT, discover its meaning, and locate the page and section in BDB where it is discussed. The older editions of BDB remain serviceable; they merely lack the correlation to Strong's.

109. (Grand Rapids: Zondervan, 1997). Each article has a number, and those without Hebrew knowledge may access its contents in two ways: by finding the word's number under its English equivalent in E. W. Goodrick and J. R. Kohlenberger, *Exhaustive Concordance of the NIV* (Grand Rapids: Zondervan, 1990), or by converting a Strong's number to a *NIDOTTE* number through the conversion chart in Goodrick-Kohlenberger.

110. (Grand Rapids: Eerdmans, 2003). The other exhaustive Hebrew lexicon is edited by D. J. A. Clines, *Dictionary of Classical Hebrew,* 8 vols. (Sheffield: Sheffield Academic Press/Continuum, 2011).

Hebrew word *berit* and that BDB discusses the word on p. 136.[111] Turning to BDB we find the basic meaning for *berit*: pact, compact, covenant. The lexicon subdivides this basic meaning into three categories: "I. between men; II. between God and man; and III. phrases (as in covenant making, covenant keeping, and covenant violation)." If we further scrutinize the first category, we find a variety of nuances of covenants between people: "(1) treaty or alliance, as in Abram's alliance with the Amorites (Gen 14:13); (2) a constitution or ordinance between a monarch and subjects (2 Sam 5:3); (3) a pledge (2 Kgs 11:4); (4) alliance or friendship, as between David and Jonathan (1 Sam 18:3; 23:18); and (5) a marriage alliance (Prov 2:17; Mal 2:14)." BDB delineates the other two categories with equal thoroughness.

It appears that *berit* can have the sense of a bilateral arrangement in which two parties draw up a mutually agreeable pact or relationship. But it can also denote a unilateral arrangement that God (or a victorious monarch) determines and imposes. For example, God unilaterally established a covenant with Abraham (Gen 17:3–10; Exod 6:4), though Israel was required to keep its terms to enjoy God's promised blessings.

Surveying *HALOT*,[112] students will find definitions similar to those in BDB but also a more elaborate discussion of the various uses and some bibliographic references. The author assesses the possible etymology of *berit* along with possible connections to Akkadian words. He adds crucial elements to the discussion of *berit*: how the covenant is maintained and how it can be neglected or broken.

The discussion in *NIDOTTE* rounds out these findings.[113] McConville gives some attention to the relationship of *berit* to Akkadian, and while the term occurs only in Hebrew, the ANE provides many examples of treaties and law codes that help fill out the background for the concept. This background identifies six elements of Hittite suzerain-vassal treaties that help us understand those in Deuteronomy: titulary (the parties to the covenant), historical prologue (their past relations), stipulations, document clause (requirements for preserving the document), god list (witnesses to the treaty), and blessings and curses (invoked for keeping or breaking the treaty). Thus for Israel we see that Israel's suzerain Yahweh has invoked a treaty that demands certain commitments from the people for it to be preserved. Importantly, McConville observes, "The historical prologue is relevant here, because it puts the treaty/covenant into the context of a continuous relationship."[114] He also spells out in more detail the kinds of covenants between God and his people in the OT, e.g., the Noachic, Abrahamic, Mosaic, and Davidic covenants. He includes a section surveying the concept of covenants in the prophets observing that, though they use it rarely, they

---

111. Alternatively, one would discover *berit* from reading a tool such as *The NIV Interlinear Hebrew-English Old Testament*, ed. J. R. Kohlenberger, III (Grand Rapids: Zondervan, 1987); or J. J. Owens, *Analytical Key to the Old Testament.*, 4 vols. (Grand Rapids: Baker, 1990–93).

112. "בְּרִית:," *HALOT* 1:157–59.

113. G. J. McConville, "בְּרִית," *NIDOTTE* 1:747–55.

114. *NIDOTTE* 1:747.

often substitute different ideas to capture the essence of God's relationship with his people, as in marriage in Hosea or election in Amos. In the prophets we also encounter the question of whether the covenant ceased at the exile, though ultimately they deny that possibility but present a renewed vision of God's restoration and the promise of the new covenant (see Jer 31:31–34). The article concludes with a short section on post-OT uses, as at Qumran, a short trajectory of the idea into the NT, and an extensive bibliography.[115]

At this point the student has a good grasp of the range of meaning of *berit*. In places it may overlap with the meaning of the word "contract," into which two parties enter and agree to certain obligations and benefits. But it also may mean a treaty that a victorious king imposes on a vanquished foe. It refers, too, to a pact or arrangement that God decides upon in order to provide for and bless people. In this instance, he requires their obedience and trust in response, or he may cancel the covenant. The distinctly biblical idea that emerges is one of a personal God who freely enters into a gracious relationship with his people. Even though his people fail, he will ultimately accomplish his purposes for them.

Moving to the NT, students who know Greek will find two lexicons most valuable for studying its words: *A Greek-English Lexicon of the New Testament and Other Early Christian Literature,* 3rd ed., by W. Bauer, F. Danker, W. F. Arndt, and F. W. Gingrich (BDAG),[116] and *A Greek-English Lexicon of the New Testament Based on Semantic Domains,* 2 vols., by J. P. Louw and E. A. Nida (L&N).[117] While both provide excellent help in finding the range of meaning for Greek words, BDAG provides the more extensive references for each entry, often including every NT occurrence of a word. L&N, on the other hand, provides essential definitions and insight about a word's field of meaning that are lacking in BDAG and other lexicons.

The Greek word *kyrios* (lord) can serve to compare the two lexicons. In surveying the uses of this word during the Hellenistic period, BDAG divides the range of meaning into two main categories. The general designation includes: (1) owner: "one who is in charge by virtue of possession, owner"—master or lord; and (2) one who is in a position of authority, "Lord" or the title of respect, "sir." Used in religious contexts, "lord" is used of God, of deified kings, Jesus, and other supernatural beings like angels.[118]

L&N conveniently lists the range of meaning in the index volume (II) under the entry of *kyrios*: Lord, owner, ruler, and sir.[119] The domain reference numbers indicate that each meaning comes from a different domain. "Lord" belongs to the domain

---

115. More thorough still is the discussion in *TDOT*, 2:253–78, which supplies the fullest discussion in English. The main entries for this twenty-five-page essay include: "I. etymology; II. meaning; III. semantic range; IV. covenantal ceremony; V. covenant and law"; etc. The bibliography is more extensive, yet heavily leaning to German scholarship.

116. (Chicago: Univ. of Chicago Press, 2000). See the more extensive comments about these excellent sources in the bibliography. We also provide additional help in utilizing the wealth of information they provide.

117. (New York, etc.: United Bible Societies, 1988).

118. BDAG, 576–79.

119. L&N, 2:149.

of words indicating supernatural beings and powers (12.9). The definition in vol. 1 identifies this as a title for God or Christ, indicating "one who exercises supernatural authority over mankind."[120] The second meaning, "owner," occurs in the domain of words that express ownership or possession (57.12). Here the definition of *kyrios* is "one who owns and controls property, including especially servants and slaves, with important supplementary semantic components of high status and respect"; "owner," "master," and "lord" are good glosses.[121] *Kyrios*, meaning "ruler," occurs in the group of words used to indicate control or rule and in the subdomain focusing on ruling or governing other people (37.51). The proposed translations, "ruler," "master," "lord" communicate its meaning as "one who rules or exercises authority over others."[122] When *kyrios* means "sir" (87.53), it belongs to the domain of words indicating status and the subdomain of words expressing high status or rank. Thus, it was "a title of respect used in addressing or speaking of a man—sir, mister."[123] Looking these up in vol. 1 discloses both the specific domain to which each of these meanings belong, and a precise definition of each meaning.

After this canvass of the lexicons, the student next attempts to identify the semantic domain to which a specific use of the word most likely belongs. In the case of a "covenant," does the occurrence of *berit* fall into the domain of "imposed, unilateral arrangements" or "mutually negotiated treaties"—to put them in stark terms? How are we to understand the use in Job 31:1, "I made a *covenant* with my eyes not to look lustfully at a young woman"? Though the use is figurative, it appears that the speaker *imposed*, by means of personal discipline, a restriction on what his eyes would see.

Or what does the following text imply in speaking about the Servant of the Lord: "I will keep you and will make you to be a *covenant* for the people and a light for the Gentiles" (Isa 42:6)? Is this the "new covenant" that God promises to provide (see Jer 31:31–34; cf. Heb 8:8–12)? Is it an imposed arrangement or one mutually enacted? Might God cancel its benefits as he did with Israel and the first covenant? These may be difficult decisions but these questions demonstrate the issues the interpreter must investigate.

Using the NT example of *kyrios*, in Acts 9:5 Paul addresses the voice he hears with the question, "Who are you, *lord?*" Here the interpreter must decide whether this use is a title of respect (i.e., "sir" indicating high status), whether Saul (or the writer) intends a higher sense ("Lord," perhaps even with a supernatural connotation), or whether the writer has in mind a double entendre.

In addition to understanding a word's range of meaning, the interpreter needs to know how the specific meaning of the word in the passage relates to the other words in its field of meaning. By discovering the particular meaning of a word within its field of meaning, the interpreter learns the general sphere of ideas to which this

---

120. Ibid., 1:139.
121. Ibid., 1:559.
122. Ibid., 1:478.
123. Ibid., 1:739.

meaning of the word belongs; the relationship that exists between this word and the other words used in this semantic field; and perhaps what distinguishes this word from the others in its semantic field.

One aspect of word studies brings the two testaments together. Since Greek had replaced Hebrew as the spoken language of the Jewish community in Alexandria in the second century BC, Jews there produced the Septuagint.[124] Subsequently, the Jews living in the Roman world used this Greek translation, and it became the Bible of the early Christians during the first century AD. Because of their experience of the OT through this Greek translation, the NT writers used many Greek words with meanings not normally found in the everyday secular use of the same terms, much like Christians today might use terms like "fellowship" or "redemption" with meanings not normally understood by secular people.[125] Religious and theological ideas developed in the OT became attached to the words, adding new nuances to their meanings.

The Septuagint use of *kyrios* (lord) is one of many examples of this kind of influence on NT words. This word appears over 9,000 times in the LXX with the majority—6,156 to be exact—translating the divine name "Yahweh."[126] The use of *kyrios* to translate the Hebrew term for "Lord," *adonay*, which the OT sometimes used as a title for God, was quite natural. However, the translation of God's sacred name "Yahweh" by *kyrios* reflects the Jewish aversion to uttering the divine name lest they be guilty of desecrating it. Given how consistently the LXX translated the Hebrew "Yahweh" as *kyrios*, many scholars affirm the high probability that references to Jesus as "Lord" in the NT carry strong connotations of deity.[127]

---

124. The title Septuagint (from the Latin for seventy), thus abbreviated LXX, originates in the legend that seventy (or seventy-two) Jewish scholars produced the translation. For accounts, see Philo, *Vita Mosis* 2. 5.-7.25–44; Josephus, *Ant.* 12.2.1–15; Justin, *Apology* 1.31; and Irenaeus, *Against Heresies* 3.21.2.

125. E. Ferguson gives other common examples when he writes, "The distinctive religious meaning of many New Testament words (e.g., *ekklēsia, baptisma, presbyteros, psallō, cheirotonia*) is to be found not from etymology or classical usage but from the adaptations already made by Greek-speaking Jews" (*Backgrounds of Early Christianity* [Grand Rapids: Eerdmans, 1987], 346–47). The Greek words he cites mean, respectively, church (assembly), baptism (immersion), elder, sing psalms, and lifting up of one's hand.

126. The KJV occassionally rendered this Hebrew word "Jehovah." According to W. A. Elwell and B. J. Beitzel, "Jehovah," in *Baker Encyclopedia of the Bible* (Grand Rapids: Baker, 1988), 1106, Jehovah is the "Name for God formed by adding the vowels of the Hebrew word *Adonai* to the consonants of the Hebrew divine name, *YHWH*. . . . It is thought that in about AD 1520 Petrus Galatinus conceived the idea of combining the two names, thus creating the new form *YeHoWaH* from which the English term Jehovah comes. Although this form was foreign to the Hebrew language, it gained wide acceptance and was included as the translation for God's name in the KJV and ASV."

127. C. E. B. Cranfield says concerning Paul's use of *kyrios* at Rom 10:9, "Paul applies to Christ, without—apparently—the least sense of inappropriateness, the *kyrios* of LXX passages in which it is perfectly clear that the *kyrios* referred to is God Himself." He goes on, "We take it that, for Paul, the confession that Jesus is Lord meant the acknowledgment that Jesus shares the name and the nature, the holiness, the authority, power, majesty and eternity of the one and only true God," in *The Epistle to the Romans*, ICC, 2 vols. (Edinburgh: T&T Clark, 1979), 2:529. Confirming this conclusion in commenting on the use of *kyrios* at Acts 2:36, F. F. Bruce notes, "To a Jew, there was only one name 'above every name'—the Ineffable Name of the God of Israel, represented in synagogue reading and in the LXX text by the Title 'Lord.' And that the apostles meant to give Jesus the title 'Lord' in this highest sense of all is indicated by the way in which they do not hesitate on occasion to apply to Him passages of OT scripture referring to Yahweh," in *The Book of Acts*, NICNT, 2nd ed. (Grand Rapids: Eerdmans, 1988), 68. Finally, speaking of Paul's use of "Lord" in 1 Cor 12:3, G. D. Fee observes, that the affirmation of Jesus as Lord "meant absolute allegiance to Jesus as one's deity and set believers apart from both Jews, for whom such a confession was blasphemy,

Another example of the insights gained from a study of the LXX influence is the NT use of the word "firstborn" (Greek: *prōtotokos*). When the title "firstborn" applies to Jesus in Luke 2:7, it carries the literal meaning of the first child born to his mother: "She gave birth to her firstborn, a son." But this literal sense does not *fit* the two theological uses of the word in the titles for Christ in Colossians, "the firstborn of all creation" (1:15; NRSV and most translations) and "the firstborn from the dead" (1:18; NRSV). While some have suggested that "firstborn of all creation" means that Jesus was the first created being and, therefore, is not God,[128] strong evidence from the LXX usage suggests an entirely different meaning that fits the context more naturally. In their discussion of the word *prōtotokos* (firstborn) L&N argues, "In Jewish society the rights and responsibilities of being a firstborn son resulted in considerable prestige and status. The firstborn son, for example, received twice as much in inheritance as any other offspring."[129]

This prestige associated with being the firstborn in the Jewish culture gave rise to a figurative meaning for firstborn indicating superiority or higher status. This meaning of the Greek "firstborn" belongs to the semantic domain indicating status and to the subcategory of words expressing high status or rank. Thus, L&N translates Colossians 1:15, "existing superior to all creation."[130] The NIV seeks to capture this connotation by the phrase "firstborn *over* all creation." This finding gains further support from the LXX use of "firstborn" as a messianic title in Psalm 89:27, defined by Hebrew parallelism in precise superiority language,

> I will appoint him my firstborn (LXX: *prōtotokos*; Hebrew: *bekor*),
>   the most exalted of the kings of the earth.

Contextual information in Colossians 1 confirms that Paul used firstborn as a title to stress Jesus' superiority and supreme sovereignty over all creation. The references to his kingdom and the purpose statement in verse 18, "so that in everything he might have the supremacy," corroborate that the superiority of Christ over creation is the meaning of firstborn in this passage. These contextual factors make it clear that the phrase "firstborn from among the dead" (Col 1:18), the second occurrence of firstborn in this passage, also communicates this idea of superiority. Clearly, the LXX usage of the word "firstborn" has influenced Paul's choice of this messianic

and pagans, especially those in the cults, whose deities were called 'lords,'" in *The First Epistle to the Corinthians*, NICNT, rev. ed. (Grand Rapids: Eerdmans, 2014), 645.

128. This is a standard explanation propounded today by the Jehovah's Witnesses, for example. They say, "Being God's first creation, he was with the Father in heaven from the beginning of all creation. Jehovah God used him in the creating of all other things that have been created," in *From Paradise Lost to Paradise Regained* (Brooklyn: Watchtower Bible & Tract Society, 1958), 126–27. ". . . The Bible shows that there is only one God . . . 'greater than His son,' . . . And that the Son, as the First-born, Only-begotten and 'the creation by God,' had a beginning" (164). Among many refutations of their use of "firstborn," see B. M. Metzger, "The Jehovah's Witnesses and Jesus Christ: a Biblical and Theological Appraisal," *Theology Today* 10 (1953): 65–85. Reprinted in pamphlet form (Lancaster, PA: Lancaster Press, 1953), Metzger's article evaluates the Witnesses' doctrine of Christ and their *New World Translation*.

129. L&N, 1: 117.

130. Ibid., 1:117, 738.

title to show Christ's primacy over both creation and those who will experience resurrection from the dead.

Thus, the serious student of the NT must ask whether a given word's meaning reflects Septuagint influence that shifted its meaning beyond what was current among Greek speakers at the time. To discover any such influences, note the main meanings of the Hebrew words that the Greek word used to translate in the LXX. The final step always requires studying the specific NT context to test any potential LXX influence. The best help for evaluating Septuagintal usage and potential influence on the NT comes primarily from two sources: Moisés Silva, ed., *New International Dictionary of New Testament Theology and Exegesis*, 5 volumes (*NIDNTTE*),[131] and G. Kittel and G. Friedrich, ed., *Theological Dictionary of the New Testament*, 10 volumes (*TDNT*).[132]

The final area that we need to explore to determine the potential meaning of a word is its *nonbiblical* use in the everyday speech, literature, and inscriptions at the time the biblical book was written. Knowing the popular meaning of a word in the daily life of the people often gives insight into the frame of reference by which both writer and recipients understood the term.

For such insights into the language of the OT one should consult *HALOT* and *TDOT*. Returning to our discussion of *berit*, *TDOT* mentions that the appearance of G. Mendenhall's article, "Covenant Forms in Israelite Tradition," led to a rash of further studies on treaties in the ancient Near East.[133] These show the close relationship between the treaties of fourteenth and thirteenth century BC Hittite kings with their vassal rulers and the covenants enacted by Joshua during the conquest and settlement of Israel (and especially Josh 24). These findings, reported in *TDOT* 2:266–69 shed great light on the biblical records and may help us understand both the religious and political ramifications of the covenantal idea in the OT. The elements of the Hittite treaties also seem to be reflected in the organization of Exodus 19–24 and perhaps the book of Deuteronomy.[134]

While students can find specific examples of everyday use of Hellenistic Greek for NT studies in J. H. Moulton and G. Milligan, *The Vocabulary of the Greek New Testament*,[135] the work is dated and sketchy, and now its most valuable insights are

---

131. (Grand Rapids: Zondervan, 2014).

132. (Grand Rapids: Eerdmans, 1964–78). A one-volume abridgment, sometimes called "little Kittel" makes the essentials available in a more compact form: G. Kittel and G. Friedrich, *Theological Dictionary of the New Testament*, ed. G. A. Bromiley (Grand Rapids: Eerdmans, 1986). Again, see the bibliography for further insight on these and other tools.

133. *Biblical Archaeologist* 17 (1954): 50–76. See also G. Mendenhall, *Law and Covenant in Israel and the Ancient Near East* (Pittsburg: Biblical Colloquium, 1955).

134. Beyond that, Weinfeld notes, "Deuteronomy abounds with terms originating in the diplomatic vocabulary of the ancient Near East. Such expressions as 'hearken to the voice of,' 'be perfect with,' 'go after,' 'serve,' 'fear' (revere), 'put the words on one's heart,' 'not turn to the right hand or to the left,' etc., are found in the diplomatic letters and state treaties of the second and first millenniums B.C., are especially prominent in the vassal treaties of Esarhaddon, which are contemporaneous with Deuteronomy" (*TDOT*, 2:268–69). See J. G. McConville, *Deuteronomy*, Apollos Old Testament Commentary (Downers Grove: InterVarsity, 2002), and P. C. Craigie, *The Book of Deuteronomy*, NICOT (Grand Rapids: Eerdmans, 1976).

135. (Grand Rapids: Eerdmans, 1930).

incorporated into *NIDNTTE* and *TDNT*.[136] As an example, from *NIDNTTE* one learns that the Greek word for "lord" (*kyrios*) was not a title Greeks used for their gods in the early classical period of their language. The servile relation of the slave to his or her master [*doulos* (slave) to *kyrios* (master)] was so repulsive to the early Greeks that they did not consider "lord" a suitable divine title. However, starting with the first century BC *kyrios* began to be used as a title with reference to the gods. The ancient practice of calling both gods and kings "Lord" (because kings were viewed as representatives of the gods) began to penetrate the Mediterranean world. The emperor Augustus (63 BC–AD 14) was called god and lord in Egypt, and the title *kyrios* was applied to Herod the Great. Though Augustus and Tiberius (AD 14–37) discouraged the practice of attributing deity to them by the title "Lord," their successors Caligula (37–41) and Nero (54–68) promoted it and encouraged the imperial title "Lord and God." With the arrogant Domitian (81–96), claiming divine imperial status by the title, "Lord and God" reached a climax.[137] At the same time, the prevailing first-century Christians' attitude of submission expressed by calling themselves "slaves" of the "Lord" Jesus Christ conflicted with the traditional Greek religious mindset and put these believers on a direct collision course with the growing trend toward emperor worship.

An intriguing development for NT studies appears in the use of the Greek word for *covenant* (*diathēkē*). In Romans 11:27 Paul uses covenant of God's unilateral commitment to establish a relation with people (cf. Heb 8:10; Acts 3:25). *Diathēkē* also means the agreement or pact between people that carries benefits and obligations (Gal 3:15). However, the range of the Greek *diathēkē* went beyond the Hebrew *berit* and included the sense of "to make a will or testament."[138] The writer of Hebrews employs *diathēkē* in this sense of "will" in 9:16–17, creating a fascinating play on the same word used to mean "covenant" in the immediate context of 9:15 and 18.

In addition to lexicons the student should consult *concordances*. These alter the focus from word meanings and definitions in a range of sources to actual usage in the Bible, and from the range of possibilities to specific biblical contexts.[139] This may seem to duplicate the work of the lexicographers, but a brief review in a concordance will provide the student with an important firsthand sense of the range of meaning and uses. Having said this, students may decide to consult concordances even prior to their investigations of the dictionaries and lexicons. Such a search will provide an inductive appreciation of the apparent alternatives. Since we can determine the intended meaning of a word only from assessing the related ideas within its context,

---

136. Also, consult H. Balz and G. Schneider, eds., *Exegetical Dictionary of the New Testament*, 3 vols. (Grand Rapids: Eerdmans, 1990–92).

137. "κύριος, et al." *NIDNTTE*, 2:768–78.

138. This appears to be its primary sense in classical Greek. See H. G. Liddell and R. Scott, *A Greek English Lexicon*, 9th ed. (Oxford: Clarendon, 1940; supplement 1996), 394–95.

139. Students able to search biblical words electronically in essence can assemble concordance information in a few seconds. We will forbear here to illustrate with our examples *berîth* [covenant] and *kyrios* [lord]. See the bibliography for helps in selecting appropriate concordances.

we need to check an author's use of a given word in other places in the same writing and in other works. We can obtain further insight by reviewing how other authors use a word in the Bible. One author may use a word in a distinctive way that sets his use apart from that of other authors. For OT words, we should especially observe whether a word's usage seems concentrated in certain books with unique content (e.g., Leviticus, Lamentations), in books of prose or poetry (e.g., Judges or Songs, respectively), or in books associated with the priestly, prophetic, or wisdom traditions. Sometimes a distinct pattern of usage is discernible that gives the interpreter evidence that clarifies the meaning in the passage under consideration. At other times one discovers wide variety in its usage by an author or OT tradition. But even this has value because it helps to inform the interpreter concerning the types of contexts in which certain meanings of the word occur.

Interpreters must remember that the concept of contextual circles of meaning applies here, too. That is, word-uses closer to the passage under study have greater weight than word-uses at the periphery. So how the author uses words in the same paragraph and book has more relevance than how that author uses the same words in other books. From there we would consider how other authors in the same testament use the words, then how another author uses these words elsewhere in the Bible, and finally how extrabiblical writers use the words.

3. *Select the Meaning that Best Fits the Context*

Once students have discovered the possible meanings of a word, they must select the one that fits best in the passage under study. They must exercise care to avoid simply (and illegitimately) imposing one of the possible senses onto a specific use. This temptation is especially great where one meaning fits the interpreter's theology or desired outcome. Though novices must be wary of over-confidence, within reason students may probe the lexicons, and be willing even to call into question the category of meaning in which the experts have located a specific text. Though students are wise to trust the best resources,[140] at least this tactic will assure that interpreters have wrestled with the issues and have the necessary data to make an informed decision. Because of the complexity of word meanings, the interpreter should seek to discover all the information about a word that may help in determining its meaning in a specific passage.

Once the student knows the potential meanings of the word, *contextual factors* become the supreme arbitrator for selecting the most probable meaning. Often the general subject of the passage will strongly favor a meaning from one semantic domain. This marks the key principle: *The use of a word in a specific context constitutes the single*

---

140. We can't repeat often enough that since the goal is the *best* understanding of an author's intended meaning in a text, responsible interpreters must find and use the *best* sources in their study. Simply because a source is cheap, or in digital form, or readily available on the internet is no guarantee that it is trustworthy and accurate. Sometimes sources go out of print because they are outdated and shown to be inferior. Publishers also reprint older (and, in our view, outdated) sources because they need pay no royalties or copyright fees. Most often, the best sources are the most recent ones, and the best sources will incorporate the excellent insights of previous works.

most crucial criterion for the meaning of a word. Thus the interpreter must scrupulously evaluate the total context to decide which of the possible meanings fits best in the passage under study. The elements we have discussed up to this point become crucial determiners. Which meaning fits best given the historical-cultural background of the passage? Which best fits the literary context? Which fits the argument of the narrative or the poetic structure (e.g., its parallel words) in the most appropriate manner? Remember, though words have a range of possible meanings through their history, individual speakers or writers decide how they will use words in specific contexts. Writers may modify meanings or employ words in unique ways. In fact, writers may deliberately use words ambiguously or with double meanings, as occurs with the Greek word *anōthen* ("again" and/or "from above") in John 3:3, 7. Did Jesus mean that people needed to be born again, born from above, or both? To repeat, *context is the single most significant determiner of the meaning of a word or phrase.*

GRAMMATICAL-STRUCTURAL RELATIONSHIPS

As important as it is to know the meanings of words, our task is not yet complete. Indeed, as we just asserted, apart from larger contexts we cannot be completely certain about what words mean. People communicate by combining words together in larger units. The grammatical and structural relationships of words and word-groups make up the final component of language communication we must assess to understand a writer's meaning. People combine words according to the structures of a given language to convey their meaning. Before we proceed to explain in subsequent chapters how the various genres of literature function, we must explore the topics of grammar and structure, at least in a general way.

Technically speaking, grammar consists of two elements: morphology and syntax.[141] *Morphology* concerns the forms of individual words—typically how words are inflected (manipulated) to indicate their function in a language. To take only one simple example, in English we may put an -s on the end of some nouns to indicate "more than one." The -s is a morpheme designating "plural" in English. So, we say, "She ate one apple, but I ate two apples."[142] Functioning like the English -s, Hebrew employs

---

141. Two fine introductions to a modern understanding of language, especially in its application to biblical studies, are Cotterell and Turner, *Linguistics*; and S. E. Porter and D. A. Carson, eds., *Linguistics and the New Testament: Critical Junctures*, JSNTSup 168 (Sheffield, UK: Sheffield Academic Press, 1999). A seminal article on the topic is E. A. Nida, "Implications of Contemporary Linguistics for Biblical Scholarship," *JBL* 91 (1972): 73–89. For more general introductions to grammar as understood by modern linguistics, see J. Lyons, *Introduction to Theoretical Linguistics* (Cambridge: Cambridge University Press, 1977); and J. Lyons, *Language and Linguistics* (Cambridge: Cambridge University Press, 1981). Perhaps this is the place to remind readers that grammar only *describes* how languages function. That is, the modern study of grammar is descriptive, not prescriptive. For grammar of particular relevance for studying Greek and Latin, see D. Fairbairn, *Understanding Language: A Guide for Beginning Students of Greek and Latin* (Washington, D.C.: The Catholic University of America Press, 2011). For an example of how specific studies of syntax can become, see, e.g., H. Dallaire, *Syntax of Volitives in Biblical Hebrew and Amarna Canaanite Prose* (Sheffield, UK: Eisenbrauns, 2014).

142. Rules for English are so difficult since it has shamelessly assimilated words from so many other languages.

im, e, or *ot* at the end of its words to make plurals. Greek is more complex yet, with different plural morphemes (these formal indicators) often associated with each case (nominative, genitive, etc.). On another level, we put -ed at the end of some verbs to mark past time: "Today I will pick a red apple, though I pick*ed* a green one yesterday."

The other component of grammar, *syntax*, describes the system each language has for combining its various constituents in order to communicate. Word order is a crucial element of syntax for the English language. "John hit the ball" means something quite different from "The ball hit John." Because the words "John" and "ball" are not marked in any other way, English indicates their functions in this example by word order.[143] Word order in Hebrew typically follows standard conventions but exhibits more variety than English permits, especially the bare-bones grammar of poetry. Thus, it can state, "John hit the ball" either as (lit.) "hit John the ball" and "the ball hit John," although the latter specifically spotlights the object that John hit. For Greek, case markings (back to morphology—the forms of words) on nouns, pronouns, adjectives, etc., indicate functions to show whether a word serves as the agent or the recipient of an action. These case markings allow for more varied word order in Greek than in English that lacks them. Students who have studied German (to cite another highly inflected language) know the importance of word endings to indicate whether a noun functions as subject, object, or indirect object. Thus, syntax expresses the way a language arranges words to form a meaningful phrase, sentence, or larger unit.

In addition, relations between clauses within a sentence or between sentences are also crucial. The relationships between phrases and clauses are also important in Greek and Hebrew. As a simple example in English, we might say, "If it rains, we will get wet," or "We will get wet if it rains." Both are permissible, and there may be some reasons to say one or the other. Likewise the biblical languages may front dependent or independent clauses for a variety of reasons. That leads us to the next point.

Most guides to exegesis and analysis tend to work on the level of the sentence, and that remains an essential task for all interpreters. More recently, however, linguists have stressed the need for analysis of larger units—paragraphs and entire discourses. Communication rarely occurs simply in isolated sentences. Often called discourse analysis or text linguistics, this program is bearing good fruit.[144] In one sense language

---

While we put an -s on apple to indicate plural, it takes -es for box, -en for ox, -ies and the removal of y for sky, -i after removing -us for cactus, -a in place of -um for stadium, a change of the final -i to -e for crisis, the replacement of -f by -ves for hoof, but not a thing for sheep or deer.

143. Of course, in poetry some of these rules for word order may change, showing they are not really rules at all—only conventions. Thus, when one enters a different genre one expects new criteria for combining elements. We discuss poetry in the next chapter.

144. On the NT side, see S. E. Porter and J. T. Reed, eds., *Discourse Analysis and the New Testament: Approaches and Results*, JSNTSup 170 (Sheffield: Sheffield Academic, 1999); cf. the extensive bibliography in D. F. Watson, "Structuralism and Discourse Analysis," in *Dictionary of the Later New Testament and Its Developments*, ed., R. P. Martin, and P. H. Davids (Downers Grove: InterVarsity, 1997), 1134–35. For excellent introductions see S. E. Runge, *Discourse Grammar of the Greek New Testament: A Practical Introduction for Teaching and Exegesis* (Peabody, MA: Hendrickson, 2010); and S. Levinsohn, *Discourse Features of New Testament Greek* (Dallas: Summer Institute

combines various elements, as building blocks, to construct meaningful communication. In simple terms, combining morphemes (minimal elements of meaning, like the plural marker -s in English) produces words; putting words together produces phrases, clauses, and sentences; and syntactically combining sentences results in paragraphs, passages, or discourses. These are all dimensions of syntactical analysis.

This process of putting words together to communicate successfully involves many factors. Word order, the forms of words, the combinations of words, and the use of connecting words (such as conjunctions and prepositions) mark the various relationships between the words and sentences in a passage. All of these contribute to meaning. This underscores the absolute necessity of interpreting every biblical passage consistent with its grammar (morphology and syntax). Since grammar is a basic component in how writers organize words to express their thoughts and how audiences decipher the meaning from the words, grammatical analysis is an essential aspect of correct interpretation.

The Importance of Grammatical Relationships

To understand the meaning of any statement one must understand how words, phrases, sentences, and larger units interact (or are interrelated). Each word's contribution to the thought expressed stems from its relationship with the rest of the words in the sentence. Returning to our simple statement above, a minor rearrangement of the words, "John hit the ball," to "The ball hit John," changes the meaning drastically. Both sentences use the identical words, but they communicate different meanings depending upon whether "John" or "ball" functions as the subject or object. If these two short sentences involved a fastball thrown by a major league baseball pitcher, the consequences for the batter would differ significantly! Perhaps you have heard of the sign over the butcher's shop: "Try our sausages. None like them." In other words—grammar matters.

Grammatical study is strategic for correct interpretation because the biblical languages sometimes convey nuances that are hard to capture in an English translation. First John begins with an explicit assertion of the reality of Christ's physical body. Attempting to counteract a docetic gnostic teaching that claimed Jesus only appeared to have a physical body, the author affirms that his message about Jesus is based upon that "which we *have heard*, which we *have seen* with our eyes." Both verbs occur in the Greek perfect tense, which expresses a resulting state of affairs that is ongoing. Blass, DeBrunner, and Funk (BDF) call it "the continuance of completed

of Linguistics, 2000). Applications to the OT include R. D. Bergen, ed., *Biblical Hebrew and Discourse Linguistics* (Dallas: Summer Institute of Linguistics; Winona Lake, IN: Eisenbrauns, 1994); W. R. Bodine, ed., *Discourse Analysis of Biblical Literature: What It Is and What It Offers* (Atlanta: Scholars Press, 1995); R. E. Longacre, *Joseph, A Story of Divine Providence: A Text Theoretical and Textlinguistic Analysis of Genesis 37 and 39–48* (Winona Lake: Eisenbrauns, 1989); and E. Talstra, "Text Grammar and Hebrew Bible. I. Elements of a Theory," *Bibliotheca Orientalis* 35 (1978): 169–74. Outside of strictly biblical usage, see J. P. Gee, *An Introduction to Discourse Analysis: Theory and Method* (London and New York: Routledge, 1999).

action."[145] By using the perfect tenses, the author asserts that what he had heard and seen produced a new state of affairs in which he now lives. This is no mere historical reporting of past events.

In similar fashion the command in 1 John 4:1, "Dear friends, *do not believe* every spirit, but test the spirits to see whether they are from God," uses a present imperative of prohibition, a grammatical construction often employed to forbid the continuation of something already happening.[146] In this context, "Stop believing every spirit" might well express the grammar more precisely. The grammar here may suggest that the Christians gullibly accepted some allegedly spirit-induced utterances.[147] The negative command in 1 John 3:13, "*Do not be surprised,* my brothers and sisters, if the world hates you" might well carry the same force, suggesting that confusion troubled some believers and needed to stop.

What about use of the conjunction "if" in this same verse? This "if" clause does not mean, "maybe the world hates you and maybe it doesn't." In using this type of conditional Greek clause, the writer does not question that the believers were experiencing hatred; for the sake of his argument, he assumes the existence of that hatred.[148] On the other hand, an "if" whose premise is uncertain (as in "If it rains, we will get wet") occurs in Matthew 5:13. Jesus tells his followers, "You are the salt of the earth. But *if* the salt loses its saltiness, how can it be made salty again?" Jesus does not assume salt (the disciples) will lose its saltiness or that it will retain it. This remains an open issue. These differences in the significance of the conditional

---

145. F. Blass and A. Debrunner, *A Greek Grammar of the New Testament and Other Early Christian Literature,* trans. and rev. R. W. Funk (Chicago and London: University of Chicago Press, 1961), 175. On the "perfective/ stative" aspect, which describes the significance of the perfect tense, S. E. Porter says, "the action is conceived of by the language user as reflecting a given (often complex) state of affairs," in *Idioms of the Greek New Testament* (Sheffield, UK: Sheffield Academic Press, 1992), 21–22. The important topic of "verbal aspect" in Greek has received much attention and some disagreement. See C. R. Campbell, *Basics of Verbal Aspect in Biblical Greek* (Grand Rapids: Zondervan, 2008). For a study of aspect to explain the intricacies of Greek verb tenses in the book of Revelation, see D. L. Mathewson, *Verbal Aspect in the Book of Revelation* (Leiden: Brill, 2010).

146. BDF § 336 (3), 172. Cf. N. Turner, *Syntax,* in *A Grammar of New Testament Greek,* by J. H. Moulton, 4 vols. (Edinburgh: T. & T. Clark, 1963), 3:74–76. On the other hand, we must be alert to the fact that this grammatical construction does not always forbid an action in progress; it may do so in less than half of its occurrences in the NT as J. L Boyer, "A Classification of Imperatives: A Statistical Study," *GTJ* 8 (1987): 40–45, has shown. He found that in only 74 of the 174 instances of the negated present imperative in the NT did the writer call for the termination of ongoing activity. Porter, *Idioms,* 224–26; D. B. Wallace, *Greek Grammar Beyond the Basics* (Grand Rapids: Zondervan, 1996), 724–25; and many other grammarians affirm this conclusion.

147. At the same time, students must always take care not to "overexegete" such grammatical fine points. It would be inappropriate apart from further contextual evidence to posit too confidently the existence of this problem or how pervasive it was. Clearly, the prohibition seeks to prevent and, if necessary, stop false beliefs. Again, the grammar allows for or opens up the potential for the nuance "stop." Context determines its presence or absence.

148. At the risk of oversimplification, we note here that some older grammarians of Greek mistook the meaning of the first class condition. That is, this Greek usage does not necessarily mean that the premise (if-clause) is actually true. It merely indicates that the writer/speaker assumes its truth for the sake of the argument. It may or may not be factually true; the context rules again. In his research, Boyer discovered that the "if" in such first class conditions could be accurately translated "since" (indicating its obvious truthfulness) in only 37 percent of its NT uses. Another 12 percent are false premises, while the remaining 51 percent are indeterminate. See J. L. Boyer, "First Class Conditions: What Do They Mean?" *GTJ* 2 (1981): 75–114; cf. Porter, *Idioms,* 255–59; and Wallace, *Greek Grammar,* 690–94.

conjunction "if" go back to different Greek conjunctions or adverbs (*ei, ean*), but will not be readily apparent in English translations.

If we consider Hebrew, we encounter a language whose verbs function quite differently from English. In certain contexts imperfect (incomplete action) and perfect (completed action) may indicate past, present, or future actions. Rather than use a negative particle with the imperative as in Greek, Hebrew instead pairs the particle with an imperfect or a jussive (e.g., "You shall not kill," meaning "Don't kill"). However, it does employ features that appear similar to those we find in Greek or English—nouns, adjectives, participles, prepositions, and infinitives, to name a few. One feature of Hebrew employs an infinitive before a finite verb. For example, "hear (infinitive) and hear (finite verb)" and "see and see" literally render the words in Isaiah 6:9, as in the RSV: "Hear and hear, but do not understand; see and see, but do not perceive." However, this feature of Hebrew grammar is a way to indicate "surely, indeed, certainly." Thus, "hear and hear" may be a direct translation,[149] but it obscures the meaning. Better is the NIV: "Be ever hearing . . . be ever seeing" or the NRSV: "Keep listening . . . keep looking."

As with Greek, Hebrew also has the capacity to use different kinds of conditions whose nuances students must study carefully. Conditions may be assumed fulfilled, contrary to fact, or more or less probable.[150] Another common Hebrew grammatical feature, the construct state, consists of one word—noun or adjective—occurring with another noun, adjective, pronoun, or clause. The result appears as "X of Y." The relation between the two is a matter of the interpreter's understanding of the context since the construction may indicate various ideas. The English reader may not always realize that the translator made the decision how to render the construct. For example, the phrase "wisdom of Solomon" (1 Kgs 4:30) stands for the wisdom that Solomon displays.[151] On the other hand, "mourning of an only son" (Amos 8:10) in context clearly means *not* the mourning that the son does, but that others mourn *for* an only son.[152] Or the construct state may be descriptive: "scales of righteousness" (Lev 19:36) must mean "honest scales" (NIV) or "just balances" (ESV).[153] Psalm 23:2 literally reads, "He makes me lie down in pastures of grass." "Grass" or "grassiness" somehow characterizes the pastures. Most English versions translate this as "green pastures." At other times the relationship is one of apposition—where the second term in effect renames or defines the first—as in "the land of Canaan" (Num 34:2) or "daughter of Zion" (Isa 1:8).

---

149. We use the word "direct" instead of the more common but tricky term "literal" since linguists and translators prefer it, and it avoids confusion. A truly literal translation of one language into another would be largely unreadable. The more direct (or formally equivalent) translations seek to remain closer to the structure and wording of the source. Recall our prior discussion in ch. 4.

150. For a more complete discussion, see B. K. Waltke and M. O'Connor, *An Introduction to Biblical Hebrew Syntax* (Winona Lake, IN: Eisenbrauns, 1990), 636–38.

151. This is analogous to the Greek subjective genitive.

152. This parallels the Greek objective genitive.

153. This parallels the Greek descriptive genitive.

These limited examples illustrate that English versions do not always clarify certain nuances in the biblical languages or how much translations result from interpretive decisions by translators. They illustrate, as well, that when translations differ, an English reader may be at a loss to understand why. One may be more direct in the sense of closely paralleling the original's words, but another may better capture an original nuance. Moreover, as we observed earlier, "direct" may or may not be more "accurate" if grasping the intended meaning is our goal. A better goal may be equivalent effect or, in terms we used before, a faithful replica of the speech act.

Therefore, reliable biblical interpretation requires careful evaluation of the grammatical nuances of the original language texts of the Hebrew and Aramaic OT and the Greek NT. Ideally, every interpreter should know these biblical languages. Many grammatical features are apparent only in the original languages. Even the best of translations do not and probably should not bring them out. Where good modern translations do express clearly some grammatical nuances, they involve a greater or lesser degree of interpretation, for scholars do not always agree on the significance of certain grammatical constructions in a given passage. Knowing the biblical languages equips the interpreter to weigh the contextual evidence to identify the grammatical explanation that fits the text best. People who do not know Hebrew or Greek must always remember that they work at a disadvantage. Every student who aspires to become a biblical scholar must strive for competence in the biblical languages.

However, we are realistic enough to admit that it is impractical to expect all interpreters to know the biblical languages. Stage of life, the pressures and responsibilities of living, calling, language aptitude, access to a program of instruction—all these and more make this ideal impossible for many Bible students.[154] Yet we sincerely believe that *all believers are competent to study the Bible.* Those without knowledge of the biblical languages must compensate for their limitation by having a good grasp of English grammar, by using the best direct English translations of the Bible, and by using reliable commentaries and other resources produced by scholars who can explain the grammar. On the last point, by comparing several sources on a specific passage, one can determine whether an alleged grammatical analysis has general consensus. Further, the contextual evidence cited in support of a suggested grammatical point will enable the reader to understand the issues involved better.[155]

Accurately understanding a passage requires analyzing its structure and the significance of important grammatical constructions. While some grammatical insights

---

154. What is *not* an adequate reason for avoiding learning the biblical languages is the claim that computer programs now make all the insights of the biblical languages available to students. While we are avid users of several software programs (Logos, BibleWorks, and Accordance are the chief ones), they are no substitute for understanding how the languages actually function. Being able to label a feature of Greek or Hebrew is not equivalent to understanding what it means or how it functions.

155. Again we draw our readers' attention to Carson, *Exegetical Fallacies,* which contains a short but helpful section on "Grammatical Fallacies" (65–86). Though focusing on the Greek NT, Carson raises numerous cautions that could well apply to the OT. For example, all interpreters should heed his warning about reading more into tenses than is there.

cannot be discovered apart from the original language texts, the willing student can uncover a surprising amount of important grammatical information by carefully analyzing the English text and then double-checking the commentaries. This is especially true of the structure. Analyzing the structure for meaningful grammatical insights requires an English translation that carefully preserves the original language sentence pattern. Many find the New American Standard Bible (NASB),[156] the New Revised Standard Version (NRSV),[157] or the English Standard Version (ESV),[158] most valuable for this type of study. While many modern translations break up longer, complex sentences in the original languages into several brief sentences in English, the NASB often keeps the long involved sentences with their many subordinate clauses.

Obviously, the modern trend to shorter sentences contributes to smoother reading and higher comprehension. We highly recommend the versions that seek better ways to communicate the Bible's message. For example, a dynamic equivalent translation seeks to convey in English what a biblical writer would have said were he speaking English in *his own time*. The *Good News Bible* is a prime example of this tactic.[159] Another highly recommended version of this type is the *New Living Translation* (NLT). For the NT, J. B. Phillips takes another approach.[160] He seeks to say in modern (British) English what the biblical writer would say were he writing *today.* So looking at Luke 13:11, where the GNB has "a woman who had an evil spirit" (how a modern English speaker would have phrased this idea in Jesus' time), Phillips has "a woman who had been ill from some psychological cause" (how Phillips imagines the author would express the idea were he alive today).[161] E. Peterson's *The Message*[162] takes an even more paraphrastic approach than Phillips. Whereas the NIV renders Luke 13:19, "It is like a mustard seed, which a man took and planted in his garden. It grew and became a tree, and the birds of the air perched in its branches," *The Message* has, "It's like a pine nut that a man plants in his front yard. It grows into a huge pine tree with thick branches and eagles build nests in it." Both seek to recast the literal words and structures of the Hebrew and Greek languages into modern idioms and ways of expression, though their translation theory governs how they do it.[163]

However, the gain in readability in some modern translations comes with price

---

156. NASB updated ed. (La Habra, CA: The Lockman Foundation, 1995).

157. NRSV, copyright 1989, Division of Christian Education of the National Council of the Churches of Christ in the USA. The NRSV seeks to use the modern idiom and to be more inclusive in its use of language than some other translations.

158. ESV, copyright 2001, 2007, 2011 by Crossway Bibles, a division of Good News Publishers.

159. 2nd ed. (New York: American Bible Society, 2001); also called *Today's English Version*. The American Bible Society also publishes the *Contemporary English Version* (1995), also not a paraphrase but a translation of the original manuscripts.

160. *The New Testament in Modern English* (London: Bles, 1960).

161. Of course, in this example Phillips may also demythologize the original text interpreting a "spirit of sickness" (lit.) to be a psychological malady rather than an evil spirit.

162. E. H. Peterson, *The Message: The Bible in Contemporary Language* (Colorado Springs: NavPress, 2002).

163. See ch. 4 above for our fuller discussion of Bible translation. In addition, the journal *Bible Translator* consistently addresses issues of interest to those involved in this task. Also consult the various essays in S. E. Porter and M. J. Boda, ed. *Translating the New Testament: Text, Translation, Theology* (Grand Rapids: Eerdmans, 2009).

tags: some original meaning, not to mention nuances, is lost (an evil spirit differs from a psychological malady, and a mustard seed is not a pine nut), and one may fail to appreciate the text's original nuances. Most often and for most people, paraphrases are worth the price. But for serious grammatical study, more direct versions are superior. Studying biblical passages in the original languages forces the interpreter to interact with the text's own meanings and its sentence structures to determine how subordinate clauses and phrases relate to the main statement of the sentence and/or to each other. For this dimension of study, the more direct the English translation, the better. Different kinds of translations have their place in other phases of one's study.[164]

Steps for Discovering Structural Relationships

Structural analysis involves several simple steps—simple, that is, if one understands basic English grammar. Of course, we cannot make that assumption for everyone. We often do things in our own language without understanding what we have done or why. We can also unknowingly commit grammatical errors. People express ideas in language in the ways they learned. So even analyzing an English text requires conscious effort.[165] To explain the thought flow of a given passage often requires paying attention to and thinking carefully about what we read. Sometimes the relationships that exist in a passage are so obvious that we ignore their contribution to its total meaning.

Natural Divisions

First, the interpreter must *discover the natural divisions* of the section for study. The direction this takes will depend upon the kind of literature, and we provide specific help for various genres in the chapters that follow. But to illustrate, in historical narratives major sections may encompass many chapters in our current Bibles (for example, the story of Joseph encompasses Gen 37–50), and the interpreter needs to divide a large section into its smaller elements. The same holds true for NT Gospels or Epistles. Each section will require analysis to discern the writer's flow of thought within it. In poetry, of course, the individual poem constitutes the unit for analysis—some shorter, others longer. Wisdom literature requires more care, for the units may be more difficult to classify. A segment may consist of one proverb, an isolated psalm (e.g., Ps 37), a speech (e.g., Job 23:1–24:25), an entire book, or Jesus' Sermon on the Mount. Apocalyptic is the most troublesome; it puts modern readers in the most unfamiliar territory. But the dream of Daniel 7:1–14 is one unit; its interpretation in 7:15–28 is another.

---

164. Readers will recognize this as a brief summary of what we said about these issues in our section on texts and translations in ch. 4.

165. One fine source of help is B. Aarts, *Oxford Modern English Grammar* (New York: Oxford University Press, 2011). Not designed for English majors or specialists, the book seeks to explain standard English grammar to students and readers. A briefer summary of basic English grammatical categories—preparing students to undertake Greek, though it would help anyone review grammar—is found in the initial chapter of J. Wenham, *Elements of New Testament Greek*, 2nd ed. (Cambridge: Cambridge University Press, 2002).

Flow of Thought

Usually the interpreter seeks to understand one passage, at least one at a time. After discovering the main sections, the next step involves tracing the flow of thought in the passage for study.[166] Ask how does the writer's logic progress?[167] First, one must isolate, where appropriate, the individual paragraphs.[168] Paragraphs typically develop a unit of thought, often incorporating a topic sentence that the paragraph develops. Then the interpreter proceeds to analyze the building blocks of paragraphs—sentences—and how their assertions or propositions develop the writer's argument or narration.[169] Placing proper proportionate weight on each element in a sentence involves distinguishing the main statement (independent clause) or statements from any subordinate (dependent) clause or clauses that qualify it.

One helpful approach to understanding the basic structure of a passage involves a method for identifying the main statement(s) in each sentence, then identifying the subordinate clause(s) in each sentence, and determining how each modifies or qualifies the ideas expressed in the main statement(s). The following limited analysis of a paragraph of James 1 illustrates this procedure. We underline each main clause with a solid line. Those not underlined are subordinate clauses or phrases. The functions of some clauses or phrases are given in italics above each.

command	*addressees*	*temporal clause*
(2) <u>Consider it pure joy,</u>	my brothers and sisters,[171]	whenever you face trials of many kinds,

reason clause		
(3) because you know that the testing of your faith produces perseverance.		

command	*purpose clause*	*description*
(4) <u>Let perseverance finish its work</u>	so that you may be mature and complete,	not lacking anything.

---

166. Many books present methods of structural analysis to represent visually the configuration of a passage. W. C. Kaiser calls his approach a syntactical display or block diagram and illustrates his method using English, Hebrew, and Greek in *Toward An Exegetical Theology*, 99–104; 166–81. See also G. D. Fee, *New Testament Exegesis*, 3rd ed. (Philadelphia: Westminster John Knox, 2002), 41–58; and Osborne, *The Hermeneutical Spiral*, 45–49. Students must determine which method suits their individual needs. The objective is to understand the thought-flow or argument of a passage, however one can attain it. Often visualizing the structure provides useful insights into how the elements are related to each other.

167. This is an overview of steps that we develop later specifically for individual genres in ch. 9. Hence, each step will not necessarily be applicable for each genre. Clearly, what we next say about paragraphs does not apply to a proverb.

168. For specific help on locating paragraphs see Beekman and Callow, *Translating*, 279–81. In his discussion of discourse analysis, Porter lists several features that signal the boundaries between individual units of a discourse: shifts in grammatical person (e.g., first to third) and shifts in verb tenses (*Idioms*, 301–2).

169. A guide to understanding Hebrew sentences is F. I. Andersen, *The Sentence in Biblical Hebrew* (The Hague/Paris: Mouton; Berlin/New York: Walter de Gruyter, 1974); cf. also the appropriate sections of C. L. Seow, *A Grammar for Biblical Hebrew: Revised Edition* (Nashville: Abingdon, 1995).

170. Literally, the Greek word is *adelphoi,* "brothers," which, of course, refers to all the Christian readers of the letter, not males exclusively. Inclusive language versions, as the NIV here, show that in their translations.

conditional clause	command	
(5) If any of you lacks wisdom,	<u>you should ask God,</u>	

description	assertion	
who gives generously to all without finding fault,	<u>and it will be given to you</u>.	

temporal clause	command	reason clause
(6) But when you ask,	<u>you must believe and not doubt,</u>	because the one who doubts is like a wave of the sea, blown and tossed by the wind.

command

(7) <u>Those who doubt should not think they will receive anything from the Lord;</u>

assertion

(8) <u>they are a double-minded and unstable in all they do.</u>

The main clause of the first sentence is "Consider it pure joy." Three subordinate elements then qualify this statement. For each subordinate (dependent) clause or phrase the student must determine: (1) what word it modifies, (2) what type of clause or phrase it is (a chart showing possible types follows below), and (3) how this affects the meaning of the sentence. Most clause types answer one of the six well-known journalistic questions: *who, what, why, when, where,* or *how.* In the first sentence the first subordinate phrase, "my brothers and sisters," qualifies the understood subject "you" of the verb "consider," while the remaining two clauses modify the verb. The first subordinate element, the phrase "my brothers and sisters," indicates *who* is to count it all joy; the second, the clause "whenever you face trials of many kinds," shows *when* this is to be done; and the final one answers the question *why,* giving the reason for "considering it all joy."

To discover how each element influences the meaning of the sentence, the student should ask, "What would this statement mean without each subordinate clause or phrase?" Without the phrase "my brothers and sisters" in James 1:2, the recipient might not know who were to respond to trials with an attitude of joy. The second clause identifies the specific occasion when joy must be exhibited. Without the last clause, a reader would be thoroughly perplexed since joy is not an attitude normally associated with trials. This clause argues for a genuine reason for joy even in experiences of adversity that do not automatically stimulate that response.[171] The knowledge that difficult experiences contribute to the development of perseverance provides legitimate grounds for joy. This passage does not advocate some sadistic enjoyment of hardship.

In the second sentence of this passage, verse 4, two subordinate clauses follow the main statement, "Let perseverance finish its work." The first clause, introduced

---

171. In Greek, joy (*chara*) expresses a positive subjective feeling, a sense of well-being that normally comes from a positive objective cause. D. J. Moo, *The Letter of James*, PNTC (Grand Rapids: Eerdmans; Leicester, England: Apollos, 2000), 53, says that James' point "is that trials should be an occasion for genuine rejoicing."

with "so that . . ." modifies the verb, "let finish," and expresses the purpose (why?) for allowing perseverance to finish its work. The sentence ends with the phrase, "not lacking anything," which modifies the words "mature and complete" at the end of the subordinate clause. Answering the question, "What?" this phrase further explains the meaning of being mature and complete by describing it negatively.

The third sentence in v. 5 presents a more complicated structure. It begins with a subordinate clause followed by a compound main clause that is broken up by another subordinate clause. The compound main clause reads, "you should ask God [for wisdom] . . . and it [wisdom] will be given to you." The opening subordinate clause, "If any of you lacks wisdom," is a conditional clause that qualifies the verb "should ask." It indicates the specific condition in which one should offer this prayer—the one lacking wisdom in the midst of trials. The subordinate clause that divides the main clause, "who gives generously to all without finding fault," is a descriptive (adjectival in the chart below) clause that modifies "God." To what kind of God do we pray? This reminder of God's benevolent character encourages the reader to pray for wisdom in times of trial.

While an analysis of the structure of the remaining sentences in this paragraph would further illustrate the process and value of this approach, we leave that for the reader. The chart below provides a full list of the types of subordinate clauses that may occur. They indicate the kinds of logical relations possible in the structures of sentences.

TYPE[172]	JOURNALISTIC QUESTION	SAMPLE CONSTRUCTIONS
Adverbial[173]		
1. temporal	when?	when, after, before
2. local	where?	beside, above, below
3. causal	why?	because, for, since
4. purpose	why?	that, so that, in order that
5. result	what?	so, so that, hence
6. conditional	when?	if, provided, unless

---

172. Here we provide classifications mainly in relationship to English. Were students to conduct their analyses in the original language texts, certain of these categories would look different in places, as each language has unique ways to communicate. A worthy detailed analysis of Hebrew grammar is Waltke and O'Connor, *Introduction*. The best comparable source for Greek is Wallace, *Greek Grammar*. For other standard Greek grammars consult: BDF; Turner, *Syntax*; and Porter, *Idioms*.

173. Adverbial clauses modify or qualify verbs, or occasionally adjectives, in the ways listed. For example, the first shows *when* the action of the verb occurs, the second *where*, the seventh shows the circumstances despite which the action occurs, etc.

174. Noun clauses, as the name suggests, function as nouns. In the sentence, "Professors who love to ski seek teaching posts in Colorado," the entire clause "professors who love to ski" functions as the subject of the verb "seek." It operates like a noun in the sentence structure.

175. In similar fashion, adjectival clauses or phrases modify or describe nouns or pronouns.

TYPE[172]	JOURNALISTIC QUESTION	SAMPLE CONSTRUCTIONS
7. concessive	how?	although, in spite of the fact
8. comparative	how?	as, just as, likewise
Noun[174]		
9. subject	who or what?	who, which, that
10. object	who or what?	whom, what, that
11. apposition	who or what?	whom, what, that
12. direct address	who?	(identifies persons, objects)
Adjectival[175]		
13. modifier	who or what?	who, which, that

Is all this analysis worth the trouble? We sincerely believe so, for asking such structural questions enables the interpreter to identify the flow of the text's argument or narration, the associations, and the inter-relationships not otherwise evident. The interpreter is able to perceive the logic of a writer's flow of thought, breaks in thought, unusual features, and directions that readers easily miss without the time and effort spent to analyze the structure in these ways.

Verbs

The next step in the grammatical study of a passage focuses on the *impact of the verbs.* The complex verb systems of the biblical languages influence the meaning of sentences in several different ways. Understood in conjunction with their contexts, verbs designate the mood, aspect, time, kind, and voice of the action or state expressed.[176] The *mood* of the verb in each indicates whether the writer is making a statement, asking a question, giving a command, expressing a possibility, or making a wish. The interpreter must understand each sentence consistent with the mood expressed. It makes a big difference whether a sentence asserts a fact, merely expresses a possibility, or asks a question.[177] Interestingly, in James' paragraph above, the predominant mood is the imperative. Each of the five sentences contains a command or appeal. The only assertions of fact come in verses 5 and 8. After commanding the person who lacks wisdom to pray, James asserts in 1:5, "and it will be given to you"—a statement that carries the force of a promise. Verse 8 certifies the nature of the person who doubts

---

176. Waltke and O'Connor (*Introduction*, 344) provide an illuminating look at the Hebrew verbal system in their analysis of the form *wayakûhā*, literally translated "And they smote it" (Judg 1:8; most English versions have "set it on fire"). They note that this one form, the combination of a conjunction and a verb, expresses: (1) the action of smiting; (2) the subject of the action; (3) the object; (4) active voice; (5) case frame (verb is transitive); (6) type of action (Hebrew *hiphil*)—causative rather than simple action; (7) time of action—smiting already past; (8) quality of action—it has an endpoint; and (9) mood—action is an independent assertion.

177. Compare these: "This dog bites"; "This dog may bite"; and "Will this dog bite?"

God. While a careful reading of the English text makes most of these mood uses clear, students should verify their observations with good commentaries.

Influenced by the field of linguistics, an increasing number of biblical interpreters recognize the need to classify verbs according to their *aspect*.[178] Although tense in English mainly concerns *time,* in other languages—Hebrew and Greek are examples— the tense of a verb primarily indicates aspect (or "kind of action").[179] That is, in the biblical languages tense specifies the kind of action from the *perspective of the writer*. It indicates whether the writer or speaker conceives of the action of the verb as a completed state (perfective or stative), still in process (imperfective or progressive), or an unspecified whole—a simple occurrence (aoristic). English typically employs perfect or simple past tenses to convey perfective / stative action: "She *has read* that book"; or "She *read* that book." English marks an ongoing (imperfective) action with present or past progressive forms: "She *is reading/was reading* that book." "She *reads* books" can express and unspecified (aoristic) kind of action. How the writer actually frames the action (aspect) may or may not conform to reality, but that is not the issue. The Greek tense specifies how the writer presents the nature of the action.[180] For finding the time of the action, see below.

For example, note the author's words in John 1:29: "On the next day, he *sees* Jesus coming to him, and he *says* . . ." This is our direct translation where the italicized words highlight what grammarians call the "historical present." For his desired effect of creating a sense of vividness for his readers, John presents past actions as now happening (continuous action).[181]

Hebrew verbal systems also allow for another phenomenon under the category of aspect: causative constructions. At times a writer depicts an agent not simply as performing an action; the agent actually causes the action to occur. In English we

---

178. For assessments of aspect in the Greek language of the NT see C. R. Campbell, *Basics of Verbal Aspect*; S. E. Porter, *Verbal Aspect in the Greek of the New Testament with Reference to Tense and Mood* (New York: Peter Lang, 1989); B. M. Fanning, *Verbal Aspect in New Testament Greek* (Oxford: Clarendon, 1990); and K. L. McKay, *A New Syntax of the Verb in New Testament Greek: An Aspectual Approach* (Bern et al.: Peter Lang, 1994). A briefer analysis occurs in Porter, *Idioms,* 20–45; and Wallace, *Greek Grammar,* 499–504, and the pages on which he discusses each specific tense. Inevitably, disagreements remain among these grammarians concerning the specific applications of aspect theory.

179. Technically, grammarians divide the topic of tense into aspect, *Aktionsart,* and to a much lesser extent, time. Both aspect and *Aktionsart* pertain to the nature of the verbal action—whether it is ongoing, completed with results, or a simple occurrence. "Aspect" designates how the author or speaker presents the nature of the action in a linguistic context. It defines how the speaker or author conceives of the action. *Aktionsart* refers to the actual, objective nature of a verbal action (see Fanning, *Verbal Aspect,* 31, 85; Porter, *Verbal Aspect,* 88; Wallace, *Greek Grammar,* 499). Strictly speaking, Hebrew does not have tenses in the English language sense of categories for specifying the time of the action of a verb. But the language does employ forms for perfect and imperfect action. In specific contexts both may denote past, present, or future time. See Waltke and O'Connor, *Introduction,* 347–50, 461–66, 481–95.

180. For example, we may say, "It has been raining all day." We specify an imperfective kind of action (continuous), even though in reality it has rained only off and on during the day—with long spells of no rain at all.

181. Most English versions obscure this effect. The NIV has, ". . . John saw Jesus coming toward him and *said* . . ." To conform to modern English the NASB has a similar translation, but it indicates such instances of the historical present by appending an asterisk to the verb. The KJV most directly renders the Greek: ". . . John seeth Jesus coming unto him . . ."

employ additional verbal forms to convey causation: "They *make* me eat spinach." Or we may add a prefix to a verb. Compare "They closed the door" to "They *en*closed the yard" (They caused the yard to be closed in). The Hebrew language has special adjustments to the *verb* form to alter "They eat spinach" to "They cause to eat spinach." In Greenberg's words, "The *hif'il* is commonly causative: the subject makes the object do the action or be in the state expressed by the *qal* verb; *qal* 'he remembered,' *hif'il* 'he reminded' (lit., 'made remember')."[182]

Besides aspect and kind of action, verb forms indicate other details that contribute to correct interpretation. In places, verbs (or various other syntactical techniques) may mark the *time* of action (past, present, or future). And a verb's *voice* shows whether its subject performs the action (active voice: "Mary *cut* the pie"), is acted upon (passive voice: "The pie *was cut* by Mary"), or acts in reference to itself (middle voice in Greek often indicated by reflexive pronouns in English: "Mary *cut for herself* a piece of pie").[183] Or the verb may have no voice but merely specify a state of being, as in, "Our cat Tully *is* very large." Because verbs convey all of these types of information, the careful interpreter must evaluate each one closely in light of the context and weigh all the nuances the verbal form indicates as to the time and kind of action. For those who do not know the biblical languages, there is no substitute, again, for multiple translations and reliable commentaries that evaluate the verbal elements.

Connectives

The discussion of important grammatical elements must include *connectives*. Connectives (usually conjunctions, but also relative pronouns) occur at the beginning of sentences to link them with what precedes and within sentences to indicate the relationship between the words, phrases, and clauses through which ideas are conveyed.[184] The previous discussion of the relationship between main and subordinate clauses already underscored the significance of connectives as indicators of how the different parts of a sentence fit together. Although connectives are often small and seemingly insignificant, they exert an influence on meaning that far exceeds their size. Like joints and junctions in a plumbing system of pipes, they regulate the flow of a text's argument. The following chart presents the vast scope of connectives that the interpreter must note in order to understand precisely the meaning of a passage.[185]

---

182. M. Greenberg, *Introduction to Hebrew* (Englewood Cliffs, NJ: Prentice-Hall, 1965), 43. *Qal* and *hif'il* refer to different Hebrew verbal stems. Their meanings need not detain us at this point.

183. The Greek language has "voices" similar to English. Hebrew employs "binyans," similar to conjugations, which also indicate voice. The three voices in Hebrew correspond to active, passive, and reflexive. See Waltke and O'Connor, *Introduction*, 354–55.

184. English, Hebrew, and Greek use a variety of connectives to indicate subordination. Hebrew often coordinates items by using *waws*. (Readers without Hebrew can ignore that comment.) For those wanting further insight see R. J. Williams, *Hebrew Syntax: An Outline*, 3rd ed., rev. and exp. J. C. Beckman (Toronto: University of Toronto Press, 2007), 152–71 and Waltke and O'Connor, *Introduction*, 632–55.

185. For particles and conjunctions in Greek see BDF §§ 438–57; Porter, *Idioms*, 204–17; and Dana and Mantey, *Grammar*, 239–67. Andersen, *Sentence*, and Seow, *Grammar*, 54–63; 104–15; 210; 324–25, survey the various ways Hebrew accomplishes connections.

TYPES	MEANING	SAMPLE CONNECTIVES
Temporal or Chronological	Time	after, as long as, before, now, meanwhile, since, then, until, when, whenever, while
Local or Geographical	Place	where, beside, upon, above, under, below, on, over, at
	Direction	to, toward, from
Logical	Continuative	and, also, besides, both . . . and, furthermore, moreover, likewise, not only . . . but also, whereupon
	Contrast	although, but, however, much more, nevertheless, not only . . . but also, yet, otherwise, still, whereas
	Purpose	in order that, that, so that
	Result	so that, as a result, hence, consequently, so, then
	Inference	therefore, thus, then, wherefore
	Reason	as, because, for, inasmuch as, since, whereas, why
	Condition	as if, as though, if, lest, provided, providing, unless
	Concession	although, yet, in spite of, though, unless, while
Modal	Agency/Means	by, through, by means of
	Manner	as
	Comparison	also, as, as . . . so, just as . . . so, indeed, in fact, likewise, so also, so as, moreover, than
	Example	for, for example, indeed, in fact, namely
Emphatic	Emphasis	indeed, only, finally

Adjectives and Adverbs

Several remaining grammatical items require the attention of the careful interpreter, namely *adjectives and adverbs.* These modifiers regulate the meaning of a noun or verb in some significant way. It's one thing to walk; it's another to walk *slowly.* Waltke and O'Connor cite Hosea 1:6 to display a wide use of adverbs in Hebrew.[186] They translate: "Call her name *Not*-Pitied, *for indeed* I will *not* continue *any longer* to have pity on the House of Israel." Each italicized word represents a Hebrew adverb, one giving time, several negating, and one providing emphasis. That is, "any longer" suggests

186. Waltke and O'Connor, *Introduction,* 657.

that God had shown compassion on Israel, but would "not" do so "any longer." As a result, the prophet characterizes the nation as those "Not-pitied *any longer.*" The termination of God's pity merits an emphatic "indeed." Another example illustrates several adjectives: "They will hear of your *great* name and your *strong* hand and your *outstretched* arm" (1 Kgs 8:42). Each provides additional color to the noun it modifies. These Hebrew adjectives are similar to those used in English and Greek. Often, though, Hebrew performs the function of description through construct phrases to which we referred earlier (as in "the royal seed" [lit. seed of royalty; 2 Kgs 25:25], the "royal throne" [lit. throne of royalty; 1 Kgs 1:46], or even through apposition, "the deceitful tongue" [lit. tongue of deceit; Ps 120:2]).[187]

In James 1:2 discussed above, the writer significantly strengthens the initial command by the inclusion of the Greek adjective "all" (Greek *pasan*), translated "pure" in the NIV.[188] To "Consider it *pure* joy whenever you face trials of many kinds" is far more demanding than just to "Consider it joy." Without the adjective "pure," this command would be unclear about the quality or amount of obligatory joy. Similarly, the adverb "generously" in verse 5 adds a vital dimension to God's giving. He does not simply give, James insists; God gives *generously* to all who ask him for wisdom.

Pronouns

Students must not underestimate the significance of another seemingly routine grammatical item: the *use of pronouns* and whether they (and nouns) are *singular or plural*. It is important to determine the antecedents of all pronouns to learn to whom or to what they refer. The marking of pronouns, both their case usage and whether singular or plural, is often clearer in Hebrew and Greek than in English. Hebrew marks personal pronouns as to number, person, and gender. In addition, Hebrew employs demonstrative pronouns (this, that), interrogatives and indefinites (who, what, whoever, how, why, where), and relative pronouns (who, whom, which). Greek, likewise, employs a wide array of pronoun types: personal, relative, demonstrative, intensive (as in the *same* man or the man *himself*), possessive (his, her, my), reflexive (yourself), reciprocal (love *one another*), interrogative, and indefinite.

Whereas the pronoun "you" may be either singular or plural in English, Greek (as well as Hebrew) makes a clear distinction. (Hebrew also has masculine and feminine forms for "you" in both singular and plural). Twice in 1 Corinthians Paul identifies believers as the temple of the Holy Spirit. Warning against the serious dangers of sexual immorality in 6:18–19, he reminds them that each Christian's physical body is a temple of God indwelt by the Holy Spirit. However, Paul's reference to God's temple earlier in 1 Corinthians 3:16–17 pictures the corporate group of believers—namely, the

---

187. Ibid., 255–56.

188. The NIV "pure" here is preferable to the potentially ambiguous "all" where "all" may appear to be a direct object of the verb consider. The point is not to consider all [things] as joy; rather, consider [it] pure joy whenever trials come.

entire church—as God's temple indwelt by the Spirit. Second-person plural pronouns make this distinction clear. Paul uses the same temple analogy in two distinct ways: to refer both to individuals and to the entire church. Unfortunately, many sincere believers have missed the point of Paul's warning in chapter 3 not to destroy God's temple. Thinking of their individual body as God's temple, they understand Paul's admonition as a call to personal piety; they do not perceive Paul's true corporate intent—a plea not to allow divisions to destroy the church.[189] Similarly, at the conclusion of both letters to Timothy the writer says, "Grace be with *you*." We might mistakenly think these are Paul's concluding benedictions to an individual, Timothy. Actually, the Greek pronouns are plural, so in fact, he invokes God's blessing upon the entire church.[190] For a Hebrew example, the fact that Jeremiah 5:4 reports the prophet's thoughts ("I thought, 'These are only the poor . . .'") suggests that he is also the "you" commissioned in v. 1—except that "you" in v. 1 is plural "indicating that Jeremiah is part of a larger search party."[191]

The specific distinctions that Greek *relative pronouns* make between singular and plural, as well as between masculine, feminine, and neuter, provide a precision not available in our generic English "who" and "what."[192] Direct English translations of Jesus' genealogy in Matthew do not clarify that Jesus is the child of only Mary, not of both Joseph and Mary. Matthew 1:16 reads, ". . . and Jacob the father of Joseph, the husband of Mary, of *whom* Jesus was born, who is called the Messiah" (NRSV). Yet, the Greek text uses a feminine singular relative pronoun that restricts "whom" to Mary alone.[193]

Many such grammatical details that exist in the biblical languages do not always appear in English translations—even the so-called "literal" ones (what we have called "direct" or "formally equivalent" translations). By their very nature, translations are limited in their ability to bring out all nuances of the original languages. No two languages ever mirror each other exactly. Hence, accuracy and thorough understanding demand that students check all interpretations against the original languages to be certain they are consistent with the grammar of the text. As we have repeatedly urged, students must surround themselves with a range of good translations and key biblical commentaries that provide insight into the nuances of grammar.[194]

---

189. Cf. Fee, *1 Corinthians*, 2nd ed., 157–62; 291–94.

190. Southern American English has a colloquial mechanism for plural you: "y'all." "Ye" served as the plural pronoun of the second person in the subjective case in Old English (beginning ca. AD 1000). Other languages today can also distinguish between singular and plural "you." Those familiar with the KJV or Shakespeare will recognize the many older ways to refer to the second person: you, ye, thee, thy, thine, thou.

191. J. R. Lundbom, *Jeremiah 1–20*, AB 21a (New York: Doubleday, 1999), 376.

192. So the one pronoun "who" can serve in all these ways: "Who is my neighbor?" (singular); "Who are those children?" (plural); "She is the woman who taught me Greek." (feminine singular); "The men who race cars live down the street" (masculine plural). Like English, Hebrew also employs undeclined relative pronouns, e.g., *'šr* and *š*.

193. The NIV avoids the ambiguity by saying, ". . . the husband of Mary, and Mary was the mother of Jesus who is called the Messiah."

194. The bibliography lists the best resources.

8

GENERAL RULES OF
HERMENEUTICS:
BIBLICAL POETRY

omprising about one-third of the entire Bible, poetry is its second most common literary feature.[1] Poetry abounds even outside the so-called poetical books like Psalms, Job, Song of Songs, and Lamentations. OT narrative books periodically present long sections of poetry, and most prophetic oracles take poetic form.[2] Also, contrary to a common impression, poetry dots the pages of the NT, in original forms as well as in quotations of the OT.[3] Indeed, against present practice, the printing of more of those texts as poetry rather than as prose in modern Bibles would enable readers better to appreciate their poetic nature.[4] Small wonder that Ryken warns, "There is *no* book in the Bible that does not require the ability to interpret poetry to some degree, because every book includes some figurative language."[5]

The purpose of this chapter is to prepare interpreters both to enjoy and to interpret the Bible's poetic literature well. As Longman notes, since "the Bible is an affective book that communicates much of its meaning by moving the feelings and the will of its readers," readers must be careful not to "depoeticize its form" by ignoring its literary conventions.[6] An understanding of its unique literary dynamics will not only

---

1. F. W. Dobbs-Allsopp, "Poetry, Hebrew," in *The New Interpreter's Dictionary of the Bible Volume 4 Me-R*, ed. K. D. Sakenfeld (Nashville: Abingdon, 2009), 558.

2. For examples of poetry amid narratives, see Exod 15:1–18; Judg 5; 1 Sam 2:1–10; 2 Sam 22; 23:1–7. For the most definitive study of the phenomenon thus far, see J. W. Watts, *Psalm and Story: Inset Hymns in Hebrew Narrative*, JSOTSup 139 (Sheffield: Sheffield Academic Press, 1992). For more recent developments, cf. J. W. Watts, "Biblical Psalms outside the Psalter," in *The Book of Psalms: Composition and Reception*, ed. P.W. Flint and P.D. Miller, Jr., VTSup 99 (Leiden and Boston: Brill, 2005), 288–309.

3. Though some are questionable, likely sections include Matt 11:17; 13:13; Luke 1:46–55, 67–79; 2:29–32; 6:20–26; 7:31; John 1:1–18; Rom 11:33, 36; Eph 5:14; Phil 2:6–11; Col 1:15–20; 1 Tim 3:16; 2 Tim 2:11–13; 1 John 2:12–14; Rev 4:11; 5:9–10; 7:15–17; 11:17–18; 12:10–12; 13:10; 15:3–4; 16:5–7; 18; 19:1–8; cf. P.W. Comfort, *The Poems and Hymns of the New Testament* (Eugene, OR: Wipf & Stock, 2010); S. C. Grabiner, *Revelation's Hymns: Commentary on the Cosmic Conflict*, LNTS 511(London and New York: Bloomsbury T&T Clark, 2015).

4. So L. Ryken, *Words of Life: A Literary Introduction to the New Testament* (Grand Rapids: Baker, 1987), 101–2.

5. Ryken, *How to Read the Bible as Literature* (Grand Rapids: Academie Books, 1984), 87. According to N. K. Gottwald ("Poetry, Hebrew," *IDB*, K-Q: 829), only seven OT books—Leviticus, Ruth, Ezra, Nehemiah, Esther, Haggai, and Malachi—seem to lack any poetic lines.

6. T. Longman, III, "Biblical Poetry," in *A Complete Literary Guide to the Bible*, ed. L. Ryken and T. Longman, III (Grand Rapids: Zondervan, 1993), 81.

heighten the pleasure of reading the poetry but also enable interpreters to "hear" the poets' thoughts more clearly.[7] Fortunately, as we shall see, though scholars still debate many important issues, recent scholarly study of Hebrew poetry has uncovered for us a rich lode of insights to mine in studying the poetry of both testaments.

THE DYNAMICS OF POETRY

What is poetry? Poetry consists of written compositions typified by terseness, vivid words, verbal inventiveness, a base in the single poetic line, and a high degree of structure.[8] Put differently, poetry displays a higher degree of organization, sound-play, and evocative language than prose. We say to a "higher degree" because many prose texts also have poetic elements. Indeed, one should not think of poetry and prose as completely distinct, unrelated categories; rather, they represent the ends of a literary continuum. The more intense, dense, and compact a literary piece is, the closer it approaches the poetry side of the continuum.[9]

The opening lines of the poem "The Eve of St. Agnes" by John Keats illustrate the basic elements of poetry:[10]

> St. Agnes' Eve—Ah, bitter chill it was!
> The owl, for all his feathers, was a-cold;
> The hare limp'd trembling through the frozen grass,
> And silent was the flock in woolly fold . . .

Structurally, what dominates the piece is not a grammatical sentence or paragraph but the poetic line. Each line is terse—so terse, in fact, that none fills out a full line of the printed page. Read aloud, each shows a natural rhythm of accented and unaccented syllables (and SI-lent WAS the FLOCK in WOOL-ly FOLD).

In turn, the rhythmic structure dictates an economy of language. The poet has carefully carved his thoughts into a few precise words that fit the rhythmic scheme; there are no wasted words—words just thrown in to fill blank space or to impress

---

7. Occasionally that understanding may also help us solve thorny textual problems or interpret difficult verses. See the example from Amos 6:12 in W. S. LaSor, D. A. Hubbard, and F. W. Bush, *Old Testament Survey*, 2nd ed. (Grand Rapids: Eerdmans, 1996), 231.

8. For the defining importance of the poetic line, see Dobbs-Allsopp, "Poetry, Hebrew," 551; cf. R. Alter, *The Art of Biblical Poetry* (New York: Basic Books. 1985), x ("the best words in the best order"); A. Berlin, *The Dynamics of Biblical Parallelism* (Grand Rapids: Eerdmans, 2008), 5, 16 (a high degree of "terseness and parallelism"). For detailed discussion of criteria, see W. G. E. Watson, *Classical Hebrew Poetry*, JSOTSup 26 (Sheffield: JSOT, 1984), 46–62.

9. Cf. D. L. Petersen and K. H. Richards, *Interpreting Hebrew Poetry* (Minneapolis: Fortress, 1992), 13–14; but cf. Dobbs-Allsopp, "Poetry, Hebrew," 551: "Aside from lineation there are no intrinsic markers or clear-cut boundaries between poems and nonpoems, but only a cluster of intersecting and always local variables that signal the presence of poetry." Of course, the border between poetry and prose can often be difficult to pinpoint; cf. the treatment of the problem in S. E. Gillingham, *The Poems and Psalms of the Hebrew Bible*, Oxford Bible Series (Oxford: Oxford University Press, 1994), 18–43.

10. For the full text, see O. Williams, ed., *Immortal Poems of the English Language* (New York: Washington Square Press, 1952), 333–43. What follows draws its inspiration and some content from C. S. Lewis, *Christian Reflections* (Grand Rapids: Eerdmans, 1967), 129–35.

the reader. As for sound, the most obvious feature is the poem's rhyme. The final words of every other line rhyme ("was" / "grass"; "a-cold" / "fold").[11] More subtly, observe the repetition of the sound "f" in the words "for," "feathers," "frozen," "flock," and "fold." The poet has crafted rhyme and repetition into his lines so they sound pleasant when read aloud.

Finally, several things are striking about the poem's language. First, the poet offers concrete images to convey an abstract idea. He could have simply stated his main idea like "It was very cold on St. Agnes' Eve." Instead, he described the cold through three images—an owl, a hare (a rabbit), and a flock of sheep. How cold was it? It was so cold that the owl's feathers could not keep him warm, the rabbit could barely hop, and the flock could not even bleat a "baah." Now, that's cold![12]

Indeed, this leads us to a second observation. Through vivid language ("bitter chill," "limp'd," "frozen grass," "woolly fold"), the poet wants us to experience his topic—to *feel* the cold of that particular night. So his words appeal not so much to our reason as to our imagination. They paint imaginary pictures that allow us to experience the topic—its feel, sights, smells, touch, or taste. Our imagination sees the freezing owl, the limping rabbit, and the silent sheep; we feel that evening's "bitter chill." In sum, "poetry is a language of images that the reader must experience as a series of imagined sensory situations."[13]

But some may object that prose often betrays an underlying rhythm and employs similarly vivid language. They may ask, then, how poetry differs from prose. At this point it is best to distinguish between poetic language (i.e., rhythmic sentences and concrete imagery) and poetry. Prose does make use of poetic language, particularly prose that is written for public presentation. The distinct attributes of poetry, however, are its sparseness and its restricted structure; these are not intrinsic to prose. Though prose may be compact and carefully structured, its structure is formed of sentences and paragraphs. The structure of poetry, by contrast, consists of tightly arranged lines and compact language.[14] Further, compared to prose, poetry features a higher concentration of metaphors and images—what we often call "poetic language."

How does biblical poetry compare to the poetry most familiar to us? Consider the overview of Hebrew poetry that this clever limerick offers:

> Hebrew poems are not just a mess,
> nor is this, we hope, a mere guess.

---

11. In describing poetry, the / sign means "parallels" or "corresponds to . . . ." Later we will use // to signal the end of a poetic unit of parallel lines (e.g., two or more such lines joined by /).

12. Cf. the observation by Lewis (*Christian Reflections*, 131) that adjectives dominate poetic language.

13. Ryken, *How to Read*, 91 (his italics omitted).

14. So Berlin, *Dynamics*, 16, with reference to the constitutive structure of biblical poetry, parallelism (to be discussed later); cf. Petersen and Richards, *Interpreting Hebrew Poetry*, 14 ("parallelism, rhythm, and style"). Against J. L. Kugel (*The Idea of Biblical Poetry* [Baltimore: Johns Hopkins, 1981], 85, 94–95), who wrongly denies the idea of "biblical poetry." Kugel mistakenly equates "poetry" with "meter," overlooking the former's more typical feature, mimesis; cf. R. Raphael, "That's No Literature, That's My Bible: On James Kugel's Objections to the Idea of Biblical Poetry," *JSOT* 27 (2002): 37–45.

They may not have rhyme,
but you'll find every time
that the poets composed under stress.[15]

As was true of the Keats poem explored above, the Bible's poetry is "not just a mess" but has sound (but not rhyme), structure, and language. The interpreter's task is to understand each of these three features and, hence, to be able to interpret biblical poems with insight and understanding. This table summarizes the features that distinguish poetry from prose:

How to Tell Prose from Poetry

FEATURE	POETRY	PROSE
Basic Unit	Single line	Sentence
Unit's Length	Symmetrical	Variable
Language	Evocative Inventive (e.g., ambiguity, allusion) Rare, Archaic Word- and Sound-plays	Variable Word and Sound-plays
Grammar	Concise, Simple Sentences Few Prose Particles Ellipsis	Complex Sentences Many Prose Particles
Syntax	End-of-Line Pause Spatial Compression Parallelism Frame	Variable
Average Length	Two to Four Lines	Variable
Rhythm	Free, Variable Product of End-Pause and Parallelism	Variable
Semantics	Semantic Overlap of Words Intense Word Interplay	Variable
Reading Rate	Slow	Fast

The Sounds of Hebrew Poetry

Rhyme and Meter

First we will consider the feature of *sound*.[16] Traditional English poetry uses two aspects of sound: rhyme and meter. *Rhyme* occurs when a poet pairs at least two words

---

15. Watson, *Classical Hebrew Poetry*, 100. For a useful survey of the poetic devices used by Jesus, see R. H. Stein, *The Method and Message of Jesus' Teachings*, rev. ed. (Philadelphia: Westminster, 1994), 7–32. The classic catalog of biblical poetic techniques remains E. W. Bullinger, *Figures of Speech Used in the Bible* (Grand Rapids: Baker, 1968 [orig. 1898]).

16. Obviously, this subject relates primarily to readers who can access the original Hebrew and Greek texts.

with identical sounds at the end of successive or alternating lines (e.g., "The owl, for all his feathers, was *a-cold* / And silent was the flock in woolly *fold*" [italics added]). *Meter* involves the rhythmic alternation between accented and unaccented syllables within each poetic line. By printing the accented syllables in capital letters, we can readily see the accentual alternation of the line just quoted from Keats:

> The OWL, for ALL his FEA-thers, WAS a-COLD
> And SI-lent WAS the FLOCK in WOOL-ly FOLD.

Observe that in this example an accent falls specifically on every other syllable, and that each line has a total of five accents.[17]

Hebrew poetry differs from English poetry in its uses of sound. For example, it lacks the rhyme that English speakers deem so basic to poetry.[18] That is, Hebrew poets did not normally structure poetic lines so that their final words rhymed. On the other hand, they occasionally used rhyming sounds with great effect.[19] The most common use is end-rhyme in which the poet rhymes the final sounds of successive lines using suffixes or endings. For example, all four lines of Isaiah 33:22 end with the same sound, the suffix—*nu/–enu* ("our" or "us"). The other use is word-pair rhyme in which the poet rhymes two or more words in a row. Observe the three rhymed words that conclude this example from Isaiah 22:5:

ki yom	*mehumah*	*umebusah*	*umebukah*
For it is a day	of tumult	and trampling	and terror.[20]

Does Hebrew poetry have regular meter? In recent decades, a lively discussion, spurred in part by studies of extrabiblical Semitic poetry, has produced a divided scholarly house on the question. On one extreme, some scholars virtually deny that biblical poetry has any meter at all.[21] Others argue that it does indeed have meter and explain it by counting letters or syllables, by alleging uses of stressed syllables, or

---

Nevertheless, an awareness of these additional dimensions of OT poetry will enable Bible readers to benefit from the occasional comments on the original languages in major reference books. For an example of where sound also figures in NT poetry, see below.

17. Drawing on analogies from ancient Greek poetry, scholars have assigned technical labels to kinds of poetic meter. They call the alternation of unaccented and accented syllables ("in WOOL-ly FOLD") *iambic*; its opposite (i.e., accented followed by unaccented syllables) *trochee*. With five accents in each line, the Keats poem follows a common meter called *iambic pentameter*.

18. Cf. the clever chapter title "It May Not Rhyme, But It's Still . . . Hebrew Poetry," in L. M. Fields, *Hebrew for the Rest of Us: Using Hebrew Tools without Mastering Biblical Hebrew* (Grand Rapids: Zondervan, 2008), 258–72. Of course, though it may lack rhyme, we concede that free verse still qualifies as poetry.

19. Cf. the discussion in Watson, *Classical Hebrew Poetry*, 229–34. See also our discussion below of the related phenomena, assonance and alliteration.

20. Watson, *Classical Hebrew Poetry*, 232, who provides other examples of both types of rhyme (231–32).

21. Most recently, D. R. Vance, *The Question of Meter in Biblical Hebrew Poetry* (Lewiston, NY: Edwin Mellen Press, 2001), 496 ("one may safely conclude that the poetry of the Hebrew Bible does not contain meter"); Kugel, *The Idea of Biblical Poetry*, 301; cf. also Berlin, *Dynamics*, 4. While conceding the periodic presence of poetic stress, Alter believes "the term meter should probably be abandoned for biblical verse" (*The Art of Biblical Poetry*, 9).

by analyzing syntax.[22] The problem is that, thus far, no system adequately explains all the poetic phenomena available. At one point or another each has to squeeze or stretch the poetry to fit its preconceived systematic mold.[23]

In our view, Hebrew poetry follows neither lock-step, sing-song meter nor an unanchored free verse. Instead, it follows what Hrushovski calls a *free rhythm,* that is, the flexible use of accented syllables within certain broad limits.[24] It shows such flexibility in several respects. First, a given poetic line may have two, three, or four words with accented syllables. Second, its parallel line(s) may or may not have the same number of such words. Scholars commonly use numbers to describe the accented syllables in a poetic couplet. For example, they would call a couplet in which each line has three stresses 3:3. If the second line had two or four stresses, it would be 3:2 or 3:4, respectively. Third, the number of unaccented syllables between accented ones varies, although at least one must intervene. Fourth, the number of parallel lines forming a poetic unit may vary from two to four but normally not more than four. Finally, unlike European metrical poetry, a given Hebrew poem need not consistently follow one rhythmical pattern throughout.

On the other hand, biblical poetry does operate within certain assumed poetic limitations—that is, within its own "poetics." First, regardless of how many accents it has, each line or pair of lines constitutes either a phrase or a syntactical or logical unit. In other words, each will express either one complete thought or two related ones.[25] Second, the lines typically occur in groups of twos or threes of equal or similar length (i.e., 3:3; 3:2; 3:4). Hebrew poetry avoids overly long or short line-pairs (e.g., 5:1; 4:1, etc.). Third, as noted above, two accented syllables never occur in a row; at least one unaccented syllable intervenes. Fourth, also as noted above, normally the

---

22. The latest defense of the syllable-counting approach is J. P. Fokkelman, *Major Poems of the Hebrew Bible: At the Interface of Hermeneutics and Structural Analysis,* vol. 2 (Assen: Van Gorcum Press, 2000); cf. D. N. Freedman and J. C. Geoghegan, "Quantitative Measurement in Biblical Hebrew Poetry," in *Ki Baruch Hu: Ancient Near Eastern, Biblical, and Judaic Studies in Honor of Baruch A. Levine,* ed. R. Chazan, W. W. Hallo, and L. Schiffman (Winona Lake, IN: Eisenbrauns, 1999), 229–49. Vance (*The Question of Meter,* 41–222) offers an exhaustive discussion and critique of all ancient and modern theories; cf. more briefly, Watson (*Classical Hebrew Poetry,* 97–110) and Berlin (*Dynamics,* 18–30). The writings of O. Loretz argue for a letter-counting method (for bibliography, see Watson, *Classical Hebrew Poetry,* 105–6). Appealing to syntactical analysis are M. O'Connor, *Hebrew Verse Structure* (Winona Lake, IN: Eisenbrauns, 1980) and T. Collins, *Line-Forms in Hebrew Poetry: A Grammatical Approach to the Stylistic Study of the Hebrew Prophets,* Studia Pohl: Series Maior 7 (Rome: Biblical Institute Press, 1978).

23. Even Fokkelman, who claims that ancient poets counted syllables and used such counts to shape their poems, deems it "highly unlikely that the debate will ever reach a consensus"; cf. J. P. Fokkelman, *Reading Biblical Poetry* (Louisville: Westminster John Knox, 2001), 23. But he also proposes two "escape routes" around the impasse (23–24).

24. B. Hrushovski, "Prosody, Hebrew," *Encyclopaedia Judaica,* 18 vols. (Jerusalem: Keter Pub.; New York: Macmillan, 1972), 13:1201; cf. Dobbs-Allsopp, "Poetry, Hebrew," 551 ("a general [though variable] symmetry in length that contrasts noticeably with the randomness of clause and sentence length in biblical Hebrew prose"); cf. the concurrence of Alter, *The Art of Biblical Poetry,* 8; Longman, "Biblical Poetry," 83; Gillingham, *Poems and Psalms,* 67–68; Petersen and Richards, *Interpreting Hebrew Poetry,* 43–47. We owe much of what follows to the discussions in Hrushovski (cols. 1200–1203) and Watson, *Classical Hebrew Poetry,* 97–103.

25. The Hebrew texts signal the end of the line by a grammatical stop (a phenomenon called "end-stopping"; cf. Watson, *Classical Hebrew Poetry,* 332–33). The commas or semicolons in English translations commonly indicate such stops.

number of parallel lines never exceeds four. Fifth, the key structural determiners are the recurrence of end-stopping and parallelism.[26] Finally, Hebrew poetry seems to have certain fixed patterns that occur in certain literature. For example, the 3:2 pattern is typical of funeral dirges (see further development in ch. 9).[27]

Does knowledge of Hebrew rhythm help us interpret OT poetry more accurately? The answer is a qualified yes. First, it should make us cautious about adopting alterations in the present Hebrew text because of meter. Since the nineteenth century, it has been common practice for scholars to suggest such minor changes by tailoring the Hebrew to fit an alleged, expected metrical pattern. Their goal is a good one—to recover the wording of (or, at least, that closest to) the original Hebrew text (i.e., the method called textual criticism). Though less popular than before, the practice still appears in commentaries and other books.[28] Given the flexibility of Hebrew meter, however, Bible readers should carefully evaluate such textual suggestions before adopting them outright.

Second, an awareness of Hebrew rhythm allows us to capture additional dimensions of a text.[29] Indeed, even readers without knowledge of Hebrew can sense those added dimensions. Granted, as a translation, an English Bible provides no glimpse of the accents of the actual Hebrew words, but a relatively literal, word-for-word English translation (e.g., KJV, NASB, ESV) does reveal the relative lengths of the Hebrew poetic lines. In turn, line lengths may point to one aspect of a poem's rhythm, namely, its tempo (the speed at which one should read it). Again, that tempo may say something about the speed of the actions that the words portray.

For example, long lines or several long words convey the idea of slowness (cf. Ps 19:7–9 [MT 19:8–10];[30] Lam 3:6a, 15), while short lines or series of short words suggest staccato-like rapidity (cf. Judg 5:22; Jer 46:3–4). At the same time, a sudden,

---

26. Dobbs-Allsopp, "Poetry, Hebrew," 551, who comments: "A clausal or sentential whole (frame) is articulated and then reiterated once or twice over, producing a pulsing series of progressions—one step forward, reiteration, and then another step forward, reiteration again, and sometimes twice over (in the case of triplets), and so on. The recursion of parallelism redoubles the syntactic frame, and in the process reinforces the projection of wholeness and the felt fullness of the stop at the end."

27. For those who know Hebrew, Watson (*Classical Hebrew Poetry*, 99–103) provides details about how to identify stresses and meter. Recently, Sabo has voiced reservations about whether dirges have a unique, rhetorical "rhythm" rather than specific "meter"; cf. P.J. Sabo, "Poetry Amid Ruins," in *Poets, Prophets, and Texts in Play: Studies in Biblical Poetry and Prophecy in Honour of Francis Landy*, ed. E. Ben Zvi, LHBOTS 597 (London and New York: Bloomsbury T&T Clark, 2015), 149–51. In his view, the unique rhythm in Lamentations creates the effect of "limping" or "sobbing" (terms quoted from D. Hillers and R. Garr, respectively). For a strongly argued case against the assumption that dirges have a unique meter, see Vance, *The Question of Meter*, 485–87; R. de Hoop, "Lamentations: the Qinah-Meter Questioned," in *Delimitation Criticism: A New Tool in Biblical Scholarship*, ed. M. Korpel and J. Oesch (Assen: Van Gorcum, 2000), 80–104. The metrical study of Lamentations by Freedman and Geoghegan ("Quantitative Measurement," 238–39) confirms the presence of the 3:2 "falling rhythm" but argues that its parallelism with "rising rhythm" and "balanced lines" suggest that dirge "content and falling rhythm should not be tied together too closely."

28. Cf. the occasional appeal to "m cs" (i.e., *metri causa*, "because of meter") in the textual notes of the current Hebrew text, *Biblia Hebraica Stuttgartensia*. Of course, if Hebrew poetry lacks meter (so Vance, *The Question of Meter*, and Kugel, *The Idea of Biblical Poetry*) such appeals plainly err.

29. We are indebted for most of what follows to the fine discussion in Watson, *Classical Hebrew Poetry*, 111–13.

30. The abbreviation "MT." in brackets identifies the Masoretic Text (Hebrew) verse numbers whenever they differ from the numbers in our English Bibles, not to be confused with the abbreviation Heb for NT book of Hebrews.

surprising change in line length alters the tempo of reading from fast to slow or vice versa, casting the spotlight on those lines—a kind of poetic "special effects." The shift compels the reader to pay special attention.

Consider an example from the prophet Nahum. He describes the fall of Nineveh, capital of Israel's hated enemy, Assyria:

> The crack of whips
>> the clatter of wheels,
> galloping horses
>> and jolting chariots!
> Charging cavalry,
>> flashing swords
>> and glittering spears!
> Many casualties,
>> piles of dead,
> bodies without number,
>> people stumbling over the corpses—
> all because of the wanton lust of a prostitute,
>> alluring, the mistress of sorceries,
> who enslaved nations by her prostitution
>> and peoples by her witchcraft. (Nah 3:2–4)[31]

The short, compact lines convey both rapid action and quick close-ups of specific aspects of a broad scene. They create a vivid sense of action happening in all directions. But by elongating the concluding lines, the writer suddenly slows down the action to a complete halt. The sudden stop in the action directs the reader's focus to one thing: Nineveh's lust. The last lines hammer home the point: Nineveh dies because of her prostitution (i.e., her political seduction of other nations).

In sum, careful study of a good literal English translation gives even the nonspecialized reader a partial glimpse of the Hebrew original. That glimpse provides clues to a poem's tempo and to its meaning.

The Sounds of Poetic Words

Besides rhythm, biblical poets also used the sounds of words to create poetic effects. Knowing these various uses is an extremely helpful aid to proper interpretation of biblical poems.[32]

---

31. Occasionally, the translation in a commentary captures the rhythm of the Hebrew. For a good example see the rendering of Nahum and Habakkuk in O. P. Robertson, *The Books of Nahum, Habakkuk, and Zephaniah*, NICOT (Grand Rapids: Eerdmans, 1990).

32. For a full discussion, see Watson, *Classical Hebrew Poetry*, 222–50, on whom much of what follows depends; cf. also Berlin, *Dynamics*, 103–26. As we said earlier, full appreciation of word sounds in the Bible requires knowledge of Hebrew and Greek. The present treatment here, however, aims to prepare readers for comments about words in standard reference books on the Bible. To hear the full effect of the examples below, readers will need to pronounce the transliterated Hebrew texts.

The Sounds of Poetic Words	
Assonance	Repetition of *vowel* sounds • "How now brown cow."
Alliteration	Repetition of *consonants* • "Peter Piper picked a peck of pickled peppers."

Assonance is the repetition of the same or closely similar vowel sounds in a series of words. Its primary purpose is to give a feeling of unity to a poetic unit, whether a single phrase, a single line, or a series of parallel lines. By calling attention to itself, assonance also serves a secondary purpose—to give special emphasis to the words that use it. It does so by linking the sounds of the words with their meaning in the same poetic unit. To use a contemporary example, in the days of the Soviet Union one might have said, "I would rather live under communism than die in a nuclear war." But assonance makes the simple phrase "Better Red than dead" far more striking and memorable. The repeated "eh" sound (b*e*tter, r*e*d, d*e*ad) provides unity, emphasis, and memorability.

In its simplest form assonance features the recurrence of a single vowel sound. For example, observe the heavy use of-a-sounds in this couplet:

Transliteration	*maddua yarash malkam et-gad* *weammo bearayw yashab*[33]
Translation	Why then has Molech taken possession of Gad? Why do his pople live in its towns? (Jer 49:1b)

The Bible also offers more complex uses of assonance that combine several sounds in the same unit. A good example is the repetition of *o*, *a*, and *i* sounds in this line:

Transliteration	*lo–aamin ki–yaazin qoli*[34]
Translation	I do not believe he would give me a hearing. (Job 9:l6b)

Alliteration offers a similar use of sounds: the repetition of the same or similar-sounding consonants within a poetic unit. Alliteration serves purposes similar to those of assonance—to give its poetic unit (usually a line) a sense of wholeness as well as special emphasis. Also, it is common for a key word to be dominant in biblical poems, and alliteration around that word also serves to highlight it.[35] Finally, by

---

33. Cf. the use of "e" (Jer 49:8), "i" (Ps 113:8), "o" (Isa 58:12; Job 5:21), "u" (Lam 4:15).

34. One word of clarification about assonance: as Petersen and Richards point out (*Interpreting Hebrew Poetry*, 5–6, 34), the sounds of the present Hebrew text may not correspond exactly to those of the original. The reason is that originally the Hebrew text had only consonants; later scribes called "Masoretes" added the vowels so that future generations would not forget the language. Thus, our perception of assonance assumes a close similarity, if not identity, between the present Hebrew text and its original; cf. Berlin, *Dynamics*, 104, who limited her treatment of sound-play to consonants.

35. For examples and discussion of other functions, see Watson, *Classical Hebrew Poetry*, 228. In a prose text, observe the repetition of the key thematic word *šûb* ("to return") throughout Ruth 1.

linking sound with sense, alliteration makes the words more memorable. That is why even children can remember the line "Peter Piper picked a peck of pickled peppers."

Hebrew poets use this word device in various ways. Sometimes they alliterate the first letter of each word of a phrase or line ("word-initial alliteration"). Notice, for example, the repetition of initial sh-sounds in the second line of this couplet:

Transliteration	*im–yhwh lo–yishmar–ir* *shawe shaqad shomer*[36]
Translation	Unless the LORD watches over the city, the *guards stand watch in vain.* (Ps 127:1b, our italics)

The most common form of alliteration is the repetition of similar sounds over parallel lines. Notice the recurrence of the-k-and-ts-sounds in this example:

Transliteration	*ketsits yatsa wayyimmal* *wayyibrakh katstsel welo yaamod*
Translation	They *spring up* like *flowers* and wither away; like fleeting *shadows*, they do not endure. (Job 14:2)[37]

In the first line the ts sound occurs twice in the first word (*ketsits*) then reappears a third time in the second word (*yatsa*). This repetition gives the line a unity of sound. Further, in the second line the consonantal combination k-ts of *ketsits* ("like a blossom") recurs in the phrase *katstsel* ("like . . . shadows"), thereby giving the entire poetic pair a cohesive sound. In other cases, the alliteration appears over a series of lines. For example, in Joel 2:15–16a the letter q appears eight times in eight lines, four times as the initial letter of a line.[38]

Frequently, poets employ both assonance and alliteration in the same series of words. For example, consider the word pair *lintosh welintots* ("to uproot and tear down"), a pleasing phrase in Jeremiah's prophetic commission (Jer 1:10). Except for the final letters, the two words sound exactly alike (*we* is the conjunction "and"). Similarly, the phrase *beqeren ben-shamen* concludes the introduction to Isaiah's memorable "Song

---

36. Notice also that the repetition builds on the line's key word *šmr*. Cf. the repetition of initial "i" and "y" sounds in the line's preceding parallel.

37. Watson's translation (*Classical Hebrew Poetry*, 227).

38. Watson, *Classical Hebrew Poetry*, 227. Cf. Nah 1:10 where a series of initial "s" sounds "may actually parody the lisp of a drunk" (Longman, III, "Biblical Poetry," 87). A common, extended form of alliteration is the alphabetic acrostic in which each verse begins with succeeding letters of the alphabet (Pss 9; 10; 25; 111; 119; Prov 31:10–31; Lam 1–4; Nah 1:2–8; etc.); cf. conveniently, C. J. Fantuzzo, "Acrostic," *Dictionary of the Old Testament: Wisdom, Poetry, and Writings*, ed. T. Longman III and P. Enns (Downers Grove, IL: IVP Academic, 2008), 1–4 [henceforth *DOTWPW*]; P.J. Botha, "'Wealth and Riches are in His House' (Psalm 112:3): Acrostic Wisdom Psalms and the Development of Antimaterialism," in *The Shape and Shaping of the Book of Psalms: The Current State of Scholarship*, ed. N. L. deClaissé-Walford, AIL 20 (Atlanta: SBL Press, 2014), 105–28; H. Minkoff, "As Simple as ABC: What Acrostics in the Bible Can Demonstrate," *BRev* 13 (1997): 27–31, 46–47.

of the Vineyard" (Isa 5:1). All three words end with the same sound (*-en*), making the phrase almost rhyme.[39]

The opening line in Greek of the NT book of Hebrews also combines assonance and alliteration to great effect:

Polumerōs kai polutropōs palai ho theos lalēsas tois patrasin en tois prophētais
"Many times and in many ways, long ago God spoke to our ancestors by the prophets . . ." (Heb 1:1, our translation)

Besides the repetition of initial "p" sounds, the first two adverbs ("many times," "in many ways") both begin with the sound *polu-* and end with *-ōs*. The cluster of sounds subtly enhances the line's rhetorical power and sets a poetic tone for the book's opening paragraph (vv. 1–4).[40]

The Rev. Martin Luther King, Jr. is well remembered for urging us to judge people "not by the *color* of their skin but by the *content* of their *character*" (our italics). What makes that line memorable is its repetition of alliterative words with initial "c" sounds ("color," "content," "character") to underscore the superiority of character content over skin color in assessing others. It skillfully employed *wordplay* (also called paronomasia, or more commonly, a "pun"), a familiar rhetorical sound device that Hebrew poetry also uses effectively.[41] In the most common form, a poet pairs up two or more words that differ in one of their three consonants. For example, observe how Isaiah concluded his song about Israel as a vineyard that Yahweh planted to produce good fruit (Isa 5:7):

> And he [Yahweh] looked for justice (*mishpat*),
> but saw bloodshed (*mishpach*);
> for righteousness (*tsedaqah*),
> but heard cries of distress (*tseaqah*).

Slightly more sophisticated is the "root-play," a pun in which one word's consonants reappear in later words but in a different order. Consider the clever play on the reversible roots *b-w-sh* and *sh-w-b* in Psalm 6:10 [MT 6:11] (our translation):

> All my enemies will be overwhelmed with shame (*yeboshu*) and anguish;
> they will turn back (*yashubu*),
> and suddenly be put to shame (*yeboshu*).

---

39. In a prose context, a similar combination gives the last line of Ruth 1:6 (*latet lahem lahem*, "giving them food") added emphasis and memorability.

40. This example slightly adapted from D.A. Black, "Translating New Testament Poetry," in *Scribes and Scripture: New Testament Essays in Honor of J. Harold Greenlee*, ed. D.A. Black (Winona Lake, IN: Eisenbrauns, 1992), 120–21. For a larger poetic treatment of vv. 1–4, see his "Hebrews 1:1–4: A Study in Discourse Analysis," *WTJ* 49 (1987): 175–94. Cf. R. B. Dupertuis, "Poetry in the NT," *NIDB* 4:550; S. Farris, "Hymns, NT," *NIDB* 2:923.

41. The classic study remains I. M. Casanowicz, *Paronomasia in the Old Testament* (Boston: J. S. Gushing et al., 1894); but cf. more conveniently, K. Heim, "Wordplay," *DOTWPW*, 925–29; L.J. De Regt, "World Play in the OT," *NIDB*, 5:898–900; Greenstein, "Wordplay, Hebrew," *ABD* 6:968–72; and Watson, *Classical Hebrew Poetry*, 237–50. Together, assonance, alliteration, and wordplay are examples of phonological parallelism at work.

Coming in the psalm's final verse, the pun gives the text's conclusion a special rhetorical flourish.

Sometimes the pun plays on changes in vowels between words of the same consonants (i.e., the same root). For example, when Jeremiah told God, "I see a branch of an almond tree (*shaqed*)," Yahweh's reply picked up on the root (*sh-q-d*): "I am watching (*shoqed*) to see that my word is fulfilled" (Jer 1:11–12).[42] At other times poets employ a double meaning or double entendre wordplay. This involves the repetition of the same word but with a different meaning in each case. Observe how the Preacher repeated the same formula (*eyn lahem menahem*, "there was no one to . . .") but with a different meaning for *menahem*:

> I saw the tears of the oppressed,
> and I saw that there was no one to *comfort* them.
> Strength was on the side of their oppressors,
> and there was no one to *avenge* them. (Eccl 4:1, NEB, our italics)

The NT also provides a ready example of play on similar-sounding words in Jesus' statement to Peter: "And I tell you, you are Peter (*petros*), and on this rock (*petra*) I will build my church" (Matt 16:18). The similar sounds lead the hearer to compare the two words, while their differences in sound and sense serve to convey Jesus' meaning. "Peter" translates (actually transliterates) the Greek word *petros* ("stone") and "rock" translates *petra* ("fixed rock, rock shelf"), the wordplay on Peter's name suggesting that Christ will found his church on Peter (as the early chapters of Acts then play out).[43]

Word repetition is another common type of wordplay. In this case the poet simply repeats a word or words, perhaps in slightly different forms, throughout a series of poetic lines. The prophet Isaiah skillfully used this device in the opening lines of his "Song of the Vineyard" (Isa 5:1). Observe the recurrence of the words "sing" / "song" (*shir*), "lover" (*lididi, dodi*), and "vineyard" (*kerem*):

> I will *sing* (*shir*) for the one I love (*lididi*)
> a *song* (*shir*) of my *lover* (*dodi*) about his vineyard (*kerem*):
> My loved one (*lididi*) had a vineyard (*kerem*)
> on a fertile hillside. (Isa 5:1, our translation)[44]

Finally, poets sometimes use *onomatopoeia,* that is, words whose own sounds imitate the actual sounds of the actions they portray. The English language has many onomatopoetic words. So we say that a bee "buzzed" around our head, that a

---

42. Cf. Isaiah's play on the root *'kl*, i.e., *tō'kēlû* "you shall eat," *tē'ukkelû* "you shall be eaten" (Isa 1:19–20).

43. D. A. Hagner, *Matthew 14–28*, WBC 33b (Dallas: Word, 1995), says, ". . . Peter is also the 'rock' upon which Jesus the Messiah will build his community" (469). Note also that five verses later (v. 23) Jesus extends the wordplay, rebuking the "rock" for threatening to become a "stumbling block." This pun confirms that the "rock" Jesus identifies is in fact Peter himself, not the latter's confession and certainly not Christ as some allege.

44. After Berlin, *Dynamics*, 113.

baby "babbled," or that a drainpipe "gurgled." Each word imitates the sound made by a bee, baby, or drainpipe. Similarly, one can almost hear the sounds of galloping horses in the second line of this battle scene (Judg 5:22):

Then thundered the horses' hoofs—

galloping,	galloping go	his mighty steeds.
middharot	*daharot*	*abbiraw*[45]

To cite an example from the NT, in James 5:1 the author invites the rich to "weep and wail." The first word (*klausate*) may describe audible weeping, but the second term (*ololyzontes*) is certainly an onomatopoeic word that sounds like howling. Some suggest that the verb *battalogeō* ("keep on babbling") in Matthew 6:7 is also onomatopoetic for it sounds like babbling.

Now the use of such literary devices is valid and valuable in and of itself for it highlights the beauty and creativity both of human language and of the poets who skillfully shape it into poetry to entice and delight readers. But how does a knowledge of Hebrew sounds contribute to proper interpretation? Consider that by the clever use of sounds, biblical poets called special attention to their words. While amusing and pleasurable in itself, such showcasing of sounds also signals the poets' intentions. It casts a spotlight on the words that the writer sought to emphasize, and, thus, may point to the poem's meaning. In some cases, wordplay underscores the poem's theme. Certainly, the repetition of "Praise him" (*halleluhu*) in some psalms shows their theme to be the praise of Yahweh (see Ps 148:3–5; 150; cf. Rev 19:1, 3, 4, 6). In other cases, wordplay highlights a strategic contrast. To retrieve an earlier example, by reversing the letters *b-w-sh* and *sh-w-b*, the psalmist stressed the reversal of fortune for which his prayer pled (Ps 6:10 [MT 6:11]). Hearing the sound of the poet's words is indeed a useful tool in interpreting biblical poetry.

THE STRUCTURE OF HEBREW POETRY

Parallelism

Scholars refer to the structure of Hebrew poetry as *parallelism of members,* a phenomenon that also shaped the writings of NT writers.[46] The term "parallelism" has, unfortunately, spawned a common misunderstanding.[47] Many people understand

---

45. Cf. Isaiah's imitation of birds chirping (Isa 10:14) and gibberish language (28:10, 13).

46. Cf. J. L. Bailey and L. D. Vander Broek, *Literary Forms in the New Testament: A Handbook* (Louisville: Westminster John Knox, 1992), 77 ("[t]he use of parallelism in the New Testament most certainly has its origin in Hebrew poetry"). On the other hand, Dobbs-Allsopp, "Poetry, Hebrew," 552, estimates that "as much as a third" of biblical poetry lacks parallel lines.

47. Historically, this discovery goes back to R. Lowth's inaugural lectures as professor of poetry at Oxford in the eighteenth century (cf. R. Lowth, *Lectures on the Sacred Poetry of the Hebrews* [London: S. Chadwick & Co., 1847]). For a recent critical reassessment of Lowth's work, however, see J. Jarick, ed., *Sacred Conjectures: The Context and Legacy of Robert Lowth and Jean Astruc,* LHBOTS 457 (London: T&T Clark, 2007). Later discoveries showed the practice of parallelism to be widespread among Semitic poets; for Ugaritic examples, see M. S. Smith, *Ugaritic*

it to mean that a second poetic line merely restates or contrasts the point of the previous line in different words. They assume that an equal sign (=) links the lines together. Actually, *parallelism is that phenomenon whereby two or more successive poetic lines dynamically strengthen, reinforce, and develop each other's thought.* As a kind of emphatic additional thought, the follow-up lines further define, specify, expand, intensify, or contrast the first. As Berlin puts it, "Parallelism focuses the message on itself but its vision is binocular. Like human vision it superimposes two slightly different views of the same object and from their convergence it produces a sense of depth."[48] Concerning the effect of the movement from line to line, Alter adds insightfully, "In the abundant instances, . . . the characteristic movement of meaning is one of heightening or intensification . . . of focusing, specification, concretization, even what could be called dramatization."[49]

In other words, succeeding parallel lines do not simply restate the opening line; rather, they add to or expand its thought. Isaiah 1:10 illustrates this dynamic:

> Hear the word of the LORD, you rulers of Sodom;
> Listen to the instruction of our God, you people of Gomorrah!
> (our translation)

The correspondences between these two lines are obvious. Their grammatical structures are exactly alike—imperative + direct object and a vocative. Individual words also correspond to each other in meaning: "hear" / "listen to"; "word of the LORD" / "instruction of our God"; and "rulers of Sodom" / "people of Gomorrah."

As we said above, however, the second line is not simply a restatement of the first in different words; both lines betray subtle differences. For example, though some words overlap in meaning, they are not actually synonyms. "Instruction" (Heb. *torah*) is not really another way of saying "word" (*dabar*) nor is "people" (*am*) the exact counterpart of "rulers" (*qatsin*). The Bible associates "word" with the message of a prophet and "instruction" with the teaching about the law by a priest (see Jer 18:18). Similarly, "Sodom" and "Gomorrah" are not simply two names for the same town; they designate separate, though proximate, cities (cf. Gen 10:19; 14; 18). At the same time, when mentioned together (usually the case) they designate "twin cities of sin."

Narrative Poetry, WAW 9 (Atlanta: Scholars Press, 1997). Cf. R. Abbott, "Forked Parallelism in Egyptian, Ugaritic and Hebrew Poetry," *TynBul* 62.1 (2011): 41–64, who argues that tricola (co-called "forked parallelisms") were common thematic indicators in early Hebrew, Ugaritic, and Egyptian poetry and chronologically antedate the later predominance of bicola in the MT.

48. Berlin, *Dynamics*, 99; cf. Berlin., "Parallelism," *NIDB*, 4:379–81; cf. Dobbs-Allsopp, "Poetry, Hebrew," 553 ("The parallel frame coerces auditors into considering two images together and giving rise to a new perception in the process"). Cf. J. M. LeMon and B. A. Strawn, "Parallelism," *DOTWPW*, 502–15; and specifically for proverbs, K. M. Heim, *Poetic Imagination in Proverbs: Variant Repetitions and the Nature of Poetry*, BBRSup 4 (Winona Lake, IN: Eisenbrauns, 2013), 11–19, 29–35.

49. Alter, *The Art of Biblical Poetry*, 19.

In our view, this combination of similarity and difference serves Isaiah's rhetorical purpose.[50] On the one hand, the mention of both fabled, neighboring cities underscores that all Isaiah's listeners are sinful (like residents of Sodom and Gomorrah). On the other hand, the change from "word" to "instruction" indicates a subtle but significant development in Isaiah's train of thought. "Word" signals that what follows is a divine revelation, while "instruction" tells the hearers to accept Isaiah's message as they would teaching by a priest.

This well-known saying of Jesus likewise combines similarity and difference rhetorically:

> Love your enemies,
> do good to those who hate you,
> bless those who curse you,
> pray for those who mistreat you. (Luke 6:27b)[51]

Both grammatically and semantically, the four lines are parallel. Each comprises an imperative and its direct object whose meanings apparently overlap (e.g., "love" // "do good," "enemies" // "those who hate you," etc.). A closer look, however, reveals subtle nuances in succeeding lines. The latter further clarify the meaning of the first: "enemies" are not military invaders but "those who hate you"; they are people who "curse" and "mistreat" believers. To "love" them means to "do good" to them (i.e., to do whatever benefits them), to "bless" them (i.e., to wish them God's blessing), and to "pray" on their behalf.

These examples underscore the current consensus that the relationships between lines of biblical poetry are amazingly complex.[52] The careful Bible reader will determine what relationship exists between the poetic lines in each text taking care not to assume a simplistic notion that their unity boils down to one or two main principles—e.g., that they are either synonymous or antithetical. Rather, one must reckon the double logic of parallelism—that it simultaneously invokes the "logic of synonymity and the logic of progression . . . ."[53]

Basic Units of Parallelism

Traditionally, scholars subdivided parallelism into three types—synonymous, antithetical, and synthetic—depending on whether the succeeding line restated, contrasted,

---

50. Similarly, in critiquing Kugel and Alter for understanding parallelism as based primarily on differences, LeMon and Strawn ("Parallelism," 310) stress that in parallelism *"sameness* is every bit as important as *difference*. [. . .] *Both* sameness *and* difference matter. To neglect one and favor the other is to mistake something crucial about the nature of Hebrew prosody . . . ."

51. This example comes from Gillingham, *Poems and Psalms*, 84. We commend her excellent discussion of parallelism in Jesus' poetic aphorisms (82–88).

52. LeMon and Strawn, "Parallelism," 512; cf. the illustrative example in Kugel, *The Idea of Biblical Poetry*, 2–7, and Alter's warning against inferring too quickly, *The Art of Biblical Poetry*, 18.

53. Longman, "Biblical Poetry," 84.

or developed the first, respectively.[54] Recent study, however, has tended to avoid those categories as overly simplistic and misleading.

So, below we will follow a common, useful scheme simply to suggest more adequately the ways in which parallelism works. Our purpose is two-fold: (1) to sensitize readers to the potential communicative power of parallelism, and (2) to help them thread their way through what otherwise might seem an impenetrable thicket of complexity. To do this we will first need to consider how scholars describe poetic lines. With this knowledge we will be able to describe poetic lines precisely and, more important, to visualize the similarities and differences between them. In turn, these preliminary steps will enable us to understand how the lines interrelate.

The technical term for a single line of poetry is *stich* (pronounced "stick").[55] Two parallel lines form a unit that scholars designate either as a *couplet* or a *distich*. Three parallel lines form a triplet or *tristich*. Just as the Bible's subdivision into chapters and verses allows us to identify its subparts, so scholars commonly assign a capital letter to each stich deemed parallel to the next line(s). Thus, the first line of a tristich would be "A" and the next two lines "B" and C," respectively. They also use small letters for the subparts within a single stich. Consider this example in which two stichs, designated A and B, are fairly synonymous (Ps 77:1):

	a	*b*	*c*
A	I cried out	to God	for help;
	a'	*b'*	*c'*
B	I cried out	to God	to hear me.

Both stichs have three parts labeled *a, b,* and *c* in A, and *a', b',* and *c'* in B. Two schematic principles are at work here:

1. In each stich the same lower case letter designates elements that have the same meaning (are semantically parallel) or that play the same grammatical role in the sentence (are syntactically parallel).
2. The addition of ' to a letter (e.g., *a'*, called "*a* prime") shows that it belongs to the second stich.[56]

Thus, one would describe the structure of stich A as *a b c,* stich B as *a' b' c'*; and that of the whole verse as *a b c / a' b' c'*.

As a second example consider this verse in which the stichs express a contrast (Prov 14:34):

---

54. Cf. conveniently Petersen and Richards, *Interpreting Hebrew Poetry*, 24–27. As they point out, the traditional definition of synthetic parallelism has proved to be very problematic.

55. From Gk. *stichos* "row, line (of writing)"; plural *stichoi* (pronounced "STICK-oy"). Other scholars prefer the term "colon" (plural "cola"); Alter (*The Art of Biblical Poetry*, 9) opts for "verset," while Petersen and Richards favor "colon" or "line" (*Interpreting Hebrew Poetry*, 23).

56. Were there a third parallel line, each of its components would bear a double prime (e.g., *a"*). Those of a fourth parallel line (a rare but possible occurrence) would have *a* triple prime (e.g., *a'''*).

	a	*b*	*c*
A	Righteousness	exalts	a nation,
	-a	*-b*	*-c*
B	but sin	condemns	any people.

Syntactically, the two lines are parallel, but semantically they express opposite meanings. To indicate that contrast, we prefix the letters describing stich B with a minus sign (-). Hence, we describe its structure as *-a-b-c* and that of the entire verse as *a b c / -a-b-c*.

Frequently, however, a second (or third) stich may omit items found in the first, a phenomenon called *ellipsis*. For example, it is common for the second stich (B) to assume the presence of the verb from the first stich but not to repeat it. This omission leaves the second stich without a verb. Study this example (Amos 8:10):[57]

	a	*b*	*c*
A	I will turn	your religious festivals	into mourning,
		b'	*c'*
B	and	all your singing	into weeping.

The second stich (B) assumes but omits a verb such as "I will turn" present in the first stich (A). Presumably, the wording chosen for the second stich dictated the omission of the verb. That omission does not mean, however, that the second stich is shorter than the first.[58]

In other cases, the second stich (B) may omit the verb and add elements unparalleled in the first (Ps 50:4; cf. Amos 9:10):

	a	*b*	
A	He summons	the heavens above,	
		b'	*c*
B	and	the earth,	that he may judge his people.

The second stich omits (but assumes) the verb "he summons" but also adds a phrase (*c*) that, quite significantly, specifies the purpose of that summons. In other words, rather than simply restate the point of A, here the second one further *develops* it by stating its purpose.[59] This example has the structure *a b / b' c*.

---

57. We owe the first example to LaSor, et al., *Old Testament Survey*, 233, the second to Kugel, *The Idea of Biblical Poetry*, 6. For "ellipsis" Alter prefers the term "hidden repetition" (*The Art of Biblical Poetry*, 23; cf. his illuminating discussion of the phenomenon, 24–26).

58. In Mary's Magnificat (Luke 1:52), though A ends with a prepositional phrase, B omits it: "He [God] has brought down the powerful from their thrones, / and lifted up the lowly (. . .)." The parallelism is *abcd / a'b'c'*; cf. Bailey and Vander Broek, *Literary Forms*, 163–64.

59. Because *c* does not repeat anything from line A, it is not called *c* prime. Notice also the development from "heavens" to "earth," that is, from the upper extreme of the created cosmos to the lower one. Such paired extremes (heaven and earth) are called *merismus* (see below).

How Parallelism Works

The relationships that bind parallel stichs range across a continuum of increasing complexity—a complexity that is not adequately described by the traditional categories of parallelism (i.e., synonymous, antithetical, synthetic). At one end of the continuum are the rare cases of synonymous parallelism in which the second stich simply restates the first in different words (Prov 19:5):

> A false witness will not go unpunished,
> 　　and he who pours out lies will not go free.[60]

The parallels are obvious: "false witness" / "he who pours out lies" and "not go unpunished" / "will not go free." There is no perceptible development from the first line to the second. At the other end of the continuum are cases in which line B shows no similarity at all to the first (Ps 115:18):

> It is we who extol the LORD,
> 　　both now and forevermore.

In this case, B completes the first grammatically; the two stichs form a single sentence.[61] As we shall see, most biblical poetry falls somewhere between these two extremes. In order to determine where a stich should be placed on the continuum we need to understand the dynamics of parallelism—how it works. This understanding is crucial for an accurate analysis of poetry.

What Makes Parallelism Work?	Parallelism Combines Features of: Grammar / Words and their Meanings / Sounds
	Parallelism sets side-by-side features of language in creative and intriguing ways to elicit interest

As Berlin has shown, parallel lines may interrelate grammatically, lexically, semantically, and phonologically.[62] Some parallels are interrelated by only one of these factors, others by all three. The *grammatical factor* is the structural skeleton of parallelism. It concerns the elements of grammar (tense, mood, case, number, etc.) that appear in each line of a parallel pair. For example, in comparing stichs one might observe a change in nouns from singular to plural or in verbs from present to future tense. Stich A might make a statement while its parallel (stich B)

---

60. Cf. Alter, *The Art of Biblical Poetry*, 22; Job 27:4. Here belong also the even more extreme, rare exact parallelisms, that is, repeated refrains like "for his loyalty is forever" (Ps 136) or "praise him" (Ps 150); cf. Berlin, *Dynamics*, 130.

61. Cf. Berlin, *Dynamics*, 90, n. 42.

62. Here we offer a simplified overview of Berlin's excellent, detailed treatment (*Dynamics*, 31–126; cf. also the summary paradigm, 29).

asks a question; another stich might state something positively, while its parallel states it negatively.[63]

If grammar provides the skeleton, the *lexical-semantic factor* provides the flesh and blood.[64] This aspect focuses on the relationship between the specific words in each parallel line. For example, like their linguistic kinsfolk at ancient Ugarit, Hebrew poets often built their poetry around word pairs, sets of words commonly associated together.[65] This explains why parallel lines commonly develop around pairs of synonyms (eat/drink, earth/dust) or antonyms (right/left, there is/there are not).[66] At the same time, it also permits a poet to juxtapose two nonassociated words creatively for poetic effect (for examples, see below).

The *phonologic factor* refers to the use of words of similar sounds (e.g., assonance, alliteration, and wordplay or paronomasia) either within a single stich or in parallel ones. English speakers commonly use this delightful device for rhetorical effect. One popular joke, for example, tells of a man condemned to hang for continuously making puns. As he stood on the scaffold, the merciful crowd commuted his sentence, to which he replied, "No noose is good news!" Of course, to access this aspect in the OT the reader must read the Hebrew aloud, listening for similar sounds. Nevertheless, English Bible readers need to understand this phenomenon because biblical commentators often refer to it. Occasionally, footnotes in English translations point out puns on Hebrew names (in NIV, e.g., Jer 1:12; 19:7; Mic 1:10–15; etc.).

Types of Parallelism

How do parallel lines of Hebrew poetry interrelate? Here we follow the three main variations of parallelism proposed by Gillingham to nuance further Kugel's basic definition "A, then B."[67] We have gleaned some examples from recent studies and arranged them systematically within Gillingham's categories. Our purpose is to train the reader's eye to identify parallelism and to provide some terms to describe how the lines function and interrelate—key elements in interpreting poetry.

---

63. Cf. the examples provided by Berlin, *Dynamics*, 56–57, 59: "For in Death there is no mention of you / In Sheol who can acclaim you?" (Ps 6:5 [MT 6:6]). "My son, do not forget my teaching / And let your heart guard my commandments" (Prov 3:1).

64. Berlin, *Dynamics*, 64.

65. Cf. W.G.E. Watson, *Traditional Techniques in Classical Hebrew Verse*, JSOTSup 170 (Sheffield: Sheffield Academic Press, 1994), 262–312; Y. Avishur, *Stylistic Studies of Word-Pairs in Biblical and Ancient Semitic Literatures* (Neukirchener-Vluyn: Neukirchener, 1984). For catalogues of this phenomenon, see M. Dahood, "Ugaritic-Hebrew Parallel Pairs," *Ras Shamra Parallels* [=*RSP*] (Rome: Biblical Institute Press, 1972), 1:71–382 (ed. L. R. Fisher); *RSP* (1975), 2:1–39 (ed. L. R. Fisher); *RSP* (1981), 3:1–206 (ed. S. Rummel). For its interpretation, see Berlin, *Dynamics*, 64–102.

66. Watson, *Classical Hebrew Poetry*, 131–32 (cf. also his fine overview, 128–44).

67. Gillingham, *Poems and Psalms*, 78–82; cf. Heim's recent approbation of her method, most importantly, "her recognition that there are different kinds of parallelism . . . and that Hebrew parallelism allows for difference as well as similarity" (*Poetic Imagination*, 28). The subcategories below, however, are our own, based on examples gleaned from Berlin, Alter, and Kugel. We are grateful to Professor M. D. Carroll R. for supplying examples used below from the book of Amos.

Main Types of Parallelism		
Type	**Definition**	**Line Relationship**
A = B	A equals B	**A** and **B** are interchangeable **B** echoes / contrasts **A**
A > B	A is greater than B	**A** states the main idea **B** qualifies it further
A < B	B is greater than A	**A** prefaces the main idea **B** states the main idea to complement / complete **A**

1. The first variation of parallelism (A = B) occurs when A and B are interchangeable in some fashion—i.e., B either echoes or contrasts A.[68] In Jesus' famous words in Matthew 11:30, for example, B simply echoes A (i.e., *abc / a'b'c'*):

		a	*b*	*c*
A		My yoke	is	easy,
		a'	*b'*	*c'*
B	and	my burden	is	light

On the other hand, Proverbs 11:20 (NCV) illustrates how A=B also may signal a contrast:

		a	*b*	*c*
A		The LORD	hates	those with evil hearts
			-b	*-c*
B	but		is pleased with	those who are innocent.

The ellipsis of the subject ("the LORD") and the contrast in B produces the parallelism *a b c / -b-c*. The verse sharply contrasts Yahweh's response to two kinds of people. He "hates" the wicked but "is pleased with" the righteous. This comprises an antithetical contrast because it speaks of opposites that share no common ground. In the Bible, good and evil are opposites engaged in deadly combat. Because of his nature, Yahweh cannot delight in the wicked nor detest the righteous. In passing, one should notice the double-edge this proverb wields—it both encourages and warns. On the one hand, it encourages the righteous to keep up their blameless lives. On the other, it warns the wicked to abandon their hateful conduct.

Occasionally, parallel lines may convey a contrast that is not antithetical. For this reason, we have defined this category as one of "contrast," not "antithesis."[69] Consider Judges 5:25:

---

68. This variation combines the older categories of synonymous and antithetical parallelism. As examples, Gillingham cites Job 10:12; Isa 62:1; Amos 9:2; Ps 33:6–7; Matt 5:42//Luke 6:30; Mark 10:38//Matt 20:22; Luke 11:17 (in our view, wrongly); Mark 13:24–25//Matt 24:29; Luke 6:27, 37–38//Matt 7:1–2; Luke 15:32; 16:10; cf. Gillingham, *Poems and Psalms*, 78–80, 84–85. For other examples of contrast, see Amos 6:3, 6; 8:8.

69. So Berlin, *Dynamics*, 95.

		a	b		c
A		He	asked for		water,
		a'	b'	d	c'
B	and	she	gave	him	milk.

The line contrasts the water, which the Canaanite general Sisera sought, and the milk, which the Kenite woman, Jael, served him. Unlike the previous example, there is no antithesis here, for water and milk are acceptable alternatives, not direct opposites. In sum, parallelism of contrast involves both simple contrast and actual antithesis.

2. In the second variation of parallelism (A > B), A states the main idea while B qualifies it, thus more fully bringing the thought of A to completion. For example, biblical poetry often displays a parallelism of *subordination* in which the second stich is grammatically subordinate to its parallel. In Psalm 111:6, for example, stich B describes the *means* by which Yahweh accomplished what stich A stated:[70]

> A He has shown his people the power of his works,
> B giving them the lands of other nations.

In other words, A leaves the reader with a question: how did Yahweh show his people his power? The B stich answers it: he displayed it by taking territory owned by other nations and giving it to his people.

It is also common for one stich to state the *reason* for the claims of the other, as Exodus 15:21 shows:

A	Sing to the LORD,	(statement)
B	for he is highly exalted.	(reason)
C	Both horse and driver	(example)
D	he has hurled into the sea.[71]	

Correct interpretation requires the reader carefully to follow the logic of each line. "Sing to the LORD" states the main idea, demanding that one burst into song. But why should one sing Yahweh's praise? Because he is a "highly exalted" God (cf. also Ps 13:6). That is, he is the cosmic ruler of heaven and earth—fully entitled to such high honor. But the verse answers one last question: What evidence confirms his exalted position? The answer follows: "Both horse and driver he has hurled into the sea"—an allusion to Yahweh's stunning defeat of Pharaoh at the Red Sea. In sum, in this case the poet qualifies the command with a reason and then supports the reason with an example (see also Ps 106:1; 107:1). To understand the poet's meaning properly, one must walk through the lines, sorting out each one as we did above.

---

70. So Berlin, *Dynamics*, 81; cf. Amos 4:1b-c; 5:15a; Gillingham, *Poems and Psalms*, 80–81 and 85–86, who offers other examples (Gen 4:24; Prov 30:8; Isa 45:12; Jer 2:15; Matt 6:12//Luke 11:4; Matt 7:7–8//Luke 11:9–10; Matt 7:17; Mark 2:27; Luke 12:48, 49–50; 18:14).

71. In this example, C is grammatically subordinate to D, emphatically supplying the latter with a direct object. It, thus, exemplifies the third type of parallelism (A < B) explained below.

In other cases, one stich specifies the *time* of its parallel:

A   By the rivers of Babylon
            we sat and wept   (statement)
B   when we remembered Zion. (Ps 137:1)   (temporal clause)[72]

Here the poet describes how exiled Israelites sat down and wept in Babylon. The temporal clause defines the time when they wept—when they remembered Zion, the holy mountain in their homeland. Implicitly, however, the temporal clause also states the reason for the people's grief—memory of beloved Zion.[73]

3. The third variation of parallelism (A < B) occurs when A prefaces the main idea while B states the main idea in a way that complements or completes A. Unlike Psalm 137:1 above, in Psalm 114:1–2 the *parallelism of time* (A) is two-fold (lines A // B); they precede and set the scene for the complementary main statement (B [lines C // D]):

A	When	Israel	came	out of Egypt,	(two-fold temporal clause)
B		Jacob			from a people of foreign tongue,
C		Judah	became	God's sanctuary,	(two-fold main clause)
D		Israel			his dominion.

The preface A // B connects the main statement temporally and geographically with Israel's historic exodus from Egypt. It invokes synonymous names for the nation ("Israel" // "Jacob") and remembers "Egypt" not as the site of terrible oppression but of an alien (i.e., non-Semitic) language. The main statement (C // D) focusses on the event's two outcomes: "Judah" became "God's sanctuary" (i.e., the nation's religious center), while "Israel" (here probably the whole nation) became "his dominion" (i.e., his royal domain). The rest of Psalm 114 recounts the dramatic reactions to the event by the Red Sea, the Jordan River, and the mountains (vv. 3–6), and ends with a call for the whole earth to react—to tremble at the thought of God's presence (vv. 7–8).

In cases of parallelism of *continuation*, for example, succeeding parallel lines present a progression of thought. For example, observe how Isaiah 40:9 creates the illusion of simple repetition but actually portrays progress:[74]

A.   You who bring good news to Zion,

---

72. Cf. Ps 14:7b, "When the LORD restores the fortunes of his people [temporal clause] / let Jacob rejoice and (let) Israel he glad!" [call to rejoice]. In this case, the statement also expresses the *result* of the temporal clause.

73. Cf. cases where one stich is a prepositional phrase subordinate to the other: "There on the poplars / we hung our harps" (Ps 137:2; so Alter, *The Art of Biblical Poetry*, 19). Cf. Judg 5:25b.

74. Cf. Berlin, *Dynamics*, 90–91, who, however, offers a more technical linguistic discussion; cf. also Isa 16:5; Amos 1:5, 8; Eph 5:14; 2 Tim 2:11–13. Gillingham's examples of the A < B variation (*Poems and Psalms*, 81–82 and 86–87) include Isa 40:3; Ps 29:1, 10; 77:17; Jer 31:21; and Judg 5:4–5, 26–27; Matt 7:11//Luke 11:13; Matt 8:20//Luke 9:58; Matt 10:32–33//Luke 12:8–9; Matt 15:11; Luke 9:24//Matt 16:25//Mark 8:35. Cf. also Amos 1:4–5; 5:5–6, 15.

    B. go up on a high mountain.
    C. You who bring good news to Jerusalem,
    D. lift up your voice with a shout,
    E. lift it up, do not be afraid;
    F. say to the towns of Judah,
    G. "Here is your God!"

At first glance, repeated phrases and parallel words create the impression that succeeding lines restate the first in other words.[75] Actually, the text paints the actions of the messenger in the order in which they would normally occur. First, he would ascend a high mountain to address a large area, and then he would shout out his message. Only then would he say, "Here is your God!"—reserved here for the climactic last line. Hence, to understand such examples, the reader must look past the illusion of repetition and think through the logic of each line to discover how each interacts with its predecessor. Failure to work through this process will result in a misreading of the text.

In a parallelism of *comparison*, parallel lines form a simile, that is, a comparison. (For similes, see below; Amos 2:13). Psalm 103:13 illustrates this common parallelism:

    A. As a father has compassion on his children,
    B. so the LORD has compassion on those who fear him.

Here the psalmist describes the LORD's compassion by comparing it to that of a father toward his children. He explains the unknown (or lesser known)—the LORD's compassion—by appeal to something well (or at least better) known—the compassion of a father. Through the comparison, the poet puts flesh on what otherwise would remain an abstract idea ("the LORD has compassion"). Implicitly, he recalls the reader's own childhood experiences—how mercifully his or her father had glossed over glaring goofs with a smile and a hug. The reader now visualizes the LORD's mercy along similar lines. And that is the point—"the LORD has compassion." But this couplet also subtly explains who are the LORD's children—not just ethnic Israelites, but "those who fear him."

Sometimes, however, the comparison is implicit rather than explicit. We say "implicit" because in these cases the Hebrew text lacks the explicit signals of the simile—the words "like" or "as." Instead, it simply aligns two stichs side-by-side without clarifying their connection (i.e., a metaphor). Consider how Psalm 125:2 reads literally:

    A. Jerusalem—mountains surround it;
    B. And YHWH surrounds his people.[76]

Why did the psalmist arrange these two stichs together? How do they interrelate? Obviously, he juxtaposed "mountains" and "YHWH" (Yahweh) because they somehow

---

75. I.e., "you who bring good tidings," "lift up (your voice)," "Zion" / "Jerusalem."

76. The example and translation come from Berlin, *Dynamics*, 101 (cf. the entire discussion and other examples, 100–1).

compare. What do they have in common? Both protect Jerusalem from the attacks of her enemies. Hence, the couplet compares the protection both offer. As before, the poet speaks of an abstract idea in a concrete way. The line about Jerusalem's mountains serves as a simile for the protection given by Yahweh. Recognizing this, the NIV rightly makes the implicit simile explicit by using the English grammatical marker "as":

> As the mountains surround Jerusalem
> so the LORD surrounds his people . . . [77]

Pondering Yahweh's protection, one imagines it to be a huge, towering wall of solid rock—something impossible for enemies to penetrate. To understand the poet's meaning, the reader must determine how mountains and the LORD compare, and whether the psalmist's real focus is on the mountains or on the LORD (obviously, the latter). When interpreting comparisons, the reader must take care to avoid being preoccupied with the simile distinction (the meaning of "mountains" or "father"), as if that were the poet's meaning. Rather, the reader must seek to understand the main point (the LORD's compassion or protection) in light of the simile's portrait.

A comparison also underlies examples where poets invoke the traditional argument "from the lesser to the greater." Jesus' saying in Matthew 7:11 exemplifies this:[78]

A. If you, then, though you are evil, know how to give good gifts to your children,

B. how much more will your Father in heaven give good gifts to those who ask him!

The lines compare the generosity of earthly fathers, who are "evil," with that of "your Father in heaven," who presumably is "righteous." The comparison argues that if the former (the "lesser") give their children gifts, the latter ("the greater") will do so even more generously if asked. Clearly, B gives the main point after the introduction by A.

In the parallelism of *specification,* each succeeding stich makes more specific what the opening stich states in general terms. In other words, the movement is from general to specific.[79] There are various forms of specification. Sometimes it has to do with spatial or geographic entities. Isaiah 45:12 illustrates this type (NRSV, our italics):

A. I made the *earth* (general)

B. and created *humankind upon it*; (specific)

C. it was my hands that stretched out the *heavens*, (general)

D. and I commanded all their *host*. (specific)

---

77. Cf. also Prov 26:9.

78. Cf. Gillingham, *Poems and Psalms,* 86.

79. We owe much of what follows to Alter, *The Art of Biblical Poetry,* 9–26; cf. his comment (19): "The rule of thumb . . . is that the general term occurs in the first verset [i.e., stich] and a more specific instance of the general category in the second verset." Cf. Amos 5:15a.

In these two distichs, Yahweh affirms that he created the universe.[80] Observe how each first line (A, C) concerns a general geographical realm (the earth, the heavens) while the second (B, D) focuses in on something more specific within that realm, namely, its inhabitants. This movement, from general to specific, narrows the reader's attention to a smaller perspective. At the same time, lines CD continue the thought of AB concerning the theme "Yahweh is sovereign creator." They do so by shifting the site of that sovereignty from earth (AB) to the heavens where he "commanded" (and "commands") their mighty army ("their host")—the means through which God can rescue Israel.

In other cases of this type, succeeding stichs provide an explanation of the opening line. Consider, for example, how the lines in Isaiah 48:20b–21 explain the opening line by giving specifics:

A. Say, "The Lord has redeemed his servant Jacob.
B.   And they did not thirst in the deserts where he led them;
C.   water from a rock he made flow for them.
D.   He split a rock and water gushed out."[81]

The first line (A) offers the general statement "the Lord has redeemed Israel"; those that follow (B, C, D) explain that redemption. Further, the following lines become increasingly more specific, each implicitly answering a question arising from its immediate parallel. Alter describes this technique as an "explanatory chain":

What does it mean that God "redeemed" Israel (first verset [i.e., line])? They were not thirsty in the desert (second verset). How could they not have been thirsty?—because He made water flow from a rock (third verset). How did He make water flow from a rock?—by splitting it so the water gushed (fourth verset).[82]

The poet might have taken the subject of Israel's redemption in many directions. His comments might have recalled, for example, the defeat of Pharaoh at the Red Sea, the wondrous provision of manna, Israel's freedom from slavery, or the meeting with God at Mt. Sinai. Instead, he focused on one episode—the day Yahweh split a rock to give Israel water (cf. Num 20:11). Again, proper interpretation carefully considers the development of thought between the opening and subsequent lines.

In another variety of the parallelism of specification, the second stich specifies the first in a dramatic fashion; the general terms of stich A are followed by striking language in B. Notice, for example, the dramatic effect achieved by a simple change in a verb:

---

80. In context, the strophe provides evidence to banish his people's doubt about his ability to bring them home from exile (see vv. 11–13). The argument (technically, "from the greater to the lesser") runs: "If my power made the whole massive cosmos, it can certainly redeem Israel from human hands."

81. Our translation; italics as in Alter, *The Art of Biblical Poetry*, 20.

82. Alter, The Art of Biblical Poetry, 20.

A. May the desert tribes *bow before him*

B. and his enemies *lick the dust.* (Ps 72:9, our italics)

The context is prayer for a successful reign by Israel's king, perhaps on the occasion of his coronation.[83] The speaker (possibly a priest) affirms one aspect of that hoped-for success: the king's wide dominion. Typically, stich A makes a general statement that desert tribes will submit to the king's rule. In ancient custom to "bow before" someone was to show that person great honor. Stich B, however, gives two specifics: it details that these tribes are not royal friends but "enemies," and it graphically portrays their bowing—they "lick the dust." The startling language dramatically states the completeness and humiliation of their surrender.

In yet another variety, the second stich may specify the purpose of the first. Consider Proverbs 4:1, for example:

	a	*b*
A	Listen, my sons,	to a father's instruction;
	a'	*c*
B	pay attention	[to a father's instruction] and gain understanding.

The parallelism between "listen" (*a*) and "pay attention" (*a'*) creates the impression that B (*a' c*) simply restates A. The ellipsis of *b* ("to a father's instruction"), however, permits the poet some rhythmic space to add a purpose clause (*c*, "to gain understanding"). Thus, *a' c* goes beyond a mere restatement of *a b*—it specifies the latter's purpose (Why should a son listen to his father's teaching? To gain understanding). The complementary nature of the second stich must be recognized for a proper interpretation. A correct paraphrase of the proverb would be: a wise son listens to his father's teaching so that he may gain understanding.

The last major use of the A < B variation of parallelism is the parallelism of *intensification*. Intensification occurs when the second stich of a couplet restates the first in a more pointed, extreme, or forceful way. To paraphrase the dynamics, we might say the second develops the first by saying, "Not only that but more so!"[84] The effect of this intensified language is to heighten the poetic power of the entire distich. The most obvious example of intensification is the use of numbers in parallelism. Consider this verse from Moses' farewell address to Israel shortly before his death:

A. How could *one* man chase a *thousand,*

B. or *two* put *ten thousand* to flight . . . ? (Deut 32:30)

---

83. Cf. E. S. Gerstenberger, *Psalms, Part 1: With an Introduction to Cultic Poetry*, FOTL 14 (Grand Rapids: Eerdmans, 1988) 19; Pss 2, 110.

84. Alter, *The Art of Biblical Poetry*, 11, who compares it to the *a fortiori* logical argument; cf. Kugel's summary formula "A is so, *what's more*, B is so" (*The Idea of Biblical Poetry*, 8). This compares to what some scholars call "climactic parallelism"; so L. Ryken, *Words of Delight: A Literary Introduction to the Bible* (Grand Rapids: Baker, 1987), 181–82. For other examples, see Amos 1:11; 2:2b; 2:14–16; 5:16b-17; 9:2–4.

Obviously, the numbers "one" and "two" or "thousand" and "ten thousand" are not synonyms but paired lesser-to-greater amounts. Moses' question invokes two hypothetical military manpower ratios, the second greater than the first, to highlight the great odds against victory. Now, after the 1:1000 ratio in A, the word "two" in B primes the reader to expect a doubled ratio of 2:2000. Instead, "ten thousand" unexpectedly increases the odds ten times to achieve a climatic poetic effect: to heighten the image of the stunning military rout to which Moses refers.[85]

Intensification occurs in other ways as well. Observe, for example, the contrast of intensity between the verbs in this verse:

A. Your granaries *will be filled* with abundance,
B. with new wine your vats will *burst*. (Prov 3:10, Alter's translation, our italics)

In content, the lines supplement each other: A is about grain, B is about wine. Taken together, they make the single point that God will amply provide for those who honor him (i.e., both food and drink). There is an emotive contrast, however, between the verbs "be filled" and "burst." The former describes a passive state; the latter paints a dramatic picture of action with a touch of hyperbole. That is, Israel will have so much wine that her vats will burst! Other poets achieve the same effect by stringing together parallel nouns.

Consider, also, these lines (Ps 88:11–12 [MT 88:12–13]; cf. Isa 59:9–10):

A. Is your love declared in the grave,
B. your faithfulness in Destruction (*abaddon*)?
C. Are your wonders known in the place of darkness,
D. or your righteous deeds in the land of oblivion?

In context, the psalmist presses Yahweh to save him from death. Surprisingly, he argues that God should do so because only the living, not the dead, are able to praise Yahweh. As Alter notes, however, the language combines two sets of parallel words, one fairly synonymous, the other signaling development. The near synonyms are "love" / "faithfulness" and "wonders" / "righteous deeds." The other set, however, "carries forward a progressive imaginative realization of death. . . ."[86] The poet first pairs the common term "grave" with the poetic synonym "Destruction" (*abaddon*). The latter steps up the emotive intensity slightly by pointing out the grim fate—extinction—that the grave cruelly imposes.

Then, he parallels another everyday word (darkness) with a second poetic expression for the underworld (the land of oblivion). "Darkness" goes beyond "grave," however,

---

85. Cf. also "seven" / "seventy-seven" in Lamech's boast (Gen 4:24). A more common phenomenon is to parallel a number with a number larger by one (e.g., "three" / "four," Amos 1:3, 6, 9; Prov 30:15, 18; etc.; "seven"/ "eight," Mic 5:5 [Heb 4]; Eccl 11:2). Scholars describe this device with the formula "n / n + 1." For a full discussion of numerical parallelism, see Watson, *Classical Hebrew Poetry*, 144–49.

86. Alter, *The Art of Biblical Poetry*, 14.

because it introduces the sensory experience of death, thereby making the fate more personal. Finally, "land of oblivion" both summarizes the previous lines and brings them to an emphatic close. It implies that "death is a realm where human beings are utterly forgotten and extinct, and where there can be no question of God's greatness being recalled."[87]

Now, in some texts the reader may have difficulty distinguishing the dimension of intensification from that of specification since the two overlap somewhat. We must also allow the possibility that both phenomena may be present in a single passage. This may be the case, for example, in this well-known line from Paul's short hymn to Christ (Phil 2:6–11): "he humbled himself by becoming obedient to death—even death on a cross" (v. 8b).[88] Paul affirms that Jesus' humble obedience to God led him voluntarily to accept death, but the last line ("even death on a cross") offers both specification of *how* he died (i.e., by execution as a criminal, not of natural causes) and emotional intensification in the word "cross" (i.e., an image of "the ultimate in human degradation").[89]

With any poem the reader must scrutinize succeeding poetic lines to define precisely what relationship links them. As Petersen and Richards point out, "The juxtaposition of an A and B provides the opportunity for an almost infinite number of correspondences."[90]

By way of summary, parallelism presents readers a wide range of colorful and creative ways of expression. In our analysis, we have detected numerous ways parallelism works. Perhaps it would help, at the conclusion of this section, to display these ways in outline form. We have described three major ways that parallelism works (A=B, A>B, and A<B), which can be further delineated into seven categories. Then, we suggested subdivisions for two of the categories. In presenting the summary below, we reiterate that it in no way exhausts the multitude of possible types and functional subtypes which Hebrew poetry may show.

---

87. Alter, *The Art of Biblical Poetry*, 14.

88. There is general agreement that these verses comprise an early Christian hymn, but there is no consensus as to its strophic structure and its authorship (the possibilities: Paul, another early Christian, a borrowing from non-Christian sources); for full discussion, see R. P. Martin, *A Hymn of Christ: Philippians 2:5–11 in Recent Interpretation and in the Setting of Early Christian Worship* (Downers Grove: InterVarsity, 1997); and G. F. Hawthorne, *Philippians*, WBC 43, rev. and exp. by R. P. Martin (Nashville: Thomas Nelson, 2004), 90–135. For a theological exposition of the hymn in the context of Paul's understanding of the cross, see G. B. Caird, *Paul: An Introduction to His Thought*, Outstanding Christian Thinkers Series (London: Geoffrey Chapman, 1994), 105–09. Cf. M. S. Park, *Submission within the Godhead and the Church in the Epistle to the Philippians: An Exegetical and Theological Examination of the Concept of Submission in Philippians 2 and 3*, LNTS 361 (New York: T&T Clark, 2007). For the passage's importance for Christology in Philippians, cf. the chapter on Philippians in G. D. Fee, *Pauline Christology: An Exegetical-Theological Study* (Peabody, MA: Hendrickson Publishers, 2007).

89. Hawthorne, *Philippians*, 123, who also observes how grammatically the "intensive or explicative [Greek] conjunction *de* ("even") . . . calls special attention to this most striking element in the humiliation of Christ" (122); cf. Martin, *Hymn of Christ*, 228 ("the lowest point in the dramatic parabola").

90. Petersen and Richards, *Interpreting Hebrew Poetry*, 35.

Types and Subtypes of Hebrew Parallelism		
Type	Definition	Subtypes
A = B	A equals B	1. Echo 2. Contrast

A > B	A is greater than B	3. Subordination
		    Means
		    Reason
		    Time

A < B	B is greater than A	4. Time
		5. Continuation
		6. Comparison
		7. Specification
		    Spatial
		    Explanation
		    Dramatic Effect
		    Purpose
		8. Intensification

Other Poetic Structures

To conclude our survey of Hebrew poetic structure, we introduce other distinct structural devices that are common among biblical poets. As its name implies, *staircase* (or *stairstep) parallelism* is a couplet (or tristich) in which the succeeding lines develop in steps.[91] That is, they add things not found in the opening couplet, frequently with the use of ellipsis. Observe the stairstep structure of these three examples:

A.   Return,   Virgin Israel,

B.   return   to your towns. (Jer 31:21b)

A.   Awake,   my soul!

B.   Awake,   harp and lyre!

C.   I will awaken   the dawn. (Ps 57:8 [MT 57:9])[92]

A.   In him was *life*,

B.   and   that *life* was the *light* of all mankind.

C.   The *light* shines in the *darkness*,

D.   and   the *darkness* has not overcome it.

     (John 1:4–6, our italics)[93]

---

91. Cf. LeMon and Strawn, "Parallelism," 511; Watson, *Classical Hebrew Poetry*, 150–56.

92. These examples (but not their translation) come from Watson, *Classical Hebrew Poetry*, 151; cf. also Watson, *Traditional Techniques*, 313–91.

93. Expanded and adapted from Ryken, *Words of Life*, 101, who observes how "the last key word in a line becomes the first main word in the next line."

In the example from John 1, "life" marks A as the first staircase step and becomes the initial key word in the next step (B). To "life" B adds "light," which then becomes the initial key word in the third step (C), while C concludes with "darkness" which provides the initial key word for the final step (D). Paired words link pairs of lines (i.e., "life" [A//B], "light" [B//C], "darkness" [C//D]) and lay out a stairstep development of thought through the addition of new key words in succeeding lines. In short, by combining repetition and variation, follow-up lines extend the thought of the first forming a verbal staircase. The concluding element actually completes the thought. The poetic effect is for each line to build on its predecessor, the last line serving as a kind of climax.

Chiasm (or chiasmus) is another common structural device in which the word order of a parallel line is the reverse of its predecessor (*a b / b' a'*). Lines drawn between the parallel elements would form an X—the Greek letter *chi* from which the device draws its name. Often the chiasm can be observed only in the Hebrew or Greek text (cf. Job 6:15; Ps 137:5–6a; Amos 5:7, 14–15, 24), but sometimes it is reflected in the English translation. Observe this example from Luke 1:71–74 (our translation). Note how the lines hinge on the central affirmation of God's covenant. The words "enemies" and "ancestor(s)" indicate the parallels.

a	salvation from our *enemies*
	and from the hand of all who hate us–
b	to show mercy to our *ancestors*
c	and to remember his holy covenant,
b'	the oath he swore to our *ancestor* Abraham:
a'	to rescue us from the hand of our *enemies*,
	and to enable us to serve him without fear

Study the word order reversal and X pattern (*abc / b'c'a'* and *abc / c'b'a'*) of these examples:

a	*b*	*c*	
In Judah	God	is known;	
	b'	*c'*	*a'*
	his name	is great	in Israel. (Ps 76:1, NRSV)

a	*b*	*c*	
The sabbath	was made	for humankind,	
c'		*a'*	
and not *humankind* ( )		for the *sabbath* . . . (Mark 2:27, NRSV, our italics)[94]

---

94. Adapted from Bailey and Vander Broek, *Literary Forms*, 178.

The chiasm in the first example hinges on the reversal of the parallel elements "in Judah"/ "in Israel" and "is known" / "is great." In the second, the words "sabbath" and "humankind" exchange places. Usually, chiasm is more than just a decorative device. Poets use it to convey something about the meaning of the lines concerned. For example, a poet might use chiasm to underscore the contrast between the content of two stichs (to show a reversal of fate or to stress their antithesis [cf. antithetical proverbs]). The Bible reader, thus, must analyze how each case of chiasm affects the meaning of the biblical text.[95]

The use of chiasm is not limited to individual parallel lines. We also find examples of *extended chiasm* in the Bible, that is, chiastic structures that underlie entire passages and even entire books.[96] When extended chiasm occurs, the second half of a text or book corresponds to its first half except in reverse order. Each corresponding section has parallel content, and in the case of single texts, often the very same or similar words.

Further, the climax of an extended chiasm falls in the structural center of the text, the one section that lacks a parallel. The climax constitutes the structural hinge or turning point that joins the text's two halves. This is precisely where we find the main point of the passage. Finally, a text's secondary emphasis appears in its frames, that is, in the sections at the beginning and the end (i.e., A and A').

Jeremiah 2:5–9 offers an example of extended chiasm in a single text. Observe the correspondence between parallel parts (e.g., A/A', B/B', etc.), the inverse order of the second half, and the turning point (E in all caps).[97] To highlight the links between sections, we have set key words in italics:

---

95. For further discussion with examples, see P. Overland, "Chiasm," *DOTWPW*, 54–57; Gillingham, *The Poems and Psalms*, 78–82; Watson, *Classical Hebrew Poetry*, 201–8. Chiasm also occurs in lines of prose texts (e.g., Gen 4:4–5; Ruth 1:14; et al.). On chiasm in the NT see J. L. Bailey and L. D. Vander Broek, *Literary Forms*, 49–54, 178–83.

96. Cf. Amos 2:11–12; 5:1–17. Extended chiasm was a common literary technique in the ancient Near East. J. W. Welch, ed., *Chiasmus in Antiquity: Structures, Analyses, Exegesis* (Hildesheim: Gerstenberg, 1981; repr. Provo: Research Press, 1998 with updated bibliography) provides the best critical collection of suggested biblical and extra-biblical examples. J. Lundbom, *Jeremiah: A Study in Hebrew Rhetoric*, 2nd ed. (Winona Lake, IN: Eisenbrauns, 1997), 82–146, explores the topic in Jeremiah, and I. H. Thomson, *Chiasmus in the Pauline Letters*, JSNTSup 111 (Sheffield: Sheffield Academic Press, 1995) does the same for the Pauline Epistles. For other NT examples, see N. W. Lund, *Chiasmus in the New Testament* (repr. Peabody, MA: Hendrickson, 1992); V. Rhee, "The Role of Chiasm for Understanding Christology in Hebrews 1:1–14," *JBL* 131 (2012): 341–62; L. Kierspel, "'Dematerializing' Religion: Reading John 2–4 as a Chiasm," *Bib* 89/4 (2008): 526–54. For OT examples, see Y. Berger, "Chiasm and Meaning in 1 Chronicles," *JHebS* 14 (2014): 1–31; R. Yudkowsky, "Chaos or Chiasm? The Structure of Abraham's Life," *JBQ* 35 (2007): 109–14.

97. The example (slightly modified) comes from W. G. E. Watson, "Chiastic Patterns in Biblical Hebrew Poetry," in *Chiasmus in Antiquity*, 141.

This Yahweh has said:

A What did your *fathers* find wrong with me,   2:5
   to keep their distance from me?
   B Chasing "Delusion" and being deluded
     C *Never saying*:   2:6
       "*Where is Yahweh*"
       D who brought us from the *land,* Egypt
         steered us through the desert   2:7
         through the *land* of steppe and chasm,
         through the *land* both hot and dark,
         through the *land* no one crosses,
           where no man lives.
          E I BROUGHT YOU TO AN ORCHARD LAND,
           TO EAT ITS LOVELY FRUIT
        D' But, on arrival you fouled my *land.*
         my bequest you made disgusting.
     C' The priests *never said*:   2:8
       "*Where is Yahweh?*"
       Law-experts did not know me,
       pastors rebelled against me;
   B' prophets prophesied by Baal,
     and after "no-go(o)ds" ran.
A' So, my case against you rests,   2:9
  Yahweh's word,
  against your *grandchildren* is my case.

The parallels between most of the corresponding sections are evident. C' repeats the wording of C while D' recalls the emphasis on land in D. B' clarifies the word "delusion" in B as a reference to idolatry, while the familial terms "fathers" (A) and "grandchildren" (A') parallel each other. Without a parallel, E forms the structural hinge and states the text's main point: that Yahweh (not Baal) brought Israel to a fruitful (not barren) land. The frames A/A' state that Yahweh condemns all Israel, both ancestors and descendants. Obviously, an understanding of the structure provides a key starting point for interpreting passages such as this. It helps readers to isolate the text's main point, and that in turn enables them to interpret the whole text—i.e., to study how the surrounding content supports that point.

Extended chiasm may also underlie the overall structure of a biblical book. For example, study the detailed, parallel structure proposed by Robert Alden for the Songs of Songs:[98]

---

98. Reproduced with the permission of R. L. Alden in D. E. Garrett, *Proverbs, Ecclesiastes, Song of Songs*, NAC 14 (Nashville: Broadman, 1993), 376. For a suggested, simple chiasm underlying the Book of Revelation, see Lund, *Chiasmus in the New Testament*, 325–26, and his discussion (326–30); for a suggested chiastic structure underlying the book of Kings, see Y. T. Radday, "Chiasmus in Hebrew Biblical Narrative," in Welch, ed., *Chiasmus in Antiquity*,

A 1:1–4a "Take me away"
  B 1:4b Friends speak
    C 1:5–7 "My own vineyard"
      D 1:8–14 "Breasts," "silver," "we will make"
        E 1:15–2:2 "House"
          F 2:3–7 "His left arm" "daughters of Jerusalem . . . so desires," "apple," "love"
            G 2:8–13 "Fragrance," "come my darling," "blossoming"
              H 2:14–15 "Vineyards," "show me"
                I 2:16–17 "My lover is mine"
                  Ja 3:1–5 "The watchmen found me"
                    Jb 3:6–11 Description of carriage, "gold," "Lebanon," "daughters of Jerusalem"
                      Jc 4:1–7 Description of girl, "Your eyes . . . hair . . . teeth"
                        K 4:8–15 "Myrrh," "spice," "honey," "honeycomb," "wine," "milk"
                          L 4:16 "Into his garden"
                          L' 5:1a "Into my garden"
                        K' 5:1bc "Myrrh," "spice," "honey," "honeycomb," "wine," "milk"
                    J'a 5:2–9 "The watchmen found me"
                  J'b 5:10–6:1 "Gold," "Lebanon," "daughters of Jerusalem"
                J'c 6:4–11 Description of girl, "Your eyes, . . . hair . . . teeth"
              I' 6:2–3 "My lover is mine"
            H' 6:13–7:9a [10a] "Vines," "wine," "that we may gaze on you"
          G' 7:9b–13 [10b–14] "Fragrance," "come my darling," "blossom"
        F' 8:1–5 "His left arm," "daughters of Jerusalem . . . so desires," "apple," "love"
      E' 8:6–7 "House"
    D' 8:8–9 "Breasts," "silver," "we will build"
    C' 8:10–12 "My own vineyard"
  B' 8:13 "Friends"
A' 8:14 "Come away"

According to this structure the book's main focus is on *L//L'* and the motif of intimate human love ("Into his/my garden"). This glimpse of the book's overall structure provides a starting point for further interpretation of the Song of Songs.[99] A closer look at what its center (*L//L'*) says about human physical love becomes the key to understanding the main themes of the entire book since they presumably support or expand on it. Finally, knowledge of the central motif and main themes in turn would help illumine interpretation of individual sections within the book as a whole.[100]

---

62 (cf. his discussion of chiasm in Kings, 61–67). Cf. also D. S. Williams, "Once Again: The Structure of the Narrative of Solomon's Reign" *JSOT* 86 (1999): 49–66.

  99. We deeply regret that our beloved colleague, Professor Robert L. Alden, did not live to provide us his own exposition of this structure.

  100. For suggested chiastic structures in shorter NT texts, see N. T. Wright, "Poetry and Theology in Colossians

Merismus is another literary device that appears in both prose and poetry. *Merismus* occurs when a writer mentions the extremes of some category in order to portray it as a totality—that is, those opposites and everything in between them.[101] One common form of *merismus* is the use of polar word pairs in a single phrase. In some cases the phrase's wording expressly states a continuum. For example, consider these lines from the prophet Jeremiah:

> No longer will they teach their neighbors . . . , "Know the LORD,"
> because they will all know me, from the *least* of them to the *greatest* . . .
> (Jer 31:34b, our italics)

The prophet wanted to stress that under the new covenant everyone would know the Lord. To reinforce his point he invoked the extremes of the category "important people" through the *merismus* "from the least [important] . . . to the greatest." Paraphrased, the latter means, "from unimportant to important people—and everyone in between." In other cases, only the word "and" joins the two extremes. For example, the Bible's familiar opening line uses *merismus*: "In the beginning God created the *heavens* and the *earth*" (Gen 1:1, our italics). The phrase "heavens and earth" invokes the extremes of the category "universe" to affirm that God created them and everything in between.[102]

A second common *merismus* employs polar word pairs in parallel stichs. Study how the psalmist displayed God's greatness in this double *merismus*:

> In his hands are the *depths of the earth,*
>   and the *mountain peaks* belong to him.
> The *sea* is his, for he made it,
>   and his hands formed the *dry land.* (Ps 95:4–5, our italics)

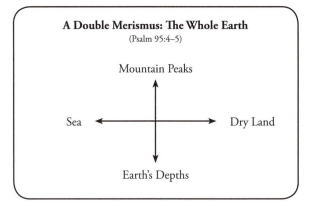

A Double Merismus: The Whole Earth
(Psalm 95:4–5)

Mountain Peaks

Sea ←——————→ Dry Land

Earth's Depths

1.15–20," *NTS* 36 (1990): 449; Bailey and Vander Broek, *Literary Forms*, 49–54 (Pauline letters), 178–83 (the Gospels and Acts).

101. Watson, *Classical Hebrew Poetry*, 321–24; cf. Amos 9:2–4.

102. This phenomenon closely resembles another device called hendiadys (Gk. *hen dia dys*, "one through two"). Hendiadys joins two words by "and" to convey a single idea; cf. Isa 51:19 ("ruin and destruction" meaning "destructive ruin"). More precisely, the two nouns mutually define each other; hence, one serves as an adjective modifying the other. For discussion, see Watson, *Classical Hebrew Poetry*, 324–28.

To achieve a comprehensive effect, the psalmist portrays two pairs of extremes of the category "earth," each in a parallel stich. The first pair describes earth's vertical extremes ("depths"/"peaks"), the other its horizontal ends ("sea"/"dry land"). The total effect is to affirm forcefully that God owns everything on earth, and in context this offers evidence of his greatness.

The final structural device we mention also occurs in both prose and poetry: *inclusio*—framing a poem (or narrative) by repeating words or phrases from its opening lines at its conclusion.[103] This repetition provides a unity and finality the poem would not have otherwise.[104] For example, Psalm 8 opens and closes with these lines that form an inclusio around it:

> LORD, our Lord,
>> how majestic is your name in all the earth! (Ps 8:1a, 9)[105]

The observation of this inclusio is important for two reasons: it signals that the psalm's main theme is the majesty of Yahweh on earth, and it suggests that one must understand all remaining verses (1b–8) in light of that theme. In other words, they illustrate or amplify it. Take, for example, the lengthy section about humanity (vv. 3–8). It marvels at a strange mystery—that God cared enough about puny humans to appoint them as rulers over his own created works. The thematic inclusio indicates, however, that humanity's elevation to greatness is simply an expression—perhaps even a reflection—of God's greater majesty. In other words, God displayed his own greatness by condescending to raise insignificant mortals to a position of great importance.[106] Or notice how Matthew 19:30 includes the words, "But many who are first will be last, and many who are last will be first," virtually repeated, though reversed in a kind of chiasm, in Matthew 20:16: "So the last will be first, and the first will be last." By employing this inclusio Matthew intends readers to understand the intervening parable of the landowner who hired workers for his field throughout the day in light of this principle—the reversal of values in the kingdom of God.

THE LANGUAGE OF POETRY

In addition to unique structure and sound, biblical poetry also uses distinct *language*. Unfortunately, a preoccupation with the phenomenon of parallelism too often creates the impression that parallelism alone is the essence of biblical poetry. But as Ryken observes,

---

103. For prose examples, see 1 Sam 3:1, 21; Ruth 1:6, 22; Matt 4:23–25; 9:35. Poets invoke inclusios in both longer and shorter poems; cf. the extensive treatment of them in Lundbom, *Jeremiah*, 36–81. In Amos 7:9–17 the word "sword" limits the context and encourages the reader to trace the thematic development within those limits.

104. Watson calls this the envelope figure (*Classical Hebrew Poetry*, 282–87); cf. E. S. Gerstenberger, "The Lyrical Literature," in *The Hebrew Bible and Its Modern Interpreters*, ed. D. A. Knight and G. M. Tucker (Philadelphia: Fortress; Chico, CA: Scholars Press, 1985), 423; Berlin, *Dynamics*, 132.

105. Observe also the operation of parallelism here, i.e., how the distich conveys a single sentence composed of *a* as a vocative, *b* as an exclamation. Cf. Pss 103:1a, 2a, 22b; 118:1, 29; 145–150.

106. Closely akin to the inclusio is the use of refrains, that is, the repetition of a phrase within a poem, e.g., Ps 136 ("his love endures forever"); Songs 2:8 [MT 2:7]; 3:5; 8:4 ("Do not arouse or awaken love until it so desires"); Amos 4:6, 8, 9, 10, 11 ("but you have not returned to me"); cf. Watson, *Classical Hebrew Poetry*, 295–99.

Parallelism . . . is not the most essential thing that a reader needs to know about biblical poetry. Much more crucial . . . is the ability to identify and interpret the devices of poetic language.[107]

We hope to prepare the reader to do just that—"to identify and interpret the devices of poetic language." We will treat two aspects of poetic language: imagery and poetic devices.

Imagery

Initially, we must understand the nature of poetic language. Poets are essentially artists who paint pictures with words. From their poetic palette they draw *images*—"words that evoke a sensory experience in our imagination."[108] If well chosen, those words conjure up vivid mental pictures and stir up powerful emotions. By appealing to our senses and emotions, they compel us to see and experience their word-pictures. Thus, to be effective an image must be concrete, not abstract. For the abstraction, "The Lord takes good care of me," the biblical poet substitutes, "The LORD is my shepherd, I shall lack nothing" (Ps 23:1). He paints a simple but warm picture of care at its best: a shepherd who ensures that his sheep get everything they need. Further, effective images also have an element of surprise, either by introducing a new, unknown image or by giving an old one a new twist. Certainly, Jeremiah startled his hearers when he described the state funeral that God had planned for King Jehoiakim:

> He will have the burial of a donkey
> —dragged away and thrown
> outside the gates of Jerusalem. (Jer 22:19)[109]

Normally, respectful Hebrews did not speak of their kings with such outspoken disgust! And no doubt the disciples warmed when Jesus applied the caring shepherd image to himself ("I am the good shepherd"). But then he surprised them by adding, "The good shepherd lays down his life for his sheep" (John 10:11), affirming a stunning self-sacrifice not typical of most shepherds. In both examples, the surprise element is what makes the use of images so effective. Poets constantly speak in the concrete, familiar terms of daily life—of clouds and rain, rocks and rivers, flowers and grass, lions and lambs, mothers and fathers. It is that familiarity and vividness that makes their words so appealing and so memorable.

Devices of Poetic Language

Similes and Metaphors

Similes and metaphors are two poetic devices that are significant in biblical poetry.[110] A *simile* is a figure of speech that compares two things using the words "like" or

---

107. Ryken, *How to Read*, 90, who commends the essay by C. S. Lewis ("The Language of Religion," in *Christian Reflections* [Grand Rapids: Eerdmans, 1967], 129–41) as a good introduction to poetic language.

108. Ryken, *How To Read*, 90.

109. Watson, *Classical Hebrew Poetry*, 252; cf. Jer 9:21; 17:11.

110. Composers of biblical prose also use poetic devices. For example, Luke uses similes to report how the Holy Spirit came upon Jesus "in bodily form *like* a dove" (Luke 3:22) and that the crowd at Pentecost heard "a sound *like* the blowing of a violent wind . . ." (Acts 2:2).

"as."[111] OT poetry uses several kinds of simile. A simple simile draws a single correspondence between two items in a single sentence. Consider these three examples (italics ours):

> Now then, I will crush you
> *as a cart* crushes
> when loaded with grain. (Amos 2:13; cf. 3:12; 5:24)

> *Like a lily* among thorns
> is my darling among the young women. (Song 2:2)

> What shall I compare the kingdom of God to?
> It is *like yeast* that a woman took and mixed into about sixty pounds of
> flour until it worked all through the dough. (Luke 13:20–21)

In the first case, Yahweh compares his imminent crushing judgment to the ground being crushed by the wheels of a heavily loaded cart. He will roll over Israel, crushing her into the dust. In the second case, the lover brags about how much prettier his girlfriend is than other young women; she stands out in a crowd—like a solitary lily in a field of unattractive thorns. Finally, Jesus compares the kingdom to yeast that leavens bread—a subtle, invisible force that transforms everything.

The parallelism typical of biblical poetry easily lends itself to the use of paired similes. These are similes that are part of parallel lines. Study these examples (italics ours):

> The mountains melt beneath him,
> and the valleys split apart,
> *like wax* before the fire,
> *like water* rushing down a slope. (Mic 1:4)

> . . . he [the righteous king] is *like the light* of morning at sunrise
> on a cloudless morning,
> *like the brightness* after rain
> that brings grass from the earth. (2 Sam 23:4; cf. Amos 3:12; 5:24)

Micah's two similes graphically display what horrible devastation God's arrival will wreak on mountains and valleys: first they disintegrate from solids into liquids ("like wax . . ."), then they quickly cascade away into oblivion ("like water . . ."). More positively, David's pair of similes compares the blessings of a righteous king to the "light" of a cloudless dawn and the "brightness after rain," both symbols of relief and renewed hope after darkness and storms; his righteousness guarantees that good days lie ahead ("that brings grass . . .").

Frequently, biblical poets string together series of three or more similes to heighten

---

111. Hebrew forms similes with the preposition *ke/kemo,* the conjunction *kaasher,* the verb *mashal* ("to be like"), and the formula *ke . . . ken* ("like . . . so [is]"); cf. Watson, *Classical Hebrew Poetry,* 257–62, from whom some of what follows derives; and Petersen and Richards, *Interpreting Hebrew Poetry,* 50–60. Greek forms similes with *hōs* (Matt 28:3; 1 Thes 2:7; Rev 1:14, 15) *hōsei* (Matt 3:16; Acts 6:15; Heb 1:12), and *hōmoios* (Luke 12:36; Gal 5:21; Rev 18:18), all meaning "like" or "as."

the effect. Examine the four-item series of similes in this description of Yahweh's future judgment of Israel (italics ours):

> So I will be *like a lion* to them,
> *like a leopard* I will lurk by the path.
> *Like a bear* robbed of her cubs,
> I will attack them and rip them open;
> *like a lion* I will devour them—
> a wild animal will tear them apart. (Hos 13:7–8)

Pairing similes or stringing them together in series is an extremely effective poetic device. Each simile compares to the brush strokes of a painter on a canvas: the more there are, the richer the portrait. Observe the progression of thought and increasing terror effected by the simile series.[112] The first mention of the lion sparks instinctive human fear but does not specify the animal's actions. With the lurking leopard, however, the prophet clarifies the danger and increases the reader's feelings of fear: at any moment Yahweh can spring upon Israel from his hiding place. The bear adds even more clarity and more terror: Yahweh is driven by outrage, so he will rip Israel to pieces, killing her. The lion delivers the final blow—Yahweh will devour Israel's national carcass, leaving only useless carrion behind. In sum, the string of similes forecasts terrible judgment for Israel. Yahweh will pounce on her (lion), taking her by surprise (leopard), killing her for personal injury (bear), and eating her bloody remains (lion). Hosea certainly demonstrates how powerful similes can be. "Like a lion" also functions as an inclusio.

That same power flows from a series of vivid similes in Matthew's report of Jesus' resurrection:

> [The angel's] appearance was *like lightning*, and his clothes were white *as snow*.
> The guards were so afraid of him that they shook and became *like dead men*.
> (Matt 28:3–4, our italics)

The evangelist's simile series creates a clear mental image of the scene: the bright, angelic sight froze normally brave guards into terrified corpses. Similarly, a chain of two parallel similes enables Jesus' listeners better to ponder what the kingdom of God is like (Matt 13:44–46)—like a surprise treasure discovered in a field or a pearl of inestimable value.

Finally, biblical poets often developed an extended simile, making a simple comparison then amplifying it with a lengthy commentary on the poetic image invoked. For example, review how Jeremiah compared an Israelite who depends on Yahweh to a fruitful tree:

---

112. Here we follow the insights of Petersen and Richards, *Interpreting Hebrew Poetry*, 55–57. Cf. T. L. Brensinger, *Simile and Prophetic Language in the Old Testament* (Lewiston: Mellen Biblical Press, 1996); J. C. Exum, "Of Broken Pots, Fluttering Birds, and Visions in the Night: Extended Simile and Poetic Technique in Isaiah," *Beyond Form Criticism: Essays in Old Testament Literary Criticism*, ed. P. R. House, Sources for Biblical and Theological Study 2 (Winona Lake, IN: Eisenbrauns, 1992), 349–72.

But blessed are those who trust in the LORD,
whose trust is in the LORD.

Simile:	They will be *like a tree* planted by water, sending out its roots by the stream.
Comment:	It shall not fear when heat comes, and its leaves shall stay green; in the year of drought it is not anxious, and it does not cease to bear fruit. (Jer 17:7–8, NRSV)[113]

To interpret such examples properly, the reader must first define the image invoked (e.g., a tree rooted by a stream) and then observe what the writer says about that image. In this case, Jeremiah stresses how, rooted beside a reliable water source, the tree calmly faces deprivations and thrives. The point is that the believer's trust gives him or her a calm confidence of thriving amid turmoil. Though not stated explicitly, the text implies that Yahweh will surely meet the believer's needs. In these instances, readers must be careful to interpret the image in light of the commentary. Here the reader might ask how the tree's being rooted by a stream illustrates the nature and benefits of trusting in Yahweh: why do the "roots" create such fearless confidence in the face of daunting circumstances?

Like a simile, *a metaphor* also draws a comparison between two things; however, the metaphor draws the correspondence more bluntly. Omitting the words "like" or "as," it states straightforwardly "A *is* B."[114] So, the psalmist solemnly affirms:

Your word *is* a lamp to my feet
and a light on my path. (Ps 119:105, our italics)

The writer compares God's word to a lamp illuminating a dark path. As a lamp lights the path ahead so a traveler may stay safely on it, so the word illuminates believers on what lifestyle pleases God. In another example, the prophet Zephaniah describes the civic leaders of Jerusalem:

Her officials within her are *roaring lions*;
her rulers are *evening wolves*,
who leave nothing for the morning. (Zeph 3:3, our italics)

---

113. Cf. also his comparison of someone who trusts in human strength to a bush in a desert (vv. 5–6); Ps 1:1–3; Ezek 31:2–9.

114. Ryken, *How To Read*, 91. Much of what follows derives from Ryken, *Words of Delight*, 166–69; and Watson, *Classical Hebrew Poetry*, 263–72. For slightly broader treatments, see I. Paul, "Metaphor and Exegesis," in *After Pentecost: Language and Biblical Interpretation*, ed. C. Bartholomew, C. Greene, and K. Möller, Scripture and Hermeneutics Series 2 (Carlisle, UK: Paternoster, 2001), 387–402; and B. Green, *Like A Tree Planted: An Exploration of Psalms and Parables through Metaphor* (Collegeville, MN: Liturgical Press, 1997). For NT metaphors, see the compendious treatment in A. Byatt, *New Testament Metaphors* (Edinburgh: Pentland Press, 1995).

What a vivid picture of political tyrants! They are hungry animals recklessly roving Jerusalem day and night, terrifying her inhabitants, and preying on her weak. Their appetite so drives them that they never delay their destruction.[115]

Finally, recall this psalmist's portrait of God:

> The *eyes* of the LORD are on the righteous,
>   and his *ears* are attentive to their cry;
> but the *face* of the LORD is against those who do evil,
>   to blot out their name from the earth. (Ps 34:15–16, our italics)

He pictures God as a human being with eyes, ears, and a face—a type of metaphor called an *anthropomorphism*.[116] The point is not that God has an actual body just like humans, but that God constantly tunes his senses to the needs of his people and will confront those who try to harm them.

How do metaphors work? Implicitly, metaphors compare two things that, although *different*, share something in common; in some way the two words or concepts overlap in meaning.[117] The comparison of two basically dissimilar things give the metaphor its striking effect. For example, study the line "The eyes of the LORD are on the righteous" just cited from Psalm 34:15. Here the comparison is between human eyes and the Lord. What do these have in common? They share the trait of focused attention. As human eyes "watch" things with keen interest, so Yahweh "watches"—pays close attention to—his beloved people.

Similarly, the line "Her officials are roaring lions" (Zeph 3:2) implicitly compares city officials with wild animals. In this case, the overlap between these two concepts is less obvious. Without exhausting the possibilities, we suggest that they share great hunger and humanly unstoppable power. The two traits of the animals are physical—a ravenous appetite for prey and overwhelming physical strength. The traits of the leaders are more abstract—a ravenous greed for financial gain and unlimited political power to obtain it.

Like similes, metaphors may also occur in series and in extended form. For example, Jacob's blessing of his children (Gen 49) strings together a series of metaphors, one for each son. Judah is a lion's cub (v. 9), Zebulun a safe harbor (v. 13), Issachar a donkey (v. 14), Dan a viper (v. 17), Naphtali a doe (v. 21), Joseph a fruitful vine (v. 22), and Benjamin a ravenous wolf (v. 27). By painting each son metaphorically, the poet pictures their varied tribal destinies. As a whole, the series

---

115. Cf. also Micah's graphic description of Israel's leaders as cannibals (Mic 3:1b-3) and Amos's sarcastic portrait of Israelite upperclass women as "cows of Bashan" (Amos 4:1). Along a slightly different line, cf. the stinging metaphor "You brood of vipers!" thrown on several occasions by both John the Baptist and Jesus at the Pharisees (Matt 3:7; 12:34; 23:33).

116. Psalm 18:8–16 teems with anthropomorphisms. God has nostrils, a mouth (vv. 8, 15), feet (v. 9), and a voice (v. 13). Verse 16 also implies that he has hands. See also images of God as roaring lion (Amos 1:2; 3:8), water spring (Jer 2:13), rock (Ps 18:2), and mother hen (Ps 91:4).

117. Watson, *Classical Hebrew Poetry*, 263.

of metaphors also offers an impressive poetic collage of Israel's complex future as a nation.

In addition, the Bible teems with examples of extended metaphors. Consider this lengthy description of female beauty:

> Your lips drop sweetness as the honeycomb, my bride;
>> milk and honey are under your tongue.
> The fragrance of your garments
>> is like the fragrance of Lebanon.
> You are a garden locked up, my sister, my bride;
>> you are a spring enclosed, a sealed fountain.
> Your plants are an orchard of pomegranates
>> with choice fruits. . . . (Song 4:11–13)

This lengthy description appeals to all the reader's senses. It enables one to taste, smell, and see this great beauty. Its effect is cumulative and comprehensive.[118]

Permit us, however, to warn readers against the "overinterpretation" of similes and metaphors. Overinterpretation occurs when a reader draws meanings from an image that the poet never intended. For example, we once heard someone speak on Psalm 92:12, "The righteous flourish like a palm tree . . ." Ignoring the specific point made by the context, he expounded thirteen (!) ways the righteous resemble palm trees. Jesus' metaphorical statement "You are the salt of the earth" (Matt 5:13) frequently suffers from similar overinterpretation. One hears commentators interpret it in light of various modern uses of salt (as a seasoning) rather than in light of its surrounding context and use in Bible times (a preservative). Such "insights" owe more to the creativity of the interpreters than the meaning of the biblical text. In short, this is not interpretation at all but eisegesis—"reading in" a meaning not intended by the text.

The best guard against overinterpretation is to adhere to the rule of context—both literary and historical-cultural. We must understand poetic images in light of their use in the immediate context and of what would have come to people's minds in *biblical* times. Since images commonly invoke only a few points of comparison, the proper interpretation requires that we understand them within this limited range rather than read in meanings not intended by the writer.

Other Poetic Language Devices

The devices of simile and metaphor certainly dominate biblical poetry, but readers must also be aware of several other common figures of speech.

---

118. For other extended metaphors, see the descriptions of Egypt as a crocodile (Ezek 29:3–5), Jerusalem's judgment as a full cup (Ezek 23:32–34), and Tyre as a shipwreck (Ezek 27:25–36).

Other Poetic Language Devices

DEVICE	DEFINITION	EXAMPLES
Personification	Non-Human Item in Human Terms	Psalm 98:8 Romans 6:19
Apostrophe	Direct Address to Someone/Something as if Actually Present	Psalm 2:10 James 5:1
Hyperbole	Conscious Exaggeration for Effect	Job 37:1 Galatians 5:12
Metonymy	Substitution of Word/Idea for Closely Associated Word/Idea	Psalm 23:5 Matthew 23:37
Synecdoche	Part of Idea/Item Represents the Whole	Amos 8:10 Matthew 14:30
Irony	Tongue-in-Cheek Statement of the Opposite of Intended Meaning	1 Kings 18:27 1 Corinthians 4:8–10

By *personification* a poet writes about something nonhuman—an inanimate object or abstract idea—as if it were human.[119] This figure of speech enables the poet to make the subject vivid and concrete. Biblical poets use it in several ways. Sometimes they employ personification to bring an abstract idea to life. Consider this example:

> Send me your light and your faithful care,
>> let them guide me;
> let them bring me to your holy mountain,
>> to the place where you dwell. (Ps 43:3)

Here the poet portrays the abstract concepts "light" and "faithful care" as people—guides who will help him find the temple. Of course, the implication is that to find the temple is to meet God since he lives there.

Similarly, Proverbs 8 presents the abstract idea "wisdom" as a woman calling out to passersby in the streets:

> To you, O people, I call,
>> and my cry is to all that live.
> Hear, for I will speak noble things,
>> and from my lips will come what is right;
> I walk in the way of righteousness,
>> along the paths of justice,
> endowing with wealth those who love me
>> and filling their treasuries. (Prov 8:4, 6, 20–21, NRSV)[120]

---

119. Ryken, *Words of Delight*, 178.
120. Later, the "woman" gives her credentials—her participation in the creation of the universe (vv. 22–31).

The picture of a woman brings the abstract idea of wisdom to life. It enables us to understand it in personal terms—the direct, passionate pleadings of a concerned stranger if not a mother, sister, beloved aunt, or favorite neighbor. The address by a person enables us to relate to wisdom more personally than we would otherwise.

Other personifications picture objects as people:

> Let the rivers clap their hands,
> > let the mountains sing together for joy. (Ps 98:8)

Obviously, rivers do not have hands to clap nor mountains voices to lift in song. But the psalmist treats them as if they had those human traits to evoke the tumultuous joy that should greet the arrival of King Yahweh. Another form of personification is to portray a nation, tribe, or city as a person:

> Gilead stayed beyond the Jordan.
> > And Dan, why did he linger by the ships?
> Asher remained on the coast
> > and stayed in his coves. (Judg 5:17).[121]

In Romans 6:19 Paul counsels his readers to offer the members of their bodies "as slaves to righteousness leading to holiness." In this way he personifies the positive traits of "righteousness" and "holiness" as the new benevolent master to whom they ought to enslave themselves (i.e., to render God complete devotion).

The device of *apostrophe* closely resembles that of personification. Indeed, poets frequently employ both in the same context (see the examples below). Apostrophe is "a direct address to someone or something absent as though it were present."[122] Typically, it appears suddenly in a context, as if the poet, overcome by emotions, blurts out his address. The thing addressed may be an abstract idea or an inanimate object. Apostrophe serves a twofold purpose: to give vent to strong feelings and to generate a sense of excitement.

We occasionally use apostrophe ourselves. For example, arriving home from work, parents discover that their kids have left the family kitchen a mess. As if the offenders were present, the parents say, "You kids are in big trouble now!" Again, safely out of earshot of the boss a frustrated employee might explode, "I'm going to get you for this, boss!" Examine the addressees and emotions evident in these three biblical examples:

> Therefore, you kings, be wise;
> > be warned, you rulers of the earth. (Ps 2:10)

Cf. R. E. Murphy, "The Personification of Wisdom," in *Wisdom in Ancient Israel: Essays in Honour of J. A. Emerton,* ed. J. Day, R. P. Gordon, and H. G. M. Williamson (Cambridge: Cambridge University Press, 1995), 222–33.

121. The OT frequently personifies Jerusalem (often called "Zion") in various ways (e.g., Pss 48:11 [MT 48:12]; 97:8; Isa 12:6; 37:22; et al.); cf. K. M. Heim, "The Personification of Jerusalem and the Drama of Her Bereavement in Lamentations," *Zion, City of Our God,* ed. R. S. Hess and G. J. Wenham (Grand Rapids: Eerdmans, 1999), 129–69.

122. Ryken, *Words of Delight,* 177–78.

> Where, O death, is your victory?
>> Where, O death, is your sting? (1 Cor 15:55; cf. Hos 13:14)

> Now listen, you rich people, weep and wail
>> because of the misery that is coming on you. (Jas 5:1)

In the first example, the psalmist addresses the kings of the earth, none of whom was probably present on the occasion of this psalm. Also, his address marks a noticeable literary shift in the context: it follows a report of God's decree establishing the Davidic monarchy (Ps 2:7–9). In the second, Paul breaks off his discourse on Christian hope to address "death"—presumably absent—as a mighty warrior. In the third, James comforts his poor, oppressed readers by condemning their (absent) oppressors. Appearing suddenly in the context, each conveys strong emotional feelings and generates a sense of excitement.[123]

Occasionally all of us resort to the common device of *hyperbole.* "I shopped 'til I dropped," we say to describe our physical exhaustion. A frazzled parent might reprimand, "I've told you a *thousand times* to make your bed!" Hyperbole is "conscious exaggeration for the sake of effect."[124] Its purpose is to state something the poet feels strongly—the joy of salvation, the bitterness of death, the awfulness of judgment. Hence, as Ryken notes, it stretches the literal truth for the sake of emotional impact. Study these examples:

> At this my heart pounds
>> and leaps from its place. (Job 37:1)[125]

> I am poured out like water,
>> and all my bones are out of joint.
> My heart has turned to wax;
>> it has melted away within me. (Ps 22:14)

> Saul and Jonathan—
>> in life they were loved and admired,
>> and in death they were not parted.
> They were swifter than eagles,
>> they were stronger than lions. (2 Sam 1:23)

As for those agitators, I wish they would go the whole way and emasculate themselves! (Gal. 5:12)

Obviously, the four speakers offer exaggerated descriptions of their situations. In the Job passage Elihu's heart did not literally jump out from his chest. He simply

---

123. Cf. the excitement generated by the catalogue of apostrophes in Ps 148. For more examples, see Bullinger, *Figures of Speech*, 901–5.

124. Ryken, *Words of Delight*, 177; cf. Watson, *Classical Hebrew Poetry*, 316–21.

125. Job 37:1 exemplifies the parallelism of intensification that we discussed earlier; that is, the hyperbole of the second stich gives more intensity than the first.

exaggerated—"It pounded so hard it popped out!"—to show his excitement at God's greatness. Similarly, the psalmist's entire skeleton did not really get out of joint nor did his heart suddenly become melted wax. Through exaggeration he emphasizes, "I've got no fight left in me." By the same token, David's exaggerated tribute to Saul and Jonathan underscored their great physical prowess. And Paul actually has no urgent desire that Jews in Galatia, who want new Christians there to undergo circumcision voluntarily, model even greater devotion by volunteering for castration. He's simply "had it" with their improper agitation and the distraction it has created among sincere new believers.

Biblical poets also use numbers to express hyperbole:

> Your city that marches out a *thousand* strong
>> will have only *a hundred* left;
> your town that marches out a *hundred* strong
>> will have only *ten* left. (Amos 5:3, our italics; cf. Isa 4:1)

The prophet is not presenting precise statistics here. He is exaggerating the numbers, both high and low, to portray Israel's high casualty rate—that the coming divine judgment will be catastrophic for the nation. Nor does Jesus advocate mutilation in calling his disciples to gouge out their eyes or literally to cut off their hands (Matt 5:29–30; cf. Gal 5:12). He exaggerates to urge his disciples to take the dangers of sin so seriously that they avoid it at all costs.

The Bible abounds with examples of extended hyperbole in which the exaggeration continues at length (see Jer 5:16–17; Nah 3:15b–17; Job 3:4–9).[126] Similarly, the evangelist clearly exaggerates the extent of the crowds coming to Jesus when he says, "People went out to him from Jerusalem and all Judea and the whole region of the Jordan. Confessing their sins, they were baptized by him in the Jordan River" (Matt 3:5–6). His hyperbole aims to convey the excitement that Jesus' ministry generated at the time.

The device called *metonymy* features the substitution of a word or idea for one closely associated with it. The substitute serves as a verbal stand-in representing the other. Note these examples of metonymy (cf. the metonymic word in italics):[127]

> You prepare a *table* before me
>> in the presence of my enemies. (Ps 23:5a)

> The high places of *Isaac* will be destroyed
>> and the sanctuaries of Israel will be ruined. (Amos 7:9a)

> Truthful *lips* endure forever,
>> but a lying *tongue* lasts only a moment. (Prov 12:19)

---

126. For an example that uses hyperbole, apostrophe, and personification, see Ps 114 and Ryken's comments (*Words of Delight*, 179–80).

127. We owe these examples to M. S. Terry, *Biblical Hermeneutics* (n.p.: Arkose Press, 2015), 161–62. For more examples, see Bullinger, *Figures of Speech*, 538–612.

The psalm does not say that God will make the psalmist a brand new piece of furniture to impress his enemies; rather, "table" substitutes for the bountiful meal that a host spreads across it for a guest. Similarly, biblical history identifies Isaac as a patriarchal ancestor of Israel. So, in Amos 7:9 "Isaac" rightly becomes another way of saying "Israel" (Isaac/Israel). Or Matthew 23:37 reports that Jesus often longed to gather and shelter *Jerusalem* which, by metonymy, stands for all Jews. Again, Proverbs 12:19 does not teach that liars will suddenly lose their tongues. Instead, the physical organs of speech, "lips" and "tongue," represent the speakers who lie or tell the truth—and receive the consequences each deserves. In sum, the device of metonymy represents something indirectly by substituting something else associated with it.

A similar principle underlies a related device called *synecdoche*. In synecdoche, a part of something serves to represent the whole idea or item. This device allows the writer to focus the reader's attention on something specific as a symbol of something larger. Study these examples with the synecdochal word in italics:[128]

> I will turn your religious *festivals* into mourning,
>   and all your *singing* into weeping. (Amos 8:10)

> I put no trust in my *bow*,
>   my *sword* does not bring me victory . . . (Ps 44:6 [MT 44:7])

> And it shall come to pass afterward,
>   that I will pour out my spirit on all *flesh* . . . (Joel 2:28 [MT 3:1], RSV)

But when he saw the *wind*, he was afraid and, beginning to sink, cried out, "Lord, save me!" (Matt 14:30)

In Amos 8:10, "singing" parallels the word "festivals" in the preceding line. Singing constituted one important part of Israelite feasts, so "singing" rightly represents the whole series of festival activities. Along the same line, "bow" and "sword" (Ps 44:6 [7]) symbolize the larger category of weapons. Again, in Joel 2:28 [3:1] one constituent of human nature, "flesh," represents the whole person. Thus, "all flesh" really means "all people," a conclusion confirmed by the following verse ("my servants, both men and women"). Matthew writes that Peter's outlook changed when he saw the wind, a synecdoche for the storm, and with failing faith began to sink (Matt 14:29–30).

Besides identifying metonymy and synecdoche, the interpreter must consider the writer's purpose in using them. In other words, what effect does each example intend to convey? We suggest, for example, that the phrase "you prepare a table in the presence of my enemies" (Ps 23:5a) aims to conjure up more than the general idea of food. In context "table" portrays the idea of God's plenteous provision of food despite the enemies' attempts to cut off such supplies—provision in line with the "I will

---

128. We have gleaned OT examples from Alter, *The Art of Biblical Poetry*, 73–74; and Bullinger, *Figures of Speech*, 614–56. Cf. also Terry, *Biblical Hermeneutics*, 162–63.

lack nothing" of v. 1. Similarly, Amos 8:10 specifies "singing" rather than another festival activity like "praying" because the former symbolizes joy and celebration. Thus, "(joyous) singing" serves to contrast the "mourning" and "weeping" that the coming divine judgment will inflict.

Finally, we mention the device of *irony* in which a writer says the very opposite of what he or she means. In contemporary terms, the poet speaks tongue-in-cheek; a moment later the reader expects to hear an emphatic "Just kidding!" At times, irony becomes sarcasm whereby the speaker pokes fun at the object of his or her words. Though not all drawn from poetry, the following verses illustrate the use of irony:

> Go to Bethel and sin;
>> go to Gilgal and sin yet more.
> Bring your sacrifices every morning,
>> your tithes every three years. (Amos 4:4b; cf. v. 5; 6:13)

> And the LORD said to me, "Throw it to the potter"
> —the handsome price at which they valued me! (Zech 11:13)

At noon Elijah began to taunt them [i.e., the priests of Baal]. "Shout louder!" he said. "Surely he is a god! Perhaps he is deep in thought, or busy, or traveling. Maybe he is sleeping and must be awakened." (1 Kgs 18:27)[129]

Amos knew the city of Bethel as a center of Israelite pagan worship ("Go to Bethel and sin"). Hence, despite his command to "bring your sacrifices . . . ," he really wants Israel *not* to go, that is, to repent of its pagan practices. Similarly, the phrase "handsome price" intends to convey just the opposite meaning—the price asked is insultingly low. Further, Elijah does not believe that Baal is a god actually preoccupied with other activities. His words, in fact, sarcastically state the opposite: Baal has not answered the prayers of his priests because he does *not* exist; hence, he can*not* do anything.[130]

Finally, a NT passage that drips with irony is 1 Corinthians 4:8–10 where Paul says,

Already you have all you want! Already you have become rich! You have begun to reign—and that without us! How I wish that you really had begun to reign so that we also might reign with you! For it seems to me that God has put us apostles on display at the end of the procession, like those condemned to die in the arena. We have been made a spectacle to the whole universe, to angels as well as to human

---

129. Two of the above examples (1Kgs 18:27; Zech 11:13) come from Terry, *Biblical Hermeneutics*, 165–66. For others, see Bullinger, *Figures of Speech*, 807–15.

130. Recent studies have explored the use of irony in whole books; cf. M. D. Nanos, *The Irony of Galatians: Paul's Letter in First-Century Context* (Minneapolis: Fortress, 2002); G. M. Feagin, *Irony and the Kingdom in Mark: A Literary-Critical Study* (Lewiston, NY: Mellen Biblical Press, 1997). For the OT, see L. R. Klein, *The Triumph of Irony in the Book of Judges*, JSOTSup 68 (Sheffield: Almond Press, 1988); E. M. Good, *Irony in the Old Testament*, 2nd ed. (Sheffield: Almond Press, 1981 [1965]).

beings. We are fools for Christ, but you are so wise in Christ! We are weak, but you are strong! You are honored, we are dishonored!

Certainly, such effective irony would have shamed the Corinthian Christians into repenting of their arrogance. At least that was Paul's desire.[131]

Interpreting Poetic Language

To interpret the meaning conveyed through poetic devices, we suggest that the reader take the following steps.[132] First, *identify* the kind of figure of speech present (i.e., simile, metaphor, personification, etc.). Remember that more than one device may be present in the same biblical text. For example, a verse may employ hyperbole through both a simile and a metaphor.

Second, *interpret* the figure of speech by distilling its figurative meaning from its literal meaning. By "literal meaning," we mean the actual physical object denoted, the ideas that object conjures up, and the emotional connotations the reader associates with it. By "figurative meaning," we mean the aspect of the literal meaning that the poet desires to highlight. The reader will have to decide which of the literal meaning's many associated ideas and connotations best fit the emphasis of the context.

For example, one psalmist describes his enemies this way:

> I am in the midst of lions;
> I am forced to dwell among ravenous beasts—
> men whose teeth are spears and arrows,
> whose tongues are sharp swords. (Ps 57:4)

From the first two lines, one might see the poet as literally cornered by terrible beasts. Men with "teeth" and "tongues" in the last two lines, however, indicate an allusion to verbal slander. Literally, the metaphors "spears and arrows" and "sharp swords" refer to common weapons of ancient warfare. The latter have three main features: (1) the enemy launches them from a distance (spears and arrows) or from nearby (sharp swords); (2) they inflict painful, if not fatal, wounds by piercing the body; (3) an ordinary person has no defense against them.

These observations point to the metaphor's figurative meaning, that is, what those weapons suggest about slander. They portray it as harsh, "pointed" words that wound their victim. They conjure up images of a victim flinching with continuous pain. The words also imply that slander sometimes strikes suddenly, "out of the blue"—probably an allusion to the secrecy of slander. Furthermore, by striking suddenly, slander leaves its victim defenseless; there is no way to protect against it. In sum, literal weapons figuratively illumine the psalmist's portrait of verbal slander.

Finally, the reader should determine the *function* of the figure in its context. In

---

131. Other examples where Paul famously employs irony include Rom 2:17–24 and 2 Cor 11:7–17.
132. Cf. Ryken, *How to Read*, 94–96; Ryken, *Words of Delight*, 161–62, 177–78.

other words, why did the poet use this particular figure? What did it contribute to the meaning he desired to convey?

Let us apply these steps briefly to Psalm 18:2 [MT 18:3] as an example:

> The LORD is my rock, my fortress and my deliverer;
> > my God is my rock, in whom I take refuge,
> He is my shield and the horn of my salvation,
> > my stronghold.

The kind of figure the psalmist used here is metaphor. As for the literal meaning, the verse pictures several common, concrete images: "rock," "fortress," "shield," "horn," and "stronghold." Together they suggest ideas of immovability, impenetrable protection, and great strength ("horn").[133] Emotionally, their connotations are positive; the reader would view them as "saviors" in a day of near-death.

This analysis helps us see the figurative meaning. What fortresses and shields have in common with Yahweh is great strength and protection. Thus, the figurative meaning is that Yahweh is the psalmist's protection, the one whose awesome strength surrounds him. Finally, we suggest that within Psalm 18 the figures function to sound one of the psalm's main themes—God's protection—a theme the psalmist's own testimony (Ps 18:4–19) confirms.[134]

This table summarizes the steps to take in assuring that you understand the language of the poet.

How to Interpret Poetic Language
1. Identify the Figure(s) of Speech Present
2. Identify Its Emotional Connotations (Positive/Negative)
3. Distill the Figurative Meaning from the Literal One
4. Determine the Figure's Function (i.e., Why used here?)

LARGER UNITS OF POETRY

Sense Units

Thus far, our discussion may have created the impression that all Hebrew poetry consists of only a few lines. Obviously, a glance at the psalms quickly confirms that this is not the case![135] The Bible's parallel lines actually form part of larger structural

---

133. Of course, this step requires the reader to have a good understanding of the biblical world. For example, we must discover what "horn" connoted in Bible times, not today. We recommend the regular use of Bible dictionaries and encyclopedias as excellent sources of background on figures of speech. Recall our prior explanation of word studies and historical and cultural backgrounds in ch. 7.

134. Careful readers must also watch for poetic language in nonpoetic passages (e.g. Gen 4:7; Matt 23:37; Jas 1:15); cf. Ryken, *Words of Delight*, 180.

135. The NT writers do not include long poems such as we find in the OT psalms, but we do find examples of extended hymnic material such as Col 1:15–20 and Phil 2:6–11.

units we will call *sense units*.[136] A sense unit constitutes the major subdivision of an entire poem. Just as a house may have one or more rooms, so a poem has at least one sense unit but may have many more of varying sizes.

The key indicators of a poem's sense units are as follows: (1) changes in content, grammar, literary form, or speaker; (2) the concentration of keywords in a section; and (3) the appearance of refrains or repeated statements.[137] Psalm 32 provides an example of sense units and their indicators. With your Bible open, compare the following chart.[138]

Sense Unit	Verses	Indicators
1	1–2	form: impersonal "blessed is the person" formula content: sin, forgiveness function: to provide general thematic introduction
2	3–5	transition: "for" change of speaker: "I" form: report of personal experience content: experience of forgiveness function: to illustrate the forgiveness theme
3	6–7	transition: "for" form: exhortation (v. 6), affirmation of confidence (v. 7) addressee: God ("you" singular) content: prayer, protection, deliverance function: to urge people to pray
4	8–10	form: instruction (cf. prohibition [v. 9], proverb [v. 10]) addressee: Israel ("you" singular) content: teaching about trust in Yahweh function: to teach the benefit of trust
5	11	form: call to rejoice addressee: righteous Israelites ("you" plural) content: rejoicing, gladness, singing function: to call for response to entire psalm

136. We borrow the term from Petersen and Richards (*Interpreting Hebrew Poetry*, 60–63) as an alternative to popular but ambiguous terms like "stanza" and "strophe" (against Watson, *Classical Hebrew Poetry*, 160–67). Fokkelman favors the term "stanza" (*Reading Biblical Poetry*, 117–40) and offers an illuminating discussion of this larger unit with examples.

137. These same indicators may also signal the main literary divisions of prose passages.

138. Cf. Gerstenberger, *Psalms, Part 1*, 140–43.

Sense units are basic to the structure of a poem, so if we want to decipher this structure we must first identify the poem's sense units. With a piece of notepaper in hand, read the poem watching for the key indicators mentioned above. When these indicators change significantly, indicating a break between sections, write the verses of the sense unit just concluded. Continue this analysis until the entire poem's sections are identified. After identifying the sense units, the reader should isolate any subsections within those sense units. Read the poem a second time, identifying the subsections within each sense unit. Write the verses for each subsection under the verses for each sense unit.

Finally, beside the verses for each sense unit/subunit, write a short label that describes its literary form. Be sure that the label describes the literary *form* rather than the *content*. The difference is this: a content label describes *what* a sense unit says (its content); a literary label describes *how* it says what it says (its literary form). For example, Psalm 73:1 ("Surely God is good to Israel/to those who are pure in heart") constitutes a sense unit whose content is about God's goodness to Israel. Its form, however, is that of an affirmation. By the same token, in content Amos 5:6a ("Seek the LORD and live") is about devotion to God, but its form is a call to worship.

To illustrate this procedure, consider how you would describe these three sections of Psalm 32:

> vv. 3, 5   When I kept silent, my bones wasted away
> through my groaning all day long. [. . .]
> Then I acknowledged my sin to you
> and did not cover up my iniquity.
> I said, "I will confess my transgressions to the LORD."
> And you forgave the guilt of my sin.
>
> 9   Do not be like the horse or the mule,
> which have no understanding
> but must be controlled by bit and bridle
> or they will not come to you.
>
> 11   Rejoice in the LORD and be glad, you righteous;
> sing, all you who are upright in heart!

Obviously, the excerpt of vv. 3 and 5 describes the ending of personal trouble through the confession and forgiveness of sin. One might depict the *content* as "The trouble and forgiveness of sin" or "Confession of sin ends trouble." Observe, however, that this is not an impersonal, abstract discussion of human suffering caused by sin. Rather, it offers a personal report given by an individual about a past experience of forgiven sin. The proper literary label (*form*) would be something like "Personal report: trouble and forgiveness."

Taken by itself, the content of v. 9 easily wins labels like "An appeal for self-control" or "An example of stubbornness." Since it follows up v. 8, however ("I will instruct you . . . in the way you should go"), one might describe its content more precisely as "Stubborn resistance to good teaching." Literarily, however, notice that v. 9 is not a description but a prohibition ("Do not be like the horse or the mule . . .") that the speaker urges upon his audience. So, one should label it literarily as a "Prohibition." As for v. 11, its content readily calls to mind a label like "Rejoicing and singing." Again, however, observe the form: two commands with which the speaker exhorts the audience ("Rejoice . . . sing"). Literarily, then, one should describe it as an "Exhortation" or "Call to Worship."

After completing the descriptions of sense units and their subparts, we suggest two final steps. First, one should write a *literary outline* based on those descriptions. The purpose of such an outline is to present the poem's literary structure in visual form. The outline, then, can become the basis for analyzing the poem's literary and thematic development. A literary outline of Psalm 32 might look like this:[139]

I. Superscription 1a
II. The Psalm 1b–11
   A. Declaration 1b–2
   B. Personal report: trouble and forgiveness 3–5
      1. Description: trouble 3–4
      2. Description: forgiveness 5
   C. Exhortation and confession 6–7
      1. Exhortation. 6
      2. Confession 7
   D. Instruction. 8–10
      1. Statement of intention 8
      2. Instruction itself. 9–10
         a. Prohibition 9
         b. Proverb 10
   E. Closing exhortation 11

Notice our consistent use of literary terms rather than descriptions of content. As indicated, we describe vv. 3–5 as a "Personal report" because that is its form (the comment "trouble and forgiveness," however, adds some clarification). Because the exhortation of v. 11 concludes the psalm, we call it a "Closing exhortation." Our "Prohibition" (v. 9), however, forms only part of a larger section (vv. 8–10), along with a proverb (v.10) and a declaration of intention to give instruction (v. 8). Since v. 8 introduces what follows as instruction (vv. 9–10), we label the entire section as "Instruction."

---

139. The following is a modification of Gerstenberger, *Psalms, Part 1*, 140. For a fuller treatment of this method and its application to poetic and nonpoetic texts, see volumes in the Forms of Old Testament Literature (FOTL) series (Eerdmans) and G. M. Tucker, *Form Criticism of the Old Testament* (Philadelphia: Fortress, 1971).

Second, using the literary outline as a guide, the reader should analyze the poem's structure. To do so, study the outline to answer questions like the following:

1. What comes first in the poem? What comes last? Why?
2. What comes in the middle of the poem? Why?
3. What organizing principle underlies its structure (e.g., liturgical practices, thematic development, etc.)?
4. What is (are) the poem's main theme(s)?
5. How does each sense unit contribute to its thematic development?
6. What literary form best describes the poem as a whole (e.g., report, call to praise, exhortation, warning, etc.)?
7. What is the poem's intention or purpose (i.e., What did the poet hope to accomplish?)?
8. What is its main point?

In sum, analysis of a poem's structure is more than an academic exercise. Applied carefully, it provides readers with a helpful tool of interpretation. In fact, one may also apply this same method—the preparation of a literary outline—to nonpoetic texts. In such cases, however, the outline would describe its subparts not as poetic sense units but as *narrative* ones. Our method provides a way for readers to break a text down into its constituent parts. Awareness of those parts gives readers the basis for tracing the thematic development of a passage and for determining its main themes and main point.

Part IV

UNDERSTANDING
BIBLE GENRES

9

GENRES OF THE
OLD TESTAMENT

We agree with Leland Ryken that "when the Bible employs a literary method, it asks to be approached as literature and not as something else."[1] That's why we devote this chapter and the following one to introducing the main literary genres of the Bible. To underscore their importance, however, permit us to present a brief exercise for readers to complete. Please read the four texts below and identify the following features in each: its literary structure, genre, life setting, and intention. When done, compare your answers with our subsequent comments concerning the four.

Text #1: Oh, the grand old Duke or York,
    He had ten thousand men;
    He marched them up to the top of the hill,
    And he marched them down again.

    And when they were up, they were up,
    And when they were down, they were down.
    But when they were only half-way up,
    They were neither up nor down.

Text #2: Do you solemnly swear that you will tell the truth, the whole truth, and nothing but the truth, so help you God? (Implied Response: I do.)

Text #3: Give a man a fish, and you feed him for a day. Teach a man to fish, and you feed him for a lifetime.

Text #4: We hold these truths to be self-evident, that all men are created equal, that they are endowed by their Creator with certain unalienable Rights, that among these are Life, Liberty and the pursuit of Happiness. That to secure these rights, Governments are instituted among Men, deriving their just powers from the consent of the governed, That whenever any Form of Government becomes destructive of these ends, it is the Right of the People to alter or to abolish it, and to institute new Government, laying its foundation on such

---

1. Cf. L. Ryken, *How to Read the Bible as Literature* (Grand Rapids: Zondervan, 1984), 11–12.

principles and organizing its powers in such form, as to them shall seem most likely to effect their Safety and Happiness.

THE NATURE OF GENRE

The genre of Text #1 is a children's song whose typical setting is a gathering of children for activities (e.g., a classroom, park, camp, etc.). Its structure has two parts: the story of the wise king's troop-marching practices told by an unnamed storyteller (lines 1–4) and the application of the story to the audience (lines 5–8). The stress on "up" / "down"/ "halfway" hints that actual motions accompany the singing ("up" = standing; "down" = sitting; "halfway" = in between). Given the setting and genre, the song's likely intention is simply to entertain the assembled children.

The setting of Text #2 is a courtroom, its genre a report of the ritual by which a bailiff swears in a witness. The bailiff addresses the witness in two parts: the bailiff's command that the addressee assume the customary physical posture of oath-taking (line 1–2) followed by the formulaic question for the witness to answer (lines 3–6; the formulaic "I do" is implied in lines 7–8). The ritual's intention is to elicit the witness's promise to testify truthfully.

Text #3 is a popular saying whose setting is a local community. Its structure has two parts: the first states the benefit of giving someone food (lines 1–3), while the second states the benefit of teaching someone to fish (lines 4–6). Each part has the same inner structure: an implied condition ("If you give / teach . . .") followed by its consequences ("feed . . . for a day" / "feed . . . for a lifetime"). Their contrasting language implies the superiority of the second over the first, so we propose that the text's intention is to teach that the wisest action is one that has the greatest positive impact.

Finally, the genre of Text #4 is an affirmation by a group ("we hold . . .") of certain firm principles. Its setting can be described with unusual precision—July 4, 1776 at Philadelphia, Pennsylvania—and its speakers are representatives of the British colonies in America. Structurally, part one is the opening short summary affirmation (line 1), part two the amplification of its object—three absolute principles (lines 2–13). Its intention is to articulate the affirmation. Of course, Text #4 is not a complete text; it is the opening paragraph of a longer historical document whose genre as a whole is a declaration—the Declaration of Independence. This example teaches us something important—that writers and speakers may combine genres together to compose a larger document of another genre. Put differently, a given text's genre may comprise other genres subordinate to the genre of the whole text.

Now, why are we able easily to identify most, if not all, of these texts? Each kind of literature has its own frame of reference, ground rules, strategy, and purpose, and the text examples above are probably already familiar to most readers—they're part of the culture in which we grew up. In reading them, we have what John Barton once called literary competence: "linguistic competence" (the ability to understand what is written on a page) and "genre recognition" (the cultural familiarity instinctively to discern the cues of a particular genre and its background). That recognition indicates the kind of literature present and signals what to expect or not to expect from it. But for us to read the Bible poses a challenge because of the geographical and chronological distance between us and it. We didn't grow up in Mesopotamia, Egypt, or Canaan back then, do not read their ancient languages, much less have the cultural background to pick up the genre clues in their literatures.

But two things save us from what might otherwise be a deadend of literary *in*competence. First, as scholars have recently recognized, we share common human experiences with people who lived long ago and far away. We resonate with children who like to sing and act out motions; we know that law follows certain set procedures; we ourselves have received and passed down wisdom from our ancestors; and we know the importance of historical documents. Second, we have the advantage of modern literary tools that, if properly applied, allow us to tune into ancient texts closely—with practice and experience over time to improve our level of literary competence. The Bible is, in fact, written literature—compositions of prose and poetry in various sizes and shapes written by human beings in human language. God chose to convey his revelation to humans in a way they could understand—by written literature. To interpret it properly, then, we must use literary tools for they alone enable us to understand the Bible holistically. They sharpen our mind so we can discover its ideas; they tune our imagination so its truth can grip us emotionally. They steer us clear of misreadings.

We assert that the Bible student who knows the formation, function, and background of each literary type (genre) is in the best position to interpret correctly and to avoid serious misunderstandings. So, as with poetry, the discussion below draws on the remarkable recent advances in our understanding of the Bible's rich and varied literary landscape. This chapter mines the insights of Old Testament *form criticism* to illumine our understanding of the structure, literary type or genre, original life-setting, and intention of much OT literature.[2] It consults the study of *poetics* to help clarify *how* texts, especially OT narratives, work by identifying their devices and literary dynamics.[3] It also draws on the methodological ally of poetics, the so-called *new literary criticism*, for further illumination.[4]

---

2. Good recent introductions to OT form criticism are M. A. Sweeney, "Form Criticism," in *Dictionary of Old Testament: Wisdom, Poetry, and Writings* (henceforth, *DOTWPW*), ed. T. Longman III and P. Enns (Downers Grove: IVP Academic, 2008), 227–41; and J. Barton, *Reading the Old Testament* (Louisville: Westminster John Knox, 1996), 30–44. For a survey of major biblical genres, see M. D. Johnson, *Making Sense of the Bible: Literary Type as an Approach to Understanding* (Grand Rapids: Eerdmans, 2002). Cf. the in-depth discussion of the method in M. A. Sweeney and E. Ben Zvi, *The Changing Face of Form Criticism for the Twenty-First Century* (Grand Rapids: Eerdmans, 2003); and D. L. Petersen, "Brevard Childs and Form Criticism," in *Old Testament Theology: Reading the Hebrew Bible as Christian Scripture*, ed. C. R. Seitz and K. H. Richards (Atlanta: Society of Biblical Literature, 2013), 9–19.

3. Such markers include, for example, plot, characterization, descriptions, style, narrative pacing, point of view, the use of wordplays or word repetition, the inclusion/exclusion of key details, etc. For poetics, cf. the ground-breaking study of R. Alter, *The Art of Biblical Narrative*, rev. ed. (New York: Basic Books, 2011); and M. Sternberg, *Poetics of Biblical Narrative: Ideological Literature and the Drama of Reading* (Bloomington: Indiana University Press, 1985).

4. For one view of the new literary criticism, see D. J. A. Clines and J. C. Exum, "The New Literary Criticism," in *The New Literary Criticism and the Hebrew Bible*, ed. J. C. Exum and D. J. A. Clines (Valley Forge, PA: Trinity Press International, 1993), 11–25. Instead of *poetics*, some scholars prefer the term "narrative criticism"; cf. P. E.

To enhance the reader's literary competence in both the OT and the NT, this chapter and the following one will survey briefly the Bible's main literary forms. Their purpose is threefold: (1) to provide reliable first steps in thinking "literarily" about the Bible; (2) to teach a preliminary literary vocabulary to aid in interpretation; and (3) to help readers both to enjoy the Bible's riches more and to understand it better. In so doing, we hope they will experience what Jasper describes:

> By concentrating on the literary qualities of the biblical texts, the reader encounters with new immediacy their power and mystery. Like all great texts of literature, they are seen as both historical *and* contemporary, as living with history.[5]

NARRATIVES

Everyone loves a good story. From the bedtime "Once upon a time . . ." of childhood to the newest Hollywood film, we enjoy losing ourselves in the imaginative worlds of books, plays, and the big screen. Bible writers love stories, too; that is why narratives are the most common literature found in the Bible—one-third of the OT.[6] In reality, rather than a single type of "Old Testament narrative," the OT has narratives of many kinds.

Recall some memorable biblical scenes: the knife in Abraham's hand a frozen instant from slaying Isaac; the raging Red Sea waters pliantly obeying Moses' uplifted little rod; God's thunderous voice rolling down Mt. Sinai to Israel's frightened ears; deadeye David's shot that toppled Goliath like a tree. Recall some memorable biblical characters: clever Rebecca scheming to win young Jacob the firstborn's blessing; crafty Laban outfoxing love-struck Jacob on his wedding night; bold Moses telling God "no" when told of his destruction plans; grieving Rizpah shooing away buzzards and jackals from her two sons' corpses. For great stories and vivid characters, Hollywood has nothing on the Bible! More important, we often see ourselves in them.

To learn to read its stories clearly—i.e., to have the requisite literary competence—is the first step to hearing God's clear voice speaking through them.[7] After all, unlike

---

Satterthwaite, "Narrative Criticism: The Theological Implications of Narrative Techniques," in *NIDOTTE*, 1:125–33. Other useful summaries of a literary approach include V. P. Long, "Reading the Old Testament as Literature," in *Interpreting the Old Testament: A Guide for Exegesis*, ed. C. C. Broyles (Grand Rapids: Baker, 2001), 85–123; and J. P. Fokkelman, *Reading Biblical Narrative: An Introductory Guide* (Louisville: Westminster John Knox, 1999).

5. D. Jasper, "Literary Readings of the Bible," in *The Cambridge Companion to Biblical Interpretation*, ed. J. Barton (Cambridge: Cambridge University Press, 1998), 27. We gratefully acknowledge the helpful comments of Professor M. D. Carroll R. concerning an earlier version of this chapter.

6. Y. Amit, "Narrative Art of Israel's Historians," in *Dictionary of Old Testament: Historical Books* (henceforth, *DOTHB*), ed. B. T. Arnold and H. G. M. Williamson (Downers Grove: InterVarsity, 2005), 708. For a survey of the main narrative types, see Johnson, *Making Sense of the Bible*, 35–47. Cf. also Ryken, *How to Read*, 33–73. Though Bible readers commonly call OT narratives "history," we prefer to distinguish the two because we believe that "history" describes the content of the material; "narrative," its literary form.

7. Cf. Ryken, *How to Read*, 33: "Narrative is the dominant form in the Bible . . . What this means to readers of the Bible is that the more they know about how stories work, the more they will enjoy and understand vast portions of the Bible." And, perhaps more importantly, the stories will work on us, as R. Jacobson, "We Are Our Stories: Narrative Dimension of Human Identity and its Implications for Christian Faith Formation," *WW* 34 (2014): 123–30, argues.

historians, their purpose is more to instruct than to inform; more to teach later generations about God-honoring conduct than to make sure they have the facts straight. But
two points of clarification seem in order here. First, though most narratives display
some marks of the storyteller's craft, the amount of conscious literary art will vary
from narrative to narrative. Some will display great literary art, while others will
narrate the facts with little embellishment.[8] The writers include only what serves to
communicate their key themes. Second, to speak of biblical narratives as "stories"
does not by itself imply that they are not historical. As Goldingay rightly observed,
"The historical 'having happened-ness' of the story matters."[9]

In our view, to speak of a biblical text as "story" means to highlight the literary
form in which its implied historical claims address us. Further, despite some scholarly
claims to the contrary, history-writing is not in and of itself a literary genre; rather,
history is a topic or theme (i.e., events in the past), and the concern to report history
in writing may find expression in various genres, even fictional ones.[10] However
superb their literary art, biblical narratives "are more than history, not less than
history."[11] Proper literary competence requires readers to appreciate their historical
content and literary form.

Old Testament Narrative Genres

Earlier we noted that the OT has many different types of narratives, so what
follows surveys those genres. Some of the descriptive categories below reflect
standard scholarly terminology, some offer our own classifications, and some borrow
descriptions used for comparable ancient and modern narratives.[12] Readers should
regard these terms as descriptive, not technical. Further, genre categories describe
two levels—both an individual biblical passage as well as the larger context it
serves. The reason is that one genre (e.g., a narrative) may contain several other
specific genres within it (e.g., a historical story, an anecdote, a battle report, etc.).

---

8. Cf. Ryken's helpful distinction (*How to Read*, 33) between biblical stories that, like entries in a historical
chronicle, simply tell *about* an event and full-fledged stories (e.g., David, Job) that *present* an event in full detail.
For the thesis that the ethical intent of biblical narratives arises from their narrative art, see G. J. Wenham, *Story as
Torah: Reading the Old Testament Ethically*, OTS (Edinburgh: T. & T. Clark, 2000).

9. J. Goldingay, "How Far Do Readers Make Sense? Interpreting Biblical Narratives," *Them* 18 (1993): 5.

10. See below for our discussion of a genre whose literary features support its description as "a history." For full,
balanced discussion of the relationship between "story" and "history," see V. P. Long, *The Art of Biblical History*, Foundations
of Contemporary Interpretation 5 (Grand Rapids: Zondervan, 1994), 56–119; and D. M. Howard, Jr., *An Introduction
to the Old Testament Historical Books* (Chicago: Moody, 1993), 44–58; cf. also T. Butler, "Narrative Form Criticism,"
in *A Biblical Itinerary: In Search of Method, Form, and Content*, ed. E. E. Carpenter, JSOTSup 240 (Sheffield: Sheffield
Academic, 1997), 57 ("Form criticism . . . does not place a historical judgment upon the materials . . ."). We prefer this
understanding to the distinction between "narrative" and "history" in D. B. Sandy and R. L. Giese, Jr. *Cracking Codes:
A Guide to Interpreting Literary Genres of the Old Testament* (Nashville: Broadman and Holman, 1995), 69–112.

11. J. Goldingay, *Models for Interpretation of Scripture* (Grand Rapids: Eerdmans, 1995), 32.

12. For additional details, see the comprehensive surveys and concluding glossaries in G. W. Coats, *Genesis*,
FOTL 1 (Grand Rapids: Eerdmans, 1983), 1–10 ("Introduction to Narrative Literature"); B. O. Long, *1 Kings*, FOTL
9 (Grand Rapids: Eerdmans, 1984), 1–8 ("Introduction to Historical Literature"), 243–65; and, less comprehensively,
Ryken, *How to Read*, 75–85.

Similarly, one genre (e.g., a song) may be a component of a larger genre (e.g., a historical story).

Reports	Heroic Narrative
• Anecdote	• Epic
• Battle Reports	• Cosmic
• Construction Reports	• Ancestral
• Dream Reports	• Prophet Story
• Epiphany Reports	• Comedy
• Dream Epiphany Reports	• Farewell
• Historical Stories	• Speech
• A History	
• Memoir	

Reports

The simplest biblical narrative, the basic building block of the Bible's narrative complexes, is the *report*: a "brief, self-contained narration, usually in third-person style, about a single event or situation in the past."[13] It narrates the facts of what happened in a straightforward style without literary embellishment. OT examples include reports about tribal settlements in Canaan (Judg 1:16–17), royal construction projects (1 Kgs 7:2–8; 12:25), and military campaigns (1 Kgs 14:25–26; 2 Kgs 24:20b–25:7). Occasionally, reports serve an aetiological purpose, explaining how a certain place acquired its name—i.e., how a certain oak tree came to be called the Oak of Weeping (Gen 35:8 [NIV Allon Bacuth]) or a certain watering hole came to be known as Bitter (Exod 15:23 [NIV Marah]).

The OT has several kinds of reports. An *anecdote* is a report that details an event or experience in the life of a person—in other words, more private biography rather than public history. It may report conversations as when Elijah symbolically summons Elisha to become his disciple (1 Kgs 19:19–21) and may use imaginative descriptions. Another example of an anecdote is the report of gift-cities that King Solomon gave to King Hiram of Tyre (1 Kgs 9:10–14), a report that ends by tracing the area's apparently derogatory name Cabul (perhaps "like nothing" or "bound") to the incident.[14]

A *memoir* is a report written in the first-person about incidents in the life of an individual. Its purpose is not to flesh out the writer's autobiography, but to portray the

---

13. Long, "Historical Literature," 5; cf. Coats, "Narrative Literature," 10. Long labels a short report a "notice," a longer one an "account." For ancient analogies, see the Siloam inscription and report of Egyptian expeditions in *ANET*, 227–28, 229–30, 321, etc. For more on reports discussed below, see Long, "Historical Literature," 244, 247, 248. For the genre *birth report*, see T. D. Finlay, *The Birth Report Genre in the Hebrew Bible*, FAT II 12 (Tübingen: Mohr Siebeck, 2005).

14. Coats, "Narrative Literature," 10; Long, "Historical Literature," 243–44. An *annal* is a report, often part of royal records, that details chronologically events concerning an institution like the monarchy or the temple. According to Long ("Historical Literature," 243), the OT has no annals, although some texts may be based on them (e.g., 1 Kgs 3:1; 9:15–23; 2 Chr 11:5–12).

era in which he or she lived. Scholars believe the memoirs of Ezra (Ezra 7:27–9:15) and Nehemiah (Neh 1:1–7:73a; 12:27–31) comprise part of the books that bear their names.[15]

A *battle report* recounts a military clash between opposing forces and its outcome, whether of victory or defeat. Among the Bible's many battle reports are defeats of the Amorites (Num 21:21–24), Moabites (Judg 3:26–30), Arameans (2 Sam 10:15–19), two Midianite kings (Judg 8:10–12), and the Canaanite city of Ai (Josh 7:2–5). A *construction report*, on the other hand, recounts the construction of important buildings or objects and describes their size, materials, and decoration in great detail (Exod 36:8–37:16 [the tabernacle]); 1 Kgs 6–7 [the Jerusalem temple]).

Told in first- or third-person, the *dream report* details an individual's experience of a dream. Two stylistic features help identify this genre: repetition of the verb "to dream" and use of the phrase "and behold" (Heb. *wehinneh)* to demarcate major changes in the dream's subject matter. Usually a separate, subsequent scene interprets the experience for the awakened dreamer. OT dream reports include those concerning Joseph (Gen 37:5–11), his two prisoner friends (40:9–11, 16–17), the Egyptian Pharaoh (41:1–8), and a Midianite soldier (Judg 7:13–14).[16]

An *epiphany report*, by contrast, reports an experience in which God or the angel of the Lord appears to someone, often to convey a message. Typically, the verb "to appear, become visible" (Heb. *raah*, niph.) signals the beginning of such epiphanies. They played an important role in the lives of Abraham (Gen 12:7; 17:1–21; 18:1–33), Isaac (26:2–5, 24), Moses (Exod 3:2–12), Samson's parents (Judg 13), and King Solomon (1 Kgs 3:4–15; 9:1–9).[17] The report of Jacob's experience at Bethel is a *dream epiphany* since it involves God's appearance in a dream (Gen 28:12–16; cf. 48:3–4; Matt 2:19–20).[18]

The genre *historical stories* are reports written with more literary elaboration than an ordinary report.[19] They develop a rudimentary plot (moving from tension to resolution), record dialogues and speeches by characters, and include dramatic literary touches. Like the simple report, they aim to recount an event, but they do so with an appealing written flair. Two excellent examples are the stories of Saul's emergence as king (1 Sam 11:1–11) and of Ahab's confrontation with the prophet Micaiah ben Imlah (1 Kgs 22:1–37; see also Judg 9:1–21; 1 Kgs 12:1–20; 20:1–43).

---

15. Cf. E. M. Yamauchi, "Ezra and Nehemiah, Books of," *DOTHB*, 290–91; H. G. M. Williamson, *Ezra, Nehemiah*, WBC 16 (Waco, TX: Word, 1985), xxiv-xxxii; but cf. R. North, "Nehemiah," *ABD* 4:1070 ("hardly likelihood of any 'Ezra-Memoir' at all").

16. Cf. also the dreams of Nebuchadnezzar in the narrative sections of the book of Daniel (Dan 2:1–11; 4:1–18). Cf. the range of studies compiled recently by E. R. Hayes and L.-S. Tiemeyer, eds., *'I Lifted My Eyes and Saw': Reading Dream and Vision Reports in the Hebrew Bible*, LHBOTS (London and New York: Bloomsbury T&T Clark, 2014). For a broad, comparative study of dream phenomena, see J.-M. Husser, *Dreams and Dream Narratives in the Biblical World*, The Biblical Seminar 63 (Sheffield: Sheffield Academic, 1999).

17. For the suggestion that a ritual of royal induction inspired the report of Solomon's dream, see B. Lang, *The Hebrew God: Portrait of an Ancient Deity* (New Haven: Yale University Press, 2001), 8–11; cf. Husser, *Dreams and Dream Narratives*, 124–28.

18. Cf. Husser, *Dreams and Dream Narratives*, 128–32. Inexplicably, Long reckons all divine appearances as dream epiphanies even when the context either says nothing about a dream or, in the cases of Abraham (Gen 18) and Moses (Exod 3), actually specifies their nondream circumstances ("Historical Literature," 248).

19. Long, "Historical Literature," 6–7.

Finally, authors or editors may compile a series of reports and consciously struc-ture them to underscore connections between events and to sound certain themes. The result is a *history*, a lengthy document that focuses on a particular subject or historical era.[20] Explicitly or implicitly, the authors/editors convey their evaluation of the sequence of events reported in order to apply instruction or legitimation from the past to situations or institutions in the author/editor's own day. This genre includes the book of Kings and the book of Chronicles.[21]

Principles of Interpretation—Reports

Follow the following principles for interpreting reports:

1. In interpreting a simple report the reader should focus on its main subject and how it contributes to the themes of the larger context.

2. Since reports tend to stress factual matters (i.e., what happened, who did what, etc.), they tend not to provide obvious devotional content. Hence, readers must deduce their theological themes from the larger context that surrounds them. For example, Joshua 12 lists the Canaanite kings that Yahweh defeated to give Israel the promised land. Literally, it sounds like a ceremonial counting of results (". . . the king of X . . . one, the king of Y . . . one . . ."), and the lesson for some readers might be, "Wow, never cross Yahweh!" But in the context of the victories that Joshua 1–11 recounts, the implied themes of Joshua 12 are: God's awesome power to help his people, his promising-keeping, his worthiness of Israel's gratitude. By contrast, the interpretation of reports in which God participates (e.g., dream reports, epiphany reports) sounds their themes more directly, depending less on the context. For example, Jacob's dream report (Gen 28) stressed God's personal relationship with Jacob and assured him of God's presence on his journey. Such themes certainly have implications for today.

3. Typical of narratives, reports make their points indirectly. The reader must ask: What is this text trying to say? What subtle signals has the writer woven into the account to convey the message? The student will probably find more interpretive clues in historical stories and histories than in simple reports. For example, 1 Kings 22 obviously portrays the prophet Micaiah ben Imlah as the

---

20. As noted above, Long, "Historical Literature," 7–8, who notes (8), "The OT is unrivaled in the ancient Near East for its use of this literary genre." Scholars commonly assume that palace scribes responsible for recording affairs of state prepared such histories.

21. Lively scholarly debate on the matter continues, but the theory that Deuteronomy to 2 Kings once comprised a larger historical work, the "Deuteronomistic History" (DH) edited during Israel's exile in Babylon (sixth century BC), still seems valid; cf. S. L. McKenzie, "Deuteronomistic History," *NIDB*, 2:107 ("[t]he theory . . . remains dominant, though there is widespread disagreement about the specifics of authorship, date, and purpose"); and S. L. Richter, "Deuteronomistic History," *DOTHB*, whose in-depth discussion (219–30) concludes that "there is a Deuteronomistic History, and that it is historiographic in nature"(228). For a more critical view, see T. C. Römer, *The So-Called Deuteronomistic History: A Sociological, Historical, and Literary Introduction* (London and New York: T&T Clark, 2007). Concerning the compilation and purpose of Chronicles, see conveniently L. C. Jonker, *1 & 2 Chronicles*, UBC (Grand Rapids: Baker, 2013), 6–22.

courageous hero persecuted by a corrupt Ahab. In so doing, it condemns Ahab's nominal Mosaic religion and, by implication, all other examples of less than fully committed faith.[22] For application, one might ask, "In what ways have cultural pressures sapped vitality from my faith so that it seems more nominal than before?"

4. Reports strung together in series (commonly called "histories") are like choirs—a series of individual voices joined to sound common themes. To find those themes, the reader must analyze the emphases of the individual reports to see what they share in common. For example, compared to Kings, Chronicles focuses on Judah, David's patronage of Israel's worship, and the importance of the temple. Kings evaluates the Israelite monarchy as a spiritual disaster—a case-history of the past mistakes the exiles must not repeat when they return home. By contrast, Chronicles seeks to highlight its positive spiritual legacy, its establishment of proper temple worship. Written for post-exilic Judah, the book reviews Israel's history in order to urge its audience faithfully to worship Yahweh and obediently to keep the Torah.[23]

Heroic Narrative

A more common OT genre is the *heroic narrative*.[24] This comprises a series of episodes that focus on the life and exploits of a hero whom people later consider significant enough to remember. Typically, such heroic narratives include some account of the person's birth, marriage, life work, and death. They place particular emphasis on the hero's displays of virtue and extraordinary heroism. As Ryken observes,

> Such stories spring from one of the most universal impulses of literature—the desire to embody accepted norms of behavior or representative struggles in the story of a character whose experience is typical of people in general.[25]

Heroic narratives may seek to inculcate such behavioral norms by both positive and negative examples. A hero who failed offers as powerful a lesson about important life values as one who succeeded.

The life of Moses (Exodus-Deuteronomy) offers the best OT example of this genre.[26] At length, it depicts his birth, marriage, sense of vocation, exploits as leader

---

22. For discussion of this narrative with particular interest in its literary use of anonymity, see R. L. Hubbard, Jr., "'Old What's His Name': Why the King in 1 Kings 22 Has No Name," in *God's Word for Our World*, 2 vols., JSOTSup 388–89, ed. J. H. Ellens, et al. (London and New York: T&T Clark International, 2004), 2:294–314.

23. W. Riley, *King and Cultus in Chronicles*, JSOTSup 160 (Sheffield: JSOT, 1993), 202–4; conveniently, W. S. LaSor, D. A. Hubbard, and F. W. Bush, *Old Testament Survey*, 2nd ed. (Grand Rapids: Eerdmans. 1996), 545–49.

24. Ryken, *How to Read*, 75–80. For this category, Coats ("Narrative Literature," 6) and Long ("Historical Literature," 250) prefer the term "heroic saga," but we question the definition and appropriateness of the term "saga"; cf. Butler, "Narrative Form Criticism," 56: "If Israel told materials as family history or as promise narratives, why load ambiguous titles such as saga or legend to such materials?"

25. Ryken, *How to Read*, 75.

26. Cf. F. F. Greenspahn, "From Egypt to Canaan: A Heroic Narrative," in *Israel's Apostasy and Restoration: Essays in Honor of Roland K. Harrison*, ed. A. Gileadi (Grand Rapids: Baker, 1988), 1–8; G. W. Coats, *Moses: Heroic Man, Man of God*, JSOTSup 57 (Sheffield: JSOT, 1987). In the NT, the Gospel accounts of the life of Jesus show

and lawgiver, and his death.[27] Certainly, his life embodies both the struggles of Israel's national life during that period and the ideal of consummate loyalty to God. Again, one may consider the book of Judges as a collection of heroic narratives.[28] The stories of Deborah (Judg 4–5), Gideon (Judg 6–8), and Samson (Judg 13–16) particularly show traits of this genre. They symbolize Israel's dual struggles during that period: invasions from outside and idolatry inside. Their successes and failures embody Israel's own national struggles with political survival and faithfulness to God.[29]

The *epic* represents a subvariety of heroic narrative since it tells the heroic exploits of a virtuous hero.[30] Two unique traits set it apart: its greater length and its magnification of the hero's exploits to a greater scale of importance. An epic displays a strong nationalistic interest with the hero representing the destiny, not just of a family, but of a whole nation. In other words, it narrates events that the entire nation admires in retrospect as epoch-making. Hence, its themes are large-scale ones—conquest, kingdom, warfare, and dominion. Since epics portray a nation's formative history, they abound with historical allusions.[31]

In addition, the epic involves supernatural settings, events, and characters. Events play themselves out in a cosmic arena, which includes both heaven and earth, and supernatural agents participate directly in human history on earth. Again, the plot of an epic is mildly episodic (it presents separate incidents rather than a chain of connected events) and often aims at a central feat or quest by the hero.

Genesis 1–11 offers a *cosmic epic* because it narrates the formative story not just

---

traces of this genre, although they focus more on his teaching than on his biography. See our discussion of the gospel genre in the following chapter.

27. Knierim even argues that the genre of the whole Pentateuch is the biography of Moses with particular emphasis on his unique role as mediator at Mt. Sinai; cf. R. P. Knierim, "The Composition of the Pentateuch," SBLSP 24 (Atlanta: Scholars, 1985), 409–15. That the character of Moses still makes fascinating biography is evident in J. Kirsch, *Moses: A Life* (New York: Ballantine Books, 1998).

28. So Ryken, *How to Read,* 80, conceding, however, that "certain features of the book resemble epic" (on which, see below); cf. the similar terminological ambivalence in S. Niditch, *Judges*, OTL (Louisville: Westminster John Knox, 2008), 3, who uses "heroes" in a specifically folkloric sense. Cf. C. L. Echols, "Can the Samson Narrative Properly be Called Heroic?," in *Leshon Limmudim: Essays on the Language and Literature of the Hebrew Bible In Honour of A.A. Macintosh*, ed. D. A. Baer and R. P. Gordon, LHBOTS 593 (London: Bloomsbury T&T Clark, 2013), 63–76 (after detailed discussion, Echols answers, "Yes.").

29. Within the book of Judges, however, their lives contribute to its main theme, i.e., Israel's need for a king to stave off invasions, to end tribal rivalries, and to ensure religious fidelity (Judg 17:6; 18:1; 19:1; 21:25); cf. T. C. Butler, *Judges*, WBC 8 (Nashville: Thomas Nelson, 2009), lxiii, lxxvii ("Israel needs a king"; "Judges points the leadership question forward toward monarchy, not backward to the theocracy of Joshua's day"); T. Schneider, *Judges*, Berit Olam (Collegeville, MN: Liturgical Press, 2000), 284–85. Along with Butler and Schneider, two insightful treatments of Judges include M. Wilcock, *The Message of Judges: Grace Abounding* (Downers Grove: InterVarsity, 1992) and K. R. R. Gros Louis, "The Book of Judges," in *Literary Interpretations of Biblical Narratives*, 2 vols., ed. K. R. R. Gros Louis, et al. (Nashville: Abingdon, 1974), 1:141–62.

30. Ryken, *How to Read,* 78–81. For a broader literary study, see D. A. Miller, *The Epic Hero* (Baltimore: Johns Hopkins University Press, 2000). Admittedly, in this chapter we apply the term "epic" to prose narratives even though it normally describes poetic ones; cf. the recent comparative study of biblical and extrabiblical epics in M. S. Smith, *Poetic Heroes: The Literary Commemorations of Warriors and Warrior Culture in the Early Biblical World* (Grand Rapids: Eerdmans, 2014).

31. For discussion of ancient Near Eastern epics and their implications for biblical epics, see conveniently J. H. Walton, *Ancient Israelite Literature in Its Cultural Context: A Survey of Parallels between Biblical and Ancient Near Eastern Texts* (Grand Rapids: Zondervan, 1989), 46–49, 58–65.

of a nation but of the cosmos and its human inhabitants.[32] Supernatural elements abound, for God participates directly with Adam and Eve in the garden (Gen 3) and with Noah in the great flood (Gen 6–9). Later, he scatters people across the earth and separates them into distinct language groups (Gen 11). The genealogies of Adam (Gen 5) and Noah (Gen 10) also evidence a variation of the nationalistic motif: interest in the origins of earth's major ethnic groups.[33]

Historical allusions include references to the beginning of human occupations (Gen 4:20–22), the giant race called the Nephilim (Gen 6:4; cf. Num 13:32–33), and the foundation of ancient cities (Gen 10:10–12; cf. 11:2–3).[34] In these texts the hero is not an individual but a series of individuals, yet, in context, they serve to represent early humanity as a whole. Again, recall that toward the end of this epic, the narrative focus narrows to the Semites, the racial ancestors of the Hebrews (Gen 11:10–32).

Genesis 12–36 presents an *ancestral epic*.[35] It certainly shows nationalistic themes—the destiny of Israel and her ownership of the land of Canaan. Indeed, the programmatic promise to Abram (Gen 12:1–3) predicts Israel's destiny as the instrument of blessing for all other ethnic groups. Though not prominent, supernatural elements are nevertheless present. Yahweh actively participates, appearing to the patriarchs (Gen 17:1; 18:17–33; 26:2; 35:1, 7), raining down destruction on Sodom, and giving elderly Sarah a son (21:1–2; cf. also Lot's angelic rescuers [19:1, 15] and Jacob's mysterious wrestling match [31:22–32]).

As for historical allusions, in our view Abraham's defeat of Kedorlaomer's military coalition (Gen 14:1–16) recalls an ancient event long-remembered in the region.[36] Granted, the patriarchal narratives involve a sequence of four heroes rather than one. Nevertheless, their story traces Israel's national roots and defines her national destiny. Further, the

---

32. Cf. Coats, "Narrative Literature," 5–6 ("the primeval saga"). An ancient Near Eastern parallel, the "Epic of Atrahasis," follows a similar narrative structure; it, thus, lends some cultural support to our categorization of Gen 1–11 as epic; cf. A. R. Millard, "A New Babylonian 'Genesis' Story," in *"I Studied Inscriptions from before the Flood": Ancient Near Eastern, Literary, and Linguistic Approaches to Genesis 1–11*, ed. R. S. Hess and D. T. Tsumura, Sources for Biblical and Theological Study 4 (Winona Lake, IN: Eisenbrauns, 1994), 114–28. For a translation of the epic, see V. H. Matthews and D. C. Benjamin, *Old Testament Parallels: Laws and Stories from the Ancient Near East*, 3rd ed. (New York: Paulist Press, 2006), 33–42.

33. For background, see J. H. Walton, "Genealogies," *DOTHB*, 309–16. For the function of the genealogies within Genesis, see F. Crüsemann, "Human Solidarity and Ethnic Identity: Israel's Self-Definition in the Genealogical System of Genesis," in *Ethnicity and the Bible*, ed. M. G. Brett, BibInt 19 (Leiden: E. J. Brill, 1996), 57–76. R. S. Hess, "The Genealogies of Genesis 1–11 and Comparative Literature," in Hess and Tsumura, *"I Studied Inscriptions,"* 58–72, discusses the forms of biblical genealogies within their ancient context.

34. For the interpretation of Gen 6:1–4, see B. K. Waltke (with C. J. Fredricks), *Genesis: A Commentary* (Grand Rapids: Zondervan, 2001), 115–17, who suggests that the Nephilim descend from demon-possessed ancient royal tyrants; cf. also Millard, "A New Babylonian 'Genesis Story,'" in Hess and Tsumura, *"I Studied Inscriptions,"* 122–23. Waltke (*Genesis*, 165–75) discusses the ethnographical information in Genesis 10.

35. Cf. Coats, "Narrative Literature," 6 ("family saga"); B. C. Birch, W. Brueggemann, T. E. Fretheim, and D. L. Petersen, *A Theological Introduction to the Old Testament* (Nashville: Abingdon, 1999), 68 ("The stories involve fathers and mothers, sons and daughters, aunts and uncles—simply put, families").

36. Cf. G. J. Wenham, *Genesis 1–15*, WBC 1 (Waco: Word, 1987), 319 ("the evidence . . . suggests that this chapter is based on one of the oldest literary sources in Genesis"); Coats, "Narrative Literature," 317 (cf. also pp. 118–22), whose genre glossary lists Gen 14:1–24 under "annals" with the definition "a report from the archives of the royal court"; but cf. O Margalith, "The Riddle of Genesis 14 and Melchizedek," *ZAW* 112 (2000): 501–8 (a "para-myth" reflecting wars in the late thirteenth c. BC); and C. Westermann, *Genesis 12–36: A Commentary*, CC (Minneapolis: Augsburg, 1985), 193 ("It cannot be traced back to a definite historical event in the form in which it is preserved").

idea of promise that drives the plot of Gen 12–36 (Gen 12:1–3; etc.) favorably compares to the motif of the typical epic quest (the quest for land and national destiny).[37]

Prophet Story

The *prophet story* recounts events in the life of a prophet, particularly those that demonstrate virtues worthy of emulation and, more importantly, that theologically critique the world in which the story's readers lived.[38] Its purpose, thus, is two-fold: to edify its audience by presenting the prophet as a model of proper conduct and to discredit the larger politico-religious system for its denial of Yahweh as sovereign lord. They reflect the Bible's larger driving dynamic—a theological and ideological movement to reshape the readers' view of the world and radically to reform their values. The narratives about Elijah and Elisha (1 Kgs 17–2 Kgs 9; 2 Kgs 13:14–21) and Daniel (Dan 1–6) best illustrate prophet stories.[39] For example, Elijah and Elisha model perseverance in the face of royal political pressure and boldly challenge the tyranny and errors of state-sponsored religious apostasy. In prophet stories about Elisha miracles sometimes play a prominent role (e.g., Elisha's healing of the Shunammite woman's son [2 Kgs 4:8–37] and his rescue of the sunken ax head [6:1–7]). The miracles display Yahweh's unchallenged omnipotence and by implication expose the impotence of the popular god, Baal.

Similarly, Daniel shows faithfulness in the face of pressures from foreign overlords like Nebuchadnezzar and models an unwavering confidence in God's sovereign protection of his people. At the same time, the book of Daniel offers a powerful critique of the terrible oppressions of empires and of the dangerous self-delusions of emperors.[40] The book of Jonah also fits in this category, although it instructs through a negative example. In our view, its literary style intentionally imitates the prophetic

---

37. With good reason, Johnson (*Making Sense of the Bible*, 35) says the OT comprises "large epics" woven into "the grand narrative of the Bible"—the story from creation to the postexilic period. He also calls Joshua to 2 Kings an "epic"; cf. Ryken, *How to Read*, 80 (the book of Joshua as "the conquest epic"; also the rise of King David [1 Sam 16–2 Sam 8]). For a scholarly study of David, see V. L. Johnson, *David in Distress: His Portrait through the Historical Psalms*, LHBOTS 505 (London and New York: T&T Clark, 2009); cf. also W. Brueggemann, *David's Truth in Israel's Imagination and Memory*, 2nd ed. (Minneapolis: Fortress, 2002); and M. J. Steussy, *David: Biblical Portraits of Power* (Columbia, SC: University of South Carolina Press, 1999).

38. While most scholars use the term "prophetic story," the older term "prophetic legend" occasionally appears; cf. M. A. Sweeney, *Isaiah 1–39*, FOTL 16 (Grand Rapids: Eerdmans, 1996), whose "Introduction to Prophetic Literature" (18–22) lists as major narrative types both "prophetic story" and "prophetic legend" (20–21). For a recent overview of the prophetic stories, see T. L. Leclerc, *Introduction to the Prophets: Their Stories, Sayings and Scrolls* (New York: Paulist Press, 2007); cf. the subcategories proposed by A. Rofé, *The Prophetical Stories* (Jerusalem: Magnes Press, 1988). We are particularly grateful to Professor M. D. Carroll R. for his helpful comments on an earlier version of this section.

39. Cf. Gros Louis's illuminating comparison of Elijah and Elisha to Shakespeare's Hamlet is still worth reading; cf. K. R. R. Gros Louis, "Elijah and Elisha," in *Literary Interpretations*, 1:177–90. Cf. also U. Simon, *Reading Prophetic Narratives*, ISBL (Bloomington: Indiana University Press, 1997); J. Goldingay, "Story, Vision, Interpretation: Literary Approaches to Daniel," in *The Book of Daniel in the Light of New Findings*, ed. A. S. van der Woude (Leuven: Uitgeverij Peeters, 1993), 295–314; and D. Gunn and D. N. Fewell, *Narrative in the Hebrew Bible* (Oxford: Oxford University Press, 1993), 174–88 (an insightful literary treatment of Dan 3).

40. Cf. T. S. Cason, "Confessions of An Impotent Potentate: Reading Daniel 4 Through the Lens of Ritual Punishment Theory," *JSOT* 39 (2014): 79–100; H. Avalos, "Nebuchadnezzar's Affliction: New Mesopotamian Parallels for Daniel 4," *JBL* 133 (2014): 497–507; J. E. Goldingay, "The Stories in Daniel: A Narrative Politics," *JSOT* 37 (1987): 99–116. For the ideological critique in Amos, see M. D. Carroll R., *Contexts for Amos: Prophetic Poetics in Latin American Perspective*, JSOTSup 132 (Sheffield: Sheffield Academic, 1992).

stories about Elijah. Again, it clearly has a didactic aim—in our view, to teach the reader about God-honoring attitudes toward non-Israelites (see Jonah 4:10–11).[41] Like Jonah, Israel was running from its mission to bring the light of God to the nations.

Principles of Interpretation—Heroic Narratives and Prophet Stories

To interpret heroic narratives and prophet stories, we suggest the following principles:

1. Interpretation should focus on the life of the main character, whether an individual, a family, or a nation. The two questions to consider are: How does the hero's life model a relationship with God and with other people? And what aspects of the original reader's worldview does it seek to critique or discredit?

2. Since heroes portray values, the student must ask what values a given hero represents. For example, several texts elevate Abraham as an example of dogged faith (cf. Gen 15:6; 22:12). Thus, he exhibits the kind of trust in God expected of ancient Israel and of modern Christians, too. The portrait of Ahab, by contrast, seems mainly negative. What conduct did it aim to cultivate in Israel, and what might it teach modern readers? The student should also ask, How do those values challenge and seek to reshape the values dominant in the biblical and the modern worlds?

3. Besides the values presented, interpretive priority should be given to finding the large themes involved (election, conquest, religious apostasy, etc.). For example, the life of Elisha portrays Israel's disloyal rejection of Yahweh in favor of Baal, while Daniel's life displays the challenges of remaining loyal in the face of strong cultural pressures. By implication, both underscore how important loyalty is to the covenant requirements for Israel to experience God's blessing and how God's servants must sometimes challenge any leadership promoting other values.

4. Application of these narratives should focus on analogous situations between the biblical characters and Christians today. For example, one theme in the ancestral epic presents God miraculously overcoming infertility to keep the patriarchal line alive (cf. Gen 21; 29–30). But the application is not that God always provides believers with children. For reasons known only to him, God may choose *not* to give them children in some situations. A better analogy is that the epic reminds Christians of God's firm commitment to carry out his salvation plan today. It is better because it draws on a biblical truth that never changes rather than on one subject to God's mysterious will.

Comedy

To modern readers, the term *comedy* probably conjures up images of television shows like *Seinfeld* or *The Big Bang Theory*. In literature, however, a comedy is a narrative whose

---

41. L. C. Allen, *The Books of Joel, Obadiah, Jonah, and Micah*, NICOT (Grand Rapids: Eerdmans, 1976), 175, 190–91 ("the unwelcome truth of God's sovereign compassion for foreigners and beasts"); cf. also recently S. P. Riley, "When the Empire Does Not Strike Back: Reading Jonah in Light of Empire," *Wesleyan Theological Journal* 47 (2012): 116–26. For literary treatments of Jonah, see Gunn and Fewell, *Narrative in the Hebrew Bible*, 129–46; and P. Trible, *Rhetorical Criticism: Context, Method, and the Book of Jonah*, GBS OT Series (Minneapolis: Fortress, 1994).

plot has a happy ending, in some cases through a dramatic reversal. It often aims to amuse, particularly through characters like buffoons, clowns, fools, rogues, and tricksters; through ridiculous or ludicrous scenes; and through satire and irony.[42] Typically, it features disguises, mistaken identity, providential coincidences, surprising turns-of-events, escapes from disaster, and the conquest of obstacles. Comedies often conclude with a marriage, a celebratory feast, reconciliation with opponents, or victory over enemies.

We classify the book of Esther as a comedy.[43] Its plot turns tragedy into triumph, involves the conquest of obstacles (Haman's treachery and King Ahasuerus's ignorant complicity); disguise (Esther's hidden Jewish identity; Esth 2:10, 20); providential coincidence (the timing of Ahasuerus's insomnia; 6:1–11); surprise (the unmasking of Haman's plot; 7:1–6); sudden reversal of fortune (chs. 8–9); and a concluding feast (Purim; 9:18–19).[44] Thematically, it also critiques the self-deluded pretentions of empires and emperors, and perhaps gender bias as well.

The story of Joseph (Gen 37–50) offers a second example of OT comedy.[45] From the tragedy of Joseph's exile and imprisonment in Egypt (Gen 37, 39–40) the plot ends in triumph: Pharaoh elevates him to prime minister (41:39–40), Joseph rescues Egypt and his own family from famine (42–50), and Joseph is reconciled with his brothers (42–45, 50). In between, one reads of obstacles overcome, providential events (cf. 41:51, 52; 45:7, 8; 50:21), and Joseph's hidden identity (42–44). In sum, it is a fitting example of comedy.

Principles of Interpretation—Comedy

The following principles are useful for interpreting OT comedy:

1. Since plot drives a comedy, interpretation must trace how tragedy turns to triumph. So, the student should trace how Joseph and Esther save Israel from their respective crises. In the process of tracing this development it is particularly important to define the story's crisis, the turning point, and the climax.

2. Character development merits some attention. Note the character traits of both

---

42. Cf. the nuanced discussions of comedy in J. W. Whedbee, *The Bible and the Comic Vision* (Cambridge: Cambridge University Press, 1998), 6–11; and C. H. Holman and W. Harmon, *A Handbook to Literature*, 5th ed. (New York: Macmillan Publishing Company; London: Collier Macmillan, 1986), 98–101. For OT tragedies, the negative counterpart of comedy, we suggest Gen 3 and the life of Saul (1 Sam 9–31).

43. Cf. the insightful treatment of Esther as comedy in Whedbee, *The Bible and the Comic Vision*, 171–90. For the recent critique of this classification and the suggestion that Esther is heroic narrative with comedic or farcical elements, see K. McGeough, "Esther the Hero: Going Beyond 'Wisdom' in Heroic Narratives," *CBQ* 70 (2008): 44–65. For reading Job as comedy, cf. A. Pelham, "*Job* as Comedy, Revisited," *JSOT* 35 (2010): 89–112.

44. For further details, consult recent commentaries; cf. A. Berlin, *Esther*, JPS Bible Commentary (Philadelphia: Jewish Publication Society, 2001); M. V. Fox, *Character and Ideology in the Book of Esther*, 2nd ed. (Grand Rapids: Eerdmans, 2001); and T. K. Beal, *Esther*, Berit Olam (Collegeville, MN: Liturgical Press, 1999). For recent evangelical treatments of Esther, see D. G. Firth, *The Message of Esther: God Present but Unseen* (Downers Grove: InterVarsity, 2010); and D. Reid, *Esther: An Introduction and Commentary*, TOTC (Nottingham: Inter-Varsity Press; Downers Grove: IVP Academic, 2008); slightly older but still useful is M. Breneman, *Ezra, Nehemiah, Esther*, NAC 10 (Nashville: Broadman & Holman Publishers, 1993).

45. Cf. C. Westermann, *Joseph: Studies of the Joseph Stories in Genesis*, trans. O. Kaste (Edinburgh: T&T Clark, 1996); D. A. Seybold, "Paradox and Symmetry in the Joseph Narrative," and J. S. Ackerman, "Joseph, Judah, and Jacob," in *Literary Interpretations*, 1:59–73 and 1:85–113 (respectively).

heroes and villains and how they contribute to their respective success or demise. Also observe positive and negative developments in characters. For example, Esther seems to change from a reluctant intermediary to a bold, courageous leader (cf. Esth 4; 7). At the same time, Haman appears to degenerate from supreme self-confidence to childish self-pity (Esth 3; 6). Observe also which of Joseph's brothers seem to fit the label of hero or villain.

3. Discern what role God plays in the story: is it direct or indirect? Ask whether or not the biblical writer views accidents and coincidences as acts of hidden divine providence.

4. Define the comedy's main theme(s). The Joseph story sends several clear thematic signals: God guided Joseph's ups and downs to preserve Israel's existence (Gen 45:7–9; 50:20). Esther sounds its themes more subtly, but certainly a major one would be God's preservation of his people before tyrants.

5. Application follows from the comedy's main theme(s). So, for example, Joseph and Esther echo a key biblical truth that God takes care of his people, whatever their hardships and wherever they are. Remember, however, that these dramatic reversals of fortune are no promise of spectacular divine intervention in every similar situation.

Farewell Speech

Finally, the *farewell speech* deserves mention because of the important role it plays at key junctures of OT narrative literature. The farewell speech is an address in the first-person voice reportedly given by someone shortly before his or her death.[46] Typically, the speaker refers to his or her old age or imminent death and exhorts the hearers to live along certain lines in the future.[47] The speakers are usually leaders of such great historical prominence that the speeches tend to mark momentous turning points in Israel's national life. Though expounding legal instructions, the series of speeches given by Moses in Deuteronomy represent an expanded form of the farewell speech. Or, put differently, the book comprises Moses' "ethical will"—the inheritance of instruction that he leaves to Israel.

Principles of Interpretation—Farewell Speech

The following principles will be helpful in interpreting the farewell speech:

---

46. Long, "Historical Literature," 249. The list of farewell speeches reads like an abbreviated outline of OT history: Jacob to his sons (Gen 49:29–30), Moses to Israel (Deut 29:2–30:20; 31:1–8), Joshua to Israel (Josh 23:1–16), Samuel to Israel (1 Sam 12), and David to Solomon (1 Kgs 2:1–9); cf. Paul in Acts 20:18–35; and Jesus in John 13:1–17:26. Cf. also the poetic "Last Words of David" (2 Sam 23:1–7).

47. Often a brief report of the speaker's death and burial follow the speech (Gen 49:33; Deut 34:5–6; 1 Kgs 2:10; cf. Josh 24:29–30). Though not speeches, NT Epistles written late in an apostle's life seem to carry on the same tradition (e.g., 2 Tim 4:6–8; 2 Pet 1:12–15). For the rhetoric of the farewell discourse (John 13–17), see J. C. Stube, *A Graeco-Roman Rhetorical Reading of the Farewell Discourse*, LNTS 309 (New York; London: T&T Clark, 2006).

1. The student must determine what makes the occasion of the speech historically pivotal. In other words, why did the speaker give the speech? What surrounding circumstances or pressing issues lie in the background?

2. Given the historical setting, the student must also summarize the speaker's main concern in a brief sentence. What does the aging leader urge his audience to do about it?

3. Decide what a given speech contributes to the themes of the larger context. For example, how does Samuel's speech (1 Sam 12) develop the themes of the book of 1 Samuel?

4. Look for application from the speech's momentous historical setting and its main point. The student should think of a contemporary situation that closely compares to the biblical one and then apply the speaker's main point to that situation. For example, Samuel's words would exhort us to serve God faithfully despite our fears of criticism from unbelievers.

Interpreting a Sample Narrative: Judges 7:1–15

This episode, which weaves together several narrative genres and literary devices, offers a useful example to illustrate how to interpret a narrative.[48] It is set in the context of horrible oppression by marauding tribes—Midianites, Amalekites, and people of the east—whose seven-year hegemony reduced north-central Israel to near starvation (see 6:2–6). Though suffering for unfaithfulness (6:1), Israel's ongoing distress-cry eventually moved God to send a deliverer, Gideon (6:14, later called Jerub-baal [6:32; 7:1]), who has assembled a huge army by the spring of Harod within striking distance of the enemy (7:1).

The narrative structure features two parts: two reports of God's command to reduce the force's numbers (vv. 2–3, 4–8) and a report of Gideon's secret visit to the Midianite camp (vv. 9–15). The former reduces the troop number from 20,000 to 300 by "sifting out" weak soldiers (Heb. *tsarap* "to refine, test"), while the latter features a dream report by a Midianite soldier overhead by Gideon (vv. 13–14) that emboldens him to issue the battle order (v. 15). The text's genre is a report of divine assurance of victory in battle, and its structural outline might look something like this:[49]

I. Report: Time and Place 7:1
II. The Assurance of Victory 7:2–15
   A. Yahweh's Instruction: Right-sizing the Army 7:2–8
      1. Step 1: Dismissing the Fearful. 7:2–3
      2. Step 2: Selecting the Vigilant 7:4–6

---

48. For a more complete literary reading of this text and Judges as a book, see B. G. Webb, *Judges*, NICOT (Grand Rapids: Eerdmans, 2012); B. G. Webb, *The Book of Judges: An Integrated Reading*, JSOTSup 46 (Sheffield: Sheffield Academic, 1987).

49. The study of narrative texts follows the same procedure that we introduced in the "Larger Units of Poetry" section of in ch. 8.

3. Conclusion 7:7–8
    a. Yahweh's Promise of Victory 7:7
    b. Gideon: Dismissal of Excess Troops 7:8
B. Gideon's Reconnaissance 7:9–15
   1. God's Two-fold Commission: "Go" and "Hear" . . . 7:9–11
   2. Gideon's Compliance 7:12–15
    a. Description: The Huge Enemy Camp 7:12
    b. Overheard: An Enemy's Dream Report 7:13–14
      1) Dream Report 7:13
      2) Its Interpretation 7:14
    c. Gideon's Two-fold Response 7:15
      1) Worship 7:15a
      2) In Israel's Camp: Promise of Victory 7:15b

Notice two key themes that emerge in the narration. The first concerns the lesson Israel is to learn from victory—that Yahweh's power, not huge troop strength, achieved it. The narrator sounds it in Yahweh's explanation of the reduction (v. 2), ironic in contradicting the preference of human commanders for overwhelming force. Gideon personifies the second theme—whether Gideon surrenders to his fears or boldly trusts Yahweh (vv. 10–11)—a widespread biblical theme of special relevance to an Israel wavering between reliance on Yahweh or on other gods.

The dream report (vv. 13–14) marks the episode's dramatic turning point, drama sharpened by the narrator's clever use (v. 13) of word repetition and a wordplay on a Hebrew root. He uses *hinneh* ("Look!") to highlight the providential surprise that the Midianite began to speak just as Gideon passed his tent (i.e., "Gideon entered the camp, and—Shhhh! What's that guy saying?"). He hears (our paraphrase): "Look (*hinneh*), here's my dream: See (*hinneh*), this barley loaf was 'rolling' (*hapak* hith.) in the camp . . . It struck the tent; it turned upside down (*hapak* qal) . . ." His buddy then interprets its symbolism (v. 14): the barley cake is "Gideon's sword"; the tent's upset is Midian's defeat by God through Gideon (a cake normally would bounce off or crumble). Thus reassured, Gideon rallies his small band (v. 15) and routs the enemy (vv. 16–25).

The text underscores God's power to use crumbly barley cakes (i.e., frail humans) to overturn mighty armies. It reminds readers of the many biblical words of reassurance (e.g., "I am with you," Isa 41:10; Matt 28:20) that dispel fears of inadequacy. Gideon models the proper response—trust in that power, not in other gods, and bold actions of faith.

Embedded Genres

Popular Proverbs	Curses/Riddles	Parables/Songs
Blessings	Fables	Lists

Popular Proverbs and Blessings

Some literary genres are embedded within OT narratives. When we say, "That's the way the ball bounces," we invoke a *popular proverb* (Heb. *mashal*)—a pithy, well-known saying that comments on everyday people and events. Colorfully, it says, "That's life!" Ancient Israel had similar sayings, normally prefaced by the formula "so it became a saying" or "that is why they say . . . ." For example, 1 Samuel twice reports the popular proverb, "Is Saul also among the prophets?" Apparently, that Israelite expression highlighted someone's unexpected, uncharacteristic behavior (1 Sam 10:12; 19:24).[50] Popular proverbs always occur as quotations in a larger context, although the book of Proverbs may incorporate some in its collections (Prov 18:9; 24:26; 29:5). (For the interpretation of proverbs, see below under wisdom.)

Israel also commonly invoked *blessings and curses* as part of her daily life. The formula "Blessed is/be [someone]" (Heb. *baruk* . . .) was the way Israelites wished others well (Gen 9:26; Deut 28:3; Ruth 2:19, 20). The opposite formulas, "cursed is/be [someone/thing]" (Heb. *arur* . . .) or "cursed is/be one who [is/does something]" (Heb. *arur haish asher*) seeks the opposite consequence for its object (see Gen 9:25; Deut 27:15; Judg 5:23; Jer 11:3).[51]

Riddles, Fables, and Parables

OT narratives also contain examples of riddles, fables, and parables.[52] A *riddle* (Heb. *hidah*) is a simple statement whose hidden meaning must be discovered. The classic example is the one Samson used to stump his Philistine companions: "Out of the eater, something to eat; out of the strong, something sweet" (Judg 14:14; see the answer in v. 18). The posing of clever riddles was typical fare at wedding feasts, and Samson's verbal art in that context enabled him both to head off possible physical violence by his Philistine hosts and to exert some control over a tricky political situation.[53]

---

50. Other examples: "Like Nimrod, a mighty hunter before the Lord" (Gen 10:9); "From evildoers come evil deeds" (1 Sam 24:14); "The 'blind and lame' will not enter the palace" (2 Sam 5:8); "The days go by and every vision comes to nothing" (Ezek 12:22); "Like mother, like daughter" (Ezek 16:44); "The fathers eat sour grapes, and the children's teeth are set on edge" (Jer 31:29; Ezek 18:2).

51. For Israel's understanding of this practice, see the convenient summary of J. Scharbert, "*ʾārar*," *TDOT* 1:408–12, 416–18; and J. Scharbert, "*bārak*," *TDOT* 2:302–8. The genre "imprecation" also wishes dire misfortune on someone but without invoking the curse formula and without addressing the person directly (e.g., Ps 109:6–20). Though resembling a blessing on the surface, a "beatitude" actually makes a declaration ("Blessed is the person who . . . .") rather than a wish (e.g. Ps 1:1; cf. Matt 5:3–11).

52. For a brief survey, see K. J. Cathcart, "The Trees, the Beasts, and the Birds: Fables, Parables, and Allegories in the Old Testament," in *Wisdom in Ancient Israel: Essays in Honour of J. A. Emerton*, ed. J. Day, R. P. Gordon, and H. G. M. Williamson (Cambridge: Cambridge University Press, 1995), 212–21. Besides texts we introduce below, he treats three allegories from Ezekiel—the useless vine (Ezek 15:1–8), the lioness and the vine (29:1–14), and the great tree (31:1–18)—as well as the tale of Balaam's ass (Num 22:22–35) and the ravens feeding Elijah (1 Kgs 17:1–6).

53. So C. V. Camp and C. R. Fontaine, "The Words of the Wise and their Riddles," in *Text and Tradition: The Hebrew Bible and Folklore*, ed. S. Niditch, SemeiaSt 20 (Atlanta: Scholars, 1990), 127–51. They conclude (148–49) that riddles are the stock-in-trade of Israel's wisdom tradition for use in political diplomacy. For details on the scene and its underlying hostility, see Butler, *Judges*, 336–39. Solomon and Daniel were renowned for their ability to solve riddles (1 Kgs 10:1; Dan 5:12). A. Wolters, "The Riddle of the Scales in Daniel 5," *HUCA* 62 (1991):

By contrast, *fables* teach moral truths through brief stories in which plants and animals behave like people. Modern readers immediately recall Aesop's fables—for example, the famous race between the tortoise and the hare—and fables from ancient Egypt and Mesopotamia abound. The OT offers two fine examples, both of a political sort. In one, Jotham told how trees sought a king among various trees and vines but found only the thorn bush willing to serve (Judg 9:8–15).[54] His fable warned the people of Shechem to be wary of Abimelech's leadership as king.[55] Then in 2 Kings 14:9 King Jehoash responded to the challenge of Amaziah with a little fable of a thistle that sent a message to a cedar. Meanwhile, a wild animal trampled on the thistle. Jehoash's message to Amaziah was clear: do not think too highly of yourself and blindly overestimate your strength![56]

A *parable* is a brief story with common human characters that illustrates an important truth.[57] Though OT writers used this form much less than did the rabbis and Jesus, the OT has at least two good examples, one in a narrative context and the other in a wisdom book. The prophet Nathan told King David how a greedy rich man stole a poor man's only lamb to feed a visiting guest. The story, a judicial parable alluding to David's adultery and act of murder, caused him to face his sin (2 Sam 12:1–4).[58] Similarly, the Preacher told how the wisdom of a poor man had once saved a besieged town but that afterward no one remembered him (Eccl 9:13–15; cf. 4:13–16). The lesson was that wisdom is better than strength even if people disregard it (v. 16).[59] As with the NT, OT parables always occur as part of a larger context.

155–77, suggests that the famous wall inscription of Belshazzar has three levels of meaning, all adding up to God's sovereign toppling of the proud king.

54. For discussion see Cathcart, "Trees, Beasts, and Birds," 215–16, who cites several ANE parallels; cf. also G. S. Ogden, "Jotham's Fable: Its Structure and Function in Judges 9," *BT* 46 (1995): 301–8.

55. But cf. D. Janzen, "Gideon's House as the אטד: A Proposal for Reading Jotham's Fable," *CBQ* 74 (2012): 465–75, who argues that the "bramble" is not Abimelech but Gideon and his house and that the fable highlights the insincerity of Shechem and its offer of rulership to Gideon—and that the city will pay a heavy price for this slight. By contrast, S. Tatu, "Jotham's Fable and the Crux Interpretum in Judges IX," *VT* 56 (2006): 105–24, appeals to cognate words to suggests that a thorn-tree, not a bramble, is meant and that Shechem faces a desperate, no-win situation—what he calls an "irony of dilemma" (124).

56. Cf. A. M. Vater Solomon, "Jehoash's Fable of the Thistle and the Cedar," in *Saga, Legend, Tale, Novella, Fable: Narrative Forms in Old Testament Literature*, ed. G. W. Coats, JSOTSup 35 (Sheffield: JSOT, 1985), 126–32 (cf. also her helpful introduction to the genre [114–25]); more briefly, Cathcart, "Trees, Beast, and Birds," 217–18.

57. For a survey of parables in the ancient world, see C. L. Blomberg, *Interpreting the Parables*, 2nd ed. (Downers Grove: IVP Academic, 2012), 56–57; and K. R. Snodgrass, *Stories with Intent: A Comprehensive Guide to the Parables of Jesus* (Grand Rapids: Eerdmans, 2008), 37–59. Blomberg's list of possible parables includes Judg 9:7–15; 2 Sam 14:1–17; 1 Kgs 20:39–42; 2 Kgs 14:9–10; Isa 5:1–7; Jer 13:12–14; Ezek 15:1–8; 17:1–10; 19:1–14; 31:1–18. Cf. C. Westermann, *The Parables of Jesus: In the Light of the Old Testament*, trans. F. Golka and A. H. B. Logan (Edinburgh: T&T Clark, 1990).

58. Cf. J. Schipper, "Did David Overinterpret Nathan's Parable in 2 Samuel 12:1–6?" *JBL* 126 (2007): 383–91, who argues that David recognizes the story as a parable but overinterprets it, presuming that he is the visiting traveler, not the rich man. For another, creative OT example, see J. Schipper, "From Petition to Parable: The Prophet's Use of Genre in 1 Kings 20:38–42," *CBQ* 71 (2009): 264–74.

59. Cf. Z. Weisman, "Elements of Political Satire in Koheleth 4:13–16; 9:13–16," *ZAW* 111 (1999): 554–60. He categorizes the text as a satirical, "quasi-historical anecdote" on the futility of political upheavals.

Songs

Singing played a significant role in Israel's daily life, so it is not surprising that OT narratives quote several kinds of *songs*. The ancient "Song of the Well" (Num 21:17–18) apparently was a work song sung during the digging of wells.[60] Israel also sang victory songs after winning great military battles. Hence, the "Song of the Sea" (Exod 15:1–18) celebrated Yahweh's victory over Pharaoh at the Red Sea, and the "Song of Deborah" (Judg 5) celebrated his conquest of Jabin the Canaanite king (cf. also Exod 15:21; Num 21:27–30; 2 Kgs 19:21–28). Jonah sang a song of thanksgiving from the belly of the great fish (Jonah 2:1–9), and God rescued him (v. 10).[61]

On the other hand, the loss of loved ones, particularly fallen military comrades, was the occasion for the singing (or chanting) of a funeral *dirge* (Heb. *qinah*). One key to recognizing such dirges is the opening word "How . . . !" (Heb. *eyk*). They also have a distinctive poetic meter—five stressed syllables per line—that scholars call the *qinah* (i.e., "dirge") rhythm. The best-known examples are David's laments for Saul and Jonathan (2 Sam 1:19–27) and for Abner (2 Sam 3:33–34; cf. 2 Chr 35:25).[62] (Further information on dirges in the prophets follows.)

Lists

Finally, OT narratives also often incorporate ancient *lists*. A list is a recounting of names or items whose shared characteristics allow their logical categorization.[63] In the ancient world, compiling lists was a common practice. Sometimes these lists served as a means of accounting or inventory control; at others they functioned as a primitive classification of observed phenomena.[64] OT narratives include lists reflective of similar activity in ancient Israel—e.g., lists of booty (Num 31:32–40), votive offerings (Exod 35:5b–9; cf. vv. 21–29), Israelite cities and towns (Josh 15–19), royal mercenaries (2 Sam 23:24–39), and royal officials (1 Kgs 4:2–6, 8–19).

Numbers 33 records an ancient itinerary, the list of places where Israel camped en route from Egypt to Mount Hor (see vv. 5–37).[65] The most common list, however,

---

60. Other texts mention rejoicing and singing that celebrated other occasions; see Gen 31:27; Judg 9:27; 21:21; 1 Sam 18:6–7; Isa 16:10; and the convenient table of E. Werner, "Music," *IDB*, K-Q:458. Cf. also V. H. Matthews, "Music in the Bible," *ABD* 4:930–34; I. H. Jones, "Musical Instruments," *ABD* 4:934–39. For other kinds of songs, see our discussion of poetry below.

61. His study of the song's metrical structure leads Christensen to suggest that its two stanzas may originally have been sung; cf. D. L. Christensen, "The Song of Jonah: A Metrical Analysis," *JBL* 104 (1985): 217–31.

62. Though technically not funeral dirges, Lam 1–2 and 4 offer a collection of dirges over the city of Jerusalem similar in content and rhythm to David's funeral laments. For recent scholarly doubts concerning whether the OT has the dirge genre, see our discussion in the chapter on biblical poetry.

63. Cf. B. E. Scolnic, *Theme and Context in Biblical Lists*, SFSHJ 119 (Atlanta: Scholars, 1995), especially the "Master List of Lists Proper" and "Types of Lists in the Bible" (15–18); Long, "Historical Literature," 4–5.

64. For lists from Ugarit, see C. H. Gordon, *Ugaritic Textbook*, AnOr 38 (Rome: Pontifical Biblical Institute, 1965), 17.2 (290–91). For Egyptian examples, see the lists of Ramses III (twelfth century BC) in *ANET* 261–62.

65. This genre receives in-depth treatment in A. R. Roskop, *The Wilderness Itineraries: Genre, Geography, and the Growth of Torah*, HACL 3 (Winona Lake: Eisenbrauns, 2011), who proposes connections between itineraries and royal annals and a scenario about the composition of the Torah's wilderness itineraries. Scolnic (*Lists*, 67–133) concludes that, unlike other pentateuchal narratives, Num 33 presents the wilderness period positively as "A March

is the genealogy or list of ancestors (Gen 10:1–32; 22:20–24; 25:1–4; Ruth 4:18–22; 1 Chr 2:1–3:24).[66] This list traces the descent of an individual or tribe from antiquity down to a later time. Genealogies tend to bore the modern reader, but ancient peoples regarded them as crucial legal documents. They used genealogical records to establish their claims to be king or high priest, to possess certain property, and to marry into certain families.[67]

Principles of Interpretation—Embedded Genres

The following principles will help the student to interpret embedded genres:

1. Usually, an embedded genre forms a component of a larger context rather than an independent context itself.[68]
2. Thus, the goal of interpretation is to find what that component contributes to the message of the whole.
3. To attain that goal: (a) define the main point of the embedded genre (read by itself, what does it say?); (b) define the main idea(s) of its surrounding context (what subject does the context treat and what does it say about it?);[69] and (c) analyze the relationship between the point of the embedded genre and the idea(s) of its context (why does the compiler change genres in mid-context; how is the change supposed to affect the reader; what does it contribute to the message of the whole?).

To illustrate the application of these principles, we consider two examples. The first is the genealogy of Adam's descendants (Gen 5). Besides giving their names in order, the passage seems to focus on two key statistics for each descendant—his age when he fathered a son and his total lifespan. Its main point is that many generations and many years passed between Adam and Noah. As for the context, it apparently revolves around two ideas—the negative results of the fall of humankind (Abel's murder, Gen 4) and its numerical growth (Gen 6:1). In our view, the genealogy contributes two ideas to the context. By tracing many generations, it shows the proliferation of human life between Adam and Noah—and its increasing sinfulness. It also serves

---

of Triumph" (his chapter title)—i.e., "a nation . . . presented with a view of a glorious past as an inspiration for the creation of a glorious future" (133).

66. The definitive study of genealogy, both biblical and extrabiblical, remains R. R. Wilson, *Genealogy and History in the Biblical World* (New Haven: Yale University Press, 1977); cf. also conveniently, his "Genealogy, Genealogies," *ABD* 2:929–32. Concerning genealogies and Genesis, see B. S. Childs, *Introduction to the Old Testament as Scripture* (Philadelphia: Fortress, 1979), 145–53.

67. The genealogy of Jesus (Matt 1:1–17) serves a similar purpose. By tracing Jesus' descent from David, it establishes his claim to David's royal throne, thus to his identity as Messiah; cf. J. C. Hutchison, "Women, Gentiles, and the Messianic Mission in Matthew's Genealogy," *BSac* 158 (2001): 152–64.

68. Some longer texts like songs or dirges represent exceptions to this principle. One may, in fact, study them both as independent contexts and as components of their surrounding context.

69. Here "context" actually means a series of contexts that surround the embedded genre as if the latter were the center of several concentric circles. The closest circle (the *immediate* context) probably will consist of a few verses before and after the genre. Succeeding circles (the *larger* context) may be a chapter, several chapters, or both.

as a literary bridge between them, as if to say simply, "Much time passed here, and the human condition has deteriorated."

The second example is the song Hannah sang after she gave birth to Samuel (1 Sam 2:1–10).[70] At first glance, the song seems slightly out of place in the context—an unexpected musical disruption in the narrative's flow. Its content soars far beyond the simple thanks of a once-barren woman for her infant son. Rather, it praises God's great sovereign power over history in routing his enemies and in exalting his friends. Further, it falls between reports of Samuel's dedication to Yahweh (1:21–28) and the sinfulness of Israel's priesthood (2:12–17).

What does the song contribute to the context? In our view, it signals that the sovereign God of history stands behind the emergence of Samuel (and, later, of David, too). That he routs his enemies anticipates the prophecies of divine judgment on the priesthood that follow (2:27–36; 3:11–18).

LAW

Law probably strikes most readers as a rather dull subject. They may even wonder why we would treat it here as "literature."[71] Actually, the Pentateuch embeds law within the context of narratives, even if it does not have a story-like "feel." That larger story provides the setting for what scholars believe are three major collections of laws: the Ten Commandments and the Covenant Code (Exod 20:1–23:33), the Deuteronomic Code (Deut 12–26), and the Priestly Code (Exod 25–31; 34:29–Lev 16; parts of Numbers).[72] With the oppressive, cruel social system of Egypt as background, these collections offer a comprehensive, radically different view of human community and the social values it promotes.[73] Surely, that amount of material driven by that sweeping, alternative vision of society merits some comment in an introduction to OT genres.[74] Most importantly, the laws pointed the way for Israel, through obedience, to enjoy God's fullest blessings—and to repair their relationship with Yahweh when

---

70. Cf. Childs, *Introduction,* 272–73; also R. C. Bailey, "The Redemption of YHWH: A Literary Critical Function of the Songs of Hannah and David," *BibInt* 3 (1995): 213–31.

71. In reality, Levinson makes an intriguing case for the literary nature of law based on two literary phenomena, the adjustment by editors of conflicting laws within the Bible and their pseudonymity in doing so; cf. B. M. Levinson, "The Right Chorale: From the Poetics to the Hermeneutics of the Hebrew Bible," in *Not in Heaven: Coherence and Complexity in Biblical Narrative,* ISBL (Bloomington: Indiana University Press, 1991), 129–53.

72. Most lists also include the Holiness Code (Lev 17–26), but recent studies have raised serious questions about whether those chapters ever comprised an actual "code"; cf. M. J. Selman, "Law," in *Dictionary of Old Testament: Pentateuch* (henceforth, *DOTP*), ed. T. D. Alexander and D. W. Baker (Downers Grove: InterVarsity, 2003), 497–515. For a convenient overview of the codes, see Selman, *DOTP,* 500–4; cf. also R. Sonsino, "Forms of Biblical Law," *ABD* 4:252–54. D. Patrick, *Old Testament Law* (Atlanta: John Knox, 1985), 63–261, offers a fine introduction to the topic.

73. Cf. P. D. Miller, "The Good Neighborhood: Identity and Community Through the Commandments," in *The Way of the Lord: Essays in Old Testament Theology* (Grand Rapids: Eerdmans, 2007 [repr.]), 51–67.

74. For a topical survey of law's teachings, see R. Westbrook and B. Wells, *Everyday Law in Biblical Israel: An Introduction* (Louisville: Westminster John Knox, 2009). Excellent discussions of the view of society behind the codes are still available in M. Douglas, *In the Wilderness: The Doctrine of Defilement in the Book of Numbers* (Oxford and New York: Oxford University Press, 2001); M. Douglas, *Leviticus as Literature* (Oxford/New York: Oxford University Press, 1999).

disobedience strained it. The gracious gift of laws also shaped Israel's distinct identity among their neighbors as a just, compassionate, pure, and holy people. Yahweh intended their character to advance his mission for all the world's peoples: by mirroring his divine character, they put on public display in human form Yahweh's superiority over other gods (Deut 4:5–8).[75]

Comparative study of large legal codes from the ancient Near East has considerably enriched our understanding of biblical law.[76] In this brief survey of law we will first discuss the OT's two main types of legal forms and then survey the genres of legal collections. Finally, we will suggest some principles for interpreting OT law.

Forms of Old Testament Legal Material

Casuistic Law	Legal Series
Unconditional Law	Legal Instruction

- Prohibitions
- Admonitions
- Curses
- Participial Sentences

Casuistic Law

The first main type of legal form is *casuistic law* (or "case law").[77] Its distinctive "if . . . then" grammatical structure and impersonal third-person style make it easily recognizable. The "if" clause describes the case concerned, the "then" clause describes the legal penalty for infractions (Exod 21:2, 31, 36; Deut 24:10). Consider this example:

Condition	If men quarrel and one hits the other with a stone or with his fist and he does not die but is confined to bed,
Penalty	the one who struck the blow will not be held responsible if the other gets up and walks around outside with his staff; however, he must pay the injured man for the loss of his time and see that he is completely healed. (Exod 21:18–19)

---

75. For the law's ethical implications, see J. B. Green and J. E. Lapsley, eds., *Old Testament Ethics: A Book-by-Book Survey* (Grand Rapids: Baker Academic, 2013), 1–65; and essays by C. B. Anderson, "Biblical Laws: Challenging the Priciples of Old Testament Ethics," and D. T. Olson, "Between Humility and Authority: The Interplay of Judge-Prophet Laws (Deuteronomy 16:18–17:13) and the Judge-Prophet Narratives of Moses," in *Character Ethics and the Old Testament: Moral Dimensions of Scripture*, ed. M. D. Carroll R. and J. E. Lapsley (Louisville: Westminster John Knox, 2007), 37–50 and 51–62 (respectively). Cf. also D. I. Block, *The Gospel According to Moses: Theological and Ethical Reflections on the Book of Deuteronomy* (Eugene, OR: Cascade Books, 2012); A. Stone, *At Home in a Strange Land: Using the Old Testament in Christian Ethics* (Peabody, MA: Hendrickson, 2008); and C. J. H. Wright, *Old Testament Ethics for the People of God* (Downers Grove: InterVarsity, 2004).

76. A good introduction is S. Greengus, "Biblical and ANE Law," *ABD* 4:242–52. The major extrabiblical collections are the Laws of Ur-Nammu, the Lipit-Ishtar Law Code, the Laws of Eshnunna, the Code of Hammurabi, the Middle Assyrian Laws, the Hittite Laws, and the NeoBabylonian Laws. For complete translations of the collections, see *ANET* 159–98; more conveniently, Matthews and Benjamin, *Old Testament Parallels*, 101–36. For a survey and critical assessment of the parallels, see Walton, *Ancient Israelite Literature*, 69–92.

77. Cf. Sonsino, "Forms of Biblical Law," 252–53; and Selman, *DOTP*, 504.

By stating both the condition and the penalty, legal precision carefully defines everything. That the form (and to some extent, the content) of Israelite casuistic law resembles ancient Near Eastern law suggests that the roots of this genre pre-date Israel's entrance into the arena of history.[78] With regard to content, OT casuistic law primarily treats civil or criminal cases rather than religious ones and probably derives from actual use within a legal system. Those with a penalty may originate in a law court. Interestingly, some of these laws follow a more personal relational style—second person singular ("you") addressed to someone:

> If you lend money to one of my people among you who is needy, do not treat it like a business deal; charge no interest. (Exod 22:25 [MT 22:24])[79]

Unconditional Law

The second major category is *unconditional law*, laws promulgated in unconditional, categorical directives such as commands and prohibitions.[80] Instead of finely tuned case descriptions, they issue absolute orders about right and wrong without considering any exceptions. They also feature personal direct address ("you shall / shall not") and primarily treat moral and religious matters.[81] The best-known form of unconditional law is the *prohibition* or negative command (e.g., "You shall not murder," Exod 20:13) that directly orders, "Don't do this!" Though less common, the *admonition* issues a positive command (Heb. imperative): "Honor your father and your mother . . ." (Exod 20:12; cf. v. 8). The admonition commands, "Do this!" without considering any exceptions (see a similar wisdom form below). *Curses* comprise another subgenre of unconditional law which only occurs as a legal form in the list in Deuteronomy 27:15–26 (e.g., "Cursed is the person who . . ."; cf. Gen 3:17).[82] Another unconditional subgenre draws its name from its grammatical form. The

---

78. Cf. this example from the Laws of Eshnunna (*ANET* 162, para. 30): "If a man hates his town and his lord and becomes a fugitive, (and if) another man takes his wife—when he returns, he shall have no right to claim his wife." For a comparative discussion of biblical and extrabiblical legal forms, see the essays in *Theory and Method in Biblical and Cuneiform Law: Revision, Interpolation and Development*, ed. B. M. Levinson, JSOTSup 181 (Sheffield: Sheffield Academic, 1994). B. S. Jackson, *Wisdom-Laws: A Study of the Mishpatim of Exodus 21:1–22:16* (Oxford: Oxford University Press, 2006), has argued that much of the casuistic laws consist of "wisdom-laws"—laws that show wisdom values (e.g., a preference for "self-executing rules" and avoidance of settling disputes by judicial means). He argues that many of the laws in the Covenant Code in Exodus should also be similarly understood.

79. Among casuistic laws, Patrick helpfully distinguishes between *remedial law* (laws whose apodosis prescribes a legal remedy for violations) and *primary law* (laws phrased in personal language that prescribe the rights and duties of legal relationships); cf. Patrick, *Old Testament Law*, 23; cf. Selman terms the former category "judicial law" (*DOTP*, 504).

80. This is Selman's suggested replacement (*DOTP*, 504–5) term for the older, now less satisfactory term *apodictic law* ("absolute law"). For a survey of the controversy concerning this category, see Sonsino, "Forms of Biblical Law," 252–53.

81. Only a few examples of unconditional law appear in ancient Near Eastern law codes; cf. the Code of Hammurabi (*ANET* 174, para. 187): "The (adopted) son of a chamberlain, a palace servant, or the (adopted) son of a votary, may never be reclaimed"; cf. also the Laws of Eshnunna, paragraphs 15–16 and 51–52 (*ANET* 162, 163).

82. Cf. also "Cursed are you/is your . . ." (Deut 28:16–19; cf. Gen 3:14; 4:11). For discussion and bibliography, see J. Scharbert, "*ārar*," *TDOT* 1: 408-12; C. A. Keller, "*ārar*," *THAT* 1:236–40.

participle sentence deals with capital crimes: "Whoever strikes a person mortally shall be put to death" (Exod 21:12).[83] The Hebrew participle ("Whoever . . .") describes the case while the main verb prescribes the penalty ("put to death"). Typical of unconditional law, the statement is categorical and considers no exceptions.

Last, we mention the well-known *law of retaliation* (or "lex talionis"):

> . . . if there is serious injury, you are to take life for life, eye for eye, tooth for tooth, hand for hand, foot for foot, burn for burn, wound for wound, bruise for bruise. (Exod 21:23–25; cf. Gen 9:6; Lev 24:18–22; Deut 19:21)

Like other unconditional law, it addresses the audience personally ("you are to . . ."). Its subject is premeditated crimes involving bodily harm (but see Deut 19:21). Strikingly, it articulates a broad legal principle—the equivalence of injury and penalty—rather than a specific action.[84] As with casuistic law, this genre goes back to pre-Israelite ancient legal practice and probably reflects actual use. Those that state general principles (often the case) may have originated in contexts of instruction or authority—e.g., a religious, educational, legal, or hybrid situation.

We may rightly lay to rest, however, the older view that the law of retaliation represented a "primitive" form of justice. On the contrary, it responds to a culture whose dominant legal principle was that of blood revenge—endless cycles of tit-for-tat violence (see Gen 4:23–24)—and marks "an effort to introduce the principle of proportionality into Israel's law."[85]

Legal Series

Laws rarely occur in isolation, so a consideration of legal literature must include types of legal collections. Scholars call a text with a small number of laws phrased in a similar style a *series* of laws. Unconditional laws typically occur in series and thereby take on an almost poetic quality when read.[86] Probably the best-known OT series is the Ten Commandments (Exod 20:2–17; Deut 5:6–21). They typify a unique ten-member series or decalogue (cf. Deut 10:4) like the one Exodus 34 claims to have (see v. 28; one is hard pressed, however, to count exactly ten commandments). Though certainty eludes us, such texts may reflect an ancient practice that viewed

---

83. Grammatically, the participle is the subject of the verbal clause "must be put to death." Cf. also Exod 22:19; Gen 26:11; Lev 20:10; 24:16, 21; Num 35:21.

84. The point, quite simply, is: "justice must be maintained." E.g., the Code of Hammurabi, para. 196: "If a seignior has destroyed the eye of a member of the aristocracy, they shall destroy his eye" (*ANET* 175); cf. Greengus, "Biblical and ANE Law," 248–49. For recent discussion of the talion form, see J. Van Seters, "Some Observations on the lex talionis in Exod 21:23–25," in *Recht und Ethos im Alten Testament—Gestalt und Wirkung*, ed. S. Beyerle, G. Mayer, and H. Strauss (Neukirchen-Vluyn: Neukirchener, 1999), 27–37.

85. B. C. Birch, *Let Justice Roll Down: The Old Testament, Ethics, and Christian Life* (Louisville: Westminster John Knox, 1991), 163–64. In essence it says, "Only *one* eye for an eye, only *one* tooth for a tooth," etc.

86. Patrick, *Old Testament Law*, 20–22; cf. series of prohibitions (Exod 20:13–17; Lev 18:6–24; 19:11–18, 26–29; cf. Hos 4:2; Jer 7:9), participle laws (Exod 21:15–17; 31:14–15; Num 35:16:18), and curses (Deut 27:15–26; 28:16–19).

such series as an ideal law code. They certainly were easy to recite by counting from one to ten on one's fingers.[87]

Here's an example from the Covenant Book (see below) of a series composed of participial sentences strung in sequence (in italics):

> *Anyone who strikes a person with a fatal blow is to be put to death.*
>
> However, if it is not done intentionally, but God lets it happen, they are to flee to a place I will designate.
>
> But if anyone schemes and kills someone deliberately, that person is to be taken from my altar and put to death.
>
> *Anyone who attacks their father or mother is to be put to death.*
>
> *Anyone who kidnaps someone is to be put to death*, whether the victim has been sold or is still in the kidnapper's possession.
>
> *Anyone who curses their father or mother is to be put to death.* (Exod 21:12, 15–17; cf. Lev 24:15–20)

Countable series like this may have originally been at home in some Israelite educational context.

Casuistic laws are grammatically more complex and wordy than unconditional laws. Hence, the OT organizes them, not in series, but in *topical groups*. A brief review of one context replete with casuistic laws, the so-called Covenant Book in Exodus, makes this evident. There we find sections of laws that prescribe social policy for the treatment of servants (Exod 21:2–11), bodily injuries (21:18–32), and property losses (22:1–15).[88]

Legal Instruction

The Pentateuch has two lengthy instruction genres. As its name implies, *priestly instruction* comprises an ancient Minister's Manual aimed to instruct priests in professional matters such as ritual procedures. To recognize this genre, the reader must determine from both the context (e.g., Lev 6:9) and the content that the text addresses the tasks of priests. Examples of priestly instruction include Leviticus 6–7 (about offerings)

---

87. Cf. recently, P. D. Miller, "The Place of the Decalogue in the Old Testament and Its Law," in *The Way of the Lord*, 3–16; H. G. Reventlow and Y. Hoffman, eds., *The Decalogue in Jewish and Christian Tradition*, LHBOTS 509 (New York: T&T Clark, 2011). Concerning the significance of the Decalogue, see S. M. Hauerwas and W. H. Willimon, *The Truth About God: The Ten Commandments in Christian Life* (Nashville: Abingdon, 1999).

88. Recently, Wright has argued provocatively that the Covenant Book (or Code) represents an updating or revision specifically of the Code of Hammurabi completed during the Assyrian period (740–650 BC); cf. D. P. Wright, *Inventing God's Law: How the Covenant Code of the Bible Used and Revised the Laws of Hammurabi* (Oxford; New York: Oxford University Press, 2009); D. P. Wright, "The Origin, Development, and Context of the Covenant Code (Exodus 20:23–23:19)," in *The Book of Exodus: Composition, Reception, and Interpretation*, ed. T. B. Dozeman, C. A. Evans, and J. N. Lohr, VTSup 164 (Leiden; Boston: Brill, 2014), 220–44. How widely Wright's thesis will win acceptance remains to be seen, but a review by B. Wells (*The Journal of Religion* 90 [2010]: 558–60) notes the ambiguity of the evidence Wright musters. For previous discussion, see F. Crüsemann, *The Torah: Theology and Social History of Old Testament Law* (Minneapolis: Fortress, 1996), 109–200; J. M. Sprinkle, *"The Book of the Covenant": A Literary Approach*, JSOTSup 174 (Sheffield: Sheffield Academic, 1994).

and Leviticus 21 (about priestly purity). Given their intended audience, it is best to interpret them as texts that concern the duties and expectations specifically of leaders.

The other instructional genre is *ritual* or instruction for lay people about how to perform rituals properly—for example, how to bring offerings and what to offer (Lev 1–5). To recognize this genre, the reader must determine from the context and content of the passage whether it addresses a lay audience.[89]

Principles of Interpretation—Law

OT law poses an interpretive challenge for the Bible student, mainly because of a common misunderstanding of the nature of biblical law. To the modern mind, the word "law" conjures up images of massive, intricate legal codes and a spirit of "legalism." Yet in reality, for all its detail the OT's legal sections do not constitute a comprehensive legal code. Many OT laws (e.g., the Ten Commandments) fail to specify a penalty for violations and to task an authority with enforcing compliance. They seem simply to assume an honor system of self-enforcement by the Israelites themselves.

Instead of a code in a modern sense, OT laws present a select sample of illustrative cases or topics whose legal principles were to guide Israelite individuals, the larger community, and lawmakers in making decisions and in living out Israel's worldview. Taken together, they articulated what today we might call "national policy." Their purpose was to teach the Israelite fundamental values—what it means to live all of life in the presence of God—not to provide them with a handy legal reference tool.[90] In short, their aim was instructional rather than judicial. Further, OT law is best understood in a covenant framework. It articulates the stipulations of the covenant made between God and Israel at Mt. Sinai; thus, OT law represents the personal demands of Israel's sovereign Lord, not an abstract system of morality or a technical legal code.[91]

In light of this, readers must interpret law relationally—as the guidelines that govern Israel's ongoing life with her gracious God. In return for his protection and blessing, God expects his people to obey what the law commands—in short, to maintain their covenant relationship with God on a healthy footing. The Ten Commandments (Exod 20; Deut 5) express the broad, overarching ethical principles whose details

---

89. An earlier generation of scholars referred to such instructions for laity as *torah* ("instruction") and for priests as *da'at* ("professional knowledge").

90. Birch, *Justice*, 171–172; R. L. Hubbard, Jr., *The Book of Ruth*, NICOT (Grand Rapids: Eerdmans, 1988), 50. In fact, the nature of ancient law remains a matter of ongoing discussion; cf. the essays in Levinson, *Theory and Method*; and C. M. Carmichael, *The Origins of Biblical Law: The Decalogues and the Book of the Covenant* (Ithaca/London: Cornell University Press, 1992).

91. So R. E. Averbeck, "Law," in *Cracking Codes*, 134–35; Birch, *Justice*, 145–46 (cf. also his discussion [146–57] of "The God Who Makes Covenant"); cf. also E. A. Martens, "How Is the Christian to Construe Old Testament Law?" *BBR* 12 (2002): 199–216. Here we accept ancient treaty-making as the background of the Mosaic covenant as in G. Wenham, "Grace and Law in the Old Testament," in *Law, Morality, and the Bible*, ed. B. N. Kaye and G. Wenham (Downers Grove: InterVarsity, 1978), 9–13.

the subsequent legal codes flesh out.[92] Thus, Bible students must interpret them as foundational ethical principles to maintain relationship with a loving Lord and to cultivate a covenant community, not as a legal code.[93] Their complex contents aim to create a distinctive people of God, one whose community structure and ethics accurately mirror the nature of its Lord.

For readers of this book the question is: *How does the law apply to Christians today?* In reply, we affirm two fundamental interrelated assumptions about the nature of OT law.[94] First, we believe that God intends it to serve as a paradigm of timeless ethical, moral, and theological principles. In other words, the law is more than a temporary, dispensable cultural phenomenon. Actually, it plays a key role in Israel's priestly ministry as a "light to the nations" (Isa 49:6; cf. Exod 19:5–6). Christians who dismiss it as outmoded and irrelevant deprive themselves of the teachings God conveyed through it. They miss an additional resource for understanding what it might mean to be Christ-like.

Second, to interpret law properly the student must discover the timeless truth it conveys. In some cases the truth lies right on the surface unobscured by culture. Prohibitions like "Do not murder" and "Do not steal" (Exod 20:13, 15; Deut 5:17, 19) need no cross-cultural translation; they clearly identify murder and stealing as wrong. Similarly, the timeless aspect of the instructions about equitable legal procedure (Exod 23:1–8) is fairly obvious: witnesses should tell the truth, not cater to the crowd (vv. 1–3); opponents at law should treat each other civilly (vv. 4–5); and judges should judge by evidence and refuse bribes (vv. 6–8). In other instances the underlying, universal truth may be difficult to perceive behind its present cultural form—ancient Israelite law—so careful interpretation is necessary. Consider, for example, the perplexing laws that decree a woman's menstrual bleeding makes her and everything she touches unclean (Lev 15:19–30).[95] These laws seem rather harsh and unfair, in effect making women untouchable one week out of every four. We wonder what timeless principle could possibly underlie them.

To answer this question we need to consider the Israelite cultural background. Israelite women married early, had children early, weaned their children late (at ages

---

92. Birch, *Justice*, 168; G. Wenham, "Law and the Legal System in the Old Testament," in Kaye and Wenham, *Law, Morality, and the Bible*, 28–29. For an excellent description of the community the law intended to shape, see Birch, *Justice*, 172–84. Pastors will find help for their pulpit ministry from C. J. H. Wright, "Preaching from the Law," in *Reclaiming the Old Testament for Christian Preaching*, ed. G. J. R. Kent, P. J. Kissling, and L. A. Turner (Downers Grove: IVP Academic, 2010), 47–63.

93. For a topical treatment of five types of law, C. J. H. Wright, *An Eye for An Eye. The Place of Old Testament Ethics Today* (Downers Grove: InterVarsity, 1983), 153–59. We prefer his more sociologically based categories to the traditional division of OT law into civil, ceremonial, and moral types. For a broader treatment of ethics, including discussion of crucial contemporary issues, see C. J. H. Wright, *Walking in the Ways of the Lord: The Ethical Authority of the Old Testament* (Downers Grove: InterVarsity, 1995); C. S. Rodd, *Glimpses of a Strange Land: Studies in Old Testament Ethics*, OTS (Edinburgh: T&T Clark, 2001).

94. Wright, *Eye*, 40–45, 156–57, 161–62, 170–71.

95. Here we draw on the comments of G. J. Wenham, *The Book of Leviticus*, NICOT (Grand Rapids: Eerdmans, 1979), 219–24. Anyone who was "unclean" could not, among other things, join the community in public worship.

two or three), and tended to have large families (cf. Ps 127:4–5). Thus, a monthly menses was much less common among married Israelite women than it is today. In actuality, unmarried, adolescent women were those most directly and frequently affected by these laws. We suggest, then, that these laws, in effect, sought to regulate teenage passions and discourage sexual relations between young, unmarried Israelites.[96] If so, the underlying truth appears to be that sexual relations outside of marriage displease God and may adversely affect the orderly relations between Israelite families.

From early on Christians have often spoken of Christ as the key to interpreting the OT. Jesus himself established precedent for this view when he declared, "Do not think that I have come to abolish the Law or the Prophets. I have not come to abolish them but to fulfill them" (Matt 5:17). Clearly, the Gospel writers believed that Christ fulfilled many prophecies; five such fulfillment quotations appear in Matthew 1–2 alone. But here Jesus refers to "the Law" as well as to the prophets, presumably meaning all the Hebrew Scriptures, and Matthew goes on to illustrate Jesus' code of ethics in contrast to the OT Law. Therefore, to fulfill a law must mean to bring to completion everything for which that law was originally intended (cf. v. 18: "until everything is accomplished").[97]

In some cases, as with sacrifices and various ceremonies (cf. Col 2:16–17), that point of completion was Christ's death and resurrection. Throughout his ministry, Jesus challenged fundamental principles of both oral and written *Torah*, especially those relating to Sabbath and dietary laws. At the same time, he never broke any of the written law while it remained God's will for his people (i.e., before the cross, resurrection, and sending of the Holy Spirit at Pentecost inaugurated the age of God's new covenant).[98] In other cases, as with many moral injunctions, the point of completion will not occur until Christ's return.

Matthew 5:17, therefore, suggests the following hermeneutical principle for applying the OT in the NT age: *All of the OT applies to Christians, but none of it applies apart from its fulfillment in Christ.*[99] Thus, our view falls in the middle ground between the views of classic covenant theology (all the OT applies except what the NT repeals) and in classic dispensationalism (none of the OT applies except what the NT repeals). The former would logically lead to prohibitions against most modern farming practices and clothing fashions (Deut 22:9–12), while the latter would logically lead to the

---

96. So Wenham, *Leviticus*, 224. Conceivably, other factors also come into play in this instance (e.g., ritual taboos associated with bodily emissions).

97. For the thesis that Paul understood Christ as the "termination," not just the "goal," of the law, see J. P. Heil, "Christ, the Termination of the Law (Romans 9:30–10:8)," *CBQ* 63 (2001): 484–98. On the wider topic of the Law in the Gospels and Paul, see conveniently R. S. Hendel, "The Law in the Gospel: The Law Is an Essential Precondition for the Gospel," *BRev* 14 (1998): 20, 52; and B. S. Rosner, *Paul and the Law: Keeping the Commandments of God*, New Studies in Biblical Theology (Downers Grove: IVP Academic, 2013).

98. Cf. especially R. Banks, *Jesus and the Law in the Synoptic Tradition*, SNTSMS 28 (Cambridge, UK: Cambridge University Press, 2005 [repr.]); D. J. Moo, "Jesus and the Authority of the Mosaic Law," *JSNT* 20 (1984): 3–49. See also the nuanced discussion in W. R. G. Loader, *Jesus' Attitude Toward the Law*, WUNT 97 (Tübingen: J. C. B. Mohr [Paul Siebeck], 1997).

99. Cf. esp. D. A. Dorsey, "The Law of Moses and the Christian: A Compromise," *JETS* 34 (1991): 321–34.

acceptance of sorcerers, mediums, and spiritists (despite Deut 18:9–13)! For in neither case does the NT say anything one way or the other about these specific practices. Instead, we suggest that all of the OT laws as "useful for teaching, rebuking, correcting and training in righteousness" (2 Tim 3:16), but only as one discovers how those laws are fulfilled in Christ.

How may we determine how Christ fulfills them? We suggest that where the NT specifically cites a particular law, the interpreter's task is eased considerably. We obey the laws of sacrifice by trusting in Christ as our once-for-all sacrifice (Heb 9:1–10:25), not by bringing sheep or goats to be slain each Sunday in church. The kosher laws were designed to set the Israelites apart from the other nations, so we obey this principle as we pursue a Christ-like lifestyle that avoids sin (2 Cor 6:17), even though Christ declared that all foods are clean (Mark 7:19). The symbol of baptism parallels the principle behind the law of circumcision (Col 2:11b–12a), though the rites are not identical in all aspects. For example, Christians baptize women as well as men, and most likely the NT envisioned only people old enough to repent from sin rather than infants as recipients (Col 2:11–12).

Where the NT does not address a particular law, we must discover if it fits a category of law the NT does address. For example, orthodox Jews today view the command "you shall not boil a kid in its mother's milk" (Exod 23:19; 34:26; Deut 14:21) as a dietary law that prevents them from serving milk and meat dishes at the same meal. Even if this was the law's original intention, this command takes its place with the other kosher laws that no longer apply literally to Christians' diets since Jesus has declared all foods clean (Mark 7:19).[100] Alternately, it may have been a command meant to dissociate the Israelites from certain pagan, religious practices, much like the otherwise unrelated warnings, "Do not cut the hair at the sides of your head or clip off the edges of your beard. Do not cut your bodies for the dead or put tattoo marks on yourselves" (Lev 19:27–28).[101] Any practices, whether relating to diet or personal appearance, that represent pagan worship (as in the self-mutilation practices of several world religions and occult sects today) remain strictly forbidden for believers. But if Christians partake of goat's meat and milk or get tattooed for some nonreligious reason, they do not transgress God's commands.

To summarize, OT law relates to Christians in light of the NT in the following ways:

- Some laws retain literal validity for Christians. For example, Jesus reaffirmed the OT injunctions to love the Lord wholeheartedly and to love one's neighbor (Matt 5:21–48; 22:40; cf. Deut 6:5; Lev 19:18). Similarly, Paul

---

100. Though quoted three times (for texts, see above), the background of the prohibition against boiling a kid in its mother's milk remains uncertain. The best one can say is that it prohibits a practice thought to compromise Israel's exclusive relationship with Yahweh; so J. I. Durham, *Exodus*, WBC 3 (Waco, TX: Word, 1987) 462; cf. D. L. Christensen, *Deuteronomy 1:1–21:9*, 2nd ed., WBC 6a (Nashville: Nelson, 2014), 289–90, 294–95.

101. Association with pagan mourning rites seems the most likely rationale; cf. J. Milgrom, *Leviticus 17–22*, AB 3a (New York: Doubleday, 2000), 1690–93; E. S. Gerstenberger, *Leviticus: A Commentary*, OTL (Louisville: Westminster John Knox, 1996), 276–77.

invoked the OT legal requirement of two or three witnesses to establish guilt in the case of accusations against Christian leaders (1 Tim 5:19; cf. Deut 17:6; 19:15; 2 Cor 13:1). Any other laws that the NT applies to Christians remain valid.

- In some cases, the NT actually makes the OT law stricter. For example, in the case of marriage, the seventh commandment forbids adultery, and the OT permits divorce and remarriage (Exod 20:14; Deut 5:18; 24:1–4). But unlike the OT, Jesus regards divorce and remarriage (and, by implication, polygamy) as adultery (Luke 16:18; Matt 19:3–12; Mark 10:2–12). Further, Jesus permitted divorce only when marital infidelity had occurred (Matt 19:9); Paul, only in the case of desertion by an unbeliever (1 Cor 7:15–16). The truth behind both OT and NT laws was the value of preserving stable marriages.[102] Finally, Jesus intensifies the command against murder by forbidding anger (the root cause that may lead to murder; Matt 5:21–22) and forbids not only adultery but also lust (another root cause; Matt 5:27–28).

- Some laws no longer have literal validity because of NT teachings (i.e., their fulfillment in Christ renders their literal practice obsolete).[103] Thus, Christians no longer need to follow literally the OT sacrificial system (Heb 10:1–10), to obey its food laws (Mark 7:19; cf. Acts 10:9–16), or to perform circumcision (Gal 5:2–6). But see the next point.

- Laws that no longer apply literally still teach important timeless truths. Thus, the OT sacrificial system graphically reminds Christians that God takes sin seriously, requires a severe penalty, yet graciously offers forgiveness. Similarly, the clean animals in OT food laws probably symbolized Israel as the chosen people, in contrast to her ritually "unclean" pagan neighbors. Hence, eating reminded Israelites (and, by implication, Christians) of their gracious election by God and their resulting duty to pursue God-like holiness.[104] Even the cultic law concerning the sabbatical fallow year (Lev 25; Deut 15) proves instructive, underscoring that compassionate humanitarian service ultimately represents service for God.[105]

Understanding Jesus as the fulfillment of the law also has implications for interpreting NT ethics more generally. Kingdom demands, like the Mosaic law, flow from and respond to the redemption of God's people but do not "earn" anyone's salvation.

---

102. Wenham, "Law and the Legal System," 36–37, who comments, however, "in practice the differences [between OT and NT teachings] were quite slight."

103. Cf. J. J. Davis, *Foundations of Evangelical Theology* (Grand Rapids: Baker, 1984), 257–58.

104. Wenham, "Law and the Legal System," 30.

105. Wright, *Eye*, 156–57. Cf. also Paul's application of Deut 25:4 ("Do not muzzle an ox while it is treading out the grain") to the right of Christian leaders to earn their living by ministry (1 Cor 9:7–12); and his teaching that love underlies—and, thereby, its practice fulfills—the law (Rom 13:8–10). For additional discussion of the application of law, see J. D. Hays, "Applying the Old Testament Law Today," *BSac* 21 (2001): 21–35.

But failure to observe OT laws often led to specific sanctions and punishments; failure by the nation at large eventually led to loss of peace, prosperity, and land. Because Jesus' single sacrifice has fulfilled all of God's demands in Scripture for justice, few NT ethical texts suggest that keeping or transgressing God's commandments today lead to the identical material blessings or punishments.[106] One example is Paul's warning to the Corinthian Christians that their abuse of the Lord's Supper explains "why many among you are weak and sick, and a number of you have fallen asleep" (1 Cor 11:30).

Although the story of the woman caught in adultery almost certainly was not in John's original text, a good case can be made for its authenticity as a true story about what Jesus did and said.[107] In it he establishes a precedent for forbidding the application of OT sanctions even for such a fundamental moral issue as adultery. A possible exception appears in the case of murder. Because what we would call "first-degree homicide" was the only sin for which a ransom could not be substituted for a sacrifice (Num 35:31),[108] some Christians believe capital punishment for murder remains appropriate in the Christian era. But many others point to Christ's once-for-all sacrifice as obliterating the need for further sanctions—whether physical or spiritual—for all sin.

As for specific *principles of interpretation,* we recommend the following:

1. Whatever its literary type, the collection or series in which an individual law appears serves as its literary context. Thus, the student should investigate surrounding laws for interpretive clues.
2. The student should endeavor to understand the original meaning and purpose of laws in light of their cultural background. Since many readers lack such knowledge, we recommend that they liberally consult Bible dictionaries, commentaries, and other background sources. See the bibliography at the end.
3. Apply laws primarily to the NT counterpart of the original audience. For example, laws aimed at Israel as a whole make proper application to Christians in general. Since the NT affirms the "priesthood of all believers," both priestly and ritual instructions would also apply to Christians in general, not just to clergy.
4. Whether a given law applies literally, in principle, or both, depends upon how it compares to laws in the categories discussed above. The reader may use the latter as guidelines for making application.

---

106. For a standard, full treatment of NT ethics, see J. B. Green, ed., *The New Testament and Ethics: A Book-by-Book Survey* (Grand Rapids: Baker Academic, 2013); B. Witherington III, *The Indelible Image: The Theological and Ethical Thought World of the New Testament,* 2 vols. (Downers Grove: IVP Academic, 2009–10); G. H. Stassen and D. P. Gushee, *Kingdom Ethics: Following Jesus In Contemporary Context* (Downers Grove: InterVarsity, 2003).

107. See esp. G. M. Burge, "A Specific Problem in the New Testament Text and Canon: The Woman Caught in Adultery (John 7:53–8:11)," *JETS* 27 (1984): 141–48. For more recent interpretation, see L. J. Kreitzer and D. W. Rooke, eds., *Ciphers in the Sand: Interpretations of the Woman Taken in Adultery (John 7:53–8:11),* Biblical Seminar Series (Sheffield: Sheffield Academic, 2000).

108. See esp. W. C. Kaiser, Jr., *Toward Old Testament Ethics* (Grand Rapids: Zondervan, 1983), 165–68.

A Sample Legal Text: Exodus 21:7–11

A brief study of this text—in form, casuistic law—permits us to apply the above discussion.[109] Set within a larger slave law (vv. 1–11), vv. 7–11 concern the redemption of an Israelite woman whose father, presumably driven by financial necessity, has sold her into a slave-marriage. Structurally, the text first defines the case (Heb. *ki*; "When . . . , she shall not . . . ," v. 7), then details its subconditions (Heb. *im*; "if . . . , then . . . ," vv. 8–11). A structural outline of this text might look something like this:

I. Case Definition: Basic condition for release 21:7
II. List: Subconditions and their legal outcomes for the slave 21:8–11

Now a male slave needs no redemption because he automatically goes free after six years of service (v. 2), so the instruction mandates the redemption of a female slave—the paying off of the debt to free her—under two conditions: 1) she no longer "pleases" the man; 2) he has given her legal status as a wife (v. 8). On the other hand, she enjoys standing as a "daughter" if the man has given her to his son as wife (v. 9).

Two things are striking about this law. First, it gives the woman remarkable protection against abuse by her displeased husband. It forbids him from selling her to a foreigner or from denying her spousal rights to food, clothing, and sexual relations (vv. 8–11). Second, the reason for her right to redemption is his breach of faith (i.e., "since he has dealt unfairly [Heb. *bagad*] with her"; v. 8b). The law makes the loss of favor his responsibility; indeed, the root *bagad* ("to deal treacherously") seems to imply a breach of faith on his part that opens the possibility of her freedom.

Several implications flow from this legal instruction. First, the law bases marriage in understandings and commitments inherent in the relationship rather than in one member's "likes" or "dislikes." Second, in protecting a socially vulnerable woman, it implies God's commitment to protect the vulnerable from abuse. Now, the NT shares that commitment to the lowly, so to apply the OT law today would entail two things: on the one hand, an honest examination of one's relationships for possible abuse of people, and, on the other, a look-around for any abused or vulnerable people nearby whom one might offer protection, if not advocacy.

Deuteronomy

In a sense, the book of *Deuteronomy* represents a collection of laws, yet as a unique literary genre it requires special consideration. Deuteronomy offers a comprehensive restatement of the Mosaic law. Excluding the brief narrative opening (1:1–5) and lengthy conclusion (chs. 31–34), the book consists of Moses' farewell speeches to the Israelites while they were camped east of the Jordan River (1:6–4:40; 5–26; 27:11–28;

---

109. For further discussion and bibliography, see R. L. Hubbard, Jr., "The Divine Redeemer: Toward a Biblical Theology of Redemption," in *Reading the Hebrew Bible for A New Millennium: Form, Concept, and Theological Perspective*, 2 vols., ed. W. Kim, et al., Studies in Antiquity and Christianity (Harrisburg: Trinity Press International, 2000), 1:189–91.

29:2–30).[110] Scholars commonly describe the rhetoric of these speeches as *parenesis*—a style of speech that intends to persuade the audience to adopt a certain course of action.[111]

Further, the structure of the book closely resembles that of suzerain-vassal treaties like those of the Hittites and Assyrians (second and first millennia BC, respectively).[112] Such treaties dictated the relationship between a major power (the suzerain) and its subject nation (the vassal). Like those treaties, Deuteronomy has a historical prologue (1:6–4:43), a list of stipulations (chs. 5–26), mention of witnesses to the agreement ("heaven and earth," 4:26; 30:19; 31:28), and blessings and curses (chs. 27–28).

On the other hand, in one significant respect Deuteronomy differs from the ancient treaties: in the latter, the Hittite or Assyrian king addresses the subject nation; in the former Moses, not King Yahweh, addresses Yahweh's subject, Israel. Thus, though treaty-like in form, Deuteronomy is best read as the testament of Moses—a series of exhortations that articulate his ethical will as if he were addressing his successor, whether Israel as a whole, a later king, or both.[113]

Principles of Interpretation—Deuteronomy

We suggest that readers interpret Deuteronomy according to these guidelines:

1. Deuteronomy is best heard as Moses' impassioned speeches to God's people threatened by temptations to compromise their exclusive commitment to God.
2. Its crucial historical background is the potential corrupting influence of the Canaanite religion on Israel. The foreboding shadow of Baal worship haunts much of its content, a fact that should shape our interpretation of it.
3. Approach the laws of Deuteronomy as Moses' passionate exhortations—i.e., a series of farewell speeches just prior to his death and Israel's entry into Canaan—rather than as abstract, technical legal instruction. At its heart lies the theological issue of religious accommodation to idolatry, an issue still relevant today.
4. The literary nature of each section should dictate the interpretive approach to it. For example, poetic sections (chs. 32–33) require treatment appropriate to poetry; laws, those proper for legal materials, etc. Similarly, application should follow guidelines for each genre.

110. Useful introductions to the book are available in J. G. McConville, "Deuteronomy, Book of," *DOTP*, 182–93; R. E. Clements, *Deuteronomy*, OT Guides (Sheffield: JSOT, 1989); and Christensen, *Deuteronomy 1:1–21:9*, lvii–lxxix. Cf. also C. J. H. Wright, *Deuteronomy*, UBC (Grand Rapids: Baker Academic, 2012 [1996]).

111. So Long, "Historical Literature," 255, citing Deut 6–11; Zech 1:3–6; Josh 24:2–15; 1 Kgs 8:56–61.

112. T. Rata, "Covenant," *DOTP*, 99–105. Though somewhat dated, D. J. McCarthy, *Old Testament Covenant* (Richmond, VA: John Knox, 1972), 10–34, still offers a good introduction; cf. also J. J. M. Roberts, "The Ancient Near Eastern Environment," in *The Hebrew Bible and Its Modern Interpreters*, ed. D. A. Knight and G. M. Tucker (Chico: Scholars, 1985), 93–94. For translations of Egyptian and Hittite treaties, see *ANET* 199–206.

113. Of course, Moses' exhortations restate the covenant just before Israel enters the promised land, so scholars often refer to it as the Moab Covenant because of its geographical setting; cf. S. D. McBride, "Deuteronomy, Book of," *NIDB*, 2:112–13. In passing, we observe that a few OT narratives report ancient Israelite legal processes. Awareness of their legal nature will enable the reader to understand them better. These include an investigative procedure called an ordeal (Num 5:11–31), several criminal trials (Gen 31:25–42; 2 Sam 1:1–16; 4:5–12), and a civil process about prior rights (Ruth 4:1–12).

POETRY

After narratives, poetry is the most common literary form in the Bible. Virtually all biblical books, even those not traditionally called "poetical," contain some poetry.[114] Now poetry is not a genre per se but a literary style—the alternative to prose. So, to study poetry we will survey the major literary types of OT poetry and conclude with suggested principles of interpretation.[115]

Types of Old Testament Poetry

Prayers	**Songs**
Protest	Thanksgiving
Royal Protest	Liturgies
Imprecation	Royal Thanksgiving
Penitential Psalm	Wisdom Psalms
Dirge	Hymn
	Personal Hymn
	Coronation Hymn
	Zion Hymn
	Yahweh-Kingship Hymn
	Love Song
	Royal Wedding Song

Prayers

Prayers are specially worded, extended statements spoken (not sung) to God by individuals or groups. The *protest* constitutes the most common genre of prayer in the psalms.[116] Whether prayed by an individual or the corporate worshiping community, a protest is a heart-felt petition for Yahweh to deliver from some humanly

---

114. J. B. Gabel, C. B. Wheeler, and A. D. York, *The Bible as Literature: An Introduction*, 4th ed. (New York; Oxford: Oxford University Press, 2000), 34. For example, Exodus and Judges each have a lengthy victory song, the "Song of Moses" (Exod 15:1–18; cf. v. 21) and the "Song of Deborah" (Judg 5; see also 1 Sam 2:1–10; 2 Sam 23:1–7; Jonah 2:1–10).

115. Cf. ch. 8, "the General Rules of Hermeneutics: Biblical Poetry." For an introduction to all psalm genres, consult N. deClaissé-Walford, R. A. Jacobson, and B. LaNeel Tanner, *The Book of Psalms*, NICOT (Grand Rapids: Eerdmans, 2014), 13–38; and the "Index of Form-Critical Categorizations" in *Interpreting the Psalms: Issues and Approaches*, ed. P. S. Johnston and D. Firth, (Downers Grove: InterVarsity, 2005), 295–300. T. Longman III, "The Psalms and Ancient Near Eastern Prayer Genres," in *Interpreting the Psalms*, ed. Johnston and Firth, 41–62, compares psalms with other ancient prayers. For a wide-ranging treatment of the Psalms by Jewish and Christian scholars, cf. S. Gillingham, ed., *Jewish and Christian Approaches to the Psalms: Conflict and Convergence* (Oxford: Oxford University Press, 2013). For a multicultural perspective on the Psalms, see S. B. Reid, *Listening in: A Multicultural Reading of the Psalms* (Nashville: Abingdon, 1997).

116. "Protest" represents our update of the more familiar terms, "complaint" and "lament," per the suggestion of J. Goldingay, *Psalms*, BCOTWP, 3 vols. (Grand Rapids: Baker Academic, 2006–8), 1:60–64. To some, "complaint" evokes the sense "griping" (a negative, misleading term), and we limit "lament" more narrowly to expressions of grief over something irreversible like death or dismemberment. But cf. introductions to "complaints" / "laments" in C. Broyles, "Lament, Psalms of," *DOTWPW*, 384–99; P. S. Johnston, "The Psalms and Distress," in Johnston and Firth, *Interpreting the Psalms*, 63–84; R. E. Murphy, *The Gift of the Psalms* (Peabody, MA: Hendrickson, 2000

unsolvable crisis. For an individual the crisis might be severe illness, misfortune, or false accusations; for the community, it might be a drought, plagues, or invasions by enemies.[117] Most scholars assume that protests were prayed at a sanctuary, such as the temple in Jerusalem, as part of a larger ritual process. Unlike dirges or laments, in which speakers vent deep grief and hopeless despair, protests voice deep suffering but assume that the crisis can be resolved by God's intervention.[118]

Psalm 22 provides an excellent example of the typical protest psalm.[119] It opens with an invocation of God's name(s) as a way of making contact with Yahweh (vv. 1–2). It includes an affirmation of confidence (vv. 3–5) by which the petitioner affirms trust in God. The protest element (vv. 6–8) describes in general terms the affliction threatening the individual or community. In the petition (vv. 19–21) the worshiper specifically asks for God's help in resolving the problem. Finally, protests often close with a thanksgiving element—in this case, a hymn of thanksgiving (vv. 22–26)—in which the petitioner offers thanks in advance of receiving his petition.[120] When the king either speaks or is spoken of, we designate that psalm a *royal protest* (see Pss 89; 144).[121] A structural outline of Psalm 22 might look like this:[122]

I. Protest 22:1–21
   A. Invocation, Protest 22:1–2
   B. Report: Struggle 22:3–11
      1. Confidence 22:3–5
      2. Protest 22:6–8

[repr.]), 11–14; and E. S. Gerstenberger, *Psalms 1*, FOTL 14 (Grand Rapids: Eerdmans, 1988), 11–14 ("Introduction to Cultic Poetry"), 108.

117.For the communal protests, see R. J. Bautch, *Developments in Genre Between Post-Exilic Penitential Prayers and the Psalms of Communal Lament*, AcBib 7 (Atlanta: Society of Biblical Literature, 2003); and the fine study by P. W. Ferris, Jr., *The Genre of Communal Lament in the Bible and the Ancient Near East*, SBLDS 127 (Atlanta: Scholars, 1992).

118. With great insight, W. Brueggemann (*The Message of the Psalms* [Minneapolis: Augsburg, 1984], 18–23) calls the protests psalms of disorientation because the psalmist's experience of suffering seems to imply a disturbed relationship with God. These disorientation psalms contrast the psalms of orientation (i.e., songs of praise) and of new orientation (i.e., thanksgiving songs after restoration from suffering). For the use of psalms in prayer, see S. L. Jaki, *Praying the Psalms: A Commentary* (Grand Rapids: Eerdmans, 2001).

119. For brief treatment of another protest (Ps 77), see T. Longman, III, "Lament," in Sandy and Giese, *Cracking Codes*, 210–12. For an illuminating, in-depth study of protests, see also D. Dombkowski Hopkins, *Journey through the Psalms*, rev. ed. (St. Louis: Chalice Press, 2002), 77–132.

120. Other common elements include a confession of sin or assertion of innocence (e.g., Ps 7:3–5; 51:3–5) and an imprecation against enemies (e.g., Ps 5:11; 109:6–20). C. Mandolfo, *God in the Dock: Dialogic Tension in the Psalms of Lament*, JSOTSup 357 (Sheffield: Sheffield Academic, 2002), studies another phenomenon, the transition from first and second to third person speakers within the same protests, and concludes (197–206) that they reflect actual dialogues in cultic settings.

121. Protests also occur in Jer 10–20 and in Job; cf. K. M. O'Connor, *The Confessions of Jeremiah: Their Interpretation and Role in Chapters 1–25*, SBLDS 97 (Atlanta: Scholars, 1988); R. G. Murphy, *Job: A Short Reading* (New York: Paulist Press, 1999). For reassessments of the nature and canonical function of royal psalms, see conveniently, W. H. Bellinger, Jr., *Psalms: A Guide to Studying the Psalter*, 2nd ed. (Grand Rapids: Baker Academic, 2012), 111–28; A. Grant, "The Psalms and the King," in Johnston and Firth, *Interpreting the Psalms*, 101–18; S. R. A. Starbuck, *Court Oracles in the Psalms: The So-Called Royal Psalms in their Ancient Near Eastern Context*, SBLDS 172 (Atlanta: SBL, 1999).

122. Modified after Gerstenberger, *Psalms, Part 1*, 18.

   3. Confidence 22:9–10
   4. Petition 22:11
  C. Main Protest 22:12–18
  D. Petition 22:19–21
II. Thanksgiving, Praise 22:22–31
  A. Thanksgiving Hymn 22:22–26
   1. Vow 22:22
   2. Call to Praise 22:23–24
   3. Vow 22:25
   4. Blessing 22:26
  B. Hymn of Praise 22:27–31

A few protest psalms include an imprecation as part of the petition. Hence, such texts are sometimes called *imprecatory psalms*.[123] The horrible things that the imprecations request from God trouble some readers (e.g., "For the curses and lies they utter, consume them in wrath, consume them until they are no more," Ps 59:12b–13; cf. Pss 10:15; 109:6–15; 137:7–9; 139:19–22). We suggest, however, that students should understand their extreme language as hyperbole—emotional exaggerations by which the psalmist hopes to persuade Yahweh to act. In other words, the psalmist wants God to know how strongly he feels about the matter.

They thus serve an important two-fold function: to expose the world's cruel violence and oppression lest it be ignored and continue unopposed; and to give its victims the words in which to express their legitimate despair and outrage. Further, as prayers they occur within an ongoing relationship with God; they direct their fury to the right person, the God of justice and vengeance. They affirm that the sufferers' pain touches God's heart and that God will meet their needs and avenge their suffering according to his will. At the same time, one must read imprecatory psalms in light of the Bible's criticism of blind vengeance (e.g., Rom 12:9, 21) and, hence, not appeal to them to justify revenge.[124]

The *penitential psalms* are seven especially poignant psalms in which a deeply contrite individual seeks God's mercy for her or his sin, relief from the physical and emotional distress it has caused, and restoration to the joyful intimacy with God formerly enjoyed.[125] They give us today words to express our own sincere repentance and desire for mercy and gracious restoration.

---

123. Cf. N. L. deClaissé-Walford, "The Theology of the Imprecatory Psalms," in *Soundings in the Theology of Psalms: Perspectives and Methods in Contemporary Scholarship*, ed. R. A. Jacobson (Minneapolis: Fortress, 2011), 77–92; and the treatment of Ps 137 by P. D. Miller, "The Hermeneutics of Imprecation," in *The Way of the Lord*, 193–202; and the insightful chapter in H. C. Bullock, *Encountering the Psalms* (Grand Rapids: Baker, 2001), 227–38.

124. Cf. Miller, "Hermeneutics of Imprecation," 193–202; Bullock, *Psalms*, 237–38. For further suggestions concerning their liturgical use, see Miller, "Hermeneutics of Imprecation," 201–2.

125. These are Pss 6, 32, 38, 51, 102, 130 and 143. Cf. L.-S. Tiemeyer, "The Doubtful Gain of Penitence: The Fine Line between Lament and Prayer," in *Spiritual Complaint: The Theology and Practice of Lament*, ed. M. J. Bier and T. Bulkeley (Eugene, OR: Wipf & Stock, 2013), 102–23.

A *dirge* is a funeral lamentation spoken as part of ancient mourning rites. Its main components are expressions of moaning or wailing, a description of some disaster, and a call for others to weep and wail.[126] Obviously, the emotional mood is one of utter despair over an irreversible loss. Though dirges are absent from the Hebrew Psalter, their influence is evident on several psalms (Pss 35:13–14; 44; 74). Parts of the book of Lamentations, however, have dirges that lament not the loss of a person, but the destruction of a city and its population (see Lam 1–2, 4). Indeed, the book may reflect an ancient custom of mourning the loss of a city.[127]

Recognition of the Bible's dirges is beneficial in several ways. First, it enables the interpreter to read the text with a specific scenario in mind: wailing mourners bitterly rending their clothes or donning sackcloth. Second, it underscores the hopelessness of the situation the text describes. Death remains a tragedy with no conceivable human remedy. The reader, thus, must sense the emotional despair in Lamentations, even though the author's appeal to God for rescue does offer hope (cf. 1 Thes 4:13). Third, it legitimizes the expression of human grief among Christians today. By honoring grief practices of old, the Bible stamps them as "normal" for God's people who suffer similar losses today.[128]

Songs

The singing of songs—especially those sung in worship at the temple—played a prominent role in the life of God's people. Apparently, even Israel's neighbors highly valued her musical expertise, for the Assyrian king Sennacherib proudly listed male and female musicians among the items of tribute given to him by king Hezekiah of Jerusalem (eighth century BC).[129]

The *thanksgiving song* (Heb. *todah*) is closely associated with the protest. Through such songs, the individual or community voiced joyful gratitude to God for deliverance from previous misery. They, as it were, made good on their previous promises of thanks.[130] Significantly, speakers directly address their remarks both to Yahweh and to others participating in the ceremony.

Psalm 30 illustrates the two elements at the heart of this song: the praise of Yahweh

---

126. Gerstenberger, *Psalms 1*, 10–11. For the best examples, see our comments about genres embedded in OT narratives (pp. 433–38).

127. See P. Michalowski, ed., *The Lamentation over the Destruction of Sumer and Ur*, Mesopotamian Civilizations 1 (Winona Lake: Eisenbrauns, 1989); *ANET* 455–63; Matthews and Benjamin, *Old Testament Parallels*, 247–55. For a discussion of the relationship between Sumerian antecedents and Lamentations, see Walton, *Ancient Israelite Literature in Its Cultural Context*, 160–63. Recent larger treatments of Lamentations are available in K. M. O'Connor, *Lamentations and the Tears of the World* (Maryknoll, NY: Orbis, 2002); and T. Linafelt, *Surviving Lamentations: Catastrophe, Lament, and Protest in the Afterlife of a Biblical Book* (Chicago: University of Chicago Press, 2000).

128. Dombkowski Hopkins (*Journey through the Psalms*, 105–32) offers an insightful, pastoral treatment of the process of lament with examples of ways in which congregations might incorporate it in worship today.

129. See the Prism of Sennacherib, *ANET*, 287–88. Further, Ps 137:3 ("Sing us one of the songs of Zion!") may imply that the Babylonians found Israelite music appealing, just as many people find delight in modern Hebrew music.

130. Bellinger, Jr., *Psalms: A Guide to Studying the Psalter*, 79–110; Murphy, *The Gift of the Psalms*, 10–11; Dombkowski Hopkins, *Journey Through the Psalms*, 133–40, who also cites Ps 30 as an example; cf. Gunkel, *Psalms,*

for his help (vv. 1, 12b) and the invitation for others to join in thanking and praising Yahweh (vv. 4–5). A third key element is an account of salvation that reports what Yahweh has done to merit praise (vv. 2–3, 6–12a). As with protests, when the king either speaks or is spoken of, we designate such a text as a *royal thanksgiving song* (see Pss 18; 21).

The *hymn* (or song of praise) closely resembles the thanksgiving song and comprises a major genre in the Psalter. Originally part of a large, colorful Israelite festivity, a hymn is a song that praises Yahweh.[131] (For hymns in the prophets and Job, see below.) Psalm 96 exemplifies the two main structural components of a hymn: the summons to praise, addressed to other worshipers and probably sung by a song leader or choir (vv. 1–3; cf. vv. 7–13); and the actual praise of Yahweh (vv. 4–6).[132] In some cases, an individual offers praise for some personal experience of Yahweh's greatness, so we call that a *personal hymn* (see Pss 8; 77; 103–104; 139; et al.).[133]

Brueggemann helpfully distinguishes two types of praise.[134] "Declarative praise" underscores God's actions on behalf of Israel or an individual. It cites concrete reasons for praise—something great done by God in the past that Israelite traditions remember—and often connects the psalm's present context with Israel's experience of liberation and receipt of divine mercy. In reality, such praise issues in thanksgiving, hence bridging the hymn and thanksgiving genres. "Descriptive praise," by contrast, features general summons to laud God for his character qualities—e.g., majesty, sovereignty, holiness, creativity, etc. Its focus falls exclusively on praise without directly voicing thanksgiving. Awareness of this distinction enables readers to tune in more closely to the unique world of each psalm-type.

Several other hymns were limited to ceremonies that either involved the king or celebrated the uniqueness of Jerusalem. Indeed, for that very reason, many scholars have called them "royal psalms" (occasionally, "messianic psalms"). For example, Psalms 2 and 110 (and possibly 72) are *coronation hymns* sung or read during ceremonies at the accession of a new king to power (see 2 Kgs 11:4–12).[135] A *Zion hymn*

199–221. According to Gerstenberger (*Psalms, Part 1*, 15) the offertory formula "I give you thanks" means "I am handing over to you my thank offering" (Pss 118:21; 138:1–2; cf. Isa 12:1).

131. Cf. Murphy, *The Gift of the Psalms*, 9–10; Dombkowski Hopkins, *Journey Through the Psalms*, 32–58; Gunkel, *Psalms*, 22–65. According to the book of Chronicles, families of temple singers, not the congregation, sang such hymns (1 Chr 15:16–22; 16:5–7; 2 Chr 5:12).

132. For other examples of hymns, see Pss 8; 19; 65; 66; 67; 68; 95; 96; 100; 104; 105; et al. According to Wolters, Proverbs 31's many hymnic characteristics commend it as a heroic hymn; cf. A. Wolters, "Proverbs 31:10–31 as Heroic Hymn: A Form-critical Analysis," in *Poetry in the Hebrew Bible: Selected Studies from Vetus Testamentum*, ed. D. E. Orton (Leiden/Boston: E. J. Brill, 2000), 186–97.

133. Hymns were also common elsewhere in the ANE; cf. J. L Foster (translator) and S. T. Hollis (editor), *Hymns, Prayers, and Songs: An Anthology of Ancient Egyptian Lyric Poetry*, WAW 8 (Atlanta: Scholars, 1995); Matthews and Benjamin, *Old Testament Parallels*, 153–56.

134. W. Brueggemann, *Israel's Praise: Doxology Against Idolatry and Ideology* (Minneapolis: Augsburg Fortress Publishers, 1988), 89–122. Brueggemann associates each type of praise with unique world views and ideologies.

135. For discussion, see Starbuck, *Court Oracles in the Psalms*, 122–68; Gunkel, *Psalms*, 99–120. Cf also G. H. Wilson, "King, Messiah, and the Reign of God: Revisiting the Royal Psalms and the Shape of the Psalter," in *The Book of Psalms: Composition and Reception*, ed. P. W. Flint and P. D. Miller, Jr., VTSup 99 (Leiden; Boston: Brill, 2005), 391–406.

is one that praises Mount Zion as the residence of Yahweh, the main site of Israelite worship, and Jerusalem as a royal city (see Pss 46; 48; 76; 84; 122; 132). Presumably, on various festive occasions Israel commemorated such divinely sanctioned truths about Jerusalem. Also at home in such liturgical festivities was the *Yahweh-kingship hymn* that extols his supreme rulership as well as his association with the Davidic dynasty (Pss 47; 93; 96–99).[136]

Finally, the OT contains a few *love songs*. For example, Psalm 45 is a royal *wedding song* that was probably sung at royal marriage ceremonies.[137] Verse 2 eulogizes the king's beauty (cf. 1 Sam 9:2; 16:12) while vv. 10–12 address the bride. Recognition of this genre enables the reader to understand references to the ceremony's participants and proceedings (vv. 9, 14, 15). The reader can imagine a splendid scene—one not unlike modern royal weddings—repeated over the centuries when monarchs ruled Israel. More important, it helps the reader learn something of the behavior and policy God expected of those rulers.

The Song of Songs offers the Bible's best-known love songs.[138] Though its origin is a matter of dispute, the book probably is a collection of love poetry some of which may have been used at weddings (see 3:6–11). Recognizing this aspect of the literary style enhances proper interpretation. It allows the book to be read as an anthology of poems united around common themes, not as a narrative or drama with plot and development. It also allows the interpreter to take the book's eroticism with full seriousness—as glorification of human sexual love within the context of marriage.[139]

Liturgies

Israel worshiped together as a community in the temple in Jerusalem and undoubtedly used *liturgy* on such occasions. A liturgy is a text used in worship in which two or more speakers participate in response to each other. The most common speakers include priests as worship leaders and the whole congregation speaking as "we" or "us." Less frequently, individual lay persons speak as "I" and prophets give messages from Yahweh.

---

136. Cf. Ryken, *How to Read*, 117, who uses the term "Worship psalms" for "Zion songs." What we call "Yahweh-kingship-hymns," Gunkel (*Psalms*, 66–81) and Dombkowski Hopkins (*Journey Through the Psalms*, 140–47) designate as "enthronement psalms." For the larger theme, see M. Z. Brettler, *God is King: Understanding an Israelite Metaphor*, JSOTSup 76 (Sheffield: JSOT, 1989).

137. Starbuck, *Court Oracles in the Psalms*, 114 ("written for a royal wedding, but its historical specificities have been leveled without a trace"); Gerstenberger, *Psalms, Part 1*, 186–90, with additional bibliography and discussion of alternate views.

138. Song of Songs renders the book's Hebrew title (lit., "the best song"; cf. "Song of Solomon" in many older Bible versions). For recent treatments, see I. M. Duguid, *The Song of Songs: An Introduction and Commentary*, TOTC (Downers Grove: InterVarsity, 2015); R. S. Hess, *Song of Songs*, BCOTWP (Grand Rapids: Baker Academic, 2005); and T. Longman, III, *Song of Songs*, NICOT (Grand Rapids: Eerdmans, 2001). For extrabiblical parallels, see W. G. E. Watson, "Some Ancient Near Eastern Parallels to the Song of Songs," in *Words Remembered, Texts Renewed: Essays in Honour of John F. A. Sawyer*, ed. J. Davies, G. Harvey, and W. G. E. Watson (Sheffield: Sheffield Academic, 1995), 253–71; M. V. Fox, *The Song of Songs and the Ancient Egyptian Love Songs* (Madison, WI: University of Wisconsin Press, 1985).

139. Cf. C. E. Walsh, *Exquisite Desire: Religion, the Erotic, and the Song of Songs* (Minneapolis: Fortress, 2000), who explores the erotic aspects of the OT and how they relate to Israel's experience of God. For a topical treatment, see T. Gledhill, *The Message of the Song of Songs*, BST (Downers Grove: InterVarsity, 1994).

For instance, observe the different participants evident in the following excerpt from Psalm 118, a "thanksgiving liturgy" that celebrates a great national victory:[140]

Call to praise (*priests*)	Give thanks to the LORD, for he is good; his love endures forever. Let Israel say:
Response (*congregation*)	"His love endures forever . . ."
Call (*priests*)	Let the house of Aaron say:
Response (*congregation*)	"His love endures forever . . ."
Testimony (*an individual*)	In my anguish I cried to the LORD, and he answered by setting me free. All the nations surrounded me, but in the name of the LORD I cut them off.
Petition/Thanks (*congregation*)	O LORD, save us; O LORD, grant us success. The LORD is God, and he has made his light shine upon us.
Thanksgiving (*an individual*)	You are my God, and I will give you thanks; you are my God, and I will exalt you.
Call to praise (*priests*)	Give thanks to the LORD, for he is good; his love endures forever. (Ps 118:1–3, 5, 10, 25–26, 28–29; cf. Pss 66; 75; 136)[141]

Wisdom Psalms

Long ago scholars recognized that certain psalms seemed to belong not to Israel's public worship life but to the private educational sphere of her wisdom teachers (see Jer 18:18).[142] Their language, style, and themes more closely resemble the books of

---

140. Cf. E. S. Gerstenberger, *Psalms, Part 2 and Lamentations*, FOTL 15 (Grand Rapids: Eerdmans, 2001), 300–8, who categorizes the psalm a "Thanksgiving of the Individual." Israel might originally have recited this liturgy during a procession that ended at the temple gate (see vv. 19–21). If so, the phrase "from the house of the LORD we bless you" (v. 26) and the reference to the "horns of the altar" (v. 27) suggest that the procession was at that point inside the temple grounds. But Gerstenberger (*Psalms, Part 2*, 307) understands the psalm's present setting to be the "exilic and postexilic thanksgiving rites within Jewish congregations of 'righteous' Yahweh believers" led by an "officiant" instead of a "priest" (301).

141. Pss 15 and 24:3–6 may reflect an ancient "entrance liturgy," a ceremony with a question-and-answer format performed originally at the temple gate where worshipers affirmed their readiness to enter into the sanctuary; cf. Gerstenberger, *Psalms, Part 1*, 89. The worshipers ask a series of questions that the priest answers from inside the gate with a *torah* instruction; cf. Isa 33:14–16; Mic 6:6–8. Ps 95 features a congregational processional (vv. 1–7a) followed by an exhortation (vv. 7b-11), perhaps by a prophet or priest (but cf. Gerstenberger, *Psalms, Part 2*, 182 ("Yahweh-Kingship Hymn; Sermon"); see Ps 12 with an oracle of salvation in vv. 5–6 and the sermon in Ps 50:7–23.

142. Bellinger, Jr., *Psalms: A Guide to Studying the Psalter*, 129–40; Gerstenberger, *Psalms, Part 1*, 19–21. Concerning the "wisdom school" and its literature, see J. L. Crenshaw, *Old Testament Wisdom: An Introduction*, rev. ed. (Louisville: Westminster John Knox, 2010); K. Dell, "Wisdom in Israel," in *Text in Context*, ed. A. D. H. Mayes (New York; Oxford: Oxford University Press, 2000), 348–75; B. K. Waltke and D. Diewert, "Wisdom Literature," in *The Face of OT Studies*, ed. D. W. Baker and B. T. Arnold (Grand Rapids: Baker; Leicester: InterVarsity, 1999), 295–332. Cf. the series of articles in *DOTWPW*, 842–84.

Proverbs and Ecclesiastes than the Psalter's woeful protests and joyous thanksgivings. More meditative in mood and didactic in intention, they focus on ethical issues such as the justice of human suffering and God's apparent injustice in tolerating it. Theologically, their interest lies more in God as creator and cosmic ruler than as Israel's redeemer and lord.

Hence, we call such psalms *wisdom psalms*. Uncertainty over what literary elements constitute such a genre, however, has produced scholarly disagreement as to which psalms fit it. The strongest case can be made for Psalms 1, 19, 33, 39, 49, 127.[143] Psalm 1, for example, shows the common wisdom theme of the contrasting fates of the wicked and the righteous.[144] The comparison of the righteous to a tree planted by flowing streams also has a parallel in Egyptian wisdom literature, which suggests that it is a common wisdom motif. When the psalmist beholds God's glory in the heavens (Ps 19), he reflects wisdom's love of creation and its empirical approach to discovering truth. By including a lengthy section of instruction (vv. 12–19), Psalm 33 betrays the priority of wisdom, which is to teach a God-pleasing lifestyle, and Psalm 127 sounds like Ecclesiastes when it stresses the vanity of human efforts.

Principles of Interpretation—Poetry

From this survey of poetic genres we suggest the following interpretive principles:

1. Poems originated as complete units, so the student should interpret them in their entirety rather than as isolated verses. They should be read as poetry skillfully crafted by poets who "speak" by creating images in our imagination and by evoking emotional responses.[145]

2. Similarly, we should keep an eye out for hyperboles, especially in love songs ("there is no flaw in you," Song 4:7), as language exaggerated for effect rather than literal application. Interpretation must reckon with them accordingly.

3. The student must take into account the structure of a poem, its genre, and the development of its thought. To do so, the student will need to determine its major sections, the main point each makes, and the contribution of each to

---

143. Cf. the "Index of Form-Critical Categorizations" in *Interpreting the Psalms*, ed. Johnston and Firth, 295–300. Wisdom influence has also been suggested in Pss 32:8–9; 94:8–11; and possibly 104:13–18. To our list Murphy would add Pss 32, 34, 37, 112, and 128 and affirm "wisdom influence" in Pss 25:8–10, 12–14; 31:24–25; 39:5–7; 40:5–6; 62:9–11; 92:7–9; 94:8–15; cf. R. Murphy, "A Consideration of the Classification of 'Wisdom Psalms,'" in *Congress Volume. Bonn, 1962*, VTSup 9 (Leiden: Brill, 1962), 156–67 (reprinted in *Studies in Ancient Israelite Wisdom*, ed. J. L. Crenshaw [New York: KTAV, 1976, 456–67). For additional discussion of background and of several illustrative psalms, see Dombkowski Hopkins, *Journey through the Psalms*, 59–76.

144. Cf. recently, I. Saint Brianchaninov, "'Blessed is the Man': A Commentary on Psalm 1," *The Orthodox Word* 50 (2014): 185–96; M. J. Whiting, "Psalms 1 and 2 as a Hermeneutical Lens for Reading the Psalter," *EvQ* 85 (2013): 246–62.

145. To understand their poetry, see our chapter on biblical poetry. For the relationship between poetic imagery and theology, see W. P. Brown, *Seeing the Psalms: A Theology of Metaphor* (Louisville: Westminster John Knox, 2002). For how the psalms assess and imagine life and politics, see W. Brueggemann, *Israel's Praise*; and W. Brueggemann, *The Message of the Psalms: A Theological Commentary*, Augsburg Old Testament Studies (Minneapolis: Augsburg, 1984).

the message of the whole. (For an example on how to do this, see our earlier discussion of the nature of poetry.)

4. Application must conform to the situation behind each genre and its usual purpose, especially whether communal or individual. In other words, apply corporate lamentations to the Christian community and individual ones to the Christian individual. Song of Songs 8:6–7 affirms how incredibly powerful love is—unquenchable, unmovable, and priceless. Some readers might think it describes God's love for his people, but actually its theme is how strong human love is. That theme challenges individual readers to rejoice in love's joys through thick and thin and to maintain good relationships with spouses and friends. As for texts involving leaders (e.g., kings, priests, prophets, etc.), they are best applied to leaders in the Christian community. In general, we advise the student to resist the temptation to draw quick devotional applications that risk violating the text and its context. Instead, first, pause over the scripture, asking "Given the context, what is this writer trying to say?" The answer to that question points the reader in the right direction to answer the second question, "What does this text say to me?"

Principles of Interpretation—Psalms

Recent scholarship suggests that we may read the Psalter as an actual "book" comparable to other biblical books rather than just as a miscellaneous, loose collection. Structurally, it comprises Books I–V, within which are incorporated collections of psalms (e.g., the Songs of Ascent [Pss 120–134]). The chart below supplies a big picture of the book's contents, and we commend its use in implementing our suggested principles of interpretation.

The Books of the Psalms: An Overview[146]

1. In cases where a psalm's genre and original historical context are clearly identifiable (e.g., the Temple, royal palace, sites around Jerusalem, the Babylonian exile, postexilic Judah), we recommend interpreting and applying it in line with that context.

2. In all other cases, the student should accept the Book within the Psalter as a psalm's "same book context" and the psalms that immediately surround it as its immediate context. Use the chart below to determine the given Book's main themes and the historical era with which its themes compare.

3. Compare it to psalms of the same genre but also with psalms of other genres that share common themes with it. Indeed, the latter psalms may actually have more in common with it for purposes of interpretation than psalms of

---

146. The chart gleans from data from deClaissé-Walford, Jacobson, and LaNeel Tanner, *Psalms*, 26–28, 38, 55–57, 393–99, 581–84, 674, 685–91, 809–11. But their integration into it is our own.

Book	First Psalm Genre	Final Psalm Genre	Principal Genres	Historical Era	Davidic Title	Themes
Book I Psalms 1–41	Thematic Introduction (1) Royal Psalm (seam) (2)	Thanksgiving Song	Protests (59%) Praise Hymns (20%) Others (21%)	Reigns of David and Solomon	95%	God's Torah God's Anointed King God's Goodness vs. Present Suffering
Book II Psalms 42–72	Protest	Royal Psalm (seam) Doxology Ending	Protests (65%) Praise Hymns (19%) Others (16%)	Reigns of David and Solomon	58%	David: Man of Turmoil David: Man of Faith Celebration of His Reign
Book III Psalms 73–89	Royal Reflection: From Faith to Doubt to New Faith	Protest (Royal Psalm as seam) Doxology Ending	Protests (47%) Praise Hymns (35%) Others (18%)	Divided Kingdoms & Their Destructions	6%	Community in Crisis Echoes of Exodus to Settlement Theodicy
Book IV Psalms 90–106	Community Cry for Help	Praise Hymn	Protests (24%) Praise Hymns (29%) Others (47%)	The Babylonian Exile	12%	Faith, Identity Review God With Israel Anywhere God as Cosmic King The Present as New Wilderness Israel (not King) as Responsible Hope via Echoes of Moses, the Wilderness
Book V Psalms 107–150	Community Praise Hymn	Praise Hymn Doxology Ending	Protests (23%) Praise Hymns (52%) Others (25%) Thematic Conclusion	The Return Post-Exile	32%	David's Reprise Praise of God's Sovereignty Faith Restoration Torah as Anchor Renewed Trust in Yahweh

the same genre. In no case is the student to presume that psalms of the same genre have the same author.

4. Contemporary use should coincide with the poem's original purpose, occasion, and speakers. So, the student should reserve wedding songs for weddings and protests for times of extreme hardship. Similarly, communal poems are best used in corporate worship or in small groups. (Of course it is permissible to appropriate principles and lessons from them that may apply to individuals, say, in private worship, while recognizing the distinction.)

5. In public contexts, we also advise that psalms that feature several speakers be read with the equivalent number and type of speakers. Also, we highly commend the creative use of the processions and rituals implied by some texts as a way to visualize them and, thus, enrich a worship service.[147]

6. Individual protest psalms speak to situations of individual suffering and may be applied accordingly. Royal psalms relate best to the modern counterparts of Israel's kings: the leaders of the Christian community. At least initially, the student should be wary of extracting instant devotional applications rather than pausing, first, to ponder seriously the text within its original context.

7. Interpret corporately any psalms spoken by the community (communal protests, liturgies, songs, etc.). They voice the petitions and praise of Israel as a nation, not those of an individual Israelite. Their equivalent today is the Christian community.

8. Be advised that "by David" probably means "in David's honor" or "in David's spirit" and, hence, affirms David as Israel's Poet-Par-Excellence, but not that David is the author of every psalm that mentions his name. Be aware also that the historical allusions to David's life represent interpretations by later scribes rather than by the psalm's original author.

9. "Enemies" figure prominently in the psalms, and their modern equivalents might be opponents of the gospel, inner hurts or burdens that weigh us down, or struggles that retard our spiritual growth.

10. Christians believe that Christ is the new David who fulfills the latter's kingship. Thus, we may apply the royal psalms typologically to the kingly role that the NT recognizes in Jesus as Lord. The OT kings, thus, serve as types that anticipate the reign of their greatest Descendant. Secondarily, and more tentatively, we might also apply appropriate principles of leadership from the royal psalms to church leaders today while recognizing, we insist, the crucial inherent differences between ancient monarchs and church leaders.

---

147. Excellent resources are available to foster the use of the psalms in private and corporate worship; e.g., J. D. Witvliet, *The Biblical Psalms in Christian Worship: A Brief Introduction and Guide to Resources*, Calvin Institute of Christian Worship Liturgical Studies (Grand Rapids: Eerdmans, 2007); S. B. Reid, ed., *Psalms and Practice: Worship, Virtue, and Authority* (Collegeville, MN: Liturgical Press, 2001); and N. T. Wright, *The Case for the Psalms: Why They Are Essential* (New York: HarperOne, 2013).

PROPHECY

When Israel grievously strayed into idolatry, God sent prophets to announce his plans for his people. Though their proclamation often produced "foretelling" (i.e., predictions about the future), its main staple was "forthtelling" (i.e., announcements of imminent divine judgment in the present or near future). Today we read their proclamations in the books of the OT prophets, the written record of their words and deeds, a record that reflects the great rhetorical and literary creativity of both the prophets themselves and the disciples who compiled them.

Thus, to understand the prophets will require us to reckon both with the completed books that bear their names—what we today call their "final shape"—as well as with individual passages of various genres—narratives and poetry—to determine *what* they say, *how* they say it, and *why* they say it that way.[148] We will need to apply insights gained in the earlier chapters on prose and poetry. What follows surveys the major individual genres of prophecy as defined by form criticism. Our approach, however, accepts the literary fact that we access the prophets only through the present biblical books bearing their names, books probably edited by others.[149] We also concede that, because editorial activity stands between us and the actual prophets and their words, our interpretations are more tentative and humble than would be the case had we more direct sources (if that were possible).

But the phenomenon of inner-biblical allusion introduced in chapter 2 empowers us to speak historically about the prophets and their words. It suggests that they and their proclamations made it into our Bibles because the Israelite community had recognized their authority long ago. Among later scribes, the national disasters of 722 and 587 BC quickly confirmed which prophets got it right and which did not. So, they copied and compiled the words of the former, adding occasional biographical narratives. That recognition of authority is why our Bibles have the Book of Jeremiah but no "Book of Hananiah" (Jer 28).

Thus, notwithstanding the complexity introduced by subsequent editorial work, we affirm that, just as the Gospels convey the *ipsissima vox* ("the very voice") of Jesus, so the prophetic books still convey "the very voice" of the prophets. We, thus, will first sample some major prophetic genres and subgenres—what Sweeney calls "prophetic speech"[150]—and later incorporate the literary genre "prophetic book" in our suggested principles of interpretation.

---

148. Three useful introductions to prophecy are H. C. P. Kim and L. Stulman, *You Are My People: An Introduction to Prophetic Literature* (Nashville: Abingdon Press, 2010); P. L. Redditt, *Introduction to the Prophets* (Grand Rapids: Eerdmans, 2008); D. B. Sandy, *Plowshares and Pruning Hooks: Rethinking the Language of Biblical Prophecy and Apocalyptic* (Downers Grove: InterVarsity, 2002). For further discussion of the interpretive issues surrounding prophetic books and the original words of prophets, see conveniently Sweeney, "Prophetic Literature," 10–15 and (concerning the "book" genre) 16–18.

149. Here we acknowledge our debt to rhetorical and canonical criticisms, two recent methods introduced in our earlier chapter on the history of interpretation. Their unique contribution is the shift in focus of recent research to larger complexes of oracles with prophetic books, if not to the whole books themselves.

150. Sweeney, "Prophetic Literature," 22. For scholarly exploration of the transition from speaking prophets

Basic Types of Prophecy

Prophecy of Disaster	Woe Speech	Against Foreign Nations
Prophecy of Salvation	Dirge	Vision Report
Commission	Hymn	Narratives
Call to Hear	Liturgy	Apocalyptic
	Disputation	

Prophecy of Disaster

The most common genre among the prophets is the *prophecy of disaster*, an announcement of imminent or future disaster either to an individual or to an entire nation.[151] Typically, its structure includes an indication of the situation, a messenger formula ("Thus says the LORD"), and a prediction of disaster. The "indication of the situation" states the problems that occasion the message, the prediction details the disaster to come, and the messenger formula authenticates the word as coming from God.[152] A "therefore" (Heb. *laken*) commonly introduces the prediction section.

Often prophecies of disaster have other elements: at the beginning they may include a prophetic *commission* ("Go and say," etc.) and a *call to hear* ("Hear this word!" etc.); they may also give reasons for the disaster introduced by "because of this" (Heb. *al-asher*) or "for" (Heb. *ki*). An oracle given by Elijah to King Ahaziah and reported within a prophetic story (see below) offers a simple illustration of this genre:

Prophetic commission	Go up and meet the messengers of the king of Samaria and ask them,
Indication of the situation	"Is it because there is no God in Israel that you are going off to consult Baal-Zebub, the god of Ekron?"
Messenger formula	Therefore this is what the LORD says:
Prediction	"You will not leave the bed you are lying on. You will certainly die!" (2 Kgs 1:3–4; cf. Jer 28:12–14, 15–16; Mic 1:2–7)

In this example, the indication of the situation subtly suggests the reason for the disaster. By consulting Baal-Zebub instead of Yahweh, Ahaziah implied that Israel

---

to written books, see D. V. Edelman and E. Ben Zvi, eds., *The Production of Prophecy: Constructing Prophecy and Prophets in Yehud* (London; Oakville, CT: Equinox, 2009). Two websites provide excellent charts of form critical genres: http://biblical-studies.ca/pdfs/Guide_to_Prophetic_Forms.pdf (a handy summary of Sweeney's list) and http://people.bethel.edu/~pferris/ot103/pdfs/ProphetSpeechChart.pdf.

151. Sweeney, "Prophetic Literature," 23–24, who prefers the term "prophetic judgment speech" and who distinguishes (23–25) other subgenres of "prophetic announcement"; cf. also the classic study of C. Westermann, *Basic Forms of Prophetic Speech* (Louisville: Westminster John Knox, 1991); and the review of Westermann in B. T. Arnold, "Forms of Prophetic Speech in the Old Testament: A Summary of Claus Westermann's Contributions," *AsTJ* 27 (1995): 30–35, 39.

152. The messenger formula was the standard phrase that identified the source of a message given by a messenger on behalf of someone (Gen 32:4; Exod 5:10; Judg 11:15; 1 Kgs 2:30; et al.). It carried the same authority that a signature or official stamp does today.

had no god or at least that Yahweh was unable to heal his injury. The prediction announces that Ahaziah would pay for that insult with his life. Many prophecies of disaster, however, are structurally more complex than this simple example. Most lack the prophetic commission, while many have other elements: descriptions, commands to invading armies to attack, calls for their victims to mourn, etc. Also, most disaster prophecies are longer, and the order of their component parts may vary considerably.

Nevertheless, the careful student, familiar with the form's essential elements, will clearly recognize the additional elements and varying structure. The important thing is to determine (a) the disaster announced and (b) the reason(s) for it. Notice, for example, the similarities and variations in the following example:

Messenger formula	This is what the Sovereign LORD, the Holy One of Israel, says:
Indication of the situation	"In repentance and rest is your salvation, in quietness and trust is your strength, but you would have none of it.
Prediction	You said, 'No, we will flee on horses.' Therefore you will flee! You said, 'We will ride off on swift horses.' Therefore your pursuers will be swift! A thousand will flee at the threat of one; at the threat of five you will all flee away, till you are left like a flagstaff on a mountaintop, like a banner on a hill." (Isa 30:15–17)

Unlike the earlier example, here the indication of the situation comes between the messenger formula and the prediction. Also, compare the twofold repetition of the "therefore" to its single use in the first example. Note also how the prophet cleverly quotes statements of those addressed and rebuts them through his announcement. Again, the key is to find the prediction and the indications of the situation, and to observe other significant elements.

Prophecy of Salvation

Prophets also announced restoration for individuals and nations. So the prophecy of disaster has a positive counterpart—to announce hope for the future. In structure, the *prophecy of salvation* resembles the disaster prophecy, but its content is as positive as the latter's is negative.[153] A prophetic narrative in Jeremiah 28 provides a simple example of this form given by the prophet Hananiah who showed "good form" but bogus content.

---

153. Sweeney, "Prophetic Literature," 25–27 ("prophecy of salvation") with various subgenres. Cf. the classic study of this genre by C. Westermann, *Prophetic Oracles of Salvation in the Old Testament*, trans. K. Crim (Louisville: Westminster John Knox, 1991) and the assessment of Westermann in Arnold, "Forms of Prophetic Speech," 35–39.

Messenger formula	This is what the LORD Almighty, the God of Israel, says:
Prediction: Basic statement	"I will break the yoke of the king of Babylon.
Amplification	Within two years I will bring back to this place all the articles of the LORD's house that Nebuchadnezzar king of Babylon removed from here and took to Babylon. I will also bring back to this place Jehoiachin son of Jehoiakim king of Judah and all the other exiles from Judah who went to Babylon," declares the LORD,
Emphatic restatement	"for I will break the yoke of the king of Babylon." (Jer 28:2–4; cf. Isa 2:1–5; Amos 9:11–15 etc.)

As indicated, the structure exactly parallels that of the prophecy of disaster. Similarly, the salvation prophecy may include additional elements, may continue for great length, and may show a variable order of components. As was true of the negative counterpart, the basic goal is to identify the future hope announced, in this case, the return of Judah's king and the temple's articles from Babylon.

Woe Speech

The prophets also announced doom through the *woe speech*.[154] Its distinguishing feature is the opening interjection "Woe to those who/you who . . ." followed by participles describing those addressed. The description details the evil deeds that make them worthy of woe. The woe speech concludes with a prediction of divine punishment, usually without the "therefore, thus says the LORD" introductory formula.

The form's opening interjection (Heb. *hoy*; "woe!") and description have raised the question about where it originated in Israelite society. Did the prophets invent it or borrow some pre-existing form? Probably, the woe speech represents the prophets' adaptation of the ancient funeral lament.[155] But these speeches are more than just ordinary laments for the dead. Rather, they resemble the laments for murder victims in which the laments condemn the killers for the outrage. If so, one must hear the woe speeches as expressions of prophetic outrage at the sinful behavior they condemn.

In the following example of the woe speech, notice the opening interjection, the description of the doomed addressees and their crimes, and the disaster predicted (our translation):

154. Sweeney, "Prophetic Literature," 28 (with bibliography); cf. Westermann, *Basic Forms*, 190–94. Cf. W. A. M. Beuken, "Woe to Powers in Israel That Vie to Replace YHWH's Rule on Mount Zion! Isaiah Chapters 28–31 from the Perspective of Isaiah Chapters 24–27," in *Isaiah in Context: Studies in Honour of Arie van der Kooij on the Occasion of His Sixty-Fifth Birthday*, ed. M. N. van der Meer, et al., VTSup 138 (Leiden; Boston: Brill, 2010), 25–43. The classic study remains W. Janzen, *Mourning Cry and Woe Oracle*, BZAW 125 (Berlin: deGruyter, 1972). For examples, see Amos 5:18–20; 6:1–7; Isa 5:8–10, 11–14, 18–19, 20, 21, 22–25; 10:1–3; 28:1–4; 29:1–4, 15; 30:1–5; 31:1–5.

155. Janzen, *Mourning Cry*; G. M. Tucker, "Prophecy and the Prophetic Literature," in Knight and Tucker, *Hebrew Bible*, 340; contra Westermann, *Basic Forms*, 194–99 (woes derived from ceremonies of curses against enemies). Alternatively, the woe may mark the negative counterpart of the blessing saying ("Happy is the person who . . ."); cf. E. Gerstenberger, "The Woe-Oracles of the Prophets," *JBL* 81 (1962): 249–63; and J. W. Whedbee, *Isaiah and Wisdom* (Nashville: Abingdon, 1971), 80–110.

Declaration of woe	Woe to those who plan iniquity, those who plot evil on their beds!
Explanation: offenses Basic statement	At morning's light they carry it out because it is in their power to do it.
Amplification	They covet fields and take them, and houses, and take them away. They defraud people of their homes, they rob them of their inheritance.
Messenger formula	Therefore, the LORD says:
Prediction	"I am planning disaster against this people, from which you cannot save yourselves. You will no longer walk proudly, for it will be a time of calamity. In that day people will ridicule you; they will taunt you with this mournful song: 'We are utterly ruined; my people's possession is divided up. He takes it from me! He assigns our fields to traitors.' Therefore you will have no one in the assembly of the LORD to divide the land by lot." (Mic 2:1–5)

Given this genre's likely cultural background, the opening "Woe!" might imply that Micah mourns the people he has in mind. But his sharp indictment of their greedy schemes quickly dispels any impression of sympathy. In fact, according to his prediction, the opposite lies in store after disaster strikes: yes, people will sing them a "mournful song"—but in ridicule, faking phony lamentation as a gleeful taunt whose true message is "Good riddance!" The genre's literary effect is to underscore the judgment as a "done deal" and (by sarcasm) to undercut audience sympathy.

Prophetic Dirge

Along similar lines, the prophets occasionally recited a *dirge* or funeral lament over Israel (for this form, see above under poetry).[156] They addressed the nation as if she were a corpse ready for burial. In other words, the literary effect of using the dirge here is to portray her awful future as a *fait accompli*. Amos provides a sample of these potent passages:

Call to hear	Hear this word, Israel, this lament I take up concerning you:
The Dirge	"Fallen is Virgin Israel, never to rise again, deserted in her own land, with no one to lift her up."

---

156. Cf. Sweeney, "Prophetic Literature," 518–19.

Messenger formula	This is what the Sovereign LORD says to Israel:
Prediction	"Your city that marches out a thousand strong will have only a hundred left; your town that marches out a hundred strong will have only ten left." (Amos 5:1–3; cf. Isa 14:4–23; Ezek 19:1–14; 26:17–18; 27:1–36)

Amos sees Israel as a tragic figure, a virgin who dies unmarried and alone. The prediction says that forces defending Israel will suffer ninety percent casualties. Through the dirge Amos speaks as if this had already happened. What a powerful way to announce the certainty and horror of Israel's imminent national demise!

Prophetic Hymn

Occasionally, the prophets used genres drawn from Israel's worship practices. Examples of the *hymn* appear occasionally in the prophetic books (for hymns, see above under poetry; for hymns in Job, see below).[157] The following short example illustrates how Amos includes brief hymnic pieces that extol Yahweh:

> He who forms the mountains,
>> who creates the wind,
> and who reveals his thoughts to mankind,
>> who turns dawn to darkness,
> and treads on the heights of the earth—
>> the LORD God Almighty is his name! (Amos 4:13 NRSV; cf. 5:8–9; 9:5–6)

Amos ended the previous section (vv. 6–12) by announcing that Israel should "prepare to meet your God" in judgment (v. 12) since she had turned a deaf ear to Yahweh's earlier efforts to confront her. The hymnic lines quoted above give the announcement a climactic rhetorical flourish, painting a vivid picture of Yahweh's majesty to underscore the certainty of judgment.[158]

On the other hand, Isaiah used longer hymn pieces to illustrate the song of praise Israel would sing when Yahweh finally brought her exiled citizens home:

Introduction	In that day you will say:

157. Some prefer the term "doxology"; so Sweeney, "Prophetic Literature," 29, 519, 521; cf. R. W. Byargeon, "The Doxologies of Amos: A Study of Their Structure and Theology," *The Theological Educator* 52 (1995): 47–56; and the classic study of J. L. Crenshaw, *Hymnic Affirmations of Divine Justice: The Doxologies of Amos and Related Texts in the Old Testament*, SBLDS 24 (Missoula, MT: Scholars, 1975).

158. As Carroll R. points out (*Contexts for Amos*, 206–21), the irony of this imminent "meeting" with Yahweh the awesome creator is that Israel had sought to meet him and to gain his blessing at the sanctuaries of the Northern Kingdom (vv. 4–5) but had missed meeting him in the series of disasters (vv. 6–11). Cf. the importance of doxologies in concluding individual psalms and the Psalter's Books.

The hymn	"Give praise to the LORD, proclaim his name; make known among the nations what he has done, and proclaim that his name is exalted. Sing to the LORD, for he has done glorious things; let this be known to all the world. Shout aloud and sing for joy, people of Zion, for great is the Holy One of Israel among you." (Isa 12:4–6; cf. vv. 1–3; 25:1–8, 9–12; 26:1–19; 42:10–13; 49:13)

By citing a praise hymn to be sung upon return from exile, the prophet not only finds words worthy of their awesome divine subject but also taps into the joy his audience would associate with such songs. In short, after dreary exile, this will be a day for singing!

Prophetic Liturgy

The prophets also used various kinds of *liturgies* as part of their message (for liturgy, see poetry above).[159] As noted previously, a liturgy is a text used in worship in which two or more speakers participate in response to each other. Isaiah 63:7–64:12, for example, contains a lengthy, sad liturgy that asks Yahweh finally to end his angry punishment of exiled Israel. It involves two speakers: the prophet reminiscing about Yahweh's great past deeds (63:7–14) and a communal protest pleading for God's mercy (63:15–64:12).

Jeremiah 14 offers a second example of a communal protest set in a time of severe national drought. Given the background of communal protests, the text takes an unexpected turn. Normally, when Israel prayed for help during similar national disasters, she expected Yahweh to answer positively—usually through a prophet—with a prophecy of salvation. In the following excerpts, observe Israel's protest and how Yahweh answers it:

Introduction	This is the word of the LORD that came to Jeremiah concerning the drought:
Description	"Judah mourns, her cities languish; they wail for the land, and a cry goes up from Jerusalem. The nobles send their servants for water; they go to the cisterns but find no water. They return with their jars unfilled; dismayed and despairing, they cover their heads.

---

159. Cf. Isa 12; Joel 1–2; Habakkuk; and Nahum. Sweeney, "Prophetic Literature," 29–30, notes that prophetic liturgies "apparently reflect the cultic setting in which prophetic literature was performed and perhaps produced"; cf. S. Mowinckel, *The Psalms in Israel's Worship*, 2 vols., trans. D. R. Ap-Thomas, Biblical Resources Series (Grand Rapids: Eerdmans; Dearborn: Dove Booksellers, 2004 [repr.]), 2:53–73 ("The Prophetic Word in the Psalms and the Prophetic Psalms").

Protest	Although our sins testify against us, do something, LORD, for the sake of your name. You are among us, O LORD, and we bear your name; do not forsake us! For we have often rebelled; we have sinned against you."
Messenger formula	This is what the LORD says about this people:
Message	"They greatly love to wander; they do not restrain their feet. So the LORD does not accept them; he will now remember their wickedness and punish them for their sins." (Jer 14:1–3, 7, 10; cf. Joel 1–2)

There are two things to highlight here. First, notice Yahweh's answer: he flatly denied Israel's petition for relief. Israel expected a prophecy of salvation but received one of disaster instead. The reversal of expectation has the literary effect of heightening the shock (and the horror) of God's reply. Second, unlike Isaiah 63–64, here the liturgy and divine response serve as a prophecy of disaster. They function as an announcement ("the word of the LORD") about the drought—it will continue as Israel's punishment.

This example reinforces a point we made earlier about interpreting a genre: one must interpret both what it says by itself as well as how it functions in the context. Here the liturgy and response say that Israel prayed and Yahweh answered. Introduced by "this is the word of the Lord," it *functions* as a prophecy of disaster.

The book of Habakkuk offers another variety of liturgy, a *dialogue of protest* (for protests, see poetry above). By way of background, scholars believe that normally God answered individual protests with a prophecy of salvation promising relief from the distress. That same protest-answer structure underlies the opening section of Habakkuk (1:2–2:4) with two significant differences.

Psalmic protests have a single protest without any recorded answer from Yahweh, but Habakkuk has two protests (1:2–4; 1:12–2:1) and an answer reported for each (1:5–11; 2:2–4). For that reason we call this subgenre a dialogue of protest.[160] Jeremiah also lifted protests to God, in his case, in response to persecution for his preaching. The "confessions of Jeremiah" record his intensely personal pleas for protection from enemies and vindication of his prophetic ministry. Like Habakkuk, he received direct divine answers to his protests (Jer 11:18–23; 12:1–6; 15:10–11, 15–21).[161]

---

160. Cf. Sweeney, "Prophetic Literature," 30. The interpretive difficulty as to whether the second answer ends at 2:4 or 2:5 does not affect our point here.

161. For other confessions without divine answers, see Jer 17:14–18; 18:18–23; 20:7–13; cf. the lament in 20:14–20 and its parallel genre in Job 3. For recent discussion of the confessions, see C. Bultmann, "A Prophet in Desperation? The Confessions of Jeremiah," in *The Elusive Prophet: The Prophet as a Historical Person, Literary Character and Anonymous Artist*, ed. J. C. de Moor, OtSt 45 (Leiden: Brill, 2001), 83–93; O'Connor, *The Confessions of Jeremiah*. Cf. recent essays on the topic in E. K. Holt and C. J. Sharp, eds., *Jeremiah Invented: Constructions and Deconstructions of Jeremiah*, LHBOTS 595 (London and New York: Bloomsbury T&T Clark, 2015), 63–91.

Prophetic Disputation

Occasionally, the prophets employed a rhetorical form called the *disputation* (or "debate") that apparently originated in Israel's wisdom tradition (for its importance in Job, see below). In a disputation, the speaker tries to persuade the audience to accept the validity of some truth, at times "rational and reasoned, passionate and angry, or a combination of the two."[162] Its purpose is to facilitate the discussion of an issue from two or more perspectives. In disputes that reach some resolution (and they need not always), the genre serves to endorse that conclusion as superior to the others presented. Typical prophetic disputations have three parts: statement of the thesis under dispute, statement of the proposed counterthesis, and the actual argumentation in its favor. Disputations play a significant role in Job and comprise most of the book of Malachi, but the prophet Amos provides an apt, short illustration:

Series of Questions	Do two walk together unless they have agreed to do so? Does a lion roar in the thicket when it has no prey? Does it growl in its den when it has caught nothing? Does a bird swoop down to a trap on the ground when no bait is there? When a trumpet sounds in a city, do not the people tremble? When disaster comes to a city, has not the LORD caused it?
Conclusion	Surely the Sovereign LORD does nothing without revealing his plan to his servants the prophets.
Lesson	The lion has roared—who will not fear? The Sovereign LORD has spoken— who can but prophesy? (Amos 3:3–8; cf. 9:7)

This example highlights several features that distinguish the disputation from the prophecy of disaster. First, here the prophet himself speaks as a fellow Israelite, not in the first person as the direct voice of Yahweh. Second, the speaker does not announce new revelation; he simply argues for a point, in this case, that nothing

---

162. Cf. T. Longman III, "Disputation," *DOTWPW*, 108–12 (quote 108). The major study remains A. Graffy, *A Prophet Confronts his People*, AnBib 104 (Rome: Biblical Institute Press, 1984); but cf. also D. F. Murray, "The Rhetoric of Disputation: Re-examination of a Prophetic Genre," *JSOT* 38 (1987): 95–121. Sweeney ("Prophetic Literature," 28, 519) offers a convenient summary and list of texts.

happens without a cause. Third, disputations commonly use rhetorical questions to involve the audience and conclude with a lesson.[163]

In this case, Amos rhetorically draws his audience into discussion with three initial, non-threatening questions about daily life all with the same obvious answer ("Of course not!"). But the next two suddenly threaten the hearer with a frightening invasion sent by Yahweh, and they require an affirmative answer ("Of course!"). Now alert and anxious, the audience receives the lesson: "I [Amos] prophesy because I've heard God's voice of judgment."[164] Its guilt and spiritual blindness exposed, Israel must confront the horrible consequences before Israel's holy God in the rest of the book of Amos.

Prophecies against Foreign Nations

Many prophetic books have lengthy collections of *prophecies against foreign nations*.[165] Technically, these do not constitute a separate literary genre but employ genres of various kinds. Prominent among them is the "war oracle," a genre that probably goes back to Israel's ancient tradition of holy war where it aimed to curse her enemies.[166] This tradition taught that Yahweh, the divine warrior, went out in battle to defeat his (and Israel's) enemies (Exod 15:3; Num 10:35; Josh 10:42; etc.). Originally, God gave military leaders the go-ahead for their operations and assured them of victory through a war oracle. For example, in 1 Kgs 20:28 God spoke to Ahab during an Aramean attack against Israel:

> This is what the LORD says: "Because the Arameans think the LORD is a god of the hills and not a god of the valleys, I will deliver this vast army into your hands, and you will know that I am the LORD."

The prophets, however, press war oracles into service as prophecies of disaster against foreign nations. Their twofold purpose is to announce the enemy's defeat

---

163. For disputations in Job and its ancient Near Eastern parallels, cf. Longman III, *DOTWPW*, 108–12. For other disputations, see Isa 10:8–11; 28:23–28; Jer 2:23–28; 3:1–5; 8:1, 8–9; Mic 2:6–11; and most of the book of Malachi. Cf. also the illuminating exposition of the disputation in Isa 28 by Whedbee, *Isaiah and Wisdom*, 51–68. For the disputation in Nahum, see M. A. Sweeney, "Concerning the Structure and Generic Character of the Book of Nahum," *ZAW* 104 (1992): 364–77.

164. Literarily, the metaphor of the roaring lion connects the disputation with 1:2 and 3:12 and, thus underscores its importance for the message. Carroll R. (*Contexts for Amos*, 182–92) discusses other literary features.

165. See Amos 1–2; Isa 13–21, 23, 34; Jer 46–51; Ezek 25–32, 35, 38–39; Joel 3:1–16; Obad; et al. For recent studies, see E. K. Holt, H. C. P. Kim, and A. Mein, eds., *Concerning The Nations: Essays on the Oracles against the Nations in Isaiah, Jeremiah and Ezekiel*, LHBOTS 612 (London: Bloomsbury, 2015); for comparative study, cf. C. B. Hays, *Hidden Riches: A Sourcebook for the Comparative Study of the Hebrew Bible and the Ancient Near East* (Louisville: Westminster John Knox, 2014), 257–64; L. Lanner, *"Who Will Lament Her?" The Feminine and the Fantastic in the Book of Nahum*, LHBOTS 434 (New York: T&T Clark, 2006); D. H. Ryou, *Zephaniah's Oracles against the Nations*, BibInt 13 (Leiden: Brill, 1995).

166. Cf. Deut 20:1–4; 1 Kgs 22; D. L. Christensen, *Prophecy and War in Ancient Israel: Studies in the Oracles Against the Nations*, Bibal Monograph Series 3 (Sheffield: Sheffield Academic, 1989), 18–72, 281; Sweeney, "Prophetic Literature," 26–27. In addition, the war oracle includes the following subgenres: summons to battle, summons to flight, summons to mourn, battle curses, announcements of victory or defeat, and victory and taunt songs (cf. Christensen, *Prophecy and War*, 15). T. Longman III and D. G. Reid, *God Is a Warrior* (Grand Rapids: Zondervan, 1995) conveniently survey the biblical tradition of Yahweh war.

and to reassure Israel that God protects her security. After observing the presence of war oracle motifs in a text, the student must determine how the prophet is using them.

For example, the war oracle in Zechariah 9:1–8 announces doom for Israel's historic enemies. In succession, the prophet describes awful destruction for Damascus, Tyre, and the Philistine cities (vv. 1–7). It concludes, however, with a promise concerning Jerusalem (v. 8):

> But I will encamp at my temple
> > to guard it against marauding forces.
> Never again will an oppressor overrun my people,
> > for now I am keeping watch.

The defeat of her enemies frees Jerusalem from threats, and God's promise of protection guarantees her security. Here the function of the war oracle is to reassure Jerusalem of a secure future. That, in turn, lays the groundwork for the following prophecy (vv. 9–13) about the advent of a great king. It ultimately functions, however, to support the appeal for exiled Judeans to return (v. 12). In sum, the war oracle reassures them that a God-given peace has replaced Jerusalem's violent past so they may come home without fear.[167]

Prophetic Vision Report

OT prophets were also known as "seers," probably because they sometimes saw visions (1 Sam 9:9; Amos 1:1; 7:12; Mic 3:6–7; cf. Num 23–24). Thus, some prophetic books include *prophetic vision reports*.[168] These are autobiographical reports of things the prophet saw or heard in a vision that convey God's message. The following features make this genre readily recognizable: the words "see" or "made to see" (Heb. *raah*, qal and hiph., respectively) and the phrase "and behold" (*wehinneh*) followed by a description of the vision.

Based on variations in content and style, we can distinguish three types of vision reports. The "oracle-vision" features a question-and-answer dialogue between Yahweh and the prophet about something the latter sees that provides the occasion for an oracle. For example, Jeremiah's glimpse of two baskets of figs—one with good figs, the other with bad ones—becomes the occasion for God to contrast the good and bad future fates, respectively, of Israelites exiled in Babylon and those surviving in Jerusalem (Jer 24; cf. 1:11–14; Amos 7:7–8; 8:1–2; Zech 5:1–4; Gen 15). The "dramatic

---

167. To good rhetorical effect, the prophets occasionally turn this genre against Israel or Judah, addressing them among doomed nations (see Amos 1–2; Isa 13–23).

168. Sweeney, "Prophetic Literature," 18–19; cf. B. O. Long, *1 Kings*, 263-64. For recent in-depth studies, see L.-S. Tiemeyer, *Zechariah and His Visions: An Exegetical Study of Zechariah's Vision Report*, LHBOTS 626 (London and New York: Bloomsbury T&T Clark, 2015); and E. R. Hayes and L.-S. Tiemeyer, eds., *'I Lifted My Eyes and Saw': Reading Dream and Vision Reports in the Hebrew Bible*, LHBOTS 584 (London and New York: Bloomsbury T&T Clark, 2014).

word vision" depicts a scene in heaven that portends some future event on earth that the prophet presumably is to announce. It closely resembles the vocation reports (on which see below) of Isaiah (Isa 6) and Ezekiel (Ezek 1–3).

For example, the Lord showed Amos the locusts and fiery disaster he was preparing for Israel's imminent judgment (Amos 7:1–6; cf. 1 Kgs 22:17–22; Jer 38:21–22). In the "revelatory-mystery vision," an angelic guide dialogues with the prophet about the bizarre symbolic imagery he sees. The purpose of the conversation is to reveal the veiled secrets of God's future plans. So Zechariah conversed with an angel about his vision of a man with a measuring line and learned about plans for Jerusalem to be rebuilt (Zech 2:1–4; cf. 4:1–6; Dan 8; 10–12).

Prophetic Narratives

Two narrative literary types commonly appear in the prophetic books. Best known, the *vocation reports* narrate the personal experience by which God called and commissioned someone as a prophet (Isa 6; Jer 1; Ezek 1–3; cf. Amos 7:14–15; Hos 1:2).[169] Structurally, they share the following features: a confrontation with God, a commissioning, an objection by the prophet, God's reassurance, and a sign. This genre may have derived from the ancient requirement for ambassadors or messengers to present their credentials to the party to whom they had been sent (see Gen 24:35–48).

In the prophetic books, vocation reports serve a similar purpose: they authenticate the prophet's authority and message by showing that God had indeed sent him. Literarily, they also serve to underscore the theological themes central to a given prophet's message. The OT shows two types of vocation reports. Some report a vision of God's court like other vision reports (Isa 6; Ezek 1–3; 1 Kgs 22:19–23). The other type details how someone heard the coming of the word (Jer 1:4–10; Exod 3–4; Judg 6:11–14).

The second narrative genre in prophetic books is divine *instruction about symbolic actions* that the prophet is to perform.[170] Typically, such narratives include: a command to perform an action, a report of the performance, and its interpretation through a followup prophetic word or vision (2 Kgs 13:14–19; Hos 1:2–9).[171] Jeremiah 19 provides

---

169. Sweeney, "Prophetic Literature," 20 ("Vocation Account"); cf. W. Hsu, "Views of the Person in the Prophetic Books: A Study of Call Narratives," *Taiwan Journal of Theology* 36 (2013): 71–93; the still foundational studies of B. O. Long, "Prophetic Call Traditions and Reports of Visions," *ZAW* 84 (1972): 494–500, and N. Habel, "The Form and Significance of the Call Narratives," *ZAW* 77 (1965): 297–323. "Vocation Reports" replaces the older, now discarded term "call narratives." Concerning their purpose, see B. O. Long, "Prophetic Authority as Social Reality," in *Canon and Authority: Essays in Old Testament Religion and Theology*, ed. B. O. Long and G. W. Coats (Philadelphia: Fortress, 1977), 3–20.

170. See Hos 1, 3; Isa 7:3; 8:1–4; 20:1–6; Jer 13:1–11; 16:1–4, 5–7, 8–9; 32:1–15; Zech 11:4–16. Cf. Sweeney, "Prophetic Literature," 19–20; and K. G. Friebel, *Jeremiah's and Ezekiel's Sign-Acts*, JSOTSup 283 (Sheffield: Sheffield Academic, 1999). Cf. recent studies of examples from Ezekiel by J. B. Whitley, "The Literary Expansion of Ezekiel's 'Two Sticks' Sign Act (Ezekiel 37:15–28)," *HTR* 108 (2015): 307–24; and R. Benton, "Narrator, Audience, and The Sign-Acts of Ezekiel 3–5," in *Festschrift in Honor of Professor Paul Nadim Tarazi*, 2 vols., ed. N. Roddy (New York: Peter Lang, 2013), 2:135–40, 162–64.

171. There is also a simpler form that has only a command and the interpretation (Isa 8:1–4; Jer 16:2–4) or report and interpretation (1 Kgs 11:29–31; Jer 28:10–11). For even simpler examples, see Isa 7:3; 20:1–6; 1 Kgs 19:19–21.

an excellent example. The Lord commissioned Jeremiah to take a pottery jug, smash it before Jerusalem's leaders in the Hinnom Valley, and proclaim a message. That action symbolized the crushing disaster that God would soon send against the city. The sight of such symbolic gestures would undoubtedly unsettle its witnesses because they assumed that, like the prophet's words, the actions set Yahweh's future plans in motion (cf. 2 Kgs 13:14–19).[172] Within a prophetic book they literarily illustrate its main message and give it added rhetorical force.

General Principles for Interpreting Old Testament Prophecy

Martin Luther once said of the prophets:

> They have a queer way of talking, like people who, instead of proceeding in an orderly manner, ramble off from one thing to the next, so that you cannot make head or tail of them or see what they are getting at.[173]

Several aspects of the prophetic books probably mystify and frustrate readers. As Rofé observed, "Readers are held back by what at first glance seems disorder within the books."[174] They may find it difficult to decide when one message ends and the next begins, and the books create the impression of repetition with little evident thematic development. Many prophetic messages also strike them as hopelessly obscure. What is one to make, they wonder, of all those spooky creatures flying or crawling over the earth?[175]

To overcome such obstacles, a good starting point is to understand the nature of prophecy and of prophetic books. Fundamentally, *prophecy is a biblical phenomenon by which God conveyed messages to his people through human speakers or writers.* It assumes that God has something important he wants people to understand—that he wishes to communicate not obfuscate—whether spoken orally by a living prophet or by a finished prophetic book. The books of the prophets not only preserved their legacy—their original words and deeds—but also rhetorically ordered their messages to address later generations, including us. Careful reading of the prophets and consultation with recent commentaries can suggest that the books do have compositional order rather than chaos.

---

172. Tucker, "Prophecy and the Prophetic Literature," in Knight and Tucker, *Hebrew Bible*, 342; but cf. W. D. Stacey, *Prophetic Drama in the Old Testament* (London: Epworth, 1990), who argues that these reports exemplify and enhance the effect of the prophet's message but do not cause events; and K. Friebel, "A Hermeneutical Paradigm for Interpreting Prophetic Sign-Acts," *Did* 12 (2001): 24–45 (they comprise "rhetorical nonverbal communication"). The symbolic action of Jesus in cursing the figless tree parallels the example of Jer 19 (Mark 11:12–14, 20–21, par.).

173. Quoted by G. von Rad, *Old Testament Theology*, 2 vols. (New York: Harper & Row, 1965), 2:33, n. 1.

174. A. Rofé, *Introduction to the Prophetic Literature*, BibSem 31 (Sheffield: Sheffield Academic, 1997), 7.

175. At the same time, there is no shortage of recent writers who confidently cross reference current events (especially those in the Middle East) with, say, the goat's fourth horn of Daniel (Dan 8) or Ezekiel's Gog (Ezek 38–39). Such identifications, of course, do enjoy one distinct advantage: the more obscure the prophet, the less ground modern readers have to dispute the interpreter's views! But to date all such depictions have proved false in some respect, which should warn us against imitating them or paying them too much attention.

Thus, to grasp the relevance of their "forthtelling" (i.e., announcements about the present) and "foretelling" (i.e., future predictions), the reader must reckon with the rhetorical strategies that shaped the books and their contents. What follows suggests some principles to help readers savor spiritual benefits from the rich feast of OT prophecy.[176]

Interpreting Prophetic "Forthtelling"

To defend his own preaching, Jeremiah reminded his opponent, Hananiah, that all the prophets who preceded them announced imminent doom rather than hope just as he did (Jer 28:8–9). In other words, most prophecy involves *forthtelling*—messages for a prophet's own audience about their own day or the near future. To understand those messages, we suggest the following interpretive considerations.[177]

First, the reader must understand the historical situation in which a given prophet spoke. One needs to review the events and the state of Israel's religious life during his lifetime by consulting a book on the history of Israel.[178] Besides an assessment of the period, such books also point the reader to crucial biblical texts to be read as well. In a historical review, important questions to answer include:

- What were Israel's relations with surrounding nations like at the time?
- How good was its economy, and who were benefiting and/or not benefiting from it?
- What was the quality of Israel's religious life?

This step is essential in two respects: first, it frames the background for interpretation of prophetic texts; and second, it provides the historical basis for contemporary application (see below).

Second, the reader needs to determine the kind of judgment announced by a prophetic text. For example, the immediacy and urgency of this message must have scared Jeremiah's audience:

---

176. Some scholars have suggested that a few prophetic books (e.g., Isaiah) were originally compiled to be read aloud to audiences as a kind of "oral performance." Students would do well to keep that possible background scenario in mind as they interpret them. For a fine survey of prophetic rhetoric, see J. R. Lundbom, *The Hebrew Prophets: An Introduction* (Minneapolis: Fortress, 2010), 165–207. Cf. C. J. Sharp, *Irony and Meaning in the Hebrew Bible*, ISBL (Bloomington: Indiana University Press, 2009); M. E. Shields, *Circumscribing the Prostitute: the Rhetoric of Intertexuality, Metaphor and Gender in Jeremiah 3.1–4.4*, JSOT 387 (London and New York: T&T Clark International, 2004); K. Möller, *A Prophet in Debate: The Rhetoric of Persuasion in the Book of Amos*, JSOTSup 372 (Sheffield and New York: Sheffield Academic, 2003); Z. Weisman, *Political Satire in the Bible*, SBLDS 32 (Atlanta: Scholars, 1998).

177. Cf. the useful guidelines for interpretation in T. C. Butler, "Announcements of Judgment," in *Cracking Codes*, 166–68, and their illustration in a brief study of Jeremiah 8 (168–73). Cf. also A. Chalmers, *Interpreting the Prophets: Reading, Understanding and Preaching from the Worlds of the Prophets* (Downers Grove: IVP Academic, 2015), 145–62 (for preaching); and T. E. Fretheim, "Interpreting the Prophets and Issues of Social Justice," in *The Bible and the American Future*, ed. R. L. Jewett, et al. (Eugene, OR: Cascade, 2009), 92–107.

178. Excellent resources for history include I. Provan, V. P. Long, and T. Longman, III, *A Biblical History of Israel*, 2nd ed. (Louisville: Westminster John Knox, 2015); and J. Bright, *A History of Israel*, 4th ed. (Louisville: Westminster, John Knox, 2000). For a brief overview of the main periods, see Chalmers, *Interpreting the Prophets*, 34–66. For Israel's religion, see R. S. Hess, *Israelite Religions: An Archaeological and Biblical Survey* (Grand Rapids: Baker Academic, 2007). See the bibliography at the end for more resources.

Raise the signal to go to Zion!
    Flee for safety without delay!
For I [Yahweh] am bringing disaster from the north,
    even terrible destruction. (Jer 4:6)

His proclamation concerns the coming of a terrifying military invasion, and it is important to identify the army (if possible) to which the prophet alludes (in this case, probably Babylon). But other prophecies announce future exile from Israel's homeland (e.g., Amos 4:2–3; 5:27; Isa 5:13; Mic 1:16) and horrible natural disasters as the list of past judgments sent by Yahweh in Amos 4:6–10 illustrates (i.e., famine, drought, blight and mildew on crops, and a plague of locusts).

Normally, the syntactical marker "therefore . . ." (Heb. *laken*) introduces descriptions of judgment as a distinct section toward the end of an announcement (e.g., Amos 2:13–16; Isa 5:5–6; Jer 7:12–15), but they may occur earlier (e.g., Amos 4:2–3, 12–13). Consideration of the means, both natural and historical, through which God has sent judgment in the past confronts the reader with the theological reality that God treats his people's sin with deadly seriousness, and sometimes God judges them for it.

Third, the reader must pay close attention to the reasons given for the judgment announcement. Usually, words like "for," "because," and "since" grammatically mark what follows as a statement of God's reason(s) for his actions, and such statements may precede, follow, or be interwoven within messages. Consider the preexilic prophet Hosea's explication of Yahweh's indictment against Israel:

There is no faithfulness, no love,
    no acknowledgement of God in the land.
There is only cursing, lying and murder,
    stealing and adultery;
They break all bounds,
    and bloodshed follows bloodshed. (Hos 4:1b–2)

This description, which explicitly cites violations of at least three of the Ten Commandments (cf. Exod 20:13–15; Deut 5:17–19), contextually serves to indict the priests for failing to instruct Israel in what Yahweh expects (Hos 4:4–8). Statements that explain the rationale for judgment may occur in a distinct section (e.g., Amos 2:6–12), be interspersed throughout a passage (e.g., Hos 4:6, 8), or appear in direct address or descriptions without the explicit markers noted above (e.g. Amos 4:1; Mic 3:2–3). If not based on specific OT laws, the rationales for judgment rest on expected standards of conduct deeply rooted in Israel's covenant with Yahweh. Careful definition of the reasons within the covenant's relational framework is important because it forms the basis for the application of the passage to contemporary Christian life. Indeed, sometimes they sound so painfully contemporary that readers may wish they did *not* understand them!

In application, the principle of analogy provides the bridge from Israel in the past to Christians in the present. Having carefully defined Israel's sin(s), the reader now may seek analogies to them in modern life. To use the above example from Hosea 4, one might ask in what ways contemporary Christians show "no faithfulness, no love, no acknowledgment of God." In what ways might cursing, lying, murder, stealing, murder, and bloodshed typify our lives—and how might we change our ways?[179]

Two words of caution merit mention, however. First, since Israel was a nation, it is tempting to apply the messages of the prophets to the situations of modern nations. Since the prophets reflect what God values and hates, certainly some application of those values to nations in general is permissible. But, unlike other nations, Israel was specifically a *covenant* people bound by a relationship with God that entailed a lifestyle aligned with his will. Thus, for Christians the most proper application of the prophets is not to modern nations but to the modern covenant people, the Christian church, a collective, spiritual people bound to Israel's God through Christ and committed to a God-pleasing lifestyle. If the covenant ethos guided Israel, for Christians the gospel ethos marks the standard by which to measure how their values, priorities, and lifestyle line up with God's desires for them. That ethos leads them to follow the personal example and teachings of Jesus and to cultivate the fruits of the Spirit as well.

A second caution: some readers may wrongly infer from OT prophecy that divine judgment might follow their individual sins. Instead, one must remember that divine judgment fell on Israel not for a few sins, but after a long history of their sinfulness, rebellion, and resistance to repentance (see Jer 7:12–15). Thus, the implication of prophetic announcements of judgment is not that God will punish *every* sin but that he may intervene against a persistent, proud, sinful lifestyle (cf. 1 Cor 11:30 quoted above).

Though less numerous, OT prophets also proclaimed prophecies of salvation, primarily about return from exile and restoration to the land after judgment.[180] For example, some prophecies of salvation spoke comfort to Israel during its painful exile in Babylon:

> Why do you complain, Jacob? Why do you say, Israel,
>   "My way is hidden from the LORD;
> my cause is disregarded by my God"?
>   Do you not know? Have you not heard?
> The LORD is the everlasting God,
>   the Creator of the ends of the earth. [. . .]

---

179. Butler ("Announcements of Judgment," 167) rightly clarifies that OT announcements of judgment should not be used as "bribes" to benefit a given preacher or congregation, nor do they in any way limit God's freedom to judge or not to judge according to his own will.

180. The foundational treatment of these prophecies remains C. Westermann, *Prophetic Oracles of Salvation in the Old Testament* (Louisville: Westminster John Knox, 1991). But cf. also Sweeney, "Prophetic Literature," 25–26; W. A. Van Gemeren, "Oracles of Salvation," in *Cracking Codes*, 131–55.

> He gives strength to the weary
> > and increases the power of the weak. (Isa 40:27–29)

Addressing the exiles' fear that God has abandoned them, the prophet reassures them that God's strength will sustain them even where they are.

But most oracles of salvation proclaim God's promise that exiled Israel will one day return home, as Jeremiah 30:10–11a illustrates:

> "So do not be afraid, Jacob my servant;
> and do not be dismayed, O Israel,"
> > declares the LORD.
> "I will surely save you out of a distant place,
> > your descendants from the land of their exile.
> Jacob will again have peace and security,
> > and no one will make him afraid.
> I am with you and will save you,"
> > declares the LORD. (cf. 24:5–7; 29:10–14; 30:10–11a; 32:1–15)

The prophet's message, poignantly addressing the exiles by the revered ancestral name "Jacob," is twofold: it comforts God's discouraged people ("have no fear") and promises them divine deliverance from captivity and a return home ("I am going to save you"; "Jacob shall return").[181] Both Isaiah 40 and Jeremiah 30 aim to promote the exiles' perseverance through despair until the return occurs, as it in fact did a few decades later in 538 BC.

The application of such messages builds on the principle of analogy noted above.[182] The reader, first, needs to understand Israel's exile—its causes, its purposes, its events, and its results—then ask what modern experiences of "exile" compare to it. Finally, a review of the text's specific words of encouragement opens the way to reflections on how those words encourage Christian perseverance in our exile experiences.[183]

---

181. So Van Gemeren, "Oracles," in *Cracking Codes*, 153, who observes that, by addressing Israel as "Jacob," Jeremiah roots the promise in the ancient promises to the patriarchs (e.g., Gen 35:9–12).

182. The fact that the texts' historical fulfillment clearly occurred in the sixth century BC permits our interpreting them in such a spiritual sense. With any prophecy of salvation, however, the possibility remains of another fulfillment later, provided—and this is the crucial point—later Scriptures either so interpret it or support such an interpretation (on this see below).

183. For other principles of interpretation, see Van Gemeren, "Oracles," in *Cracking Codes*, 146–52. As one might expect, the "forthtelling" of the postexilic prophets spoke to the crucial issues of their day, especially the need to rebuild the temple in Jerusalem (Haggai and Zechariah, late sixth c. BC) or to repent of lackadaisical religious life (Malachi, fifth c. BC). Their interpretation applies the same approach as discussed concerning the preexilic and exilic periods. For an introduction to their books, background, and message, see conveniently R. J. Coggins, *Haggai, Zechariah, Malachi*, OT Guides (Sheffield: Sheffield Academic, 1996). For recent commentaries, see A. R. Petterson, *Haggai, Zechariah & Malachi*, ApOTC 25 (Nottingham: Apollos; Downers Grove: InterVarsity, 2015); C. L. and E. M. Meyers, *Haggai, Zechariah 1–8* and *Zechariah 9–14*, AB 25B and 25C (Garden City: Doubleday, 1987, 1993); P. L. Redditt, *Haggai, Zechariah, and Malachi*, NCB (Grand Rapids: Eerdmans, 1995).

Interpreting Prophetic "Foretelling"

The above discussion concerned messages that either addressed Israel in the past or reached their fulfillment in the OT era. The former indicted God's people for rebellious idolatry and cruel injustices, while the latter concerned exilic and postexilic issues. But consider the implications of prophecies like these:

> On this mountain [Zion] the LORD of hosts will make for all peoples
> > a feast of rich food, a feast of well-aged wines,
> > of rich food filled with marrow, of well-aged wines strained clear.
> And he will destroy on this mountain
> > the shroud that is cast over all peoples,
> > the sheet that is spread over all nations;
> > he will swallow up death forever.
> Then the Lord GOD will wipe away the tears from all faces,
> > and the disgrace of his people he will take away from all the earth,
> > for the LORD has spoken. (Isa 25:6–8 NRSV)

> I will save my flock, and they shall no longer be ravaged;
> > and I will judge between sheep and sheep.
> I will set up over them one shepherd, my servant David,
> > and he shall feed them: he shall feed them and be their shepherd. (Ezek 34:22–23 NRSV)

Isaiah 25 announces a future banquet, not for Israel but for "all peoples"; it also foresees the final end of death and human grief. It clearly anticipates events that far exceed anything seen by Israel during the OT period (and the NT era, too!). Ezekiel 34 promises that David will "shepherd" and "feed" God's flock (i.e., rule as king). Now, the last known king of Israel was Jehoiachin who was exiled to Babylon where he probably died (see 2 Kgs 24:12, 15; 25:27–30), although those who returned from exile may have regarded Zerubbabel as one sent to restore the Davidic kingship.[184] Even if the latter is true, subsequent OT books show little interest in the matter.[185]

---

184. Two matters are at issue: first, whether messages given Zerubbabel by Haggai and Zechariah (e.g., Hag 2:20–23; Zech 4:6–10) view him as a royal figure; and, second, whether at the time local populations might legitimately regard as "king" someone whom the Persian empire recognized by the title "governor" (Hag 1:1, 14; 2:2, 21). M. J. Boda, *Zechariah*, NICOT (Grand Rapids: Eerdmans, 2016), 408–09, believes that Zechariah 6 views Zerubbabel as a royal figure who will restore the Davidic monarchy. For the contrary view, see G. Goswell, "The Fate and Future of Zerubbabel in the Prophecy of Haggai," *Bib* 91 (2010): 77–90. Cf. the still useful, earlier discussion in H. G. M. Williamson, "Exile and After: Historical Study," in *The Face of Old Testament Studies: A Survey of Contemporary Approaches*, ed. D. W. Baker and B. T. Arnold (Grand Rapids: Baker Academic, 1999), 253–54.

185. E.g., G. H. Jones, *1 and 2 Chronicles*, OTG (Sheffield: Sheffield Academic, 1993), 109 ("there was no king in the post-exilic community known to the Chronicler"). Ezra and Nehemiah invoke David retrospectively as patron of the temple and its personnel (Ezra 3:10; 8:20; Neh 12:24, 36, 45, 46), record his descendants (Ezra 8:2), use his name in geographical locations (Neh 3:15, 16; 12:37), but say nothing about a contemporary royal figure. Only Zechariah 12 assumes the presence of the "house of David" (but never "King David") in Jerusalem when a future international attack against the city happens (vv. 7, 8, 10, 12; cf. also 13:1; 9:9), but the date of Zechariah 9–14 is problematic (for a balanced discussion, see Boda, *Zechariah*, 23–26, 516–22; cf. Coggins, *Haggai, Zechariah,*

If it is to find any fulfillment, the restoration of the Davidic monarchy must find it after the OT closes.

How, then, do we interpret "foretelling" (i.e., predictive) prophecies that apparently go beyond the OT period? The simple answer is that we must interpret them in light of the NT. On that premise, students need to bear in mind several general characteristics of biblical prophecy. First, the OT prophets understood that *history has two major periods—the present age and the age to come*—although they did not always make a hard-and-fast distinction between the two. Most OT prophecies concern the present age, even those that predict events in the distant future. But introductory phrases like "in the latter days," "in that day," or "days are coming" often signal a prophecy about the age to come—in NT perspective, the future, final messianic age when Christ reigns on earth (e.g., Isa 2:2; 11:10, 11; Jer 23:5; 31:31; Zech 14:1; etc.) and possibly thereafter (Isa 24:21). There are exceptions to this general rule, however (e.g., Jer 30:3; Amos 4:2; etc.), so only the content of a text can determine which prophetic age it concerns.

Second, it is helpful to understand that the OT prophets have a *telescopic view* of the future. From Denver, Colorado, the Rocky Mountains appear on the western horizon as a series of distant peaks close together, though in reality the peaks are many miles from each other. Similarly, the prophets saw the future as a single succession of events (i.e., the view of distant "peaks" from Denver), but the NT shows that, in fact, large time gaps intervene between them (i.e., distance between "peaks" when viewed from above).[186] Isaiah 9:6–7 (MT 9:5–6) provides a good example:

> "For to us a child is born,
>> to us a son is given . . .
> He will reign on David's throne . . .
>> from that time on and forever."[187]

Isaiah foresees the birth of a royal son who will reign on David's throne forever. The text assumes that the birth and reign occur during the son's lifetime—that he will succeed his father closely. Christians read "forever" as a clue that, besides an immediate fulfillment in Isaiah's time (cf. chs. 7–8), this text anticipates the birth and reign of David's greatest son, Jesus the Messiah, the one whose coming inaugurates the "last days." Unlike Isaiah, who sees the birth and reign of this future Davidic ruler as telescoped (i.e., chronologically close rather than separated), the NT teaches that the present so-called church age comes between Christ's birth and his future earthly reign.

The point is that, because the prophets viewed the age to come telescopically as a

---

Malachi, 60–71). It is striking, however, that Zechariah 9–14 exalts only one king, Yahweh (Zech 14:9, 16, 17; cf. Mal 1:14). The mention of David in Isa 55:3 is probably not postexilic.

186. G. Fee and D. Stuart, *How to Read the Bible for All Its Worth*, 4th ed. (Grand Rapids: Zondervan, 2014), provide a good visual illustration of this telescopic concept (201).

187. Concerning the birth announcement formula ("to X is born a son"), see R. L. Hubbard, "Ruth iv 17: A New Solution," *VT* 38 (1988): 295–98; S. B. Parker, "The Birth Announcement," in *Ascribe to the Lord: Biblical and Other Essays in Memory of Peter C. Craigie*, ed. L. Eslinger and G. Taylor, JSOTSup 67 (Sheffield: JSOT, 1988), 133–49.

whole scene without obvious time gaps, our interpretive task is to align the content of OT prophecies with the NT's perspective. According to the NT, the first coming of Jesus introduced the future age to come into the present age. The work of Christ and the church represents an invasion of that future age of judgment and salvation into the present one.[188] Hence, we must interpret OT prophecies about the age to come in terms of the historical turning point that Jesus initiated.

To be specific, while OT prophets saw the coming age as a whole, the NT presents it as having several major phases. Opinions among Christians may differ as to the number and definition of such phases, but it has at least two periods, the present church age (this age) and the period (age to come) initiated by Christ's second coming.[189] Hence, when plotting the fulfillment of OT prophecies about the future, we must carefully analyze their content to see where they fit in this larger schema.

A third characteristic of biblical prophecy is that an OT prophecy may have two fulfillments: one near the prophet's lifetime and one long past it.[190] We know of these *multiple fulfillments* because the NT itself reapplies already-fulfilled prophecy to a later event. For example, God promises David that his son, Solomon, will succeed him as king (2 Sam 7:12–16). In v. 14, God even promises Solomon that "I will be his father, and he will be my son." When Solomon later became king (1 Kgs 1–2), this prophecy found its fulfillment. But Hebrews 1:5 also applies 2 Samuel 7:14 to Jesus, not just as son of David, but as son of God. Sound theology undergirds the idea of such multiple fulfillments—belief that God rules all human history and can bring about both "sons."[191]

Fourth, NT teaching associates all *prophetic fulfillments with Christ's first and second comings.* That teaching leads us *not* to expect fulfillments in between those two events. Thus, one should not suggest that a certain contemporary event "fulfills biblical prophecy" unless one can also demonstrate that current events also imply the imminent return of Jesus. Lacking the latter, Bible students should treat such alleged fulfillments as speculations, not biblical interpretation, since to this point they have all proved erroneous despite being confidently proclaimed.

Finally, one must remember that *many prophecies are conditional not absolute.*[192]

---

188. On this subject, see G. E. Ladd, *A Theology of the New Testament*, rev. ed. by D. A. Hagner (Grand Rapids: Eerdmans, 1993), 60–67, including several useful diagrams (66–67); G. E. Ladd, *The Presence of the Future* (Grand Rapids: Eerdmans, 2000 [1974]). Cf. also N. T. Wright, *Jesus and the Victory of God* (Minneapolis: Fortress, 1996), 467–74.

189. So-called premillennialists also regard a third major historical period, the thousand-year reign of Christ (or millennium) inaugurated by his second coming, as part of the age to come. For a summary of this view, see R. G. Clouse, R. N. Hosack, and R. V. Pierard, *The New Millennium Manual: A Once and Future Guide* (Grand Rapids: Baker, 1999), 46–49.

190. In most cases, the original prophets probably were unaware of a possible future fulfillment, but using Matthew's citations of Isaiah, Blomberg argues that Isaiah actually foresaw both an immediate and a future fulfillment; cf. C. L. Blomberg, "Interpreting Old Testament Prophetic Literature in Matthew: Double Fulfillment," *TrinJ* 23 (2002): 17–33.

191. The same principle may help us explain Matthew's application (Matt 1:22–23) of Isaiah's prophecy about Emmanuel's virgin birth (Isa 7:14). For discussion of the Matthew text, see D. A. Hagner, *Matthew 1–13*, WBC 33a (Dallas: Word, 1993), 15–16, 20–22; and C. L. Blomberg, *Matthew*, NAC 22 (Nashville: Broadman, 1992), 59–61. For the Isaiah text, see conveniently J. N. Oswalt, *The Book of Isaiah, Chapters 1–39*, NICOT (Grand Rapids: Eerdmans, 1986), 207–13.

192. Cf. the helpful discussion in Sandy, *Plowshares and Pruning Hooks*, 43–47; and J. B. Green, *How to Read Prophecy* (Downers Grove: InterVarsity, 1984), 100–103.

By this we mean that their fulfillment hangs on two crucial factors: the sovereignty of God (i.e., his freedom to do or not do as he wishes) and the status of the relationship between the people and God (i.e., their rebellion or repentance). In Jeremiah 18 God articulated the principle that underlies all of his prophetic dealings:

> If at any time I announce that a nation or kingdom is to be uprooted, torn down and destroyed, and if that nation I warned repents of its evil, then I will relent and not inflict on it the disaster I had planned. And if at another time I announce that a nation or kingdom is to be built up and planted, and if it does evil in my sight and does not obey me, then I will reconsider the good I had intended to do for it. (vv. 7–10)

God says that an evil nation may escape judgment already announced against it by sincerely repenting, and that by rebelling a nation on whom he has already announced blessing may receive judgment instead.

The case of Jerusalem in Jeremiah's day illustrates the second scenario (i.e., blessing to judgment). Jeremiah announced the condition of the city's survival—repentance (Jer 26:1–6; cf. 7:1–15; 36:1–7)—but Jerusalem rejected the offer, and God destroyed the capital two decades later (Jer 52). The fate of Jonah and the city of Nineveh illustrates the first scenario (i.e., judgment to blessing). Jonah's message seemed straightforward and unconditional: "Forty more days and Nineveh will be destroyed" (Jonah 3:4). But the forty days came and went without destruction falling on the city because the people repented and received God's mercy (3:5–10). In both cases, though he had already announced his plans, God exercised his sovereignty by altering them because of the status of the relationship with the humans concerned.[193]

The Many Ways of Fulfillment

Given the discussion above, it is not surprising that biblical prophecy finds fulfillment in many ways.[194] As we shall argue, that larger pattern provides us with useful options to apply to our interpretation of prophecy.

1. As we might expect, some prophecies commonly find historical fulfillment in subsequent events. We might also call this a literal fulfillment. In some cases, the fulfillment follows a short time later. For example, Elisha predicted that, though cut off from outside supplies by a Syrian siege, Samaria would have inexpensive food by the next day (2 Kgs 7:1–2; cf. 19:20–36). Other prophecies find historical fulfillment within their respective biblical periods. Thus, an unnamed prophet prophesied that Josiah would desecrate the idolatrous altar at Bethel (1 Kgs 13:1–3), and three hundred years later he did (2 Kgs 23:15–16). Similarly, Jesus successfully predicted his own death (Matt 16:21; 27)

---

193. Similarly, G. V. Smith, "Prophet; Prophecy," *ISBE*, rev. ed., 3:1002. Green (*How to Read Prophecy*, 100–2) even believes—rightly, in our view—that the same condition applies to the promises to Abraham (Gen 12:1–3; 15; 17).

194. Cf. Green, *How to Read Prophecy*, 83–108.

and the destruction of Jerusalem (Luke 19:41–44).[195] Then, too, some OT prophecies reach historical fulfillment in the NT period. So the preaching of John the Baptist prepared the way for Jesus just as Isaiah had said (Isa 40:3–5; Luke 3:3–6), and Jesus announced that his ministry fulfilled the messianic mission foreseen by Isaiah (Isa 61:1, 2; Luke 4:16–21).[196]

2. At the same time, the rhetorical structure of some OT prophetic books reflects what one might call *frustrated* or *suspended fulfillment*. In other words, their present form leads readers through a series of surprising, incomplete fulfillments that, in the end, rhetorically point to a fulfillment beyond the book's own historical perspective. The present books of Isaiah and Amos exemplify this rhetorical strategy, addressing the prophet's original message to a much later audience.[197] For example, books associated with two eighth-century prophets clearly reference later events. Isaiah refers to Cyrus the Persian by name (559–530 BC; Isa 44:28; 45:1, 13; cf. Ezra 1–4), to the destroyed temple in Jerusalem in retrospect (587 BC; 47:6), and to the Babylonian exile as a present reality (587–538 BC; 42:18–25; 43:14; 48:20; 49:21). Similarly, Amos 9:14–15 presumes Israel to be in exile at that moment and promises their return (hence, pre-538 BC). Concerning the prediction about the restoration of the Davidic monarchy see below and Amos 9:11–12.

3. The NT also indicates that OT prophecies may reach historical fulfillment in unique, less-than-literal, ways. They may, for example, find a *historical/figurative fulfillment*. Given our discussion of typology above, consider Jesus' application of Zechariah 13:7 ("Strike the shepherd, and the sheep will be scattered") to the flight of his disciples after his arrest (Matt 26:31). According to Zechariah (Zech 13:7–9), God would severely judge Israel by killing both the shepherd (her leader) and his scattered sheep (the people of Israel). Two-thirds of them will die, but God will refine the remaining third and enter into a covenant with them (v. 9). Obviously, for Jesus this involves no precise historical fulfillment. Granted, one may rightly regard Jesus as the shepherd (cf. John 10), and one might even say that God did "judge" him. The problem is that, according to Zechariah, God judged the shepherd for his own sins, while Jesus, completely sinless, suffered God's judgment for the world's sin (cf. Gal 3:13; 1 Pet 2:24–25).

---

195. Here we assume with many scholars that the Synoptic Gospels probably were written prior to AD 70 (though in the case of Matthew, not long before) and, thus, record genuine predictive prophecies. For further defense see, inter alia, D. A. Carson and D. J. Moo, *An Introduction to the New Testament*, 2nd ed. (Grand Rapids: Zondervan, 2005), 152–56, 179–82, 207–10. For an alternative evangelical view, see P. J. Achtemeier, J. B. Green, and M. M. Thompson, *Introducing the New Testament* (Grand Rapids: Eerdmans, 2001), 69–74.

196. Cf. also Mic 5:2 and Matt 2:4-b.

197. For further discussion of Isaiah, see D. G. Firth and H. G. M. Williamson, eds., *Interpreting Isaiah: Issues and Approaches* (Downers Grove: IVP Academic 2009); and for Isaiah and Amos, see M. D. Carroll R., "The Power of the Future in the Present: Eschatology and Ethics in O'Donovan and Beyond," in *A Royal Priesthood: The Use of the Bible Ethically and Politically*, ed. C. Bartholomew, A. Wolters, and J. Chaplin (Grand Rapids: Zondervan, 2002), 116–43.

Further, when the disciples scattered, God did not kill eight of them and bless the remaining four. Thus, Zechariah 13:7 apparently found its fulfillment historically in the death of Jesus and the flight of the disciples, but only in a figurative sense.

4. Other OT prophecies reach what we call a *historical/spiritual fulfillment*. For example, Amos 9:11–12 prophesied about the restoration of the Davidic monarchy and its rule over Edom and other nations that ended ca. 560 BC (2 Kgs 25:37–30). The context gives the reader no reason to expect anything but a historical fulfillment, but in Acts 15:16–17 James says the fulfillment of Amos 9 is the admission of non-Jewish believers to the company of Jesus' followers.[198] He does so by interpreting Amos's prediction of David's future political rule as representing Christ's spiritual rule over non-Jewish Christians. In sum, James sees the prophecy fulfilled in a historical/spiritual way—historical in that it happened in history to God's people and spiritual in that it also involves Gentiles.[199]

5. Some OT prophecies receive *unexpected/historical fulfillment* in the NT.[200] They may take on new meaning in time and their fulfillment may also involve a surprise—something that goes beyond the original prophecy. Jesus himself best illustrates this element of surprise. Though some significant pre-Christian interpreters understood the suffering servant of Isaiah 52–53 to refer to an eschatological figure, the fact that Jesus' disciples rejected his predictions of his death (e.g., Mark 8:27–33) suggests that most of Jesus' Jewish contemporaries probably did not, and, hence, OT prophecy did not prepare them for his crucifixion.[201] They expected a conquering Messiah (cf. Isa 9; 11),

---

198. For the textual problems, see the NIV footnote and the thorough discussions in C. K. Barrett, *A Critical and Exegetical Commentary on Acts of the Apostles*, ICC, 2 vols. (Edinburgh: T&T Clark, 1998), 2:724–29. For discussion of the Amos text, see J. Jeremias, *The Book of Amos: A Commentary*, OTL (Louisville: Westminster John Knox, 1998), 161–70.

199. Similarly, since OT history records no fulfillment of Jeremiah's prophecy about the new covenant (Jer 31:31–34), one might expect its fulfillment in the last days. But Hebrews rightly interprets its fulfillment in the church and sealed by Jesus' atoning death (see 8:8–12; 10:15–17; cf. 1 Cor 11:25)—i.e., a historical/spiritual fulfillment. From Rom 11 one might argue that prophecies like Amos 9 and Jer 31 might still have a future *historical* fulfillment involving Israel, but we contend that the NT seems to assume that such prophecies have already been fulfilled through Christ and the church—the latter, a single people composed of Jews and Gentiles (cf. Isa 19:19–25; Rom 2:28–29; Gal 6:16; Eph 2:11–16; 1 Pet 2:9–10). On the other hand, Rom 11:11–32 does foresee future Israel's being grafted back into God's olive tree—in our view, a future outpouring of faith in Israel as a whole nation. Paul's contacts with Jews both in Palestine and in the diaspora around the Mediterranean suggest that the "Israel" he has in mind is probably similarly dispersed rather than tied to a specific geographical location. If so, nothing in Rom 11 supports the assumption that that "Israel" has unique rights to particular geography; cf. C. E. B. Cranfield, *A Critical and Exegetical Commentary on the Epistle to the Romans*, 2 vols., ICC (Edinburgh: T&T Clark, 1980–1983), 2:576–79. For a similar view that leaves open the possibility of future fulfillments, see D. L. Bock, "The Reign of the Lord Christ," in *Dispensationalism, Israel and the Church: The Search for Definition*, ed. C. A. Blaising and D. L. Bock (Grand Rapids: Zondervan, 1992), 36–67.

200. Green, *How to Read Prophecy*, 103–5.

201. For convincing evidence that some pre-Christian writings interpreted the servant of Isa 53 as a suffering eschatological figure, see Martin Hengel with Daniel P. Bailey, "The Effective History of Isaiah 53 in the Pre-Christian Period," in *The Suffering Servant: Isaiah 53 in Jewish and Christian Sources*, ed. B Janowski and P. Stuhlmacher

not a suffering one. So they stumbled over the cross of Christ; meant to be a bridge, it became a barrier to their belief (1 Cor 1:23).[202] Does this mean that God is unpredictable? Not at all. Enough continuity exists between the original prophecy and its unexpected fulfillment for readers to recognize their connection, as did the disciples after Easter vis-à-vis the crucifixion. Instead, such surprises suggest that God has the right to exceed the expectations of his ancient words in light of the new historical situation and in line with his redemptive purposes for his creation.

Stephen Travis offers a helpful human illustration of this point. He compares God to a loving parent who, knowing his children's expectations, delights in outdoing them. A little girl may expect a doll for Christmas, but the doll she receives—one that walks, talks, weeps, and wets—far exceeds her expectations. She gets what she wanted—a new doll—so continuity connects her expectations with their fulfillment. She does not feel deceived by the difference between them but happily surprised.[203] Likewise, God's fulfillment of some prophecies may exceed the expectations his people have of them.

An important implication flows from this illustration, one not always heeded in popular writings: readers must interpret predictive prophecy tentatively rather than dogmatically. We should not approach prophecy as if it were a script written for God and from which God cannot deviate. As sovereign Lord, God has the freedom to bring about the fulfillment or non-fulfillment of OT prophecies as he wishes. This does not imply divine unpredictability, as if God arbitrarily changes his mind simply because he feels like it. Certainly, God's sovereign purposes do not change, and we may expect him to adhere to much of the prophetic design. We still regard the prophecies that involve the major milestones in God's plan for history—e.g., the return of Christ, God's final triumph over his enemies, and the creation of a new heavens and a new earth—as unconditional and therefore untainted by any Christian apostasy. Their grounding rests solidly upon God's sovereign, unchangeable, larger will for his creation, not upon an exact course events en route to its realization.

So, as the Apostle Paul's wrote, we live "by faith, not by sight" (2 Cor 5:7). With complete confidence Christians may rightly anticipate the future advent

---

(Grand Rapids: Eerdmans, 2004), 75–145. That the idea may also go back to Jewish ideas of the martyrdom of the righteous, see C. A. Evans, "Messianism," in *Dictionary of New Testament Background*, ed. C. A. Evans and S. E. Porter (Downers Grove: InterVarsity, 2000), 700; and R. L. Hubbard, Jr., "Redemption," in *New Dictionary of Biblical Theology*, ed. T. D. Alexander and B. Rosner (Leicester: Inter-Varsity, 2000), 719, 720.

202. Similarly, in the NT the OT promise of land to Abraham takes on new meaning. For Christians the promised land is not earthly Palestine but "a better country—a heavenly one" (Heb 11:16; cf. vv. 8–15). If so, a review of evangelical approaches to that land promise today seems in order. Cf. the stimulating essays in S. J. Munayer and L. Loden, eds., *The Land Cries Out: Theology of the Land in the Israeli-Palestinian Context* (Eugene, OR: Cascade, 2012); G. M. Burge, *Whose Land? Whose Promise?: What Christians Are Not Being Told about Israel and the Palestinians*, rev. ed. (Cleveland: Pilgrim Press, 2013); and C. Chapman, *Whose Promised Land?: The Continuing Crisis over Israel and Palestine* (Grand Rapids: Baker Books, 2002).

203. S. H. Travis, *I Believe in the Second Coming of Jesus* (Grand Rapids: Eerdmans, 1982), 140.

of these great events. But as in the past, God may delight to ad-lib some unexpected lines, so Bible students should interpret prophecy tentatively rather than dogmatically. Our God is a God of surprises, and he may still have some left!

Now, some readers may wonder how NT writers can interpret apparently literal OT prophecies so nonliterally (examples 2 through 5 above). In our view, the writers make a fundamental theological assumption, one that also frames the way readers should interpret prophecy today. Put simply, NT writers believed that Jesus Christ and the Christian church represent the fulfillment of Israel's God-given mission in history.

The NT writers regard Jesus as the new David (cf. Isa 11:1–5; Jer 23:5–6) and the church as the new Israel. They do not deny that Israel still exists, nor do they say it has no prophetic future (e.g., Rom 10:1–4; 11). But they stand convinced that Jesus and the church—with both Jewish and Gentile members—fulfill Israel's prophetic hopes and, hence, constitute God's one, true elect people (see Eph 1–2).[204] That explains why their term for "church" is *ekklēsia* ("assembly"), the same word the Septuagint used to describe Israel as a spiritual community.[205] That also explains why Paul called believers of all ethnic backgrounds the children of Abraham (Rom 4:11–12; Gal 3:6–9).

6. Finally, some OT and NT prophecies remain *unfulfilled*. In our view, these pertain to the second coming of Christ and the events at the end of the age. The world, for example, still awaits the idyllic state of perfect harmony that Isaiah foresaw. Nations have not yet given up warfare (Isa 2:4), and lambs still wisely avoid lying beside wolves (11:6). We do not believe these have been "spiritually" fulfilled in the church. Christians have yet to hear the sound of archangel and trumpet signaling the return of Christ (1 Thes 4:13–18), and they still anticipate the great wedding supper of the Lamb (Rev 19:1–11). In our view, the presence and ministry of the church does not sufficiently account for the diversity of prophecies given to Israel according to the OT. Surely some are realized spiritually in the church, but others seem more concretely and ethnically tied to historical, physical Israel. Thus, history awaits the day when the people of ethnic Israel will receive God's mercy and the full realization of all their ancient hopes (Rom 11). Unfulfilled prophecy offers believers great things to anticipate—to borrow a phrase from Jeremiah, "hope and a future" (Jer 29:11; cf. Rom 15:4).

---

204. For one perspective on God's true elect people, see W. W. Klein, *The New Chosen People: A Corporate View of Election*, rev. and expanded ed. (Eugene, OR: Wipf & Stock, 2016). Paul understood the church as the body of Christ (e.g., Eph 4:12; 1 Cor 10:16; 12:27).

205. For details on this key word, see J. Roloff, "*ekklēsia*," *EDNT*, 1:410–15; and K. L. Schmidt, "ἐκκλησία," *TDNT*, 3:501–36; cf. its OT background in G. Carpenter, "*qāhāl*," *NIDOTTE*, 3:888–92. An excellent treatment of the theme of Christianity's connections with ancient Judaism is M. R. Wilson, *Our Father Abraham: Jewish Roots of the Christian Faith* (Grand Rapids: Eerdmans, 1989). Cf. also B. D. Chilton and J. Neusner, *Classical Christianity and Rabbinic Judaism: Comparing Theologies* (Grand Rapids: Baker Academic, 2004).

Specific Principles for Interpretation—Prophecy

In summary, we suggest several basic principles for the proper interpretation of prophecy:

1. The best starting point for interpretation is to read a whole prophetic book at one or two sittings. That may sound like a lot, especially for the Major Prophets, but it is the best way to become familiar with its contents, especially its main themes, and to begin to sense its overall rhetorical strategy. For example, a careful reading of Isaiah might reveal the importance of the prophet's visions (Isa 2:1–4; chs. 6–39) and the calls for later readers to respond with action (2:5) or to draw encouragement from them (chs. 40–66). One might also notice that the vineyard metaphor, a symbol of Israel, recurs (e.g., 1:8; 3:14; 5:1–7; 27:2–6) and may suggest possible links to the NT (e.g., John 15).

2. After these readings (or during subsequent readings), it is a good discipline to record one's observations (with sample references). Notice the book's recurring themes, prominent metaphors, indicators of its probable intention or purpose, possible audience, and overall rhetorical strategy. The key question is: Why does the book develop the way it does? Further study may lead one to refine or supplement these observations, but they provide a good starting point.

3. After some reflection, list ways in which the book's worldview may differ, if not challenge, the ways Christians see the world today. Here the key question is: In what ways might the book wish to transform, perhaps even radically, our worldview today?

4. In light of the book's context, the reader may then focus on smaller contexts (i.e., a section of verses, a whole chapter, or several chapters, etc.). Notice *what* it says (i.e., its themes), *how* it says it (i.e., its literary forms, metaphors, thought development, etc.), and what it is about the "how" that gives the "what" its rhetorical power. The ultimate goal should be to understand the major point(s) that each section stresses, what it contributes to the whole book, and what transformations it seeks to make in readers.

5. Concerning fulfillments of prophecy, the Bible itself offers the best guide to determining which prophecies were fulfilled during the OT and NT periods, and suggests patterns for interpreting OT prophecies today. The question is: Given its nature, when did/will a given prophecy most likely reach fulfillment—in the OT, NT periods, or in the future?

6. In most cases, OT prophecies about Israel and Zion find their fulfillment spiritually in the church. But those that seem to pertain more to a physical nation of Israel may anticipate a future historical fulfillment.

7. With a highly symbolic apocalyptic[206] text, the student should, first, strive to

---

206. For more on this, see the next section below.

understand the meaning of its main symbols and, then, to decide on the whole text's major thematic points. Ask, for example:

- What light does the use of a given symbol in the OT or in extrabiblical literature cast on its possible meaning in this prophecy?
- What is the purpose of the prophecy as a whole (i.e., to condemn empire builders, to encourage perseverance by God's people, to warn of coming accountability, etc.)?
- What does it say about the nature of God or about Israel's sin?

8. As for application, we suggest that the student find a situation in modern life that seems analogous to the situation addressed either by a whole book or by at least one section. To be analogous, at least several key characteristics of the modern situation must closely compare with those of the biblical one. For example, it should:

- Concern the same kinds of people (e.g., political or religious leaders, the people as a whole, merchants, average laborers, foreigners, etc.); and
- involve the same problematic issue (e.g., power or powerlessness, idolatry, greed, callousness to need, lack of faith, selfishness, etc.).

After confirming the validity of a proposed analogy, the question to ask is: What does this prophetic section say about that analogous situation? Put differently, if the ancient prophet were to speak to your church as a guest, from what you know of his message, what do you think he would say?

A Sample Prophetic Text: Isaiah 5:1–7

A close reading of this text, often called Isaiah's "Song of the Vineyard," allows us to apply the above principles to an example of prophetic "forthtelling." Cleverly, the prophet weaves together a love song (vv. 1–2), two direct addresses by Yahweh (vv. 3–6), and the prophet's concluding explanation (v. 7) to form a judicial allegory (vv. 1–7).[207] A structural outline of this text would look something like this:

I. The Love Song. 5:1–6
   A. Introduction of the Singer (Isaiah) 5:1a
   B. The Song Itself 5:1b–4
      1. Report: Yahweh's Generosity 5:1–2
      2. Interruption: Yahweh to Audience 5:3–4
         a. Request: "Judge between me and vineyard" 5:3
         b. Two-fold Question 5:4
            1) "What more could have been done?" 5:4a
            2) "Why the bad grapes?" 5:4b
   C. Yahweh's Announcement 5:5–6

---

207. Cf. Sweeney, "Prophetic Literature," 121–24.

    1. Declaration: Intent to Act 5:5a

    2. List of Actions. 5:5b–6

       a. Removal of Protective Hedge (with Result) 5:5b1

       b. Destruction of Its Wall (with Result) 5:5b2

       c. "I will make it a wasteland" 5:6a

       d. "I will withhold the rain" 5:6b

II. Identification of the Parties (Isaiah) 5:7

  A. The Vineyard & Vines = Israel and Judah 5:7a

  B. The Contrast: Yahweh's Harvest 5:7b

    1. Bloodshed instead of Justice 5:7b1

    2. Distress Cries instead of Righteousness 5:7b2

As allegory, elements of its story symbolize historical parties, and the whole serves to make a point; the language of "judge between" (Heb. *shaphat be*; cf. Deut 25:1; Isa 2:4) signals its judicial subject matter. Rhetorically, the prophet plays on two possible senses of the vineyard metaphor—the warm memories of a lovely bride in the song (e.g., Songs 2:15; 4:16–17) and of Israel as Yahweh's own personal "vine" in the addresses (e.g., Ps 80:8–13). The love song so lures the audience into the prophet's rhetorical hand that they cannot escape hearing the aggrieved landowner, whose actual identity Isaiah hides until near the end (v. 6). As we will see, Isaiah also musters parallelism and aural poetic devices to give his words added power.

The love song warmly lauds the landowner's devotion and generosity (vv. 1–2): his selection of a fertile hill, his labors clearing away its stones, his planting of choice vines, his construction of a protective watchtower, his expectant digging of a wine vat. But the song suddenly stops after reporting the resulting crop—useless "bad grapes." Confused and uneasy, the audience now hears the vineyard owner, as if just barging in unannounced, ask them to "judge between me and my vineyard" (vv. 3–4)—to decide the "innocent" and "guilty" parties in the dispute. His first rhetorical question (v. 4) defends his innocence, and his second ("Why . . . bad grapes?") implies a guilty vineyard.

By now, the audience probably realizes that the metaphorical vineyard is not a bride but Israel and Judah. But before the listeners can say a word, the owner—still unidentified, though they probably suspect Yahweh—announces his own intention to remove its protection, leaving it vulnerable to attack (v. 5). Notice how the parallelism makes the announcement sound all the more ominous and the vineyard owner all the more determined (v. 5b, our translation): "I'll remove its hedge, and it'll burn" // "I'll tear down its wall, and it'll be trampled."

Verse 6 skillfully wields Hebrew poetics to detail the future scenario (our translation):

Summary	I will make it a waste;
Amplification: A Contrast	it shall not be pruned or hoed,
	but briers and thorns will overgrow it;[208]
Intensification	I will also command the clouds
	not to rain any rain upon it.[209]

To loss of owner protection against outsiders (v. 5) the prophet adds loss of owner care against overgrowth (v. 6a)—in sum, total abandonment. Now, briers and thorns can survive with minimal moisture, but v. 6b intensifies the waste motif with a final, fatal step of abandonment: the owner will prohibit rainfall on it. A vineyard that cannot even grow weeds is truly abandoned! More importantly, this line immediately confirms listener suspicions that the owner is Yahweh since Israelites knew that rain clouds did his bidding (e.g., Ps 104:3, 13–15; Zech 10:1). The point of the allegory is now clear: outraged at his "wild grapes," Yahweh will leave Israel to destruction.

Now Isaiah himself speaks a concluding word of explanation (v. 7). By parallelism and chiasm, he identifies the vineyard ("the vineyard . . . is the nation of Israel" // "and the people of Judah the vines [Yahweh] delighted in"), then climactically wields ellipsis, wordplays, and two contrasting parallelisms to distinguish Yahweh's expectations from his people's "bad grapes" (our translation):

he [Yahweh]	hoped for	justice	(*mishpat*),
	but look—	bloodshed	(*mishpah*)!
		righteousness	(*tsedaqah*),
	but listen—	a cry!	(*tseaqah*)

Notice how, though synonymous in meaning, the second contrast ("righteousness" / "cry [of distress]") actually is sequential to the first ("justice" / "bloodshed"); the victim of injustice responds by crying out for divine justice and rescue. In short, Yahweh will leave Israel to destruction because they preferred injustice (forbidden to God's people) to justice (modeled by God, expected of his people).

Certainly, this text reminds modern Christians how deadly seriously God regards the pursuit of justice by his people. Notice that God "planted" Israel and expected a harvest of "justice," but when the harvest produced "wild grapes," he destroyed it. This seems to imply that God views our doing of justice as the proper fruit (i.e., one purpose) of our salvation; in other words, God transforms us in Christ not just to spare us eternal damnation but that we might work for justice today. Also, Jesus

---

208. Notice that the poet combines alliteration and assonance both to unify individual stichs and to highlight their contrasting content. Assonance in the first line (*lo yizzamer welo yeader* "not pruned or hoed") plays on the repetition of *lo* ("not") and "a" and "e" sounds, while alliteration plays on the initial "y" and final "r" sounds. In its parallel (*weala shamir washayit* "but briers and thorns will overgrow") assonance puns on first-syllable "a" and final-syllable "i" sounds, while alliteration repeats "sh" sounds.

209. Again, notice how the prophet puns aurally on two words from the Heb. root *mtr* ("to rain"): *mehamtir* ("[not] to cause rain") and *matar* ("rain"), in sum, "to not cause *rain* to *rain* on it."

clearly echoes Isaiah 5 in the parable of the wicked tenants (Matt 21:33–46; Mark 12:1–12): the vineyard metaphor and the owner's actions (i.e., "planted, dug, built a watch tower") clearly recall wording from Isaiah 5:2.[210] Rhetorically, Jesus compares his opponents to rebellious ancient Israel and, thus, implicitly confronts them (and us) with the hazards of not accepting Jesus as God's Messiah and not living their (and our) lives in complete obedience to his will.

Apocalyptic Prophecy

Thus far we have presented the genres of what we might call *prophecy proper*. Though formally diverse, prophecy proper shares two features in common. First, it communicates the "word" of God directly, as if God himself were speaking. The so-called messenger formula, "Thus says the LORD," introduces Yahweh's own speeches to his people (given, of course, by the human prophet). Second, it presupposes that God works within ordinary human history. So prophecy proper announces the coming of God's judgment or salvation through the actions of human armies (e.g., the Assyrians, Babylonians, or Persians). Statistically, prophecy proper encompasses most of the OT prophetic material.

But the OT also includes a second major type of prophecy called *apocalyptic* (Gk. *apokalypsis*, "revelation"; cf. Rev 1:1). Though the line between prophecy proper and apocalyptic often blurs, the following comparative chart highlights the features that set the latter apart.[211]

Prophecy vs. Apocalyptic

Prophecy	Apocalyptic
Repentance from sin	Sin too great, destruction inevitable
God's displeasure with his evil people	People's displeasure with evil, desire for God's intervention
Call for God's people to repent	Call for a faithful remnant to persevere
Divine intervention by natural or human means	Direct divine intervention by supernatural means
Direct speech by God	Mysterious, symbolic, indirect speech by intermediary
Prediction of imminent and future events	Prediction of cosmic, final solutions

Apocalyptic describes prophecies in which God "reveals" his hidden future plans, usually through dreams or visions with elaborate and at times strange symbolism or

---

210. For detailed discussion of the connections, see J. L. Story, "Hope in the Midst of Tragedy (Isa 5:1–7; 27:2–6; Matt 21:33–46 par.)," *HBT* 31 (2009): 178–95; W. J. C. Weren, "The Use of Isaiah 5, 1–7 in the Parable of the Tenants," *Bib* 79 (1998): 1–26; and C. A. Evans, "On the Vineyard Parables of Isaiah 5 and Mark 12," *BZ* 28 (1984): 82–86.

211. Simplified from D. B. Sandy and M. G. Abegg, Jr., "Apocalyptic," in *Cracking Codes*, 178–79; cf. their helpful discussion (179–81) and also that by Green, *How to Read Prophecy*, 31, 49–67; J. J. Collins, "Apocalyptic Literature," in *Dictionary of New Testament Background*, ed. Evans and Porter, 40–45; and J. J. Collins, *The Apocalyptic Imagination: An Introduction to Jewish Apocalyptic Literature*, 2nd ed., Biblical Resources Series (Grand Rapids: Eerdmans, 1998). See also "Revelation as Apocalyptic" in the next chapter.

numbers. The form of apocalyptic (i.e., dreams, visions, symbols) makes its communication less direct than the spoken word of prophecy proper. This explains in part why it poses such an interpretive challenge.

More important, apocalyptic has a unique view of God's relationship to human history. Rather than work within it, the apocalyptic God radically intervenes from outside it. Behind this lay a profound religious crisis among the Israelites. The events of human history had plunged them into such despair that they doubted whether God still controlled it. In reply, apocalyptic held out hope of God's sovereign intervention beyond history, an intervention so radical as to usher in an utterly new era. Daniel 7–12 and Revelation offer the best biblical examples of apocalyptic, but apocalyptic influence is also evident in the "Little Apocalypse" (Isa 24–27), Ezekiel 38–39, Joel 2:28–3:21, and Zechariah 1–6 and 9–14 (cf. Matt 24–25).[212]

Principles of Interpretation—Old Testament Apocalyptic

The apocalyptic genre presents unique challenges to the interpreter. The following principles of interpretation will help readers meet those challenges.[213]

1. Set a modest goal: rather than trying to understand everything, try simply to grasp as much as possible about what a text says. Apocalyptic probably presents some of the Bible's most difficult passages to interpret. Even Daniel himself found one such vision "beyond understanding" (Dan 8:27; 12:8).

2. It is best to take the symbolism and numbers seriously but not literally. Symbolism and imagination fascinated ancient peoples more than did statistical accuracy. For example, it is significant that Daniel sees four *beasts* rather than, say, four *grapes* in Daniel 7. They symbolize four kingdoms that threaten to ravage the world (v. 17), and the beast metaphor (imagine its connotations!) shows how the book "thinks" and "feels" about empires. But we need not make anything out of the fact that the first one is a lion, the second a bear, and so on. For the same reason, the various groups of "sevens" in Daniel 9:24–27 probably represent complete periods of time—whether long or short—rather than groups of actual seven-year periods. We recommend that readers consult a Bible dictionary or encyclopedia about biblical symbols and numbers to understand their symbolic significance.[214] Above all, ponder the metaphorical and emotional connotations of the symbols. For example, contrast the rhetorical

---

212. Technically, the term apocalyptic denotes a type of literature, a historical movement, and a view of history. For a convenient survey of genres unique to apocalyptic literature, including apocryphal apocalypses, see J. J. Collins, *Daniel with an Introduction to Apocalyptic Literature*, FOTL 20 (Grand Rapids: Eerdmans, 1984), 2–24. For a discussion of apocalypticism as a movement, see P. D. Hanson, "Apocalyptic Literature," in *Hebrew Bible*, ed. Knight and Tucker, 465–88.

213. Cf. Sandy and Abegg, "Apocalyptic," in *Cracking Codes*, 187–90; for the principles for interpreting symbolism and numbers, see Green, *How to Read Prophecy*, 74–81.

214. For example, see articles like "Biblical Numbers." One may also consult L. Ryken, et al., eds., *Dictionary of Biblical Imagery* (Downers Grove: InterVarsity, 1998) and commentaries on Daniel; cf. J. J. Collins, *Daniel*, Herm (Minneapolis: Fortress, 1993); and J. Goldingay, *Daniel*, WBC 30 (Dallas: Word, 1989). On numbers in Revelation,

world created by portraying empires as beasts with that portraying "one like a human being coming with the clouds of heaven" (7:13).

3. Read OT apocalyptic in connection with NT apocalyptic like Matthew 24 (pars.) and Revelation. The latter either will indicate the fulfillment of the former prophecies or will supplement their predictions.[215]

4. Observe the prophet's pastoral concern for his audience. As we noted above, the roots of apocalyptic lie in a crisis of Israel's faith in God's control over history. Its primary purpose, therefore, is to encourage suffering saints. For example, Daniel repeatedly stresses that the "saints" (i.e., Israelite believers) will survive their present hardships to enjoy ruling history's final kingdom (see Dan 7:18, 21–22, 27; 8:25; cf. 12:1–4). He does so to encourage Jews suffering under foreign domination.

5. Ultimately, the student needs to move beyond the details to determine the main points. The key question is: What is the text about as a whole? What does it say about temples, empires and their victims? So, whatever one makes of Daniel's beasts and weeks, his point is that God abhors oppressive empires, has planned their demise, and will one day end the present agony of his people. Similarly, Zechariah stresses the vindication of Jerusalem and Judah before all her historical enemies (e.g., Zech 12–14).

6. Applications should derive from the text's main points. Implicitly, Daniel and Zechariah call their readers to persevere through lengthy persecution. So, they also call Christians today to the same faithfulness to God in the face of social opposition if not outright oppression.

7. Above all, learn to enjoy reading this imaginative and uplifting literature. As Sandy and Abegg note, "like cliffs for the climber and caviar for the connoisseur, apocalyptic can provide special delights for those who learn to appreciate it."[216]

WISDOM

Our earlier discussion of the wisdom psalms introduced ancient Israel's educators, the so-called wisdom teachers. Here we survey the many genres of the OT "wisdom literature," the larger category that includes the books of Proverbs, Job, and Ecclesiastes.[217] Readers must remember that the roots of wisdom thought lie in creation theology. A person acquires wisdom not by receiving divine revelation but by recording observations about

---

see esp. F. J. Murphy, *Fallen Is Babylon: The Revelation to John*, The New Testament in Context (Harrisburg: Trinity Press International, 1998), 24–27.

215. For help, see G. K. Beale, *The Use of Daniel in Jewish Apocalyptic Literature and in the Revelation of St. John* (Eugene, OR: Wipf & Stock, 2010 [repr.]); and A. B. Mickelsen, *Daniel and Revelation* (Nashville: Thomas Nelson, 1984).

216. Sandy and Abegg, "Apocalyptic," 177.

217. In the Apocrypha, the wisdom books are Ben Sira and the Wisdom of Solomon. For an overview of wisdom, see N. deClaissé-Walford, "Wisdom in the Ancient Near East," *DOTWPW*, 862–65; K. J. Dell, "Wisdom in the OT," *NIDB*, 5:869–75; D. J. Estes, "Wisdom and Apocalyptic," *DOTWPW*, 847–58; J. L. Crenshaw, *Old Testament Wisdom: An Introduction*, rev. ed. (Louisville: Westminster John Knox, 1998); and R. E. Murphy, *The Tree of Life: An Exploration of Biblical Wisdom Literature*, 2nd ed. (Grand Rapids: Eerdmans, 1996). Cf. also W. P. Brown, *Character in Crisis: A Fresh Approach to the Wisdom Literature of the Old Testament* (Grand Rapids: Eerdmans, 1996); and G. von Rad, *Wisdom in Israel* (Nashville: Abingdon, 1972).

what works or fails to work in daily life in the world created by God. Based on creation, wisdom provides an indirect, limited form of revelation. Its principles are tentative because they may be overridden by the mysterious freedom of God (e.g., Job), by the teaching of other direct revelation, or by other factors outside one's control (see below).

Further, OT wisdom offers sharply different perspectives on life—e.g., the calm certainty of Proverbs versus the dogged skepticism of Ecclesiastes—so its books are best read canonically, not in isolation. One glimpses the full rainbow of biblical wisdom only by reckoning with its several perspectives. Finally, its literary nature also requires readers to apply principles for interpreting both poetry and narratives treated earlier. To understand it one must carefully tease out the dynamics of its parallelisms, the meanings of its metaphors, and its subtle use of drama, characterization, and plot. As Alter rightly warns, the subtle literary craft of wisdom literature means that "if we are not good readers we will not get the point of the sayings of the wise."[218]

Types of Wisdom Literature

Proverbs	Instruction	Disputation Speech
Descriptive	Example Story	Hymn
Prescriptive Better-Than	Reflection	Avowal of Innocence
Numerical		
Antithetical		

Proverbs

Probably the best-known form of wisdom literature is the *proverb*: "a concise, memorable statement of truth" learned over extended human experience.[219] Grammatically, a proverb occurs in the indicative mood and thus makes a simple declaration about life as it is. Imagine, for example, the many cases observed over centuries that produced this proverb:

> A quick-tempered person does foolish things,
> and the one who devises evil schemes is hated. (Prov 14:17)

Proverbs show great variety in form and content. *Descriptive proverbs* state a simple observation about life without reckoning with exceptions or applications:

> Some give freely, yet grow all the richer;
> Others withhold what is due, and only suffer want. (Prov 11:24 NRSV;
> cf. also 15:23; 17:27–28; 18:16)

On the other hand, a *prescriptive proverb* does more than observe something significant about life. It states its truth with a specific aim to influence human behavior. For example, Proverbs 19:17 surely invites obedience when it says,

---

218. R. Alter, *The Art of Biblical Poetry* (New York: Basic Books, 1985), 168.

219. Ryken, *How to Read*, 121. Cf. T. Hildebrandt, "Proverb, Genre of," *DOTWPWP*, 528–39; and Murphy, *Wisdom Literature*, 4, who classifies the proverb as a subtype of "saying."

> Whoever is kind to the poor lends to the Lord,
>> and will be repaid in full. (NRSV; cf. Prov 14:31; 15:33; 22:22–23)[220]

It is the specific promise of benefit, often by God's intervention, that distinguishes the prescriptive proverb from its descriptive counterpart. By extending that promise, it subtly appeals for reader obedience.

Some proverbs make their point by using comparisons; we describe them as *better-than proverbs*.[221] The proverb "Better is a dinner of vegetables where love is than a fatted ox and hatred with it" (Prov 15:17 NRSV) lauds the importance of love in the home (cf. 16:8, 16, 19; 17:1; 21:9; etc.). Such comparisons seek to underscore the superiority of certain character traits or personal conduct over others. *Numerical proverbs*, by contrast, cleverly drive their truths home by using the formula x / x + 1 in the title. For example:

> There are three things that are too amazing for me,
>> four that I do not understand:
> the way of an eagle in the sky,
>> the way of a snake on a rock,
> the way of a ship on the high seas,
>> and the way of a man with a young woman. (Prov 30:18–19)

In this case, "x" is three and "x + 1" is four.[222] The title introduces the subject—things too amazing to understand—while the subsequent list enumerates four examples. The greatest emphasis, however—the *truly* amazing thing—falls on the last item ("the way of a man with a maiden"). The previous ones merely serve to heighten the wonder or disgust over it. In such cases, proper interpretation must focus, not on the entire list, but on the final element and how it differs from or even surpasses the others.[223]

The most common proverb is the *antithetical proverb*, the form that dominates the large collection in Proverbs 10–15. By painting a stark contrast, such proverbs attempt to commend wise conduct highly and to make foolishness completely unappealing. Since antithesis is the key to this form, proper interpretation requires the reader to focus on the contrast presented. One must isolate the two traits or types of people that the proverb sets side-by-side and then decide which of the opposites the proverb commends and why.

For instance, note these two examples:

---

220. Our "descriptive" and "prescriptive" proverbs correspond to Murphy's "experiential (or observational) saying" and "didactic saying," respectively (*Wisdom Literature*, 4–6).

221. Cf. the survey of proverbial forms in Hildebrandt, *DOTWPW*, 533–35. The numerical sayings may serve a mnemonic function or derive from the ancient practice of lists found in ancient onomastica.

222. This formula occurs in texts both within and outside of the wisdom literature (Amos 1:3–2:8; Prov 30:15b–16, 21–23, 29–31). Also, other schemas occur: one/two (Job 33:14–15; cf. Ps 62:11–12); two/three (Sir 26:28; 50:25–26); six/seven (Prov 6:16–19; Job 5:19–22); and nine/ten (Sir 25:7–11). For an Akkadian example of six/seven, see the "Dispute between the Tamarisk and the Date Palm," *ANET* 593 (lines 17–18).

223. There are several lists of two (Prov 30:7–8; Job 13:20–22) and four items (Prov 30:24–28; Sir 25:1–2) that share the feature(s) stated in the title. Evidently, this form aims to treat the title's subject comprehensively by giving several illustrations of it. Cf. Murphy, *Wisdom Literature*, 180.

> Those who are hot-tempered stir up strife,
>> but those who are slow to anger calm contention. (Prov 15:18 NRSV)

> Anxiety weighs down the heart,
>> but a kind word cheers it up. (Prov 12:25)

The first example compares quick-tempered and patient people; it commends patience over an ill temper. The reason, of course, is that fiery people cause dissension while patient ones bring calm. The second example contrasts an anxious heart with a kind word. It commends the latter as the soothing antidote for the former.[224]

Principles of Interpretation—Proverbs

An initial, general word of clarification about how to apply proverbs properly is in order.[225] Put simply, proverbs teach probable truth, not absolute truth. By nature, proverbs are not absolute promises from God that guarantee the promised outcome if one follows them. Rather, they point out patterns of conduct that, if followed, give one the best chance of success, all things being equal. In other words, they offer general principles for successful living rather than a comprehensive "legal code for life." Further, proverbs place a higher premium on etching themselves on one's memory than on theoretical accuracy. That is, their primary goal is to state an important, simple truth about life in easy-to-remember terms. Hence, they do not intend to cover every imaginable circumstance. Readers must decide which proverbs apply to specific contemporary situations.

Consider this example: "All hard work brings a profit, but mere talk leads only to poverty" (Prov 14:23). This proverb teaches that, generally speaking, good effort, not good promises, pays off in the end. But the principle does not reckon with other factors that might hinder success, despite one's best efforts—economic recessions, company bankruptcies, or hailstorms, for example. As a result, to interpret proverbs properly, we must balance our understanding of each one, first, in light of other proverbs in the Bible, and, second, in light of other scriptural teachings. In the end, we must make a judgment call as to which piece of wisdom best applies to our specific situation.

But what do we do with those proverbs that our own experience seems to contradict? For example, Proverbs 13:4 promises:

> The appetite of the lazy craves, and gets nothing,
>> while the appetite of the diligent is richly supplied. (NRSV)

Obviously, the proverb commends diligent work over lazy daydreaming. But how does it square with reality today? Hardworking Christian farmers in places like the Philippines and Peru barely eke out a living, much less find their "appetite . . . richly

---

224. Lest we leave the mistaken impression that proverbs only occur in Proverbs, we note in passing that they also appear in sections of Ecclesiastes (4:6, 13; 5:10–12; 7:1–12; 9:11–12, 17–18; 10:1–2, 6, 8–9; 11:4; etc.). For NT examples, see Matt 11:30; Gal 6:7; Jas 3:6 (so Ryken, *How to Read*, 121–22).

225. Cf. Fee and Stuart, *How to Read the Bible*, 233–57.

supplied." Poor soil, inhospitable climate, and political conflict all conspire against them (other factors mentioned above). Has God failed to keep his "promise" in their case? In response, we must highlight several factors that readily apply to other proverbs as well.

First, as we noted above, a proverb expresses a truth observed to work in most cases. It may be limited to the sage's personal experience and certain specific contexts. It does not deny that exceptions occur; it merely omits them from consideration. Thus, in application, we cannot simply pick-and-choose proverbs that sound good; rather, we must carefully ensure that their original context and our proposed application context closely match up. Second, we must take care not to interpret a proverb by modern Western standards of desires. The proverb does not refer to nice homes, new cars, ski trips, and ocean cruises. Probably, it envisions rather simple desires—a small house, enough food (by ancient standards!), and a happy, harmonious family. Third, the reality of a fallen world must factor into our interpretation (cf. Gen 3:17–19). Sadly, the world struggles with the results in nature and history of Adam's rebellion. Poor soil, poor climate, and poor politics are some of its symptoms. Thus, though the proverb may be true in most cases ("all things being equal"), our fallen world may prevent its full realization—all things are not equal.

Further, the starting point for understanding any proverb is its literary traits—its parallelism, metaphors, wordplays, and even its narrative features. Analysis of its careful literary formulation opens the doorway to our understanding of its contents. Finally, the wide-ranging content of biblical proverbs may be best studied through topical surveys (e.g., family relations, business dealings, etc.) or character studies (e.g., the fool, the lazy person, the wicked, etc.).

Instruction

Israel's wisdom sages also spoke in the imperative mood in the genre *instruction*.[226] Instruction may be simply a brief exhortation such as Proverbs 8:33: "Listen to my instruction and be wise; and do not ignore it." The "sayings of the wise" (Prov 22:17–24:22) contain another variety of the short instruction in which a prohibition ("Do not . . .") is supported by a motive clause ("for" or "because"). Sometimes this shorter type makes explicit the truth urged indirectly by other proverbs:

> Do not exploit the poor because they are poor
>   and do not crush the needy in court,
> for the LORD will take up their case
>   and will exact life for life. (Prov 22:22–23, directly prohibiting what
>   14:31 implies; cf. 16:3 and 20)

As this example illustrates, the purpose of instruction is to persuade the hearer to adopt or abandon certain conduct or attitudes. The frequent motive clauses (e.g.,

---

226. Murphy, *Wisdom Literature*, 6, 50–51.

"for the LORD will take up their case . . .") give the reasons for compliance, making the teaching all the more persuasive.

On the other hand, instruction may take a longer form, for example, the series of lengthy instructions that constitute the heart of Proverbs 1–9.[227] The wisdom teacher urges his "child(ren)" at length (e.g., 1:8; 2:1; 4:1; 7:1; etc.) to follow the way of wisdom. An unusual feature of these instructions is that they occasionally include a unique subgenre called the *wisdom speech*.[228] Here they personify wisdom as a woman who openly and passionately proclaims her message in the public streets and squares (1:20–33; 8:1–36; 9:1–6; cf. folly as a woman [9:13–17]; Job 28).

Principles of Interpretation—Instruction

The following principles of interpretation are based on the literary format of the instruction genre:

1. The student should carefully observe that this literary form's commands or prohibitions present absolute demands for obedience not tentative suggestions for consideration. Readers must respond to them with seriousness.
2. The student must approach wisdom speeches as if listening to a woman passionately pleading with passing crowds to follow her advice. That very passion underscores the seriousness of her advice—how crucial for people to obey it, and how menacing is the danger that stalks those who do not. One should hear the passage as the urgent plea of an alarmed friend, not as an abstract treatise.
3. The student should pay special attention to any motive clauses present for they offer the rationale for the instruction given.
4. Having read the passage, the student might capture its form and content by completing this sentence: "This very concerned woman urges me to . . . because . . . ."

Example Story and Reflection

The wisdom books also contain two somewhat autobiographical genres. In an *example story*, the writer narrates a personal experience or other illustration from which he or she has distilled an important truth to pass on.[229] Formally, example stories often open with formulas like "I saw and considered . . ." or "I passed by . . ." followed by the story proper. They conclude with a statement concerning the moral to be drawn. Proverbs 24:30–34 illustrates this genre:

---

227. For structural details, see Murphy, *Wisdom Literature*, 49; for additional background on Prov 1–9, including the possible influence of Egyptian wisdom and Israelite prophecy on the collection, see pp. 50–52. Cf. also the treatments by K. J. Dell, *The Book of Proverbs in Social and Theological Context* (Cambridge; New York: Cambridge University Press, 2006), 18–50; C. E. Yoder, *Wisdom as a Woman of Substance: A Socioeconomic Reading of Proverbs 1–9 and 31:10–31*, BZAW 304 (Berlin; New York: de Gruyter, 2001); S. L. Harris, *Proverbs 1–9: A Study of Inner-Biblical Interpretation*, SBLDS 150 (Atlanta: Scholars, 1995).

228. Egyptian parallels suggest that these may be hymns in praise of wisdom, but in our view they are best seen as speeches since, Egyptian analogies notwithstanding, they lack the obvious traits of hymns.

229. Murphy, *Wisdom Literature*, 176. For the use of this genre in the NT, see J. T. Tucker, *Example Stories: Perspectives on Four Parables in the Gospel of Luke*, JSNTSup 162 (Sheffield: Sheffield Academic, 1998).

Opening	I passed by the field of one who was lazy, by the vineyard of a stupid person;
Example Story	and see, it was all overgrown with thorns; the ground was covered with nettles, and its stone wall was broken down. Then I saw and considered it; I looked and received instruction.
The Moral	A little sleep, a little slumber, a little folding of the hands to rest, and poverty will come upon you like a robber, and want, like an armed warrior.[230] (NRSV)

This example story begins with observations about the terrible disrepair of a certain lazy person's field and vineyard. From reflections ("I saw and considered . . .") flow the moral, i.e., that laziness ends in the cruel surprise of inescapable poverty. For the reader the obvious implication is that hard work is better than sloth regardless of how alluring sleeping late or long naps might be.

The second autobiographical genre is the *reflection*.[231] In a reflection, the writer reports personal musings and conclusions about a truth, often citing firsthand observations, example stories, and lengthy thought. Though loosely structured, reflections have the following formal features: (1) opening formulas like "I saw and considered . . ." or "I passed by . . ."; (2) the quotation of proverbs, use of rhetorical questions, or citation of example stories; and (3) a concluding moral.

The reflection dominates the book of Ecclesiastes (e.g., 1:12–2:26) though with a less obvious structure than the above example.[232] Section after section opens with "I have seen" or "I looked and saw" (1:14; 3:16; 4:1; 5:13; 6:1; et al.). Then, mixing prose and poetic musings, example stories, and proverbial quotations, the writer wrestles with the futility of life. The book's literary tone is realistic, sober, and disarmingly honest—a tone that readily draws readers into its world because of its freshness and integrity. Finally, at intervals he draws the morals from his observations (2:24–25; 3:22; 5:18–20).

Principles of Interpretation—Example Story and Reflection

Based on the format of the example story and reflection we suggest the following guidelines for interpretation:

1. The key is to determine how individual components support the concluding moral. For example, the reflection in Ecclesiastes 4:7–12 extols the value of

---

230. Cf. Murphy, *Wisdom Literature*, 130, 176. For other examples, see Prov 4:3–9; 7:6–27; Eccl 4:13–16; 9:13–16; cf. Ps 37:25, 35–36.

231. Murphy, *Wisdom Literature*, 130, 181. Scholars generally believe this autobiographical style originated in Egypt where examples abound.

232. For discussion of this intriguing book, see Dell, "Wisdom in Israel," in *Text and Context*, ed. Mayes, 364–67; cf. also the introduction in T. Longman, III, *Ecclesiastes*, NICOT (Grand Rapids: Eerdmans, 1997).

human companionship. The example story of a rich but lonely single person (v. 8) poses the problem—how miserable to be alone. The lengthy discourse (vv. 9–12) illustrates the moral—that life is better when two people share it than when one lives alone.

2. Longer texts or series of texts (e.g., Prov 1, 5, 7–9) offer a special opportunity to consider their narrative aspects—their development of plot, themes, and character. Such narrativity allows readers to understand the text through both mind and imagination.

3. Readers should observe how each text works literarily, considering its structure, thematic development, mood, and theological assumptions.

4. The concluding morals merit particular attention because they express the writer's main point. The example from Proverbs 24 above, for example, concluded that laziness ends in economic disaster. The writer warns of the dangers of laziness and, by implication, praises hard work.

5. Applications of an example story or reflection need to flow from the concluding moral. So Ecclesiastes 4 challenges believers to cultivate friendships, for God has ordained them to make human life less miserable. For Christians, a local church community or its subgroups provide one good opportunity for this.

6. Ultimately, in reading Ecclesiastes students should, on the one hand, fully appreciate its unique literary style and grapple with its realistic perspective, and, on the other, interpret its teaching canonically in light of other biblical revelation.

Disputation Speeches

A massive literary masterpiece, the book of Job incorporates many genres.[233] Setting aside Job's narrative framework (Job 1–2; 42:7–17), the rest of the book consists of the genre *disputation*. As we noted above, in a disputation a speaker seeks to persuade the audience of some truth. In contrast to prophetic examples (see above) that report only the prophet's side, Job reports the arguments of both Job and his friends.[234] Specifically, we hear the lengthy *disputation speeches* in which the speakers debate the

---

233. So far, attempts to define the genre of the book as a whole have not won a consensus. Among the options are the following: a frame tale (M. Cheney), dramatization of a lament (C. Westermann), a judicial process (H. Richter), paradigm of the answered lament (H. Gese), comedy (J. W. Whedbee), and *sui generis* (D. Wolfers); cf. Dell, "Wisdom in Israel," in *Text and Context*, ed. Mayes, 361–62; Murphy, *Wisdom Literature*, 16–19. Among possible ancient Near Eastern parallels, Job most closely resembles a work called the *Babylonian Theodicy* (so Murphy, *Wisdom Literature*, 10). For the text, see *ANET* 601–4; for a careful comparative analysis, see Walton, *Ancient Israelite Literature in Its Cultural Context*, 184–87.

234. After Job's opening soliloquy (chap. 3), we hear Eliphaz (chaps. 4–5, 15, 22), Bildad (chaps. 8, 18, 25), Zophar (chaps. 1, 20), and the latecomer Elihu (chaps. 32–37). In between, Job offers his rebuttals (chaps. 6–7, 9–10, 12–14, 16–17, 19, 21, 23–24, 26, 27–28), closing with a climactic soliloquy (chaps. 29–31). For more on disputations in Job and their argumentative nature, see T. Longman III, "Disputation," *DOTWPW*, 108–12; Murphy, *Wisdom Literature*, 175–76. For cultural background, see K. van der Toorn, "The Ancient Near Eastern Literary Dialogue as a Vehicle of Critical Reflection," in *Dispute Poems and Dialogues in the Ancient and Mediaeval Near East*, ed. G. J. Reinink and H. L. J. Vanstiphout (Louvain: Departement Oriëntalistiek [Peeters], 1991), 59–75.

cause of Job's suffering. In the end, however, the Lord's dramatic, irrefutable speeches (chs. 38–39, 40–41) reduce Job to humble acquiescence (42:1–6).

Occasionally, the book's disputation speeches incorporate into their argument literary forms from Israel's worship. In Job 16, for example, Job sounds like a psalmist when he voices a *protest* or passionate cry of despair (for this see above under poetry). He describes the attack of his enemy—God himself—and affirms his innocence:

> Surely, God, you have worn me out;
>> you have devastated my entire household . . .
> My face is red with weeping,
>> deep shadows ring my eyes;
> yet my hands have been free of violence
>> and my prayer is pure. (Job 16:7, 16–17)

Then Job lifts a petition—a pained cry for justice through an advocate pleading his case in heaven:

> Earth, do not cover my blood;
>> may my cry never be laid to rest!
> Even now my witness is in heaven;
>> my advocate is on high.
> My intercessor is my friend
>> as my eyes pour out tears to God,
> on behalf of a man he pleads with God
>> as one pleads for a friend. (Job 16:18–21)

In the end, however, Job despairs that, barring an answer from God, death is his only future:

> If the only home I hope for is the grave,
>> if I spread out my bed in the realm of darkness, . . .
> where then is my hope—
>> who can see any hope for me?
> Will it go down to the gates of death? (Job 17:13, 16a; cf. 30:1–31)

As to interpretation, protests remind the reader of the speaker's frame of reference: acute affliction suffered unjustly and the assumption that an appeal to God might bring rescue. This background helps underscore why Job's fate is especially bitter: God himself, not his human peers, is Job's implacable enemy; and, rather than rescue Job, God remains silent.

Also, disputations include a *hymn* or *hymnic elements*. We can recognize them by their lengthy description of things that the Lord does on an ongoing basis (in Hebrew, primarily with participles). Observe this psalmic song of praise to Yahweh's greatness:

He moves mountains without their knowing it
    and overturns them in his anger . . .
He alone stretches out the heavens
    and treads on the waves of the sea.
He is the Maker of the Bear and Orion,
    the Pleiades and the constellations of the south.
He performs wonders that cannot be fathomed,
    miracles that cannot be counted. (Job 9:5, 8–10; cf. also 5:9–16;
      11:7–12; 12:13–25; 25:2–6; 26:5–14; cf. 38:31; Amos 5:8.)

From Israel's worship practices also comes the *avowal of innocence*, a statement by which an individual attempts to prove his or her innocence. For example, one may voluntarily take on an oath of horrible consequences to be suffered if guilty.[235] Job does this as the capstone of his impassioned, closing soliloquy (Job 31):[236]

If I have walked with falsehood
    or my foot has hurried after deceit . . .
then may others eat what I have sown,
    and may my crops be uprooted.
If I have denied the desires of the poor
    or let the eyes of the widow grow weary,
if I have kept my bread to myself,
    not sharing it with the fatherless . . .
if I have seen anyone perishing for lack of clothing,
    or the needy without garments, . . .
if I have raised my hand against the fatherless,
    knowing that I had influence in court,
then let my arm fall from the shoulder,
    let it be broken off at the joint. (Job 31:5, 8, 16–17, 19, 21–22)

Job lists the conditions ("If I . . .")—the alleged guilt—then the dire punishment to follow if those conditions apply. His willingness to risk disaster argues for his innocence since no guilty person who takes God's vengeance seriously would dare do so.

Principles of Interpretation—Job

The following principles for interpretation apply to the various genres found in the book of Job:

---

235. Cf. Ps 7:3–5. Alternatively, the speaker may simply deny any guilt through a series of "I did" or "I did not" statements (see Pss 17:3–5; 26:4–6; Jer 15:16–17). The repetition of emphatic denials gives the avowal its persuasive power. We do not encounter this type of avowal in Job (but see 9:29–31). For oaths, see T. W. Cartledge, *Vows in the Hebrew Bible and the Ancient Near East*, JSOTSup 147 (Sheffield: Sheffield Academic, 1994).

236. Murphy (*Wisdom Literature*, 38) compares it to "a final statement before a judge"; cf. M. B. Dick, "Job 31, the Oath of Innocence, and the Sage," *ZAW* 95 (1983): 31–53. S. C. Mott, "The Ideal Righteous Person in the Hebrew Bible," *Christian Social Action* 9 (1996): 35, offers insightful reflections on Job 31.

1. Since disputation speeches dominate the book, the student should determine what truth(s) dominates each speaker's attempts at persuasion.[237]
2. The book's narrative framework identifies Job as the hero. He is the most righteous person alive (1:8); in the end God sides with Job against his opponents (42:7–9) and doubly restores his losses (42:10–17). Thus, the student should pay particular attention to Job's self-defense and beware that the seemingly good advice of his companions often reflects a position diametrically opposite from God's.
3. When other genres support the disputation speeches, we need to analyze how they work, why the poet included them, and what they contribute thematically. For example, from the occasional use of hymns it would be misleading to read Job as a kind of musical play in which the debaters periodically break into song! In the above example, by portraying God's irresistible power, the hymnic section provides evidence—evidence made more powerful by its musical form—to support the preceding line, "who has resisted him, and succeeded?" (v. 4b). In the end, Job drew the obvious inference: such power threatens to overwhelm any human who attempts to argue with it (vv. 14–20).
4. Job's avowal of innocence (ch. 31) provides a crucial interpretive clue to understand the book. By forcefully affirming his innocence, Job denies that his own guilt has caused his suffering. Chapters 1–2 seem to confirm this claim by portraying Job's righteousness and God's recognition of it. In the psalms, avowals of innocence support the psalmist's plea for God to issue a legal verdict in his favor. Thus, the form also implies that the goal of Job's avowal is to receive legal vindication from God.[238]
5. In light of the above, the student must decide from careful consideration of God's long, poetic soliloquy—the only presentation of his point of view—what his main point is and to what degree it answers Job's disputations. From Job's responses (chs. 38:1–42:6) one must ponder whether Job is truly innocent and what the book teaches about the cause and purpose of his (and our) suffering.[239] Consequently, we suggest that the book's lesson is that the ultimate root of *some* (not all) human suffering lies in the mysterious, hidden purposes of God for his people.[240]

---

237. The size of Job commends the excellent overviews of its contents available in Alter, *Biblical Poetry*, 85–110; G. H. Wilson, *Job*, UBC (Grand Rapids: Baker Academic, 2007); R. N. Whybray, *Job* (Sheffield: Sheffield Academic, 1998); and J. E. Hartley, *The Book of Job*, NICOT (Grand Rapids: Eerdmans, 1988).

238. Job frequently uses motifs drawn from Israel's legal system (e.g., Job 9:14–16; 9:29–10:1; 18:18–21; etc.), though not major legal genres. Hence, it pays to read such sections in light of that legal background. Ps 7:3–5 provides another excellent example. For a discussion of Ps 7 and its legal background, see R. L. Hubbard, Jr., "Dynamistic and Legal Processes in Psalm 7," *ZAW* 94 (1982): 267–80.

239. Cf. the insightful treatment of the whirlwind scene in Alter, *Biblical Poetry*, 94–110. Several earlier passages may anticipate God's soliloquy from the whirlwind (e.g., Job 9:5–10; 12:7–25; 28; 11:7–9 [Zophar]; 15:7–8 [Eliphaz]; 37:14–24 [Elihu]). We are grateful to Professor M. D. Carroll R. for this suggestion.

240. Cf. LaSor, et al., *Old Testament Survey*, 493–94. Dell, "Wisdom in Israel," in *Text and Context*, ed. Mayes, 363–64, surveys alternative views on Job's theological themes.

6. The book's ending provides a crucial clue to the interpretation of the whole book. God vindicates and rewards Job and criticizes the arrogance of his friends. Job encourages believers to trust God for similar, ultimate vindication from unjust suffering, whether it comes in this life or the next.

7. As with Ecclesiastes and Proverbs, whatever main theme one concludes from Job must be understood alongside the perspectives of the other wisdom books and in light of later revelation.

A Sample Wisdom Text: Proverbs 30:24–28

Close consideration of the following wisdom text will help illustrate the proper application of the above principles:[241]

> [24]Four things on earth are small,
>   yet they are exceedingly wise:
> [25]the ants are a people without strength,
>   so they provide their food in the summer;
> [26]the badgers are a people without power,
>   so they make their homes in the rocks;
> [27]the locusts have no king,
>   yet all of them march in rank;
> [28]the lizard can be grasped in the hand,
>   yet it is found in kings' palaces.

Literarily, these lines string together four proverbs (vv. 25–28) under an introduction (v. 24) to form a parable within the "words of Agur" (Prov 30). The proverbs run through four small but very wise non-human creatures to teach humans how to behave properly. The first three model cardinal virtues extolled by wisdom (vv. 25–27), while the last underscores the surprising rewards their quiet adaptation to the created order reaps (v. 28). Contextually, their quiet adaptation sharply contrasts the four upstarts whose conduct disrupts the social order (vv. 21–23).

Strikingly, the first two lines each boldly invoke people as a metaphor (e.g., people symbolize ant conduct rather than the reverse). Ants are "people" who lack brute physical strength (Heb. *az*) so they show the virtue of wisely timed hard work, storing food to survive the usual winter shortage (v. 25). Badgers are "people" who lacks the ant's army-like numerical strength (Heb. *atsum*) so they reside in rocks to protect their small, more defenseless numbers behind inaccessible terrain (v. 26). They show the virtue of seeking appropriate shelter.

Locusts lack a king, but they still stay in step together, thereby modeling the virtue of self-disciplined community (v. 27). Finally, the lizard illustrates how wisdom

---

241. Translation and comment below draw on B. K. Waltke, *The Book of Proverbs*, NICOT (Grand Rapids: Eerdmans, 2005), 461–62, 496–99.

rewards its practitioners: though easily controllable by size, his wise adaptation gains him unexpected eminence in society's highest levels—free run of the palace.

Agur draws no explicit moral, but in context the parable seems to promote the theme of the wisdom of adaptability to creation—of accepting the "givens" of one's limitations and adjusting one's life accordingly. Applications of this text need to consider our present limitations—the world as it is—and ways in which we might adapt to it by living out wisdom's virtues (timely hard work, proper shelter, community) today. We might also ask how what is it about those virtues that serve to please God and bring him glory. Finally, applications might describe some of the rewards or benefits for such God-pleasing adaptability. Along such lines we implement wisdom's foundational theme, the "fear of the Lord."

CONCLUSION

This survey shows that the OT is a fertile literary garden. Its major species are narrative, law, poetry, prophecy, and wisdom, and everywhere varieties of literary devices flourish within them. Some texts reflect the rich inheritance the people of Israel received from their cultural ancestors in the ancient Near East, while others derive from Israel's own creative cultural life. Our goal has been to cultivate in our readers "literary competence"—the ability to read a text in light of its own background and purpose—by suggesting principles of interpretation keyed to the diverse nature of OT literature. We hope that they provide a helpful map to walk readers through its wonderful literary terrain and to enhance both their understanding of the OT's ideas and their sheer pleasure in meandering through its fascinating world.

HOW TO WRITE A STRUCTURAL OUTLINE

In our discussion of individual texts we have occasionally included a structural outline. We believe that composing such outlines is an important tool in interpreting texts. We commend it as a first step in the process of interpretation and here provide a brief guide on how to write a structural outline. You can write a structural outline of any biblical text, regardless of genre following these steps.

Steps	Matters to Consider
1. Delimit your text	• Where does it begin and end—and why? • Look for markers or text-clues to decide.
2. Identify its subgenres	• At first glance, what seem to be its main sections? • List them, identifying each by their genre.

Steps	Matters to Consider
3. Decide how the subgenres relate	• Given the context, which genres go together (i.e., form subparts of a larger literary part within the text) and which stand alone? • Avoid the temptation to simply list the genres. • Try out a few possibilities before deciding.
4. Prepare an outline	• Use whatever outline format you prefer. • Remember to use *genre* (not *content*) terms for each part. • (But for some subparts, simply summarize their content.) • See the example below (and others above) for help with this step.
5. Define the text's genre	• What is the genre of the whole text? • In some cases, one subgenre will determine the genre of the whole. It may occur early in the text, at an observable turning point in the middle, or toward the end.
6. State the text's intention	• Write a sentence with this format: "The intention of this text is to . . . [use an infinitive]." • Remember: this states your conclusion as to the text's purpose or function. • It answers the question: Why did God include this text in the Bible? • Strive to find a single (not multiple) intention.
7. Interpret your outline	• What do you observe in the outline? • What comes first and what comes last? • Are there any patterns (e.g., repetitions, restatements, metaphors)? • Visualize the metaphors. What do they connote? What do they contribute? • Trace the flow or logic of the text: read through it, paraphrasing how each part develops its thought or message. • Remember: the goal of this process is interpretation.

Now we'll demonstrate how they work in a sample text, Isaiah 31:1–9, which reads:

> ¹Woe to those who go down to Egypt for help,
>   who rely on horses,
> who trust in the multitude of their chariots
>   and in the great strength of their horsemen,
> but do not look to the Holy One of Israel,
>   or seek help from the Lord.
> ²Yet he too is wise and can bring disaster;
>   he does not take back his words.
> He will rise up against that wicked nation,
>   against those who help evildoers.
> ³But the Egyptians are mere mortals and not God;
>   their horses are flesh and not spirit.
> When the Lord stretches out his hand,

those who help will stumble,
 those who are helped will fall;
all will perish together.

⁴This is what the LORD says to me:

"As a lion growls,
 a great lion over its prey—
and though a whole band of shepherds
 is called together against it,
it is not frightened by their shouts
 or disturbed by their clamor—
so the LORD Almighty will come down
 to do battle on Mount Zion and on its heights.
⁵Like birds hovering overhead,
 the LORD Almighty will shield Jerusalem;
he will shield it and deliver it,
 he will 'pass over' it and will rescue it."

⁶Return, you Israelites, to the One you have so greatly revolted against. ⁷For in that day every one of you will reject the idols of silver and gold your sinful hands have made.

⁸"Assyria will fall by no human sword;
 a sword, not of mortals, will devour them.
They will flee before the sword
 and their young men will be put to forced labor.
⁹Their stronghold will fall because of terror;
 at the sight of the battle standard their commanders will panic,"
declares the LORD,
 whose fire is in Zion, whose furnace is in Jerusalem.

To complete Step #1 (Text Delimitation) requires a brief reading of the immediate context, Isaiah 30 and 32. The latter continues the theme of future hope with which Isaiah 31 ends, but the central character is a coming righteous king—a figure mentioned in 30:33 and 32:1 but completely absent from Isaiah 31. The mention of Assyria's destruction (30:41) forges a thematic link between chapter 30 and 31, but in our view two markers signal a break (or pause) between chapters 30, 32, and 31: the king's absence just mentioned and, most importantly, the latter's opening woe declaration. That formula typically inaugurates the oracle to follow, so if the king's prominence in ch. 32 (and changed content) suggests a break between chs. 31 and 32, the woe formula sets off out text as a context of its own from ch. 30.

As for Step #2 (Identification of Genres), based on our treatment of genres above, this would be our list:

Declaration of Woe (v. 1)
Prophecy of Salvation (vv. 4–5)
Call to Repentance (v. 6)
Prophecy of Salvation (vv. 7–9)

That leaves the genre of vv. 2–3 up for consideration. Notice that, unlike vv. 4–5 where the Messenger Formula introduces a word from Yahweh to Isaiah, the speaker in vv. 2–3 (Isaiah, in our view) simply comments on how radically Yahweh's wisdom compares to—and radically differs from!—the wisdom of those buying horses from Egypt. (Given the context, the purchases are presumably for national defense against the Assyrian threat—by the way, in clear violation of Deut 17:16). Yahweh can rise up and bring disaster on an evil nation, a remark that implies that the horse purchases in question mirror a lack of faith in Yahweh's ability to do that. While the genre "Comment" would work, the topic of wisdom leads us to prefer the wisdom genre "Instruction."

In our view, to complete Step #3 (Genre Interrelationship) requires us to decide on whether the instruction (vv. 2–3) and call to repentance (v. 6) stand alone or form a larger section that requires recognition as a genre. Since the instruction follows up on the woe declaration (v. 1), and since the messenger formula definitely sets off what follows, we incorporate vv. 2–3 with v. 1. In our view, the woe declaration dominates, making the instruction that comments on it subordinate to it. So, the genre of vv. 1–3 is a declaration of woe. One clue leads us to decide what to do with the call to repentance (v. 6). Syntactically, the word "For" links v. 6 with vv. 7–9, and that link means that v. 6 cannot stand alone. The hopeful prospect of Assyrian defeat that vv. 7–9 hold out is the reason—indeed, the motive—for Judah to repent. The question now is, what genre do vv. 6–9 comprise? As with vv. 1–3, we believe that the genre of vv. 6–9 is a call to repentance, since the syntax subordinates vv. 7–9 to v. 6. If so, our outline of this text would have at least two main parts, The declaration of woe (vv. 1–3) and the call to repentance (vv. 6–9).

What to do with vv. 4–5 is the most difficult matter to decide. To have a third section between the previous two, a prophecy of salvation (vv. 4–5), is certainly possible. In the end, we decided to join them to what follows mainly for one rhetorical reason—that that structure surrounds the text's main thrust, repentance, with prophecies of salvation, thereby doubling the motivation for it. But, we concede that a three-part outline for Isaiah 31 is certainly reasonable. Here is ours (Step # 4):

I. Declaration of Woe (Isaiah) 31:1–3
   A. Declaration Itself 31:1
   B. Instruction: A Contrast 31:2–3

1. As for Yahweh 31:2
   a. Wise, True-to-His-Word 31:2a
   b. Promise: Disaster for the Wicked. 31:2b
2. As for the Egyptians 31:3
   a. Two-Fold Contrast 31:3a
      1) They: Mortal Not God. 31:3a.1
      2) Their Horses: Flesh Not spirit. 31:3a.2
   b. Implication: Yahweh Unstoppable 31:3b
II. Call to Repentance (Isaiah) 31:4–9
  A. Prophecy of Salvation. 31:4–5
   1. Messenger Formula. 31:4a
   2. The Message: Two Images–Two Promises 31:4b–5
     a. Lion: Yahweh to Defend Zion 31:4b
     b. Birds: Yahweh to Rescue Jerusalem 31:5
  B. Call to Repentance (Isaiah). 31:6–7
   1. Call Itself 31:6
   2. Reason ("For . . ."): Prophecy of Salvation. 31:7–9
     a. Prediction: Judah's Repentance 31:7
     b. Announcement: Defeat of Assyria 31:8–9
      1) Means: Divine Not Human 31:8
      2) Result: Terror of Commanders 31:9

Once the outline is before us, we determine (Step #5) the genre of the whole to be a "Call to Repentance" and state its intention (Step #6) as "to motivate Judah's repentance by reassuring prophecies of salvation backed by Yahweh's wise character." We shall leave Step #7 for our readers to complete on their own as a fitting end to this introduction of structural analysis—of course, using the guidance provided in the above table.

10

GENRES OF THE
NEW TESTAMENT

The NT does not contain as many literary genres or forms as the OT. Still, four major genres appear with various subforms embedded in them. As in the OT, principles of interpretation may vary according to genre or form.

GOSPELS

The Greek word *euangelion* (gospel) means "good news." Before the NT was written, the term often referred to news such as the announcement of an emperor's military victory. In the NT the term refers to the good news of the message proclaimed by Jesus. Mark may well have been the first person to use the term in this way (cf. Mark 1:1, 14–15; 8:35; 10:29; 14:9). After Matthew, Mark, Luke, and John had all written their accounts of the life of Jesus, Christians came to refer also to those narratives as Gospels. But the older sense still lingered on so the people who first began to collect the four Gospels together entitled them "The Gospel according to so-and-so." Each document reflected the one unified message from Jesus, which was now also about him and witnessed in four different accounts.[1]

Noncanonical documents also came to have the label "gospel" attached to them. But none of these adopted the same genre as the four canonical Gospels. Some, like the Coptic Gospel of Thomas, were not narratives but collections of numerous sayings allegedly from Jesus, loosely strung together with almost no connections between them. Others took narrative form but focused only on one small portion of Jesus' life, such as his childhood (e.g., the Infancy Gospel of Thomas) or his death and resurrection (e.g., the Gospel of Peter and the Gospel of Nicodemus). Still others resembled extended treatises on Jesus' postresurrection teaching for his disciples (e.g., the Gospels of Philip and Mary). Most of these documents clearly came from unorthodox factions of early Christianity, usually related to Gnosticism. They contain various teachings or beliefs that are legendary and/or incompatible with the claims of the canonical Gospels.[2]

---

1. Cf. M. F. Bird, *The Gospel of the Lord: How the Early Church Wrote the Story of Jesus* (Grand Rapids: Eerdmans, 2014), 254–69. M. Hengel (*The Four Gospels and the One Gospel of Jesus Christ* [Harrisburg: Trinity Press International, 2000], 48–53) suggests that Mark himself called his document a Gospel and that the other evangelists imitated him.

2. The two main collections of noncanonical works in which these various gospels appear are E. Hennecke, *New Testament Apocrypha: vol. 1: Gospels and Related Writings*, rev. and ed. W. Schneemelcher, trans. R. M. Wilson,

Therefore, in the earliest centuries of Christianity the word "gospel" did not refer primarily to a literary genre in any formal sense. It is obvious, however, from even a cursory study of the four Gospels that these books all have much in common both in form and in content. Therefore, we will classify them together and seek to identify their genre more closely.

Throughout most of the church's history, Christians have thought of the Gospels as *biographies* of Jesus. But in the modern era this identification has been widely rejected. After all, Mark and John say nothing about Jesus' birth, childhood, or young adult years. Luke and Matthew include selected incidents related to his birth and one episode about his teachings in the temple at age twelve, but otherwise they too are silent. On the other hand, all four Gospels devote a disproportionately large space to the last few weeks and days of Christ's life. What is more, the main events of Jesus' ministry appear in different order in the different Gospels, and rarely are we told how much time elapsed between any two events.

As a result, modern scholars have looked for other generic labels to apply to the Gospels. A few have identified them with well-known genres of Greco-Roman fiction. Some have called the Gospels *aretalogies*: accounts of episodes from the life of a "divine man," usually embellishing and exaggerating the feats of a famous hero or warrior of the past. Some have applied the language of playwrights to them, associating the Gospels with *comedies* (stories with a triumphant ending) or *tragedies* (stories in which the protagonist is defeated, despite having shown signs of greatness). Perhaps they form *epic* narratives, like Homer's *Iliad* and *Odyssey* or Virgil's *Aeneid*. A few link these books with *parables*, seeing an entire Gospel as a metaphorical discourse designed both to reveal and to conceal. And occasionally, despite their similarities, one or more Gospels are treated as representing a different genre from the others. Matthew, for example, has been viewed as a midrash of Mark and Q (material common to Matthew and Luke not found in Mark): an interpretive retelling of sacred tradition in which straightforward history is elaborated and embellished with various fictitious additions in order to communicate important theological beliefs. More commonly, John is set apart from the three Synoptic Gospels as more *drama* than history or biography.[3] More conservatively, it has been analyzed as a Hebrew trial (*rib*) in which God brings a lawsuit against his people.[4]

2nd ed. (Louisville: Westminster John Knox; London: James Clarke, 1990); and J. M. Robinson, ed., *The Nag Hammadi Library*, 3rd ed. (Leiden: Brill, 1996). Also see R. Kasser, M. Meyer, and G. Wurst, eds., *The Gospel of Judas* (Washington, D.C.: National Geographic, 2006). This fragmentary document deals with Jesus' last week and turns Judas into the hero rather than the villain, as in Sethian Gnosticism.

3. For a more detailed description and critique of each of these views, with bibliographic references to representative advocates, see C. L. Blomberg, *The Historical Reliability of the Gospels*, 2nd ed. (Leicester and Downers Grove: InterVarsity, 2007), 298–303; cf. C. L. Blomberg, *The Historical Reliability of the New Testament* (Nashville: B & H, 2016). For another recent and thorough survey of proposals, see J. A. Diehl, "What is a Gospel? Recent Studies in the Gospel Genre," *CBR* 9 (2011): 171–99.

4. See esp. G. L. Parsenios, *Rhetoric and Drama in the Johannine Lawsuit Motif*, WUNT 258 (Tübingen: Mohr Siebeck, 2010). At the same time, R. Bauckham (*The Testimony of the Beloved Disciple: Narrative, History, and Theology in the Gospel of John* [Grand Rapids: Baker, 2007], 93–112) shows significant parallels with Greco-Roman historiography as well.

Problems exist with each of these suggestions, however, so that none has commanded a consensus. A common view in modern scholarship has suggested that the four evangelists in essence created a new genre when they composed their Gospels. But a substantial number of studies have again linked the Gospels with *Hellenistic biography*. Earlier readers were thrown off track because conventions for writing biography in the ancient Greco-Roman world did not always correspond to modern standards. Hellenistic biographers did not feel compelled to present all periods of an individual's life or to narrate everything in chronological order. They selected events carefully in order to teach certain moral lessons or promote a particular ideology, and they frequently focused on a person's death because they believed the way people died revealed much about their character. Luke's prologue (Luke 1:1–4), in fact, closely resembles the introductions to the historical writings of ancient Jews, Greeks, and Romans such as Josephus, Herodotus, Tacitus, Arrian, Dio Cassius, and Sallust.[5]

Of course, if a gospel is about Jesus, by that criterion it will differ from other Hellenistic biographies. Robert Guelich offers a judicious survey of modern proposals concerning gospel genre and concludes with his own:

> *Formally*, a gospel is a narrative account concerning the public life and teaching of a significant person that is composed of discreet [sic] traditional units placed in the context of Scriptures. . . . *Materially*, the genre consists of the message that God was at work in Jesus' life, death, and resurrection effecting his promises found in the Scriptures.[6]

This seems best to us, too. "Formally," then the Gospels have parallels in other literature; "materially" they prove uniquely Christian. Perhaps it is best, therefore, to call them *theological biographies*.[7]

Implications for Interpretation
Historical Trustworthiness

Historiography in Writing Gospels
Different standards for quotations in the ancient world
Selective inclusion
Thematic organization, not necessarily chronological
Gospels are portraits of Jesus, not snapshots
As to Jesus' words: we have his *ipsissima vox*, not his *ipsissima verba* [his authentic voice, not his very words]

---

5. On the Gospels as biographies, see esp. R. A. Burridge, *What Are the Gospels?*, 2nd ed. (Grand Rapids: Eerdmans, 2004). On Luke 1:1–4, see B. Witherington, *The Acts of the Apostles: A Socio-Rhetorical Commentary* (Grand Rapids: Eerdmans; Carlisle: Paternoster, 1998), 24–39.

6. R. Guelich, "The Gospel Genre," in *The Gospel and the Gospels*, ed. P. Stuhlmacher (Grand Rapids: Eerdmans, 1991), 206.

7. Cf. I. H. Marshall, "Luke and His 'Gospel,'" in *The Gospel and the Gospels*, 273–82; and L. Alexander, "What Is a Gospel?" in *The Cambridge Companion to the Gospels*, ed. S. C. Barton (Cambridge: Cambridge University Press, 2006), 28.

There is a widespread belief that only a small portion of the canonical Gospels preserves accurate historical information about the actual words and deeds of Jesus and his companions. This has led to the development of *tradition criticism* and its "criteria of authenticity" for tracing the growth of the Jesus-tradition. In this view, the tradition ranges from fairly authentic sayings and factual narratives to the more complex combinations of history and legend or myth found in the final form of the canonical gospels. For many scholars, only what they deem to be the earliest stage or most authentic material is normative for Christians today.[8] Others postulate varying degrees of normativity based on the layer and the tradition to which a given verse or text can be assigned.[9] The Jesus Seminar gained notoriety in the 1990s for its two books that color-coded all of the sayings and narratives of Jesus in the *five* Gospels (including the gnostic Gospel of Thomas) and concluded that only 18 percent of the sayings and 16 percent of the narratives of Jesus actually reflected something he said or did in reasonably accurate form.[10]

Now to be sure, we must not force the Gospels anachronistically to measure up to modern conventions for writing history or biography. Instead, they must be evaluated according to the standards of their day.[11] They employ frequent paraphrase rather than direct quotation (neither Greek nor Aramaic used quotation marks or felt a need for them). Readers today encounter much interpretation, abbreviation and digests of long speeches and narratives, topical as well as chronological arrangement of accounts, and careful selection of material to fit a writer's particular theological emphasis. But once all this is recognized, the Gospel materials actually measure up quite well by the most valid criteria of authenticity.[12]

So, for example, we should not be surprised when Mark and Luke report that the voice from heaven at Jesus' baptism declared "you are my Son whom I love" (Mark 1:11; Luke 3:22), while Matthew's account has "This is my Son whom I love" (Matt 3:17). Matthew has probably reworded Mark to emphasize that the heavenly voice spoke not only for Jesus' benefit but also for the crowd's. Or again, Matthew

8. The classic and perhaps most skeptical twentieth-century work that sought to trace *The History of the Synoptic Tradition* was the book by R. Bultmann with that title (London: SCM; New York: Harper & Row, 1963; Peabody: Hendrickson, 1994 [Ger. orig. 1921]). The best example of a work treating the earliest stages of the tradition as most normative is the far less skeptical book by J. Jeremias, *New Testament Theology: Vol. 1: The Proclamation of Jesus* (London: SCM; Philadelphia: Westminster, 1971).

9. E.g., J. D. Crossan (*The Historical Jesus: The Life of a Mediterranean Jewish Peasant* [San Francisco: Harper Collins, 1991]) parcels out the Gospel traditions into four strata. The later the stratum, the less likely he believes it to be historical and the less significant for determining the permanent relevance of Jesus for Christians (see esp. 426).

10. R. W. Funk, R. W. Hoover, and the Jesus Seminar, *The Five Gospels: The Search for the Authentic Words of Jesus* (New York; London: Macmillan, 1993); R. W. Funk and the Jesus Seminar, *The Acts of Jesus: The Search for the Authentic Deeds of Jesus* (San Francisco: HarperSanFrancisco, 1998).

11. On which, see esp. C. Hemer, *The Book of Acts in the Setting of Hellenistic History*, WUNT 49, ed. C. H. Gempf (Tübingen: Mohr, 1989), 63–91. Cf. S. Byrskog, *Story as History—History as Story*, WUNT 123 (Tübingen: Mohr, 2000).

12. See esp. C. S. Keener, *The Historical Jesus of the Gospels* (Grand Rapids: Eerdmans, 2009); and D. L. Bock and R. L. Webb., eds., *Key Events in the Life of the Historical Jesus: A Collaborative Exploration of Context and Coherence* (Tübingen: Mohr Siebeck, 2009; Grand Rapids: Eerdmans, 2010).

and Luke differ as to which of Satan's temptations of Jesus they place second and which third—jumping off the temple to be rescued by the angels or worshiping Satan to receive all the kingdoms of the earth (cf. Matt 4:1–11 with Luke 4:1–13). But Luke does not use any chronological connectives in his account, only the Greek words *de* (but) and *kai* (and). Luke has probably placed what occurs as Matthew's second temptation last so that the climax of Jesus' temptations, as with his ministry overall, would end with Jesus at the temple in Jerusalem, a motif that Luke stresses.

Sometimes the differences between parallels prove more substantial. At first sight, Matthew 10:37 appears to tone down Luke 14:26 drastically. Luke writes, "If anyone comes to me and does not hate father and mother, wife and children, brothers and sister—yes, even their own life—such a person cannot be my disciple." But Matthew has, "Anyone who loves their father or mother more than me is not worthy of me." Matthew accurately paraphrases what Luke reports more literally. In Semitic language and thought, "hate" had a broader range of meanings than it does in English, including the sense of "leaving aside," "renunciation," or "abandonment." "I prefer this to that" was often stated as "I like this and hate that."

Another famous alleged contradiction between Gospels involves the story of raising Jairus' daughter. In Mark 5:21–43 Jesus is summoned to Jairus's home twice, once before and once after the child has died. Matthew 9:18–26 reports only one summons—at the beginning of the passage in which Jairus says the child has already died. By contemporary standards of reporting this would be an inaccuracy, but in light of ancient tendencies to abbreviate and "telescope" such reports significantly (combining separate stages of an episode into one), no one would likely have charged Matthew with falsifying his report.

We could offer many other illustrations.[13] All of these types of changes are natural and common in ancient biographies and should cause no concern. But it is quite a different matter to allege that entire sayings or narratives in the Gospels were created out of whole cloth and do not correspond in any recognizable fashion to what Jesus said and did. Such claims go far beyond what the evidence actually suggests.[14]

Reading Horizontally and Vertically

Gordon Fee and Douglas Stuart helpfully summarize the task of interpreting the Gospels' unique blend of history and theology with the concepts of thinking horizontally and vertically.[15] Because many narratives of the teachings and actions of Jesus occur in more than one Gospel, the serious student should consult a synopsis

---

13. On the general historical trustworthiness of the Gospels, with these and numerous additional examples of resolutions of alleged contradictions among parallels, see Blomberg, *Historical Reliability of the Gospels*, esp.152–240.

14. R. T. France, "The Authenticity of the Sayings of Jesus," in *History, Criticism and Faith*, ed. C. Brown (Downers Grove: InterVarsity, 1976), 130–31. Cf. A. Kirk, "Orality, Writing, and Phantom Sources: Appeals to Ancient Media in Some Recent Challenges to the Two Document Hypothesis," *NTS* 38 (2012): 21–22.

15. G. D. Fee and D. Stuart, *How to Read the Bible for All Its Worth*, 4th ed. (Grand Rapids: Zondervan, 2014), 140–48.

or harmony of the Gospels that prints parallel accounts in parallel columns.[16] Then the student can *read and think horizontally*—across the page—and compare the ways in which the different Gospel writers treat a certain passage. Often the distinctive emphases of a given evangelist appear most clearly in those portions of an episode that he alone has chosen to record. The student should apply this procedure to individual passages, to major sections of narrative, and to the Gospels as complete units. Thus, for example, the reader will discover that Matthew's version of the parable of the wicked tenants uniquely stresses the transfer of God's kingdom from Israel to the church (Matt 21:43), a theme that reappears throughout his Gospel (e.g., 8:10–12; 11:20–30; 13:10–12; 22:1–14; 25:31–46; and 10:5–6 vs. 28:18–20). In the resurrection narratives, only Mark highlights the fear and misunderstanding of Jesus' followers (Mark 16:8), a motif he, too, distinctively underlines elsewhere (e.g., 4:13; 4:40; 6:52; 8:21; 8:33; 9:14–29; 10:35–45). And a reading of all of Luke discloses his particular interest in showing Jesus as the friend of sinners and outcasts in Jewish society—most notably Samaritans, Gentiles, tax collectors, prostitutes, poor people, and women. See, for example, the otherwise unparalleled stories of the Good Samaritan (Luke 10:25–37), Mary and Martha (10:38–42), the Prodigal Son (15:11–32), the Rich Man and Lazarus (16:19–31), the nine Jewish and one Samaritan Leper (17:11–19), and the Pharisee and Tax Collector (18:9–14).

Interpretation and application of a given passage in the Gospels, then, should stress the particular emphases of the Gospel in which the passage occurs rather than blurring its distinctives by immediately combining it with other parallels. God chose to inspire not a harmony of the Gospels but four distinct ones, and we should respect his choice rather than undermine it by our interpretation.[17]

May we assume the first readers of an individual Gospel would recognize these distinctives before they had the other written Gospels with which to compare them? Yes, we may, because a common body of information about Jesus circulated by word of mouth (often called the *kerygma*, from the Greek for "proclamation"). Thus, Christians among one Gospel's readers would have easily recognized some of the ways in which that Gospel differed from the "standard" kerygma. This also means that the Gospel writers could assume that the people to whom they wrote already had a fair amount of prior knowledge about Jesus and the Christian faith (cf. also Luke 1:4).[18] So, it is

---

16. The most complete edition with perhaps the most attractive layout, yet remarkably affordable, is K. Aland, ed., *Synopsis of the Four Gospels*, rev. ed. (New York: American Bible Society, 2010). It is also available in Greek/English and Greek only editions.

17. It is still widely believed that Mark was the first Gospel written, that Matthew and Luke both relied on Mark as well as other sources including "Q" (other material common to Matthew and Luke), and that John was not as directly dependent on any of the other canonical writings. This approach to source criticism means that Matthew's and Luke's differences from Mark and from each other are more likely to be significant than Mark's or John's differences from either Matthew or Luke or each other. But these views have been challenged, and the methods we encourage here do not depend on any one particular source-critical hypothesis. Readers interested in pursuing the debate should consult R. L. Thomas, ed., *Three Views on the Origins of the Synoptic Gospels* (Grand Rapids: Kregel, 2002); and B. Viviano, *What Are They Saying about Q?* (New York: Paulist, 2013).

18. This is true even for John, as stressed by R. Bauckham, "John for Readers of Mark," in *The Gospels for All*

appropriate in thinking horizontally to use one Gospel to interpret another, so long as one does not mask the distinctives of each. For example, by comparing Matthew 27:56, Mark 15:40, and John 19:25, it is reasonable to deduce that Zebedee's wife's name was Salome and that she and Jesus' mother, Mary, were sisters. Jesus would then have been cousins with his two disciples John and James. This information, if true, might well have been widely known in early Christianity so that no one Gospel writer felt a need to spell it out. But we cannot prove any of this. Any application of the stories of Jesus' death that focused more on these possible relationships than on the actual information in the Gospels would be misguided.

← HORIZONTALLY →				
	Matthew	Mark	Luke	John
	1	1	1	1
V E R T I C A L L Y				6:1–15 5000 fed
		6:32–44 5000 fed	9:10–17 5000 fed	
	14:13–21 5000 fed			
	28	16	24	21

Thinking vertically, therefore, should take priority over thinking horizontally. By this we mean that any passage in the Gospels should be interpreted in light of the overall structure and themes of that Gospel despite the nature of any parallel accounts that appear in other Gospels. In other words, it is more important to read down the columns of a synopsis than across them. Frequently the Gospel writers group passages topically or thematically rather than chronologically. If we overlook these connections, we risk reading in a false interpretation. For example, Luke places the story of Jesus' preaching in the Nazareth synagogue at the beginning of his description of the Galilean ministry (Luke 4:16–30), even though chronologically it happened much later (cf. where the story occurs in Mark 6:1–6; Matt 13:53–58). This is probably because he sees the episode as programmatic of the nature of Jesus' ministry and the response it would receive. Luke 4:14b–15 makes it clear that much time had already elapsed since Jesus began preaching in Galilee. Luke 5:1–11 moves (backward in time) to the calling of some of the disciples (cf. Matt 4:18–22; Mark 1:16–20) with the temporally indefinite introduction "while the people pressed upon

Christians, ed. R. Bauckham (Grand Rapids: Eerdmans, 1998), 147–71. Cf. also Edward W. Klink, *The Sheep of the Fold: The Audience and Origin of the Gospel of John*, SNTSMS 141 (Cambridge: Cambridge University Press, 2010).

him to hear the word of God . . . ." (v. 1). But the modern reader, accustomed to strict chronology in biographies, could easily make the mistake of assuming 4:16–30 took place before 5:1–11 and conclude that Jesus called his disciples as a result of his rejection in Nazareth![19]

Similar examples occur throughout the Gospels. Matthew 8–9 presents ten of Jesus' miracles from various stages in his ministry. Luke 9:51–18:14 is probably not the "travel narrative" or "Perean ministry" as it is so often labeled; rather, it is a thematically structured collection of Jesus' teachings all spoken under the shadow of the cross, which he knew would soon end his life (9:51).[20] Mark 2:1–3:6 groups together a series of pronouncement and conflict stories (on which, see below). In fact, thematic groupings in the Gospels are so common that it is best not to assume that two episodes that appear next to each other are in chronological order unless the text actually says so (by specifying, e.g., "After this . . ."). And English Bibles may not always help because they sometimes translate Greek words for "and" or "therefore" as "then" or "now" as if the connections were temporal.

In other instances, even when passages occur in chronological order, the Gospel writers seem likely to have included and omitted material because of thematic parallels or contrasts. Thus Mark 8:31–9:32 presents, in turn, Jesus' predictions of his coming suffering, his transfiguration, and the failure of his disciples to exorcise a demon. In so doing Mark appears to juxtapose the theme of Jesus' imminent death with a foretaste of his coming glory and to contrast Jesus' sovereignty and authority with the disciples' weakness and misunderstanding. Or again, the sequence of three parables in Matthew 24:43–25:13 graphically illustrates the point of 24:36 that no one can know when Christ will return. He may come back entirely unexpectedly (24:44), or sooner than people think (24:48), or much later (25:4). Even as straightforward a chronological account as Matthew's infancy narrative (Matt 1–2) seems more interested in excerpting those events that show Jesus as the fulfillment of Scripture (1:23; 2:6, 15, 18, 23) and as the true king of Israel (as against Herod the usurper) than in presenting anything like a comprehensive survey of the events surrounding Jesus' birth.[21]

Thinking horizontally and thinking vertically amounts to studying the Gospels along the lines of modern *redaction criticism*. Redaction criticism is best defined as the attempt "to lay bare the historical and theological perspectives of a biblical writer by analyzing the editorial (redactional) and compositional techniques and interpretations employed in shaping and framing the written and/or oral traditions at

---

19. On Luke 4:16–30, see esp. W. W. Klein, "The Sermon at Nazareth (Luke 4:14–22)," in *Christian Freedom: Essays in Honor of Vernon C. Grounds,* ed. K. W. M. Wozniak and S. J. Grenz (Lanham: University Press of America, 1986), 153–72.

20. Cf. esp. C. L. Blomberg, "Midrash, Chiasmus and the Outline of Luke's Central Section," in *Gospel Perspectives III: Studies in Midrash and Historiography,* ed. R. T. France and D. Wenham (Sheffield: JSOT, 1983; Eugene, OR: Wipf & Stock, 2004), 217–61.

21. Cf. esp. C. L. Blomberg, "The Liberation of Illegitimacy: Women and Rulers in Matthew 1–2," *BTB* 21 (1991): 145–50.

hand (see Luke 1:1–4)."[22] When we compare parallel accounts and find a particular evangelist's distinctives and then see those same themes emphasized throughout that Gospel, we may feel rather confident that we have discovered a key point the Gospel writer wished to make. To be sure, redaction criticism has been widely abused, turning distinctives into contradictions, but this is a problem with its practitioners not with the method itself.[23]

The Gospels' First Audiences

Thinking about the theological emphases and distinctives of each Gospel leads naturally to a consideration of their original readers or audiences. Presumably, Matthew, Mark, Luke, and John each highlighted different aspects of the life of Christ mainly because those aspects were particularly relevant to the individuals and congregations to whom they were writing. Redaction criticism has expended much effort in trying to reconstruct the situations of these early Christian communities. This enterprise is by nature more speculative than that of comparing parallels to determine theological distinctives. Probably, certain parts of each Gospel were included simply because they formed part of the common kerygma or because they were important for all Christians (or interested "inquirers") irrespective of their specific circumstances at the moment.[24]

Nevertheless, numerous proposals about the evangelists' original audiences seem probable. For example, in his emphasis on the disciples' fear and misunderstanding Mark most likely intended to reassure and encourage a Gentile-Christian audience, possibly in Rome, as imperial persecution against Christians intensified. This hypothesis dovetails with the meager external evidence we have concerning the composition of Mark. If Jesus' disciples were prone to failure yet God was still able mightily to use them, Christians feeling weak and inadequate in another time and place could take heart, too. Preachers and teachers today may thus choose to focus particularly on Mark as they seek to encourage beleaguered Christian communities.[25]

Similarly, John uniquely plays down the status of John the Baptist (1:19–28, 29–34; 3:22–39). Now, Acts 19:1–7 describes a strange group of "disciples" in Ephesus, the

---

22. R. N. Soulen and R. K. Soulen, *Handbook of Biblical Criticism*, 4th ed. (Louisville: Westminster John Knox, 2011), 178.

23. See esp. D. A. Carson, "Redaction Criticism: On the Legitimacy and Illegitimacy of a Literary Tool," in *Scripture and Truth,* ed. D. A. Carson and J. D. Woodbridge (Grand Rapids: Zondervan, 1983; Grand Rapids: Baker, 1992), 119–42. For a brief overview of the distinctive theologies of each of the four evangelists, see C. L. Blomberg, *Jesus and the Gospels: An Introduction and Survey,* 2nd ed. (Nashville: B&H; Leicester: Inter-Varsity, 2009), 131–35, 146–50, 163–70, 186–93. For outlines sensitive to thematic patterns, cf. pp. 130, 145–46, 162–63, 185–86.

24. For a brief survey of the most plausible proposals, see Blomberg, *Jesus and the Gospels,* 135–38, 150–53, 170–73, 193–97. *The Gospels for All Christians* (ed. Bauckham) argues that all of the Gospels were initially intended to address the church in general. There is some plausibility to this, but it does not require jettisoning the notion that specific congregations were particularly in view, as the initial or primary recipients. See C. L. Blomberg, "The Gospels for Specific Communities *and* All Christians," in *The Audience of the Gospels: The Origin and Function of the Gospels in Early Christianity,* LNTS 353, ed. E. W. Klink III (London and New York: T&T Clark, 2010), 111–33.

25. See esp. E. Best, *Disciples and Discipleship: Studies in the Gospel according to Mark* (Edinburgh: T&T Clark, 1986). Cf. K. Brower, "'We Are Able': Cross-bearing Discipleship and the Way of the Lord in Mark," *HBT* 29 (2007): 177–201.

traditional location of the churches to whom the apostle John later wrote, who knew only of John the Baptist and not of Jesus. Later Christian writings (most notably the third-century Pseudo-Clementine Recognitions) speak of a second-century sect in the same area that worshiped John. Quite plausibly, the Fourth Gospel's information about the Baptist was designed to temper any improper exaltation of John at the expense of worshiping Christ, which might have crept into Ephesian churches. And if it was wrong to glorify the human leader of whom Jesus had said, "among those born of women there is no one greater than John" (Luke 7:28), then surely it is inappropriate to exalt human leaders of God's people in any age. Contemporary Christians might choose, therefore, to highlight the Fourth Gospel's portrait of John the Baptist when struggling against church leaders who direct too much attention to themselves and too little to Christ.[26]

Recognizing that the disciples in the Gospels represent believers in any age also helps us avoid certain hermeneutical errors of the past. For example, medieval Catholicism sometimes argued that Jesus taught a two-tiered ethic. His more stringent demands, such as vows of poverty, were reserved for fulltime Christian workers like priests, nuns, or monks—the so-called religious. The contemporary Russian church has sometimes held the view, made understandable by decades of persecution, that Jesus intended the Great Commission (Matt 28:18–20) only for the apostles and not for all believers. Dispensationalists, particularly in the U.S., have sometimes maintained that because Jesus' disciples were Jewish one cannot assume his instructions to them also apply to Gentile Christians. But Scripture provides no support for any of these contentions, and the vast majority of Christian interpreters of all theological traditions down through the centuries have rightly rejected them.

Key Theological Issues

As discussed earlier, students must interpret every text in light of its historical background and literary context. Students need to interpret those parts of Scripture that contain numerous writings by the same author (notably with the Epistles of Paul) or multiple accounts of the teaching of one individual (as with the Gospels) in light of larger theological contexts. To interpret the Gospels correctly in view of the basic message of Jesus' teaching, we must correctly understand two theological issues: Jesus' views on the kingdom and the nature of his ethic.

The Kingdom of God

The central theme of Jesus' teaching is the announcement of the arrival of the kingdom of God. This kingdom refers more to a power than to a place, more to a reign than to a realm. "Kingship" perhaps better captures this sense of "authority to rule." But interpreters continue to debate to what extent Jesus believed that God's kingship had actually arrived during his lifetime and to what extent he saw it as still future.

---

26. Cf. further R. E. Brown, *The Community of the Beloved Disciple* (New York: Paulist, 1979), 69–71.

Others differ over whether God's rule concentrates on empowering his people or on redeeming the cosmos. A related question asks whether the Christian's primary task is to encourage personal transformation or social reform. A correct understanding of the relationship of the kingdom to the church and to Israel also seems vital.

Space prevents consideration of the strengths and weaknesses of each major position adopted on these questions. We agree with a fair consensus of interpreters who believe that the kingdom of God arrived in part at Christ's first coming but awaits its full consummation at his return (cf., e.g., Mark 1:15; Matt 12:28; Luke 17:20–21 with Matt 6:10; 25:1–13; and Acts 1:6–8). This is the view often known as *inaugurated eschatology*.[27] Like an inauguration at the beginning of a president's term of office, Jesus inaugurated God's kingdom at the beginning of his reign, even though much more awaits fulfillment. Because he could personally preach to only a handful of the world's population, Jesus' priority during his lifetime was to gather around himself a community of followers who would live out the principles of God's kingdom. These followers, as they made new disciples, could eventually demonstrate God's will for all the world concerning human life in community and society.

Personal conversion—repentance from sin and faith in Jesus Christ as Savior and Lord—alone secures eternal life and prevents eternal punishment and separation from God; so it must take priority over social transformation (Mark 1:15; Matt 9:2; Luke 9:23–27; John 3:16). But challenging sinful, systemic structures forms a crucial part of God's purposes for his world as well and must not be neglected (Luke 4:18–19; 7:22–23; Matt 8:17). The kingdom does not equal the church. The church is the group of believers in all ages over whom God reigns, who demonstrate to the world the presence of his kingdom. Nor was the kingdom something offered exclusively to Israel, rejected, and then replaced by the church. What Jesus referred to as the mystery of the kingdom was not a shift from Israel to the church but the surprising fact that the kingdom of God had arrived without applying the irresistible power many had expected.[28]

Andrew Kirk ties together these strands of thought with a comprehensive formulation of Jesus' kingdom priorities:

> The kingdom sums up God's plan to create a new human life by making possible a new kind of community among people, families, and groups. [It combines] the possibility of a personal relationship to Jesus with man's responsibility to manage

---

27. This term has been associated especially with the numerous writings of G. E. Ladd. Perhaps his best work on the kingdom was *The Presence of the Future* (Grand Rapids: Eerdmans, 1974). The issue was comprehensively surveyed again in J. P. Meier, *A Marginal Jew: Rethinking the Historical Jesus*, 5 vols. to date, AYBRL (New York: Doubleday, 1991–), 2:237–506. For a more recent, succinct presentation, see B. Witherington III, *Imminent Domain: The Story of the Kingdom* (Grand Rapids: Eerdmans, 2009). Witherington prefers to refer to the kingdom as "the Dominion of God."

28. In addition to Ladd, cf. esp. S. McKnight, *A New Vision for Israel* (Grand Rapids and Cambridge: Eerdmans, 1999), 70–155; and M. A. Beavis, *Jesus and Utopia: Looking for the Kingdom of God in the Roman World* (Minneapolis: Fortress, 2006).

wisely the whole of nature; the expectation that real change is possible here and now; a realistic assessment of the strength of opposition to God's intentions; the creation of new human relationships and the eventual liberation by God of the whole of nature from corruption.[29]

Students need to keep in mind all these aspects when they interpret Jesus' teaching and actions, including those in which Jesus does not necessarily mention the kingdom explicitly.

Consider, for example, the beatitudes of Matthew 5:3–12 and Luke 6:20–26. It is probably significant that both versions begin and end with present tense blessings ("theirs/yours *is* the kingdom of heaven/God"), but sandwich between these present promises future tense promises ("they/you *shall* be satisfied"). People who live in the way Jesus describes in the beatitudes (poor, mourning, meek, etc.) are spiritually blessed in the present through life in Christ and his church, but they can expect full compensation for their suffering only in the life to come. Again, a correct understanding of kingdom theology prevents driving an improper wedge between Matthew 5:3 ("Blessed are the poor in spirit") and Luke 6:20 ("Blessed are you poor"). Those who are blessed are both the materially and the spiritually poor. The probable Hebrew concept underlying the Greek term used here is that of the *anawim*—the pious poor "who stand without pretense before God as their only hope."[30]

So, too, when we read in Matthew 6:33 and Luke 12:30, "seek first [God's] kingdom and his righteousness and all these things [adequate food, drink, and clothing] shall be yours as well," we must avoid two opposite misinterpretations. One error assumes that Jesus has guaranteed health and wealth (or even a minimally decent standard of living) for all who put him first in their lives. Many faithful believers throughout church history and particularly in the Majority World today simply do not experience these blessings. And it is almost diabolical to accuse all such believers of having insufficient faith. On the other hand, we dare not so spiritualize the text that it no longer makes any demands on God's children to help their destitute brothers and sisters in material ways. In Mark 10:29–30 Jesus promises his followers who give up their homes for the sake of discipleship that they will receive "houses" and "lands" "a hundredfold now in this time" as well as eternal life in the age to come. In other words, Jesus anticipated that his followers would share material possessions with each other![31]

The Present Nature of the Kingdom of God / Heaven
Already but Not Yet
Inaugurated but Not Consummated
Spiritual, Not Political

29. A. Kirk, *The Good News of the Kingdom Coming* (Downers Grove: InterVarsity, 1983), 47.

30. R. A. Guelich, *The Sermon on the Mount* (Waco: Word, 1982), 75.

31. Cf. C. L. Blomberg, "On Wealth and Worry: Matthew 6:19–34—Meaning and Significance," *CTR* 6 (1992): 73–89; D. M. May, "Mark 3:20–35 from the Perspective of Shame/Honor," *BTB* 17 (1987): 83–87.

Perhaps the simplest summary of Jesus' theology of the kingdom is the slogan "already but not yet." Christians struggling with faltering ministries or difficult personal circumstances, as well as those currently experiencing many victories and triumphs, need consistently to temper their despair or enthusiasm by reminding themselves of both halves of this slogan. Does Jesus' perspective suggest that some Christians should go into politics to help change the world? Yes, and he promises they can often expect to have a positive effect, although they may never know to what extent. Should a believer pray for healing from illness? Of course, and sometimes God will answer positively but always on his terms, though often he chooses to work through human frailty instead (1 Cor 12:8–9). Can Christians expect victory over sins that keep plaguing them? Yes—at least in some measure, usually over a substantial period of time, but painful relapses may recur, and God guarantees ultimate victory only on the other side of eternity.

The Ethics of Jesus

Understanding Jesus' kingdom theology enables interpreters to make good sense of his ethical demands. Interpreters have regularly puzzled over their stringency. Nowhere is this more obvious than in the Sermon on the Mount. Did Jesus seriously expect his followers to view hatred as murder, lust as adultery, never to retaliate when abused, and actually to love their enemies (Matt 5:21–48)? We have already noted the *traditional Catholic* response: only select disciples are expected to follow these more austere rules. *Lutherans* often viewed Jesus' ethics as "law" (rather than "gospel") meant to point out the hopelessness of our sinful condition and drive us to our knees in repentance and faith in Christ. Against both these views, we note that Jesus addressed his words to all his disciples, as well as to the crowds of would-be followers who flocked to hear him (Matt 5:1). *Anabaptists* frequently took these commands as seriously applying to public life and to all people on earth, so they renounced all violence and became pacifists. Tolstoy adopted a similar response on a personal level, as do many Mennonites and others today. But Jesus nowhere teaches that his kingdom principles should form the basis for civil law. *Nineteenth-century liberals* often preached a "social gospel" of human progress and moral evolution apart from the personal transformation of conversion to Christ, but twentieth-century worldwide warfare squelched much of their optimism. *Existentialists* see in Jesus' teaching precedent for decisive calls to ethical action without viewing any of his teaching as absolute. *Dispensationalists* have traditionally reserved Jesus' kingdom ethic for the millennial age and have not found it directly relevant for Christians now. But this requires a greater disjunction between Israel and the church than Scripture allows. Jesus' choice of twelve disciples, for example, almost certainly was deliberate—to match the twelve tribes of Israel and portray the community of his followers as the new locus of God's saving activity.[32]

---

32. Contemporary progressive dispensationalism has distanced itself from many of its traditional tenets such

None of these approaches, furthermore, does justice to the interpretive framework of Jesus' inaugurated eschatology. Most of Jesus' teachings apply to all believers in all situations, unless Scripture itself clearly imposes certain limitations. When Jesus concludes the section of the Sermon on the Mount alluded to above, he declares, "Be perfect [whole, mature; Greek *teleios*[33]], therefore, as your heavenly Father is perfect [whole, mature]" (Matt 5:48). This remains the standard or ideal of discipleship for all Christians. We will not attain wholeness in this life, but we can arrive at a measure of maturity. Jesus' standards should be our constant goal ("already but not yet"). He intended his ethic for *all* believers, not just a select few. But inasmuch as his ethic is primarily for *believers*, we dare not impose it on those outside the faith. We cannot expect unbelievers to follow or appreciate God's will, though (through common grace) we are sometimes pleasantly surprised when they do. We must not try to coerce an unregenerate world to conform to his standards, though surely believers ought to use all legal measures available to foster an ethical society.[34]

Occasionally, however, contextual material in the Gospels themselves clearly limits the application of certain teachings of Jesus. For example, some of the severe restrictions Jesus placed on the Twelve when he sent them out on their first mission (Luke 9:3–5) were later rescinded (22:35–38). Jesus did not intend his command to the rich young ruler to sell all he had and give the proceeds to the poor (Luke 18:22) to apply to all disciples because shortly afterwards Jesus praises Zacchaeus for giving (only!) half of his possessions to the poor (19:8). Then he tells a parable praising two servants who wisely invested their master's money for his benefit rather than giving it away (19:11–27). Likewise, the statement about divorce and remarriage in Matthew 19:9 could not have had every possible exception in view when Jesus declared that all who divorce "except for marital unfaithfulness" and marry another commit adultery. Later Paul felt free to add a second exception based on a new situation Jesus did not face in his lifetime—an unbeliever wishing to leave a Christian spouse (1 Cor 7:15–16).[35] But apart from a defensible hermeneutical principle, it is irresponsible for interpreters to assume that a certain teaching of Jesus does not apply to us in our current circumstances.

The Forms within the Gospels

As already noted for the OT, different literary genres (entire works) have different interpretive principles, and we must often treat individual forms (smaller self-contained

---

as this. The fullest survey of interpretations of the Sermon on the Mount is C. Baumann, *The Sermon on the Mount: The Modern Quest for Its Meaning* (Macon: Mercer, 1985).

33. BDAG suggest the meaning here is "being fully developed in a moral sense" (996).

34. The best detailed unfolding of Jesus' ethics from the perspective of inaugurated eschatology is A. Verhey, *The Great Reversal: Ethics and the New Testament* (Grand Rapids: Eerdmans, 1984). From this perspective, elaborating on Christian ethics more generally, see esp. G. H. Stassen and D. P. Gushee, *Kingdom Ethics: Following Jesus in Contemporary Context* (Downers Grove: InterVarsity, 2003).

35. The last of these examples is the most controversial. But see C. L. Blomberg, "Marriage, Divorce, Remarriage and Celibacy: An Exegesis of Matthew 19:3–12," *TrinJ* 11 (1990): 161–96.

units of material) in unique ways. In the Gospels, the three most prevalent and distinctive forms that merit special attention are the parable, the miracle story, and the pronouncement story.[36]

Parables

The stories Jesus told, such as the Good Samaritan, the Prodigal Son, and the Sower, rank among the most famous and popular parts of all Scripture. Modern readers often express surprise to learn how differently these parables have been interpreted in the history of the church. Until this century, most interpreters treated the parables as detailed allegories, assuming that most or all of the individual characters or objects in a parable stood for something other than themselves, namely, spiritual counterparts that enabled the story to be read at two levels. So, for example, in the story of the Prodigal Son (Luke 15:11–32), the ring that the father gave the prodigal might represent Christian baptism; and the banquet, the Lord's Supper. The robe could reflect immortality; and the shoes, God's preparation for journeying to heaven.[37]

Seldom, however, did two allegorical interpretations of the same parable agree, and what a particular detail was said to represent often seemed arbitrary and even anachronistic (neither Christian baptism nor the Lord's Supper had yet been instituted when Jesus told the parable of the Prodigal). At the end of the nineteenth century, the German liberal Adolf Jülicher wrote a massive exposé of these inconsistencies and proposed a diametrically opposite alternative. He argued that parables are in no way allegories, and no detail "stands for" anything else. Rather, they make only one point apiece, as they teach rather general truths about spiritual realities. Thus, the entire story of the Prodigal can be reduced to the lesson of "the boundless joy of God's forgiveness." The richness of detail merely adds realism, vividness, and local color.[38]

Twentieth-century interpreters increasingly sought ways to swing the pendulum back from Jülicher without returning to the allegorical excesses of his predecessors.[39]

---

36. Form criticism has, of course, attempted to do much more than simply analyze constituent literary forms within the Gospels to interpret them rightly. E.g., it has often attempted to reconstruct the oral history of those forms. See esp. E. V. McKnight, *What is Form Criticism?* (Philadelphia: Fortress, 1969). But the analysis of forms has been its most objective and successful enterprise, and the only one that concerns us here. For a more up-to-date survey and critique of the method, see N. Perrin, "Form Criticism," in *Dictionary of Jesus and the Gospels*, ed. J. B. Green; 2nd ed. (Downers Grove: InterVarsity, 2013), 288–94. For further on the variety of forms in the gospels see J. L. Bailey and L. D. Vander Broek, *Literary Forms in the New Testament* (Louisville, KY: Westminster John Knox, 1992), 91–183.

37. The fullest history of interpretation, including these examples, is W. S. Kissinger, *The Parables of Jesus: A History of Interpretation and Bibliography* (Metuchen, NJ: Scarecrow, 1979). For a more recent survey of major approaches, see D. B. Gowler, *What Are They Saying about the Parables?* (New York: Paulist, 2000).

38. A. Jülicher, *Die Gleichnisreden Jesu*, 2 vols. (Freiburg: Mohr, 1899), 2:362. That no one has published a translation of Jülicher in English is one of the strangest omissions of modern biblical scholarship.

39. The two most significant twentieth-century studies of the parables were C. H. Dodd, *The Parables of the Kingdom* (London: Nisbet, 1935); and J. Jeremias, *The Parables of Jesus*, 3rd ed. (London: SCM; Philadelphia: Westminster, 1972 [Ger. orig. 1947]). Dodd's definition of a parable became a classic: "a metaphor or simile drawn from nature or common life, arresting the hearer by its vividness or strangeness, and leaving the mind in sufficient doubt about its precise application to tease it into active thought" (p. 16). But Jeremias reminded us that underneath the Greek *parabolē* lay the Hebrew *māšāl*, which had a very broad semantic range including "figurative forms of

Most rejected his rather bland moralizations and tied the central truths of the parables more directly to Jesus' proclamation of God's kingdom. Many recognized that the parables often break the bounds of realism and shockingly subvert conventional expectation. Thus, no ancient, Middle-Eastern, well-to-do head of household would have run to greet a wayward son (a most undignified action) or interrupt him before he completed his speech of repentance, but God goes to greater extents than human fathers in trying to seek and save the lost. Because the majority of the parable (like parables more generally) draws on ordinary experiences of life to illustrate analogous truths about spiritual life, the unrealistic portion stands out all the more in comparison.

A growing minority of interpreters once again regards as appropriate a limited amount of allegorical interpretation. It is hard to make any sense of Jesus' story of the Prodigal without assuming that the father in some sense represents God (or even Christ); that the prodigal stands for all the wayward and rebellious (like the tax collectors and "sinners" of 15:1); and that the older brother represents the self-righteous hypocrite (like the Pharisees and scribes of 15:2). The literary context of a parable must be consulted, contra Jülicher and many contemporary existentialists, as a reliable guide to the meaning of the parable itself. At the same time, many have been reluctant to abandon the quest for one central truth per passage. But with respect to that issue, we return to the Prodigal Son. Is the main point the possibility of repentance for even the most rebellious? Or is it an emphasis on the lavish forgiveness God offers all his children? Or is it perhaps a warning against imitating the hard-heartedness of the older brother?[40]

We find the way forward through an appreciation of the parables as narrative fiction. Longer examples of this genre (novels or short stories) regularly communicate meaning through their main characters. They encourage readers to identify with one or more of these characters and experience the plot of the story from their various points of view. Rabbinic parables functioned very similarly. When we analyze the parables in terms of main characters, we discover that approximately two-thirds of Jesus' stories are *triadic* in structure. That is, they present three main characters (or groups of characters). More often than not, one is a master figure (king, master, father, shepherd) and two are contrasting subordinates (servants, sons, sheep). Consider, for example, the bridegroom with his two quite different groups of bridesmaids (Matt 25:1–13), the shepherd with his one lost and ninety-nine safe sheep (Luke 15:3–7), or the sower with his three portions of unfruitful seeds/soil versus his one fruitful section

---

speech of every kind: parable, similitude, allegory, fable, proverb, apocalyptic revelation, riddle, symbol, pseudonym, fictitious person, example, theme, argument, apology, refutation, jest" (p. 20).

40. Two important evangelical literary critics who recognized allegory and multiple points in the parables were L. Ryken (see esp. his *How to Read the Bible as Literature* [Grand Rapids: Zondervan, 1984], 139–53, 199–203) and J. Sider, *Interpreting the Parables* (Grand Rapids: Zondervan, 1995). K. R. Snodgrass (*Stories with Intent: A Comprehensive Guide to the Parables of Jesus* [Grand Rapids: Eerdmans, 2008]) prefers to label them analogies, but his exegesis remains strikingly close to those who consider them limited allegories. Particularly helpful in distinguishing the realistic from the surprise elements in parables is K. Bailey (see esp. his *Poet and Peasant* and *Through Peasant Eyes* [Grand Rapids: Eerdmans, 1983]—2 vols. bound as one).

(Mark 4:3–9). In other cases the characters or groups of characters relate differently, but still there are three (the man who was robbed and beaten, the pair of clerics who ignore him, and the Samaritan who helps him, Luke 10:29–37). Or we may consider the king, the servant for whom he forgives an enormous debt, and that servant's underling who does not receive cancellation of even a paltry sum (Matt 18:23–35).

In about one-third of the parables, the narrative proves shorter and the structure simpler. Sometimes they contrast two characters without a master figure—wise and foolish builders (Matt 7:24–27), Pharisee and tax collector (Luke 18:9–14). Or a master and one subordinate may appear, as with the parable of the unprofitable servant (Luke 17:5–8). In still other instances, we find a monadic structure. Here only one character appears—as in the parables of the mustard seed and leaven (Luke 13:18–21), the tower-builder and the warring king (Luke 14:28–33), and the hidden treasure and the pearl of great price (Matt 13:44–46).

In light of our illustrations of the problems of interpreting the Prodigal Son, it seems reasonable to suggest that readers should consider each parable from the perspective of each of the main characters. The three major suggestions for the "one point" of Luke 15:11–32, in fact, result from doing precisely this. A focus on the prodigal teaches about repentance; following the father's actions reveals God's lavish love and forgiveness; and attending to the older brother warns against hardheartedness. All three of these points reflect part of the parable's meaning.[41]

It seems that many interpreters have already unconsciously adopted this approach. Robert Stein, for example, sums up the "one" point of the parable of the Great Supper (Luke 14:16–24) as follows:

> It is impossible in reading this parable not to interpret the guests and their replacements as representing the attitudes of the Pharisees/scribes/religious leaders and the outcasts of Israel . . . the parable was not allegorical, because it posits only one main point of comparison. The point is that the kingdom of God has come and that those who would have been expected to receive it (the religious elite) did not do so, whereas the ones least likely to receive it (the publicans, poor, harlots, etc.) have.[42]

But this point is actually articulated in three independent clauses. Stein's interpretation seems perfectly correct, but it is inaccurate to call it one point and thereby to deny a certain allegorical nature to the parable.

Of course, there may be ways of combining the two or three points of dyadic and triadic parables into one simple sentence. Where this works, it is probably desirable to do so in order to illustrate the thematic unity of the passage and the relationship between the various lessons learned from reading the story through the eyes of its

---

41. For all the details of the approach we are suggesting here, see C. L. Blomberg, *Interpreting the Parables*, 2nd ed. (Downers Grove: InterVarsity; and Nottingham: Apollos, 2012).

42. R. H. Stein, *An Introduction to the Parables of Jesus* (Philadelphia: Westminster, 1981), 89; cf. S. Kistemaker, *The Parables: Understanding the Stories Jesus Told*, 2nd ed. (Grand Rapids: Baker, 2002), 40, on the sower. Both texts nevertheless remain excellent introductory works for studying parables.

different characters. Thus, from the parable of the Two Sons (Matt 21:28–32) we might deduce three lessons from the three characters: (1) like the father sending his sons to work, God commands all people to carry out his will; (2) like the son who ultimately disobeyed, some promise but do not perform rightly and so are rejected by God; and (3) like the son who ultimately obeyed, some rebel but later submit and so are accepted. Then a possible way of combining these three points emerges: "Performance takes priority over promise." This formulation helps preachers and teachers communicate the message of the parable in a much more memorable form! One might harmonize this short proposition with the longer series of three points by speaking of one main point with three subpoints or by equating the short summary with the parable's plot and the longer sentences with its various points of view.

Not all of the parables, especially some of the longer more complex narratives, yield a simple, unified lesson so easily. It is arguably better, then, to preserve a more detailed and possibly cumbersome formulation than to compose a pithy summary that risks losing some of the message of the text. So, for example, with the Good Samaritan, interpreters should strive to preserve all three strands of meaning that have often been perceived. From the example of the priest and Levite comes the principle that religious status or legalistic casuistry does not excuse lovelessness; from the Samaritan we learn that we must show compassion to those in need; from the man in the ditch emerges the lesson that even an enemy is a neighbor. Or, in the case of the parable of the Wicked Tenants, four key characters or groups of characters teach us: (1) God is extremely patient in waiting for his rebellious people to do his will; (2) a day will come, however, when that patience is exhausted and he will destroy those who remain rebellious; (3) his purposes will not then be thwarted for he will raise up new, obedient followers; and (4) this turning point will occur at the time of the Jews' rejection and crucifixion of Christ (Mark 12:1–12).

Although there are other important things we could say about parables, one point is crucial. As metaphorical discourse, parables create an impact through their choice of imagery and narrative form, which is largely lost when one tries to communicate their meaning with one or more propositions. Yet against the so-called new hermeneutic (see ch. 2), it is both possible and important to translate parables into propositional language. Otherwise, modern readers may not understand their meaning at all![43] But with the new hermeneutic, it is equally appropriate and helpful to consider retelling a parable in modern garb to recreate the effect it would have had on its original audience. After two millennia of domestication, these texts sometimes convey to modern readers the exact opposite of what Jesus originally intended. Today even the most biblically illiterate Westerner "knows" that a Samaritan is compassionate and

---

43. The best and fullest exposition of the parables from this perspective of the new hermeneutic is B. B. Scott, *Hear Then the Parable* (Minneapolis: Fortress, 1989). But it needs to be read in light of the massive methodological critique by A. C. Thiselton, *The Two Horizons: New Testament Hermeneutics and Philosophical Description* (Grand Rapids: Eerdmans, 1980).

that Pharisees are "bad guys." But this is precisely *not* what any first-century Jew would have thought—Samaritans were the hated half-breeds and Pharisees the most popular of the religious leaders. To have the proper impact on a typical conservative white American congregation in the twenty-first century, a preacher ought to consider retelling the story with the man in the ditch as a white Anglo-Saxon Protestant, the priest and Levite as two upstanding local evangelical Presbyterian and Southern Baptist pastors, and the Samaritan as a fundamentalist Arab Muslim (or perhaps an atheist African-American lesbian!). Such preachers who have particularly racist, sexist, or nationalist congregations ought also to consider if faithfulness to the Bible in this fashion might cost them their jobs and whether they are prepared to pay this price![44]

Miracle Stories

Another unique form in the Gospels is the miracle story. A biblical miracle "is a strikingly surprising event, beyond what is regarded as humanly possible, in which God is believed to act, either directly or through an intermediary."[45] Common motifs include the description of someone's distress, a cry for help, the response of the miracle worker, the miracle itself, the reaction of the crowd and the response of the miracle worker to that reaction. Numerous other features, with many variations, also frequently appear.[46]

Since the Enlightenment, all except for conservative interpreters have tried either to rationalize or to demythologize these stories. The older, rationalist approach sought to explain the apparently supernatural events of the Gospels as scientifically natural ones. The feeding of the 5,000 involved the large crowd sharing small crumbs of bread in anticipation of Jesus' institution of the Eucharist. Jesus appeared to walk on the water because he was wading out on a sandbar just beneath the water's surface.

By the mid-nineteenth century this approach was generally rejected as misguided. Scholars viewed the miracle stories as myths—fictitious accounts designed to glorify and exalt Jesus and promote his divinity. In the twentieth century, form critics and existential theologians developed the idea of demythologizing—seeking the theological message of a miracle story that people could still believe and apply in a scientific age that had discarded the supernatural. In other words, they looked for what remained after they peeled away the "myth." Thus, while Jesus may not have miraculously healed people of illnesses or exorcised demons, nevertheless he did enable people to embrace psychosomatic wholeness and to reject all manifestations of evil that threatened their personal well-being.[47]

---

44. The inspiration for the contemporization of the Good Samaritan comes from Fee and Stuart's similar example (*How to Read the Bible for All Its Worth*, 4th ed. (Grand Rapids: Zondervan, 2014], 166). Bailey *(Peasant Eyes,* 48) comments from the perspective of a Western missionary in the Middle East that in twenty years he did not have "the courage to tell to the Palestinians a story about a noble Israeli, nor a story about the noble Turk to the Armenians."

45. E. Eve, *The Jewish Context of Jesus' Miracles*, JSNTSup 231 (New York; London: Sheffield Academic Press, 2002), 1.

46. For the fullest analysis, see G. Theissen, *The Miracle Stories of the Early Christian Tradition* (Edinburgh: T&T Clark, 1983).

47. For a survey and critique of various approaches to the miracles in view of the Enlightenment, see esp. C.

Science, of course, has never disproved the supernatural. Because of the uncertainties inherent in Einstein's theory of relativity and Heisenberg's indeterminacy principle, quantum physics has left a number of twenty-first-century scientists far more cautious about pronouncing the impossibility of God's existence and direct intervention in human history. Meanwhile, evangelical Christians never abandoned their belief in biblical miracles as historical events.[48] Ironically, however, much conservative *application* of the Gospel miracles has differed little from more liberal demythologizing. Conservatives do not reject the miraculous; they merely consign it to Bible times! *Jesus* may have supernaturally stilled the storm, but *we* would be foolish to expect him to intervene in the affairs of weather today. When in the mid-1980s evangelist and politician Pat Robertson claimed he helped veer a hurricane away from the Eastern seaboard of the U.S. through prayer, he was ridiculed by at least as many fellow evangelicals as by others. Instead, we are told, the correct application of this miracle story is that Jesus "stills the storms of our lives," enabling us to be at peace in the midst of crises. With such an interpretation the distinctively supernatural element of the account remains irrelevant!

Interpreters from numerous theological traditions have increasingly recognized a better approach.[49] The miracle stories in the Gospels function first *christologically* to demonstrate who Jesus was, and then *salvation-historically* to corroborate his claims that the kingship of God was breaking into human history. Thus, when Jesus exorcised one demoniac, he declared, "If I drive out demons by the Spirit of God, then the kingdom of God has come upon you" (Matt 12:28). When John the Baptist sent messengers from prison to ask Jesus if he really was the Messiah who was to come, he told them to tell their master, "the blind receive sight, the lame walk, those who have leprosy are cured, the deaf hear, the dead are raised," and "blessed is the person who does not fall away on account of me" (11:5–6). The storm-stilling miracle, therefore, shows Jesus as exercising divine prerogatives. Like Yahweh himself in the OT, Jesus is Lord of wind and waves (cf. Jonah 1–2 and Ps 107:23–32). The Gospel accounts agree that this miracle forced Jesus' disciples to raise the question of his identity (Matt 8:27; Mark 4:41; Luke 8:25). And while this particular miracle does not occur in John, the Fourth Gospel consistently affirms miracles to be signs (evidences of Jesus as Son of God) meant to bring people to belief in Christ (e.g., John 2:11; 7:31; 10:25; 20:31).[50]

Brown, *Miracles and the Critical Mind* (Exeter: Paternoster; Grand Rapids; Eerdmans, 1984). H. E. G. Paulus and D. F. Strauss were two of the nineteenth-century giants of the rationalistic and mythological schools of interpretation, respectively. In the twentieth century, R. Bultmann's program of demythologizing stands out above all others.

48. By far the best scholarly defense today is C. S. Keener, *Miracles: The Credibility of the New Testament Accounts*, 2 vols. (Grand Rapids: Baker, 2011). Keener also meticulously chronicles the several hundred best-attested and best-documented miracles on every continent on earth in recent decades, noting parallels to every kind of miracle that appears in the New Testament.

49. Cf. esp. G. H. Twelftree, *Jesus the Miracle Worker* (Downers Grove: InterVarsity, 1999); Meier, *A Marginal Jew*, 2:509–1038; and R. Latourelle, *The Miracles of Jesus and the Theology of Miracle* (New York: Paulist, 1988).

50. At the same time, John is quick to point out that people should not have to have signs in order to believe. Cf. esp. 4:48 and 20:29.

Some of the more unusual miracle stories suddenly make sense when interpreted in light of the rule of God that Jesus' person and work introduced. Turning water into wine symbolized the joyful newness of the kingdom against the old constraints of Judaism (John 2:1–11); cursing the fig tree provided a vivid object lesson of the destruction of Israel if she persisted in rejecting her Messiah (Mark 11:12–14, 20–25); and Jesus' walking on the water disclosed his identity to his disciples—Yahweh himself. We should probably understand Mark's enigmatic words, "He was about to pass by them," to mean, "He was about to reveal himself to them" (6:48; cf. God's self-revelation to Moses in Exod 33:22; 34:6).[51] Then Jesus' subsequent announcement, "It is I" (more literally "I am"—Greek *egō eimi*—v. 50), forms an allusion to the divine name revealed to Moses in Exodus 3:14.[52]

Contemporary application of Gospel miracles should thus be more evangelistic than pietistic. Jesus' stilling of the storm should provoke people to ask who such a man was and is—with the correct answer being the divine Messiah. And in an age when reports of apparently supernatural healings, exorcisms, and even occasional nature miracles are increasingly common, we may risk quenching the Spirit by refusing to pray for the risen Christ to repeat the miraculous in our day—not primarily to benefit believers but to help in converting the unsaved. Not surprisingly, many of the most dramatic modern-day miracles occur precisely in those parts of the world long dominated by non-Christian and even occult beliefs and practices (and sadly, more and more parts of the Western world are lapsing back into such paganism). Although the kingdom arrived decisively in first-century Israel, the process of establishing God's rule in the entire world has been a gradual, intermittent one that remains incomplete. We must always guard against counterfeit miracles, to be sure. But Christians today can expect to apply the Gospel miracle stories in valid ways by praying for similar manifestations of God's power in Jesus' name to demonstrate his deity and his superiority over all other objects of worship.[53]

Pronouncement Stories

A third important and distinctive Gospel form receives various labels: apothegm, paradigm, pronouncement story, conflict story, and chreia. All of these terms have their own history and refer to slightly differing groups of texts. But "pronouncement story" is the most common and self-explanatory term.

Common in the Gospels, it designates a short, self-contained narrative that functions primarily to introduce a key climactic saying (or pronouncement) of Jesus. These

---

51. For a discussion of the interpretive options see W. L. Lane, *The Gospel of Mark*, NICNT (Grand Rapids: Eerdmans, 1974), 236.

52. For these three examples and related ones, see esp. C. L. Blomberg, "The Miracles as Parables," in *Gospel Perspectives VI: The Miracles of Jesus*, ed. D. Wenham and C. L. Blomberg (Sheffield: JSOT, 1986; Eugene, OR: Wipf & Stock, 2004), 327–59.

53. A well-balanced statement of contemporary application of the miracles appears in L. B. Smedes, ed., *Ministry and the Miraculous: A Case Study at Fuller Theological Seminary* (Waco: Word, 1987). Also helpful at a slightly more popular level is J. Deere, *Surprised by the Power of the Spirit* (Grand Rapids: Zondervan, 1993).

pronouncements are usually proverbial in nature. As proverbs (see the discussion above in OT wisdom literature), they inculcate wise generalizations in the form of concise memorable phrases and should not be interpreted as absolute truths. Most of them highlight the radical newness of Jesus' message and ministry that quickly aroused the opposition of Jewish readers; hence, they are also called "conflict stories." Some resemble the Greco-Roman literary form "chreia": "a brief statement or action with pointedness attributed to a definite person" designed to epitomize a key aspect of that individual's life or teaching.[54]

Mark 2:13–17 offers a classic example of a pronouncement story. The call of Levi builds to a climax with Jesus' final pronouncement against his Pharisaic critics: "It is not the healthy who need a doctor, but the sick. I have not come to call the righteous, but sinners" (v. 17). Obviously these are generalizations; healthy people did at times need physicians for preventative medicine, and Jesus did occasionally minister among those who considered themselves righteous, which is probably what the Greek *dikaioi* here means (cf. Luke 14:1–24). But both of these situations were exceptions and not the rule.

At the same time, Jesus' claims challenged (and still challenge) conventional ideas of ministry. Neither in Jesus' day nor in ours do most religious people consider preaching and healing among the outcasts of society to be priorities. Not surprisingly, Mark includes this pronouncement/conflict story in a series of five (Mark 2:1–12, 13–17, 18–22, 23–28; 3:1–6) that concludes with the ominous note, "then the Pharisees went out and began to plot with the Herodians how they might kill Jesus" (3:6). This story, finally, captures concisely the heart of Jesus' mission and message—seeking and saving the lost despite increasing opposition. Another series of pronouncement stories appears in Mark 11:27–33; 12:13–17, 18–27, 28–34, and 35–37. In each case we should focus on the climactic saying, avoid turning it into a timeless truth, and recognize its radical challenge to the religious status quo.

Other Forms

Scholars have identified numerous other forms in the Gospels. Many of these have OT parallels—legal maxims, beatitudes and woes, announcement and nativity stories, calling and recognition scenes, farewell discourses, and so on.[55] Most figures of speech are prevalent in the Gospels. In fact, some estimate that Jesus couched over

---

54. B. L. Mack and V. K. Robbins, *Patterns of Persuasion in the Gospels* (Sonoma: Polebridge, 1989; Eugene, OR: Wipf & Stock, 2008), 11, quoting Aelius Theon.; Cf. esp. A. J. Hultgren, *Jesus and His Adversaries: The Form and Function of the Conflict Stories in the Synoptic Tradition* (Minneapolis: Augsburg, 1979) and M. C. Moeser, *The Anecdote in Mark, the Classical World and The Rabbis*, JSNTSup 227 (London; New York: Sheffield Academic Press, 2002).

55. The most useful treatments of all the constituent literary forms in the Gospels are Bailey and Vander Broek, *Literary Forms*, 89–188; and K. Berger, *Formgeschichte des Neuen Testaments* (Heidelberg: Quelle und Meyer, 1984). Berger covers all NT forms and genres with a comprehensive categorization of individual texts. For forms in the entire Bible, presented at a basic level, see L. Ryken, *A Complete Handbook of Literary Forms in the Bible* (Wheaton: Crossway, 2014).

90 percent of his teaching in poetic or figurative language. This would appeal to the crowds and prove easy to remember.[56] Although we cannot go into more detail here, the student who masters the principles we have outlined can proceed with confidence to interpret the majority of the accounts and passages in the Gospels.[57]

ACTS

As might be expected, Acts—the second volume of Luke's two-part work—bears a strong resemblance to the Gospel genre. Acts 1:1 harks back to the Gospel of Luke in a way that suggests its prologue (Luke 1:1–4) applies to both parts. If theological biographies best captures the essence of the Gospels, then *theological history*—a narrative of interrelated events from a given place and time, chosen to communicate theological truths—best characterizes Acts.[58] Instead of focusing on one main character as in a biography, Acts broadens its scope to present key episodes in the lives of several early church leaders.[59] Still, the title "Acts of the Apostles" is misleading because eleven of the Twelve disappear soon after the opening chapters. Most of Luke's narrative centers on Peter and Paul; subordinate characters such as the deacons, Stephen and Philip, garner the next greatest amount of attention. The "Acts of the Holy Spirit" might be a more descriptive title inasmuch as Luke sees the coming of the Spirit at Pentecost and his subsequent filling of believers as the key to the birth and growth of the fledgling Christian community.

As they do with the Gospels, many interpreters of Acts succumb to false dichotomies between theology and history. On the one end of the spectrum, conservative scholars of Acts have been preoccupied with archaeology and other kinds of research, hoping to substantiate the historical trustworthiness of Acts. But in successfully doing so, they have often lost sight of the theological emphasis foremost in Luke's mind.[60] Liberal scholars have often proved more sensitive to Luke's theological insights, but in so doing they have unnecessarily alleged that he contradicts the other evangelists,

56. Cf. the helpful survey in R. H. Stein, *The Method and Message of Jesus' Teaching*, 2nd ed. (Philadelphia: Westminster Press, 1994), 7–32.

57. Of more detailed studies, perhaps the most helpful for beginning students are S. McKnight, *Interpreting the Synoptic Gospels* (Grand Rapids: Baker, 1989); and G. M. Burge, *Interpreting the Gospel of John*, 2nd ed. (Grand Rapids: Baker, 2013). Cf. also J. T. Pennington, *Reading the Gospels Wisely: A Narrative and Theological Introduction* (Grand Rapids: Baker, 2012).

58. R. Maddox, *The Purpose of Luke-Acts* (Edinburgh: T&T Clark, 1982), 16; W. C. van Unnik, "Luke's Second Book and the Rules of Hellenistic Historiography," in *Les Actes des Apôtres: Traditions, redaction, theologie*, ed. J. Kremer (Gembloux: Duculot, 1979), 37–60. For three other complementary genre identifications indicated by their article titles, see D. W. Palmer, "Acts and the Ancient Historical Monograph" (pp. 1–29); L. C. A. Alexander, "Acts and Ancient Intellectual Biography" (pp. 31–63); and B. S. Rosner, "Acts and Biblical History" (pp. 65–82)—all in *The Book of Acts in Its Ancient Literary Setting*, ed. B. W. Winter and A. D. Clarke (Grand Rapids: Eerdmans, 1993).

59. It is tempting to follow Sean A. Adams (*The Genre of Acts and Collected Biography*, SNTSMS 156 [Cambridge: Cambridge University Press, 2013]) and speak of Acts as collected biography, but none of the individuals highlighted in Acts has even an entire selective biography composed about them.

60. The classic example is W. Ramsay, *St. Paul the Traveler and Roman Citizen*, rev. and upd. M. Wilson (Grand Rapids: Kregel, 2001 [orig. London: Hodder and Stoughton, 1895]); cf. Hemer, *Acts*.

the Epistles of Paul, and historical facts.[61] A third approach plays down both Luke's theology and historical accuracy in favor of emphasizing those features of Acts that would have proved entertaining and adventurous for ancient audiences. This approach views Acts akin to a popular novel or historical romance that includes many details simply to enhance its readers' enjoyment and delight.[62]

Implications for Interpretation

We believe that it is possible (and desirable) to embrace all three of these perspectives as part of the genre of Acts without pitting any one against the others. The cumulative evidence for the historicity of Acts—its wealth of detail about people, places, and customs—is too overwhelming to be ignored.[63] But, as in his Gospel, Luke did not compile history for history's sake; rather, he compiled it to teach his readers what he believed God was accomplishing in the world and what God was commanding believers to do in and through the events he narrated. Like the authors of the other "acts" (*praxeis*) of the Greco-Roman world (including later apocryphal "acts" of various apostles of more dubious historical worth),[64] Luke wrote in a lively and entertaining way. So we must not assume that every minor detail necessarily conveys theological import. For example, the story of Paul's sea journey and shipwreck in Acts 27 is rich in nautical detail and high adventure that seems primarily designed to heighten the drama and suspense while also highlighting God's sovereign protection of Paul to enable him to fulfill his calling—cf. 23:11.

"The Acts of the Holy Spirit": A Theological History
A theological retelling of how the Holy Spirit moved among Jesus' followers to establish and spread the church.
Interpretation involves: archaeology, historical criticism, theology analysis, and literary criticism

Thinking Vertically

It is likely that Luke composed Acts much as he did his Gospel: by combining information from shorter written accounts of various events with what he had learned by word of mouth, often from eyewitnesses. In addition, in several places his writing

61. The standard resource is E. Haenchen, *The Acts of the Apostles* (Oxford: Blackwell; Philadelphia: Westminster, 1971). More recently, cf. J. D. Crossan, *The Birth of Christianity* (Harper: San Francisco, 1999).

62. See esp. R. I. Pervo, *Profit with Delight. The Literary Genre of the Acts of the Apostles* (Philadelphia: Fortress, 1987); R. I. Pervo, *Acts*, Herm (Minneapolis: Fortress, 2008). For evangelical appropriation, see L. Ryken, *Words of Life: A Literary Introduction to the New Testament* (Grand Rapids: Baker, 1987), 77–87. As with the Gospels, there are those who have likened Acts to epic fiction, but ancient epic narratives were usually much longer and virtually always in poetry.

63. See esp. the massive presentation of the supportive data throughout Hemer, *Acts*; and C. S. Keener, *Acts*, 4 vols. (Grand Rapids: Baker, 2012), 1:90–382.

64. The collection of apocryphal acts appears in E. Hennecke, *New Testament Apocrypha: Vol. 2: Writings Related to the Apostles; Apocalypses and Related Subjects*, rev. and ed. W. Schneemelcher, trans. R. M. Wilson, 2nd ed. (Louisville: Westminster John Knox; Cambridge: James Clarke, 1992 [1964]).

shifts from third- to first-person plural narrative (from "he" or "they" to "we" did such-and-such), which suggests that on those occasions he was personally present for the events he described.[65] But Luke has thoroughly reworked and integrated his material into a coherent whole. Thus, it is highly speculative in Acts to undertake either source criticism or that brand of redaction criticism that requires comparison between the canonical form and earlier sources.[66] If we had parallel books of Acts as we have parallel Gospels, it might well be a different matter, but we do not. So we cannot create a synopsis to enable us to *think horizontally*.

On the other hand, we have a wealth of data to enable us to *think vertically*. The overall outline of Acts is clearer than the outline of any of the four Gospels. We see Acts 1:8 as theologically programmatic for Luke's purposes.

> But you will receive power when the Holy Spirit comes on you; and you will be my witnesses in Jerusalem, and in all Judea and Samaria, and to the ends of the earth. (Acts 1:8)

He wishes to narrate selected episodes related to the geographical and cultural expansion of Christianity in order to present the gospel as a message for all peoples. Thus, he begins his story by describing virtually all of the first followers of Jesus as Jews who lived in Jerusalem, the political and cultural capital of Israel. But the story ends a mere thirty or so years later with the gospel firmly planted in Rome, the political and cultural center of the empire that dominated Europe and the Middle East in the first century. Within that short span of time, Christianity had been transformed from an almost exclusively Jewish sect to a predominantly Gentile, empire-wide religion.

In six instances, Luke marks off what appear to be major divisions in his narrative that punctuate this expansion of Christianity (6:7; 9:31; 12:24; 16:5; 19:20; 28:31). Each of these summary statements refers to the word of the Lord as growing and spreading. So a very plausible outline of Acts might well look like this:

I. The Christian Mission to Jews . . . . (1:1–12:24)
   A. The Church in Jerusalem . . . . (1:1–6:7)
   B. The Church in Judea, Samaria, and Galilee . . . . . . (6:8–9:31)
   C. Further Advances in Palestine and Syria . . . . (9:32–12:24)
II. The Christian Mission to Gentiles . . . . (12:25–28:31)

---

65. See esp. C. Hemer, "First Person Narrative in Acts 27–28," *TynBul* 36 (1985): 79–109, against the view that this is merely a fictitious device. W. S. Campbell (*The "We" Passages in the Acts of the Apostles: The Narrator as Narrative Character*, Studies in Biblical Literature [Atlanta: SBL, 2007]) demonstrates the narrative role of such passages in Acts and other Greco-Roman histories as defending and projecting "the narrator's personal knowledge as eyewitness or researcher, and, therefore, his credentials for telling the story accurately" (p. 90). Campbell does not weigh in on the accuracy of that projection for Acts itself but shows that at least readers would not have thought they were reading a fictional genre.

66. Scholarly speculations nevertheless abound. See the survey in J. A. Fitzmyer, *The Acts of the Apostles*, AB (New York; London: Doubleday, 1998), 80–89.

A. First Missionary Journey of Paul
and the Jerusalem Council . . . . (12:25–16:5)
B. Wide Outreach through Paul's Two Other
Missionary Journeys . . . . (16:6–19:20)
C. To Jerusalem and then to Rome . . . . (19:21–28:31)[67]

To interpret correctly a particular episode in Acts, therefore, we should first correlate it to its place in Luke's unfolding outline and developing themes. This will help us to perceive Luke's primary purposes and to pass up secondary elements in the episode that he did not intend to resolve. Two excellent examples appear in Acts 8. The two main episodes of this chapter involve: (1) the conversion and baptism of the Samaritans, with their ringleader Simon Magus (8:5–25); and (2) the conversion and baptism of the Ethiopian eunuch on the road to Gaza (8:26–39). In light of modern debates about water baptism, baptism in the Spirit, and eternal security, readers of Acts today usually raise such questions as: Why didn't the Spirit come immediately when the Samaritans believed Philip's preaching? Was Simon Magus ever really saved, and, if so, did he lose his salvation? Is it significant that Philip baptizes the Ethiopian eunuch as soon as they come upon a sufficiently large body of water?

Although all of these are legitimate questions, they are *our* questions. Probably none was in Luke's mind as he penned this chapter of Acts. This passage occurs in the section of his outline that concentrates on how the gospel began to leave exclusively Jewish territory. Thus, the two most striking features of Acts 8 become the reception of Philip's message first by *Samaritans* and then by a *eunuch*, both considered ritually unclean by orthodox Jews. The main applications of Acts 8 for Christian living today, therefore, should not center on the timing of the arrival of the Holy Spirit and its effects, nor on debates about how much water one needs for baptism, or how quickly it should follow on conversion. Rather, these texts should call all Christians today to determine who the Samaritans and eunuchs are in our world. Christian ministry must not neglect today's "untouchables" or outcasts—AIDS victims, the homeless, unwed mothers, drug addicts, gang members, and the like.[68]

Thinking vertically also involves treating *Luke-Acts* as one unit. Identifiable redactional or theological emphases in Luke's Gospel will probably recur in Acts, so students should give special attention to these.[69] The theme of Jesus' compassion for outcasts identified above certainly fits in this category. So, too, does Luke's emphasis on the role of the Holy Spirit and of prayer in believers' lives. Thus, we should not pass over lightly those texts in which the church in a given community gathers and prays for God's guidance, seeking to be "of one accord" (1:14; 2:46; 4:24; 5:12). In

---

67. R. N. Longenecker, "Acts," in *Expositor's Bible Commentary Revised*, 13 vols., ed. T. Longman III and D. E. Garland (Grand Rapids: Zondervan, 2007), 10:708–12, with slight modification.

68. See, e.g., Witherington, *Acts of the Apostles*, 279–301.

69. W. L. Liefeld, *Interpreting the Book of Acts* (Grand Rapids: Baker, 1996), 79–98, identifies ten key theological themes.

an age when some conservative Christians strongly voice their desire to imitate the "New Testament church," very few follow a process of decision making that seeks unanimity or near-unanimity through prolonged prayer meetings of an entire body of believers. Yet that is the consistent pattern of Acts!

By comparing Luke and Acts we may discern structural or thematic parallels even apart from any comparison of Luke with the other Gospels. Frequently, the disciples in Acts closely imitate some facet of our Lord's life as described in Luke. Consider, for example, some of the first Christian miracles. The story of Aeneas (9:32–35) very closely resembles Jesus' healing of the paralytic in Luke 5:17–26, right down to the very wording, "get up and take your mat . . . ." Peter's raising of Tabitha from the dead (Acts 9:36–43) uncannily parallels Jesus' raising of Jairus' daughter (Luke 8:40–42, 49–5 6). In fact, the Aramaic commands to the two dead women probably varied by only one letter—*Talitha koum* ("little girl, arise") and *Tabitha koum* ("Tabitha, get up")![70]

Or compare the closing chapters of Luke and Acts. The Gospel ends with a long and detailed focus on Jesus' passion and death. In fact, Luke 9:51 introduces the theme of Jesus journeying toward Jerusalem and the cross earlier than does any other Gospel. Acts, too, slows down its narrative substantially to focus on Paul's final, fateful journey to Jerusalem and the sufferings and imprisonments that await him there, in Caesarea and in Rome. Like Jesus, Paul determines at one specific point to begin journeying toward Jerusalem (Acts 19:21). Luke may or may not have written his account after Paul's eventual death, but he certainly sees parallels in the closing stages of the lives of both Jesus and Paul. These kinds of similarities between Luke and Acts suggest that Luke saw the life of a faithful disciple as often imitating that of Christ, both in its spiritual power and in the necessity of suffering. What was true for Paul should therefore be true for us. Unfortunately, we rarely find the combination of the themes of power and suffering in contemporary Christianity; those who successfully emphasize the one usually tend to play down the other.[71]

The Significance of Pentecost

Proper interpretation of Acts also requires an appreciation of the significance of the events of Acts 2. This marks the crucial turning point between the age of the Mosaic covenant and the age of the new covenant that was made possible by Jesus' atoning death, vindicating resurrection, and exaltation to the right hand of the Father (Acts 1:1–11). Careful exegesis necessitates a mediating view between, say, the extremes of traditional Dispensationalism and unqualified covenant theology. In other words, the student must avoid interpretations that exaggerate either the continuity or the discontinuity between the two ages.[72]

---

70. Cf. C. K. Barrett, *Acts: A Shorter Commentary* (Edinburgh: T&T Clark, 2002), 148.

71. For excellent evangelical summaries of Acts' major theological contributions, see I. H. Marshall and D. Peterson, eds., *Witness to the Gospel: The Theology of Acts* (Grand Rapids: Eerdmans, 1998).

72. Dispensationalism has taken great strides away from the excesses of past generations toward a more centrist position. Covenant theology, too, has made similar though often not as significant overtures. A helpful volume

> No, this is what was spoken by the prophet Joel: "'In the last days', God says, 'I will pour out my Spirit on all people. Your sons and daughters will prophesy, your young men will see visions, your old men will dream dreams.'" (Acts 2:16-17)

Luke's understanding of Peter's speech concerning the fulfillment of Joel's prophecy (Acts 2:14–21; cf. Joel 2:28–32) strongly suggests that a new, previously unavailable spiritual empowerment will henceforth characterize the lives of Jesus' followers. For example, the baptism and indwelling of all believers by the Spirit (2:38–39; cf. 1 Cor 12:13) and the phenomenon of tongues (2:5–12; 10:44–46; 19:4–7) mark a significant break from OT times. Though they do not recognize it immediately or without conflict, these first Christians come to believe that Jewish and Gentile believers alike no longer need observe laws of the OT apart from their fulfillment in Christ (10:1–11:18; 15:1–29). Thus, one must be careful, for example, not to assume that Acts 1:22–26 offers a model for how Christians should make decisions. Although casting lots was a common and proper practice in the OT era (cf. Lev 16:8; Num 26:55; Neh 10:34), it never reappears in the NT. Indeed, the giving of the Spirit that immediately follows this episode probably is meant to replace methods such as lots for Christian decision making.[73]

On the other hand, interpreters must guard against driving too great a wedge between the days before and after Pentecost. Though we may not cast lots today, we should not accuse the first disciples of having erred when they practiced this method. The notion that Paul was God's true choice for Judas's replacement rather than Matthias finds no exegetical support in any NT text.[74] And the concern for prayer and unity that preceded the use of lots clearly continues on beyond Pentecost.

In not exaggerating the discontinuity between old and new ages, the student must also beware of minimizing the positive value of Acts on the grounds that it reflects a transitional period between covenants.[75] Of course, Acts does describe transitions. Where the disciples had not yet fully come to appreciate their freedom in Christ, we must be cautious about imitating their behavior, as, for example, when the Hebraic Jews in Jerusalem insist that Paul continue to support the sacrificial cult (Acts 21:17–26).[76] But such caution comes from sensitivity to Luke's own clues as a narrator as to what God approved and what he did not. As with many sections of

---

contrasting key perspectives in both camps is J. S. Feinberg, ed., *Continuity and Discontinuity: Perspectives on the Relationship between the Old and New Testaments* (Westchester: Crossway, 1988).

73. That Luke views this lot-casting as appropriate is well argued by D. L. Bock, *Acts*, BECNT (Grand Rapids: Baker, 2007), 89–90. For the Spirit's guidance replacing its use, see A. Fernando, *Acts*, NIVAC (Grand Rapids: Zondervan, 1998), 79.

74. Rightly, W. J. Larkin, *Acts*, IVPNTC 5 (Leicester and Downers Grove: InterVarsity, 1995), 47. *Contra*, e.g., G. C. Morgan, *The Acts of the Apostles* (NY: Revell, 1924), 19–20. This position nevertheless still proves popular in church circles nearly a century later!

75. As classically in an older dispensationalism (see, e.g., M. R. de Haan, *Pentecost and After* [Grand Rapids: Zondervan, 1964; Grand Rapids: Kregel, 1996], 8), but as widely practiced by others, too, and still popular at the lay level.

76. On the whole theme of "The Law in Acts," see C. L. Blomberg, "The Christian and the Law of Moses," in Marshall and Peterson, ed., *Witness to the Gospel*, 397–416.

OT historical narrative, students need to look for hints in the text itself concerning what it presents as a good, bad, or neutral example. Narrative often teaches more indirectly than didactic literature, but that makes it no less normative, once we correctly discern the text's original intent.[77] At the very least, then, the reader must guard against seeing Acts 21:17–26 as too positive a model inasmuch as the whole plot backfires (vv. 27–36).

But this does not hold true for Luke's descriptions of early Christian "communism." Though some (usually staunch capitalists!) argue that the experiments in communal sharing of 2:44–45 and 4:32–37 were misguided failures, Luke appears instead to present them as positive models. He words the results as follows: "And the Lord added to their number daily those who were being saved" (2:47), and "much grace was upon them all. There were no needy persons among them" (4:33b–34a).[78]

It is equally misguided to identify turning points within the book to show that the message of salvation should be offered to Jews no longer. Of course, on several occasions Paul turns from Jews to Gentiles because of the repeated rejection and hostility he receives from the Jewish people (13:46–48; 18:5–7; 19:8–10; 28:23–28). But the very fact that he repeats this pattern several times, as he moves from city to city, prevents us from alleging that any given episode indicates a more general strategy of abandoning the Jews in favor of an exclusively Gentile mission. Even the final turning from Jews to Gentiles in Rome that concludes Acts (28:23–38) does not justify any inferences about appropriate evangelistic strategy elsewhere. After all, in his farewell speech to the Ephesian elders—which he presents as a model for the ministry of subsequent Christian leaders (20:18–35)—Paul emphasizes proclamation "to both Jews and Greeks" (v. 21). And 19:10, 17–18 make clear that even after Paul shifted preaching venues in Ephesus, Jews continued to hear the gospel and to believe.[79] These observations thus rule out all of the older, more extreme forms of Dispensationalism that viewed as normative for Gentile Christians only those parts of the NT that occurred after one of the alleged turning points in Acts.

Acts as Narrative

Acts as Narrative implies that we must employ the tactics for interpreting stories: plot structure, climax, character development, intrigue, twists. We have already stated that narrative often teaches more indirectly than didactic literature without becoming any less normative. Fee and Stuart correctly added to their older maxim that "unless Scripture explicitly tells us we must do something, what is only narrated

---

77. See esp. L. Ryken, *The Literature of the Bible* (Grand Rapids: Zondervan, 1974), 45–106. On the topic of what is normative versus descriptive in applying Acts, see W. L. Liefeld, *Interpreting the Book of Acts*, GNTE (Grand Rapids: Baker, 1995), 113–28.

78. On this theme, cf. esp. R. J. Cassidy, *Society and Politics in the Acts of the Apostles* (Maryknoll: Orbis, 1987; Eugene, OR: Wipf & Stock, 2015).

79. J. A. Weatherly, *Jewish Responsibility for the Death of Jesus in Luke-Acts*, JSNTSup 106 (Sheffield: Sheffield Academic Press, 1994).

or described does not function in a normative way," the additional clarification, "unless it can be demonstrated on other grounds that the author intended it to function in this way."[80] We wish to put it even more strongly. Second Timothy 3:16 provides the grounds to assume students can learn some kind of lesson from every passage in the Bible, even in narrative literature. We have already illustrated in some detail how parables, for example, often contrast characters whose behavior is meant to be imitated or avoided. Sometimes a parable's context makes that point clear (e.g., Luke 10:37; 18:1; 13:3–5). This suggests that in other cases we should draw similar conclusions. Nevertheless, one must proceed much more cautiously when direct commands are absent. How then should we interpret Acts? Primarily, we need to study the entire book to determine if specific events form a consistent pattern throughout or if the positive models Luke presents vary from one situation to another. The former will suggest that Luke was emphasizing a normative, consistent principle; the latter, that applications *may* change from one time and place to the next.[81]

Descriptive	What the author describes in the narrative; what happened
Prescriptive	What the author intends as normative truth for his readers

Examples abound. Gamaliel's advice to the Sanhedrin concerning the Twelve ("Leave these men alone! Let them go! For if their purpose or activity is of human origin, it will fail. But if it is from God, you will not be able to stop these men; you will only find yourselves fighting against God." Acts 5:38–39) fortunately secured the disciples' freedom. But when Paul encountered "magical" religion in Ephesus (comparable to what we would call the occult), he employed a different strategy: strongly exhorting people to abandon such practices and to burn the scrolls containing incantations (19:17–20). Today, Islam is the largest and most powerful non-Christian religion in the world. Historically, Christians have largely ignored it, but after 1,400 years it has hardly gone away. So, while God in his sovereignty graciously used Gamaliel's "logic" to help the disciples, we dare not imitate it in every instance. In other words, Acts' inclusion of Gamaliel's advice does not make it normative for Christians.

Models of church government and organization in Acts disclose an even more bewildering variety of forms. Congregationalists, Presbyterians, and Episcopalians all legitimately point to passages in Acts to support their views of church structure and leadership. In 6:1–6 the entire congregation chooses the apostles' helpers. In 13:1–3 a select group of church leaders chooses Barnabas and Saul for their missionary ministry. And in Acts 20:17–38 Paul resembles a bishop who convenes all the Ephesian elders for instruction. Each of these models in turn draws on various Jewish

---

80. Fee and Stuart, *How to Read the Bible for All Its Worth*, 124.

81. Particularly helpful in discerning timeless from situation-specific principles in Acts is Liefeld, *Interpreting Acts*, 113–27, though readers may dispute one or two of his conclusions.

or Greco-Roman precedents. Luke views all of these models as appropriate examples of valid leadership under various circumstances in various cultures. To apply them today, one needs to look for analogous circumstances in our cultures.[82] It is probably not mere coincidence that a decision affecting everyone in a local congregation was discussed by all; that one limited to the personal ministries of church leaders was dealt with by that smaller group; and that general instruction for people in several congregations came from one who had authority over all of them.

On the other hand, sometimes patterns of ministry and mission remain constant throughout Acts. A good example is how Luke understands the filling of the Holy Spirit. Every time believers are filled with the Spirit—and this happens repeatedly to the same person or group (2:4; 5:8, 31; 9:17; 13:9)—they are enabled to proclaim the Word of God boldly or to do mighty works in Jesus' name. In his letter to the Ephesians, Paul describes different results of the Spirit's filling: praising, worshiping, and thanking God, and submitting to other believers (Eph 5:18–21). But these descriptions are complementary rather than contradictory. A proper doctrine of Scripture will not subordinate Acts to Paul simply because the one is narrative and the other didactic literature. Neither will it subordinate Paul to Acts because of an inherent preference by some for the phenomena of Acts (such as speaking in tongues).[83] The Spirit inspired *all* of Scripture; no one genre trumps the others.

The phrase "baptism in [or "of"] the Spirit" occurs only twice in Acts, but its seven uses in the NT are likewise all consistent. In every instance but one, it refers to the initiating experience of the Spirit creating the church at Pentecost (Matt 3:11; Mark 1:8; Luke 3:16; John 1:33; Acts 1:5, 11:16), and the other usage declares that *all* the Corinthian Christians (and many of them were quite immature) had received this experience (1 Cor 12:13; cf. 1:7). On the other hand, only three times in all of the NT do tongues appear at someone's conversion or baptism (Acts 2:4, 10:46, 19:6). Therefore, while tongues remain a gift for God's Spirit to give as *he* chooses (1 Cor 12:11), speaking in tongues cannot serve as a criterion of salvation or even of Christian maturity. If we are to use the expression as does the NT, baptism in or of the Spirit cannot be equated with receiving any specific gift or post-conversion blessing (legitimate as those experiences may be), but must signify the Spirit's coming to live in a new believer at conversion.[84]

Probably the most important examples of consistent patterns within Acts relate to Luke's main theme—the expansion of the Gospel from Jewish to Gentile territory. Amid the great diversity of sermons that Peter and Paul preach throughout the pages

---

82. E.g., the Greek *ekklēsia* ("assembly" of citizens), the Jewish synagogue elders, and the Roman territorial magistrates.

83. Generally well balanced throughout is M. M. B. Turner, *The Holy Spirit and Spiritual Gifts: In the New Testament Church and Today*, rev. ed. (Peabody, MA: Hendrickson, 1998). More broadly, cf. A. C. Thiselton, *The Holy Spirit in Biblical Teaching, through the Centuries, and Today* (Grand Rapids: Eerdmans, 2013).

84. See esp. James D. G. Dunn, *Baptism in the Holy Spirit* (Philadelphia: Westminster, 1970). Cf. also J. M. Hamilton, Jr., *God's Indwelling Presence: The Holy Spirit in the Old and New Testaments* (Nashville: B & H, 2006).

of Acts, we can discern a common kerygma (proclamation of salvation). The first Christians consistently focus on the death, resurrection, and exaltation of Jesus as the core of their message. Because of who Jesus was and what he did, all people must now repent in order to receive forgiveness of sins. To be sure, this message occurs elsewhere in the NT but, even if it did not, its consistent appearance in Acts would make it normative.[85]

Even the diversity within the sermons in which this kerygma appears points to another consistent feature of early Christian preaching: concern for contextualizing the gospel. When preaching to Jews, Peter and Paul appeal to the fulfillment of Scripture (2:14–39; 3:12–26; 13:16–41). When addressing the Stoics and Epicureans, Paul explains to them their "unknown god" (17:22–31). When he speaks to the superstitious believers in mythology in Lystra, Paul appeals to the testimony of the creator as found in rain and harvest (14:14–18). In each case these preachers sought to establish common ground with their audiences in order to gain the greatest possible acceptance of their message. In each case, too, they made sure to include a distinctive witness to the true and living God, usually explicitly in terms of the person and work of Christ. Christians in all ages can learn much about cross-cultural ministry from these models and would do well to emulate them.[86]

EPISTLES

Implications for Interpretation

General Considerations

At first glance, genre criticism of the Epistles might seem to have little to say. An epistle is a letter. The NT letters are less literary, formal, and artistic than many classical Greek treatises but still generally longer, more carefully structured, and more didactic than typical personal correspondence.[87] As writings from apostles and other

---

85. The classic study of the core kerygma is C. H. Dodd, *The Apostolic Preaching and Its Developments* (New York: Harper and Row, 1951). Cf. the discussion in G. E. Ladd, *A Theology of the New Testament*, rev. and ed. D. A. Hagner (Grand Rapids: Eerdmans, 1993), 364–78.

86. A particularly helpful study of the patterns of ministry and preaching throughout Acts is M. Green, *Evangelism in the Early Church*, 2nd ed. (Grand Rapids: Eerdmans, 2003). The issue of the historicity of the speeches of Acts has generated extensive scholarly debate. Some rather uncritically cite the ancient Greek historian, Thucydides, as Luke's exemplar to prove both substantial trustworthiness and substantial fabrication! It is *not* clear, however, that there is only one Thucydidean view of reporting speeches. He apparently followed memory and eyewitness sources carefully at times and on other occasions made up speeches while striving for historical verisimilitude. See S. E. Porter, "Thucydides 1.22.1 and Speeches in Acts: Is There a Thucydidean View?" *NovT* 32 (1990): 121–42. On the speeches of Acts, the most thorough and balanced study is C. H. Gempf, "Historical and Literary Appropriateness in the Mission Speeches of Paul in Acts" (PhD thesis, University of Aberdeen, 1988). But for those who subscribe to the authority of the final form of Scripture, not considering its prehistory or tradition criticism, few hermeneutical issues hinge on the solution to this debate.

87. For details of ancient letter writing, cf. S. K. Stowers, *Letter Writing in Greco-Roman Antiquity* (Philadelphia: Westminster, 1986); E. R. Richards, *Paul and First-Century Letter Writing: Secretaries, Composition and Collection* (Downers Grove: InterVarsity, 2004); and H.-J. Klauck, *Ancient Letters and the New Testament: A Guide to Context and Exegesis* (Waco: Baylor University Press, 2006).

early church leaders to various Christian communities and individuals, the Epistles primarily teach theology and offer ethical instruction. From one point of view, then, the interpreter's task is easier here than anywhere else in Scripture. For, presumably, the writers of the Epistles believed the doctrines they promulgated and obeyed the instructions they promoted. For example, a survey of Romans reveals Paul's concern to teach God's plan of salvation—from humanity's universal sinfulness (1:18–3:20), to justification in Christ (3:21–5:20), to sanctification by the Spirit and glorification in the future (Rom 6–8). Key ethical topics include holistic transformation of body and mind (12:1–2), faithful use of spiritual gifts (12:3–8), Christian love and submission (12:9–13:14), and exercising or restraining one's freedom (14:1–15:13). Little wonder many people have come to faith in Christ and grown in their walk with him simply by reading Romans—without a hermeneutics textbook!

A more careful analysis, however, reveals complexities in the Epistles. Though the most deliberately and directly didactic of all the NT genres, epistles are also the most "occasional." In other words, the authors wrote the Epistles for specific occasions to address individual audiences who were facing unique problems. Interpreters must reconstruct those original "occasions" and purposes as precisely as possible in order to separate timeless principles from situation-specific applications. The same readers who found Romans so straightforward may puzzle quite a bit more when they come to 1 Corinthians 11 regarding Paul's instructions about men's and women's head coverings and the proper observance of the Lord's Supper. In many cultures Christians today seem to pay little attention to what people do or do not wear on their heads in church or to how long their hair is, and few churches, if any, offer their communicants enough wine for anyone to worry about getting drunk. In fact, many prefer to substitute nonfermented juice for wine.[88]

While we discuss this problem of separating universal principles from context-bound or culturally limited applications more thoroughly in chapter 12, it is particularly acute for the interpretation of epistles. Sometimes the historical context enables the interpreter to determine how to proceed; sometimes the text of the epistle itself offers clues. For example, the text on the Lord's Supper (1 Cor 11:27–29) permits Christians to draw general principles applicable to situations in which drunkenness poses no danger. Whenever one eats or drinks "in an unworthy manner" (v. 27), one profanes the body and blood of Christ. The problem with the Corinthians' gluttony and drunkenness was, foremost, that it undermined the theological truth of the unity of the body of Christ when it deprived others of getting enough to eat and drink (v. 21). So whenever members of a Christian congregation disregard each other's needs (and so subvert the body of Christ), they are not prepared to partake of the Lord's Table worthily. Notice that this application differs considerably from the

---

88. C. Kraft recounts the provocative story of his missionary work in Nigeria in which new believers could not understand why Western Christians "obeyed the Biblical commands against stealing but not those about head-coverings" (*Christianity in Culture*, 2nd ed. [Maryknoll: Orbis, 2005], 107).

common but mistaken notion that people should refrain from communion when they personally feel "unworthy." The Greek term is an adverb, not an adjective—we must not eat "unworthily."[89]

These last examples illustrate one further general hermeneutical consideration for the Epistles: interpreters must locate them as specifically as possible in a particular historical context. Fortunately, at least with the Pauline Epistles, a close reading of a given letter from start to finish usually discloses specific details about that letter's audience and relevant circumstances.[90] Comparison with information in Acts often yields additional data,[91] and the study of other ancient writers' descriptions of the various cities in which the apostolic churches were situated may help to round out the picture.[92] Thus, we can learn much about Paul's opponents in Philippi from references in the letter itself (Phil 1:15–18; 3:2–11). We may appreciate the superstitious, pagan attitudes Paul encountered in Galatia by reading background material in Acts (cf. Acts 14:11–13 with Gal 3:1). And we can understand why Paul wrote extensively about sexual morality in 1 Corinthians (5:1–13; 6:12–20; 7:1–40) when we learn from other historical sources that the massive temple to Aphrodite, which towered over the city of Corinth from a nearby cliff-top, had at one time employed over 1,000 "sacred prostitutes"—male and female!

Of course, not all of the Epistles can be so easily set in their historical contexts. Galatians, for instance, polarizes interpreters who debate whether it was written to North or South Galatia and whether it is to be dated "early" or "late" (i.e., before or after the Apostolic Council of Acts 15). The comparison between Acts 14 and Galatians 3 made above works only if one adopts an early date and Southern provenance.[93] Hebrews (written anonymously) and most of the so-called general Epistles (James, 1 and 2 Peter, 1, 2, and 3 John, and Jude) tell us very little about their destinations or dates. And many scholars view as pseudonymous (i.e., written in the name of an apostle or other leading Christian figure by someone else) several of the letters ascribed to Paul (most notably Ephesians, Colossians, 1, 2 Timothy and Titus), as well as those of James, Peter, and Jude, perhaps dating from a generation or more after the lifetime of that individual.[94] Such a view relegates any discussion of provenance to enlightened speculation at best.

This issue of *pseudonymity*, therefore, deserves a few comments here. Authorship

---

89. See, e.g., A. C. Thiselton, *The First Epistle to the Corinthians*, NIGTC (Carlisle: Paternoster; Grand Rapids: Eerdmans, 2000), 890.

90. Recall our detailed instructions above for researching historical background issues.

91. Once the general trustworthiness of Acts is shown to be probable (on which see above).

92. See esp. C. E. Fant and M. G. Reddish, *A Guide to Biblical Sites in Greece and Turkey* (Oxford: Oxford University Press, 2003); cf. also P. Walker, *In the Steps of Paul: An Illustrated Guide to the Apostle's Life and Journeys* (Grand Rapids: Zondervan, 2008).

93. For details and a defense of this position, see R. N. Longenecker, *Galatians*, WBC 41 (Dallas: Word, 1990), lxi–lxxxviii; and D. J. Moo, *Galatians*, BECNT (Grand Rapids: Baker, 2013), 2–18.

94. As in most standard critical introductions to the NT, e.g., D. Burkett, *An Introduction to the New Testament and the Origins of Christianity* (Cambridge: Cambridge University Press, 2002); or M. E. Boring, *An Introduction to the New Testament: History, Literature, Theology* (Louisville: Westminster John Knox, 2012).

may make quite a difference in how one interprets, say, 1 Timothy 2:8–15. For various reasons many scholars deny that Paul could have written the Pastorals (1, 2 Timothy and Titus). Instead, they view these three letters as the product of a disciple of Paul a generation later who wrote when the church was becoming more institutionalized and chauvinistic (or "repatriarchalized"). By that time, Christians had allegedly lost sight of the totally egalitarian positions of Jesus and Paul (cf. esp. Gal 3:28) and were lapsing back into the bad habits of the surrounding culture. Such a view, then, allows Christians to disregard the prohibitions in 1 Timothy 2:12 against women teaching or having authority over men in church.[95]

Some scholars have freely embraced pseudonymity when they perceived "contradictions" between the theologies of various epistles attributed to the same writer or noted marked changes in style or ethos. On the other hand, other scholars have rejected pseudonymity as incompatible with the inspiration or authority of Scripture. If an epistle begins, "Paul, an apostle . . . ," they argue, no one but Paul could have written it.

Neither of these approaches, however, can withstand close scrutiny. The linguistic and theological differences among the Epistles have been overblown. Given the limited amount of material we have from any one Scripture writer, and given the different styles authors will adopt for different circumstances, we doubt that a modern reader could ever conclusively say that the person whose name appears in the opening verse could not have written a given epistle.[96]

But neither must we read such texts uncritically. No one today protests that the *Congressional Record* errs when it attributes to a particular senator a speech that was written by an aide and possibly was never even delivered on the Senate floor. We understand the literary convention. Nor do readers of an autobiography of a famous public figure accuse its publishers of fraud when they discover in the preface that a ghostwriter actually wrote the celebrity's memoirs. Many books written by preachers today fit this category. In many instances "authors" do not even identify their ghostwriters, nor is the convention made explicit in any place in the book. Is this problematic? The crucial question to ask, therefore, is whether or not pseudonymity would have been an accepted literary convention within first-century Christianity. The proliferation of popular intertestamental Jewish writings suggests that pre-Christian Judaism may have come to accept this device. Yet the battle with gnostic and other heretical Christian writings, from the mid-second century on, demonstrates that later Christians regularly rejected it. But what of the first century? The jury is still out; the evidence is meager on both sides.[97]

---

95. It is possible to be fully egalitarian and evangelical while maintaining Pauline authorship, by arguing that there are historical or textual reasons for seeing 1 Tim 2:12 as situation specific in its original intention. Here we identify the view that dismisses its authority because it was written by an inferior author.

96. With respect to the Pastorals see esp. L. T. Johnson, *The First and Second Letters to Timothy*, AB 35A (New York; London: Doubleday, 2001), 55–99. Johnson gives a vigorous defense of Pauline authorship of these letters.

97. The fullest recent treatment of the diversity of forms of pseudonymity in the ancient Mediterranean world

One likely way to advance the discussion would occur if one could show that a particular epistle conforms to a demonstrably pseudonymous genre. Of several hypotheses, perhaps the most persuasive comes from Richard Bauckham, who relates 2 Peter to the consistently pseudonymous *testamentary* genre.[98] To Bauckham, 2 Peter 1:15 presents this epistle as "Peter's" final instructions to his followers shortly before his death. But, he observes, this is precisely the function of testaments written a generation or more later by a follower of a great individual, telling readers of that day what he believed the person would say if he were present. On this view, Peter's audience, knowing full well that Peter was long dead, would not have accused the epistle's author of any deception but would have recognized the attribution of authorship as a key to the letter's genre. An OT parallel of sorts is Deuteronomy, compiled after Moses' death, which is narrated in its final chapter. Even as late as AD 200, Tertullian explained that "it is allowable that that which pupils publish should be regarded as their master's work" (*Against Marcion* 4:5). But, of course, testaments could be written by people in their own names as well, and not every feature of 2 Peter conforms to the genre; so even Bauckham's case must be declared only "possible" rather than conclusive. More importantly, this type of theory of pseudonymity does not diminish in any way the authority of the epistle; it remains just as normative for believers irrespective of authorship. After all, these alleged pseudonymous writings enjoy canonical status.

Specific Considerations

To interpret the NT Epistles correctly we need to compare them with other Greco-Roman letters of antiquity. A fairly typical structure, which even first-century students were exhorted to follow, began with a salutation (identification of author, recipients, and some kind of greeting) and a prayer or expression of thanks for the well-being of the recipients. Then one proceeded to the body of the epistle, which set forth the major reason(s) for writing. If the writer had advice or exhortation to give, this came after the body. A closing farewell rounded out the document.[99]

Understanding these conventions enables the interpreter to recognize what is typical and atypical in the NT Epistles. The opening prayers and thanksgivings, while certainly more theological than an average "secular" letter, in fact performed what all writers considered a common courtesy. On the other hand, when Galatians has no thanksgiving (had Paul written one, it would have come between 1:5 and 6), and when 1 Thessalonians has two (1 Thess 1:2–10; 2:13–16), readers should sit up and take notice. Paul stresses the severity of the Galatians' lapse into legalism by ignoring

is J. Frey, et al., eds., *Pseudepigraphie und Verfasserfiktion in frühchristlichen Briefen/Pseudepigraphy and Author Fiction in Early Christian Literature*, WUNT 246 (Tübingen: Mohr Siebeck, 2009). B. D. Ehrman (*Forged: Writing in the Name of God—Why the Bible's Authors Are Not Who We Think They Are* [New York: HarperOne, 2011]) thus considerably exaggerates how confident anyone can be that (a) any of the NT writings *are* pseudonymous, and (b) that if they are it must have been a deceptive practice.

98. R. J. Bauckham, *Jude, 2 Peter*, WBC 50 (Waco: Word, 1983), 131–63.

99. For a helpful discussion see C. J. Roetzel, *The Letters of Paul*, 5th ed. (Louisville: Westminster John Knox, 2009), 59–72.

standard conventions and plunging directly into the heart of his complaint against them. Conversely, Paul has more words of sustained praise for the Thessalonians than for any other apostolic congregation. So, it is not surprising that he should include an unconventional, added section of thanksgiving.

Sub-Genres of Greco-Roman Letters	
Type	NT Example
• Exhortation Letter: Parenesis	1 Thessalonians
• Diatribe	Romans
• Letter of Introduction/Recommendation	Philemon
• Apologetic Letter of Self-Commendation	2 Corinthians 1–7
• Family Letter	Philippians

Scholars also divide Greco-Roman letters into various subgenres. An epistle like 1 Thessalonians illustrates the "parenetic" or *exhortational letter*. All the praise that Paul lavishes on the Thessalonians fits the strategy of this kind of writing. He gives them some very pointed moral instruction in 4:1–12 (particularly on sexual and business ethics), and he corrects crucial points of theology in 4:13–5:11 (regarding Christ's second coming). But he tactfully prepares his readers for this exhortation by establishing his friendship with them and by emphasizing how well they are progressing and how little they really need any further instruction.[100]

A second subgenre is the *diatribe*: a conversational method of instruction in which the writer considers and answers hypothetical objections from opponents. Most of Romans 1–11 fits reasonably well into this classification. So when Paul frequently tackles objections to his presentation of the gospel (Rom 2:1, 9; 4:1; 6:1, 15; 7:7), readers need not assume that such objectors were actually present in the Roman church. More likely, Paul was anticipating the types of questions his letter might elicit and answering them before they ever arose.[101]

Still another subgenre of epistle is the *letter of introduction or recommendation*, designed to introduce the bearer of the letter to its recipients before requesting a certain favor. Often the writer of the letter was a close friend or relative of the recipient(s) who was promising to return the favor in some way. Philemon exemplifies this genre. Paul asks Philemon to welcome home his runaway slave Onesimus without punishing him, promises to pay any damages Philemon incurred, and reminds Onesimus of the debts he owes Paul. The entire epistle is a masterpiece of tact and persuasion as Paul steers a delicate course between pleading and demanding. Since the letter of recommendation was a well-established genre of writing, Paul could expect Philemon to comply with his requests.[102]

---

100. Cf. A. J. Malherbe, *The Letters to the Thessalonians*, AB 32B (New York; London: Doubleday, 2000).

101. S. K. Stowers, *The Diatribe and Paul's Letter to the Romans*, SBLDS 57 (Chico, CA: Scholars, 1981).

102. D. E. Aune, *The New Testament in Its Literary Environment* (Philadelphia: Westminster, 1987), 211–12; Stowers, *Letter Writing in Greco-Roman Antiquity*, 155.

Not every proposed subgenre in the criticism of the Epistles is as clear-cut as the examples of 1 Thessalonians, Romans, and Philemon. Nevertheless, a number of other suggestions possess value for honing our hermeneutical approach. Most of 2 Corinthians 1–7 likely forms an *apologetic letter of self-commendation*, a well-known Greco-Roman form of rhetorical self-defense. Although Paul recoils at the vacuous rhetoric of his opponents in Corinth, he nevertheless crafts a carefully structured and highly rhetorical response.[103] Chapters 10–13 are particularly steeped in irony and a kind of legitimate boasting of which rhetoricians particularly approved.[104] Recognizing Paul's strategy prevents a misreading of 1 Corinthians 2:1–5. Paul does not reject all the standards of "secular" wisdom of his day; he merely rejects anything that intractably opposes the gospel of the cross of Christ. With the Spirit's guidance he happily employs effective rhetorical devices to persuade his audiences of his views. Good Christian communication in any age should do the same.

Some have tended to view Philippians as disjointed, even as a composite product of several epistles gathered haphazardly into one scroll. But more likely, this epistle illustrates the structure of the *family letter*, combining, in sequence: an address and greeting (1:1–2), a prayer for the recipients (1:3–11), reassurance about the sender (1:12–26), a request for reassurance about the recipients (1:27–2:18), information about the movement of intermediaries (2:19–30), an exchange of greetings with third parties (4:2–22), and a closing wish for health (4:23). Paul then departs from convention and adds a polemic against false teachers (3:1–4:1) and various other exhortations and thank yous (4:2–20). The Philippians have recently sent him money, for which he expresses his gratitude, but they have also come under attack, which causes him distress. Because these two sections deviate from the norm, they would have stood out and received the most attention. Paul probably departed from the standard form of a family letter precisely to highlight these two special concerns.[105]

Another way of categorizing epistles considers the kinds of rhetoric they employ. The ancient Greeks and Romans distinguished three major types: *judicial* (seeking to convince an audience of the rightness or wrongness of a past action), *deliberative* (trying to persuade or dissuade certain individuals concerning the expediency of a future action), and *epideictic* (using praise or blame to urge people to affirm a point of view or set of values in the present). A full-blown rhetorical address would contain all of the following features, though often one or more sections might be missing:

exordium — stated the cause and gained the audience's attention and sympathy
narratio — related the background and facts of the case

103. L. L. Belleville, "A Letter of Apologetic Self-Commendation: 2 Cor. 1:8–7:16," *NovT* 31 (1989): 142–63. For the entire letter as an *apologia*, see M. J. Harris, *The Second Epistle to the Corinthians*, NIGTC (Grand Rapids: Eerdmans, 2005), 46.

104. Cf. esp. C. Forbes, "Comparison, Self-Praise and Irony: Paul's Boasting and the Conventions of Hellenistic Rhetoric," *NTS* 32 (1986): 1–30.

105. Cf. further L. Alexander, "Hellenistic Letter-Forms and the Structure of Philippians," *JSNT* 37 (1989): 87–101. Others often put Philippians in the broader category of a friendship letter.

propositio	stated what was agreed upon and what was contested
probatio	contained the proofs based on the credibility of the speaker and appealed to the hearers' feelings and/or logical argument
refutatio	refuted opponents' arguments
peroratio	summarized argument and sought to arouse hearers' emotions.[106]

Many of the NT Epistles reasonably approximate this structure. As a basis for outlining NT Epistles, it can help the student understand how each part of a letter is functioning. For example, 2 Thessalonians 2:1–2 forms the thesis or *propositio(n)* around which all of the letter is built—the day of the Lord is not as immediately at hand as some in the church have been led to think.[107] Galatians 3:1–4:31 gathers together the proofs (*probatio*) for Paul's proposition concerning justification by faith in 2:15–21. These reveal the diversity of arguments an ancient writer or speaker might employ to try to persuade. They also suggest strategies that we may still use effectively today. These include arguments from undeniable personal experience (the Galatians' reception of the Spirit, 3:1–5 vs. their previous non-Christian lives, 4:8–11); from Scripture (Gen 15:6; Deut 27:26; Hab 2:4; Lev 18:5; and Deut 21:23 in Gal 3:6–14); from common human practice (in making covenants, guarding prisoners, and granting inheritances, 3:15–18, 21–22; 4:1–7); from Christian tradition (particularly in baptism, 3:26–29); from friendship (4:12–20); and from an analogy (with the establishment of the Abrahamic covenant, 4:21–31).[108]

Determining the rhetoric of an epistle often proves more difficult when authors mix two or three kinds together. Almost all NT letters function *deliberatively* because a primary purpose was to tell believers how to act or how not to act. Still, one may be able to distinguish an emphasis, say, between 2 and 3 John.[109] Third John seems primarily *epideictic*—"the elder" praises Gaius for his Christian lifestyle and hospitality. Although he encourages him to continue faithfully, Gaius does not need to be persuaded of the correctness of his behavior. But in 2 John, the elder employs primarily deliberative rhetoric, advising "the elect lady" on the correct course of action in light of the heretics who have seceded from the community.

We, too, do well to know our audiences—when to praise and when to persuade. Faithful Christians do not need more sermons that tell them why they should do what they already know they ought to do. Where there is often abundant motivation by guilt, we could do with a little more praise! Conversely, in evangelistic contexts and in an increasingly secularized, paganized, and postmodern world (or church), we dare

---

106. G. A. Kennedy, *New Testament Interpretation through Rhetorical Criticism* (Chapel Hill: University of North Carolina Press, 1984), 24.

107. F. W. Hughes, *Early Christian Rhetoric and 2 Thessalonians,* JSNTSup 30 (Sheffield: JSOT, 1989), 56–57.

108. H.-D. Betz, *Galatians,* Herm (Philadelphia: Fortress, 1979), 19–22; we have modified some of his labels.

109. Cf. D. F. Watson, "A Rhetorical Analysis of 2 John according to Greco-Roman Convention," *NTS* 35 (1989): 104–30; with D. F. Watson, "A Rhetorical Analysis of 3 John: A Study in Epistolary Rhetoric," *CBQ* 51 (1989): 479–501.

not assume that people comprehend or accept the logic and content of basic Christian beliefs or morals. We need to contend for them with carefully thought-out strategies.

Rhetorical analysis also demonstrates the unity of epistles previously thought to be composites. We have already observed this with Philippians and 2 Corinthians 1–7 above. A third example is Romans. Scholars used to identify the long list of greetings in chapter 16 as a misplaced appendix, perhaps belonging instead at the end of the letter to the Ephesians. This view was rendered improbable by Karl Donfried a quarter-century ago.[110] More plausibly, Romans concludes this letter with epideictic rhetoric and the subgenre of an *ambassadorial letter*.[111] That is to say, Paul paves the way for an anticipated visit to Rome by commending his understanding of the gospel to the church there and by explaining the purposes of his travels. It is in his best interests to establish a good hearing for his message by referring to individuals in the Roman church with whom he is acquainted. As with Priscilla and Aquila, this probably took place when they had met or worked together elsewhere in the empire.

Distinctives of Hebrews and the General Epistles

Hebrews and three of the General Epistles—James, 1 John, and Jude—vary from traditional letter genres: Hebrews does not begin like a letter, James does not end like one, and 1 John has neither a salutation nor a closing. Hebrews describes itself as "a word of encouragement or exhortation" (Heb 13:22). Since this phrase occurs elsewhere in the NT only in Acts 13:15 where it designates a sermon, its author may well have designed Hebrews as a written sermon or homily. Among other things, this means that the numerous warnings against apostasy (2:1–4; 3:7–4:11; 6:4–12; 10:19–39; 12:14–29) are most likely not hypothetical. The writer of Hebrews seriously believed that some in his congregation were in danger of abandoning their profession of Christian faith, and he wanted to warn them against it.[112]

Perhaps the most significant study of the genre of a non-Pauline epistle is Peter Davids's analysis of James as a complex *chiasmus* (for this device, see the discussion above). Three themes stand out: trials and temptations, wisdom and speech, and wealth and poverty. James 1 introduces each of these themes twice, while chs. 2–5 present them in greater detail in inverse order.[113] Even if this outline requires modification at points, it refutes two widely held notions about the letter. First, James is not simply a collection of teachings loosely strung together, like the book of Proverbs or other ancient wisdom literature. Second, James' main concern is not faith versus works (though that has been the primary preoccupation of commentators ever since Martin

---

110. K. P. Donfried, *The Romans Debate*, rev. ed. (Peabody: Hendrickson, 2015 [orig. 1991]).

111. R. Jewett, "Romans as an Ambassadorial Letter," *Int* 36 (1982): 5–20. Cf. R. Jewett, *Romans*, Herm (Minneapolis: Fortress, 2007), 42–46.

112. On the genre and exegesis of Hebrews, see esp. W. L. Lane, *Hebrews*, 2 vols., WBC 47A–47B (Dallas: Word, 1991). Nuancing this and speaking of a letter with homiletic elements or composed of a series of smaller homiletic components is R. T. France, "Hebrews," in *Expositor's Bible Commentary Revised*, 13:20, 25–27.

113. P. H. Davids, *The Epistle of James*, NIGTC (Exeter: Paternoster; Grand Rapids: Eerdmans, 1982).

Luther). Though this concern is significant, James' indictment of a faith that produces no works (2:18–26) is actually subordinate to the larger and more crucial topic: the appropriate use of one's material resources (see 2:14–17). Opponents of "lordship salvation" and promoters of "the American way of life" would do well to ponder at greater length the implications of 2:15–16 in the context of the rhetorical question of v. 14 (which anticipates the answer, no).[114]

First John neither begins nor ends like a letter. Out of several proposals, perhaps the best designates this document a *deliberative homily*.[115] Like Hebrews, it resembles a sermon more than a letter. Like other forms of deliberative rhetoric, it was designed to persuade. In this case, John calls the Ephesian churches to side with him and embrace true Christian doctrine and practice over against the false teachers who promoted heresy and ungodliness, and who had begun to split the church (2:19). If John had any outline in mind as he wrote, it has defied the best attempts of commentators to discover it. But perhaps he was composing instead a series of meditations around the themes of "the tests of life"—Jesus as fully human and fully divine, obedience to God's commandments, and love for one another—so that we should not try to impose more structure than was ever intended.[116]

Jude may well illustrate the more distinctively Jewish genre and interpretive techniques of midrash (see ch. 5),[117] though without introducing any fictitious details. Verses 3–4 state Jude's purpose in a nutshell: ". . . I felt compelled to write and urge you to contend for the faith that was once for all entrusted to God's holy people. For certain individuals whose condemnation was written about long ago have secretly slipped in among you . . . ." Verses 5–19 do not argue the case but merely present a series of illustrations of what this condemnation will be like. Here Jude draws heavily on Jewish Scripture and tradition. He likens the false teachers to three OT exemplars and then interprets these comparisons (vv. 5–10). Then he repeats the process with three more OT types (vv. 11–13). Turning to intertestamental sources, he cites and interprets the "prophecy" of 1 Enoch (vv. 14–16). Arriving finally at the NT age, Jude recalls and comments on the prophecies of the apostles (vv. 17–19). The effect was rhetorically powerful, even if it seems troublesome to the modern reader. The harshness of Jude's polemic was actually mild by the standards of his day.

A fuller overview of recent proposals concerning the genres and rhetoric of various epistles could multiply our examples. The Eerdmans Socio-Rhetorical Commentary series develops these kinds of outlines in considerable detail.[118] We recommend,

---

114. See further throughout C. L. Blomberg and M. J. Kamell, *James*, ZECNT (Grand Rapids: Zondervan, 2008).

115. Aune, *The New Testament in Its Literary Environment*, 218. Cf. G. Strecker, *The Johannine Letters. Herm* (Minneapolis: Fortress, 1996), 3.

116. R. Law, *The Tests of Life* (Edinburgh: T&T Clark, 1909).

117. Bauckham, *Jude, 2 Peter*, 3–6.

118. Most of which have been written by Ben Witherington, III (on Mark, Acts, 1 and 2 Corinthians, and Galatians), but also by David DeSilva (on Hebrews) and Craig Keener (on Matthew). See also Witherington's *New Testament Rhetoric: An Introduction to the Art of Persuasion in and of the New Testament* (Eugene, OR: Cascade, 2009).

however, that students proceed cautiously, because many of the proposals are quite recent and comparatively untested. Several scholars have pointed out that one cannot automatically move from forms of oral speechmaking to written letters, and that we cannot be sure Paul and the other NT Epistle writers would have even known of all these forms.[119] Nevertheless, the letters were all originally written to be read aloud, and early Christian preachers like Chrysostom recognized some of these rhetorical forms in the NT.[120] So where there seems to be a particularly apt fit between form and contents, we may proceed with a given proposal with some confidence.

Individual Forms in the Epistles

Form criticism of the Epistles is not nearly as common as that of the Gospels or what we identified in the OT. For the most part, NT letter writers did not rely on existent materials nor did they use self-contained forms. But important exceptions do occur. Perhaps the four most significant forms for a study of hermeneutics are creeds or hymns, domestic codes, slogans, and virtue and vice lists.

Creeds and Hymns

In several places in the Epistles, short, paragraph-length sections of a letter present key summaries of doctrine, usually of Christology, in a fashion that resembles ancient poetry, hymnody, and confessions of faith. Scholars generally agree, therefore, that the epistle writers borrowed and/or modified units of material that were already well known and valued in the worship of the early church. Commonly cited examples in Paul include Philippians 2:6–11; Colossians 1:15–20; and 1 Timothy 3:16. Peter perhaps used confessional forms in at least three instances: 1 Peter 1:18–21; 2:21–25; and 3:18–22. Criteria for recognizing these creeds include the presence of a carefully structured poetic style (rhythm and parallelism) that suddenly intrudes into ordinary prose; a self-contained unit of thought introduced with a relative pronoun as a rationale for various instructions; unusual language and vocabulary; and concise statements of doctrine listed sequentially.[121]

Of course, all this involves a substantial measure of speculation, but where proposals of hymns or creeds seem reasonable, several implications follow. We may discern information that reflects what the church over a wide area deemed important in some of its earliest years. We may acknowledge liturgical aspects of early Christian worship, possibly including the discovery of baptismal liturgies.[122] And at times we

---

119. Cf. S. E. Porter, "The Theoretical Justification for Application of Rhetorical Categories to Pauline Epistolary Literature," in *Rhetoric and the New Testament*, ed. S. E. Porter and T. H. Olbricht (Sheffield: JSOT, 1993), 100–22; and J. A. D. Weima, "What Does Aristotle Have to Do With Paul? An Evaluation of Rhetorical Criticism," *CTJ* 32 (1997): 458–68.

120. J. Fairweather, "The Epistle to the Galatians and Classical Rhetoric," *TynBul* 45 (1994): 1–38, 213–43.

121. For an even more detailed list, see M. Barth, *Ephesians*, 2 vols., AB 34A–34B (Garden City: Doubleday, 1974), 1:7–8.

122. The standard introduction is J. N. D. Kelly, *Early Christian Creeds*, 3rd ed. (London: Longmans, 1972; London and New York: Continuum, 2006).

may make educated guesses about distinctions between tradition and redaction. For example, Philippians 2:6–11 falls relatively neatly into two stanzas that portray the condescension (vv. 6–8) and exaltation (vv. 9–11) of Jesus. Each of these in turn may subdivide into three strophes of three lines each, each line containing three stressed syllables. But one phrase breaks this symmetry: "even death on a cross" (end of v. 8). When we recognize that the cross occupied the center of Paul's preaching (1 Cor 2:2), it seems plausible that Paul incorporated into his letter a preexistent Christian hymn or creed to which he added one crucial line[123]—the line he wanted to stress.

The Domestic Code

Numerous ancient Jewish and Greco-Roman sources contain sections of instruction for individuals in a relationship of authority or submission. Often these instructions focused on relationships within the extended household: husbands and wives, parents and children, masters and slaves. Scholars thus refer to these materials as "domestic" or "household" codes, following Martin Luther's use of the German term *Haustafeln*. Colossians 3:18–41; Ephesians 5:22–6:9; and 1 Peter 2:13–3:7 form three clear examples of this form. Probably the most significant discovery that emerges from a comparison of canonical and extra-canonical *Haustafeln* concerns the radical nature of the value the Christians placed on the subordinate partner in each relationship. Modern readers debate at great length to what extent Christian wives, children, slaves, and even citizens should still submit to those people and institutions traditionally seen as authorities over them. But few if any ancient readers would have concentrated on this. They took submission for granted but were probably shocked to read of the strict limitations imposed on the authority of husbands, parents, and masters. Perhaps if the church today paid more attention to obeying these latter commands, the former ones would not seem so oppressive.[124]

Slogans

First Corinthians offers interpreters a relatively unique challenge. In this NT epistle Paul states that he is responding to a specific set of questions and controversies (posed both orally and in writing) from the church (1 Cor 1:11; 7:1). Hence, the outline of 1 Corinthians reads like a checklist of Paul's answers to these various problems: for example, on incest (5:1–12), lawsuits (6:1–11), sexual immorality more generally (6:12–20), marriage and divorce (7:1–40), and so on. In the process, Paul quotes views

123. E. Lohmeyer, *Kyrios Jesus: Eine Untersuchung zu Phil. 2,5–11* (Heidelberg: Winter, 1928). Numerous other analyses of Phil 2:6–11 caution against valuing this one too highly, but it still seems to us quite plausible. The most influential English-language study of this passage, which agrees that the end of v. 8 is Paul's key addition to an existing hymn, is R. P. Martin, *A Hymn of Christ: Philippians 2:5–11 in Recent Interpretation and in the Setting of Early Christian Worship* (Downers Grove: InterVarsity, 1997).

124. On NT *Haustafeln*, see esp. D. Balch, *Let Wives Be Submissive: The Domestic Code in 1 Peter*, SBLMS 126 (Chico, CA: Scholars, 1981); and J. P. Hering, *The Colossian and Ephesian* Haustafeln *in Theological Context*, AUS 7.260 (New York: Peter Lang, 2007). For an extensive bibliography on this topic see W. W. Klein, *The Book of Ephesians: An Annotated Bibliography* (New York; London: Garland, 1996), 268–77.

held by some at Corinth that he wishes to dispute. He can endorse these "slogans" up to a point but substantially qualifies them. We may refer to this as Paul's "yes-but" logic. In several instances, these slogans are clear enough that recent NT translations employ quotation marks (6:12; 6:13; and 10:23). Obviously, Paul himself could not have taught that "everything is permissible for me" (6:12) without substantial qualification!

Paul's Use of Slogans in 1 Corinthians
"I have the right to do anything" (6:12)
"Food for the stomach and the stomach for food, and God will destroy them both" (or only "Food for the stomach and the stomach for food") (6:13)
"It is good for a man not to have sexual relations with a woman" (7:1)
"We know that we 'all possess knowledge'" (8:1)

In other instances, we may not feel quite so confident, but the hypothesis of a number of Corinthian slogans remains probable. Given the likely influence of a quasi- or proto-gnostic influence at Corinth, it is reasonable to interpret 8:1 with the NIV as a Corinthian quotation: "We all possess knowledge." Also 7:1 likely introduces a slogan, "it is good for a man not to have sexual relations with a woman."[125] Origen (ca. AD 200), for example, already considered this a slogan. In fact, all of ch. 7 falls into place once one recognizes that Paul is responding to an ascetic wing of the church that was overly zealous about celibacy. Paul's main point throughout, then, becomes, "Don't change your state in life or be too eager to preserve it just to avoid having sex." Notwithstanding various exceptions that he discusses, Paul tells the Corinthians that: married couples should not deprive each other of sex (vv. 2–7); widows and widowers should consider remaining unmarried only if they can do so without self-destructive lusting (vv. 8–9); divorce is not a legitimate way to avoid sex (vv. 10–16); and it is good for those who have never married to consider celibacy though marriage is not a sinful option (vv. 25–38). Personally, Paul clearly prefers celibacy, but he also recognizes that God has gifted only a limited number of believers for this lifestyle. So, he acknowledges some validity to the pro-celibacy advocates in Corinth but substantially qualifies their enthusiasm. The occasional setting of 1 Corinthians accounts for Paul's tone and emphases and helps readers to understand better how the same apostle could sound so enthusiastic about marriage in Ephesians (5:25–33), a letter, interestingly, that was likely intended for a much wider audience.[126]

These various Corinthian slogans share several common features: they are short and concisely worded (as slogans typically are); they reflect views with which Paul can agree in part but which prove significantly misleading if interpreted without qualification; and they represent a common perspective found in the form of ancient

---

125. The NIV, NRSV, ESV, NET, and HCSB all now put these statements in quotation marks.

126. This assessment of 1 Cor 7 and of slogans elsewhere in the epistle is heavily indebted to G. D. Fee, *The First Epistle to the Corinthians*, NICNT, 2nd ed. (Grand Rapids: Eerdmans, 2014), 297–393.

Greek philosophy that eventually developed into Gnosticism. Recognition of these common features may enable interpreters to evaluate other proposals for slogans in 1 Corinthians. One of the most popular in recent decades, though apparently never seriously advocated before the last century, involves 14:33–35, where Paul writes: ". . . as in all the congregations of the Lord's people. Women should remain silent in the churches. They are not allowed to speak, but must be in submission, as the law says." Proponents understand Paul's comments about women being silent and in submission as another aberrant Corinthian view, which vv. 36–38 then reject. But vv. 33b–35 satisfy none of the criteria just noted for a slogan. The words are not concise or proverbial. If vv. 36–38 form Paul's response, then he does not endorse vv. 33b–35 even in part. And the perspective attributed to the Corinthians would be the opposite of the more egalitarian thrust of proto-Gnosticism. Numerous other options may account for vv. 33b–35, including some that support a modern egalitarian interpretation, but the proposal that these verses form a slogan is one of the least likely of all.[127]

Vice and Virtue Lists

A final example of common forms within the NT Epistles consists of lists of qualities or actions that typify morality or immorality from a Christian perspective. Jews and pagans often compiled similar lists. Examples from the NT include Romans 1:29–31; 1 Corinthians 6:9–10; Galatians 5:19–23; James 3:17–18; and 2 Peter 1:5–7. Comparison with extrabiblical parallels again reveals the NT distinctives as well as one or two principles of hermeneutics. For example, the ancient Greek world regularly condoned gay and lesbian sex. Paul's uniform disapproval of it (cf. Rom 1:24–32; 1 Cor 6:9; 1 Tim 1:10), which fits the entire Bible's disapproval, would have stood out and caused offense then as it so often does today. But faithfulness to the gospel requires that all sins be identified as such in any age, even as we try to be as gracious and loving as possible in the process.[128] It is sometimes objected that we don't treat all sins in the vice lists equally, so that, for example, we scarcely hear any teaching against greed or covetousness (Rom 1:29; Eph 5:3; Col 3:5). The appropriate way of dealing with the inconsistency, of course, is not to ignore all sin but to warn against all of it. Plus, it is important to recall that not all sins are equally serious. Jesus talks

---

127. In our opinion, the most convincing exegesis is that of Thiselton, *First Epistle to the Corinthians*, 1150–61.

128. See esp. R. A. J. Gagnon, *The Bible and Homosexual Practice: Texts and Hermeneutics* (Nashville: Abingdon, 2001). Cf. also R. E. Gane, N. P. Miller, and H. P. Swanson, eds., *Homosexuality, Marriage, and the Church: Biblical, Counseling, and Religious Liberty Issues* (Berrien Springs, MI: Andrews University Press, 2012). At the risk of stating the obvious, just because a given nation or society declares something legal (or illegal) does not change a Christian's obligation. If, e.g., gay marriage is legal in a country, and as long as there are mechanisms for civil (and perhaps even religious) ceremonies that ensure all citizens their rights, no clerics of any religion should ever be forced to violate their consciences by performing a wedding of people they do not believe should marry. If all citizens have equal access to public education, no religious institution should be required to enroll people whose beliefs or practices violate their statements of faith and lifestyle. But if pressure is brought to bear on a believer—i.e., when the laws of humans conflict with the laws of God—believers must follow God's laws (Exod 1:15–21; Dan 3:4–12; Acts 4:19–20).

about the weightier matters of the law—justice, mercy, and faith—as opposed to minute tithing practices (Matt 23:23). All sin separates us from God and puts us in danger of eternal separation from him (Matt 5:21–22). But not all sin merits equal punishment (Luke 12:47–48).

Another principle of vice and virtue lists is that the first and last items on a list often proved the most important, but the order of items in between did not necessarily follow any particular sequence.[129] So we should probably take love as the preeminent fruit of the Spirit and the highest goal of the life of faith, since it is first or last on several NT virtue lists (Gal 5:22; 2 Pet 1:7; cf. 1 Cor 13). We should also recognize that godly wisdom must be morally pure above all else, since it appears first on James' virtue list (Jas 3:17).

Key Theological Questions for the Pauline Epistles

As noted above, when an author writes as many different books over a period of time as did Paul, distinctive theological questions arise. The two most pressing have often been: (1) Is there a unifying center of Pauline theology? and (2) Does Paul's theology develop from one period of time to another so that he changes his mind on any significant issue(s)?

Is There a Center of Pauline Theology?

Because of Luther's influence, for centuries most Protestants assumed that Paul's foremost concern was to stress justification by faith over all forms of works-righteousness. Over time, however, certain planks in Luther's platform eroded. For example, there is no evidence that Paul struggled as a Jew with a guilty conscience, increasingly more frustrated with his inability to please God through good works. Quite the contrary, he thought that he was "blameless" under the law (Phil 3:6) and "advancing in Judaism beyond many" of his age (Gal 1:14).[130] The debate over Romans 7:14–25 continues to rage, but one conclusion seems clear: Paul does not there describe a personal battle he waged before his conversion. Either this details his post-conversion perception of what had previously occurred, or perhaps more likely, it describes the struggle between his old and new natures (or the power of the flesh vs. the power of the Spirit) that he continued to experience as a Christian.[131]

Luther's "center," however, generally held firm though an occasional voice would propose a different, though often complementary, unifying theme (e.g., reconciliation or being "in Christ").[132] Sometimes a scholar or two would question whether Paul's

---

129. Bauckham, *Jude, 2 Peter,* 172–93.

130. See esp. K. Stendahl, "The Apostle Paul and the Introspective Conscience of the West," *HTR* 56 (1963): 199–215.

131. See respectively, D. J. Moo, *The Epistle to the Romans,* NICNT (Grand Rapids: Eerdmans, 1996), 442–51; and C. E. B. Cranfield, *A Critical and Exegetical Commentary on the Epistle to the Romans,* 2 vols., ICC (Edinburgh: T&T Clark, 1975), 1:340–47.

132. Cf., respectively, R. P. Martin, *Reconciliation: A Study of Paul's Theology* (Atlanta: Knox, 1981); and W. D. Davies, *Paul and Rabbinic Judaism,* 4th ed. (Philadelphia: Fortress, 1980), 221–22.

theology was even consistent enough to have a unifying center.[133] But largely through the writings of E. P. Sanders and his followers since 1977, a quite "new perspective on Paul" has taken center stage.[134] Many scholars today contend that "merit theology" or works-righteousness did not characterize first-century Judaism, so that Paul's main contrast with Judaism cannot be faith (or grace) versus works. Rather, Jews believed in "covenantal nomism." That is, obeying the Law saved no one, but obedience kept one or identified one as a member of the exclusive covenant community God had established with Israel. Accordingly, Paul's radical challenge to Judaism was his (to the Jews) radical universalism: the message that one could come to God in Christ apart from the Torah. On this view, Paul's complaint with Jewish practices such as circumcision, the dietary laws, or the Sabbath ordinances was that most Jews had turned them into badges of national pride and identity, rather than that they were trying to save themselves by performing these rituals. On this view the incorporation of Gentiles into the church on equal terms with Jews thus replaces justification by faith as a unifying core of Paul's thought. For Paul, the gospel is the declaration that Jesus is truly Lord over all the universe and that God can be counted on to be faithful to fulfill all his promises for it.[135]

Obviously, the way one interprets much of what Paul wrote will depend on how one assesses this kind of debate over the core of his theology. A still more recent trend has been to read much of the NT, but especially Paul, against the backdrop of Roman imperial claims and actions. To borrow the oft-repeated slogan made best known by N. T. Wright, "if Jesus is Lord, then Caesar is not."[136] Thus, the three largest, most recent English-language commentaries on the Greek text of Romans consistently come to quite different conclusions: T. R. Schreiner goes with the older Lutheran consensus; J. D. G. Dunn enthusiastically advocates the new perspective; and R. Jewett see the primary issue as the imperial background.[137] Probably the truth lies in some combination of the three.[138] We introduce the debate here primarily to remind interpreters again that much depends on the theological grids they presuppose when

---

133. E.g., H. Lüdemann, *Die Anthropologie des Apostels Paulus und ihre Stellung innerhalb seiner Heilslehre* (Kiel: Universitäts Buchhandlung, 1872). Among current scholars, see esp. H. Räisänen, *Paul and the Law*, 2nd ed. (Eugene, OR: Wipf & Stock, 2010).

134. See esp. E. P. Sanders, *Paul and Palestinian Judaism* (Philadelphia: Fortress, 1977); and E. P. Sanders, *Paul: The Apostle's Life, Letters, and Thought* (Minneapolis: Fortress, 2015). For an excellent survey of subsequent developments, see J. D. G. Dunn, *The New Perspective on Paul* (Tübingen: Mohr Siebeck, 2005; Grand Rapids: Eerdmans, 2008). Finally, for an extremely useful assessment see N. T. Wright, *Paul and His Recent Interpreters* (Minneapolis: Fortress, 2015).

135. See now the magisterial theology of Paul by N. T. Wright, *Paul and the Faithfulness of God*, 2 vols. (London: SPCK; Minneapolis: Fortress, 2013).

136. E.g., N. T. Wright, *Paul: In Fresh Perspective* (London: SPCK; Minneapolis: Fortress, 2005), 56.

137. T. R. Schreiner, *Romans*, BECNT (Grand Rapids: Baker, 1998); J. D. G. Dunn, *Romans*, 2 vols., WBC 38A–38B (Waco: Word, 1988); and Jewett, *Romans*.

138. Cf. D. A. Carson, P. T. O'Brien, and M. A. Seifrid, eds., *Justification and Variegated Nomism*, 2 vols., WUNT 2.140 (Tübingen: Mohr Siebeck; Grand Rapids: Baker, 2001–4); M. F. Bird, *The Saving Righteousness of God* (Milton Keynes: Paternoster; Eugene, OR: Wipf & Stock, 2007); and M. Zetterholm, *Approaches to Paul: A Student's Guide to Recent Scholarship* (Minneapolis: Fortress, 2009), 225–41.

they approach a text. While we have made this point more generally elsewhere, it is acute for the Epistles of Paul, since nowhere else in Scripture do so many different documents come from the same writer. If a minor point of one document develops into a major point for all, or vice-versa, interpretation will be skewed.

Is There Development in Paul's Writings?

The proliferation of Pauline Epistles leads to a second theological question. Did Paul ever change his mind or progress in understanding on a particular issue within the span of his canonical letters? Evangelicals have typically rejected this idea where it implied contradiction within the NT even while regularly appealing to progressive revelation to account for God's clear policy changes between the old and new covenants. But what of Paul's harsh words against Peter and the Judaizers in Galatians 2:11–21 when compared with his policy of bending over backwards to be "all things to all people" in 1 Corinthians 9:19–23? And doesn't he believe in 1 Thessalonians 4:13–18 that he will live to see Christ's return, whereas later he recognizes he might die first (2 Cor 1:8–11; Phil 1:20–28)?

One cannot exclude the possibility of development in Paul simply by an appeal to a certain view of Scripture. Not only does revelation progress both within and between the testaments, but a prophet of the Lord may reverse his message completely in a matter of minutes based on a new word from God (cf., e.g., 2 Kgs 10:1–6). But having said this, we believe the case for development in Paul's letters remains unproven. In each case better explanations account for the data than do hypotheses of development. For example, Galatians 2 and 1 Corinthians 9 differ because at Galatia the eternal lives of Paul's hearers were at stake. Any attempt to earn salvation through works only damns a person, so Paul resists the idea adamantly. To the Corinthians, however, he talks about morally neutral practices that establish common ground in order to win the gospel a good hearing. Actually, a unity underlies the two passages: Paul will do whatever it takes, without being immoral or unethical, to bring people to saving faith through the grace of Jesus Christ. In the case of 1 Thessalonians 4 and 2 Corinthians 1, interpreters have probably misunderstood Paul's earlier comments. The "we" of 1 Thessalonians 4:15 does not necessarily include Paul. Grammatically, the phrase "we who are still alive, who are left till the coming of the Lord" may simply mean, "whichever Christians are still alive . . ."[139]

On the other hand, one may fairly speak of a development in Paul between 1 and 2 Thessalonians. In 1 Thessalonians 4:13–5:11 Paul warns the Thessalonians against fearing that Christ's return would be overly delayed. In 2 Thessalonians 2:1–12 he cautions them not to think that it has already taken place. Quite possibly, 2 Thessalonians 2:2 indicates that they had overreacted to his first letter.[140] But no

---

139. On the issue of development as well as on other major hermeneutical issues for Paul's writings, see esp. T. R. Schreiner, *Interpreting the Pauline Epistles*, 2nd ed. (Grand Rapids: Baker, 2011).

140. I. H. Marshall, *1 and 2 Thessalonians*, NCB (Grand Rapids: Eerdmans, 1983), 24, 187.

contradiction divides these two epistles; he simply affirms that one must maintain a crucial balance between assuming the second coming is too near or that it is too distant. We must evaluate each proposal concerning development in Paul, therefore, on its own merits. Can we articulate the alleged development without it resulting in a necessary contradiction in Paul's thought? Does it fit the best interpretation of each of the key texts involved? Does it make best sense of the historical contexts in which the various documents were written? Only after we answer these questions can we make confident pronouncements.

REVELATION

Even the great Reformer, John Calvin, admitted his uncertainty about what to do with the book of Revelation. He did not write a commentary on it even though he completed volumes on almost all the rest of the NT. Interpreters through the centuries have shared Calvin's perplexity, and many of the writers of popular commentaries and guides to its prophecies might have done better to follow in his footsteps! Still, genre criticism can help the careful student sift the more likely from the less likely interpretations among the maze of opinions that compete for attention. Perhaps the most important key is to recognize that Revelation combines parts of three distinct genres: epistle, prophecy, and apocalyptic.[141]

Revelation as an Epistle

Revelation 1:4 states clearly that the author wrote this book to seven churches in Asia Minor. Chapters 2–3 contain seven mini-letters with commendation and/or condemnation for each church. Thus, Revelation includes various characteristics of epistles. For example, interpreters will need to try to reconstruct as accurately as possible the historical circumstances of each church.[142] Most of the details of the letters to the seven churches make better sense when read against this background. For example, ancient Laodicea was well known for its material wealth, the medicinal ointment it produced, and its woolen industry. But the pathetic state of its church led John to encourage believers there to purchase "gold . . . , white clothes . . . and salve to put on your eyes" (3:18). As we noted briefly earlier, archaeology has shed light on the water supply of Laodicea. The city depended on water that came through aqueducts from either the cold mountain streams near Colossae or the natural hot springs near Hierapolis. Either way, the water was lukewarm by the time it arrived in town. So John calls the church there not to resemble its water supply but to be

---

141. On which, see esp. D. E. Aune, *Revelation*, 3 vols., WBC 52A–52C (Dallas: Word, 1997–1998), 1:lxx–xc.

142. The two best resources for this enterprise, the first a classic and the second an important modern update, are W. M. Ramsay, *The Letters to the Seven Churches of Asia* (London: Hodder and Stoughton, 1904; Minneapolis: James Family Publishing, 1978); and C. J. Hemer, *The Letters to the Seven Churches of Asia in their Local Setting*, JSNTSup 11 (Sheffield: JSOT, 1986; Grand Rapids: Eerdmans, 2000). On a more popular level, see J. R. Michaels, *Interpreting the Book of Revelation* (Grand Rapids: Baker, 1992), 35–50.

either refreshingly cold or therapeutically hot. The common view that "cold" here means "clearly opposed to the gospel" or "completely insensitive" is almost certainly the exact opposite of what John meant![143]

Revelation Shares Features in Common with Other NT Epistles
• Identifies its author, recipients, and location (1:4 but also chs. 2–3)
• Greetings (1:4)
• Conclusion (22:21)

Sometimes we are not able to determine the original meaning of John's allusions so easily. The white stone of 2:17 might have been an admission ticket, a jury's vote of "not guilty," or an amulet with a divine name. "Satan's throne" in Pergamum (2:13) might have referred to a temple to the Greek god Zeus, or to the imperial center for emperor worship, or to the shrine to Asklepios, the Greek god of healing. But in each instance the general sense of something highly desirable or undesirable is clear enough.[144]

Studying Revelation as an epistle written to identifiable believers under specific circumstances is also appropriate for material outside chapters 2 and 3. Primarily, the book intends to encourage Christians undergoing persecution, *not* to confuse or divide its readers over fine points of eschatology. In fact, many of John's visions of the future called to mind contemporary events in the Roman Empire near the end of the first century. The judgment of the third seal in 6:6 closely resembles the famine of AD 92. A day's supply of wheat and barley became so scarce as to consume an entire day's wage. But the olive trees and grapevines, whose roots grew deeper, were not as affected by the relatively short-lived drought. So, it seems that God wanted the readers of Revelation to envision the coming judgment as similar to the famine they had recently experienced.[145]

Or again in 9:7–11, the bizarre description of the locusts of the fifth trumpet probably called to mind the distinctive appearance of the Parthian hordes that periodically attacked Rome in its northeastern-most outposts. Unlike the Romans, the Parthians relied heavily on a

> corps of mounted archers, whose tactics were to shoot one volley as they charged and another over their horses "tails." There was therefore some factual basis for John's surrealist pictures of "horses able to wound with their mouths and their tails."[146]

---

143. Cf. further M. J. S. Rudwick and E. M. B. Green, "The Laodicean Lukewarmness," *ExpTim* 69 (1957–58): 176–78; S. E. Porter, "Why the Laodiceans Received Lukewarm Water," *TynBul* 38 (1987): 143–49.

144. For full lists of options, see G. R. Osborne, *Revelation*, BECNT (Grand Rapids: Baker, 2002), 141, 148–9.

145. Cf. G. E. Ladd, *A Commentary on the Revelation of John* (Grand Rapids: Eerdmans, 1972), 101: "these words place a limitation on the degree of scarcity."

146. G. B. Caird, *The Revelation of St. John the Divine*, BNTC (London: Black; New York: Harper & Row, 1966), 122.

Just as the Parthians offered the severest threat known in first-century times to the seeming invincibility of the Roman empire, so Satan's endtime armies will prepare for the greatest battle ever conceived in human history (though ch. 19 describes how this "battle" ends before it is scarcely begun!).

Interpreting Revelation in light of the events of its day should caution overly zealous interpreters against looking for detailed correspondence between the events predicted and contemporary news items in the twenty-first (or any other) century. Many items familiar to first-century audiences contribute to the overall imagery without necessarily corresponding to any specific "endtimes" referent. Christian scholars generally agree that the writers of the popular endtimes paperbacks have missed the message! A perennially best-selling work of nonfiction in the United States since it was published in 1970 has been Hal Lindsey's *The Late Great Planet Earth*, yet over and over again he violates fundamental hermeneutical principles.[147] He asserts that in Revelation 9:7–11 John was describing armed helicopters and their tailgunners! Now to be sure, Lindsey draws some striking parallels between John's locusts and modern-day flying machines, but in so doing he ignores the meaning that would have occurred to John's original readers in favor of one that could never have been imagined until a few decades ago. This violates the most basic principle of hermeneutics: seek the meaning of the text. What is more, his interpretation unwittingly demythologizes the text. Instead of depicting supernatural, demonic creatures coming out of the Abyss (vv. 2–3) ruled by Satan their king (v. 11), Lindsey reduces John's vision to one about mere human warfare.

Lindsey and many others would avoid such errors by observing a basic rule of hermeneutics that interpreters are prone to abandon when studying Revelation: *the text cannot mean something that would have been completely incomprehensible to its original audience.*[148] Nor may an interpreter appeal to Daniel 12:9 in support of a different view. True, Daniel did not understand everything he prophesied (v. 8), and God did reply through an angel, "the words are closed up and sealed until the time of the end." But we must register three crucial observations. First, the only thing Daniel did not explicitly understand was "the outcome of all this." He did not ask for an explanation of what he had been told, but for further information about what had not been revealed. Second, concerning what had been revealed, he was told only that "none of the wicked will understand," but "those who are wise [i.e., not wicked] will understand" (v. 10). Third, Revelation differs from Daniel in that, as the completion of new covenant revelation, God brings his plan of salvation-history to the threshold of the end. All stands ready for Christ to return. So John is told exactly the opposite

---

147. (Grand Rapids: Zondervan, 1970). A similar approach is now popularized by the extraordinarily best selling *Left Behind* novels by T. LaHaye and J. Jenkins. For a powerful critique of this approach, see C. Hill, *In God's Time: The Bible and the Future* (Grand Rapids: Eerdmans, 2002).

148. Fee and Stuart (*How to Read the Bible for All Its Worth*, 263) put it this way: "the primary meaning of Revelation is what John intended it to mean, which in turn must also have been something his readers could have understood it to mean."

from what Daniel was instructed: "Do not seal up the words of the prophecy of this book, because the time is near" (Rev 22:10).

Revelation as Prophecy

Frederick Mazzaferri has shown how the closest generic parallels to Revelation appear in Isaiah, Jeremiah, and particularly Ezekiel. John stands in the tradition of the major prophets of the OT—forthtelling as well as foretelling.[149] Scholars have long debated four major interpretations of the time-orientation of Revelation. The *preterist* approach sees all events through ch. 19 as past; the *futurist*, as all still future (at least from ch. 6 on); the *historicist*, as tracing the development of the entire church age; and the *idealist*, as a symbolic presentation of the timeless struggle between good and evil.[150] When Revelation, with its liberal dose of symbolism appearing throughout, is viewed as similar to OT prophecy, a combination of preterist and futurist interpretations emerges as best. The climactic manifestation of the events that usher in Christ's return (chs. 6–19) remains yet future, but the events will nevertheless resemble (even if on a larger scale) the victories and judgments that God's people and the world have experienced many times since creation—including during John's own time. John's words proclaimed a message of comfort and urged his first century readers to endure hardship (preterist). His prophecy also shows how God's people will need to persevere throughout this age as God brings it to its climactic end (futurist).

Not surprisingly, then, the seven seals closely resemble the signs that Jesus said must occur even though "the end is not yet" (Matt 24:6): warfare, murder, famine, and earthquakes—disasters that have afflicted people through most ages of human history. The seven trumpets and bowls call to mind God's plagues against the Egyptians in Moses' day (hail and fire, water turning to blood, darkness, and sores or boils on people; cf. Exod 7–11). Clearly God is more concerned to warn his people with imagery familiar to them than with literal photographs of what everything will look like. So, we cannot be certain how these prophecies of judgment will be fulfilled. But as prophecy they point to real events at the end of the church age that have not yet occurred. *The prophecies predict literal events, though the descriptions do not portray the events literally.*

Thus, we may not know exactly who the two witnesses of 11:3–6 are, but we know that God's Word will continue to be proclaimed with great power in the last days. If we should happen to be living in the final generation, this should encourage us to continue witnessing boldly for Christ. Again, we probably should not waste too much time trying to guess what great world figure or empire will play the role of the beast of 13:1–4. Numerous guesses have littered the pages of church history,

---

149. F. D. Mazzaferri, *The Genre of the Book of Revelation from a Source-Critical Perspective*, BZNW 54 (Berlin: de Gruyter, 1989). Also review our discussion of the OT genre of prophecy above.

150. For further delineations of these various options, see the introductions to most standard commentaries on the Apocalypse. Some of the best introductory treatments include R. Mounce, *The Book of Revelation*, 2nd ed., NICNT (Grand Rapids: Eerdmans, 1998); C. S. Keener, *Revelation*, NIVAC (Grand Rapids: Zondervan, 2000); and S. Kistemaker, *Exposition of the Book of Revelation*, NTC (Grand Rapids: Baker, 2001).

and all of them so far have proved wrong.[151] But in the end we can expect some ruler and/or government to usurp the prerogatives of God and persecute his people, even as others have so many times throughout history.

If Revelation is prophecy, then only an antisupernatural bias will permit one to agree with Adela Yarbro Collins when she writes, "a hermeneutic which takes historical criticism seriously can no longer work with an interventionist notion of God."[152] In other words, she believes that modern readers cannot seriously expect the world to end with God's supernatural intervention by means of the various plagues and the tribulation described in Revelation. Certainly, she insists, we do not expect the universally visible and bodily return of Jesus Christ from heaven. Yet an understanding of Revelation as prophecy must affirm precisely this, however much different schools of interpretation disagree concerning other details (most notably concerning the millennium and the rapture).[153]

Revelation as Apocalyptic

Probably the most significant and yet perplexing of the three genres in Revelation is the last one. The title of the book, derived from its first line, designates the document as the *apokalypsis*: "the *revelation* of Jesus Christ, which God gave him to show his servants what must soon take place" (1:1). Apocalyptic literature was prevalent in the world of the NT (cf. the earlier discussion of OT apocalyptic). Contemporary Jewish writings like 4 Ezra and 2 Baruch, and to a lesser extent 1 Enoch, exemplified this genre. Daniel 7–12 and Zechariah 9–14 provide the closest OT parallels. Later Christian writings like the Apocalypse of John the Theologian and the Apocalypse of Peter offer still further illustrations.[154]

Characteristics of apocalyptic literature include a description of the events surrounding the end of world history, often said to have come from God by means of angelic or otherworldly intermediaries. Visions and dreams appear regularly. God's

---

151. See the fascinating survey in B. McGinn, *Anti-Christ. Two Thousand Years of the Human Fascination with Evil* (San Francisco: HarperSanFrancisco, 1994). Cf. also F. X. Gumerlock, *The Day and the Hour: Christianity's Perennial Fascination with Predicting the End of the World* (Atlanta: American Vision, 2000).

152. A. Y. Collins, "Reading the Book of Revelation in the Twentieth Century," *Int* 40 (1986): 242.

153. The fullest recent survey of issues surrounding apocalyptic literature is J. J. Collins, ed., *The Oxford Handbook of Apocalyptic Literature* (Oxford: Oxford University Press, 2014). Two evangelical symposia helpfully lay out the major perspectives and give each contributor a chance to respond to each other. R. G. Clouse, ed., *The Meaning of the Millennium: Four Views* (Downers Grove: InterVarsity, 1977), presents advocates for *postmillennialism* (Christ returns after the 1,000 years described in Rev 20:4), *amillennialism* (the millennium is symbolic for either the whole church age or the new heavens and earth of chs. 21–22), and *premillennialism* (Christ returns before the millennium)—which then subdivides into *historic* and *dispensational* forms. In R. Reiter, ed., *Three Views on the Rapture*, 2nd ed. (Grand Rapids: Zondervan, 1996), P. D. Feinberg, G. L. Archer, and D. J. Moo debate whether Christians alive just prior to Christ's return are bodily removed (or "raptured") from the earth before, during, or after the judgments of God described in chs. 6(7)–16.

154. Good studies of apocalyptic literature include F. Murphy, *Apocalypticism in the Bible and Its World* (Grand Rapids: Baker, 2012); and B. Sandy, *Plowshares and Pruning Hooks: Rethinking the Language of Biblical Prophecy and Apocalyptic* (Downers Grove: InterVarsity, 2002). The fullest collection of texts is J. H. Charlesworth, ed., *Old Testament Pseudepigrapha: Vol. 1* (Garden City: Doubleday, 1983; Peabody, MA: Hendrickson, 2010).

supernatural intervention into this age at the end of time rescues a sinful world in a way that no human ideology or schemes can accomplish. Elaborate and sometimes bizarre symbolism depicts past, present, and future events in a way that requires a careful decoding of the elements of the text. Battles between the forces of good and evil often appear with the good eventually triumphing. One of the primary purposes of apocalypses, therefore, is to encourage a beleaguered religious community in times of oppression or persecution.

What Apocalyptic Does
• Promises God's intervention into his people's dire circumstances, assuring them of his ultimate victory over their enemies
• Warns that in the meantime, things may go from bad to worse
• Portrays its message in other-worldly terms
• Assures, encourages, and warns God's people in the midst of their trials

More formal definitions of apocalypses are not easy to agree on. One widely endorsed, technical definition comes from John Collins in conjunction with a "working group" of scholars from the Society of Biblical Literature:

"Apocalypse" is a genre of revelatory literature with a narrative framework in which a revelation is mediated by an other-worldly being to a human recipient, disclosing a transcendent reality which is both temporal insofar as it envisages eschatological salvation, and spatial insofar as it involves another, supernatural world.[155]

On the other hand, Leon Morris nicely summarizes eight key *differences* between Revelation and typical apocalypses:

1. regular references to the book as prophecy;
2. typically prophetic warnings and calls for repentance;
3. lack of pseudonymity;
4. an optimistic worldview;
5. no retracing of past history in the guise of prophecy;
6. realized eschatology (the end times have begun with the first coming of Christ);
7. little interpretation by angels; and
8. belief that the Messiah has already come and made atonement.[156]

In large measure, we may account for these differences by distinctives of Christian rather than Jewish theology and by the fact that Revelation is prophetic as well as apocalyptic.

---

155. J. J. Collins, "Introduction: Morphology of a Genre," *Semeia* 14 (1979): 9. Cf. also his *The Apocalyptic Imagination: An Introduction to Jewish Apocalyptic Literature*, 2nd ed. (Grand Rapids: Eerdmans, 1998), 5.

156. L. Morris, *The Book of Revelation*, TNTC, rev. ed. (Leicester: Inter-Varsity; Grand Rapids: Eerdmans, 1987), 25–27.

To the extent that Revelation shares features of other apocalypses, however, several important interpretive implications follow.[157] Most importantly, we must recognize that Revelation employs highly symbolic and figurative imagery that we dare not interpret too literally. Virtually every reader recognizes this in the most obvious instances as when John specifically explains that the seven stars are angels (or messengers) and that the seven lampstands are churches (1:20); that the bowls of incense are the prayers of the saints (5:8); that the dragon is the devil (12:9); that ten horns are ten kings (17:12); and that the great prostitute is a city that rules over the kings of the earth (17:18). Symbols are a stock in trade of the genre.

Nevertheless, it is amazing how some readers do not recognize that other images in the book are equally symbolic. Instead, many insist that references to a temple (e.g., 11:1) must refer to a literal, rebuilt temple in Jerusalem; that the battle of Armageddon (Hebrew for Mt. Megiddo, 16:16) must occur at that specific geographical site in northern Israel; or that the mark of the beast (13:16–17) has to be some actual visible sign that distinguishes unbelievers from believers.[158]

A far more legitimate approach is to study each scene and each image in light of what Revelation itself tells about them, in light of relevant OT backgrounds, and in view of other historical information of which John's first-century audience would have been aware. Knowing that John pictures the churches as lampstands (1:20) and understanding the background of olive trees in OT texts (e.g., Psalm 52:8; Jeremiah 11:16; and Zechariah 4:3, 11) provide the modern reader clues for how to understand the two witness in Revelation 11:1–13—who are "the two olive trees and the two lampstands" (11:4). Perhaps they are not individuals at all, but the witnessing church. Deciphering the imagery of Revelation then becomes much like interpreting an editorial cartoon in a newspaper. A reader of an American paper in 1989, for example, who saw a picture of a large bear extending an olive branch in his paw to a bald eagle, would recognize the portrait of Russian overtures of peace to the United States. Similarly, we may see the woman who flies to the desert to escape the attacks of the serpent (who is also a dragon making war on her offspring) as the church being protected by God even as individual believers are persecuted and sometimes martyred by Satan and those on earth who serve him (13:13–17).

It is crucial, therefore, to discover the symbolic elements of Revelation and seek to determine what they represent. We suggest no shortcuts or simplistic answers. Interpreters must become familiar with the relevant historical background and the most likely theological significance of various details. As with parables, certain parts of an apocalyptic vision may function only to add life, color, or drama to the picture. Here,

---

157. Perhaps the best introductory guide for interpreting Revelation is B. M. Metzger, *Breaking the Code: Understanding the Book of Revelation* (Nashville: Abingdon, 1993). Cf. also R. Lowery, *Revelation's Rhapsody: Listening to the Lyrics of the Lamb: How to Read the Book of Revelation* (Joplin, MO: College Press, 2006).

158. A good list of symbols explained by Revelation, by the OT, or left unexplained, appears in M. C. Tenney, *Interpreting Revelation* (Grand Rapids: Eerdmans, 1957), 186–93.

if ever, students must consult a representative sampling of the better commentaries on Revelation, and, where these disagree, students must try to decide which approach is most self-consistent and most likely to have made sense to John's original audience.[159] The more time the student spends reading other apocalypses (especially examples in the OT), the more confidence he or she will gain in the process. Though we give only a small sampling of illustrations here, we hope they will clarify the proper procedures.

One image for which OT background is helpful is the bittersweet scroll of 10:9–11, which closely resembles the scroll Ezekiel was commanded to eat (Ezek 2:9–3:9). There it clearly referred to the message of both judgment and hope that God commanded his prophet to speak to his people. This fits perfectly in Revelation as well.

Or consider those who had been redeemed from the earth "who did not defile themselves with women" (14:4). At best this sounds like the comment of someone who does not believe in sex; at worst like the comment of a misogynist (woman-hater). Actually the OT brims with imagery of sexual faithfulness and faithlessness as symbols of spiritual loyalty or idolatry (e.g., Hos 2:4; Jer 5:7; Ezek 16:32). Thus, we see John figuratively referring to those who remained spiritually pure.

A final, more controversial example involves the three and one-half years (alternately referred to as forty-two months or 1260 days) of great tribulation (Rev 11:2; 12:6, 14; 13:5). This figure seems to come straight out of the book of Daniel where it refers to the period between the end of sacrifice and desolation of God's temple and the end of the age (9:27; cf. 12:7 and 12:11–12, where the number of days is slightly augmented). In view of Jesus' use of this imagery in Matthew 24:15–31, the "tribulation" may well have begun with the destruction of the temple in AD 70. If so, it refers to virtually the entire church age.[160] Alternately, it may refer to a still future event that will bring on the last and most horrible events before Christ returns. Most important either way, three and one-half is half of seven—the sacred, perfect, and complete number throughout Scripture (harking back to the seven days of creation). Merely three and one-half—the period of tribulation years—it is not perfect or good. It is not God's final word, but only an imperfect, incomplete parody of the perfection to come. Whether or not it spans a *literal* three and one-half year period is impossible to determine. And of course if the period refers to the entire church age, then it is much longer!

This last example brings up the complex topic of numerical symbolism in Revelation. Seven, twelve, and 1,000, and other numbers related to them, play a prominent role in the book. The famous 144,000 of 7:4 and 14:1 offers a classic example. One hundred and forty-four thousand is twelve times twelve times 1,000—the number of the tribes

---

159. To those mentioned in previous footnotes we add esp. G. K. Beale, *The Book of Revelation*, NIGTC (Carlisle: Paternoster; Grand Rapids: Eerdmans, 1999); G. R. Osborne, *Revelation*, BECNT (Grand Rapids: Baker, 2002); and C. R. Koester, *Revelation*, AB 38 (New Haven: Yale University Press, 2014). Incisive popular-level exposition appears in E. H. Peterson, *Reversed Thunder: The Revelation of John and the Praying Imagination* (San Francisco: Harper and Row, 1988); and B. K. Blount, *Can I Get a Witness? Reading Revelation through African-American Culture* (Louisville: Westminster John Knox, 2005).

160. Carson, "Matthew," in *Expositor's Bible Commentary Revised*, 9:559.

of Israel raised to the second power (or times the number of apostles; cf. 21:12, 14) and multiplied by a large round number. So, this great company of the redeemed may in fact picture the church as the fulfillment of the promises to Israel in a grand and glorious way. The notorious 666—the number of the beast (13:18)—may well be significant because each digit is one less than seven. Seven hundred and seventy-seven would be a perfect number fit for Christ, which 666 tries hard to imitate but falls notably short at every point. This makes a crucial point: each member of the "Satanic Trinity" of chs. 12–13 (the dragon and the two beasts) parodies but falls short of duplicating the characteristics of his counterpart in the "Holy Trinity" (e.g., by mimicking the crucifixion [13:3] or working signs and wonders [13:13]).[161]

In other cases, numbers function merely to indicate short or long units of measurement. One thousand years is a long and wonderful "golden age" (20:4). The armies of 200,000,000 (literally two myriads of myriads, with a myriad as 10,000 equaling the largest named number in the Greek language) comprise the largest conceivable gathering of people in John's day. And the five-month plague of the demonic locusts (9:5) amounts to a relatively limited time (also equivalent to the life cycle of the insect).

Interpreting Apocalyptic Images in Revelation
• Be alert for the OT background to fill in the significance of allusions
• Remember that a text cannot mean what it could *not* have meant to its original readers (though its subsequent *application* will change over time)
• Be alert to its major theological themes: Christ, the church (past, present, future), and the consummation of the age-long conflict between God and Satan

Even given all these guidelines, interpretations will still no doubt diverge greatly. So, the most crucial axiom is this: determine the major theological principles of Revelation and avoid getting bogged down in the details. Arguably, chs. 4–5 form the doctrinal center of the book, and they prove easiest to interpret: hymns of praise and adoration to God and Christ in view of the splendors of heaven; the atonement won for humanity by Jesus; and the promises of God's sovereignty and triumph mediated to his people in spite of the horrors of the end. In fact, the whole book exudes teaching on all the major doctrines of the Christian faith, not just eschatology. Interpreters must watch for these and highlight them. Even with respect to eschatology, we may agree to disagree on many details and still affirm the reality of Christ's future, visible, and universal return to judge all humanity and to assign to people one of the only two possible destinies awaiting them: the unspeakable agony of eternal punishment or the indescribable glory of eternal life, based on their acceptance or rejection of Jesus.[162] Above all, if we learn the lessons of Matthew 24:36 and Acts 1:6–8 and stop

---

161. See, respectively, Mounce, *Revelation*, 158; G. R. Beasley-Murray, *The Book of Revelation*, NCB (London: Oliphants, 1974; Grand Rapids: Eerdmans, 1981; Eugene, OR: Wipf & Stock, 2010), 220.

162. A salutary example of this unity within interpretive diversity is S. Gregg, ed., *Revelation: Four Views—A*

trying to guess if we are living in the final generation or how the latest news might fit in with this or that verse, then we can focus on the grand theological themes of the book and be encouraged about God's sovereignty, love, and justice even during our hardest times.[163]

CONCLUSION

When interpreting NT passages, then, readers must always take into account whether they are reading a gospel, the Acts, an epistle, or the book of Revelation. Each of these genres in turn contains various forms or subgenres. While the principles discussed in earlier chapters ("general hermeneutics") apply to all of Scripture, each genre or form has unique features that interpreters need to take into account as well. We cannot treat parables in exactly the same way as pronouncement stories. Teaching in Acts is often more indirect than in the Epistles, and apocalyptic differs from straightforward historical narrative. Our discussion has not been exhaustive, merely illustrative. But we have set the stage for an appreciation of the multiple dimensions of Scripture that will help us understand its meaning. When we do our work well we set the stage for fruitful and transformative uses of Scripture—the topics that we address next in Part V.

Parallel Commentary (Nashville: Nelson, 1997). Cf. also C. Marvin Pate, ed., *Four Views on the Book of Revelation* (Grand Rapids: Zondervan, 1998).

163. Particularly helpful with respect to major themes are G. Goldsworthy, *The Gospel of Revelation* (Exeter: Paternoster, 1984); and R. Bauckham, *The Theology of the Book of Revelation* (Cambridge: Cambridge University Press, 1993). An excellent work that combines methodological with thematic insights is M. Gorman, *Reading Revelation Responsibly: Uncivil Worship and Witness—Following the Lamb into the New Creation* (Eugene, OR: Cascade, 2011).

Part V

THE FRUITS OF
INTERPRETATION

11

USING THE BIBLE TODAY

The Bible has endured over the millennia, and it continues to be a bestseller even into the modern scientific and postmodern world of the twenty-first century. Millions of people across the globe find that this venerable book speaks and is useful to them. The Bible serves many important functions, and, we believe, it is most useful if people employ it according to the principles of sound and accurate biblical interpretation that we have articulated in this volume. But hermeneutics is not an end in itself. Having studied the principles of interpretation, the student might ask, "Is there a reason for understanding the Bible beyond the acquisition of knowledge?" "Is it worth going to all this effort?" We answer, yes and yes. The Scriptures constitute God's revelation to his people—his inspired word communicated to us in written form. We believe that God's people should strive to understand and respond to his message. It is a message to engage us—to encourage, motivate, guide, challenge, and instruct. Beyond and above all that, the Bible portrays the grand narrative of God's mission in the world—that he use his people to represent him and bring the good news of his salvation to all people.[1] So, due to its character as a historical book and its divine origin, in the following pages we consider some of the ways that Christians employ the Bible.[2] Then in the succeeding chapter we present principles to guide readers more specifically in applying the Bible's message concretely and practically to their lives.

Uses of the Bible
To Gain Information and Understanding
To Motivate and Enrich Worship
To Construct Liturgy
To Formulate Theology
To Preach

---

1. For an extensive treatment of this point see C. J. H. Wright, *The Mission of God: Unlocking the Bible's Grand Narrative* (Downers Grove: InterVarsity, 2006).

2. Certainly many people other than Christian believers engage the Bible in various ways. Scholars in fields such as sociology, ancient history, or archaeology—to name a few—assess it in keeping with the concerns of their disciplines. Literary critics explore the Bible as literature. Others may read it out of curiosity, or even antagonistically, in an attempt to refute its claims or believers' claims about it. We acknowledge, of course, that some of what we say will apply to Jews and their use of the Tanakh (Hebrew Bible)—what Christians call the Old Testament. Nevertheless, we focus in what follows on those uses to which Christian believers put the Bible.

Uses of the Bible
To Teach
To Provide Pastoral Care
To Promote Spiritual Formation in the Christian Life
To Enjoy its Beauty as Literature

TO GAIN INFORMATION AND UNDERSTANDING

The first use to which readers put the Bible is *to gain information and understanding.* As the foundational document of the Christian faith, the Bible functions as the primary source of data or information, not only about the history of the people of God, but also about the narrative of God's mission in the world. Christians believe that the Bible is God's written *revelation* to humans.[3] Theologians say the Bible is *special* revelation not available from any other source.[4] Thus, those who wish to learn about the Judeo-Christian faith read and study the Bible. Christians believe that through the Bible God has conveyed information to people—information about who God is, what he has done in history, what he wants people to know, how they should respond to God, and, most significantly, the story of God's relationship to humans whom he created in his image.

The Bible reports the history and religious faith of Israel, the life and teachings of Jesus, and the establishment and spread of the Christian church. In it we discover how Israel worshiped, how the prophets took the nation to task for her idolatry, and what the ancient Israelites believed about their national identity and destiny. It recites how Christians like Peter and Paul came to apprehend salvation through faith in Jesus and to spread this gospel (good news) throughout the Roman world.

Christians begin with the presupposition that through the Bible God conveys reliable information.[5] In order to comprehend this revelation, we must interpret the biblical accounts accurately; so our approach to hermeneutics governs what we learn from the Bible. A proper hermeneutic promotes our understanding and helps us to interpret the Bible's content accurately and to see the facts correctly. It protects us, for

---

3. The writer of Hebrews makes this point explicit in saying, "In the past God spoke to our ancestors through the prophets at many times and in various ways . . ." (Heb 1:1). The prophets wrote not simply their own musings or observations but messages they believed God revealed to them. Again, "Above all, you must understand that no prophecy of Scripture came about by the prophet's own interpretation of things. For prophecy never had its origin in the human will, but prophets, though human, spoke from God as they were carried along by the Holy Spirit" (2 Pet 1:20–21). The creeds of the church affirm, then, that the Bible owes its origin to divine revelation, not to human invention.

4. This complements *general* or *natural* revelation available in creation (Ps 19:1–6; Rom 1:19–20) to all people.

5. See our earlier discussion of presuppositions in ch. 5. For a consideration of various aspects of the Bible's truthfulness readers might want to consult C. L. Blomberg, *Can We Still Believe the Bible? An Evangelical Engagement with Contemporary Questions* (Grand Rapids: Brazos, 2014); and A. Köstenberger, et al., *Truth in a Culture of Doubt: Engaging Skeptical Challenges to the Bible* (Nashville: B&H, 2014).

example, from interpreting poetry or apocalyptic as if their authors necessarily intended them to convey history. It keeps us from asserting that a text's meaning is equivalent to the literal words of that text (locution) without understanding what those words were intended to accomplish for the original readers (illocution and perlocution). This enables us to discover the knowledge and insight that God wanted us to have.

TO MOTIVATE AND ENRICH WORSHIP

The second common use of the Bible is *to enrich worship*. Since the Bible reveals God's will and ways and records his mighty deeds and glorious person, his people discover in its pages motivation and opportunities for worship. Worship occurs when people respond to God's revelation of himself and how he has acted in Jesus Christ. Robert Rayburn defines worship in this expansive way:

> Worship is the activity of the new life of a believer in which, recognizing the fullness of the Godhead as it is revealed in the person of Jesus Christ and His mighty redemptive acts, he seeks by the power of the Holy Spirit to render to the living God the glory, honor, and submission which are His due.[6]

God's grace and love prompt his people to respond in various appropriate ways. When believers learn from their study of the Bible who God is and what he has accomplished on their behalf, their hearts well up in praise and adoration.

In places the poetry of the Psalms draws readers into such an experience. For example, one of the psalmists writes:

> The heavens declare the glory of God;
> the skies proclaim the work of his hands.
> Day after day they pour forth speech;
> night after night they display knowledge.
> There is no speech or language
> where their voice is not heard.

---

6. R. G. Rayburn, *O Come Let Us Worship: Corporate Worship in the Evangelical Church* (Grand Rapids: Baker, 1980; Eugene, OR: Wipf & Stock, 2010), 21. Excellent studies of the topic of worship include D. A. Carson, ed., *Worship by the Book* (Grand Rapids: Zondervan, 2002); B. Kauflin, *Worship Matters: Leading Others to Encounter the Greatness of God* (Wheaton: Crossway, 2008); H. M. Best, *Unceasing Worship: Biblical Perspectives on Worship and the Arts* (Downers Grove: InterVarsity, 2003); D. Peterson, *Engaging With God: A Biblical Theology of Worship* (Downers Grove: InterVarsity, 2002); and R. E. Webber, *The Biblical Foundations of Christian Worship* (Peabody, MA: Hendrickson, 1993). For key analyses of the worship in ancient Israel, see the classic H. H. Rowley, *Worship in Ancient Israel* (Philadelphia: Fortress, 1967; Eugene, OR: Wipf & Stock, 2010), especially "Psalmody and Music," 176–212; and S. E. Balentine, *The Torah's Vision of Worship*, Overtures to Biblical Theology (Minneapolis: Augsburg Fortress, 1999). A book that spans the testaments is J. A. Smith, *Music in Ancient Judaism and Early Christianity* (Farnham: Ashgate, 2011). On the early church's worship see L. W. Hurtado, *At the Origins of Christian Worship: The Context and Character of Earliest Christian Devotion* (Grand Rapids: Eerdmans, 2000). For a discussion of the nature of worship as portrayed in the key texts in the NT see W. W. Klein, "Can You Worship Anyplace? Reflections on How the New Testament Answers the Question," in *Midwestern Journal of Theology* 9 (2010): 96–121.

Their voice goes out into all the earth,
    their words to the ends of the world. (Ps 19:1–4)

Again, another poet proclaims:

The LORD is my light and my salvation—
    whom shall I fear?
The LORD is the stronghold of my life—
    of whom shall I be afraid? . . .
One thing I ask of the LORD,
    this only do I seek:

that I may dwell in the house of the LORD
    all the days of my life,
to gaze upon the beauty of the LORD
    and to seek him in his temple. (Ps 27:1, 4)

In other places the biblical writers expressly seek to worship God and to elicit from the readers their own adoration of God.

I will praise you, LORD, with all my heart;
    before the "gods" I will sing your praise.
I will bow down toward your holy temple
    and will praise your name
    for your unfailing love and your faithfulness,
for you have so exalted your solemn decree
    that it surpasses your fame. . . .
May all the kings of the earth praise you, LORD,
    when they hear what you have decreed. (Ps 138:1, 2, 4)

Praise the LORD, all you nations;
    extol him, all you peoples.
For great is his love toward us,
    and the faithfulness of the LORD endures forever.
Praise the LORD. (Ps 117)

The Israelites incorporated these and many other hymns into their Scriptures, and since the beginning of the church, Christians have joined them in praising God through these treasured lines.[7]

The NT authors included fewer explicit hymns in their accounts,[8] yet the pages of

---

7. A wise assessment of OT Israel's worship with a view to contemporary Christian worship is A. E. Hill, *Enter His Courts with Praise! Old Testament Worship for the New Testament Church*, 2nd ed. (Grand Rapids: Baker, 1997). For resources to support the use of Psalms today, see J. D. Witvliet, *The Biblical Psalms in Christian Worship: A Brief Introduction and Guide to Resources* (Grand Rapids: Eerdmans, 2007).

8. The number and extent of hymns actually incorporated into the NT letters are issues of some debate among

the NT demonstrate that singing and music played important roles in the worship of the emerging church. Commenting on the early church, G. Delling observes: "The Word of Christ is alive in the community in teaching and admonition and in the singing of songs for God, i.e., in these the community praises God from the heart on account of the salvation which He has given by what He has done in Christ."[9] Music, indeed, was a central focus of the Christians' communal life as K. H. Bartels emphasizes: "Next to the preaching of the word and participation in the sacrament, the heart of worship was this 'spiritual singing,' a festive recognition of God in Jesus Christ as the Lord of the congregation and of the world."[10] Using prayers or anthems—some even drawn directly from the OT—the early Christians sought to lift up their readers to praise and adore their God. Paul says, "Praise be to the God and Father of our Lord Jesus Christ, who has blessed us in the heavenly realms with every spiritual blessing in Christ." He adds, "Now to him who is able to do immeasurably more than all we ask or imagine, according to his power that is at work within us, to him be glory in the church and in Christ Jesus throughout all generations, for ever and ever! Amen" (Eph 1:3; 3:20–21).

At other times believers throughout church history have responded to what they read in Scripture with their own unique spontaneous worship. Whether or not Paul intended to evoke worship from his readers when he penned these stunning verses, they certainly must have inspired the Roman Christians to proclaim the greatness of their God:

> For I am convinced that neither death nor life, neither angels nor demons, neither the present nor the future, nor any powers, neither height nor depth, nor anything else in all creation, will be able to separate us from the love of God that is in Christ Jesus our Lord (Rom 8:38–39).

What believer can read of Jesus' loving sacrifice for his people without responding in worship and praise for God's immeasurable charity lavished upon his people "while we were still sinners" (Rom 5:8)? The Bible performs this major role for the Christian: to elicit and to shape the worship of God's people.

Hence, believers employ the Bible in worship both individually and corporately. In their *individual* use of the Bible, believers read, study, and seek to respond to

---

scholars. For one take see R. P. Martin, *A Hymn of Christ: Philippians 2:5–11 in Recent Interpretation & in the Setting of Early Christian Worship* (Downers Grove: InterVarsity, 1997). For further insight, in addition to our comments about the genre of hymns / poetry above, see S. Grabiner, *Revelation's Hymns: Commentary on the Cosmic Conflict*, LNTS 511 (London and NY: Bloomsbury: T&T Clark, 2015); R. J. Karris, *A Symphony of New Testament Hymns: Commentary on Philippians 2:5–11, Colossians 1:15–20, Ephesians 2:14–16, 1 Timothy 3:16, Titus 3:4–7, 1 Peter 3:18* (Collegeville, MN: Liturgical Press, 1996); R. P. Martin, *Worship in the Early Church*, rev. ed. (Grand Rapids: Eerdmans, 1975); V. H. Neufeld, *The Earliest Christian Confessions* (Leiden: Brill, 1963); and J. T. Sanders, *The New Testament Christological Hymns: Their Historical and Religious Background*, SNTSMS 15 (Cambridge: Cambridge University Press, 1971).

9. G. Delling, "ὕμνος, κτλ," *TDNT* 8: 498. See also the articles on hymn, psalm, and song, in M. Silva, "ὕμνος," "ψαλμός" and "ᾠδή," *NIDNTTE* 4:447–48; 4:718–20; 4:737–39.

10. K. H. Bartels, "Song, Hymn, Psalm," *NIDNTT* 3:675.

what they find within its pages. The Bible directs believing readers to praise and adoration, to confession of sins, and to prayers of thanksgiving. In response to the God revealed in the pages of the Bible, Christians seek to conform all dimensions of their lives to his will. The Bible provides inspiration and challenge; it generates religious experiences; it provides hope and sustenance. In short, the Bible furnishes the medium for individual worship. God speaks through his living and active word, and his people venerate him.

This Bible also provides the basis for *corporate* worship. As the people of Israel worshiped their God, so also the church seeks to be a believing and worshiping community. Applying OT terminology to the Body of Christ, Peter proclaims:

> But you are a chosen people, a royal priesthood, a holy nation, God's special possession, that you may declare the praises of him who called you out of darkness into his wonderful light. Once you were not a people, but now you are the people of God; once you had not received mercy, but now you have received mercy (1 Pet 2:9–10; cf. Exod 19:5–6; Hos 2:23).

In one sense, believers function as a worshiping community to announce to the unbelieving world "How Great Thou Art."[11] From what they discover in the Bible believers can obey the admonition: "Through Jesus, therefore, let us continually offer to God a sacrifice of praise—the fruit of lips that openly profess his name" (Heb 13:15). Though the term "word" (or "message") has a wide semantic range, as we now read Paul's instructions we can readily see how the "word of Christ" embraces the Bible: "Let the word of Christ dwell in you richly; teach and admonish one another in all wisdom; and with gratitude in your hearts sing psalms, hymns, and spiritual songs to God" (Col 3:16 NRSV). To believers the Scriptures attest God's presence, activity, and love, particularly as expressed in his son, Jesus Christ. The message of the Bible brings to their attention, in a concrete and graphic manner, God's personal and loving commitment to his people. And as such, the Scriptures move them to worship—individually and corporately.

TO CREATE LITURGY

The liturgy of the Christian church has always incorporated texts from the Bible. The third use of the Bible is to create liturgy. The English word "liturgy" derives from the Greek term *leitourgia*, which meant some kind of public work in Hellenistic Greek. The LXX used it for the Temple services.[12] Whether "high" or "low," the liturgy of the church employs prayers, hymns, various readings (e.g., responsive readings), psalms,

---

11. The title of a Christian hymn based on a Swedish poem and translated into English from a Russian version. The most popular version was done by missionary S. K. Hine in 1949.

12. A formal definition of liturgy is "a form or formulary according to which public religious worship, especially Christian worship, is conducted," in C. Soanes and A. Stevenson, eds., *Concise Oxford English Dictionary* (Oxford: Oxford University Press, 2004). In J. F. White's words, "Liturgy, then, is a work performed by the people for the

and the ordinances (sacraments).[13] The Scriptures inform all these elements; indeed, many feature scriptural portions directly. An obvious example is the chorus to the French Christmas carol "Angels We Have Heard on High," which quotes *Gloria in excelsis Deo*, ("Glory to God in the highest") based on Luke 2:14 in the Latin Bible. The popular hymn "Great Is Thy Faithfulness" comes right out of Lamentations 3:23. Many contemporary praise choruses take their words verbatim from the Psalms; for example, "Come let us worship and bow down," from Psalm 95:6. The chorus to the hymn "I Know Whom I Have Believed" quotes the KJV of 2 Timothy 1:12. *The Book of Common Prayer* of the Anglican Communion incorporates portions of the Bible extensively in guiding worshipers, both individually and corporately.[14] The prayer books of other Christian traditions do the same. One has only to visit churches of different denominations (e.g., Roman Catholic, Greek Orthodox, Presbyterian, Anglican, and Plymouth Brethren) to grasp how different can be their celebration of the Lord's Supper. Though all based on the pivotal passages in the Gospels and 1 Corinthians, their components, rhythm, duration, and place in the overall worship of the church vary enormously in various churches and denominations—often as the result of the groups' distinct historical developments and theology.

Unquestionably, then, the Scriptures aid our worship and perform an appropriate liturgy-forming function, in which worship is embodied and holistic—not merely a matter of the head. Liturgy enables worshipers to enact elements of the salvific drama and embody their responses to God's grace. The influence of Scripture on non-musical liturgical elements is also very significant, e.g., psalmic calls to worship, corporate Scripture reading, confession of sin and assurance of pardon, the corporate recitation of the Lord's Prayer, baptismal formulae, Lord's Supper institutions, and scriptural benedictions (pastoral or corporate).[15] At the same time, we believe it is important that worshipers comprehend and embrace the biblical passages or allusions.[16] In some uses of the Bible that we will shortly consider (preaching or teaching), the goal may well be to help hearers to discover the meaning of the texts and actions. In using

---

benefit of others . . . the quintessence of the priesthood of believers that the whole priestly community of Christians shares," in *Introduction to Christian Worship*, 3rd ed. (Nashville: Abingdon, 2000), 25.

13. For a thorough discussion of the history and practice of liturgy in the main traditions from the beginning of Church history to today's postmodern era, see F. C. Senn, *Christian Liturgy: Catholic and Evangelical* (Minneapolis: Augsburg Fortress, 1997). M. J. Hatchett, *Sanctifying Life, Time, and Space: An Introduction to Liturgical Study* (New York: Seabury Press, 1976) is also helpful. Cf. M. C. Ross, *Evangelical versus Liturgical? Defying a Dichotomy* (Grand Rapids: Eerdmans, 2014).

14. *The Book of Common Prayer* (New York: Church Publishing, 1997; Oxford: Oxford University Press, 2008). For the story of its composition see A. Jacobs, *The Book of Common Prayer: A Biography* (Princeton, NJ and Oxford: Princeton University Press, 2013). It has been the template and inspiration for many other liturgies as shown in C. Hefling and C. Shattuck, ed., *The Oxford Guide to the Book of Common Prayer: A Worldwide Survey* (Oxford, UK: Oxford University Press, 2006).

15. Especially insightful for this is D. T. Benedict, Jr. *Patterned By Grace: How Liturgy Shapes Us* (Nashville: Upper Room Books, 2007). He discusses the daily office, the Christian year, and the sacraments, among other liturgical elements.

16. P. H. Pfatteicher, *Liturgical Spirituality* (Harrisburg, PA: Trinity, 1997) stresses the need for the interior life of the Spirit, which is formed and nurtured by the church's liturgy.

the wealth of liturgical forms, those who lead should find ways to help participants understand what they are hearing or doing in following the prescribed rituals. The Bible contains no magic charms. People need to understand its meaning to profit from its message. Mindlessly following a liturgy by rote, reading a text, drinking some wine, or singing a song has little value in transforming the worshiper—which is the goal of engaging Scripture.

TO FORMULATE THEOLOGY

All humans live according to a belief system or worldview. For theists (i.e., those who believe in a god or gods) belief systems can be termed "theologies" (from the Greek words for "god," *theos*, and "word," *logos*). To formulate a theology, one affirms in an orderly fashion his or her belief system with a god or gods at the center. Christian theology understands the God featured in the Bible as the one true God. Christian theology regards the Bible as the necessary foundation and source for its development.[17] So, the fourth use of the Bible is to shape the formulation and expression of theology. At the same time, to produce or write a "theology" is a human endeavor; it articulates an individual's or a group's understanding of reality with God at the center. To answer the question "How does a Christian group understand and express its faith?" requires an explanation of its theology.[18]

Although formulating theology is an ongoing task in the life of the church, theology acts as an anchor for the church and for Christians who may feel unschooled or uncertain about the faith in a time of relativism or competing worldviews. Theology offers the church (and specific branches of Christendom) a secure understanding of itself and of how it fits into God's overall purposes in the grand narrative of redemption. Theology enables individuals, local churches, or entire denominations to grasp the significance of how they understand their own place within the broad spectrum of worldviews and ideologies.

Theology has served to protect the church against the ever-changing challenges to its existence and claims of truth since its beginning. From first-century Gnosticism to modern scientism, the church has contended with manifold alternative explanations of reality and truth.[19] Its understanding of theology has established the boundaries

---

17. Theology may incorporate other data as well for its formulation, but for our purposes in this book, we will focus on the Bible as its foundational document.

18. For a helpful discussion of the nature of doing theology and locating "systematic theology" on the theological map, see M. J. Erickson, *Christian Theology*, 3rd ed. (Grand Rapids: Baker, 2013), 8–22.

19. Our mention of these two competitors is merely representative and readily acknowledges the positive benefits of modern science in general. Full-fledged Gnosticism was a second- to-third-century AD phenomenon that arose out of a variety of religious and philosophical ancestors and became a leading competitor to Christianity. For further insight, consult B. A. Pearson, *Ancient Gnosticism: Traditions and Literature* (Minneapolis: Fortress, 2007); A. H. B. Logan, *The Gnostics: Identifying an Early Christian Cult* (London and New York: T&T Clark, 2006); and R. Roukema, *Jesus, Gnosis and Dogma* (London and New York: T&T Clark, 2010). P. A. Heelan expresses what we mean by scientism: "Analytical philosophy generally defends the fundamental position that science is a knowledge of a privileged kind, not deriving from and not responsible to the projects and values of the Western cultural world . . . ;

of orthodoxy. And whenever the church claims to be biblical in its understanding of theology, then the Bible must stand at the center and comprise the source and norm of its theological thought.[20]

Yet there is a crucial distinction between "biblical" and "systematic" theology. If what we have just said is true, then virtually all Christians would insist that any enterprise that purports to call itself "theology" must be biblical. Nevertheless, since the eighteenth century Christian theologians have followed two distinct theological approaches.[21] Biblical theology relates more closely to the development of theology within the historical development of the Bible itself. It presents the theology that the Bible itself contains. George Ladd provides this definition: "Biblical theology is that discipline which sets forth the message of the books of the Bible in their historical setting. Biblical theology is primarily a descriptive discipline . . . Biblical theology has the task of expounding the theology found in the Bible in its own historical setting, and its own terms, categories, and thought forms."[22] In this view of "biblical theology" one could speak, for example, of the theology of the postexilic prophets in contrast to that of earlier prophets. Or one might compare the theology of the Synoptic Gospels with that of the Gospel of John.

To illustrate, it is possible to discuss Paul's particular theology of *faith* and show how that compares to the notion of faith presented by James or the writer of Hebrews. In this restricted sense, biblical theologians focus upon how individual biblical writers, sections, or books framed their messages to meet the needs of their specific readers in their historical contexts. The biblical writers' theologies were both explicit and implicit. That is, at times they expressed clearly their understandings of God and his ways, but in other places their theology emerges more implicitly; we see how their theological convictions determine and shape their prescriptions for their readers. Thus, biblical theologians recognize in their formulations that the canon consists of "occasional" writings: writings for specific occasions. The designs of the original writers shape biblical theology.

Put starkly, we are indebted to the agenda of the Judaizers for motivating Paul to explain to the Galatians his view of justification by faith apart from works.[23] For

---

rather, it constitutes a socially and historically independent account of reality, more reliable than any given so far," in "Hermeneutical Phenomenology and the Philosophy of Science," in *Gadamer and Hermeneutics*, ed. H. J. Silverman (New York; London: Routledge, 1991), 214.

20. S. J. Grenz and J. R. Franke put it well in seeing "Scripture as the 'Norming Norm' of Theology," in *Beyond Foundationalism* (Louisville: Westminster John Knox, 2001), 63–75.

21. For a helpful discussion of this development, see G. Hasel, *Old Testament Theology: Basic Issues*, rev. ed. (Grand Rapids: Eerdmans, 1991), 10–17.

22. G. E. Ladd, *A Theology of the New Testament*, 2nd ed., ed. D. A. Hagner (Grand Rapids: Zondervan, 1993), 20.

23. To "Judaize" is to attempt to make Christianity more Jewish (a phenomenon that still exists in the twenty-first c.). Judaizers in the first century insisted, "Unless you are circumcised, according to the custom taught by Moses, you cannot be saved" (Acts 15:1). The Council at Jerusalem refuted this error (Acts 15). Paul also countered Judaizing tendencies in Galatians (e.g., 2:15–16; 5:2–6). For discussions of correlating Paul and James on James 2:14–26, see the pages devoted to this passage in, especially: P. Davids, *The Epistle of James*, NIGTC (Grand Rapids: Eerdmans,

Paul, *faith* goes to the heart of how one attains salvation; salvation comes through faith in Jesus Christ alone, not by following Jewish rituals—i.e., "works of the law." Yet James' dispersed readers had a different struggle with *faith*, and that situation moved James to insist that a truly living and genuine faith must be lived out in the circumstances of life. Faith must produce "works." Thus, we can speak of the contrasting views of faith in Paul's theology and that of James. This does not mean the two are contradictory; it simply means that the writers expressed their views out of concrete situations that were strikingly different. Paul and James framed their theological responses differently because each was replying to specific problems in specific churches.

Biblical theology, then, emerges from historical conditions. Its formulation depends upon the movements and circumstances of people and events—the interaction of author and recipients in the heat of fast-breaking developments.[24] As Berkeley Mickelsen puts it, "In this approach the biblical theologian must be constantly aware of the biblical languages, all known historical factors, and the freshness of the message of God through his servant to men involved in a life and death struggle with dread realities."[25]

How Biblical and Systematic Theology Differ

Yet, to define "biblical theology" is not as simple as we have just presented. As with many terms, people use them as they will, and it turns out that many writers consider what they do to be biblical theology—even while their approaches seem to have different emphases. In a helpful volume Klink and Lockett divide the discipline of biblical theology into five different schools of thought.[26] They name them in the following ways: BT1: biblical theology as historical description; BT2: biblical theology as history of redemption; BT3: biblical theology as worldview-story; BT4: biblical theology as canonical approach; and BT5: biblical theology as theological construction. The writers exemplify these schools, respectively, in the works of: (1) James Barr; (2) D. A. Carson; (3) N. T. Wright; (4) Brevard Childs; and (5) Francis Watson. Yet what joins these different schools—to greater or lesser degrees—remains their primary locus in the world of the ancient texts.

All this presents a decidedly different picture from a "systematic" theology. Millard Erickson identifies systematic theology as "that discipline which strives to give a coherent statement of the doctrines of the Christian faith, based primarily on the Scriptures, placed in the context of culture in general, worded in a contemporary idiom, and related to the issues of life."[27] Though systematic theology also makes a valid claim

1982); D. J. Moo, *The Letter of James*, PNTC (Grand Rapids: Eerdmans, 2000); and C. L. Blomberg and M. J. Kamell, *James*, ZECNT (Grand Rapids: Zondervan, 2008).

24. For a list of the best examples of biblical theologies, see the bibliography.

25. A. B. Mickelsen, *Interpreting the Bible* (Grand Rapids: Eerdmans, 1963), 344.

26. E. W. Klink, III and D. R. Lockett, *Understanding Biblical Theology. A Comparison of Theory and Practice* (Grand Rapids: Zondervan, 2012).

27. Erickson, *Christian Theology*, 8. For their part, G. R. Lewis and B. A. Demarest, *Integrative Theology*, 3 vols. (Grand Rapids: Zondervan, 1996), 1:23, say, "Systematic theology . . . aims to produce normative guidelines to spiritual

to being biblical (that is, its goal is to exhibit the theology of the Bible), its categories are not necessarily those of the biblical writers but those of the theologian's making. Traditional (and novel, at least at the time of formulation) categories comprise the doctrinal framework for the presentation of the biblical material. Often the frameworks derive from the theologians' interactions with the ongoing theological traditions,[28] philosophers, the social context in which the theologian works, and other religions or belief systems. So, for example, one may read Catholic, Reformed, or Lutheran systematic theologies and encounter categories that reflect, in part, the special concerns and issues relevant to these traditions. In other words, the theologians systematize the Bible's teaching in a framework that they feel best represents the Bible's emphases in light of their own study *and the issues with which they or their society are currently struggling.* That is to say, inevitably, systematic theologies reflect the philosophical frameworks and interpretive agendas of the systematizers and their worlds.

The Problem of Preunderstanding

We must consider another issue to clarify the nature of theology. Put in categories we have discussed above, the systematic theologians' own preunderstandings shape the categories and issues they use in their systems (though they may insist that their goal is to allow the Bible's own teaching to provide guidance).[29] As well, the theologians' own perspectives will guide their selection of the various texts within each category and as they determine the relative weight they give the Bible's various teachings on specific issues. This is readily apparent when one reads the theologies dealing with specific controversial issues, say divine sovereignty versus human responsibility.[30] People come to different positions on the Bible's teaching on this matter in part because they bring different preunderstandings to their analysis of the relevant texts and they give different weight to them.

---

reality for the present generation; it organizes the material of divine revelation topically and logically, developing a coherent and comprehensive world view and way of life." Finally, D. A. Carson ("Unity and Diversity in the New Testament: The Possibility of Systematic Theology," in *Scripture and Truth,* D. A. Carson and J. D. Woodbridge, ed. [Grand Rapids: Baker, 1992], 69–70) provides his working definition of systematic theology: "the branch of theology that seeks to elaborate the whole and the parts of Scripture, demonstrating their logical (rather than their merely historical) connections and taking full cognizance of the history of doctrine and the contemporary intellectual climate and categories and queries while finding its sole ultimate authority in the Scriptures themselves, rightly interpreted."

28. At times the attempt is to fit in with a tradition; at other times the theologian seeks to adjust, challenge, or even jettison a tradition. E.g., is universalism (all will be saved) biblical? For a work from a Catholic that is relevant to all who consider the issue, see R. Martin, *Will Many Be Saved?: What Vatican II Actually Teaches and Its Implications for the New Evangelization* (Grand Rapids: Eerdmans, 2012). Another issue might be the question of the orthodoxy (for evangelicals) of the so-called openness of God theology. See, e.g., C. Pinnock, et al., *The Openness of God: A Biblical Challenge to the Traditional Understanding of God* (Downers Grove: InterVarsity, 1995). As a result of such challenges, theologians devise theologies to include or exclude various options based on what they believe the Bible teaches.

29. We must remind readers that so-called biblical theologians also operate with their own preunderstandings. As we argued, no interpreter is free of them.

30. An instructive specimen is D. Basinger and R. Basinger, eds., *Predestination & Free Will: Four Views of Divine Sovereignty & Human Freedom* (Downers Grove: InterVarsity, 1986). In this work four writers differ in their view of the nature of God's foreknowledge. Based on their view that God determines and controls events, several argue that God knows future events without limit. Others argue for particular limitations on God's foreknowledge on the basis that God has freely chosen to give humans genuine autonomy. For energetic appeals for and against a popular theological system, see M. Horton, *For Calvinism* (Grand Rapids: Zondervan, 2011); and R. E. Olson, *Against Calvinism* (Grand Rapids: Zondervan, 2011).

In a sense, then, each generation, and perhaps each culture, needs to update its formulations of "systematic" Christian theology. This does not mean that God's truth keeps changing. Rather, it reflects the nature of the process of systematizing: it always exhibits the perspectives and concerns of those who do it. To illustrate, most Protestants will agree that the Westminster Confession of Faith presented a singularly important understanding of Christian theology. But its discussion of the covenants reflects issues, concerns, and the preunderstandings—religious and political—of Christians in seventeenth century Scotland and England.[31] Civil war had broken out in England and the king, Charles I, was forced to initiate reform. An assembly was called at Westminster to devise a creed that both Scots and English could affirm. Speaking about the "federal theology" that the Westminster Confession embodied, Dillistone observes,

> [it] seemed to provide just the system or schema that men were seeking in the period of consolidation after the revolutionary changes of the sixteenth century. A dialectical interpretation of reality does not lend itself to an easy formalization whereas a succession of contracts can be systematized within a legal framework. . . .
>
> Once a group is established and inspired with growing confidence, it tends to look for something more concrete, more definite, more constitutional and this is exactly what the developing Churches of the Reformation found in the doctrine of the Two Covenants. . . . Puritan and Calvinist alike found in this one idea the necessary framework for a new theological and ecclesiastical system.[32]

Thus, our point here is *not* that the authors of the Confession were right on some points and wrong on others, that the issues they struggled with no longer concern us, or that language of the document is archaic.[33] Rather, history shows that they formulated their declarations and addressed their own concerns, among other reasons, to counter opposing viewpoints prevalent at that time. Their affirmations were not simply objective statements of theology, or "what the Bible actually teaches." Nor, we maintain, ought we

---

31. For helpful discussions of the historical background of the Westminster Confession consult R. T. Kendall, *Calvin and English Calvinism to 1649* (Oxford: Oxford University Press, 1979); and W. M. Hetherington, *History of the Westminster Assembly of Divines* (New York: Anson D. F. Randolph & Co., 1890). "Federal theology" is the term used to describe the brand of Calvinism that developed in the late sixteenth and seventeenth centuries in England and Scotland that gave great prominence to the doctrine of the covenants (the English word "covenant" translates the Latin *foedus*, hence, federal). The concept of covenants was crucial in the socio-political world of the time—namely, what covenants protected the "rights" of the king versus those of the people. It was natural that theologians thought in terms of covenants, and the federal Calvinists came to distinguish between the covenants of grace and works. Important to our discussion is this point: neither Calvin nor the other Reformers made this distinction between a covenant of grace (a phrase used only twice in Calvin's *Institutes*) and a covenant of works (not used at all) in the manner used in the Westminster Confession. Later systematizers introduced it.

32. F. W. Dillistone, *The Structure of the Divine Society* (Philadelphia: Westminster Press, 1951), 132. Our intent here is not to open a lengthy historical discussion, nor to debate Calvinism or so-called federal theology, but just to give an example. The Nicene Creed similarly reflected its era—the fourth-century debate between Athanasius and Arius over the identity of Jesus: "begotten, not made, being of one substance with the Father . . ."

33. It is also helpful to realize that Gnosticism, Marcionism, and other early alternate views led to the a) selection of the scriptural canon on which to base theology, and b) the formulation of early creeds to define what was orthodox and what was not.

naively consider any confession to be a timeless statement of Christian theology. Though we can learn much from previous theologians and ancestors in the faith, contemporary Christians require theologians living now to express what the Christian faith means today.[34] Indeed, Grenz and Franke argue, "the truly Reformed tradition is by its very nature 'open.' And this 'openness,' in turn, preserves the dynamic nature of tradition."[35]

Must We Choose Between Biblical and Systematic Theology?

Are the two disciplines of biblical and systematic theology at odds? Must we insist upon one or the other? Evangelicals accept the unity as well as the diversity of the Scriptures, as we affirmed above.[36] The Bible's *diversity* reflects the variety of its numerous authors and the circumstances of their times, places, and situations. Its *unity* derives from its single divine Source/Author and the overall grand narrative it unveils. The two affirmations of diversity and unity provide the foundations for both biblical and systematic theologies. The approaches of biblical theology uniquely expose and highlight the inherent diversity of the Bible. The lenses of biblical theology enable us to perceive each author's or text's unique perspectives, distinctives, and emphases and to see clearly how they can speak most sensitively and creatively in parallel or similar circumstances today. Biblical theologians feel more deeply the rough edges of the Bible's teachings, for they are not obligated (at this point in their study) to harmonize or explain difficult teachings by resorting to what the Bible says elsewhere about an issue, at least in some versions of the discipline.[37] This approach takes the Bible on its own terms at each point and with each author.[38]

---

34. Arguably, the best twenty-first-century evangelical systematizers include Erickson, *Christian Theology*; Lewis and Demarest, *Integrative Theology*; S. J. Grenz, *Theology for the Community of God*, 2nd ed. (Grand Rapids: Eerdmans, 2000); A. E. McGrath, *Christian Theology: An Introduction*, 5th ed. (Oxford, UK: Blackwell, 2011); Michael Bird, *Evangelical Theology: A Biblical and Systematic Introduction* (Grand Rapids: Zondervan, 2013); and Michael Horton, *The Christian Faith: A Systematic Theology for Pilgrims on the Way* (Grand Rapids: Zondervan, 2011). Self-consciously illustrating that systematics exhibits the perspectives of the theologians, we cite J. L. González, *Mañana: Christian Theology from a Hispanic Perspective* (Nashville: Abingdon, 1990); J. R. Williams, *Renewal Theology* (Grand Rapids: Zondervan, 1990); or S. M. Horton, ed., *Systematic Theology: A Pentecostal Perspective* (Springfield, MO: Logion Press, 1994). From broader theological traditions, key works in the last century included K. Barth, *Church Dogmatics,* 12 vols., translated by G. T. Thomson, G. W. Bromiley, et al. (Edinburgh: T&T Clark; New York: Scribner, 1936–69); P. Tillich, *Systematic Theology*, 3 vols. (Chicago: University of Chicago Press, 1976); and W. Pannenberg, *Systematic Theology*, 3 vols. (Grand Rapids: Eerdmans, 1997).

35. Grenz and Franke, *Beyond Foundationalism*, 125.

36. See J. Goldingay, *Approaches to Old Testament Interpretation*, rev. ed. (Downers Grove: InterVarsity, 1990); D. A. Carson, "Unity and Diversity," 65–100; and S. Hafemann and P. House, eds., *Central Themes in Biblical Theology: Mapping Unity in Diversity* (Grand Rapids: Baker, 2007).

37. The need to harmonize unique perspectives leads many theologians to favor one biblical author's formulation over another's. Returning to our example above, Luther's preoccupation with Paul's view of justification by faith led him to question James' orthodoxy. That is, Luther believed (wrongly, we think) that James' statement in 2:24 was incompatible with Paul's theology. Perhaps in his concern to systematize, Luther felt he needed to have a precise understanding of *faith*; he preferred Paul's, not James'. The biblical theologian retains the unique emphases ("rough edges," as we said above) of both Paul and James. A similar situation exists with the conflicts between the Gospel writers (resulting in one aspect of the so-called Synoptic Problem). Of course, this does not mean that evangelical biblical theologians simply leave the matter there. They seek to show how diverse perspectives are compatible.

38. W. W. Klein, *The New Chosen People: A Corporate View of Election*, rev. and expanded ed. (Eugene, OR: Wipf & Stock, 2015), attempts to understand the important concept of God's choosing from a biblical theological perspective.

At the same time, we cannot be content with a mere collection of theological truths espoused by the various biblical authors. We need the organization and structure of the whole. At their best the systematizers bring together all the bits and pieces of the Bible's teaching on an issue and present them logically so we see how they all fit together. Since we presume divine authorship of the entire canon and that God has a unified message to present, the discipline of systematic theology can express this larger picture in a coherent fashion.

Yet the project of systematic theology faces some potential pitfalls. At their worst, the systematizers reflect only their own preunderstandings, which they read into the biblical material; their work amounts to a reader-response take on the entire Bible. It makes eisegesis the *modus operandi* of the program.

Another pitfall is the temptation to claim more precision than the actual details of the biblical texts warrant, in the interests of devising a system. Systematizers may build an entire scheme in which many of the elements derive only from their own inferences rather than on explicit evidence from the Scriptures. Or they may cling tenaciously to their own categories and defend their own theological structures at all costs.[39] These hazards are ever-present. But as we asserted above and will explain below, when informed by the best work of biblical exegetes and theologians, systematic theology can organize the biblical data into meaningful systems that provide great help and assistance to the church.[40]

How to Formulate Theology: Key Principles

Formulating Theology on the Basis of the Bible
1. Follow the conclusions of the sound exegesis of appropriate biblical passages
2. Base theology on the Bible's total teaching on an issue, not on selected or isolated texts
3. Determine and express the Bible's own emphases about an issue
4. State theological conclusions in ways that explain and illustrate their significance for the life and ministry of the church. That is, *show how theology is relevant*
5. Center theology in what God has revealed: beware of the tyranny of systems
6. Compare conclusions with the insights of others, especially those whose perspectives may differ; this includes our spiritual ancestors

---

39. It is risky to suggest examples here, for we all see more clearly the rigidity and inadequacies of others' systems rather than our own. One helpful book that exposes the influences of theological systems is G. A. Boyd and P. R. Eddy, *Across the Spectrum: Understanding Issues in Evangelical Theology*, 2nd ed. (Grand Rapids: Baker Academic, 2009).

40. At this point we will not explicitly develop two other components of the classical theological curriculum: historical and practical theology. The former traces the development of theological understanding throughout the history of the church. Excellent examples are A. E. McGrath, *Historical Theology: An Introduction to the History of Christian Thought*, 2nd ed. (Oxford: Blackwell, 2012); G. Allison, *Historical Theology: An Introduction to Christian Doctrine* (Grand Rapids: Zondervan, 2011); and R. E. Olson, *The Story of Christian Theology: Twenty Centuries of Tradition & Reform* (Downers Grove: InterVarsity, 1999). So-called practical theology focuses attention on the application of theology to real life about which will have more to say below. Highly recommended is R. S. Anderson, *The Shape of Practical Theology: Empowering Ministry with Theological Praxis* (Downers Grove: InterVarsity, 2001). Cf. R. R. Osmer, *Practical Theology: An Introduction* (Grand Rapids: Eerdmans, 2008).

So how does the Bible inform theology? Most theologians seek to express the teaching of the Bible in contemporary terms. But how do they formulate the Bible's theology? Whether it be biblical or systematic,[41] we cannot espouse a self-structured theology that promotes its own self-serving agenda. Therefore, we contend: (1) *valid theologizing must depend on the sound exegesis of the appropriate biblical texts*. To use our earlier example, if theologians wish to formulate a theology of faith, they must investigate all the passages that speak to that issue. To borrow terms from the scientific arena, theology ought to originate *inductively* out of a responsible analysis (as we have attempted to elucidate in the previous chapters) of the relevant passages of the Bible. It may not merely posit a theological datum and then seek *deductively* to defend it in various texts. Once a tenet has been established via the careful study of the biblical texts, one can deduce implications and see their potential effects in other areas. Induction and deduction both have their place, but each must inform and correct the other so that in the end theologians extract the Bible's teaching rather than impose their own.[42] Unless a system of responsible hermeneutics guides the process of exegesis and theological formulation, theology, at best, will not rise above human wisdom, and, at worst, will be false, misguided, tendentious, and even dangerous.

A second key point is implicit in these assumptions, but we must state it explicitly: (2) *a theological affirmation must reflect the Bible's total teaching, not only some select or isolated texts*. For example, suppose we want to develop a theology of women's roles in the church or about the timing of Christ's return. We cannot develop a faithful and honest theology surrounding topics such as these if we deny or discount texts that conflict with our preferred theories. If God inspired the entire Bible and if as a result its parts do not hopelessly contradict (these hark back to our presuppositions), then a valid theological statement about an issue must take into account *all* that the authors intended to say about it.

Other factors enter into the process of weighing the Bible's various teachings on an issue of theology. For example, in considering some doctrines we discover that certain texts speak more clearly to the issues than do other texts that are more tangentially related. In addition, some details appear often and in a range of places in the Bible, whereas other points may occur in only isolated or even single references. Some teachings occur in direct and didactic passages. They may even be propositional in nature as in these: "I am the Lord your God; consecrate yourselves and be holy, because I am holy" (Lev 11:44); or ". . . God is love. This is how God showed his love among us: He sent his one and only Son into the world that we might live through him" (1 John 4:8–9). The Bible presents other points by means of metaphor, "God is light; in him there is no darkness at all" (1 John 1:5), or in narrative (see how many

---

41. We will no longer employ these distinctions in what follows. Again, we assume that both approaches seek to explicate the meanings of the biblical texts regardless of how they use the results.

42. For a plea that theologians do this more transparently, see W. W. Klein, "Exegetical Rigor with Hermeneutical Humility: The Calvinist-Arminian Debate and the New Testament," in *New Testament Greek and Exegesis: Essays in Honor of Gerald F. Hawthorne*, ed. A. M. Donaldson and T. B. Sailors (Grand Rapids: Eerdmans, 2003), 23–36.

of God's attributes emerge from God's speech in Job 38–39 or in the parable of the Prodigal Son in Luke 15:11–32).

One finds biblical teaching in earlier parts of the Bible that are developed and enlarged in later revelation. We do not mean here that later parts of the Bible contradict or in every case supersede earlier sections, but that in some instances God reveals his truth progressively. In other words, some earlier truths prepared the way for people to understand and accept what God said and did in subsequent events. For example, viewed from hindsight, the OT sacrificial system was never an end in itself; rather, it prepared the way for the Lamb of God who would eventually come to take away the sins of the world (John 1:29; cf. Heb 10:1–18). Correspondingly, the OT law, important as it was for the nation of Israel, finds fulfillment in Christ and no longer applies in the same way to the church as it began to define itself following Jesus' resurrection.[43]

Our point in listing these various factors should be obvious: we must weigh evidence to arrive at adequate conclusions. The student must be conscientious and prudent about the evidence adduced in favor of a theological judgment. Clearer teaching must carry more weight than obscure texts whose points may be ambiguous. An interpreter may have more conviction about a point often repeated than about one made only once (though this does not allow the interpreter to discard any clear point in Scripture, even if made only once). Where metaphors or narratives leave conclusions more ambiguous, we dare not force them to overrule texts that speak more clearly or didactically. Likewise, where earlier revelation has progressively prepared the way for later formulations of God's truth, we must give priority to the later.[44]

Another point parallels this: (3) *legitimate theology respects and articulates the Bible's own emphases*. We have noted repeatedly the inevitable effects preunderstandings have on interpreting and theologizing. These color the content and the organization of any theological formulation. So theologians ought to strive to "major on the majors" in their theologies—to stress what the Bible portrays as most important and be willing to hold more loosely those tenets that are more peripheral. As well, theology should promote God's principal concerns in the Scriptures, rather than merely mirror contemporary agendas and priorities.[45] Contemporary issues may pose the questions;

---

43. Cf., e.g., Mark 7:19; Acts 15:7–11; Rom 10:4; Heb 8–10. At the same time, as we argued above, NT ethics do not completely jettison the law. The standard for Gentiles in Acts 15 did have roots in OT law. Jesus insisted that his program fulfilled the law (Matt 5:17–20). For helpful perspectives see F. Thielman, *The Law and the New Testament: The Question of Continuity*, Companions to the New Testament (New York: Crossroad/Herder, 1999); W. G. Strickland et al., *Five Views on Law and Gospel* (Grand Rapids: Zondervan, 1996); and T. R. Schreiner, *The Law & Its Fulfillment: A Pauline Theology of Law*, 2nd ed. (Grand Rapids: Baker, 1998). At a popular level, an outstanding resource is M. Williams, *How to Read the Bible through the Jesus Lens* (Grand Rapids: Zondervan, 2012).

44. This principle causes uncomfortable encounters between Christians and Jews. There is a movement afoot to affirm that Jews do not need Christ, for they represent God's chosen people and their way of salvation is sufficient for them. See, e.g., P. Eisenbaum, *Paul Was Not a Christian: The Original Message of a Misunderstood Apostle* (New York: HarperOne, 2009). Much NT revelation calls this into question—where Jews themselves (e.g., Peter and Paul) presented Jesus as the savior for all people, not only Gentiles, but Jews as well. Recall Acts 4:12.

45. Many popular Christian self-help books in recent decades address pressing problems and issues Christians

but the answers must be biblical. Theology always runs the risk of being faddish when popular issues determine its outcomes.

Further, if theology is to have life and significance—and fulfill its design, we would argue—theologians must do more than understand clearly and precisely what the relevant biblical texts mean. (4) *They must state theological points in ways that explain and illuminate their significance for the life and ministry of the church today.* If God's message is to transform the lives of people today, theology must display the Bible's truth in ways that disclose its Spirit-energized capacities. Theology must show how the Bible's meaning broadens to new situations, edifies believers, stimulates righteousness, and secures God's will "on earth as it is in heaven." Nothing is more boring and irrelevant than a cold and sterile statement of theology. No doubt, theology (or "doctrine") suffers some of its current bad press because of the omissions of its practitioners. When detached from life and divorced from practical implementation, theology fails to achieve its central mission—to express God's truth to his creatures and accomplish his mission to transform the world. Scripture says of itself, "All Scripture is God-breathed and is useful for teaching, rebuking, correcting and training in righteousness" (2 Tim 3:16). By definition, then, valid theology is practical, and theologians must demonstrate the concrete implications of their theological formulations.[46]

What About Church Tradition?

An additional point requires careful consideration, which we divide into two items: the Bible is the definitive source for theology; yet we must be ready to learn from our spiritual ancestors. So, for the first part, (5) *theology must be centered in what God has revealed in Scripture*, not in what people, however enlightened, devise in their own thinking. This is the Reformation rallying cry: *sola scriptura*. Though study in numerous fields—for example, archaeology, paleography, ancient history, philology and linguistics, comparative religion, anthropology, sociology, etc.—sheds significant light on the Bible, such study must never supplant what the Bible itself says. Unless theology rests upon solid biblical foundations, it exists, at best, only as a monument to human brilliance.

Yet, the downside of this important Reformation principle was Protestantism's denigration of the church's rich heritage and tradition.[47] Fortunately, many are now

---

face. For example, one dominant theme concerns marriage and the family. Many theological discussions of the family grow out of legitimate fears in the face of societal breakdowns and upheavals. They seek to support the family and elevate its importance, almost above all else. Yet we wonder if, indeed, the Bible exhibits such an emphasis upon the "traditional family," as often understood by American evangelicals. See esp. R. Clapp, *Families at the Crossroads: Beyond Traditional & Modern Options* (Downers Grove: InterVarsity, 1993); and D. E. Garland and D. R. Garland, *Flawed Families of the Bible: How God's Grace Works through Imperfect Relationships* (Grand Rapids: Brazos, 2007). Cf. R. S. Hess and M. D. Carroll R., eds., *Family in the Bible: Exploring Customs, Culture, and Context* (Grand Rapids: Baker, 2003), for a survey of various perspectives within the canon.

46. For further help on this issue see the next chapter.

47. D. B. Martin, *Pedagogy of the Bible: An Analysis and Proposal* (Louisville: Westminster John Knox, 2008),

seeing the error of this over-reaction, for, as Ferguson puts it, "Christian theology should be done in dialogue with the creeds and traditions of the church."[48] So we insist that (6) *theology must listen to the voices of our spiritual ancestors to help decipher the meaning and significance of Scripture.* Modern theologians cannot do their work as if in a vacuum, as if no Christians have ever considered these issues prior to their own time. We have much to learn from our sisters and brothers who walked the paths of faith before us. For two thousand years, in their own times and circumstances, believers have sought to transmit faithfully and live out authentically the teachings, symbols, and practices of the Christian faith (not to mention pious Jews before them).[49] We are only the latest to attempt to do so.

Of course, traditions, creeds, and church dogmas cut in two directions. On one hand, as we explained above, they can restrict interpreters and theologians severely by predetermining what is orthodox or heterodox. As the Pharisees and rabbis of Jesus' time were locked into their own comfortable traditional wines and wineskins (Luke 5:37–39), so our traditions can restrict our ability to hear what the biblical texts are saying to us. For example, contemporary Christians tend to see God as primarily loving—certainly an essential one of his attributes. But do we neglect (or even reject) the Bible's picture of God as judge, the one who is "a consuming fire" (Heb 12:29)? Do we forget that Jesus' parables sometimes end with offenders cast into the place where there is weeping and gnashing of teeth (see Matt 8:12; 13:42, 50; 22:13; 24:51; 25:30; Luke 13:28)? Love does not erase justice. Though we cannot avoid our preunderstandings and our church traditions and commitments, we must be scrupulous in subjecting our theological formulations to the confirmation of the Bible. We must foster a constant dialogue between our doctrines and the biblical text.

On the other hand, the theological insights of our spiritual predecessors can open up our thinking to ideas, implications, and conclusions that would never have occurred to us. These mentors serve as teachers and advisers about the truth of Scripture. At their best, the church's councils and creeds attempt to articulate God's truth. Though dogmas or traditions are not on the same level as passages from the Bible, they do incorporate what our spiritual forebearers understood the Bible to teach. As we attempt to do the same in our era, it makes sense to listen to their voices. We may decide to reject their teaching as being wrong or prejudiced; we may modify or rearrange it; but we lose much by simply ignoring their input. And if we ignore them, we run the great risk of missing sterling insights, committing similar errors, or wasting time redoing or rethinking what they have accomplished already for us.

---

actually calls for an overhaul in the way seminaries teach students in order to allow the church's rich tradition to inform and complement the usual historical-critical methodology. For a useful primer on learning from Christian tradition see J. J. O'Keefe and R. R. Reno, *Sanctified Vision: An Introduction to Early Christian Interpretation of the Bible* (Baltimore: Johns Hopkins University Press, 2005).

48. D. S. Ferguson, *Biblical Hermeneutics: An Introduction* (Atlanta: John Knox, 1986), 113.

49. See R. Olson, *The Story of Christian Theology.* For excerpts of significant theological writings over the centuries see A. E. McGrath, *The Christian Theology Reader*, 4th ed. (Chichester, UK: Wiley-Blackwell, 2011).

TO PREACH

Accurate interpretation informs and governs the public proclamation of God's message. Grant Osborne makes a striking statement: "The hermeneutical process culminates not in the results of exegesis (centering on the original meaning of the text) but in the homiletical process (centering on the significance of the Word for the life of the Christian today)."[50] Though significance goes beyond preaching, as we will show, we affirm this sentiment. So, the fifth use of the Bible is to preach its message.[51]

Most Christian preaching purports to be biblical. Believing that the Bible is God's revelation to his creatures, preachers seek to proclaim its message to all who will listen. By its very nature, preaching seeks to convey biblical insights and to persuade people to respond to it in appropriate ways. The origins of preaching probably go back to the post exilic period of Ezra and Nehemiah. In Nehemiah 8 the narrator explains the occasion when Ezra the scribe stood on a high wooden platform (8:4), opened and read from the Book of the Law (8:5, 8), and proceeded to explain what he had read so the people could understand its meaning (8:8). An occasion of great rejoicing resulted, "because they now understood the words that had been made known to them" (8:12). Jesus followed a similar tack when he read from the scroll of Isaiah 61 and proceeded to explain its significance to his hearers in the synagogue of Nazareth (Luke 4:16–30).[52] Accounts in the book of Acts provide additional examples of early Christian preaching (e.g., Acts 2:14–41; 13:16–41).

Nevertheless, if preaching is to be more than just religious public speaking and if it is to convey more than the wisdom of the ages or of the preacher, it must be biblically informed. *Any claim to biblical preaching must rest on what the Bible teaches or clearly implies.* If preachers seek to inform people of God's ways and his will, they must be sure that sound hermeneutical principles guide the process, i.e., that their preaching is based on the intention of the biblical texts. If on the basis of a biblical text preachers say to their listeners, "God wants you to . . . ," then they are bound ethically (and to their God-given function) to interpret God's will accurately.

We cannot stress too strongly, then, what a critical function sound biblical

---

50. G. R. Osborne, *The Hermeneutical Spiral: A Comprehensive Introduction to Biblical Interpretation*, 2nd ed. (Downers Grove: InterVarsity, 2006), 440. H. W. Robinson, *Biblical Preaching: The Development and Delivery of Expository Messages*, 3rd ed. (Grand Rapids: Baker, 2014), makes a strong case for the centrality of biblical exegesis in the task of sermon preparation and delivery. In an important reminder C. R. Wells, "New Testament Interpretation and Preaching," in *Interpreting the New Testament: Essays on Methods and Issues*, ed. D. A. Black and D. S. Dockery, (Nashville: B&H, 2001), 506–23, argues for critical thinking and methodology as essential friends, not enemies, of good preaching.

51. For the task of preaching, we highly recommend C. J. H. Wright, *How to Preach and Teach the Old Testament for All Its Worth* (Grand Rapids: Zondervan, 2016); S. Greidanus, *The Modern Preacher and The Ancient Text: Interpreting and Preaching Biblical Literature* (Grand Rapids: Eerdmans, 1994); W. L. Liefeld, *New Testament Exposition. From Text to Sermon* (Grand Rapids: Zondervan, 1984); S. D. Mathewson, *The Art of Preaching Old Testament Narrative* (Grand Rapids: Baker, 2002); and J. R. W. Stott, *Between Two Worlds: The Challenge of Preaching Today* (Grand Rapids: Eerdmans, 1978).

52. Cf. W. W. Klein, "The Sermon at Nazareth (Luke 4:14–22)," in *Christian Freedom: Essays in Honor of Vernon C. Grounds*, ed. K. W. M. Wozniak and S. J. Grenz (Lanham: University Press of America, 1986), 153–72.

interpretation performs. When people listen to preaching they want to "hear a word from God." When they cry out to know if there really is a God or how they may know him personally—when the vexing questions of human existence confound, or when issues of ultimate destiny demand answers—mere human opinions fail to satisfy or convince. And if preachers offer erroneous answers, their hearers will be misled, with possibly tragic and even eternal consequences. As people seek to find guidance and courage to live responsibly as Christians—or merely to survive in a crisis—they want to know how God can help or what God says about their situation. At such points, no self-help or human wisdom suffices.

Preachers find their role at this very point. When true to their calling, preachers possess the great privilege and awesome responsibility of comprehending the ancient text, arriving at its correct meaning, and conveying its significance to people in their own time and culture so they may apply it to their lives. Thus, preachers serve as intermediaries who take the truth of God revealed in the Bible and transmit it to their hearers today (akin to the office of the prophet). The sermon itself may stick close to the actual structure of a biblical text (what some call expository preaching), or it may gather biblical truth from various places in a topical arrangement—or numerous other formulae. The point is that biblical sermons are grounded in the intentions of the biblical texts. Before they ask questions of application or significance, preachers must do the work of grasping the meaning and purpose of the text. As we argued above, we must discern first *meaning* and then *significance*; that is the proper order for reading and preaching the Bible.

Of course much else than what we have just described alleges to be preaching. Sadly, loyal parishioners will regularly hear all kinds of topical messages or political orations that have little to do with the Bible. Or perhaps they will encounter addresses that start with a biblical quotation but then proceed to range far afield with the Bible only a distant memory (sometimes called leap frog preaching!). They may receive only psychological prescriptions, a handy list of "how tos," or other human wisdom—all of which may be more or less useful or true. Our point is that these kinds of preaching fail to qualify as biblical preaching because they do not take seriously the message contained in the Bible and, in our estimation, violate the preacher's unique calling. To use the Bible for the preacher's own agenda constitutes an abuse of both the preaching office and the Bible. Biblical preaching invites people to hear God's voice, to obey his will, and to respond to his redemptive acts on their behalf. Since only the Bible reliably records that voice, that will, and those redemptive acts, only a faithful proclamation of the Bible's message fulfills the preacher's calling.[53]

---

53. Many useful sources elucidate the task of preaching. In addition to works cited earlier, we also recommend D. Helm, *Expositional Preaching: How We Speak God's Word Today* (Wheaton, IL: Crossway, 2014); R. J. Allen, *Why Preach from Passages in the Bible?* (Louisville: Westminster John Knox, 1996); G. Goldsworthy, *Preaching the Whole Bible as Christian Scripture: The Application of Biblical Theology to Expository Preaching* (Grand Rapids: Eerdmans, 2000); E. L. Lowry, *The Homiletical Plot: The Sermon as Narrative Art Form*, rev. ed. (Louisville: Westminster John

TO TEACH

Much that we have asserted about preaching applies also to a parallel use of the Bible—teaching. Indeed, we cannot press too strict a distinction between preaching and teaching, for good preaching always involves some teaching, and good teaching always calls those taught to some response.[54] But for our purposes let us refer to teaching as specific training or instruction in matters of Christian beliefs (while not neglecting the need for acting or living out those beliefs). It includes instruction so that people know and embrace beliefs. Since in some sense the Bible functions as the Christians' "textbook," the church has always needed teachers who educate and train the saints from that book, much like Jesus who taught his disciples.[55]

Both testaments attest to the perverse human tendency to stray from following God into false religions, heresies, and apathy. But as the standard of truth, the Bible serves to keep believers on track. Today the church needs teachers[56] who conscientiously seek to explain accurately the Christian faith as it competes with the truth claims of other belief systems represented by cults, new age thinking, and other ideologies, or as it seeks to stake its claim to absolute truth in a postmodern world where almost anything goes.[57]

These represent major challenges to biblical Christianity, but it may be that nominal Christianity poses the greatest challenge of all. One segment of this group consists of people who have grown up as "Christians." They identify themselves as Christian though the Bible or Christian teaching play virtually no significant role in their values or actions. There are nominal Christians among older generations but precious few among Gen Xers and Baby Boomers. Typically, they have consciously "deconverted." Often, people have been admonished on some occasion simply to "receive Christ" without any accompanying instruction about what true discipleship requires.[58] Certainly the

---

Knox, 2000); E. R. Achtemeier, *Preaching from the Minor Prophets* (Grand Rapids: Eerdmans, 1998); and D. S. Jacobsen, *Preaching Luke-Acts* (Nashville: Abingdon, 2001).

54. The NT itself employs various terms that mark these activities. One term, *kērygma*, meant proclamation or announcement and could be understood as preaching (see 1 Cor 1:21; 2 Tim 4:17; Titus 1:3; BDAG, 543). Its corresponding verb form, *kēryssō*, meant to announce or proclaim and refers extensively to preaching in the NT (see 2 Tim 4:2; Rom 10:8; Acts 20:25; 28:31; Gal 2:2; 1 Cor 9:27; 1 Pet 3:19; 2 Cor 4:5; 11:4; etc.; BDAG, 543–44). The other term, *didachē*, specifies the activity or the content of teaching or instruction, often in the NT, Christian instruction (see Acts 2:42; 5:28; 13:12; Rom 16:17; 1 Cor 14:26; 2 John 9–10; Rev 2:24; etc.; BDAG, 241).

55. The etymological meaning of the Greek word *mathētēs* (disciple) is "learner," although in Christian usage in the NT it came to mean much more—a committed follower of Jesus Christ. It occurs exclusively in the Gospels and the Acts. D. Müller says, "Following Jesus as a disciple means the unconditional sacrifice of his whole life (Matt. 10:37 [9:37]; Luke 14:26f.; cf. Mk. 3:31–35; Luke 9:59–62) for the whole of his life (Matt. 10:24f.; Jn. 11:16). To be a disciple means (as Matt. in particular emphasizes) to be bound to Jesus and to do God's will" (Müller, "*mathētēs*," *NIDNTT* 1:488). See the article on "μανθάνω, κτλ," in *NIDNTTE* 3:219–27, with specific reference to *mathētēs*, 224–26; cf. K. Rengstorf, "μαθητής," *TDNT* 4:414–60.

56. We do not presume to limit teachers to professional scholars and clergy. The church has always depended upon the faithful work of committed lay teachers.

57. A helpful guide in this task is P. Copan, *True for You, But Not for Me: Overcoming Objections to Christian Faith*, rev. ed. (Bloomington, MN: Bethany House, 2009).

58. In Jesus' words, "If people want to follow me, they must give up the things they want. They must be willing

teaching role requires the use of responsible hermeneutics and courageous explanation to provide believers with an accurate understanding so they may "contend for the faith that was once for all entrusted to God's holy people" (Jude 3).

Of course, biblical teaching must go beyond proclaiming and defending orthodoxy—correct beliefs. It should encompass orthopraxy—correct living in the world. Christian lifestyle and service in the church and in the world require focused teaching. To live in a Christian manner, believers need to understand their identity as Christ followers and what that status requires of them. In providing instruction to their original readers, the biblical writers supplied guidance for all their successors in the faith. Both testaments contain numerous examples of Israelites and early Christians who were misinformed or stubborn about what they were to believe or how they were to live. The Israelites supposed that their sacrifices would please God, but Micah informed them what qualities God really sought in their lives: "And what does the LORD require of you? To act justly and to love mercy and to walk humbly with your God" (Mic 6:8). Israel also assumed that, as God's chosen people, it would win a great victory on the "day of the LORD," but Amos brought the people up short with the warning that that Day would bring God's judgment for their sins (Amos 5:18–20).

The NT writers also make pointed demands of Christians. Jesus taught: "You cannot serve both God and Money" (Matt 6:24). James instructed his early Christian readers: "Religion that God our Father accepts as pure and faultless is this: to look after orphans and widows in their distress and to keep oneself from being polluted by the world" (Jas 1:27). With sobering words Jesus warned: "Not everyone who says to me, 'Lord, Lord,' will enter the kingdom of heaven, but only the one who does the will of my Father who is in heaven" (Matt 7:21). Christian teachers must explain the implications of such words for believers today.

Cultural values and false teaching can lull Christians into a false sense of what God expects of them, as if he simply smiles upon whatever behavior or attitudes they adopt. Christian teachers need to understand what the biblical directives meant when first written and then explain how believers can fulfill God's expectations for his people today. Instructors need to advise believers how to serve Christ in the church and in the world. If we are to be biblical Christians, we must obtain our agenda from God's Word. Skillful hermeneutics, again, guides our quest for what is truly God's will for his people. Ferguson reminds us that it is necessary "that the teacher preserve the delicate balance between being faithful to the intent of Scripture and allowing at the same time the Scripture to give perspective and guidance on current issues and problems."[59]

---

even to give up their lives to follow me. Those who want to save their lives will give up true life, and those who give up their lives for me will have true life. It is worth nothing for them to have the whole world if they lose their souls" (Matt 16:24–26, NCV; cf. 10:37 and Luke 14:26–27). Whatever else these difficult words mean, they clearly affirm the seriousness of following Jesus.

59. Ferguson, *Biblical Hermeneutics*, 122.

TO PROVIDE PASTORAL CARE

The Bible has always been a source of positive guidance as well as comfort and consolation for God's people. While the section after this one will examine the Bible's role in personal spiritual formation and in providing instruction for godly living, here we focus on its provision of care or guidance to people in times of need. We acknowledge the truth in Jesus' words, "In this world you will have trouble" (John 16:33). He was not unreasonably negative or unduly alarmist; his words simply state the human condition—not only for humanity as a whole, but also for his disciples. Life is difficult and unpredictable. Circumstances crash in on people, sometimes due to their own weaknesses or sins, or natural disasters, but also because of the sins of others. Moreover, as if that were not enough, the world is often especially hostile to Jesus' followers. Yet Jesus added a crucial and comforting assurance to John 6:33: "But take heart! I have overcome the world." What comfort or support exists for strugglers in the midst of life's trials and tragedies, not to mention its doubts and dilemmas?

Christians have many resources available to help others in need, whether pastoral caregivers, close friends, or relatives. As Clinebell puts it, "Pastoral counseling draws on the rich wisdom and authority of the Hebrew-Christian tradition, as these are available through prayer, scripture, sacraments, liturgical practice, and the disciplines of the church."[60] The Bible stands as the major resource that empathetic helpers may use to provide relief for sufferers.[61] Using the Scriptures, we can remind those who despair or grieve, who are lonely or in agony, that God does care for them; he shepherds them through their dark valleys; he remembers that they are dust and are frail (Ps 23:4; 103:14). In the Scripture's teachings about God's love and provisions, in the stories of men and women of faith, in the songs of comfort or prayers for deliverance, God's people can discover a sympathetic God who cares. Hannah's example of persevering prayer in the midst of childlessness (1 Sam 1–2) and Job's trust in God's character despite his painful plight (recall Job said, "Though he slay me, yet will I hope in him"; Job 13:15) speak to the troubled today.

Jesus' comforting words to Martha—in the midst of his own pain over Lazarus's death—have provided hope for grieving loved ones ever since. He affirmed, "I am the resurrection and the life. The one who believes in me will live, even though they die; and whoever lives by believing in me will never die" (John 11:25–26). In life's desperate misfortunes, when pain and agony impel us to cry out for explanations,

---

60. The classic study is H. J. Clinebell and B. C. McKeever, *Basic Types of Pastoral Care and Counseling: Resources for the Ministry of Healing and Growth*, 3rd ed. (Nashville: Abingdon, 2011). The quality and quantity of resources pastoral care encompasses increases all the time—particularly with the growing application of psychology to pastoral theology. Other useful resources include: D. Benner, *Strategic Pastoral Counseling: A Short-Term Structured Model*, 2nd ed. (Grand Rapids: Baker, 2003); G. R. Collins, *Christian Counseling: A Comprehensive Guide*, 3rd ed. (Nashville: Nelson, 2007); and B. M. Roberts, *Helping Those Who Hurt: A Handbook for Caring and Crisis* (Colorado Springs: NavPress, 2009).

61. Observe, for example, how sensitively D. J. Tidball brings biblical insights and perspectives to bear in his excellent book on pastoral theology, *Skillful Shepherds* (Grand Rapids: Zondervan; Leicester: Inter-Varsity, 1986).

and even in the silences when no answers appear, we take courage in Paul's assurance: "And we know that in all things God works for the good of those who love him, who have been called according to his purpose" (Rom 8:28). Moreover, to the Corinthians he wrote, "No temptation has overtaken you except what is common to mankind. And God is faithful; he will not let you be tempted beyond what you can bear. But when you are tempted, he will also provide a way out so that you can endure it" (1 Cor 10:13). Though the Bible may not depict the exact situation or dilemma we encounter today, it teaches values and principles that promote comfort or healing or give guidance and hope.[62]

But the use of the Bible in pastoral care has its pitfalls to avoid. When dealing with the raw edges of human suffering, caregivers naturally want to give as much hope and promise as possible. In such situations they may be tempted to abuse the Bible—to make it say more than it does. Or they may simply neglect the Bible and resort to answers from modern psychology or other sources that exclude the divine perspective. We believe the Bible provides much help while at the same time insisting on responsible interpretation as much here as in all our uses of the Bible. We desperately want to assure a parent grieving over a wayward child that all will be well. Therefore, we may be tempted to turn the well-known proverb into a definitive promise: "Start children off on the way they should go, and even when they are old they will not turn from it" (Prov 22:6). However, sound hermeneutics forbids such an error because proverbs state general truths, not specific promises (recall the discussion of wisdom literature above).

Alternatively, we may seek God's will in some situation and sincerely want to follow a path that honors him. Those are fine motives, but we cannot claim Jeremiah 29:11 ("For I know the plans I have for you," declares the LORD, "plans to prosper you . . .") as a specific promise of financial gain or a reversal of misfortune. Jeremiah referred to God's unique plans for Israel's return from exile, not their plans for recouping lost wealth; we cannot apply this text across the board. Though God indeed seeks to prosper his people, we dare not read in the adverb financially.[63]

Other sections of the Bible suffer similar misuse in our well-meaning attempts to provide guidance or comfort. Indeed, such exploitation of the Scriptures is all too common. For example, some mistreat the story of the stilling of the storm on the Sea of Galilee (Matt 8:23–27).[64] Matthew intended the story to highlight the wonder and power of Jesus. The story intends to call attention to Jesus and elicit faith in him as the Lord of all. It ends with the disciples explicitly asking, "What kind of man is this? Even the winds and the waves obey him!" Yet we hear people treat the story as

---

62. Outstanding examples that seek to understand the Bible's perspective in the midst of suffering are P. Yancey, *Disappointment with God* (Grand Rapids: Zondervan, 1988); D. A. Carson, *How Long, O Lord? Reflections on Suffering and Evil*, 2nd ed. (Grand Rapids: Baker, 2006); and T. Keller, *Walking with God through Pain and Suffering* (New York: Penguin, 2013).

63. In the next chapter we provide more guidance on how to apply the biblical text responsibly.

64. See the discussion of how to interpret miracle stories above under Gospels.

if it taught, "God will calm the storms of your life." This may or may not be a true sentiment, but it does not emerge in any hermeneutically defensible way from *this* passage.[65] As Job learned, sometimes God actually *sends* storms to fulfil his purposes.

Equally, we cannot promise food or money to those going through economic hard times with Paul's words, "And my God will meet all your needs according to the riches of his glory in Christ Jesus" (Phil 4:19).[66] This is not a universal promise. Paul's words followed his glowing commendation of the Philippians who generously supported his ministry (4:15–18). They gave sacrificially, and so Paul assured them that God would not abandon Christians who demonstrate such faithfulness.[67] He would meet all their needs. Paul articulates the same principle when he says, ". . . whoever sows generously will also reap generously" (2 Cor 9:6). This is no investment strategy: if you give money to God's cause, then he will return even more money back to you. Perhaps even more tragic are those who take examples of healing in the gospels and make them into promises of God's healing for them. It is commendable to trust God; but trusting God for healing is no substitute for seeking professional medical help. We insist that it be both.

In our efforts at providing pastoral care, we should promise only those things that God has in fact *intended* to say. A responsible system of hermeneutics will restrain well intentioned but misguided help. Caregivers dare not take texts out of context or make them say what God never intended they say. They subvert the function of God's Word when they make false promises or give false assurance in the name of God and the Bible. When such mistaken words prove to be empty, those in need of help may come to discount the value of the Bible or, worse, become disillusioned with God himself and abandon the faith. Instead, the Bible offers caregivers a treasury of truths through which the voice of God may speak hope, healing, and God's sustaining presence.

TO PROMOTE SPIRITUAL FORMATION IN THE CHRISTIAN LIFE

As we have seen, people respond to the Bible's message in worship and praise, and the Bible's teachings provide comfort and hope. In addition, the Bible helps to build up the spiritual life; it provides motivation and guidance for developing a robust

---

65. For more on this pericope see R. T. France, *The Gospel of Matthew*, NICNT (Grand Rapids: Eerdmans, 2007), 336–37.

66. If this seems unreasonable, we can ask only that readers follow our succeeding discussion on determining valid applications of Scripture. The examples in this paragraph illustrate a point. We might want to add that the theology underlying these examples may support extended applications, but they must be more general and less authoritative, as we will explain below. To promise one who is suffering that "God will calm the storms of your life" based on Matt 8:23–27 may be cruelly hollow. It would be better to remind them of God's calming, reassuring presence—his promise that "surely I am with you always" (Matt 28:20; cf. Ps 23)—whether in storms or sunshine.

67. See further W. G. Hansen, *The Letter to the Philippians*, PNTC (Grand Rapids; Nottingham, UK: Eerdmans, 2009), 324–25.

spiritual life that draws a believer closer to God. We argue that personal spiritual development most adequately rests upon correct interpretation and valid uses of the Bible. It is almost axiomatic to Christians that the Bible stands at the core of spiritual growth: to grow in the Christian faith mandates some regimen of Bible study.[68] In their earnest grappling with biblical teachings and their implications, Christians have a prime resource for becoming *spiritual* men and women of God.

This returns us to one of the basic Christian presuppositions. If the Bible contains God's revelation—his written communication to his people—then in listening carefully to his voice on its pages, they encounter his very presence. The Holy Spirit uses the Spirit-inspired Bible to speak to God's people to grow them spiritually. This is not "bibliolatry"; Christians do not worship the Bible itself. We believe that the Bible stands as God's written Word to us. So as we listen faithfully and expectantly to its Spirit-mediated message, we believe that we hear his voice and sense his presence. In Scripture we sense the supervision of a loving parent whose instruction and counsel we seek and welcome.[69]

How may the Bible so form the inner being of the believer? First, the approach we have defended for understanding the intended meaning of the biblical texts provides the central input for this task. When we engage in a careful and faithful reading of the Bible—focusing on its intention—God nurtures our spiritual lives. Our hearts grasp the meanings and principles, we see the examples to follow or to avoid, we exult in God's works on our behalf, we reflect on their implications for our lives, ministries, and relationships—all these and more provide instruction for the person who seeks to walk with God. We perform our Bible study with all due diligence, using sound principles of biblical interpretation, and we embrace what we discover in our own walk with God.[70]

Yet for too many this remains on an overly cognitive a level—what Robert Mul-

---

68. Note the place given to input from the Bible in such helpful books as B. Demarest, *Satisfy Your Soul: Restoring the Heart of Christian Spirituality* (Colorado Springs: NavPress, 1999); H. Baker, *Soul Keeping. Ancient Paths of Spiritual Direction* (Colorado Springs: NavPress, 1998); W. W. Klein, *Become What You Are: Spiritual Formation According to the Sermon on the Mount* (Downers Grove: InterVarsity, 2006); A. H. Calhoun, *Spiritual Disciplines Handbook*, 2nd ed. (Downers Grove: InterVarsity, 2015); R. K. DeYoung, *Glittering Vices: A New Look at the Seven Deadly Sins and Their Remedies* (Grand Rapids: Brazos, 2009); M. Laird, *Into the Silent Land: A Guide to the Christian Practice of Contemplation* (Oxford: Oxford University Press, 2006); J. B. Smith, *The Good and Beautiful God: Falling in Love with the God Jesus Knows* (Downers Grove: InterVarsity, 2009); C. Webb, *The Fire of the Word* (Downers Grove: InterVarsity, 2011); D. Willard, *The Great Omission: Reclaiming Jesus' Essential Teachings on Discipleship* (San Francisco: HarperCollins, 2006); and M. R. Mulholland, Jr., *Shaped by the Word: The Power of Scripture in Spiritual Formation*, rev. ed. (Nashville: The Upper Room, 2001). Of course always worthy of study are such recent classics as R. J. Foster, *Celebration of Discipline*, 3rd ed. (New York: Harper and Row, 1988); and D. Bonhoeffer, *Meditating on the Word* (Cambridge, MA: Cowley, 1986).

69. Helpful on this point is T. Longman III, *Reading the Bible with Heart and Mind* (Colorado Springs: NavPress, 1997), who expresses the beauty of the connection of God and his people through the Bible.

70. On moving from Bible study to spiritual formation see B. K. Waltke, "Exegesis and the Spiritual Life: Theology as Spiritual Formation," *Crux* 30 (1994): 28–35; E. H. Peterson, *Eat This Book: A Conversation in the Art of Spiritual Reading* (Grand Rapids: Eerdmans, 2009); and N. Vest, *Knowing by Heart: Bible Reading for Spiritual Growth* (London: Darton, Longman, and Todd, 1995).

holland calls the "informational" level.[71] Therefore, we suggest a second approach also worth our pursuit. Sometimes called *lectio divina* (sacred reading), this way of reading of the Scripture charts a different course.[72] Instead of being in control by seeking (in this exercise) the author's intended meaning in the text, *lectio* aims to allow the text itself to control the process—under the prayerful guidance of the Holy Spirit. More meditative, this kind of reading does not seek so much the meaning in the text as the meaning of our lives *under* the text's mastery. In the historic four stages of this type of reading, first one *reads* in a reflective, gentle, slow manner; the goal is to listen carefully, not to get through a body of text quickly. Second, one *meditates* on the significance of the text; meditation seeks to engage what one has read with the heart, thoughts, feelings, motivations, and the like. Third, one responds to this meditation in *prayer*—heart-felt cries to God that emerge from meditation on the Word. Finally, one rests in quiet *contemplation* in the presence of God; it is a time of rest and peace with our God. These are not mechanical steps nor a set formula, or even a precise order, but a holistic attempt to engage God in his Word.

We do not suggest informational and formational approaches exist in opposition to each other. Reading the Bible for information and corresponding application is important—as we have demonstrated. But we dare not allow this informational approach (the historical meaning of texts) to crowd out the Bible's formational role, which is to allow God's Spirit to speak at the core of our being. No matter how we pursue formation in our Bible reading, it must be done! We ought not merely to know what the Bible says and means; we need to ingest it internally and transformationally. The goals of both informational and formational Bible reading are that we be motivated spiritually (i.e., Spirit-ually) and directed by internal spiritual (i.e., Spirit-ual) principles, not simply those of the culture around us.

We affirm our desire to grow spiritually and grow more Christ-like. To accomplish that goal, we need to embody the principles we discover in Scripture and seek to become more conformed to the image of Christ. In this way the Bible shapes and colors our values and attitudes. With the Spirit's aid we embrace what we learn and grow in our devotion to serving God and other people. And our sense of God's presence and work in our lives deepens; an unbelievable calm enters—we feel his delight in us.

Often "the Spirit's aid," mentioned above, takes the form of God's agents—others on the spiritual journey with us. Often learning to apply biblical principles must be caught by observing it in the lives of others. An important concept to embrace when

---

71. He distinguishes between an informational versus formational reading of Scripture. See M. R. Mulholland, Jr., *Shaped by the Word*, 47–60. A NT scholar by trade, he outlines the values of this non-cognitive approach to using the Bible in spiritual formation.

72. For useful insights and guidance on *lectio* see T. Gray, *Praying Scripture for a Change: An Introduction to Lectio Divina* (West Chester, PA.: Ascension: 2009); M. Casey, *Sacred Reading: The Ancient Art of Lectio Divina* (Liguori, MO: Triumph Books, 1996); L. S. Cunningham and K. J. Egan, *Christian Spirituality. Themes from the Tradition* (New York: Paulist Press, 1996), 38–40; and M. J. Thompson, *Soul Feast: An Invitation to the Christian Spiritual Life* (Louisville: Westminster John Knox, 1995), 17–30.

we think of spiritual formation is the need for mentors and spiritual directors.[73] The categories of mentoring (a broader term) and spiritual direction overlap, but the latter is less advice giving or coaching and more gently guiding the directee to seek to know what God is doing inside him/her—to help them listen for what God is saying or doing in their present experiences. These practices obviously overlap several topics we have covered already—teaching, preaching, or pastoral care. On one side, we must seek spiritual guides in our lives—to help impress on us God's ways and show us the "how to" of responding to God and applying the Bible to our lives. On the other side, with spiritual maturity comes the responsibility and privilege of guiding others' lives to enable them to live out the Bible's imperatives for their lives. It means applying more broadly to the entire church the principle involved in Paul's counsel to the older women in Crete: ". . . to teach what is good. Then they can urge the younger women to love their husbands and children, to be self-controlled and pure, to be busy at home, to be kind, and to be subject to their husbands, so that no one will malign the word of God" (Titus 2:3–5).[74] Those further along on the spiritual journey have a responsibility to teach godly values and virtues to those behind them. In true biblical mentoring the mentor must assure that he or she imparts *biblical principles* into the life of the mentee.[75]

In short, as we interact with Scripture we engage in a two-way conversation with the Bible's Author.[76] As we understand what God says to us, we progress in our relationship with him and gain increased motivation to grow spiritually. The more we advance in this process, the more spiritually mature we become. Indeed, as Christians, we will develop and promote a spiritual life only by regular interaction with God through such disciplines as Bible study and prayer.[77]

Personal spiritual formation can never remain a private inner issue because the

---

73. The literature on the topic of mentoring also grows rapidly. For helpful perspectives see P. R. Wilson, "Core Virtues for the Practice of Mentoring," *Journal of Psychology and Theology* 29 (2001): 121–30; P. Stanley and R. Clinton, *Connecting: The Mentoring Relationships You Need to Succeed* (Colorado Springs: NavPress, 1992); L. Zachary, *The Mentor's Guide: Facilitating Effective Learning Relationships*, 2nd ed. (San Francisco: Jossey-Bass, 2011); and B. Williams, *The Potter's Rib: Mentoring for Pastoral Formation* (Vancouver, BC: Regent College Publishing, 2005). On spiritual direction more specifically, see H. J. J. Nouwen, *Spiritual Direction: Wisdom for the Long Walk* (New York: HarperOne, 2015); G. T. Smith, *Spiritual Direction: A Guide to Giving and Receiving Direction* (Downers Grove: InterVarsity, 2014); W. A. Barry and W. J. Connolly, *The Practice of Spiritual Direction*, 2nd rev. ed. (New York: HarperOne, 2009); M. Guenther, *Holy Listening: The Art of Spiritual Direction* (Cambridge, MA.: Cowley, 1992); G. W. Moon and D. G. Benner, *Spiritual Direction and the Care of Souls: A Guide to Christian Approaches and Practices* (Downers Grove: InterVarsity, 2004); and W. A. Barry, *Spiritual Direction and the Encounter with God: A Theological Inquiry*, rev. ed. (Costa Mesa, CA.: Paulist, 2005).

74. For other NT examples of mentoring and training in Scripture see D. E. Lanier, "The Multiplication of Disciples," *Faith and Mission* 16 (1999): 5–15.

75. J. M. Houston makes this important point in "Spiritual Mentoring in an Age of Confusion," *Crux* 30 (1994): 2–11. See also D. Benner, *Sacred Companions: The Gift of Spiritual Friendship and Direction* (Downers Grove: InterVarsity, 2004).

76. One can even pray the Scriptures. See, inter alia, M. L. Smith, *The Word is Very Near You. A Guide to Praying with Scripture* (Cambridge, MA: Cowley, 1989).

77. Of course, we do not intend in any sense to limit the means to spiritual formation to Bible study and prayer. Many of the books noted in the previous footnotes pursue a more full-orbed discussion of this crucial issue. We simply want to underscore here the crucial role the Bible ought to play.

complement to spiritual *formation* is spiritual *living*, and the Bible functions significantly here, too. How do we know what lifestyle pleases God? Which actions demonstrate and grow out of the life of the Spirit versus those that are antithetical to that life? In the midst of the perplexing decisions of life, which options please God or promote his purposes for our lives? God's Word gives principles and instructions to guide us. We do not suggest that the Bible provides ten easy steps to attaining God's perfect will for our lives. The Bible does not speak specifically to all the personal decisions—either major or minor—that life demands of us each day. Neither do we suggest that it is always a simple matter to know what is the best decision in a given situation. Yet as the next chapter on application demonstrates, the Bible provides positive guidance so that we can act confidently and responsibly in compliance with God's purposes. The spiritually minded person—one whose heart and motivations are permeated with God's presence, principles, and purposes—will employ this guidance in the decisions and activities of life. To obey God requires an act of submission, and the biblically informed believer has the resources to submit in ways that fulfill God's will.[78] In our opinion, Jesus' followers must have their spiritual ears open and attuned to what God is addressing then.

How important it is then to handle the Bible with accuracy! If we desire to please God and do his will, we need a valid interpretation of the Bible. If we do not understand accurately what God intended to say in his Word, or if we read in our own subjective prejudices without any safeguards, we risk abusing the Bible for our own ends rather than using it with God's intentions. How tragic when, like poor Samuel (1 Sam 3), our ears are so spiritually ignorant or inexperienced that they can't pick out God's voice from among the cacophony calling for our attention. How tragic when, instead of following God's principles and will as taught in the Scripture, people twist or reject its teachings to condone or even promote their sin.

To illustrate, it is easy for us to condemn what we consider blatant sins, such as murder or adultery. But responsible readers must also acknowledge that the Bible insists that gossiping, greed, envy, and boasting are abhorrent offenses to God (Rom 1:29–32)! In reality, when Paul lists the kinds of lifestyles that disqualify people from entrance into God's eternal kingdom, greed is prominent on the list (1 Cor 6:9–10). How easy it is in our western affluence to turn greed and boasting into virtues (perhaps calling them "savvy business plans" or "clever marketing strategies" or even simple hard work). As consumers, we envy what others possess, we believe the advertisers who assure us that we deserve it, and we justify luxury, materialism, and often its accompanying bondage to debt.[79] Jesus told his disciples that they could not serve God and money, but many Christians beg to differ with Jesus and think they can serve

---

78. Certainly, Jesus' use of Scripture in his defense against Satan's temptations provides a ready example of applying biblical principles in the crucible of life (Matt 4:1–11 par.). The OT books Job and Psalms supply ample evidences of blunt, passionate one-on-one wrestling with God.

79. Toward a biblical theology of wealth, see C. L. Blomberg, *Christians in an Age of Wealth: A Biblical Theology of Stewardship* (Grand Rapids: Zondervan, 2013); C. L. Blomberg, *Neither Poverty nor Riches: A Biblical Theology*

both. Jesus said that the poor are blessed, but most of us disagree. Who is correct? How sad that Christians so often lack the tender compassion, patient forbearance, and gentle spirit of their Lord. We need spiritual openness to allow God's Spirit to produce in us true spiritual fruit (Gal 5:22–25).

All Christians, however sincere, face an ever-present tendency: to mold the Bible's teachings to promote their values instead of allowing the Bible to transform them. The Bible condemns many practices that we have come to accept and even recommend! Without doubt, we require a responsible hermeneutic to guide our interpretation and to assure its objectivity. We dare not make the Bible say what we want it to say or have it approve the activities that we want to pursue. The Bible, as God's revealed truth, demands that we submit to its teaching and transformation of our character, not mold it to our desires.

That means, even after the best interpretive work is complete, the ultimate question remains: will we submit to God's instructions as discovered in his Word? Not will we do the ones we prefer as we prefer to do them, but will we submit to God's expectations and welcome the transformed person he offers to make us? Spiritual formation involves the transformation of our hearts, minds, and spirits—our character and outlook, our relationship with God and our relationships with other people. If we do not allow God's Spirit to transform us, we risk God's indictment on us, as on the Israelites of old. As one example, Amos paints the picture of God's response to Israel's injustice against the poor in their midst: "I hate, I despise your religious festivals; your assemblies are a stench to me. Even though you bring me burnt offerings and grain offerings, I will not accept them. . . . Away with the noise of your songs! I will not listen to the music of your harps. But let justice roll on like a river, righteousness like a never-failing stream" (Amos 5:21–24). Spiritual formation requires inner transformation that also renovates all that we are. This is what the Spirit seeks to accomplish in concert with the Scriptures.

TO ENJOY ITS BEAUTY AS LITERATURE

In addition to all its other virtues, the Bible delights the people of God, and even many unbelievers. Its pages brim with adventure, humor, intrigue, and pageantry. In it we find aesthetic beauty but also some grim violence. Surely God gave us this marvelous message to *enjoy*! The Scriptures have come to us in various kinds of highly crafted literature. It would be difficult not to appreciate the Bible's assorted literary qualities and genius.[80] Though we do not limit the value of the Bible to being great literature, many people appropriately acknowledge the Bible as literature and expound

---

of Possessions (Downers Grove: InterVarsity, 1999); and B. Witherington III, *Jesus and Money: A Guide for Times of Financial Crisis* (Grand Rapids: Brazos, 2010).

80. See the section on "Literary Criticism" in the bibliography for resources on investigating the literary dimensions of the Bible.

its literary excellence.[81] People savor the artful narrative of the intrigues of Joseph and his brothers, and they admire Nathan's cunningly simple parable that exposes the hypocrisy of King David. They appreciate the masterful poetry in the Psalms and delight in the parables of Jesus. The Bible's diverse kinds of literature—OT epics, strange apocalyptic prophecy, tightly reasoned epistles, and the skillful sustained argumentation in Hebrews—inspire and capture our interest. The book itself arouses intellectual and emotional enjoyment. It invites us to appreciate its multifaceted beauty. But above that, the Bible's beauty and the pleasure it promotes reflects the beauty and personality of the God who inspired it. Its beauty sings his praises just as the stars and planets do (Ps 19).

SUMMARY

The Bible is a collection of remarkable writings of great consequence to all people. For believers it constitutes God's written revelation to his people. Yet, as in any kind of communication, understanding the message is critical. Whether one communicates with a wink, a word, a picture, or oral speech, if the message is misconstrued, the point is lost. Obviously, the results of a muddled message can range from inconsequential to tragic.

The Bible communicates in various ways and serves many purposes (as we have just reviewed). But if the Bible is to retain its integrity and potency as God's communication to his people, we must understand the intention of its message. We must not settle for mistaken or muddled messages. To impose our own meaning is not a valid option if we want to discern its (God's) voice. As we have argued, only a responsible system of hermeneutics gives us confidence that we have understood God's message. We must know the meaning of the Bible's message before we can expect that meaning to accomplish what God intended for its readers. That people misuse and misconstrue the Bible's teachings every day (as some have throughout the church's history) does not invalidate the relevance of hermeneutics. That God may work through or even in spite of faulty interpretation is beside the point. If a child asks for arsenic and her mother hands her an apple, things may turn out well in that instance, but we dare not argue that to understand the correct meanings of the words "arsenic" and "apple" is irrelevant. So it is in the uses of the Bible: correct meaning is paramount. We must always affirm that the best outcomes result from the most accurate interpretations— and outcomes constitute God's purpose for the Bible.

---

81. On this topic see L. Ryken, *How to Read the Bible as Literature* (Grand Rapids: Zondervan, 1984); and J. B. Gabel et al., *The Bible As Literature: An Introduction*, 5th ed. (Oxford, UK: Oxford University Press, 2005).

12

APPLICATION

In previous chapters we have described and defined how an interpreter deciphers the meaning of the text. Yet for the practicing Christian, the process that began with interpretation is incomplete if it stops at the level of meaning. One must then ask how the text applies to life. Certainly we cannot discover the proper application of a text until we have determined what it means. "Application focuses the truth of God's Word to specific, life-related situations. It helps people understand what to do or to use what they have learned."[1]

The terminology adopted for the stage of application varies. Some speak of application as part of interpretation, while others think of it as a separate step. Some talk of what the text *meant* versus what it *means*.[2] One of the most popular distinctions that evangelicals have utilized follows E. D. Hirsch's discussion of meaning versus significance.[3] "Meaning" refers to the ideas the biblical text originally intended to communicate to its readers; "significance" refers to the implications of that meaning in different, later situations. From this vantage point, therefore, the meaning of any given passage of Scripture remains consistent no matter who is reading the text, while its significance may vary from reader to reader. As we have noted in several places above, various scholars have applied speech act theory to distinguish the locutionary from the illocutionary or perlocutionary forces of a text—distinguishing, respectively, what a text says; what the author intends to achieve (including the tactics required to do that) in the text; and what are the author's intended outcomes or results in the text.[4]

But whatever the terminology employed, the issue is clear. How do we who believe the Bible remains relevant for people beyond the first audience determine that ongoing relevance? We might ask, "What bearing does the biblical message have on life today—on life in general and on my life in particular? How does God expect *me* to respond? What actions am I to *perform*?"[5]

---

1. D. Veerman, *How to Apply the Bible*, 2nd ed. (Wheaton: Tyndale, 1993), 15.

2. See esp. K. Stendahl, "Biblical Theology: Contemporary," in *Interpreter's Dictionary of the Bible*, 4 vols., ed. G. Buttrick (New York: Abingdon, 1962), 1:419–22.

3. E. D. Hirsch, Jr., *Validity in Interpretation* (New Haven: Yale University Press, 1967).

4. See esp. A. C. Thiselton, *New Horizons in Hermeneutics* (Grand Rapids: Zondervan, 1992); and K. J. Vanhoozer, *Is There a Meaning in This Text?*. More briefly, cf. R. S. Briggs, "Speech-Act Theory," in *Words and the Word: Explorations in Biblical Interpretation and Literary Theory*, ed. D. G. Firth and J. A. Grant (Downers Grove: InterVarsity, 2008), 75–110, as well as our discussion above.

5. S. C. Barton ("New Testament Interpretation as Performance," *SJT* 52 [1997]: 178–208) argues powerfully for this understanding of application as the necessary culmination of the interpretive process.

THE IMPORTANCE OF APPLICATION

Not everyone shares our conviction that God intended his people to apply the Bible outside its original setting. However, even secular relevance theory now recognizes that all human communicative acts have this potential.[6] In the case of the Christian Scriptures, two factors in the statements of the intentions of its authors explicitly support our conviction.[7] First, the Scriptures themselves repeatedly claim that people glorify God by obeying—that is by applying—his Word. After Moses reviewed the law at the end of the wilderness wandering, he concluded by promising the people blessing and prosperity if, and only if, they obeyed the laws (Deut 30:11–20). Here blessing and prosperity are conditional; they follow only if people apply the laws to their daily lives. The historical and prophetic books of the OT in large measure describe the cycles of faithfulness and faithlessness that caused the Israelites alternately to receive God's blessing and judgment. The Assyrian and Babylonian captivities thus served as vivid reminders of the serious consequences of failing to live consistently with God's Word. In the Sermon on the Mount, Jesus reiterates the necessity not merely to hear his words but to put them into practice (Matt 7:13–27). James echoes Jesus' words when he reminds his audience, "Do not merely listen to the word, and so deceive yourselves. Do what it says" (Jas 1:22).

Second, the Bible claims that its message is relevant for later generations, not just its original readers. After Moses wrote down the law and assigned the Levites as its custodians, he gave instructions for them to read it every seven years before the assembled people (Deut 31:9–13). Individual parents, however, were to teach the law to their children on a regular basis (Deut 6:7–25). After centuries of relative neglect by the people of Israel, Josiah obtained a copy of the law, recognized its continuing authority, and led the people in renewing their commitment to God's covenant (2 Kgs 22–23). Nearly two centuries later when a remnant returned to Jerusalem from captivity in Babylon, Ezra the scribe reaffirmed the relevance of the law for his generation by calling the people together to hear God's Word read and explained (Neh 7:73b–8:18). Later prophets applied to their own generations the messages given by earlier prophets. Jeremiah, for example, recalled Nathan's promises to David to assure the exiles that God would restore them to their land after seventy years in captivity (Jer 33:19–22; cf. 2 Sam 7:12–16). He also built on Isaiah's prophecy that a righteous branch would sprout from David's line (Jer 33:14–16; cf. Isa 11:1).

The NT contains equally striking evidence confirming that God's Word was designed not only for the original readers but also for subsequent generations. Note that just as Jesus commands his disciples to teach their disciples "everything I have

---

6. Tim Meadowcroft, "Relevance as a Mediating Category in the Reading of Biblical Texts: Venturing beyond the Hermeneutical Circle," *JETS* 45 (2002): 611–27.

7. For more detail, cf. W. Henrichsen and G. Jackson, *Studying, Interpreting, and Applying the Bible* (Grand Rapids: Zondervan, 1990), 259–330.

commanded you" (Matt 28:19), he also prays not only for his immediate followers but also for all those who would believe in him through their message (John 17:20). In addition, Paul warns the believers in Corinth, who were emphasizing their freedom in Christ, of the dangers of idolatry and immorality by reminding them of God's judgment on the Israelites in the wilderness. Despite recognizing that these believers lived in a different age and era in salvation history, he nevertheless states, "Now these things occurred as examples to keep us from setting our hearts on evil things as they did" (1 Cor 10:6). He makes a similar point later to Roman believers but generalizes to include all the OT: "For everything that was written in the past was written to teach us, so that through endurance and the encouragement of the Scriptures we might have hope" (Rom 15:4).

We understand that people who do not share our presuppositions about the authority of Scripture are not always as concerned to apply it. But in light of the Scripture's own witness,[8] we find it more difficult to comprehend why many who claim to be Bible-believing Christians read and study the Bible so minimally and are so little concerned to apply it correctly.[9] And even among those who do seek to implement God's word, many do not consistently heed "the whole counsel of God" (cf. Acts 20:27 ESV). Certain parts of the Psalms and Proverbs, the Gospels, and Paul's letters are well-known and applied, while much of the rest of Scripture remains virtually untouched.

This leads to an important theological conviction. *All* Scripture is both inspired and relevant ("useful for teaching, rebuking, correcting, and training in righteousness, so that the servant of God may be thoroughly equipped for every good work"— 2 Tim 3:16). This does not mean that we will find a personal application in every phrase or sentence in Scripture, because the amount and kind of application of a passage will vary from genre to genre. We must interpret and apply each text in its context as part of a larger meaningful linguistic utterance. Tightly packed didactic, epistolary texts may place demands on our lives in virtually every phrase and clause. At the other end of the spectrum, we may read several chapters of genealogical material (e.g., in 1 Chr 1–12) before finding much of relevance, and even then only broad principles—about God's providence, his plan of salvation, his concern for individuals, and so on. But every sentence, indeed every verse, appears as part of a larger, coherent unit of thought that has some relevance for us.[10]

---

8. On the significance of the Scriptures' own claim to their authority more generally, see W. A. Grudem, "Scripture's Self-Attestation and the Problem of Formulating a Doctrine of Scripture," in *Scripture and Truth*, ed. D. A. Carson and J. D. Woodbridge (Grand Rapids: Zondervan, 1983; Grand Rapids: Baker, 1992), 19–59.

9. On Bible-reading habits among American Christians, see the annual Barna Research Group reports. For 2014, see "6 Trends for 2014," accessed at https://www.barna.com/barna-update/culture/664-the-state-of-the-bible -6-trends-for-2014#.VbrnTE3JBLM.

10. See further K. J. Vanhoozer, "The Semantics of Biblical Literature: Truth and Scripture's Diverse Literary Forms," in *Hermeneutics, Authority, and Canon*, ed. D. A. Carson and J. D. Woodbridge (Grand Rapids: Zondervan, 1986; Eugene, OR: Wipf & Stock, 2005), 49–104.

AVOIDING MISTAKES IN APPLICATION

Despite the importance of application, few modern evangelical scholars have focused on this topic. In fact, most hermeneutics textbooks give it only brief coverage, and many major commentary series only mention application with passing remarks to help readers bridge the gap from the biblical world to the modern world. Perhaps many assume that sound application is more "caught than taught." This is probably true, but sound application often seems hard to find, much less to catch! Fortunately, recent studies are helping to rectify this error of omission. Anthropologists, linguists, and missiologists are engaging in intensive discussions of contextualization: how to apply the Bible cross-culturally from a Western to a non-Western context.[11]

The principles involved prove identical to those needed to apply the Bible's meaning in its original non-Western context to a Western one such as ours (or any others, for that matter).[12] Several recent commentary series are working more self-consciously and with greater sophistication to meet the need for application.[13] By far and away the most helpful of these is the NIV Application Commentary Series from Zondervan, which organizes all of its comments on each text under three headings: "original meaning," "bridging contexts," and "contemporary significance." Nevertheless, much more work remains, for Christians today still encounter widespread misapplication of Scripture. Though we could readily multiply and categorize examples in detail, we will point out three of the most common here.[14]

Total Neglect of Any Context

Many well-meaning Christians read the Bible for "instant blessings" or quick instructions for life. In the process they are prone to mistakes and errors. We list several that are common and should be avoided. The first we might term the ouija

---

11. Perhaps the most well known is C. Kraft, *Christianity in Culture*, rev. ed. (Maryknoll: Orbis, 2005); recall our earlier discussion under historical-cultural background. D. E. Flemming demonstrates how every book of the NT is itself a product of contextualization (*Contextualization in the New Testament: Patterns for Theology and Mission* [Downers Grove: InterVarsity, 2005]).

12. A point stressed by Osborne in his helpful chapters on application, both labeled, somewhat idiosyncratically, "Homiletics" and subdivided into "Contextualization" and "The Sermon" (*The Hermeneutical Spiral*, 410–33 and 434–64, respectively).

13. See, e.g., the Story of God Bible Commentary series from Zondervan and the Teach the Text series from Baker. Cf. also the Smyth & Helwys Bible Commentary. Among just slightly older series, see esp. The Bible Speaks Today from InterVarsity. Both one-volume Bible commentaries as well as whole series are now emerging from the Majority World, with an emphasis on application to their cultural contexts. See esp. the Africa Bible Commentary series (Nairobi: Word Alive; Bukuru, Nigeria: ACTS; Accra: Challenge Enterprises of Ghana; Grand Rapids: Zondervan); or B. Wintle, ed., *The South Asia Bible Commentary* (Grand Rapids: Zondervan, 2015).

14. As, e.g., in J. W. Sire, *Scripture Twisting: Twenty Ways the Cults Misread the Bible* (Downers Grove: InterVarsity, 1980), which covers errors of interpretation as well as errors of application (errors that, unfortunately, are by no means limited to the cults!). Cf. also T. Longman III (*Reading the Bible with Heart and Mind* [Colorado Springs: NavPress, 1997], 53–56), who discusses the "distorting lenses" of treating Scripture as a "treasure chest of golden truths," "grab bag of promises and comforts," a compilation of "riddles and secrets," or "a talisman with magical power"; while D. R. Bauer and R. A. Traina (*Inductive Bible Study: A Comprehensive Guide to the Practice of Hermeneutics* [Grand Rapids: Baker, 2011], 327–30) lists four fallacies to avoid—those of "the Empty Concept," of "Limited Appropriation," of "Norm Reductionism," and of "Genre Reductionism."

board approach to guidance. Christians who want to base their decisions on the will of God may be tempted to use the Bible as if it were a magical book. For example, often after a prayer for divine help they might open the Bible at random and accept the verse their eyes fall on as God's guidance for the decision they are making. While God might conceivably accommodate a sincere but misguided Christian through this method, he never promises to do so. As a result, serious mistakes with damaging consequences inevitably occur when people persist in this approach. One of us, for example, knew a young man who had to decide whether to enlist in the armed forces or go to college. Opening his Bible at random, he saw the passage in Ezekiel that speaks of people coming from Tarshish to Tyre in ships (Ezek 27:25). Although this passage contains no command for anyone to go anywhere in a ship and has nothing to do with becoming part of the armed forces, this young man interpreted the text as a call to join the Navy. In so doing he might have deprived himself of a college education by making a decision he thought was God's will. More seriously, though, he completely misunderstood what role the Bible should have in the Christian decision-making process.

A more unfortunate incident was recorded a number of years ago on the front page of the sports section of a major Chicago newspaper under the bold headline, "'God's Orders' Send Pitcher Packing." The story explained how the Christian owner of a minor league baseball team decided to release a pitcher who had requested a raise in pay. She opened her Bible at random, again to Ezekiel (no doubt because it comes roughly in the middle!), and read the phrase, "prepare thee stuff for removing" (Ezek 12:3 KJV). This became her guidance "from God" for dismissing the pitcher.[15] Had she read the context, she would have discovered that these instructions from God to Ezekiel concerned an object lesson Ezekiel was to give the Israelites. He was to pack as if going on a long trip, but he was not actually supposed to go anywhere. Had the owner of this team really wanted to imitate Ezekiel (which would still not have been a correct application of the passage!), *she* would have been the one to make preparations for leaving rather than firing someone else.[16]

Much more recently, one of us was called by a friend who had been diagnosed with cancer and told, as part of her testing, she needed to get a small medical tattoo. Horrified, she refused because she knew that "God hated tattoos." She had correctly recalled that there was a Bible passage that forbade tattoos but she knew neither its wording nor its context. Leviticus 19:28b does teach ancient Israel not to "put tattoo marks on yourself," but it does so immediately after commanding them not to cut the hair on the sides of their heads or clip the edges off their beards (vv. 27), commands almost no Christians worry about today. Then the law declares, "Do not cut your bodies for the dead" (v. 28a). Here is the key to this cluster of verses. Various ancient

---

15. G. Edes, "'God's Orders' Send Pitcher Packing," *Chicago Tribune*, June 30, 1978, sec. 6, p. 1.

16. For details of this example, along with a discussion of inappropriate uses of a fleece to determine God's will (Judg 6:37–40), see K. A. Ecklebarger, "Are We Fleecing Ourselves?" *Moody Monthly* 85 (Nov. 1984): 26–28.

Near Eastern peoples practiced these rituals as part of pagan worship, and the Israelites were not to follow suit.[17] Medicinal purposes are an entirely different, unrelated context. In the NT, Philippians 4:13 is a text that is regularly quoted without any respect to its context: "I can do all things through him who strengthens me" (ESV). In context, the "him" is Christ. But this scarcely means that Jesus will magically empower a believer to be able to leap tall buildings in a single bound or become a star athlete without long periods of training and competition.

It is sad, then, when Christians think it is appropriate to apply this verse to some spiritual task for which they are utterly unprepared, have never practiced, and for which they are not gifted. Missions pastors in particular often have to deal with people who come requesting financial support from the church because, for example, God has called them to India as evangelists. But if they have never had any cross-cultural experience, if their constitutions do not readily tolerate foreign foods (and foreign germs!) and, most importantly, if they have never shown any inclination to evangelize in their home country, the odds are extraordinarily small that God will strengthen them for a successful career of evangelistic ministry in India (or elsewhere). In context, Paul is declaring that he has learned how to be content in situations of plenty and of want, and that is how we should apply the text today. For this reason, the NIV now renders the verse as "I can do *all this* through him who gives me strength" (italics added).[18]

Partial Neglect of the Literary or Historical Context of a Passage

Fortunately, most Bible readers usually avoid the extreme errors of the ouija board approach or the total disregard of context. Much more common, however, is the proof-texting error that is often unwittingly encouraged by Bible memory systems that focus primarily on individual verses. To their credit, those who use this approach at least read entire sentences as meaningful units of thought, but often they fail to observe the larger contexts that appear to limit the application in important ways. Jeremiah 29:11 is a popular text ("'For I know the plans I have for you,' declares the LORD, 'plans to prosper you and not to harm you, plans to give you hope and a future'"), and some people even know that it appears in the context of God's promise to restore his people after exile. But it still is quoted far too often as just a catch-all verse of encouragement to troubled believers. Fortunately, there are plenty of contexts in life

---

17. See, e.g., G. J. Wenham, *The Book of Leviticus*, NICOT (Grand Rapids: Eerdmans, 1979), 272. Wenham goes on to note, however, beyond what most commentators say, that this was an inappropriate defacing of God's image in humanity—the purity of the external should correspond to the purity of the internal. Even if this is so, it is still doubtful if tattooing is automatically sinful in the NT age in which external, ritual purity laws have been abolished (see explicitly, J. Sklar, *Leviticus*, TOTC, rev. ed. [Nottingham and Downers Grove: InterVarsity, 2013], 250). But to the extent that tattooing, or any other practice, damages the body, it is not exercising good stewardship of "the temple of the Holy Spirit" (1 Cor 6:19). On the other hand, J. Milgrom (*Leviticus*, CC [Minneapolis: Fortress, 2004], 242) thinks Leviticus is abolishing Hebrew slavery by forbidding the sign that an Israelite had become a slave in perpetuity.

18. Cf. further R. R. Melick, *Philippians, Colossians, Philemon*, NAC 32 (Nashville: Broadman, 1991), 154–55; and J. S. Duvall and J. D. Hays, *Journey into God's Word: Your Guide to Understanding and Applying the Bible* (Grand Rapids: Zondervan, 2008), 92.

in which God does want to bless us in our physical and material circumstances. But we can hardly take this as a promise that he will always, or even most of the time, restore us to our homelands or give us happy circumstances in this life, even if at a *deeper, spiritual and eternal level*, the text will prove true for all his people.[19]

In other instances readers miss important contextual or historical-cultural background insights. Psalm 127:3–5, for example, reads:

> Sons are a heritage from the LORD, children a reward from him. Like arrows in the hands of a warrior are sons born in one's youth. Blessed is the man whose quiver is full of them. They will not be put to shame when they contend with their enemies in the gate.

This is a popular passage for wedding ceremonies, perhaps because Christian couples think that God is thus commanding them to have large families. If so, they need to look more carefully at the historical context. Contending with their enemies in the gate of an ancient walled city refers either to military battle or to legal action (which took place near the city gate). The language here is exclusive: "sons" does not include "daughters" because in ancient Israel girls could be neither soldiers nor legal witnesses. In an age when infant and child mortality rates were high, large families ensured that sufficient sons would survive to care for aged parents in their declining years. While there is at least one clear principle in this passage that Christians can apply (e.g., about the need to care for one's elderly parents, cf. 1 Tim 5:8), Christians dare not use this verse to assert that all couples must have large families.[20]

Insufficiently Analogous Situations

The most subtle of all misapplications of Scripture occurs when readers correctly interpret passages in their literary and historical contexts but then bring them to bear on situations where they simply do not apply. Satan's temptation of Christ well illustrates the subtlety and sinister nature of this misapplication. Using a cunning ploy, Satan quoted Psalm 91:11–12 and challenged Jesus saying, "If you are the Son of God . . . throw yourself down. For it is written, 'He will command his angels concerning you, and they will lift you up in their hands, so that you will not strike your foot against a stone'" (Matt 4:5). Here Satan asks Jesus to call upon God's miraculous ability to preserve his life. Certainly Jesus himself had such power. What is more, the psalmist states that God promises safety and protection to all who "dwell in the shelter of the Most High" (Ps 91:1). The problem here is that the devil's challenge confuses the psalmist's reference to "unintentional stumbling" with taking a *deliberate* jump off the temple pinnacle. The psalmist's intent here is not that we test God's faithfulness

---

19. J. A. Dearman (*Jeremiah and Lamentations*, NIVAC (Grand Rapids: Zondervan, 2002], 264) thus distinguishes between the "first context" in which the hope and the future are return to the promised land (Jer 30–31) and a spiritual application: "The same kind of confidence in God's saving purposes is available to any generation of people who, as Jeremiah writes, seek him 'with all [their] heart' (29:13)."

20. Cf. further L. C. Allen, *Psalms 101–50*, WBC 21 (Waco: Word, 1983), 180–1.

to his word by manufacturing situations in which we try to force him to act in certain ways. Rather, it points out his providential care for his children. Jesus thus refutes the devil with another text of Scripture that strictly forbids presuming on the grace of God (Deut 6:16).[21] No passage of Scripture can be casually or carelessly applied to any and/or every situation.

Matthew 18:20 promises that where two or three people gather in Christ's name he is present with them. Of course, because of Jesus' omnipresence in his exalted state, this is a timeless truth. Christ is present where only one of his people is all by him- or herself. Christ is also present where only a single non-Christian lives, though not indwelling that person as with believers. But when Christians use this verse to console themselves because not very many people have shown up for some service or activity, they have lost sight of the context. Originally, Jesus made this declaration in the context of promising that God would ratify decisions made by local churches when they exercise church discipline according to the regulations prescribed in vv. 15–17. The "two or three" who are gathered together in verse 20 are the "one or two witnesses" of v. 16 plus the aggrieved party, making two or three people to meet with an offending party, in hopes of helping them to repent.[22]

A FOUR-STEP METHODOLOGY FOR LEGITIMATE APPLICATION

What then should we do? It is always easier to spot fallacies in wrong methods than to formulate sound principles. The very nature of application—which varies from individual to individual in ways that meaning does not[23]—indicates that we probably cannot create a comprehensive list of foolproof principles; however, we can formulate some general and workable guidelines. The preceding examples of how *not* to apply passages remind us that all applications must be consistent with the meaning of passages arrived at by means of the sound hermeneutical principles we have already discussed in this book.[24] Legitimate application requires the use of both the general hermeneutical principles (establishing an accurate text, the correct meaning of words, the historical-cultural background, the larger literary contexts, and the like) and also special hermeneutics or genre criticism.

In other words, we must also ask of historical narratives if various characters represent good or bad examples or if they merely describe what happened as part of some larger theological point about God's working in the world. We must inquire

---

21. Cf. further C. L. Blomberg, *Matthew*, NAC 22 (Nashville: Broadman, 1992), 84–85.

22. G. R. Osborne, *Matthew*, ZECNT (Grand Rapids: Zondervan, 2010), 688.

23. A point no more strongly stressed than by W. C. Kaiser, Jr. "The Single Intent of Scripture," in *Evangelical Roots*, ed. K. Kantzer (Nashville: Nelson, 1978), 123–41, and elsewhere. Rather than speak of single intent or single meaning with multiple applications or significances, however, it seems to us better to speak of fixed meaning with varying significances. Kaiser's language could wrongly suggest that certain passages originally intended to communicate only one idea when in fact several are present.

24. Cf. B. Ramm, *Protestant Biblical Interpretation*, 3rd ed. (Grand Rapids: Baker, 1970), 185.

if prophecies were pointing to current events in the biblical writer's day, to the first coming of Christ, to his second coming, or to some combination of the three. We must inquire whether proverbs are descriptive or prescriptive and, if the latter, to what extent they teach absolutes or mere generalizations. We must also determine in what ways OT laws were fulfilled in Christ. In short, most of the principles and many of the examples already discussed in this volume suggest legitimate applications.

But we can say more. Recent evangelical analysis has come to a modest consensus that the key to legitimate application involves what many writers call "principlizing."[25] This may be defined as "an attempt to discover in a narrative [i.e., a text] the spiritual, moral, and/or theological principles that have relevance for the contemporary believer."[26] How one develops this process ranges from the relatively simple to the relatively complex. Jack Kuhatschek's excellent *Applying the Bible* boils it all down to three steps: understand the original situation, determine the broader principle that the biblical application reflects, and apply that general principle to situations we face.[27] Ramesh Richard, on the other hand, enumerates six steps that move from biblical statements to implications, extrapolations, applicational interpretations, interpretive applications, and finally to significance.[28] We propose the following four-stage model that we believe incorporates all of the major elements of these and other paradigms currently used:

1. Determine the original application(s) intended by the passage.
2. Evaluate the level of specificity of those applications to their original historical situations. If the original specific applications are transferable across time and space to other audiences and situations, apply them in culturally appropriate ways.
3. If the original applications are not transferable, identify one or more broader cross-cultural principles that the specific elements of the text reflect.
4. Find appropriate applications for today that implement those principles.

Alternative models are not always as different as they may first seem. In a curious protest against our approach, Peter Enns disputes the legitimacy of principlizing and thus uses the "bridging contexts" section of the NIV Application Commentary's format not to discuss cross-cultural principles as other volumes do, but to present the rest of the Bible's teaching on the same theme.[29] This is, of course, an important check and balance in the applicational process, as we will see below. Elmer Martens explicitly pits this approach of "biblical theology" against "principlizing."[30] But this

---

25. E. E. Johnson, *Expository Hermeneutics: An Introduction* (Grand Rapids: Zondervan, 1990), 229.

26. H. A. Virkler and K. G. Ayayo, *Hermeneutics: Principles and Processes of Biblical Interpretation*, 2nd ed. (Grand Rapids: Baker, 2007), 194.

27. (Downers Grove: InterVarsity, 1990; Grand Rapids: Zondervan, 1996), 33.

28. R. P. Richard, "Application Theory in Relation to the New Testament," *BSac* 143 (1986): 211.

29. P. Enns, *Exodus*, NIVAC (Grand Rapids: Zondervan, 2000).

30. E. A. Martens, "How Is the Christian to Construe Old Testament Law?" *BBR* 12 (2002): 199–216.

contrasts apples and oranges, as the former is not an alternate method to the latter but one important tool in determining timeless principles. Kevin Vanhoozer seems to present a quite different and exciting approach to placing ourselves in today's world in similar positions to the original audiences of the narratives and performing the drama of Scripture. But he recognizes there must be a propositional basis for the scripts we craft, however ad hoc unexpected circumstances sometimes make them become.[31] Jeannine Brown likewise prefers a participationist to a principlizing hermeneutic, while recognizing there must be principles to incarnate or enculturate.[32] The differences, it seems, are more in terminology and emphasis. Kuhatschek and Johnson want people to obey the Scriptures as much as Vanhoozer or Brown do but are focused most on how they determine what it is they are to obey. To explain these steps further, we will briefly elaborate on each.[33]

Determine the Original Application(s)

In this step the interpreter asks questions such as: How did the biblical author of a given passage want his hearers or readers to respond? What did the author intend the readers to do? To answer these questions, the interpreter asks a series of additional questions. Is there a command to obey, an example to follow or to avoid, a promise to claim, a warning to heed, a teaching to act on (even if not phrased as a direct command), or a truth to believe?[34] We can suggest other queries such as: Is there a need that prompts prayer or a blessing that motivates praise? Sometimes contemporary applications will be identical to the originally intended responses, though often they will differ in some ways. Mark Strauss reminds us also to review where the passage occurs in the overall storyline of Scripture, what its context and genre are, how it informs our understanding of God's nature, and what it teaches about what we ought to be in terms of character or attitudes and about what we ought to do in terms of actions or goals.[35]

For example, obeying the *command* not to covet a neighbor's wife or house remains as timely today as it did when Moses received it on Mount Sinai (Exod 20:17).

---

31. K. J. Vanhoozer, *The Drama of Doctrine: A Canonical Linguistic Approach to Christian Doctrine* (Louisville: Westminster John Knox, 2005); and K. J. Vanhoozer, *Faith Speaking Understanding: Performing the Drama of Doctrine* (Louisville: Westminster John Knox, 2014).

32. J. K. Brown, *Scripture as Communication: Introducing Biblical Hermeneutics* (Grand Rapid: Baker, 2007), 257–67.

33. Cf. also J. S. Duvall and J. D. Hays, *Grasping God's Word: A Hands-On Approach to Reading, Interpreting, and Applying the Bible*, 3rd ed. (Grand Rapids: Zondervan, 2012), 235–46. J. Arthurs ("The Fundamentals of Sermon Application [Part 2]," in *Interpretation and Application*, ed. C. B. Larson [Peabody: Hendrickson, 2012], 84–95) refers to the same four steps as "discover the *telos* [goal or intention] of the passage," "articulate the principles," "analyze your audience to find points of similarity," and "apply (that is, explain, prove, motivate, and equip) with concrete images."

34. T. N. Sterrett and R. L. Schultz, *How to Understand Your Bible*, 3rd ed. (Downers Grove: InterVarsity, 2010), 189–93. This is *not* the same as assuming that the Bible is nothing but a collection or list of commands to obey or promises to claim, etc., as Mark L. Strauss (*How to Read the Bible in Changing Times: Understanding and Applying God's Word Today* [Grand Rapids: Baker, 2011], 19–33) rightly stresses.

35. Strauss, *How to Read the Bible in Changing Times*, 78–79.

But this verse also prohibits coveting a neighbor's manservant, maidservant, ox, or donkey. The principle that prohibits covetousness finds its appropriate application in specific areas. The text identifies those possessions of their neighbors that the Israelites might be most tempted to desire. Most Western urban dwellers do not have to worry about the last four of these. The interpreter needs to ask what might be the relevant possessions today and include these in the application: a fancy car, a home entertainment center, or the latest computer technology, and so on. In fact the text of Exodus specifically justifies such generalization by concluding "or anything else that belongs to your neighbor."

Changing the example, to apply correctly the early church members' practices of sharing their faith, modern readers need to focus on marketplace evangelism (Acts 17:17). Many groups automatically assume that identical practices are both appropriate and necessary today. In certain contexts and certain cultures this may be true, but the interpreter must inquire why the first Christians gravitated to the central squares of Asian and European towns to preach. The answer is: public arenas were the socially acceptable places to consider new ideas (cf. Acts 17:18–21). That is where they applied the principle of evangelizing the world. Many Majority World villages today have similarly structured communities whose central plazas make ideal settings for preaching the gospel. But most Western cities have no such centralized location, and the nearest equivalent—a shopping mall, park, or an airport terminal—is not a place where people go to hear the latest news or to hear visitors publicly greet the town. In fact, because non-Christian cult members often conduct their evangelism in these arenas, Christians have to overcome a cultural stigma to witness effectively in such places. Sensitive application of Acts 17 may motivate believers to look for better, more suitable forums (in colleges and universities, through radio and television, or online through blogging, Facebook, and the like) while not neglecting legitimate opportunities for street evangelism.[36]

Asking if there is a truth to *believe* and a teaching to *act upon* from Acts 16:25–34 would certainly yield the identical answer Paul gave to the Philippian jailer: "Believe in the Lord Jesus, and you will be saved" (v. 31). This example differs from the previous two since the application is already at the level of a general principle, so we need not pursue the remaining steps in the process. However, since many readers of this passage are already believers, they simply need to consider how they can help others apply its message. Or, if they are tempted to abandon their faith, they should remind themselves that there is salvation nowhere else. These three examples have now taken us through the entire process of application, but we need to go on to itemize what we have done and give further illustrations.

---

36. For a sensitive treatment of the topic, see M. Green, *Evangelism in the Early Church*, rev. ed. (Eastbourne: Kingsway, 2003; Grand Rapids: Eerdmans, 2004). See also throughout A. Fernando, *Acts*, NIVAC (Grand Rapids: Zondervan, 1998).

Evaluate the Level of Specificity of the Original Application(s)

This step was a fairly easy task for the passages on not coveting and on believing in Jesus that we discussed. The command against coveting a neighbor's wife or husband clarified that this was a specific example of the more general prohibition against coveting what belongs to others (the precursor to theft). In the Acts 16 example of believing in Jesus, anyone familiar with the Bible or Christian teaching recognizes this as the foundational principle of the NT that is repeated in many different ways and places. But in the example of marketplace evangelism, not every reader will realize this as a specific example of a broader principle that may vary from one context to the next. Those familiar with biblical examples and commands concerning evangelism will recognize that the *methods* vary while the *mandate* to share the faith widely remains consistent. Even then, further historical and cultural background information may help readers to understand what functional equivalents to the marketplace may be available for believers in other times and places.[37]

The issues raised here revolve around a major topic in the study of hermeneutics, and, more specifically, of application. How does the interpreter know when certain biblical commands, examples, promises, warnings, and so on, are culture-bound (i.e., limited to their original context, not timeless or universal)? To answer the question, we suggest further questions: When can the interpreter rightly assume that the text presents a specific *form* (example) of a more general *principle*? When does the principle remain timeless and unchanging? How may the form of implementing that principle change from one context to the next?[38]

An excellent example of this dilemma today involves the issue of women's roles in the home and the church. On the one hand, we find the stance of the historic churches (Orthodox and Roman Catholic) and other traditionalists that have placed certain limits on women's roles. On the other hand, the impact over the last half-century of the women's liberation movement on almost all mainline Protestant churches and an increasing number of evangelical contexts has led to the toppling of many of these limits. Jobs women were forced to work during World War II also convinced many in society more generally of women's abilities in a broader range of roles than they often previously held. Although key texts (e.g., 1 Cor 11:2–16; 14:33b–38; 1 Tim 2:8–15; Eph 5:18–33; 1 Pet 3:1–7) indicate both certain timeless elements and certain culture-bound elements, sorting out which is which proves immensely difficult given the interpreters' preunderstandings.

Take 1 Timothy 2:8–15, for example. Many would agree that it is possible for

---

37. Recall our earlier discussion of the distinction between what is *descriptive* and what is *prescriptive* (or normative). The Bible may describe an incident (embodying a principle), but how that principle was implemented in that text (the description) may not prescribe *how* we ought to apply the principle.

38. Cf. esp. D. J. Estes, "Audience Analysis and Validity in Application," *BSac* 150 (1993): 219–29. Bauer and Traina (*Inductive Bible Study*, 294) speak of a "continuum of transcendence" with ends of the continuum representing "situational/circumstantially contingent statements tied to original situations" and "transcendent statements directly expressing trans-situational teachings."

men to pray in a godly fashion without necessarily "lifting up holy hands" (v. 8) and that braided hair for women is not always (or often) immoral (v. 9). The principles involved concern for praying and dressing appropriately and how that may have looked in the Ephesian church. Similarly, few would challenge that it is always appropriate for men to pray without anger or disputing (v. 8) and that women should always perform good deeds (v. 10). But what does the interpreter do with vv. 11–12, in which women are commanded to learn in quietness and full submission and not to teach or have authority over men? In addition to questions about the translation of key words in this passage and their grammatical relationship to one another, the debate over the function of vv. 13–14 looms large. To many interpreters, v. 13 grounds Paul's commands in God's order of creating man first and then woman. They see this as a natural indicator that they should apply his teaching universally. Verse 14, however, seems to base those same commands in the events of the fall, in which case we would expect the redemption in Christ to reverse its effects.

While we do not propose to take a stand on the foregoing passage,[39] we do note that many hermeneutics textbooks use passages like this to illustrate the principles they outline,[40] and if readers disagree with their particular interpretations and applications, unfortunately, they are prone to question the principles employed. We must admit that the passages involving women's and men's roles are among the most difficult in Scripture, and this accounts for the sincere disagreement of godly, well-educated, and well-intentioned interpreters. The strong social values today of justice and equality seem to conflict with these texts as well. Consequently, these passages are examples of the difficulty of positing universal application except perhaps to rule out some of the most extreme and unlikely positions. Individual preunderstandings almost inevitably color interpreters' approaches to these delicate texts.[41]

We purpose here to list a variety of criteria that will enable most interpreters to reach a fair measure of agreement on a wide variety of less complex texts, which they can employ with the more complicated passages. Before doing so, however, we must introduce one other preliminary matter. Many passages in Scripture do not clearly indicate whether they convey universal principles or only culture-specific applications. As a result, on one extreme some interpreters argue that unless something in the text

---

39. For a good juxtaposition of egalitarian and complementarian perspectives, see J. R. Beck, ed., *Two Views on Women in Ministry*, rev. ed. (Grand Rapids: Zondervan, 2005). For an excellent attempt to combine the best of both positions and be even more biblical, see M. Lee-Barnewall, *Neither Complementarian nor Egalitarian: A Kingdom Corrective to the Evangelical Gender Debate* (Grand Rapids: Baker, 2016).

40. E.g., D. A. Carson, *Exegetical Fallacies*, 2nd ed. (Grand Rapids: Baker, 1996), 108–12 (but this feature is noticeably lessened from the first edition); to varying degrees cf. also Osborne, *The Hermeneutical Spiral*, 423–25; G. D. Fee and D. Stuart, *How to Read the Bible for All Its Worth*, 4th ed. (Grand Rapids: Zondervan, 1994), 86–89; and S. McKnight, *The Blue Parakeet: Rethinking How You Read the Bible* (Grand Rapids: Zondervan, 2010), 153–207.

41. On which, see esp. R. K. Johnston, "The Role of Women in the Church and Home: An Evangelical Testcase in Hermeneutics," in *Scripture, Tradition and Interpretation*, ed. W. W. Gasque and W. S. LaSor (Grand Rapids: Eerdmans, 1978), 234–59; and A. J. Köstenberger, "Gender Passages in the New Testament: Hermeneutical Fallacies Critiqued," *WTJ* 56 (1994): 259–83. But in principle we should be able to bracket our powerful presuppositions and make progress, as recent research in fact suggests is occurring.

specifically indicates that the passage teaches a timeless truth, we should assume it to be occasional, that is, limited in its specific application to its original context.[42] On the other pole, other writers assume that the reverse is true: unless specific textual data support a culture-bound perspective, we should assume the originally intended application remains normative for all believers of all times.[43]

We detect problems, however, with both of these views. The former makes it difficult to establish the timelessness even of fundamental moral principles such as prohibitions against theft or murder;[44] the latter would seem to require us to bar children born outside marriage from our churches (Deut 23:2), to greet one another with a holy kiss (1 Thess 5:26), and to drink wine for upset stomachs (1 Tim 5:23).[45] This debate in fact reminds us of the polarization of perspectives on the application of OT law in the NT age. As with our resolution of that debate, we believe the fairest and most scriptural approach assumes neither of the above perspectives, but rather a mediating one. With 2 Timothy 3:16 and related texts, we affirm that every passage (a meaningful unit of discourse that makes one or more points that can be restated, if necessary, in a proposition) has some normative value for believers in all times and places (recall Rom 15:4). But we presuppose nothing about whether the application for us today will come by preserving unchanged the specific elements (i.e., application) of the passage or whether we will have to identify broader principles that suggest unique applications for new contexts.[46] Instead we ask a series of ten questions of the text to determine the nature of their significance for a later time or different culture.[47]

1. *Does the text present a broad theological or moral principle or does it give a specific manifestation of such a principle, which another book of Scripture elsewhere embodies in one or more different forms?* Nine-tenths of the Decalogue (minus the Sabbath command) clearly illustrates such broad moral categories (Exod 20:2–17). Much of the rest of the law gives specific ways of obeying and disobeying these principles. In the NT, both Jesus and Paul reaffirm the continuing relevance of all nine.[48] The

---

42. See the discussion of and response to this and related perspectives in J. R. McQuilkin, "Problems of Normativeness in Scripture: Cultural Versus Permanent," in *Hermeneutics, Inerrancy, and the Bible*, ed. E. D. Radmacher and R. D. Preus (Grand Rapids: Zondervan, 1984), 222–27.

43. The view McQuilkin himself presupposes ("Normativeness," 230), and that is defended by W. J. Larkin, Jr., *Culture and Biblical Hermeneutics: Interpreting and Applying the Authoritative Word in a Relativistic Age* (Grand Rapids: Baker, 1988; Eugene, OR: Wipf & Stock, 2003), 314–18.

44. McQuilkin, "Normativeness," 225–27. This may account for some clergy defenses of abortion.

45. A. Johnson, "A Response to Problems of Normativeness in Scripture: Cultural Versus Permanent," in Radmacher and Preus, eds., *Hermeneutics, Inerrancy, and the Bible*, 277–78.

46. Similarly, Osborne, *Hermeneutical Spiral*, 421.

47. The list of ten does not purport to be exhaustive but illustrative. It shares important similarities with that of Johnson, "Response," 279–80, but is by no means identical. Strauss (*How to Read the Bible in Changing Times*, 222–34) collapses some of our categories together and expands others, yielding eight very similar points. S. Liggins organizes thirteen very similar criteria under the headings of exegesis, biblical theology, systematic theology, and historical theology in "Distinguishing the Cultural from the Supracultural in the Prescriptive Material of the New Testament," *RTR* 68 (2009): 12–28.

48. For a justification of treating the Sabbath command differently, see C. L. Blomberg, "The Sabbath as Fulfilled in Christ," in *Perspectives on the Sabbath: 4 Views*, ed. Christopher J. Donato (Nashville: B&H, 2011), 305–58.

same is true of the so-called double-love command (Deut 6:4–5; Lev 19:18), which Jesus brings together in Mark 12:29–31 ("Love the Lord your God . . . and love your neighbor as yourself"). Romans 12:1–9 presents fundamental ethical obligations for believers: transformation of body and mind; use of spiritual gifts; and, again, love. A theme that recurs in the Law, Psalms, Proverbs, the Prophets, the Gospels, and the Epistles is the prohibition against partiality and the need to show mercy to the poor and dispossessed, to the outcast and the stranger.

On the other hand, numerous specific texts illustrate *applications* of this principle that may need to change if the principle is to be successfully implemented in new contexts. For example, OT law commanded farmers not to harvest the very edges of their field or go over their land a second time to glean what they missed in the initial harvest. This enabled the poor to gather freely the leftovers (Lev 19:9–10). These commands presuppose a rural, agrarian society in which the poor have access to the fields. Such an application would scarcely help the vast majority of urban poor in our world today.

Instead, those who seek to apply this text must find new ways to prevent the wasting or hoarding of surplus food in our world and to give some of this away to the poor. Restaurant owners might willingly restrict their profits for the sake of such redistribution. One Christian businessman in the Denver area, for example, tried repeatedly and finally succeeded in getting a major airline to donate its unused meals to a local clearing house for Christian charities, which in turn distributed them to needy people. We may need to find equivalents to the effort expended in gleaning so that poor people today have to expend some effort for their food rather than simply receiving it free. Many charitable food banks have allowed the poor to retain their dignity and incentive to work through charging a nominal fee for commodities. The laws of gleaning are thus relevant as a specific example of the *broader principle of concern for the poor*, even if we do not imitate exactly their ancient formal application.[49] Certainly the Scriptures themselves exhibit a diversity of responses to the problem (cf. Mark 10:21; Luke 19:8; Acts 4:32–35; Jas 1:27).

2. *Does the larger context of the same book of Scripture in which the passage appears limit the application in any way or does it promote a more universal application?* This question concerns information that might be near to the passage or separated from it in another part of the book. For example, the interpreter might read Jesus' warning to Peter that he would have to die for his faith (John 21:18–19) and wonder how widely it applies. Even if not every Christian is martyred, should all believers at least be prepared for someone to lead them "where [they] do not want to go" (v. 18b)? Reading further in the context leads the interpreter to see that Jesus predicts a quite different kind of destiny for John (vv. 20–23). In fact, some later misinterpreted Jesus' words

---

49. See further C. L. Blomberg, *Christians in an Age of Wealth: A Biblical Theology of Stewardship* (Grand Rapids: Zondervan, 2013). An excellent resource for implementing these principles is T. Sine, *Mustard Seed vs. McWorld* (Grand Rapids: Baker, 1999).

as implying that John would live until Christ's return (v. 23). But Jesus did not say that. In fact he spoke positively enough about John's future to clarify that his words to Peter applied to Peter alone and could not be generalized to include anyone else.[50]

On the other hand, the book of Ecclesiastes is more difficult to assess in places. It is clear that the author has indulged in most of life's pleasures and found them to be futile. Even though periodically he punctuates his narrative with seemingly positive principles such as, "A person can do nothing better than to eat and drink and find satisfaction in his work" (Eccl 2:24a), ambiguity clouds his statements. Although he immediately adds, "this too, I see, is from the hand of God" (v. 24b), he ends the paragraph with the conclusion, "this too is meaningless, a chasing after the wind." We detect his purpose only when we recognize chapters 11–12 as the concluding lessons that "the Preacher" has learned. Here he presents without any qualification similarly positive commands to enjoy life in wholesome ways while one is able (11:9–12:1; 12:13). This suggests that passages like 2:24a have a timeless, normative value.[51]

3. Does subsequent revelation limit or qualify the application of a particular passage even if the book in which it appears does not? Obviously, the interpreter must ask this question of every OT text. As discussed above, we can assume neither that all of the OT carries over into the NT without any change in application nor that none of it carries over unchanged. Rather, we must examine each text to discover how it has been fulfilled in Christ (Matt 5:17). But the same test must be applied to NT texts, not because we live in a new period of salvation history but because the NT itself sometimes revokes earlier commands or presents alternate models. In such cases earlier applications of the principles were not intended to be normative for every place and time.

A well-known example is Jesus' command to his disciples to take along no money or provisions for their itinerant preaching but to rely solely on the generosity of those to whom they minister (Matt 10:9–10). Later, however, Jesus refers specifically to these commands (Luke 22:35) and then says, "But now if you have a purse, take it, and also a bag . . ." (v. 36). Paul does this, too, changing or reversing early practices later on in his ministry. On occasion he relies on other Christians for financial support; at other times he makes tents to finance his ministry. The rationale in each case is what most effectively advances the cause of the gospel (1 Cor 9). It is thus inappropriate for Christians today to assume that all full-time Christian workers must be paid by other believers or that none may be so remunerated. We must ask which option will bring the most number of people to Christ (or most effectively accomplish the ministry

---

50. Cf. further D. A. Carson, *The Gospel According to John*, PNTC (Grand Rapids: Eerdmans, 1991), 679–82.

51. Though even then interpreters do not all agree. We have followed the perspective we believe to be ably defended in D. A. Garrett, *Proverbs, Ecclesiastes, Song of Songs*, NAC 14 (Nashville: Broadman, 1993); and M. A. Eaton, *Ecclesiastes*, TOTC (Downers Grove: InterVarsity, 1983). For a more pessimistic perspective that in essence sees the entire book as what is learned about "life under the sun" (this fallen world), with only the conclusion to fear God and keep the commandments as a positive takeaway, see T. Longman III, *The Book of Ecclesiastes*, NICOT (Grand Rapids: Eerdmans, 1998).

objectives). Which will avoid putting the gospel into disrepute? Which will not overly burden God's people? Given the abuses of fundraising by so many in ministries today and the downturn in giving that it often provokes, we could make a good case for promoting far more tent-making models than currently exist![52]

4. *Is the specific teaching contradicted elsewhere in ways that show it was limited to exceptional situations?* In a sense this is simply an important subquestion of the previous one. Because Scripture portrays Abraham as a paradigm of faith and obedience, we must ask how we can apply the story of his willingness to offer up his son Isaac on the altar (Gen 22). Although we will return to this example later, one thing seems clear here: God does not want us to sacrifice our children (as did many early Canaanite and a few contemporary pagan religions). Later laws make this abundantly plain (e.g., Lev 18:21; 20:2–5). We cannot know whether Abraham realized that in his day, but we need not vacillate. As the narrative shows, God never intended that Abraham kill his son. Surely the test was a unique one, not repeated elsewhere in Scripture and not to be repeated by any subsequent believers.

Another inimitable example is God's unusual call to the prophet Hosea to "Go, marry a promiscuous woman and have children with her . . . ." While some first-time readers of Hosea 1:2 might question why God appears to condone prostitution or at least tells Hosea to marry an apparently unrepentant prostitute, this situation is unique and bears closer study. To begin with, it is unclear if this text originally meant, as is usually assumed, that Gomer already was a harlot, or if it merely anticipated her later adultery.[53] But even if the former, other Scriptures unequivocally state that prostitution is sinful (Lev 19:29; 1 Cor 6:15). What then are we to make of Hosea uniting again with his wife after her later adultery (Hos 3:1)? The original command from God to marry a prostitute violates no law, but what of Hosea taking her back after further prostitution?

Of course, the shock value here corresponds to the shock God wants to create in Israel when they realize they are guilty of spiritual adultery. Jesus, centuries later, indicates that reconciliation is not always possible or necessary following marital unfaithfulness (Matt 19:9).[54] But unlike the Judaism of his day, he never mandated divorce, even in the case of infidelity. Hosea's actions were object lessons intended by God to illustrate the spiritual infidelity of his people Israel and God's unfailing love for them in spite of their disobedience (Hos 1:2; 3:1). Since God did not command this as a general principle, we cannot apply these specific instructions from Hosea to our contemporary situation. In other words, we find no mandate here either to

---

52. On this theme, cf. further W. K. Willmer, ed., *Revolution in Generosity: Transforming Stewards to be Rich toward God* (Chicago: Moody, 2008); C. L. Blomberg, *Neither Poverty nor Riches: A Biblical Theology of Possessions* (Leicester: Inter-Varsity, 1999; Downers Grove: InterVarsity, 2001).

53. For the history of interpretation and the merits of the options, see J. A. Dearman, *The Book of Hosea*, NICOT (Grand Rapids: Eerdmans, 2010), 80–88.

54. On which see further C. L. Blomberg, "Marriage, Divorce, Remarriage and Celibacy: An Exegesis of Matthew 19:2–12," *TrinJ* 11 (1990): 161–96.

marry prostitutes or to preserve marriages ruptured by adultery. Still, the Bible does defend the broader principle of faithfulness in the face of faithlessness; it may suggest that in some circumstances these actions are acceptable, perhaps even on occasion preferable. More importantly, they should cause us to seek other applications of the broader principle, such as ways of continuing to love prodigal children or friends who have wronged us, and so on.[55]

5. *Are cultural conditions identified in Scripture or assumed by its authors that make it inappropriate always to apply a given text in the same way?* One of the few things widely agreed on by interpreters of the "problem passages on women" is that veils (or long hair) on women and short hair on men (1 Cor 11:2–16) are not universal absolutes. A key to this understanding is Paul's own statement that a woman who prays or prophesies with her head uncovered might as well shave her head (v. 5), which is a "disgrace" (v. 6). These remarks drive the contemporary reader to ask what was disgraceful about shaved heads among women of Paul's day. Numerous possibilities exist. For Jewish women shaved heads may have suggested that they were guilty of adultery. For Greco-Roman women shaved heads may have indicated that they were the more masculine partner in a lesbian relationship. So unless short hair or uncovered heads send similar signals in modern-day cultures (as, for example, in certain parts of the more conservative Islamic world), the specific practice here is irrelevant. On the other hand, there is a *principle* here: any dress or grooming, behavior or conversation that suggests infidelity to God's sexual standards is as wrong for Christian women today as it was in first-century Corinth.

An examination of the rationale for Paul's commands to the men in this passage might at first glance suggest a different conclusion. In 1 Corinthians 11:14 Paul writes, "Does not the very nature of things teach you that if a man has long hair, it is a disgrace to him?" Currently, most of us, if honest, would quickly answer the question, no. But Paul's use of the term "nature" suggests that he is appealing to some timeless principle unknown to us. Here knowledge of Scripture and of some historical background helps. Paul, raised as a devout Jew, knew of one major category of Jewish man whom God praised for never cutting his hair—the one who took a Nazirite vow (Num 6:1–21). Paul himself had practiced similar vows on a temporary basis (Acts 18:18). So "the nature of things" in 1 Corinthians 11:14 must mean something like "the common custom throughout the first-century Greco-Roman world," which in turn explains why all the churches of that time had adopted this practice (v. 16). We see again the need to understand the culture of the time to find the rationale. The best recent research suggests that long hair (perhaps resembling an external head covering) on a man likely made him appear too much like Roman priests officiating at certain pagan rituals. Once again, the principle: if long hair is inextricably bound

---

55. Cf. esp. R. C. Ortlund, Jr., *God's Unfaithful Wife: A Biblical Theology of Spiritual Adultery*, rev. ed. (Nottingham: Apollos; Downers Grove: InterVarsity, 2006).

up with non-Christian religious practice in some modern culture, then it, too, should remain taboo. But if not, then hair style is not a moral issue with God.[56]

6. *Is the particular cultural form expressed in the biblical text present today, and if so does it have the same significance as it did then?* The two examples from 1 Corinthians 11 could illustrate this criterion as well. But we may move even further to examples in which certain cultural forms no longer even exist, at least not in all cultures. For example, few of us have ever considered if we should or even could bring a sheep or goat to church and slaughter it in front of the pulpit, letting the blood run down the sides! Of course, the sacrificial laws of the OT were fulfilled in Christ and no longer require our literal obedience, even if we could (Heb 4:14–10:18).

But we can still learn principles about the costliness and purity demanded by those laws as we read the opening chapters of Leviticus. Do they not say to us that we should be equally devoted to Christ and should seriously embrace moral purity (2 Cor 6:14–7:1) and sacrificial giving (2 Cor 8–9)? Just as poor people could offer less costly sacrifices in those days (Lev 12:8; cf. Luke 2:24), so Christians should not expect identical levels of giving from all believers today. In fact, the NT does not promote a fixed percentage of giving. We may better capture the spirit of NT giving through what Ronald Sider calls a "graduated tithe," by which the more one makes, the higher percentage one ought to give to the Lord's work, and especially to helping the poor (1 Cor 16:2; 2 Cor 8:12–15).[57]

Other religious practices exist among Christians in certain parts of the world but not in others. For example, few North Americans trouble themselves over the fact that they do not greet each other with a holy kiss (1 Thess 5:26). Southerners in the United States, however, do at times greet each other this way. While living in Florida, one of us had a pastor who greeted almost all the women who came to his church with a kiss on the cheek, and the practice was largely accepted and appreciated in that context. In the Middle East, however, men commonly greet other men with a kiss on each cheek. In the republics of the former Soviet Union it is traditional for men to kiss other men on their lips (though much less so among the younger generations). The ancient biblical practice most resembled modern Middle Eastern behavior, i.e. same-sex kissing on the cheek.[58] No sexual connotations were associated with it; it was the acceptable convention for greeting a good friend warmly.

The identical form of application can therefore be preserved in some contemporary cultures but not in those that are highly sexualized like most of the Western world. Opposite-sex kissing should probably be discouraged in settings where it is not already

56. On the meaning and application of 1 Cor 11:2–16, cf. further C. L. Blomberg, *1 Corinthians*, NIVAC (Grand Rapids: Zondervan, 1994), 207–26. Cf. P. B. Payne, *Man and Woman, One in Christ: An Exegetical and Theological Study of Paul's Letters* (Grand Rapids: Zondervan, 2009), 141–73.

57. See esp. R. J. Sider, *Rich Christians in an Age of Hunger*, 5th ed. (Nashville: Nelson, 2005), 187–90, even if the specific figures need modification from one setting to the next.

58. See further L. Morris, *The First and Second Epistles to the Thessalonians*, 2nd ed., NICNT (Grand Rapids: Eerdmans, 1991), 185–86.

part of the culture. The LBP offers an acceptable alternative: "shake hands warmly." *The Message* reads, "Greet all the Christians there with a holy embrace." The CEV moves to the underlying principle, with "Give the Lord's followers a warm greeting." Even more abstractly, the NLT translates, "Greet each other in Christian love."

Most readers could correctly infer the significance of 1 Thessalonians 5:26 even if they do not customarily kiss others in church. However, we might not realize that it was usually limited to men with men and women with women. In other cases, the significance of biblical practices may escape us altogether. Luke 9:62 ("No one who puts a hand to the plow and looks back is fit for service in the kingdom of God") has been transparent to many as long as people have been familiar with traditional farming methods. Today, an increasing number of people don't automatically think of a hand-held plow and don't recognize the principle that one must keep one's eyes fixed on an end point ahead of one to cut a straight furrow for seed planting. Looking backwards prevents one from walking in a straight line and produces an inefficient use of precious farmland. Service for the kingdom likewise requires consistent, attentive focus on God's ways.[59] A modern equivalent might be something like, "You better keep your eye on the basket as you lead the fast break or you may miss your layup (or slam dunk, depending on your size)!"

Perhaps the most famous example of a practice from biblical times that has largely vanished in Western cultures (though by no means in other parts of the world) is the custom of eating food sacrificed to idols. We include it because it illustrates principles widely applicable to our society. In both 1 Corinthians 8–10 and Romans 14:1–15:13 Paul enjoins his readers to exercise mutual tolerance on this and related issues. In other words, numerous morally neutral practices can lead some people but not others into sin. In the case of food sacrificed to idols, some could not disassociate eating the meat from their own past pagan practices, namely, fellowship meals with various deities (1 Cor 10:14–22). Paul counseled the "strong" brothers and sisters in Christ not to flaunt their freedoms in these areas if this would cause "weaker" ones to engage in actual sin—and potentially abandon Christ. He also admonished the weaker ones not to pass judgment on the stronger for their practices.

While modern equivalents abound,[60] perhaps the best known involves the consumption of alcohol. One Scripture passage recognizes wine, for example, as a gift from God that gladdens human hearts (Ps 104:15), but another earnestly commands believers not to get drunk (Eph 5:18). This latter verse obviously counsels moderation rather than debauchery. Some people, however, often because of their prior experiences with drinking, cannot imbibe without being tempted to consume to excess. They are wise to abstain altogether, and their friends are wise to affirm their self-discipline. Those who can avoid drunkenness may choose to drink discreetly—and in moderation;

---

59. Cf. D. E. Garland, *Luke*, ZECNT (Grand Rapids: Zondervan, 2011), 614.

60. See the lengthy and sadly amusing list in G. Friesen with R. Maxson, *Decision Making and the Will of God*, rev. ed. (Colorado Springs: Multnomah, 2004), 388, a list we could greatly expand.

however, their primary concern should be to seek the filling of the Spirit and not to hurt their weaker brothers or sisters. Those who abstain, in turn, should not pass judgment on those who choose to drink modest amounts.[61]

The same principles apply to the entire process of determining legitimate applications. Since applications may vary from individual to individual, even though meaning remains fixed, numerous biblical passages require Christians to express mutual tolerance. It is unfortunate that Christians often explain their different interpretations of the meaning of a text by saying, "This is what this passage means to me . . . ," as if that justified any preferred interpretation. Often, however, when people speak of the *meaning* of a text "for them," they may in fact be referring to what is actually a legitimate *application*, which can vary from person to person or culture to culture. For example, Deuteronomy 6:6–7 establishes the fixed *principle* (the illocution of the text) that parents have the responsibility to teach God's commands to their children. But in applying this principle to grade-school education, one couple may use it to explain why they chose homeschooling; another to justify Christian schools; and a third to support sending their children to public schools while teaching them about the Bible at home and in church.

7. Is the rationale for the application rooted in a creation ordinance, in the character of God, or in part of his redemptive plan for humanity?[62] That is, is the rationale rooted in theological, and not merely cultural arguments? If so, such principles remain timeless even while their applications may differ. Creation ordinances refer to principles for how people should live that God established prior to the fall of humanity into sin. Presumably, such principles remain part of the redemptive ideal for Christians as they are progressively renewed in God's image after their salvation. A classic example is monogamous marriage. Both Jesus (Matt 19:5) and Paul (Eph 5:31) reaffirm Genesis 2:24 as the rationale for strict standards on sexual ethics. Intervening biblical tolerance of a wide variety of divorces (Deut 24:1) or of occasional polygamy,[63] therefore, does not legitimize divorce or polygamy as valid applications of these texts of Scripture for Christians today. At times these practices might reflect the lesser of two evils, as in the case in certain non-Western cultures where a polygamous husband becomes a believer. In such instances the less evil action may be to keep the extended family

---

61. For a good study of the biblical data, see N. L. Geisler, "A Christian Perspective on Wine-Drinking," *BSac* 139 (1982): 46–56. Geisler goes on to argue for teetotaling as an appropriate contemporary Christian response to the excesses of our culture. This is one understandable response, but it is not the only legitimate application of the relevant texts (see below). For further reflection on the meaning and significance of 1 Cor 8–10, see Blomberg, *1 Corinthians*, 159–206.

62. Larkin, *Culture and Biblical Hermeneutics*, 109. K. Giles ("A Critique of the 'Novel' Contemporary Interpretation of 1 Timothy 2:9–15 Given in the Book, *Women in the Church*: Part II," *EvQ* 72 [2000]: 195–200) argues that the criterion of creation order is largely a modern German invention, though he concedes partial precedents in Luther and Calvin. The precise terminology may be new, but it is hard to see what else one should call the logic Jesus explicitly employs in Matt 19:1–12.

63. We must realize how rare polygamy was even in OT times; almost without exception it was limited to kings or very wealthy aristocrats who could afford more than one wife. See esp. W. C. Kaiser, Jr., *Toward Old Testament Ethics* (Grand Rapids: Zondervan, 1983), 182–90.

intact and spare the "extra" wives the tragic circumstances that would occur should he divorce them.[64] But that is a quite different matter from telling a Christian who has only one spouse that it could be acceptable under certain circumstances to take more than one!

Other scriptural commands reflect the nature of God himself. In Leviticus 19:1 Yahweh commands all the Israelites to "be holy because I, the LORD your God, am holy." Centuries later Peter quotes these words to justify his commands to "prepare your minds for action; be self-controlled; set your hope fully on the grace to be given you," and "do not conform to the evil desires you had when you lived in ignorance," but "be holy in all you do" (1 Pet 1:13, 14, 15). We can be sure that the pursuit of holiness (separation to God for his purposes) is a timeless, universal principle applicable for all believers everywhere, even as specific illustrations of that holiness at times vary.[65]

Galatians 3:27–28 illustrates a passage grounded in principles of redemption: "For all of you who were baptized into Christ have clothed yourselves with Christ. There is neither Jew nor Greek, slave nor free, male nor female, for you are all one in Christ Jesus." While this passage by itself cannot prove that Paul envisioned no functional distinctions between categories of people in the church, neither can it be limited to equality in opportunities for salvation. Baptism reflected an outward, liberating rite for women that put them on equal public footing with men in a way that the corresponding OT initiation ritual of circumcision could not. So, too, at the very least, the church of Jesus Christ should seek outward, public signs to affirm the full equality of the sexes and also of races and classes.[66]

8. *Is the biblical command or application at variance with standard cultural norms of its day?* If so, it likely indicates a transcultural or timeless mandate for believers. In all the discussion of women's roles, many often forget that what would have stood out as most noticeably radical in the various NT domestic codes (see above) were the commands to the *men*. A few partial parallels, for example to "husbands, love your wives" (Eph 5:25), exist in the ancient world, but none enjoins as sacrificial an abandonment of men's own rights and privileges as Paul's statement, which goes on to add, ". . . just as Christ loved the church and gave himself up for her to make her holy" (v. 26).[67] Similarly, in the Greco-Roman world few voices were as blunt and sweeping in their disapproval of gay or lesbian sex (or of heterosexual sin such as

---

64. See esp. S. W. Kunhiyop, *African Christian Ethics* (Nairobi: Word Alive; Bukuru, Nigeria: ACTS; Grand Rapids: Zondervan, 2008), 223–42.

65. Significantly, Kaiser (*Ethics*) sums up OT ethics under this very heading of holiness and then divides his thematic studies into holiness in various areas: e.g., family and society, marriage and sex, wealth and possessions, and so on. His broad understanding of holiness compares to that of Lev 19.

66. See esp. B. Witherington III, "Rite and Rights for Women—Galatians 3.28," *NTS* 27 (1981): 593–604. R. N. Longenecker reveals some of these possibilities by organizing his discussion of *New Testament Social Ethics for Today* (Grand Rapids: Eerdmans, 1984) around the three parts of Gal 3:28.

67. E. Best, *Ephesians*, ICC (Edinburgh: T&T Clark, 1998), 539–44; A. T. Lincoln, *Ephesians*, WBC 42 (Dallas: Word, 1990), 373–74.

premarital sex or adultery) as Paul's in Romans 1:18–32. This makes it unlikely that Paul's views were in any way intended to be limited to first-century Roman society.[68]

To understand how to apply the OT *lex talionis*—"an eye for an eye and a tooth for a tooth" (Exod 21:24)—we must read it against its cultural background. To us it sounds like a vindictive call for revenge, but in its day it was a radically limiting law that prevented an individual from exacting *more* than equivalent compensation and, for the most part, limited retribution to a legal court.[69] Jesus goes further and prohibits personal retaliation altogether (Matt 5:38–42). Both of these principles remain timeless, but their specific applications continue to vary. In the first century, striking someone on the right cheek (v. 39) was typically a backhanded slap intended more to insult than to injure, taking one's cloak was a form of legal collateral (v. 40), and going the extra mile referred to forced Roman conscription (v. 41). Legitimate application of these passages does not require Christians to put themselves or their loved ones in positions that deliberately risk injury or nakedness. It does require them to renounce retaliation and to find ways of loving their enemies (v. 43)—giving them what will help them become better individuals.[70]

9. *Does the passage contain an explicit or implicit condition that limits its application?* Conditional promises are valid only if the conditions are met. In the Sermon on the Mount, Jesus promised his followers: "Ask and it will be given to you, seek and you will find, knock and the door will be opened to you" (Matt 7:7). Many today treat this promise as if it were a contract from God guaranteeing that God will give to them whatever they request, particularly in the areas of health and wealth. Others add the qualification, based on passages like James 5:15, that if they ask in faith (or with "enough" faith) they can be sure this will happen.[71] But after reading this book, hopefully, no one will try to interpret Matthew 7 without first reading Matthew 6 or try to interpret James 5 without first reading James 4!

In these larger contexts of Jesus' and James' teaching, we learn about the most important condition of all for God to answer prayer: it must first be in accordance with his will (Matt 6:10; Jas 4:15). James 4 helps us to understand better why God grants some and not other requests. On the one hand, even when certain good gifts do accord with his will, God has determined to give them only if we ask (Jas 4:2). That alone should be a powerful incentive to pray. On the other hand, sometimes we ask for things with wrong, selfish motives and therefore do not receive them (v. 3). But

---

68. See esp. R. A. J. Gagnon, *The Bible and Homosexual Practice: Texts and Hermeneutics* (Nashville: Abingdon, 2002). On both heterosexual and homosexual sin, see esp. L. L. Belleville, *Sex, Lies, and the Truth: Developing a Christian Ethic in a Post-Christian Society* (Eugene, OR: Wipf & Stock, 2010).

69. A theme helpfully expanded by C. J. H. Wright into an entire book, *An Eye for an Eye: The Place of Old Testament Ethics Today* (Downers Grove: InterVarsity, 1983).

70. A theme desperately in need of additional application to the church today. See esp. G. H. Stassen, *Just Peacemaking: The New Paradigm for the Ethics of Peace and War*, rev. ed. (Cleveland: Pilgrim, 2008); and J. C. Arnold, *Why Forgive?* rev. ed. (Walden, NY: Plough, 2010).

71. For a good survey and incisive critique, see D. W. Jones and R. S. Woodbridge, *Health, Wealth & Happiness: Has the Prosperity Gospel Overshadowed the Gospel of Christ?* (Grand Rapids: Kregel, 2010).

in other cases, even when our motives are pure, we need to remember that our desires do not always conform to God's. Particularly in the area of physical healing, Jesus' reply to Paul may also apply to us: "My grace is sufficient for you, for my power is made perfect in weakness" (2 Cor 12:9). In light of these various scriptural conditions concerning prayer, Douglas Moo well defines the prayer of faith in James 5:15 as that which "always includes within it a tacit acknowledgment of God's sovereignty in all matters; that it is *God's* will that must be done."[72] First John 5:14 makes the same point even more explicitly, that "if we ask anything according to his will," he hears us.

Not only do promises in Scripture often have conditions attached, but so also does prophecy. It is not always easy to sort out which OT predictions concerning Israel's future have conditions and which do not. Historically, dispensational theology has tended to emphasize numerous apparent unconditional promises to the Jewish people, while so-called covenant theology has stressed the unfulfilled conditions attached to many of those promises.[73] The promise of land for the nation of Israel provides an excellent illustration of this debate. In Genesis 15 God reiterates his programmatic promise to Abraham made in Genesis 12:1–3 and specifies that he will give to Abraham's descendants "this land, from the river of Egypt [the Nile] to the great river Euphrates" (15:18). In neither chapter do any conditions appear, unless one interprets the call to Abraham to "go" in 12:1 as a condition, but Abraham did indeed leave his home in Ur and travel to the promised land. On the other hand, when the Israelites under Moses were ready to occupy Canaan, God declared all of the blessings of the land to be contingent on their obedience to the law (Deut 28). One plausible way to resolve this tension, which fits the rest of OT history, is to state that the promise always remains available in principle but that the opportunity for the people of each generation to appropriate that promise depends on their obedience.[74] Another resolution sees conditionality already in Genesis 17:1–2 so that the blessing was contingent on obedience even during the time of the patriarchs.

The plot thickens, however, when we ask if God's promise to Abraham and to Moses has ever been completely fulfilled. The largest known territory occupied by Israel occurred under Solomon. Apparently that included land up to the Euphrates (1 Kgs 4:24), but no Scripture indicates that it ever went all the way to that river. Still, Solomon himself could praise God by saying, "Not one word has failed of all the good promises he gave through his servant Moses" (8:56). So, if God's promise to Israel was fulfilled, then we need not necessarily look for any further fulfillment. This interpretation would obviously have direct bearing on the view that sees a modern-day Jewish nation in the land of Israel as the fulfillment of Scripture, not to

---

72. D. J. Moo, *James*, TNTC, rev. ed. (Nottingham: InterVarsity; Grand Rapids: Eerdmans, 2015), 229.

73. The debate is well represented in J. S. Feinberg, ed., *Continuity and Discontinuity: Perspectives on the Relationship between the Old and New Testaments* (Westchester: Crossway, 1988). A significant collection of essays representing the shift toward mainstream evangelicalism among the last generation of dispensationalist scholars is C. A. Blaising and D. L. Bock, eds., *Dispensationalism, Israel and the Church* (Grand Rapids: Zondervan, 1992).

74. See esp. W. C. Kaiser, Jr., *Toward an Old Testament Theology* (Grand Rapids: Zondervan, 1978), 110–13.

mention the fact that Solomon's dimensions of the land included territory currently part of Syria and Iraq.

On the other hand, even if we assume that the people of Israel never fully occupied all the land God had intended for them, this does not automatically mean we should look for a complete and literal fulfillment in our, or some subsequent, day. The NT applies to the church many OT passages that originally applied solely to Israel (see esp. 1 Pet 2:4–10). In fact, Paul specifically quotes from God's initial promises to Abraham ("All nations will be blessed through you"—Gen 12:3b) as part of the gospel, which foresaw Gentiles coming to faith in Christ (Gal 3:8). So it seems highly incongruous to take the first half of the verse out of Genesis and assume that "Israel" still means a literal Jewish nation. Although it is popular among conservative American Christians to cite Genesis 12:3a ("I will bless those who bless you, and whoever curses you I will curse") as a reason for supporting the current state of Israel, legitimate principles of application would seem to require that the "you" in this text now refers to the church of Jesus Christ. In other words, God will bless those who support Christian causes and will not bless those who attack them.[75]

But are there no unfulfilled promises to Jewish people? Some would say not, but various NT passages seem to hold out hope for a more glorious future for the Jews. The most well-known of these is Romans 11:26–27: "And so all Israel will be saved, as it is written: 'The deliverer will come from Zion; he will turn godlessness away from Jacob. And this is my covenant with them when I take away their sins'" (quoting Isa 59:20–21). Since Paul contrasts Jews and Gentiles throughout Romans 9–11, it is not likely that "all Israel" means "the church" here. Neither is it likely that Paul means every single Jewish person will be saved irrespective of his or her attitude toward Jesus.[76] The context refers to the coming Messiah (the deliverer) and speaks of banishing godlessness and of forgiving sins.

The most likely interpretation of this passage is that there will be an outpouring of faith in Messiah Jesus among large numbers of Jews at the time of Christ's return.[77] But that does not suggest that the overwhelming majority of Jews in the land of Israel, who are not currently Christians, is a necessary fulfillment of prophecy. Paul implies a clear condition in Romans 11:26–27—for Jews now to experience God's blessings they must have faith in Christ. At best, we might say that current Jews in Israel comprise a precursor of such fulfillment. What is more, nothing in this or any other NT passage refers to a *nation* of Israel—that is, a political state that occupies certain boundaries. Romans 9–11 could just as conceivably be fulfilled among Jews and Gentiles scattered

---

75. Cf. esp. B. K. Waltke with C. J. Fredricks, *Genesis* (Grand Rapids: Zondervan, 2001), 206.

76. In his discussion of Rom 11:25–36, E. P. Sanders, *Paul: The Apostle's Life, Letters, and Thought* (Minneapolis: Fortress, 2015), 687–89, leaves open the possibility, perhaps even the likelihood, that in the end God will save everyone. He says, "If God decides to save all those whom he created, he can do it, and all one can say is 'Amen'" (689). We find this difficult to square with all Paul has said in Romans to this point about the need for faith in Christ for salvation.

77. Cf. further C. E. B. Cranfield, *A Critical and Exegetical Commentary on the Epistle to the Romans*, 2 vols., ICC (Edinburgh: T&T Clark, 1975–79), 2:572–79.

throughout the world. In fact, Jesus takes language from the Psalms about Israelites living in the promised land and applies it to all true Christians inheriting the entire earth ("the meek shall inherit the earth" Matt 5:5, quoting Ps 37:11).[78]

So it is hermeneutically naive to claim that the largely secular nation of Israel today necessarily occupies any privileged position in God's scheme of things. Worse still, such a view often leads to uncritical political support for Jews against the Palestinian people, even though about 80 percent of our Christian brothers and sisters in Israel as of 2012 were Arab or Palestinian rather than Jewish.[79] We realize this may be a controversial example for some of our readers;[80] however, in light of our emphasis on the commitment of Scripture to social justice we feel it is important to raise this issue here. Hermeneutics can literally make the difference between life and death for multitudes of people on our globe!

10. *Should we adopt a "redemptive movement" hermeneutic that suggests we move beyond NT teaching?* By far the most significant and sophisticated reflection on the issue of sifting the cultural from the timeless in Scripture is the work of William Webb.[81] Webb presents eighteen potential criteria for the task under the headings "persuasive," "moderately persuasive," and "inconclusive." The heart of his argument (and the gist of a majority of his "persuasive criteria") is that just as one can trace developing understanding of various topics within successive stages of OT revelation, as well as from the OT to the NT, so also there may be places where the trajectory of biblical thought implies that Christians today should move beyond NT teaching. Webb believes Christians have already done this on the issue of slavery. He convincingly shows that the biblical data on homosexual behavior do *not* fit such a trajectory. Homosexual practice is consistently declared to be contrary to God's will throughout both testaments. But he believes biblical teaching on women is more akin to that on slavery. He does not interpret biblical teaching on gender roles, as biblical feminists do, as clearly promoting egalitarianism, but he does see development of thought moving in a direction that would support Christians today going beyond the NT to support complete interchangeability of gender roles in home and church.

Webb's study deserves a careful and thoughtful response. Most of the volume proves extraordinarily helpful. But a few nagging questions remain. Webb correctly points

---

78. On *The Gospel and the Land* in these and other passages, see esp. W. D. Davies, in his book so-titled (Berkeley: University of California Press, 1964).

79. J. Sharon, "Christian Population in Israel Growing," *Jerusalem Post* (Dec. 25, 2012), accessed at http://www.jpost.com/National-News/CBS-report-Christian-population-in-Israel-growing.

80. For a vibrant defense of the position adopted here, see esp. G. M. Burge, *Whose Land? Whose Promise? What Christians Are Not Being Told about Israel and the Palestinians*, rev. ed. (Cleveland: Pilgrim, 2013); and C. Chapman, *Whose Promised Land? The Continuing Crisis over Israel and Palestine*, 5th ed. (Oxford: Lion Hudson, 2015). Cf. also G. M. Burge, *Jesus and the Land: The New Testament Challenge to "Holy Land" Theology* (Grand Rapids: Baker Academic, 2010); and the essays in S. J. Munayer and L. Loden, eds., *The Land Cries Out: Theology of the Land in the Israeli-Palestinian Context* (Eugene, OR: Cascade, 2012).

81. W. J. Webb, *Slaves, Women, and Homosexuals: Exploring the Hermeneutics of Cultural Analysis* (Downers Grove: InterVarsity, 2001).

to 1 Corinthians 7:21 on slaves taking advantage of opportunities for freedom as the kind of seed thought that set the stage for the later abolition of slavery.[82] But there really is no analogous text encouraging women to become elders or heads over their husbands if the opportunity arises.[83] On the other hand, numerous descriptive texts presented approvingly of women in other unprecedented leadership roles suggest that perhaps Webb is correct that the NT is an advance on the OT here. Two of Webb's "persuasive criteria" appeal to extrabiblical bodies of knowledge—when the basis of an instruction cannot be sustained from one culture to another or when a component of a text "is contrary to present-day scientific evidence."[84] But both cultural practice and scientific evidence have proved remarkably changeable over time, particularly in the "softer" social sciences—the very ones involved in the gender roles debate. Once one opens the lid to going beyond Scripture, even based on trajectories seemingly present in Scripture, a Pandora's box of problems may emerge (cf. also 1 Cor 4:6).[85] It may not be a Pandora's box that has emerged with respect to one issue (e.g., gender roles), but it might in some other area (e.g., the rampant litigation in our culture of entitlement), despite the prohibitions in 1 Corinthians 6:1–11.

The only other fully persuasive criterion for sifting the timeless from the cultural that Webb presents, unrelated to our comments thus far, is that of "purpose/intent statements."[86] Scripture itself may give a reason for a command that requires a different application in a different culture precisely *to preserve* the original rationale. Thus 1 Peter regularly gives evangelistic reasons for its commands to citizens, slaves, and women to submit to the authorities over them (2:12, 15; 3:1, 16). In a world that without exception took submission to authorities as a cultural given, to deviate from this behavior as Christians would place unnecessary obstacles in the path of non-Christians coming to Christ. But what of application in a world where many take egalitarianism equally for granted? Might the same rationale argue for treating one another entirely as peers?[87] The evangelistic rationale of 1 Peter might support the *opposite* Christian practice today. What approach would better enhance Christian credibility in that context and enhance the advance the gospel in it? In this case Webb's criterion could be seen as supporting the egalitarian agenda, though its application is further complicated by the diverse mix of cultures in many parts of our world today. However one answers the question, the issue (and the criterion on which it is based) is clearly worth raising.

---

82. Webb, *Slaves, Women, and Homosexuals*, 84.

83. On the other hand, while less specific, many believe that Gal 3:28 forms precisely such a precedent.

84. Webb, *Slaves, Women, and Homosexuals*, 209, 221 (quotation).

85. E.g., early feminist claims about minimal psychological differences between the genders have been substantially toned down after further studies. A particularly detailed survey of gender roles and the social sciences appears in S. Clark, *Man and Woman in Christ* (Ann Arbor: Servant, 1980), 369–570. Helpful updates and a different overall perspective appear in M. S. van Leeuwen, *My Brother's Keeper: What the Social Sciences Do (and Don't) Tell Us about Masculinity* (Downers Grove: InterVarsity, 2002).

86. Webb, *Slaves, Women, and Homosexuals*, 105.

87. For two opposite answers to this question, see S. Dowd, "1 Peter," in *The Women's Bible Commentary*, 3rd ed., ed. C. A. Newsome, S. H. Ringe, and J. E. Lapsley (Louisville: Westminster John Knox, 2012), 462–64; and J. H. Elliott, *1 Peter*, AB 37B (New York: Doubleday, 2000), 585–99.

Identify the Cross-Cultural Principles

We have already illustrated this step with most of the examples discussed above. Can we deduce a broad principle that a specific biblical text promotes as timeless even if we cannot apply universally without alteration the particular command, example, promise, or warning of the text? If we discern such a principle, we must then devise new illustrations or applications of that principle for new situations. For example, with Paul's teaching on food sacrificed to idols, we proposed the broader principle of "freedom for Christians on morally neutral practices while they weigh how their freedom might affect fellow believers." For tattoos, the principle was not to imitate pagan religious practices that call one's allegiance to Christ into question. For women's head coverings, we generalized to encompass any forms of appearance or behavior that would suggest religious or sexual infidelity. In other words, in each case we want to know why a specific command was given or a particular practice adopted or shunned. What did it mean in its particular cultural or historical context? Sometimes Scripture tells us directly in the immediate or larger context of a passage, or at least gives hints. Sometimes we must do our own historical and cultural research, or, more typically, rely on the best work that others have done.

But we must address here another issue involved in this third step in the process of application. When Bible students generalize or principlize from a specific application, how generally should they phrase the overarching principle? Consider again the story of Abraham's near sacrifice of his son Isaac. Since God does not expect Christians to kill their children, what broader principles can we deduce from this passage? Someone might propose, for example: "Obey God in whatever he commands you, even to the point of trusting him to get you out of seemingly intractable moral dilemmas." After all, Scripture consistently reminds us of the positive, purifying value of trials and temptations (e.g., Jas 1:2–18; 1 Pet 1:3–9).

But nowhere does God promise to get us out of all situations in which we might be tempted to sin or act unwisely. In 1 Corinthians 10:13 Paul suggests that, more often than not, God leaves us in those situations but provides the power not to sin and guidance for wise actions (a power and a guidance we can choose or refuse to accept!). Moreover, the text never hints that Abraham recognized he was being tested, although in retrospect the biblical narrator explains that he was (Gen 22:1).[88] On occasion we, too, cannot be sure if difficulties in our lives reflect testing from God or temptation from the devil—or are simply the results of our own poor choices, the actions of others, or the effects of living in a fallen world.

So perhaps we should advance a still broader principle from Genesis 22: "Trust in God's sovereignty." This principle lies behind numerous passages of Scripture, most notably in the OT historical narrative. Its truth is impeccable. But then we must raise

---

88. On this literary device, in which the narrator knows more than the characters throughout Gen 22, see J. H. Sailhamer, "Genesis," in *Expositor's Bible Commentary Revised*, 13 vols., ed. D. E. Garland and T. Longman III (Grand Rapids: Zondervan, 1990), 1:210–13.

the question: Is that *all* the passage intends to teach us? A specific application for our lives based on this general principle might bear little resemblance to the specifics of the story of Abraham and Isaac. For example, we might decide to trust that God will provide us an adequate job after months of unemployment. But this application does not in any way link with the specifics of the Genesis 22 passage.

We might settle for a mediating solution, perhaps based on the reflection of Hebrews 11:17–19 that Abraham believed God could raise the dead, so he trusted that even if he killed his son, God would bring Isaac back to life. Our timeless principle then becomes, "We will not overly grieve or worry when death threatens us or fellow believers, since we know that even if it comes, we will be resurrected on the last day." This principle has solid NT support (1 Thess 4:13–18; 1 Cor 15:20–28) and fits several of the particulars of the passage in Genesis. Even if we limit ourselves to Genesis, we can conclude that Abraham took God with the utmost seriousness, believing that he was able to keep his promise about supplying numerous descendants for Abraham, through whom all nations on earth would be blessed (Gen 12:1–13)—which encourages us to trust in the other as-yet unfulfilled promises of Scripture.

Levels of Authority

This process illustrates that applications possess different *levels of authority.* The closer the modern application corresponds to the application in the biblical text, the greater the degree of confidence we have that our application is legitimate. Usually, the specific application will be close to the text only if the broader principle it teaches specifically incorporates elements from the text. More general truths, like "the sovereignty of God" in our example above, will not regularly yield specific, contemporary applications that closely resemble the original ones.

So we may not, therefore, always assert with the same level of confidence that we have correctly applied a passage. How confident can we be? (1) We have the highest level of confidence that our application is valid when we can employ the originally intended response in our situation with little or no change (and that response validly applies the timeless principle in the passage),[89] (2) We have the next level of confidence that our application is legitimate when we can derive a broader principle whose application incorporates a significant number of elements of the passage. But we have to be sure we have derived a valid, timeless principle. (3) When we back off still further to the level of applying more general truths from a passage, our applications may well reflect good Christian things to do, but we cannot be as confident that they are actual applications *of the specific text at hand.*[90] As Millard Erickson nicely phrases it, we should "look for principles of the maximum degree of specificity that meet the

---

89. It is crucial to add these words since we may directly apply an instruction in a text and actually miss the principle that instruction conveyed in the text. For example, we might very literally wash another believer's feet in applying John 13:14 and miss the point of humble service. The practice of foot washing does not convey in our culture the meaning that the practice did in Jesus' world.

90. For further discussion of these distinctions, see esp. Kuhatschek, *Applying the Bible,* 56–57.

criteria for generalizability."[91] Webb speaks helpfully of a "ladder of abstraction, in which the most abstract ideas are at the highest rungs of a ladder, whereas it is our task to climb only as high as the text requires us."[92]

We confront this issue particularly when we seek to address contemporary situations to which the Bible does not directly speak. What, for example, is a Christian position on the possession or use of weapons of mass destruction? While the Bible says nothing about nuclear, chemical or biological weapons, it does record much about war (mostly in the OT). Yet Christians disagree on whether or not war is ever appropriate in the NT age.[93] Few in the history of the church, however, have espoused full-fledged pacifism. Be this as it may, do the principles of conventional warfare necessarily carry over to an era of weapons of mass destruction? Some think not, alleging, for example, that the historic principles for a just war (trying to avoid civilian casualties, etc.) cannot be applied to even the most limited of nuclear, chemical, or biological wars.[94] But were we to grant, for the sake of argument, that all such war is immoral, does that prohibit even the *possession* of those kinds of weapons? Does their benefit as a deterrent outweigh the dangers of a catastrophic accident that could trigger such a holocaust? Obviously, we do not answer these questions by citing chapters and verses of Scripture!

That does not mean, however, that the Bible is irrelevant in a debate on WMDs.[95] Interpreters can bring broader principles or general truths to bear on the topic. They need to balance the teaching of Scripture about the sanctity of life with its concern for justice. They need to raise questions about the eternal destiny of people who might lose their lives in a military holocaust. They may also apply teaching about the role of government in enforcing the law and about Christians not demanding their rights or seeking to retaliate against wrongs done to them.

Even with smaller-scale warfare, modern technology raises important new questions. One of the key criteria in the classic Christian just war theory is the minimization of civilian casualties. One of the desirable criteria for any warring nation is the minimization of combatant casualties. The development of carefully guided unmanned drones holds the potential for furthering both of these criteria, but to date their degree of accuracy has not yet lived up to their potential. And can computer operators from

---

91. M. J. Erickson, *Evangelical Interpretation: Perspectives on Hermeneutical Issues* (Grand Rapids: Baker, 1993), 65. C. Kraft ("Interpreting in Cultural Context," *JETS* 21 [1978]: 357–67) makes much the same point using the language of "levels of abstraction."

92. Webb, *Slaves, Women and Homosexuals*, 54. Cf. also H. W. Robinson, *Biblical Preaching: The Development and Delivery of Expository Messages*, 3rd ed. (Grand Rapids: Baker, 2008), 197–98, 201–2; Strauss, *How to Read the Bible in Changing Times*, 211–17; and Bauer and Traina, *Inductive Bible Study*, 322–24.

93. See, e.g., R. G. Clouse, ed., *War: Four Christian Views* (Downers Grove: InterVarsity, 1981); R. S. Hess and E. A. Martens, eds., *War in the Bible and Terrorism in the Twenty-First Century* (Winona Lake, IN: Eisenbrauns, 2008).

94. E.g., R. J. Sider, *Completely Pro-Life: Building a Consistent Stance on Abortion, the Family, Nuclear Weapons, the Poor* (Downers Grove: InterVarsity, 1987; Eugene, OR: Wipf & Stock, 2010), 159–63.

95. Or on modern warfare more generally. For a representative range of perspectives, see J. A. Wood, *Perspectives on War in the Bible* (Macon: Mercer, 1998).

a distance take seriously enough the situation on the ground to make the most ethical decisions with enough personal investment? Conversely, might some be able to be more objective because their own lives aren't immediately at risk?[96] The issues are complex and we understand why Christians disagree. We cannot directly use specific passages in the same way that they were used in biblical times. And even the general principles we adopt will tend to be broad. So we must temper our discussion with humility. Although we may feel strongly about one side or the other in the argument, we dare not claim the same level of certainty that we have when we quote John 3:16 as the basis for trusting in Christ for salvation![97]

Find Appropriate Applications that Embody the Broader Principles

We have been illustrating this final step all along. The following diagram illustrates the process.

Having found the principles(s) that led to the specific application "back then," we seek to translate the principle(s) into appropriate and corresponding applications "now." Knowing the practice back then that implemented the underlying principle enables us to discern the appropriate practice today that implements that same principle. Thus, we may give a hearty handshake instead of a holy kiss; we may set up inexpensive food banks instead of leaving our fields to be gleaned; and we should be concerned about the effect of consuming alcohol in the presence of a recovering alcoholic, even if we are never faced with the dilemma of whether or not to eat meat sacrificed to idols. Most of these applications probably seem straightforward and reasonable to our readers.

Greater sensitivity is required, however, when Christians wish to live responsibly in cross-cultural contexts. Whether a white person of European descent ventures to minister effectively in a Muslim community in Jordan, or whether people of two different races try to get along in the same American city, differences between cultures increase the possibility of gaffes in communication. Some conservative Christians in Guatemala are stunned that American believers feel free to get (and show off)

---

96. For a representative sampling of perspectives, see Dennis R. Himes, *Drones and the Ethics of Targeted Killing* (Lanham, MD: Rowman & Littlefield, 2015); and D. Cortright, R. Fairhurst, and K. Wall, eds., *Drones and the Future of Armed Conflict: Ethical, Legal and Strategic Implications* (Chicago: University of Chicago Press, 2015).

97. A good resource for how to think Christianly about contemporary issues is H. Blamires, *The Christian Mind: How Should a Christian Think?* (Ann Arbor: Servant, 1978; Vancouver, Regent College, 2005). Excellent illustrations of applying the broad themes of creation, the fall, and redemption to ethical dilemmas appear in J. R. W. Stott, *Decisive Issues Facing Christians Today* (Grand Rapids: Baker, 1996). Less methodologically sophisticated but also quite helpful on a variety of contemporary topics is K. S. Kantzer, ed., *Applying the Scriptures* (Grand Rapids: Zondervan, 1987).

tattoos. Many Muslim-background believers find it outrageous that North American women feel free to uncover their shoulders in public and that men and women alike eat pork. Some American evangelicals cannot understand the freedom that C. S. Lewis felt in England or many north German Christians today feel to smoke. In each case scriptural texts are marshaled to support these particular applications. And what does one do when some states liberally sell legalized marijuana (as in Colorado where the authors of this book live), even while it is technically still illegal nationally? Thoughtless Christians who carelessly flaunt their freedom or quickly impose their conservatism will soon lose the respect of their acquaintances in other cultures, even if their applications could prove defensible.[98] One has to think in terms of what behavior is worthy of the gospel and of what will advance the gospel.

Scripture provides many examples of cross-cultural contextualization. When Paul encounters those who teach that circumcision is mandatory for salvation, he resists the teaching rigorously even at the risk of severe schism (Gal 2). But when this issue concerns merely a better reception for the half-Jew Timothy to minister among Jews, he happily circumcises him (Acts 16:1–5).[99] Indeed, Paul himself justifies such behavior, noting that it is a characteristic of ministry:

> For though I am free with respect to all, I have made myself a slave to all, so that I might win more of them. To the Jews I became as a Jew, in order to win Jews. To those under the law I became as one under the law (though I myself am not under the law) so that I might win those under the law. To those outside the law I became as one outside the law (though I am not free from God's law but am under Christ's law) so that I might win those outside the law. To the weak I became weak, so that I might win the weak. I have become all things to all people, that I might by all means save some. I do it all for the sake of the gospel, so that I may share in its blessings (1 Cor 9:19–23; NRSV).

If 1 Corinthians 8 and 10 stress the need for believers to consider the feelings and convictions of other believers, 1 Corinthians 9 certainly underscores the need to consider what will most likely help or hinder *unbelievers* in the process of coming to the faith.

One final difficulty preachers have in coming up with legitimate contemporary applications of biblical texts stems from the appropriate desire not to be overly repetitious. How many times have seasoned churchgoers heard a message about drawing near to God in which the same handful of spiritual disciplines—especially prayer and Bible study—are about the only applications the speaker makes? Listeners wonder if they are missing other dimensions of significance. Daniel Doriani has written

---

98. A standard evangelical work on contextualization in cross-cultural settings is D. J. Hesselgrave and E. Rommen, *Contextualization: Meanings, Methods, and Models* (Grand Rapids: Baker, 1989; Pasadena: William Carey Library, 2013). See also A. S. Moreau, *Contextualization in World Missions: Mapping and Assessing Evangelical Models* (Grand Rapids: Kregel, 2012); and M. Cook et al., eds., *Local Theology for the Global Church: Principles for an Evangelical Approach to Contextualization* (Pasadena: William Carey Library, 2010).

99. Cf. W. O. Walker, "The Timothy-Titus Problem Reconsidered," *ExpTim* 92 (1981): 231–35.

a wide-ranging volume on *Putting the Truth to Work: The Theory and Practice of Biblical Application*,[100] the heart of which addresses this question by proposing seven "biblical sources" for application and four "aspects" of application. The seven sources correspond in part, but not completely, to the diversity of literary genres, as Doriani identifies "rules, ideals, doctrines, redemptive acts in narratives, exemplary acts in narratives, biblical images, and songs and prayers."[101] One text may in fact contain several of these components. The four "aspects" Doriani labels "duty, character, goal and discernment."[102] Thus for every "biblical source" in a given passage, one may ask what one should do, what one should be (the kind of person to become), to what causes one should devote oneself, and how can one distinguish truth from error. Consciously thinking through all twenty-eight potential combinations of sources and aspects will normally give an interpreter plenty of diverse applications.

Sources → Aspects ↓	Rules	Ideals	Doctrines	Redemptive Acts in Narratives	Exemplary Acts in Narratives	Biblical Images	Songs and Prayers
Duty: what to do							
Character: what to be							
Goal: what causes to engage in							
Discernment: distinguish truth from error							

In conclusion, faithfully applying the Bible to new contexts requires that we become as earnest in our study of the contemporary world as we are of Scripture itself. That is to say, we must learn not only to exegete the Scriptures but also to exegete cultures. Many who preach or teach the Bible to others eventually learn this lesson,[103] but in fact everyone who seeks to apply the Bible to his or her life in a valid way must discover it. Thoughtfully reading and listening to news; judiciously watching movies, listening

---

100. (Phillipsburg, NJ: Presbyterian and Reformed, 2001).

101. Doriani, *Putting the Truth to Work*, 82.

102. Ibid., 98.

103. See esp. the excellent suggestions of J. R. W. Stott, *Between Two Worlds: The Art of Preaching in the Twentieth Century* (Grand Rapids: Eerdmans, 1982) on "The Call to Study" (pp. 180–210), in which he describes resources and resource people he uses to balance scrutiny of Scripture with an understanding of the modern world. Of course, with the advent of the internet searches, the problem in the twenty-first century is often not how to access information but how to access and discern what is reliable information. It is incredibly tempting for people to see what they are predisposed to believe and accept it without verification, even when it is entirely made up, as well as to see what they are predisposed to disbelieve and reject it without reason, even when it is entirely accurate. Wikipedia articles, e. g., have improved tremendously in quality, but if one can scroll down a little and discover on-line versions of peer-reviewed hard-copy dictionaries, encyclopedias, or other standard reference works, one is still much better off consulting them.

to music, and monitoring other sources of popular culture; traveling, and, if possible, living for a while in different cultures; sharing with Christians across denominational and religious lines—all these (and this is merely a representative sample) can enhance our sensitivity. A regular amount of time spent in direct contact and friendship with unbelievers is also crucial. A study of the full breadth of topics usually included in the core curricula of liberal arts colleges can be beneficial. Full discussions of how to exegete culture might require another book like this one, but we would be remiss if we did not alert our readers to the importance of the task.

THE ROLE OF THE HOLY SPIRIT

We would also be remiss if we did not remind our readers of a presupposition we stated earlier: everything we have taught in this book falls short of the intended goal if interpreters do not simultaneously pray and rely on the Holy Spirit to guide them in the hermeneutical task. We have assumed that point of departure; it is part of our preunderstanding. Yet as we pointed out earlier, an appeal to the Spirit is no substitute for sound interpretive method. Roy Zuck's excellent article on "The Role of the Holy Spirit in Hermeneutics" deserves reading from start to finish; here we can merely summarize his fourteen main points:

1. The Holy Spirit does not give new revelation on a par with Scripture.
2. He does not guarantee that our interpretations are infallible.
3. He does not give one person new insights that no one else has.
4. Many non-Christians can apply sound hermeneutics to understand the meaning of Scripture; without the Spirit, however, they refuse to apply it adequately to their lives.
5. Understanding is not the exclusive domain of biblical scholars.
6. Spiritual devotion on the part of the interpreter is crucial.
7. Lack of spiritual preparation can hinder correct interpretation.
8. There is no substitute for diligent study.
9. The Spirit does not rule out study helps.
10. He does not override common sense and logic.
11. He does not normally give sudden intuitive flashes.
12. The Spirit's role in hermeneutics is part of the process of illumination.
13. He does not make all of the Bible equally clear.
14. He does not ensure comprehensive understanding.

In short, the five crucial elements for proper interpretation and application are: (1) spiritual rebirth, (2) spiritual maturity, (3) diligent study, (4) common sense and logic, and (5) humble dependence on the Spirit for discernment.[104] Zuck's list

---

104. R. B. Zuck, "The Role of the Holy Spirit in Hermeneutics," *BSac* 141 (1984): 120–30. Cf. R. B. Zuck, *Basic*

also reminds us that the Holy Spirit never intended that we read the Bible solely in isolation from all other believers. God has guided millions of his people over the years; checking our interpretations and applications against a broad cross-section of others' readings of Scripture offers important checks and balances on what we think we have discovered or sensed the Spirit teaching.[105]

We hope this book has demonstrated the necessity for all five of these elements, even if our primary focus has been on (3) and (4). No one should imagine that this textbook presents a foolproof formula for interpreting and applying the Scriptures. That represents a lifelong process—a goal toward which we should strive. But if we have stimulated your desire for reading the Bible more, for tackling some of the more difficult or lesser known portions of it, then we are happy. If we have heightened your awareness of the kinds of questions to ask of the text as you read and to ask of others' interpretations, then we have made progress. If we have encouraged you to use some of the outstanding study tools and resources that are available to Christians today, then we have accomplished some of our goals. Nevertheless, our labor is in vain if we have not awakened a greater zeal to *obey* the Scriptures more, once they are understood, and to know and love the God who inspired them.[106] We live in an age of great biblical illiteracy and even greater biblical disobedience. As a preacher once put it, "When the darkness is very great, even a little light will do." So we conclude this focus on application by encouraging you to put into practice the principles we have outlined in this book. As you do this you will have the ability to handle correctly the Word of truth (2 Tim 2:15). Read the Word, study it, meditate on it, and then apply it. God will bless you as you do!

Bible Interpretation (Wheaton: Victor, 1991), 279–92. Also helpful in many respects is M. I. Wallace, "Performative Truth and the Witness of the Spirit," *SwJT* 35 (1993): 29–36.

105. See further Strauss, *How to Read the Bible in Changing Times*, 93–105.

106. Cf. the excellent chapter on "Obeying the Word: The Cultural Use of the Bible," in W. C. Kaiser, Jr. and M. Silva, *An Introduction to Biblical Hermeneutics: The Search for Meaning*, rev. ed. (Grand Rapids: Zondervan, 2007), 223–39. This chapter addresses a number of the issues we have discussed with respect to application.

ANNOTATED BIBLIOGRAPHY— HERMENEUTICAL TOOLS

M any books on hermeneutics provide a bibliography. Often such books list a catalogue of significant works in the field of hermeneutical theory.[1] We commend such bibliographies and urge readers to consult them for further study, but we will not follow their example. Readers interested in further study in the various areas of hermeneutics can pursue those interests by consulting the extensive footnotes provided throughout this text. (Conveniently located in the appropriate sections, these function in lieu of that kind of bibliography.) Rather, we have chosen to provide a bibliography that assists students in the actual practice of interpretation. We are convinced that biblical interpreters require the appropriate tools as much as skilled practitioners in any endeavor.

The bibliographic references are presented here in units based on usage. Brief annotations supply insight into the uses and benefits of the various entries. We have marked those books we believe to be outstanding, indispensable, or at least top priority with an asterisk [*]. As students are building their biblical libraries we suggest they purchase these books early in the process.[2] We have listed a few out of print titles because of their superior worth and because they may be found in libraries or purchased from book vendors.

Some books we include use the Hebrew and Greek languages. This distinction is noted in the annotations. Students who can acquire the use of these languages will have a decided advantage in the process of interpretation, and they should make use of these original language tools.[3] Those who are unable to learn one or both of

---

1. For example, excellent bibliographies exist in G. R. Osborne, *The Hermeneutical Spiral: A Comprehensive Introduction to Biblical Interpretation*, rev. ed. (Downers Grove: InterVarsity, 2007), 548–605. Two regularly updated bibliographies—one for the OT and one for the NT—of tools important for the practice of exegesis are published in the *Denver Journal*, an online journal sponsored by Denver Seminary. See http://www.denverseminary.edu, go to the Resources menu and click on the link for the *Denver Journal*. For comprehensive guides to commentaries, see T. Longman, III, *Old Testament Commentary Survey*, 5th ed. (Grand Rapids: Baker, 2013); D. A. Carson, *New Testament Commentary Survey*, 5th ed. (Grand Rapids: Baker, 2013); and J. F. Evans, *A Guide to Biblical Commentaries and Reference Works*, 10th ed. (Grand Rapids: Zondervan, 2016). Another source for useful biblical and theological resources is J. Glynn, *Commentary and Reference Survey*, 10th ed. (Grand Rapids: Kregel, 2007).

2. Obviously, our colleagues in other institutions—including pastors, teachers, and students—who use this textbook may have different preferences. Though individual favorites may differ, we have attempted to provide a list of sources widely accepted as the best currently available.

3. Frankly, we lament the increasing tendency to omit or drastically reduce the amount of study of the biblical languages from theological curricula, but that is another matter.

the biblical languages can usually omit purchasing most of these volumes. Readers will note, though, in our description of some of these original language tools that we suggest that even students without knowledge of Hebrew or Greek can profit considerably by using them. Where possible, students should attempt to borrow or use such books from friends or theological libraries to gauge their personal value or usefulness prior to purchasing them.

As tools, books are only as good as the scholars who wrote or compiled them. But even scholars and editors are fallible; they can misjudge evidence and draw imprecise or incorrect conclusions. Some may also have an axe to grind or be biased for various reasons (recall our discussion of preunderstandings and presuppositions). So recognizing that biblical interpretation will never be a hard and fast process like the sciences, whose tables of mathematical formulae are precise and accurate, it is wise to work with a variety of reference works to verify judgments and opinions.

This is especially important on controversial issues where reasonable scholars differ. Readers must ask pointed questions: Is the burden of proof there? Do other reputable scholars agree? Is the evidence upon which the conclusion is based clear enough to draw it? Was the evidence examined fairly and objectively? Though we might like to believe that a reference book contains only accepted truths, this is not always the case. We are certainly not advocating complete agnosticism or skepticism; clearly the state of our knowledge today exceeds that of any time in human history. The alternative—to reject all resources and tools—would be far more harmful. Rather, we hope to plant seeds of common sense and critical thinking that refuse to embrace anything less than the best possible answers to the questions of interpretation.

Of course, the references and footnotes in the preceding chapters have already suggested some of the books in the following list. Here we attempt to collate in an organized fashion the better tools for doing biblical research and interpreting the Bible responsibly and accurately. An increasing number of these resources can be found in digital formats and within software packages. We limit the list to works in English, with a few exceptions (mostly original language tools) as noted. The focus is on the *practice of interpretation*, not on its theory or defense—we have already attempted that and cited many works in the footnotes. Generally, books are listed in order from *less* advanced to *more* advanced (as precisely as possible) and from those based on the English text of the Bible to those that employ or require the original languages. Usually, OT sources precede NT sources. The annotations should make these factors clear. So, for many categories, students with the least background should begin by consulting the initial volumes. Then work down the lists as more expertise is gained and more in-depth information is required. As to style, we list individual resources in SBL bibliographic format; hence the last names of authors appear first for each entry.[4]

---

4. B. J. Collins, et al., ed. *The SBL Handbook of Style*, 2nd ed. (Atlanta: SBL Press, 2014).

ANNOTATED LISTING

Biblical Texts—English language

See the discussion in Chapter 3 on canon and translations for help here.

Biblical Texts—Original Languages

Old Testament

*Kohlenberger, J. R., ed. *The Interlinear Hebrew-English Old Testament*. Grand Rapids: Zondervan, 1987. This work presents the Hebrew text and the NIV in parallel columns. It also appends English glosses to each word of Hebrew text. Among other uses, it enables readers to locate appropriate Hebrew words for further study. Some computer-based software programs enable users to make their own interlinear texts either of single verses or whole contexts in parallel columns.

Elliger, K., and W. Rudolph, eds. *Biblia Hebraica Stuttgartensia* [BHS]. 5th ed. Stuttgart: Deutsche Bibelstiftung, 1997. Produced by a wide variety of collaborators, this is the standard text of the OT in Hebrew and is conveniently available through the various national Bible Societies. Its footnotes list the important textual variants, including occasional ones from the Dead Sea Scrolls, as well as suggested improved readings by the editors.[5] For students and pastors, we recommend the handy smaller edition of BHS, also now available in paperback. Since 2004, portions of the successor to BHS, *Biblia Hebraica Quinta* (BHQ), have appeared, with an estimated completion date of 2020.

Rahlfs A. and R. Hanhart, *Septuaginta* [LXX]. 2nd rev. ed. Stuttgart: Deutsche Bibelgesellschaft, 2006. This is the standard complete text of the OT in Greek today. In addition to its translation of the OT into Greek, the Septuagint includes the Greek text of the OT Apocrypha.[6]

New Testament

*Douglas, J. D. et al., eds. *The New Greek-English Interlinear New Testament*. 4th ed. Wheaton, IL: Tyndale, 1993; and Green, J. P., *Interlinear New Testament*. 3rd ed. Grand Rapids: Baker, 1997. Both works provide in horizontal lines literal English translations for each word in the Greek NT. Some computer-based software programs (e.g., Logos) also perform this function, often allowing students to set many variables in horizontal lines.

*Nestle-Aland, *Novum Testamentum Graece* [NA[28]]. 28th ed. Stuttgart: Deutsche Bibelstiftung, 2012. First edited by E. Nestle in 1898 and now revised and edited by B. Aland, along with others, this volume is the standard text used by NT scholars. Representing the latest scholarly consensus of the original text of the NT documents, it records virtually all the most important places in the NT where alternative readings occur in different manuscripts. Its introduction and appendices also provide a wealth of information. It cites the textual traditions in a more limited fashion than the UBS Greek NT (see next entry).

---

5. Some find the BHS abbreviations obscure, so a supplementary guide was produced by R. I. Vasholz, *Data for the Sigla of BHS* (Winona Lake, IN: Eisenbrauns, 1983). Further help is found in R. Wonneberger, *Understanding BHS: A Manual for the Users of Biblia Hebraica Stuttgartensia*, 3rd rev. ed. (Rome: Biblical Institute, 2001).

6. Cf. T. M. Law, *When God Spoke Greek: The Septuagint and the Making of the Christian Bible* (Oxford: Oxford University Press, 2013). K. H. Jobes and M. Silva, *Invitation to the Septuagint*, 2nd ed. (Grand Rapids: Baker, 2015) describe why and how to study the Septuagint. The most detailed critical edition for scholarly research, still in process, is *Septuaginta: Vetus Testamentum Graecum* (Göttingen: Vandenhoeck & Ruprecht, 1939–).

*Aland, K. et al., eds. *Greek New Testament* [UBSGNT[5] or UBS[5]]. 5th ed. Stuttgart: United Bible Societies, 2014. The Greek text is essentially identical to that of Nestle-Aland's 28th edition, apart from periodic differences in paragraphing or layout. But unlike its counterpart, the UBS textual apparatus cites only those places where it deems there are variants that significantly affect translation, providing relatively complete manuscript evidence for each alternative reading. In addition, a "rating system" helps readers see the editors' preferences for the various alternative readings. See the next entry.

Metzger, B. M. ed. *A Textual Commentary on the Greek New Testament.* 2nd ed. New York: United Bible Societies, 1994. Written as a companion volume and reading like the minutes of a committee, this manual provides the details and reasoning the textual critics used in resolving the textual problems in producing the UBSGNT, 4th ed.

Aland, K. ed. *Synopsis Quattuor Evangeliorum.* 15th ed. Stuttgart: Deutsche Bibelstiftung, 2007. This is the standard Greek synopsis for studying the Gospels. Printed in vertical columns, the Gospels can be studied in comparison to each other. For each section (pericope) of the text, appropriate parallels from the other Gospels are cited as often as they occur. The text and symbols are identical to Nestle's 26th edition. In addition to the texts of the Gospels, this synopsis cites numerous parallels in other early Christian literature, including NT Apocrypha and the works by early church fathers, plus the entire text of the Gospel of Thomas in an appendix. This tool also exists in a strictly English edition, *Synopsis of the Four Gospels*, ed. K. Aland. rev. ed. (RSV; New York: American Bible Society, 2010) and a *Greek-English Synopsis of the Four Gospels*, ed. K. Aland (RSV) diglot edition (10th ed.; New York: United Bible Societies, 1993), with texts in the two languages on facing pages. These latter editions lack the extensive parallels in Christian literature or appendices of the Greek volume.

Textual Criticism

General

The New Cambridge History of the Bible. 4 vols. Cambridge: Cambridge University Press, 2012–16. These volumes present the history of the transmission of the text of the Bible from its origins to the modern period. They provide help in sorting out the problems of the texts and ancient versions. Volume 1, *From the Beginnings to 600*, ed. J. C. Paget and J. Schaper, 2013; Volume 2, *From 600 to 1450*, ed. R. Marsden and E. A. Matter, 2012; Volume 3, *From 1450 to 1750*, ed. E. Cameron, 2016; and Volume 4, *From 1750 to the Present*, ed. J. Riches, 2015. Wegner, P. D. *A Student's Guide to Textual Criticism of the Bible.* Downers Grove: IVP Academic, 2006, offers a useful general introduction to the textual criticism of both testaments.

Old Testament

*Brotzman, E. R. *Old Testament Textual Criticism: A Practical Introduction.* 2nd ed. Grand Rapids: Baker Academic, 2016. This is a useful, accessible guide both to the BHS textual apparatus and to the process of textual criticism written by an evangelical. Its many examples will especially benefit students who know Hebrew.

See also the survey of the discipline in Wolters, A. "The Text of the OT." Pages 19–37 in *The Face of Old Testament Studies.* Edited by D. W. Baker and B. T. Arnold. Grand Rapids: Baker; Leicester: Inter-Varsity, 1998.

McCarter, P. K. *Textual Criticism: Recovering the Text of the Hebrew Bible*. Philadelphia: Fortress, 1986. A part of the Guides to Biblical Scholarship series, this brief but helpful book provides a good introduction for students to the science of OT textual criticism.

*Tov, E. *Textual Criticism of the Hebrew Bible*. 3rd rev. and exp. ed. Minneapolis: Fortress, 2012. This is the best introduction to the subject of OT textual criticism. The author is an eminent Jewish scholar whose text-critical research ranks him among the subject's leading authorities today. More technical than Brotzman or McCarter, it will primarily interest the more advanced reader. We especially commend its chapter on evaluating variant textual readings.

Würthwein, E. *The Text of the Old Testament*. 3rd ed. Rev. and exp. by A. A. Fischer. Grand Rapids: Eerdmans, 2014. Suggests a methodology for deciding which textual variant should be reckoned as the earliest.

Jellicoe, S. *The Septuagint and Modern Study*. Winona Lake, IN: Eisenbrauns, 2013. This reprint of the 1978 original volume treats the origins of the LXX, its transmission, its text, and its language. It also surveys the modern study of the LXX. Though still a valuable source, it is out of print. A good, more up-to-date replacement is Kraus, W. and R. G. Wooden, eds. *Septuagint Research: Issues and Challenges in the Study of the Greek Jewish Scriptures*. SBL Septuagint and Cognate Studies 53. Atlanta: SBL, 2006. Cf. also the chapter, "The Current State of Septuagint Research," pages 239–307 in Jobes, K. H., and M. Silva, *Invitation to the Septuagint*. 2nd ed. Grand Rapids: Baker, 2015.

Tov, E. *The Text-Critical Use of the Septuagint in Biblical Research*. 23rd ed. Rev. and exp. Winona Lake, IN: Eisenbrauns, 2015. Jerusalem Biblical Studies 8. Jerusalem: Simor, 1997. The author discusses such topics as the canon of the LXX, variants, how to reconstruct the *Vorlage*, reconstruction of other elements, variants/non-variants/pseudo-variants, the nature of the Hebrew text underlying the LXX, and the contribution of the LXX to literary criticism.

New Testament

Greenlee, J. H. *The Text of the New Testament: From Manuscript to Modern Edition*. Grand Rapids: Baker, 2008. Not an advanced or technical treatment, this book provides the beginner with an overview of the principles of textual criticism and how critics determine the original text of the NT. A very brief counterpart is Black, D. A. *New Testament Textual Criticism: A Concise Guide*. Grand Rapids: Baker, 1994. It shows how the original texts were corrupted and how textual criticism operates in an attempt to recover the originals. See also Comfort, P. W. *The Text of the Earliest New Testament Greek Manuscripts*. Wheaton: Tyndale, 2001.

*Aland, K. and B. Aland. *The Text of the New Testament*. 2nd ed. Grand Rapids: Eerdmans, 1989. A standard text, it presents the discipline and methods of the textual criticism of the NT. These German scholars lead readers through the technicalities of making decisions concerning the many manuscripts and versions to determine what were most likely the original readings (the so-called autographs) of the NT documents. They survey modern editions of the NT and the transmission of the Greek text of the NT through its history. This is an advanced text for the serious student.

Metzger, B. M. and B. D. Ehrman, *The Text of the New Testament: Its Transmission, Corruption and Restoration*. 4th ed. New York; Oxford: Oxford University Press, 2005. This is an alternative to the previous volume by the Alands. Also highly recommended, this work introduces readers both to the history and study of textual criticism and demonstrates how its techniques are actually performed. Again, this volume is not for the novice, though those interested in the subject can learn much here.

Wallace, D. B. *Laying a Foundation: A Handbook on New Testament Textual Criticism.* Grand Rapids: Zondervan, forthcoming 2018. Wallace is also the founder and executive director of the Center for the Study of New Testament Manuscripts, an ongoing project to digitize the world's ancient New Testament manuscripts, which it then makes available freely. See the website: csntm.org.

Versions and Translations

*Fee, G. D. and M. L. Strauss *How to Choose a Translation for All Its Worth: A Guide to Understanding and Using Bible Versions.* Grand Rapids: Zondervan, 2007. Excellent, introductory information about the major translations in English, the philosophies behind them, and their strengths and weaknesses.

Metzger, B. M. *The Bible in Translation: Ancient and English Versions.* Grand Rapids: Baker, 2001. Outlined here is the development of biblical translation, including a careful analysis of more than fifty versions of the Bible beginning with the earliest translations of the Old and New Testaments before proceeding to English. More selective with respect to modern English versions than the next two entries, it is very readable and concise.

Brunn, D. *One Bible, Many Versions: Are All Translations Created Equal?.* Downers Grove: InterVarsity, 2013. A mid-level explanation of the varying translation theories, with an emphasis on showing how none of the major translations rigidly fit into any one theory and how much more similar than different they are. Partisan rallying behind a certain version as best for all Bible reading and study is thus misguided.

*Lewis, J. P. *The English Bible from KJV to NIV.* 2nd ed. Grand Rapids: Baker, 1991. Not only does this volume detail the story of the English Bible up to the 1978 ed. of the NIV, but, also includes chapters on the NKJV, REV, and NRSV.

Beekman, J. and J. Callow. *Translating the Word of God.* Grand Rapids: Zondervan, 1974. A classic work that provides an illuminating primer on the process and theory of translation of the Bible into other languages. It also yields numerous insights into various grammatical features of the Greek NT.

For more advanced students, the United Bible Societies publishes an inexpensive series, Helps for Translators, on many individual biblical books in both testaments. A unique kind of commentary aimed for people actually preparing translations, each volume provides linguistic and cultural background useful to translators and discusses how best to render the original text in other languages.

Studying Words and Their Theological Significance

The sources in the following list presume that the user is able to locate the "lexical form" of Hebrew or Greek words. In a later section we include theological dictionaries and encyclopedias that students who do not want to engage the original languages may consult. For students without a sufficient knowledge of the biblical languages but who do know the alphabet to find Hebrew or Greek words, say in an interlinear OT or NT, helpful tools exist. For the OT see, e.g., Owens, J. J. *Analytical Key to the Old Testament.* 4 vols. Grand Rapids: Baker, 1990–93; or Davidson, A. B. *Analytical Hebrew-Chaldee Lexicon.* Peabody, MA: Hendrickson, 1981. Repr. of 1848 ed. For the Greek OT, see Taylor, B. ed. *Analytical Lexicon to the Septuagint*. Peabody, MA: Hendrickson, 2009. For the NT see Mounce, W. D. *The Analytical Lexicon to the Greek New Testament*. Grand Rapids: Zondervan, 1993. An alternative excellent source is Friberg, T. et al., *Analytical Lexicon of the Greek New Testament*. Grand Rapids: Baker, 2000. All of these volumes list every word occurring in the Hebrew (and Aramaic) and Greek testaments in alphabetical order. Each term is analyzed grammatically and is listed with the lexical form (sometimes called a "lemma"). The reader needs to know how to locate this form to use the following tools. Beyond these print versions, several computer software products have advanced the ability to discover, analyze, and parse original language forms to a fine art. Often links to other resources enable savvy users to search a multitude of resources.[7]

Lexicons

Hebrew, Aramaic, and Old Testament Lexicons

Holladay, W. L. *A Concise Hebrew and Aramaic Lexicon of the Old Testament: Based upon the Lexical Work of Ludwig Koehler and Walter Baumgartner*. Leiden: Brill, 1997. An abbreviated form of KBL [*HALOT*] below, this work provides briefer access to the meaning of OT words. It functions well for students beginning their study of biblical Hebrew and Aramaic.

*Brown, F., S. R. Driver, and C. A. Briggs, *A Hebrew and English Lexicon of the Old Testament* [BDB]. Repr. Peabody, MA: Hendrickson, 1996. The words are coded to *Strong's Concordance* (see below). This has been the standard Hebrew lexicon, the revision and translation of the monumental work begun by Gesenius (1810–12). Showing uncommon thoroughness, BDB gives the meanings not only of individual words but also of common phrases and idioms. It lists related roots and words that occur in the sister languages of biblical Hebrew. To help find words in BDB, some students consult Einspahr, B. *Index to Brown, Driver and Briggs Hebrew Lexicon*. Chicago: Moody, 1976. Organized just like the Bible (i.e., by books, chapters, and verses), it gives the meaning and location in BDB of all but the most common Hebrew words (for which BDB gives a biblical reference). Using this *Index* one can locate the page and section in which BDB discusses a Hebrew word, see where it occurs in the OT, and discover its meaning.

*Koehler, L. and W. Baumgartner, eds. *Hebrew and Aramaic Lexicon of the Old Testament (Lexicon in Veteris Testamenti Libros)* [*HALOT* or KBL]. 3rd ed. 5 vols. Leiden: Brill, 1994–2001; Study edition, 2 vols. Leiden: Brill, 2001. A translation of the most complete, most recent Hebrew and Aramaic German lexicon, this is the modern counterpart to BDB. *HALOT* surpasses BDB on two counts: words are listed alphabetically and not by root, and it employs Ugaritic and Qumran sources to which BDB did not have access. The descriptions are in both German and English, though the English is clearly the weaker of the two. It assumes

---

7. It is risky to list specific software products since the market for computer resources changes so rapidly. A short list of notable resources as of this writing includes Logos Bible Software (Faithlife Corp), which integrates Bible versions and an increasing number of research sources (and onto which platform many publishers locate their products) and BibleWorks, which integrates many Bible texts and modern versions in multiple languages, various dictionaries and research tools, and facilitates complex searches within the biblical texts. Gramcord (Windows) and Accordance (Macintosh and Windows) allow sophisticated searches in the Greek and Hebrew testaments.

at least an introductory knowledge of Hebrew. One must constantly use the supplement to augment the main entries. Many consider the Aramaic section superior to the Hebrew sections.

Clines, D. J. A., ed. *The Dictionary of Classical Hebrew*. Sheffield, UK: Sheffield Phoenix Press, 1993–2016. Nine volumes have appeared to this point. Designed for a contextual and usage approach to understanding the meaning of words. One unique feature is its inclusion of extra-biblical occurrences of words (e.g., Qumran, ostraca, inscriptions, etc.).

For Aramaic words, the best lexicon in English is Jastrow, M. *A Dictionary of the Targumim, the Talmud Babli and Yerushalmi, and the Midrashic Literature*. 2 vols. 2nd ed. New York: Pardes, 1950. It is accessible online at http://www.tyndalearchive. com/tabs/jastrow/. Another searchable, online resource is the *Comprehensive Aramaic Lexicon* (http://cal1.cn.huc.edu/). Most students, however, will find that the Aramaic sections of the first three above lexicons will easily meet their needs.

In reading the Septuagint, the best lexicon to use is Muraoka, T. *A Greek-English Lexicon of the Septuagint*. Leuven: Peeters, 2010.

Greek and New Testament Lexicons

*Louw, J. P. and E. A. Nida, *A Greek-English Lexicon of the New Testament Based on Semantic Domains*. 2 vols. New York: United Bible Societies, 1988. The Society of Biblical Literature published a supplement volume in 1992. As the title implies, these volumes organize the vocabulary of the NT Greek into its various semantic fields or domains of meaning. They provide an excellent source for actually defining words, seeing the range of meaning of individual words, finding the most likely sense for a given word in a context, and understanding synonyms. This lexicon has assumed its rightful place among the standard, important tools for doing Greek word studies. It is an important companion to BDAG, which follows.

*Bauer, W., F. Danker, W. F. Arndt, and F. W. Gingrich. *A Greek-English Lexicon of the New Testament and Other Early Christian Literature* [BDAG]. 3rd ed. Chicago: University of Chicago Press, 2000. This is the standard lexicon specifically devoted to the Hellenistic Greek of the NT and parallel literature. One can hardly overestimate the wealth of information encompassed in BDAG. The authors often provide succinct meanings, trace uses of the words through the Hellenistic period, and dispense perceptive evaluations of the significance of words. The latest revision adds entries for many more words and more than 25,000 additional references to classical, intertestamental, early Christian, and modern literature. Danker has also introduced a more consistent mode of reference citation, provided a composite list of abbreviations, and extended the definitions of many Greek terms. Words are listed in Greek, and one must know the lexical form (lemma) of Greek words to look them up. It is also available in some Bible software programs.

Moulton, J. H. and G. Milligan. *Vocabulary of the Greek Testament Illustrated from the Papyri and Other Non-Literary Sources* [M&M]. 2nd ed. Repr. Peabody, MA: Hendrickson, 1997. This volume provides examples of specific uses of Greek in Hellenistic times from nonliterary papyri. Begun in 1914, it has been reprinted several times. Far from exhaustive, this volume cites only those words employed in nonliterary sources and so sheds light on how they were understood in everyday use about the time of the NT. The editors provide dates for the citations and often translate them into English. The work is somewhat outdated (since many new sources have surfaced since 1930), but a revision is underway.

Lampe, G. H. W. ed. *A Patristic Greek Lexicon.* Oxford: Clarendon, 1985. This work complements NT usage by showing meanings of words in the subsequent era of the early church fathers (to about AD 826). It sometimes proves instructive to see changes in word meanings as the church developed in its first few centuries, though, of course, later meanings cannot be imposed upon NT uses.

Liddell, H. G., R. Scott, H. S. Jones, and R. McKenzie. *A Greek-English Lexicon* [LSJ]. 9th ed. with supplement. 2 vols. Oxford: Clarendon, 1925–40. Repr. 1968. New supplement 1996. This is the standard comprehensive lexicon for the entire range of the Greek language in the ancient world including the NT. It specializes in the classical period of ancient Greek (up until 330 BC) but also traces meanings into the Hellenistic period. It provides valuable help in studying the history and etymology of words that occur in the NT. The newly revised Supplement gives the dictionary a date range from 1200 BC to AD 600. It is fully cross-referenced to the main text but additions have been designed to be easily used without constant reference to the main text. Some Bible software programs include it among their electronic lexicons. Oxford also publishes *An Abridged Greek-English Lexicon* (1966), a shorter version of this outstanding resource.

Theological Dictionaries

Old Testament

Harris, R. L. et al., eds. *Theological Wordbook of the Old Testament* [*TWOT*]. 2 vols. Chicago: Moody, 1980. This book comprises a compact discussion of key Hebrew words. Its authors are all evangelical scholars, and the work is readily accessible to most readers, even those without a working knowledge of Hebrew. It attempts to investigate each Hebrew word and its cognates and synthesize the meaning of words in context in a concise format. Each entry has a number that corresponds to the numbers assigned Hebrew words in Strong's concordance (on which see below). It has been eclipsed, however, by the next entry.

*VanGemeren, W. et al., eds. *New International Dictionary of Old Testament Theology and Exegesis* [*NIDOTTE*]. 5 vols. Grand Rapids: Zondervan, 1997. Volumes 1–4 are organized alphabetically by Hebrew words; volume 5, topically around English words or biblical book titles. Many topical entries also incorporate discussion of relevant Hebrew words. The contributors are evangelicals from throughout the English-speaking world, and *NIDOTTE* represents a standard work on Hebrew words. (For the use of Brown, Silva, and Kittel for OT word studies, see below). English readers may access the Hebrew words by cross-reference numbers in the Goodrick-Kohlenberger concordance (see below), which also has a *NIDOTTE*-Strong's numbers conversion chart. VanGemeren has also edited *A Guide to Old Testament Theology and Exegesis.* Grand Rapids: Zondervan, 1999. This is a collection of *NIDOTTE*'s introductory articles.

Jenni, E. and C. Westermann, eds. *Theological Lexicon of the Old Testament.* 3 vols. Peabody, MA: Hendrickson, 1997.[8] This translation finally makes available to English readers what continues to be the standard theological dictionary of German students and pastors after nearly three decades. Written by leading European scholars, each article thoroughly treats the OT's most important theological words, their etymology, cognates, range of meanings, usage in the

---

8. The original German title was *Theologisches Handwörterbuch zum Alten Testament*, 2 vols. (München; Gütersloh: Chr. Kaiser, 1971, 1984).

OT, LXX equivalents, and use at Qumran. Its higher-critical tendencies notwithstanding, its pages teem with rich literary and theological insights worth mining by the advanced user.

Botterweck, G. J. and H. Ringgren, eds. *Theological Dictionary of the Old Testament* [*TDOT*]. 12 vols. Grand Rapids: Eerdmans, 1974–2015.[9] This is the OT counterpart to *TDNT* (see below). *TDOT* assesses key OT terms and their theological significance—occasionally going on to postbiblical developments (e.g., Qumran and the rabbis) and employing cognate languages where possible (especially, though not only, Akkadian and Ugaritic) to explain the meaning. A knowledge of Hebrew is useful, if not essential, to get the most out of this source. Its orientation is less conservative theologically than *TWOT* or *NIDOTTE*, often building upon literary-critical assumptions. Read critically, however, there is no better source for Hebrew word studies.

New Testament

Balz, H. and G. Schneider, eds. *Exegetical Dictionary of the New Testament* [*EDNT*]. 3 vols. Grand Rapids: Eerdmans, 1992.[10] This work presupposes the historical background found in such works as *TDNT*, *NIDNTT*, and *NIDNTTE* (see below). Unlike them, in *EDNT* the authors treat every word in the NT, but theologically significant words have longer entries. In particular, *EDNT* traces the development of the meanings of theologically significant words in their NT contexts to assess their significance for exegesis. An electronic version is available on Logos.

Brown, C., ed. *New International Dictionary of New Testament Theology* [*NIDNTT*]. 4 vols. Grand Rapids: Zondervan, 1975–78.[11] This is a work similar to *TDNT* and *NIDNTTE* (below) that discusses the theological significance of words over time. However, the words are organized around semantic fields of meanings, countering some of Barr's criticisms of *TDNT*. It aims to provide help for theologians, pastors, and teachers, and omits some of the depth of historical research that characterizes *TDNT*. Generally, the articles in *NIDNTT* are briefer and written from a more conservative viewpoint than *TDNT*. Overall this is a valuable resource but is now out of print since it has been superseded by its successor, *NIDNTTE* (see below). Like *TDNT*, it is useful for studying OT Hebrew words since most articles discuss the Hebrew background of NT words. The final volume consists wholly of indexes that expedite a variety of searches. For a one-volume digest, see Verbrugge, V. D. *New International Dictionary of New Testament Theology: Abridged Edition.* Grand Rapids: Zondervan, 2003. An electronic version is available.

*Silva, M., ed. *New International Dictionary of New Testament Theology and Exegesis* [*NIDNTTE*]. 5 vols. Grand Rapids: Zondervan, 2014. A thorough revision of *NIDNTT* (immediately above), it both abbreviates sections on classical Greek and Septuagintal background and adds a significant number of additional words. Silva has preserved the best of *NIDNTT* (thus note comments made above), while making needed corrections and updates. An electronic version is available.

---

9. This English edition translates the German original, *Theologisches Wörterbuch zum Alten Testament* (Stuttgart: Kohlhammer, 1970–).

10. This is the English translation of *Exegetisches Wörterbuch zum Neuen Testament*, 3 vols. (Stuttgart: Kohlhammer, 1978, 1981, 1983).

11. *NIDNTT* translates, but also provides additions and revisions to, the German work done by L. Coenen, et al., eds., *Theologisches Begriffslexikon zum Neuen Testament*, vols. I, II/1–2 (Wuppertal: Brockhaus, 1967, 1969, 1971).

Kittel, G. and G. Friedrich (since 1954), eds. *Theological Dictionary of the New Testament* [*TDNT*]. English translation by G. W. Bromiley. 10 vols. Grand Rapids: Eerdmans, 1964–1978.[12] It is also available in an electronic version. Knowledge of Greek is very helpful, though probably not essential to obtain its basic insights. Following a discussion of a word's etymology, this dictionary traces its uses in its various contexts through the ancient world—classical Greek, Hellenistic Greek, LXX Greek, and Jewish writers—all as background for the uses in the NT. If a Greek word has a Hebrew counterpart in the OT, the authors provide discussion of that too. Indeed, it is often useful for studying OT Hebrew words since many articles treat the usage of their Greek counterparts in the Septuagint. (Of course, this requires the student to find the Greek word for the Hebrew word under study). The words are organized according to their etymological roots, a cause for some criticism among reviewers and users. Though this makes locating some terms in *TDNT* a challenge, the final volume contains various indexes that facilitate various searches in this massive storehouse of research. Not all its conclusions can be taken at face value, particularly in some of the early volumes.[13] Read critically, however, there is no better source for Greek word studies. The translator of this multivolume work, G. Bromiley, has produced an abridged and edited one-volume distillation of the entire work—about one sixth of the original, also called *TDNT*. Exeter: Paternoster; Grand Rapids: Eerdmans, 1985. Known as "little Kittel," users who know little or no Greek will find it easier to use. An electronic version is available.

Spicq, C. *Theological Lexicon of the New Testament*. 3 vols. Peabody, MA: Hendrickson, 1994.[14] Excellent insights on many theologically significant words, though a one-man product— thus we list it last, not because it is more advanced or less accessible. An electronic version is available.

Concordances

Organized according to the alphabetical order of the words occurring in the Bible or a Testament, a concordance quotes the specific line in which a given word occurs and identifies the reference where the line may be found. Bible students have access to concordances in both the original and English languages. Concordances enable students to study the biblical use of individual words ("sin," "salvation," etc.) as well as phrases ("in the latter days," etc.). Most software programs (e.g., BibleWorks, Logos, Accordance, and others) allow one to produce concordances on the fly—either of root forms (e.g., all occurrences of "love" or ἀγαπάω) or specific inflected forms (e.g., "loved," "will be loved," or ἀγαπηθήσεται), and this holds true for all versions and modern and original languages.

---

12. The German original is *Theologisches Wörterbuch zum Neuen Testament*, 10 vols. (Stuttgart: Kohlhammer, 1933–79).

13. Volumes 1–4 were done between 1933 and 1942 and need updating. For an important critique of the methodology employed in *TDNT* see J. Barr, *The Semantics of Biblical Language* (Oxford: Oxford University Press, 1961), especially pp. 206–62. Barr rightly assails the untenable view that in studying specific Greek words employed in the NT one is investigating the stock of key theological concepts of the early Christians, as if there is a direct correlation between lexemes and theological concepts (207). For appropriate correctives in doing Greek word studies see M. Silva, *Biblical Words and Their Meaning: An Introduction to Lexical Semantics*, rev. ed. (Grand Rapids: Zondervan, 1995).

14. The French original is *Notes de lexicographie néo-testamentaire*, Orbis Biblicus et Orientals 22/1, 2, 3 (Fribourg, Suisse: Éditions Universitaires, 1982).

English Concordances

Concerning concordances for English Bibles, the student must acquire one (or more) that parallels the version of the Bible used for study. Now the Bible market is such that each translation has a corresponding concordance. To cite three examples, see Thomas, R. L., ed. *The Strongest NASB Exhaustive Concordance.* Grand Rapids: Zondervan, 2000; Goodrick, E. and J. R. Kohlenberger, III, eds. *The Strongest NIV Exhaustive Concordance.* Grand Rapids: Zondervan, 2004; and Kohlenberger, III, J. R., ed. *The NRSV Concordance Unabridged.* Grand Rapids: Zondervan, 1991. This latter text includes all occurrences of all words in the *NRSV,* including the apocryphal books and alternate and literal translations found in the footnotes. All these enable one to discover specific words that occur in these versions in all their biblical locations.

The old standbys for the KJV were: Young, R. *Analytical Concordance to the Bible.* Repr. Peabody, MA: Hendrickson, 1993; and Strong, J. *Exhaustive Concordance of the Bible.* New York: Hunt Eaton; Cincinnati: Cranston Curts, 1894; with some revisions and improvements by Nelson, 1997; and the much improved *The Strongest Strong's Exhaustive Concordance of the Bible.* Zondervan, 2001. They enable readers without the knowledge of the biblical languages to correlate specific Hebrew or Greek words with their corresponding English terms in the KJV and to compare in the concordance itself uses of the same Hebrew or Greek terms, not simply English translations.[15]

*As a bridge between Hebrew or Greek concordances and those based on English language versions are two works by the same editors: Kohlenberger, III, J. R. and J. A. Swanson. *The Hebrew-English Concordance to the OT.* Grand Rapids: Zondervan, 1998; and *The Greek-English Concordance to the NT.* Grand Rapids: Zondervan, 1997. Arranged the same way, they list Hebrew or Greek words alphabetically and indicate the references where they occur with brief excerpts from the KJV. These works are keyed, like the new BDB and *TWOT,* to Strong's numbering system and other reference works. Many of the computer software programs also key words to Strong's numbering system.

Hebrew and Aramaic Concordances

Davidson, A. B. *A Concordance of the Hebrew and Chaldee Scriptures.* London: Samuel Bagster, 1876. This covers all the Hebrew and Aramaic words of the OT. It is designed for students who know little or no Hebrew and cites texts in English translation.

*Even-Shoshan, A. *A New Concordance of the Old Testament.* 2nd ed. Grand Rapids: Baker, 1997. This mammoth work, more comprehensive but harder to use than Davidson's, lists every word in the Hebrew Bible alphabetically under its root. To use it requires at least a seminary-level knowledge of Hebrew because all of its citations are in Hebrew (with vowels) and its meanings are given in modern Hebrew. One important feature commends it over Mandelkern and Lisowsky (see below): it groups together identical grammatical forms,

---

15. As we have noted, various lexical reference tools have included Strong's numbering system enabling students who would not be able to do so otherwise to locate words. See descriptions of the tools themselves.

phrases, and words of similar meaning. The introduction by J. H. Sailhamer enables the beginner to take advantage of this remarkable resource.

Mandelkern, S. *Veteris Testamenti Concordantiae Hebraicae atque Chaldaicae.* Leipzig: Veit et Comp., 1876. 2nd ed., 1925. Repr. Graz: Akademischer Druck, 1955. Repr. with corrections and additions. New York: Schulsinger, 1955. Gottstein, M. H. 3rd ed. with corrections and supplements. Jerusalem/Tel Aviv: Schocken, 1959. This is a massive and outstanding work, more comprehensive but less manageable than Even-Shoshan's, but increasingly difficult to acquire. Rather than merely listing citations (which may be all a student wants), Mandelkern lists them by grammatical form (e.g., construct, conjugated verbs, etc.), a useful advantage if one seeks a Hebrew specific phrase or formula (e.g., "angel of the Lord," "X found favor in your eyes," etc.). All the wealth this work has to offer clearly belongs to the advanced student and scholar.

Greek Concordances

Hatch. E. and H. E. Redpath, *Concordance to the Septuagint and Other Greek Versions of the Old Testament.* 2 vols. Oxford: Clarendon, 1897. Volume 3, a supplement, 1906. Repr. [with supplement] in 2 vols. Graz: Akademischer Druck, 1954. Repr. Grand Rapids: Baker, 2005. This constitutes the standard concordance for the LXX. It lists each Greek word in the Greek OT and apocryphal books along with its Hebrew counterpart. Passages are given in Greek. Its drawback is the limited number of manuscripts (four, in fact) that lie behind the citations. The work, requiring a working knowledge of Greek, is indispensable for a study of the LXX, and is the standard work for finding the Hebrew words behind it. To make this work more accessible, use Muraoka, T. *A Greek/Hebrew-Aramaic Index to the Septuagint.* Grand Rapids: Baker, 2010.

Marshall, I. H., ed. *Moulton and Geden: A Concordance to the Greek Testament.* 6th ed. Edinburgh: T&T Clark; New York: Continuum, 2002. The original work published in 1897 used the Greek text of Westcott and Hort, but this complete update is based on the UBSGNT[4] / NA[27]. It is extremely complete and truly functional for it provides grammatical helps, Greek citations from the LXX and Apocrypha, and Hebrew quotes where a citation comes from the OT. Asterisks and daggers indicate whether the vocabulary items in the NT occur in classical Greek and in the Septuagint. References to the variants in the older Greek NT editions are preserved, so that the student has available every reading which might potentially be regarded as forming part of the true text of the NT. Unlike prior editions, prepositions are included in the main text of the Concordance. Where the same word occurs twice in the same verse, these occurrences are now printed on separate lines and individually verse-numbered so that it is easier to assess all the occurrences of any given word.

Aland, K. *Vollständige Konkordanz zum griechischen Neuen Testament: Unter Zugrundelegung aller kritischen Textausgaben und des Textus Receptus [VKGNT].* 2 vols. Berlin; New York: de Gruyter, 1975–83, 1978. A computer-generated, exhaustive concordance based upon the UBS[3] and NA[26], *VKGNT* is a standard Greek concordance for serious NT studies, providing all variants for the modern critical editions of the NT. Citations are full, in Greek, and include word frequencies for each word—book by book—and alphabetically. Words are categorized as to uses. A fully serviceable slimmer (and less expensive) version is also available: Bachmann, H. and H. Slaby, eds. *Concordance to the Novum Testamentum Graece of Nestle-Aland, 26th edition, and to the Greek New Testament, 3rd edition.* Berlin; New York: de Gruyter,

1987.[16] It omits citations for twenty-nine frequently occurring words, though it does list the passages for these words in an appendix. For personal use this vies with Moulton and Geden.

Since citations in all the preceding concordances occur in the original languages, students wishing to use them will need to have language facility or will need to use these volumes along with an English Bible for finding references (a time-consuming but often worthwhile project).

Bible Dictionaries and Encyclopedias

Draper, C. W., C. Draper and A. England, ed. *Holman Illustrated Bible Dictionary.* Rev. ed. Nashville: Broadman, 2003. Providing excellent definitions, it is beautifully illustrated with color photographs, maps, and charts. It is a useful semi-popular dictionary.

Powell, M. A., ed. *HarperCollins Bible Dictionary.* 3rd rev. ed. New York: HarperCollins, 2011. This dictionary reflects mainstream biblical scholarship and was authored by members of the Society of Biblical Literature. It covers the Bible and its world, the Apocrypha and Pseudepigrapha of the OT and NT, and the early church fathers.

*Freedman, D. N., ed. *Eerdmans Dictionary of the Bible.* Grand Rapids: Eerdmans, 2000. The best, most up-to-date, one-volume dictionary. Written by both mainstream and evangelical scholars, this dictionary features well-informed articles on the Bible and the full spectrum of background topics. In recent publication, this work may enjoy a slight edge over the other one-volume dictionaries in this section.

Tenney, M. C. and M. Silva, eds. *The Zondervan Encyclopedia of the Bible, Revised.* 5 vols. Grand Rapids: Zondervan, 2009. A classic, introductory-level encyclopedia revised and upgraded to a very thorough but readable collection of short articles. Lavishly illustrated.

InterVarsity Press has issued four superb dictionaries devoted to the NT and four devoted to the OT that stand as some of the finest available. Written by a wide cross-section of scholars, mostly but not exclusively evangelicals, these represent extensive and accurate summaries of the issues reflected in the topics of each volume.

*Green, J. B., ed. *Dictionary of Jesus and the Gospels.* 2nd ed. Downers Grove; Leicester: InterVarsity, 2013.

*Hawthorne, G. F., R. P. Martin, and D. G. Reid, eds. *Dictionary of Paul and His Letters.* Downers Grove; Leicester: InterVarsity, 1993.

*Davids, P. H. and R. P. Martin, eds. *Dictionary of the Later New Testament and Its Developments.* Downers Grove; Leicester: InterVarsity, 1997.

*Evans, C. A. and S. E. Porter, eds. *Dictionary of New Testament Background.* Downers Grove; Leicester: InterVarsity, 2000.

*Alexander, T. D. and D. W. Baker, eds. *Dictionary of the Old Testament: Pentateuch.* Downers Grove; Leicester: InterVarsity, 2003.

*Arnold, B. T. and H. G. M. Williamson, eds. *Dictionary of the Old Testament: Historical Books.* Downers Grove: InterVarsity, 2005.

---

16. The German title is *Konkordanz zum Novum Testamentum Graece von Nestle-Aland, 26. Auflage, und zum Greek New Testament,* 3rd edition.

*Longman, T. III and P. Enns, *Dictionary of the Old Testament: Wisdom, Poetry and Writings*. Downers Grove; Leicester: InterVarsity, 2008.

*Boda, M. J. and J. G. McConville, *Dictionary of the Old Testament: Prophets*. Downers Grove; Leicester: InterVarsity, 2012.

Another InterVarsity Press dictionary merits inclusion here: Ryken, L. et al., eds. *Dictionary of Biblical Imagery*. Downers Grove: InterVarsity, 1998. As the title indicates, the authors explain the background and significance of the images that occur throughout the Bible. Many scholars contributed articles, though the editors composed the final versions of the entries. All of these InterVarsity Press dictionaries are available in an electronic version.

Bromiley, G. W., ed. *International Standard Bible Encyclopedia* [*ISBE*]. 4 vols. Rev. ed. Grand Rapids: Eerdmans, 1979–86. This venerable work's revision makes it an ongoing standard for extensive treatment of virtually every biblical topic. This masterpiece must be consulted in any biblical study. More conservative than its counterpart *ABD* below. An electronic version is available.

Sakenfeld, K. D., ed. *New Interpreter's Dictionary of the Bible*. 5 vols. Nashville: Abingdon, 2009. Not quite as comprehensive in coverage or thorough in treatment as the *ABD*, the next entry, but more up-to-date. Also like *ABD*, it employs little of distinctively evangelical scholarship. But also very little is idiosyncratic.

*Freedman, D. N., ed. *The Anchor [Yale] Bible Dictionary* [*ABD*]. 6 vols. Garden City, NY: Doubleday, 1992. This dictionary provides the scholarly world and the general public a comprehensive treatment of all biblical subjects and topics in a readable though authoritative manner. It is both multicultural and interdisciplinary in scope and reflects the current state of mainstream biblical scholarship. Over 800 scholars contributed to this massive work. It is available in electronic versions.

Roth, C. and G. Wigoder, eds. *Encyclopedia Judaica*, 2nd ed. 22 vols. New York: Macmillan, 2006. This set is the definitive work on the Hebrew Scriptures and all things Jewish. It contains in-depth articles on a wide variety of subjects in the Hebrew Scriptures as well as information on Jewish holidays, customs, and teachings.

Grammatical Analysis

Hebrew

Williams, R. J. *Williams' Hebrew Syntax: An Outline*. 3rd ed. revised and expanded by J. C. Beckman. Toronto: University of Toronto Press, 2007. A classic, recently updated work that presents a useful, simple overview of Hebrew syntax. With its user-friendly organization and index, it remains a favorite tool of both beginning and advanced students of syntax.

Arnold, B. T. and J. H. Choi. *A Guide to Biblical Hebrew Syntax*. New York: Cambridge University Press, 2003. A concise, clear, and easy-to-use guide to the main features of Hebrew syntax. Well-organized and has a fine index. Its detailed glossary of technical terms is a delightful plus for students and ministers alike.

*Waltke, B. K. and M. O'Connor. *An Introduction to Biblical Hebrew Syntax*. Winona Lake, IN: Eisenbrauns, 1990. Based upon modern linguistic principles, it serves as both a reference grammar and a resource for self-study. Though not as user-friendly as it might be, it is an indispensable tool for the student with a seminary-level knowledge of Hebrew. It contains numerous examples and excellent indexes. Its somewhat technical language may limit its usefulness to only advanced students.

Van Der Merwe, C. H. J., J. A. Naudé, and J. H. Kroeze. *A Biblical Hebrew Reference Grammar.* Sheffield: JSOT, 1999. An affordable, well-indexed study incorporating recent insights of linguistics.

The standard reference grammar of OT Hebrew in English remains Gesenius, W. and E. Kautzsch. *Gesenius' Hebrew Grammar.* 2nd ed. Oxford: Clarendon, [1910] 1995, based on the 28th German edition of W. Gesenius, *Hebräische Grammatik* by A.E. Cowley. It is still authoritative for philology and morphology, but its treatment of syntax is outdated in many places. For the latter, see Williams and Waltke-O'Connor above. Available online in pdf format at http://tmcdaniel.palmerseminary.edu/ GeseniusGrammar.pdf.

Greek

*Mathewson, D. and E. B. Emig. *Intermediate Greek Grammar: Syntax for Students of the New Testament.* Grand Rapids: Baker, 2016. The most user-friendly of the intermediate Greek grammars and thoroughly abreast of all the most recent linguistic developments.

Porter, S. E. *Idioms of the Greek New Testament.* Sheffield, UK: Sheffield Academic Press, 1992. This is an intermediate-level grammar based on modern linguistic principles. Porter's treatment of Greek tenses as aspectual broke new ground for a non-technical work of its size when the book appeared. Includes a helpful section on discourse analysis. Some unique but also idiosyncratic features.

Mounce, W. D. *The Morphology of Biblical Greek.* Grand Rapids: Zondervan, 1994. Good for learning the basic forms of Hellenistic Greek and why every paradigm functions the way it does.

Campbell, C. R. *Advances in the Study of Greek: New Insights for Reading the New Testament.* Grand Rapids: Zondervan, 2015. Title aptly summarizes the work. Makes an excellent supplement to Mathewson and Emig or Porter above but is not a full-blown grammar in and of itself.

Runge, S. E. *Discourse Grammar of the Greek New Testament.* Peabody: Hendrickson, 2010. Best, detailed treatment of discourse analysis available, with abundant illustrations of its value for exegesis of specific New Testament texts.

*Köstenberger, A. J., B. L. Merkle and R. L. Plummer. *Going Deeper with New Testament Greek: An Intermediate Study of the Grammar and Syntax of the New Testament.* Nashville: B&H, 2016. Not quite as comprehensive as Wallace below but more user-friendly. Still very thorough but without adding rare or questionable categories. Slightly more up-to-date on verbal aspect theory than Wallace.

*Wallace, D. B. *Greek Grammar Beyond the Basics.* Grand Rapids: Zondervan, 1996. The most comprehensive intermediate-advanced grammar currently available. Extensive examples make this a goldmine for understanding how specific grammatical features function in context. An electronic version is available.

Blass, F., A. Debrunner, and R. W. Funk, *A Greek Grammar of the New Testament and Other Early Christian Literature* [BDF]. Chicago: University of Chicago Press, 1961. This was the standard advanced grammar for making exegetical decisions about the Greek text before Wallace and continues to have information available nowhere else.[17] The indexes often help the student gain assistance in specific verses or grammatical issues. Unfortunately, the work is not user-friendly, and finding specific help is not always easy. This work requires a good grasp of Greek.

Geography

Though smaller and less comprehensive, two paperback works merit mention as useful for much basic geography: Lawrence, P. *The InterVarsity Press Concise Atlas of Bible History*. Ed. R. W. Johnson. Downers Grove: IVP Academic, 2012; and Frank, H. T., ed. *Hammond's Atlas of the Bible Lands*. Springfield, NJ: Hammond World Atlas Corporation, 2007.

*Beitzel, B. *The New Moody Atlas of the Bible*. Rev. ed. Chicago: Moody Press, 2009. This is similar in size to Aharoni/Avi-Yonah and Rasmussen (see below) but seems the best atlas in its class. Conservative in viewpoint, it also has fine color maps and pictures.

Rasmussen, C. G. *The Zondervan Atlas of the Bible*. Rev. ed. Grand Rapids: Zondervan, 2010. This is an excellent volume produced from an evangelical viewpoint.

Pritchard, J. B., ed. *The HarperCollins Atlas of Bible History*. Rev. ed. New York: HarperOne, 2008. Representing a more mainline scholarly viewpoint, this is perhaps the most definitive atlas to emerge in recent decades and may become a standard. Students must decide, however, if their library can accommodate its large size.

*Aharoni, Y., M. Avi-Yonah, A. F. Rainey, and Z. Safrai, eds. *The Carta Bible Atlas*. 5th ed. Jerusalem: Carta the Israel Map Pub. Co., 2011. New edition of a standard atlas that provides individual maps for many significant Bible events. Formerly the *Macmillan Bible Atlas*, this is now distributed through Eisenbrauns. This atlas takes pride of place as one of the best available. The authors, Jewish scholars, identify biblical sites and events, though evangelicals may disagree at times with their dating. For obvious reasons, it concentrates more on Palestine and less on the Roman world and so is less helpful in studying the expansion of the early church.

Ha-El, M., P. Wright, and B. S. M. Haron. *The Essential Bible Guide: Bible Background with Maps, Charts, and Lists*. Nashville: Abingdon, 2010. A recent anthology of geography visuals keyed to crucial historical events and Bible books.

The most thorough resource for biblical geography, one destined to become a standard for advanced students and scholars, is Mittmann, S. and G. Schmitt, eds. *Tübinger Bibelatlas*. Stuttgart: Deutsche Bibelgesellschaft, 2001. Each oversized, foldout, colored map portrays a region, its cities, roads, and landmarks during a specific historical period in remarkable detail. Though prepared in Germany, the volume has both German and English captions and is available through any United Bible Societies affiliate.

---

17. BDF is a translation and revision of the 9th–10th edition of F. Blass and A. Debrunner, *Grammatik des neutestamentlichen Griechisch* (Göttingen: Vandenhoeck & Ruprecht, 1954, 1959). Translator R. Funk also had access to and employed additional notes of A. Debrunner. He also incorporated his own findings, so BDF goes beyond the printed German edition.

Schlegel, W. *Satellite Bible Atlas,* is available at http://www.bibleplaces.com/satellite-bible-atlas
-schlegel.htm. It offers 85 full-paged color maps with biblical events marked on enhanced
satellite imagery, accompanied by geographical and historical commentary.

For an excellent, complete online Bible atlas visit http://bibleatlas.org/. Alphabetical
access to maps of Bible sites (cities, mountains, regions, etc.) with links to local,
regional, and full-page views as well as Google maps. A brief encyclopedia article
summarizing the site's role in the Bible and a cross reference to Strong's concordance
accompany each map.

Access to a host of historical maps is a component of BibleWorks and Logos,
among others.

History of the Ancient World

We face a major difficulty in recommending useful volumes that will serve the
student in basic research into the history of the ancient world. Simply put, the discipline
is as vast as the terrain. Nevertheless, we suggest a basic list. Though we divide the
section into several subgroups, various works overlap.

Ancient Near Eastern and Classical Literature

*Arnold, B. T. and B. E. Beyer, *Readings from the Ancient Near East.* Encountering Biblical
Studies. Grand Rapids: Baker, 2002. This companion volume to the authors' *Encountering
the Old Testament* (see below) offers a balanced selection of ancient Near Eastern texts for
the general reader, each with a helpful background introduction.

Matthews, V. H. and D. C. Benjamin. *Old Testament Parallels: Laws and Stories from the Ancient
Near East.* 3rd ed. New York: Paulist Press, 2006. This handy paperback offers the general
reader brief introductions to and translations of the most important extrabiblical texts that
parallel materials in the Bible. Its literary glimpse of the ancient world helps the student
better understand both that world and important biblical texts.

Sparks, K. L. *Ancient Texts for the Study of the Hebrew Bible.* Grand Rapids: Baker Academic,
2005. A volume of fresh translations of ancient texts that may illumine biblical texts.
Examples are organized by broad literary categories (e.g., Hymns, Prayers, Laments; Love
Poetry; Intermediary Texts; Omens and Prophecies; etc.). Editor's concluding observations
per category follow. Strong introduction with chronological charts, maps, and discussions
of ancient scribal culture and the nature of genres.

Dalley, S., ed. *Myths from Mesopotamia.* Oxford World Classics. New York; Oxford: Oxford
University Press, 1998. This is a collection of translations of the most important mythical
texts on topics of interest to Bible students (e.g., creation, flood, etc.).

Simpson, W. K. *The Literature of Ancient Egypt: An Anthology of Stories, Instructions, Stelae,
Autobiographies, and Poetry.* Translated by R. K. Ritner. 3rd ed. New Haven: Yale University
Press, 2003. The classic, comprehensive anthology of translation of important Egyptian writings.

Coogan, M. D. and M. S. Smith, ed. *Stories from Ancient Canaan.* Louisville: Westminster John
Knox, 2012. This handy paperback gives the general reader introductory background and the
translation of several important texts from Ugarit, the center of pre-Israelite Canaanite culture.
It offers a literary glimpse of the religion with which Israel's faith had to contend in Canaan.

*Hayes, C. B. *Hidden Riches: A Sourcebook for the Comparative Study of the Hebrew Bible and Ancient Near East.* Louisville: Westminster John Knox, 2014. Organized by canonical section genre (e.g., Pentateuch, Former/Latter Prophets, Writings), this volume by an evangelical not only surveys extrabiblical literary parallels but also introduces the comparative method and gives background on each parallel text. Its contents and clear style make it a valuable resource even for the general reader.

Hallo, W. and K. L Younger, Jr., eds. *Context of Scripture.* 4 vols. Leiden: Brill, 1997–2016. This masterful set presents translations by an international team of scholars of ancient texts of interest to Bible students, including ones recently discovered. It representative selection of texts, use of biblical cross references, and judicious commentary mark it as a standard reference work for this century's scholars and advanced students.

Pritchard, J. B. ed. *The Ancient Near East: An Anthology of Texts and Pictures* [*ANEA*]. Foreward by D. E. Fleming. Princeton: Princeton University Press, 2011. This anthology combines the two venerable volumes of texts [*ANET*] and pictures [*ANEP*] into a single book. Though the translations are somewhat dated, this single paperback volume still offers the general reader an enormous collection of ancient writings organized by culture (Mesopotamia, Egypt, etc.) and literary type (law, history, wisdom, etc.) and pictures of ancient sites and artifacts.

Beyerlin, W. ed. *Near Eastern Religious Texts Relating to the Old Testament.* OTL. Philadelphia: Westminster, 1978. This is the translation of a German original that focuses specifically on ancient religious texts that illumine the OT.

Chavalas, M. W. *Ancient Near East: Historical Sources in Translation.* Blackwell Sourcebooks in Ancient History. Malden, MA; Oxford: Blackwell Publishing, 2006. Fresh, accessible translations (many by evangelicals) of ancient historiographic texts. Organized as a semester-long supplemental text for students. Translators' prefaces to their translations add a wealth of background information. A good companion to Dalley's work on Mesopotamian myths and Simpson's on Egyptian literature.

Gould, G. P. et al., eds. *The Loeb Classical Library.* Founded by J. Loeb. Cambridge, MA: Harvard University Press; London: Heinemann. In more than 450 volumes these works furnish the standard original language (Greek or Latin) editions of major classical works with English translations on facing pages. They include classical Greek writers (e.g., Plato and Aristotle), ancient historians (e.g., Thucydides, Herodotus), Jewish writers (Philo and Josephus), and postbiblical Christian and secular writers (e.g., Augustine, Eusebius, Cicero, and Ovid).

Ancient World History and Near Eastern History

Hallo, W. W. and W. K. Simpson. *The Ancient Near East: A History.* 2nd ed. Fort Worth: Harcourt Brace College Publishers, 1998. This work offers an excellent history of the ancient world aimed at the general reader with a particular focus on Mesopotamia and Egypt.

Kuhrt, A. *The Ancient Near East: 3000–330 BC.* 2 vols. New York: Routledge, 1995. This marks a thorough, scholarly survey of the history of the biblical world by a British scholar. It has already become the standard resource for university ancient history courses and offers more detail than Hallo but less than *CAH* (see below).

Van de Mieroop, M. *A History of the Ancient Near East ca. 3000–323 BC.* 2nd ed. Malden, MA: Blackwell Publishing, 2007. This is a recent, popular historical summary for students by a distinguished professor at Columbia University, author of a recent history of ancient Egypt. Numerous, helpful chronological charts of ancient dynasties and regional maps. Draws connections between the larger history and Israel but not as many as Bible readers might like.

Snell, D. C., ed. *A Companion to the Ancient Near East*. Blackwell Companions to the Ancient World. Malden, MA: Blackwell Publishing, 2005. A well-illustrated, very accessible history, although more compact than Van de Mieroop but slightly longer than Podany (see below).

Podany, A. H. *The Ancient Near East: A Very Short Introduction*. Very Short Introductions Series. Oxford: Oxford University Press, 2014. A very readable history. Ably condenses the cream of recent scholarship into 148 pages with occasional photos, charts, maps, and quotes from ancient texts. Ideal for an undergraduate course.

Podany, A. H. and M. McGee, *The Ancient Near Eastern World*. The World in Ancient Times. Oxford: Oxford University Press, 2005. A well-written glimpse of people in the ancient world, both professional and ordinary (e.g., scribes, potters, school children, lawmakers, architects) who, among other things, invented the wheel, first wrote down law, and first adopted belief in a single god.

Nissen, H. J. *The Early History of the Ancient Near East, 9000–2000 BC*. Translated by E. Lutzeier. Chicago: University of Chicago Press, 1988. Though now dated, this book still ably surveys the historical period that saw the emergence of civilization in the ancient Near East. Since Abraham probably lived ca. 2000 BC, it portrays the larger historical landscape preceding that biblical figure.

Hornblower, S., A. Spawforth, and E. Eidinow, eds. *The Oxford Classical Dictionary*. 4th ed. Oxford: Oxford University Press, 2012. This dictionary provides a reliable window into the world of the classical period.

Edwards, I. E. S., et al., eds. *The Cambridge Ancient History* [*CAH*]. 3rd ed. 5 vols. (often in two or more parts) to date. Many volumes/parts of the 2nd ed. still in print but outdated. Cambridge: Cambridge University Press, 1970–. This represents, without challenge, the most comprehensive study of the political, economic, and social world out of which emerged the OT and NT.

Von Soden, W. *The Ancient Orient: An Introduction to the Study of the Ancient Near East*. Translated by D. G. Schley. Grand Rapids: Eerdmans, 1994. This volume by a front-rank Semitic specialist still has value as an introduction to the Ancient East, its history, peoples, institutions, and culture. The general reader will appreciate its broad overview.

Old Testament History

Shanks, H., ed. *Ancient Israel: From Abraham to the Roman Destruction of the Temple*. 3rd ed. Biblical Archaeology Society, 2012. Popular writing with each chapter written by one or two experts in the field.

*Long, V. P. *The Art of Biblical History*. Vol. 5 of *Foundations of Contemporary Interpretation*. Editor M. Silva. Grand Rapids: Zondervan, 1994. Seeks to show the need to balance historicity, literary art, and theology in understanding the history writing of the Old Testament.

*Bright, J. *A History of Israel*. 4th ed. Greatly revised with an introduction by W. P. Brown. Louisville: Westminster John Knox, 2000. This text systematically presents Israel's history according to the principles of the now oft-maligned Albright school. Highly praised, the book represents an outstanding accomplishment in history-writing. At the same time, some scholars disagree with its stance in several places.

Provan, I., V. P. Long, and T. Longman III. *A Biblical History of Israel*. 2nd ed. Louisville: Westminster John Knox, 2015. This marks the significantly revised and updated second edition of the first major history of Israel written from a moderate perspective to appear in English in two decades. Its authors, three leading evangelical scholars, respond directly to criticisms of its first edition and unapologetically reassert that the OT should be taken seriously as a historical document. Traces the history from 2000 to 400 BC. Maps and fourteen tables make useful references for students.

Coogan, M. D., ed. *The Oxford History of the Biblical World*. New York; Oxford: Oxford University Press, 1998. Each essay by a mainstream scholar treats a specific period of Israel's history.

Miller, J. M. and J. H. Hayes. *A History of Ancient Israel and Judah*. Philadelphia: Westminster, 1986. Here we find a portrait of Israelite history that departs significantly from that of Bright, Provan, Long, and Longman (above). Conservative readers may find themselves less at home with its treatment of the patriarchs and the conquest of Canaan than with those of the four scholars just named.

Dever, W. G. *What Did the Biblical Writers Know and When Did They Know It? What Archaeology Can Tell Us about the Reality of Ancient Israel*. Grand Rapids: Eerdmans, 2001. Polemical but useful survey and important critique of some of current biblical historiographic and postmodern interpretations. Also see Dever, W. G. *Who Were the Israelites, and Where Did They Come From?* Grand Rapids: Eerdmans, 2003. Provocative but debatable thesis that the original "Israelites" comprised Canaanites, pastoral nomads, and escaped slaves from Egypt.

Kaiser, W. C. and P. D. Wegner. *A History of Israel*. Rev. ed. Nashville: B&H, 2017. A recently updated, well-illustrated edition of a conservative evangelical account of ancient Israel's past. See also, Merrill, E. H. *Kingdom of Priests: A History of Old Testament Israel*. 2nd ed. Grand Rapids: Baker Academic, 2008.

Miller, P. D. *The Religion of Ancient Israel*. Louisville: Westminster John Knox, 2000. A study of many important topics of Canaanite and Israelite religion by a well-known scholar.

Albertz, R. *A History of Israelite Religion in the Old Testament Period*. 2 vols. OTL. Louisville: Westminster John Knox, 1994. This detailed, comprehensive study uses a classic higher-critical reconstruction of the history of Old Testament literature with interaction with recent discussions and discoveries to describe Israel's religion. Read critically, this oft-cited work is a must-read for the informed, advanced student.

Gerstenberger, E. S. *Israel in the Persian Period: The Fifth and Fourth Centuries BCE*. Translated by S. S. Schatzmann. Biblical Encyclopedia. Atlanta: Society of Biblical Literature, 2011. A survey for advanced students of an important era of Israel's history.

Smith, M. S. *The Origins of Biblical Monotheism: Israel's Polytheistic Background and the Ugaritic Texts*. New York; Oxford: Oxford University Press, 2001. This provocative book traces the late emergence of Israelite monotheism in the context of West-Semitic polytheism, especially that evident in Ugaritic texts, of which the author is a leading authority. It follows up Smith's earlier stimulating study: *The Early History of God*. San Francisco: Harper and Row, 1990. Both aim at advanced students and scholars.

De Moor, J. C. *The Rise of Yahwism. The Roots of Israelite Monotheism*. BETL 91. Peeters, 1990. Important evidence and arguments for Israel's worship of one God in Mosaic and later times.

Arnold, B. T. *Introduction to the Old Testament and the Origins of Monotheism*. Cambridge: Cambridge University Press, 2014. An evangelical author tracks the theological theme of monotheism through a survey of the Old Testament books.

Gnuse, R. K. *No Other Gods: Emergent Monotheism in Israel*. JSOTSup 241. Sheffield: Sheffield Academic Press, 1997. Assumes that Israel gradually emerged from the culture of Palestine and argues Israel's alleged monotheistic "revolution" was actually an "evolution" that still continues.

Long, V. P., ed. *Israel's Past in Present Research: Essays on Ancient Israelite Historiography*. SBTS 7. Winona Lake, IN: Eisenbrauns, 1999. A variety of experts contribute essays on the writing and interpretation of historical data relating to the major Old Testament periods and genres.

Millard, A. R., J. K. Hoffmeier, and D. W. Baker, eds. *Faith, Tradition, and History: Old Testament Historiography in Its Near Eastern Context*. Winona Lake, IN: Eisenbrauns, 1994. Important articles on the methods and interpretation of various Old Testament passages in the light of ancient Near Eastern comparisons.

Matthews, V. H. *A Brief History of Ancient Israel*. Louisville: Westminster John Knox, 2002. Accessible, concise, condensed history of Israel from the ancestral period through both the exilic and postexilic periods. Rich in comparative materials and visuals. Useful for both undergraduates and the scholars who teach them.

Hess, R. S. *Israel's Religions: An Archaeological and Biblical Survey*. Grand Rapids: Baker Academic; Nottingham, England: Apollos, 2007. A well-informed, balanced overview of Israel's religious life during the main periods of its history by a distinguished evangelical scholar. His critical assessment of the sources, both biblical and archaeological, which illumine the history is a genuine plus.

History of Intertestamental Times

Jagersma, H. *A History of Israel from Alexander the Great to Bar Kochba*. London: SCM, 1985; Philadelphia: Fortress, 1986. An excellent introduction to the main events and characters during this period from 331 BC to AD 135.

Nicklesburg, G. W. E. *Jewish Literature between The Bible and the Mishnah: A Historical and Literary Introduction*. Minneapolis: Fortress, 1981. The title says enough: an excellent treatment of valuable primary sources (in English translation).

Skarsaune, O. *In the Shadow of the Temple: Jewish Influences on Early Christianity*. Downers Grove: InterVarsity, 2002. A detailed introduction to early Judaism and its contribution to the New Testament and early Christianity.

Scott, J. J., Jr. *Customs and Controversies*. Grand Rapids: Baker, 1995. A clear, thorough, evangelical overview of the most pertinent historical and religious background to the New Testament from the intertestamental period with special focus on social customs and ideological controversies.

*VanderKam, J. C. *An Introduction to Early Judaism*. Grand Rapids: Eerdmans, 2001. An outstanding synthesis of scholarship on historical developments, non-canonical literature, and institutional developments of Judaism in the Second Temple period.

Grabbe, L. L. *An Introduction to Second Temple Judaism: History and Religion of the Jews in the Time of Nehemiah, the Maccabees, Hillel, and Jesus*. London: Bloomsbury T&T Clark, 2010. A lengthy and technical overview of the history of Judaism from the end of the Old Testament period to the end of the New Testament period.

Hengel, M. *Judaism and Hellenism: Studies in Their Encounter in Palestine during the Early Hellenistic Period*. 2 vols. Minneapolis: Fortress, 1974. These volumes provide the author's helpful insights into the interaction between Judaism and the Greek world that set the stage for Judaism as it existed in the first century AD. Hengel's updated summary is entitled *Jews, Greeks and Barbarians: Aspects of the Hellenization of Judaism in the Pre-Christian Period*. Minneapolis: Fortress, 1980.

Collins, J. J. and D. C. Harlow, eds. *Dictionary of Early Judaism*. Grand Rapids: Eerdmans, 2010. State-of the art articles arranged alphabetically are preceded by a series of longer thematic essays. They also composed *Early Judaism: A Comprehensive Overview*. Grand

Rapids: Eerdmans, 2012. This is a collection of fifteen essays by specialists on topics that provide in-depth glimpses of facets of early Judaism.

History of New Testament Times

*Witherington, B. *New Testament History: A Narrative Account.* Grand Rapids: Baker, 2001. This work begins with the events that brought about the close of the OT era and traces Jewish and secular history right through the age of the NT events. No other work matches this for readability and concise coverage over this essential terrain.

Jeffers, J. S. *The Greco-Roman World of the New Testament Era.* Downers Grove: InterVarsity, 1999. Topically arranged chapters introduce readers to major social and cultural practices and developments, particularly for the non-Jewish portion of early Christianity: e.g., government, social class and status, economics, the military, citizenship, slavery, and so on.

Barnett, P. *Jesus and the Rise of Early Christianity: A History of New Testament Times.* Downers Grove: InterVarsity, 1999. An excellent evangelical overview of relevant historical first-century background to the life of Jesus and the first seventy years of church history. Equally clearly places all of the NT writings and events referred to in them in chronological sequence.

*Ferguson, E. *Backgrounds of Early Christianity.* 3rd ed. Grand Rapids: Eerdmans, 2003. Well organized and providing extensive additional bibliographic resources all along the way, this text gives brief but highly useful explanations of numerous aspects of the religious, political, philosophical, and social world of the NT.

McKnight, S. and J. B. Modica, eds. *Jesus is Lord, Caesar is Not: Evaluating Empire in New Testament Studies.* Downers Grove: InterVarsity, 2013. Balanced set of essays presenting and evaluating the case for the imperial cult and other Roman religious claims as a key direct or indirect backdrop for all parts of the New Testament. This discipline of empire studies has become widespread in popularity in recent decades and also widely criticized.

*Wright, N. T. *The New Testament and the People of God.* Vol. 1 of Christian Origins and the Question of God. London: SPCK; Minneapolis: Fortress, 1992. A veritable tour de force that challenges many time-honored assumptions and "assured results." Describes the history, social make-up, worldview, beliefs, hope, and symbolic world of Palestinian Judaism within its larger Greco-Roman world. Then takes up the genesis of the first Christians within that matrix. Must reading.

Barrett, C. K., ed. *The New Testament Background: Writings from Ancient Greece and the Roman Empire That Illuminate Christian Origins.* Rev. ed. San Francisco: Harper & Row, 1995. This is a wide-ranging compilation of sources that provide helpful background for a variety of NT studies. A similar work, Cartlidge, D. R. and D. L. Dungan, *Documents for the Study of the Gospels.* Rev. and expanded ed. Minneapolis: Fortress, 1994, collects texts from pagan, Jewish, and Christian authors to portray form-critical categories employed in modern research on the Gospels. One may then compare other forms with those that appear in the Gospels (e.g., parables). See also Evans, C. A. *Noncanonical Writings and New Testament Interpretation.* Peabody, MA: Hendrickson, 1993.

Klauck, H.-J. *The Religious Context of Early Christianity: A Guide to Graeco-Roman Religions.* Minneapolis: Augsburg Fortress, 2003. A full guide to the religious environment into which Christianity emerged including domestic and civic religion, popular beliefs (e.g., divination, astrology, and "magic"), mystery cults, ruler and emperor cults, philosophy, and Gnosticism.

Koester, H. *Introduction to the New Testament: History, Culture and Religion of the Hellenistic Age.* 2nd ed. Berlin/New York: de Gruyter; Minneapolis: Fortress, 1995. This first volume provides abundant information about the history of the Greek and Roman worlds. The second volume, *History and Literature of Early Christianity*, 2nd ed. Fortress: 2000, rounds out the picture. In places Koester's pet theories skew his analyses, and he has received some criticism on that score.

Schürer, E. *The History of the Jewish People in the Age of Jesus Christ (175 BC–AD 135)*. Revised and edited by G. Vermes, F. Millar, M. Black, M. Goodman, and P. Vermes. 4 vols. London: Bloomsbury T&T Clark, 2014. This massive study discusses the entire NT period from both historical and sociological perspectives. It includes extensive bibliographies. The revision has toned down many of Schürer's opinions that did not accord with the best modern scholarship.

Safrai, S., M. Stern, et al., eds. *The Jewish People in the First Century*. Section One of *Compendia Rerum Iudaicarum ad Novum Testamentum*. 2 vols. Leiden: Brill, 1988. One part of a massive project written by Christian and Jewish scholars to study the relationship between Judaism and Christianity through the centuries, this section concentrates on the first century AD These scholarly articles are of uneven quality and must be used cautiously.

Customs, Culture, Society

Pre-Christian Era

*Matthews, V. H. *Manners and Customs in the Bible: An Illustrated Guide to Daily Life in Bible Times*. 3rd ed. Grand Rapids: Baker Academic, 2006. This third edition updates its excellent predecessor and still offers the general reader a reliable, illustrated guide to the daily world of both testaments. Photographs enhance its value. In addition see Matthews, V. H., *Hebrew Prophets and Their Social World*. 2nd ed. Grand Rapids: Baker Academic, 2012. It covers the prophets' worlds chronologically and seeks to show how their social contexts shaped their messages.

Yamauchi, E. and M. R. Wilson, eds., *Dictionary of Daily Life in Biblical & Post-Biblical Antiquity*. 4 vols. Peabody, MA: Hendrickson, 2014. Edited by two distinguished evangelical scholars. Provides background on the world of the Hebrew Bible and NT from 2000 BC to approximately AD 600. Some articles treat topics not usually treated in comparable works.

*Walton, J. H., V. H. Matthews, and M. W. Chavalas. *The InterVarsity Press Bible Background Commentary: Old Testament*. Downers Grove: InterVarsity, 2000. Takes a verse-by-verse approach to providing insight into historical and cultural background matters.

Hoerth, A., G. Mattingly, and E. Yamauchi, eds. *Peoples of the Old Testament World*. Grand Rapids: Baker, 1994. An evangelical update of Wiseman, D., ed. *Peoples of Old Testament Times*. Oxford: Clarendon, 1973. This volume contains chapters on the nations with which Israel interacted. Though the authors are all scholars of international renown, they speak to the general reader. Dated but still of value.

*King, P. J. and L. E. Stager. *Life in Biblical Israel*. Library of Ancient Israel. Louisville: Westminster John Knox, 2001. With color photos and drawings, this is the best discussion of how life was lived in biblical times.

Matthews, V. H. and D. C. Benjamin. *The Social World of Ancient Israel: 1250–587 BCE*. Grand Rapids: Baker Academic, 2011 [1993]. An accessible window into the prominent social institutions of the world of early Israel and the period of the monarchy—and how an understanding of these informs biblical interpretation. Treats politics, economics, diplomacy, law, and education.

Two books introduce readers to the culture of the ancient world: Bottero, J. et al., eds. *Everyday Life in Mesopotamia*. Baltimore: Johns Hopkins University Press, 2001; and Snell, D. C. *Life in the Ancient Near East 3100–322 BC*. New Haven: Yale University Press, 1998. Briefer accounts are also available more recently in the well-written, attractive volume by Snell, D. C. *Ancient Near East: The Basics*. Oxford; New York: Routledge, 2014; as well as in several chapters of Von Soden, W. *The Ancient Orient* (see above).

de Vaux, R. *Ancient Israel: Its Life and Institutions*. Edited by D. N. Freedman. Grand Rapids: Eerdmans, 1997 [1961].[18] A classic volume for the non-specialist surveys Israel's main social and religious institutions with a wide range of subtopics for understanding life in ancient Israel (e.g., nomadism, family structures, civil institutions, the military, and religion).

Aharoni, Y. *The Land of the Bible*. Rev. ed. Philadelphia: Westminster, 1979. From the pen of a well-known Israeli archaeologist, this volume offers extensive information about the geography of ancient Israel.

Sasson, J. M., ed. *Civilizations of the Ancient Near East*. 4 vols. New York: Scribner, 1995. This is the standard, in-depth reference work concerning the major cultural groups of the ancient Near East.

The Christian Era

Esler, P. F. *The First Christians in Their Social Worlds: Social-Scientific Approaches to New Testament Interpretation*. London/New York: Routledge, 1994. This is an extremely readable introduction to a sociological approach to the study of the NT.

Hanson, K. C. and D. E. Oakman. *Palestine in the Time of Jesus. Social Structures and Social Conflicts*. 2nd ed. Minneapolis: Augsburg Fortress, 2008. An overview of social analysis and the ancient Mediterranean worldview that systematically presents major domains and institutions of family, politics, and economy, always with reference to biblical texts.

Malina, B. J. *The New Testament World: Insights from Cultural Anthropology*. 3rd ed. Louisville: Westminster John Knox, 2001. Extremely insightful, this book provides windows of understanding into certain values, practices, and perspectives of inhabitants of the first-century world.

*Keener, C. S. *The InterVarsity Press Biblical Background Commentary: New Testament*. 2nd ed. Downers Grove: InterVarsity, 2014. Takes a verse-by-verse approach to providing insight into historical and cultural background matters. Very user-friendly.

Burge, G. M., L. H. Cohick, and G. L. Green. *The New Testament in Antiquity*. Grand Rapids: Zondervan, 2009. Like Keener above, proceeds sequentially through the New Testament but more selectively, commenting in more detail on major items of cultural background book by book.

*Meeks, W. *The First Urban Christians: The Social World of the Apostle Paul*. 2nd ed. New Haven: Yale University Press, 2003. This significant, ground-breaking work takes a sociological approach to analyzing the institutions and practices of the first century world and the early Christians' presence within it.

---

18. This text translates the French original, *Les institutions de l'Ancien Testament*, 2 vols., 2nd ed. (Paris: Cerf, 1961, 1967). This English translation employs notes, corrections, and additions provided by de Vaux, and is packaged in a one-volume paperback edition.

Finegan, J. *Myth & Mystery: An Introduction to the Pagan Religions of the Biblical World*. Grand Rapids: Baker, 1989. Finegan surveys the spectrum of religious beliefs in the world during the emergence of the NT.

Theissen, G. *Sociology of Early Palestinian Christianity*. Minneapolis: Fortress, 1978. A sociological analysis of the Jesus movement, this work attempts to describe the social attitudes and behaviors typical of people in Palestine at the time of Jesus' appearance.

*De Silva, D. A. *Honor, Patronage, Kinship and Purity: Unlocking New Testament Culture*. Downers Grove: InterVarsity, 2000. Clear, evangelical introduction to the most significant distinctive cultural values of the NT world (as reflected in the title) with numerous applications to how the information makes a difference for interpreting texts.

Magness, J. *Stone and Dung, Oil and Spit: Jewish Daily Life in the Time of Jesus*. Grand Rapids: Eerdmans, 2011. Drawing on recent archaeological discoveries, the NT, Josephus, and rabbinic teachings, this book illumines the fascinating details of daily life (e.g., dining customs, Sabbath observance, fasting, toilet habits, burial customs, etc.) in ancient Palestine.

Green, J. B. and L. M. McDonald, eds. *The World of the New Testament: Cultural, Social, and Historical Contexts*. Grand Rapids: Baker Academic, 2013. A treasure trove of essays by distinguished evangelical scholars. Resembles a mini-Bible dictionary on topics of importance for NT interpretation.

Archaeology

General

Stern, E., ed. *New Encyclopedia of Archeological Excavations in the Holy Land* [*NEAEHL*]. 5 vols. Jerusalem: Israel Exploration Society; Washington: Biblical Archaeology Society, 1993, 2008. A rich mine of articles on historical sites and artifacts. Its Supplemental Volume (vol. 5) is recent (2008). For Near Eastern sites, see Meyers, ed., *OEANE* (below).

Meyers, E. M. and M. A. Chancey. *Alexander to Constantine: Archaeology of the Land of the Bible*. AYBRL 3. New Haven: Yale University Press, 2014. Comprehensive, richly illustrated book. Focus on archaeological background of early Judaism and early Christianity. Of interest to scholars, students and general readers.

Magness, J. *The Archaeology of the Holy Land: From the Destruction of Solomon's Temple to the Muslim Conquest*. Cambridge: Cambridge University Press, 2012. A survey of archaeology over a long, important era.

Murphy O'Connor, J. *The Holy Land: An Oxford Archaeological Guide*. Oxford Archaeological Guides. Oxford: Oxford University Press, 2008. An updated version of a reliable, concise archaeological guide with brief overviews for general readers and Holy Land visitors.

Hoffmeier, J. K. *Archaeology of the Bible*. Oxford: Lion Hudson, 2008. A beautifully illustrated, well balanced survey of archaeological illumination on the OT and NT by a distinguished evangelical Egyptologist. Its main drawback is its brevity (just under 200 pages).

Master, D. M., ed. *The Oxford Encyclopedia of the Bible and Archaeology*. 2 vols. New York: Oxford University Press, 2013. An excellent, up-to-date reference work.

Pre-Christian Era

Mazar, A. *Archaeology of the Land of the Bible: 10,000–586 BCE*. AYBRL 1. New Haven; London: Yale University Press, 1990.

Stern, E. *Archaeology of the Land of the Bible: 732–332 BCE.* AYBRL 2. New Haven; London: Yale University Press, 1992–2008. For volume 3 in this series see below.

Meyers, E. M., ed. *The Oxford Encyclopedia of Archaeology in the Near East.* 5 vols. [*OEANE*]. Oxford: Oxford University Press, 1997. Organized by sites and topics, this set is the definitive reference work on archaeology of the ancient world. Best source for sites outside the Holy Land.

The Christian Era

See Meyers and Chancey above. Also Frend, W. H. C. *The Archaeology of Early Christianity: A History.* Philadelphia: Fortress, 1996.

Chronology

*Walton, J. H. *Chronological and Background Charts of the Old Testament.* Rev. ed. Grand Rapids: Zondervan, 1994. Offering attractive, nontechnical chronological tables that cover biblical and ancient Near Eastern history, this text also provides other background charts to help Bible readers sort out complex biblical topics (e.g., Israel's main sacrifices, etc.). The NT counterpart is House, H. W. *Chronological and Background Charts of the New Testament.* 2nd ed. Grand Rapids: Zondervan, 2009.

Hoehner, H. W. *Chronological Aspects of the Life of Christ.* Grand Rapids: Zondervan, 1978. This is a helpful guide to the variety of issues and questions of dating events in the Gospels, though it defends the minority view that Jesus was crucified in AD 33 rather than AD 30, as a majority of scholars believe.

Barnes, W. H. *Studies in the Chronology of the Divided Monarchy of Israel.* HSM 48. Atlanta: Scholars Press, 1991. A technical study coordinating biblical chronology with Assyrian dates. Argues that the reigns for several Israelite kings may be too long.

Thiele, E. R. *The Mysterious Numbers of the Hebrew Kings.* Rev. ed. Grand Rapids: Kregel, 1995. This work has useful chronological charts for the monarchy period of Israel and Judah and detailed discussions of the major chronological problems besetting biblical dating. Its technical discussions, however, make it more useful for the advanced student than for the general reader, especially incorporating the widely accepted corrections by McFall, L. "A Translation Guide to the Chronological Data in Kings and Chronicles." *BSac* 148 (1991): 3–45.

Hayes, J. H. and P. K. Hooker. *A New Chronology for the Kings of Israel and Judah.* Atlanta: John Knox, 1988. These authors set aside Thiele's solutions and propose an alternative chronology for the same period from a less conservative perspective.

*Finegan, J. *Handbook of Biblical Chronology: Principles of Time Reckoning in the Ancient World and Problems of Chronology in the Bible.* Rev. ed. Peabody, MA: Hendrickson, 1998. The work details both principles for determining chronology in biblical studies as well as attempted solutions to specific problems of dating. It does a better job with the NT than with the OT.

*Bruce, F. F. *Paul: Apostle of the Heart Set Free.* Grand Rapids: Eerdmans, 1977. The product of many years of research and teaching, Bruce presents the best "life of Paul" (what puts it in this category) along with a wise clarification of many Pauline issues. For chronology, see also Riesner, R. *Paul's Early Period: Chronology, Mission Strategy, Theology.* Grand Rapids: Eerdmans, 1997.

Galil, G. *The Chronology of the Kings of Israel and Judah.* Leiden/New York: Brill, 1996. In this scholarly book, an Israeli scholar proposes a viable, alternative system to that of Thiele, explaining the few inconsistencies as due to the biblical author's sources.

Introductions and Surveys

These works provide information on a variety of background issues—authorship, recipients, dating, provenance, purpose, and integrity. They collect in single volumes the essential data to begin the study of a biblical book. The wise student will consult several, along with appropriate commentaries or other sources, to secure a balanced perspective, especially where several options exist for issues of interpretation. Some of these go on to survey the contents of the books.

Old Testament

Hill, A. E. and J. H. Walton. *A Survey of the Old Testament*. 2nd ed. Grand Rapids: Zondervan, 2001. This college-level survey of the OT emphasizes its content, background, and literary nature. Its perspective is somewhat more conservative than the following volume.

Arnold, B. T. and B. E. Beyer. *Encountering the Old Testament: A Christian Survey*, 3rd ed. Encountering Biblical Studies. Grand Rapids: Baker, 2015. An excellent survey of the OT aimed at the beginning student and enriched by its online additional resources.

Baker, D. W. and B. T. Arnold, eds. *The Face of Old Testament Studies: A Survey of Contemporary Approaches*. Grand Rapids: Baker, 2004. An important work surveying the academic field of Old Testament studies written and edited by evangelicals.

*Dillard, R. and T. Longman, III. *An Introduction to the Old Testament*. 2nd ed. Grand Rapids: Zondervan, 2006. A helpful, up-to-date evangelical contribution. Longman finished the project after Dillard's death. It supplies an evangelical introduction with responses to literary criticism.

*LaSor, W., F. Bush, and D. A. Hubbard. *Old Testament Survey*. 2nd ed. Grand Rapids: Eerdmans, 1996. Another outstanding introduction produced by evangelicals, this superb text treats issues of OT authority, revelation and inspiration, canon, and the formation of the OT. It also provides specific introductions and surveys of all the OT books as well as concluding background articles.

Matthews, V. H. and J. C. Moyer, *The Old Testament: Text and Context*. 3rd ed. Grand Rapids: Baker Academic, 2012. This student-oriented, appealing textbook sets the OT books against their historical background including the larger world of the ancient Near East. The authors employ the recent findings of OT scholars and considers the insights of archaeologists. The book uses charts, illustrations, and maps to excellent advantage. It uniquely orders Israel's books within the corresponding era of Israel's narrative story but sometimes rearranges their order by genre.

Arnold, B. T. *Introduction to the Old Testament*. New York; Cambridge: Cambridge University Press, 2014. Distinguished evangelical OT scholar. Besides book-by-book survey, traces the theme of monotheism through the OT.

Childs, B. S. *Introduction to the Old Testament as Scripture*. Philadelphia: Fortress, 1979. A very influential general introduction to the Bible that is still much discussed and much misunderstood. Childs here advocates canonical criticism, whereby books of the Bible and indeed the whole Bible must be interpreted in the form in which they are accepted by Jews and Christians: as canonical (i.e., inspired and authoritative works).

Birch, B. C., W. Brueggemann, T. E. Fretheim, and D. L. Petersen. *A Theological Introduction to the Old Testament*. 2nd ed. Nashville: Abingdon, 2005. Mainline scholars writing from the perspective of canonical criticism.

Coogan, M. D. *The Old Testament: A Historical and Literary Introduction to the Hebrew Scriptures*. 3rd ed. Oxford: Oxford University Press, 2013. Well-written, attractive volume by a well-known scholar. Lives up to its title. Balanced, mainline perspective.

Gottwald, N. K. *The Hebrew Bible: A Socio-Literary Introduction*. Philadelphia: Fortress, 1985, 2002. This volume's idiosyncratic sociological approach by a mainstream scholar gives the advanced reader, reading critically, a fresh angle from which to view OT books and Israel as a society. A CD-ROM with charts and aids accompanies its newest (2002) printing.

Hess, R. S. *The Old Testament: A Historical, Theological, and Critical Introduction*. Grand Rapids: Baker, 2016. A brand-new, major work by a leading evangelical scholar and our colleague. Long in the making, it has the potential of becoming a standard in the field.

Hubbard, R. L., Jr. and J. A. Dearman, *Introduction to the Old Testament*. Grand Rapids: Eerdmans, forthcoming. Well-illustrated introduction book-by-book. Aims to prepare readers to actually read the OT itself. Provides reflection questions for each book and sidebars and excursus to supply helpful background. Good bibliographies for each book.

We also must mention the fine bibliography on this topic: Hostetter, E. C. *Old Testament Introduction*. Institute for Biblical Research Bibliography. Grand Rapids: Baker, 1995.

New Testament

Witherington, B., III. *Invitation to the New Testament: First Things*. Oxford: Oxford University Press, 2012. Evangelical, up-to-date, and the easiest read. A little idiosyncratic in places in terms of what is excluded, included, or discussed in detail.

Elwell, W. A. and R. W. Yarbrough. *Encountering the New Testament: A Historical and Theological Survey*. 3rd ed. Grand Rapids: Baker, 2013; and Elwell and Yarbrough, *Readings from the First-Century World* [with CD-ROM]. Grand Rapids: Baker, 1998. The most user-friendly college freshman-level introduction. Staunchly conservative throughout.

*Powell, M. A. *Introducing the New Testament: A Historical, Literary, and Theological Survey*. Grand Rapids: Baker, 2009. Not overly detailed. Unique in that conservative and liberal positions are given equal time and explanation and the author doesn't argue for either side.

Gundry, R. *A Survey of the New Testament*. 5th ed. Grand Rapids: Zondervan, 2012. This volume includes both brief treatments of introduction as well as a survey of the contents of the NT books. Best basic level survey in terms of pure content. Its fifth edition proves its worth.

Wenham, D. and S. Walton. *Exploring the New Testament*. Vol. 1: *A Guide to the Gospels & Acts*; Marshall, I. H., S. Travis, and I. Paul. Vol. 2: *A Guide to the Epistles and Revelation*. 2nd ed. Nottingham and Downers Grove: InterVarsity, 2011. A British counterpart to Gundry in level and purpose.

Anderson, P. N. *From Crisis to Christ: A Contextual Introduction to the New Testament*. Nashville: Abingdon, 2014. Broadly evangelical publisher addressing mainline Protestant audience with special emphasis on the theological contexts that gave rise to each of the New Testament books. Strongest on the Gospels and Acts.

Carson, D. A. and D. J. Moo. *An Introduction to the New Testament*. Grand Rapids: Zondervan, 2005. This work places primary focus on the background issues of the NT books such as authorship, date, sources, purpose, destination, etc. The authors include brief outlines of each book plus brief accounts of recent studies on and the theological significance of each NT document. The bibliographies are particularly helpful. A revision is in progress.

*deSilva, D. A. *An Introduction to the New Testament: Context, Methods and Ministry Formation*. Downers Grove: InterVarsity, 2004. Covers all the expected topics but with bonus sidebars and sections on various interpretive methods in conjunction with books of the Bible that well illustrate them and reflections on spiritual formation deriving from each book as well.

Köstenberger, A. J., L. S. Kellum, and C. L. Quarles. *The Cradle, The Cross, and the Crown: An Introduction to the New Testament.* Nashville: B&H, 2009. Key Southern Baptist work, thoroughly conservative, very thorough and readable.

*Hagner, D. A. *The New Testament: A Theological and Historical Introduction.* Grand Rapids: Baker, 2012. Mature reflection of a veteran and judicious scholar. Broadly evangelical with acceptance of pseudonymity in places. Extraordinarily detailed and helpful bibliographies.

Boring, M. E. *An Introduction to the New Testament: History, Literature, Theology.* Louisville: Westminster John Knox, 2012. The most thorough of several recent liberal introductions and possibly the most likely of them to supersede Brown (see below).

*Brown, R. E. *An Introduction to the New Testament.* N.Y.: Doubleday, 1997. The non-evangelical standard that has stood the test of (recent) time. Brown is actually quite centrist across the whole theological spectrum and acknowledges views to both his left and right.

The New Testament Use of the Old Testament

Students will find this a hotly debated field with abundant articles and essays that present the various perspectives on the discussion—some of which we included in our discussions above. As well, students should consult bibliographic sources (in the following) for additional entries. The following is a list of helpful books.

*Beale, G. K. *Handbook on the New Testament Use of the Old Testament: Exegesis and Interpretation.* Grand Rapids: Baker, 2012. Well organized, clear introductory survey of all the major categories with illustrations. Based in part on Carson and Beale below. Includes a very extensive bibliography.

Longenecker, R. N. *Biblical Exegesis in the Apostolic Period.* 2nd ed. Grand Rapids: Eerdmans, 1999. This work covers not only Jewish hermeneutical methods but also discusses how the various writers of the NT may or may not have employed such tactics themselves.

Carson, D. A. and H. G. M. Williamson, eds. *It Is Written: Scripture Citing Scripture.* Cambridge: Cambridge University Press, 1988. This volume is actually a wide-ranging collection of essays on various aspects of the topic (esp. pp. 191–336) including each major NT author's distinctive use of Scripture.

*Carson, D. A. and G. K. Beale, eds. *Commentary on the Use of the Old Testament in the New.* Grand Rapids: Baker, 2007. Has quickly become the standard resource work in this discipline, commenting book-by-book on every quotation of the OT in the NT—and not a few allusions and echoes as well. Provides original contexts in the OT, how the NT is using the OT and, at times, history of other Jewish uses of the same texts. Uniformly evangelical.

Ellis, E. E. *Paul's Use of the Old Testament.* Grand Rapids: Eerdmans, 1957; Grand Rapids: Baker, 1981. Still an excellent overview of the different uses by Paul, with special attention to some of the more controversial uses. Particularly helpful in surveying Jewish methods of interpretation at the time of the writing of the NT.

France, R. T. *Jesus and the Old Testament.* London: Tyndale; Downers Grove: InterVarsity, 1971; Vancouver: Regent College, 1992. France investigates the various ways in which Jesus used the OT as recorded in the Gospels—how those uses agree with the LXX or the Hebrew text, examples of typology uses, predictive materials, and finally the influences that Jesus' may have had on others' uses.

Biblical Theology

Before listing books for each testament, we mention several reference works that span the testaments:

Alexander, T. D. and B. S. Rosner, eds. *New Dictionary of Biblical Theology*. Leicester and Downers Grove: InterVarsity, 2000. Organized topically, each article surveys its theological subject through both testaments. An American equivalent, though perhaps with not quite as uniformly high standards, is Elwell, W. A., ed. *Evangelical Dictionary of Biblical Theology*. Grand Rapids: Baker, 1996.

Mead, J. K. *Biblical Theology: Issues, Methods, and Themes*. Louisville: Westminster John Knox, 2007. A general introduction to the subject not tied to either testament.

Leading evangelical scholars treat this topic's past and future in Hafemann, S. J. ed. *Biblical Theology: Retrospect and Prospect*. Downers Grove: InterVarsity; Leicester: Apollos, 2002. In a very illuminating treatment, two scholars discuss the various ways the discipline of biblical theology is understood among its practitioners: Klink, III, E. W. and D. R. Lockett. *Understanding Biblical Theology. A Comparison of Theory and Practice*. Grand Rapids: Zondervan, 2012.

Old Testament

Martens, E. A., ed. *Old Testament Theology*. Bibliographies No. 13. Grand Rapids: Baker, 1997. Though dated, its survey of more than five hundred of the most important works, listed by subject is still useful.

Routledge, R. *Old Testament Theology: A Thematic Approach*. Downers Grove: IVP Academic, 2008. A survey of the main theological themes of the OT. Topical format. Well-written volume. An excellent overview of the subject for the general reader.

*Kaiser, Jr., W. C. *The Promise-Plan of God: A Biblical Theology of the Old and New Testaments*. Grand Rapids: Zondervan, 2008. Based on his earlier *Toward an Old Testament Theology*. Grand Rapids: Zondervan, 1991. A survey of OT theology centered on the theme of God's promise. Develops that theme chronologically through the OT and (more briefly) into the NT.

*House, P. R. *Old Testament Theology*. Downers Grove: InterVarsity, 1998. A narrative approach designed for college and seminary students, this work outlines God's nature and acts in each book of the OT.

*Goldingay, J. *Old Testament Theology*. 3 vols. Downers Grove: InterVarsity, 2003. An engaging, very readable, in-depth treatment of the subject by a distinguished evangelical scholar. Full of insightful exegesis on a host of texts and themes. Highly recommended.

Moberly, R. W. L., *Old Testament Theology: Reading the Hebrew Bible as Christian Scripture*. Grand Rapids: Baker Academic, 2013. Insightful, engaging volume by an evangelical. Treats select biblical texts thought to be representative of the OT's theology. Focus on proper hermeneutics.

*Waltke, B. K. (with C. Yu). *An Old Testament Theology: An Exegetical, Canonical, and Thematic Approach*. Grand Rapids: Zondervan, 2007. The flower of decades of reflection by a distinguished evangelical. Traces the kingdom of God as the OT's center into the NT. Rich content, narrative style, chronological organization. A treasury of thoughtful theological exegesis.

Anderson, B. W. *Contours of Old Testament Theology*. Minneapolis: Fortress, 1999. Themes of the holiness of God, covenants, torah/wisdom, and prophecy/apocalyptic are interwoven in this synthesis by an influential mainline scholar.

Brueggemann, W. *Old Testament Theology: An Introduction*. Library of Biblical Theology. Nashville: Abingdon Press, 2008. Distinguished, popular, mainline author. Insightful, engaging, relevant, topically organized content. Idiosyncratic in places. Cf. his major work below.

Preuss, H. D. *Old Testament Theology*. OTL. 2 vols. Louisville: Westminster John Knox, 1995–6. Following the tradition of classic OT theologies, Preuss sees God's acts of election and covenant and the subsequent human responses to God as the central and unifying theme of Old Testament theology.

Sailhamer, J. H. *Introduction to Old Testament Theology: A Canonical Approach*. Grand Rapids: Zondervan, 1995. An evangelical, structured study on how to do OT theology.

Childs, B. S. *Old Testament Theology in a Canonical Context*. Minneapolis: Fortress, 1986. Classic on canon with a sensitivity to the NT.

Birch, B. C., W. Brueggemann, T. E. Fretheim, and D. L. Petersen. *A Theological Introduction to the Old Testament*. Nashville: Abingdon, 1999. Written by leading mainstream scholars, this book treats the OT's main theological themes in an order approximating the canon's organization.

*Barr, James. *The Concept of Biblical Theology: An Old Testament Perspective*. London: SCM, 1999. The most important survey of OT theologies at the end of the twentieth century, although occasionally confrontational in its perspective.

Brueggemann, W. *Theology of the Old Testament: Testimony, Dispute, Advocacy*. Minneapolis: Fortress, 1997. A provocative approach that structures the discussion around the metaphor and imagery of the courtroom.

Gerstenberger, E., *Theologies in the Old Testament*. Translated by John Bowden. Minneapolis: Fortress, 2002. Uniquely features voices on theological topics in social settings (e.g., the family and clan, the village, the tribal group, and the kingdom). Surveys the range of Israelite views on God. Ecumenical perspective.

Eichrodt, W. *Theology of the Old Testament*. 2 vols. London: SCM, 1961; Louisville: Westminster John Knox, 1967. A classic OT theology topically-organized around the concept of covenant. Dated but still full of exegetical and theological insight.

Von Rad, G. *Old Testament Theology*. 2 vols. Edinburgh/London: Oliver and Boyd; New York: Harper & Row, 1962, 1965. Vol. 2 has been reissued, Louisville: Westminster John Knox, 2001, with an introduction by W. Brueggemann. Another classic that elucidates the specific theologies of individual biblical writers or of OT books. Still worth consulting for insightful exegesis and theology.

At present, OT theology is the subject of great scholarly debate on many difficult issues. Though now dated, Hasel, G. *Old Testament Theology: Basic Issues in the Current Debate*. 4th ed. Grand Rapids: Eerdmans, 1995, still offers the advanced student an overview of the complex discussion as well as his own attractive solution.

Ollenberger, B. C., ed. *The Flowering of Old Testament Theology: Flowering and Future*. Sources for Biblical and Theological Study 1. Winona Lake, IN: Eisenbrauns, 2004. This book is a reader of important essays on OT theology during the seminal period of 1930–1990.

New Testament

Caird, G. B. (completed and ed. by L. D. Hurst). *New Testament Theology.* Oxford: Clarendon, 1995. Imagines the apostolic authors all participating at a round-table theological discussion and highlights the distinctives each brings to the table. Painstakingly compiled by one of Caird's former doctoral students after his untimely death.

*Ladd, G. E. *A Theology of the New Testament.* Grand Rapids: Eerdmans, 1974. Rev. ed. by D. A. Hagner, 1993. Ladd compiles the theology of the various sections or writers in the NT as they occur canonically in the NT. So, for example, part I treats the "Synoptic Gospels" with individual chapters covering all the theologically significant issues in the Synoptics. Part II follows with "The Fourth Gospel" with its key issues. The remaining parts of the book cover "The Primitive Church," "Paul," "The General Epistles," and "The Apocalypse." Ladd's exceptional volume offers the student a trustworthy guide through the mazes of intricate issues.

*Marshall, I. H. *New Testament Theology: Many Witnesses, One Gospel.* Downers Grove: InterVarsity, 2004. Combines a sequential overview of the theological contents of each book, section by section through that book, with a thematic summary and synthesis of the major themes of each book and each group of NT books. Defends mission as the integrating theme of the testament. Extremely carefully researched and presented. Represents a Wesleyan perspective.

Schreiner, T. R. *New Testament Theology: Magnifying God in Christ.* Grand Rapids: Baker, 2008. Treats the NT topically in terms of its major integrating themes and then discusses each theme in its specific form book-by-book or section by section through the NT. Stresses the glory of God which Christ displays as the unifying theme. Represents a Reformed perspective.

*Schnelle, U. *Theology of the New Testament.* Grand Rapids: Baker, 2009. Classic German developmental or evolutionary model of NT theology but with ample amounts attributable to Jesus at the beginning of the entire process. Will probably become the non-evangelical standard for some time.

Strecker, G. *Theology of the New Testament.* Louisville: Westminster John Knox, 2000. Beginning with the theology of Paul and adopting history-of-religions presuppositions, this book proceeds through a discussion of Jesus, the message of the kingdom of God, the composition and contributions of the Gospels, the Deuteropaulines, and ends with the theology of the Catholic Epistles. Schnelle and Strecker comprise the standard liberal approaches to NT theology.

*Beale, G. K. *A New Testament Biblical Theology: The Unfolding of the Old Testament in the New.* Grand Rapids: Baker, 2011. The most detailed work of current vintage, arranged topically, thoroughly evangelical, and showing countless links between the testaments, in defense of "new creation" as the unifying theme of the NT.

*Four other monumental works merit special mention though they do not cover the entire NT in their scope: Dunn, J. D. G. *The Theology of Paul the Apostle.* Grand Rapids: Eerdmans, 1998; Dunn, J. D. G. *Jesus Remembered.* Grand Rapids: Eerdmans, 2003; Wright, N. T. *Jesus and the Victory of God.* London: SPCK; Minneapolis: Fortress, 1996; and Wright, N. T. *Paul and the Faithfulness of God.* 2 vols. London: SPCK; Minneapolis: Fortress, 2013. None of these should be missed. Both writers are extremely thorough, creative, and provocative, and represent various dimensions of the so-called new perspective on first-century Judaism and Paul.

Literary Criticism

Dyck, E., ed. *The Act of Bible Reading: A Multidisciplinary Approach to Biblical Interpretation*. Downers Grove: InterVarsity, 1996. Supplying good examples of literary readings, this anthology of different authors introduces a handful of key methods of the most introductory level of any item on this list.

*Ryken, L. *Words of Delight: A Literary Introduction to the Bible*. 2nd ed. Grand Rapids: Baker, 1993. This is one of the best introductions to the Bible from a literary perspective.[19] This edition, which combines two earlier volumes, divides the OT into three sections: biblical narrative, biblical poetry, and other literary forms in the Bible, and includes a helpful glossary of literary terms at the end. It proceeds to cover specific literary features found in the NT.

Bailey, J. L. and L. D. Vander Brock. *Literary Forms in the New Testament*. Louisville: Westminster John Knox, 1992. The work surveys the multiple literary features of the NT in three sections: the Pauline tradition, the Gospels and Acts, and other NT writings. This work not only describes the various forms but goes on to show the value of understanding them for interpretation. It provides good examples and bibliographies for further study.

Resseguie, J. L. *Narrative Criticism of the New Testament: An Introduction*. Grand Rapids: Baker, 2005. Clear, readable, introduction to plot, character, setting, rhetoric, point of view, and other major narrative devices with abundant illustrations from the New Testament.

Gabel, J. B., et al. *The Bible as Literature. An Introduction*. 5th ed. New York; Oxford: Oxford University Press, 2005. Approaches the Bible from a literary/historical perspective seeking to show how its forms and the strategies the biblical authors employ convey messages from and to real people.

Ryken, L. and T. Longman III, eds. *A Complete Literary Guide to the Bible*. Grand Rapids: Zondervan, 1993. An evangelical counterpart to Alter and Kermode below.

*Alter, R. *The Art of Biblical Narrative*. Rev. ed. New York: Basic Books, 2011; and Alter, R. *The Art of Biblical Poetry*. Rev. ed. New York: Basic Books, 2011. These two extremely popular books explain the literary dimensions of biblical narrative art and poetry. Both have become standard introductions to their respective subjects and both are available in paperback. They represent the perspectives of modern literary criticism.

Walsh, J. T. *Old Testament Narrative: A Guide to Interpretation*. Louisville: Westminster John Knox, 2009. A good, standard introduction to the Bible's important literary features (plot, characterization, setting, pace, point of view, and patterns of repetition). One appealing unique feature: an appendix with practical examples of narrative interpretation.

Amit, Y. *Reading Biblical Narratives: Literary Criticism and the Hebrew Bible*. Translated by Y. Lotan. Minneapolis: Fortress Press, 2001. This Israeli scholar introduces the literary devices and strategies in biblical narratives. She uniquely notes the narrative use of catchwords and dialogue.

Bar Efrat, S. *Narrative Art in the Bible*. Sheffield: Sheffield Academic Press, 1989. An Israeli scholar discusses the specific techniques of biblical narrative and illustrates his points with numerous biblical examples.

Gillingham, S. E. *The Poems and Psalms of the Hebrew Bible*. Oxford Bible Series. Oxford: Oxford University Press, 1994. This is the best introduction to Hebrew poetry for students. Its strengths are its many examples, its fresh insights, and its incorporation of NT examples.

---

19. See also the earlier work, L. Ryken: *How to Read the Bible as Literature* (Grand Rapids: Zondervan, 1984).

*Petersen, D. L. and K. H. Richards. *Interpreting Hebrew Poetry*. GBS. Minneapolis: Fortress, 1994. In touch with the best scholarship on biblical poetry, it provides the beginning student with an up-to-date introduction to the subject with many biblical illustrations.

Alter, R. and F. Kermode, eds. *The Literary Guide to the Bible*. Cambridge, MA: Harvard University Press, 1990. In this volume specialists discuss the literary aspects of each book of the Bible. The result is a valuable reference book that presents the best fruits of a modern literary critical approach as practiced by internationally known scholars from diverse backgrounds.

Sternberg, M. *The Poetics of Biblical Narrative*. Bloomington: Indiana University Press, 1987. The definitive technical book on OT narrative, this work makes available for a wide audience a series of influential journal articles by a noted Israeli scholar, but its highly technical discussions will probably scare away all but the most advanced students. For a very useful counterpoint see Gunn, D. M. and D. N. Fewell. *Narrative in the Hebrew Bible*. The Oxford Bible Series. Oxford University Press, 1993.

Watson, W. G. E. *Classical Hebrew Poetry*. Sheffield: JSOT, 1984. The definitive, thorough discussion of its subject. Compares OT poetry to its ancient Near Eastern counterparts. Of interest mainly to the advanced student, although with numerous examples and clear writing not technical sounding. It is now out of print. See also Watson, W. G. E. *Traditional Techniques in Classical Hebrew Verse*. JSOTSup 170. Sheffield: Sheffield Academic Press, 1994. A collection of Watson's articles and corrections to his original volume. Offers access to his mastery of Hebrew poetry.

Guides to Studying the Bible: Methods and Principles of Exegesis

Augsburg Fortress (Minneapolis) has a series entitled, Guides to Biblical Scholarship (1969–2002). Edited by D. O. Via, Jr., and spanning both testaments, the series seeks to explain to the nonspecialist the most common interpretive methods of modern biblical scholars. Some provide genuine and helpful insights; others have met dubious reactions from readers, for the methods are not uniformly sanctioned by scholars. Volumes that treat generally accepted methods (e.g., form, redaction, narrative, and textual criticism, NT theology, etc.) provide useful instructions from the perspective of mainstream critical scholarship. There is also a volume, *Postmodern Biblical Criticism* by A. K. Adam, 1995; and another *Psychological Biblical Criticism* by D. A. Kille, 2000. For a comprehensive overview of the issues surrounding biblical interpretation see Steven L. McKenzie, editor in chief. *The Oxford Encyclopedia of Biblical Interpretation*, 2 Volumes. Oxford/New York: Oxford University Press, 2013.

Old Testament

*Stuart, D. K. *Old Testament Exegesis*. 4th ed. Louisville: Westminster John Knox, 2009. This volume explains to the beginning seminary student how to exegete an OT passage. It also offers an excellent bibliography. Sadly, many busy pastors will probably find Stuart's procedures too lengthy, though there is no better book on the subject.

*Broyles, C. C., ed. *Interpreting the Old Testament. A Guide for Exegesis*. Grand Rapids: Baker, 2001. Evangelical scholars discuss methods of OT exegesis and criticism for interpreting the text.

Gorman, M. J. *The Elements of Biblical Exegesis: A Basic Guide for Ministers and Students*. Peabody, MA: Hendrickson, 2001. Presents the essential elements of the exegetical method in a succinct and incisive way. Designed for students, teachers, pastors, and others wishing to think and write about the Bible carefully, this brief hands-on guide incorporates insights from the field of biblical interpretation into its straightforward approach to the complex task of exegesis. Gives examples of exegesis papers that students might write in an exegesis course.

Hayes, J. H. and C. R. Holladay. *Biblical Exegesis. A Beginner's Handbook*. 3rd ed. Louisville: Westminster John Knox, 2007. An explanation of the process of exegesis from the perspective of mainline, critical scholars.

Steck, O. H. *Old Testament Exegesis: A Guide to the Methodology*. 2nd ed. Atlanta: Scholars Press, 1995. Translated from German by J. D. Nogalski, the book makes available to English readers a well-respected European exegetical guide. Its thorough approach makes it mainly useful to advanced students.

New Testament
Methods

*Fee, G. D. and D. K. Stuart. *How to Read the Bible for All Its Worth: A Guide to Understanding the Bible*. 4th ed. Grand Rapids: Zondervan, 2014. This is a time-tested, popular-level guide to biblical interpretation with particular emphasis on genres.

Fee, G. D. and D. K. Stuart. *How to Read the Bible Book by Book*. Grand Rapids: Zondervan, 2002. Designed to integrate the Bible as a whole; and even when the whole is narrowed to individual biblical books, this popular volume helps readers to see how each book fits into the grand story of the Bible.

Black, D. A. and D. S. Dockery, eds. *Interpreting the New Testament*. Nashville: Broadman & Holman, 2001. In this volume many scholars write chapters explaining the various dimensions of the interpretation of the NT. The authors all subscribe to a conservative view of Scripture and have produced essays especially useful for serious students.

*Green, J. B., ed. *Hearing the New Testament: Strategies for Interpretation*. 2nd ed. Grand Rapids: Eerdmans, 2010. Each chapter introduces a particular approach to NT interpretation and demonstrates how that approach can be used fruitfully by students and pastors. Five texts from different parts of the NT are used as sample texts throughout the book in order to facilitate understanding of the differences among the interpretive strategies.

Exegesis

Under the rubric, "Guides to New Testament Exegesis," ed., S. McKnight (Grand Rapids: Baker) see: McKnight, S. *Interpreting the Synoptic Gospels*, 1988; McKnight, S., ed. *Introducing New Testament Interpretation*, 1990; Schreiner, T. K. *Interpreting the Pauline Epistles*. 2nd ed., 2011; Burge, G. M. *Interpreting the Gospel of John*. 2nd ed. 2013; Liefeld, W. L. *Interpreting the Book of Acts*, 1995; Trotter, A. H. *Interpreting the Epistle to the Hebrews*, 1997; and Michaels, J. R. *Interpreting the Book of Revelation*, 1998. All are highly useful.

*Blomberg, C. L. with J. F. Markley, *Handbook of New Testament Exegesis*. Grand Rapids: Baker, 2010. A less formulaic equivalent to Fee below with more examples from actual texts. Discusses the eight key areas of historical-cultural background, literary context, word studies, grammar, interpretive problems, outline, theology, and application.

Fee, G. D. *New Testament Exegesis: A Handbook for Students and Pastors*. 3rd ed. Louisville: Westminster John Knox, 2002. Fee guides students through a process of doing Greek exegesis in various kinds of NT literature. He presents a systematic approach to exegesis for sermon preparation and includes helpful bibliographies. This is a practical guide, though some consider it unrealistic for the busy pastor.

Erickson, R. J. *A Beginner's Guide to New Testament Exegesis: Taking the Fear out of Critical Method*. Downers Grove: InterVarsity, 2005. A cross between Fee and Stuart and Blomberg with Markley (both above). Some exegetical method, some focus on genre. Lots of biblical illustrations.

Periodicals and Journals

Bibliography and Abstracts

These tools enable interpreters to locate items specific to questions or issues under investigation. Indexes in these tools further enable the interpreter to locate articles (and books) on specific biblical texts. Many such tools exist; we list only three we consider to have the most ongoing usefulness.

Old Testament Abstracts [*OTA*] is published thrice yearly by the Catholic Biblical Association of America (Washington, DC). First appearing in February 1978, it provides abstracts of periodical articles and notices of recently published books on the full range of issues relevant to the study of the OT. The entire run of *OTA* for the years 1978–2000 (Vols. 1–23) is now available on CD-ROM from the American Theological Library Association.

New Testament Abstracts [*NTA*] is also published thrice yearly by Weston School of Theology, Cambridge, MA. First appearing in 1956, it abstracts all periodical literature on topics relevant to the study of the NT. Abstracts are written in English, though reviewers abstract important articles written in all modern languages. Each issue closes with brief comments on major books recently published in NT studies. One can hardly overestimate the value of *NTA* for researching issues, topics, and texts concerning the NT.

The third is actually a collection of electronic resources. Again we must limit to a few; no doubt others will prove useful in specific areas of research. *OCLCFirstSearch* is a comprehensive and complete online reference service with a rich collection of databases. It supports research in a wide range of subject areas with well-known bibliographic and full-text databases in addition to ready-reference tools such as directories, almanacs, and encyclopedias. Databases include: *ATLA Religion Index One: Periodicals* (1975–) and *Religion Index Two: Multi-Author Works* (1960–), Evanston, IL: American Theological Library Association; PsycINFO; and ERIC; among others. These serve as excellent sources for resources in biblical studies as well as wider topics in religion. See your local library for print and online access. Other excellent online resources include:

The *Christian Periodical Index* produced by the Association of Christian Librarians: it indexes more than one-hundred selected publications; the *Philosopher's Index*: abstracts from books and journals of philosophy and related fields; and *Religious and Theological Abstracts*: provides abstracts for periodical literature in the fields of religion and theology from over 400 journals. OT and NT Abstracts are also now available in this format, at least going back to 1988. Based at the University of Innsbruck, BILDI (http://www.uibk.ac.at/bildi/bildi/search/index.html.en) offers an excellent, free search gateway for finding books and articles in biblical and theological studies.

Biblical/Theological Periodicals (with common abbreviations)

The number of journals currently published—even if we limit ourselves to biblical and theological studies—is enormous. Out of that vast number we list the following major journals because of their focus on the study of biblical texts, their popularity, their ready availability in many theological libraries, and whose articles are predominantly in English. They run the gamut from those devoted more exclusively to the technical work of scholars writing for other scholars to those oriented to nonspecialists and practitioners. Their theological orientations also differ—from those with clear boundaries, which publish only work acceptable to their constituencies, to those that publish all work they consider worthy. We list them in two general categories, giving their common abbreviations in parentheses.

For General Readers:

1. *Asia Journal of Theology (AsJT)*
2. *Bible Today (BibTod)*
3. *Biblical Archaeology Review (BAR)*
4. *Bibliotheca Sacra (BSac)*
5. *Evangelical Quarterly (EvQ)*
6. *Ex Auditu (ExAud)*
7. *Expository Times (ExpTim)*
8. *Interpretation (Int)*
9. *Journal of the Evangelical Theological Society (JETS)*
10. *Near Eastern Archaeology (NEA)*
11. *Review and Expositor (RevExp)*
12. *Southern Baptist Journal of Theology (SBJT)*
13. *Southwestern Journal of Theology (SwJT)*
14. *Stulos Theological Journal (STJ)*
15. *Themelios (Them)*
16. *Trinity Journal (TJ)*
17. *Tyndale Bulletin (TynBul)*
18. *Westminster Theological Journal (WTJ)*
19. *Word and World (WW)*

For Advanced Students and Specialists:

1. *Bible Translator (BT)*
2. *Biblica (Bib)*
3. *Biblical Interpretation (BibInt)*
4. *Bulletin for Biblical Research (BBR)*
5. *Biblical Theology Bulletin (BTB)*
6. *Catholic Biblical Quarterly (CBQ)*
7. *Calvin Theological Journal (CTJ)*
8. *Criswell Theological Review (CTR)*
9. *Currents in Biblical Research (CurBR)*
10. *Filología Neotestomentaria (FN)*
11. *Horizons in Biblical Theology (HBT)*
12. *Jewish Quarterly Review (JQR)*
13. *Journal for the Study of the Historical Jesus (JSHJ)*
14. *Journal for the Study of Paul and His Letters (JSPHL)*
15. *Journal for the Study of the NT (JSNT)*
16. *Journal for the Study of the OT (JSOT)*
17. *Journal of Biblical Literature (JBL)*
18. *Journal of Greco-Roman Christianity and Judaism (JGRChJ)*
19. *Journal of Theological Studies (JTS)*
20. *Neotestamentica (Neot)*
21. *New Testament Studies (NTS)*
22. *Novum Testamentum (NovT)*
23. *Palestine Exploration Quarterly (PEQ)*
24. *Revue Biblique (RB)*
25. *Vetus Testamentum (VT)*
26. *Zeitschrift für die alttestamentliche Wissenschaft (ZAW)*
27. *Zeitschrift für die neutestamentliche Wissenschaft (ZNW)*

Commentaries

A wealth of information resides in commentaries, which are useful in single volumes or as sets. Hundreds are currently in print from all segments of the theological spectrum and serve a variety of purposes. Bible students must be clear on their purposes in employing specific commentaries, for the commentary genre covers an array of approaches to commenting on the books. All commentaries reflect the presuppositions and theological commitments of the writers. They are written for various purposes. Some are devotional and stress personal application; others aid preachers or teachers by focusing on illustrating truth or on the "preachability" of biblical texts. Some scholars write commentaries only for other scholars and those who want precise and technical citations of parallel ancient literature and sundry such connections. Others write them so lay people, pastors, or advanced students can understand the meaning of the biblical books. Some commentaries stress history and the technical details of the ancient world; others focus on the texts' theological significance. Some writers attempt to adopt several agendas to provide help for a variety of readers' needs. Many in the following lists are available electronically on various platforms.

Commentaries present Bible students with a tremendous variety of choices. Our advice to interpreters is to know what you need and use those commentaries that will meet your needs. Since commentaries represent a major investment, choose wisely—preferably, if possible, after hands-on scrutiny. For bibliographies of commentaries, see footnote 1 (p. 637).

Two ecumenically produced series projected to cover the entire Bible collates the salient comments of ancient commentators and preachers from the so-called church fathers: Oden, T. C., gen. ed. *Ancient Christian Commentary on Scripture.* Downers Grove: InterVarsity, 1998–; and the Reformation Period: Bray, G. L., gen. ed. *Reformation Commentary on Scripture.* Downers Grove: InterVarsity, 2011–.

We list the major, current, English language series, recognizing that other series and fine individual volumes exist outside of series. We will omit older series.[20] Space simply does not permit our listing individual works. Single volume commentaries on the entire Bible suffer in that their enforced brevity often precludes significant help for interpreters.[21] *The Zondervan NIV Study Bible* (Grand Rapids: Zondervan, 2015); and *The ESV Study Bible* (Wheaton: Crossway, 2008), however, have outstanding study notes in them throughout. Note that commentary series, understandably, may contain members of varying quality. Simply because one volume is excellent (or poor) does not mean the others will follow suit. Our list will be subdivided to aid in our descriptions.

Series Commenting on the English Bible (practical emphasis)

Motyer, J. A. and J. R. W. Stott, eds. The Bible Speaks Today [BST]. Downers Grove/Leicester, UK: InterVarsity, 1968–. This is a popular-level, paperback series on selected books in both testaments. Most of the authors are British evangelicals. Not all are well written, but they consistently provide practical help for living.

---

20. To omit older series is a difficult decision, but we made it because this bibliography is already lengthy. We urge readers to consult the work of our theological predecessors. Two series are worthy of particular note: J. Calvin, *NT Commentaries* [Torrance edition] (Grand Rapids: Eerdmans), with select OT volumes; and C. F. Keil and F. Delitzsch, *Old Testament Commentary*, 10 vols. (Peabody, MA: Hendrickson, 1996).

21. If you want a one-volume commentary, the best include Dunn, J. D. G. and J. Rogerson, eds. *The Eerdmans Bible Commentary.* Grand Rapids: Eerdmans, 2003, written by an ecumenical group of scholars; Carson, D. A., et al., eds. *New Bible Commentary: Twenty-First Century Edition.* Downers Grove: InterVarsity, 1994; Bruce, F. F. *Zondervan Bible Commentary.* 3rd ed. Grand Rapids: Zondervan, 2008, by evangelicals; Mays, J. L. et al., eds. *HarperCollins Bible Commentary.* Rev. ed. San Francisco: HarperSanFrancisco, 2000; Barton, J. and J. Muddiman, eds. *The Oxford Bible Commentary.* Oxford: Oxford University Press, 2001, by mainstream scholars; and Brown, R. E., et al., eds. *The New Jerome Biblical Commentary.* 3rd ed. Englewood Cliffs, NJ: Prentice-Hall, 1999, for a Roman Catholic perspective. An important survey of each book of the Bible—providing mini-commentaries—is B&H Staff, ed. *Holman Illustrated Bible Handbook.* Nashville: B&H, 2012, a feature also (along with other articles) of Fee, G. D. and R. L. Hubbard, Jr., eds. *Eerdmans Companion to the Bible.* Grand Rapids: Eerdmans, 2011.

*Strauss, M. L. and J. H. Walton. Teach the Text Commentary Series [TTCS]. Grand Rapids: Baker, 2013–. Newly and rapidly emerging series on both testaments, lavishly illustrated. Combines commentary on basic meaning of text, passage-by-passage, insightful applications, and suggestions for teaching.

Ngewa, S., ed. Africa Bible Commentary Series [ABC]. Nairobi: Word Alive; Bukuru, Nigeria: Hippo Books; Accra, Ghana: ACTS; Grand Rapids: Zondervan. A newly emerging series designed for English-speaking Africans. But Westerners will profit both from the concise summaries of original meaning and from the incisive applications to issues of particular concern in Africa but which are by no means absent from any culture.

Keener, C. S. and M. F. Bird, eds. New Covenant Commentary Series [NCCS]. Eugene, OR: Cascade, 2009–. Short, succinct treatments of the text, fully abreast of scholarship, and including short sections on Bridging the Horizons to contemporary life. Produced by a diverse collection of scholars, several of them non-Western or minorities.

Osborne, G. R., ed. New Testament Commentary [IVPNTC]. Downers Grove/Leicester, UK: InterVarsity, 1991–. This series of brief commentaries links the pastoral heart with the scholarly mind, emphasizing the significance of the biblical text for today's church in its analyses of the NT Books.

*Miller, P. D., eds. Interpretation [Int]. Louisville: Westminster John Knox. This series covers both testaments and specialized volumes (the first on Jesus' parables) have now begun to emerge. Written by mainline scholars, these focus on the meaning and application of the texts for preachers and teachers.

*Muck, T., ed. The NIV Application Commentary [NIVAC]. Grand Rapids: Zondervan, 1994–. The series aims to cover both testaments and is almost complete. The format breaks down the comments on each section to its "original meaning," "bridging contexts" into today's world, and "contemporary significance"—to allow the text to speak with power to the modern world. Due to this approach, the comments on the original meaning are necessarily brief. Probably the premier series in this section.

Longman, T., III and S. McKnight. Story of God Bible Commentary [SGBC]. Grand Rapids: Zondervan, 2013–. Designed in part to function like the NIVAC above, but with more space allotted to applications, appropriately in story form, with more of an international focus, and with a younger and more diverse authorship of the various volumes.

Series Commenting on the English Bible with References to the Original Languages

Gasque, W. W., R. L. Hubbard, Jr., and R. K. Johnston, eds. Understanding the Bible Commentary [UBC]. Grand Rapids: Baker, 1988–2013. Formerly known as the New International Biblical Commentary [NIBC] published by Hendrickson, and before that by Harper & Row. Baker has reprinted and reissued the now complete series. Covers both testaments and features well-known scholars, including many evangelicals, writing to make the best scholarship accessible to a wide audience. They tend to be much briefer than other entries in this category.

*Firth, D. G., ed. The Tyndale Old Testament Commentaries [TOTC]. Leicester, UK/Downers Grove: InterVarsity, 1964–99.

*Schnabel, E. J. ed. The Tyndale New Testament Commentaries [TNTC]. Leicester, UK InterVarsity; Grand Rapids: Eerdmans, 1956–91. Together these series represent mainstream evangelical scholarship from both Britain and North America, written for layperson and pastor alike to present the theological significance of the biblical books. They include helpful historical introductions and prove to be reliable guides for interpretation. Many of the earlier volumes have been revised, and both the NT and OT series are complete. They are comparable to the NICOT/NT in quality, though much briefer.

Furnish, V. P., gen. ed. Abingdon New Testament Commentaries [ANTC] and Miller, P. D., gen. ed. Abingdon Old Testament Commentaries [AOTC]. Nashville: Abingdon, 1996–. Ecumenical in scope, seeks to provide compact, critical comments particularly for theological students but also for pastors and church leaders.

Talbert, C. H., ed. Reading the New Testament [RNT]. Macon, GA: Smyth & Helwys. An ecumenical series focusing specifically on the literary flow of the final form of the biblical text against its historical background. Presents cutting-edge biblical research in an accessible language that is both coherent and comprehensive.

Nash, R. S., ed. Smyth & Helwys Bible Commentaries [SHBC]. Produced by what once was the moderate wing of the Southern Baptist, now the Cooperative Baptist Fellowship. The volumes are very uneven in length, but all deal thoughtfully with contemporary horizons, especially in light of social and cultural trends after overviews of the main exegetical and theological issues in each passage.

Martens, E. A. (OT) and W. M. Swartley (NT), eds. The Believer's Church Bible Commentary [BCBC]. Scottdale: Herald, 1991–. This important Mennonite/Anabaptist set provides rather substantial comments on the English Bible text, with Hebrew and Greek employed in the background plus extensive applications to contemporary church life.

Green, J. B. and M. Turner, eds. Two Horizons New Testament Commentary [THNTC]. Grand Rapids: Eerdmans, 2005–. Unique format with a little over half being the meaning of the text in context and the second part integrating the passage with systematic theology.

Hooker, M. D., ed. Black's (or Harper's) New Testament Commentaries [BNTC; HNTC]. London: A. & C. Black; New York: Harper and Row, 1957–, some volumes reprinted by Baker and Hendrickson. These volumes were written mostly by British authors of the previous generation though volumes continue to emerge, and some early offerings are being replaced, London/New York: Continuum, 2002–. They contain excellent material designed to be accessible to readers without knowledge of Greek.

Longman, T., III (OT) and D. E. Garland (NT), eds. *Expositor's Bible Commentary, Revised* [*EBC*]. 5 vols. Grand Rapids: Zondervan, 2012. This series includes commentaries on all the books of the Bible, plus introductory articles. Authors come from the United States, Canada, England, Scotland, Australia, and New Zealand, and from many denominations, including Anglican, Baptist, Brethren, Methodist, Nazarene, Presbyterian, and Reformed, all evangelicals, and write for a wide audience. They aim to explain the meaning of the Bible, not to engage technical or obscure issues. The revised editions include original authors updating their work along with new authors, and the quality is now much more consistently good.

*Clendenen, R., gen. ed. New American Commentary [NAC]. 40 volumes. Nashville: Broadman, 1991–2014. A series sponsored by the Southern Baptists but including a few contributors beyond that circle, this series is complete. The target readers are pastors, though students and laypersons alike can profit from these thoroughly evangelical, detailed but not overly technical works.

Arnold, C. E. (NT) and J. H. Walton (OT), eds. Zondervan Illustrated Bible Backgrounds Commentary [ZIBBC]. 9 Vols. Grand Rapids: Zondervan, 2002, 2009. This set that helps readers understand the historical and cultural background of the books of the Old and New Testaments including full color photos and graphics.

Harrington, D. J., ed. Sacra Pagina [SP]. Collegeville, MN: Liturgical Press, 1991–. A multi-volume series on the NT from a Roman Catholic perspective.

* Hubbard, Jr., R. L., ed. New International Commentary on the Old Testament [NICOT]. Grand Rapids: Eerdmans, 1965–.

*Green, J. B., ed. New International Commentary on the New Testament [NICNT]. Grand Rapids: Eerdmans, 1952–. Work on these two series is ongoing. All the original NT volumes and some OT volumes are being revised by their original authors or replaced by other authors. The NT set is virtually complete, while gaps still remain on the OT side. They represent a high level of conservative evangelical scholarship, more technical than popular, though scholarly details are often relegated to footnotes. Most readers will discover these to be extremely useful tools.

Clements, R. E. and M. Black, eds. The New Century Bible Commentary [NCB]. Grand Rapids: Eerdmans; London: Marshall, Morgan & Scott, 1966–94. They fall in the middle of the theological spectrum—the NT volumes tending to be more conservative than the OT volumes. Brief at some points, they provide many fine analyses of the biblical books. They are written for a wide audience, but the series is now out of print.

Witherington, B. and B. T. Arnold, eds. The New Cambridge Bible Commentary [NCBC]. Cambridge: Cambridge University Press, 2003–. Designed to replace and improve the old Cambridge Bible Commentary, these volumes are thoroughly abreast of contemporary scholarship but reasonably succinct and comparatively lightly footnoted. A cross-section of scholars of various theological traditions, including a number of evangelicals. Has been emerging rather slowly.

Mays, J. L., et al., eds. The Old Testament Library [OTL]. Louisville: Westminster John Knox, 1962–. This series includes both commentaries on OT books as well as specialized works on a variety of topics of concern to students of the OT. Some of the commentaries are translations of German originals, some appeared previously in other series, and excellent new volumes and replacements of older ones continue to arrive regularly. Overall these books reflect good mainline scholarship, and most include theological comments useful to teachers and preachers. The New Testament Library [NTL], 2002–, a new series of clothbound commentaries, general studies, and modern classics has more recently begun to emerge fairly rapidly.

*Carson, D. A., ed. Pillar New Testament Commentaries [PNTC]. Leicester, UK: Inter-Varsity; Grand Rapids: Eerdmans, 1988–. About three-quarters complete, this series represents a major mid-range series and spans a perceived gap between most of the series in this category and those in the next. Uniformly of high quality.

Cotter, D. W., ed. Berit Olam: Studies in Hebrew Narrative and Poetry. Collegeville, MN: Liturgical Press. 1996–. The commentaries in this still emerging series, with contributions thus far by both mainline and evangelical scholars, apply the new literary criticism to produce a literary analysis of OT books.

Series Commenting on the Original Languages and Texts

Olsen, R. and R. Hausman, et al., eds. Continental Commentaries [CC]. Minneapolis: Augsburg Fortress, 1984–. This is a collection of English translations of major German works—often with important histories of investigation of issues and theological excurses. To date, most are OT volumes.

Collins, J. J., ed. Anchor Bible [AB]. New Haven: Yale University Press, 1964–. This ongoing series covers both the OT and the NT plus Apocryphal books. The original volumes were very uneven in quality and size, but replacement and new volumes are uniformly superior. Treatments of texts are divided between disconnected technical "Notes" and readable prose "Comments." Contributors include Catholics, Jews, and Protestants.

*Silva, M., ed. Baker Exegetical Commentary on the New Testament [BECNT]. Grand Rapids: Baker, 1992–. This ongoing series, written from a conservative, evangelical viewpoint, provides in-depth exegesis of the original language texts. Volumes continue to appear rapidly, virtually all of very high quality.

*Arnold, C., ed. Zondervan Exegetical Commentary on the New Testament [ZECNT]. Grand Rapids: Zondervan, 2008–; and Block, Daniel I., ed. *Zondervan Exegetical Commentary on the Old Testament*. Grand Rapids: Zondervan, 2015–. A user-friendly commentary that moves through passages in the biblical texts with their big ideas, and using a format that divides material on each text into introductory, exegetical, and application levels. Extra features include a section with the grammatical layouts translated into English in it, an exegetical outline, and the literary context of each passage.

* deClaissé-Walford, N. L. (OT) and P. H. Davids (NT), eds. Word Biblical Commentary [WBC]. Grand Rapids: Zondervan [formerly Word Books and then Thomas Nelson], 1982–. Almost complete, this series comments on all books in both testaments, and revisions of earlier volumes is ongoing. Two (or even three) volumes are devoted to several of the longer biblical books. Their format includes sections that provide textual and literary analysis, exegesis (occasionally technical), and conclusions about the meaning and significance of the texts. These are not for average readers, though almost anyone could profit from the "Explanation" sections to obtain the results of the technical exegeses.

*Goodcare, Mark and Todd Still, eds. New International Greek Testament Commentary [NIGTC]. Grand Rapids: Eerdmans, 1978–. This series reflects a high level of conservative scholarship, extremely thorough, next only to the ICC and occasionally more so, though generally written well enough and formatted so as to make the set accessible to all with a background in Greek. Extremely slowly appearing, the series is now about two-thirds complete.

Davies, G. I. and C. M. Tuckett, eds. International Critical Commentary, Old and New Testaments [ICC]. Edinburgh: T&T Clark, 1895–. Begun in the nineteenth century though never completed, the project ground to a halt when the volume on Kings appeared in 1951. The project was resumed with the revision of Romans by C. E. B. Cranfield, 2 vols. (1975, 1979), the appearance of the first volume of Jeremiah (1986), and a sluggish stream of a handful of volumes thereafter. Highly technical and stressing critical and philological matters, the volumes are written by the first rank of scholars. The new volumes are among the best and most thorough available. However, the older volumes are all very dated.

Machinist, P. and H. Koester, eds. Hermeneia: A Critical and Historical Commentary on the Bible [Herm]. Minneapolis: Augsburg Fortress, 1972–. This series has volumes on books in the OT, the NT, plus apocryphal books, early church fathers, and even one on the Sermon on the Mount. The most liberal of all the series, it also often provides the most detailed treatment of books available by front-line scholars. The works are highly technical and focus on historical and critical issues with little emphasis on theology or application. Some earlier volumes were translations of German works, but not so more recently, and those are being replaced. Due to their high level of scholarship and prohibitive cost, it is likely that only specialists will find much use for most of these. Often full of references to key background passages, however, in Jewish or Greco-Roman literature.

Final Recommendations

If students want to buy an entire commentary set (one complete or nearing completion)—given our cautions at the outset—we recommend considering:

1. Tyndale OT Commentaries and Tyndale NT Commentaries (for general readers plus pastors, teachers—for exegesis of the texts)
2. NIV Application Commentary (for general readers plus pastors, teachers—for an applicational focus)
3. Interpretation (for preachers and teachers—from a more ecumenical perspective)
4. New American Commentary (for pastors and teachers—for exegesis of the texts)
5. New International Commentary OT and New International Commentary NT (for pastors, teachers, and scholars)
6. Word Biblical Commentary (for serious teachers and scholars)
7. Pillar New Testament Commentary (for serious general readers, students, and pastors)
8. Baker Exegetical Commentary on the New Testament (for preachers, teachers, and scholars)
9. Zondervan Exegetical Commentary on the New Testament (for preachers, teachers, and scholars)

SCRIPTURE INDEX

GENESIS

1.	54
1–2.	156
1–11.	426, 427
1:1	394
1:1–2	185
1:2	42
1:26–27	62, 87
2:7	59
2:10	71
2:18	157
2:24	136, 162, 212, 622
3:14	440
3:17	440
3:17–19	497
4:4–5	391
4:7	409
4:11	440
4:20–22	427
4:23–24	441
4:24	381, 387
5.	437
6:1	437
6:1–4	209
6:4	427
6:7	212
9.	335
9:6	441
9:25	434
9:26	434
10:1–32	437
10:9	434
10:10–12	427
10:19	374
11:2–3	427
11:10–32	427
12.	335
12–15.	54
12–36	303, 427
12:1–3	482, 625
12:1–13	630
12:2–3	76
12:3	64, 626

12:6	265
12:7	423
12:10–20	121
14.	374
14:13	336
14:14	82, 265
15.	472, 482, 625
15:6	429, 548
17.	482
17:1–2	625
17:1–11	76
17:1–21	423
17:3–10	336
17:23–27	82
18.	374
18:1–33	423
19:1–38	158
19:30–38	85
20:1–18	121
21.	429
22	618, 630
22:1	305, 629
22:12	429
22:14	265
22:20–24	437
23:2	67
24:35–48	473
25:1–4	437
26:2	212
26:11	441
27:29	64
28	424
28:12–16	423
29–30	429
29:20	97
31:25–42	450
31:27	436
32:4	463
34	123
35:8	422
36:31	265
37–50.	121, 123, 351, 430
37:5–11	423

38.	305
40:9–11	423
40:16–17	423
41:1–8	423
43:3	305
43:8	305
44:14	305
44:16	305
44:18	305
45:7–9	431
46:28	305
48:3–4	423
49.	400
49:26	186
49:29	58
49:29–30	431
49:33	58, 431
50:20	181, 431

EXODUS

1:15–21	147, 554
3:2–12	423
3:14	530
4:22–23	287
5:10	463
6:2	212
6:4	336
7–11.	561
9:16	212
11:3–6	561
11:7	332
12:37	214
12:43	212
13:1–4	561
15:1–18	361, 436, 451
15:3	471
15:21	381, 436, 451
15:23	422
16:18	146
17.	81
19–24.	341
19:5–6	444, 576
20	443

20:1–23:33. 438
20:2–17 . . . . 441, 615
20:12 440
20:13 . . . . 440, 444
20:13–15 476
20:13–17 441
20:14 447
20:15 444
20:17 611
20:23–23:19 442
21:1–22:16. 440
21:2 439
21:2–11 442
21:7–11 449
21:12 . . . . 441, 442
21:15–17 . . . . 441, 442
21:18–19 439
21:18–32 442
21:23–25 441
21:24 624
21:31 439
21:36 439
22:1–15 442
22:19 441
22:25 440
23:1–8 444
23:19 446
25–31. 438
31:14–15 441
33:22 530
34 441
34:6 530
34:26 446
34:29–Leviticus 16 438
34:33–35 78
35:5–9 436
36:8–37:16. 422

LEVITICUS

1–5. 443
6–7 442
11:7 35
11:10–12 35
11:44 585
12:3 75
12:8 620
13–14. 67
14:54–57 67
15:19–30 444
16:8 537
17–26. 438
18:5 548
18:6–24 441
18:21 618
19:1 623

19:9–10 616
19:11–18 441
19:18 . . . . 446, 616
19:19 56
19:26–29 441
19:27–28 446
19:28 . . . . 56, 606
19:29 618
19:36 348
20:2–5 618
20:10 441
21. 443
24:15–20 442
24:16 441
24:18–22 441
24:21 441
25. 447
26:34–35 68

NUMBERS

6:1–21 619
10:35 471
13:32–33 427
19. 82
20:11 385
21. 81
21:17–18 436
21:21–24 422
21:27–30 436
22:22–35 434
23–24 472
23:19 212
26:55 537
31:32–40 436
34:2 348
35:16–18 441
35:21 441
35:31 448

DEUTERONOMY

1:1–5 449
1:6–4:40 449
1:6–4:43 450
4:5–8 439
4:26 450
5. 443
5–6 450
5–26 449
5:6–21 441
5:12–15 75
5:17 444
5:17–19 476
5:18 447
5:19 444
6–11. 450

6:4–5 616
6:4–9 323
6:5 446
6:6–7 622
6:7–25 603
6:16 . . . . 62, 609
9:4 256
10:4 441
10:5–7 311
12–26 438
14:21 446
15. 447
15:11 164
17:6 447
18:9–13 446
18:17–19 178
19:15 447
19:16 59
19:21 441
20:1–4 471
21:18–21 75
21:23 548
22:9–12 445
23:2 615
24:1 622
24:1–4 447
24:10 439
25:1 489
25:4 . . . . . 79, 173, 212, 255, 256
26:5–9 222
27–28. 450
27:11–28 450
27:15 434
27:15–26 . . . . 440, 441
27:26 548
28 625
28:3 434
28:16–19 . . . . 440, 441
29:2–30 . . . . 431, 450
30:11–20 603
30:12–14 256
30:19 450
31–34. 449
31:1–8 431
31:9–13 603
31:28 450
32–33 450
32:30 386
32:35 79
32:43 . . . . .190, 251, 311
34 265
34:5–6 431
34:10 67

JOSHUA

1:1–2 306
7:2–5 422
10:42 471
14:6 202
15–19 436
23:1–16 431
23:6 306
24 341
24:2–13 222
24:2–15 450
24:24 306
24:29–30 431

JUDGES

1:8 355
1:16–17 422
2:6–23 303
3–16 303
3:26–30 422
4–5 425
5 . . . . 361, 436, 451
5:4–5 382
5:17 403
5:22 373
5:23 434
5:25 . . . . 380, 382
5:26–27 382
6–8 425
6:1 432
6:2–6 432
6:14 432
6:32 432
6:37–40 606
7:1–15 432–33
7:5 332
7:13–14 423
8:10–12 422
9:1–21 423
9:7–15 435
9:23 52
9:27 436
11:15 463
11:31 138
11:36 138
13 423
13–16 . . . . 120, 425
14:14 434
17–21 303
17:6 426
18:1 426
19 53
19:1 426
21:21 436
21:25 . . . . 313, 426

RUTH

1:1 265
1:6 395
1:14 391
1:22 395
2:19 434
2:20 434
4:1–12 450
4:6–8 56
4:7 . . . . 67, 265
4:11 78
4:18–22 . . . . 265, 437

1 SAMUEL

1–2 . . . . 120, 140, 593
1:21–28 438
2:1–10 . . . . 361, 438, 451
2:12–17 438
2:27–36 438
3:1 395
3:11–18 438
3:21 395
9:2 456
9:9 472
9:17 212
9:25 302
10:1 302
10:3 302
10:5 302
10:12 434
11 189
11:1–11 423
12 . . . . 431, 432
13:14 202
15:29 213
16:12 456
16:14–16 52
16 427
16–22 133
17 57
17:43 331
18:3 336
18:6–7 436
19:24 434
23:1–7 305
23:8–39 305
23:18 336
24:1 305
24:14 . . . . 331, 434

2 SAMUEL

1–2 120
1:1–16 450
1:19–27 436

1:23 404
3:33–34 436
4:5–12 450
5:3 336
5:8 434
7:12–13 55
7:12–16 . . . . 481, 603
7:14 481
8 427
9:8 332
10:15–19 422
11:1 129
12:1–4 . . . . 270, 435
12:1–6 435
13 . . . . 139, 158
14:1–17 435
16:9 331
22 361
23:1–7 . . . . 361, 451
23:4 397
23:34–39 436
24:1 153

1 KINGS

1–2 481
1:46 359
2:1–9 431
2:10 . . . . 55, 431
2:30 463
3:1 422
3:4–15 423
4:2–6 436
4:8–19 436
4:24 625
4:30 348
6–7 422
6:1 55
7:2–8 422
8:42 359
8:56 625
8:56–61 450
9:1–9 423
9:3 212
9:10–14 422
9:15–23 422
10:1 434
11:29–31 474
12:1–20 423
12:25 422
13–14 318
13:1–3 482
14:25–26 422
15:23 55
15:31 55
17 428

17–18 61
17:1–6 434
18:27 . . . . 402, 407
19:19–21 . . . . 422, 474
20:1–43 423
20:28 471
20:38–42 435
20:39–42 435
22 . . . . 424, 471
22:1–37 423
22:17–23 473
22:19–23 52

2 KINGS
1:3–4 463
2 140
4:8 225
4:8–37 428
5 123
6:1–7 428
7:1–2 482
8:13 332
9 428
10:1–6 557
11:4 336
11:4–12 455
13:14–19 . . . . 473, 474
13:14–21 428
14:9 435
14:9–10 435
18:17 57
18:27 314
19:20–36 482
19:21–28 436
22–23 603
22:20 58
23:15 209
23:15–16 482
24:12 479
24:15 479
24:20–25:7 422
25:25 359
25:27–30 479
30–37 484

1 CHRONICLES
1:12 604
2:1–3:24 437
15:16–22 455
16:5–7 455
22–26 55
22:5 55
28–29 55
29:1 55
29:29 55

2 CHRONICLES
5:12 455
8:14 55
11:5–12 422
18:18–22 52
29:25 55
35:15 55
35:25 436
36:21 68

EZRA
1–4 483
3:10 479
7:27–9:15 422
8:2 479
8:20 479

NEHEMIAH
1:1–7 422
3:15 479
3:16 479
7:73–8:18 603
8 589
8:7–8 69
10:34 537
12:24 479
12:27–31 422
12:36 479
12:37 479
12:45 479
12:46 479

ESTHER
2:10 430
2:20 430
3 431
4 431
6 431
6:1–11 430
7 431
7:1–6 430
8–9 430
9:18–19 430

JOB
1–2 500
1:8 503
3 469
3:4–9 405
5:9–16 502
5:19–22 495
5:21 369
6:15 390
9:5 502

9:5–10 . . . . 502, 503
9:14–16 503
9:29–10:1 503
9:29–31 502
10:12 380
11:7–9 503
11:7–12 502
12:7–25 503
12:13–25 502
13:15 593
13:20–22 495
14:2 370
15:7–8 503
16:7 501
16:16–17 501
16:18–21 501
17:13 501
17:16 501
18:18–21 503
23:1–24:25 351
25:2–6 502
26:5–14 502
27:4 378
28 . . . . 498, 503
30:1–31 501
31 502
33:14–15 495
37:1 . . . . 402, 404
37:14–24 503
38–39 586
38:1–42:6 503
38:31 502
42:1–6 501
42:7 132
42:7–9 503
42:7–17 500
42:10–17 503

PSALMS
1 . . . . 48, 458
1–41 460
1:1 . . . . 62, 434
1:6 62
2 . . . . 85, 386, 455
2:2 212
2:7–9 404
2:10 . . . . 402, 403
2:11–12 186
2:12 193
3 . . . . 287, 288
5:11 452
6:5 379
6:10 . . . . 371, 373
7 503
7:3–5 . . . . 452, 502

8. . . . . 85, 455
8:1 395
8:9 395
9. 370
10. 370
10:5 62
10:15 453
12. 457
13:6 381
14:1 295
15. 457
16:8–11 259
17:3–5 502
18. 455
18:2 . . . . 400, 409
18:4–19 409
18:8–16 400
19. . . . . 455, 458, 601
19:1–6 . . . . 572, 574
19:7–9 367
21. 455
22 . . . . 261, 452–53
22:12 317
22:14 404
23. . . . . 49, 595
23:1 396
23:2 348
23:4 593
23:5 . . . . 402, 405, 406
24:3–6 457
25. 370
25:8–10 458
25:12–14 458
26:4 62
26:4–6 502
27:1 574
27:4 574
29:1 382
29:10 382
30 454–55
31:24–25 458
32. 458
32:1–11 410–12
32:3 411
32:5 411
32:9 411
33. 458
33:6–7 380
34 458
34:15–16 400
35:13–15 454
37. . . . . 351, 458
37:11 627
39. 458
39:2 62

39:5–7 458
40:5–6 458
40:6–8 311
42–72 460
43:3 402
44 454
44:6 406
45. . . . . 85, 251, 456
45:6–7 250
46 456
47. 456
48 456
48:11 403
49. 458
50:7–23 457
51:3–5 452
51:15 62
52:8 564
53:1 295
57:4 408
57:8 389
59:12–13 453
62:9–11 458
62:11–12 495
65. 455
66 . . . . 455, 457
67. 455
68 455
68:18 190
69:25 251
72. 455
72:9 386
73–89 460
73:1 411
74. 454
75. 457
76. 456
76:1 390
77 455
77:1 376
77:17 382
78. 222
80–81 381
80:8–13 489
84 456
85–86 381
88:11–12 387
89. 452
89:27 340
90–106 460
91:1 608
91:4 400
91:11–12 . . . . 62, 79, 608
92:7–9 458
92:12 401

93. 456
94:8–15 458
95. . . . . 455, 457
95:4–5 394
95:6 577
95:7–11 256
96–99 456
96 455
96:12 222
97:8 403
98:8 . . . . 402, 403
100. 455
103–104. 455
103:1 395
103:2 395
103:13 383
103:14 593
103:22 395
104. 455
104:3 490
104:13–15 490
104:13–18 458
104:15 621
105. 455
106:1 381
107–150. 460
107:1 381
107:23–32 529
109:6–15 453
109:6–20 . . . . 434, 452
109:8 251
110. . . . . 85, 386, 455
110:1 259
111. 370
111:6 381
112. 458
112:3 370
113:8 369
114. 405
114:1–2 382
115:18 378
117. 574
118. 457
118:1 395
118:1–3 457
118:5 457
118:10 457
118:21 455
118:25–29 457
118:29 395
119. 370
119:96 215
119:97–104 206
119:105 . . . . 33, 194, 399
120–134 459

120:2 359
122 456
125:2 383
127 458
127:1 370
127:3–5 608
127:4–5 445
128 458
132 456
136 . . . . 378, 395, 457
137:1 382
137:2 382
137:3 454
137:5–6 390
137:7–9 453
138:1 574
138:1–2 455
138:2 574
138:4 574
139 455
139:19–22 453
144 452
144–150 . . . . 182, 395
148 404
148:3–5 373
150 . . . . 373, 378

PROVERBS

1 500
1–9 498
2:17 336
3:6 62
3:10 387
3:34 79
4:1 386
5 500
6:16–19 495
7–9 500
8:4 402
8:6 402
8:20–21 402
8:22–31 402
8:33 497
10–15 495
11:20 380
11:24 494
12:19 . . . . 405, 406
12:25 496
13:4 496
14:17 494
14:23 496
14:31 . . . . 495, 497
14:34 376
15:17 495
15:18 496

15:23 494
15:33 495
16:3 497
16:8 495
16:16 495
16:19 495
16:20 497
17:5 196
17:27–28 494
18:9 434
18:16 494
19:5 378
19:17 494
21:9 495
22:6 594
22:17–24:22 497
22:22–23 . . . . 495, 497
24 500
24:26 434
24:30–34 498
25–29 67
25:21–22 79
26:4–5 . . . . 171, 216
26:9 384
27:17 . . . . 30, 283
29:5 434
30:7–8 495
30:8 381
30:15 387
30:15–16 495
30:18 387
30:18–19 495
30:21–23 495
30:24–28 . . . . 495, 504–5
30:29–31 495
31 297
31:10–31 . . . . 370, 455

ECCLESIASTES

1:12–2:26 499
1:14 499
2:24 617
2:24–25 499
3:1–8 148
3:16 499
3:22 499
4:1 . . . . 372, 499
4:6 496
4:7–12 499–500
4:13 496
4:13–16 435
5:10–12 496
5:13 499
5:18–20 499
6:1 499

7:1–12 496
9:11–12 496
9:13–15 435
9:17–18 496
10:1–2 496
10:6 496
10:8–9 496
11:2 387
11:4 496
11:9–12:1 617
12:13 617
13:13–14 148

SONG OF SOLOMON

2:2 397
2:8 395
2:15 489
3:5 395
3:6–11 456
4:7 458
4:11–13 401
4:16–17 489
8:4 395
8:6–7 459

ISAIAH

1:8 . . . . 348, 487
1:10 374
1:18 231
1:19–20 372
2:1–4 487
2:1–5 465
2:2 480
2:4 . . . . 308, 486, 489
2:5 487
3:14 487
4:1 405
5:1 . . . . 371, 372
5:1–7 . . . . 435, 487–91
5:5–6 476
5:8–10 465
5:11–14 465
5:13 476
5:18–25 465
6 473
6–39 487
6:9 348
7–8 480
7:3 . . . . 473, 474
7:14 . . . . 193, 251, 481
8:1–4 473
8:1–10 251
9 484
9:6–7 480

10:1–3 465
10:8–11 471
10:14 373
11. 484
11:1 603
11:1–5 486
11:6 . . . . 261, 486
11:10 480
11:11 480
12:1 455
12:1–6 468
12:6 403
13–23 . . . . 471, 472
14:4–23 467
16:5 382
16:10 436
19:19–25 484
20:1–6 . . . . 473, 474
22:5 365
23. 471
24–27 492
24:21 480
25. 479
25:1–12 468
25:6–8 479
26:1–19 468
26:2–5 423
26:24 423
27:2–6 . . . . 487, 490
28:1–4 465
28:10 373
28:13 373
28:23–28 471
29:1–4 465
29:15 465
30 507
30:1–5 465
30:15–17 464
31. 507–9
31:1–5 465
31:1–9 506
32. 507
33:14–16 457
33:22 365
34 471
35:4–6 311
35:5–6 77
36:12 314
37:22 403
40 478
40–66 487
40:3 382
40:3–5 483
40:9 382
40:20 51

40:27–29 478
41:10 433
42:6 338
42:10–13 468
42:18–25 483
43:14 483
44:28 483
45:1 483
45:12 . . . . 381, 384
45:13 483
47:6 483
48:20 483
48:20–21 385
49:6 444
49:13 468
49:21 483
51:19 394
52–53. 484
52:13–53:12. 298
55. 217
55:12 216
56–66 150
58:12 369
59:9–10 387
59:20–21 626
61:1 483
61:1–2 . . . . .77, 259, 311
61:2 483
61:11 76
62:1 380
63–64 469
63:7–64:12 468
64:4 256

JEREMIAH

1. 473
1:4–10 473
1:10 370
1:11–12 372
1:11–14 472
1:12 379
2:5–9 391
2:13 400
2:15 381
2:23–28 471
3:1–5 471
4:6 476
5:4 360
5:7 565
5:16–17 405
7:1–15 482
7:9 441
7:12–15 . . . . 476, 477
8:1 471
8:8–9 471

9:21 396
11:3 434
11:16 564
11:18–23 469
12:1–6 469
13:1–11 473
13:12–14 435
14. 468
14:1–3 469
14:7 469
14:10 469
15:10–11 469
15:15–21 469
15:16–17 502
16:1–9 473
17:7–8 399
17:11 396
17:14–18 469
18. 482
18:18 . . . . 310, 374, 457
18:18–23 469
19. 473–74
19:7 379
20:7–13 469
20:14–20 469
22:19 396
23:5 480
23:5–6 486
24. 472
24:5–7 478
25:11–12 68
26:1–6 482
28 . . . . 462, 464
28:2–4 465
28:8–9 475
28:10–11 474
28:12–16 463
29:7 143
29:10 68
29:10–14 478
29:11 . . . . 299, 486, 607
30 478
30–31 608
30:3 480
30:10–11 478
31:15 78
31:21 . . . . 382, 389
31:29 434
31:31 480
31:31–34 . . . . 172, 337, 338, 484
31:34 394
32:1–15 . . . . 473, 478
32:6–9 256
33:14–15 603
33:19–22 603

36:1–7 482
38:21–22 473
46–51 471
46:3–4 367
49:8 369
52 482

LAMENTATIONS

1–2 454
1–4 370
3:6 367
3:23 577
4 454
4:15 369

EZEKIEL

1–3 473
2:9–3:9 565
12:3 606
12:22 434
15:1–8 . . . . 434, 435
16:32 565
16:44 434
17:1–10 435
18:2 434
19:1–14 . . . . 435, 467
23:32–34 401
25–32 471
26:17–18 467
27:1–36 467
27:25 606
27:25–36 401
29:1–14 434
29:3–5 401
31:1–18 . . . . 434, 435
34 479
34:22–23 479
35 471
38–39 . . . . 471, 474, 492
39:18 317
40–48 171

DANIEL

1–6 428
2:1–11 423
3:4–12 554
4:1–18 423
5:12 434
7 492
7–12 . . . . 492, 562
7:1–14 351
7:15–28 351
7:18 493
7:21–22 493
7:27 493

8 . . . . 473, 474
8:25 493
8:27 492
9:24–27 492
9:27 565
10–12 473
12:1–4 493
12:7 565
12:8 492
12:9 560
12:11–12 565

HOSEA

1 473
1:2 . . . . 473, 618
1:6 . . . . 79, 358
1:9 79
1:10 79
2:4 565
2:23 . . . . 79, 576
3 473
3:1 618
4:1–2 476
4:2 441
4:4–8 476
4:6 476
4:8 476
6:6 79
11:1 . . . . 249, 261, 286, 287
13:7–8 398
13:14 404
14:4–8 122
14:9 67

JOEL

1–2 . . . . 468, 469
1:15–21 307
2:1 307
2:5–12 537
2:11 307
2:15–16 370
2:28 406
2:28–3:21 492
2:28–32 . . . . 311, 537
2:31 . . . . 307, 308
2:38–39 537
3:1–6 471
3:10 308
3:14 307
10:1–11:18 537
10:44–46 537
15:1–29 537
19:4–7 537

AMOS

1–2 . . . . 471, 472
1:1 472
1:2 . . . . 317, 400
1:3 387
1:3–2:5 317
1:3–2:8 495
1:4–5 382
1:5 382
1:6 387
1:8 382
1:9 387
1:11 386
2:2 386
2:6–12 476
2:11–12 391
2:13 . . . . 383, 397
2:13–16 476
2:14–16 386
3:3–8 470
3:8 400
3:12 397
4:1 . . . . 317, 381, 400, 476
4:2 480
4:2–3 476
4:4 407
4:5 407
4:6 395
4:6–10 476
4:8 395
4:9 395
4:10 395
4:11 395
4:12–13 476
4:13 467
5:1–3 467
5:1–17 391
5:3 405
5:5–6 382
5:6 411
5:7 390
5:8 502
5:8–9 467
5:14–15 390
5:15 . . . . 381, 382
5:16–17 . . . . 317, 386
5:18–20 . . . . 465, 592
5:21 317
5:21–24 600
5:24 . . . . 390, 397
5:26 323
5:27 476
6:1–7 465
6:3 380

6:6 380
6:12 362
6:13 407
7:1–6 473
7:7–8 472
7:9 . . . . 405, 406
7:9–17 395
7:12 472
7:14–15 473
8:1–2 472
8:8 380
8:10 . . . . 377, 402, 407
9:2 380
9:2–4 . . . . 386, 394
9:5–6 467
9:7 470
9:11–12 . . . . . 190, 256, 483, 484
9:11–15 . . . . 122, 465
9:14–15 483

JONAH

1–2 529
2:1–9 436
2:1–10 451
3:4 482
3:5–10 482
4:10–11 428
11:16 591

MICAH

1:2–7 463
1:4 397
1:10–15 379
1:16 476
2:3–5 466
2:6–11 471
3:2–3 476
3:6–7 472
4:3 308
5:2 483
5:5 387
6:6–8 457
6:8 . . . . 202, 592

NAHUM

1:2–8 370
3:2–4 368
3:15–17 405

HABAKKUK

1:2–2:4 469
1:6 73
1:13 73
2:4 . . . . 73, 548

ZEPHANIAH

1:2–3 242
3:2 400
3:3 399
3:14–20 122

HAGGAI

1:1 479
1:14 479
2:2 479
2:20–23 479
2:21 479

ZECHARIAH

1–6 492
1:3–6 450
2:1–4 473
3:2 400
3:3 399
4:1–6 473
4:3 564
4:6 212
4:6–10 479
4:11 564
5:1–4 472
9–14 . . . . 479, 480, 492, 562
9:1–13 472
10:1 490
11:4–16 473
11:12–13 256
11:13 407
12–14 493
12:7–8 479
12:10 479
12:12 479
13:1 479
13:7 484
13:7–9 483
14:1 480

MALACHI

1:14 480
2:14 336

MATTHEW

1–2 . . . . 181, 445, 517
1:1–17 437
1:1–18 158
1:16 360
1:23 251
2:4 483
2:15 . . . . . 249, 261, 286, 287
2:17 . . . . 78, 249
2:19–20 423

2:23 249
3:5–6 405
3:7 400
3:10 48
3:11 540
3:16 397
3:17 513
4:1–11 . . . . . 216, 276, 514, 599
4:4 79
4:5 608
4:7 79
4:18–22 516
4:23–25 395
5–7 303
5:1 522
5:3–11 434
5:3–12 521
5:4 191
5:5 627
5:13 . . . . 347, 401
5:14 . . . . 46, 64
5:16 . . . . 46, 64
5:17 . . . . 445, 617
5:17–20 586
5:17–40 172
5:18 215
5:21–22 . . . . 447, 555
5:21–48 . . . . 446, 522
5:27–28 447
5:29–30 405
5:38–42 624
5:42 380
5:48 523
6:7 373
6:10 . . . . 520, 624
6:12 381
6:22–24 138
6:24 592
6:33 521
7:1 299
7:1–2 380
7:7 624
7:7–8 381
7:11 . . . . 382, 384
7:13–27 603
7:17 381
7:21 592
7:24–27 526
8–9 517
8:10–12 515
8:12 588
8:17 520
8:20 382
8:23–27 594
8:27 529

9:2 520
9:13 79
9:17 281
9:18–26 514
9:35 395
9:37 591
10:5–6 515
10:9–10 617
10:24 591
10:25 259
10:32–33 382
10:37 . . . . 514, 591
10:42 64
11:4–5 311
11:5–6 529
11:17 361
11:20–30 515
11:28–30 167
11:30 . . . . 380, 496
12:8 79
12:28 529
12:34 400
13:3–8 270
13:10–12 515
13:13 361
13:42 588
13:44 133
13:44–46 . . . . 398, 526
13:50 588
13:53–58 516
14:13–21 516
14:21 215
14:29–30 406
14:30 402
15:11 382
16:18 372
16:21 482
16:24–26 592
16:25 382
18:20 . . . . 299, 609
18:23–35 526
19–20 252
19:1–12 622
19:2–12 618
19:3–12 . . . . 447, 523
19:5 . . . . 212, 622
19:9 . . . . 447, 523, 618
19:30 395
20:1–16 252
20:16 395
20:22 380
21:28–32 527
21:33–46 . . . . 122, 490
21:43 515
22:1–14 . . . . 122, 515

22:13 588
22:40 446
23:5 323
23:23 555
23:33 400
23:37 . . . . 402, 406, 409
24–25 492
24:6 561
24:15–31 565
24:29 380
24:36 . . . . 517, 566
24:43–25:13 517
24:44 517
24:51 588
25:1–3 . . . . 520, 525
25:3 42
25:30 588
25:31–46 515
25:40 64
25:45 64
26:31 483
27 482
27:9–10 256
27:56 516
28:3 397
28:3–4 398
28:18–20 . . . . 151, 515, 519
28:19 604
28:19–20 . . . . 158, 272
28:20 . . . . 433, 595

MARK

1:1 510
1:8 540
1:11 513
1:14–15 510
1:15 . . . . 77, 520
1:16–20 516
1:20 139
1:26 52
2:1–3:6 517
2:1–28 531
2:13–17 531
2:17 174
2:27 390
3:1–6 531
3:20–35 521
3:31–34 223
3:31–35 . . . . 136, 591
4:3–9 526
4:13 515
4:40 515
4:41 529
5:21–43 514
6:1–6 516

6:3 223
6:30–44 129
6:32–44 516
6:48 530
6:52 515
7:3–5 57
7:19 . . . . 446, 447, 586
8:1–10 129
8:21 515
8:27–33 484
8:31–9:32 517
8:33 515
8:35 . . . . 382, 510
8:36 147
9:14–29 515
9:39–40 289
10:2–12 447
10:21 616
10:29 510
10:29–30 521
10:35–45 515
10:38 380
11:12–14 . . . . 474, 530
11:20–21 474
11:20–25 530
11:27–33 531
12:1–12 . . . . 490, 527
12:13–37 531
12:28 520
12:29–31 616
13:24–25 380
14:7 164
14:9 510
14:12–26 129
15:40 516
16:8 515
16:9–20 188
16:18 193

LUKE

1–2 181
1:1–4 55, 306, 308, 512, 518, 532
1:4 515
1:14 535
1:28 88
1:46–55 361
1:52 377
1:59 75
1:67–79 361
1:71–74 390
2:7 340
2:14 577
2:21 75
2:24 620
2:29–32 361

2:46 535
3:16 540
3:22 . . . . 396, 513
4:1–13 . . . . 216, 276, 514
4:6 298
4:9–12 62
4:14–15 516
4:14–22 517
4:16–21 . . . . 259, 483
4:16–30 . . . . .516, 517, 589
4:18–19 520
4:18–21 . . . . 77, 311
4:24 535
5:1–11 . . . . 516, 517
5:12 535
5:17–26 536
5:37–39 588
6:7 534
6:20–26 . . . . 361, 521
6:27 . . . . .375, 380
6:30 380
6:37–38 380
7:21–23 77
7:22–23 520
7:28 519
7:31 361
7:36–50 160
8:25 529
8:40–42 536
8:49–56 536
9:3–5 523
9:10–17 516
9:23–27 520
9:24 382
9:31 534
9:51 536
9:51–18:14 517
9:58 382
9:59–62 591
9:62 621
10:7 . . . . 173, 212
10:25 52
10:25–37 515
10:29–37 526
10:30 58
10:37 539
10:38–42 515
11:4 381
11:5–8 137
11:8 191
11:9–10 381
11:13 . . . . 259, 382
11:17 380
11:28 33
12:8–9 382

12:24 534
12:28 259
12:30 521
12:36 397
12:47–48 555
12:48–50 381
13:3–5 539
13:11 350
13:18–21 526
13:19 350
13:20–21 397
13:28 588
13:32 314
14:1–24 531
14:16–24 526
14:26 . . . . 514, 591
14:26–27 592
15:1 525
15:1–2 303
15:2 525
15:3–7 525
15:3–32 303
15:11–32 133, 515, 524, 526, 586
15:32 380
16:1–13 320
16:5 534
16:10 380
16:18 447
16:19–31 515
16:21 332
17:5–8 526
17:11–19 515
17:20–21 520
18:1 539
18:9–14 . . . . 515, 526
18:14 381
18:22 523
19:8 . . . . 523, 616
19:11–27 523
19:20 534
19:41–44 483
21:20–24 61
22:19 35
22:19–20 186
22:20 173
22:35 617
22:35–38 523
23:43 . . . . 168, 274
24:25–27 . . . . 260, 262
24:27 40
24:44 170
28:31 534

JOHN

1:1 . . . . 284, 287

1:1–2 185
1:1–18 361
1:4–6 389
1:19–28 518
1:29 . . . . 356, 586
1:29–34 518
1:33 540
2:1–11 530
2:11 529
3:1–15 120
3:3 . . . . 253, 344
3:7 344
3:14 81
3:16 520
3:22 272
3:22–39 518
4:1–2 272
5:14 625
6:1–15 516
6:33 593
7:3–5 223
7:31 529
7:50–52 120
7:53–8:11 . . . . 188, 448
10. 483
10:11 396
10:25 529
10:35 . . . . 212, 215
11:25–26 593
13–17 431
13:1–17:26 431
13:14 630
13:14–15 35
13:27 299
14–16 207
14:6 235
14:26 172
14:27 328
15 487
15:26 172
16:33 . . . . 328, 593
17:17 215
17:20 604
17:22–23 289
19:25 516
19:38 120
19:39 120
20:30–31 306
20:31 529
21:18–19 616
21:25 55

ACTS

1:1 532
1:1–6:7 534

1:1–11 536
1:1–12:24 534
1:5 540
1:6–8 . . . . 520, 566
1:8 534
1:20 251
1:22–26 537
2:2 396
2:4 540
2:14–21 537
2:14–36 311
2:14–39 541
2:14–41 589
2:16 259
2:16–17 537
2:20 307
2:25–28 257
2:25–34 259
2:30 178
2:36 339
2:38 272
2:41 272
2:42 591
2:42–47 146
2:44–45 538
2:47 538
3:12–26 541
3:25 342
4:12 . . . . 235, 586
4:19–20 554
4:25 212
4:32 147
4:32–5:11 146
4:32–35 616
4:32–37 538
4:35 146
5:8 540
5:14 146
5:28 591
5:31 540
5:38–39 539
6:1–6 539
6:1–7 150
6:8–9:31 534
6:15 397
8 535
8:12 272
8:20 194
8:38 272
9:5 338
9:17 540
9:18 272
9:32–12:24 534
9:32–43 536
10:9–16 447

10:46 540
10:47–48 272
11:16 540
11:29 146
12:25–16:5 535
12:25–28:31 534
13:1–3 539
13:9 540
13:12 591
13:15 549
13:16–41 . . . . 541, 589
13:22 202
13:46–48 538
14:11–13 543
14:14–18 541
15 . . . . 178, 543, 579, 586
15:16–17 . . . . 256, 484
15:17 190
16 613
16:1–5 633
16:6–19:20 535
16:10–17 55
16:14–15 136
16:15 272
16:25–34 612
16:31–34 136
16:33 . . . . 272, 280
17 612
17:22–31 541
17:28 167
18:5–7 538
18:8 272
18:18 619
19:1–7 518
19:5 272
19:6 540
19:8–10 538
19:17–20 . . . . 538, 539
19:21 536
19:21–28:31 535
20:5–15 55
20:17–38 539
20:18–35 . . . . 431, 538
20:25 591
20:27 604
21:1–18 55
21:12 58
21:17–26 537–38
23:11 533
27 533
27:1–28:16 55
28:23–38 538
28:31 591
38–39 272

ROMANS

1:18–3:20 542
1:18–32 624
1:19–20 572
1:24–32 554
1:29 554
1:29–31 554
1:29–32 599
2:1 546
2:9 546
2:17–24 408
2:28–29 . . . . 64, 484
3:4 59
3:21–5:20 542
3:22 309
3:25 191
4:1 546
4:11–12 486
4:16 64
5:8 575
6–8 542
6:1 546
6:15 546
6:19 . . . . 402, 403
7:7 546
7:14–25 555
8:28 . . . . 299, 594
8:35–39 299
8:38–39 575
9–11 626
9:17 212
9:21 167
9:25 79
9:26 79
9:30–10:8 445
10:1–4 486
10:4 586
10:6–8 256
10:8 591
10:9 339
11 . . . . 484, 486
11:11–32 484
11:26–27 626
11:27 342
11:33 361
11:36 361
12:1–2 542
12:1–9 616
12:2 . . . . 240, 285, 318
12:3–8 542
12:9 453
12:9–13:14 542
12:17–21 79
12:21 453

13:1–5 322
13:8–10 447
14:1–15:13 . . . . 542, 621
15:4 . . . . . 65, 225, 486, 604, 615
16:4 191
16:17 591

1 CORINTHIANS

1:7 540
1:10–17 141
1:11 552
1:21 591
1:23 485
2:1–5 547
2:2 552
2:6–16 206
2:9 256
2:13 212
2:14 . . . . 202, 203
3:10 57
3:16–17 . . . . 57, 359
4:6 628
4:8–10 . . . . 402, 407
5:1 305
5:1–2 552
5:1–13 543
5:9 180
6:1 305
6:1–11 . . . . 552, 628
6:9 554
6:9–10 . . . . 554, 599
6:12 . . . . 305, 553
6:12–20 . . . . 543, 552
6:13 553
6:15 618
6:18–19 359
6:19 . . . . 57, 607
7:1 . . . . 58, 304, 552, 553
7:1–40 . . . . 543, 552
7:15–16 . . . . 447, 523
7:21 . . . . 161, 628
8–10 . . . . 621, 622
8:1 553
9 . . . . 557, 617
9:1–18 138
9:5 223
9:7–12 447
9:8–10 255
9:9 . . . . 79, 256
9:10 80
9:14 173
9:19–23 . . . . 557, 633
9:27 591
10:6 604
10:13 . . . . 594, 629

10:14–22 621
10:16 486
10:23 553
11 620
11:2 298
11:2–16 . . . . . .209, 333, 613, 619
11:4–6 35
11:13 35
11:14 619
11:14–16 56
11:20–21 141
11:24–25 187
11:25 484
11:27–29 542
11:30 . . . . 448, 477
12–14 141
12:3 339
12:8–9 522
12:10 40
12:11 540
12:13 . . . . 537, 540
12:27 486
12:31 298
13 . . . . 49, 555
14:26 591
14:33–35 554
14:33–38 613
14:36–38 554
15:3–5 64
15:3–8 222
15:13–23 236
15:17 232
15:17–20 222
15:20–28 630
15:55 404
16:2 620

2 CORINTHIANS

1 557
1–7 . . . . 546, 549
1:8–7:16 547
1:8–11 557
1:12 329
2:1 298
3:6 173
3:14–16 78
3:15–18 206
4:5 591
5:7 485
6:13 304
6:14–7:1 . . . . 304, 620
6:16 212
6:17 446
7:2 . . . . 298, 304
8–9 . . . . 146, 620

8:12–15 620
9:6 595
9:7 147
11:4 591
11:7–17 408
12:9 625
13:1 447

GALATIANS

1:13 329
1:14 555
2 . . . . 557, 633
2:2 591
2:11–14 310
2:11–21 557
2:15–16 579
2:15–21 548
2:16 309
3:1 543
3:1–4:31 548
3:1–5 548
3:6–9 486
3:6–14 548
3:8 . . . . 309, 626
3:11 309
3:13 483
3:15 342
3:15–18 548
3:16 76
3:21–22 548
3:24 309
3:26–29 548
3:27–28 623
3:28 . . . . 156, 544, 628
3:29 . . . . 64, 76
4:1–7 548
4:8–11 548
4:12–20 548
4:21–31 548
5:2–6 . . . . 447, 579
5:12 . . . . 402, 404, 405
5:19–23 554
5:21 397
5:22 555
5:22–25 600
6:7 496
6:16 . . . . 64, 178, 484

EPHESIANS

1–2 486
1:3 575
2:3 329
2:11–16 484
2:14–16 575
3:20–21 575

4:8 190
4:12 486
4:22 329
4:24 44
5:3 554
5:14 . . . . 361, 382
5:18 621
5:18–21 540
5:18–33 613
5:22–6:9 552
5:22–33 156
5:25 623
5:31 622

PHILIPPIANS
1:1–2 547
1:3–11 547
1:12–26 547
1:15–18 543
1:20–28 557
1:23 168
1:27 329
1:27–2:18 547
2:5–11 . . . . 552, 575
2:6–11 . . .361, 388, 409, 551, 552
2:19–30 547
3:1–4:1 547
3:2 332
3:2–11 543
3:6 555
4:2 298
4:2–20 547
4:2–22 547
4:3 28
4:8 . . . . 210, 238
4:10–20 138
4:13 . . . . 300, 607
4:19 595
4:23 547

COLOSSIANS
1:15 340
1:15–20 . . . . .361, 409, 551, 575
1:18 340
2:11–12 446
2:16–17 445
3:5 554
3:16 576
3:18–41 552

1 THESSALONIANS
1:2–10 545
2:7 . . . . 186, 397
2:13–16 545
4. 557

4:1–12 546
4:13 454
4:13–5:11 . . . . 546, 557
4:13–18 . . . . 486, 557, 630
4:15 . . . . 329, 557
5:26 . . . . 615, 620, 621

2 THESSALONIANS
2:1–2 548
2:1–12 557
2:2 557

1 TIMOTHY
1:10 554
2:8–5 613
2:8–15 . . . . 544, 613
2:9–15 . . . . 158, 622
2:11–15 . . . . .156, 157, 159
2:12 158
3. 141
3:16 . . . . .361, 551, 575
5:8 608
5:17–18 79
5:18 . . . . 173, 212
5:19 447
5:23 615

2 TIMOTHY
1:12 577
2:11–13 . . . . 361, 382
2:15 636
3:16 . 59, 178, 212, 446, 539, 587,
                                         615
3:16–17 266
3:17 604
4:2 591
4:6–8 431
4:17 591

TITUS
1:2 . . . . 213, 215
1:3 591
1:12 167
2:3–5 598
3:4–7 575
3:5 206

HEBREWS
1:1 572
1:1–4 371
1:5 481
1:6 . . . . .251, 310–11
1:8–9 251
1:12 397
2:1–4 549

2:14–26 550
3. 409
3:1 406
3:7–4:11 549
3:7–11 256
4. 387
4:12–13 217
4:14–10:18 620
5–6 480
6. 379
6:4–12 549
6:18 213
7. . . . . 395, 406
8–10. . . . . 367, 586
8:8–12 . . . . 338, 484
8:8–13 173
8:10 342
9. 389
9:15–18 342
10:1–18 586
10:15–17 484
10:19–39 549
11. . . . . 371, 373
11:6 202
11:16 485
11:17–19. 630
12. 403
12–13. 387
12:14–29 549
12:29 588
13:15 576
13:17 31
13:22 549
22:24 440

JAMES
1:2 353
1:2–18 629
1:3 307
1:5 355
1:5–8 307
1:13 213
1:15 409
1:22 603
1:27 . . . . 592, 616
2:1 307
2:3 202
2:14 307
2:14–26 . . . . 308, 579
3:6 496
3:17 555
3:17–18 554
4:2 624
4:15 624
5:1 . . . . .373, 402, 404
5:15 . . . . 307, 624, 625

1 PETER

1:3–9	629
1:13–15	623
1:18–21	551
2:4–10	626
2:9–10	484, 576
2:12	628
2:13–3:7	552
2:15	628
2:21–25	551
2:24	47, 332
2:24–25	483
3:1	628
3:1–7	613
3:16	628
3:18	575
3:18–19	225
3:18–22	209, 551
3:19	591
3:20–21	261
5:5	79
5:6	79

2 PETER

1:5–7	554
1:7	555
1:12–15	431
1:15	545
1:16	224
1:20–21	212, 266, 572
1:21	60
3:15–16	308
3:16	173, 212
3:21	261

1 JOHN

1:5	585
2:12–14	361
3:13	347
4:1	347
4:8–9	585

2 JOHN

9–10	548, 591

JUDE

3	592

REVELATION

1:1	491, 562
1:4	558, 559
1:14	397
1:15	397
1:20	564
2:13	559
2:17	559
2:24	591
3:14–22	316
3:18	558
4:11	361
5:8	564
5:9–10	361
6:6	559
7:4	565
7:15–17	361
9:5	566
9:7–11	559, 560
10:9–11	565
11:1	564
11:1–13	564
11:2	565
11:17–18	361
12:6	565
12:9	564
12:10–12	361
12:14	565
13:5	565
13:10	361
13:13	566
13:13–17	564
13:18	264, 566
14:1	565
14:4	565
15:3–4	361
16:5–7	361
16:16	564
17–18	153
17:12	564
17:18	564
18	361
18:18	397
19:1	373
19:1–8	361
19:1–11	486
19:3	373
19:4	373
19:6	373
19:9	212
20:1–10	275
20:4	566
21:12	565
21:14	565
22:10	561
22:18–19	248
22:21	559

EXTRA BIBLICAL LITERATURE INDEX

DEUTEROCANONICAL WORKS

Sirach

25:1–2 495
25:7–11 495
26:28 495
50:25–26 495
51:23–27 167

Baruch

3:36–37 168

1 Maccabees

9:27 170

2 Maccabees

2:13–15 171
12:44–45 168

JOSEPHUS

Against Apion

1.38–41 169
1.40–41 167

Jewish Antiquities

4.8.13 323
12.2.1–15 339

TALMUD

Baba Batra

14b 171

Sanhedrin

22a 167

ANCIENT TEXTS

Dead Sea Scrolls

4Q397 170
4QSam 189

SUBJECT INDEX

Acts
  genre of, 532–41
  horizontal thinking of, 534
  interpretation of, 533–41
  as narrative, 538–41
  outline of, 534–35
  Pentecost and, 532, 536–41
  vertical thinking of, 533–34
adjectives, 358–59
adverbs, 358–59
advocacy groups
  cultural criticism, 145, 148–55
  feminist hermeneutics, 34, 144–45, 155–63, 234
  LGBT hermeneutics, 145, 161–64
  liberation hermeneutics, 111, 145–48
Alexandrian thinkers, 83–85
allegorical method, 70–72, 82–94
allegory, 70–72, 82–94, 218, 488–90
alliteration, 369–71
Ambassadorial letter, 549
anagogical sense, 89, 91
ancestral epic, 427
anecdotes, 422
anthropomorphism, 400
antithetical proverbs, 495–96. *See also* Proverbs
apocalyptic literature, 142, 251, 562–67. *See also* literature
apocalyptic prophecy, 491–93. *See also* prophecy
Apocrypha, 87, 166–75
apostles, 77–86, 168–69, 174, 178–79
apostolic fathers, 81–83
apostolic period, 77–80
apostrophe, 402–4
application
  analogous situations, 608–9
  authority levels, 630–32
  avoiding mistakes in, 605–9
  of Bible to life, 64–65, 602–36
  of broader principles, 604, 610, 613–19, 629–35
  cross-cultural applications, 605–7, 610, 629–35
  evaluating, 610–28
  Holy Spirit and, 635–36
  identifying cross-cultural principles, 629–35

  importance of, 603–4
  incorrect analogies, 608–9
  interpretation and, 77, 79, 602–36
  meaning of, 602–3
  methodology for, 609–35
  original applications, 611–28
  specificity of, 610–28
  terminology for, 602–3
aretalogies, 511
assonance, 369–71
audience, 49–53
author, 49–53, 123–25
author-centered meaning
  biblical literary studies and, 268–69, 293–300
  definition of, 265–66
  as goal of interpretation, 263–66, 293–94
  historicity and, 269–71
  reader-oriented interpretation and, 266–68
authorial intention, 118, 125, 130, 245, 247
autographs, 182–89
avowal of innocence, 502–3. *See also* wisdom
    literature

baptism
  in Holy Spirit, 535, 540
  of infants, 273–74
  interpretation and, 272–74, 285, 289
  of Jesus, 214, 279, 513
  salvation and, 188, 261
battle reports, 422
Bible
  analogous situations, 608–9
  applying to life, 64–65, 602–36
  authority of, 213–17
  avoiding mistakes with, 605–9
  beauty of, 600–601
  as canon of Holy Scripture, 221–22
  constructing liturgies with, 576–78
  diversity of, 218–20, 308, 486, 540–41, 583
  enriching worship with, 573–76
  formulating theology with, 578–88
  gaining information from, 105–6, 571–73
  incorrect analogies, 608–9

inner-biblical allusion, 69–77
literary context of, 305–12, 605–9
as literature, 119–26, 268–69, 293–300, 600–601
neglecting context of, 605–9
pastoral care with, 572, 593–95, 598
preaching with, 589–90
presuppositions about, 211–22
promoting spiritual formation with, 593, 595–600
as spiritual document, 217, 221–22
teaching with, 591–92
truth of, 213–17
understanding, 40–42, 52, 202–8, 220–21, 571–73
unity of, 106, 120–21, 181–82, 218–20
using today, 571–601
for worship, 35, 573–76
bible genres, 417–567. *See also* genres
biblical canon, 165–97. *See also* canon
biblical poetry, 361–413. *See also* poetry
Biblical Theology Movement, 106, 109
blessings, 433–34

canon. *See also* Bible
criteria for, 178–80
criticism, 109, 180–90
development of, 166–77
English translations, 192–96
of Holy Scripture, 221–22
of New Testament, 172–78
of Old Testament, 166–72
order of, 171–72, 177–78
textual criticism of, 184–90
translations and, 165–97
canon criticism, 109, 180–90
casuistic law, 439–42, 449
catena, 88–89
characterization, 119–20, 125, 494, 500, 538
chiasm, 390–94
chreia, 530, 531
church councils, 81, 86–88, 96
church membership, 202, 208–9, 273, 612
church tradition, 80–83, 93–94, 180, 223–24, 587–88
comedy, 429–31
communication, 45–49
conflicting views, 289–90
conjunctions, 357–58
connectives, 357–58
connotative meaning, 47–48, 331–32. *See also* meaning
conservative reader-response, 129–31
construction reports, 422
contextualization, 314–15, 318–23
contextual meaning, 47–48, 332–33, 343–44. *See also* meaning

cosmic epic, 426
couplets, 366, 369–70, 376, 383–86, 389
covenantal nomism, 556
creeds, 50–51, 114, 239, 249, 285, 551–52
critical realism, 127, 131, 237, 280
crucifixion, 47, 108, 232–35, 484–85, 527, 566
cultural criticism, 145, 148–55
cultural distance, 56–57
cultural-historical background
caution regarding, 319–21
contextualization of, 314–15, 318–23
examining passages, 321–24
expression of, 318–19
mindset on, 313–14, 317
original background of, 315–16
original impact of, 317
perspective on, 313–15, 319–22
principles for interpretation, 315–21
of prose, 312–24
retrieving, 321–24
significance of, 313–15

Dead Sea Scrolls, 72, 169–70, 184, 251, 259
deconstruction, 131–34
demythologize, 105–6, 528–29, 560
denotative meaning, 47–48, 331–32. *See also* meaning
descriptive proverbs, 494. *See also* Proverbs
Deuteronomy laws, 449–51
developmentalism, 99
dialectical theology, 105–6
Didache, 81, 174
Diognetus, 81
dirges, 451, 454, 466–67
disaster, prophecy of, 463–64
dispensationalism, 241, 445, 519, 522, 536–38
disputation speeches, 470–71, 500–503
distance
cultural distance, 56–57
geographical distance, 57–58
of language, 58–59
of time, 53–56
distichs, 376, 385–86, 395
diversity, 218–20, 308, 486, 540–41, 548, 583, 634
divine factor, 59–61
domestic code, 552
dream reports, 422–23

ellipsis, 377, 380, 386, 389
embedded genres. *See also* genres
blessings, 433–34
fables, 434–35
interpretation of, 437–38
lists, 436–37
parables, 434–35

proverbs, 433–34
riddles, 434
songs, 436
end times, 274–76
epics, 425–27
epiphany reports, 423
Epistles
creeds in, 551–52
domestic codes in, 552
forms within, 551–55
general considerations, 541–45, 549–51
genre of, 541–58
hymns in, 551–52
interpretation of, 541–45
lists in, 551, 554–55
Pauline Epistles, 178, 543, 555–58
Revelation as, 558–61
slogans in, 552–54
special considerations, 545–49
eschatology, 274–75, 285, 520–23, 559–66
eternal relevance, 59–60
ethics of Jesus, 522–23
example story, 498–500. *See also* wisdom literature
existentialism, 104–9, 204, 232, 522, 525

fables, 434–35
faith, rule of, 87, 218
farewell speech, 431–32
feminist hermeneutics, 34, 144–45, 155–63, 234
flow-of-thought, 295–96, 351–55
foreign nations prophecies, 471–72
foretelling, 479–82
form criticism, 103–7, 118–22, 229, 419–21, 462, 551
forthtelling, 475–78
free rhythm, 366. *See also* rhythm
fulfillment, 482–86

genres
Acts genre, 532–41
blessings, 433–34
comedy, 429–31
embedded genres, 433–38
Epistles, 541–58
fables, 434–35
farewell speech, 431–32
Gospels, 510–32
heroic narratives, 421, 425–29
law, 438–51
lists, 436–37
literary genres, 103, 209, 219, 281, 293–94, 304–5, 417–20, 434, 510–11
narrative genres, 419–38
nature of, 417–19
of New Testament, 510–67

of Old Testament, 417–509
parables, 434–35
poetry, 451–61
prophecy, 462–93
prophet story, 428–29
proverbs, 433–34
reports, 421–25
Revelation, 558–67
riddles, 434
songs, 436, 451, 454–56
structural outlines, 432–33, 449–53, 488–89, 505–9
understanding, 417–567
wisdom literature, 179, 351, 458, 493–509
geographical distance, 57–58
God
faith in, 202–5
kingdom of, 519–22
message of, 34–35, 59–65, 209–14, 241–42, 266, 311–12, 472, 580, 587–89, 601
revelation inspired by, 211–13
word of, 31–33, 39–41, 53, 59–62, 104, 108, 164, 203, 207, 212–14, 237–41, 284, 308, 312–15, 399, 491, 517, 540, 561, 592–99, 602–4
Gospels
audiences of, 518–19
ethics of Jesus and, 522–23
explanation of, 510–12
forms within, 523–32
genre of, 510–32
history of, 512–19
horizontal thinking of, 514–18
interpretation of, 512–19
kingdom of God and, 519–22
meaning of, 510–11
miracle stories in, 98, 141–42, 524, 528–30
original readers of, 518–19
parables in, 52, 320–21, 332, 434–35, 525–28, 601
pronouncement stories in, 524, 530–31, 567
theological issues, 519–23
vertical thinking of, 514–18
grammatical-historical analysis, 117, 129, 144, 255–62
grammatical-structural relationships
of adjectives, 358–59
of adverbs, 358–59
of conjunctions, 357–58
of connectives, 357–58
discovering, 351–60
flow-of-thought, 351–55
importance of, 346–51
natural divisions of sections, 351
of pronouns, 359–60
in prose, 344–60

sections for study, 351
of sentences, 345–60
of verbs, 355–57

Hebrew poetry, 361–413. *See also* poetry
Hellenistic Judaism, 70–72. *See also* Judaism
hermeneutical spiral, 127, 228, 240–43, 277–80, 286
hermeneutics
    advocacy groups, 144–64
    cultural criticism, 145, 148–55
    definition of, 39–40, 42–43
    explanation of, 39–43
    feminist hermeneutics, 34, 144–45, 155–63
    goal of, 61–65, 224–26
    hermeneutical spiral, 127, 228, 240–43, 277–80, 286
    LGBT hermeneutics, 145, 161–64
    liberation hermeneutics, 111, 145–48
    need for, 39–65
    new hermeneutics, 40, 108–9, 233, 527–28
    of poetry, 361–413
    presuppositions about, 224–26
    of prose, 293–360
    redemptive-movement hermeneutic, 115, 627
    rules of, 293–360, 362–413
    of transformation, 115
heroic narratives
    ancestral epic, 427
    cosmic epic, 426
    description of, 421
    epics, 425–27
    historical allusions, 426–27
    interpretation of, 429
    prophet story, 428–29
historical allusions, 426–27
historical-critical methods
    concerns about, 60, 99–101
    explanation of, 50, 99
    of interpretation, 50, 60, 90, 99–105, 134–35, 232–35
    social-scientific approaches and, 134–35, 152–53
historical-cultural background
    caution regarding, 319–21
    contextualization of, 314–15, 318–23
    examining passages, 321–24
    expression of, 318–19
    mindset on, 313–14, 317
    original background of, 315–16
    original impact of, 317
    perspective on, 313–15, 319–22
    principles for interpretation, 315–21
    of prose, 312–24
    retrieving, 321–24
    significance of, 313–15

historical-grammatical analysis, 117, 129, 144, 255–62
historical reports, 423
historicity, 106, 229–33, 269–71, 533
Holy Scripture, 211–15, 221–22
Holy Spirit
    baptism in, 535, 540
    guidance of, 51, 255, 597
    illumination of, 41–42, 93–94, 202, 206–9
    praying to, 635–36
    relying on, 206–7, 635–36
    role of, 39, 217, 221, 535–36, 635–36
    witness of, 94, 176
hymns, 455–56, 467–68, 501–3, 551–52. *See also* songs
hyperbole, 402, 404–5

illocution, 46–52, 63, 244–57, 263–69, 276–78, 286–88
illocutionary purposes, 131, 214–16, 244, 257, 602
imagery, 122, 363, 396, 473, 527, 560–65
implied author, 123
implied reader, 123
imprecatory psalms, 451, 453
inaugurated eschatology, 520, 523
inclusio, 395, 398
inductive Bible study, 114, 228–30, 322, 342
inner-biblical allusion
    Hellenistic Judaism, 70–72
    post-biblical interpretation, 69–77
    Qumran community, 72–73
    rabbinic Judaism, 73–77
    transitions, 69–77
innocence, avowal of, 502–3. *See also* wisdom literature
interpretation
    apostolic period, 77–80
    application and, 77, 79, 602–36
    approaches to, 117–64
    art of, 42–43
    assessment of, 276–80
    author-centered meaning, 263–71, 293–300
    baptism and, 272–74, 285, 289
    benefits of, 571–601
    challenges of, 53–65
    communication and, 45–47
    conflicting views on, 289–90
    constructing meaning, 271–80
    correct interpretation, 210–26, 293–94
    divine factor, 59–61
    of Epistles, 541–45
    eternal relevance of, 59–60
    of genres, 417–567
    goal of, 61–65, 201–42, 244–90
    of Gospels, 512–19

historical-critical interpretation, 50, 60, 90, 99–105, 134–35, 232–35
historical-cultural interpretation, 315–21
history of, 66–116
inner-biblical allusion, 66–69
Jewish interpretation, 66–77
levels of meaning, 246–63
literal-contextual interpretation, 77, 79
literal interpretation, 77
literary approaches to, 48, 110, 117–34
meaning of message, 45–49, 246–63, 304
methods for, 202, 209–10
Middle Ages, 88–91
modern period, 99–116
of narratives, 424–33
need for, 39–65
objectivity in, 241–43
patristic period, 80–88
philosophical approaches, 229–36
of poetry, 361–413
post-biblical interpretation, 69–77
post-Reformation period, 96–98
presuppositions for, 60, 201, 210–26
preunderstandings for, 201, 226–43
principles of, 298–300, 315–21
of prose, 293–360
qualifications for, 202–10
reader-oriented interpretation, 266–68, 271–80
Reformation period, 92–96
rules of, 293–360, 362–413
science of, 42–43
social-scientific approaches to, 117, 134–64
speech acts and, 244–49, 255–57, 263–69, 349
testing validity of, 287–88
textual meaning, 263–71
traditional interpretation, 83, 86–91, 157–58
transitions, 69–77
typological interpretation, 78, 93, 258–62, 286–88
validating, 133, 280–90, 321–22, 470–88
interpreter
goal of, 61–65, 201–42, 244–90
presuppositions for, 201, 210–26
preunderstandings of, 201, 226–43
qualifications of, 202–10
role of, 44–45, 201–43
interpretive gloss, 89
intertextuality studies, 112–13, 219
irony, 402, 407–8, 430, 435, 467

Jesus
baptism of, 214, 279, 513
crucifixion of, 47, 108, 232, 235, 484–85, 527, 566
death of, 64, 219, 262, 309, 445, 484, 510–12, 516, 540–41

ethics of, 522–23
messiahship of, 77–80
ministry of, 54–55, 100–110, 278, 311, 323, 405, 511, 516
parables of, 52, 320–21, 332, 434–35, 525–28, 601
quest for, 107–10
resurrection of, 174–76, 188, 219, 222, 235, 262, 275–76, 309, 341, 398, 445, 510–12, 540–41, 586, 593–94
sayings of, 82–83, 174–77, 182, 187, 265, 375, 384, 608
teachings of, 100–108, 172–77, 477
words of, 33, 51–54, 174–77, 182, 187, 289, 299, 593, 603, 616–17
Jewish interpretation. *See also* Interpretation
Hellenistic Judaism, 70–72
inner-biblical allusion, 66–69
post-biblical interpretation, 69–77
Qumran community, 72–73
rabbinic Judaism, 73–77
Job, interpretation of, 502–4
Judaism
birthday of, 69
Hellenistic Judaism, 70–72
inner-biblical allusion, 66–69
rabbinic Judaism, 73–77

kerygma, 105, 235, 515, 518, 541
kingdom of God, 519–22. *See also* God

language, distance of, 58–59
language-event, 108–9, 235
language of poetry, 395–409. *See also* poetry
law
casuistic law, 439–42, 449
Deuteronomy laws, 449–51
interpretation of, 443–51
legal instruction, 442–43
legal material, 439–40
legal series, 441–42
Old Testament legal material, 439–40
sample legal text, 449
unconditional law, 440–41
lawsuit, 511
lectio divina, 115–16, 597
LGBT hermeneutics, 145, 161–64
liberal theology, 101, 104
liberation hermeneutics, 111, 145–48
liberation theology, 145–50, 155–58, 234
lists, 436–37, 551, 554–55
literal-contextual interpretation, 77, 79. *See also* interpretation
literal fulfillment, 77, 482, 626
literal interpretation, 77. *See also* interpretation

literal sense, 50, 80, 84–94
literary context. *See also* genres
    of Bible, 305–12, 605–9
    circles of, 300–312
    flow-of-thought, 295–96, 351–55
    immediate context, 301–5
    importance of, 295–98
    logical order, 303–4
    meaning of words, 296–98
    paragraphs, 297–98
    principles of, 295–300
    of prose, 294–312
    psychological transfer, 304
    sentences, 297–98
    sequence, 301–3
    strategy for, 300
    structure, 301–3
    theme, 301–7
    transitions, 304–5
    unit relationships, 297–98
literary criticism, 48, 110, 117–34. *See also* literary
        interpretations
literary genres, 103, 209, 219, 281, 293–94, 304–4,
        417–20, 434, 510–11. *See also* genres
literary interpretations. *See also* interpretation
    deconstruction, 131–34
    literary criticism, 48, 110, 117–34
    narrative criticism, 119–26
    postmodernism, 126–34
    poststructuralism, 126–34
    reader-response criticism, 128–31
literary outline, 412–13
literary strategy, 300
literature
    apocalyptic literature, 142, 251, 562–67
    Bible as, 119–26, 268–69, 600–601
    wisdom literature, 179, 351, 458, 493–509
liturgies, 451, 456–57, 468–69, 576–78
locution, 46–52, 214–16, 225, 235, 244–45,
        254–69, 276–78
logical order, 96, 303–4
love songs, 456. *See also* songs

meaning
    of application, 602–3
    assessment of, 276–80
    author-centered meaning, 263–71, 293–300
    baptism and, 272–74
    connotative meanings, 47–48, 331–32
    constructing, 271–80
    contextual meanings, 47–48, 332–33, 343–44
    defining, 249
    denotative meanings, 47–48, 331–32
    end times and, 274–76
    levels of, 246–63

literary context and, 295–98
    of message, 45–49, 246–63, 304
    millennium and, 274–76
    potential meanings, 246–63
    reader-oriented interpretation, 266–68, 271–80
    referential meanings, 47–48, 332
    textual meaning, 47–49, 246–71
    validating, 280–90
    views on, 289–90, 602–3
    of words, 296–98, 324–44
memoirs, 422
merismus, 394
message. *See also* interpretation
    applying, 64–65, 602–36
    discerning, 63–65
    effect of, 317
    of God, 34–35, 59–65, 209–14, 241–42, 266,
        311–12, 472, 580, 587–89, 601
    intention of, 300
    meaning of, 45–49, 246–63, 304
    obeying, 202, 205–6
metaphors, 157–58, 266, 363, 396–401, 408, 487,
        494, 497, 586
meter, 364–67. *See also* poetry
metonymy, 402, 405–6
Middle Ages, 88–91
midrash, 75–76, 82, 258–63, 550
millennium, 274–76
miracle stories, 98, 141–42, 524, 528–30
misconceptions, avoiding, 63–64
modern period
    nineteenth century, 99–102
    post-World War I, 104–6
    post-World War II, 106–11
    twentieth century, 102–3
    twenty-first century, 111–16
monotheism, 153, 219, 311
moral sense, 85, 89
morphology, 344–46
motifs, 119–20, 472, 528

narrative criticism, 119–26
narrative genres. *See also* genres
    comedy, 429–31
    epics, 425–27
    farewell speech, 431–32
    heroic narratives, 421, 425–29
    interpretation of, 424–33
    prophetic narratives, 473–74
    prophet story, 428–29
    reports, 421–25
    sample narrative, 432–33
neo-orthodoxy, 105–6, 156, 214
new hermeneutics, 40, 108–9, 233, 527–28. *See also*
        hermeneutics

New Testament
    Acts genre, 532–41
    canon of, 172–78
    Epistles, 541–58
    genres of, 510–67
    Gospels, 510–32
    Revelation, 558–67
numerical proverbs, 495. *See also* Proverbs

obedience, 202, 205–6
Old Testament
    canon of, 166–72
    casuistic law, 439–42, 449
    Deuteronomy laws, 449–51
    genres of, 417–509
    legal instruction, 442–43
    legal material, 439–40
    legal series, 441–42
    narrative genres, 421–33
    poetry, 451–61
    prophecy, 462–93
    unconditional law, 440–41
onomatopoeia, 372–73

parables, 52, 320–21, 332, 434–35, 525–28, 601
paragraphs
    context of, 297–98
    in prose, 294–305, 343–46, 352–55
    sentences in, 294–302, 328–32, 345–60
parallelism. *See also* poetry
    of comparison, 383–84
    complexity of, 378–79
    of continuation, 382–83
    of contrast, 380–81
    explanation of, 373–79
    of intensification, 386–87
    of members, 373–74
    of specification, 384–86
    staircase parallelism, 389–90
    of subordination, 381–82
    of time, 382
    types of, 379–89
    units of, 375–77
paronomasia, 371–72, 379. *See also* wordplay
pastoral care, 572, 593–95, 598
patristic period, 81–88
Pauline Epistles, 178, 543, 555–58. *See also* Epistles
Pauline theology, 555–58
penitential psalm, 451, 453
Pentecost, 259, 307, 445, 532, 536–41
perlocution, 46–50, 56, 63, 244–54, 263–69, 286–89
perlocutionary purposes, 131, 215, 244–45, 254, 257, 602
personification, 402–3, 408
pesher, 73, 258–63
pietism, 97–98, 530

plot, 119–21, 125, 494, 500, 525–27, 538
poetry
    alliteration, 369–71
    anthropomorphism, 400
    apostrophe, 402–4
    assonance, 369–71
    chiasm, 390–94
    devices of, 396–401
    dynamics of, 362–73
    features of, 364
    genres of, 451–61
    hyperbole, 402, 404–5
    imagery, 396
    inclusio, 395
    interpretation of, 361–413, 458–59
    irony, 402, 407–8
    language of, 395–409
    literary outline of, 412–13
    liturgies, 451, 456–57
    merismus, 394
    metaphors, 396–401, 408
    meter, 364–67
    metonymy, 402, 405–6
    Old Testament poetry, 451–61
    onomatopoeia, 372–73
    parallelism, 373–90
    personification, 402–3, 408
    poetic effects, 368–73
    prayers, 451–54
    rhyme, 364–65, 371
    rhythm, 362–63, 366–69, 436
    similes, 396–401
    songs, 436, 451, 454–56
    sounds of, 364–73
    structure of, 363, 373–95, 409–13, 458–59
    synecdoche, 402, 406–7
    translation, 369–72
    transliteration, 369–72
    types of, 362–73, 451–61
    units of, 375–77, 409–13
    wisdom psalms, 451, 457–58
    word repetition, 372–73
post-biblical interpretation, 69–77. *See also* interpretation
postmodernism, 126–34
post-Reformation period, 96–98
poststructuralism, 126–34
prayers. *See also* worship
    dirges, 451, 454
    imprecatory psalms, 451, 453
    liturgies, 451, 456–57
    penitential psalm, 451, 453
    protest prayer, 451–53
    royal protest prayer, 451–52
    songs, 454–56

preaching with Bible, 589–90
prescriptive proverbs, 494–95. *See also* Proverbs
presuppositions
    about Bible, 211–22
    about goal of hermeneutics, 224–26
    about methodology, 222–24
    for correct interpretation, 210–26
    facts of, 225–26
    for interpretation, 60, 201, 210–26
preunderstandings
    categories of, 227–28
    changes in, 239–41
    Christian preunderstandings, 237–38
    definition of, 227–28
    of interpreter, 201, 226–43
    objectivity and, 241–43
    philosophical approaches, 229–36
    problem of, 581–83
    role of, 228–31
    testing, 236–37
pronouncement stories, 524, 530–31, 567
pronouns, 359–60
prophecy
    apocalyptic prophecy, 491–93
    dirges, 466–67
    of disaster, 463–64
    disputation, 470–71
    against foreign nations, 471–72
    foretelling, 479–82
    forthtelling, 475–78
    fulfillment, 482–86
    hymns, 467–68
    interpretation of, 474–93
    liturgies, 468–69
    narratives, 473–74
    prophecy proper, 491
    Revelation as, 561–62
    of salvation, 464–65
    sample prophecy, 488–91
    types of, 463–64
    vision reports, 472–73
    woe speech, 465–66
prophetic narratives, 473–74
prophet story, 428–29
prose
    adjectives in, 358–59
    adverbs in, 358–59
    conjunctions in, 357–58
    connectives in, 357–58
    cultural background of, 312–24
    flow-of-thought in, 295–96, 351–55
    grammatical relationships, 344–60
    historical background of, 312–24
    interpretation of, 293–360
    literary context of, 294–312

    paragraphs in, 294–305, 343–46, 352–55
    pronouns in, 359–60
    sentences in, 294–302, 328–32, 345–60
    structural relationships, 344–60
    verbs in, 355–57
    word meanings, 324–44
protest prayer, 451–53
Proverbs
    antithetical proverbs, 495–96
    better-than proverbs, 495
    descriptive proverbs, 494
    interpretation of, 496–97
    numerical proverbs, 495
    popular proverbs, 433–34
    prescriptive proverbs, 494–95
    types of, 494–97
Psalms
    imprecatory psalms, 451, 453
    interpretation of, 459–61
    overview of, 459–61
    penitential psalm, 451, 453
    protest prayer, 451–53
    royal protest prayer, 451–52
    songs, 454–56
    wisdom psalms, 451, 457–58, 493–94
pseudepigrapha, 167
pseudonymity, 438, 543–45, 563
psychological transfer, 304
puns, 371–72, 379

qualifications
    church membership, 202, 208–9
    faith in God, 202–5
    illumination of Holy Spirit, 202, 206–8
    of interpreter, 202–10
    methods for interpretation, 202, 209–10
    obedience, 202, 205–6
Qumran community, 72–73
Qur'an, 188–89

rabbinic Judaism, 73–77
radical Reformation, 95
rationalism, 97–98, 101, 204
reader-oriented interpretation, 266–68, 271–80
reader-response criticism, 128–31
real author, 123–25
real reader, 123–25
reception history, 113
redaction criticism, 107, 117, 123, 180–83, 517–18, 534
redemptive-movement hermeneutic, 115, 627
referential meaning, 47–48, 332. *See also* meaning
reflection, 498–500. *See also* wisdom literature
Reformation period, 92–96
reports
    anecdotes, 422

battle reports, 422
construction reports, 422
dream reports, 422–23
epiphany reports, 423
historical reports, 423
interpretation of, 424–25
memoirs, 422
vision reports, 472–73
Revelation
as apocalyptic literature, 562–67
as Epistle, 558–61
genre of, 558–67
inspiration of, 211–13
as prophecy, 561–62
rhetoric, 71, 118, 145, 268, 450, 547–50
rhetorical criticism, 118
rhyme, 364–65, 371. *See also* poetry
rhythm, 362–63, 366–69, 436. *See also* poetry
riddles, 434
royal protest prayer, 451–52
rule of faith, 87, 218

salvation, and baptism, 188, 261
salvation, prophecy of, 464–65
scholasticism, 90–92, 95–97
scientific method, 99, 229
scientism, 228–29, 578–79
semantic fields, 325–30, 338–39
sense units, 409–13
sensus plenior, 255–57, 263
sentences
context of, 297–98
grammatical-structural relationships of, 345–60
in prose, 294–302, 328–32, 345–60
types of, 352–55
Septuagint, 70, 87, 167–69, 189, 310, 334, 339–41
sequence, 219, 259–63, 301–3
Sermon on the Mount, 351, 522–23, 603, 624
similes, 396–401
slogans, 552–54
social history, 135–40
social-scientific interpretations, 117, 135–64, 152–53
social-scientific theories, 135, 140–44
sola scriptura, 93, 95–96, 578
songs, 436, 451, 454–56
source criticism, 100, 107, 122, 152, 534
speech act theory
categories of, 45–47
elements of, 45–47, 244–45
illocutionary purposes and, 131, 214–16, 254, 257, 602
interpretation and, 244–49, 255–57, 263–69, 349
mindset and, 313–14
perlocutionary purposes and, 131, 215, 254, 257, 602
sensus plenior and, 255–57
spiritual document, 217, 221–22. *See also* Bible

spiritual formation, 593, 595–600
staircase parallelism, 389–90. *See also* parallelism
stichs, 376–78, 383–85, 391, 394
structural-grammatical relationships
of adjectives, 358–59
of adverbs, 358–59
of conjunctions, 357–58
of connectives, 357–58
discovering, 351–60
flow-of-thought, 351–55
importance of, 346–51
natural divisions of sections, 351
of pronouns, 359–60
in prose, 344–60
sections for study, 351
of sentences, 345–60
of verbs, 355–57
structural outlines, 432–33, 449–53, 488–89, 505–9
supernatural, 60, 99, 102, 142, 203–5, 222–29
syncretism, 318–19
synecdoche, 402, 406–7
syntax, 191, 209, 258, 344–46, 366
systematic theology, 92, 104, 579–83

Talmud, 74, 171
Targum, 69–70, 190
teaching with Bible, 591–92
textual criticism, 184–90, 210, 367
textual meaning, 47–49, 246–71. *See also* meaning
thanksgiving song, 454–55. *See also* songs
theme, 119–21, 125, 301–7, 500
theology
church tradition and, 587–88
dialectical theology, 105–6
formulating, 578–88
liberal theology, 101, 104
liberation theology, 145–50, 155–58, 234
Pauline theology, 555–58
preunderstanding and, 581–83
principles of, 584–87
systematic theology, 92, 104, 583–85
time, distance of, 53–56
traditional interpretation, 83, 86–91, 157–58. *See also* interpretation
tradition criticism, 513
transitions, 69–77, 304–5
translations, 165–97, 369–72
transliteration, 369–72
triplets, 376
tristichs, 376, 385–86, 389
Twelve Apostles, 174, 178–79. *See also* apostles, Didache
typological interpretation, 78, 93, 258–62, 286–88. *See also* interpretation
typology, 80–81, 97, 218, 260–63, 277–79, 483

unconditional law, 440–41
units of poetry, 375–77, 409–13. *See also* poetry
unity, 106, 120–21, 181–82, 218–20

validity of interpretation, 133, 280–90, 321–22,
    470–88. *See also* interpretation
verbs, 355–57
vice lists, 551, 554–55
virtue lists, 551, 554–55
vision reports, 472–73
Vulgate, 87–88, 92–93, 96, 192, 298

wedding songs, 456. *See also* songs
wisdom literature
    criticism of, 179
    disputation speeches, 470–71, 500–503
    example story, 498–500
    genres of, 351, 458
    hymns, 501–3
    innocence, 502–3
    instruction, 497–98
    interpretation of, 494–505
    proverbs, 494–97
    reflection, 498–500
    sample wisdom text, 504–5
    structural outlines, 505–9
    types of, 493–509

wisdom psalms, 451, 457–58, 493–94
woe speech, 465–66
womanist, 163, 234
wordplay, 133, 371–73, 379, 433, 490, 497
words
    analysis of, 332–33
    as arbitrary signs, 325–27
    changing meanings of, 330–32
    connotative meanings of, 47–48, 331–32
    contextual meanings of, 47–48, 332–33, 343–44
    defining, 296–98, 324–28
    denotative meanings of, 47–48, 331–32
    features of, 325–32
    figurative meanings of, 331–32
    literary context of, 296–98
    meanings of, 296–98, 324–44
    nature of, 325–32
    overlapping meanings of, 328–29
    in prose, 324–44
    range of meanings for, 333–43
    referential meanings of, 47–48, 332
    study of, 332–44
worship. *See also* prayers
    Bible and, 35, 573–76
    corporate worship, 217, 451–52, 461, 576
    enriching, 573–76
    temple worship, 55, 425

AUTHOR INDEX

Aarts, B., 351
Abbott, R., 374
Abegg, M. G., Jr., 72, 491, 492, 493
Achtemeier, M., 234
Achtemeier, P. J., 483, 591
Adam, A. K. M., 131
Adamo, P. C., 88
Adams, Sean A., 532
Aesop, 119, 435
Aland, B., 184
Aland, K., 184
Alden, Robert L., 392, 393
Alexander, L. C. A., 512, 532, 547
Alexander, T. D., 265
Allen, L. C., 428, 608
Allen, R. J., 590
Allison, D. C., Jr., 80
Allison, G. R., 50, 584
Alter, R., 270, 362, 366, 374,
    375, 376, 377, 378, 385, 386,
    387, 388, 406, 419, 494, 503
Amador, J. O. H., 157
Amit, Y., 120, 124, 268, 420
Andersen, F. I., 352, 357
Anderson, C. B., 439
Anderson, P. N., 110
Anderson, R., 584
Aquinas, Thomas, 87, 88, 91,
    93–94, 98
Archer, G. L., 562
Archer, K. J., 102
Armerding, C., 212
Arndt, W. F., 337
Arnold, B. T., 143, 463, 464
Arnold, C. E., 318
Arnold, J. C., 624
Aronson, Jason, 272
Arthurs, J., 611
Auerbach, E., 125
Augustine, 87, 89–91, 238
Aune, D. E., 269, 546, 550, 558
Austin, J. L., 244
Avalos, H., 212, 428

Averbeck, R. E., 443
Avishur, Y., 379
Ayayo, K. G., 111, 610

Bailey, J. L., 373, 377, 390, 391,
    394, 524, 531
Bailey, K. E., 320, 525, 528
Bailey, Randall C., 112, 149, 438
Bainton, R., 93
Baker, D. L., 78
Baker, D. W., 190, 223
Baker, H., 596
Balch, D. L., 143, 552
Balentine, S. E., 573
Balla, P., 180
Balz, H., 342
Banks, R., 445
Bar-Efrat, S., 134
Barker, Kit, 195, 257
Barnabas, 81–82, 173–74, 179, 539
Barr, James, 215, 330, 580
Barrett, C. K., 75, 77, 79, 304,
    484, 536
Barron, R. E., 115
Barry, W. A., 598
Bartchy, S. S., 161
Bartels, K. H., 575
Barth, Karl, 104, 105, 214, 583
Barth, M., 551
Barthes, Roland, 49, 248
Bartholomew, C. G., 111, 114,
    219, 244
Barton, J., 128, 172, 232, 236,
    268, 419
Barton, S. C., 602
Bassler, J. M., 120
Bateman, H. W., 277
Bauckham, R., 511, 515, 516,
    545, 550, 555, 567
Bauer, D. R., 114, 605, 631
Bauer, Walter, 223, 337
Baum, A. D., 55
Baumann, C., 523

Baumgarten, M., 101
Baumgartner, W., 335
Baur, F. C., 100, 101, 102
Bautch, R. J., 452
Beal, T. K., 430
Beale, G. K., 78, 107, 219, 250,
    260, 264, 276, 309, 493, 565
Beardsley, M. C., 118, 242
Beasley-Murray, G. R., 274, 566
Beavis, M. A., 520
Bechtel, L. M., 158
Beckman, J. C., 357
Beckwith, Roger, 167, 170, 171
Bedouelle, G., 96
Beecher, W. J., 101
Beekman, J., 191, 352
Begrich, J., 103
Beitzel, B. J., 339
Bell, A. A., Jr., 139
Bellah, R., 57
Belleville, L. L., 162, 547, 624
Belli, H., 147
Bellinger, W. H., Jr., 452, 454, 457
Benedict, D. T., Jr., 577
Benjamin, D. C., 137, 138, 139,
    426, 439, 454, 455
Bennema, C., 119
Benner, D. G., 593, 598
Benton, R., 473
Bergant, D., 139
Berger, Y., 391, 531
Berlin, A., 119, 270, 362, 363, 365,
    366, 369, 372, 374, 378, 379,
    380, 381, 382, 383, 395, 430
Berstein, M., 72
Best, E., 57, 518, 623
Best, H. M., 573
Betz, H.-D., 548
Beuken, W. A. M., 465
Beza, Theodore, 95, 96
Bilezikian, G., 156
Billings, B. S., 187
Birch, B. C., 107, 427, 441, 443,

444

Bird, M. F., 510, 556, 583
Black, D. A., 331, 371
Blaiklock, E. M., 126
Blaising, C. A., 277
Blamires, H., 632
Blass, F., 346, 347
Blenkinsopp, J., 141
Block, D. I., 52, 439
Blomberg, Craig L., 56, 103, 107,
    120, 123, 125, 146, 158, 160,
    189, 195, 203, 204, 205, 212,
    214, 217, 218, 249, 251, 253,
    266, 281, 294, 304, 313,
    435, 481, 511, 514, 517, 518,
    521, 523, 526, 530, 537, 550,
    572, 580, 599, 609, 615, 616,
    618, 620, 622
Bloom, H., 182
Blount, B. K., 565
Boccaccini, G., 73
Bock, Darrell L., 61, 167, 190,
    250, 255, 262, 277, 290,
    484, 513, 537
Boda, M. J., 350, 479
Boer, R., 146
Boerman, D., 98
Bonhoeffer, D., 596
Bonner, G., 87
Booth, R. R., 273
Borg, M. J., 224
Borgen, P., 71
Boring, M. E., 543
Borsch, F. H., 320
Botha, P. J., 370
Botterweck, G. J., 335
Bourkin, Y., 123
Boyd, G. A., 205, 234, 584
Boyer, J. L., 347
Bray, G., 91, 96, 99, 100, 101, 102
Breed, B. W., 113
Breneman, M., 430
Brensinger, T. L., 398
Brettler, M. Z., 456
Briggs, C. A., 102, 335
Briggs, R. S., 131, 244, 602
Bright, J., 475
Bromiley, G. W., 104, 214, 273,
    334, 583
Brooke, George J., 72, 259
Brotzman, E. R., 184, 187
Brower, K., 518
Brown, C., 528
Brown, D., 87
Brown, F., 335

Brown, Jeannine K., 46, 117, 244,
    245, 313, 611
Brown, R., 256, 519
Brown, S., 256
Brown, W. P., 215, 458, 493
Brownlee, W. H., 73
Brownson, J. V., 234
Broyles, C., 451
Bruce, F. F., 172, 174, 175, 179,
    222, 259, 297, 334
Brueggemann, W., 107, 220, 427,
    452, 455, 458
Brunn, D., 192
Brunner, Emil, 105
Bullinger, E. W., 364, 404, 405,
    406, 407
Bullock, H. C., 453
Bultmann, C., 469
Bultmann, Rudolf, 44, 104–5,
    107–8, 232, 330, 513, 529
Bunsen, C. C. J. von, 101
Burdick, D. W., 330
Burge, G. M., 64, 448, 485, 532,
    627
Burkett, D., 543
Burridge, R. A., 512
Bush, F. W., 167, 362, 425
Buss, M. J., 123
Bussell, H. L., 45
Butler, C., 127
Butler, T. C., 334, 421, 425, 426,
    434, 475, 477
Byargeon, R. W., 467
Byatt, A., 399
Byrskog, S., 513

Cain, A., 88
Caird, G. B., 46, 388, 559
Calhoun, A. H., 596
Callahan, A. D., 154
Callahan, J. P., 221
Callow, J., 191, 352
Calvin, John, 94–96, 159, 558,
    582, 622
Cameron, E., 93
Camp, C. V., 434
Campbell, Alexander, 100, 102
Campbell, C. R., 331, 347, 356
Campbell, W. S., 534
Caragounis, C. C., 58
Carmichael, C. M., 443
Carnell, E. J., 64, 236, 237
Carpenter, G., 486
Carrington, J. L., 92
Carroll, R. P., 141

Carroll R., M. D., 139, 152, 323,
    379, 419, 428, 467, 471, 483,
    503, 587
Carson, D. A., 50, 133, 179, 193,
    195, 207, 211, 229, 232, 235,
    253, 254, 330, 331, 349, 483,
    518, 565, 580, 581, 583, 594,
    614, 617
Carter, C. E., 135
Carter, W., 137
Cartledge, M. J., 113
Cartledge, T. W., 502
Casanowicz, I. M., 371
Casey, M., 597
Cason, T. S., 428
Cassian, John, 90
Cassidy, R. J., 146, 538
Cathcart, K. J., 434, 435
Cavalcanti, T., 158
Ceresko, A. R., 145
Cervantes, 119
Chadwick, O., 92, 96
Chafer, L. S., 277
Chalmers, A., 475
Chapman, C., 485, 627
Chapman, S. B., 169
Charles, J. D., 173
Charlesworth, J. H., 176
Charry, E. T., 115
Cheney, M., 500
Cheng, P. S., 163
Childers, J., 115
Childs, Brevard S., 106, 107, 109,
    113, 114, 172, 180, 181, 182,
    437, 438, 580
Chilton, B. D., 69, 74, 486
Chisholm, R. C., 315
Christensen, D. L., 436, 446,
    450, 471
Chrysostom, John, 85
Ciampa, R. E., 56
Cicero, 119
Citino, D., 134
Clapp, R., 587
Clark, S. L. R., 70, 628
Clement of Rome, 81, 84, 173–74
Clements, R. E., 141, 450
Clinebell, H. J., 593
Clines, David J. A., 120–21, 132,
    335, 419
Clinton, R., 598
Clouse, R. G., 481
Coats, G. W., 121, 421, 422, 425,
    426, 427
Cobb, J. B., 232

Coggins, R. J., 478, 479
Cohen, S. J. D., 73
Cohn, R., 181
Collins, A. Y., 142, 562
Collins, G. R., 593
Collins, J. J., 77, 127, 169, 491, 492, 563
Collins, R. F., 119
Collins, T., 366
Cone, J. H., 146
Connolly, W. J., 598
Coogan, M. D., 120
Cook, E. M., 72
Copan, P., 235, 591
Corner, M., 145
Cosgrove, C. H., 152
Costas, O. E., 148
Cotterell, P., 325, 344
Cottret, B., 94
Cowan, S. B., 213
Cozelmann, H., 107
Craigie, P. C., 341
Cranfield, C. E. B., 339, 484, 555, 626
Cremer, A. H., 101
Crenshaw, J. L., 457, 467, 493
Crim, K., 464
Croatto, J. S., 147
Crosman, R., 235
Crossan, John Dominic, 133, 224, 320, 513, 533
Crüsemann, F., 442
Culler, J., 131
Culpepper, R. A., 121, 124
Cunningham, L. S., 597

Dahood, M., 379
Dallaire, H., 344
Daly, M., 156
Danby, H., 76
Danker, F., 337
Darwin, Charles, 99
Davids, P. H., 549, 579
Davies, P. R., 72
Davies, W. D., 555, 627
Davis, J. J., 447
De Lubac, H., 89
De Regt, L. J., 371
Dearman, J. A., 608, 618
DeBrunner, A., 346, 347
DeClaissé-Walford, N., 182, 451, 453, 459, 493
Deere, J., 530
Delitzsch, Franz, 101
Delitzsch, Friedrich, 103

Dell, K. J., 457, 493, 498, 499, 500, 503
Delling, G., 575
Demarest, B. A., 580, 596
Dempster, S., 171
Dentan, R. C., 195
Derrida, Jacques, 131, 248
DeSilva, David, 550
Dever, W. G., 142, 204, 229
DeVries, Simon J., 52
Dewey, J., 124
DeYoung, J., 256
DeYoung, K., 234
DeYoung, R. K., 596
Di Berardino, A., 115
Dibelius, M., 104
Dick, M. B., 502
Diehl, J. A., 511
Diewert, D., 457
Dillard, R. B., 169
Dillistone, F. W., 582
Dobbs-Allsopp, F. W., 361, 362, 366, 367, 373, 374
Dockery, D., 77, 86, 213
Dodd, C. H., 105, 524, 541
Dombkowski Hopkins, D., 452, 454, 456, 458
Donfried, K. P., 549
Doriani, Daniel, 633–34
Dorival, G., 84
Dorsey, D. A., 445
Doty, W. G., 108
Douglas, J. D., 334
Douglas, M., 140, 143, 438
Dowd, S., 628
Driver, S. R., 101, 106, 335
Drosin, M., 221
Dube, M. W., 151, 163
Duguid, I. M., 456
Dunbar, D. G., 172, 174
Dungan, D. L., 85, 92, 98, 100, 177, 265
Dunn, J. D. G., 107, 214, 220, 540, 556
Dupertuis, R. B., 371
Durham, J. I., 446
Duvall, J. S., 607, 611

Eaton, M. A., 617
Ebeling, G., 108, 232
Ecklebarger, K. A., 606
Eco, U., 128
Eddy, P. R., 205, 584
Edes, G., 606
Edwards, Jonathan, 97

Edwards, M., 84
Edwards, R. A., 123
Egan, K. J., 597
Ehrman, Bart D., 60, 61, 177, 184, 545
Eichhorn, J. G., 99
Einspahr, B., 335
Eisenbaum, P., 586
Eliezer, R., 75
Elliott, J. H., 117, 135, 138, 141, 628
Ellis, E. E., 169
Elwell, W. A., 339
Enns, Peter, 215, 218, 250, 262, 370, 419, 610
Epperly, B. G., 233
Erasmus, 87, 92–93, 98
Erickson, M. J., 275, 578, 580, 583, 631
Esler, P. F., 135
Estes, D. J., 493, 613
Estienne, Robert, 185
Eusebius, 175
Evans, C. A., 82, 176, 250, 260, 262, 485, 491
Evans, M. J., 157
Evans, R., 113
Eve, E., 528
Ewald, H., 101
Exum, J. C., 158, 398, 419

Fagen, R. S., 323
Fairbairn, D., 83, 84, 344
Fairweather, J., 551
Fanning, B. M., 356
Fant, C. E., 543
Fantuzzo, C. J., 370
Farmer, William R., 152, 178
Farnell, F. D., 285
Farris, S., 371
Feagin, G. M., 407
Fearghail, F. Ó., 72
Fee, G. D., 58, 59, 196, 339, 352, 360, 388, 480, 496, 514, 528, 539, 553, 560, 614
Feinberg, J. S., 232
Feinberg, P. D., 562
Felder, Cain Hope, 154
Feldman, L. H., 72
Ferguson, D. S., 227, 228, 235, 588
Ferguson, E., 81, 273, 339, 588, 592
Fernández, D. R., 153
Fernando, A., 537, 612
Ferris, P. W., Jr., 452

Fewell, D. N., 124, 268, 428, 429
Fields, L. M., 365
Finlay, T. D., 422
Finney, M. T., 138
Firth, D. G., 430, 451, 452, 483
Fischer, A. A., 184
Fish, Stanley E., 43, 130, 248, 253
Fishbane, M., 67
Fitzmyer, J. A., 117, 154, 320, 534
Flemming, D., 319, 605
Flesher, P. V. M., 69
Fleteren, F. van, 87
Flint, Peter W., 72
Fokkelman, J. P., 270, 366, 410, 419
Fontaine, C. R., 434
Forbes, C., 547
Ford, J. M., 146
Forrester, D. B., 148
Foster, R. J., 596
Fowler, Robert M., 128, 129
Fox, M. V., 430, 456
France, R. T., 260, 514, 517,
    549, 595
Franke, J. R., 213, 214, 579, 583
Fredricks, C. J., 121, 626
Freedman, D. N., 308, 323, 334,
    366, 367
Frend, W. H. C., 83
Fretheim, T. E., 107, 427, 475
Friebel, K. G., 473, 474
Fried, J., 88
Friedrich, G., 341
Friesen, G., 621
Froehlich, K., 84
Frye, N., 134
Fuchs, E., 108
Funk, R. W., 60, 176, 223, 232,
    346, 347, 513
Furnish, V. P., 304

Gabel, J. B., 134, 451, 601
Gadamer, H. G., 108, 113, 205,
    226, 227, 230, 232
Gaffin, R. B., Jr., 261
Gager, J. G., 141
Gagnon, R. A. J., 112, 162, 234,
    554, 624
Gakuru, G., 67
Galatinus, Petrus, 339
Garland, D. E., 203, 587, 621
Garland, D. R., 587
Garr, R., 367
Garrett, D., 265, 392, 617
Garsiel, M., 129
Gee, J. P., 346

Geisler, N. L., 61, 285, 622
Gempf, C. H., 125, 541
Geoghegan, J. C., 366, 367
George, S. K., 148
Gerstenberger, E. S., 218, 386,
    395, 410, 412, 452, 454, 455,
    457, 465
Gese, H., 500
Giese, R. L., Jr., 421
Giles, K., 622
Gillingham, S. E., 147, 268, 362,
    366, 375, 379, 380, 381,
    382, 384, 391
Gilmour, M. J., 112
Gingrich, F. W., 337
Githuku, S., 153
Gladd, B. L., 107
Gleason, R. C., 94
Gledhill, T., 456
Goethe, 119
Goheen, M. W., 114, 219
Goldberg, N. R., 156
Goldin, J., 258
Goldingay, John, 121, 215, 218,
    219, 262, 311, 420, 421, 428,
    451, 492, 583
Goldsworthy, G., 567, 590
Gombis, T. G., 190
González, J., 90, 97, 99, 150, 583
Good, E. M., 407
Goodacre, M., 107
Goodrick, E. W., 335
Gootjes, A., 94
Goppelt, L., 78, 260
Gordon, C. H., 436
Gorman, M., 567
Goswell, G., 479
Gottwald, Norman K., 140, 154,
    155, 361
Gowler, D. B., 524
Grabiner, S. C., 361, 575
Graffy, A., 470
Graham, Billy, 289
Grant, A., 452
Grant, R. M., 84, 98
Graves, Michael, 218, 251
Gray, T., 597
Green, B., 399
Green, E. M. B., 559
Green, G. L., 173
Green, J. B., 481, 482, 483, 484,
    491
Green, M., 541, 612
Green, W. H., 101
Greenberg, M., 357

Greene-McCreight, K., 262
Greengus, S., 439
Greenlee, J. H., 184
Greenspahn, F. E., 170, 333, 425
Greenspoon, L., 70
Greer, R. A., 79, 81, 258
Greidanus, S., 315, 589
Grenz, S. J., 127, 213, 214, 234,
    275, 579, 583
Griffin, D. R., 232
Grizzle, T., 113
Groothuis, D. R., 127, 236
Gros Louis, K. R. R., 426, 428
Grudem, Wayne A., 157, 159,
    195, 212, 266, 604
Guelich, Robert A., 512, 521
Guenther, M., 598
Gumerlock, F. X., 562
Gunkel, Hermann, 103, 454, 455
Gunn, D. M., 120, 124, 268,
    428, 429
Gushee, D. P., 448, 523
Gutiérrez, G., 145

Haan, M. R. de, 537
Habel, N., 473
Hadjiev, T. S., 107
Haenchen, E., 533
Hagen, K., 94
Hagner, D. A., 72, 78, 174, 204,
    223, 252, 309, 372, 481
Hahneman, G. M., 175
Hakola, R., 120
Hall, B., 93, 95
Hall, C. A., 80, 87
Hall, D. R., 217
Hallaschka, M., 107
Hallmann, J., 162
Hamborg, R., 111
Hamilton, J. M., Jr., 540
Hamilton, V. P., 139, 186
Hanks, T. D., 145, 147
Hansen, W. G., 595
Hanson, K. C., 139
Hanson, P. D., 142, 492
Hanson, R. P. C., 80
Harland, P. A., 143
Harmon, W., 430
Harnack, Adolf von, 100, 101, 179
Harrelson, W., 195
Harrington, D. J., 125, 166
Harris, H. H., III, 190
Harris, M. J., 251, 304, 547
Harris, R. L., 178
Harris, S. L., 67, 498

Harrison, C., 86
Harrisville, R. A., 99, 100, 101, 104, 109
Hartley, J. E., 503
Hasel, G., 579
Hatchett, M. J., 577
Hauerwas, S., 95, 208, 230, 442
Hauser, A. J., 94–95
Hawk, L. D., 268
Hawthorne, G. F., 388
Hayes, E. R., 423
Hayes, R. B., 67
Hays, C. B., 471
Hays, J. D., 447, 607, 611
Heacock, A. R., 112
Heaney, S. E., 146
Heard, W., 147
Heelan, P. A., 578
Hegel, G. W. F., 99
Heidegger, Martin, 104, 230, 232
Heil, J. P., 445
Heim, K. M., 371, 374, 379, 403
Heine, R., 84
Heitzenrater, R. P., 97
Helm, D., 590
Helyer, L. R., 70
Hemer, C. J., 316, 513, 532, 533, 534, 558
Hendel, R., 128, 445
Hendriksen, William, 275, 276
Hengel, M., 70, 177, 484, 510
Hengstenberg, E. W., 101
Hennecke, E., 533
Henrichsen, W., 603
Henry, C. F. H., 213
Herbert, A. C., 137
Hering, J. P., 552
Hermas, 81, 174
Herzog, William R., II, 143–44
Hess, Richard S., 54, 143, 426–27, 456, 475, 587
Hesselgrave, D. J., 633
Hetherington, W. M., 582
Hibbard, J. T., 112
Hiebert, P. G., 134
Hildebrandt, T., 494, 495
Hill, A. E., 574
Hill, C. E., 175, 176, 560
Hillers, D., 367
Himes, Dennis R., 632
Hine, S. K., 576
Hirsch, E. D., Jr., 43, 238, 247, 281, 602
Hoag, Gary G., 159
Hobbes, Thomas, 98

Hodgson, P. C., 100
Hoffmann, M., 92
Hoffmeier, J. K., 223
Hofmann, J. C. K. von, 101
Hollerman, J. H., 138
Holman, C. H., 430
Holmberg, B., 144
Holmes, Arthur, 238
Holmes, M. W., 82, 173
Holter, K., 152
Homer, 71, 511
Hoop, R. de, 367
Hoover, R. W., 176, 513
Hopkins, J. H., 52, 53
Horgan, M. P., 73
Hornsby, T. J., 112, 160
Horsley, R. A., 137
Horton, Michael, 581, 583
Hosack, R. N., 481
House, P. R., 52, 172
Houston, J. M., 598
Howard, D. M., Jr., 421
Howard, T. L., 261
Howard, W. F., 311
Hrushovski, B., 366
Hsu, W., 473
Hubbard, D. A., 167, 362, 425
Hubbard, Robert L., Jr., 67, 194, 265, 424, 443, 449, 480, 485, 503
Huber, I., 128
Hughes, F. W., 548
Hultgren, A. J., 320, 531
Humphreys, W. L., 123
Hundley, R. C., 147
Hunter, A. M., 219
Hurtado, Larry W., 151–52, 573
Hurty, S., 256
Husser, J.-M., 423
Hutchison, J. C., 437

Ignatius, 81
Instone-Brewer, D., 73
Ireland, D. J., 320
Irenaeus, 175
Isasi-Díaz, A. M., 163
Iser, Wolfgang, 123, 128

Jackson, Basil, 44
Jackson, Bernard S., 440
Jackson, G., 603
Jacobs, A., 577
Jacobs, I., 75
Jacobsen, D. S., 591
Jacobson, R. A., 182, 420, 451, 459

Jaki, S. L., 452
Janzen, D., 435
Janzen, W., 465
Jasper, D., 419
Jeanrond, W. G., 253
Jefford, C. N., 81
Jenkins, J., 560
Jenson, P. P., 138
Jeremias, J., 182, 274, 484, 513, 524
Jerome, 87, 89–90
Jewett, P. K., 274
Jewett, R., 549, 556
Jobes, K. H., 70, 189, 310
Jobling, D., 119
Johnson, A., 615
Johnson, D. E., 276
Johnson, E. E., 610
Johnson, J., 135
Johnson, L. T., 173, 544
Johnson, M. D., 419, 420, 427, 611
Johnson, V. L., 427
Johnston, P. S., 451, 452
Johnston, R. K., 614
Jones, D. W., 287, 624
Jones, G. H., 479
Jones, I. H., 436
Jones, S. L., 162
Jonker, L. C., 424
Judah, R., 76
Juel, D. H., 76, 77
Jülicher, Adolf, 524, 525
Junior, N., 149

Kähler, M., 101, 105
Kaiser, O., 166
Kaiser, W. C., Jr., 111, 220, 250, 255, 262, 312, 352, 448, 609, 622, 625, 636
Kaltner, J., 111
Kamell, M. J., 550, 580
Kamesar, A., 87
Kampen, J., 152
Kannengiesser, C., 80
Kaplan, A., 272
Karris, R. J., 575
Kasher, R., 258
Kauflin, B., 573
Keats, John, 362, 364, 365
Kee, Howard C., 140, 141
Keegan, T. J., 131
Keener, Craig S., 126, 204, 213, 513, 529, 533, 550, 561
Keener, H. J., 114
Keil, C. F., 101
Kelber, Werner, 132

Keller, C. A., 440
Keller, T., 594
Kellum, L. S., 179
Kelly, J. N. D., 88, 551
Kendall, R. T., 582
Kennedy, G. A., 548
Kennedy, P., 101
Kent, J., 97
Kerr, F., 91
Kessler, J., 218
Kierkegaard, Søren, 104
Kierspel, L., 391
Kim, H. C. P., 462
Kim, S., 137
Kim, Y. S., 115
King, Martin Luther, Jr., 146, 371
King, P. J., 139
Kirk, A., 147, 514, 520, 521
Kirsch, J., 425
Kissinger, W. S., 524
Kistemaker, S. J., 276, 526, 561
Kitchen, K. A., 204, 212
Kittel, G., 341
Klauck, H.-J., 541
Klein, L. R., 407
Klein, William W., 57, 194, 213,
    249, 290, 486, 517, 552, 573,
    583, 585, 589, 596
Kline, M. G., 179
Klingbeil, G. A., 204
Klink, Edward W., 516, 580
Knierim, R. P., 425
Knight, D. A., 229, 465, 474
Knight, G. W., III, 212
Koehler, L., 335
Koester, C. R., 565
Kohlenberger, J. R., 335, 336
Kominsky, J. S., 142
Komoszewski, J. E., 187
Köstenberger, A. J., 158, 179, 207,
    572, 614
Kraemer, D., 171
Kraft, C., 542, 605, 631
Kraft, R. A., 82
Kreitzer, B., 115
Krentz, E., 103
Kristanto, B., 126
Kroeger, C. C., 157, 158, 159
Kroeger, R. C., 158, 159
Kruger, M. J., 176, 179, 212
Kugel, J. L., 69, 70, 72, 74, 258,
    363, 365, 367, 375, 377,
    379, 386
Kuhatschek, Jack, 610, 611, 630
Kuhn, T. S., 117

Kunhiyop, S. W., 623
Kunjummen, J. D., 256
Kurewa, J. W. Z., 315

Ladd, George E., 264, 275, 309,
    481, 520, 541, 559, 579
Laffey, A. L., 160
LaHaye, T., 560
Laird, M., 596
Lamarche, P., 70
Lampe, G., 260
Lane, W. L., 530, 549
Lang, B., 423
Lange, J. P., 101
Langton, Stephen, 185
Lanier, D. E., 598
Lanner, L., 471
Larkin, W. J., Jr., 240, 242, 256,
    319, 537, 615, 622
Larsson, T., 104
Lash, N., 205, 206
LaSor, William S., 167, 256, 257,
    362, 377, 425, 503
Latourelle, R., 529
Law, R., 550
Law, T. M., 70
Leclerc, T. L., 428
Lee, C. C., 150
Lee-Barnewall, Michelle, 159, 614
Leeuwen, M. S. van, 628
Leiman, Sid Z., 170, 171
Leithart, P. J., 228, 271
Lemche, N. P., 143
Lemcio, E. E., 182, 183
LeMon, J. M., 374, 375, 389
Lentricchia, F., 268
Levering, M., 87
Levine, Amy-Jill, 285
Levinsohn, S., 345
Levinson, B. M., 438, 443
Lewis, B. S., 102
Lewis, C. S., 362, 363, 395, 633
Lewis, G. R., 580, 583
Lewis, J. P., 169, 192
Lewis, L. G., 161
Lewis, P., 88
Lichter, S. L., 423
Licona, M. L., 205
Liddell, H. G., 342
Liefeld, W. L., 535, 538, 539, 589
Lightfoot, J. B., 101
Lightstone, J. N., 75
Linafelt, T., 454
Lindsey, Hal, 560
Linnemann, E., 222, 320

Little, D. L., 102
Loader, W. R. G., 445
Lockett, D. R., 580
Logan, A. H. B., 578
Lohmeyer, E., 552
Löhr, W., 82
Long, B. O., 421, 472, 473
Long, V. P., 204, 419, 421, 423,
    431, 475
Longacre, R. E., 346
Longenecker, R. N., 76, 77, 79,
    259, 535, 543, 623
Longman, T., III, 54, 120, 134,
    169, 204, 268, 334, 361,
    366, 370, 375, 419, 425, 451,
    452, 456, 470, 471, 475, 500,
    596, 605, 617
Loretz, O., 366
Louw, J. P., 325, 337
Lowery, R., 564
Lowry, E. L., 590
Lowth, R., 373
Lucas, George R., 232
Lüdemann, H., 556
Lührmann, D., 308
Lund, N. W., 391, 392
Lundbom, J. R., 360, 391, 395, 475
Lundin, Roger, 229, 230, 252
Luther, Martin, 93–96, 474,
    552, 622
Lynch, J. H., 88
Lyons, J., 46, 328, 344

MacCullough, D., 92, 93, 94,
    95, 96
Mack, B. L., 531
Maddox, R., 532
Mafico, T. L. J., 153
Mailloux, Stephen, 125
Malherbe, A. J., 546
Malina, B. J., 57, 117, 134, 135, 144
Mandolfo, C., 452
Manson, T. W., 105
Marcion, 174
Margalith, O., 427
Marguerat, D., 123
Markley, J. F., 294, 313
Marsden, R., 89
Marshall, I. H., 173, 180, 205,
    214, 224, 309, 314, 512, 557
Martens, E. A., 443, 610
Martin, D. B., 284, 587
Martin, J., 101
Martin, R. P., 388, 552, 555, 574,
    575, 581

Marx, Karl, 99, 146–47
Marxsen, W., 107
Mason, S., 72
Matera, F. J., 179
Mathewson, D. L., 320, 347
Mathewson, S. D., 315, 589
Matthews, V. H., 137, 138, 139, 426, 439, 454, 455
Maxson, R., 621
May, D. M., 136, 521
Maynard-Reid, P. U., 148
Mazzaferri, Frederick, 561
McBride, S. D., 450
McCarthy, D. J., 450
McComiskey, T. E., 54
McConville, G. J., 336, 341, 450
McCracken, P. V., 69
McDonald, L. M., 167, 221
McDonald, M. W., 94
McGavran, D., 136
McGeough, K., 430
McGiffert, A. C., 102
McGinn, B., 562
McGrath, A. E., 583, 584, 588
McKay, K. L., 356
McKeever, B. C., 593
McKenzie, S. L., 111, 204, 423
McKim, D. K., 214
McKnight, E. V., 40, 105, 134, 234, 235, 267, 524
McKnight, S., 520, 532, 614
McNally, R. E., 88, 89
McNamara, M. J., 69
McQuilkin, J. Robertson, 255, 615
Meadowcroft, Tim, 603
Meeks, Wayne, 143
Meier, J. P., 139, 176, 205, 223, 520, 529
Meinhold, A., 67
Melick, R. R., 607
Melugin, R. F., 54
Melville, Herman, 123
Mendenhall, G. E., 140, 341
Metzger, B. M., 167, 172, 177, 178, 180, 182, 186, 192, 195, 298, 340, 564
Meyer, Ben F., 127
Meyer, M., 83
Meyer, T., 101
Meyers, C. L., 478
Meyers, E. M., 478
Michaelis, J. D., 98
Michaels, J. R., 558
Michie, D., 124
Mickelsen, A. B., 493, 580

Milgrom, J., 446, 607
Millard, Alan R., 56, 223, 426, 427
Miller, D. A., 426
Miller, G. J., 95
Miller, P. D., 102, 438, 442, 453
Milligan, G., 330, 341
Minkoff, H., 370
Miranda, José P., 146
Miscall, Peter D., 133
Moeser, M. C., 531
Mollenkott, V. R., 157
Möller, K., 475
Mondesért, C., 71
Moo, Douglas J., 179, 250, 256, 257, 260, 261, 353, 445, 483, 543, 555, 562, 580, 625
Moon, G. W., 598
Moore, S. D., 129, 133, 134, 254
Morales, L. M., 107
Moreau, A. S., 633
Morgan, G. C., 537
Morgan, Robert, 231–32, 236, 248, 268
Morris, Leon, 216, 563, 620
Mott, S. C., 502
Moulton, J. H., 311, 330, 341, 347
Mounce, Robert H., 264, 276, 561, 566
Mounce, W. D., 334
Mowinckel, S., 468
Muilenburg, J., 118
Mulholland, M. R., Jr., 596, 597
Müller, D., 591
Muller, R. A., 92, 95, 284
Murphy, F. J., 492, 562
Murphy, R. E., 403, 451, 454, 455, 458, 493, 494, 495, 496, 497, 498, 499, 500, 502
Murphy, R. G., 452
Murray, D. F., 470
Murray, S., 95

Nanos, M. D., 407
Nash, R. H., 147
Nassif, B., 84, 85
Neil, W., 97, 98, 99
Neill, S., 104, 105
Nel, P. J., 327
Netland, H. A., 235
Neufeld, V. H., 575
Neusner, J., 74, 75, 76, 486
Newsom, C. A., 157
Nicholson, E., 100
Nicole, R., 213

Nicolson, A., 192
Nida, E. A., 191, 325, 337, 344
Niditch, S., 54, 425
Nielsen, L. O., 91
Nienhuis, D. R., 183
Nikolsky, R., 74
Ninow, F., 78
Noble, P. R., 130, 182
Nogalski, J., 103
Noll, K. L., 130
Noll, M. A., 102
Nolland, J., 224
Norris, C., 131
Norris, R. A., Jr., 86
North, R., 422
Noth, M., 140
Nouwen, H. J. J., 598
Nuñez, E. A., 147
Nurmela, R., 67

Oakman, D. E., 139
O'Brien, B. J., 164, 230
O'Brien, P. T., 190
Ocker, C., 88, 89, 90, 91
O'Connor, K. M., 452, 454, 469
O'Connor, M., 92, 348, 354, 355, 356, 357, 358, 359, 366
Oden, T. C., 80
Ogden, G. S., 435
O'Keefe, J. J., 78, 85, 86, 251, 284, 588
Olbricht, T. H., 102
Olofsson, S., 186
Olson, D. T., 439
Olson, R. E., 72, 90, 91, 92, 93, 94, 95, 97, 581, 584, 588
O'Neal, G. M., 114
Ortlund, R. C., Jr., 619
Osborn, E., 84
Osborne, Grant R., 63, 66, 111, 128, 240, 246, 264, 275, 352, 559, 565, 589, 609, 614, 615
Osiek, C., 157
Osmer, R. R., 584
Oss, D. A., 256
Oswalt, J. N., 481
Overholt, T. W., 135, 138
Overland, P., 391
Owens, J. J., 336
Ozment, S., 96

Padilla, R. C., 240
Paget, J. C., 80, 83, 84
Palmer, D. W., 532
Pannenberg, W., 583

Park, M. S., 388
Parker, S. B., 480
Parker, T. H. L., 94
Parsenios, G. L., 511
Patrick, D., 438, 440, 441
Patte, D., 119
Paul, I., 399
Paulus, H. E. G., 529
Payne, P. B., 620
Pearson, B. A., 578
Pelham, A., 430
Pelikan, J., 81, 83, 239
Pennington, J. T., 532
Pentiuc, E. J., 66
Perdue, L. G., 106
Perrin, N., 107, 266, 524
Pervo, R. I., 533
Petersen, D. L., 107, 362, 363,
    366, 369, 376, 388, 397,
    398, 410, 419, 427
Petersen, Norman R., 126
Peterson, D., 573
Peterson, Eugene, 194, 318, 350,
    565, 596
Petterson, A. R., 478
Pfatteicher, P. H., 577
Phillips, G. A., 133
Phillips, J. B., 285, 318, 350
Pierard, R. V., 481
Pilch, J. J., 144
Pinnock, C. H., 234, 581
Pitkin, B., 94
Plaskow, J., 159
Poirier, J. C., 102
Polycarp, 81, 173, 174
Porter, S. E., 104, 105, 111, 119,
    130, 260, 331, 347, 350, 354,
    356, 357, 541, 551, 559
Porton, G. G., 74
Powell, M. A., 117, 120, 126,
    270, 334
Poythress, V. S., 195, 242
Provan, I., 204, 475
Pui-lan, K., 163
Pyper, H. S., 127

Quarles, C. L., 179, 258

Rad, G. von, 260, 474, 493
Radday, Y. T., 393
Rae, M. A., 262
Räisänen, H., 556
Ramm, B., 207, 282, 609
Ramsay, W. M., 532, 558
Raphael, R., 363

Raschke, C., 127
Rata, T., 450
Rayburn, Robert G., 573
Reddish, M. G., 543
Redditt, P. L., 462, 478
Reid, D. G., 430, 471
Reid, S. B., 451
Rengstorf, K., 591
Reno, R. R., 50, 78, 86, 251,
    284, 588
Resseguie, James L., 120, 128, 270
Reuchlin, Johann, 92
Reuther, Rosemary, 155, 156
Rhee, V., 391
Rhoads, D., 124
Richard, R. P., 610
Richards, E. R., 164, 230, 541
Richards, K. H., 362, 363, 366,
    369, 376, 388, 397, 398, 410
Richardson, A., 101, 104, 105, 238
Riches, J., 102
Richter, H., 500
Ricoeur, 230
Riley, S. P., 428
Riley, W., 425
Ringe, S. H., 157
Ringgren, H., 335
Roach, W. C., 61
Roberts, A. R., 84
Roberts, B. M., 593
Roberts, J. J. M., 450
Roberts, T. J., 125
Robertson, D. A., 125
Robertson, O. P., 368
Robertson, Pat, 529
Robins, V. K., 531
Robinson, H. Wheeler, 142, 315,
    589, 631
Robinson, J. C., 104, 105, 111
Robinson, J. M., 107, 108
Robinson, S. E., 176
Rodd, C. S., 444
Roetzel, C. J., 545
Rofé, A., 428, 474
Rogers, J. B., 214, 234
Rogerson, J. W., 101, 142
Rohrbaugh, R. L., 144
Roloff, J., 486
Römer, T. C., 423
Rommen, E., 633
Roskop, A. R., 436
Rosner, B. S., 56, 445, 532
Ross, M. C., 577
Rotelle, J. E., 87
Roukema, R., 83, 578

Routledge, R., 218
Rowland, C., 145
Rowley, H. H., 573
Rudwick, M. J. S., 559
Rüger, H. P., 166
Rummel, E., 92
Runge, S. E., 345
Russell, Letty, 156
Ryken, Leland, 48, 49, 120, 192,
    252, 268, 361, 363, 386, 389,
    395, 396, 399, 402, 403, 404,
    405, 408, 409, 420, 421, 425,
    426, 427, 456, 492, 494, 525,
    531, 533, 538, 601
Ryou, D. H., 471

Sabo, P. J., 367
Sailhamer, J. H., 182, 261, 629
Saint Brianchaninov, I., 458
Samely, A., 75
Sanders, E. P., 556, 626
Sanders, J. A., 109, 181, 183, 250
Sanders, J. T., 575
Sandy, D. Brent, 46, 51, 54, 214,
    215, 244, 269, 421, 462, 481,
    491, 492, 493, 562
Sandy-Wunsch, J., 97, 99
Satterthwaite, P. E., 419
Sawyer, J. F. A., 325
Sawyer, M. J., 187
Schaberg, J., 158
Scharbert, J., 434, 440
Schiffman, L. H., 70
Schipper, J., 149, 435
Schmidt, K. L., 486
Schneider, G., 342
Schneider, T., 426
Schnelle, U., 179
Schniedewind, W. M., 56
Schreiner, T. R., 158, 274, 309,
    556, 557, 586
Schreiter, J., 284
Schroter, J., 110
Schultz, R. L., 611
Schunack, G., 260
Schüssler Fiorenza, Elisabeth,
    156–57
Schweitzer, A., 107
Scobie, C. H. H., 219
Scolnic, B. E., 436
Scott, R., 342
Searle, J., 244
Seeley, D., 132
Seesemann, H., 330

Segovia, F. F., 149, 150
Segundo, J. L., 146
Seitz, C., 78
Seitz, C. R., 183
Seitz, C. S., 260
Selderhuis, H. J., 94
Selman, M. J., 438, 439, 440
Senn, F. C., 577
Seow, C. L., 352, 357
Seters, J. van, 144, 441
Seung, T. K., 131
Shakespeare, William, 119, 360,
    428
Shanks, H., 178
Sharon, J., 627
Sharp, C. J., 475
Shead, S., 325
Shepherd, C. E., 114
Shields, B. E., 100, 102
Shields, M. E., 475
Sider, R. J., 620, 631
Silberman, Lou H., 229
Silva, D. A. de, 139, 166
Silva, M., 39, 70, 111, 189, 310,
    325, 328, 330, 334, 341,
    575, 636
Simon, Richard, 98
Sine, T., 616
Sire, J. W., 605
Sklar, J., 607
Slonim, R., 272
Small, K. E., 189
Smalley, B., 89, 90
Smart, J. D., 106
Smith, B. D., 141
Smith, G. T., 598
Smith, G. V., 482
Smith, H. P., 102
Smith, J. A., 573
Smith, J. B., 596
Smith, J. K. A., 113
Smith, M. J., 163
Smith, M. L., 598
Smith, M. S., 153, 373, 426
Smith, W. Robertson, 101, 102
Snodgrass, Klyne R., 260, 261,
    266, 278, 320, 435, 525
Soares-Prabhu, G. M., 151
Solivan, S., 113
Sommer, B. D., 165, 170
Sonsino, R., 438, 439, 440
Sophocles, 119
Soulen, R. K., 518
Soulen, R. N., 518
Spanje, T. E. van, 150

Sparks, H. D. F., 88
Sparks, Kenton L., 215
Spencer, A. B., 118, 156, 157
Spener, Philip Jacob, 97
Spinks, D. C., 50
Spinoza, Bernard, 98
Spittler, R., 316
Sprinkle, J. M., 442
Spurgeon, C. H., 207
Stacey, W. D., 474
Stager, L. E., 139
Stanley, P., 598
Starbuck, S. R. A., 452, 455, 456
Starling, David, 240
Stassen, G. H., 448, 523, 624
Stein, R. H., 49, 55, 129, 265,
    364, 526, 532
Steinmetz, David C., 50, 254
Stemberger, G., 69
Stendahl, K., 43, 555, 602
Sternberg, M., 123, 124, 129, 419
Sterrett, T. N., 611
Steussy, M. J., 427
Stone, A., 439
Stone, Barton W., 102
Stone, K., 112
Story, J. L., 490
Stott, J. R. W., 315, 589, 632, 634
Stowers, S. K., 541, 546
Strauss, D. F., 529
Strauss, Mark L., 196, 611, 615,
    631, 636
Strawn, B. A., 374, 375, 389
Strecker, G., 550
Strickland, W. G., 586
Stuart, D. K., 54, 59, 287, 480,
    496, 514, 528, 539, 560, 614
Stube, J. C., 431
Stuhlmacher, P., 219, 283
Stulman, L., 462
Sugirtharajah, R. S., 150–51, 234
Sumpter, P., 114
Sundberg, A. C., Jr., 167, 169
Sundberg, W., 99, 100, 101, 104,
    109, 168
Swanson, J., 89
Swartley, W., 45, 53, 207, 283, 284
Sweeney, M. A., 103, 112, 419,
    428, 462, 463, 464, 465,
    466, 467, 468, 469, 470, 471,
    472, 473, 477, 488
Sykes, N., 95, 97, 98

Talbert, C. H., 117
Talstra, E., 346

Tamez, E., 148, 149, 153
Tannehill, R. C., 124
Tanner, B. LaNeel, 182, 451, 459
Tate, M. E., 62
Tate, W. R., 246, 271
Tatu, S., 435
Taylor, V., 105
Templeton, D. A., 125
Tenney, G. C., 330, 334
Tenney, M. C., 564
Terry, M. S., 405, 406, 407
Tertullian, 86, 173, 175, 545
Theissen, G., 141, 528
Thielman, F. S., 180, 309, 586
Thiselton, A. C., 40, 57, 58, 80,
    110, 111, 112, 131, 203, 205,
    226, 227, 228, 229, 230,
    232, 240, 244, 252, 254, 315,
    527, 540, 543, 554, 602
Thomas, R. L., 60, 61, 515
Thompson, J. L., 92, 94, 284
Thompson, M. D., 93, 94, 116, 210
Thompson, M. J., 597
Thompson, M. M., 483
Thomson, G. T., 583
Thomson, I. H., 391
Thuesen, P. J., 193
Tidball, D. J., 136, 593
Tiemeyer, L.-S., 423, 453, 472
Toal, M. F., 88
Tolbert, M. A., 130
Tolstoy, Leo, 522
Torre, M. A. de la, 149
Tov, E., 184, 185, 189
Tovey, D., 270
Towner, P. H., 173
Tracy, David, 45, 84, 98, 229
Traina, R. A., 114, 605, 631
Travis, Stephen H., 485
Treier, D. J., 114, 278
Trethowan, T., 233
Trible, P., 158, 429
Trigg, J. W., 81, 84
Tsumura, D. T., 52, 54, 427
Tucker, G. M., 412, 465, 474
Tucker, J. M., 102
Tucker, J. T., 498
Tuckett, C., 176
Turner, M., 325, 344, 354
Turner, M. M. B., 540
Turner, N., 347
Twain, Mark, 106
Twelftree, G. H., 529

Unnik, W. C. van, 532